The International Critical Commentary

on the Holy Scriptures of the Old and New Testaments.

PLANNED AND FOR YEARS EDITED BY

THE LATE REV. PROFESSOR SAMUEL ROLLES DRIVER, D.D., D.LITT.

THE REV. ALFRED PLUMMER, M.A., D.D.

THE LATE REV. PROFESSOR CHARLES AUGUSTUS BRIGGS, D.D., D.LITT.

GENESIS

JOHN SKINNER, D.D.

TO

MY WIFE

THE INTERNATIONAL CRITICAL COMMENTARY

A CRITICAL AND EXEGETICAL COMMENTARY ON GENESIS

BY

JOHN SKINNER, D.D., HON. M.A. (CANTAB.)

PRINCIPAL AND PROFESSOR OF OLD TESTAMENT LANGUAGE AND LITERATURE, WESTMINSTER COLLEGE, CAMBRIDGE

SECOND EDITION

EDINBURGH

T. & T. CLARK, 38 GEORGE STREET

PRINTED IN SCOTLAND BY
MORRISON AND GIBB LIMITED
EDINBURGH AND LONDON
FOR
T. & T. CLARK LTD., EDINBURGH

0 567 05001 7

FIRST EDITION 1910
SECOND EDITION . . . 1930
LATEST IMPRESSION . . 1976

PREFACE TO FIRST EDITION.

IT is a little over six years since I was entrusted by the Editors of "The International Critical Commentary" with the preparation of the volume on Genesis. During that time there has been no important addition to the number of commentaries either in English or in German. The English reader still finds his best guidance in Spurrell's valuable *Notes* on the text, Bennett's compressed but suggestive exposition in the *Century Bible*, and Driver's thorough and masterly work in the first volume of the *Westminster Commentaries*; all of which were in existence when I commenced my task. While no one of these books will be superseded by the present publication, there was still room for a commentary on the more elaborate scale of the "International" series; and it has been my aim, in accordance with the programme of that series, to supply the fuller treatment of critical, exegetical, literary, and archæological questions, which the present state of scholarship demands.

The most recent German commentaries, those of Holzinger and Gunkel, had both appeared before 1904; and I need not say that to both, but especially to the latter, I have been greatly indebted. Every student must have felt that Gunkel's work, with its æsthetic appreciation of the genius of the narratives, its wider historical horizons, and its illuminating use of mythological and folklore parallels, has breathed a new spirit into the investigation of Genesis, whose influence no writer on the subject can hope or wish to escape. The last-mentioned feature is considerably emphasised in the third edition, the first part of which (1909) was published just too late to be utilised for this volume. That I have not neglected the older standard commentaries of Tuch, Delitzsch, and Dillmann, or less comprehensive expositions like that of Strack, will be apparent from the frequent acknowledgments in the notes. The same remark applies to many books of a more general kind (mostly cited in the list of "Abbreviations"), which have helped to elucidate special points of exegesis.

The problems which invest the interpretation of Genesis are, indeed, too varied and far-reaching to be satisfactorily treated within the compass of a single volume. The old controversies as to the compatibility of the earlier chapters with the conclusions of modern science are no longer, to my mind, a living issue; and I have not thought it necessary to occupy much space with their discussion. Those who are of a different opinion may be referred to the pages of Dr. Driver, where they will find these matters handled with convincing force and clearness. Rather more attention has been given to the recent reaction against the critical analysis of the Pentateuch, although I am very far from thinking that that movement, either in its conservative or its more radical manifestation, is likely to undo the scholarly work of the last hundred and fifty years. At all events, my own belief in the essential soundness of the prevalent hypothesis has been confirmed by the renewed examination of the text of Genesis which my present undertaking required. It will probably appear to some that the analysis is pushed further than is warranted, and that duplicates are discovered where common sense would have suggested an easy reconciliation. That is a perfectly fair line of criticism, provided the whole problem be kept in view. It has to be remembered that the analytic process is a chain which is a good deal stronger than its weakest link, that it starts from cases where diversity of authorship is almost incontrovertible, and moves on to others where it is less certain; and it is surely evident that when the composition of sources is once established, the slightest differences of representation or language assume a significance which they might not have apart from that presumption. That the analysis is frequently tentative and precarious is fully acknowledged; and the danger of basing conclusions on insufficient data of this kind is one that I have sought to avoid. On the more momentous question of the historical or legendary character of the book, or the relation of the one element to the other, opinion is likely to be divided for some time to come. Several competent Assyriologists appear to cherish the conviction that we are on the eve of fresh discoveries which will vindicate the accuracy of at least the patriarchal traditions in a way that will cause the utmost astonishment to some who pay too little heed to the findings of archæological experts. It is naturally difficult to estimate the worth of such an anticipation; and it is advisable to keep an open mind. Yet even here it is possible to adopt a position which will not be readily undermined. Whatever triumphs may be in store for the archæologist,—though he should prove that Noah and Abraham and Jacob and Joseph are all real historical personages,—he will hardly succeed in dispelling the atmosphere of mythical imagination, of legend, of poetic idealisation, which are the life and soul of the narratives of Genesis. It will still be necessary, if we are to retain our faith in the inspiration of this part of Scripture, to recognise that the Divine Spirit has enshrined a part of His Revelation to men in such forms as these. It is only by a frank acceptance of this truth that the Book of Genesis can be made a means of religious edification to the educated mind of our age.

As regards the form of the commentary, I have endeavoured to include in the large print enough to enable the reader to pick up rapidly the general sense of a passage; although the exigencies of space have compelled me to employ small type to a much larger extent than was ideally desirable. In the arrangement of footnotes I have reverted to the plan adopted in the earliest volume of the series (Driver's *Deuteronomy*), by putting all the textual, grammatical, and philological material bearing on a particular verse in consecutive notes running concurrently with the main text. It is possible that in some cases a slight embarrassment may result from the presence of a double set of footnotes; but I think that this disadvantage will be more than compensated to the reader by the convenience of having the whole explanation of a verse under his eye at one place, instead of having to perform the difficult operation of keeping two or three pages open at once.

In conclusion, I have to express my thanks, first of all, to two friends by whose generous assistance my labour has been considerably lightened: to Miss E. I. M. Boyd, M.A., who has rendered me the greatest service in collecting material from books, and to the Rev. J. G. Morton, M.A., who has corrected the proofs, verified all the scriptural references, and compiled the Index. My last word of all must be an acknowledgment of profound and grateful obligation to Dr. Driver, the English Editor of the series, for his unfailing interest and encouragement during the progress of the work, and for numerous criticisms and suggestions, especially on points of philology and archæology, to which in nearly every instance I have been able to give effect.

JOHN SKINNER.

CAMBRIDGE,
April 1910.

PUBLISHERS' NOTE TO SECOND EDITION.

DR. SKINNER had prepared a new Introduction, and had revised the Bibliography for the Second Edition, but died before these could be submitted to him in proof form. The Rev. G. S. Gunn, M.A., Juniper Green, Midlothian, kindly came to our assistance and undertook the work of correcting and editing them.

T. & T. CLARK.

EDINBURGH,
February 1930.

CONTENTS.

ABBREVIATIONS.

1. SOURCES (see pp. xlii ff.), TEXTS, AND VERSIONS.

E	Elohist, or Elohistic Narrative.
J	Yahwist, or Jahwistic Narrative.
JE . . .	Jehovist, or the combined narrative of J and E.
P or PC . .	The Priestly Code.
P^g . . .	The historical kernel or framework of P (see p. lviii).
R^E, R^J, R^P . . .	Redactors within the schools of E, J, and P, respectively.
R^{JE} . . .	The Compiler of the composite work JE.
R^{JEP} . . .	The Final Redactor of the Pentateuch.
EV[V] . . .	English Version[s] (Authorised or Revised).
Jub. . . .	*The Book of Jubilees.*
MT . . .	Massoretic Text.
OT . . .	Old Testament.
Aq. . . .	Greek Translation of Aquila.
Θ	,, ,, ,, Theodotion.
Σ	,, ,, ,, Symmachus.
Gr.-Ven. . .	Codex 'Græcus Venetus' (14th or 15th cent.).
𝔊	The Greek (Septuagint) Version of the OT (ed. A. E. Brooke and N. M'Lean, Cambridge, 1906).
$𝔊^L$ . . .	Lucianic recension of the LXX, edited by Lagarde, *Librorum Veteris Testamenti canonicorum pars prior Græce*, etc. (1883).
$𝔊^{A, B, E, M, etc.}$.	Codices of 𝔊 (see Brooke and M'Lean, p. v).
𝔏	Old Latin Version.
𝔖	The Syriac Version (Peshiṭtâ).
𝔐	The Samaritan Recension of the Pent. (Walton's 'London Polyglott').
$𝔗^O$ . . .	The Targum of Onkelos [2nd cent. A.D.] (ed. Berliner, 1884).
$𝔗^J$ . . .	The Targum of Jonathan [8th cent. A.D.] (ed. Ginsburger, 1903).
𝔙	The Vulgate.

2. COMMENTARIES

Ayles . . . H. H. B. Ayles, *A Critical Commentary on Genesis ii. 4–iii. 25* (1904).

Ba[ll] . . . C. J. Ball, *The Book of Genesis : Critical Edition of the Hebrew Text printed in colours . . . with Notes* (1896). See *SBOT*.

Ben[nett] . . W. H. Bennett, *Genesis* (Century Bible).

Calv[in] . . *Mosis Libri V cum Joh. Calvini Commentariis. Genesis seorsum*, etc. (1563).

De[litzsch] . . F. Delitzsch, *Neuer Commentar über die Genesis* (5th ed. 1887).

Di[llmann] . . *Die Genesis. Von der dritten Auflage an erklärt von A. Dillmann* (6th ed. 1892). The work embodies frequent extracts from earlier edns. by Knobel: these are referred to below as "Kn.-Di."

Dr[iver] . . *The Book of Genesis with Introduction and Notes*, by S. R. Driver (7th ed. 1909).

Gu[nkel] . . *Genesis übersetzt und erklärt*, von H. Gunkel (2nd ed. 1902).

Ho[lzinger] . . *Genesis erklärt*, von H. Holzinger (1898).

IEz. . . . Abraham Ibn Ezra (†*c.* 1167).

Jer[ome], *Qu.* . Jerome (†420), *Quæstiones sive Traditiones hebraicæ in Genesim.*

Kn[obel] . . A. Knobel.

Kn.-Di. . . See Di[llmann].

König . . . *Genesis, eingeleitet übersetzt und erklärt.*

Ra[shi] . . Rabbi Shelomoh Yiẓḥaḳi (†1105).

Spurrell . . G. J. Spurrell, *Notes on the Text of the Book of Genesis* (2nd ed. 1896).

Str[ack] . . *Die Genesis übersetzt und ausgelegt*, von H. L. Strack (2nd. ed. 1905).

Tu[ch] . . . Fr. Tuch, *Commentar über die Genesis* (2nd ed. 1871).

3. WORKS OF REFERENCE AND GENERAL LITERATURE.

Barth, *ES* . . J. Barth, *Etymologische Studien zum sem. insbesondere zum hebr. Lexicon* (1893).

„ *NB* . . *Die Nominalbildung in den sem. Sprachen* (1898–91).

Barton, *SO* . . G. A. Barton, *A Sketch of Semitic Origins* (1902).

Baumgärtel . *Elohim ausserhalb des Pent.*

B.-D. . . . S. Baer and F. Delitzsch, *Liber Genesis* (1869). The Massoretic Text, with Appendices.

BDB . . . F. Brown, S. R. Driver, and C. A. Briggs, *A Hebrew and English Lexicon of the OT* (1906).

Benz[inger], *Arch.*[2] I. Benzinger, *Hebräische Archäologie* (2nd ed. 1907).

Ber. R. . . The Midrash *Bereshith Rabba* (tr. into German by A. Wünsche, 1881).

Bochart, *Hieroz.*.	S. Bochartus, *Hierozoicon, sive bipertitum opus de animalibus Sacræ Scripturæ* (ed. Rosenmüller, 1793–96).
Bu[dde], *Urg.* .	K. Budde, *Die biblische Urgeschichte* (1883).
Buhl, *GP* . .	Fr. Buhl, *Geographie des alten Palaestina* (1896).
,,	*Geschichte der Edomiter* (1893).
Burck[hardt] .	Burckhardt, *Notes on the Bedouins and Wahábys.*
,,	*Travels in Syria and the Holy Land.*
Che[yne], *TB[A]I*	T. K. Cheyne, *Traditions and Beliefs of Ancient Israel* (1907).
CIS . . .	*Corpus Inscriptionum Semiticarum* (1881–).
Cook, *Gl.* . .	S. A. Cook, *A Glossary of the Aramaic Inscriptions* (1898).
Cooke, *NSI.* .	G. A. Cooke, *A Textbook of North-Semitic Inscriptions* (1903).
Co[rnill], *Einl.* .	C. H. Cornill, *Einleitung in das AT* (see p. xlv, *n.*).
,, *Hist.* .	*History of the People of Israel* (tr. 1898).
Curtiss, *PSR* .	S. I. Curtiss, *Primitive Semitic Religion to-day* (1902).
Dahse . . .	*Textkritische Materialien zur Hexateuchfrage* (1912).
Dav[idson] . .	A. B. Davidson, *Hebrew Syntax.*
,, *OTTh*	*The Theology of the OT* (1904).
DB . . .	*A Dictionary of the Bible*, ed. by J. Hastings (1898–1902).
Del[itzsch], *Hwb.*	Friedrich Delitzsch, *Assyrisches Handwörterbuch* (1896).
,, *Par.*.	*Wo lag das Paradies? Eine biblisch-assyriologische Studie* (1881).
,, *Prol.*	*Prolegomena eines neuen hebräisch-aramäischen Wörterbuchs zum AT* (1886).
,,	See *BA* below.
Doughty, *AD* .	C. M. Doughty, *Travels in Arabia Deserta* (1888).
Dri[ver], *LOT* .	S. R. Driver, *An Introduction to the Literature of the OT* (9th ed. 1913).
,, *Sam.* .	*Notes on the Hebrew Text of the Books of Samuel* (1890).
,, *T.* .	*A Treatise on the use of the Tenses in Hebrew* (3rd ed. 1892).
EB . . .	*Encyclopædia Biblica*, ed. by T. K. Cheyne and J. Sutherland Black (1899–1903).
EBL . . .	See Hilprecht.
Ee[rdmans] . .	B. D. Eerdmans, *Alttestamentliche Studien:* i. *Die Komposition der Genesis.* ii. *Die Vorgeschichte Israels.*
Eichrodt . .	*Die Quellen der Genesis von neuem untersucht* (1916).
Eissfeldt . .	*Hexateuch. Synopse* (1922).
Erman, *LAE* .	Ad. Erman, *Life in Ancient Egypt* (tr. by H. M. Tirard, 1894).
,, *Hdbk.* .	*A Handbook of Egyptian Religion* (tr. by A. S. Griffith, 1907).

Ew[ald], *Gr.* . H. Ewald, *Ausfürliches Lehrbuch der hebräischen Sprache des alten Bundes* (8th ed. 1870).

" *HI* . *History of Israel* [Eng. tr. 1871].

" *Ant.* . *Antiquities of Israel* [Eng. tr. 1876].

Field . . . F. Field, *Origenis Hexaplorum quæ supersunt; sive Veterum Interpretum Græcorum in totum V.T. Fragmenta* (1875).

Frazer, *AAO* . J. G. Frazer, *Adonis Attis Osiris: Studies in the History of Oriental Religion* (1906).

" *GB* . . *The Golden Bough: a Study in Magic and Religion* (2nd ed. 1900).

" *Folklore in the OT* (1907).

v. Gall, *CSt.* . A. Freiherr von Gall, *Altisraelitische Kultstätten* (1898).

G.-B. . . . Gesenius' *Hebräisches und aramäisches Handwörterbuch über das AT* (14th ed. by Buhl, 1905).

Geiger, *Urschr.* . A. Geiger, *Urschrift und Uebersetzungen der Bibel in ihrer Abhängigkeit von der innern Entwcikelung des Judenthums* (1857).

Ges[enius], *Th.* . W. Gesenius, *Thesaurus philologicus criticus Linguæ Hebræ et Chaldææ V.T.* (1829–58).

G.-K. . . . Gesenius' *Hebräische Grammatik*, völlig umgearbeitet von E. Kautzsch (26th ed. 1896) [Eng. tr. 1898].

Glaser, *Skizze* . E. Glaser, *Skizze der Geschichte und Geographie Arabiens*, ii. (1890).

Gordon, *ETG* . A. R. Gordon, *The Early Traditions of Genesis* (1907).

Gray, *HPN*. . G. B. Gray, *Studies in Hebrew Proper Names* (1896).

" . . . *A Critical Introduction to the Old Testament* (1913).

Gressmann . . *Texte und Bilder.*

Gu[nkel], *Schöpf.* H. Gunkel, *Schöpfung und Chaos in Urzeit und Endzeit* (1895).

" . . . *Schriften des AT in Auswahl übersetzt.*

" . . . *Festschrift* (1923).

" . . . *Preussiche Jahrbücher* (1919).

Guthe, *GI* . . H. Guthe, *Geschichte des Volkes Israel* (1899).

Harrison, *Prol.* . Jane E. Harrison, *Prolegomena to the Study of Greek Religion* (2nd ed. 1908).

Hilprecht, *EBL* . H. V. Hilprecht, *Explorations in Bible Lands during the 19th cent.* [with the co-operation of Benzinger, Hommel, Jensen, and Steindorff] (1903).

Hölscher . . *Gesch. d. isr. und jüd. Religion* (1922).

Hol[zinger], *Einl.* or *Hex.* H. Holzinger, *Einleitung in den Hexateuch* (1893).

Hom[mel], *AA* . F. Hommel, *Aufsätze und Abhandlungen arabistisch-semitologischen Inhalts* (i–iii, 1892–).

" *AHT.* *The Ancient Hebrew Tradition as illustrated by the Monuments* (1897).

Hom[mel], *AOD*.	*Die altorientalischen Denkmäler und das AT* (1902).
,, *Gesch.*	*Geschichte Babyloniens und Assyriens* (1885).
,, *SAChrest.*	*Süd-arabische Chrestomathie* (1893).
Hupf[eld], *Qu.* .	H. Hupfeld, *Die Quellen der Genesis und die Art ihrer Zusammensetzung* (1853).
Jastrow, *RBA* .	M. Jastrow, *The Religion of Babylonia and Assyria* (1898).
JE . . .	*The Jewish Encyclopædia.*
Jen[sen], *Kosm.* .	P. Jensen, *Die Kosmologie der Babylonier* (1890).
Je[remias], *ATLO*²	A. Jeremias, *Das Alte Testament im Lichte des alten Orients* (2nd ed. 1906).
*KAT*² . . .	*Die Keilinschriften und das AT*, by Schrader (2nd ed. 188).
*KAT*³ . . .	*Die Keilinschriften und das AT.* Third ed., by Zimmern and Winckler (1902).
Kennett . .	*Deuteronomy and the Decalogue* (1926).
Kent, *SOT* . .	C. F. Kent, *Narratives of the Beginnings of Hebrew History* [Students' Old Testament] (1904).
KIB . . .	*Keilinschriftliche Bibliothek*, ed. by Eb. Schrader (1889–).
Kit[tel], *BH* .	R. Kittel, *Biblia Hebraica* (Genesis) (1905).
,, *GH* .	*Geschichte der Hebräer* (1888–92).
,, *GVI* .	*Gesch. Volk. Israel.*
Kön[ig], *Lgb.* .	F. E. König, *Historisch-kritisches Lehrgebäude der hebräischen Sprache* (2 vols., 1881–95).
,, *S* . .	*Historisch-comparative Syntax der hebr. Sprache* (1 97).
KS . . .	E. Kautzsch and A. Socin, *Die Genesis mit aüsserer Unterscheidung der Quellenschriften.*
Kue[nen], *Ges.Abh.*	A. Kuenen, *Gesammelte Abhandlungen* (see p. xlv, *note*).
,, *Ond.* .	*Historisch-critisch Onderzoek* . . . . (see p. xlv, *note*).
Lag[arde], *Ank.* .	P. A. de Lagarde, *Ankündigung einer neuen Ausgabe der griech. Uebersetzung des AT* (1882).
,, *Ges. Abh.* .	*Gesammelte Abhandlungen* (1866).
,, *Mitth.* .	*Mittheilungen*, i–iv (1884–91).
,, . .	*Orientalia*, 1, 2 (1879–80).
,, *Sem.* . .	*Semitica*, 1, 2 (1878).
,, *Symm.* .	*Symmicta*, 2 pts. (1877–80).
,, *OS* . .	*Onomastica Sacra* (1870).
Lane, *Lex.* . .	E. W. Lane, *An Arabic-English Lexicon* (1863–93).
,, *ME* . .	*An Account of the Manners and Customs of the Modern Egyptians* (5th ed. 1860).
Len[ormant], *Or.*	F. Lenormant, *Les Origines de l'histoire* (i–iii, 1880–84).
Levy, *Ch. Wb.* .	J. Levy, *Chaldäisches Wörterbuch über die Targumim* . . . (3rd ed. 1881).
Lidz[barski], *Hb.* or *NSEpigr.*	M. Lidzbarski, *Handbuch der nordsemitischen Epigraphik* (1898).

Löhr . . .	*Untersuchungen zum Hexateuch-problem : 1. Der Priesterkodex in der Genesis* (1924).
Lu[ther], *INS* .	See Meyer, *INS*.
Marquart . .	J. Marquart, *Fundamente israel. und jüd. Geschichte* (1896).
Meyer, *Entst.* .	E. Meyer, *Die Entstehung des Judenthums* (1896).
,, *GA*^{1} .	*Geschichte des Alterthums* (Bd. i. 1884).
,, *GA*^{2} .	,, ,, ,, (2nd ed. 1909).
,, *INS*. .	*Die Israeliten und ihre Nachbarstämme*, von E. Meyer, mit Beiträgen von B. Luther (1906).
Müller, *AE* . .	W. Max Müller, *Asien und Europa nach altägyptischen Denkmälern* (1893).
Naville . .	*Archæology of the Old Testament : Was the Old Testament Written in Hebrew ?* (1913).
,, . .	*The Text of the O.T.* (Schweich Lectures, 1915).
Nestle, *MM* .	E. Nestle, *Marginalien und Materialien* (1893).
Nö[ldeke], *Beitr.*.	Th. Nöldeke, *Beiträge zur semitischen Sprachwissenschaft* (1904).
,, *Unters.*	*Untersuchungen zur Kritik des AT* (1869).
Oehler, *ATTh* .	G. F. Oehler, *Theologie des AT* (3rd ed. 1891).
OH . . .	*Oxford Hexateuch* = Carpenter and Harford-Battersby, *The Hexateuch* (see p. xlv, *note*).
Ols. . . .	J. Olshausen.
Orr, *POT* . .	J. Orr, *The Problem of the OT* (1906).
OS . . .	See Lagarde.
P[ayne] Sm[ith], *Thes.*	R. Payne Smith, *Thesaurus Syriacus* (1879, 1901).
Peters . . .	*Early Hebrew Story.*
Petrie . . .	W. Flinders Petrie, *A History of Egypt.*
Pro[cksch] . .	O. Procksch, *Das nordhebräische Sagenbuch : die Elohimquelle* (1906).
Reuss . . .	*Gesch. der. heil. Scrift. des. AT*^{2} (1890).
Riehm, *Hdwb.* .	E. C. A. Riehm, *Handwörterbuch des biblischen Altertums* (2nd ed. 1893–94).
Robinson, *BR* .	E. Robinson, *Biblical Researches in Palestine* (2nd ed., 3 vols., 1856).
Sayce, *EHH* .	A. H. Sayce, *The Early History of the Hebrews* (1897).
,, *HCM* .	*The Higher Criticism and the Verdict of the Monuments* (2nd ed. 1894).
SBOT . . .	*The Sacred Books of the OT, a crit. ed. of the Heb. Text printed in Colours,* under the editorial direction of P. Haupt.
Schenkel, *BL* .	D. Schenkel, *Bibel-Lexicon* (1869–75).
Schr[ader], *KGF*	Eb. Schrader, *Keilinschriften und Geschichtsforschung* (1878).
,,	See *KAT* and *KIB* above.
Schultz, *OTTh* .	H. Schultz, *Old Testament Theology* (Eng. tr. 1892).

Schürer, *GJV* .	E. Schürer, *Geschichte des jüdischen Volkes im Zeitalter Jesu Christi* (3rd and 4th ed. 1898–1901).
Schw[ally] . .	Fr. Schwally, *Das Leben nach dem Tode* (1892).
,,	*Semitische Kriegsaltertümer*, i. (1901).
Sellin . .	*Introduction to the OT* (Eng. tr. 1923).
Sievers . .	*Studien zur hebräischen Metrik*, i. (1901).
Skinner . .	*Divine Names in Genesis* (1914).
Smend, *ATRG* .	R. Smend, *Lehrbuch der alttestamentlichen Religionsgeschichte* (2nd. ed. 1899).
,, . . .	*Die Erzählung des Hexateuch* (1912).
GASm[ith], *HG* .	G. A. Smith, *Historical Geography of the Holy Land* (1895).
Rob. Smith, *KM*²	W. Robertson Smith, *Kinship and Marriage in Early Arabia* (2nd ed. 1903).
,, *OTJC*²	*The Old Testament in the Jewish Church* (2nd ed. 1892).
,, *Pr.*² .	*The Prophets of Israel* (2nd ed. 1895).
,, *RS*² .	*Lectures on the Religion of the Semites* (2nd ed. 1894).
Spiegelberg . .	W. Spiegelberg, *Aegyptologische Randglossen zum AT* (1904).
,,	*Der Aufenthalt Israels in Aegypten im Lichte der aeg. Monumente* (3rd ed. 1904).
St[ade] . . .	B. Stade, *Ausgewählte akademische Reden und Abhandlungen* (1899).
,, *BTh* .	*Biblische Theologie des AT*, i. (1905).
,, *GVI* .	*Geschichte des Volkes Israel* (1887–89).
Steuern[agel], *Einw.*	C. Steuernagel, *Die Einwanderung der israelitischen Stämme in Kanaan* (1901).
,, . .	*Einleitung* (1912).
TA . . .	Tel-Amarna Tablets [*KIB*, v; Knudtzon, *Die el-Amarna Tafeln* (1908–)].
Thomson, *LB* .	W. M. Thomson, *The Land and the Book* (3 vols. 1881–86).
Tiele, *Gesch.* .	C. P. Tiele, *Geschichte der Religion im Altertum*, i. (German ed. 1896).
Tristram, *NHB* .	H. B. Tristram, *The Natural History of the Bible* (9th ed. 1898).
Welch . . .	*The Code of Deuteronomy* (1924).
We[llhausen], *Comp.*²	J. Wellhausen, *Die Composition des Hexateuchs und der historischen Bücher des AT* (2nd ed. 1889).
,, *De gent.* .	*De gentibus et familiis Judæis quæ 1 Chr. 2. 4 enumerantur* (1870).
,, *Heid.* .	*Reste arabischen Heidentums* (2nd ed. 1897).
,, *Prol.*⁶ .	*Prolegomena zur Geschichte Israels* (6th ed. 1905).
,, . . .	*Skizzen und Vorarbeiten.*
,, *TBS* .	*Der Text der Bücher Samuelis* (1871).
Wi[nckler], *AOF*.	H. Winckler, *Altorientalische Forschungen* (1893–).

Wi[nckler]. *ATU* . *Alttestamentliche Untersuchungen* (1892).
,, *GBA* . *Geschichte Babyloniens und Assyriens* (1892).
,, *GI* . *Geschichte Israels in Einzeldarstellungen* (i. ii., 1895, 1900).
,, See *KAT*³ above.
Wundt . . *Völkerpsychologie.*
Zunz, *GdV* . . Zunz, *Die gottesdienstlichen Vorträge der Juden* (2nd ed. 1892).

4. PERIODICALS, ETC.

AJSL . . . *American Journal of Semitic Languages and Literatures* (continuing *Hebraica*).
AJTh . . . *American Journal of Theology* (1897–).
ARW . . . *Archiv für Religionswissenschaft.*
BA . . . *Beiträge zur Assyriologie und semitischen Sprachwissenschaft,* herausgegeben von F. Delitzsch und P. Haupt (1890–).
BS . . . *Bibliotheca Sacra and Theological Review* (1844–).
Deutsche Litteraturzeitung (1880–).
ET . . . *The Expository Times.*
Exp. . . . *The Expositor.*
GGA . . . *Göttingische gelehrte Anzeigen* (1753–).
GGN . . . *Nachrichten der königl. Gesellschaft der Wissenschaften zu Göttingen.*
Hebr. . . . *Hebräica* (1884–95). See *AJSL.*
JBBW . . [Ewald's] *Jahrbücher der biblischen Wissenschaft* (1849–65).
JPh . . . *The Journal of Philology* (1872–).
J[*S*]*BL* . . *Journal of* [the Society of] *Biblical Literature and Exegesis* (1881–).
JQR . . . *The Jewish Quarterly Review.*
JRAS . . . *Journal of the Royal Asiatic Society of Great Britain and Ireland* (1834–).
JTS . . . *The Journal of Theological Studies* (1900–).
Lit[*erarisches*] *Zentralbl*[*att für Deutschland*] (1850–).
M[*B*]*BA* . . *Monatsberichte der königl. preuss. Akadamie der Wissenschaften zu Berlin.* Continued in *Sitzungsberichte* der k. p. Ak. . . . (1881–).
MVAG . . *Mittheilungen der vorderasiatischen Gesellschaft* (1896–).
NKZ . . . *Neue kirkliche Zeitschrift* (1890–).
OLz . . . *Orientalische Litteraturzeitung* (1898–).
PAOS . . . *Proceedings* [*Journal*] *of the American Oriental Society* (1851–).
PEFS . . . Palestine Exploration Fund : *Quarterly Statements.*
PSBA . . . *Proceedings of the Society of Biblical Archæology* (1878–).

SBBA . . .	See *MBBA* above.
SK . . .	*Theologische Studien und Kritiken* (1828–).
ThLz . . .	*Theologische Litteraturzeitung* (1876–).
ThT . . .	*Theologisch Tijdschrift* (1867–).
TSBA . . .	*Transactions of the Society of Biblical Archæology.*
ZA . . .	*Zeitschrift für Assyriologie* (1886–).
ZATW . .	*Zeitschrift für die alttestamentliche Wissenschaft* (1881–).
ZDMG . .	*Zeitschrift der deutschen morgenländischen Gesellschaft* (1845–).
ZDPV . . .	*Zeitschrift des deutschen Palästina-Vereins* (1878–).
ZKF . . .	*Zeitschrift für Keilschriftsforschung* (1884–85).
ZVP . . .	*Zeitschrift für Völkerpsychologie und Sprachwissenschaft* (1860–).

5. OTHER SIGNS AND CONTRACTIONS.

NH . .	'New Hebrew'; the language of the Mishnah, Midrashim, and parts of the Talmud.
v.i. . . .	*vide infra* } Used in references from commentary
v.s. . . .	*vide supra* } to footnotes, and *vice versa*.
*	Frequently used to indicate that a section is of composite authorship.
†	After OT references means that all occurrences of the word or usage in question are cited.
√	Root or stem.
. . .	Sign of abbreviation in Heb. words.
וגו׳. . . .	= וגומר = 'and so on': used when a Heb. citation is incomplete.

INTRODUCTION.

§ 1. *Name, canonical position, and general scope of the book.*

The Book of Genesis is the first of 'the five fifths of the Law' (חמשה חומשי התורה), *i.e.* the five sections into which the Pentateuch is divided in the Hebrew as in all other Bibles. In the English Bible it bears a twofold title: "The First Book of Moses called [RV 'commonly called'] Genesis." The first designation, which follows Luther's translation, expresses the traditional view of its authorship, but as a title has no ancient authority. In the second the name 'Genesis' comes directly from the Vulgate (*Liber Genesis*), ultimately from the Septuagint, where the usual heading is simply Γένεσις.* This name is correctly explained by Philo † as referring to the opening theme of the book, the creation of the world, as in the titles of the second and fourth books (Ἔξοδος, Ἀριθμοί). So also in Syriac (*sephrâ dabʿrîthâ*), and sometimes in Talmud and Midrash (ספר היצירה).‡ In common Jewish usage the several

---

* The commonest titles, as given in the Cambridge Septuagint, are Γένεσις (EM+13 cursives), and Γένεσις κόσμου (A, y). Among other titles, occurring but once each, we find ἡ βίβλος τῶν γενέσεων (r), which seems to be taken from 2^{4a} 𝕲 and 5^{1}, and suggests that the scribe had in view the series of *Tôlĕdôth* which commences there (see p. lxv).—Only two codd. (o, e) name Moses as the author.

† *De Abrah.*, *init.*: Τῶν ἱερῶν νόμων ἐν πέντε βίβλοις ἀναγραφέντων, ἡ πρώτη καλεῖται καὶ ἐπιγράφεται Γένεσις ἀπὸ τῆς τοῦ κόσμου γενέσεως, ἣν ἐν ἀρχῇ περιέχει, λαβοῦσα τὴν πρόσρησιν· καίτοι κτλ.

‡ Origen, in Euseb. *HE*, vi. 25: "The book which among us Christians bears the name Γένεσις is called by the Hebrews after the beginning of the book Βρησιθ"; Jerome, *Prol. gal.* and *Quæst. in Gen.*; cf. Philo above.

books of the Pent. are designated by their first words; hence Genesis is usually cited as בראשית, 'In the beginning.' *

Genesis thus forms the introductory section of the great historical and legislative work, traditionally ascribed to Moses, known as the Law (תורה), which again is the first division of the tripartite Hebrew Canon (תורה נביאים וכתובים). The *Tôrāh* must have attained canonical authority soon after its completion in the age of Ezra and Nehemiah, and certainly *before* the date of the Samaritan schism (*c.* 430 (?), 330 (?) B.C.).† Of the division into five books the earliest express notices are Philo, *De Abrah.* (see above), and Josephus, *c. Ap.* i. 29; but it is found in the Samaritan Pent. as well as the LXX, and may very well be as old as the final redaction of the Pent.‡ In the case of Genesis at all events the division is strikingly appropriate. Four centuries of complete silence lie between its close and the beginning of Exodus, where we enter on the history of a nation as contrasted with that of a family, and the centre of interest is shifted from individual biography to public and political events. This may suggest that the patriarchal traditions preserved in Genesis are of a different quality, and have a different origin from those of Exodus and the succeeding books. Be that as it may, Genesis is a complete and well-rounded whole, and except Deuteronomy there is no book of

---

* According to Blau (*Buchwesen*, p. 48), it was also called by the Talmudists and Massoretes 'The Book of the Patriarchs,' ספר הישרים, wrongly identified with ספר הישר in Jos. 10^{13}, 2 Sa. 1^{18}.

† See Ryle, *Canon of the OT*, chs. iv. v.; Wildeboer, *Origin of the Canon of the OT* [E.T.]^{2}, 27 ff., 101 ff.; Buhl, *Kanon und Text des AT*, 8 f.; Budde, art. 'Canon,' in *EB*; and Woods, 'OT Canon,' in *DB*.—The above statement takes no account of the extremely radical tendency in criticism represented by Hölscher in his *Gesch. d. isr. und jud. Religion* (1922) and other writings. He brings down the completion of the Law to the 4th cent. B.C. (p. 157) and the date of the Samaritan schism to about 57 B.C. (p. 172). Such positions are a challenge to current conceptions of the history of the Canon which must be met; but they are too remote from the purpose of this commentary, and from the standpoint from which it it written, to call for discussion here.

‡ So Kuenen, *Onderzoek*, i. pp. 7, 331; Blau, *l.c.* and most. Procksch, on the other hand, thinks the division originated among the Jews of Alexandria (*Comm.* p. 2).

the Pentateuch which lends itself so readily to monographic treatment.

From a wider point of view than that contemplated in its title Genesis may be described as the Book of Hebrew 'Origins.' In its later and longer part (chs. 12–50) it is a collection of narratives concerning the immediate ancestors of the Hebrew people, showing how they were gradually separated from the surrounding nations and became a chosen race, and at the same time how they were related to those tribes and nationalities most nearly connected with them. This is preceded (in chs. 1–11) by an account of the origin of the world, the beginnings of human history and civilisation, and the distribution of the various races of mankind. The whole converges steadily on the line of descent from which Israel sprang, and through which it became conscious of its special mission and destiny in the world. It is significant, as already remarked, that it stops just at the point where family history ceases with the death of Joseph, to give place after a long interval to the history of a nation: perhaps even more significant that it does not close without a prophetic forecast of the glorious future which awaits it under the kingdom, and beyond that the dim vision of a Messianic kingdom in which the promise will be fulfilled that through this people all nations of the earth shall be blessed (chs. 49^{8-12} 12^{3} etc.).

A. The Narrative Material of Genesis.*

§ 2. *History or Legend?*

The first question which arises with regard to these 'origins' is whether they are in the main of the nature of

* This part of the Introduction follows lines first projected by Gunkel, who initiated the synthetic method of studying the composition of Genesis. While most critical commentaries start from the book as a whole, and proceed by way of literary analysis to separate the various documents of which it is composed, Gunkel, starting from the individual story as the ultimate unit, traces the growth of legendary cycles through the amalgamation of such stories in the course of oral transmission, and finally the formation of the larger written collections into which the literary analysis had resolved the book. Each method

history or of legend *—whether (to use the expressive German terms) they are *Geschichte*, things that happened, or *Sage*, things said. There are certain broad differences between these two kinds of narration which ought to enable us to determine to which class the traditions of Genesis belong.

History in the technical sense is the written record of actual events, based as far as possible on documents contemporary, or nearly contemporary, with the facts narrated. If it deals with contemporary incidents, it seeks to transmit to posterity as accurate an account as may be of the real course of events, of their causal sequence, and their relations to time and place. If written long after the events, it endeavours by all available means to obtain authentic information regarding the circumstances of the actions described, and the character and motives of the principal actors; and thus to form a consistent objective conception of the actual occurrences free from the passions and prejudices that may have coloured the accounts of the original authorities. History, moreover, concerns itself primarily with great public affairs,—wars and conquests, the rise and fall of nations, the deeds of kings and statesmen, and such like. It is usually at a later stage of development that the impulse to veracious and disinterested narration is directed to the sphere of private and domestic life, and produces memoirs and biographies which may rank among the most valuable of historical documents.—That the Israelites, from a comparatively early period, knew how to write history in this sense we can see from many passages in the historical books of the Old Testament,—especially the long story of David's court in 2 Sa. 9–20, 1 Ki. 1, 2. There we have a graphic and circumstantial narrative of the struggles for the crown, free from bias or exaggeration, and told with a convincing realism which gives the impression of first-hand information derived from

has its advantages, and there is no reason why they should not be combined, as I have attempted to do in the following pages.

* The word 'legend' is here used in the widest sense as including all statements regarding the past which have reached us after a long period of oral tradition. 'Folk-tale' would be more accurate, but is too un-English for frequent repetition. 'Saga' (which has also been employed) is an outlandish word not easily naturalised in our language.

the evidence of eye-witnesses. As a specimen of true historical literature (as distinct from mere annals or chronicles) it has no parallel in antiquity till we come down to the works of Herodotus and Thucydides in Greece.

Quite different from historical writing of this kind is the *Volkssage*,—the mass of popular narrative *talk* about the past, which exists in greater or less profusion amongst all uncultured races. Every nation, as it emerges into historic consciousness, finds itself in possession of a store of traditional material of this kind, either circulating among the common people, or woven by bards and poets into a picture of a legendary heroic age. Such legends, though they survive the beginnings of authentic history, belong essentially to a pre-literary and uncritical stage of society, when the popular imagination works freely on reminiscences of the great events and personalities of the past, producing an amalgam in which tradition and phantasy are inseparably mingled. Ultimately they are themselves reduced to writing, and give rise to a species of literature which may readily be mistaken for history, but whose true character will usually disclose itself to a patient and sympathetic examination. And while legend is not history, it has in some respects a value greater than history. For it reveals the soul of a people, its instinctive selection of the types of character which represent its moral aspirations, its conception of its own place and mission in the world; and also, to some indeterminate extent, the impact on its subconscious life of the historic experiences in which it first woke up to the consciousness of national unity and destiny.*

Now we are not entitled to assume *a priori* that Israel is an exception to the general rule that a legendary age forms the ideal background of history: whether it be so or not must be ascertained from the evidence of its records. Should it prove to be no exception, we shall not assign to its legends a lower significance as an expression of the national spirit than to the heroic legends of the Greek or Teutonic races. It is no question of the truth or religious value of the book that we

* Comp. Gordon, *Early Traditions*, p. 84: "As a real expression of the living spirit of the nation, a people's myths are the mirror of its religious and moral ideals, aspirations, and imaginations."

are called to discuss, but only of the kind of truth and the particular medium of revelation which we are to find in it. One of the most unfortunate of theological prepossessions is that which identifies revealed truth with matter-of-fact accuracy in science and in history. Legend is after all a species of poetry, and it is hard to see why a revelation which has freely availed itself of so many other kinds of poetry—song, drama, allegory, parable—should disdain that form of it which is the most influential of all in the life of a primitive people. As a vehicle of religious ideas, poetic narrative possesses obvious advantages over literal history: the spirit of religion, deeply lodged in the heart of a nation, will so permeate and fashion its legendary lore as to make it a plastic embodiment of the imperishable truths which have come to it through its experience of God.*

The legendary character of the Genesis traditions appears in such features as these: (1) The narratives are the literary deposit of an oral tradition which, if it rests on any substratum of historic fact, must have been carried down through many centuries,—in the case of the primæval traditions through many millenniums. With regard to these last there can be no serious question of reliable historical tradition. But even in the case of the patriarchal stories, there lies between the events and the time of Moses an interval (according to the traditional chronology) of more then 400 years of which no memory has survived. Few will maintain that the patriarchs prepared written memoranda for the information of their descendants; † and the narrators nowhere profess their indebtedness to such records. Hebrew historians freely refer to written authorities where they used them (Kings, Chronicles); but no instance of this practice occurs in Genesis. Now oral tradition is the natural vehicle of popular legend, as writing is of history. And experience shows that apart from written records there is no exact knowledge of a remote past. Making every allowance for the superior retentiveness of the oriental memory, it is still impossible to suppose that an accurate recollection of bygone incidents should have survived twenty generations or more of oral transmission. Nöldeke (*Amalekiter*, p. 25 f.) has proved, indeed, that the historical memory of the pre-Islamic Arabs was so defective that all knowledge of great nations like the Nabatæans and Thamudites had been lost

---

* See Gunkel, *Schriften des AT in Auswahl übersetzt*, p. 17: "Nor will religion suffer from the conclusion that this book contains legends (*Sagen*): poetic narration is in fact much better adapted to form the vehicle of ideas, including religious ideas, than prose."

† On Naville's theory of cuneiform originals, see pp. xxxviii–xlii.

within two or three centuries.*—(2) The literary quality of the narratives stamps them as partly products of the artistic imagination. The very picturesqueness and truth to life which are sometimes appealed to in proof of their authenticity are, on the contrary, characteristic marks of legend (Di. 218). We may assume, for example, that the scene at the well of Ḥarran (ch. 24) actually took place; but that the description owes its graphic power to the remembrance of the exact words spoken and the precise actions performed on the occasion cannot be supposed: these are due to the revivifying work of the imagination of successive narrators. But imagination, uncontrolled by the critical faculty, does not confine itself to restoring the colours of a faded picture; it introduces new colours, insensibly modifying the picture till it becomes impossible to tell how much belongs to the real situation and how much to later fancy. The clearest proof of this is the existence of parallel narratives of an event which only happened once, but which emerges in tradition in different forms (*e.g.* the two accounts of the Flood in chs. 6–8; chs. $12^{10ff.}$ ‖ $20^{1ff.}$ ‖ $26^{6ff.}$; 16 ‖ $21^{8ff.}$; 15 ‖ 17; etc.).—(3) The subject matter of the tradition is of the kind congenial to the folk-tale all the world over, and altogether different from transactions on the stage of history. The proper theme of history, as has been said, is great public and political events; but legend delights in *genre* pictures, private and personal affairs, trivial anecdotes of domestic everyday life, and so forth,—matters which interest common people and come home to their daily experience. That most of the stories of Genesis are of this description needs no proof; and the fact is very instructive.† A real history of the patriarchal period would tell of migrations of peoples, of religious movements, of wars of invasion and conquest; and accordingly all modern attempts to vindicate the historicity of Genesis

* The instances cited by König (*Comm.* p. 82) of the memorising capacity of early ages—Rig-Veda, Arabic Hamâsa, Homeric poems—are examples of a trained professional memory brought to bear on the *ipsissima verba* of poetic compositions, and furnish no real analogy to the case before us. It is conceivable that in the later stages of the tradition the narratives were reproduced word for word by expert rhapsodists or story-tellers; but in the earlier stages no such professional class can have existed; while the variations in detail in parallel narratives (see below) prove that from the beginning the exact words were *not* preserved.—When König further (pp. 83, 93) protests against citing the 'descriptive pencil-strokes' of the stories as evidence of their non-historical character, he seems to me to misunderstand the position of his opponent (Gunkel). It is quite true that the historically credible element in the tradition must be sought in the broad outlines which are common to all its forms. But the 'pencil-strokes' are there, and being there they show that the narratives are legendary, and not in the literal sense history. That is all that Gunkel is contending for.

† Cf. Winckler, *Abraham als Babylonier*, p. 7.

proceed by way of translating the narratives into such terms as these. But this is to confess that the narratives themselves are not history. They have been simplified and idealised to suit the taste of an unsophisticated audience, so that the strictly historic element, down to a bare residuum, has evaporated. The single passage which preserves the ostensible appearance of history in this respect is ch. 14; and that chapter presents such a contrast to the rest of the patriarchal tradition that it only serves to throw into stronger relief the essentially legendary character of the tradition as a whole (see p. 271 ff.).—(4) The final test—though to any one who has learned to appreciate the spirit of the narratives it goes against the grain to apply it—is the hard matter-of-fact test of self-consistency and credibility. It is not difficult to show that Genesis relates incredibilities which no reasonable appeal to miracle suffices to remove. With respect to the origin of the world, the antiquity of man on the earth, the distribution and relations of peoples, the beginnings of civilisation, etc., its statements are at variance with the scientific knowledge of our time; * and no person of educated intelligence accepts them in their plain natural sense. We know that angels do not cohabit with mortal women, that the Flood did not cover the highest mountains of the world, that the ark could not have accommodated all the species of animals then existing, that the Euphrates and Tigris never had a common source, that the Dead Sea was not first formed in the time of Abraham, etc. There is admittedly a great difference in respect of credibility between the primæval (chs. 1–11) and the patriarchal (12–50) traditions. But even the latter, when taken as a whole, yield many impossible situations. Sarah was more than sixty-five years old when Abraham feared that her beauty might endanger his life in Egypt (ch. 12); she was over ninety when the same fear seized him in Gerar (17^{17}, 20). Abraham at the age of ninety-nine laughs at the idea of having a son (17^{17}), yet forty years later he marries and begets children (25). Both Midian (25^{2}) and Ishmael were grand-uncles of Joseph; but their descendants appear as tribes trading with Egypt in his boyhood (37). Amalek was a grandson of Esau (36^{12}); yet the Amalekites are settled in the south of Palestine in the time of Abraham (14^{7}). It is true that these incongruities are mostly due to an artificial chronological scheme, and disappear when the book is resolved into its separate strata. Still even in their substance the patriarchal stories occasionally betray their legendary origin by the manner in which they introduce supernatural incidents. The apparition of three divine visitants to Abraham in ch. 18, and the weird account of Jacob's wrestling with a god in $32^{24ff.}$, are narratives of profound spiritual import, but make no appeal to us as authentic historical records. Such contradictions and violations of historic probability and scientific possibility are intelligible, and not at all disquieting, in a collection of legends, while they are inconsistent with the supposition that Genesis is literal history.

* See Driver, *Gen.*[7] xxxi ff., 19 ff.

It is not implied in the position here taken up that the tradition is devoid of historic truth. History, legendary history, legend, myth, form a descending scale, with a progressive dilution of the historical element; and the lines between the first three are vague and fluctuating. In what proportions they are represented in Genesis we shall consider later (§ 6), after we have examined more fully the obviously legendary character of the oral tradition. The previous discussion will have served its purpose if it has shown that the religious message of the Book of Genesis comes to us not in the form of literal history, but through the medium of poetic legendary narratives, reflecting the beliefs and ideals by which the spiritual life of Israel was sustained at an early stage of its development.

§ 3. *Myth and legend—Foreign myths—Types of mythical motive.*

Are there myths in Genesis, as well as legends in the narrower sense? The practically important distinction between the two is that the legend does, and the myth does not, start from the plane of historic fact. The myth is originally a story of the gods, suggested by the more imposing phenomena of nature, while legend attaches itself to the personages and movements of real history. Thus the Flood-story is a legend if Noah be a historical figure, and the kernel of the narrative a real event; it would be a myth if it were based on observation of a solar phenomenon, and Noah a representative of the sun-god (see p. 180 f.). It is true that the utility of this distinction is largely neutralised by a tendency to transfer mythical traits from gods to human beings, so that the most indubitable traces of mythology will not of themselves warrant the conclusion that the hero is not a historical personage. It is nevertheless essential to the right understanding of the narratives to recognise the presence of a mythical element if such can be shown to exist.

For attempts to distinguish between myth and legend, see Tuch, pp. I–XV; Gu. p. XIV f.; Höffding, *Phil. of Rel.* (Eng. tr.), 199 ff.; Gordon, *ETG*, 77 ff.; Procksch, *NS*, 1; König, 226. Dr. Gordon distinguishes between spontaneous (nature) myths and reflective (ætiological) myths (see p. xii); and while recognising the existence of the latter in Genesis, considers that the former type is hardly represented in the OT at all. The distinction is valuable, though it seems doubtful if ætiology is ever (at least in Genesis) an independent source of myths, while as a parasitic development it attaches itself to myth and legend alike.

In ancient Israel the mythopœic impulse was from the first repressed by the monotheistic bent of its religion, and no traces of a native mythology, in the sense of stories of the gods, can be detected in its traditions. There are, however, two forms under which a mythical or semi-mythical element appears in the narratives of Genesis. (1) In filling up the prehistoric background of their national history the Hebrews were largely dependent on the traditions circulating among the more civilised peoples of antiquity (Babylonia especially); and in these traditions mythology of the most pronounced character found ample scope. This foreign influence is most apparent in the primæval traditions of chs. 1–11, where a mythical origin can be proved by direct comparison with oriental parallels, and is confirmed by slight touches of mythological thinking which survive in the biblical records. The discovery of the Babylonian versions of the Creation- and Deluge-narratives leaves no reasonable doubt that these are the originals from which the Genesis accounts are derived (see pp. 45 ff., 177 f.). A similarly close relation obtains between the ante-diluvian genealogy of ch. 5 and Berossus's list of the ten Babylonian kings who reigned before the Flood (p. 137 f.). The story of Paradise has its nearest analogies in Iranian tradition; but there are Babylonian echoes which suggest that it belonged to the common stock of Eastern mythology (p. 90 ff.). Both here and in ch. 4 a few coincidences with Phœnician tradition point to the Canaanite civilisation as the channel through which such myths came to the knowledge of the Israelites. All these (as well as the stories of the birth of the Giants in ch. $6^{1\text{-}4}$ and the Tower of Babel in ch. 11) were originally genuine myths—stories of the gods; and if they no longer answer to that description it is because the Hebrew monotheism has expelled the polytheistic conception of deity apart from which true mythology cannot exist. The few passages where a trace of polytheism still appears (1^{26} $3^{22. 24}$ $6^{1ff.}$ $11^{1ff.}$) only serve to show how completely the faith of Israel has transformed and purified the crude ideas of pagan mythology and made them the vehicle of the highest religious teaching.

The naturalisation of Babylonian myths in Israel has usually been explained by the literary school of criticism as due to the direct use of Babylonian documents, and brought down to a date near to that of our written Pent. sources.* Largely through the influence of Gunkel, a different view has come to prevail, viz. that we are to think rather of a gradual process of assimilation to the religious ideas of Israel in the course of oral transmission, the myths having first passed into Canaanite tradition during the second millennium B.C., and thence to the Israelites after their settlement in Canaan.† Although, as König rightly insists (*GATR*, 334 ff. ; *Gen.* 3 f.), the influence of Babylonian culture on Canaan has frequently been over-estimated, and although some of the arguments advanced in its favour are not conclusive, there is no doubt that the theory of progressive adaptation of foreign material in the course of oral tradition affords the best explanation both of the affinities and the differences between the Hebrew legends and their Babylonian originals. It is at all events unsafe to assume that the myths could not have been assimilated by Israelite theology before the belief in Yahwe's sole deity had been firmly established through the teaching of the prophets. Monotheism had roots in Hebrew antiquity reaching much further back than the age of written prophecy, and the present form of the narratives is more intelligible as the product of an earlier phase of religion than that of the literary prophets. We may not be able to determine the precise channels or the approximate date of this infusion of Babylonian elements into the religious tradition of Israel ; but that it took place much earlier than the dates usually assigned to the Pentateuchal documents is certainly the more probable opinion.

It is remarkable that while the patriarchal legends exhibit no clear traces of specifically Babylonian mythology, they contain a few examples of mythical narrative to which analogies are found in other quarters. The visit of the three deities to Abraham (see p. 302 f.), and the destruction of Sodom (311 f.), are incidents of obviously mythical origin (stories of the gods) ; and to both, classical and other parallels exist. The account of the births of Esau and Jacob embodies a mythological motive (p. 359), which is repeated in the case of Zerah and Perez (p. 455 f.). The whole story of Jacob and Esau presents

---

* Budde, *Urg.* (1883), 515 f. ; Kuenen, *ThT* (1884), 167 ff. ; Kosters, *ib.* (1885), 325 ff., 344 ; Stade, *ZATW* (1895), 159 f., (1903), 175 f., *BTh*, 238 ff.

† *Schöpf. u. Chaos* (1895), 143 ff. ; *Gen.*³ (1910), 72 f. ; cf. Dri. 31, *KAT*³, 560.

points of contact with that of the brothers Hypsouranios (Šamemrum) and Usōos in the Phœnician mythology (Usōos = Esau: see pp. 360, 124). There appears also to be a Homeric variant of the incest of Reuben (p. 427). These are amongst the most perplexing phenomena which we encounter in the study of Hebrew tradition (see Gu.[3] LXI f.); and we can scarcely as yet conjecture the hidden sources from which such widely diffused legends have sprung, or the channels through which they made their way into the folklore of Israel.

(2) A second form of mythical motive, very common in Genesis, is that of *ætiological* or *explanatory* myths: *i.e.* those which account for some familiar fact of experience by a story of the olden time. Both the questions asked and the answers given are frequently of the most naïve and childlike description: they have, as Gunkel says, all the charm which belongs to the artless but profound speculations of an intelligent child (*Gen*[3]. p. xx.).

The classical example is the story of Paradise and the Fall in chs. 2, 3, which contains one explicit instance of ætiology (2^{24}, why a man cleaves to his wife), and implicitly a great many more: why we wear clothes and detest snakes, why the serpent crawls on his belly, why the peasant has to drudge in the fields, and the woman to endure the pangs of child-birth, etc. (p. 95). The account of creation explains why there are so many kinds of plants and animals, why man is lord of them all, why the sun shines by day and the moon by night, etc.; why the Sabbath is kept. The Flood-story tells us the meaning of the rainbow, and of the regular recurrence of the seasons; the Babel-myth accounts for the existing diversity of language among men. The story of Jacob's wrestling tells why Israelites do not eat the sciatic nerve.—Examples of pure ætiology occur mostly in the first eleven chapters; but the general idea pervades the patriarchal history, specialised under the headings which follow.*

(*a*) The *ethnological* motive plays a considerable part in the narratives; *i.e.*, the attempt to explain the known characteristics of different tribes or nations or races, and their relations to one another, by something that happened in the distant past. Thus, the subjugation of Canaan and the wide territory of Japheth are traced back to a curse and blessing pronounced by Noah in consequence of the behaviour of his three sons on a particular occasion ($9^{22ff.}$); the insecure wandering life of a certain Bedouin tribe is explained by the fratricide which brought down the divine curse on the ancestor of the tribe ($4^{12ff.}$); the recognition of Gilead as the boundary between Israel and the Arameans by a treaty made between Jacob and Laban, and monuments set up in

* The classification, which is not quite exhaustive, is taken with some simplication from Gu.[3], p. XXI ff.

memory of it (31^{52}); Reuben's loss of the leadership in Israel by a crime committed against his father, and the sentence uttered in Jacob's dying words (35^{22} $49^{3f.}$); and so forth.—This motive is naturally grafted on to a main stock of an essentially different kind, viz. the *ethnographic legend*, which rests on a basis of historic fact, and represents real movements and relationships of tribes or nations under the guise of individual biography (see below, p. xxix). Between the two it is impossible to draw a clear line of division.

(*b*) Next comes the important class of *cult-myths*. Many of the patriarchal legends are designed to explain the sacredness of the principal national sanctuaries, while a few contain notices of the origin of particular ritual customs (circumcision, ch. 17 [but cf. Ex. $4^{24ff.}$]; the abstinence from eating the sciatic nerve, 32^{32}). To the former group belong such incidents as Hagar at Laḥairoi (16), Abraham at the oak of Mamre (18), his planting of the sacred tamarisk at Beersheba (21^{33}), Jacob at Bethel—with the reason for anointing the sacred stone, and the institution of the tithe—($28^{10ff.}$), and at Peniel ($32^{24ff.}$); and many more. The general idea is that the places were hallowed by an appearance of the deity in the patriarchal period, or at least by the performance of an act of worship (erection of an altar, etc.) by one of the ancestors of Israel. In reality the sanctity of these spots was in many cases of immemorial antiquity, being rooted in primitive forms of Semitic religion; and at times the narrative suffers it to appear that the place was holy before the visit of the patriarch (see on 12^{6}). It is probable that inauguration-myths had grown up at the chief sanctuaries while they were still in the possession of the Canaanites. We cannot tell how far such legends were transferred to the Hebrew ancestors, and how far the traditions are of native Israelite growth.

(*c*) Of less interest is the *etymological* motive which so frequently appears as a side issue in legends of wider scope. Speculation on the meaning and origin of names is fascinating to the primitive mind, and in default of a scientific philology the most far-fetched explanations are accepted. That it was so in ancient Israel could easily be shown from the etymologies of Genesis. It is just conceivable that the derivation given may occasionally be correct (though there is hardly a case in which it is plausible); but in the great majority of cases the real meaning of the name stands out in palpable opposition to the alleged account of its origin. Moreover, it is not uncommon to find the same name explained in two different ways (many of Jacob's sons, ch. 30), or to have as many as three suggestions of its historic origin (Ishmael, 16^{11} 17^{20} 21^{17}; Isaac, 17^{17} 18^{12} 21^{9}). To claim literal accuracy for incidents of this kind is manifestly impossible.

(*d*) There is yet another element which, though not mythical or legendary, belongs to the imaginative side of the narratives, and must be taken account of in interpreting them. This is the element of *poetic idealisation*. Whenever a character enters the world of legend, whether through the gate of history or through that of ethnographic personification, it is apt to be conceived as a type; and as the story passes from mouth to mouth the typical features are emphasised, while those which have no such significance tend to be effaced or forgotten. Then the dramatic instinct comes into play—the artistic impulse to perfect the story as a lifelike picture of human nature in interesting situations and action. To see how far this process was carried, we have but to compare the conception of Jacob's sons in the so-called Blessing of Jacob (ch. 49) with their appearance in the younger narratives of Joseph and his brethren. In the former case the sons are tribal personifications, and the characters attributed to them are those of the tribes they represent. In the latter, these characteristics have almost entirely disappeared, and the central interest is now the pathos and tragedy of Hebrew family life. Most of the brothers are without character or individuality; but the accursed Simeon and Levi are respected members of the family, and the 'wolf' Benjamin has become a helpless child whom the father will hardly let go from his side. This, no doubt, is the supreme instance of romantic or 'novelistic' treatment which the book contains; but the same idealising tendency is at work elsewhere, and must constantly be allowed for in endeavouring to reach the historic or ethnographic facts from which the legends start.

§ 4. *Style and form of the legends—Prose or poetry?*

In all popular narration the natural unit is the short story, which does not tax too severely the attention of a simple audience, and which retains its outline and features unchanged as it passes from mouth to mouth.* A considerable part of the Book of Genesis consists of narratives of this description—single tales, of varying length but mostly very short, each complete in itself, with a clear beginning and a satisfying conclusion. As we read the book, unities of this description detach themselves from their context, and round themselves into independent wholes; and it is only by studying them in their isolation, and each in its own light, that we can fully appreciate their beauties, and understand in some measure the circumstances of their origin. The primæval history and the history of Abraham are composed entirely of single incidents

---

* Wellhausen, *Comp. d. Hex.*[3], p. 8: "Die Ueberlieferung im Volksmund kennt nur einzelne Geschichten"; *Proleg.*[6] 334: "Die Individualität der einzelnen Erzählung ist das Wesentliche und das Ursprüngliche, der Zusammenhang ist Nebensache und erst durch die Sammlung und schriftliche Aufzeichnung hineingebracht."

of this kind: think of the story of the Fall (ch. 3), of Cain and Abel (4^{1-15}), of the Flood (6^{13}–8^{22}), of Noah's drunkenness (9^{20-27}), of the Tower of Babel (11^{1-9}); and again of Abraham in Egypt (12^{10-20}), of the flight and expulsion of Hagar (16. 21^{8-21}), of the sacrifice of Isaac (22^{1-19}), of Rebecca's betrothal to Isaac (24), etc. These no doubt differ greatly in extent, from eight to ten verses up to a lengthy chapter; but judged by modern literary standards they are all short, and, what is more important, all self-contained units. When we pass the middle of the book, however, the mode of narration begins to change. The biography of Jacob is much more consecutive than that of Abraham; though even here the separate incidents stand out in their original distinctness of outline: *e.g.* the barter of the birthright (25^{27-34}), the vision at Bethel (28), the meeting with Rachel at the well (29^{2-12}), the wrestling at Peniel (32^{24-32}), the outrage on Dinah (34), etc. It is not till we come to the history of Joseph that the principle of biographical continuity gains the upper hand. Joseph's story is indeed made up of a number of incidents; but they are made to merge into one another, so that each derives its interest from its relation to the whole, and ends (except the last) on a note of suspense and expectation rather than of rest. This may be partly due to the greater popularity and more frequent repetition of the stories of Jacob and Joseph; but at the same time it bears witness to a marked development of the art of story-telling, and one in which we may recognise some degree of literary aptitude and activity.—We have thus to distinguish two types of narrative: the *single short story*, which is the more primitive form of the tradition, and the *composite narrative*, in which several legends, either relating to the same person or similar in character, are strung together, and worked up more or less completely into a higher unity. In some narratives, however (such as ch. 24, etc.), there is a blending of the two types, so that they cannot be absolutely assigned either to the one class or to the other.

The short stories of Genesis are exquisite works of art, as unique and perfect in their kind as the parables of Jesus are in theirs. They are clearly no random productions of fireside talk, but original creations of individual genius (Gu.[3], pp. xxx, l). Their artistic distinction lies first of all in their effective use of the simplest means and the fewest possible words to produce the desired impression. The situations dealt with are all extremely simple ; there are rarely more than two persons on the stage at one time, and these persons play their parts with a convincing realism which charms and satisfies the listeners. Through the concentration of interest on a single issue each tale is rounded off into an artistic unity, and when it is finished the hearers relax their attention and feel that there is nothing more to be said. Take two examples. In ch. 22 Abraham is commanded by God to sacrifice his only son. The sympathy of the hearers is aroused by the opening announcement, and is kept on the stretch by the description of the preparations, of the three days' journey, of the dialogue between father and son, of the deliberate arrangements for the final act. At the last moment God interposes, the tragedy is averted, and Isaac is spared. They return together to Beersheba. The story is ended ; the listeners breathe a sigh of relief. Throughout there are really only two human actors, Abraham and Isaac, the two servants do not count ; the mother is not even mentioned. And how reticent the story is as to the feelings even of these two ! No word of the father's anguish ; no appeal for pity on the part of Isaac ! We see what happened : that is enough. Yet the effect, even on our minds, is overpowering.—Or again, in ch. 24 (a transitional narrative) Abraham on his death-bed wishes to procure a wife for Isaac, and sends his oldest servant on this errand to Ḥarran. We are told how wonderfully he prospered in his mission, and how he brought the bride home. In the meantime the old father has died ; Isaac takes Rebecca as his wife, and is comforted for the death of his father. That is the end. Here the *dramatis personæ* are more numerous—although as a rule, only two of them are in action at once—and there is certainly no parsimony of speech. Yet the narrative is complete in itself : it needs no previous knowledge of Abraham's history to be intelligible, and it requires no sequel.

Next to their concentrated simplicity the most characteristic feature of the short stories is their objectivity. The early narrators had little skill, and their hearers little interest, in psychological analysis. They had, indeed, a keen perception of character and emotional states, but they never describe them directly as a modern novelist would do : at most a mere word : 'he was angry' (4^{5} 30^{2} 31^{36} etc.), 'he was afraid' (26^{7} 28^{17} 32^{7} etc.), 'he loved (her) him' (24^{67} 29^{18} 34^{3} 37^{3}) etc. Character is made to reveal itself in word and action, but especially in action. They follow the dramatic rule that characterisation is subordinated to action. We are not told, *e.g.*, how Hagar felt when she was ill-treated by her mistress, but simply that she ran away (16^{6}), what Rebecca thought when she met Isaac, but that she put on her veil (24^{65}), that Lot was selfish and greedy, but that he chose the best portion ($13^{10f.}$), that Laban was dazzled by the stranger's gold, but that he effusively invited him into the house ($24^{30f.}$), and so on.—The natural vehicle for the expression of character and feeling is speech, and of this the narrators freely avail themselves, although with a reserve which at times surprises us. The long Deluge-story does not record a single word of Noah ; nothing is said by Shem,

Japheth and Canaan in $9^{18ff.}$, or by Sarah in Egypt (12^{10-20}) or Rebecca in Gerar (26); Abraham makes no reply when he is promised a son (18^{10}) or commanded to sacrifice Isaac (22^2). The general rule, (although there are exceptions) appears to be that words are only introduced when they further the action. Thus Adam and Eve are speechless when they hear their sentence, because how they feel makes no difference to their fate; on the other hand, Cain's exposulation ($4^{13f.}$) procures a mitigation of his punishment.—Where speech is necessary it is introduced with telling effect; sometimes merely for the purpose of revealing what is in the mind of the speaker, as in soliloquies (2^{18} 6^7 18^{12} 26^7). The psychology of temptation has never been more finely delineated than in the conversation between the woman and the serpent in $3^{1ff.}$.—In all this we see the effort of the narrator to let the story speak for itself. His own sympathies and judgments are rigorously suppressed; and it is rarely that a moral verdict on the conduct of the actors is indicated. This does not mean that the narratives have not a moral purpose, but only that it is not explicit. It is in the mind of the narrator, and the *rapport* between him and his audience enables the latter to divine the deeper lessons embodied in the tales.

When we pass to narratives of the second type—*i.e.* composite narratives, of which the biography of Joseph is the most perfect example—we find that the characteristics of the short story have largely disappeared. The separate scenes are no longer self-contained units (as they still are in the histories of Abraham and Jacob), but stages in a process. The incident of Joseph's temptation by his master's wife, *e.g.*, is not complete in itself, for Joseph's innocence is not established (39^{7-19}); nor is the interpretation of the dreams of Pharaoh's servants: the chief butler forgets (40^{23})! It is so throughout: everything points onward to the final *dénouement* in the reconciliation of Joseph with his brethren. Again, the compression of the short stories has given place to an extremely discursive style; speech becomes elaborate and diffuse (comp. the pleading of Judah in $44^{18ff.}$), the swift movement of the older legends is sacrificed to the principle of retardation of interest by postponement of the crisis. For this purpose scenes are duplicated—there are two visits of Joseph's brethren to Egypt, twice are valuables concealed in their sacks ($42^{25ff.}$ $44^{1ff.}$), etc.—or the same events are twice recorded, once in direct narration and again rehearsed in speech (24). These and many other features reflect the more refined taste of a later and probably a literary age, with greater gifts of expression, a wider range of thought, and a more cultivated æsthetic sense. Since the same diffuse style characterises the earliest historical writing of the OT, we may with due reserve assume that the two developments are contemporary, and assign the redaction of the Joseph-stories to the age of David or Solomon. The short stories must be very much older (Gunkel^3, p. LV).

There are a few items in the Book of Genesis to which the above characterisation does not apply: viz. curt local notices like $32^{2f.}$ $33^{18ff.}$ $35^{8.14}$ $35^{16ff.}$; and genealogies (4^{17-22} 5 10 11^{10-26} 22^{20} etc.). It seems doubtful if the genealogies ever belonged to the oral tradition at all.*

Are the legends, then, to be treated as poetry or as prose? One aspect of this question has been discussed between Gunkel and König in their respective commentaries (Gu[2] XVI, [3] XII f.; Kön. pp. 96–99). But the main issue between these two authorities is not a matter of style at all, but simply of historic literalism. Gunkel holds that legend (*Sage*) is essentially of the nature of poetry, inasmuch as its aim is not to record what actually happened, but "to delight, to elevate, to inspire, to touch." König denies this absolutely, and insists on the strict prosaic matter-of-factness of the narratives. I have already (p. vi) given my opinion on this subject, and in saying that the legends are 'a species of poetry' I mean nothing more than that the creative imagination has played a great part in their composition. Imagination is one element of poetry, but it is not the whole. Intensity of emotion and elevation of language are equally characteristic, and in these respects the stories do not even rise to the level of impassioned prose.

A much more practical question is whether the book of Genesis is written in metre. The first to suggest that this is the case was Prof. Ed. Sievers of Leipzig, whose great services to the study of Hebrew metre are universally acknowledged. After a preliminary investigation of the principles of Hebrew metre (*Studien zur hebräischen Metrik*, i. 1901), in which he laid down laws now generally accepted, he proceeded in a second series of Studies (1904–5) to resolve the whole of Genesis into verse. Now, since there are many passages of Genesis which have always been recognised as poetical, and to conform to the broad characteristics of Hebrew poetry, it is clear that if metre is found in the rest of Genesis it will be of a kind to which the ordinary rules of Hebrew prosody cannot be applied. The entire absence of parallelism, and the frequent resource to the licence of *enjambement* (beginning a clause in one verse and completing it in the next) are in opposition to two fundamental

---

* The above paragraphs are indebted to the elaborate and illuminating appreciation of the *Kunstform der Sagen* given by Gunkel in his *Comm.*[3] pp. XXIII–LVI; and more briefly in *ATA* i. pp. 23–34.

laws of poetic style in Hebrew. This is not necessarily a fatal objection to the theory; but it is a consideration which enjoins great caution in any attempt to trace poetic rhythm in Genesis. Grave misgivings are also raised by the freedom claimed in counting accented and unaccented syllables, in varying the metre, and in altering the text—a freedom which in the hands of a skilled metricist may well reduce the most refractory text to any prescribed metrical scheme. But the most serious objection to the system is that it implies a divorce between poetic form and poetic feeling and diction. Of the latter there is not a trace in what have been considered the prose parts of Genesis. Nowhere is there an ornamental expression, hardly ever a figure of a picturesque description, never a syntax which departs from the order of logical prose composition. There is no sign that the order of words is dictated by the exigencies of rhythm, or that an otiose epithet is used to fill up the rhythmic measure: all is in the simple and natural manner of prose. Of no poetry in the world, probably, could this be said; and therefore, with all deference to the distinguished scholars who accept Sievers' method, and (with reserve) his results, I think we are justified in maintaining a sceptical attitude towards both.

A tentatively favourable opinion of the work of Sievers was expressed by Gunkel in the second edition of his commentary (1902, p. XXIX f.) and by Procksch in *NIS* (pp. 210 ff.). Gunkel in his third edition (1910, pp. xxvii ff.) has now pronounced definitely against it; * while Procksch in his commentary on Genesis follows it to some extent, and holds that some parts at least of the book are metrical. But even this restricted use of the method does not appear to yield convincing results. Let us examine the first passage in which Procksch finds the metre to be regular, $3^{1-19.\ 23}$—a favourable sample of the application of the theory. This passage he divides into 31 heptameters (*Siebener*) —lines of seven accents *with movable cæsura*—the measure which Sievers considers to be the distinctive epic verse in Hebrew. Now (*a*) the counting of syllables is admittedly and unavoidably variable, and unfortunately Procksch does not give a transliteration of the text so as to show how he groups the vocables, or where he places the cæsura. But to my ear a natural scansion yields seven syllables in certainly not more than 14 of the 31 lines: sometimes only 6, more frequently 8, in one line as many as 10 or 11. (*b*) The division into lines is itself arbitrary, and in the highest degree awkward. *Enjambement* occurs

* So also König, *Gen.* pp. 28–33.

9 times: particularly harsh cases in v.[6], where עִמָּהּ is cut off from לָאִשָּׁה; in v.[7], where כִּי ends the line, and v.[15], where the line-ending comes between וּבֵין זַרְעֲךָ and וּבֵין זַרְעָהּ. The phrase 'And he said' (or the like) comes 7 times at the beginning of the line (its natural position) and 4 times at the end: a writer conscious of metre would surely have found means to avoid this incongruity. A line like this:

Then spáke God Yahwè to the wóman, What is this thou hast dóne?
And ánswered the wóman—

does not read very poetically in English, and we may doubt if it would have sounded any better in Hebrew. The nearest approach to this kind of versification I can think of in English is the rhythm of Longfellow's *Courtship of Miles Standish* (hexameters). There, no doubt, *enjambement* is frequent, but on the other hand the metre is *exact*, and the style is *not* that of ordinary prose. In fine, if this is the best that can be done on Sievers' principles by so accomplished a Hebraist as Procksch, we are almost forced to the conclusion that such rhythm is nothing but a disconcerting irrelevance to the reading of the text, and certainly an unsafe guide in textual emendation or literary analysis. Gunkel admits that there may be a prose rhythm in Hebrew (whose laws have yet to be investigated); but if that be so the theory of Sievers can only serve to put us off the track of it.

§ 5. *Preservation and collection of the legends.*

We have now seen that the narratives of Genesis have taken their present shape under the joint operation of two factors: *first*, the conscious exercise of artistic genius by individual makers, to which they owe their perfection of form; and *secondly*, the gradual and undesigned modifications which they must have undergone in the process of oral repetition. When we try to understand the relation of these two factors to each other, and to the art of writing, we are faced by a number of difficult and intricate problems, of which perhaps no final solution can be found. Does the work of the individual artist lie far back in the history of oral transmission, leaving a long interval between the first fashioning of the stories and their reduction to written form; or does it stand at the end, as the last link of the oral and the first of the written tradition? If we suppose the former to have been the case, how can we conceive the legends to have preserved their original outlines during this long interval? Were they cast adrift on the stream of popular talk, with nothing to secure their identity except the distinction of their original form, and afterwards collected from the lips of the people? Or were they taken in hand from the outset by a special class whose business it was to conserve the purity of the tradition, and under whose auspices the traditional material was moulded into its present form? And again, how is this whole process related to the use of writing? Was the work of collecting and systematising the tradition primarily a literary one, or had it already commenced at the stage of oral narration?—The complete answer to such questions must be postponed till we can approach them from the side of the critical analysis of the book; but there are some general considerations in favour of assigning a large share in the organisation of the tradition to the stage of oral transmission which may fitly be stated here. The treatment will serve to illustrate two contrasted attitudes which will probably always persist among expounders of the book of Genesis.

We shall begin with the single narratives. Judging by modern ideas it seems most natural to suppose that these owe their extant literary form mainly to the authors of the first written documents in which they found a place. Many critics, accordingly, look on these authors as men of original genius who stamped their individuality on the popular stories in the act of committing them to writing, and cast them into the finished form which they now exhibit. Others, however, think that the stories circulated orally for a long time before they came to be written, retaining their form almost unaltered through the wonderful retentiveness of the popular memory among early peoples. When we look closely at certain variants which occur in the patriarchal history we seem to find indications that the latter view contains at least a large measure of truth.

We find, for example, that the story of Hagar's separation from Abraham's household is told in two forms (chs. 16 and 21^{8-22}). The leading motives are the same in both—the origin of the Ishmaelite nation and its affinity with Israel, and the sacredness of a certain well—but in spirit and tone, as well as in details, the two narratives are markedly different (see p. 324). The differences are not such as can be naturally accounted for by deliberate literary effort to accommodate the legend to the feeling of a more refined age; they must have arisen gradually and unconsciously as the story was told again and again under changing conditions of social culture; and the perfect artistic form may in each case be due to an individual story-teller who never put pen to paper. The same impression is produced by a comparison of the three versions of the incident of the abduction of a patriarch's wife by a foreign king (12^{10-20} 20^{1-18} 26^{7-11}; see p. 364 f.). Here again there is an obvious toning down of the harsher features of the original story, which must have been accomplished slowly in the oral stage of transmission. Yet in the location of the incident at Gerar (instead of Egypt), and in the name of the king, the two later versions have retained the more primitive tradition, so that direct literary dependence of these upon the oldest seems quite impossible. It appears clear from these instances that the stories remained more or less fluid for a long time in the stage of oral narration, and were picked up by the collectors of traditional lore in different stages of their development. That finishing touches were added in the act of writing them down goes without saying.

We must look next at the process by which the legends were grouped, and try to see how far this was a literary process, and how far it may have been effected in oral tradition. There are, as already pointed out (pp. xiv-xv), three distinguishable stages in this process. The first is the loose formation of legendary cycles by stringing together related legends, as seen best in the history of Abraham. In the second stage the single episodes can still be isolated, but they tend to shade into one another, and to form a continuous history: so in the biography of Jacob. In the third stage, represented by the story of Joseph, the fusion is complete; each separate incident is subordinated to the 'plot' which gives unity to the whole. Now this process lies before us in the Book of Genesis in two parallel recensions (which by anticipation we shall call J and E); and it is a singular fact that the progressive unification of the narrative proceeds *pari passu* in the two series, being least in evidence in the story of Abraham, more advanced in that of Jacob, and practically complete in that of Joseph. It is difficult to suggest an adequate explanation of this concurrent movement towards consecutiveness of narration, and for our immediate purpose it is not necessary. There may no doubt have been many other recensions which have been lost; * but it is none the less remarkable that the only two we possess exhibit

* Hos. $12^{3, 4}$, for example, seems to refer to a somewhat different version of Jacob's wrestling at Peniel from what we read in Genesis.

this parallelism both in subject-matter and in form. Since it is on several grounds improbable (see § 8 and p. liv) that either document is directly dependent on the other, it would seem to follow that the popular tradition has been systematised, and a sort of national epic composed, at a time prior to the composition of J and E. This again implies some centralised control over the co-ordination of the narratives; for obviously no effective grouping of tradition could take place through promiscuous popular recital. By whom, or at what time, could this control have been exercised? Here we step at once into the region of conjecture. We may suppose, with Gunkel ([3], p. xxi), Kittel (*GVI*[2], p. 394 n.), and others, that there were in ancient Israel, as among the Greeks and Arabs and many ancient and modern peoples, professional story-tellers, exercising their function at festivals and other public gatherings for the instruction or entertainment of the people, that these were organised into guilds, each with its own recension of the national traditions, and that our J and E are two such recensions which have survived. But this theory does not account for the origin of the common basis which underlies both, and a collaboration of the two schools is difficult to imagine, especially if (as is commonly held) the one document emanates from Judah and the other from North Israel.—Again, we might think of the prophetic guilds, which from the time of Samuel downwards were nurseries of enthusiasm for the national cause, as the centres in which the national tradition assumed a definite shape.—Or, with Procksch (*NHS*, 392 f.) we may attribute the consolidation of the tradition to the priesthood of the central sanctuary at Shiloh; although it is surprising on that view that Shiloh is not one of the many sanctuaries whose inauguration is recorded in Genesis.—And it must be owned that none of these theories, or any other that I can suggest, quite satisfactorily explains the divergent forms in which single legends have been preserved in the two documents.

The one thing that seems to emerge with certainty from these speculations is that a long time must be allowed for the processes of collection and codification which preceded the composition of our earliest written sources. This necessarily takes us back to a very early period. It is true that the rise of anything in the nature of a national epic presupposes a strong consciousness of national unity. But in Israel the national ideal was older than its realisation in the form of a state, and therefore we have no reason for placing the systematising of the tradition later than the establishment of the monarchy. From the time of Samuel at least all the essential conditions were present, and a lower limit than that will hardly meet the requirements of the case.

At what stage the collection of the narratives became a literary process it is, of course, impossible to determine with any precision. The use of writing would be introduced gradually, first of all as an aid to the memory of the narrator; and it is unlikely that narration from memory would long survive after the art of writing became common. This was the case in the age of David and Solomon; and we may surmise that from that time the oral tradition died out, ultimately leaving the written record in sole possession of the field. The story of Joseph bears strong evidence of literary composition, and could hardly have reached its present extent and continuity through any other medium. Earlier stages of codificaton might have been brought about orally; but even there it is probable that minor collections, legendary cycles, and long single stories, had been committed to writing. In this way we may suppose that 'traditional books' * would be formed, handed down from one generation to another, annotated, expanded, revised, and copied; and thus collections resembling our oldest pentateuchal documents would come into existence.

§ 6. *Historical aspects of the tradition.*

That the traditions of Genesis contain an element of authentic history is not only possible, but antecedently probable. Legend is not necessarily fiction; and although the narratives cannot be treated as historical documents in the strict sense, it would be strange if among the varied ingredients which enter into their composition there were not some true recol-

* See Prof. Gilbert Murray, *Rise of the Greek Epic*, pp. 92 ff.

lection of events of a remote past. We have now to consider to what extent this may be actually the case.*

There are three ways in which an oral, and therefore legendary, tradition may yield solid historical results: *first*, through the retention in the popular memory of the impression caused by real events and personalities; *secondly*, by the recovery of historic (ethnographic) material from the biographic form of the narratives; and *thirdly*, through the confirmation of contemporary archæological evidence. It is convenient to take these in reverse order, and begin with †—

1. *The historical background of the patriarchal traditions.*—The period covered by the patriarchal narratives of Genesis may be put very roughly as the first half of the second millennium (2000–1500) B.C.‡ Now in the opinion of an

---

* With this whole section compare the exhaustive discussion in Kittel, *GVI*[2], i. 386–455.

† The discussion in this section is confined to the patriarchal tradition, because it is only with regard to it that the question of essential historicity arises. Every one admits that the primæval history (chs. 1–11) stands on a different footing, and very few would claim for it the authority of a continuous tradition.

‡ The upper limit depends on the generally accepted assumption, based (somewhat insecurely, as it seems to me) on ch. 14, that Abraham was a contemporary of Ḫammurabi, the sixth king of the first Babylonian dynasty. The most probable date of Ḫammurabi is *c.* 2100 B.C.; it cannot be placed later than *c.* 1950. The lower limit is determined by the Exodus, which must be assigned (if Ex. 1^{11} is genuine) to the reign of Merneptah of the Nineteenth Egyptian dynasty (*c.* 1234–1214). Allowing a sufficient time for the sojourn of Israel in Egypt, we come back to about the middle of the millennium as the approximate close of the patriarchal period. The Hebrew chronology (see Driver, *Gen.*[7] [1910] xxv ff.) gives to Abraham a date about 2100, and to the Exodus about 1490, making the residence of the patriarchs in Canaan 215 years; since, however, the chronological scheme rests on artificial calculations (see pp. 135 f., 234), we need not restrict our survey to the narrow imits which it assigns to the patriarchal sojourn in Palestine. Indeedl the chronological uncertainties are so numerous that it is desirable to embrace an even wider field than the five centuries mentioned above. Thus the Exodus is sometimes put back (in defiance of Ex. 1^{11}) to *c.* 1450 B.C. (Hommel, *ET*, x. [1899], 210 ff.; Orr, *POT*, 422 ff.); while Eerdmans would bring it down to *c.* 1125 (*Vorgesch. Isr.*, 74; *Exp.*, Sept. 1908, 204). Joseph is by some (Marquart, Wi. al.) identified with a minister of Amenophis IV (*c.* 1380–1360), by Eerdmans with

influential school of writers this period of history has been so illumined by recent discoveries that it is no longer possible to doubt the essential historicity of the patriarchal tradition.* It is admitted that no external evidence has come to light of the existence of such persons as Abraham, Isaac, Jacob, and Joseph, or even (with the partial exception of Joseph) of men playing parts at all corresponding to theirs. But it is maintained that contemporary documents reveal a set of conditions into which the patriarchal narratives fit perfectly, and which are so different from those prevailing under the monarchy that the situation could not possibly have been imagined by an Israelite of that later age. That recent archæology has thrown a flood of unexpected light on the period in question is beyond all doubt. It has proved that Palestinian culture and religion were profoundly influenced from Babylonia long before the supposed date of Abraham; that Egyptian influence was hardly less powerful; and that the country was more than once subject to Egyptian authority. It has given us a most interesting glimpse from about 2000 B.C. of the natural products of Canaan, and the manner of life of its inhabitants (*Tale of Sinuhe*). At a later time the *Tel-Amarna letters* show the Egyptian dominion threatened by the advance of Hittites from the north, and by the incursion of a body of nomadic adventurers called *Habiru* (see p. 218). It tells us that there was a place in Canaan named *Ya'kob-ēl*, and possibly another named *Yôseph-ēl*, in the first half of the 15th cent. (pp. 360, 389 f.), that *Yišir-ēl* was a tribe living in Palestine about 1500 B.C., and that Hebrews (*'Apriw*) were a foreign population in Egypt from the time of Ramses II. to that of Ramses IV.† All this is of the utmost value, and *if* the patriarchs lived in this age, then this is the background against which we have to set their biographies. But the real question

a Semitic ruler at the very end of the Nineteenth dynasty (*c.* 1205). See p. 501 f.

* Jeremias, *ATLO*, 365: "Wir haben gezeigt, dass das Milieu der Vätergeschichten in allen Einzelheiten zu den altorientalischen Kulturverhältnisse stimmt, die uns die Denkmäler für die in Betracht kommenden Zeit bezeugen."

† See Heyes, *Bib. u. Aeg.*, 146 ff.; Eerdmans, *l.c.* 52 ff.; *Exp.*, Sept. 1908, 197.

is whether there is such a correspondence between the biographies and their alleged background that the former would be unintelligible apart from the latter. One would gladly welcome evidence that this is the case; but one cannot escape the impression that the remarkable thing about these narratives is just the absence of definite background, and their compatibility with the general conditions of ancient Eastern life.* The case for the historicity of the tradition based on correspondences with contemporary evidence appears to me to be greatly overstated.

The line of argument referred to in the last paragraph is to the following effect: Certain legal customs presupposed by the patriarchal stories are now known to have prevailed (in Babylon) in the age of Ḫammurabi; these customs had ceased in Israel under the monarchy; consequently the narratives could not have been invented by legend-writers of that period (Je. *ATLO*², 355 ff.). The strongest case is the parallel supplied by Cod. Ḫamm. 146 to the position of Hagar as concubine-slave in ch. 16 (see p. 285). Here everything turns on the presumption that this usage was unknown in Israel during the regal period, and it is pressing the *argumentum e silentio* too far to assert that if it had been known it would certainly have been mentioned in the later literature. It must be remembered that Genesis contains almost the only pictures of intimate family life in the OT, and that it refers to many things not mentioned later because there was no occasion to speak of them. Twin-births, for example, are twice mentioned in Gn. and never in the rest of the OT. The fact that the custom of the concubine-slave has persisted in Mohammedan countries down to modern times warns us against such sweeping negations.—Again, we learn (*ib.* 358) that the simultaneous marriage with two sisters was permitted by ancient Babylonian law, but proscribed in Hebrew legislation as incestuous. But the law in question (Lv. 18^{18}) is late; and its enactment in the PC rather implies that the

* A striking illustration of this washing out of historical background is the contrast between the Genesis narratives and the Egyptian *Tale of Sinuhe* (translated in Gressmann's *Texte und Bilder*, from which Jeremias (*ATLO*², 298 ff.) quotes at length in demonstration of their verisimilitude. While the latter is full of graphic and detailed information about the people among whom the writer lives, the former (except in chs. 14, 34, 38) have hardly any allusions (24^{3} $37^{25f.}$) to the aboriginal population of Palestine proper. Luther (*INS*, 156 f.) has even maintained that the original J conceived Canaan as at this time an uninhabited country! Without going so far as that, we must take the facts which suggest such a view as an indication of the process of 'etiolation' which the narratives have undergone in the course of oral transmission.

practice against which it is directed survived in Israel till the time of the Exile.—The distinction between the *mohar*, or purchase-price of a wife, and the gift to the bride (*ib.*) should not be cited : the *mohar* is an institution everywhere prevailing in early pastoral societies ; its name is not Babylonian ; it is known to Hebrew jurisprudence (Ex. 22^{16}); and even its transmutation into personal service is in accordance with Arab practice (p. 383 below).* In short, it does not appear that the examples given differ from another class of usages, " die nicht spezifisch altbabylonisch sind, sondern auch spätern bez. intergentilen Rechtszuständen entsprechen, die aber . . . wenigstens teilweise eine interessante Beleuchtung durch den Cod. Ḫamm. erfahren." The 'interessante Beleuchtung' is freely admitted.

Still less has the new knowledge of the political situation in Palestine contributed to the direct confirmation of the patriarchal tradition, although it has brought to light facts which have to be taken into account in interpreting that tradition. The silence of the narratives as to the protracted Egyptian dominion over the country is remarkable, and only to be explained by a fading of the actual situation from memory in a long course of oral transmission. The existence of Philistines in the south of Palestine in the time of Abraham is an anachronism into which J but not E has fallen. On the whole it must be said that archæology has in this region created more problems than it has solved. The occurrence of the name Yaḳob-el in the time of Thothmes III., of Asher (*'J-s-rw* ?) under Seti I. and Ramses II., and of Israel under Merneptah ; the appearance of Hebrews (*Ḫabiru*) in the 15th cent., and in Egypt (*'Apriw* ?) from Ramses II. to Ramses IV., present so many difficulties to the adjustment of patriarchal figures to their original background. We do not seem as yet to be within sight of a construction which will bring these data into line with the Hebrew tradition. In time no doubt a solution will be arrived at.

From a very different point of view the essential historicity of the patriarchal tradition is maintained by Gressmann and Gunkel.† They point out that the proper *habitat* of the first three patriarchs is not Canaan itself (except in occasional notices), but the pastoral regions to the south and east of that country, beyond the pale of civilisation. There is therefore no effacing of the political background, because there was none to efface. The life depicted is that of nomads, or rather semi-nomads (Maʿāze), breeders of sheep and goats, living mostly in tents, moving within restricted areas, possessing no land, though occasionally practising husbandry (26^{12}). From the nature of their calling they were a shrewd and peaceable folk,

---

* See S. A. Cook, *Cambridge Biblical Essays*, 79 f.

† Gressmann, *ZATW*, 1910, 25 ff. ; Gunkel, *Gen.*[3] lix ff.

in contrast to the warlike spirit of the later Israel: their religion also—an El-religion—was distinct both from the Baal-religion of the Canaanites, and the Yahwe-religion of the post-Mosaic period. This manner of life is so faithfully reflected in the legends as to prove that the ancestors of Israel actually lived under such conditions. Hence it follows that the narratives preserve a true memory of the time before the occupation of Palestine, and in this way "possess great historical value."

That the patriarchal narratives embody a genuine tradition in this sense is conclusively shown by the considerations thus advanced. It is not so clear, however, that they cover the whole ground. For one thing, the picture of patriarchal life is not quite uniform. Half-nomads do not as a rule keep camels, which are peculiar to the true Bedouin; yet the wealth of Abraham and of Jacob consists largely in camels (12^{16} $24^{10ff.}$ 30^{43} 31^{17} 32^{7}). No doubt, as Gressmann says, half-nomads *might* have camels; and every one knew that they were necessary for long desert journeys; but how can we tell that the camels were not invented for that very reason? In any case, the Abraham of ch. 22, who travels with his ass and two servants, is differently conceived from the wealthy sheikh who in ch. 24 equips a caravan of ten camels for the journey to Mesopotamia.—But a more serious question is whether the ancestors of Israel were really all of them the unwarlike shepherds described in the narratives of Genesis. There are two references in the history of Jacob (chs. 34 and 48^{22}) which convey the opposite impression. Gunkel gets rid of these by assigning them to the time of the Conquest, pronouncing them to be the latest in Genesis. Kittel, on the other hand (*GVI*², i. 406 f., ii. 72), gives reasons for thinking they belong to the pre-Exodus period. Until this point is settled (see below, pp. 422, 507), it is premature to assert that the original form of the tradition is preserved in the pastoral legends of Abraham, Isaac, and Jacob. We cannot suppose that Simeon and Levi were the only belligerent tribes among the Hebrews who entered Palestine; and if the occupation was in any degree effected by force of arms, there must after all have been a very considerable effacement of historical background.

2. *Ethnographic theories.*—The second method by which it is attempted to extract history from the legends is by treating the heroes of them as personifications or eponymous ancestors of tribes or peoples, whose history and mutual relations are exhibited under the guise of personal biography. The general principle involved in this method is a sound one, and is recognised in the narratives themselves.

The pre-natal struggle of Jacob and Esau prefigures the rivalry of 'two nations' (25^{23}); Ishmael is the prototype of the wandering

Bedouin (16^{12}); Cain and Lamech of some fierce nomad tribes ($4^{15. 23ff.}$); Jacob and his sons represent the unity of Israel and its division into twelve tribes; and so on. This mode of thinking was specially congenial to Semites from their habit of speaking of peoples as *sons* (*i.e.* members) of the collective entity denoted by the tribal or national name; whence arose the notion that these entities were the real progenitors of the tribes and peoples so designated. That in some cases the representation was correct need not be doubted: there are examples among the Arabs and other races of small tribes named after their ancestor, and of larger groups named after a leader of real historic memory (Nöldeke, *ZDMG*, 1886, 158 f.). But that this is the case with all eponymous persons is quite incredible; and moreover it is never true that the fortunes of a tribe are an exact parallel to the personal history of their reputed ancestor, even if he existed.

This line of interpretation has given rise to a great variety of theories, some of which recognise, and others deny, the personality of the patriarchs. The theories in question fall into two classes: those which regard the patriarchal legends as ideal projections into the past of relations subsisting, or conceptions formed, after the final settlement in Canaan; * and those which seek to obtain from them some real historical information about the period before the Exodus. Since the former class deny a solid tradition of any kind beneath the patriarchal narratives, we may here pass them over, and confine our attention to those which do allow a substratum of truth in the legends of the pre-Exodus period.

As a fair and moderate specimen of this class of theories we may take the following from Cornill's *History of Israel*, pp. 29 ff.: Abraham was a real person, who headed a migration from Mesopotamia to Canaan about 1500 B.C. Through the successive hiving off of Moab, Ammon, and Edom, the main body of immigrants was so reduced that it might have been submerged but for the arrival of a fresh contingent from Mesopotamia under the name Jacob (the names, except Abraham's, are all tribal or national). This reinforcement consisted of four groups, of which the Leah-group was the oldest and strongest. The tribe of Joseph then aimed at the hegemony, but was overpowered by the other tribes, and forced to take refuge in Egypt. The Bilhah-group, thus deprived of its former support, was assailed by the Leah-tribes led by Reuben; but the attempt was foiled, and so Reuben lost his birthright. Subsequently the whole of the tribes were driven to seek shelter in Egypt, where Joseph took a noble revenge by

---

* So Wellh., *Prol.*[6] 319 ff. [Eng. tr. 318 ff.], *Isr. u. jüd. Gesch.* 11 ff.; Stade, *GVI*, i. 112 ff., *ZATW*, i. 112 ff., 347 ff.

allowing them to settle by its side in the frontier province of Goshen.*

It will be seen that the construction hangs mainly on two ideas: *tribal affinities*, typified by various phases of the marriage relation, and *migrations*. As regards the first, we have seen that there is a true principle at the root of the method. If two eponymous ancestors are represented as twin brothers, we may be sure that the peoples they stand for were conscious of very close affinity. If a male eponym is married to a female, we may presume that the two tribes were amalgamated. If one clan is spoken of as a wife and another as a concubine, we may conclude that the latter was somehow inferior to the former. But beyond a few simple analogies of this kind (each of which, moreover, requires to be rigorously tested) the method ceases to be reliable; and the attempt to apply it to all the family relationships of the patriarchs would only lead to confusion. The idea of *migration* is still less trustworthy. Certainly not every journey recorded in Genesis (*e.g.* that of Joseph from Hebron to Shechem and Dothan ($37^{14ff.}$) can be explained as a migratory movement. Even when the ethnographic background is certain, the personal journeys may be merely corollaries of the relations between the tribes (*e.g.* Jacob's to Ḥarran, p. 357). The case of Abraham is no doubt a strong one; for if his figure has any ethnographic significance at all, his Exodus from Ḥarran (or Ur) can hardly be interpreted otherwise than as a migration of Hebrew tribes from that region. We cannot feel the same confidence with regard to Joseph's being carried down to Egypt: it is extremely improbable that this has anything to do with an enforced movement of the tribe of Joseph in advance of the rest (see p. 441).

When we pass from genealogies and marriages and journeys to pictorial narrative the breakdown of the ethnographic method becomes complete. The obvious truth is that no tribal relationships can supply an adequate motive for the wealth

---

* Luther (*ZATW*, 1901, 36 ff.) gives a conspectus of four leading theories (Wellh., Stade, Gunkel, Cornill). To these might be added Steuernagel, *Einwanderung d. Isr. Stämme*; Peters, *Early Hebrew Story*, 45 ff.; Procksch, *NHS*, 330 ff.; Kittel, *GVI*², i. 442 ff.

of detail that meets us in the richly coloured patriarchal legends; and the theory stultifies itself when it assigns ethnological significance to incidents which originally had no such meaning. Each writer selects those features which fit into his own system, and neglects those which would embarrass it. Each system may have some plausible and attractive points; but each, to avoid absurdity, has to exercise a judicious restraint on the application of its principles. The consequence is endless diversity in detail, and little agreement even in general outline.*

It is evident that these constructions can never reach a satisfactory result unless they find support in the history of the period as known from contemporary sources. The second millennium B.C. is believed to have witnessed one great movement of Semitic tribes to the north, viz. the Aramæan. About the middle of the millennium we find notices of the Aramæans as nomads in what is now the Syro-Arabian desert. Shortly afterwards the Ḫabiru make their appearance in Palestine. It is a natural conjecture that these were branches of the same migration, and that we have here the explanation of the tradition which affirms the common descent of the Hebrews and Aramæans. The question then arises whether we can connect this fact with the patriarchal tradition, and if so with what stratum of that tradition. Abraham is excluded by the chronology, unless (with Corn.) we bring down his date to *c.* 1500, or (with Steuer.) regard his migration as a traditional duplicate of Jacob's return from Laban. But if Jacob is suggested, we encounter the difficulty that he must have been settled in Canaan several generations before the age of the Ḫabiru (see below, p. 218). In the case of Abraham there may be a conflation of two traditions—one tracing his nativity to Ḥarran and the other to Ur; and it would thus be conceivable that he is the symbol of two migrations, one of which might be contemporaneous with the arrival of the Ḫabiru, and the other might be as early as the age of Ḫammurabi. But these are speculations no whit more reliable than those dealt with above. We may hope that further discoveries will bring to light facts which may enable us to decide more definitely than is possible

---

* Guthe (*GVI*, 1–6) has formulated a set of five rules which he thinks can be used with tact in retranslating the genealogical phraseology into historical terms. There is probably not one of them which is capable of strict and general application.—What Grote has written about the allegorical interpretation of the Greek legends can be applied word for word to these theories: "The theorist who adopts this course of explanation finds that after one or two simple and obvious steps, the way is no longer open, and he is forced to clear a way for himself by gratuitous refinements and conjectures" (*Hist. of Greece*, ed. 1888, p. 2).

at present how far the patriarchal tradition can be explained on ethnographic lines.

To the whole class of theories considered above (those which try to go behind the Exodus) Luther (*ZATW*, 1901, 44 f.) objects that they demand a continuous occupation of Palestine from the time when the legends were formed. He hints at a solution which has been adopted in principle by Meyer (*INS*, 127 ff., 415, 433), and which has much to recommend it. It is that two independent accounts of the origin of the nation are preserved: the Genesis-tradition, carrying the ancestry of the people back to the Aramæans, and the Exodus-tradition, which traces the origin of the nation no higher than Moses and the Exodus. There are indications that in an earlier phase of the patriarchal tradition the definitive conquest of Canaan was attributed to Jacob and his sons (chs. 34. 38. 48^{22}); on Meyer's view this does not necessarily imply that the narratives refer to a time subsequent to Joshua. A kernel of history may be recognised in both strands of tradition on the assumption (not in itself a violent one) that only a part of Israel was in Egypt, and came out under Moses, while the rest remained in Palestine. The extension of the Exodus-tradition to the whole people was a natural consequence of the consolidation of the nation under David; and this again might give rise to the story of Jacob's migration to Egypt with *all* his sons.

3. *The patriarchs as historical figures.*—We have now to inquire how far the patriarchal tradition has preserved the memory of real persons and events whose intrinsic significance made an indelible impression on the mind of the people. After what has been said, it is vain to expect that more than a *nucleus* of historic fact can be recovered from popular tales current in the earliest period of the monarchy. It is not unreasonable, however, to believe that such a historic nucleus exists, and is the point round which the mass of ethnographic and other material has crystallised. Indeed, so far as the narratives are in the strict sense *legends* (see p. v), this is their essential characteristic, that they conserve the tradition of actual occurrences.*

* Cf. Höffding, *Phil. of Rel.* 199 ff.: "Its essence [that of legend] consists in the idea of a wonderful personality who has made a deep impression on human life—who has excited admiration, furnished an example, and opened new paths. Under the influence of memory, a strong expansion of feeling takes place: this in turn gives rise to a need for intuition and explanation, to satisfy which a process of picture-making is set in motion. . . . In legends . . . the central interest is in the subject-matter, in the centripetal power, which depends on an intensification of memory rather than on any naïve personification

For the sake of brevity the discussion must here be concentrated on (*a*) the personality of the patriarchs, and (*b*) their historical and religious significance.

(*a*) We may take it as a safe maxim that tradition does not invent names. On any view we have to account for the entrance of such figures as Abraham, Isaac, Jacob, and Joseph into the world of Hebrew legend; and certainly one possible avenue of entrance is that they were real men, who lived and were remembered. What alternative explanations can be given? There are three that have been advocated:

i. That they are eponymous names of tribes, either extant in historical times or extinct. We have already seen that in principle this is an admissible theory, and that it contains an element of truth. But we have also seen that even where it is true it does not exclude the possibility that the eponymous heroes were real individuals, after whom the tribes were named. We shall consider presently which view is the more probable in the case of the Hebrew patriarchs.

ii. That the names were originally those of deities, who have been degraded to the rank of human heroes. The idea that these deities were creations of native Hebrew mythology (Goldziher) is now quite abandoned; and although the opinion is still held that they were borrowed from the Canaanites (Meyer, al.) or Babylonians Winckler, al.), it rests on such precarious speculations that we need not examine it here (see below).

iii. A third explanation has recently come into vogue, under the influence of Wundt's theory, that the primitive folk-tale (*Märchen*) is the original form of all mythological and legendary narrative.* This principle is applied to the patriarchal stories of Genesis by Gressmann and Gunkel † in a way that is best illustrated by an example. Thus, according to Gressmann (*l.c.* 9 ff.), the kernel of the Abrahamic legend is a *Märchen* embodying the motive of the *entertainment of the disguised deity*, of which several parallels are known (see Gunkel, *Gen.*[3] 193 f.). This primitive story, which has its home everywhere and nowhere, is fixed down to a particular locality (Hebron) and a particular person (Abraham), and thus becomes a legend (*Sage*); and then attracts to itself other legends formed in a similar manner, and associated with the same personal name. So with the Jacob-Esau,

---

and colouring. . . ."—Also Winckler, *KAT*[3], 204: "Es ist nämlich immer wahrscheinlicher, dass ein grosses für die Entwicklung des Volkes massgebend gewordenes Ereigniss in seiner Geschlossenheit dem Gedächtniss besser erhalten bleibt als die Einzelheiten seines Herganges."

* *Völkerpsychologie*, ii. 3. 1–592.

† Gressmann, *ZATW*, 1910, 1–34; *Gunkel Festschrift* (1923), 1–55; Gunkel, *Preussische Jahrbücher*, 1919; *ZDMG*, lxxvi.

Jacob-Laban, and Joseph narratives. In the original *Märchen*, however, these names had no historic significance: they were simply chosen at random from those familiar to the people, like 'Hans' and Grete,' and 'Mary had a little lamb.' Afterwards, when a considerable number of legends had gathered round a few names, they came to be regarded as the ancestors of Israel and the neighbouring peoples. Now it is just this process of grouping the stories round a few personal names that the theory fails to explain. That material of the kind described enters into the patriarchal tradition must be freely admitted; but that the whole tradition can be dissolved into *Märchen*-types must be as firmly denied. In the first place, there is no evidence that names like Abraham, Isaac, Jacob, and Joseph were as familiar in ancient Israel as Hans and Friedrich among the Germans, or James and Mary with us. And further, it is overlooked that stories of the kind in question tend inevitably to attach themselves to persons of historic importance (see Kittel, *GVI*, 423 ff.). How insecurely the theory is based is shown by the fact that Gressmann, who in 1910 was convinced that Joseph was nothing more than the hero of a *Glücksmärchen* (p. 18), now holds (in 1923) with equal confidence that he is an historic personage, a political leader who formed the confederacy called after him "the house of Joseph" (p. 5). Eissfeldt also (*Gunkel Festschrift*, 56 ff.) maintains in opposition to his master, Gunkel, that in the Jacob legends the ethnographic idea is fundamental and the "novelistic" element secondary: in other words, that Jacob is primarily the personification under another name of the people of Israel. As an explanation of the name Jacob he suggests tentatively that it may have been a political nickname for Israel, like the German Michael or the English John Bull. He does not say what he makes of the place-name *Yaḳob-el* in the list of Thotmes III.

The philological and archæological evidence bearing on the significance of the patriarchal *names* may be summarised as follows: (1) Isaac, Jacob, and Joseph form a class by themselves. (α) In spite of the dissent of König (p. 560 f.), all analogy is in favour of the view that they are abbreviations of *Yiẓhaḳ-el*, *Ya'aḳob-el*, and *Yôseph-el* (cf. *Yiphtaḥ* and *Yiphtaḥ-el*, etc.). Names of this type are exceedingly common in Hebrew, and also among the West-Semitic personal names of the Ḫammurabi period in Babylonia (see Ranke, in *ZATW*, 1910, 6 f.). Etymologically they are explicable only as verbal sentences with *El* as subject (e.g. *Yiẓhaḳ-el*='God laughs,' not 'the laughing God'). This point is decisive against the view that they were originally divine names. (β) Such names frequently denote tribes. This is certainly the case with Joseph; and the name *Ya'aḳob-el* in a list of place-names in Palestine of the time of Thotmes III. (*c.* 1490) shows that it must have been true of Jacob also. But Jacob (*Yaḳubum*, *Yaḳub-el*, *Yaḫḳub-el*) occurs some six times as a personal name in Babylonian contract-tablets of the time of Ḫammurabi. Now it is difficult to say whether it is more probable that the individual was named after his tribe, or the tribe after a famous individual; but it is at least true that in the majority of cases the names are more intelligible as applied in the first instance to individuals than to tribes.—(2) The name Abr(ah)am stands by itself. It represents no ethnological entity, and occurs historically only as a personal name. The solitary (possible) allusion to the biblical Abram in the monuments (see p. 244) is entirely consistent with this acceptation. *Abram* is commonly identified with *Abiram*, occurring twice as an individual name in the OT, probably a theophorous (certainly not a divine) name. The identification seems to be rendered questionable by the form *Abaram* (*A-ba-am-ra-am, A-ba-ra-ma, A-ba-am-ra-am*) as a pure Babylonian (not West Semitic) name of the time of Ammizaduga (244), which, however, only strengthens the proof that it is a personal name. On the form *Abraham* see again p. 244 : here I venture to add the conjecture that if *râma*=רחם, אברהם may be an intermediate softening of the guttural.—The balance of evidence, therefore, is adverse to the mythological and ethnographic theories : as to its bearing on the *Märchen*-theory, everything depends on the unproved assumption that these names were common at the time when the *Märchen* were passing into the form of *Sagen*.

(*b*) The idea enshrined in the patriarchal tradition would seem to be the conviction in the mind of Israel that as a nation it originated in a great religious movement,—that the divine call which summoned Abraham from his home and kindred introduced a new era in God's dealings with mankind, and gave Israel its mission in the world (Is. $41^{8f.}$). We have now to ask, Is this conception historically credible ?

We may answer, in the first place, that if Abraham had the miportance thus assigned to him, the fact is just of the kind that might be expected to impress itself indelibly on a tradition dating from the time of the event. We have in it the influence of a great personality, giving birth to the consciousness of a nation ; and this fact is of a nature to evoke that centripetal 'intensification of memory' which Höffding emphasises as the distinguishing mark and preserving salt of legend as contrasted with myth and *Märchen*. In the second place, we can say that the appearance of a prophetic personality, such as Abraham is represented to have been, is a phenomenon with many analogies in the history of religion. The ethical idea of God which is at the foundation of the religion of Israel could only enter the world through a personal organ of revelation. There is little force in the common argument that the mission of Moses would be unintelligible apart from that of Abraham ; but on the other hand we have no reason to doubt the statement that Moses came to his countrymen in the name of the God of their fathers, and therefore built on the foundation laid by Abraham. Nothing, in short, forbids us to see in Abraham the first of that long series of prophets through whom God communicated to Israel the knowledge of Himself. Nor is there anything in the religion of Abraham which the mind of an early age could not grasp.* The keynote of his piety is faith in the unseen,—faith in the divine impulse which drove him forth to a land which he never possessed, faith in the future of the religion through which all nations were to be blessed. He moves before us on the page of Scripture as the man through whom faith, the living principle of true religion, became a force in human life. It is difficult to think that so great a conception grew out of nothing. As we read the story, we may well trust the instinct which tells us that here we are face to face with an act of the living God in history, and an act whose significance was never lost in Israelite tradition.†

The significance of the Abrahamic migration in relation to the general movements of religious thought in the East is dealt with in the first part of Winckler's pamphlet, *Abraham als Babylonier, Joseph als Aegypter* (1903). The elevation of Babylon, in the reign of Ḫammurabi, to be the first city of the empire, and the centre of Babylonian culture, meant, we are told, a revolution in religion, inasmuch as it involved the deposition of Sin, the old moon-god, from the supreme place in the pantheon in favour of the 'Deliverer Marduk,' the tutelary deity of Babylon. Abraham, an adherent of the older faith, opposed the reformation; and after vainly seeking support for his protest at Ur and Ḫarran, the two great centres of the worship of Sin, migrated to Canaan, beyond the limits of Ḫammurabi's empire, to worship God after his fashion. This brilliant theory appears to rest mostly on a combination of things that are not in the Bible with things that are not in the monuments. The only positive point of contact between the two data of the problem is the fact that the Biblical tradition does connect Abraham with two chief centres of the Babylonian worship of the moon-god. But what we chiefly desiderate is some evidence that the cult of Sin had greater affinities with monotheism than the cult of Marduk, the god of the vernal sun.—To a similar effect Jeremias,

---

* Gunkel affirms it to be "certain" that legend is not in a position to preserve for so many centuries a conception of the personal piety of Abraham (p. LXXIX). And yet he believes that legend *did* preserve a trustworthy memory of the religion of the patriarchal period (p. LX f.). Why should the one be more incredible than the other?

† Comp. Procksch, *Gen.*, pp. 519 ff.

*ATLO*², 327 ff.: "A reform movement of protest against the religious degeneration of the ruling classes" was the motive of the migration (p. 333), perhaps connected with the introduction of a new astronomical era, the Taurus-epoch (which, by the way, had commenced nearly 1000 years before! cf. p. 66). The movement assumed the form of a *Hegira*, under Abraham as Mahdi, who preached his doctrine as he went, making converts in Ḥarran, Egypt, Gerar, Damascus, and elsewhere, finally establishing the worship of Yahwe at the sanctuaries of Palestine.—This is to rewrite the Abrahamic legend, in a sense considerably different from the old.

On Naville's Theory of Cuneiform Originals.—The archæological argument for the historicity of Genesis has recently assumed a remarkable form in the hands of the eminent Egyptologist Prof. Ed. Naville, who has propounded a theory of the origin of the Pentateuch by which he claims to have cut the ground from under the feet of the 'Higher Critics.' Briefly stated, the theory is as follows.* When Abraham left Babylonia for Canaan, to find freedom of worship for the religious sect of which he was the head, he naturally took with him the religious books which such a sect must have possessed. These books must have been written on baked clay tablets in the literary language of Babylonia, and in the cuneiform character. Six of these tablets are preserved in the Book of Genesis, corresponding to (1) ch. 1^{1}–2^{4a} (Creation of Heaven and Earth); (2) 2^{4b}–5^{1a} (Creation of Man, Paradise, The Fall, Cain and Abel, etc.); (3) 5^{1b}–6^{9a} (Generations of Men as far as Noah); (4) 6^{9b}–9^{29} (The Deluge, etc.); (5) 10^{1-32} (Posterity of Noah); (6) $11^{1ff.}$ (Tower of Babel and Genealogy of Abraham). These six were partly copied, partly rewritten, by Moses, but remained separate till the time of Ezra. The rest of Genesis consists of recollections preserved and partly put in writing by Abraham's descendants, until Moses collected and rewrote them.† With the Book of Exodus the events begin of which Moses was a witness, and the remainder of the Pent. he wrote himself—still, of course, in Babylonian cuneiform. In the form of disconnected tablets the records remained till Ezra arranged them in their present order, at the same time translating them into the Aramaic language and script. Lastly, "the Rabbis" (we are not told who or when), desiring to give a national character and appearance to their sacred books, translated them from Aramaic into what we call Hebrew, which was simply the vernacular of Jerusalem, although (strangely enough) it was also the idiom spoken by their

---

* *Archæology of the Old Testament: Was the OT written in Hebrew?* (1913); *The Text of the OT* [Schweich Lectures, 1915]; Articles in *Revue de Theologie et de Philosophie*, Sept., Oct., 1916, and *Revue de l'histoire des religions*, 1918; *The Higher Criticism in relation to the Pentateuch* [Eng. tr. by Prof. J. R. Mackay, 1923]. See a review of the last-named work by S. A. Cook in *JTS*, July 1924, pp. 432 ff.

† So *Archæology*, p. 55. In the Schweich Lectures the author has advanced to the surmise that Abraham kept a secretary who recorded events at the time.

ancestors Abraham, Isaac, and Jacob. For this purpose they altered the Aramaic characters sufficiently to form a new script which might stand by itself and might be called their own.

It will be seen that all this is pure conjecture, unsupported by a single scriptural statement or a single fact of archæology. The only question is whether it is reasonable conjecture, based on reliable data or inference from known facts. M. Naville repeatedly informs us that his whole theory rests on two important archæological discoveries made in Egypt: the discovery (in 1888) at Tel Amarna of Babylonian tablets belonging to the 14th cent. B.C.; and the discovery (in 1904) at Elephantine of Aramaic papyri of the 5th cent. B.C. No critic has ever hesitated to recognise the importance of these dis coveries; although certainly no critic will accept Naville's deductions from them. From the Tel Amarna correspondence he infers that Babylonian was the literary language of Palestine (as of the whole of Western Asia) at the time they were written (and indeed for centuries before). Now by a 'literary language' Naville means a language such as book-English is to a community speaking the Scottish dialect—a written language intelligible to common people, but not used by them in ordinary intercourse. That the language of the tablets was not the literary language of Palestine in that sense is proved by numerous glosses inserted to explain a Babylonian word by its native equivalent. When such words as 'perish,' 'behind,' 'ship,' 'belly,' 'mountain,' 'remember,' 'arm,' 'living,' 'kill,' 'horse,' 'official,' 'sheep,' 'field,' 'gate,' * require explanation in this way (in each case by a word closely resembling Hebrew, and in most cases utterly unlike its Babylonian equivalent) it is clear that the scribes are writing a foreign language. What the tablets do reveal is that the Babylonian language was the medium of diplomatic correspondence, conducted by trained officials, at the petty courts of Palestine, just as was the case, by Naville's admission, at the court of Egypt. The same explanation applies to the (probably contemporary) cuneiform tablets found at Ta'anak, and also to a fragment of a letter discovered at Lachish. The two contract tablets found at Gezer stand on a different footing. They belong to the middle of the 7th cent., the reign of Asshurbanipal, who is known to have settled Assyrian colonists in the cities of central Palestine (Ezr. 4^{10}). The appearance of cuneiform writing under these circumstances is nothing surprising. (There was also discovered at Gezer a Calendar-Inscription, written in Hebrew and in the so-called Phœnician alphabet. M. Naville asserts that this is not Jewish!).—So again, from the Elephantine papyri Naville draws the sweeping conclusion that Aramaic was the literary and popular language of Palestine at the time when these Jewish colonists migrated to Egypt. That this is incorrect is proved by 2 Ki. 18^{26}, which clearly shows that Aramaic was not understood by the populace of Jerusalem in the days of Hezekiah and Isaiah. It also proves that Naville is wrong in his belief that the prophets wrote in the Aramaic language and

---

* See *KAT*³, p. 652.

alphabet. The prophetic writings are as a rule reproductions or digests of their spoken discourses, and must therefore have been in the language understood by the people, which was *not* Aramaic. That they were not in the Aramaic script follows from the fact that, so far as is known, the Aramaic script was not then in existence.

Here it is necessary to examine some of M. Naville's peculiar views on the history of the Semitic alphabet. His opinion that that alphabet was unknown in the time of Moses is one that can neither be proved nor disproved. It is true that the so-called Phœnician or Old Hebrew form of it first appears in the 9th cent. on the Moabite stone, and the nearly contemporary *ostraka* of the time of Omri and Ahab, discovered at Samaria; both of which Naville considers to be due to Phœnician influence at the Israelite court. He never mentions the fact that there is a South-Semitic form of the alphabet (found on Arabian inscriptions) which is not lineally descended from the Phœnician, but nevertheless springs from the same origin. We do not know when this script was introduced into Arabia; but Prætorius thinks it may have been about 1200 B.C. or even earlier. Moreover, there has recently been discovered in the Sinaitic peninsula an ancient writing in which expert epigraphists think they can recognise a transition from the Egyptian to the Old Hebrew alphabet. It is therefore quite possible that some form of Semitic script was known to the *literati* of Egypt in the time of Moses (see also the argument of Kittel in *GVI*², i. p. 179).—Naville, however, holds that the Phœnician alphabet was known in Israel from the time of Solomon, though he will not allow that it was ever used in Judah for literary purposes, or at any rate for sacred books. Why? Because, being of heathen origin and the script of the hated Samaritans, it must have been shunned by all piously disposed writers in Judah! Hence when they discarded the old cuneiform they were obliged to adopt the Aramaic alphabet. Now the Aramaic type of the alphabet is itself a late development from the Phœnician, of which there are no traces in Palestine till near the Christian era.* The Aramaic inscriptions found at Zinjirli (8th cent.: therefore contemporary with the first writing prophets) are written in a character indistinguishable from that of the Moabite stone; and there are only slight differences in the Aramaic dockets to cuneiform documents, and inscriptions on Assyrian weights, belonging to the following century. The earliest known traces of the distinctively Aramaic type of writing are found in Egypt in the 5th cent. (Saqqarah stele and Elephantine papyri). From that time its development can be traced in a series of inscriptions which show a gradual approximation to the square alphabet in which the Hebrew Bible is now written (see Driver, *Sam.*,

* Naville appears to think it is an independent development from the cuneiform. In *The Higher Criticism*, p. 98, we read: "The Aramaic *language*, which appears to be evolved from the cuneiform, comes to light in the eighth century in countries where people had, before then, always witnessed the cuneiform." There 'language' must surely be a mistake for 'alphabet' or 'script.'

pp. xii–xxiii). Hence we must conclude that if Judean writers, for any purpose whatsoever, used any other script than the cuneiform it must have been the old Hebrew alphabet, in which it has always been held that the older parts of the OT were written. That it was actually written in that character is proved not only by the Samaritan Pentateuch (regarding which Naville holds a view which no critic will accept), but also by a curious fact which he does not mention. Origen tells us that in accurate MSS the divine name יהוה was written in archaic characters unlike those in use in his own day, adding that Ezra was believed to have changed the character after the Exile. The first of these statements has been strikingly confirmed by the discovery of fragments of the literal Greek translation of Aquila, in which the tetragrammaton is regularly written in a corrupt form of the Old Hebrew alphabet (see Burkitt, *Fragments of the Books of Kings in Aquila's Translation*). How can this be explained except as a survival from MSS wholly written in that characer? That Aquila of all men should have gone out of his way to borrow from 'the hated Samaritans' the letters of the divine name is a preposterous notion which no man of sound judgment can possibly entertain.

These observations are confined to the archæological substructure of M. Naville's speculations, and I believe they are enough to show that it breaks down at every point where it can be brought to the test of facts. Space prevents me from following him into the region of Old Testament criticism, where he often betrays his ignorance of critical positions, and attributes to individual scholars opinions of which they are quite innocent. We see how he proposes to cut the ground from under the feet of the higher critics. He has devised a theory which condemns them to work on a translation at two removes from the original; which obliterates at one stroke all those nice philological and literary distinctions on which their analysis depends; while it explains the contradictions which they point out by the arrangement of tablets which were at first separate and independent. What advantage such a theory possesses over the construction of the higher critics for defenders of the authority of Scripture like Prof. Mackay is not very apparent. But at all events the Hebrew Bible is a fact, and the cuneiform tablets have as yet no existence except in the imagination of M. Naville. And even if it were only a translation, the literary and philological distinctions are there, and have to be explained. Varieties of style in the OT have been admitted by Naville (under pressure), and he accounts for them by the idiosyncrasies of different translators from the Aramaic into the Hebrew. Every Hebrew scholar knows that that is an absurdly inadequate explanation; but such as it is, M. Naville cannot refuse us permission to apply it within the Pent. as he is prepared to apply it without. And when we find, for example, that in the fourth of his imaginary tablets (the story of the Flood) there are two strands of narrative marked by as great diversity of style as exists between almost any two OT writers, what are we to conclude? "Each tablet," says Naville, "cannot be a mosaic of authors living at an interval of several centuries." No! But still less can the contents of the supposed tablet be the work of two translators rendering alternate paragraphs, verses, half-verses, each in his own style. The only possible conclusion is that there never was a tablet at all.

There is one fundamental assumption of the theory to which I must advert in closing. It is a sound principle which M. Naville lays down when he says that a book must be accepted as the work of its professed author until the contrary is proved. Who then is the professed author of the Pent.? That Genesis is anonymous Naville admits, but he asserts that the Pent. as a whole, of which Genesis is a part, expressly claims Mosaic authorship. As a matter of fact it nowhere professes to have been written by Moses. It mentions certain items which were written by Moses (Ex. 17^{13} 24^{7} 34^{27}, Nu. $17^{2f.}$ 33^{2}); in particular it states that he wrote the law of Deuteronomy (Dt. 31^{22}) and put it by the side of the ark ($31^{24ff.}$). These statements may be historically true or they may not: the question is not whether Moses wrote certain things, but whether he wrote the statements that he did so. Since he is always spoken of in the third person, the natural inference surely is that he wrote just what he is said to have written and no more. Naville acknowledges that Moses did not write the account of his own death. He can hardly be blind to the possibility that the person who wrote that may have written all else that we read about Moses in the third person.

B. Structure and Composition of the Book.*

§ 7. *The Critical Analysis.*

That the Book of Genesis is a composite work is now so generally recognised that it would be hard to name a writer of importance who denies it. The current theories of its composition are indeed endlessly varied; but, from Naville with his cuneiform tablets at one extreme to Eerdmans with his polytheistic and monotheistic editions at the other, they all admit some kind of diversity in the structure of the book. There is only one theory, however, which has been slowly built up by the labours of successive generations of scholars, which can claim for its main outlines anything like a consensus of opinion at the present time. In its recent forms it is usually known as the Graf-Wellhausen hypothesis of the composition of the Pent., and since it is the view adopted in this commentary it is necessary to give some account of its

* See note on p. iii.

history here. The theory has reached its present form through four well-marked stages.

i. The first positive clue to the composition of Genesis was the discovery by Astruc * in 1753 that the alternation of the divine names אלהים and יהוה marks a division of a great part of Genesis into two documents (*mémoires* written respectively by an *Élohiste* and a *Jéhoviste.* This discovery, adopted and put on a broader basis of stylistic and material observations by Eichhorn, initiated the *First Documentary Hypothesis.* Eichhorn carried the analysis as far as Ex. 2, but stopped there because, on the traditional assumption of the Mosaic authorship (or editorship), he did not expect to find traces of compilation in the history of Moses' own time. We shall see later that there is a more important reason why this particular clue to the analysis could not be carried farther than the early chapters of Exodus.

ii. The next stage, the *Fragmentary Hypothesis,* seems at first sight to be a retrograde step; but it contained an element of truth, and served a good purpose by bringing the whole of the material under review. Extending the investigation into the other books of the Pent., Geddes (1792–7) and Vater (1802–26) were so impressed by the multifariousness of their contents that they resolved the whole Pent. into a number of separate sections which could not be shown to have any original connection with one another.

iii. From this temporary aberration (if it may be called so) criticism was recalled by the maiden work of Ewald, *Die Komposition der Genesis* (1823), in which he demonstrated the unity of plan which characterises the book. In that essay Ewald failed to distinguish between unity of plan and unity of authorship; but eight years later he recognised the difference, and adopted a somewhat independent form of the *Supplementary Hypothesis,* which reconciled the assumption of a diversity of sources with the fact of clearly designed arrangement of the material. On this hypothesis, which was first propounded by Stähelin in 1830, and of which the classical exposition is Tuch's fine commentary on Genesis (1838), the Pent. is composed of a *Grundschrift* (Elohistic as far as Ex. 6), into which Jehovistic passages have either been inserted by an editor (Stähelin) or composed *ad hoc* (Bleek, Tuch). The fact which gave plausibility to the theory is that frequently Elohistic and Jehovistic material are so interwoven that, on the assumption of the unity and superior antiquity of the former, the latter might easily pass for supplementary to the other. The error involved in this assumption had been exposed as early as 1798 by Ilgen, who had distinguished two Elohists in addition to the Jehovist; but

iv. It was reserved for Hupfeld (*Die Quellen der Genesis,* 1853) to produce the final demonstration of this fact, and so to introduce the *New Documentary Hypothesis.* He showed, to the ultimate satisfaction of all critics, that besides the Elohistic *Grundschrift* there was a second

* *Conjectures sur les mémoires originaux dont il paroît que Moyse s'est servi pour composer le livre de la Genèse.*

Elohistic document (now known as E) closely akin to and running parallel with the Yahwistic (J), and that both E and J had once been independent consecutive narratives. An accurate delimitation of the first Elohistic document (now called P) then became possible, and in 1869 its outlines were drawn by Nöldeke with a clearness to which subsequent investigation has had little to add.

The chief turning-point in the evolution of the theory, however, was reached in 1866, when the question of the priority of the so-called *Grundschrift* was raised by Graf. Several scholars before him (notably Reuss in 1833 and Vatke in 1835) had anticipated the view which he maintained, that this was really the youngest document of the Pent., but without attracting much support. Graf, who had not at first emancipated himself from the trammels of the Supplementary Hypothesis, argued only for the late date of the legislative parts of P, leaving the narrative parts as still the *Grundschrift* of Genesis. Being convinced by argument of the impossibility of this separation, he abandoned the Supplementary Hypothesis in favour of Hupfeld's theory; but, choosing the opposite horn of the dilemma, he brought the whole document down to the post-Exilic period. In this form the theory was at once accepted by Kuenen (1869), later by Kayser (1874) and Duhm (1875); and finally was expounded by Wellhausen (1876–78) with a cogency which has associated his name with that of Graf as joint-founders of what has become the prevalent critical hypothesis.

It does not lie within our present purpose to describe the collateral investigations which have gone to the establishment of this view of the Pent. One important contribution, however, must be mentioned, viz. the discovery of the unique character and position of Deuteronomy in the Pent., and its identification with the Law-book found in the Temple in the eighteenth year of Josiah. This was essentially the achievement of De Wette (1806), whose valuable work lay more in the department of historical than of literary criticism. Although the result has little direct bearing on the criticism of Genesis, it furnished a prominent landmark in the Pent. problem as yielding a fixed date by reference to which the age of the other documents can broadly be determined. It is quite rightly regarded as one of the main pillars of the dominant theory.*

The leading positions at which literary criticism has arrived with regard to Genesis are, therefore, briefly these: (1) The oldest sources are J and E, closely parallel documents, dating from the best age of Hebrew literature, distinguished from one another by their use of the divine names, by peculiarities of style, and by perceptible differences of representation. (2) These

* And as such has been recently assailed by Dr. Kennett, *Deuteronomy and the Decalogue* (1920); Hölscher in *ZATW* (1921); Dr. Welch, *The Code of Deuteronomy* (1924); and others.

documents were combined into a composite narrative (JE) by a redactor (RJE). (3) The remaining source P is a product of the Exilic or post-Exilic period, though it embodies older material. Originally an independent work, its formal and schematic character fitted it to be the framework of the Pentateuchal narrative; and this has determined the procedure of the final redactor (RJEP), by whom excerpts from JE have been used to fill up the skeleton outline which P gave of the primitive and patriarchal history.

The above sketch will suffice to put the reader in possession of the critical position occupied in the commentary. The evidence by which they are supported will partly be given in the next four §§, and more fully in the commentary itself; but for a full statement of the case we must here refer to special books devoted to the subject.*

§ 8. *Composite structure of J and E—Individuals or Schools?*

In J and E we have, according to what has been said above, the two earliest written recensions of a tradition which had at one time existed in the oral form. When we compare the two documents, the first thing that strikes us is their close correspondence in outline and contents. The most important difference is that E's narrative does not embrace the primitive period, but commences with Abraham. But from the point where E strikes into the current of the history (at ch. 20, with a few earlier traces in ch. 15), there are few incidents in the

* The most lucid and instructive account of the progress of criticism, up to its date, is found in Merx's *Nachwort* to the 2nd edition of Tuch's commentary (dated 1868).—See further, Kuenen, *Historisch-critisch onderzoek* . . .[2], i. (1885), and *Gesammelte Abhandlungen* [Eng. tr. *The Hexateuch* (1886)]; Wellhausen, *Composition des Hexateuchs* . . .[3] (1889), and *Prolegomena zur Geschichte Israels*[6] (1905); Reuss, *Geschichte der heiligen Schriften des ATs*[2] (1890); Robertson Smith, *The OT in the Jewish Church*[2] (1892); Driver, *Introduction to the Literature of the OT*[9] (1913); Holzinger, *Einleitung in den Hex.* (1893); Cornill, *Einleitung* (1908); König, *Einl.* (1893); Carpenter and Harford-Battersby, *Comp. of the Hex.* (1902) [=vol. i. of *The Hexateuch* (1900)]; Budde, *Gesch. der althebr. Litteratur* (1906); Sellin, *Introduction to the OT* (Eng. tr. 1923); Steuernagel, *Einleitung* (1912); Gray, *A Critical Introd. to the OT* (1913); Kittel, *GVI*[2], i. 244–333.

one document to which the other does not contain a parallel.* What is still more remarkable is that the *manner* of narration changes *pari passu* in the two documents (see p. xxii above). This extraordinarily close parallelism both of matter and form shows that both documents drew from a common body of tradition, and even suggests that that tradition had already been partly reduced to writing.

Here we come back (see § 5) to the difficult problem of the process by which the oral tradition was first consolidated and then reduced to writing. From the side of analysis the question presents itself in this form: Are the sources J and E the work of two *individual* authors, or the joint-work of two *schools* of writers, each representing certain common conceptions and observing a common literary style. Now that both J and E are composite documents, in which different strata of tradition are embodied, is universally recognised.† But there is no agreement as to the kind of collaboration involved, or the theory which best accounts for all the phenomena. Many scholars are impressed by the unity of plan and conception which characterises the two documents, and maintain that (in the case of J especially) the stamp of a powerful and original personality

---

* The precise extent to which this is true depends, of course, on the validity of the finer processes of analysis, with regard to which there is room for difference of opinion. On the analysis followed in the commentary the only episodes in E to which there is no trace of a parallel in J, after ch. 15, are: the sacrifice of Isaac, 22; Esau's selling of the birthright, 25^{29-34} (?); the theophany at Mahanaim, $32^{2.3}$; the purchase of land at Shechem, 33^{18-20}; and the various incidents in $35^{1-8.\ 14-20}$. Those peculiar to J are: the theophany at Mamre, 18; the destruction of Sodom, 19^{1-28}; Lot and his daughters, 19^{30-38}; the birth of Jacob and Esau, 25^{21-28}; the Isaac narratives, 26; Jacob's meeting with Rachel, 29^{2-14}; Reuben and the love-apples, $30^{14ff.}$; the incest of Reuben, $35^{21.\ 22a}$; Judah and Tamar, 38; Joseph's temptation, 39^{7-20}; the cup in Benjamin's sack, 44; Joseph's agrarian policy, 47^{13-26} (?); and the genealogies of 22^{20-24} 25^{1-6}.

† In J composite structure has been most clearly made out in chs. 2–11 (see pp. 2–4). On different legendary cycles in the patriarchal narratives, see pp. 240–242, 355–357.—In the case of E the evidence of composite authorship is found chiefly in the Books of Exodus, Numbers, and Joshua, and is there quite decisive: in Genesis also we have imperfectly assimilated fragments of a more ancient tradition in 34. 35^{1-7} 48^{22}, and perhaps in some other passages.

is so obvious that it is absurd to speak of the activity of a school.* Others again are satisfied with the hypothesis of *literary* schools, manipulating written documents under the influence of the tendencies which were characteristic of the school. Gunkel goes a step farther with his conception of J and E as first of all guilds of oral narrators, whose stories gradually took written shape within their respective circles, and were put together in the collections as we now have them. It is difficult to balance fairly the evidence for and against individual authorship, and it will always be more or less a matter of subjective judgment; but it seems to me that Gunkel is right in emphasising the complexity rather than the unity of the documents. He is careful to point out that his theory does not exclude the action of an outstanding personality in shaping either the oral or the literary phase of the tradition; and it is in this direction that we must look for a satisfactory explanation of the origin of the documents J and E.

The way in which individual and collective authorship might be combined is illustrated by a brilliant literary conjecture of Duhm, applied with equal felicity by Budde (*Gesch. der althebr. Litteratur* (1906), pp. 38ff., 62ff.) to the genesis of the document J. It starts from the suggestion that the historical narrative of 2 Sa. 10–20, 1 Ki. 1. 2 (which Budde very plausibly regards as a continuation of the Pent. J), was written by Abiathar, the priest who was degraded at Solomon's accession (1 Ki. $2^{26f.}$), or by some one intimately associated with him. This man is considered by Budde to have been the founder of the Yahwistic school. His successors, down to the 8th cent., working backwards from the time of David and Saul, in four successive stages—the heroic age of the Judges, the period of Moses and the Exodus, the patriarchal age, and the mythical primæval period—gradually welded the traditional lore of Israel into the compact scheme presented by J. But might we not conceive the process reversed? Abiathar was the sole survivor of the ancient priesthood of Shiloh, the natural custodians (see p. xxiii) of the national tradition. Is it not just as likely that the Yahwistic school already existed at that sanctuary, and that Abiathar, who carried away with him an ephod in his flight from Nob, also took with him the written memoirs of that school; so that he and his friends, instead of being the founders of the school, may have been the editors who put its records into their final shape? This of course is pure hypothesis, based on a single ingenious conjecture; and it is not put forward as more than a concrete illus-

* So Luther, *INS*, 107–170; Kittel, *GVI*², i. 278 ff.; Procksch, *NHS*, 206, 284–308, *Gen.* 16, 281 ff.; Sellin, *Introd.* 57 ff.

tration of how a work like J might have originated. At the same time, the fact that the whole of J *can* be dated as far back as the time of Solomon (see p. **lv**) creates a certain presumption in its favour. (I cannot agree with Budde that the story of the Fall was written under the influence of the literary prophets.)—We may suppose a similar process in the case of E: some unknown author of a later date may have done for a divergent form of the original tradition what Abiathar is supposed to have done for J.

The most recent contribution to the analysis of the Pentateuch goes to an extreme in the opposite direction. Eissfeldt (*Hexateuch-Synopse*, 1922), carrying farther the work of Smend (*Die Erzählung des Hexateuch*, 1912), analyses the narrative material of the Hexateuch into *four* sources, each the work of a single author, and each dependent on its predecessor in the order L, J, E, P. The first and oldest, L (=*Laienquelle*), is in the primæval history nearly identical with the stratum previously known as J^1, and in the rest of the Hexateuch is disentangled from connections formerly assigned mostly to J, but sometimes also to E or P. By thus substituting a four-document hypothesis for the prevalent three-document theory, Eissfeldt claims to have simplified the problem of Hexateuchal criticism, and amongst other things to have got rid of the notion of composite or collective authorship. Since it has been impossible to take note of Eissfeldt's analysis in the commentary, I give here a list of the passages in Genesis assigned by him to the source L:

Chs. 2. 3* (a recension of the stories of Paradise and the Fall, || J); $4^{1.\,17-24}$ (Cainite genealogy); 6^{1-4} (origin of the giants); 9^{21-27} (Noah's drunkenness); 11^{1-9} (Tower of Babel); 12^{1-9}* (Abraham's migration, || J and P); 13^{2-13}* (separation of Abraham and Lot, || P); 13^{14-18} (promise of the land to Abraham, || J, E, P); 18^{1-22}* (visit of three deities to Abraham, || J); 19^{1-26}* (overthrow of Sodom, || J); 19^{30-38} (Lot and his daughters); 25^{1-6} (Abraham's issue by Keturah); 25^{21-26}* (birth of Esau and Jacob, || P); 25^{29-34} (Esau sells his birthright); 25^{11b} 26^{1-11}* (Isaac compromises his wife's honour, || J [12^{10-20}], E [20]); 29^{1-10}* (meeting of Jacob and Rachel, || J, E); 29^{14-30}* (Jacob's marriage, || E, P); 30^{29-43}* (Jacob becomes rich at Laban's expense, || J); 31^{1-3} (Yahwe's command to Jacob to return to Canaan, || E); 31^{19-52}* (Jacob's flight from Laban and subsequent treaty, || J, E); 32^{24-32} (Jacob's wrestling with a demon: his name changed to Israel); $33^{18.\,19}$* (Jacob's residence in Shechem, || J, E, P); 34^1–35^5* (seduction of Dinah, and sack of Shechem, || E); $35^{21.\,22}$ (Reuben's incest); 36* (genealogies, || J, E, D); 38 (Judah and Tamar); 49^{2-27} (blessing of Jacob [|| P ?]).

Although the reasons for the analysis are not always satisfactory, it seems to me that Eissfeldt has succeeded in isolating a stratum of tradition standing out from the main narrative, composed mostly of legends of a crude and primitive type, and including (with one exception, $48^{21.\,22}$ E) all those which presuppose a continuous occupation of Palestine from the time of the patriarchs (see p. xxix above). To this extent his results are suggestive and valuable. But it is by no means clear on the evidence that this stratum formed a separate collection, or was made by a single individual, or even existed apart from the document J. A testing case is 25^{29-34}. According to Eissfeldt, this narrative is L's parallel to the JE account in ch. 27 of Jacob's fraudulent securing of the blessing from Isaac, and Esau's final renunciation of the possession of Canaan. That is very likely its original significance, although the point has been obscured by the redaction. But 27^{36} makes it perfectly clear that the incident was incorporated in the narrative of J; for the exegesis by which Eissfeldt tries to get rid of that difficulty (p. 14) is arbitrary and unconvincing. Since more than half of the sections assigned to L are interwoven with parallels from J, and practically only one (ch. 34) with E apart from the intervention of J, there seems a strong probability that L really represents an ancient layer of tradition preserved in the school of J, and partly incorporated in the main document emanating from that school.*

§ 9. *Characteristics of J and E—their relation to Prophecy.*

The most important difference between J and E is the use (for the pre-Mosaic period) of the divine name *Yahwe* by the former, and of *Elohim* by the latter. This is more than a mere matter of phraseology: in the case of E it rests on a view of religious development which connected the revelation of the name Yahwe with the mission of Moses (Ex. 3^{13-15}),—a view shared by P (Ex. 6^{2-12}). In this belief, whether it is traditional or purely theoretical, we have an adequate explanation of the consistent avoidance of the name Yahwe in these two documents throughout the Book of Genesis.

If it were the case that E continues by preference the use of 'א *after* Ex. 3^{15}, some more general explanation would be required; but that, though often asserted, seems very doubtful: (on Eissfeldt's analysis, *e.g.*, the use of 'י greatly preponderates in E to the end of the Pent.). The assumed preferential use of 'א has been explained in various ways. Eerdmans (*Altt. Studien*, i. 39 f.) sees in it a survival of the ancient polytheism of Israel. Procksch, on the other hand (*NHS*, 199; *Gen.* 283), regards it as the expression of E's absolute monotheism, due to the influence of the work of Elijah; but since the inspiring motive of Elijah's crusade was jealousy for *Yahwe* the God of Israel, that seems hardly probable. König (*Gen.* 61) thinks it points to a time when proper names were compounded with *El* and very seldom with *Yahwe*; *i.e.*, the period of the Judges and the early monarchy. Except for its indirect bearing on the date of E, the

* For a fuller account of Eissfeldt's theory, see a review by the present writer in *JTS* (1923).

question does not greatly affect the interpretation of Genesis, and need not be further considered here.

1. J maintains on the whole a more uniform literary style than E. By general admission it contains the best examples of narrative prose in the OT, and in Genesis it rarely if ever falls below the highest level. But while E hardly attains the same perfection of form, there are many passages, especially in the longer narratives, in which it is difficult to assign to the one a superiority over the other. J excels in picturesque 'objectivity' of description—in the power to paint a scene with few strokes, and in the delineation of life and character: his dialogues in particular are inimitable "for the delicacy and truthfulness with which character and emotions find expression in them" (Driver, *LOT*, 119). E frequently strikes a deeper note of subjective feeling, especially of pathos; as in the account of Isaac's sacrifice (22), of the expulsion of Hagar ($21^{8ff.}$), the dismay of Isaac and the tears of Esau on the discovery of Jacob's fraud ($27^{35ff.}$), Jacob's lifelong grief for Rachel (48^{7}), or his tenderness towards Joseph's children (48^{14}). But here again no absolute distinction can be drawn: in the story of Joseph, *e.g.*, the vein of pathos is as marked in J as in E. Where parallels are sufficiently distinct to reveal a tendency, it is found in several instances that J's objectivity of treatment has retained the archaic spirit of a legend which in E is transformed by the more refined feeling of a later age. An example is J's picture of Hagar as a hardy, intractable Bedawi woman, as contrasted with E's modernised version of the story, with its affecting picture of the mother and child perishing in the desert. So again E (20) introduces an extenuation of Abraham's falsehood about his wife which is wanting in the older narrative of J ($12^{10ff.}$).

2. The distinction between J and E appears further in the marked preference of each document for particular words and phrases, which often enable us to assign a passage to the one source or the other.

The divine names.—While the possibility of textual error has always to be borne in mind, there are very few cases in Genesis where the use of יהוה and אלהים in MT is at variance with other indications. In E contexts י׳ occurs in $22^{11.\ 14(bis)}$ 28^{21} 31^{49}, where its presence seems due to the intentional action of a redactor (see pp. 330 f., 379, 402). In J 'א frequently occurs (*a*) in an appellative sense; and Baumgärtel (*Elohim ausserhalb des Pent.*, pp. 23 ff.) has perhaps shown that this sense has a wider range than has commonly been recognised (*e.g.* in $30^{2.8}$ 33^{10b} 35^{5} 42^{28} 'א is not *necessarily* distinctive of E). (*b*) Where the contrast between the divine and the human is emphasised (32^{29}). (*c*) In conversations with, or references to, heathen, real or supposed (9^{27} 39^{9} $41^{22b.38}$ $43^{23.39}$ 44^{16}; but see on the other hand $26^{28f.}$). (*d*) In 3^{1-5} 4^{25} (a special case: see pp. 2, 53).

For *the inhabitants of Canaan*, J uses כנעני, $10^{18b.19}$ 12^{6} (R ?) $24^{3.37}$ 50^{11}+ (with פרזי, 13^{7} (R ?) 34^{30}); E אמרי, 15^{16} 48^{22}+.*

For the name of the third patriarch, J uses *Israel* after 35^{22} (exc. 46^{5b}); E consistently uses *Jacob* (exc. 46^{2} $48^{8.11.21}$ [50^{25} ?]).

The following are selected lists of expressions (in Genesis) characteristic of J and E respectively:

J: אֲבִי and ושם אחיו in genealogies: the former $4^{20.21}$ 10^{21} 11^{29} 22^{21}; the latter 4^{21} 10^{25} (cf. 22^{21} 25^{26} $38^{29f.}$).—זְקֻנִים (of a late-born son), $21^{2a.7}$ [24^{36}] 37^{3} 44^{20}.—מצא חן 6^{8} 18^{3} 19^{19} 30^{27} 32^{6} $33^{8.10.15}$ 34^{11} 39^{4} $47^{25.29}$ 50^{4}+.—טרם (without ב), 2^{5} 19^{4} $24^{15.45}$+.—ידע (in sexual sense), $4^{1.17.25}$ $19^{5.8}$ 24^{16} 38^{26} (also in P).—ילד (=' beget ') 4^{18} $10^{8.13.15.26}$ 22^{23} 25^{3}.—יש, $24^{23.42.49}$ 28^{16} $39^{4.5.8}$ 42^{2} $43^{4.7}$ $44^{19.20.26}$ 47^{6b}+ (42^{1} E ?).—Derivatives of √ עצב $3^{16.16.17}$ 5^{29} 6^{6} 45^{5a}.—הפעם 2^{23} 18^{32} $29^{34.35}$ 30^{20b} 46^{30}+.—צעיר, צעירה (for the younger of two brothers or sisters), $19^{31.34.35.38}$ 25^{23} 29^{26} 43^{33} 48^{14}.—קרא בשם י׳ 4^{26} 12^{8} 13^{4} 21^{33} 26^{25}+.—רוץ לקראת 18^{2} [19^{1}] 24^{17} 29^{13} 33^{4}.—שפחה 12^{16} $16^{1.5.6.8}$ 24^{35} $30^{7.10.12.43}$ $32^{6.23}$ $33^{1.2.6}$ (20^{14} 30^{18} R: also common in P); see on אמה below.—השקיף 18^{16} 19^{28} 26^{8}+.—מעט with following gen., 18^{4} $24^{17.43}$ $43^{2.11}$ 44^{25}.—*Particles*: בעבור, 3^{17} 8^{21} $12^{13.16}$ $18^{26.29.31.32}$ 21^{30} 26^{24} $27^{4.10.19.31}$ 46^{34}.—כי־על־כן, 18^{5} 19^{8} 33^{10} 38^{26}+.—לבלתי, 3^{11} 4^{15} 19^{21} 38^{9}+ (in E and P once each).—נא in J about 40 times, in E about 6 times (in Gn.).

E: אמה, 20^{17} $21^{10.12.13}$ 30^{3} 31^{33}+ (see שפחה above).—גרול and קטן (' elder ' and ' younger '), $29^{16.18}$ $42^{13.15.20.32.34}$ (cf. $41^{51f.}$).—כלכל 45^{11} 47^{12} 50^{21}.—משכרת, 29^{15} $31^{7.41}$.—A very characteristic idiom of E is the vocative (often doubled: 22^{11} 46^{2}+) with the answer הנני, $22^{1.7.11}$ $27^{1b.18}$ 31^{11} 37^{13} 46^{2}+.—E is further distinguished by a number of rare or archaic forms or words: אמנה, 20^{12}+, Jos. 7^{20}; דגה, 48^{16}+; זבר, 30^{20}; חמת, $21^{14.15.19}$+; טחה, 21^{16}+; כן, ' honest,' $42^{11.19.31.33.34}$; מנים, $31^{7.41}$+; נין ונכד, 21^{23} (Is. 14^{22}, Jb. 18^{19}+); עקר, 22^{9}+; פלל, 48^{11}; פתרון, פתר, $40^{5ff.8ff.}$ $41^{8ff.}$; צנום, 41^{23}; קשיטה 33^{19}+ Jos. 24^{32} (Jb. 42^{11})+; by a partiality for rare inf. forms (31^{28} 46^{3} 50^{20} 48^{11}+), and long forms of the pro-nominal suff. (21^{29} [31^{6}] 41^{21} 42^{36}).

3. The religious and theological standpoint of the two documents is in the main identical; but a difference appears in

---

* The cross (+) means that the usage is continued in the other books of the Hexateuch.

one or two features. Both evince a tolerant attitude towards the worship of the local sanctuaries while ignoring its cruder emblems, and this toleration is carried somewhat farther in E than in J.

Thus, while neither countenances the *asherah* or sacred pole, E alludes without offence to the *mazzebah* or sacred pillar ($28^{18.22}$ $31^{13.45ff.}$ 35^{20}); whereas J never mentions the *mazzebah* as an adjunct of the worship of Yahwe. It is a singular fact that while both record the erection of altars by the patriarchs, they are very reticent as to the actual offering of sacrifice: E refers to it only twice (22. 46^{1}), and J never at all in the patriarchal history (cf. $4^{3ff.}$ $8^{20ff.}$). That this indicates an indifference (Gunkel) or conscious opposition (Luther) to the cultus can hardly be supposed, since the altar had no use or significance except as a means of sacrifice.

The most striking diversity appears in the representation of the Deity, and especially of the manner of his revelation to men.

The antique form of the theophany, in which Yahwe (or the angel of Yahwe) appears visibly in human form, and in broad daylight, is peculiar to J (chs. 16. 18. 19), and corresponds to the anthropomorphic representations found in the earlier chapters (2. 3. 7. 8. $11^{5.7}$). E records no daylight theophanies, but prefers the less sensible forms of revelation—the dream or night-vision (15^{1} $20^{3.6}$ 21^{12} [cf. $21^{14ff.}$] $22^{1ff.}$ $28^{10ff.}$ $31^{11.24}$ 46^{2}),* or the voice of the angel from heaven (21^{17}). In this respect E represents a more advanced stage of theological reflexion than J.

The national feeling in both sources is buoyant and hopeful: the *scheue heidnische Stimmung*, the sombre view of life which marks the primæval history of J disappears when the history of the immediate ancestors of Israel is reached. The pessimistic strain which some writers find characteristic of E has no expression in Genesis, and belongs to secondary strata (as Jos. 24) with which we are not concerned.

4. Here we come to a question of great importance for the religious history of Israel, namely, the relation of J and E to the literary prophecy of the 8th and following centuries. It is usual to speak of the combined JE as the *Prophetical* narrative

---

* I do not include the dreams of the Joseph-stories, which stand on a somewhat different footing (p. 345). Nocturnal revelations occur, however, in J (26^{24} 28^{13}); but whether in the oldest parts of the document is not certain.

of the Pent., in distinction from P the *Priestly* narrative ; and in so far as the name is employed to emphasise that contrast it is entirely suitable. As sometimes used, however, it carries the implication that the documents—or that one to which the epithet is applied—show traces of the influence of the later prophets from Amos downwards. That view seems to be quite erroneous. It is true that J and E have many ideas and convictions in common with the writing prophets : the monotheistic conception of God, the ethical view of his government, and perhaps an opposition to certain features of the popular cultus (*asheras*, *maẓẓebas*, *teraphim*, etc.). But we have no reason to believe that these and similar doctrines were first enunciated by the prophets of the 8th cent. Nor does the fact that Abraham as a man of God is described by E as a *Nabi'* (20^{7}, cf. Dt. 34^{10}) imply that the figure of an Amos or a Hosea was before the mind of the writer. The 9th cent. witnessed a powerful prophetic movement which, commencing in N. Israel, extended into Judah ; and any prophetic influences discoverable in Genesis are more likely to be due to that movement than to the later development which is so much better known to us. But indeed it is questionable if any prophetic influence at all, other than those inherent in the religion from its foundation by Moses, is necessary to account for the religious tone of the narratives of Genesis. The important fact is that the distinctive ideas of written prophecy find no echo in those parts of J and E with which we have to do.* These are : the conviction of the impending destruction of the Israelitish nationality by a divine judgment, the polemic against foreign deities, the denunciation of oppression and social wrong, and the absolute repudiation of cultus as a means of securing Yahwe's favour. Not only are these conceptions absent from our documents, but it is difficult to think they were in the air when the documents were written. For although very different

* Budde finds a proof of Hosea's influence on the school of E in the *theocratic* standpoint represented in 1 Sa. 7 f. 10^{17-24} 12, which he assigns to that document. But the conclusion will only hold good for the later strata of the document, and cannot be extended to its older parts. The national optimism of a passage like Nu. 23^{18-24} is almost certainly pre-prophetic (see below, p. liv).

religious ideas may exist side by side in the same community, it is hardly credible that J and E could have maintained their confident hope in the future of the nation in face of the arraignment of prophecy. This consideration gains in force from the fact that secondary strata of E and redactional additions to JE, which do come within the sweep of the later prophetic movement, show that these circles were responsive to the sterner message of the prophets.

§ 10. *Date and place of origin—Redaction of JE.*

The question of the relative age of J and E is of little importance except on the theory that one of them is directly dependent on the other. Those who take that view are unanimous in assigning the priority to J; * and even among those who hold that the documents are independent this opinion is now generally accepted.† But on the hypothesis (see § 8) that J and E represent not individual writers but schools, whose literary activity may have extended over several generations, and drew on an oral tradition which may have been in process of codification long before that, it is obvious that neither their relative nor their absolute dates can be determined with mathematical precision. And it is only on this hypothesis that we can explain the conflicting indications of priority which confront us in the narratives of J and E. The conclusion to which a comparison of their contents leads is that sometimes J and sometimes E has preserved the more ancient form of the tradition, but that J as a whole is the older document.

In attempting to fix an absolute date for J or E, all we can hope to do is to discover a lower limit, later than which the document, or the part of it with which we have to deal, could not have originated. Such a limit we have already found in the rise of written prophecy in the middle of the 8th cent. (pp. lii–liii). We have now to inquire whether it is possible to fix an earlier period as the *terminus ad quem* for the composition of either document.

---

* As Wellhausen, Meyer, Luther, Sellin, Smend, Eissfeldt.

† Gunkel, Procksch; König holds that E is the older.

By the great majority of critics J is now assigned to the 9th cent. B.C.* Of the considerations which are thought to point to that period the only one that calls for special mention is the supposed affinity of the original **Yahwist** with the Rechabite and prophetic movement in North Israel and the nomadic ideal of life and religion which there found expression.† There does not seem to me to be any justification for this view; and apart from it every argument for the 9th cent. appears to hold good with even greater cogency for the 10th, to which (the reign of Solomon) the composition of J has been assigned by some scholars.‡

Among the indications which point to a date not later than Solomon are: the strong consciousness of national solidarity, and confidence in Israel's destiny (Gen. $12^{2ff.}$); pride in the Davidic kingdom (49^{10}); the absence of any allusion to the disruption of the kingdom, the friendly feeling expressed towards the northern tribes ($49^{22ff.}$), and the recognition of the sanctity of Bethel and Shechem (see Procksch, *NHS*, 286 ff., *Gen.* 16 f.; Sellin, *Introd.* 56 f.). On the other hand, the historic allusions which have been thought to indicate a later date prove on examination to be indecisive. If $31^{44ff.}$ $49^{23ff.}$ contained references to the wars between Israel and Aram under Omri and his successors, the document would have to be dated not earlier than the 9th cent.; but Gunkel has shown that interpretation to be improbable. Again, if 27^{40b} referred to the revolt of Edom in the reign of Joram, the same conclusion would follow; but (to say nothing of the doubtful genuineness of that half-verse) the allusion may be to the restoration of the Edomite kingdom by Hadad in the time of Solomon (1 Ki. 11^{25}). The curse on Canaan ($9^{25ff.}$) does not assume the final subjugation of the Canaanites by Israel, and if it did it would only prove a date not earlier than Solomon.—The date, however, cannot be determined from Genesis, or even from the Pent. alone; and it seems to me that a strong argument for an early date is found in Jud. 1, which is now generally assigned to J.§ In that chapter which, though not strictly historical, contains the oldest Hebrew tradition of the conquest of Canaan, the *incompleteness* of the conquest is emphasised in a way which strongly suggests that the writer lived at a time when the absorption by Israel of the Canaanite population had only recently taken place. This may have been the case in the reign of Solomon (1 Ki. 9^{21}), but hardly much later than that. The statement of v.[21] that the men of Judah were *unable* to expel the

---

* So We. Kue. Sta. Kit. Gu. al.

† Luther, Smend, Eissfeldt.

‡ König, Procksch, Sellin.

§ By Eissfeldt to L and J; by König, however, to E.

Jebusites from Jerusalem would seem actually to have been written before David's capture of Zion (2 Sa. $5^{6ff.}$); at all events the note that the Jebusites dwelt there with the Judæans 'unto this day' is not likely to have been true very long after the time of Solomon.—On the whole, the evidence appears to confirm the conjecture that the Yahwistic document was edited by the writers to whom we owe the contemporary history of David's court in the latter part of the Book of Samuel and the first two chapters of Kings (see p. xlvii).

It is more difficult to fix an approximate date for E. If this source is continued beyond the Hexateuch as far as 2 Sam. 7 (Budde, al.), it is probable that its later passages were written under the influence of 8th-century prophecy; if it runs on to the end of Kings (Hölscher), it could not have been completed before the Exile. But neither of these theories would require us to date the whole document by its latest sections; in the Hex., and especially in Genesis, there are so many signs of earlier authorship that we should be justified in regarding E as a 'traditional book' (see p. xxiv), kept up to date by a succession of writers, who were careful to preserve the integrity of the older narrative.

The first question that arises is whether (in the Hex.) the narrative presupposes the division of the kingdom after the death of Solomon. This is maintained by Procksch, but denied by Sellin and König; and certainly it seems precarious to find proof of the affirmative either in Joseph's dream of kingship (37^8), or the prayer for union with Judah (Dt. 33^7), or the description of Joseph as the *Nāzîr* of his brethren (Dt. 33^{16}). On the other hand, Pro. is able to point out several features converging on the early part of the 8th cent.: the conscious monotheism of the document, and the conception of Abraham (20^7) and Moses (Dt. 34^{10}) as prophets after the model of Elijah or Elisha forbid an earlier date, while the tolerance of the *maẓẓeba*, and of the popular cultus as a whole, preclude a later. If (as Pro. and Sel. agree) the book was known to Hosea it must have been in existence before the middle of the century. Other critical estimates do not differ very greatly from this: Di. and Reuss place it in the 9th cent., We., Kue., Ho., Kit., about the middle of the 8th.* We must leave it at that.

It is commonly held that J represents a *Judæan* and E an *Ephraimite* recension of the patriarchal tradition. There lies, however, behind both a common body of tradition which is

* Smend, however, brings it down to the 7th cent., after the fall of the northern kingdom.

native to northern, or rather to central, Israel, and must have taken shape there. The favourite wife of Jacob is Rachel, the mother of Joseph and Benjamin; and Joseph himself is the brightest figure in all the patriarchal gallery. The sacred places common to both recensions—Shechem, Bethel, Peniel, Beersheba—are, except the last, all in Israelite territory; and Beersheba was a favourite resort of pilgrims from the north (Am. 5^{5} 8^{14}). But when we look at the differences between the documents we find a good deal of evidence for the Judæan origin of J and the Ephraimite of E.

Whereas E never evinces the slightest interest in any sanctuary except those mentioned above, J makes Hebron the scene of its most remarkable theophany, and associates its sanctity with the name of Abraham. E alone records the place of Rachel's grave (35^{19}), of those of Deborah (^{8}), of Joseph (Jos. 24^{32}), and Joshua (^{30})—all in the northern territory. The sections peculiar to J (p. xlvi) are nearly all of local Judæan interest: in 18 the scene is Hebron; in 19^{1-28} the Dead Sea basin; $19^{30ff.}$ deals with the origin of the neighbouring peoples of Moab and Ammon; 38 is based on the internal tribal history of Judah. Finally, while Joseph's place of honour was too firmly established to be challenged, it is J who, in opposition to the older tradition, transfers the birthright and the hegemony from Reuben to Judah ($49^{8ff.}$ $35^{22f.}$, the Joseph narratives).—These indications make it at least probable that J and E belong respectively to the southern and the northern kingdoms.

The composite work JE is the result of a redactional operation which must have been completed before the other components (D and P) were incorporated in the Pent.* The redactor (R^{JE}) has done his work (in Genesis) with remarkable care and skill, and has produced a consecutive narrative whose strands it is frequently difficult to unravel. He has left traces of his hand in a number of harmonising touches designed to remove discrepancies between J and E, although it is not always possible to distinguish these from later glosses and interpolations (cf. $16^{9f.}$ $31^{44ff.}$ (*pass.*) 39^{1} 41^{50} 46^{1} $50^{10f.}$). It has commonly been supposed that this redaction took place before the publication of Deuteronomy, although it has been made probable that J and E lay before the writers of Deut. as separate books. It must at all events have been a distinct

* So Nö. We. and most; against Hupf. Di. Meyer, Kit. al.

operation from the final amalgamation of Pentateuchal documents after the Exile.

§ 11. *The Priestly Code and the Final Redaction.*

The third component of the Book of Genesis is the Priestly Code, or rather the great historical work which is at once the kernel of the Code and the framework of the Pent.—the document designated by Wellhausen Q (*Quatuor foederum liber*), by Kuenen P^2,* and now generally known as P^g. While P as a whole is manifestly the work of a school or succession of writers, P^g, although compiled from pre-existing material (see pp. 8, 35, 40, 130, 169, 428 f., al.), bears the impress of a single mind, and must be treated as a unity.

The reconstruction of this document, down to its smallest fragments, is a critical operation the result of which is accepted with remarkable unanimity by all who hold the documentary hypothesis. The following are the sections assigned to it in the first edition of the present work:

1^{1}–2^{3} [^{4a}] $5^{1-28.\ 30-32}$ 6^{9-22} $7^{6.\ 11.\ 13-16a.\ 17a.\ 18-21.\ 24}$ $8^{1.\ 2a.\ 3b-5.\ 13a.\ 14-19}$ $9^{1-17.\ 28f.}$ $10^{1a.\ 2-7.\ 20.\ 22f.\ 31f.}$ $11^{10-27.\ 31f.}$ $12^{4b.\ 5}$ $13^{6.\ 11b.\ 12ab\alpha}$ $16^{1a.\ 3.\ 15f.}$ 17^{1-22} 19^{29} $21^{1b.\ 2b-5}$ 23^{1-20} $25^{7-11a.\ 12-17.\ 19f.\ 26b}$ $26^{34f.}$ 27^{46} 28^{1-9} $29^{24.\ 28b.\ 29}$ $30^{4a.\ 9b.\ 22a}$ $31^{18a\beta\gamma\delta b}$ $33^{18a\beta}$ $35^{6a.\ 9f.\ 11-13a.\ 15.\ 22b-26.\ 27-29}$ 36* $37^{1f.}$ 41^{46a} $42^{5.\ 6a}$ $46^{6f.\ (8-27)}$ $47^{5*.\ 6a.\ 7-11.\ 27b.\ 28}$ 48^{3-6} $49^{1a.\ 28b-33a\alpha b}$ 50^{1-1}.†

---

* Kue.'s P^1 is the so-called Law of Holiness (P^h), which is older than the date usually assigned to P^g.

† The above analysis (for which of course I claim no originality) agrees very closely with four others which have since been published: by Procksch, Eichrodt, König, and Eissfeldt. Eissfeldt differs only by omission of 21^{1b} 25^{11a} 30^{22a} $45^{5.\ 6a}$, and addition of 35^{13b} 48^{7}. Eichrodt omits all the *Tôlĕdôth* headings, ch. 23 (and with it all references to the cave of Machpelah), and the list of Jacob's sons in 46^{8-27}; omits further 7^{17a} 9^{4-6} $13^{12b\alpha}$ $17^{12b.\ 13a}$ $30^{4a.\ 9b.\ 22a}$ $33^{18a\beta}$ 35^{6a} $37^{2b\beta}$ $42^{5.\ 6a}$ $47^{7.\ 8.\ 10}$; queries 13^{6} $16^{1a.\ 3}$ $29^{24.\ 28b.\ 29}$ 35^{22b-26} $46^{6f.}$; and includes 10^{1b} $31^{18a\alpha}$ 50^{22b}. Kön. and Pro. retain the *Tôlĕdôth* headings, the Machpelah references, and 46^{8-27}: otherwise they vary only by a verse here and there, except that Pro. includes in P $45^{1b.\ 17.\ 18a\alpha\beta.\ 19.\ 21a\alpha.\ 25b.\ 27a\alpha\beta b}$. It will easily be seen that with regard to these minutiæ there is room for difference of opinion; but taking all differences together we have 90 per cent. of agreement to 10 per cent. of uncertainty, which is a quite sufficient basis for a judgment on the character—documentary or otherwise—of the passages above enumerated. As a basis of discussion it is accepted in the main by Löhr (see below).

The passages thus isolated are united by certain common features, which sharply distinguish them from the rest of the Book of Genesis. These may be classified under three heads.

1 *Historical outlook.*—The historical interest of P^g centres in the institution of the Israelitish theocracy, whose symbol is the Tabernacle erected after its heavenly antitype by Moses at Sinai (Ex. $25^{8f.}$). For this event the whole previous history of mankind is a preparation. The Mosaic dispensation is the last of four world-ages: from the Creation to the Flood, from Noah to Abraham, from Abraham to Moses, and from Moses onwards. Each period is inaugurated by a divine revelation, and the last two by the disclosure of a new name of God: *El Shaddai* to Abraham (17^1) and *Yahwe* to Moses (Ex. 6^3). Each period also is marked by the institution of some permanent element of the theocratic institution: the Sabbath ($2^{2f.}$); permission of animal slaughter coupled with a ritual restriction on the use of the blood ($9^{1ff.}$); circumcision (17); and lastly the fully developed Mosaic system. Not till the last stage is reached is sacrificial worship permissible. Accordingly neither altars nor sacrifices are ever mentioned in the pre-Mosaic history; and even the distinction between clean and unclean animals is supposed to be unknown at the time of the Flood. It is noteworthy that the profane, as distinct from the sacrificial, slaughter of animals, which the Deuteronomic legislation treats as an innovation, is here carried back to the covenant with Noah.

2. *Religious and theological conceptions.*—Beneath this imposing historical scheme we find a view of religion which lays an exclusive emphasis on its formal or institutional aspect. Religion is resolved into a series of positive enactments on the part of God, and observance of these on the part of man. The old cult-legends (p. xiii), which traced the origin of existing ritual usages to historic incidents in the lives of the fathers, are swept away, and every practice to which religious value is attached is referred to a direct command of God. In the deeper problems of religion the writer evinces no interest; and of subjective piety his narrative hardly furnishes an illustration. It is true that in these respects P^g only represents in an extreme form the antique conception of religion which is shared by

f

J and E : at the same time the more imaginative treatment of religious matters by the older writers often reveals an apprehension of the fundamental questions of religion (chs. 3, 6^{5} 8^{21} $18^{23ff.}$ 45^{8} etc.), and succeeds in depicting the piety of the patriarchs as an experience of personal fellowship with God (cf. 22 $24^{12ff.}$ $32^{9ff.}$ $48^{15ff.}$ etc.). A characteristic distinction between JE and P is seen further in the studious avoidance by the latter of anthropomorphic and anthropopathic expressions (slight exceptions in $1^{26f.}$ $2^{2f.}$ [cf. Ex. 31^{17b}]). Revelation takes the form of simple speech : angels, dreams, and visions are never alluded to. Theophanies are hinted at but not described : God is said to 'appear' to men and to 'go up from' them ($17^{1.\ 22f.}$ $35^{9.\ 13}$ 48^{3}, Ex. 6^{3}), but the manner of his appearance is never indicated save in the crowning manifestation at Sinai (Ex. 34^{26b} $40^{34f.}$). A similar inconcreteness, no doubt, sometimes characterises the theophanies of J and E ; but a comparison of the parallels 17 || 15, or $35^{9ff.}$ || $28^{10ff.}$, makes it clear that P's consistent tendency springs from a deliberate purpose to exclude sensuous imagery from the representation of Godhead.

3. *Literary style and phraseology*.—The style of P^{g} reflects, broadly speaking, the qualities of the legal mind, in its stereotyped terminology, its precise and exhaustive statement, its monotonous repetitions, and its desire to leave no loophole for misunderstanding. The jurist's love of order and method appears in a great facility in the construction of schemes and schedules—genealogical tables, systematic enumerations, etc.—as well as in the carefully planned disposition of the narrative as a whole. On the other hand it is a style markedly deficient in the higher elements of literature. Though capable at times of rising to an impressive dignity (1. 47^{7-11}), it is apt to degenerate into a tedious iteration of set phrases and rigid formulæ (see Nu. 7). The power of picturesque description, or dramatic delineation of life and character, is absent : the writer's imagination is of a mechanical type, which to realise its object requires the help of exact quantitative specification. Even in ch. 23, the most lifelike narrative in the document, the characteristic formalism asserts itself in the measured periodic movement of the action, and the recurrent use of standing expressions from

the opening to the close. That such a style might be the property of a school we see from the case of Ezekiel, whose book shows strong affinities with P ; but of all the Priestly writings P^g is the one in which the literary bent of the school is best exemplified, and (it may be added) is seen to most advantage.

The following is a selection (from Dri. *LOT*^{9}, 131 ff.) of distinctive expressions of P occurring in Genesis, which shows its affinities with later literature, and especially with Ezekiel :

אלהים as the name of God, uniformly in Gn., except 17^{1} 21^{1b}.—מין, ‘ kind ’ : $1^{11. 12. 21. 24. 25}$ 6^{20} 7^{14} (Lv. 11, Dt. 14 ; only again Ezk. 47^{10}).—שָׁרַץ, ‘ to swarm ’ : $1^{20. 21}$ 7^{21} 8^{17} 9^{7}+ (outside of P only Ps. 105^{30}, Ezk. 47^{9}).—שֶׁרֶץ, ‘ swarming things ’ : 1^{20} 7^{21}+ (only in P and Dt. 14^{19}).—פרה ורבה : $1^{22. 28}$ 8^{17} $9^{1. 7}$ 17^{20} 28^{3} 35^{11} 47^{27} 48^{4} (Ex. 1^{7}, Lv. 26^{9} ; elsewhere only Jer. 3^{16} [inverted] 23^{3}, Ezk. 36^{11}).—לאכלה : $1^{29. 30}$ 6^{21} 9^{3}+ (elsewhere only in Ezk. [10 times] and [as inf.] Jer. 12^{9}).—תולדות : 10^{32} 25^{13}+ (elsewhere 1 Ch. 5^{7} $7^{2. 4. 9}$ 8^{28} $9^{9. 34}$ 26^{31}). The phrase [ו]אלה תולדות occurs in P 11 times in Gn. (see p. lxvi) and in Nu. 3^{1} ; elsewhere only Ru. 4^{18}, 1 Ch. 1^{29}.—גוע : 6^{17} 7^{21} $25^{8. 17}$ 35^{29} 49^{33}+ (elsewhere poetical : Zec. 13^{8}, Ps. 88^{16} 104^{29}, La. 1^{19}, and 8 times in Jb.).—אִתְּךָ, עִמְּךָ, etc. (in enumerations) : 6^{18} $7^{7. 13}$ $8^{6. 18}$ 9^{8} 28^{4} $46^{6. 7}$+.—אחריכם, etc. (after ‘ seed ’) : 9^{9} $17^{7. 8. 9. 10. 19}$ 35^{12} 48^{4}+.—עצם היום הזה : 7^{13} $17^{23. 26}$+ ; only in P and Ezk. 2^{3} 24^{2} 40^{1} (Jos. 10^{27} redactional).—למשפחותם—יכם— : 8^{19} $10^{5. 20. 31}$ 36^{40}+ (very often in P : elsewhere only Nu. 11^{10} [JE], 1 Sa. 10^{21}, 1 Ch. 5^{7}. $6^{47. 48}$).—ברית עולם : 9^{16} $17^{7. 13. 19}$+, only in P.—במאד מאד : $17^{2. 6. 20}$+ Ex. 1^{7} ; elsewhere only Ezk. 9^{9} 16^{13}.—רכוש : 12^{5} 13^{6} 31^{18} 36^{7} 46^{6}+ ; elsewhere Gn. 14 (5 times) 15^{14} ; and 15 times in Ch. Ezr. Dn.—רָכַשׁ : 12^{5} 31^{18} 36^{6} 46^{6}+.—נפש (=‘ person ’) : 12^{5} 36^{6} $46^{15. 18. 22. 25. 26. 27}$+ (“ much more frequent in P than elsewhere ”).—לדרתם—יכם : $17^{7. 9. 12}$+ 36 times (only in P).—מגורים : 17^{8} 28^{4} 36^{7} 37^{1} 47^{9}+ Ex. 6^{4} ; elsewhere Ezk. 20^{38}, Ps. 55^{16} 119^{54}, Jb. 18^{19}+.—אחזה : 17^{8} $23^{4. 9. 20}$ 36^{43} 47^{11} 48^{4} 49^{30} 50^{13}+. Often in Ezk. (15 times); elsewhere only Ps. 2^{8}, 1 Ch. 7^{28} 9^{2} [=Neh. 11^{3}]. 2 Ch. 11^{14} 31^{1}+.—מקנה : $17^{12. 13. 23. 27}$ 23^{18}+ (confined to P, except Jer. $32^{11. 12. 14. 16}$).—עמים : (=‘ father’s kin ’) : 17^{14} $25^{8. 17}$ 35^{29} 49^{33}+ (also Ezk. 18^{18} ; elsewhere Ju. 5^{14}?, Ho. 10^{14}+).—תושב : 23^{4}+ 10 times (also 1 Ki. 17^{1}?, 1 Ch. 29^{15}, Ps. 39^{13}).—קנין : 31^{18} [34^{23}] 36^{6}+ (outside of P, only Ezk. $38^{12f.}$, Ps. 104^{24} 105^{21}, Pr. 4^{7}).

In the choice of synonymous expressions, P exhibits an exclusive preference for הוליד in the sense of ‘ beget ’ over ילד (J), and for the form אני of the 1st pers. pron. (אנכי only Gn. 23^{4}).

Geographical designations peculiar to P are : *Ḳiryath-'Arba'* (for Hebron) 23^{2} 35^{27}+ ; *Machpelah*, $23^{9. 17. 19}$ 25^{9} 49^{30} 50^{13}+ ; *Paddan-Aram*, 25^{20} $28^{2. 5. 6. 7}$ 31^{18} $35^{9. 26}$ 46^{15}+.—To these may be added ארץ כנע, 11^{31} 12^{5} 13^{12} 16^{3} 17^{8} $23^{2. 19}$ 31^{18} 33^{18} 35^{6} 37^{1}+ ; the name is found in JE only in the Joseph-section (chs. 42. 44. 45. 47). P^g has כנען without ארץ only in בנות כנען (28^{1} 36^{2}).

It is a fundamental tenet of the modern documentary hypothesis that the sections and fragments grouped together above under the symbol P are excerpts from an independent document, which is a *source* as well as the framework of Genesis. In opposition to this it is maintained by a number of scholars that these passages are of varied origin and authorship, and have come into the text partly as traditional material (Eerdmans, Löhr), partly as redactional supplements and insertions by later hands (Orr, Dahse).*

There are four facts which tell strongly in favour of the prevalent theory: (*a*) The distinctive style and recurrent stereotyped phraseology of the passages (see p. **lx**). This, as Löhr observes, can only prove identity of authorship, not continuity of narration; but just in so far as it proves the one it creates a presumption in favour of the other; and this is confirmed by—(*b*) The consecutiveness of the history which results from piecing the fragments together. That there are *lacunæ* is beyond dispute, but these are not greater than can readily be accounted for by the exigencies of the redaction (see p. **lxiv**). In chs. 1–11 no *hiatus* whatever can be detected. In the history of Abraham (12–25^{18}) there is again no reason to suspect omissions; with the transposition of a single verse (19^{29}) to follow 13^{12}, the fragments form a skeleton biography, expanding in two places (17. 23) into circumstantial description of incidents which had a peculiar interest for the writer. In the sections on Jacob and Joseph (25^{19}–50), the omissions are more numerous and more important. We miss accounts of the birth of Jacob and Esau, of Jacob's arrival in Paddan-Aram, of his marriage with Leah and Rachel, of Joseph's birth, his career in Egypt, his reconciliation with his brothers, etc. All this has to be supplied *by us* from JE; but the probability is that P^g had reduced the biographies, as in the case of Abraham, to a meagre epitome, of which a very few sentences have been suppressed by the redactor. Löhr thinks it inconceivable that a document which in one place (the Flood-story) has broken up the rival source (J) into fragments should in other places dwindle away into a slender thread of narrative. There is no difficulty, if once we understand that the writer described elaborately events which were important for his purpose, and for the rest contented himself with a bare chronological summary as a framework to fit them into. (*c*) In every instance where P^g amplifies the history its representations are at variance with the older documents. Its cosmogony is so different from J's account of the Creation that it is meaningless to speak of the one as a supplement

* Cf. Orr, *The Problem of the OT*, 1906; Eerdmans, *Die Komposition der Gen.*, 1908; Dahse, *Textkritische Materialien zur Hexateuchfrage*, 1912; Löhr, *Untersuchungen zum Hexateuchproblem: I. Der Priesterkodex in der Gen.*, 1924. See also Eichrodt, *Die Quellen der Gen. von neuem untersucht*, 1916 (a detailed examination mainly of Eerdmans and Dahse), and (on Dahse's theory of P) my *Divine Names in Genesis*, 1914, pp. 188 ff.

to the other, and the two Flood-stories are hardly less irreconcilable. Of the two parallel accounts of the covenant with Abraham (17 P^g, and 15 JE) it is clear that the first supersedes and excludes the other. P's reason for Jacob's journey to Mesopotamia ($28^{1.9}$) is quite inconsistent with that given by JE in 27 (p. 374 f.). In JE Esau takes up his abode in Seir before Jacob's return from Mesopotamia (32^3); in P he does not leave Canaan till after the burial of Isaac. P's account of the enmity between Joseph and his brothers is truncated, but enough is preserved to show that it differed materially from that of JE (p. 444). It is difficult to make out where Jacob was buried according to J and E, but it certainly was not at Machpelah as in P^g (p. 538 f.). And so on. How far these differences rest on separate tradition, and how far they can be explained by the known tendencies of the Code, it is not easy to tell. In the primæval history there is obviously no direct dependence of P on J; but in the patriarchal narratives the differences are perhaps all explicable from P's desire to suppress or minimise discords in the patriarchal households. In any case, it is incredible that a supplementer should thus contradict his original at every turn, and yet leave it to tell its own story. (*d*) Lastly, the unity of plan which runs through the series is a very strong argument not merely for identity of authorship, but also for documentary independence and continuity.—On these grounds I hold that the attempt to dissolve the integrity of the Priestly Code is in the main a retrograde step in Pentateuchal criticism, although I fully admit that some of the objections urged against the dominant theory are valid and call for adjustments and modifications in detail. I cannot help thinking that much of the effort directed against it labours under an inability to see the wood for trees. About the *trees* there is a good deal to be learned from the work of Eerdmans, Dahse, and Löhr; but in my judgment the great critics of the last century, though their work was not final, had a truer sense of perspective.

The date usually assigned to the PC is *c.* 500 B.C. It is later than the promulgation of Deuteronomy (621 B.C.), because it assumes without question the centralisation of worship at one sanctuary, which in Dt. is only an ideal to be realised by a radical reform of established usage. That the Code as a whole is later than Ezekiel follows from the fact that the distinction between priests and Levites, of which we find the origin and justification in Ezk. 44^{6-16}, is already presupposed (Nu. 3, 4, 8, etc.). It is possible, however, that that distinction belongs to a stratum of legislation not included in P^g, in which case P^g might well be earlier than Ezk., or even than the Exile.

That P^g is earlier than the Exile is the view of Procksch, who regards it as the work of a Jerusalem priest, composed in the end of the

7th cent. (*NHS*, 322 ; *Gen.*[2] 434). He sees in it an essentially historical book, of considerable literary merit, embracing hardly any legislation except perhaps the Law of Holiness (P^h=Lv. 17–26), and recognising the priestly status of the entire tribe of Levi (Nu. 17^{16-24}), just as in Dt. and P^h in its original form. As indications of pre-Exilic composition he points to the Table of Nations in ch. 10, which bears internal evidence of having been drawn up long before the 5th cent. (see p. 191 below), and the promise of kings issuing from Abraham and Jacob (17^{16} 35^{11}), which he thinks could only have been written under the monarchy. These considerations hardly prove more than the *possibility* of so early a date, and the question does not greatly concern us here. For the understanding of Genesis it is enough to know that P^g, both in its religious conceptions and in its attitude to the national tradition, represents a phase of thought much later than J and E (cf. Kittel, *GVI*[2], i. §§ 26, 27).

The last important stage in the formation of the Pent. is the amalgamation of P with the older documents—in Gen., the amalgamation of P^g with JE. The aim of the redactor was to preserve the *ipsissima verba* of his sources as far as was consistent with the production of a harmonious narrative; and he appears to have made it a rule to find a place for every fragment of P that could possibly be retained. It is not improbable that this rule was strictly observed by him, and that the *lacunæ* which occur in P^g after ch. 25 are due to the activity of later scribes in smoothing away redundancies and unevennesses from the text. That such changes might take place after the completion of the Pent. we see from $47^{5ff.}$, where 𝔊 has preserved a text in which the dovetailing of sources is much clearer than in MT.—If, according to a common critical opinion, the Priestly Code, or part of it (P^g+P^h), was the Law-book read by Ezra as the basis of the new community of Judaism (Neh. $8^{1ff.}$), the final redaction must have been made later than B.C. 444, but earlier than the hiving off of the Samaritan community, which borrowed the Pentateuch from the Jews (*c.* 430 ? 330 ?). But that again is a matter of little moment for the interpretation of Genesis.

Of greater interest and significance than the date or method of this redaction is the fact that it was called for by the religious feeling of post-Exilic Judaism. Nothing else would have brought about the combination of elements so discordant as the legendary narratives of JE and the systematised history of the PC. We cannot doubt that the spirit of the Priestly writers was hostile to the older form of the tradition, or that if the tendencies represented by the Code had prevailed the stories which are to us the most precious parts of the Book of Genesis would have found no place in the Bible of Judaism. It is not the only case where the spiritual instinct of the Church has judged more wisely than the theology of the schools. We know that deeper influences than the legalism and institutionalism of P's manifesto—necessary as these were in their place and time—were at work in the post-Exilic Church: the individualism of Jeremiah, the universalism of the second Isaiah, the devotion and lyric fervour of the Psalmists, and the daring speculation of the writer of Job. To these we may add the vein of simple piety which turned aside from the abstractions and formulas of the Priestly document, to find its nutriment in the immortal stories which spoke home to the heart then as they do to ours to-day.*

§ 12. *Plan and Divisions of the Book.*

It is clear from what has been said that the unity of the book of Genesis must be the unity of a composite work. It also shows how we can reconcile diversity of sources with clearly designed arrangement of material. Three main documents, following substantially the same order of events, have been combined by successive redactions; one of these documents, being little more than an epitome of the history, was specially fitted to supply a framework into which the rest of the narrative could be fitted, and was selected by the final redactor for this purpose; so that the plan which we discover in the book is mainly the plan of one particular writer. This conception adequately explains all the literary unity which the book of Genesis exhibits.

A clue to the main divisions of the book is found in the redactor's practice of inserting the collateral genealogies (*Tôlĕdôth*) at the end of the principal sections ($11^{10-27\ [30]}$; 25^{12-18}; 36).† This yields a

---

* See Gunkel³, p. xcix.

† The genealogies of $4^{17-24.\ 25f.}$ and 22^{20-24} do not count here: these

natural and convenient division into four approximately equal parts :

I. The Primæval History of Mankind : i.–xi.*
II. The History of Abraham : xii. 1–xxv. 18.
III. The History of Jacob : xxv. 19–xxxvi. 43.
IV. The Story of Joseph and his Brethren : xxxvii.–l.

Many writers on Genesis have held that the editor marked the headings of the various sections by the formula [וְ]אֵלֶּה תוֹלְדוֹת, which occurs eleven times in the book : 2^{4a} 5^{1} (זֶה סֵפֶר ת׳) 6^{9} 10^{1} 11^{10} 11^{27} 25^{12} 25^{19} 36^{1} 36^{9} 37^{2}. Transposing 2^{4a} to the beginning, and disregarding 36^{9} (both arbitrary proceedings), we obtain ten sections ; † and these were actually adopted by De. as the divisions of his commentary. But the scheme is of no practical utility,—for it is nonsense to speak of 11^{10-26} or 25^{12-18} as sections of Genesis on the same footing as 25^{19}–35^{29} or 37^{2}–50^{26},—and theoretically it is open to objection. Here it is sufficient to point out the incongruity that, while the histories of Noah and Isaac fall under their own *Tôlĕdôth*, those of Abraham, Jacob, and Joseph fall under the *Tôlĕdôth* of their respective fathers. See further, p. 40 f. below.‡

---

are not *Tôlĕdôth*, and do not belong to the document used as a framework. Ch. 10 (the Table of Peoples) would naturally stand at the close of a section ; but it had to be removed from its proper position to make room for the story of the Dispersion (11^{1-9}). It may be objected, however, that the *Tôlĕdôth* of Adam (ch. 5) ought to mark a main division : that was very probably the original intention, but for practical purposes it is better to treat the primæval period as one section.

* Strictly speaking, the first part ends perhaps at 11^{27} or ^{30} ; but the present division into chapters has its advantages, and it is not worth while to depart from it.

† Procksch would reduce the number to seven by deleting 2^{4a} 6^{9} 11^{10} 36^{1}.

‡ The problem of the *Tôlĕdôth* headings has been keenly discussed in recent writings, and is still unsettled. The view adopted in this commentary, that they come from a book of genealogies incorporated in P (so Procksch², p. 459) seems as feasible a solution as any ; but the arguments against their originality in P (Eerdmans, Smend, Eichrodt, and Löhr) have considerable force, and it is not improbable that *some* of them (certainly 2^{4a}) are redactional additions. The integrity of the scheme as a constituent of P is maintained by Budde against Smend in *ZATW* (1914), 241 ff., and by König in his commentary.

COMMENTARY.

THE PRIMÆVAL HISTORY.

CHS. I–XI.

IT has been shown in the Introduction (p. xxxiii) that the most obvious division of the book of Genesis is into four nearly equal parts, of which the first (chs. 1–11) deals with the Creation of the world, and the history of primitive mankind prior to the call of Abraham. These chapters are composed of excerpts from two of the main sources of the Pent., the Priestly Code, and the Yahwistic document. Attempts have been made from time to time (*e.g.* by Schrader, Dillmann, and more recently Winckler) to trace the hand of the Elohist in chs. 1–11; but the closest examination has failed to produce any substantial evidence that E is represented in the Primitive History at all. By the great majority of critics the non-Priestly traditions in this part of Genesis are assigned to the Yahwistic cycle: that is to say, they are held to have been collected and arranged by the school or individual to whose literary activity we owe the document known as J.

To the Priests' Code, whose constituents can here be isolated with great certainty and precision, belong: 1. The Cosmogony (1^{1}–2^{4a}); 2. The List of Patriarchs from Adam to Noah (5); 3. An account of the Flood (6^{9}–9^{29} *); 4. A Table of Peoples (10 *); 5. The Genealogies of Shem (11^{10-26}), and Terah (11^{27-32} *), ending with Abraham. There is no reason to suppose either that the original P contained more than this, or, on the other hand, that P was written to supplement the older tradition, and to be read along with it. It is in accordance with the purpose and tendency of the document that the only events recorded in detail—the Creation and the Flood—are those which inaugurate two successive World-ages or Dispensations, and are associated with the origin of two fundamental observances of Judaism—the Sabbath (2^{3}), and the sanctity of the blood ($9^{4ff.}$).

In marked contrast to the formalism of this meagre epitome is the

* The asterisk denotes that the passages so marked are interspersed with extracts from another source. The detailed analysis will be found in the commentary on the various sections.

rich variety of life and incident which characterises the Yahwistic sections, viz.: 1. The Creation and Fall of Man (2^{4b}–3^{24}); 2. Cain and Abel (4^{1-16}); 3. The Genealogy of Cain (4^{17-24}); 4. A fragmentary Sethite Genealogy ($4^{25f.}$ . . . 5^{29} . . .); 5. The marriages with divine beings (6^{1-4}); 6. An account of the Flood (6^{5}–8^{22}*); 7. Noah's Curse and Blessing (9^{20-27}); 8. A Table of Peoples (10*); 9. The Tower of Babel (11^{1-9}); 10. A fragment of the Genealogy of Teraḥ (11^{28-30}). Here we have a whole gallery of varied and graphic pictures, each complete in itself and essentially independent of the rest, arranged in a loosely chronological order, and with perhaps a certain unity of conception, in so far as they illustrate the increasing wickedness that accompanied the progress of mankind in civilisation. Even the genealogies are not (like those of P) bare lists of names and figures, but preserve incidental notices of new social or religious developments associated with particular personages ($4^{17.\ 20-22.\ 26}$ 5^{29}), besides other allusions to a more ancient mythology from which the names have been drawn ($4^{19.\ 22.\ 23f.}$).

Composition of J.—That a narrative composed of so many separate and originally independent legends should present discrepancies and discontinuities is not surprising, and is certainly by itself no proof of literary diversity. At the same time there are many indications that J is a composite work, based on older collections of Hebrew traditions, whose outlines can still be dimly traced. (1) The existence of two parallel genealogies (Cainite and Sethite) at once suggests a conflate tradition. The impression is raised almost to certainty when we find that both are derived from a common original (p. 138 f.). (2) The Cainite genealogy is incompatible with the Deluge tradition. The shepherds, musicians, and smiths, whose origin is traced to the last three members of the genealogy, are obviously not those of a bygone race which perished in the Flood, but those known to the author and his contemporaries (p. 115 f.). (3) Similarly, the Table of Nations and the story of the Confusion of Tongues imply mutually exclusive explanations of the diversities of language and nationality: in one case the division proceeds slowly and naturally on genealogical lines, in the other it takes place by a sudden interposition of almighty power. (4) There is evidence that the story of the Fall was transmitted in two recensions (p. 52 f.). If Gunkel be right, the same is true of J's Table of Peoples, and of the account of the Dispersion; but there the analysis is less convincing. (5) In 4^{26} we read that Enosh introduced the worship of Yahwe. The analogy of Ex. $6^{2f.}$ (P) affords a certain presumption that the author of such a statement will have avoided the name יהוה up to this point; and as a matter of fact אֱלֹהִים occurs immediately before in v.^{25}. It is true that the usage is observed in no earlier Yahwistic passage except 3^{1-5}, where other explanations might be thought of. But throughout chs. 2 and 3 we find the very unusual compound name יהוה אלהים, and it is a plausible conjecture that one recension of the Paradise story was distinguished by the use of Elohim, and that Yahwe was inserted by a harmonising Yahwistic editor (so Bu. Gu. al.: see p. 53).

To what precise extent these phenomena are due to documentary differences is a question that requires to be handled with the utmost caution and discrimination. It is conceivable that a single author should have compiled a narrative from a number of detached legends which he reported just as he found them, regardless of their internal consistency. Nevertheless, there seems sufficient evidence to warrant the conclusion that (as Wellhausen has said) we have to do not merely with *aggregates* but with *sequences*; although to unravel perfectly the various strands of narrative may be a task for ever beyond the resources of literary criticism. Here it will suffice to indicate the principal theories.—(*a*) We. (*Comp.*² 9–14) seems to have been the first to perceive that 4^{1-16a} is a late expansion based (as he supposed) on 4^{16-24} and on chs. 2, 3; that originally chs. 2–4 existed not only without 4^{1-16a}, but also without $4^{25f.}$ and 5^{29}; and that chs. 2. 3. 4^{16-24} 11^{1-9} form a connexion to which the story of the Flood is entirely foreign and irrelevant.—(*b*) The analysis was pushed many steps further by Budde (*Biblische Urgeschichte*, pass.), who, after a most exhaustive and elaborate examination, arrived at the following theory: the primary document (J^1) consisted of $2^{4b-9\ 16-25}$ $3^{1-19.\ 21}$ 6^3 3^{23} $4^{1.\ 2b\beta.\ 16b.\ 17-24}$ $6^{1.\ 2.\ 4}$ 10^9 11^{1-9} 9^{20-27}. This was recast by J^2 (substituting אלהים for יהוה down to 4^{26}), whose narrative contained a Cosmogony (but no Paradise story), the Sethite genealogy, the Flood-legend, the Table of Nations, and a seven-membered Shemite genealogy. These two recensions were then amalgamated by J^3, who inserted dislocated passages of J^1 in the connexion of J^2, and added 4^{1-15} 5^{29} etc. J^2 attained the dignity of a standard official document, and is the authority followed by P at a later time. The astonishing acumen and thoroughness which characterise Budde's work have had a great influence on critical opinion, yet his ingenious transpositions and reconstructions of the text seem too subtle and arbitrary to satisfy any but a slavish disciple. One feels that he has worked on too narrow a basis by confining his attention to successive overworkings of the same literary tradition, and not making sufficient allowance for the simultaneous existence of relatively independent forms.—(*c*) Stade (*ZATW*, xiv. 274 ff. [= *Ak. Reden u. Abh.* 244–251]) distinguishes three main strata: (1) chs. 2. 3. 11^{1-9}; (2) $4^{25f.\ 17-22}$ 9^{20-27} 10^9? $6^{1.\ 2}$?; (3) the Flood-legend, added later to the other two, by a redactor who also compiled a Sethite genealogy ($4^{25f.}$ . . . 5^{29} . . .) and inserted the story of Cain and Abel, and the Song of Lamech ($4^{23f.}$).—(*d*) Gunkel (*Gen.*² 1 ff.) proceeds on somewhat different lines from his predecessors. He refuses in principle to admit incongruity as a criterion of source, and relies on certain verses which bear the character of connecting links between different sections. The most important is 5^{29} (belonging to the Sethite genealogy), where we read: "This (Noah) shall comfort us from our labour and from the toil of our hands on account of the ground which Yahwe has cursed." Here there is an unmistakable reference backward to 3^{17}, and forward to $9^{20ff.}$. Thus we obtain a faultless sequence, forming the core of a document where יהוה was not used till 4^{26}, and hence called J^e, consisting of: one recension of the Paradise story; the (complete) Sethite genealogy; and Noah's discovery of wine. From this sequence are excluded obviously: the second recension of the Paradise story; the Cainite genealogy; and (as Gu. thinks) the Flood-legend, where Noah appears in quite a different character: these belong to a second document (J^j). Again, $9^{18f.}$ form a connecting link between the Flood and the Table of Nations; but Gu. distinguishes two Yahwistic strata in the Table of Nations and assigns one to each of his documents: similarly with the section on the Tower of Babel. The legend of Cain and Abel is regarded (with We. Bu. Sta. al.) as an editorial expansion.

In this commentary the analysis of Gu. is adopted in the main; but with the following reservations: (1) The account of the Flood cannot be naturally assigned to J^j, because of its admitted incompatibility with the assumption of the Cainite genealogy (see above). Gu., indeed, refuses to take such inconsistencies into account; but in that case there is no reason for giving the Flood to J^j rather than to J^e. There is no presumption whatever that only two documents are in evidence; and the chapters in question show peculiarities of language which justify the assumption of a separate source (Sta.), say J^d. (2) With the Flood passage goes the Yahwistic Table of Peoples ($9^{18f.}$). The arguments for two Yahwists in ch. 10 are hardly decisive; and J^e at all events had no apparent motive for attaching an ethnographic survey to the name of Noah. (3) Gunkel's analysis of 11^{1-9} appears on the whole to be sound; but even so there is no ground for identifying the two components with J^e and J^j respectively. On the contrary, the tone of both recensions has a striking affinity with that of J^j: note especially (with We.) the close resemblance in form and substance between 11^6 and 3^{22}. Thus:

$J^j = 3^{20-22.\ 24}\ 4^{17-24}\ 6^{1-4}\ 11^{1-9}$;
$J^e = 2^{4b}–3^{19*.23}\ 4^{25f.}\ .\ .\ .\ 5^{29}\ .\ .\ .\ 9^{20-27}$;
$J^d = 6^5–8^{22*}\ 9^{18f.}\ 10^{*}$;
$J^r = 4^{1-16*}$.

Such constructions, it need hardly be added, are in the highest degree precarious and uncertain; and can only be regarded as tentative explanations of problems for which it is probable that no final solution will be found.

I. 1–II. 3.—*Creation of the World in Six Days: Institution of the Sabbath.*

A short Introduction describing the primæval chaos ($1^{1.\ 2}$) is followed by an account of the creation of the world in six days, by a series of eight divine fiats, viz.: (1) the creation of light, and the separation of light from darkness, $^{3-5}$; (2) the division of the chaotic waters into two masses, one above and the other below the 'firmament,' $^{6-8}$; (3) the separation of land and sea through the collecting of the lower waters into "one place," $^{9.\ 10}$; (4) the clothing of the earth with its mantle of vegetation, $^{11-13}$; (5) the formation of the heavenly bodies, $^{14-19}$; (6) the peopling of sea and air with fishes and birds, $^{20-23}$; (7)

the production of land animals, [24. 25]; and (8) the creation of man, [26–31]. Finally, the Creator is represented as resting from His works on the seventh day; and this becomes the sanction of the Jewish ordinance of the weekly Sabbath rest (2^{1-3}).

Character of the Record.—It is evident even from this bare outline of its contents that the opening section of Genesis is not a scientific account of the actual process through which the universe originated. It is a world unknown to science whose origin is here described,—the world of antique imagination, composed of a solid expanse of earth, surrounded by and resting on a world-ocean, and surmounted by a vault called the 'firmament,' above which again are the waters of a heavenly ocean from which the rain descends on the earth (see on vv.[6–8]).* That the writer believed this to be the true view of the universe, and that the narrative expresses his conception of how it actually came into being, we have, indeed, no reason to doubt (Wellhausen, *Prol.*[6] 296). But the fundamental difference of standpoint just indicated shows that whatever the significance of the record may be, it is not a revelation of

* The fact referred to above seems to me to impose an absolute veto on the attempt to harmonise the teaching of the chapter with scientific theory. It may be useful, however, to specify one or two outstanding difficulties of detail. (1) It is recognised by all recent harmonists that the definition of 'day' as 'geological period' is essential to their theory: it is exegetically indefensible. (2) The creation of sun and moon *after* the earth, after the alternation of day and night, and even after the appearance of plant-life, are so many scientific impossibilities. (3) Palæontology shows that the origin of vegetable life, if it did not actually follow that of animal life, certainly did not *precede* it by an interval corresponding to two 'days.' (4) The order in which the various living forms are created, the manner in which they are grouped, and their whole development compressed into special periods, are all opposed to geological evidence. For a thorough and impartial discussion of these questions see Driver, *Genesis*, 19–26. It is there shown conclusively, not only that the modern attempts at reconciliation fail, but (what is more important) that the point at issue is not one of science, but simply of *exegesis*. The facts of science are not in dispute; the only question is whether the language of Genesis will bear the construction which the harmonising scientists find it necessary to put upon it.

physical fact which can be brought into line with the results of modern science. The key to its interpretation must be found elsewhere.

In order to understand the true character of the narrative, we must compare it with the *cosmogonies* which form an integral part of all the higher religions of antiquity. The demand for some rational theory of the origin of the world as known or conceived is one that emerges at a very early stage of culture; and the efforts of the human mind in this direction are observed to follow certain common lines of thought, which point to the existence of a cosmological tradition exerting a widespread influence over ancient speculation on the structure of the universe. There is ample evidence, as will be shown later (below, p. 45 ff.), that the Hebrew thinkers were influenced by such a tradition; and in this fact we find a clue to the inner meaning of the narrative before us. The tradition was plastic, and therefore capable of being moulded in accordance with the genius of a particular religion; at the same time, being a tradition, it retained a residuum of unassimilated material derived from the common stock of cosmological speculation current in the East. What happened in the case of the biblical cosmogony is this: that during a long development within the sphere of Hebrew religion it was gradually stripped of its cruder mythological elements, and transformed into a vehicle for the spiritual ideas which were the peculiar heritage of Israel. It is to the depth and purity of these ideas that the narrative mainly owes that character of sobriety and sublimity which has led many to regard it as the primitive revealed cosmogony, of which all others are grotesque and fantastic variations (Dillmann, p. 10).

The religious significance of this cosmogony lies, therefore, in the fact that in it the monotheistic principle of the Old Testament has obtained classical expression. The great idea of God, first proclaimed in all its breadth and fulness by the second Isaiah during the Exile, is here embodied in a detailed account of the genesis of the universe, which lays hold of the imagination as no abstract statement of the principle could ever do. The central doctrine is that the world is *created*,—that it originates in the will of God, a personal Being transcending the universe and existing independently of it. The pagan notion of a Theogony—a generation of the gods from the elementary world-matter—is entirely banished. It is, indeed, doubtful if the representation goes so far as a *creatio ex nihilo*, or whether a pre-existent chaotic material is postulated (see on v.[1]); it is certain at least that the *kosmos*, the ordered world with which alone man has to do, is wholly the product of divine intelligence and volition. The spirituality of the First Cause of all things, and His absolute sovereignty over the material He employs, are further emphasised in the idea of the *word* of God—the effortless expression of His thought and purpose—as the agency through which each successive effect is produced; and also in the recurrent refrain which affirms that the original creation in each of its parts was 'good,' and as a whole 'very good' (v.[31]), *i.e.* that it perfectly reflected the divine thought which called it into existence. The traces of mythology and anthropomorphism which occur in the body of the narrative belong to the traditional material on which the author operated, and do not affect his own theological standpoint, which is defined by the doctrines just enumerated. When to these we add the doctrine of man, as made in the likeness of God, and marked out as the crown and goal of creation, we have a body of religious truth which distinguishes the cosmogony of Genesis from all similar compositions, and entitles it to rank among the most important documents of revealed religion.

The Framework.—The most noteworthy literary feature of the record is the use of a set of stereotyped formulæ, by which the separate acts of creation are reduced as far as possible to a common expression. The structure of this 'framework' (as it may be called) is less uniform than might be expected, and is much more regular in 𝔊 than in MT. It is impossible to decide how far the irregularities are due to the original writer, and how far to errors of transmission. Besides the possibility of accident, we have to allow on the one hand for the natural tendency of copyists to rectify apparent anomalies, and on the other hand for deliberate omissions, intended to bring out sacred numbers in the occurrences of the several formulæ.*

The facts are of some importance, and may be summarised here: (*a*) The fiat (*And God said, Let* . . .) introduces (both in MT and 𝕲) each of the eight works of creation (vv.[3. 6. 9. 11. 14. 20. 24. 26]). (*b*) *And it was so* occurs literally 6 times in MT, but virtually 7 times: *i.e.* in connection with all the works except the sixth (vv.[[3]. 7. 9. 11. 15. 24. 30]); in 𝕲 also in v.[20]. (*c*) The execution of the fiat (*And God made* . . .—with variations) is likewise recorded 6 times in MT and 7 times in 𝕲 (vv.[7. [9]. 12. 16. 21. 25. 27]). (*d*) The sentence of divine approval (*And God saw that it was good*) is pronounced over each work except the second (in 𝕲 there also), though in the last instance with a significant variation: see vv.[4. [8]. 10. 12. 18. 21. 25. 31]. (*e*) The naming of the objects created (*And God called* . . .) is peculiar to the three acts of separation (vv.[5. 8. 10]). (*f*) *And God blessed* . . . (3 times) is said of the sixth and eighth works and of the Sabbath day (vv.[22. 28] 2[3]). (*g*) The division into days is marked by the closing formula, *And it was evening, etc.*, which, of course, occurs 6 times (vv.[5. 8. 13. 19. 23. 31]), being omitted after the third and seventh works.

The occurrence of the ויהי כן *before* the execution of the fiat produces a redundancy which may be concealed but is not removed by substituting *so* for *and* in the translation (*So God made*, etc.). When we observe further that in 5 cases out of the 6 (in 𝕲 5 out of 7) the execution is described as a *work*, that the correspondence between fiat and fulfilment is often far from complete, and finally that 2[2a] seems a duplicate of 2[1], the question arises whether all these circumstances do not point to a literary manipulation, in which the conception of creation as a series of *fiats* has been superimposed on another conception of it as a series of *works.* The observation does not carry us very far, since no analysis of sources can be founded on it; but it is perhaps a slight indication of what is otherwise probable, viz. that the cosmogony was not the free composition of a single mind, but reached its final form through the successive efforts of many writers (see below).†

The Seven Days' Scheme.—The distribution of the eight works over six days has appeared to many critics (Ilgen, Ewald, Schrader, We. Di. Bu. Gu. al.) a modification introduced in the interest of the Sabbath law, and at variance with the original intention of the cosmogony. Before entering on that question, it must be pointed out that

---

* A familiar instance is the 'ten sayings' of *Pirḳê 'Abôth*, 5, 1: בעשרה מאמרות נברא העולם, where the number 10 is arrived at by adding to the 8 fiats the two other occurrences of ויאמר in MT (vv.[28. 29]).

† See, now, Sta. *BTh.* i. 349 and Schwally in *ARW*, ix. 159–175, which have appeared since the above paragraph was written. Both writers point out the twofold conception of the creation which runs through the chapter; and Schwally makes out a strong case for the composition of the passage from two distinct recensions of the cosmogony.

the adjustment of days to works proceeds upon a clear principle, and results in a symmetrical arrangement. Its effect is to divide the creative process into two stages, each embracing four works and occupying three days, the last day of each series having two works assigned to it. There is, moreover, a remarkable, though not perfect, parallelism between the two great divisions. Thus the *first* day is marked by the creation of light, and the *fourth* by the creation of the heavenly bodies, which are expressly designated 'light-bearers'; on the *second* day the waters which afterwards formed the seas are isolated and the space between heaven and earth is formed, and so the *fifth* day witnesses the peopling of these regions with their living denizens (fishes and fowls); on the *third* day the dry land emerges, and on the *sixth* terrestrial animals and man are created. And it is hardly accidental that the second work of the *third* day (trees and grasses) corresponds to the last appointment of the *sixth* day, by which these products are assigned as the food of men and animals. Broadly speaking, therefore, we may say that "the first three days are days of preparation, the next three are days of accomplishment" (Dri. *Gen.* 2). Now whether this arrangement belongs to the original conception of the cosmogony, or at what stage it was introduced, are questions very difficult to answer. Nothing at all resembling it has as yet been found in Babylonian documents; for the division into seven tablets of the *Enuma eliš* series has no relation to the seven days of the biblical account.* If therefore a Babylonian origin is assumed, it seems reasonable to hold that the scheme of days is a Hebrew addition; and in that case it is hard to believe that it can have been introduced without a primary reference to the distinctively Israelitish institution of the weekly Sabbath. It then only remains to inquire whether we can go behind the present seven days' scheme, and discover in the narrative evidence of an earlier arrangement which either ignored the seven days altogether, or had them in a form different from what we now find.

The latter position is maintained by We. (*Comp.*[2] 187 ff.), who holds that the scheme of days is a secondary addition to the framework as it came from the hand of its Priestly author (Q). In the original cosmogony of Q a division into seven days was recognised, but in a different form from what now obtains; it was moreover not carried through in detail, but merely indicated by the statement of 2[2] that God finished His work on the seventh day. The key to the primary arrangement he finds in the formula of approval, the absence of which after the second work he explains by the consideration that the separation of the upper waters from the lower and of the lower from the dry land form really but one work, and were so regarded by Q. Thus the seven works of creation were (1) separation of light from darkness; (2) separation of waters (vv.[6-10]); (3) creation of plants; (4) luminaries; (5) fish and fowl; (6) land animals; (7) man. The statement that God finished His work on the seventh day We. considers

* See below, p. 43 ff. On the other hand there are Persian and Etruscan analogies; see p. 50.

to be inconsistent with a six days' creation, and also with the view that the seventh was a day of rest; hence in ch. 2, he deletes [2b] and [3b], and reads simply: "and God finished His work which He made on the seventh day, and God blessed the seventh day and sanctified it."—This theory has been subjected to a searching criticism by Bu. (*Urgesch.* 487 ff.; cf. also Di. 15), who rightly protests against the subsuming of the creation of heaven and that of land and sea under one rubric as a 'separation of waters,' and gets rid of the difficulty presented by 2[2a] by reading *sixth* instead of *seventh* (see on the verse). Bu. urges further that the idea of the Sabbath as a day on which work might be done is one not likely to have been entertained in the circles from which the Priestly Code emanated,* and also (on the ground of Ex. 20[11]) that the conception of a creation in six days followed by a divine Sabbath rest must have existed in Israel long before the age of that document.—It is to be observed that part of Bu.'s argument (which as a whole seems to me valid against the specific form of the theory advanced by We.) only pushes the real question a step further back; and Bu. himself, while denying that the seven days' scheme is secondary to P, agrees with Ew. Di. and many others in thinking that there was an earlier Hebrew version of the cosmogony in which that scheme did not exist.

The improbability that a disposition of the cosmogony in eight works should have obtained currency in Hebrew circles without an attempt to bring it into some relation with a sacred number has been urged in favour of the originality of the present setting (Holzinger, 23 f.). That argument might be turned the other way; for the very fact that the number 8 has been retained in spite of its apparent arbitrariness suggests that it had some traditional authority behind it. Other objections to the originality of the present scheme are: (*a*) the juxtaposition of two entirely dissimilar works under the third day; (*b*) the separation of two closely related works on the second and third days; (*c*) the alternation of day and night introduced before the existence of the planets by which their sequence is regulated (thus far Di. 15), and (*d*) the unnatural order of the fourth and fifth works (plants before heavenly bodies). These objections are not all of equal weight; and explanations more or less plausible have been given of all of them. But on the whole the evidence seems to warrant the conclusions: that the series of works and the series of days are fundamentally incongruous, that the latter has been superimposed on the former during the Heb. development of the cosmogony, that this change is responsible for some of the irregularities of the disposition, and that it was introduced certainly not later than P, and in all probability long before his time.

Source and Style.—As has been already hinted, the section belongs to the Priestly Code (P). This is the unanimous opinion of all critics who accept the documentary analysis of the Hexateuch, and it is abundantly proved both by characteristic words and phrases, and general features of style. Expressions characteristic of P are (besides the divine name אלהים): ברא (see on v.[1]), זכר ונקבה [27], חיתו ארץ

* See Jerome's polemical note, in *Quæst.*, *ad loc.*

[חית ה'] 24. 25. 30, לאכלה 29. 30, מין 11. 12. 21. 24. 25, מקוה 10, פרה ורבה 22. 28, רָמַשׂ, רֶמֶשׂ
21. 24. 25. 26. 28. 30, שֶׁרֶץ, שָׁרַץ 20. 21, and תולדות in 2[4a].—Comp. the lists in Di. p. 1; Gu. p. 107, and *OH*, i. 208-220; and for details see the Commentary below.—Of even greater value as a criterion of authorship is the unmistakable literary manner of the Priestly historian. The orderly disposition of material, the strict adherence to a carefully thought out plan, the monotonous repetition of set phraseology, the aim at exact classification and definition, and generally the subordination of the concrete to the formal elements of composition: these are all features of the 'juristic' style cultivated by this school of writers,—"it is the same spirit that has shaped Gn. 1 and Gn. 5" (Gu.).—On the artistic merits of the passage very diverse judgments have been pronounced. Gu., whose estimate is on the whole disparaging, complains of a lack of poetic enthusiasm and picturesqueness of conception, poorly compensated for by a marked predilection for method and order. It is hardly fair to judge a prose writer by the requirements of poetry; and even a critic so little partial to P as We. is impressed by "the majestic repose and sustained grandeur" of the narrative, especially of its incomparable exordium (*Prol.*[6] 297). To deny to a writer capable of producing this impression all sense of literary effect is unreasonable; and it is perhaps near the truth to say that though the style of P may, in technical descriptions or enumerations, degenerate into a pedantic mannerism (see an extreme case in Nu. 7), he has found here a subject suited to his genius, and one which he handles with consummate skill. It is a bold thing to desiderate a treatment more worthy of the theme, or more impressive in effect, than we find in the severely chiselled outlines and stately cadences of the first chapter of Genesis.

In speaking of the style of P it has to be borne in mind that we are dealing with the literary tradition of a school rather than with the idiosyncrasy of an individual. It has, indeed, often been asserted that this particular passage is obviously the composition 'at one heat' of a single writer; but that is improbable. If the cosmogony rests ultimately on a Babylonian model, it "must have passed through a long period of naturalisation in Israel, and of gradual assimilation to the spirit of Israel's religion before it could have reached its present form" (Dri. *Gen.* 31). All, therefore, that is necessarily implied in what has just been said is that the *later stages* of that process must have taken place under the auspices of the school of P, and that its work has entered very deeply into the substance of the composition.—Of the earlier stages we can say little except that traces of them remain in those elements which do not agree with the ruling ideas of the last editors. Bu. has sought to prove that the story had passed through the school of J before being adopted by that of P; that it was in fact the form into which the cosmogony had been thrown by the writer called J^2. Of direct evidence for that hypothesis (such as would be supplied by allusions to Gn. 1 in other parts of J^2) there is none: it is an inference deduced mainly from these premises: (1) that the creation story shows traces of overworking which presuppose the existence of an older Heb. recension; (2) that in all other sections of the prehistoric tradition P betrays his dependence on J^2; and (3) that J^2 in turn is markedly dependent on Babylonian sources (see *Urgesch.* 463–496, and the summary on p. 491 f.). Even if all these observations be well founded, it is obvious that they fall far short of a demonstration of Bu.'s thesis. It is a plausible conjecture so long as we assume that little was written beyond what we have direct or indirect evidence of (*ib.* 463[1]); but when we realise how little is known of the diffusion of literary activity in ancient Israel, the presumption that J^2 was the particular writer who threw the Hebrew cosmogony into shape becomes very slender indeed.

1. We are confronted at the outset by a troublesome question of syntax which affects the sense of every member of v.^{1}. While all ancient Vns. and many moderns take the verse as a complete sentence, others (following Rashi and Ibn Ezra) treat it as a temporal clause, subordinate either to v.^{3} (Rashi, and so most) or v.^{2} (Ibn Ezra, apparently). On the latter view the verse will read: *In the beginning of God's creating the heavens and the earth*: בְּרֵאשִׁית being in the const. state, followed by a clause as gen. (cf. Is. 29^1, Hos. 1^2 etc.; and see G–K. § 130 *d*; Dav. § 25). In a note below reasons are given for preferring this construction to the other; but a decision is difficult, and in dealing with

1.—ראשית] The form is probably contracted from רַאשִׁית (cf. שְׁאֵרִית), and therefore not derived directly from ראש. It signifies primarily the *first* (or *best*) part of a thing: Gn. 10^{10} ('nucleus'), 49^3 ('first product'), Dt. 33^{21}, Am. 6^6 etc. (On its ritual sense as the first part of crops, etc., see Gray's note, *Num.* 226 ff.). From this it easily glides into a temporal sense, as the *first stage* of a process or series of events: Ho. 9^{10} ('in its first stage'), Dt. 11^{12} (of the year), Jb. 8^7 40^{19} (a man's life), Is. 46^{10} (starting point of a series), etc. We. (*Prol.*^{6} 386) has said that Dt. 11^{12} is the earliest instance of the temporal sense; but the distinction between 'first part' and 'temporal beginning' is so impalpable that not much importance can be attached to the remark. It is of more consequence to observe that at no period of the language does the temporal sense go beyond the definition already given, viz. the first stage of a process, either explicitly indicated or clearly implied. That being so, the prevalent determinate construction becomes intelligible. That in its ceremonial sense the word should be used absolutely was to be expected (so Lv. 2^{12} [Nu. 18^{12}] Neh. 12^{44}: with these may be taken also Dt. 33^{21}). In its temporal applications it is always defined by gen. or suff. except in Is. 46^{10}, where the antithesis to אחרית inevitably suggests the intervening series of which ר׳ is the initial phase. It is therefore doubtful if בְּר׳ could be used of an absolute beginning detached from its sequel, or of an indefinite past, like רִאשֹׁנָה or בַּתְּחִלָּה (see Is. 1^{26}, Gn. 13^3).—This brings us to the question of

v.[1] it is necessary to leave the alternative open.—*In the beginning*] If the clause be subordinate the reference of ראשית is defined by what immediately follows, and no further question arises. But if it be an independent statement *beginning* is used absolutely (as in Jn. 1[1]), and two interpretations become possible: (*a*) that the verse asserts the creation (*ex nihilo*) of the primæval chaos described in v.[2]; or (*b*) that it summarises the whole creative process narrated in the chapter. The former view has prevailed in Jewish and Christian theology, and is still supported by the weighty authority of We. But (1) it is not in accordance with the usage of ראשית (see below); (2) it is not required by the word 'create,'—a created chaos is perhaps a contradiction (Is. 45[18] לֹא־תֹהוּ בְרָאָהּ), and We. himself

syntax. Three constructions have been proposed: (*a*) v.[1] an independent sentence (*all* Vns. and the great majority of comm., including Calv. De. Tu. We. Dri.). *In sense* this construction (taking the verse as superscription) is entirely free from objection: it yields an easy syntax, and a simple and majestic opening. The absence of the art. tells against it, but is by no means decisive. At most it is a matter of pointing, and the sporadic Greek transliterations Βαρησηθ (Field, *Hexap.*), and Βαρησεθ (Lagarde, *Ankünd.* 5), alongside of Βρησιθ, may show that in ancient times the first word was sometimes read בָּר׳. Even the Mass. pointing does not necessarily imply that the word was meant as const.; ר׳ is never found with art., and De. has well pointed out that the stereotyped use or omission of art. with certain words is governed by a subtle linguistic sense which eludes our analysis (*e.g.* בָּרִאשֹׁנָה, מֵרֹאשׁ, מִקֶּדֶם: cf. Kön. *S.* § 294 g). The construction seems to me, however, opposed to the essentially *relative* idea of ר׳,—its express reference to *that of which* it is the beginning (see above). (*b*) v.[1] protasis: v.[2] parenthesis: v.[3] apodosis;—*When God began to create . . .—now the earth was . . .—God said, Let there be light.* So Ra. Ew. Di.* Ho. Gu. al.—practically all who reject (*a*). Although first appearing explicitly in Ra. († 1105), it has been argued that this represents the old Jewish tradition, and that (*a*) came in under

* Who, however, considers the present text to be the result of a redactional operation. Originally the place of v.[1] was occupied by 2[4a] in its correct form: אלה תולדות השמים והארץ בְּבָרְאָם אלהים. When this was transposed it was necessary to frame a new introduction, and in the hands of the editor it assumed the form of v.[1] (similarly, Sta. *BTh.* i. 349). I am unable to adopt this widely accepted view of the original position of 2[4a] (see on the verse), and Di.'s intricate hypothesis would seem to me an additional argument against it.

admits that it is a remarkable conception; and (3) it is excluded by the object of that verb: *the heavens and the earth.* For though that phrase is a Hebrew designation of the universe as a whole, it is only the *organised* universe, not the chaotic material out of which it was formed, that can naturally be so designated. The appropriate name for chaos is 'the earth' (v.^{2}); the representation being a chaotic earth from which the heavens were afterwards made ($^{6f.}$). The verse therefore (if an independent sentence at all) must be taken as an introductory heading to the rest of the chapter.*—*God created.*] The verb בָּרָא contains the central idea of the passage. It is partly synonymous with עָשָׂה (cf. vv.$^{21.\,27}$ with ^{25}), but 2^{3} shows that it had a specific shade of meaning. The idea cannot be defined with precision, but

the influence of 𝔊 from a desire to exclude the idea of an eternal chaos preceding the creation.† But the fact that 𝔗^{O} agrees with 𝔊 militates against that opinion. The one objection to (*b*) is the 'verzweifelt geschmacklose Construction' (We.) which it involves. It is replied (Gu. al) that such openings may have been a traditional feature of creation stories, being found in several Bab. accounts, as well as in Gn. 2^{4b-6}. In any case a lengthy parenthesis is quite admissible in good prose style (see 1 Sa. $3^{2a\beta-3}$, with Dri. *Notes*, *ad loc.*), and may be safely assumed here if there be otherwise sufficient grounds for adopting it. The clause as gen. is perfectly regular, though it would be easy to substitute inf. בְּרֹא (mentioned but not recommended by Ra.). (*c*) A third view, which perhaps deserves more consideration than it has received, is to take v.^{1} as protasis and v.^{2} as apodosis, '*When God began to create the heavens and the earth, the earth was, etc.*' (IEz. ? but see Cheyne, in *Hebr.* ii. 50). So far as sense goes the sequence is eminently satisfactory; the ויאמר of v.^{3} is more natural as a continuation of v.^{2} than of v.^{1}. The question is whether the *form* of v.^{2} permits its being construed as apod. The order of words (subj. before pred.) is undoubtedly that proper to the circumst. cl. (Dri. *T.* § 157; Dav. § 138 (*c*)); but there is no absolute rule against an apod. assuming this form after a time-determination (see Dri. *T.* § 78).

* The view that v.^{1} describes an earlier creation of heaven and earth, which were reduced to chaos and then re-fashioned, needs no refutation.

† See Geiger, *Urschr.* 344, 439, 444. The *Mechilta* (on Ex. 12^{40}: Winter and Wünsche's Germ. transl. p. 48) gives v.^{1} as one of thirteen instances of things 'written for King Ptolemy'; and Gei. infers that the change was deliberately made for the reason mentioned. The reading alleged by *Mech.* is אלהים ברא בראשית, which gives the *sense* but not the *order* of 𝔊. The other variations given are only partly verified by our texts of 𝔊; see on $1^{26f.}$ 2^{2} 11^{7} 18^{12} 49^{6}.

the following points are to be noted: (*a*) The most important fact is that it is used exclusively of *divine* activity—a restriction to which perhaps no parallel can be found in other languages (see We. *Prol.*[6] 304). (*b*) The idea of *novelty* (Is. $48^{6f.}$ 41^{20} $65^{17f.}$, Jer. 31^{21}) or *extraordinariness* (Ex. 34^{10}, Nu. 16^{30} [J]) of result is frequently implied, and it is noteworthy that this is the case in the only two passages of certainly early date where the word occurs. (*c*) It is probable also that it contains the idea of *effortless* production (such as befits the Almighty) by word or volition* (Ps. 33^{9}). (*d*) It is obvious (from this chapter and many passages) that the sense stops short of *creatio ex nihilo*,—an idea first explicitly occurring in 2 Mac. 7^{28}. At the same time the facts just stated, and the further circumstance that the word is always used with acc. of product and never of material, constitute a long advance towards the full theological doctrine, and make the word 'create' a suitable vehicle for it.

Close parallels (for it is hard to see that the ויהי makes any essential difference) are Gn. 7^{10} (J), 22^{1} (E), or (with impf.), Lv. 7^{16b} (P). The construction is not appreciably harsher than in the analogous case of 2^{5}, where it has been freely adopted.—ברא] enters fully into OT usage only on the eve of the Exile. Apart from three critically dubious passages (Am. 4^{13}, Is. 4^{5}, Jer. 31^{21}), its first emergence in prophecy is in Ezk. (3 times); it is specially characteristic of II Is. (20 times), in P 10 times, and in other late passages 8 times. The proof of pre-exilic use rests on Ex. 34^{10}, Nu. 16^{30} (J), Dt. 4^{32}. There is no reason to doubt that it belongs to the early language; what can be fairly said is that at the Exile the thought of the divine creation of the world became prominent in the prophetic theology, and that for this reason the term which expressed it technically obtained a currency it had not previously enjoyed. The primary idea is uncertain. It is commonly regarded as the root of a Piel meaning 'cut,' hence 'form by cutting,' 'carve,' 'fashion,' (Ar. *baraʸ*, Phœn. ברא [*CIS*, i. 347^{4}]: see BDB, *s.v.*; Lane, *Lex.* 197 b; Lidzbarski, *NS Epigr.* 244 [with ?]); but the evidence of the connexion is very slight. The only place where בֵּרֵא could mean 'carve' is Ezk. $21^{24\,bis}$; and there the text is almost certainly corrupt (see Corn., Toy, Kraetschmar, *ad loc.*). Elsewhere it means 'cut

---

* The same thought was associated by the Babylonians with their word *banû* (see phil. note); but the association seems accidental; and its significance is exaggerated by Gu. when he says "the idea of creation is that man may form with his hands, the god brings to pass through his word" (*Schöpf.* 23). *Banû* is quite synonymous with *ipisû* (make), and is not restricted to the divine activity.

2. Description of Chaos.—It is perhaps impossible to unite the features of the description in a single picture, but the constitutive elements of the notion of chaos appear to be Confusion (תהו ובהו), Darkness, and Water (מים, תהום). The weird effect of the language is very impressive. On the syntax, see above.—*waste and void*] The exact meaning of this alliterative phrase—*Tōhû wā-Bōhû*—is difficult to make out. The words are nouns; the connotation of תהו ranges from the concrete 'desert' to the abstract 'non-entity'; while בהו possibly means 'emptiness' (*v.i.*). The exegetical tendency has been to emphasise the latter aspect, and approximate to the Greek notion of chaos as empty

---

down' (Ezk. 23^{47}) or 'clear ground by hewing down trees' (Jos. $17^{15.18}$ [J])—a sense as remote as possible from fashion or make (Di., G-B. *s.v.*; We. *Prol.*^{6} 387). The Ar. *bara'a* (used chiefly of creation of animate beings) is possibly borrowed from Heb. Native philologists connect it, very unnaturally, with *bari'a*, 'be free'; so that 'create' means to *liberate* (from the clay, etc.) (Lane, 178 b, c): Di.'s view is similar. Barth (*ZA*, iii. 58) has proposed to identify ברא (through mutation of liquids) with the Ass. vb. for 'create,' *banû*; but rejects the opinion that the latter is the common Semitic בנה 'build' (*KAT*^{3}, 498^{1}), with which ברא alternates in Sabæan (Müller in *ZDMG*, xxxvii. 413, 415).

2. תהו ובהו] 𝔊 ἀόρατος καὶ ἀκατασκεύαστος; Aq. κένωμα κ. οὐθέν; Σ. ἀργὸν κ. ἀδιάκριτον; Θ. κενὸν (or οὐθὲν) καὶ οὐθέν; 𝔙 *inanis et vacua*; 𝔗^{O} צריא וריקניא ('desolate and empty'); 𝔖 ܬܘܗ ܘܒܘܗ. The fragmentary Jer. Tg. has a double trans.: "And the earth was תהיא ובהיא, and (cf. 𝔗^{O}) *desolate* from the sons of men, and *empty* of work." תהו occurs along with בהו in Jer. 4^{23}, Is. 34^{11}; תהו alone in 17 pass. besides. The meaning varies between two extremes: (*a*) a (trackless) *desert* (Jb. 12^{24} [=Ps. 107^{40}] 6^{18}, Dt. 32^{10}), and (*b*) *unsubstantiality* (שאין לו ממש, IEz.) or 'nonentity,' a sense all but peculiar to II Is. (also 1 Sa. 12^{21}, and *perhaps* Is. 29^{21}), but very frequent there. The primary idea is uncertain. It is perhaps easier on the whole to suppose that the abstract sense of 'formlessness,' or the like, gave rise to a poetic name for desert, than that the concrete 'desert' passed over into the abstract 'formlessness'; but we have no assurance that either represents the actual development of the idea. It seems not improbable that the OT usage is entirely based on the traditional description of the primæval chaos, and that the word had no definite connotation in Heb., but was used to express any conception naturally associated with the idea of chaos—'formlessness,' 'confusion,' 'unreality,' etc.—בהו] (never found apart from תהו) may be connected with *bahiya*='be empty'; though Ar. is hardly a safe guide in the case of a word with a long history behind it. The identification with Βααυ, the mother of the first man in Phœn. mythology (see p. 49 f.), is

space (Gu.). But our safest guide is perhaps Jeremiah's vision of Chaos-come-again (4^{23-26}), which is simply that of a darkened and devastated earth, from which life and order have fled. The idea here is probably similar, with this difference, that the distinction of land and sea is effaced, and the earth, which is the subj. of the sentence, must be understood as the amorphous watery mass in which the elements of the future land and sea were commingled.—*Darkness* (an almost invariable feature of ancient conceptions of chaos) *was upon the face of the Deep*] The *Deep* (תְּהוֹם) is the subterranean ocean on which the earth rests (Gn. 7^{11} 8^{2} 49^{25}, Am. 7^{4} etc.); which, therefore, before the earth was formed, lay bare and open to the superincumbent darkness. In the Babylonian Creation-myth the primal chaos is personified under the name *Ti'āmat*. The Heb. narrative is free from mythological associations, and it is doubtful if even a trace of personification lingers in the name תהום. In Babylonian, *ti'āmatu* or *tāmtu* is a generic term for 'ocean'; and it is conceivable that this literal sense may be the origin of the Heb. conception of the Deep (see p. 47).—*The Spirit of God was brooding*] not, as has sometimes been supposed, a *wind* sent from God to dry

probable.—תהום] is undoubtedly the philological equivalent of Bab. *Ti'āmat*: a connexion with Ar. *Tihāmat*, the Red Sea littoral province (Hoffmann in *ZATW*, iii. 118), is more dubious (see Lane, 320 b, c; Jensen, *KIB*, vi. 1, 560). In early Heb. the word is rare, and always (with poss. exception of Ex. $15^{5.8}$) denotes the subterranean ocean, which is the source from which earthly springs and fountains are fed (Gn. 49^{25}, Dt. 33^{13}, Am. 7^{4}, and so Dt. 8^{7}, Gn. 7^{11} 8^{2} (P); cf. Hom. *Il.* xxi. 195), and is a remnant of the primal chaos (Gn. 1^{2}, Ps. 104^{6}, Pr. 8^{27}). In later writings it is used of the sea (pl. seas), and even of torrents of water (Ps. 42^{8}); but, the passages being poetic, there is probably always to be detected a reference to the world-ocean, either as source of springs, or as specialised in earthly oceans (see Ezk. 26^{19}). Though the word is almost confined to poetry (except Gn. 1^{2} 7^{11} 8^{2}, Dt. 8^{7}, Am. 7^{4}), the only clear cases of personification are Gn. 49^{25}, Dt. 33^{13} (*Tĕhôm* that coucheth beneath). The invariable absence of the art. (except with pl. in Ps. 106^{9}, Is. 63^{13}) proves that it is a proper name, but *not* that it is a personification (cf. the case of שְׁאוֹל). On the other hand, it is noteworthy that תהום, unlike most Heb. names of fluids, is fem., becoming occasionally masc. only in later times when its primary sense had been forgotten (cf. Albrecht, *ZATW*, xvi. 62): this might be

up the waters (𝔗O, IEz., and a few moderns), but the divine Spirit, figured as a bird brooding over its nest, and perhaps symbolising an immanent principle of life and order in the as yet undeveloped chaos. Comp. Milton, *Paradise Lost*, i. 19 ff., vii. 233 ff. It is remarkable, however, if this be the idea, that no further effect is given to it in the sequel. (1) The idea of the Spirit as formative principle of the kosmos, while *in the line* of the OT doctrine that he is the source of life (Ps. 33^{6} $104^{29f.}$), yet goes much beyond the ordinary representation, and occurs only here (possibly Is. 40^{13}). (2) The image conveyed by the word *brooding* (מְרַחֶפֶת) is generally considered to rest on the widespread cosmogonic speculation of the world-egg (so even De. and Di.), in which the organised world was as it were hatched from the fluid chaos. If so, we have here a fragment of mythology not vitally connected with the main idea of the narrative, but introduced for the sake of its religious suggestiveness. In the source from which this myth was borrowed the brooding power might be a bird-like deity * (Gu.), or an abstract principle like the Greek Ἔρως, the Phœn. Πόθος, etc.: for this the Heb. writer, true to his monotheistic faith, substitutes the Spirit of God, and thereby transforms a "crude material representation . . . into a beautiful and suggestive figure" (Dri. *Gen.* 5).

due to an original female personification.—מרחפת] Gk. Vns. and 𝔙 express merely the idea of motion (*ἐπεφέρετο, ἐπιφερόμενον, ferebatur*); 𝔗O מנשבא ('blow' or 'breathe'); 𝔖 ܡܪܚܦܐ. Jerome (*Quæst.*): "incubabat sive confovebat in similitudinem volucris ova calore animantis." It is impossible to say whether 'brood' or 'hover' is the exact image here, or in Dt. 32^{11},—the only other place where the Pi. occurs (the Qal in Jer. 23^{9} may be a separate root). The Syriac vb. has great latitude of meaning; it describes, *e.g.*, the action of Elisha in laying himself on the body of the dead child (2 Ki. 4^{34}); and is used of angels *hovering* over the dying Virgin. It is also applied to a waving of the hands (or of fans) in certain ecclesiastical functions, etc. (see Payne Smith, *Thes.* 3886).

* In Polynesian mythology the supreme god Tangaloa is often represented as a bird hovering over the waters (Waitz - Gerland, *Anthrop.* vi. 241).

The conceptions of chaos in antiquity fluctuate between that of empty space (Hesiod, Arist. Lucr., etc.) and the 'rudis indigestaque moles' of Ovid (*Met.* i. 7). The Babylonian representation embraces the elements of darkness and water, and there is no doubt that this is the central idea of the Genesis narrative. It is singular, however, that of the three clauses of v.[2] only the second (which includes the two elements mentioned) exercises any influence on the subsequent description (for on any view the 'waters' of the third must be identical with the *Tĕhôm* of the second). It is possible, therefore, that the verse combines ideas drawn from diverse sources which are not capable of complete synthesis. Only on this supposition would it be possible to accept Gu.'s interpretation of the first clause as a description of empty space. In that case *the earth* is probably not inclusive of, but contrasted with, *Tĕhôm*: it denotes the space *now* occupied by the earth, which being empty leaves nothing but the deep and the darkness.

3-5. First work: Creation of light. — [*And*] *God said*] On the connexion, see above, pp. 13 ff.; and on the significance of the *fiat*, p. 7. — *Let there be light*] The thought of light as the first creation, naturally suggested by the phenomenon of the dawn, appears in several cosmogonies; but is not expressed in any known form of the Babylonian legend. There the creator, being the sun-god, is in a manner identified with the primal element of the kosmos; and the antithesis of light and darkness is dramatised as a conflict between the god and the Chaos monster. In Persian cosmogony also, light, as the sphere in which Mazda dwells, is uncreated and eternal (Tiele, *Gesch. d. Rel.* ii. 295 f.). In Is. 45[7] both light and darkness are creations of Yahwe, but that is certainly not the idea here. Comp. Milton's *Parad. Lost*, iii. 1 ff.:

> "Hail, holy Light! offspring of heaven first-born;
> Or, of the Eternal co-eternal beam," etc.

4. *saw that the light was good*] The formula of approval does not extend to the darkness, nor even to the coexistence of light and darkness, but is restricted to the light. "Good" expresses the contrast of God's work to the chaos of which darkness is an element. Gu. goes too far in suggesting that the expression covers a 'strong anthropomorphism'

---

3. ויהי אור corresponds to the ויהי כן of subsequent acts.—4. האור כי טוב]

(the possibility of failure, happily overcome). But he rightly calls attention to the bright view of the world implied in the series of approving verdicts, as opposed to the pessimistic estimate which became common in later Judaism.—*And God divided, etc.*]. To us these words merely suggest alternation in time; but Heb. conceives of a *spatial* distinction of light and darkness, each in its own 'place' or abode (Jb. $38^{19f.}$). Even the separate days and nights of the year seem thought of as having independent and continuous existence (Jb. 3^{6}).

The Heb. mind had thus no difficulty in thinking of the existence of light before the heavenly bodies. The sun and moon *rule* the day and night, but light and darkness exist independently of them. It is a mistake, however, to compare this with the scientific hypothesis of a cosmical light diffused through the nebula from which the solar system was evolved. It is not merely light and darkness, but day and night, and even the alternation of evening and morning (v.[5]), that are represented as existing before the creation of the sun.

5. *And God called, etc.*] The name—that by which the thing is summoned into the field of thought—belongs to the full existence of the thing itself. So in the first line of the Babylonian account, "the heaven was not yet named" means that it did not yet exist.—*And it became evening, etc.*] Simple as the words are, the sentence presents some difficulty, which is not removed by the supposition that the writer follows the Jewish custom of reckoning the day from

---

with attracted obj.: see G-K. § 117*h*; Dav. § 146.—5. יום in popular parlance denotes the period between dawn and dark, and is so used in [5a]. When it became necessary to deal with the 24-hours' day, it was most natural to connect the night with the *preceding* period of light, reckoning, *i.e.*, from sunrise to sunrise; and this is the prevailing usage of OT (יום ולילה). In post-exilic times we find traces of the reckoning from sunset to sunset in the phrase לילה ויום (*νυχθήμερον*), Is. 27^{3} 34^{10}, Est. 4^{16}. P regularly employs the form 'day and night'; and if Lv. 23^{32} can be cited as a case of the later reckoning, Ex. 12^{18} is as clearly in favour of the older (see Marti, *EB*, 1036; König, *ZDMG*, lx. 605 ff.). There is therefore no presumption in favour of the less natural method in this passage.—קָרָא] *Mil'el*, to avoid concurrence of two accented syll.—לָיְלָה] (also *Mil'el*) a reduplicated form (לַיְלֵי; cf. Aram. ליליא): see Nöldeke, *Mand. Gr.* § 109; Prätorius, *ZATW*, iii. 218; Kön. ii. § 52 c. —יום אחד] 'a first day,' or perhaps better 'one day.' On אחד as ord. see G-K. §§ 98 *a*, 134 *p*; Dav. § 38, *R.* 1; but cf. Wellh. *Prol.*[6] 387.

sunset to sunset (Tu. Gu. Ben. etc.). The Jewish day may have begun at sunset, but it did not end at sunrise; and it is impossible to take the words as meaning that the evening and morning *formed* the first (second, etc.) day. Moreover, there could be no evening before the day on which light was created. The sentence must refer to the *close* of the first day with the first evening and the night that followed, leading the mind forward to the advent of a new day, and a new display of creative power (De. Di. Ho. al.). One must not overlook the majestic simplicity of the statement.

The interpretation of יום as *æon*, a favourite resource of harmonists of science and revelation, is opposed to the plain sense of the passage, and has no warrant in Heb. usage (not even Ps. 90^4). It is true that the conception of successive creative periods, extending over vast spaces of time, is found in other cosmogonies (De. 55); but it springs in part from views of the world which are foreign to the OT. To introduce that idea here not only destroys the analogy on which the sanction of the sabbath rests, but misconceives the character of the Priestly Code. If the writer had had æons in his mind, he would hardly have missed the opportunity of stating how many millenniums each embraced.

6–8. Second work: The firmament.—The second fiat calls into existence a *firmament*, whose function is to divide the primæval waters into an upper and lower ocean, leaving a space between as the theatre of further creative developments. The "firmament" is the dome of heaven, which to the ancients was no optical illusion, but a material structure, sometimes compared to an "upper chamber" (Ps. 104^{13}, Am. 9^6) supported by "pillars" (Jb. 26^{11}), and resembling in its surface a "molten mirror" (Jb. 37^{18}). Above this are the heavenly waters, from which the rain descends through "windows" or "doors" (Gn. 7^{11} 8^2, 2 Ki. $7^{2.19}$) opened and shut by God at His pleasure (Ps. 78^{23}). The general idea of a forcible separation of heaven and earth

6. רָקִיעַ (𝔊 στερέωμα, 𝔙 *firmamentum*) a word found only in Ezk., P, Ps. 19^2 150^1, Dn. 12^3. The absence of art. shows that it is a *descriptive* term, though the only parallels to such a use would be Ezk. $1^{22f.\,25f.}$ 10^1 (cf. Phœn. מרקע='dish' [*Blechschale*]: *CIS*, i. 90^1; see Lidzb. 370, 421). The idea is *solidity*, not thinness or extension: the sense 'beat thin' belongs to the Pi. (Ex. 39^3 etc.); and this noun is formed from the Qal, which means either (intrans.) to 'stamp with the foot' (Ezk. 6^{11}), or

is widely diffused; it is perhaps embodied in our word 'heaven' (from *heave?*) and O.E. 'lift.' A graphic illustration of it is found in Egyptian pictures, where the god Shu is seen holding aloft, with outstretched arms, the dark star-spangled figure of the heaven-goddess, while the earth-god lies prostrate beneath (see Je. *ATLO*², 7).* But the special form in which it appears here is perhaps not fully intelligible apart from the Bab. creation-myth, and the climatic phenomena on which it is based (see below, p. 46).

Another interpretation of the firmament has recently been propounded (Winckler, *Himmels- u. Weltenbild*, 25 ff.; *ATLO*², 164, 174) which identifies it with the Bab. *šupuk šamē*, and explains both of the Zodiac. The view seems based on the highly artificial Bab. theory of a point-for-point correspondence between heaven and earth, according to which the Zodiac represents a heavenly earth, the northern heavens a heavenly heaven (atmospheric), and the southern a heavenly ocean. But whatever be the truth about *šupuk šamē*, such a restriction of the meaning of רקיע is inadmissible in Heb. In Ps. 19², Dn. 12³ it might be possible; but even there it is unnecessary, and in almost every other case it is absolutely excluded. It is so emphatically in this chapter, where the firmament is *named* heaven, and birds (whose flight is not restricted to 10° on either side of the ecliptic) are said to fly 'in front of the firmament.'

9, 10. Third work: Dry land and sea.—The shoreless lower ocean, which remained at the close of the second

---

(trans.), 'stamp firm,' 'consolidate' (Is. 42⁵ etc.). It is curious that the vb. is used of the creation of the earth, never of heaven, except Jb. 37¹⁸.—ויהי מבדיל] on ptcp. expressing permanence, see Dri. *T.* § 135, 5.—בֵּין: Kön. *S.* § 319 n.—וַיַּבְדֵּל] 𝔊 supplies as subj. ὁ θεός.—7. ויהי כן] transposed in 𝔊 to end of v.⁶, its normal position,—if indeed it be not a gloss in both places (We.).—8. 𝔊 also inserts here the formula of approval: on its omission in Heb., see above, pp. 8, 9.

9. יִקָּווּ] in this sense, only Jer. 3¹⁷. For מָקוֹם read with 𝔊 מִקְוֶה = 'gathering-place,' as in v.¹⁰. Nestle (*MM*, 3) needlessly suggests for the latter מִקְרֶה, and for יקוו, יִקָּרוּ.†—מִתַּחַת] not 'from under' but simply 'under' see v.¹⁰); G–K. § 119 *c*².—וְתֵרָאֶה] juss. unapocopated, as often near the principal pause; G–K. § 109 *a*.—At the end of the v. 𝔊 adds: *καὶ συνήχθη τὸ ὕδωρ τὸ ὑποκάτω τοῦ οὐρανοῦ εἰς τὰς συναγωγὰς αὐτῶν καὶ ὤφθη ἡ ξηρά*: *i.e.* וַיִּקָּווּ הַמַּיִם אֲשֶׁר מִתַּחַת הַשָּׁמַיִם אֶל־מִקְוֵיהֶם וַתֵּרָא הַיַּבָּשָׁה. The addition is adopted by Ball, and the pl. *αὐτῶν* proves at least that it rests on a Heb. original, *ὕδωρ* being sing. in Greek (We.).—10. יַמִּים] the pl. (cf.

---

* Comp. also the Maori myth reported in Waitz, *Anthrop.* vi. 245 ff.; Lang, *Custom and Myth*, 45 ff.

† Since withdrawn.

day, is now replaced by land and sea in their present configuration. The expressions used: *gathered together* . . . *appear*—seem to imply that the earth already existed as a solid mass covered with water, as in Ps. 104[5.6]; but Di. thinks the language not inconsistent with the idea of a muddy mixture of earth and water, as is most naturally suggested by v.[2]. Henceforth the only remains of the original chaos are the subterranean waters (commonly called *Tĕhôm*, but in Ps. 24[2] 'sea' and 'streams'), and the circumfluent ocean on which the heaven rests (Jb. 26[10], Ps. 139[9], Pr. 8[27]), of which, however, earthly seas are parts.

We.'s argument, that vv.[6-10] are the account of a single work (above, p. 9 f.), is partly anticipated by IEz., who points out that what is here described is no true creation, but only a manifestation of what was before hidden and a gathering of what was dispersed. On the ground that earth and heaven were made on one day (2[4]), he is driven to take ויאמר as plup., and assign vv.[9.10] to the second day. Some such idea may have dictated the omission of the formula of approval at the close of the second day's work.

11–13. Fourth work: Creation of plants. — The appearing of the earth is followed on the same day, not inappropriately, by the origination of vegetable life. The earth itself is conceived as endowed with productive powers —a recognition of the principle of development not to be explained as a mere imparting of the power of annual renewal (Di.); see to the contrary v.[12] compared with v.[24]. —**11.** *Let the earth produce verdure*] דֶּשֶׁא means 'fresh young herbage,' and appears *here* to include all plants in

---

Gn. 49[13], Dt. 33[19], Ps. 46[3f.] [where it is construed as sing.] 24[2] etc.) is mostly poetic and late prose; it is probably not numerical, but pl. of extension like מַיִם, שָׁמַיִם, and therefore to be rendered as sg.

11. תַּדְשֵׁא דֶּשֶׁא] lit. 'vegetate vegetation,' the noun being acc. cognate with the vb.—'תּ is ἀπ.λεγ.; on the pointing with *Metheg* (Baer-De. p. 74) see Kön. i. § 42, 7. 𝔖 (ܬܦܩ) must have read תוצא as v.[12].—דֶּשֶׁא עֵשֶׂב] 𝔊 (βοτάνην χόρτου) and 𝔙 treat the words as in annexion, contrary to the accents and the usage of the terms. It is impossible to define them with scientific precision; and the twofold classification given above—herb and tree—is more or less precarious. It recurs, however, in Ex. 9[25] 10[12.15] (all J), and the reasons for rejecting the other are, first,

the earliest stages of their growth; hence the classification of flora is not *three*fold—grass, herbs, trees (Di. Dri. al.)—but *two*fold, the generic דשא including the two kinds עֵשֶׂב and עֵץ (De. Gu. Ho. etc.). The distinction is based on the methods of reproduction; the one kind producing seed merely, the other fruit which contains the seed.—The v. continues (amending with the help of 𝕲): *grass producing seed after its kind, and fruit-tree producing fruit in which* (*i.e.* the fruit) *is its* (the tree's) *seed after its* (the tree's) *kind.—after its kind*] *v.i.—upon the earth*] comes in very awkwardly; it is difficult to find any suitable point of attachment except with the principal verb, which, however, is too remote.

14–19. Fifth work: The heavenly luminaries.—On the parallelism with the first day's work see above, p. 8f. The vv. describe only the creation of sun and moon; the clause *and the stars* in v.[16] appears to be an

---

the absence of וְ before עשב; and, second, the syntactic consideration that דשא as cognate acc. may be presumed to define completely the action of the vb.—דשא denotes especially fresh juicy herbage* (Pr. 27[25]) and those grasses which never to appearance get beyond that stage. עשב, on the other hand (unlike 'ד), is used of human food, and therefore includes cultivated plants (the cereals, etc.) (Ps. 104[14]).—עץ] read וְעֵץ with 𝔐𝕲𝔙𝔖, and 3 Heb. MSS (Ball).—למינו, למינהו] On form of suff. see G-K. § 91 *d*. 𝕲 in v.[11] inserts the word after זרע (rendering strangely κατὰ γένος καὶ καθ' ὁμοιότητα,—and so v.[12]), and later in the v. (κατὰ γέν. εἰς ὁμ.) transposes as indicated in the translation above.—מין] a characteristic word of P, found elsewhere only in Dt. 14[13. 14. 15. 18] (from Lv. 11), and (dubiously) Ezk. 47[10],—everywhere with suff. The etymology is uncertain. If connected with תְּמוּנָה (form, likeness), the meaning would be 'form' (Lat. *species*); but in usage it seems to mean simply 'kind,' the sg. suff. here being distributive: "according to its several kinds." In Syr. the corresponding word denotes a family or tribe. For another view, see Frd. Delitzsch, *Prol.* 143 f.—**12.** ותוצא] One is tempted to substitute the rare ותרשא as in v.[11] (so Ball).—After עץ 𝕲 adds פרי: Ball deletes the פרי in v.[11].

14. יהי מארת] (‖ יהי אור in v.[3]). On the breach of concord, see G-K. § 145 *o*; Dav. § 113 *b*.—מאור] a late word, is used of heavenly bodies in Ezk. 32[8], Ps. 74[16]; it never means 'lamp' exactly, but is often applied collectively to the seven-armed lampstand of the tabernacle; once it is

---

* In Ar. this sense is said to belong to *'ušb*, but Heb. עשב has no such restriction.

addition (*v.i.*). The whole conception is as unscientific (in the modern sense) as it could be—(*a*) in its geocentric standpoint, (*b*) in making the distinction of day and night prior to the sun, (*c*) in putting the creation of the vegetable world before that of the heavenly bodies. Its religious significance, however, is very great, inasmuch as it marks the advance of Hebrew thought from the heathen notion of the stars to a pure monotheism. To the ancient world, and the Babylonians in particular, the heavenly bodies were animated beings, and the more conspicuous of them were associated or identified with the gods. The idea of them as an animated host occurs in Hebrew poetry (Ju. 5[20], Is. 40[26], Jb. 38[7] etc.); but here it is entirely eliminated, the heavenly bodies being reduced to mere *luminaries*, i.e. either embodiments of light or perhaps simply 'lamps' (*v.i.*). It is possible, as Gu. thinks, that a remnant of the old astrology lurks in the word *dominion*; but whereas in Babylonia the stars ruled over human affairs in general, their influence here is restricted to that which obviously depends on them, viz. the alternation of day and night, the festivals, etc. Comp. Jb. 38[33], Ps. 136[7–9] (Jer. 31[35]). It is noteworthy that this is the only work of creation of which the purpose is elaborately specified.—*luminaries* (מְא[ו]רֹת)] *i.e.* bearers or embodiments of light. The word is used most frequently of the sevenfold light of the tabernacle

---

used of the eyes (Pr. 15[30]), and once of the divine countenance (Ps. 90[8]).—ברקיע הש׳] the gen. is not partitive but explicative: Dav. § 24 (*a*).—𝔊 inserts at this point: *εἰς φαῦσιν τῆς γῆς, καὶ ἄρχειν τῆς ἡμέρας κ. τ. νυκτὸς, καί.*—לאתת] In Jer. 10[2] אתות השמים are astrological portents such as the heathen fear, and that is commonly taken as the meaning here, though it is not quite easy to believe the writer would have said the sun and moon were *made* for this purpose.* If we take אות in its ordinary sense of 'token' or 'indication,' we might suppose it defined by the words which follow. Tuch obtains a connexion by making the double ו=*both . . . and* ("as signs, both for [sacred] seasons and for days and years"): others by a *hendiadys* ("signs *of* seasons"). It would be less

---

* The prophetic passages cited by Dri. (*Gen.* 10[1]) all contemplate a reversal of the order of nature, and cannot safely be appealed to as illustrations of its normal functions.

(Ex. 25[6] etc.); and to speak of it as expressing a markedly prosaic view of the subject (Gu.) is misleading.—*in the firmament, etc.*] moving in prescribed paths on its lower surface. This, however, does not justify the interpretation of רקיע as the Zodiac (above, p. 22).—*to separate between the day, etc.*]. Day and night are independent entities; but they are now put under the *rule* of the heavenly bodies, as their respective spheres of influence (Ps. 121[6]).—*for signs and for seasons, etc.*] מוֹעֲדִים (seasons) appears never (certainly not in P) to be used of the natural seasons of the year (Ho. 2[11], Jer. 8[7] are figurative), but always of a time conventionally agreed upon (see Ex. 9[5]), or fixed by some circumstance. The commonest application is to the *sacred seasons* of the ecclesiastical year, which are fixed by the moon (cf. Ps. 104[19]). If the natural seasons are excluded, this seems the only possible sense here; and P's predilection for matters of cultus makes the explanation plausible.—אֹתֹת (signs) is more difficult, and none of the explanations given is entirely satisfactory (*v.i.*).—**16.** *for dominion over the day . . . night*] in the sense explained above; and so v.[18]. —*and the stars*] Since the writer seems to avoid on principle the everyday names of the objects, and to describe them by their nature and the functions they serve, the clause is probably a gloss (but *v.i.*). On the other hand, it would be too bold an expedient to supply an express naming of the planets after the analogy of the first three works (Tu.).

The laboured explanation of the purposes of the heavenly bodies is confused, and suggests overworking (Ho.). The clauses which most excite suspicion are the two beginning with והיו (the difficult [14b] and [15aα]);—note in particular the awkward repetition of למארות וגו'. The

---

violent to render the first ו *und zwar* (*videlicet*): "as signs, *and that* for seasons," etc.; see BDB, *s.* ו 1. b, where some of the examples come, at any rate, very near the sense proposed. Olshausen arrives at the same sense by reading לְמוֹ' simply (*MBA*, 1870, 380).—**16.** ואת הכ'] Dri. (*Hebr.* ii. 33) renders "and the lesser light, as also the stars, to rule," etc. The construction is not abnormal; but would the writer have said that the stars rule the night?—**18.** וְלַהבדיל] On the comp. sheva see Kön. i. § 10, 6 e.

functions are stated with perfect clearness in $^{16-18}$: (*a*) to give light upon the earth, (*b*) to rule day and night, and (*c*) to separate light from darkness. I am disposed to think that ^{14b} was introduced as an exposition of the idea of the vb. מֹשֵׁל, and that $^{15a\alpha}$ was then added to restore the connexion. Not much importance can be attached to the insertions of 𝔊 (*v.i.*), which may be borrowed from v.$^{17f.}$.

20–23. Sixth work: Aquatic and aërial animals.—*Let the waters swarm with swarming things—living creatures, and let fowl fly, etc.*] The conjunction of two distinct forms of life under one creative act has led Gu. to surmise that two originally separate works have been combined in order to bring the whole within the scheme of six days. Ben. (rendering *and fowl that may fly*) thinks the author was probably influenced by some ancient tradition that birds as well as fishes were produced by the water (so Ra. and IEz. on 2^{19}). The conjecture is attractive, and the construction has the support of all Gk. Vns. and 𝔙; but it is not certain that the verb can mean "*produce* a swarm." More probably (in connexions like the present: see Ex. 7^{28} [J] [EV 8^3], Ps. 105^{30}) the sense is simply *teem with*, indicating the place or element in which the swarming creatures abound, in which case it cannot possibly govern עוֹף as obj.—שֶׁרֶץ has a sense something like 'vermin': *i.e.* it never denotes 'a swarm,' but is always used of the creatures that

---

20. ישרצו . . . שרץ] On synt. see Dav. § 73, *R.* 2. The root has in Aram. the sense of 'creep,' and there are many passages in OT where that idea would be appropriate (Lv. $11^{29.\ 41-43}$ etc.); hence Rob. Smith (*RS*², 293), 'creeping vermin generally.' But here and Gn. 8^{17} 9^7, Ex. 1^7 7^{28}, Ps. 105^{30} it can only mean 'teem' or 'swarm'; and Dri. (*Gen.* 12) is probably right in extending that meaning to all the pass. in Heb. Gn. $1^{20f.}$, Ex. 7^{28}, Ps. 105^{30} are the only places where the constr. with cog. acc. appears; elsewhere the animals themselves are subj. of the vb. The words, except in three passages, are peculiar to the vocabulary of P.—But for the fact that שֶׁרֶץ never means 'swarm,' but always 'swarming thing,' it would be tempting to take it as *st. constr.* before נפש חיה (𝔊, Aq. 𝔙). As it is, נ' ח' has all the awkwardness of a gloss (see 2^{19}). The phrase is applied once to man, 2^7 (J); elsewhere to animals,—mostly in P (Gn. $1^{21.\ 24.\ 30}$ $9^{10.\ 12.\ 15.\ 16}$, Lv. $11^{10.\ 46}$ etc.).—ועוף יעופף] The order of words as in v.^{22} (והעוף ירב), due to emphasis on the new subj. The use of descriptive impf. (𝔊, Aq. ΣΘ𝔙) is mostly poetic, and for reasons given above must here be refused.—על פני] = 'in

appear in swarms (*v.i.*).—נֶפֶשׁ חַיָּה] lit. 'living soul'; used here collectively, and with the sense of נפש weakened, as often, to 'individual' or 'being' (ct. v.^{30} and see on 2^{7}). The creation of the aquatic animals marks, according to OT ideas, the first appearance of life on the earth, for life is nowhere predicated of the vegetable kingdom.—*over the earth in front of the firmament*] *i.e.* in the atmosphere, for which Heb. has no special name.—**21.** *created*] indistinguishable from *made* in v.^{25}.—*the great sea monsters*] The introduction of this new detail in the execution of the fiat is remarkable. הַתַּנִּינִם here denotes actual marine animals; but this is almost the only passage where it *certainly* bears that sense (Ps. 148^{7}). There are strong traces of mythology in the usage of the word: Is. 27^{1} 51^{9} (Gu. *Schöpf.* 30–33), Ps. 74^{13} (?); and it may have been originally the name of a class of legendary monsters like Ti'āmat. The mythological interpretation lingered in Jewish exegetical tradition (see below).—**22.** *And God blessed them, etc.*] In contrast with the plants, whose reproductive powers are included in their creation (v.$^{11ff.}$), these living beings are endowed with the right of self-propagation by a separate act—a benediction (see v.^{28}). The distinction is natural.—*be fruitful, etc.*] "There is nothing to indicate that only a

---

front of': see BDB, *s.* פנה, II. 7, a,—𝔊 inserts ויהי כן at the end of the v.—**21.** התנינם] It is naturally difficult to determine exactly how far the Heb. usage of the word is coloured by mythology. The important point is that it represents a power hostile to God, not only in the pass. cited above, but also in Job 7^{12}. There are resemblances in the Ar. ***tinnīn***, a fabulous amphibious monster, appearing now on land and now in the sea (personification of the waterspout? *RS*^{2}, 176), concerning which the Arabian cosmographers have many wonderful tales to relate (Mas'ūdī, i. 263, 266 ff.; Kazwīnī, Ethé's tr. i. 270 ff.). Ra., after explaining literally, adds by way of Haggada that these are 'Leviathan and his consort,' who were created male and female, but the female was killed and salted for the righteous in the coming age, because if they had multiplied the world would not have stood before them (comp. En. 60^{7-9}, 4 Esd. 6^{49-52}, *Ber. R.* c. 7).*—ואת כל־נפש הח׳] Cf. 9^{10},

---

* In Bab. ***tannînu*** is said to be a mythological designation of the earth (Jen. *Kosm.* 161; Jer. *ATLO*^{2}, 136^{7}; King, *Cr. Tab.* 109^{24}); but that throws no light on Heb.

single pair of each kind was originally produced' (Ben.); the language rather suggests that whole species, in something like their present multitude, were created.

24, 25. **Seventh work: Terrestrial animals.**—24. *Let the earth bring forth living creatures*] נפש חיה (again coll.) is here a generic name for *land* animals, being restricted by what precedes—'living animals that spring from the earth.' Like the plants (v.^{12}), they are boldly said to be produced by the earth, their bodies being part of the earth's substance ($2^{7.19}$); this could not be said of fishes in relation to the water, and hence a different form of expression had to be employed in v.^{20}.—The classification of animals (best arranged in v.^{25}) is threefold: (1) wild animals, חַיַּת הָאָרֶץ (roughly, *carnivora*); (2) domesticated animals, בְּהֵמָה (*herbivora*); (3) reptiles, רֶמֶשׂ הָאֲדָמָה, including perhaps creeping insects and very small quadrupeds (see Dri. *DB*, i. 518). A somewhat similar threefold division appears in a Babylonian tablet—'cattle of the field, beasts of the field and creatures of the city' (Jen. *KIB*, vi. 1. 42 f.; King, *Cr. Tab.* 112 f.).—25. *God saw that it was good*] The formula distinctly marks the separation of this work from the creation of man, which follows on the same day. The absence of a benediction corresponding to

---

Lv. 11^{10}; 'נ though without art. is really determined by כל (but see Dri. *T.* § 209 (1)).—אשר שרצו] 'א, acc. of definition, as שֶׁרֶץ in v.^{20}.—**22.** פְּרוּ וּרְבוּ] highly characteristic of P (only 3 times elsewhere).

24. The distinctions noted above are not strictly observed throughout the OT. בהמה (from a root signifying 'be dumb'—Ar. and Eth.) denotes collectively, *first*, animals as distinguished from man (Ex. 9^{19} etc.), but chiefly the larger mammals; *then*, domestic animals (the dumb creatures with which man has most to do), (Gn. 34^{23} 36^{6} etc.). Of *wild* animals specially it is seldom used alone (Dt. 32^{24}, Hab. 2^{17}), but sometimes with an addition (אֶרֶץ, שָׂדֶה, יַעַר) which marks the unusual reference. As a noun of unity, Neh. $2^{12.14}$. See BDB, *s.v.*—חַיְתוֹ אֶרֶץ] an archaic phrase in which ו represents the old case ending of the nom., *u* or *um* (G–K. § 90 *n*). So Ps. 79^{2}; חיתו in other combinations Is. 56^{9}, Zeph. 2^{14}, Ps. 104^{11}; Ps. 50^{10} 104^{20}. In sense it is exactly the same as the commoner חַיַּת הָאָרֶץ ($1^{25.30}$ $9^{2.10}$ etc.), and usually denotes *wild* animals, though sometimes animals in general (ζῶον).—רמש and שרץ naturally overlap; but the first name is derived from the manner of movement, and the second from the tendency to swarm (Dri. *l.c.*).

vv.[22. 28] is surprising, but it is idle to speculate on the reason.

26–28. Eighth work: Creation of man.—As the narrative approaches its climax, the style loses something of its terse rigidity, and reveals a strain of poetic feeling which suggests that the passage is moulded on an ancient creation hymn (Gu.). The distinctive features of this last work are: (*a*) instead of the simple jussive we have the cohortative of either self-deliberation or consultation with other divine beings; (*b*) in contrast to the lower animals, which are made each after its kind or type, man is made in the image of God; (*c*) man is designated as the head of creation by being charged with the rule of the earth and all the living creatures hitherto made.—**26.** *Let us make man*] The difficulty of the 1st pers. pl. has always been felt.

Amongst the **Jews** an attempt was made to get rid of it by reading נַעֲשֶׂר as ptcp. Niph.—a view the absurd grammatical consequences of which are trenchantly exposed by IEz. The older Christian comm. generally find in the expression an allusion to the Trinity (so even Calvin); but that doctrine is entirely unknown to the OT, and cannot be implied here. In modern times it has sometimes been explained as pl. of self-deliberation (Tu.), or after the analogy of the 'we' of royal edicts; but Di. has shown that neither is consistent with native Heb. idiom. Di. himself regards it as based on the idea of God expressed by the pl. אלהים, as 'the living personal synthesis of a fulness of powers and forces' (so Dri.); but that philosophic rendering of the concept of deity appears to be foreign to the theology of the OT.

---

26. בצלמנו כדמותנו] 𝕲 κατ' εἰκόνα ἡμετέραν καὶ καθ' ὁμοίωσιν. *Mechilta* (see above, p. 14), gives as 𝕲's reading בצלם ובדמות.—On the בְּ 'of a model,' cf. Ex. 25^{40}; BDB, *s.v.* III. 8.—צלם] Ass. *ṣalmu*, the technical expression for the statue of a god (*KAT*[3], 476^{8}); Aram. and Syr. צַלְמָא, = 'image'; the root is not *ẓalima*, 'be dark,' but possibly *ṣalama*, 'cut off' (Nöldeke, *ZATW*, xvii. 185 f.). The idea of 'pattern' or 'model' is confined to the P pass. cited above; it stands intermediate between the concrete sense just noted (an artificial material reproduction: 1 Sa. 6^{5} etc.) and another still more abstract, viz. 'an unreal semblance' (Ps. 39^{7} 73^{20}).—דְּמוּת is the abstr. noun *resemblance*; but also used concretely (2 Ch. 4^{3}, like Syr. ܕܡܘܬܐ); Ar. *dumyat* = 'effigy.' The ו is radical (form דְּמָוּת, cf. Ar.); hence the ending וּת is no proof of Aramaic influence (We. *Prol.*[5] 388); see Dri. *JPh.* xi. 216.—ובכל־הארץ] Ins. חַיַּת with 𝕾 (*v.s.*). Other Vns. agree with MT.

The most natural and most widely accepted explanation is that God is here represented as taking counsel with divine beings other than Himself, viz. the angels or host of heaven: cf. 3^{22} 11^{7}, Is. 6^{8}, 1 Ki. 22^{19-22} (so Philo, Ra. IEz. De. Ho. Gu. Ben. al.). Di. objects to this interpretation, *first*, that it ascribes to angels some share in the creation of man, which is contrary to scriptural doctrine; * and, *second*, that the very existence of angels is nowhere alluded to by P at all. There is force in these considerations; and probably the ultimate explanation has to be sought in a pre-Israelite stage of the tradition (such as is represented by the Babylonian account: see below, p. 46), where a polytheistic view of man's origin found expression. This would naturally be replaced in a Heb. recension by the idea of a heavenly council of angels, as in 1 Ki. 22, Jb. 1, 38^{7}, Dn. 4^{14} 7^{10} etc. That P retained the idea in spite of his silence as to the existence of angels is due to the fact that it was decidedly less anthropomorphic than the statement that man was made in the image of the one incomparable Deity.—*in our image, according to our likeness*] The general idea of likeness between God and man frequently occurs in classical literature, and sometimes the very term of this v. (εἰκών, *ad imaginem*) is employed. To speak of it, therefore, as "the distinctive feature of the Bible doctrine concerning man" is an exaggeration; although it is true that such expressions on the plane of heathenism import much less than in the religion of Israel (Di.). The idea in this precise form is in the OT peculiar to P ($5^{1.3}$ 9^{6}); the conception, but not the expression, appears in Ps. 8^{6}: later biblical examples are Sir. $17^{3ff.}$, WS. 2^{23} (where the 'image' is equivalent to immortality), 1 Co. 11^{7}, Col. 3^{10}, Eph. 4^{24}, Ja. 3^{9}.

The origin of the conception is probably to be found in the Babylonian mythology. Before proceeding to the creation of Ea-bani, Aruru forms a mental image (*zikru*: see Jen. *KIB*, vi. 1, 401 f.) of the God Anu (*ib.* 120, l. 33); and similarly, in the Descent of Ištar,

* Comp. Calvin: "Minimam vero tam præclari operis partem Angelis adscribere abominandum sacrilegium est."

Ea forms a *zikru* in his wise heart before creating Aṣūšunamir (*ib.* 86. l. 11). In both cases the reference is obviously to the bodily form of the created being. See, further, *KAT*[3], 506; *ATLO*[2], 167.

The patristic and other theological developments of the doctrine lie beyond the scope of this commentary; * and it is sufficient to observe with regard to them—(1) that the 'image' is not something peculiar to man's original state, and lost by the Fall; because P, who alone uses the expression, knows nothing of a Fall, and in 9^6 employs the term, without any restriction, of post-diluvian mankind. (2) The distinction between εἰκών (*imago*) and ὁμοίωσις (*similitudo*)—the former referring to the essence of human nature and the latter to its accidents or its endowments by grace—has an apparent justification in 𝔊, which inserts καὶ between the two phrases (see below), and *never mentions the 'likeness' after* 1^{26}; so that it was possible to regard the latter as something belonging to the divine idea of man, but not actually conferred at his creation. The Heb. affords no basis for such speculations: cf. $5^{1.3}$ 9^6.—(3) The view that the divine image consists in dominion over the creatures (Greg. Nyss., Chrysostom, Socinians, etc.) is still defended by Ho.; but it cannot be held without an almost inconceivable weakening of the figure, and is inconsistent with the sequel, where the rule over the creatures is, by a separate benediction, conferred on man, already made in the image of God. The truth is that the image marks the distinction between man and the animals, and so qualifies him for dominion: the latter is the consequence, not the essence, of the divine image (cf. Ps. $8^{6ff.}$, Sir. 17^{2-4}).—(4) Does the image refer primarily to the spiritual nature or to the bodily form (upright attitude, etc.) of man? The idea of a corporeal resemblance seems free from objection on the level of OT theology; and it is certainly strongly suggested by a comparison of 5^3 with 5^1. God is expressly said to have a 'form' which can be seen (תְּמוּנָה, Nu. 12^8, Ps. 17^{15}); the OT writers constantly attribute to Him bodily parts; and that they ever advanced to the conception of God as formless spirit would be difficult to prove. On the other hand, it may well be questioned if the idea of a spiritual *image* was within the compass of Heb. thought. Di., while holding that the central idea is man's spiritual nature, admits a reference to the bodily form in so far as it is the expression and organ of mind, and inseparable from spiritual qualities.† It might be truer to say that it denotes primarily the bodily form, but includes those spiritual attributes of which the former is the natural and self-evident symbol.‡—Note the striking parallel in Ovid, *Met.* i. 76 ff.

Man (אָדָם) is here generic (the human race), not the

* A good summary is given by Zapletal, *Alttestamentliches*, 1–15.

† So Augustine, *De Gen. cont. Man.* I. 17: "Ita intelligitur per animum maxime, attestante etiam erecta corporis forma, homo factus ad imaginem et similitudinem Dei."

‡ Cf. Engert, *Die Weltschöpfung*, 33.

proper name of an individual, as 5[3]. Although the great majority of comm. take it for granted that a single pair is contemplated, there is nothing in the narrative to bear out that view; and the analogy of the marine and land animals is against it on the whole (Tu. and Ben.).—*fish of the sea, etc.*] The enumeration coincides with the classification of animals already given, except that *the earth* occurs where we should expect *wild beast of the earth.* חַיַּת should undoubtedly be restored to the text on the authority of 𝔖.—27. *in his image, in the image of God, etc.*] The repetition imparts a rhythmic movement to the language, which may be a faint echo of an old hymn on the glory of man, like Ps. 8 (Gu.).—*male and female*] The persistent idea that man as first created was bi-sexual and the sexes separated afterwards (mentioned by Ra. as a piece of Haggada, and recently revived by Schwally, *ARW*, ix. 172 ff.), is far from the thought of the passage. — 28. A benediction is here again the source of fertility, but this time also of dominion: Gu. regards this as another fragment of a hymn.

29–31. The record of creation closes with another (tenth)

---

27. בצלמו] 𝔊 om. The curious paraphrase of Σ appears to reflect the Ebionite tendency of that translator: *ἐν εἰκόνι διαφόρῳ ὄρθιον ὁ θεὸς ἔκτισεν αὐτόν* (Geiger, *Jüd. Ztschr. f. Wiss. u. Leben*, i. 40 f.). See, however, Nestle, *MM*, 3 f., who calls attention to the *ὄρθιον* in 𝔊 of 1 Sa. 28[14], and considers this word the source of the idea that the upright form of man is part of the divine image. But 𝔊 in 1 Sa. probably misread זקן as זקף.—אתו] *constructio ad formam*: אֹתָם *constr. ad sensum*, אדם being collective: see G-K. § 132*g*.—זכר ונקבה] The phrase confined to P except Dt. 4[16]; נ׳ alone in Jer. 31[21] (a gloss?). Although the application to a single pair of individuals predominates in the Law, the coll. sense is established by Gn. 7[16], and is to be assumed in some other cases (Nu. 5[3] etc.). On its etymology see Ges. *Th.*, *s.v.*, and (for a different view) Schwally, *ZATW*, xi. 181 f. — 28. ויאמר להם] 𝔊 *λέγων*; perhaps original.—וכבשֻׁהָ] The only instance of a verbal suff. in this chapter: a strong preference for expression of acc. by את with suff. is characteristic of the style of P (We. *Prol.*[6] 389).—הרמשת] ptcp. with art. = relative cl.: see Dav. § 99, *R.* 1. The previous noun is defined by כל, as in v.[21] (ࠌ inserts the art.).—After שמים 𝔖 read ובבהמה (so Ball). 𝔊 has for the end of the v.: *καὶ πάντων τῶν κτηνῶν καὶ πάσης τῆς γῆς καὶ πάντων [τῶν ἑρπετῶν] τῶν ἑρπόντων ἐπὶ τῆς γῆς.*

29. נתתי] = 'I give'; Dav. § 40*b*; Dri. *T.* § 13.—זרע (over Athnach)]

divine utterance, which regulates in broad and general terms the relation of men and animals to the vegetable world. The plants are destined for food to man and beast. The passage is not wholly intelligible apart from 9^{2ff}, from which we see that its point is the restriction on the use of animal food, particularly on the part of man. In other words, the first stage of the world's history—that state of things which the Creator pronounced very good—is a state of peace and harmony in the animal world. This is P's substitute for the garden of Eden.

A distinction is made between the food of man and that of animals: to the former (*a*) seeding plants (probably because the seed is important in cultivation, and in cereals is the part eaten), and (*b*) fruit-bearing trees; to the latter *all the greenness of herbage*, *i.e.* the succulent leafy parts. The statement is not exhaustive: no provision is made for fishes, nor is there any mention of the use of such victuals as milk, honey, etc. Observe the difference from chs. 2. 3, where man is made to live on fruit alone, and only as part of the curse has herbs (עשב) assigned to him.—**31.** The account closes with the divine verdict of approval, which

---

wrongly omitted by 𝔊.—אכלה] found only in P and Ezk., and always preceded by לְ. It is strictly fem. inf., and perhaps always retains verbal force (see Dri. *JPh.* xi. 217). The ordinary cognate words for food are אֹכֶל and מַאֲכָל.—**30.** ולכל וגו׳ The construction is obscure. The natural interpretation is that ^{30} expresses a contrast to ^{29}—the one specifying the food of *man*, the other that of *animals*. To bring out this sense clearly it is necessary (with Ew. al.) to insert נתתי before את־כל־ירק. The text requires us to treat לכם יהיה לאכלה in ^{29} as a parenthesis (Di.) and את־כל־ירק as still under the regimen of the distant נתתי.—רוֹמֵשׂ] 𝔊 ἑρπετῷ τῷ ἕρποντι—assimilating.—נֶפֶשׁ] here used in its primary sense of the *soul* or animating principle (see later on 2^7), with a marked difference from vv.$^{20f. 24}$.—ירק עשב] so 9^3, = יֶ׳ דֶּשֶׁא Ps. 37^2. יֶרֶק (verdure) alone may include the foliage of trees (Ex. 10^{15}); יֶ׳ הַשָּׂדֶה = 'grass' (Nu. 22^4). The word is rare (6 t.); a still rarer form יֵרָק may sometimes be confounded with it (Is. 37^{27} = 2 Ki. 17^{26}?).—**31.** יום הששי] The art. with the num. appears here for the first time in the chap. On the construction, see Dri. *T.* § 209 (1), where it is treated as the beginning of a usage prevalent in post-biblical Heb., which often in a definite expression uses the art. with the adj. alone (כנסת הגדולה, etc.). Cf. G–K. § 126 *w* (with footnote); Ho. *Hex.* 465; Dri. *JPh.* xi. 229 f.

here covers a survey of all that has been made, and rises to the superlative 'very good.'

Vv.[29f.] differ significantly in their phraseology from the preceding sections: thus זֹרֵעַ instead of מַזְרִיעַ ([11. 12]); העץ אשר בו פרי עץ זרע זרע instead of the far more elegant עץ עשה פרי אשר זרעו בו; the classification into beasts, birds, and reptiles (ct. [24. 25]); נפש חיה of the inner principle of life instead of the living being as in [20f. 24]; ירק עשב instead of דשא. These linguistic differences are sufficient to prove literary discontinuity of some kind. They have been pointed out by Kraetschmar (*Bundesvorstg.* 103 f.), who adds the doubtful material argument that the prohibition of animal food to man nullifies the dominion promised to him in vv.[26. 28]. But his inference (partly endorsed by Ho.) that the vv. are a later addition to P does not commend itself; they are vitally connected with 9[2ff.], and must have formed part of the theory of the Priestly writer. The facts point rather to a distinction in the sources with which P worked,—perhaps (as Gu. thinks) the enrichment of the creation-story by the independent and widespread myth of the Golden Age when animals lived peaceably with one another and with men. The motives of this belief lie deep in the human heart—horror of bloodshed, sympathy with the lower animals, the longing for harmony in the world, and the conviction that on the whole the course of things has been from good to worse—all have contributed their share, and no scientific teaching can rob the idea of its poetic and ethical value.

II. 1–3. The rest of God.—The section contains but one idea, expressed with unusual solemnity and copiousness of language,—the institution of the Sabbath. It supplies an answer to the question, Why is no work done on the last day of the week? (Gu.). The answer lies in the fact that God Himself rested on that day from the work of creation, and bestowed on it a special blessing and sanctity.—The writer's idea of the Sabbath and its sanctity is almost too realistic for the modern mind to grasp: it is not an institution which exists or ceases with its observance by man; the divine rest is a fact as much as the divine working, and so the sanctity of the day is a fact whether man secures the benefit or not. There is little trace of the idea that the Sabbath was made for man and not man for the Sabbath; it is an ordinance of the kosmos like any other part of the creative operations, and is for the good of man in precisely the same sense as the whole creation is subservient to his welfare.

1. *And all their host*] The 'host of heaven' (צְבָא הַשָּׁמַיִם) is frequently mentioned in the OT, and denotes sometimes the heavenly bodies, especially as objects of worship (Dt. 4^{19} etc.), sometimes the angels considered as an organised army (1 Ki. 22^{19} etc.). The expression 'host of the earth' nowhere occurs; and it is a question whether the pl. suff. here is not to be explained as a *denominatio a potiori* (Ho.), or as a species of attraction (Dri.). If it has any special meaning as applied to the earth, it would be equivalent to what is elsewhere called מְלֹא הארץ (Is. 6^{3} 34^{1}, Dt. 33^{16} etc.)—the *contents* of the earth, and is most naturally limited to those things whose creation has just been described.* In any case the verse yields little support to the view of Smend and We., that in the name 'Yahwe of Hosts' the word denotes the complex of cosmical forces (Smend, *AT Rel.-gesch.* 201 ff.), or the demons in which these forces were personified (We. *Kl. Proph.* 77).—2. *And God finished, etc.*] The duplication of v.[1] is harsh, and

---

1. צבא] Lit. 'host' or 'army'; then 'period of service' (chiefly military). 𝔊 *κόσμος* and 𝔙 *ornatus* look like a confusion with צְבִי. Used of the host of heaven, Dt. 4^{19} 17^{3}, Is. 24^{21} 40^{26}, where 𝔙 has in the first case *astra*, in the others *militia*; 𝔊 *κόσμος* in all.—2. ויכל] For the alleged negative sense of Piel (see above), examine Nu. 17^{25}, or (with מן) 1 Sa. 10^{13}, Ex. 34^{33} etc.—מלאכה] the word "used regularly of the work or business forbidden on the Sabbath (Ex. $20^{9.10}$ 35^{2}, Jer. $17^{22.24}$ al.)" (Dri.); or on holy convocations (Ex. 12^{16}, Lv. 16^{29} $23^{28ff.}$, Nu. 29^{7}). It has the prevailing sense of regular occupation or business, as Gen. 39^{11}, Jon. 1^{8}.—השביעי[1]] ⅏𝔊𝔖 *Jub.*, *Ber. R.* הששי, given as 𝔊's reading in *Mechilta* (cf. p. 14 above).—וישבת] The omission of continued subj. (אלהים) might strengthen We.'s contention that the clause is a gloss (see p. 10 above): it occurs nowhere else in the passage except *possibly* 1^{7}. The verb שבת (possibly connected with Ar. *sabata* = 'cut off,' or Ass. *šabātu* = 'cease,' 'be completed': but see *KAT*[3], 593 f.) appears in OT in three quite distinct senses: (*a*) 'cease to be,' 'come to an end'; (*b*) 'desist' (from work, etc.); (*c*) 'keep Sabbath' (denom.). Of the last there are four undoubted cases, all very late: Lv. 25^{2} 23^{32} $26^{34f.}$, 2 Ch. 36^{21}. But there are five others where this meaning is at least possible: Gn. $2^{2.3}$, Ex. 16^{30} 23^{12} 34^{21} 31^{17}; and of these Ex. 23^{12} 34^{21} are pre-exilic. Apart from these doubtful passages, the sense

---

* Cf. Neh. 9^{6} "the heavens, the heavens of the heavens, and all their host, the earth and all that is upon it, the seas and all that is in them."

strongly suggests a composition of sources.—*on the seventh day*] 𝔐𝔊𝔖 read *sixth day* (so also *Jubilees*, ii. 16, and Jerome, *Quæst.*), which is accepted as the original text by many comm. (Ilg. Ols. Bu. al.).* But *sixth* is so much the easier reading that one must hesitate to give it the preference. To take the vb. as plup. (Calv. al.) is grammatically impossible. On We.'s explanation, see above, p. 9f. The only remaining course is to give a purely negative sense to the vb. *finish*: *i.e.* 'desisted from,' 'did not continue' (IEz. De. Di. Dri. al.). The last view may be accepted, in spite of the absence of convincing parallels.—*and he rested*] The idea of שָׁבַת is essentially negative: cessation of work, not relaxation (Dri.): see below. Even so, the expression is strongly anthropomorphic, and warns us against exaggerating P's aversion to such representations.†—3. *blessed* . . .

'desist' (*b*) is found only in Ho. 7^4, Jb. 32^1 (Qal); Ex. 5^5, Jos. 22^{25}, Ezk. 16^{41} 34^{10} (Hiph.); of which Ho. 7^4 (a corrupt context) and Ex. 5^5, alone are *possibly* pre-exilic. In all other occurrences (about 46 in all; 9 Qal, 4 Niph., 33 Hiph.) the sense (*a*) 'come to an end' obtains; and this usage prevails in all stages of the literature from Am. to Dn.; the pre-exilic examples being Gn. 8^{22}, Jos. 5^{12} (?) (Qal); Is. 17^3 (Niph.); Am. 8^4, Ho. 1^4 2^{13}, Is. 16^{10} (?) 30^{11}, Dt. 32^{26}, 2 Ki. $23^{5.11}$, Jer. 7^{34} 16^9 36^{29} (Hiph.). These statistics seem decisive against Hehn's view (*l.c.* 93 ff.) that שׁבת is originally a denom. from שַׁבָּת. If all the uses are to be traced to a single root-idea, there can be no doubt that (*b*) is primary. But while a dependence of (*a*) on (*b*) is intelligible (cf. the analogous case of חָדַל), 'desist' from work, and 'come to an end' are after all very different ideas; and, looking to the immense preponderance of the latter sense (*a*), especially in the early literature, it is worth considering whether the old Heb. vb. did not mean simply 'come to an end,' and whether the sense 'desist' was not imported into it under the influence of the denominative use (*c*) of which Ex. 23^{12} 34^{21} might be early examples. [A somewhat similar view is now expressed by Meinhold (*ZATW*, 1909, 100 f.), except that he ignores the distinction between 'desist' and 'come to an end,' which seems to me important.]—3. ברא לעשות . . .] The awkward construction is perhaps adopted because ברא could not directly govern the subst. מלאכה. 𝔊 has ἤρξατο . . . ποιῆσαι.

---

* Expressly mentioned as 𝔊's reading in *Mechilta*: see above, p. 14, and Geiger, *l.c.* 439.

† In another passage of P, Ex. 31^{17}, the anthropomorphism is greatly intensified: "God rested and refreshed Himself" (lit. 'took breath').—See Jast. (*AJTh.* ii. 343 ff.), who thinks that God's 'resting' meant originally "His purification after His conquest of the forces hostile to

sanctified] The day is blessed and sacred in itself and from the beginning; to say that the remark is made in view of the future institution of the Sabbath (Dri.), does not quite bring out the sense. Both verbs contain the idea of selection and distinction (cf. Sir. 36 [33] 7-9), but they are not synonymous (Gu.). A blessing is the effective utterance of a good wish; applied to things, it means their endowment with permanently beneficial qualities (Gn. 27^{27}, Ex. 23^{25}, Dt. 28^{12}). This is the case here: the Sabbath is a constant source of well-being to the man who recognises its true nature and purpose. To *sanctify* is to set apart from common things to holy uses, or to put in a special relation to God.—*which God creatively made*] see the footnote.—Although no closing formula for the seventh day is given, it is contrary to the intention of the passage to think that the rest of God means His work of providence as distinct from creation: it is plainly a rest of one day that is thought of It is, of course, a still greater absurdity to suppose an interval of twenty-four hours between the two modes of divine activity. The author did not think in our dogmatic categories at all.

The origin of the Hebrew Sabbath, and its relation to Babylonian usages, raise questions too intricate to be fully discussed here (see Lotz, *Quæst. de hist. Sabbati* [1883]; Jastrow, *AJTh.* ii. [1898], 312 ff.; *KAT*³, 592 ff.; Dri. *DB*, *s.v.*, and *Gen.* 34; Sta. *BTh.* § 88, 2). The main facts, however, are these: (1) The name *šab[p]attu* occurs some five or six times in cuneiform records; but of these only two are of material importance for the Sabbath problem. (*a*) In a syllabary (II R. 32, 16 a, b) *šabattu* is equated with *ûm nûḫ libbi*, which has been conclusively shown to mean 'day of the appeasement of the heart (of the deity),'—in the first instance, therefore, a day of propitiation or atonement (Jen. *ZA*, iv. 274 ff.; Jast. *l.c.* 316 f.). (*b*) In a tablet discovered by Pinches in 1904, the name *šapattu* is applied to the fifteenth day of the month (as full-moon-day?) (Pin. *PSBA*, xxvi. 51 ff.; Zimmern, *ZDMG*, lviii. 199 ff., 458 ff.). (2) The only trace of a Babylonian *institution* at all resembling the Heb. Sabbath is the fact that in certain months of the year (Elul, Marchešvan, but possibly the rest as well) the 7th, 14th, 21st and 28th days, and also the 19th (probably as the 7×7th from the beginning of the previous month), had the character of *dies nefasti* ('lucky day, un-

---

the order of the world," and was a survival of the mythological idea of the appeasement of Marduk's anger against Ti'âmat. The vb. there used is *nâḫu*, the equivalent of Heb. נוח, used in Ex. 20¹¹.

lucky day'), on which certain actions had to be avoided by important personages (king, priest, physician) (IV R. 32 f., 33). Now, no evidence has ever been produced that these *dies nefasti* bore the name *šabattu*, and the likelihood that this was the case is distinctly lessened by the Pinches fragment, where the name is applied to the 15th day, but not to the 7th, although it also is mentioned on the tablet. The question, therefore, has assumed a new aspect; and Meinhold (*Sabbath u. Woche im AT* [1905], and more recently [1909], *ZATW*, xxix. 81 ff.), developing a hint of Zim., has constructed an ingenious hypothesis on the assumption that in Bab. *šabattu* denotes the day of the full moon. He points to the close association of new-moon and Sabbath in nearly all the pre-exilic references (Am. 8^{5}, Hos. 2^{13}, Is. 1^{13}, 2 Ki. $4^{22f.}$); and concludes that in early Israel, as in Bab., the Sabbath was the full-moon festival and nothing else. The institution of the weekly Sabbath he traces to a desire to compensate for the loss of the old lunar festivals, when these were abrogated by the Deuteronomic reformation. This innovation he attributes to Ezekiel; but steps towards it are found in the introduction of a weekly day of rest during harvest only (on the ground of Dt. 16^{9}; cf. Ex. 34^{21}), and in the establishment of the sabbatical year (Lv. 25), which he considers to be older than the weekly Sabbath. The theory involves great improbabilities, and its net result seems to be to leave the actual Jewish Sabbath as we know it without any point of contact in Bab. institutions. It is hard to suppose that there is no historical connexion between the Heb. Sabbath and the *dies nefasti* of the Bab. calendar; and if such a connexion exists, the chief difficulties remain where they have long been felt to lie, viz., (*a*) in the substitution of a weekly cycle running continuously through the calendar for a division of each month into seven-day periods, probably regulated by the phases of the moon; and (*b*) in the transformation of a day of superstitious restrictions into a day of joy and rest. Of these changes, it must be confessed, no convincing explanation has yet been found. The established sanctity of the number seven, and the decay or suppression of the lunar feasts, might be contributory causes; but when the change took place, and whether it was directly due to Babylonian influence, or was a parallel development from a lunar observance more primitive than either, cannot at present be determined. See Hehn, *Siebenzahl u. Sabbat*, 91 ff., esp. 114 ff.; cf. Gordon, *ETG*, 216 ff.

4a. *These are the generations, etc.*] The best sense that can be given to the expression is to refer the pronoun to

---

4a. תולדות] only in pl. const. or with suff.; and confined to P, Ch. and Ru. 4^{18}. Formed from Hiph. of ילד, it means properly 'begettings'; not, however, as noun of action, but concretely (='progeny'); and this is certainly the prevalent sense. The phrase א׳ ת׳ (only P [all in Gn. except Nu. 3^{1}], 1 Ch. 1^{29}, Ru. 4^{18}) means primarily "These are the descendants"; but since a *list* of descendants is a genealogy, it is practically the same thing if we render, "This is the genealogical register." In the great majority of instances (Gn. [5^{1}] 10^{1} 11^{10} 11^{27} 25^{12}

what precedes, and render the noun by 'origin': 'This is the origin of,' etc. But it is doubtful if תולדות can bear any such meaning, and altogether the half-verse is in the last degree perplexing. It is in all probability a redactional insertion.

The formula (and indeed the whole phraseology) is characteristic of P; and in that document it invariably stands as introduction to the section following. But in this case the next section (2^{4b}–4^{26}) belongs to J; and if we pass over the J passages to the next portion of P (ch. 5), the formula would collide with 5^{1}, which is evidently the proper heading to what follows. Unless, therefore, we adopt the improbable hypothesis of Strack, that a part of P's narrative has been dropped, the attempt to treat 2^{4a} in its present position as a superscription must be abandoned. On this ground most critics have embraced a view propounded by Ilgen, that the clause stood originally before 1^{1}, as the heading of P's account

---

$36^{1.9}$, 1 Ch. 1^{29}, Ru. 4^{18}) this sense is entirely suitable; the addition of a few historical notices is not inconsistent with the idea of a genealogy, nor is the general character of these sections affected by it. There are just three cases where this meaning is inapplicable: Gn. 6^{9} 25^{19} 37^{2}. But it is noteworthy that, except in the last case, at least a fragment of a genealogy follows; and it is fair to inquire whether 37^{2} may not have been originally followed by a genealogy (such as 35^{22b-26} or 46^{8-27} [see Hupfeld, *Quellen*, 102–109, 213–216]) which was afterwards displaced in the course of redaction (see p. 423, below). With that assumption we could explain every occurrence of the formula without having recourse to the unnatural view that the word may mean a "family history" (G–B. *s.v.*), or "an account of a man and his descendants" (BDB). The natural hypothesis would then be that a series of תולדות formed one of the sources employed by P in compiling his work: the introduction of this genealogical document is preserved in 5^{1} (so Ho.); the recurrent formula represents successive sections of it, and 2^{4a} is a redactional imitation. When it came to be amalgamated with the narrative material, some dislocations took place: hence the curious anomaly that a man's history sometimes appears under his own *Tôlĕdôth*, sometimes under those of his father; and it is difficult otherwise to account for the omission of the formula before 12^{1} or for its insertion in 36^{9}. On the whole, this theory seems to explain the facts better than the ordinary view that the formula was devised by P to mark the divisions of the principal work.—בהבראם] 'in their creation' or 'when they were created.' If the *lit. minusc.* has critical significance (Tu. Di.) the primary reading was inf. Qal (בְּבָרְאָם); and this requires to be supplemented by אלהים as subj. It is in this form that Di. thinks the clause originally stood at the beginning of Gen. (see on 1^{1}). But the omission of אלהים and the insertion of the ה *minusc.* are no necessary consequences of the transposition of the sentence; and the small ה may be merely an error in the archetypal MS, which has been mechanically repeated in all copies.

of the creation.* But this theory also is open to serious objection. It involves a meaning of תולדות which is contrary both to its etymology and the usage of P (see footnote). Whatever latitude of meaning be assigned to the word, it is the fact that in this formula it is always followed by gen. of the progenitor, never of the progeny: hence by analogy the phrase must describe that which is generated by the heavens and the earth, not the process by which they themselves are generated (so Lagarde, *Or.* ii. 38 ff., and Ho.). And even if that difficulty could be overcome (see Lagarde), generation is a most unsuitable description of the process of creation *as conceived by P*. In short, neither as superscription nor as subscription can the sentence be accounted for as an integral part of the Priestly Code. There seems no way out of the difficulty but to assume with Ho. that the formula in this place owes its origin to a mechanical imitation of the manner of P by a later hand. The insertion would be suggested by the observation that the formula divides the book of Gen. into definite sections; while the advantage of beginning a new section at this point would naturally occur to an editor who felt the need of sharply separating the two accounts of the creation, and regarded the second as in some way the continuation of the first. If that be so, he probably took ת׳ in the sense of 'history' and referred אֵלֶּה to what follows. The analogy of 5^1, Nu. 3^1 would suffice to justify the use of the formula before the ביום of [4b].—It has been thought that 𝕲 has preserved the original form of the text: viz. זה ספר ת׳ וגו׳ (cf. 5^1); the redactor having, "before inserting a section from the other document, accidentally copied in the opening words of 5^1, which were afterwards adapted to their present position" (Ben.). That is improbable. It is more likely that 𝕲 deliberately altered the text to correspond with 5^1. See Field, *Hex.*, *ad loc.*; Nestle, *MM*, 4.

Babylonian and other Cosmogonies.

1. The outlines of Bab. cosmogony have long been known from two brief notices in Greek writers: (1) an extract from Berossus (3rd cent. B.C.) made by Alexander Polyhistor, and preserved by Syncellus from the lost Chronicle of Eusebius (lib. i.); and (2) a passage from the Neo-Platonic writer Damascius (6th cent. A.D.). From these it was apparent that the biblical account of creation is in its main conceptions Babylonian. The interest of the fragments has been partly enhanced, but partly superseded, since the discovery of the closely parallel 'Chaldæan Genesis,' unearthed from the debris of Asshurbanipal's library at Nineveh by George Smith in 1873. It is therefore unnecessary to examine them in detail; but since the originals are not very accessible to English readers, they are here reprinted in full (with emendations after *KAT*[3], 488 ff.):

(1) Berossus: *Γενέσθαι φησὶ χρόνον ἐν ᾧ τὸ πᾶν σκότος καὶ ὕδωρ εἶναι, καὶ ἐν τούτοις ζῷα τερατώδη, καὶ ἰδιοφυεῖς* [em. Richt., cod. *εἰδιφυεῖς*] *τὰς ἰδέας ἔχοντα ζωογονεῖσθαι· ἀνθρώπους γὰρ διπτέρους γεννηθῆναι, ἐνίους δὲ*

* On Dillmann's modification of this theory, see above on 1^1.

καὶ τετραπτέρους καὶ διπροσώπους· καὶ σῶμα μὲν ἔχοντας ἕν, κεφαλὰς δὲ δύο, ἀνδρείαν τε καὶ γυναικείαν, καὶ αἰδοῖα δὲ [corr. v. Gutschm., cod. τε] δισσά, ἄρρεν καὶ θῆλυ· καὶ ἑτέρους ἀνθρώπους τοὺς μὲν αἰγῶν σκέλη καὶ κέρατα ἔχοντας, τοὺς δὲ ἵππου πόδας [corr. v. Gutschm., cod. ἱππόποδας], τοὺς δὲ τὰ ὀπίσω μὲν μέρη ἵππων, τὰ δὲ ἔμπροσθεν ἀνθρώπων, οὓς [ὡς? v. Gutschm.] ἱπποκενταύρους τὴν ἰδέαν εἶναι. Ζωογονηθῆναι δὲ καὶ ταύρους ἀνθρώπων κεφαλὰς ἔχοντας καὶ κύνας τετρασωμάτους, οὐρὰς ἰχθύος ἐκ τῶν ὄπισθεν μερῶν ἔχοντας, καὶ ἵππους κυνοκεφάλους καὶ ἀνθρώπους, καὶ ἕτερα ζῷα κεφαλὰς μὲν καὶ σώματα ἵππων ἔχοντα, οὐρὰς δὲ ἰχθύων· καὶ ἄλλα δὲ ζῷα παντοδαπῶν θηρίων μορφὰς ἔχοντα. Πρὸς δὲ τούτοις ἰχθύας καὶ ἑρπετὰ καὶ ὄφεις καὶ ἄλλα ζῷα πλείονα θαυμαστὰ καὶ παρηλλαγμένας [em. v. Gutschm., cod. παρηλλαγμένα] τὰς ὄψεις ἀλλήλων ἔχοντα· ὧν καὶ τὰς εἰκόνας ἐν τῷ τοῦ Βηλου ναῷ ἀνακεῖσθαι, ἄρχειν δὲ τούτων πάντων γυναῖκα ᾗ ὄνομα Ὁμορκα [corr. Scaliger, cod. Ὁμορωκα] εἶναι· τοῦτο δὲ Χαλδαϊστὶ μὲν Θαμτε [corr. W. R. Smith, *ZA*, vi. 339, cod. Θαλατθ], Ἑλληνιστὶ δὲ μεθερμηνεύεται θάλασσα κατὰ δὲ ἰσόψηφον σελήνη. Οὕτως δὲ τῶν ὅλων συνεστηκότων, ἐπανελθόντα Βηλον σχίσαι τὴν γυναῖκα μέσην, καὶ τὸ μὲν ἥμισυ αὐτῆς ποιῆσαι γῆν, τὸ δὲ ἄλλο ἥμισυ οὐρανόν, καὶ τὰ ἐν [σὺν? v. Gutschm.] αὐτῇ ζῷα ἀφανίσαι, ἀλληγορικῶς δέ φησι τοῦτο πεφυσιολογῆσθαι· ὑγροῦ γὰρ ὄντος τοῦ παντὸς καὶ ζῴων ἐν αὐτῷ γεγεννημένων [A]* τοιῶνδε [em. v. Gutschm., cod. τὸν δὲ] Βηλον, ὃν Δία μεθερμηνεύουσι, μέσον τεμόντα τὸ σκότος χωρίσαι γῆν καὶ οὐρανὸν ἀπ᾽ ἀλλήλων, καὶ διατάξαι τὸν κόσμον. Τὰ δὲ ζῷα οὐκ ἐνεγκόντα τὴν τοῦ φωτὸς δύναμιν φθαρῆναι, ἰδόντα δὲ τὸν Βηλον χώραν ἔρημον καὶ ἀκαρποφόρον [em. Gunkel, cod. καρποφόρον] κελεῦσαι ἑνὶ τῶν θεῶν τὴν κεφαλὴν ἀφελόντι ἑαυτοῦ τῷ ἀποῤῥυέντι αἵματι φυρᾶσαι τὴν γῆν καὶ διαπλάσαι ἀνθρώπους καὶ θηρία τὰ δυνάμενα τὸν ἀέρα φέρειν. Ἀποτελέσαι δὲ τὸν Βηλον καὶ ἄστρα καὶ ἥλιον καὶ σελήνην καὶ τοὺς πέντε πλανήτας. Ταῦτά φησιν ὁ πολυΐστωρ Ἀλέξανδρος τὸν Βηρωσσὸν ἐν τῇ πρώτῃ φάσκειν [B]* τοῦτον τὸν θεὸν ἀφελεῖν τὴν ἑαυτοῦ κεφαλὴν καὶ τὸ ῥυὲν αἷμα τοὺς ἄλλους θεοὺς φυρᾶσαι τῇ γῇ, καὶ διαπλάσαι τοὺς ἀνθρώπους· διὸ νοερούς τε εἶναι καὶ φρονήσεως θείας μετέχειν.

(2) Damascius: Τῶν δὲ βαρβάρων ἐοίκασι Βαβυλώνιοι μὲν τὴν μίαν τῶν ὅλων ἀρχὴν σιγῇ παριέναι, δύο δὲ ποιεῖν Ταυθε καὶ Ἀπασων, τὸν μὲν Ἀπασων ἄνδρα τῆς Ταυθε ποιοῦντες, ταύτην δὲ μητέρα θεῶν ὀνομάζοντες, ἐξ ὧν μονογενῆ παῖδα γεννηθῆναι τὸν Μωυμιν, αὐτὸν οἶμαι τὸν νοητὸν κόσμον ἐκ τῶν δυοῖν ἀρχῶν παραγόμενον. Ἐκ δὲ τῶν αὐτῶν ἄλλην γενεὰν προελθεῖν, Λαχην [cod. Δαχην] καὶ Λαχον [cod. Δαχον]. Εἶτα αὖ τρίτην ἐκ τῶν αὐτῶν, Κισσαρη καὶ Ἀσσωρον, ἐξ ὧν γενέσθαι τρεῖς, Ἀνον καὶ Ἰλλινον καὶ Ἀον· τοῦ δὲ Ἀου καὶ Δαυκης υἱὸν γενέσθαι τὸν Βηλον, ὃν δημιουργὸν εἶναί φασιν.†

---

* The sections commencing with [A] and [B] stand in the reverse order in the text. The transposition is due to von Gutschmid, and seems quite necessary to bring out any connected meaning, though there may remain a suspicion that the two accounts of the creation of man are variants, and that the second is interpolated. Je. *ATLO*², 134, plausibly assigns the section from ἀλληγορικῶς to φθαρῆναι to another recension (restoring [B] to its place in the text).

† The Greek text of Berossus will be found in Müller, *Fragm. Hist. Græc.* ii. 497 f.; that of Damascius in *Damascii philos. de prim. princ.* (ed. Kopp, 1826), cap. 125. For translations of both fragments, see

2. The only cuneiform document which admits of close and continuous comparison with Gn. 1 is the great Creation Epos just referred to. Since the publication, in 1876, of the first fragments, many lacunæ have been filled up from subsequent discoveries, and several duplicates have been brought to light; and the series is seen to have consisted of seven Tablets, entitled, from the opening phrase, *Enuma eliš* (='When above').* The actual tablets discovered are not of earlier date than the 7th cent. B.C., but there are strong reasons to believe that the originals of which these are copies are of much greater antiquity, and may go back to 2000 B.C., while the myth itself probably existed in writing in other forms centuries before that. Moreover, they represent the theory of creation on which the statements of Berossus and Damascius are based, and they have every claim to be regarded as the authorised version of the Babylonian cosmogony. It is here, therefore, if anywhere, that we must look for traces of Babylonian influences on the Hebrew conception of the origin of the world. The following outline of the contents of the tablets is based on King's analysis of the epic into five originally distinct parts (*CT*, p. lxvii).

i. *The Theogony.*—The first twenty-one lines of Tab. I. contain a description of the primæval chaos and the evolution of successive generations of deities:

When in the height heaven was not named,
And the earth beneath did not bear a name,
And the primæval Apsu,[1] who begat them,
And chaos, Ti'āmat,[2] the mother of them both,—
Their waters were mingled together,
. . . .
Then were created the gods in the midst of (heaven), etc.

First Laḫmu and Laḫamu,[3] then Ansar and Kisar,[4] and lastly (as we learn from Damascius, whose report is in accord with this part of the tablet, and may safely be used to make up a slight defect) the supreme triad of the Bab. pantheon, Anu, Bel, and Ea.[5]

[1] Damascius, Ἀπασων. [2] Dam. Ταυθε, Ber. Θαμτε (em., see above). [3] Dam. Λαχη and Λαχος (em.). [4] Ἀσσωρος and Κισσαρη. [5] Ἀνος, Ἰλλινος (In-lil = Bel), and Ἀος.

KAT[3], 488 ff.; G. Smith, *Chaldean Genesis* (ed. Sayce), pp. 34 ff., 43 f. (from Cory, *Ancient Fragments*); Gu. *Schöpf.* 17 ff.; Nikel, *Gen. u. Keilschr.* 24 f., 28.

* The best collection and translation of the relevant texts in English is given in L. W. King's *Seven Tablets of Creation*, vol. i. (1902); with which should be compared Jen. *Mythen und Epen*, in *KIB*, vi. 1 (1900), and now (1909) Gressmann, *Altorient. Texte und Bilder z. AT.*, i. 4 ff. See also Jen. *Kosmologie* (1890), 268–301; Gu. *Schöpf.* (1894) 401–420, and the summaries in *KAT*[3], 492 ff.; Lukas, *Grundbegriffe in d. Kosm. d. alt. Völker* (1893), 2 ff.; Jast. *Rel. of Bab. and Ass.* (1898) 410 ff.; Jer. *ATLO*[2], 132 ff.; *EB*, art. CREATION.

ii. *The Subjugation of Apsu by Ea.*—The powers of chaos, Apsu, Tiamat, and a third being called Mummu (Dam. Μωυμις), take counsel together to 'destroy the way' of the heavenly deities. An illegible portion of Tab. I. must have told how Apsu and Mummu were vanquished by Ea, leaving Tiamat still unsubdued. In the latter part of the tablet the female monster is again incited to rebellion by a god called Kingu, whom she chooses as her consort, laying on his breast the 'Tables of Destiny' which the heavenly gods seek to recover. She draws to her side many of the old gods, and brings forth eleven kinds of monstrous beings to aid her in the fight.

iii. *The conflict between Marduk and Tiamat.*—Tabs. II. and III. are occupied with the consultations of the gods in view of this new peril, resulting in the choice of Marduk as their champion; and Tab. IV. gives a graphic description of the conflict that ensues. On the approach of the sun-god, mounted on his chariot and formidably armed, attended by a host of winds, Tiamat's helpers flee in terror, and she alone confronts the angry deity. Marduk entangles her in his net, sends a hurricane into her distended jaws, and finally despatches her by an arrow shot into her body.

iv. *The account of creation* commences near the end of Tab. IV. After subduing the helpers of Tiamat and taking the Tables of Destiny from Kingu, Marduk surveys the carcase, and 'devised a cunning plan':

He split her up like a flat fish into two halves;
One half of her he stablished as a covering for the heaven.
He fixed a bolt, he stationed a watchman,
And bade them not to let her waters come forth.
He passed through the heavens, he surveyed the regions (thereof),
And over against the Deep he set the dwelling of Nudimmud.[1]
And the lord measured the structure of the Deep
And he founded E-šara, a mansion like unto it.
The mansion E-šara which he created as heaven,
He caused Anu, Bel, and Ea in their districts to inhabit.

Berossus says, what is no doubt implied here, that of the other half of Tiamat he made the earth; but whether this is meant by the founding of E-šara, or is to be looked for in a lost part of Tab. V., is a point in dispute (see Jen. *Kosm.* 185 ff., 195 ff.; and *KIB*, vi. 1, 344 f.). Tab. V. opens with the creation of the heavenly bodies:

He made the stations for the great gods;
The stars, their images, as the stars of the Zodiac, he fixed.
He ordained the year and into sections he divided it;
For the twelve months he fixed three stars.

. . . .

The Moon-god he caused to shine forth, the night he entrusted to him.
He appointed him, a being of the night, to determine the days;

---

[1] Ea.

Every month without ceasing with the crown he covered (?) him,
(saying,)
"At the beginning of the month, when thou shinest upon the land,
Thou commandest the horns to determine six days,
And on the seventh day," etc. etc.

The rest of Tab. V., where legible, contains nothing bearing on the present subject; but in Tab. VI. we come to the creation of man, which is recorded in a form corresponding to the account of Berossus:

When Marduk heard the word of the gods,
His heart prompted him, and he devised (a cunning plan).
He opened his mouth and unto Ea (he spake),
(That which) he had conceived in his heart he imparted (unto him):
"My blood will I take and bone will I (fashion),
I will make man, that man may . . . (. . .)
I will create man, who shall inhabit (the earth),
That the service of the gods may be established," etc. etc.

At the end of the tablet the gods assemble to sing the praises of Marduk; and the last tablet is filled with a

v. *Hymn in honour of Marduk.*—From this we learn that to Marduk was ascribed the creation of vegetation and of the 'firm earth,' as well as those works which are described in the legible portions of Tabs. IV.-VI.

How far, now, does this conception of creation correspond with the cosmogony of Gn. 1? (1) In both we find the general notion of a watery chaos, and an etymological equivalence in the names (*Ti'āmat, Tĕhôm*) by which it is called. It is true that the Bab. chaos is the subject of a double personification, Apsu representing the male, and Tiamat the female principle by whose union the gods are generated. According to Jen. (*KIB*, 559 f.), Apsu is the fresh, life-giving water which descends from heaven in the rain, while Tiamat is the 'stinking,' salt water of the ocean: in the beginning these were mingled (Tab. I. 5), and by the mixture the gods were produced. But in the subsequent narrative the rôle of Apsu is insignificant; and in the central episode, the conflict with Marduk, Tiamat alone represents the power of chaos, as in Heb. *Tĕhôm.*—(2) In *Enuma eliš* the description of chaos is followed by a theogony, of which there is no trace in Gen. The Bab. theory is essentially monistic, the gods being conceived as emanating from a material chaos. Lukas, indeed (*l.c.* 14 ff., 24 ff.), has tried to show that they are represented as proceeding from a supreme spiritual principle, Anu. But while an independent origin of deity may be consistent with the opening lines of Tab. I., it is in direct opposition to the statement of Damascius, and is irreconcilable with the later parts of the series, where the gods are repeatedly spoken of as children of Apsu and Tiamat. The biblical conception, on the contrary, is probably dualistic (above, pp. 7, 15), and at all events the supremacy of the spiritual principle (*Elohim*) is absolute. That a theogony must have originally stood between vv.[2] and [3] of Gn. 1 (Gu.) is more than can be safely affirmed. Gu. thinks it is the necessary sequel to the idea of the world-egg in the end of v.[2]. But he himself regards that idea as foreign to the main narrative; and if in the original source something must have come out of the egg, it is more likely to have been the world itself (as in the Phœnician and Indian cosmogonies) than a series of divine emanations.—(3) Both accounts assume, but in very different ways, the existence of light before the creation of the heavenly bodies. In the Bab. legend the assumption is disguised by the imagery of the myth: the fact that Marduk, the god of light, is himself the demiurge, explains the omission of light from the category of created things. In the biblical account that motive no longer operates, and accordingly light takes its place as the first creation of the Almighty.—(4) A very important parallel is the conception of heaven as formed by a separation of the waters of the primæval chaos. In *Enuma eliš* the *septum* is formed from the body of Tiamat; in Gen. it is simply a *rāḳîʿa*—a solid structure fashioned for the purpose. But the common idea is one that could hardly have been suggested except by the climatic conditions under which the Bab. myth is thought to have originated. Jen. has shown, to the satisfaction of a great many writers, how the imagery of the Bab. myth can be explained from the changes that pass over the face of nature in the lower Euphrates valley about the time of the vernal equinox (see *Kosm.* 307 ff.; cf. Gu. *Schöpf.* 24 ff.; Gordon). Chaos is an idealisation of the Babylonian winter, when the heavy rains and the overflow of the rivers have made the vast plain like a sea, when thick mists obscure the light, and the distinction between heaven and sea seems to be effaced. Marduk represents the spring sun, whose rays pierce the darkness and divide the waters, sending them partly upwards as clouds, and partly downwards to the sea, so that the dry land appears. The 'hurricane,' which plays so important a part in the destruction of the chaos-monster, is the spring winds that roll away the dense masses of vapour from the surface of the earth. If this be the natural basis of the myth of Marduk and Tiamat, it is evident that it must have originated in a marshy alluvial region, subject to annual inundations, like the Euphrates valley.—(5) There is, again, a close correspondence between the accounts of the creation of the heavenly bodies (see p. 21 f.). The Babylonian is much fuller, and more saturated with mythology: it mentions not only the moon but the signs of the Zodiac, the planet Jupiter, and the stars. But in the idea that the function of the luminaries is to regulate time, and in the destination of the moon to rule the night, we must recognise a striking resemblance between the two cosmogonies.—(6) The last definite point of contact is the creation of man (p. 30 f.). Here, however, the resemblance is slight, though the deliberative 1st pers. pl. in Gn. 1[26] is probably a reminiscence of a dialogue like that between Marduk and Ea in the *Enuma eliš* narrative.—(7) With regard to the order of the works, it is evident that there cannot have been complete parallelism between the two accounts. In the tablets the creation of heaven is followed naturally by that of the stars. The arrangement of the remaining works, which must have been mentioned in lost parts of Tabs. V. and VI., is, of course, uncertain; but the statement of Berossus suggests that the creation of land animals followed instead of preceding that of man. At the same time it is very significant that the separate works themselves, apart from their order: Firmament, Luminaries, Earth, Plants, Animals, Men,—are practically identical in the two documents: there is even a fragment (possibly belonging to the series) which alludes to the creation of marine animals as a distinct class (King, *CT*, lix, lxxxvi). Gordon (*Early Traditions of Gen.*) holds that the differences of arrangement can be reduced to the single transposition of heavenly bodies and plants (see his table, p. 51).

In view of these parallels, it seems impossible to doubt that the cosmogony of Gn. 1 rests on a conception of the process of creation fundamentally identical with that of the *Enuma eliš* tablets.

3. There is, however, another recension of the Babylonian creation story from which the fight of the sun-god with chaos is absent, and which for that reason possesses a certain importance for our present purpose. It occurs as the introduction to a bilingual magical text, first published by Pinches in 1891.* Once upon a time, it tells us, there were no temples for the gods, no plants, no houses or cities, no human inhabitants:

> The Deep had not been created, Eridu had not been built;
> Of the holy house, the house of the gods, the habitation had not been made.
> All lands were sea (*tāmtu*).

Then arose a 'movement in the sea'; the most ancient shrines and cities of Babylonia were made, and divine beings created to inhabit them. Then

> Marduk laid a reed† on the face of the waters;
> He formed dust and poured it out beside the reed,
> That he might cause the gods to dwell in the habitation of their heart's desire.
> He formed mankind; the goddess Aruru together with him created the seed of mankind.

Next he formed beasts, the rivers, grasses, various kinds of animals, etc.; then, having 'laid in a dam by the side of the sea,' he made reeds and trees, houses and cities, and the great Babylonian sanctuaries. The whole description is extremely obscure, and the translations vary widely.

---

* *JRAS*, 1891, 393 ff.; translated in King, *CT*, 131 ff.; *KIB*, 39 ff.; *ATLO*², 129 ff.; *Texte u. Bilder*, i. 27 f.; Sayce, *Early Israel*, 336 f. Cf. the summary in *KAT*³, 498.

† So King; but Je. 'a reed-hurdle' (*Rohrgeflecht*); while Jen. renders: 'Marduk placed a canopy in front of the waters, He created earth and heaped it up against the canopy'—a reference to the firmament (so *KAT*³).

The main interest of the fragment lies in its non-legendary, matter-of-fact representation of the primæval condition of things, and of the process of world-building. Of special correspondences with Gn. 1 there are perhaps but two: (*a*) the impersonal conception of chaos implied in the appellative sense of *tāmtu* (*Tĕhôm*) for the sea; (*b*) the comparison of the firmament to a canopy, if that be the right interpretation of the phrase. In the order of the creation of living beings it resembles more the account in Gn. 2; but from that account it is sharply distinguished by its assumption of a watery chaos in contrast to the arid waste of Gn. 2^{5}. It is therefore inadmissible to regard this text as a more illuminating parallel to Gn. 1 than the *Enuma eliš* tablets. The most that can be said is that it suggests the possibility that in Babylonia there may have existed recensions of the creation story in which the mythical motive of a conflict between the creator and the chaos-monster played no part, and that the biblical narrative goes back directly to one of these. But when we consider that the Tiamat myth appears in both the Greek accounts of Babylonian cosmogony, that echoes of it are found in other ancient cosmogonies, and that in these cases its imagery is modified in accordance with the religious ideas of the various races, the greater probability is that the cosmogony of Gn. 1 is directly derived from it, and that the elimination of its mythical and polytheistic elements is due to the influence of the pure ethical monotheism of the OT.—Gu. in his *Schöpfung und Chaos* was the first to call attention to possible survivals of the creation myth in Hebrew poetry. We find allusions to a conflict between Yahwe and a monster personified under various names (Rahab, the Dragon, Leviathan, etc.—but never *Tĕhôm*); and no explanation of them is so natural as that which traces them to the idea of a struggle between Yahwe and the power of chaos, preceding (as in the Babylonian myth) the creation of the world. The passages, however, are late; and we cannot be sure that they do not express a literary interest in foreign mythology rather than a survival of a native Hebrew myth.*

4. The Phœnician cosmogony, of which the three extant recensions are given below,† hardly presents any instructive points of comparison

---

* The chief texts are Is. $51^{9f.}$, Ps. $89^{10ff.}$, Jb. $26^{12f.}$ (Rahab); Ps. $74^{12ff.}$, Is. 27^{1} (Leviathan); Jb. 7^{12} (the Dragon), etc. See the discussion in *Schöpf.* 30–111; and the criticisms of Che. *EB*, i. 950 f., and Nikel, pp. 90–99.

† Eus. *Præp. Evang.* i. 10 (ed. Heinichen, p. 37 ff.; cf. Orelli, *Sanch. Berytii Fragm.* [1826]), gives the following account of the cosmogony of Sanchuniathon (a Phœnician writer of unknown date, and even of uncertain historicity) taken from Philo Byblius:

"Τὴν τῶν ὅλων ἀρχὴν ὑποτίθεται ἀέρα ζοφώδη καὶ πνευματώδη, ἢ πνοὴν ἀέρος ζοφώδους, καὶ χάος θολερὸν, ἐρεβῶδες. Ταῦτα δὲ εἶναι ἄπειρα, καὶ διὰ πολὺν αἰῶνα μὴ ἔχειν πέρας. Ὅτε δέ, φησιν, ἠράσθη τὸ πνεῦμα τῶν ἰδίων ἀρχῶν, καὶ ἐγένετο σύγκρασις, ἡ πλοκὴ ἐκείνη ἐκλήθη Πόθος. Αὕτη δὲ ἀρχὴ κτίσεως ἁπάντων· αὐτὸ δὲ οὐκ ἐγίνωσκε τὴν αὑτοῦ κτίσιν, καὶ ἐκ τῆς αὐτοῦ συμπλοκῆς τοῦ πνεύματος, ἐγένετο Μώτ. Τοῦτό τινές φασιν ἰλύν, οἱ δὲ, ὑδατώδους μίξεως

with Gn. 1. It contains, however, in each of its recensions, the idea of the world-egg—a very widespread cosmological speculation to which no Babylonian analogies have been found, but which is supposed to underlie the last clause of Gn. 1². In Sanchuniathon, the union of 'gloomy, breath-like Air' with 'turbid dark Chaos' produces a miry watery mixture called Μωτ, in which all things originate, and first of all certain living beings named 'watchers of heaven' (צְפֵי שָׁמַיִם). These appear to be the constellations, and it is said that they are 'shaped *like the form of an egg*,' i.e., probably, are arranged in the sky in that form. In Eudemos, the first principles are Χρόνος, Πόθος, and Ὀμίχλη: the two latter give birth to Ἀήρ and Αὔρα, and from the union of these again

---

σῆψιν. Καὶ ἐκ ταύτης ἐγένετο πᾶσα σπορὰ κτίσεως, καὶ γένεσις τῶν ὅλων. Ἦν δέ τινα ζῶα οὐκ ἔχοντα αἴσθησιν, ἐξ ὧν ἐγένετο ζῶα νοερὰ, καὶ ἐκλήθη Ζωφασημὶν [Ζωφησαμιμ] τοῦτ' ἔστιν οὐρανοῦ κατόπται. Καὶ ἀνεπλάσθη ὁμοίως [+ ᾠοῦ, see Or.] σχήματι· καὶ ἐξέλαμψε Μὼτ ἥλιός τε καὶ σελήνη, ἀστέρες τε καὶ ἄστρα μεγάλα" . . . "Καὶ τοῦ ἀέρος διαυχάσαντος, διὰ πύρωσιν καὶ τῆς θαλάσσης καὶ τῆς γῆς ἐγένετο πνεύματα, καὶ νέφη, καὶ οὐρανίων ὑδάτων μέγισται καταφοραὶ καὶ χύσεις. Καὶ ἐπειδὴ διεκρίθη, καὶ τοῦ ἰδίου τόπου διεχωρίσθη διὰ τὴν τοῦ ἡλίου πύρωσιν, καὶ πάντα συνήντησε πάλιν ἐν ἀέρι τάδε τοῖσδε, καὶ συνέῤῥαξαν· βρονταί τε ἀπετελέσθησαν καὶ ἀστραπαὶ, καὶ πρὸς τὸν πάταγον τῶν βροντῶν τὰ προγεγραμμένα νοερὰ ζῶα ἐγρηγόρησεν καὶ πρὸς τὸν ἦχον ἐπτύρη, καὶ ἐκινήθη ἔν τε γῇ καὶ θαλάσσῃ ἄῤῥεν καὶ θῆλυ." . . . Ἑξῆς τούτοις ὀνόματα τῶν ἀνέμων εἰπὼν, Νότου καὶ Βορέου, καὶ τῶν λοιπῶν, ἐπιλέγει· "Ἀλλ' οὗτοί γε πρῶτοι ἀφιέρωσαν τὰ τῆς γῆς βλαστήματα, καὶ θεοὺς ἐνόμισαν, καὶ προσεκύνουν ταῦτα, ἀφ' ὧν αὐτοί τε διεγίνοντο, καὶ οἱ ἑπόμενοι, καὶ οἱ πρὸ αὐτῶν πάντες, καὶ χοὰς καὶ ἐπιθύσεις ἐποίουν." Καὶ ἐπιλέγει· "Αὗται δ' ἦσαν αἱ ἐπίνοιαι τῆς προσκυνήσεως, ὅμοιαι τῇ αὐτῶν ἀσθενείᾳ, καὶ ψυχῆς ἀτολμίᾳ. Εἶτά φησι γεγενῆσθαι ἐκ τοῦ Κολπία ἀνέμου, καὶ γυναικὸς αὐτοῦ Βάαυ, τοῦτο δὲ νύκτα ἑρμηνεύειν, Αἰῶνα καὶ Πρωτόγονον θνητοὺς ἄνδρας, οὕτω καλουμένους." . . . [the sequel on p. 124 below].

The other versions are from Eudemos (a pupil of Aristotle) and a native writer Mōchos: they are preserved in the following passage of Damascius (cap. 125; ed. Kopp, p. 385):

Σιδώνιοι δὲ κατὰ τὸν αὐτὸν συγγραφέα (*i.e.* Eudemos) πρὸ πάντων Χρόνον υποτίθενται καὶ Πόθον καὶ Ὀμίχλην. Πόθου δὲ καὶ Ὀμίχλης μιγέντων ὡς δυοῖν ἀρχῶν Ἀέρα γενέσθαι καὶ Αὔραν, Ἀέρα μὲν ἄκρατον τοῦ νοητοῦ παραδηλοῦντες, Αὔραν δὲ τὸ ἐξ αὐτοῦ κινούμενον τοῦ νοητοῦ ζωτικὸν προτύπωμα. Πάλιν δὲ ἐκ τούτων ἀμφοῖν Ὦτον [rd. ᾠὸν] γεννηθῆναι κατὰ τὸν νοῦν οἶμαι τὸν νοητόν. Ὡς δὲ ἔξωθεν Εὐδήμου τὴν Φοινίκων εὑρίσκομεν κατὰ Μῶχον μυθολογίαν, Αἰθὴρ ἦν τὸ πρῶτον καὶ Ἀὴρ αἱ δύο αὗται ἄρχαι, ἐξ ὧν γεννᾶται Οὐλωμὸς, ὁ νοητὸς θεὸς, αὐτὸ οἶμαι τὸ ἄκρον τοῦ νοητοῦ· ἐξ οὗ ἑαυτῷ συνελθόντος γεννηθῆναί φησι Χουσωρὸν, ἀνοιγέα πρῶτον, εἶτα ᾠόν· τοῦτον μὲν οἶμαι τὸν νοητὸν νοῦν λέγοντες, τὸν δὲ ἀνοιγέα Χουσωρὸν, τὴν νοητὴν δύναμιν ἅτε πρώτην διακρίνασαν τὴν ἀδιάκριτον φύσιν, εἰ μὴ ἄρα μετὰ τὰς δύο ἀρχὰς τὸ μὲν ἄκρον ἐστὶν ἄνεμος ὁ εἷς, τὸ δὲ μέσον οἱ δύο ἄνεμοι Λίψ τε καὶ Νότος· ποιοῦσι γάρ πως καὶ τούτους πρὸ τοῦ Οὐλωμοῦ· ὁ δὲ Οὐλωμὸς αὐτὸς ὁ νοητὸς εἴη νοῦς, ὁ δὲ ἀνοιγεὺς, Χουσωρὸς, ἡ μετὰ τὸ νοητὸν πρώτη τάξις, τὸ δὲ ᾠὸν ὁ οὐρανός· λέγεται γὰρ ἐξ αὐτοῦ ῥαγέντος εἰς δύο, γενέσθαι οὐρανὸς καὶ γῆ, τῶν διχοτομημάτων ἑκάτερον.

proceeds 'an *egg*.' More striking is the expression of the idea in Mochos. Here the union of Αἰθήρ and Ἀήρ produces Οὔλωμος (עולם), from which proceed Χουσωρος, 'the first opener,' and then 'an *egg*.' It is afterwards explained that the egg is the heaven, and that when it is split in two (? by Χουσωρος) the one half forms the heaven and the other the earth. It may introduce consistency into these representations if we suppose that in the process of evolution the primæval chaos (which is coextensive with the future heaven and earth) assumes the shape of an egg, and that this is afterwards divided into two parts, corresponding to the heaven and the earth. The function of Χουσωρος is thus analogous to the act of Marduk in cleaving the body of Tiamat in two. But obviously all this throws remarkably little light on Gn. 1[2].—Another supposed point of contact is the resemblance between the name Βααυ and the Heb. בֹּהוּ. In Sanchuniathon Βααυ is explained as night, and is said to be the wife of the Kolpia-wind, and mother of Αἰών and Πρωτόγονος, the first pair of mortals. It is evident that there is much confusion in this part of the extract; and it is not unreasonably conjectured that Αἰών and Πρωτόγονος were really the first pair of emanations, and Kolpia and Baau the chaotic principles from which they spring; so that they may be the cosmological equivalents of Tōhû and Bōhû in Gn. There is a strong probability that the name Βααυ is connected with Bau, a Babylonian mother-goddess (see *ATLO*[2], 161); but the evidence is too slight to enable us to say that specifically Phœnician influences are traceable in Gn. 1[2].

5. A division of creation into six stages, in an order similar to that of Gn. 1, appears in the late book of the Bundehesh (the Parsee Genesis), where the periods are connected with the six annual festivals called Gahanbars, so as to form a creative year, parallel to the week of Gn. 1. The order is: 1. Heaven; 2. Water; 3. Earth; 4. Plants; 5. Animals; 6. Men. We miss from the enumeration: Light, which in Zoroastrianism is an uncreated element; and the Heavenly bodies, which are said to belong to an earlier creation (Tiele, *Gesch. d. Rel. im Altert.* ii. 296). The late date of the Bundehesh leaves room, of course, for the suspicion of biblical influence; but it is thought by some that the same order can be traced in a passage of the younger Avesta, and that it may belong to ancient Iranian tradition (Tiele, *l.c.*, and *ARW*, vi. 244 ff.; Caland, *ThT*, xxiii. 179 ff.).—The most remarkable of all known parallels to the six days' scheme of Gn. is found in a cosmogony attributed to the ancient Etruscans by Suidas (*Lexicon, s.v.* Τυρρηνία). Here the creation is said to have been accomplished in six periods of 1000 years, in the following order: 1. Heaven and Earth; 2. the Firmament; 3. Sea and Water; 4. Sun and Moon; 5. Souls of Animals; 6. Man (see K. O. Müller, *Die Etrusker*, ii. 38; *ATLO*[2], 154 f.). Suidas, however, lived not earlier than the 10th cent. A.D., and though his information may have been derived from ancient sources, we cannot be sure that his account is not coloured by knowledge of the Hebrew cosmogony.

II. 4b–III. 24.—*The Creation and Fall of Man* (J).

The passage forms a complete and closely articulated narrative,* of which the leading motive is man's loss of his original innocence and happiness through eating forbidden fruit, and his consequent expulsion from the garden of Eden. The account of creation in $2^{4b\text{ff.}}$ had primarily, perhaps, an independent interest; yet it contains little that is not directly subservient to the main theme developed in ch. 3. It is scarcely to be called a cosmogony, for the making of 'earth and heaven' (2^{4b}) is assumed without being described; the narrative springs from an early phase of thought which was interested in the beginnings of human life and history, but had not advanced to speculation on the origin of heaven and earth (cf. Frankenberg in Gu.[2] 24). From ch. 1 it differs fundamentally both in its conception of the primal condition of the world as an arid, waterless waste ($2^{5\text{f.}}$: ct. 1^{2}), and in the order of creative works: viz. Man (^{7}), Trees (^{9}), Animals ($^{18-20}$), Woman ($^{21-23}$). Alike in this arrangement and in the supplementary features—the garden ($^{8.\ 10\text{ff.}}$), the miraculous trees (^{9b}), the appointments regarding man's position in the world ($^{15-17}$), and the remarkable omissions (plants, fishes, etc.)—it is governed by the main episode to which it leads up (ch. 3), with its account of the temptation by the serpent ($^{1-5}$), the transgression ($^{6.\ 7}$), the inquest ($^{8-13}$), the sentences ($^{14-19}$), and the expulsion from Eden ($^{22-24}$).

The story thus summarised is one of the most charming idylls in literature: ch. 3 is justly described by Gu. as the 'pearl of Genesis.' Its literary and æsthetic character is best appreciated by comparison with ch. 1. Instead of the formal precision, the schematic disposition, the stereotyped diction, the aim at scientific classification, which distinguish the great cosmogony, we have here a narrative marked by child-like simplicity of conception, exuberant though pure imagination, and a captivating freedom of style. Instead of lifting God far above man and nature, this writer revels in the most exquisite anthropomorphisms; he does not shrink from speaking of God as walking in His garden in the cool of the day (3^{8}), or making experiments for the welfare of His first creature ($2^{18\text{ff.}}$), or arriving at a knowledge of man's sin by a searching

---

* Cf. especially $2^{4b\beta}$ with $3^{19.\ 23}$; $2^{9.\ 16\text{f.}}$ with $3^{1-5.\ 11.\ 17.\ 22}$; $2^{8b.\ 15}$ with $3^{23\text{f.}}$; 2^{19} with $3^{1a.\ 14}$; 2^{21-23} with 3^{12}; (2^{24} with 3^{16b}); 2^{25} with $3^{7.\ 10\text{f.}}$.

examination ($3^{9ff.}$), etc. While the purely mythological phase of thought has long been outgrown, a mythical background everywhere appears; the happy garden of God, the magic trees, the speaking serpent, the Cherubim and Flaming Sword, are all emblems derived from a more ancient religious tradition. Yet in depth of moral and religious insight the passage is unsurpassed in the OT. We have but to think of its delicate handling of the question of sex, its profound psychology of temptation and conscience, and its serious view of sin, in order to realise the educative influence of revealed religion in the life of ancient Israel. It has to be added that we detect here the first note of that sombre, almost melancholy, outlook on human life which pervades the older stratum of Gn. 1–11. Cf. the characterisation in We. *Prol.*[6] 302 ff.; Gu. p. 22 ff.

Source.—The features just noted, together with the use of the divine name יהוה, show beyond doubt that the passage belongs to the Yahwistic cycle of narratives (J). Expressions characteristic of this document are found in קדמת 2^{14}, הפעם 2^{23}, מה־זאת 3^{13}, ארור $3^{14.17}$, עצבון $3^{16.17}$, בעבור 3^{17}; and (in contrast to P) יצר, 'create,' instead of ברא, חית השדה instead of ח' הארץ, נשמת חיים instead of רוח ח' (see on 7^{22}); and the constant use of acc. suff. to the verb.

Traces of Composition.—That the literary unity of the narrative is not perfect there are several indications, more or less decisive. (1) The geographical section 2^{10-14} is regarded by most critics (since Ewald) as a later insertion, on the grounds that it is out of keeping with the simplicity of the main narrative, and seriously interrupts its sequence. The question is whether it be merely an isolated interpolation, or an extract from a parallel recension. If the latter be in evidence, we know too little of its character to say that 2^{10-14} could not have belonged to it. At all events the objections urged would apply only to $^{11-14}$; and there is much to be said, on this assumption, for retaining ^{10} (or at least ^{10a}) as a parallel to v.^{6} (Ho.).—(2) A more difficult problem is the confusion regarding the two trees on which the fate of man depends, a point to which attention was first directed by Bu. According to 2^{9b} the tree of life and the tree of the knowledge of good and evil grew together in the midst of the garden, and in 2^{17} the second alone is made the test of the man's obedience. But ch. 3 (down to v.^{21}) knows of only one tree in the midst of the garden, and that obviously (though it is never so named) the tree of knowledge. The tree of life plays no part in the story except in $3^{22.24}$, and its sudden introduction there only creates fresh embarrassment; for if this tree also was forbidden, the writer's silence about it in 2^{17} 3^{3} is inexplicable; and if it was not forbidden, can we suppose that in the author's intention the boon of immortality was placed freely within man's reach during the period of his probation? So far as the main narrative is concerned, the tree of life is an irrelevance; and we shall see immediately that the part where it does enter into the story is precisely the part where signs of redaction or dual authorship accumulate.—(3) The clearest indication of a double recension is found in the twofold account of the expulsion from Eden: $3^{23.24}$. Here ^{22} and ^{24} clearly hang together; ^{20} and ^{21} are as clearly out of their proper position; hence [23] may have been the original continuation of [19], to which it forms a natural sequel. There is thus some reason to believe that in this instance, at any rate, the 'tree of life' is not from the hand of the chief narrator.—(4) Other and less certain duplicates are: $2^{6} \| 2^{10\,(11-14)}$ (see above), $^{8a} \| ^{9a}$ (the planting of the garden); and ^{8b} ^{15a} (the placing of man in it); $2^{23} \| 3^{20}$ (the naming of the woman).—(5) Bu. (*Urg.* 232 ff.) was the first to suggest that the double name יהוה אלהים (which is all but peculiar to this section) has arisen through amalgamation of sources. His theory in its broader aspects has been stated on p. 3, above; it is enough here to point out its bearing on the compound name in Gn. 2 f. It is assumed that two closely parallel accounts existed, one of which (J^e) employed only אלהים, the other (J^j) only יהוה. When these were combined the editor harmonised them by adding אלהים to יהוה everywhere in J^j, and prefixing יהוה to אלהים everywhere in J^e except in the colloquy between the serpent and the woman (3^{1-5}), where the general name was felt to be more appropriate.* The reasoning is precarious; but if it be sound, it follows that 3^{1-5} must be assigned to J^e; and since these vv. are part of the main narrative (that which speaks only of the tree of knowledge), there remain for J^j only $3^{22.\,24}$, and possibly some variants and glosses in the earlier part of the narrative.—On the whole, the facts seem to warrant these conclusions: of the Paradise story two recensions existed; in one, the only tree mentioned was the tree of the knowledge of good and evil, while the other certainly contained the tree of life (so v. Doorninck, *ThT*, xxxix. 225 f.) and possibly both trees;† the former supplied the basis of our present narrative, and is practically complete, while the second is so fragmentary that all attempt to reconstruct even its main outlines must be abandoned as hopeless.

---

* So Gu. A still more complete explanation of this particular point would be afforded by the somewhat intricate original hypothesis of Bu. He suggested that the primary narrative (J^1) in which יהוה was regularly used, except in 3^{1-5}, was re-written and supplemented by J^2 who substituted אלהים for יהוה; the two narratives were subsequently amalgamated in rather mechanical fashion by J^3, with the result that wherever the divine names differed both were retained, and where the documents agreed אלהים alone appears (*Urg.* 233 f.). Later in the volume (471 ff.) the hypothesis is withdrawn in favour of the view that J^2 contained no Paradise story at all.—A similar explanation is given by v. Doorninck (*l.c.* 239), who thinks the retention of אלהים in 3^{1-5} was due to the redactor's desire to avoid the imputation of falsehood to Yahwe!

† The point here depends on the degree of similarity assumed to have obtained between the two recensions. Gu., who assumes that the resemblance was very close, holds that in J^j probably both trees were concerned in the fall of man. But the text gives no indication that in J^j the knowledge of good and evil was attained by eating the fruit of a tree: other ways of procuring unlawful knowledge are conceivable; and it is therefore possible that in this version the tree of life alone occupied a position analogous to that of the tree of knowledge in the other (see, further, Gressmann, *ARW*, x. 355 f.).

4b–7.—The creation of man.—On the somewhat involved construction of the section, see the footnote.—**4b.** *At the time when Yahwe Elohim made, etc.*] The double name יְהוָה אֱלֹהִים, which is all but peculiar to Gn. 2 f., is probably to be explained as a result of redactional operations (*v.i.*), rather than (with Reuss, Ayles, al.) as a feature of the isolated source from which these two chapters were taken.—*earth and heaven*] The unusual order (which is reversed by 𝔐𝔊𝔖) appears again only in Ps. 148[13].—5. *there was as yet no bush, etc.*] Or (on Di.'s construction) *while as yet there was no, etc.* The rare word שִׂיחַ denotes elsewhere (21[15] [E], Jb. 30[4. 7]) a desert shrub (so Syr., Arab.); but a wider sense is attested by Ass. and Phœn. It is difficult to say whether here it means wild as opposed

---

4b–7. The sudden change of style and language shows that the transition to the Yahwistic document takes place at the middle of v.[4]. The construction presents the same syntactic ambiguity as 1[1-3] (see the note there); except, of course, that there can be no question of taking [4b] as an independent sentence. We may also set aside the conjecture (We. *Prol.*[6] 297 f.; KS. al.) that the clause is the conclusion of a lost sentence of J, as inconsistent with the natural position of the time determination in Heb. [4b] must therefore be joined as prot. to what follows; and the question is whether the apod. commences at [5] (Tu. Str. Dri. al.), or (with [5f.] as a parenthesis) at [7] (Di. Gu. al.). In syntax either view is admissible; but the first yields the better sense. The state of things described in [5f.] evidently lasted some time; hence it is not correct to say that Yahwe made man at the time when He made heaven and earth: to connect [7] directly with [4b] is "to identify a *period* (v.[6]) with a *point* (v.[7]) of time" (Spurrell).—On the form of apod., see again Dri. *T.* § 78.—4. בְּיוֹם always emphasises contemporaneousness of two events (cf. 2[17] 3[5]); the indefiniteness lies in the subst., which often covers a space of time (= 'when': Ex. 6[28] 32[34], Jer. 11[4] etc.).—יהוה אלהים] in Hex. only Ex. 9[30]; elsewhere 2 Sa. 7[22. 25], Jon. 4[6], Ps. 72[18] 84[9. 12], 1 Ch. 17[16], 2 Ch. 6[41]. 𝔊 uses the expression frequently up to 9[12], but its usage is not uniform even in chs. 2. 3. The double name has sometimes been explained by the supposition that an editor added אלהים to the original יהוה in order to smooth the transition from P to J, or as a hint to the Synagogue reader to substitute אלהים for יהוה; but that is scarcely satisfactory. A more adequate solution is afforded by the theory of Bu. and Gu., on which see p. 53. Barton and Che. (*TBAI*, 99 f., take it as a compound of the same type as *Melek-Aštart*, etc., an utterly improbable suggestion.—5. שיח is probably the same as Ass. *šiḫtu*, from √ = 'grow high' (Del. *Hdwb.*), and hence might include trees, as rendered by 𝔖𝔗.—On עשב, see on 1[11]. The gen. השדה, common

to cultivated plants (Hupf. Gu.), or perennials as opposed to annuals (Ho.).—For the earth's barrenness two reasons are assigned: (1) the absence of rain, and (2) the lack of cultivation. In the East, however, the essence of husbandry is irrigation; hence the two conditions of fertility correspond broadly to the Arabian (and Talmudic) contrast between land watered by the Baal and that watered by human labour (Rob. Sm. RS^2, 96 ff.).—*to till the ground*] This, therefore, is man's original destiny, though afterwards it is imposed on him as a curse,—an indication of the fusion of variant traditions. אֲדָמָה, both here and v.^{6}, has probably the restricted sense of 'soil,' 'arable land' (cf. 4^{14}).—6. *but a flood* (or *mist*, *v.i.*) *used to come up* (periodically)] "The idea of the author appears to be that the ground was rendered capable of cultivation by the overflow of some great river" (Ayles).

It is certainly difficult to imagine any other purpose to be served by the 'flood' than to induce fertility, for we can hardly attribute to the writer the trivial idea that it had simply the effect of moistening the soil for the formation of man, etc. (Ra. al., cf. Gu. Che. *TBAI*, 87). But this appears to neutralise $^{5b\alpha}$, since rain is no longer an indispensable condition of vegetation. Ho., accordingly, proposes to remove ^{6} and to treat it as a variant of $^{10-14}$. The meaning might be, however, that the flood, when supplemented by human labour, was sufficient to fertilise the *'ădāmāh*, but had, of course, no effect on the steppes, which were dependent on rain. The difficulty is not removed if we render 'mist'; and the brevity of the narrative leaves other questions unanswered; such as, When was rain first sent on the earth? At what stage are we to place the creation of the cereals? etc.

---

to both, denotes open country, as opposed sometimes to cities or houses, sometimes to enclosed cultivated land (De. 96).—On טֶרֶם with impf. see G-K. § 107 *c*; Dri. *T.* § 27 *β*. The rendering 'before' (𝔊 [one of the deviations mentioned in Mechilta—see on 1^1] 𝔙) would imply בְּטֶרֶם, and is wrong.—6. אֵד] 𝔊 πηγή, Aq. ἐπιβλυσμός, 𝔙 *fons*, 𝔖 ܡܒܘܥܐ, 𝔗^{O} עננא. Che. conj. יְאֹר; others עַיִן (after Vns.). The word has no etymol. in Heb., and the only other occurrence (Jb. 36^{27}) is even more obscure than this. 'Cloud' (𝔗) or 'mist' is a natural guess, and it is doubtful if it be anything better. The meaning 'flood' comes from Ass. *edû*, applied to the annual overflow of a river (Del. *Hdwb.*),—note the freq. impf. Gu. thinks it a technical semi-mythological term of the same order as *Tĕhôm*, with which Ra. seems to connect it; while IEz. interprets 'cloud,' but confounds the word with אֵיד, 'calamity' (Zeph. 1^{15}); so Aq., who renders the latter by ἐπιβλυσμός in Pr. 1^{26}, Jb. 30^{12} (see *Rev. R.* § 13).—On the tenses,

If the above explanation be correct, there is a confusion of two points of view which throws an interesting light on the origin of the story. The rain is suggested by experience of a dry country, like Palestine. The flood, on the other hand, is a reminiscence of the entirely different state of things in an alluvial country like the Euphrates valley, where husbandry depends on artificial irrigation assisted by periodic inundations. While, therefore, there may be a Babylonian basis to the myth, it must have taken its present shape in some drier region, presumably in Palestine. To say that it "describes . . . the phenomena witnessed by the first colonists of Babylonia," involves more than 'mythic exaggeration' (Che. *EB*, 949).

7. *Yahwe Elōhîm moulded man*] The verb יָצַר (avoided by P) is used, in the ptcp., of the potter; and that figure underlies the representation. An Egyptian picture shows the god Chnum forming human beings on the potter's disc (*ATLO*², 146).—The idea of man as made of clay or earth appears in Babylonian; but is indeed universal, and pervades the whole OT.—*breath of life*] Omit the art. The phrase recurs only 7^{22} (J), where it denotes the animal life, and there is no reason for supposing another meaning here. "Subscribere eorum sententiæ non dubito qui de animali hominis vita locum hunc exponunt" (Calvin).—*man became a living being*] נֶפֶשׁ here is not a constituent of human nature, but denotes the personality as a whole.

The v. has commonly been treated as a *locus classicus* of OT anthropology, and as determining the relations of the three elements of human nature—flesh, soul, spirit—to one another. It is supposed to

---

see G-K. § 112 *e*; Dri. *T*. § 113, 4 (*β*).—7. אדם . . . אדמה] Both words are of uncertain etymology. The old derivation from the vb. 'be red' (. . . πυῤῥόν· ἐπειδήπερ ἀπὸ τῆς πυῤῥᾶς γῆς φυραθείσης ἐγεγόνει: Jos. *Ant*. i. 34) is generally abandoned, but none better has been found to replace it (recent theories in Di. 53 f.). According to Nöldeke (*ZDMG*, xl. 722), אדם appears in Arab. as *'ānām* (cf. Haupt, *ib*. lxi. 194). Frd. Del.'s view, that both words embody the idea of tillage, seems (as Di. says) to rest on the ambiguity of the German *bauen*; but it is very near the thought of this passage: man is made from the soil, lives by its cultivation, and returns to it at death.—עפר] Acc. of material, G-K. § 117 *hh*. Gu. regards it as a variant to האדמה from J¹.—נפש חיה] This appears to be the only place where the phrase is applied to man; elsewhere to animals ($1^{20.24}$ etc.). נ׳, primarily 'breath,' denotes usually the vital principle (with various mental connotations), and ultimately the whole being thus animated—the person. The last is the only sense consistent with the structure of the sentence here.

teach that the soul (נֶפֶשׁ) arises through the union of the universal life-principle (רוּחַ) with the material frame (בָּשָׂר): cf. *e.g.* Grüneisen, *Ahnenkultus*, 34 f. No such ideas are expressed: neither בשר nor רוח is mentioned, while נפש is not applied to a separate element of man's being, but to the whole man in possession of vital powers. "All that seems in question here is just the giving of vitality to man. There seems no allusion to man's immaterial being, to his spiritual element. . . . Vitality is communicated by God, and he is here represented as communicating it by breathing into man's nostrils that breath which is the sign of life" (Davidson, *OTTh.* 194). At the same time, the fact that God imparts his own breath to man, marks the dignity of man above the animals: it is J's equivalent for the 'image of God.'

8–17. The garden of Eden.—That the planting of the garden was subsequent to the creation of man is the undoubted meaning of the writer; the rendering *plantaverat* (𝔙: so IEz.) is grammatically impossible, and is connected with a misconception of מקדם below.—*a garden in Eden*] This is perhaps the only place where Eden (as a geographical designation) is distinguished from the garden (cf. $2^{10.15}$ $3^{23.24}$ 4^{16}, Is. 51^{3}, Ezk. 28^{13} $31^{9.16.18}$ 36^{35}, Jl. 2^{3}, Sir. 40^{27}). The common phrase גַּן עֵדֶן would suggest to a Hebrew the idea 'garden of delight,' as it is rendered by 𝔊 (often) and 𝔙 (*v.i.*). There is no probability that the proper name was actually coined in this sense. It is derived by the younger Del. and Schrader from Bab. *edinu*, 'plain,' 'steppe,' or 'desert' (Del. *Par.* 80; *KAT*², 26 f.; *KAT*³, 539); but it is a somewhat precarious inference that the garden was conceived as an oasis in the midst of a desert (Ho.).—מִקֶּדֶם] '*in the* (far) *East*'; *i.e.* from the Palestinian standpoint of the author; not, of course, to be identified with any other עֵדֶן within the geographical horizon of the Israelites (see 2 Ki. 19^{12} [= Is. 37^{12}], Ezk. 27^{23}, Am. 1^{5}).

Besides the passages cited above, the idea of a divine garden appears also in Gn. 13^{10}, Ezk. 31^{8}. Usually it is a mere symbol of

---

8. גן] 𝔊 παράδεισος (cf. פרדס, Ca. 4^{13}, Ec. 2^{5}, Neh. 2^{8}: probably from Pers.), and so 𝔙𝔖.—עֵדֶן] is regularly treated as *nom. prop.* by 𝔗ᴼ 𝔖, by 𝔙 only 4^{16} (everywhere else as appellative: *voluptas*, *deliciæ*). 𝔊 has Ἐδεμ only in $2^{8.10}$ 4^{16}; elsewhere τρυφή[s], except Is. 51^{3} (παράδεισος).—מקדם] Lit. 'in front' (on the מן see Kön. *Lgb.* ii. p. 318; BDB, 578^{b}): in the hist. books it always means 'east' or 'eastward'; but in prophs. and Pss. it usually has temporal sense ('of old'); and so it is misunder-

luxuriant fertility, especially in respect of its lordly trees (Ezk. $31^{8f. 16. 18}$); but in Ezk. 28^{13} it is mentioned as the residence of a semi-divine being. Most of the allusions are explicable as based on Gn. 2 f.; but the imagery of Ezk. 28 reveals a highly mythological conception of which few traces remain in the present narrative. If the idea be primitive Semitic (and גַּן is common to all the leading dialects), it may originate in the sacred grove (*Hima*) "where water and verdure are united, where the fruits of the sacred trees are *taboo*, and the wild animals are *'anīs*, *i.e.* on good terms with man, because they may not be frightened away" (We. *Prol.*[6] 303[2]; cf. *Heid.* 141; Barton, *SO*[1], 96). In early times such spots of natural fertility were the haunts of the gods or supernatural beings (*RS*[2], 102 ff.). But from the wide diffusion of the myth, and the facts pointed out on p. 93 f. below, it is plain that the conception has been enriched by material from different quarters, and had passed through a mythological phase before it came into the hands of the biblical writers. Such sacred groves were common in Babylonia, and mythological idealisations of them enter largely into the religious literature (see *ATLO*[2], 195 ff.).

9. ***all sorts of trees . . . food***] The primitive vegetation is conceived as consisting solely of trees, on whose fruit man was to subsist; the appearance of herbs is a result of the curse pronounced on the ground ($3^{17f.}$).—*and the tree of life* (was) ***in the midst***] On Bu.'s strictures on the form of the sentence, *v.i.* The intricate question of the two trees must be reserved for separate discussion (pp. 52 f., 94); for the present form of the story both are indispensable. The tree

---

stood here by all Vns. except 𝔊 (𝔙 *in principio*, etc.).—9. כל־עץ] G-K. § 127 *b.*—הדעת] The use of art. with inf. const. is very rare (Dav. § 19), but is explained by the frequent use of דעת as abstr. noun. Otherwise the construction is regular, טוב ורע being acc., not gen. of obj.—Budde (*Urg.* 51 f.) objects to the splitting up of the compound obj. by the secondary pred. בתוך הגן, and thinks the original text must have been ובתוך הגן עץ הדעת וגו׳; thus finding a confirmation of the theory that the primary narrative knew of only one tree, and that the tree of knowledge (p. 52; so Ba. Ho. Gu. al.). In view of the instances examined by Dri. in *Hebraica*, ii. 33, it is doubtful if the grammatical argument can be sustained; but if it had any force it ought certainly to lead to the excision of the second member rather than of the first (Kuen. *ThT*, 1884, 136; v. Doorninck, *ib.*, 1905, 225 f.; Eerdmans, *ib.* 494 ff.). A more important point is the absence of את before the def. obj. The writer's use of this part. is very discriminating; and its omission suggests that [9b] is really a nominal clause, as rendered above. If we were to indulge in analysis of sources, we might put [9b] (in whole or in part) after [8a], and assign it to that secondary stratum of narrative which undoubtedly spoke of a tree of life (3^{22}).

of life, whose fruit confers immortality (3^{22}; cf. Pr. 3^{18} 11^{30} 13^{12} 15^{4}; further, Ezk. 47^{12}, Rev. 22^{2}), is a widely diffused idea (see Di. 49; Wünsche, *Die Sagen vom Lebensbaum u. Lebenswasser*). The tree of knowledge is a more refined conception; its property of communicating knowledge of good and evil is, however, magical, like that of the other; a connexion with oracular trees (Lenormant, *Or.* i. 85 f.; Baudissin, *Stud.* ii. 227) is not so probable. As to what is meant by 'knowing good and evil,' see p. 95 ff.

The primitive Semitic tree of life is plausibly supposed by Barton (*SO*[1], 92 f.) to have been the date-palm; and this corresponds to the sacred palm in the sanctuary of Ea at Eridu (IV R. 15*), and also to the conventionalised sacred tree of the seals and palace-reliefs, which is considered to be a palm combined with some species of conifer. Cf. also the sacred cedar in the cedar forest of *Gilg.*, *Tabs.* IV. V. For these and other Bab. parallels, see *ATLO*[2], 195 ff.

10. *a river issued* (or *issues*) *from Eden*] The language does not necessarily imply that the fountain-head was outside the garden (Dri. Ben.); the vb. יָצָא is used of the rise of a stream at its source (Ex. 17^{6}, Nu. 20^{11}, Ju. 15^{19}, Ezk. 47^{1}, Zec. 14^{8}, Jl. 4^{18}). Whether the ptcp. expresses past or present time cannot be determined.—*from thence it divides itself*] The river issues from the garden as a single stream, then divides into four branches, which are the four great rivers of the world. The site of Paradise, therefore, is at the common source of the four rivers in question (pp. 62–66 below). That is the plain meaning of the verse, however inconsistent it may be with physical geography.—**11.** *Pîšôn*] The name occurs (along with Tigris, Euphrates, Jordan, and Gihon)

10. יפרד] Freq. impf.? So Dri. *T.* §§ 30 *a*, 113, 4 *β*; G–K. § 107 *d* ('always taking place afresh'), Dav. § 54 (*b*). That seems hardly natural. Is it possible that for once מִשָּׁם could have the effect of אָז in transporting the mind to a point whence a new development takes place? (Dav. § 45, *R.* 2).—רָאשִׁים] Not 'sources' but 'branches'; as Arab. *ra's en-nahr* (as distinct from *ra's el-'ain*) means the point of divergence of two streams (Wetzstein, quoted by De., p. 82). So Ass. *rîš nâri* or *rîš nâr*, of the point of divergence (*Ausgangsort*) of a canal (Del. *Par.* 98, 191).—**11.** האחד] See on 1^{5}.—הוא הסבב] On the determination of pred., Dav. § 19, *R.* 3; cf. G–K. § 126 *k* (so v.[13f.]).—החוילה] If the art. be genuine, it shows that the name was significant ('sandland,'

in Sir. 24^{25}, but nowhere else in OT. That it was not a familiar name to the Hebrews is shown by the topographical description which follows. On the various speculative identifications, see De. and Di., and p. 64 f. below.—*the whole land of Ḥăvîlāh*] The phraseology indicates that the name is used with some vagueness, and considerable latitude. In $10^{7.29}$ 25^{18} etc., Ḥavilah seems to be a district of Arabia (see p. 202); but we cannot be sure that it bears the same meaning in the mythically coloured geography of this passage.—**12.** Two other products of the region are specified; but neither helps to an identification of the locality.—*bĕdōlaḥ*] a substance well known to the Israelites (Nu. 11^7), is undoubtedly the fragrant but bitter gum called by the Greeks βδέλλιον or βδέλλα. Pliny (*NH*, xii. 35 f.) says the best kind grew in Bactriana, but adds that it was found also in Arabia, India, Media, and Babylonia.—*the šōham stone*] A highly esteemed

from חול?); but everywhere else it is wanting, and 𝔐 omits it here.—**12.** וּזֲהַב] On metheg and hat.-pathach, see G-K. §§ 10 *g*, 16 *e*, *f*; Kön. i. § 10, 6 *e* δ (cf. 1^{18}).—הִוא] The first instance of this *Qrê perpetuum* of the Pent., where the regular הִיא is found only Gn. 14^2 20^5 38^{25}, Lv. 2^{15} 11^{39} $13^{10.21}$ 16^{31} 21^9, Nu. $5^{13f.}$. Kön. (*Lgb.* i. p. 124 ff.) almost alone amongst modern scholars still holds to the opinion that the epicene consonantal form is genuinely archaic; but the verdict of philology and of Hex. criticism seems decisive against that view. It must be a graphic error of some scribe or school of scribes: whether proceeding from the original *scrip. def.* הִא or not does not much matter (see Dri. and White's note on Lv. 1^{13} in *SBOT*, p. 25 f.).—טוב] 𝔐 + מְאֹד.—הבדלח] Of the ancient Vns. 𝔊 alone has misunderstood the word, rendering here ὁ ἄνθραξ (red garnet), and in Nu. 11^7 (the only other occurrence) κρύσταλλος. 𝔖 ܒܪܘܠܚܐ can only be a clerical error. That it is *not* a gem is proved by the absence of אבן.—אבן השהם] 𝔊 ὁ λίθος ὁ πράσινος (leek-green stone); other Gk. Vns. ὄνυξ, and so 𝔙 (*onychinus*); 𝔖 ܒܪܘܠܐ, 𝔗^O בורלא. Philology has as yet thrown no light on the word, though a connexion with Bab. *sâmtu* is probable.* Myres (*EB*, 4808 f.) makes the interesting suggestion that it originally denoted malachite, which is at once *striped* and *green*, and that after malachite ceased to be valued tradition wavered between the onyx (striped) and the beryl (green). Petrie, on the other hand (*DB*, iv. 620), thinks that in early times it was green felspar, afterwards confused with the beryl. It is at least noteworthy that Jen. (*KIB*, vi. 1, 405) is led on independent grounds to identify *sâmtu* with malachite. But is malachite found in any

* Nestle has suggested a connexion with שׁוּם 'leek' (πράσινος).

gem (Jb. 28^{16}), suitable for engraving (Ex. 28^{9} etc.), one of the precious stones of Eden (Ezk. 28^{13}), and apparently used in architecture (1 Ch. 29^{2}). From the Greek equivalents it is generally supposed to be either the onyx or the beryl (*v.i.*). According to Pliny, the latter was obtained from India, the former from India and Arabia (*NH*, xxxvii. 76, 86).—**13.** *Gîḥôn*] The name of a well on the E of Jerusalem (the Virgin's spring: 1 Ki. 1^{33} etc.), which IEz. strangely takes to be meant here. In Jewish and Christian tradition it was persistently identified with the Nile (Si. 24^{27}; 𝔊 of Jer. 2^{18} [where שִׁחוֹר is translated Γηών]; Jos. *Ant.* i. 39, and the Fathers generally). The great difficulty of that view is that the Nile was as well known to the Hebrews as the Euphrates, and no reason appears either for the mysterious designation, or the vague description appended to the name.—*land of Kûš*] Usually Ethiopia; but see on 10^{6}.—**14.** *Ḥiddeḳel*] is certainly the Tigris, though the name occurs only once again (Dn. 10^{4}).—*in front of 'Aššûr*] Either between it and the spectator, or to the east of it: the latter view is adopted by nearly all comm.; but the parallels are indecisive, and the point is not absolutely settled. Geographically the former would be more correct, since the centre of the Assyrian Empire lay E of the Tigris. The second view can be maintained only if אַשּׁוּר be the city

---

region that could be plausibly identified with Ḥavilah?—**13.** גיחון] Probably from √ גיח (Jb. 38^{8} 40^{23}) = 'bursting forth.'—**14.** שֵׁם] 𝔊 om.—חדקל] Bab. *Idigla*, *Diglat*, Aram. דִּגְלַת and ܕܶܩܠܰܬ, Arab. *Diğlat*; then Old Pers. *Tigrâ*, Pehlevi *Digrat*, Gr. Τίγρις and Τίγρης. The Pers. *Tigrâ* was explained by a popular etymology as 'arrow-swift' (Strabo); and similarly it was believed that the Hebrews saw in their name a compound of חַד, 'sharp,' and קַל, 'swift,'—a view given by Ra., and mentioned with some scorn by IEz. Hommel's derivation (*AHT*, 315) from *ḫadd*, 'wādī,' and דִּקְלָה (= 'wādī of Diḳlah,' Gn. 10^{27}), is of interest only in connexion with his peculiar theory of the site of Paradise.—קדמת] Rendered 'in front' by 𝔊 (κατέναντι), 𝔖 (ܠܘܩܒܠ) and 𝔙 (*contra*); as 'eastward' by Aq. Σ. (ἐξ ἀνατολῆς) and 𝔗ᴼ (למדנחא). This last is also the view of Ra. IEz. and of most moderns. But see Nö. *ZDMG*, xxxiii. 532, where the sense 'eastward' is decisively rejected. The other examples are 4^{16}, 1 Sa. 13^{5}, Ezk. 39^{11}†.—פרת] Bab. *Purâtu*, Old Pers. *Ufrâtu*, whence Gr. Εὐφράτης.

which was the ancient capital of the Empire, now *Ḳalʿat Šerḳāt* on the W bank of the river. But that city was replaced as capital by Kalḫi as early as 1300 B.C., and is never mentioned in OT. It is at least premature to find in this circumstance a conclusive proof that the Paradise legend had wandered to Palestine before 1300 B.C. (Gressmann, *ARW*, x. 347).—*Euphrates*] The name (פְּרָת) needed no explanation to a Hebrew reader: it is *the* נָהָר *par excellence* of the OT (Is. 8[7] and often).

The site of Eden.—If the explanation given above of v.[10] be correct,—and it is the only sense which the words will naturally bear,—it is obvious that a real locality answering to the description of Eden exists and has existed nowhere on the face of the earth. The Euphrates and Tigris are not and never were branches of a single stream; and the idea that two other great rivers sprang from the same source places the whole representation outside the sphere of real geographical knowledge. In [10-14], in short, we have to do with a semi-mythical geography, which the Hebrews no doubt believed to correspond with fact, but which is based neither on accurate knowledge of the region in question, nor on authentic tradition handed down from the ancestors of the human race. Nevertheless, the question where the Hebrew imagination located Paradise is one of great interest; and many of the proposed solutions are of value, not only for the light they have thrown on the details of [10-14], but also for the questions they raise as to the origin and character of the Paradise-myth. This is true both of those which deny, and of those which admit, the presence of a mythical element in the geography of [10-14].

1. Several recent theories seek an exact determination of the locality of Paradise, and of all the data of [10-14], at the cost of a somewhat unnatural exegesis of v.[10]. That of Frd. Del. (*Wo lag das Paradies?*, 1881) is based partly on the fact that N of Babylon (in the vicinity of Bagdad) the Euphrates and Tigris approach within some twenty miles of each other, the Euphrates from its higher level discharging water through canals into the Tigris, which might thus be regarded as an offshoot of it. The *land* of Eden is the plain (*edinu*) between the two rivers from Tekrit (on the Tigris: nearly a hundred miles N of Bagdad) and ʿAna (on the Euphrates) to the Persian Gulf; the *garden* being one specially favoured region from the so-called 'isthmus' to a little S of Babylon. The *river* of v.[10] is the Euphrates; Pishon is the Pallakopas canal, branching off from the Euphrates on the right a little above Babylon and running nearly parallel with it to the Persian Gulf; Giḥon is the *Shaṭṭ en-Nil*, another canal running E of the Euphrates from near Babylon and rejoining the parent river opposite Ur; Ḥiddeḳel and Euphrates are, of course, the lower courses of the Tigris and Euphrates respectively, the former regarded as replenished through the canal system from the latter. Ḥavilah is part of the great Syrian

desert lying W and S of the Euphrates; and Kush is a name for northern and middle Babylonia, derived from the Kaššite dynasty that once ruled there. In spite of the learning and ingenuity with which this theory has been worked out, it cannot clear itself of an air of artificiality at variance with the simplicity of the passage it seeks to explain. That the Euphrates should be at once the undivided Paradise-stream and one of the 'heads' into which it breaks up is a glaring anomaly; while v.[14] shows that the narrator had distinctly before his mind the upper course of the Tigris opposite Assur, and is therefore not likely to have spoken of it as an effluent of the Euphrates. The objection that the theory confuses rivers and canals is fairly met by the argument that the Bab. equivalent of נָהָר is used of canals, and also by the consideration that both the canals mentioned were probably ancient river-beds; but the *order* in which the rivers are named tells heavily against the identifications. Moreover, the expression 'the *whole* land of Ḥavilah' seems to imply a much larger tract of the earth's surface than the small section of desert enclosed by the Pallakopas; and to speak of the *whole* of northern Babylonia as 'surrounded' by the *Shaṭṭ en-Nil* is an abuse of language.—According to Sayce (*HCM*, 95 ff.; *DB*, i. 643 f.), the garden of Eden is the sacred garden of Ea at Eridu; and the river which waters it is the Persian Gulf, on the shore of which Eridu formerly stood. The four branches are, in addition to Euphrates and Tigris (which in ancient times entered the Gulf separately), the Pallakopas and the Choaspes (now the *Kerkha*), the sacred river of the Persians, from whose waters alone their kings were allowed to drink (Her. i. 188). Besides the difficulty of supposing that the writer of v.[10] meant to trace the streams *upwards* towards their source above the garden, the theory does not account for the order in which the rivers are given; for the Pallakopas is W of Euphrates, while the Choaspes is E of the Tigris.* Further, although the description of the Persian Gulf as a 'river' is fully justified by its Bab. designation as *Nâr Marratum* ('Bitter River'), it has yet to be made probable that either Babylonians or Israelites would have thought of a garden as watered by 'bitter' (*i.e.* salt) water.—These objections apply with equal force to the theory of Hommel (*AA*, iii. 1, p. 281 ff., etc., *AHT*, 314 ff.), who agrees with Sayce in placing Paradise at Eridu, in making the single stream the Persian Gulf, and one of the four branches the Euphrates. But the three other branches, Pishon, Giḥon, and Ḥiddeḳel, he identifies with three N Arabian wādīs,—W. Dawāsir, W. Rummā, and W. Sirhān (the last the 'wādī of Diḳlah' = *ḥad-deḳel* [see on v.[14] above], the name having been afterwards *transferred* to the Tigris).

2. Since none of the above theories furnishes a satisfactory solution of the problem, we may as well go back to what appears the natural

---

* This objection is avoided by the modified theory of Dawson, who identifies Pishon with the Karun, still further E than the Kerkha. But that removes it from all connexion with Ḥavilah, which is one of the recommendations of Sayce's view.

interpretation of v.[10], and take along with it the utopian conception of four great rivers issuing from a single source. The site of Paradise is then determined by the imaginary common source of the two known rivers, Euphrates and Tigris. As a matter of fact, the western arm of the Euphrates and the eastern arm of the Tigris do rise sufficiently near each other to make the supposition of a common source possible to ancient cosmography; and there is no difficulty in believing that the passage locates the garden in the unexplored mountains of Armenia. The difficulty is to find the Pishon and the Giḥon. To seek them amongst the smaller rivers of Armenia and Trans-Caucasia is a hopeless quest; for a knowledge of these rivers would imply a knowledge of the country, which must have dispelled the notion of a common source. Van Doorninck has suggested the Leontes and Orontes (*ThT*, xxxix. 236), but a Hebrew writer must surely have known that these rivers rose much nearer home than the Euphrates and Tigris. There is more to be said for the opinion that they represent the two great Indian rivers, Ganges and Indus, whose sources must have been even more mysterious than those of the Euphrates and Tigris, and might very well be supposed to lie in the unknown region from Armenia to Turkestan.* The attraction of this view is that it embraces all rivers of the first magnitude that can have been known in western Asia (for, as we shall see, even the Nile is not absolutely excluded); and it is no valid objection to say that the Indian rivers were beyond the horizon of the Israelites, since we do not know from what quarter the myth had travelled before it reached Palestine. Yet I find no modern writer of note who accepts the theory in its completeness. De. and Di. identify the Pishon with the Indus, but follow the traditional identification of Giḥon with the Nile (see p. 61 above). But if the biblical narrator believed the Nile to rise with Euphrates and Tigris, it is extremely likely that he regarded its upper waters as the Indus, as Alexander the Great did in his time; † and we might then fall back on the old identification of Pishon with the Ganges.‡ But it must be admitted that the names Ḥavilah and Kush are a serious

---

* Strabo reports the belief of the ancients that all Indian rivers rise in the Caucasus (xv. 1. 13). The fact that in mediæval Arabian geographers *Ĝeiḥun* is a proper name of the Oxus and the Cilician Pyramus, and an appellative of the Araxes and the Ganges, might seem at first sight to have a bearing on the question at issue; but its importance is discounted by the possibility that the usage is based on this passage, due to Jewish and Christian influences in the Middle Ages.

† From the presence in both of crocodiles: Arrian, *Anab.* vi. 1, 2 f.; cf. Strabo, xv. 1. 25, and the similar notion about the Nile and Euphrates in Pausanias, ii. 5. 2.

‡ Josephus and most of the Fathers. Strangely enough, there seems to be no suggestion of the Indus earlier than Kosmas Indicopleustes (ii. 131). Is this because the identity of Nile and Indus was a fixed idea?

difficulty to this class of theories. The latter, indeed, may retain its usual OT meaning if Giḥon be the upper Nile, either as a continuation of the Indus or a separate river; but if it be the Indus alone, Kush must be the country of the Kaššites, conceived as extending indefinitely E of Babylonia. Ḥavilah has to be taken as a name for India considered as an extension of NE Arabia, an interpretation which finds no support in the OT. At the same time, as Di. observes, the language employed ('the whole land of Ḥ.') suggests some more spacious region than a limited district of Arabia; and from the nature of the passage we can have no certainty that the word is connected with the Ḥavilah of Gn. 10.—An interesting and independent theory, based on ancient Babylonian geographical documents, has been propounded by Haupt. The common source of the four rivers is supposed to have been a large (imaginary) basin of water in N Mesopotamia: the Euphrates and Tigris lose themselves in marshes; the Pishon (suggested by the Kerkha) is conceived as continued in the *Nâr Marratum* (Persian Gulf) and the Red Sea, and so 'encompasses' the whole of Ḥavilah (Arabia); beyond this there was supposed to be land, through which the Giḥon (suggested by the Karun) was supposed to reach Kush (Ethiopia), whence it flowed northwards as the Nile. The theory perhaps combines more of the biblical data in an intelligible way than any other that has been proposed; and it seems to agree with those just considered in placing the site of Eden at the common source of the rivers, to the N of Mesopotamia.*

3. It seems probable that the resources of philology and scientific geography are well-nigh exhausted by theories such as have been described above, and that further advance towards a solution of the problem of Paradise will be along the line of comparative mythology. Discussions precisely similar to those we have examined are maintained with regard to the Iranian cosmography—whether, *e.g.*, the stream Ranḥa be the Oxus or the Yaxartes or the Indus; the truth being that Ranḥa is a mythical celestial stream, for which various earthly equivalents might be named (see Tiele, *Gesch. d. Rel.* ii. 291 f.). If we knew more of the diffusion and history of cosmological ideas in ancient religions, we should probably find additional reason to believe that Gn. 2^{10-14} is but one of many attempts to localise on earth a representation which is essentially mythical. Gu. (^{1} 33, ^{2} 31), adopting a suggestion of Stucken, supposes the original Paradise to have been at the North pole of the heavens (the summit of the mountain of the gods: cf. Ezk. 28^{14}), and the river to be the Milky Way, branching out—[but does it?]—into four arms (there is some indication that the two arms between Scorpio and Capricornus were regarded in Babylonia as the heavenly counterparts of Euphrates and Tigris: see *KAT*^{3}, 528). It is not meant, of course, that this was the idea in the mind of the biblical writer, but only that the conception of the mysterious river of Paradise with its four branches *originated* in mythological speculation of this kind. If this be the case, we need not

* The summary is taken from Dri. p. 59 f.; the original article, in *Ueber Land und Meer*, 1894–95, I have not been able to consult.

be surprised if it should prove impossible to identify Pishon and Giḥon with any known rivers: on the other hand, the mention of the well-known Tigris and Euphrates clearly shows that the form of the myth preserved in Gn. 2^{10-14} located the earthly Paradise in the unknown northerly region whence these rivers flowed. And the conclusion is almost inevitable that the myth took shape in a land watered by these two rivers,—in Babylonia or Mesopotamia (see Gressmann, *ARW*, x. 346 f.).

15. *to till it and to guard it*] To reject this clause (Bu.), or the second member (Di.), as inconsistent with $3^{17ff.}$ are arbitrary expedients. The ideal existence for man is not idle enjoyment, but easy and pleasant work; "the highest aspiration of the Eastern peasant" (Gu.) being to keep a garden. The question from what the garden had to be protected is one that should not be pressed.—**16 f.** The belief that man lived originally on the natural fruit of trees (observe the difference from 1^{29}) was widespread in antiquity, and appears in Phœnician mythology.* Here, however, the point lies rather in the restriction than the permission,—in the imposition of a *taboo* on one particular tree.—For the words *of the knowledge of good and evil* it has been proposed to substitute "which is in the midst of the garden" (as 3^3), on the ground that the revelation of the mysterious property of the tree was the essence of the serpent's temptation and must not be anticipated (3^5) (Bu. Ho. Gu. al.). But the narrative ought not to be subjected to such rigorous logical

15. The v. is either a resumption of ^{8b} after the insertion of $^{10-14}$, or a duplicate from a parallel document. It is too original to be a gloss; and since there was no motive for making an interpolation at ^{8b}, the excision of $^{10-14}$ seems to lead necessarily to the conclusion that two sources have been combined.—את־האדם] 𝕲 + ὃν ἔπλασεν (as v.[8]).—ויניחהו] On the two Hiphils of נוח and their distinction in meaning, see G–K. § 72 *ee*, and the Lexx.—עדן] 𝕲^L and most cursives render τῆς τρυφῆς: 𝕲^A and uncials omit the word.—לעבדה וגו׳] Since גן is nowhere fem., it is better to point לעבדֹה ולשמרֹה (see Albrecht, *ZATW*, xvi. 53).—**16.** האדם] 𝕲 Ἀδαμ, 𝔙 *ei*. Except in v.[18], the word is regularly, but wrongly, treated as *nom. pr.* by these two Vns. from this point onwards.—**17.** מות תמות] Σ. θνητὸς ἔσῃ. In 𝕲 the vbs. of this v. are all pl. (as $3^{3.4}$).

* Eus. *Præp. Ev.* i. 10 (from Philo Byblius): εὑρεῖν δὲ τὸν Αἰῶνα τὴν ἀπὸ τῶν δενδρῶν τροφήν.

tests; and, after all, there still remained something for the serpent to disclose, viz. that such knowledge put man on an equality with God.—*in the day . . . die*] The threat was not fulfilled; but its force is not to be weakened by such considerations as that man from that time became mortal (Jer. al.), or that he entered on the experience of miseries and hardships which are the prelude of dissolution (Calv. al.). The simple explanation is that God, having regard to the circumstances of the temptation, changed His purpose and modified the penalty.

18–25. Creation of animals and woman.—The Creator, taking pity on the solitude of the man, resolves to provide him with a suitable companion. The naïveté of the conception is extraordinary. Not only did man exist before the beasts, but the whole animal creation is the result of an unsuccessful experiment to find a mate for him. Of the revolting idea that man lived for a time in sexual intercourse with the beasts (see p. 91), there is not a trace.—**18.** *a helper*] The writer seems to be thinking (as in 2^{5}), not of the original, but of the present familiar conditions of human life.—כְּנֶגְדּוֹ] (only here) lit. 'as in front of him,' ***i.e.*** *corresponding to him.*—**19.** The meaning cannot be that the animals had already been created, and are now brought to be named (Calv. al. and recently De. Str.): such a sense is excluded by grammar (see Dri. *T.* § 76, *Obs.*), and misses the point of the passage.—*to see what he would call it*] To watch its effect on him, and (eventually) to see if he would recognise in it the associate he needed,—as one watches

---

18. אעשה] May be cohort. (G–K. § 75 *l*); 𝔊𝔙 render as 1st p. pl. (as 1^{26}).—עזר] (usually 'succour') = 'helper' (*abstr. pro concr.*) is used elsewhere chiefly of God (Dt. $33^{7.\,26}$, Ps. 33^{20} $115^{9ff.}$ etc.); possible exceptions are Ezk. 12^{14} (if text right), Ho. 13^{9} (if em. with We.): see BDB.—כנגדו] 𝔊 *κατ' αὐτόν* (but v.^{20} *ὅμοιος αὐτῷ*); Aq. *ὡς κατέναντι αὐτοῦ*; Σ. *ἀντικρὺς αὐτοῦ*; 𝔙 *similis sibi* (*ejus*, v.^{20}); 𝔖 ܐܟܘܬܗ; 𝔗^{O} כקיבליה.—**19.** 𝔐𝔊 ins. עוד after אלהים.—Omission of את־ before כל־חית is remarkable in this ch. (see on v.^{9}), and is rectified by 𝔐.—נפש חיה] The only construction possible would be to take לו as *dat. eth.*, and נ' ח' as direct obj. to יקרא; but that is contrary to the writer's usage, and yields a jejune sense. Even if (with Ra.) we transpose and read 'every living thing which the man called [by a name], that was its name,' the discord of gender would

the effect of a new experience on a little child.—*whatever the man should call it*, *that* (was to be) *its name*] The spontaneous ejaculation of the first man becomes to his posterity a name: such is the origin of (Hebrew) names.—The words נֶפֶשׁ חַיָּה are incapable of construction, and are to be omitted as an explanatory gloss (Ew. al.).—**20.** The classification of animals is carried a step further than in ^{19} (domestic and wild animals being distinguished), but is still simpler than in ch. 1. Fishes and 'creeping things' are frankly omitted as inappropriate to the situation.—**21.** It has appeared that no fresh creation 'from the ground' can provide a fit companion for man: from his own body, therefore, must his future associate be taken.—תַּרְדֵּמָה] is a hypnotic trance, induced by supernatural agency (cf. Duhm on Is. 29^{10}). The purpose here is to produce anæsthesia, with perhaps the additional idea that the divine working cannot take place under human observation (Di. Gu.).—*one of his ribs*] A part of his frame that (it was thought) could easily be spared. There is doubtless a deeper significance in the representation: it suggests "the moral and social relation of the sexes to each other, the dependence of woman upon man, her close relationship to him, and the foundation existing in nature for . . . the feelings with which each should naturally regard the other" (Dri.). The Arabs use similarly a word for 'rib,' saying *hūa lizḳī* or *hūa bilizḳī* for 'he is my bosom companion.' On the other hand, the notion that the first human being was androgynous, and afterwards separated into man and woman (see Schw. *ARW*, ix. 172 ff.), finds no countenance in the passage.—**22.** *built up the rib*

be fatal, to say nothing of the addition of שֵׁם.—**20.** ולעוף] Rd. with MSS 𝔊𝔙𝔖𝔗 ולכל־עוף (Ba.).—וּלְאָדָם] Here the Mass. takes Adam as a proper name. De. al. explain it as generic='for a human being' (Gu.); Ols. emends וְהָאדם. The truth is that the Mass. loses no opportunity presented by the *Kethîb* of treating אדם as *n. pr.* Point וְלָאָדָם.—לא מצא] Tu. al. take God as subj.; but it may be pass. expressed by indef. subj. (G-K. § 144 *d, e*)='there was not found.'—**21.** תרדמה] 𝔊 *ἔκστασιν*; Aq. *καταφοράν*; Σ. *κάρον*; 𝔖 ܫܠܝܐ ('tranquillity'); 𝔙 *sopor*; 𝔗^{O} and some Gr. Vns. (Field) have 'sleep' simply. The examples of its use (15^{12}, 1 Sa. 26^{12}, Is. 29^{10}, Jb. 4^{13} 33^{15}, Pr. 19^{15}†), all except the last, confirm

. . . *into a woman*] So in the Egyptian "Tale of the two brothers," the god Chnum 'built' a wife for his favourite Batau, the hieroglyphic determinative showing that the operation was actually likened to the building of a wall (see Wiedemann, *DB*, Sup. 180).—**23.** By a flash of intuition the man divines that the fair creature now brought to him is part of himself, and names her accordingly. There is a poetic ring and rhythm in the exclamation that breaks from him.—*This at last*] Lit. 'This, this time' (*v.i.*): note the thrice repeated זאת.—*bone of my bones, etc.*] The expressions originate in the primitive notion of kinship as resting on "participation in a common mass of flesh, blood, and bones" (Rob. Sm. *RS*², 273 f.: cf. *KM*², 175 f.), so that all the members of a kindred group are parts of the same substance, whether acquired by heredity or assimilated in the processes of nourishment (cf. 29^{14} 37^{27}, Ju. 9^{2}, 2 Sa. 5^{1} 19^{13}). The case before us, where the material identity is expressed in the manner of woman's creation, is unique.—*shall be called Woman*] English is fortunate in being able to reproduce this assonance (*'Îš*, *'Iššā*) without straining language: other translations are driven to *tours de force*

Duhm's view that hypnotic sleep is indicated. It is true that in the vb. (Niph.) that sense is less marked.—**23.** זאת הפעם] The construction rendered above takes זאת as subj. of the sent. and הפעם = 'this time,' the art. having full demonstrative force, as in $29^{34f.}$ 30^{20} 46^{30}, Ex. 9^{27} (so 𝔊 ΣΘ𝔙; De. Di. Gu. al.). The accents, however, unite the words in one phrase 'this time,' after the rather important analogy of זֶה פְּעָמַיִם (27^{36} 43^{10}), leaving the subj. unexpressed. This sense is followed by 𝔖𝔗^{OJ}, and advocated by Sta. (*ZATW*, xvii. 210 ff.); but it seems less acceptable than the other.—אִישׁ, אִשָּׁה] The old derivation of these words from a common √ אנשׁ is generally abandoned, אישׁ being assigned to a hypothetical √ אושׁ = 'be strong' (Ges. *Th.*). Ar. and Aram., indeed, show quite clearly that the √ seen in the pl. אֲנָשִׁים (and in אֱנוֹשׁ) and that of אִשָּׁה (אִנְשָׁה) are only apparently identical, the one having *s* where the other has *ṯ*. The masc. and fem. are therefore etymologically distinct, and nothing remains but a very strong assonance. The question whether we are to postulate a third √ for the sing. אִישׁ does not greatly concern us here; the arguments will be found in BDB, *s.v.* See Nö. *ZDMG*, xl. 740 ("Aber אִישׁ möchte ich doch bei אנשׁ lassen"). In imitation of the assonance, Σ. has *ἄνδρις*, 𝔙 *Virago*. Θ. λῆψις, represents אֶשָּׂא, 'I will take': a curious blunder which is fully elucidated by

(*e.g.* Jer. *Virago*; Luther, *Männin*). Whether even in Heb. it is more than an assonance is doubtful (*v.i.*).—**24.** An ætiological observation of the narrator: *This is why a man leaves . . . and cleaves . . . and they become, etc.*] It is not a prophecy from the standpoint of the narrative; nor a recommendation of monogamic marriage (as applied in Mt. $19^{4ff.}$, Mk. $10^{6ff.}$, 1 Co. 6^{16}, Eph. 5^{31}); it is an answer to the question, What is the meaning of that universal instinct which impels a man to separate from his parents and cling to his wife? It is strange that the man's attachment to the woman is explained here, and the woman's to the man only in 3^{16}.

It has been imagined that the v. presupposes the primitive custom called *beena* marriage, or that modification of it in which the husband parts from his own kindred for good, and goes to live with his wife's kin (so Gu.: cf. *KM*², 87, 207); and other instances are alleged in the patriarchal history. But this would imply an almost incredible antiquity for the present form of the narrative; and, moreover, the dominion of the man over the wife assumed in 3^{16b} is inconsistent with the conditions of *beena* marriage. Cf. Benz. *EB*, 2675: "The phrase . . . may be an old saying dating from remote times when the husband went to the house (tent) of the wife and joined her clan. Still the passage may be merely the narrator's remark; and even if it should be an old proverb we cannot be sure that it really carries us so far back in antiquity."—See, however, Gressmann, *ARW*, x. 353^1; van Doorninck, *ThT*, xxxix. 238 (who assigns 2^{24} and 3^{16} to different recensions).

one flesh] If the view just mentioned could be maintained, this phrase might be equivalent to 'one clan' (Lv. 25^{49}); for "both in Hebrew and Arabic 'flesh' is synonymous with 'clan' or kindred group" (*RS*², 274). More probably it refers simply to the *connubium*.—**25.** *naked . . . not ashamed*] The remark is not merely an anticipation of the

---

the quotation from Origen given in Field, p. 15^{32}.—For מאיש, 𝔐𝔊𝔗^{O} read מֵאִישָׁהּ, which is by no means an improvement.—לֻקֳחָה־זּאת] See G–K. §§ 10 *h*, 20 *c*.—24. והיו] Add שְׁנֵיהֶם with 𝔊𝔙𝔖𝔗^{J} and NT citations. 𝔐 has והיה משניהם, referring to the offspring.—25. עֲרוּמִּים] עָרוֹם 'naked,' to be carefully distinguished from עָרוּם (√ ערם) 'crafty,' in 3^1, is either a by-form of עֵירֹם (√ עור = 'be bare') in $3^{10f.}$, or (more probably) a different formation from √ ערה ('be bare'). See BDB, *s.vv.*—יתבששו] The Hithpal. (only here) probably expresses reciprocity ('ashamed before one another'); the impf. is frequentative.

account given later of the origin of clothing (3^7, cf. ^{21}). It calls attention to the difference between the original and the actual condition of man as conceived by the writer. The consciousness of sex is the result of eating the tree: before then our first parents had the innocence of children, who are often seen naked in the East (Doughty, *AD*, ii. 475).

V.[25] is a transition verse, leading over to the main theme to which all that goes before is but the prelude. How long the state of primitive innocence lasted, the writer is at no pains to inform us. This indifference to the non-essential is as characteristic of the popular tale as its graphic wealth of detail in features of real interest. The omission afforded an opportunity for the exercise of later Midrashic ingenuity; *Jub.* iii. 15 fixes the period at seven years, while R. Eliezer (*Ber. R.*) finds that it did not last six hours.

III. 1–7. The temptation. — Attention is at once directed to the quarter where the possibility of evil already lurked amidst the happiness of Eden—the preternatural subtlety of the serpent: *But the serpent was wily*] The wisdom of the serpent was proverbial in antiquity (Mt. 10^{16}: see Bochart, *Hieroz.* iii. 246 ff.), a belief probably founded less on observation of the creature's actual qualities than on the general idea of its divine or demonic nature: *πνευματικώτατον γὰρ τὸ ζῶον πάντων τῶν ἑρπετῶν* (Sanchuniathon, in Eus. *Præp. Ev.* i. 10). Hence the epithet עָרוּם might be used of it *sensu bono* (φρόνιμος), though the context here makes it certain that the bad sense (πανοῦργος) is intended (see below). —*beyond any beast, etc.*] The serpent, therefore, belongs to the category of 'beasts of the field,' and is a creature of Yahwe; and an effort seems to be made to maintain this view throughout the narrative (v.[14]). At the same time it is a being possessing supernatural knowledge, with the power of speech, and animated by hostility towards God. It is this last feature which causes some perplexity. To say that the thoughts which it instils into the mind of the woman were on the serpent's part not evil, but only extremely sagacious, and became sin first in the human consciousness (so Merx, Di. al.), is hardly in accordance with the spirit of the narrative. It is more probable that behind the sober description of the serpent as a mere creature of Yahwe,

there was an earlier form of the legend in which he figured as a god or a demon.

The ascription of supernatural characters to the serpent presents little difficulty even to the modern mind. The marvellous agility of the snake, in spite of the absence of visible motor organs, its stealthy movements, its rapid death-dealing stroke, and its mysterious power of fascinating other animals and even men, sufficiently account for the superstitious regard of which it has been the object amongst all peoples.* Accordingly, among the Arabs every snake is the abode of a spirit, sometimes bad and sometimes good, so that *ǧānn* and *ġūl* and even *Shaiṭān* are given as designations of the serpent (We. *Heid.* 152 f.; cf. Rob. Sm. *RS*², 120¹, 129 f., 442).† What is more surprising to us is the fact that in the sphere of religion the serpent was usually worshipped as a *good* demon. Traces of this conception can be detected in the narrative before us. The demonic character of the serpent appears in his possession of occult divine knowledge of the properties of the tree in the middle of the garden, and in his use of that knowledge to seduce man from his allegiance to his Creator. The enmity between the race of men and the race of serpents is explained as a punishment for his successful temptation; originally he must have been represented as a being hostile, indeed, to God, but friendly to the woman, who tells her the truth which the Deity withheld from man (see Gres. *l.c.* 357). All this belongs to the background of heathen mythology from which the materials of the narrative were drawn; and it is the incomplete elimination of the mythological element, under the influence of a monotheistic and ethical religion, which makes the function of the serpent in Gn. 3 so difficult to understand. In later Jewish theology the difficulty was

---

* Comp. the interesting sequel to the sentence from Sanchuniathon quoted above: . . . *καὶ πυρῶδες ὑπ' αὐτοῦ παρεδόθη παρ' ὃ καὶ τάχος ἀνυπέρβλητον διὰ τοῦ πνεύματος παρίστησι, χωρὶς ποδῶν τε καὶ χειρῶν, ἢ ἄλλου τινὸς τῶν ἔξωθεν, ἐξ ὧν τὰ λοιπὰ ζῶα τὰς κινήσεις ποιεῖται· καὶ ποικίλων σχημάτων τύπους ἀποτελεῖ, καὶ κατὰ τὴν πορείαν ἑλικοειδεῖς ἔχει τὰς ὁρμὰς, ἐφ' ὃ βούλεται τάχος· καὶ πολυχρονιώτατον δέ ἐστιν, οὐ μόνον τῷ ἐκδυόμενον τὸ γῆρας νεάζειν, ἀλλὰ καὶ αὔξησιν ἐπιδέχεσθαι μείζονα πέφυκε . . . Διὸ καὶ ἐν ἱεροῖς τοῦτο τὸ ζῶον καὶ ἐν μυστηρίοις συμπαρείληπται κτλ.* (Orelli, p. 44).

† Cf. Nö. *ZVP*, i. 413: "Das geheimnissvolle, dämonische Wesen der Schlange, das sie vor allen grösseren Thieren auszeichnet, die tückische, verderbenbringende Natur vieler Arten, konnte in dem einfachen semitischen Hirten leicht den Glauben erzeugen, in ihr wohne etwas Göttliches, den Menschen Bannendes und Bezauberndes. So finden wir die Schlange im Eingang des alten Testaments, so ist sie im Alterthum, wie noch jetzt, ein Hauptgegenstand orientalischer Zauberei. So glaubte auch der Araber, die Schlange (wie einige andere schädliche Thiere) sei kein gewöhnliches Geschöpf, sondern ein Dschinn, ein Geist. Schon die Sprache drückt dies dadurch aus, dass sie mit *Džānn*, einem Worte welches mit *Džinn* eng verwandt ist, eine Schlangenart bezeichnet, etc."

solved, as is well known, by the doctrine that the serpent of Eden was the mouthpiece or impersonation of the devil. The idea appears first in Alexandrian Judaism in Wisd. 2^{24} ('by the envy of the devil, death entered into the world'): possibly earlier is the allusion in *En.* lxix. 6, where the seduction of Eve is ascribed to a Satan called Gadreel. Cf. *Secrets of En.* xxxi. 3 ff., *Ps. Sol.* 4^{9}; also *Ber. R.* 29, the name נָחָשׁ הַקַּדְמֹנִי (*Sifrê* 138 b), and in the NT Jn. 8^{44}, 2 Co. 11^{3}, Ro. 16^{20}, Ap. 12^{9} 20^{2} (see Whitehouse, *DB*, iv. 408 ff.). Similarly in Persian mythology the serpent Dahâka, to whose power Yima, the ruler of the golden age, succumbs, is a creature and incarnation of the evil spirit Angro-Mainyo (*Vend.* i. 8, xxii. 5, 6, 24; *Yaçna* ix. 27; cf. Di. 70). The Jewish and Christian doctrine is a natural and legitimate extension of the teaching of Gn. 3, when the problem of evil came to be apprehended in its real magnitude; but it is foreign to the thought of the writer, although it cannot be denied that it may have some affinity with the mythological background of his narrative. The religious teaching of the passage knows nothing of an evil principle *external* to the serpent, but regards himself as the subject of whatever occult powers he displays: he is simply a creature of Yahwe distinguished from the rest by his superior subtlety. The Yahwistic author does not speculate on the ultimate origin of evil; it was enough for his purpose to have so analysed the process of temptation that the beginning of sin could be assigned to a source which is neither in the nature of man nor in God. The personality of the Satan (the Adversary) does not appear in the OT till after the Exile (Zec. Jb. Ch.).

The serpent shows his subtlety by addressing his first temptation to the more mobile temperament of the woman (Ra. al.), and by the skilful *innuendo* with which he at once invites conversation and masks his ultimate design.—*Ay, and so God has said, etc.!*] Something like this seems to be the force of אַף כִּי (*v.i.*). It is a half-interrogative, half-reflective exclamation, as if the serpent had brooded long over the paradox, and had been driven to an unwelcome conclusion.—*Ye shall not eat of any tree*] The range of the prohibition is purposely exaggerated in order to provoke inquiry and criticism. The use of the name אֱלֹהִים is

---

1. והנחש היה] The usual order of words when a new subject is introduced, G-K. § 142 *d*; Dav. § 105.—ערום] 𝔊 φρονιμώτατος, Aq. Θ. πανοῦργος, Σ. πανουργότερος, 𝔙 *callidior.* The good sense (which appears to be secondary, cf. Ar. '*arama*='be ill-natured') is confined to Prov.; elsewhere (Jb. 5^{12} 15^{5}) it means 'crafty,' 'wily.' The same distinction is observed in all forms of the √ except that in Jb. 5^{13} עָרְם has the good sense. The resemblance to ערומים in 2^{25} is perhaps accidental.—ויאמר] 𝔊𝔖 + הנחש.—אף כי] as a compound part. generally means 'much more

commonly explained by the analogy of other passages of J, where the name יהוה is avoided in conversation with heathen (39[9] etc.), or when the contrast between the divine and the human is reflected upon (32[29]). But J's usage in such cases is not uniform, and it is doubtful what is the true explanation here (see p. 53).—**2, 3.** The woman's first experience of falsehood leads to an eager repudiation of the serpent's intentional calumny, in which she emphasises the generosity of the divine rule, but unconsciously intensifies the stringency of the prohibition by adding the words: *nor shall ye touch it*] A Jewish legend says that the serpent took advantage of this innocent and immaterial variation by forcing her to touch the fruit, and then arguing that as death had not followed the touch, so it would not follow the eating (*Ber. R.*, Ra.). Equally futile inferences have been drawn by modern comm., and the surmise that the clause is redactional (Bu. *Urg.* 241) is hypercritical.—*the tree . . . midst*] See p. 66 f.—4. *Ye shall assuredly not die*] On the syntax, *v.i.* The serpent thus advances to an open challenge of the divine veracity, and thence to the imputation of an unworthy motive for the command, viz. a jealous fear on God's part lest they should become His equals.—

(or less),' 'not to mention,' etc., as in 1 Sa. 14[30], 1 Ki. 8[27], Pr. 11[31] etc. In some cases the simple אף has this sense, and the כי (='when,' 'if') introduces the following clause (1 Sa. 23[3], 2 Sa. 4[10f.] etc.). It would be easy to retain this sense in v.[1] ('How much more *when* God has said,' etc.), if we might assume with many comm. that some previous conversation had taken place; but that is an unwarrantable assumption. The rendering on which Dri. (BDB) bases the ordinary meaning of אף כי—''*Tis indeed that*'—requires but a slight interrogative inflexion of the voice to yield the shade of meaning given above: 'So it is the case that God,' etc.? The Vns. all express a question: 𝔊 τί ὅτι, Aq. μὴ ὅτι, Σ. πρὸς τί, 𝔙 *cur*, 𝔖 ܠܡܐ ܫܪܝܪܐܝܬ, 𝔗ᴼ בקושטא (='really'?).—לא . . . מכל]='not of any': G-K. § 152 *b*.—2. מפרי] 𝔊 מִכֹּל, 𝔖 מפרי כל.—3. ומפרי] Not 'concerning the tree.' There is an *anakolouthon* at אמר אלהים, and the emphatically placed מפרי is resumed by ממנו.—העץ] 𝔐 + הַזֶּה.—תמתון] On the ending, see G-K. §§ 47 *m*, 72 *u*.—4. לא מות תמתון] On the unusual order, see Dav. § 86 (*b*); G-K. § 113 *v*. It is often explained as a negation of the threat in 2[17], adopting the same form of words; but the phrase had not been used by the woman, and the exact words are *not* repeated. More probably its effect is to concentrate the emphasis on the neg. part. rather than on

5. *But God knoweth, etc.*] And therefore has falsely threatened you with death. The gratuitous insinuation reveals the main purpose of the tempter, to sow the seeds of distrust towards God in the mind of the woman.—*your eyes shall be opened*] The expression denotes a sudden acquisition of new powers of perception through supernatural influence (21^{19}, Nu. 22^{31}, 2 Ki. 6^{17}).—*as gods*] or 'divine beings,' rather than 'as God': the rendering 'as angels' (IEz.) expresses the idea with substantial accuracy. The likeness to divinity actually acquired is not equality with Yahwe (see Gu. on v.[22]).—*knowing good and evil*] See p. 95 ff.—"The facts are all, in the view of the narrator, correctly stated by the serpent; he has truly represented the mysterious virtue of the tree; knowledge really confers equality with God (3^{22}); and it is also true that death does not immediately follow the act of eating. But at the same time the serpent insinuates a certain construction of these facts: God is envious, inasmuch as He grudges the highest good to man:—*φθονερὸν τὸ θεῖον*, an antique sentiment familiar to us from the Greeks" (Gu.).—6. The spiritual part of the temptation is now accomplished, and the serpent is silent, leaving the fascination of sense to do the rest. The woman looks on the tree with new eyes; she observes how attractive to taste and sight its fruit seems, and how desirable *for obtaining insight* (so most) or *to contemplate* (𝔊𝔙𝔖; so Tu. Ges. De. Gu. al.). The second translation is the more suitable—for how could she tell by sight that the fruit would impart wisdom?—although the vb. is not elsewhere used in Heb. for mere looking (*v.i.*).—*gave also to her husband*] "The process in the man's case was no doubt the same as that just described, the woman taking the place of the serpent" (Ben.). That Adam sinned with his eyes open in order not to be separated from his wife has

---

the verbal idea (cf. Am. 9^8, Ps. 49^8).—5. כאלהים] 𝔊 ὡς θεοί, 𝔗^O כרברבין.—6. העץ[2]] 𝔊𝔙 om.—להשכיל] 𝔊 κατανοῆσαι, 𝔙 *adspectu*, and 𝔖 ܠܡܚܙܐ ܒܗ all take the vb. as vb. of sight; 𝔗^O לאסתכלא ביה is indeterminate (see Levy, *Chald. Wb.* 163 a). In OT the word is used of mental *vision* (insight, or attentive consideration: Dt. 32^{29}, Ps. 41^2, Pr. 21^{12} etc.); in NH and

been a common idea both among Jews and Christians (*Ber. R.*, Ra. IEz. Milton, etc.), but is not true to the intention of the narrative.—7. *the eyes . . . opened*] The prediction of the serpent is so far fulfilled; but the change fills them with guilty fear and shame.—*they knew that they were naked*] The new sense of shame is spoken of as a sort of *Werthurtheil* passed by the awakened intelligence on the empirical fact of being unclothed. A connexion between sexual shame and sin (Di.) is not suggested by the passage, and is besides not true to experience. But to infer from this single effect that the forbidden fruit had aphrodisiac properties (see Barton, *SO*[1], 93 ff.; Gressmann, p. 356) is a still greater perversion of the author's meaning; he merely gives this as an example of the new range of knowledge acquired by eating of the tree. It is the kind of knowledge which comes with maturity to all,—the transition "from the innocence of childhood into the knowledge which belongs to adult age" (Dri.).—*foliage of the fig-tree*] To the question, Why fig-leaves in particular? the natural answer is that these, if not very suitable for the purpose, were yet the most suitable that the flora of Palestine could suggest (Di. Dri. Ben. al.). An allusion to the so-called fig-tree of Paradise, a native of India (probably the plantain), is on every ground improbable;—"ein geradezu philisterhafter Einfall" (Bu.). For allegorical interpretations of the fig-leaves, see Lagarde, *Mitth.* i. 73 ff., who adds a very original and fantastic one of his own.

8–13. The inquest.—Thus far the narrative has dealt with what may be called the natural (magical) effects of the eating of the tree—the access of enlightenment, and the disturbance thus introduced into the relations of the guilty pair to each other. The ethical aspect of the offence comes

---

Aram. it means 'to look at,' but only in Hithp. (Ithp.). On the other view the Hiph. is intrans. (='for acquiring wisdom': Ps. 94^8) rather than caus. (='to impart wisdom': Ps. 32^8 etc.).—Gu. considers the clause ונחמד העץ לה' a variant from another source.—ותקח] 𝔊[L] + האשה.—ויאכל] 𝔐𝔊 ויאכלו.—7. עירמים] See on 2^{25}.—עלה] coll.; but some MSS and 𝔐 have עָלֵי (so 𝔊𝔖, 𝔗[oz]).

to light in their first interview with Yahwe; and this is delineated with a skill hardly surpassed in the account of the temptation itself.—8. *they heard the sound*] קול used of footsteps, as 2 Sa. 5^{24}, 1 Ki. 14^{6}, 2 Ki. 6^{32}: cf. Ezk. $3^{12f.}$, Jl. 2^{5}.—*of Yahwe God as He walked*] The verb is used (Lv. 26^{12}, Dt. 23^{15}, 2 Sa. 7^{6}) of Yahwe's majestic marching in the midst of Israel; but it mars the simplicity of the representation if (with De.) we introduce that idea here.—*in the cool* (lit. 'at the breeze') *of the day*] *i.e.* towards evening, when in Eastern lands a refreshing wind springs up (cf. Ca. 2^{17} 4^{6}: but *v.i.*), and the master, who has kept his house or tent during the 'heat of the day' (18^{1}), can walk abroad with comfort (24^{63}). Such, we are led to understand, was Yahwe's daily practice; and the man and woman had been wont to meet Him with the glad confidence of innocence. But on this occasion they *hid themselves, etc.*—9. *Where art thou?*] (cf. 4^{9}). The question expresses ignorance; it is not omniscience that the writer wishes to illustrate, but the more impressive attribute of sagacity.—10. *I feared . . . naked*] With the instinctive cunning of a bad conscience, the man hopes to escape complete exposure by acknowledging part of the truth; he alleges nakedness as the ground of his fear, putting fear and shame in a false causal connexion (Ho.).—11. *Hast thou eaten, etc.?*] All unwittingly he has disclosed his guilty secret: he has shown himself possessed of a knowledge which could only have been acquired in one way.—12. The man cannot even yet bring himself to make a clean breast of it; but with a quaint mixture of cowardice and effrontery he throws the blame

---

8. מתהלך] acc. of condition: Dav. § 70 (*a*).—לרוח היום] 𝔊 τὸ δειλινόν, 𝔙 *ad auram post meridiem*, 𝔖 ܠܡܦܢܝܗ ܕܝܘܡܐ, 𝔗^O^ למנח יומא. On this use of ל (='towards'), see BDB, *s.v.* 6 a; and cf. 8^{11} 17^{21}, Is. 7^{15}, Jb. 24^{14}. With רוח cf. Ar. *rawāḥ = tempus vespertinum*. Jewish exegesis (*Ber. R.*) and Calv. suppose the morning (sea) breeze to be meant, as is probably the case in Ca. 2^{17} 4^{6}, and would seem more in accordance with Palestinian conditions. But it is manifestly improbable here.—עץ] coll., as often. $𝔊^{L}$ om.—9. איכה] G–K. § 100 *o*. 𝔊 supplies 'Adam' before, and 𝔖 after, the interrog.—10. שמעתי] 𝔊 + περιπατοῦντος (as v.[8]).—11. לבלתי] See G–K. § 114 *s*.—Before μὴ φαγεῖν 𝔊 has τούτου

directly on the woman, and indirectly on God who gave her to him.—**13.** The woman in like manner exculpates herself by pleading (truly enough) that she had been deceived by the serpent.—The whole situation is now laid bare, and nothing remains but to pronounce sentence. No question is put to the serpent, because his evil motive is understood: he has acted just as might have been expected of him. Calv. says, "the *beast* had no sense of sin, and the *devil* no hope of pardon."

14–19. This section contains the key to the significance of the story of the Fall. It is the first example of a frequently recurring motive of the Genesis narratives, the idea, viz., that the more perplexing facts in the history of men and peoples are the working out of a doom or 'weird' pronounced of old under divine inspiration, or (as in this case) by the Almighty Himself: see 4^{15} $8^{21ff.}$ $9^{25ff.}$ 16^{12} $27^{27ff. 39f.}$ $48^{19ff.}$, ch. 49; cf. Nu. 23 f., Dt. 33. Here certain fixed adverse conditions of the universal human lot are traced back to a primæval curse uttered by Yahwe in consequence of man's first transgression. See, further, p. 95 below.—The form of the oracles is poetic; but the structure is irregular, and no definite metrical scheme can be made out.

14, 15. The curse on the serpent is legible, partly in its degraded form and habits (^{14}), and partly in the deadly feud between it and the human race (^{15}).—**14.** *on thy belly, etc.*] The assumption undoubtedly is that originally the serpent moved erect, but not necessarily that its organism was changed (*e.g.* by cutting off its legs, etc. *Rabb.*). As a matter of fact most snakes have the power of erecting a considerable part of their bodies; and in mytho-

---

μόνου.—**13.** מה־זאת] So commonly with עשה; with other vbs. מה־זה (G–K. § 136 *c*; Dav. § 7 (*c*)).

14. מכל] On this use of מן (=*e numero*), see G–K. § 119 *w*, and cf. Ex. 19^5, Dt. 14^2 33^{24}, Ju. 5^{24} etc. Sta.'s argument (*ZATW*, xvii. 209) for deleting מכל הבהמה ו, on the ground that the serpent belongs to the category of חית השדה but not to בהמה, is logical, but hardly convincing.—גחן] Probably from √ גחן (Aram.)='curve' or 'bend' (De., BDB), occurs again only Lv. 11^{42}, of reptiles. 𝔙 renders *pectus*, 𝔊 combines *στῆθοι*

logical representations the serpent often appears in the upright position (Ben.). The idea probably is that this was its original posture: how it was maintained was perhaps not reflected upon.—*dust shalt thou eat*] Cf. Mic. 7^{17}, Is. 65^{25}. It is a prosaic explanation to say that the serpent, crawling on the ground, inadvertently swallows a good deal of dust (Boch. *Hieroz.* iii. 245; Di. al.); and a mere metaphor for humiliation (like Ass. *ti-ka-lu ip-ra*; *KIB*, v. 232 f.) is too weak a sense for this passage. Probably it is a piece of ancient superstition, like the Arabian notion that the *ğinn* eat dirt (We. *Heid.* 150).—*all the days of thy life*] i.e. *each* serpent as long as it lives, and the *race* of serpents as long as it lasts. It is not so certain as most comm. seem to think that these words exclude the demonic character of the serpent. It is true that the punishment of a morally irresponsible agent was recognised in Hebrew jurisprudence (9^5, Ex. $21^{28f.}$, Lv. $20^{15f.}$). But it is quite possible that here (as in v.[15]) the archetypal serpent is conceived as re-embodied in all his progeny, as acting and suffering in each member of the species.—**15.** The serpent's attempt to establish unholy fellowship with the woman is punished by implacable and undying enmity between them.*—*thy seed and her seed*] The whole brood of

---

and *κοιλία*.—**15.** זֶרַע] in the sense of 'offspring,' is nearly always collective. In a few cases where it is used of an individual child (4^{25}? 21^{13}, 1 Sa. 1^{11}) it denotes the immediate offspring as the pledge of posterity, never a remote descendant (see Nö. *ARW*, viii. 164 ff.). The Messianic application therefore is not justified in grammar.—הוא] the rendering *ipsa* (𝔙) is said not to be found in the Fathers before Ambrose and Augustine (Zapletal, *ATliches*, 19). Jer. at all events knew that *ipse* should be read.—ישופך . . . תשופנו] The form שוף recurs only Jb. 9^{17}, Ps. 139^{11}, and, in both, text and meaning are doubtful. In Aram. and NH the √ (ע״ו or ע״ע) has the primary sense of 'rub,' hence 'wear down by rubbing'='crush'; in Syr. it also means to crawl. There are a few exx. of a tendency of ע״ו vbs. to strengthen themselves by insertion of א (Kön. i. 439), and it is often supposed that in certain pass.

---

* "Fit enim arcano naturæ sensu ut ab ipsis abhorreat homo" (Calv.). Cf. (with Boch. *Hieroz.* iii. 250) "quam dudum dixeras te odisse æque atque angues" (Plaut. *Merc.* 4); and ἐκ παιδὸς τὸν ψυχρὸν ὄφιν τὰ μάλιστα δέδοικα (Theoc. *Id.* 15).

serpents, and the whole race of men.—*He shall bruise thee on the head, etc.*] In the first clause the subj. (הוּא) is the 'seed' of the woman individualised (or collectively), in the second (אַתָּה) it is the serpent himself, acting through his 'seed.' The current reading of 𝔙 (*ipsa*) may have been prompted by a feeling that the proper antithesis to the serpent is the woman herself. The general meaning of the sentence is clear: in the war between men and serpents the former will crush the head of the foe, while the latter can only wound in the heel. The difficulty is in the vb. שׁוּף, which in the sense 'bruise' is inappropriate to the serpent's mode of attack. We may speak of a serpent *striking* a man (as in Lat. *feriri a serpente*), but hardly of *bruising*. Hence many comm. (following 𝔊 al.) take the vb. as a by-form of שָׁאַף (strictly 'pant'), in the sense of 'be eager for,' 'aim at' (Ges. Ew. Di. al.); while others (Gu. al.) suppose that by paronomasia the word means 'bruise' in the first clause, and 'aim at' in the second. But it may be questioned whether this idea is not even less suitable than the other (Dri.). A perfectly satisfactory interpretation cannot be given (*v.i.*).

The Messianic interpretation of the 'seed of the woman' appears in 𝔗J and Targ. Jer., where the v. is explained of the Jewish com-

---

(Ezk. 36^{3}, Am. 2^{7} 8^{4}, Ps. $56^{2.3}$ 57^{4}) שׁוּף is disguised under the by-form שׁאף. But the only places where the assumption is at all necessary are Am. 2^{7} 8^{4}, where the א may be simply *mater lectionis* for the *â* of the ptcp. (cf. וְקָאם, Ho. 10^{14}); in the other cases the proper sense of שָׁאַף ('pant' or metaph. 'long for') suffices. The reverse process (substitution of שׁוף for שׁאף) is much less likely; and the only possible instance would be Jb. 9^{17}, which is too uncertain to count for anything. There is thus not much ground for supposing a confusion in this v.; and De. points out that vbs. of hostile *endeavour*, as distinct from hostile achievement (הִכָּה, רצח, etc.), are never construed with double acc. The gain in sense is so doubtful that it is better to adhere to the meaning 'crush.' The old Vns. felt the difficulty and ambiguity. The idea of crushing is represented by Aq. *προστρίψει*, Σ. *θλίψει*, 𝔊 Coisl. mg. *τρίψει* (see Field) and Jer. (*Quæst.*) *conterere*; 'pant after' by 𝔊A al. *τηρήσει*[s] (if not a mistake for *τρήσει*[s] or *τειρήσει*[s]). A double sense is given by 𝔙 *conteret . . . insidiaberis*, and perhaps 𝔖 ܢܫܘܦ . . . ܬܡܚܝܘܗܝ; while 𝔗O paraphrases: הוא יהא דכיר מה דעבדת ליה מלקדמין ואת תהי נטר ליה לסופא.

munity and its victory over the devil "in the days of King Messiah." The reference to the person of Christ was taught by Irenæus, but was never so generally accepted in the Church as the kindred idea that the serpent is the instrument of Satan. Mediæval exegetes, relying on the *ipsa* of the Vulg., applied the expression directly to the Virgin Mary; and even Luther, while rejecting this reference, recognised an allusion to the virgin birth of Christ. In Protestant theology this view gave way to the more reasonable view of Calvin, that the passage is a promise of victory over the devil to mankind, united in Christ its divine Head. That even this goes beyond the original meaning of the v. is admitted by most modern expositors; and indeed it is doubtful if, from the standpoint of strict historical exegesis, the passage can be regarded as in any sense a *Protevangelium*. Di. (with whom Dri. substantially agrees) finds in the words the idea of man's vocation to ceaseless moral warfare with the 'serpent-brood' of sinful thoughts, and an implicit promise of the ultimate destruction of the evil power. That interpretation, however, is open to several objections. (1) A message of hope and encouragement in the midst of a series of curses and punishments is not to be assumed unless it be clearly implied in the language. It would be out of harmony with the tone not only of the Paradise story, but of the Yahwistic sections of chs. 1–11 as a whole: it is not till we come to the patriarchal history that the "note of promise and of hope" is firmly struck. (2) To the mind of the narrator, the serpent is no more a symbol of the power of evil or of temptation than he is an incarnation of the devil. He is himself an evil creature, perhaps a demonic creature transmitting his demonic character to his progeny, but there is no hint that he represents a principle of evil apart from himself. (3) No victory is promised to either party, but only perpetual warfare between them: the order of the clauses making it specially hard to suppose that the victory of man was contemplated. Di. admits that no such assurance is expressed; but finds it in the general tenor of the passage: "a conflict ordained by God cannot be without prospect of success." But that is really to beg the whole question in dispute. If it be said that the words, being part of the sentence on the serpent, must mean that he is ultimately to be defeated, it may be answered that the curse on the serpent is the enmity established between him and the human race, and that the feud between them is simply the manifestation and proof of that antagonism.—It is thus possible that in its primary intention the oracle reflects the protest of ethical religion against the unnatural fascination of snake-worship. It is psychologically true that the instinctive feelings which lie at the root of the worship of serpents are closely akin to the hatred and loathing which the repulsive reptile excites in the healthy human mind; and the transformation of a once sacred animal into an object of aversion is a not infrequent phenomenon in the history of religion (see Gres. *l.c.* 360). The essence of the temptation is that the serpent-demon has tampered with the religious instinct in man by posing as his good genius, and insinuating distrust of the goodness of God; and his punishment is to find himself at eternal war with the race whom he has seduced from their allegiance to their Creator. And that is very much the light in which serpent-worship must have appeared to a believer in the holy and righteous God of the OT.—The conjecture of Gu., that originally the 'seed of the woman' and the 'seed of the serpent' may have been mythological personages (cf. *ATLO*², 217 f.), even if confirmed by Assyriology, would have little bearing on the thought of the biblical narrator.

16. The doom of the woman: consisting in the hardships incident to her sex, and social position in the East. The pains of childbirth, and the desire which makes her the willing slave of the man, impressed the ancient mind as at once mysterious and unnatural; therefore to be accounted for by a curse imposed on woman from the beginning.—*I will multiply, etc.*] More strictly, 'I will cause thee to have much suffering and pregnancy' (see Dav. § 3, *R.* (2)). It is, of course, not an intensification of pain to which she is already subject that is meant.—For הֵרֹנֵךְ, 𝔊 read some word meaning 'groaning' (*v.i.*); but to prefer this reading on the ground that Hebrew women esteemed frequent pregnancy a blessing (Gu.) makes a too general statement. It is better (with Ho.) to assume a *hendiadys*: 'the pain of thy conception' (as in the explanatory clause which follows).—*in pain . . . children*] The pangs of childbirth are proverbial in OT for the extremity of human anguish (Is. 21^{3} 13^{8}, Mic. 4^{9}, Ps. 48^{6}, and oft.: Ex. 1^{19} cannot be cited to the contrary).—*to thy*

16. אל] Read וְאֶל־, with 𝔐𝔊𝔖.—הרבה ארבה] So 16^{10} 22^{17}. On the irreg. form of inf. abs., see G-K. § 75 *ff.*—עצבון] (3^{17} 5^{29}† [J]). 𝔊 λύπας (= עַצְּבוֹתֵךְ ?).—והרנך] (√ הרה): 𝔐 והריונך (Ru. 4^{13}, Ho. 9^{11}). Ols. (*MBA*, 1870, 380) conj. בְּהריונך, to avoid the harsh use of וְ. 𝔊 *τὸν στεναγμόν σου* probably = הגיונך ; יְגוֹנֵךְ ('sorrow') has also been suggested (Gu.); and צָרָתֵךְ (Di. Ho. al.). The other Vns. follow MT.—בעצב] 𝔐 בעצבון ; 𝔊 likewise repeats *ἐν λύπαις*.—תשוקה] Probably connected with Ar. *šauḳ*, 'ardent desire' (Rahlfs "עָנִי *und* עָנָו," p. 71); cf. שׁקק, Is. 29^{8}, Ps. 107^{9}. Aq. *συνάφεια*, Σ. *ὁρμή*. Although it recurs only 4^{7} and Ca. 7^{11}, it is found in NH and should not be suspected. 𝔊 *ἡ ἀποστροφή σου* and 𝔖 ܬܘܦܢܝܟܝ point to the reading תְּשׁוּבָתֵךְ, preferred by many, and defended by Nestle (*MM*, 6) as a technical expression for the relation here indicated, on the basis of 𝔊's text of 2 Sa. 17^{3}. His parallel between the *return* of the woman to her source (the man) and the return of the man to *his* source (the ground, v.[19]) is perhaps fanciful.

husband . . desire] It is quite unnecessary to give up the rare but expressive תְּשׁוּקָה of the Heb. for the weaker תְּשׁוּבָה. of 𝔊, etc. (*v.i.*). It is not, however, implied that the woman's sexual desire is stronger than the man's (Kn. Gu.); the point rather is that by the instincts of her nature she shall be bound to the hard conditions of her lot, both the ever-recurring pains of child-bearing, and subjection to the man.—*while he* (on his part) *shall rule over thee*] The idea of tyrannous exercise of power does not lie in the vb.; but it means that the woman is wholly subject to the man, and so liable to the arbitrary treatment sanctioned by the marriage customs of the East. It is noteworthy that to the writer this is not the ideal relation of the sexes (cf. $2^{18.\,23}$). There is here certainly no trace of the matriarchate or of polyandry (see on 2^{24}).

17–19. The man's sentence.—The hard, unremitting toil of the husbandman, wringing a bare subsistence from the grudging and intractable ground, is the standing evidence of a divine curse, resting, not, indeed, on man himself, but on the earth for his sake. Originally, it had provided him with all kinds of fruit good for food,—and this is the ideal state of things; now it yields nothing spontaneously but thorns and briars; bread to eat can only be extorted in the sweat of the brow,—and this is a curse: formerly man had been a gardener, now he is a *fellaḥ*. It does not appear that death itself is part of the curse. The name death is avoided; and the fact is referred to as part of the natural order of things,—the inevitable 'return' of man to the ground whence he was taken. The question whether man would have lived for ever if he had not sinned is one to which the narrative furnishes no answer (Gu.).—**17.** *And to the man*] *v.i.* The sentence is introduced by a formal recital of the offence.—*Cursed is the ground*] As

17. Point וְלָאדָם; there is no conceivable reason why **אדם** should be a proper name here (cf. 2^{20} 3^{21}).—לאמר . . . ממנו] 𝔊 reads *τούτου μόνου* (see v.[11]) *μὴ φαγεῖν, ἀπ' αὐτοῦ ἔφαγες.*—בעבורך] 𝔊 (*ἐν τοῖς ἔργοις σου*), Σ. 𝔙 read בַּעֲבֹדָתְךָ, Θ. *ἐν τῇ παραβάσει σου* (בְּעֶבְרְךָ). The phrase is characteristic of J; out of 22 instances in the Hex., only about 3 can be assigned

exceptional fertility was ascribed to a divine blessing (27^{28} etc.), and exceptional barrenness to a curse (Is. 24^{6}, Jer. 23^{10}), so the relative unproductiveness of the whole earth in comparison with man's expectations and ideals is here regarded as the permanent effect of a curse.—*in suffering* (bodily fatigue and mental anxiety) *shalt thou eat* [of] *it*] See 5^{29}. The 'laborious work' of the husbandman is referred to in Sir. 7^{15}; but this is not the prevailing feeling of the OT; and the remark of Kno., that "agriculture was to the Hebrew a divine institution, but at the same time a heavy burden," needs qualification. It is well to be reminded that "ancient Israel did not live constantly in the joy of the harvest festival" (Gu.); but none the less it would be a mistake to suppose that it lived habitually in the mood of this passage.—**18.** *the herb of the field*] See on 1^{11}. The creation of this order of vegetation has not been recorded by J. Are we to suppose that it comes into existence simply in consequence of the earth's diminished productivity caused by the curse? It seems implied at all events that the earth will not yield even this, except under the compulsion of human labour (see 2^{5}).—**19.** *in the sweat of thy brow, etc.*] A more expressive repetition of the thought of $^{17b\beta}$. The phrase *eat bread* may mean 'earn a livelihood' (Am. 7^{12}), but here it must be understood literally as the immediate reward of man's toil.—*till thou return, etc.*] hardly means more than 'all the days of thy life' (in v.^{17}). It is not a threat of death as the punishment of sin, and we have no right to say (with Di.) that vv.$^{16-19}$ are simply an expansion of the sentence of 2^{17}. That man was by nature immortal is not taught in this passage; and since the Tree of Life in v.^{22} belongs to another recension, there is no evidence that the main narrative regarded even endless life as within man's

---

to E (none to P).—תאכלנה] The government of direct acc. seems harsh, but is not unexampled: see Jer. 36^{16}.—**18.** 𝔊 omits initial ו: so 𝔙 *Jub.*—קוץ ודרדר] Hos. 10^{8}; דרדר occurs nowhere else in OT. It is still used in Syria (*dardār*) as a general name for thistles.—**19.** זעת] (√יזע, *wada'a*) is ἅπ. λεγ.; cf. יֶזַע, Ezk. 44^{18}.—לחם] 𝔊 *Jub.* לחמך.

reach. The connexion of the closing words is rather with 2^7: man was taken from the ground, and in the natural course will return to it again.—*and to dust, etc.*] Cf. Jb. 10^9 34^{15}, Ps. 90^3 146^4, Ec. 3^{20} 12^7 etc.: *ἐκ γαίας βλαστῶν γαῖα πάλιν γέγονα.*

The arrangement of the clauses in $^{17-19}$ is not very natural, and the repeated variations of the same idea have suggested the hypothesis of textual corruption or fusion of sources. In *Jub.* iii. 25 the passage is quoted in an abridged form, the line 'Cursed . . . sake' being immediately followed by 'Thorns . . . to thee,' and ^{18b} being omitted. This is, of course, a much smoother reading, and leaves out nothing essential; but ^{17b} is guaranteed by 5^{29}. Ho. rejects ^{18b}, and to avoid the repetition of אכל proposes תעברנה instead of תאכלנה in ^{17}. Gu. is satisfied with v.$^{17f.}$ as they stand, but assigns $^{19a\alpha}$ (to לחם) and ^{19b} to another source (J^j), as doublets respectively of $^{17b\beta}$ and $^{19a\beta}$. This is perhaps on the whole the most satisfactory analysis.—The poetic structure of the vv., which might be expected to clear up a question of this kind, is too obscure to afford any guidance. Sievers, *e.g.* (II. 10 f.) finds nothing, except in v.^{19}, to distinguish the rhythm from that of the narrative in which it is embedded, and all attempts at strophic arrangement are only tentative.

20–24. The expulsion from Eden.—20. The naming of the woman can hardly have come in between the sentence and its execution, or before there was any experience of motherhood to suggest it. The attempts to connect the notice with the mention of child-bearing in $^{15f.}$ (De. al.), or

---

20. חוה] 𝔊 Εὔα [Εὖα] (in 4^1), Aq. Αὖα, 𝔙 *Heva*, Jer. *Eva* (Eng. *Eve*); in this v. 𝔊 translates Ζωή, Σ. Ζωογόνος. The similarity of the name to the Aram. word for 'serpent' (חִוְיָא ,חִוְיָא, Syr. ܚܘܝܐ, Syro-Pal. ܚܘܐ [Mt. 7^{10}]); cf. Ar. *ḥayyat* from *ḥauyat* [Nö.]) has always been noticed, and is accepted by several modern scholars as a real etymological equivalence (Nö. *ZDMG*, xlii. 487; Sta. *GVI*, i. 633; We. *Heid.* 154). The ancient idea was that Eve was so named because she had done the serpent's work in tempting Adam (*Ber. R.*; Philo, *De agr. Noe*, 21; Clem. Alex. *Protrept.* ii. 12. 1). Quite recently the philological equation has acquired fresh significance from the discovery of the name חות on a leaden Punic *tabella devotionis* (described by Lidz. *Ephemeris*, i. 26 ff.; see Cooke, *NSI*, 135), of which the first line reads: "O Lady *ḤVT*, goddess, queen . . . !" Lidz. sees in this mythological personage a goddess of the under-world, and as such a serpent-deity; and identifies her with the biblical Ḥavvah. Ḥavvah would thus be a 'depotentiated' deity, whose prototype was a Phœnician goddess of the Under-world, worshipped in the form of a serpent, and bearing the

with the thought of mortality in [19] (Kn.), are forced. The most suitable position in the present text would be before (so *Jub.* iii. 33) or after 4^1; and accordingly some regard it as a misplaced gloss in explanation of that v. But when we consider (*a*) that the name *Ḥavvāh* must in any case be traditional, (*b*) that it is a proper name, whereas הָאָדָם remains appellative throughout, and (*c*) that in the following vv. there are unambiguous traces of a second recension of the Paradise story, it is reasonable to suppose that v.[20] comes from that recension, and is a parallel to the naming of the woman in 2^{23}, whether it stands here in the original order or not. The fact that the name Eve has been preserved, while there is no distinctive name for the man, suggests that חוה is a survival from a more primitive theory of human origins in which the first mother represented the unity of the race.—*the mother of every living thing*] According to this derivation, חַוָּה would seem to denote first the idea of life, and then the source of life—the mother.* But

title of 'Mother of all living' (see Gres. *l.c.* 359f.). Precarious as such combinations may seem, there is no objection in principle to an explanation of the name Ḥavvah on these lines. Besides the Ḥivvites of the OT (who were probably a serpent-tribe), We. cites examples of Semitic princely families that traced their genealogy back to a serpent. The substitution of human for animal ancestry, and the transference of the animal name to the human ancestor, are phenomena frequently observed in the transition from a lower to a higher stage of religion. If the change took place while a law of female descent still prevailed, the ancestry would naturally be traced to a woman (or goddess); and when the law of male kinship was introduced she would as naturally be identified with the wife of the first man. It need hardly be said that all this, while possibly throwing some light on the mythical background of the biblical narrative, is quite apart from the religious significance of the story of the Fall in itself.—אם כל־חי] Rob. Sm. renders 'mother of every *ḥayy*,'—*ḥayy* being the Arab. word which originally denoted a group of female kinship. Thus "Eve is the personification of the bond of kinship (conceived as exclusively mother-kinship), just as Adam is simply 'man,' *i.e.* the personification of mankind" (*KM*², 208). The interpretation has found no support.

* So Baethgen, *Beitr.* 148, who appends the note: "Im holsteinischen Plattdeutsch ist 'Dat Leben' euphemistischer Ausdruck für das pudendum muliebre"—a meaning by the way which also attaches to Ar. *ḥayy* (Lane, *Lex.* 681 b).

the form חוה is not Heb., and the real meaning of the word is not settled by the etymology here given (*v.i.*).—כָּל־חָי commonly includes all animals (8^{21} etc.), but is here restricted to mankind (as Ps. 143^{2}, Jb. 30^{23}). Cf. however, *πότνια θηρῶν*, 'Lady of wild things,' a Greek epithet of the Earth-mother (Miss Harrison, *Prol.* 264).—**21.** Another detached notice describing the origin of clothing. It is, of course, not inconsistent with v.^{7}, but neither can it be said to be the necessary sequel to that v.; most probably it is a parallel from another source.—*coats of skin*] "The simplest and most primitive kind of clothing in practical use" (Dri.).

An interesting question arises as to the connexion between this method of clothing and the loss of pristine innocence. That it exhibits God's continued care for man even after the Fall (Di. al.) may be true as regards the present form of the legend; but that is hardly the original conception. In the Phœn. legend of Usōos, the invention is connected with the hunting of wild animals, and this again with the institution of sacrifice: . . . *ὃς σκέπην τῷ σώματι πρῶτος ἐκ δερμάτων ὧν ἴσχυσε συλλαβεῖν θηρίων εὗρε . . . ἅμα τε σπένδειν αὐταῖς ἐξ ὧν ἤγρευε θηρίων* (*Præp. Ev.* i. 10; Orelli, p. 17 f.). Since sacrifice and the use of animal food were inseparably associated in Semitic antiquity, it may be assumed that this is conceived as the first departure from the Golden Age, when men lived on the spontaneous fruits of the earth. Similarly, Rob. Sm. (*RS*^{2}, 306 ff.) found in the v. the Yahwistic theory of the introduction of the sacrifice of *domestic* animals, which thus coincided, as in Greek legend, with the transition from the state of innocence to the life of agriculture.

22–24. The actual expulsion.—**22.** *Behold . . . one of us*] This is no 'ironica exprobatio' (Calv. al.), but a serious admission that man has snatched a divine prerogative not meant for him. The feeling expressed (cf. 11^{6}) is akin to what the Greeks called the 'envy of the gods,' and more remotely to the OT attribute of the zeal or jealousy of Yahwe, —His resentment of all action that encroaches on His

---

21. Point לָאָדָם, as in v.^{17}.—**22.** כאחד] Constr. before prep.; G-K. § 130 *a*.—מִמֶּנּוּ] The so-called oriental punctuation (which distinguishes 1st pl. from 3rd sg. masc. suffix) has מִמֶּנּוּ, 'from us' (B-D. p. 81). 𝔗^{O} (יחידי בעלמא מינה) and Σ (*ὁμοῦ ἀφ' ἑαυτοῦ*) treat the form as 3rd sing.: cf. Ra.'s paraphrase: "alone below, as I am alone above."—לדעת] 'in [respect of] knowing': gerundial inf.; Dav. § 93; G-K. § 114 *o*; **Dri.**

divinity (see p. 97). In v.[5] the same words are put in the mouth of the serpent with a distinct imputation of envy to God; and it is perhaps improbable that the writer of that v. would have justified the serpent's insinuation, even in form, by a divine utterance. There are several indications (*e.g.* the phrase 'like one of us') that the secondary recension to which v.[22] belongs represents a cruder form of the legend than does the main narrative; and it is possible that it retains more of the characteristically pagan feeling of the envy of the gods.—*in respect of knowing, etc.*] Man has not attained complete equality with God, but only God-likeness in this one respect. Gres.'s contention that the v. is self-contradictory (man has become like a god, and yet lacks the immortality of a god) is therefore unfounded.—*And now, etc.*] There remains another divine attribute which man will be prompt to seize, viz. immortality: to prevent his thus attaining complete likeness to God he must be debarred from the Tree of Life. The expression *put forth his hand* suggests that a single partaking of the fruit would have conferred eternal life (Bu. *Urg.* 52); and at least implies that it would have been an easy thing to do. The question why man had not as yet done so is not impertinent (De.), but inevitable; so momentous an issue could not have been left to chance in a continuous narrative. The obvious solution is that in this recension the Tree of Life was a (or *the*) forbidden tree, that man in his first innocence had respected the injunction, but that now when he knows the virtue of the tree he will not refrain from eating. It is to be observed that it is only in this part of the story that the idea of immortality is introduced, and that not as an essential endowment of human nature, but as contingent on an act which would be as efficacious after the Fall as before it.—On the *aposiopesis* at the end of the v., *v.i.*—**23** is clearly a doublet of [24]; and the latter is the natural continuation of [22]. V.[23] is

T. § 205.—The pregnant use of פֶּן (='I fear lest') is common (Gn. 19[19] 26[9] 38[11] 44[34], Ex. 13[17] etc.). Here it is more natural to assume an *anakolouthon*, the clause depending on a cohortative, converted in v.[23]

a fitting conclusion to the main narrative, in which it probably followed immediately on v.^{19}.—**24.** *He drove out the man and made [him] dwell on the east of . . . [and stationed] the Cherubim, etc.*] This is the reading of 𝔊 (*v.i.*), and it gives a more natural construction than MT, which omits the words in brackets. On either view the assumption is that the first abode of mankind was east of the garden. There is no reason to suppose that the v. represents a different tradition as to the site of Eden from 2^{8} or $2^{10ff.}$. It is not said in 2^{8} that it was in the *extreme* east, or in 2^{10} that it was in the extreme north; nor is it here implied that it was further west than Palestine. The account of the early migration of the race in 11^{2} is quite consistent with the supposition that mankind entered the Euphrates valley from a region still further east.—*the Cherubim and the revolving sword-flame*] Lit. 'the flame of the whirling sword.' It has usually been assumed that the sword was in the hand of one of the cherubim; but probably it was an independent symbol, and a representation of the lightning. Some light may be thrown on it by an inscription of Tiglath-pileser I. (*KIB*, i. 36 f.), where the king says that when he destroyed the fortress of Ḫunusa he made 'a lightning of bronze.' The emblem appears to be otherwise unknown, but the allusion suggests a parallel to the 'flaming sword' of this passage.

The Cherubim.—See the notes of Di. Gu. Dri.; *KAT*^{3}, 529 f., 631 ff.; Che. in *EB*, 741 ff.; Je. *ATLO*^{2}, 218; Haupt, *SBOT*, *Numbers*, 46; *Polychrome Bible*, 181 f.; Furtwängler, in Roscher's *Lex.* art. GRYPS.—The derivation of the word is uncertain. The old theory of a connexion with γρύψ (*Greif*, griffin, etc.) is not devoid of plausibility, but lacks proof. The often quoted statement of Lenormant (*Orig.* i. 118), that *kirubu* occurs on an amulet in the de Clercq collection as a name

---

into a historic tense.—גם] 𝔊𝔖 om.—**24.** 𝔊 *καὶ ἐξέβαλεν τὸν Ἀδὰμ καὶ κατῴκισεν αὐτὸν ἀπέναντι τοῦ παραδείσου τῆς τρυφῆς, καὶ ἔταξεν τὰ χερουβὶν κτλ.* = ויגרש את־האדם וישכן מקדם לגן עדן וַיָּשֶׂם את־הכרובים וגו׳ Ball rightly adopts this text, but inserts אתו after וישכן, against J's usage. There is no need to supply any pron. obj. whatever: see 2^{19} 18^{7} 38^{18}, 1 Sa. 19^{13} etc. For the first three words 𝔖 has simply ܘܐܦܩܗ, and for וישכן ܘܐܣܝܡ (with the cherubim, etc., as obj.). המתהפכת] Hithpa. in the sense of 'revolve,' Ju. 7^{13}, Jb. 37^{12}; in Jb. 38^{14} it means 'be transformed.'

of the winged bulls of Assyrian palaces, seems to be definitely disproved (see Je. 218).—A great part of the OT symbolism could be explained from the hypothesis that the Cherubim were originally wind-demons, like the Harpies of Greek mythology (Harrison, *Prol.* 178 ff.). The most suggestive analogy to this verse is perhaps to be found in the winged genii often depicted by the side of the tree of life in Babylonian art. These figures are usually human in form with human heads, but sometimes combine the human form with an eagle's head, and occasionally the human head with an animal body. They are shown in the act of fecundating the date-palm by transferring the pollen of the male tree to the flower of the female; and hence it has been conjectured that they are personifications of the winds, by whose agency the fertilisation of the palm is effected in nature (Tylor, *PSBA*, xii. 383 ff.). Starting with this clue, we can readily explain (1) the function of the Cherub as the living chariot of Yahwe, or bearer of the Theophany, in Ps. 18^{11} (2 Sa. 22^{11}). It is a personification of the storm-wind on which Yahwe rides, just as the Babylonian storm-god Zû was figured as a bird-deity. The theory that it was a personification of the thunder-cloud is a mere conjecture based on Ps. $18^{11f.}$, and has no more intrinsic probability than that here suggested. (2) The association of the winged figures with the Tree of Life in Babylonian art would naturally lead to the belief that the Cherubim were denizens of Paradise (Ezk. $28^{14.16}$), and guardians of the Tree (as in this passage). (3) Thence they came to be viewed as guardians of sacred things and places generally, like the composite figures placed at the entrances of Assyrian temples and palaces to prevent the approach of evil spirits. To this category belong probably in the first instance the colossal Cherubim of Solomon's temple (1 Ki. $6^{23ff.}$ $8^{6f.}$), and the miniatures on the lid of the ark in the Tabernacle (Ex. $25^{18ff.}$ etc.); but a trace of the primary conception appears in the alternation of cherubim and *palm-trees* in the temple decoration (1 Ki. $6^{29ff.}$, Ezk. $41^{18ff.}$; see, further, 1 Ki. $7^{29ff.}$, Ex. $26^{1.31}$). (4) The most difficult embodiment of the idea is found in the Cherubim of Ezekiel's visions—four composite creatures combining the features of the ox, the lion, the man, and the eagle (Ezk. $1^{5ff.}$ $10^{1ff.}$). These may represent primarily the 'four winds of heaven'; but the complex symbolism of the *Merkābāh* shows that they have some deeper cosmic significance. Gu. (p. 20) thinks that an older form of the representation is preserved in Apoc. $4^{6ff.}$, where the four animal types are kept distinct. These he connects with the four constellations of the Zodiac which mark the four quarters of the heavens: Taurus, Leo, Scorpio (in the earliest astronomy a scorpion-*man*), and Aquila (near Aquarius). See *KAT*³, 631 f.

The Origin and Significance of the Paradise Legend.

1. *Ethnic parallels.*—The Babylonian version of the Fall of man (if any such existed) has not yet been discovered. There is in the British Museum a much-debated seal-cylinder which is often cited as evidence that a legend very similar to the biblical narrative was current in Babylonia. It shows two completely clothed figures seated on either

side of a tree, and each stretching out a hand toward its fruit, while a crooked line on the left of the picture is supposed to exhibit the serpent.* The engraving no doubt represents some legend connected with the tree of life; but even if we knew that it illustrates the first temptation, the *story* is still wanting; and the details of the picture show that it can have had very little resemblance to Gn. 3.—The most that can be claimed is that there are certain remote parallels to particular features or ideas of Gn. 2^{4}–3^{24}, which are yet sufficiently close to suggest that the ultimate source of the biblical narrative is to be sought in the Babylonian mythology. Attention should be directed to the following:—

(*a*) The *account of Creation* in $2^{4ff.}$ has undoubted resemblances to the Babylonian document described on p. 47 f., though they are hardly such as to prove dependence. Each starts with a vision of chaos, and in both the prior existence of heaven and earth seems to be assumed; although the Babylonian chaos is a waste of waters, while that of Gn. $2^{5f.}$ is based rather on the idea of a waterless desert (see p. 56 above). The *order* of creation, though not the same, is alike in its promiscuous and unscientific character: in the Babylonian we have a hopeless medley—mankind, beasts of the field, living things of the field, Tigris and Euphrates, verdure of the field, grass, marshes, reeds, wild-cow, ewe, sheep of the fold, orchards, forests, houses, and cities, etc. etc.—but no separate creation of woman.—The creation of *man* from earth moistened by the blood of a god, in another document, may be instanced as a distant parallel to 2^{7} (pp. 42, 45).

(*b*) The *legend of Eabani*, embedded in the Gilgameš-Epic (Tab. I. Col. ii. l. 33 ff.: *KIB*, vi. 1, p. 120 ff.), seems to present us (it has been thought) with a 'type of primitive man.' Eabani, created as a rival to Gilgameš by the goddess Aruru from a lump of clay, is a being of gigantic strength who is found associating with the wild animals, living their life, and foiling all the devices of the huntsman. Eager to capture him, Gilgameš sends with the huntsman a harlot, by whose attractions he hopes to lure Eabani from his savagery. Eabani yields to her charms, and is led, a willing captive, to the life of civilisation:

> When she speaks to him, her speech pleases him,
> One who knows his heart he seeks, a friend.

But later in the epic, the harlot appears as the cause of his sorrows, and Eabani curses her with all his heart. Apart from its present setting, and considered as an independent bit of folk-lore, it cannot be denied that the story has a certain resemblance to Gn. 2^{18-24}. Only, we may be sure that if the idea of sexual intercourse with the beasts be implied in the picture of Eabani, the moral purity of the Hebrew writer never stooped so low (see Jastrow, *AJSL*, xv. 198 ff.; Stade, *ZATW*, xxiii. 174 f.).

(*c*) Far more instructive affinities with the inner motive of the story

* Reproduced in Smith's *Chaldean Genesis*, 88; Del. *Babel und Bibel* (M'Cormack's trans. p. 48); *ATLO*², 203, etc. Je. has satisfied himself that the zigzag line *is* a snake, but is equally convinced that the snake cannot be tempting a man and a woman to eat the fruit.

of the Fall are found in the myth of *Adapa and the South-wind*, discovered amongst the Tel-Amarna Tablets, and therefore known in Palestine in the 15th cent. B.C. (*KIB*, vi. 1, 92–101). Adapa, the son of the god Ea, is endowed by him with the fulness of divine wisdom, but denied the gift of immortality:

"Wisdom I gave him, immortality I gave him not."

While plying the trade of a fisherman on the Persian Gulf, the south-wind overwhelms his bark, and in revenge Adapa breaks the wings of the south-wind. For this offence he is summoned by Anu to appear before the assembly of the gods in heaven; and Ea instructs him how to appease the anger of Anu. Then the gods, disconcerted by finding a mortal in possession of their secrets, resolve to make the best of it, and to admit him fully into their society, by conferring on him immortality. They offer him food of life that he may eat, and water of life that he may drink. But Adapa had previously been deceived by Ea, who did not wish him to become immortal. Ea had said that what would be offered to him would be food and water of death, and had strictly cautioned him to refuse. He did refuse, and so missed immortal life. Anu laments over his infatuated refusal:

"Why, Adapa! Wherefore hast thou not eaten, not drunken, so that
Thou wilt not live . . . ?" "Ea, my lord,
Commanded, 'Eat not and drink not!'"
"Take him and bring him back to his earth!"

This looks almost like a travesty of the leading ideas of Gn. 3; yet the common features are very striking. In both we have the idea that wisdom and immortality combined constitute equality with deity; in both we have a man securing the first and missing the second; and in both the man is counselled in opposite directions by supernatural voices, and acts on that advice which is contrary to his interest. There is, of course, the vital difference that while Yahwe forbids both wisdom and immortality to man, Ea confers the first (and thus far plays the part of the biblical serpent) but withholds the second, and Anu is ready to bestow both. Still, it is not too much to expect that a story like this will throw light on the mythological antecedents of the Genesis narrative, if not directly on that narrative itself (see below, p. 94).

What is true of Babylonian affinities holds good in a lesser degree of the ancient mythologies as a whole: everywhere we find echoes of the Paradise myth, but nowhere a story which forms an exact parallel to Gn. 2. 3. The Græco-Roman traditions told of a 'golden age,' lost through the increasing sinfulness of the race,—an age when the earth freely yielded its fruits, and men lived in a happiness undisturbed by toil or care or sin (Hesiod, *Op. et Dies*, 90–92, 109–120; Ovid, *Met.* i. 89–112, etc.); but they knew nothing of a sudden fall. Indian and Persian mythologies told, in addition, of sacred mountains where the gods dwelt, with bright gold and flashing gems, and miraculous trees conferring immortality, and every imaginable blessing; and we have seen that similar representations were current in Babylonia. The nearest approach to definite counterparts of the biblical narrative are found in Iranian legends, where we read of Meshia and Meshiane, who lived at first on fruits, but who, tempted by Ahriman, denied the good god, lost their innocence, and practised all kinds of wickedness; or of Yima, the ruler of the golden age, under whom there was neither sickness nor death, nor hunger nor thirst, until (in one tradition) he gave way to pride, and fell under the dominion of the evil serpent Dahaka (see Di. p. 47 ff.). But these echoes are too faint and distant to enable us to determine the quarter whence the original impulse proceeded, or where the myth assumed the form in which it appears in Genesis. For answers to these questions we are dependent mainly on the uncertain indications of the biblical narrative itself. Some features (the name *Ḥavvah* [p. 85 f.], and elements of ch. 4) seem to point to Phœnicia as the quarter whence this stratum of myth entered the religion of Israel; others (the Paradise-geography) point rather to Babylonia, or at least Mesopotamia. In the present state of our knowledge it is a plausible conjecture that the myth has travelled from Babylonia, and reached Israel through the Phœnicians or the Canaanites (We. *Prol.*[6] 307; Gres. *ARW*, x. 345 ff.; cf. Bevan, *JTS*, iv. 500 f.). A similar conclusion might be drawn from the contradiction in the idea of chaos, if the explanation given above of 2^6 be correct: it looks as if the cosmogony of an alluvial region had been modified through transference to a dry climate (see p. 56). The fig-leaves of 3^7 are certainly not Babylonian; though a single detail of that kind cannot settle the question of origin. But until further light comes from the monuments, all speculations on this subject are very much in the air.

2. *The mythical substratum of the narrative.*—The strongest evidence of the non-Israelite origin of the story of the Fall is furnished by the biblical account itself, in the many mythological conceptions, of which traces still remain in Genesis. "The narrative," as Dri. says, "contains features which have unmistakable counterparts in the religious traditions of other nations; and some of these, though they have been accommodated to the spirit of Israel's religion, carry indications that they are not native to it" (*Gen.* 51). Amongst the features which are at variance with the standpoint of Hebrew religion we may put first of all the fact that the abode of Yahwe is placed, not in Canaan or at Mount Sinai, but in the far East. The strictly mythological background of the story emerges chiefly in the conceptions of the garden of the gods (see p. 57 f.), the trees of life and of knowledge (p. 59), the serpent (p. 72 f.), Eve (p. 85 f.), and the Cherubim (p. 89 f.). It is true, as has been shown, that each of these conceptions is rooted in the most primitive ideas of Semitic religion; but it is equally true that they have passed through a mythological development for which the religion of Israel gave no opportunity. Thus the association of trees and serpents in Semitic folk-lore is illustrated by an Arabian story, which tells how, when an untrodden thicket was burned down, the spirits of the trees made their escape in the shape of white serpents (*RS*[2], 133); but it is quite clear that a long interval separates that primitive superstition from the ideas that invest the serpent and the tree in this passage. If proof were needed, it would be found in the suggestive combinations of the serpent and the tree in

Babylonian and Phœnician art; or in the fabled garden of the Hesperides, with its golden fruit guarded by a dragon, always figured in artistic representations as a huge snake coiled round the trunk of the tree (cf. Lenormant, *Origines*, i. 93 f.: see the illustrations in Roscher, *Lex.* 2599 f.). How the various elements were combined in the particular myth which lies immediately behind the biblical narrative, it is impossible to say; but the myth of Adapa suggests at least some elements of a possible construction, which cannot be very far from the truth. Obviously we have to do with a polytheistic legend, in which rivalries and jealousies between the different deities are almost a matter of course. The serpent is himself a demon; and his readiness to initiate man in the knowledge of the mysterious virtue of the forbidden tree means that he is at variance with the other gods, or at least with the particular god who had imposed the prohibition. The intention of the command was to prevent man from sharing the life of the gods; and the serpent-demon, posing as the good genius of man, defeats that intention by revealing to man the truth (similarly Gu. 30). To the original heathen myth we may also attribute the idea of the envy of the gods, which the biblical narrator hardly avoids, and the note of weariness and melancholy, the sombre view of life,—the 'scheue heidnische Stimmung,'—which is the ground-tone of the passage.

It is impossible to determine what, in the original myth, was the nature of the tree (or trees) which man was forbidden to eat. Gres. (*l.c.* 351 ff.) finds in the passage traces of three primitive conceptions: (1) the tree of the knowledge of good and evil, whose fruit imparts the knowledge of magic,—the only knowledge of which it can be said that it makes man at once the equal and the rival of the deity; (2) the tree of knowledge, whose fruit excites the sexual appetite and destroys child-like innocence (3^{7}); (3) the tree of life, whose fruit confers immortality (3^{22}). The question is immensely complicated by the existence of two recensions, which do not seem so hopelessly inseparable as Gres. thinks. In the main recension we have the tree of knowledge, of which man eats to his hurt, but no hint of a tree of life. In the secondary recension there is the tree of life (of which man does not eat), and *apparently* the tree of knowledge of which he had eaten; but this depends on the word גַּם in 3^{22}, which is wanting in 𝔊, and may be an interpolation. Again, the statement that knowledge of good and evil really amounts to equality with God, is found only in the second recension; in the other it is doubtful if the actual effect of eating the fruit was not a cruel disappointment of the hope held out by the serpent. How far we are entitled to read the ideas of the one into the other is a question we cannot answer. Eerdmans' ingenious but improbable theory (*ThT*, xxxix. 504 ff.) need not here be discussed. What is meant by knowledge of good and evil in the final form of the narrative will be considered under the next head.

3. *The religious ideas of the passage.*—Out of such crude and seemingly unpromising material the religion of revelation has fashioned the immortal allegory before us. We have now to inquire what are the religious and moral truths under the influence of which the narrative assumed its present form, distinguishing as far as possible the ideas

which it originally conveyed from those which it suggested to more advanced theological speculation.

(1) We observe, in the first place, that the ætiological motive is strongly marked throughout. The story gives an explanation of many of the facts of universal experience,—the bond between man and wife (2^{24}), the sense of shame which accompanies adolescence (3^{7}), the use of clothing (3^{21}), the instinctive antipathy to serpents (3^{15}). But chiefly it seeks the key to the darker side of human existence as seen in a simple agricultural state of society,—the hard toil of the husbandman, the birth-pangs of the woman, and her subjection to the man. These are evils which the author feels to be contrary to the ideal of human nature, and to the intention of a good God. They are results of a curse justly incurred by transgression, a curse pronounced before history began, and shadowing, rather than crushing, human life always and everywhere. It is doubtful if death be included in the effects of the curse. In v.[19] it is spoken of as the natural fate of a being made from the earth; in v.[22] it follows from being excluded from the tree of life. Man was capable of immortality, but not by nature immortal; and God did not mean that he should attain immortality. The death threatened in 2^{17} is immediate death; and to assume that the death which actually ensues is the exaction of that deferred penalty, is perhaps to go beyond the intention of the writer. Nor does it appear that the narrative seeks to account for the origin of sin. It describes what was, no doubt, the first sin; but it describes it as something intelligible, not needing explanation, not a mystery like the instinct of shame or the possession of knowledge, which are produced by eating the fruit of the tree.

(2) Amongst other things which distinguish man's present from his original state, is the possession of a certain kind of knowledge which was acquired by eating the forbidden fruit. This brings us to the most difficult question which the narrative presents: what is meant by the knowledge of good and evil?* Keeping in mind the possibility that the two recensions may represent different conceptions, our data are these: In 3^{22} knowledge of good and evil is an attainment which (*a*)

---

* In OT usage, knowledge of good and evil marks the difference between adulthood and childhood (Dt. 1^{39}, Is. $7^{15f.}$), or second childhood (2 Sa. 19^{36}); it also denotes (with different verbs) judicial discernment of right and wrong (2 Sa. 14^{17}, 1 Ki. 3^{9}), which is an intellectual function, quite distinct from the working of the conscience. The antithesis of good and evil may, of course, be ethical (Am. $5^{14f.}$, Is. 5^{20} etc.); but it may also be merely the contrast of pleasant and painful, or wholesome and hurtful (2 Sa. 19^{36}). Hence the phrase comes to stand for the whole range of experience,—"a comprehensive designation of things by their two polar attributes, according to which they interest man for his weal or hurt": cf. 2 Sa. 14^{17} with [20] 'all things that are in earth' (Gn. 24^{50} 31^{24}). We. maintains that the non-ethical sense is fundamental, the expressions being transferred to virtue and vice only in so far as their consequences are advantageous or the reverse. Knowledge of good and evil may thus mean knowledge in general,--knowing one thing from another.

implies equality with God, (*b*) was forbidden to man, (*c*) is actually secured by man. In the leading narrative (*b*) certainly holds good (2^{17}), but (*a*) and (*c*) are doubtful. Did the serpent speak truth when he said that knowledge of good and evil would make man like God? Did man actually attain such knowledge? Was the perception of nakedness a first flash of the new divine insight which man had coveted, or was it a bitter disenchantment and mockery of the hopes inspired by the serpent's words? It is only the habit of reading the ideas of 3^{22} into the story of the temptation which makes these questions seem superfluous. Let us consider how far the various interpretations enable us to answer them.—i. The suggestion that magical knowledge is meant may be set aside as inadequate to either form of the biblical narrative: magic is not godlike knowledge, nor is it the universal property of humanity.—ii. The usual explanation identifies the knowledge of good and evil with the moral sense, the faculty of discerning between right and wrong. This view is ably defended by Bu. (*Urg.* 69 ff.), and is not to be lightly dismissed, but yet raises serious difficulties. Could it be said that God meant to withhold from man the power of moral discernment? Does not the prohibition itself presuppose that man already knew that obedience was right and disobedience sinful? We have no right to say that the restriction was only temporary, and that God would in other ways have bestowed on man the gift of conscience; the narrative suggests nothing of the sort.—iii. We. (*Prol.*[6] 299 ff.) holds that the knowledge in question is insight into the secrets of nature, and intelligence to manipulate them for human ends; and this as a quality not so much of the individual as of the race,—the knowledge which is the principle of human civilisation. It is the faculty which we see at work in the invention of clothing (3^{21}?), in the founding of cities (4^{17}), in the discovery of the arts and crafts ($4^{19ff.}$), and in the building of the tower ($11^{1ff.}$). The undertone of condemnation of the cultural achievements of humanity which runs through the Yahwistic sections of chs. 1–11 makes it probable that the writer traced their root to the knowledge acquired by the first transgression; and of such knowledge it might be said that it made man like God, and that God willed to withhold it permanently from His creatures.—iv. Against this view Gu. (11 f., 25 f.) urges somewhat ineptly that the myth does not speak of arts and aptitudes which are learned by education, but of a kind of knowledge which comes by nature, of which the instinct of sex is a typical illustration. Knowledge of good and evil is simply the enlargement of capacity and experience which belongs to mature age,—ripeness of judgment, reason,—including moral discernment, but not identical with it.—The difference between the last two explanations is not great; and possibly both are true. We.'s seems to me the only view that does justice to the thought of 3^{22}; and if $4^{16ff.}$ and 11^{1-9} be the continuation of this version of the Fall, the theory has much to recommend it. On the other hand, Gu.'s acceptation may be truer to the teaching of $3^{1ff.}$. Man's primitive state was one of childlike innocence and purity; and the knowledge which he obtained by disobedience is the knowledge of life and of the world which distinguishes the grown man from the child. If it be objected that such knowledge is a good thing, which God could not have forbidden to man, we may be content to fall back on the paradox of Christ's idea of childhood: "Except ye turn, and become as little children, ye shall in no wise enter into the kingdom of heaven."

(3) The next point that claims attention is the author's conception of sin. Formally, sin is represented as an act of disobedience to a positive command, imposed as a test of fidelity; an act, therefore, which implies disloyalty to God, and a want of the trust and confidence due from man to his Maker. But the essence of the transgression lies deeper: God had a reason for imposing the command, and man had a motive for disobeying it; and the reason and motive are unambiguously indicated. Man was tempted by the desire to be as God, and Yahwe does not will that man should be as God. Sin is thus in the last instance presumption,—an overstepping of the limits of creaturehood, and an encroachment on the prerogatives of Deity. It is true that the offence is invested with every circumstance of extenuation,—inexperience, the absence of evil intention, the suddenness of the temptation, and the superior subtlety of the serpent; but sin it was nevertheless, and was justly followed by punishment.—How far the passage foreshadows a doctrine of hereditary sin, it is impossible to say. The consequences of the transgression, both privative and positive, are undoubtedly transmitted from the first pair to their posterity; but whether the sinful tendency itself is regarded as having become hereditary in the race, there is not evidence to show.

(4) Lastly, what view of God does the narrative present? It has already been pointed out that 3^{22} borders hard on the pagan notion of the 'envy' of the godhead, a notion difficult to reconcile with the conceptions of OT religion. But of that idea there is no trace in the main narrative of the temptation and the Fall, except in the lying insinuation of the serpent: the writer himself does not thus 'charge God foolishly.' His religious attitude is one of reverent submission to the limitations imposed on human life by a sovereign Will, which is determined to maintain inviolate the distinction between the divine and the human. The attribute most conspicuously displayed is closely akin to what the prophets called the 'holiness' of God, as illustrated, *e.g.*, in Is. $2^{12ff.}$. After all, the world is God's world and not man's, and the Almighty is just, as well as holy, when He frustrates the impious aspiration of humanity after an independent footing and sphere of action in the universe. The God of Gn. 3 is no arbitrary heathen deity, dreading lest the sceptre of the universe should be snatched from his hand by the soaring ambition of the race of men; but a Being infinitely exalted above the world, stern in His displeasure at sin, and terrible in His justice; yet benignant and compassionate, slow to anger, and 'repenting Him of the evil.' Through an intensely anthropomorphic medium we discern the features of the God of the prophets and the Old Testament; nay, in the analogy of human fatherhood which underlies the description, we can trace the lineaments of the God and Father of Jesus Christ. That is the real *Protevangelium* which lies in the passage: the fact that God tempers judgment with mercy, the faith that man, though he has forfeited innocence and happiness, is not cut off from fellowship with his Creator.

Ch. IV.—*Beginnings of History and Civilisation.*

Critical Analysis.—Ch. 4 consists of three easily separable sections: (*a*) the story of Cain and Abel ($^{1-16}$), (*b*) a Cainite genealogy ($^{17-24}$),* and (*c*) a fragment of a Sethite genealogy ($^{25.\,26}$). As they lie before us, these are woven into a consecutive history of antediluvian mankind, with a semblance of unity sufficient to satisfy the older generation of critics.† Closer examination seems to show that the chapter is composite, and that the superficial continuity conceals a series of critical problems of great intricacy.

1. We have first to determine the character and extent of the Cainite genealogy. It is probable that the first link occurs in v.$^{1ff.}$, and has to be disentangled from the Cain legend (so We. Bu.); whether it can have included the whole of that legend is a point to be considered later (p. 100). We have thus a list of Adam's descendants through Cain, continued in a single line for seven generations, after which it branches into three, and then ceases. It has no explicit sequel in Genesis; the sacred number 7 marks it as complete in itself; and the attempts of some scholars to remodel it in accordance with its supposed original place in the history are to be distrusted. Its main purpose is to record the origin of various arts and industries of civilised life; and apart from the history of Cain there is nothing whatever to indicate that it deals with a race of sinners, as distinct from the godly line of Seth. That this genealogy belongs to J has hardly been questioned except by Di., who argues with some hesitation for assigning it to E, chiefly on the ground of its discordance with vv.$^{25.\,26}$. Bu. (p. 220 ff.) has shown that the stylistic criteria point decidedly (if not quite unequivocally) to J;‡ and in the absence of any certain trace of E in chs. 1–11, the strong presumption is that the genealogy represents a stratum of the former document. The question then arises whether it be the original continuation of ch. 3. An *essential* connexion cannot, from the nature of the case, be affirmed. The primitive genealogies are composed of desiccated legends, in which each member is originally independent of the rest; and we are not entitled to assume that an account of the Fall necessarily attached itself to the person of the first man. If it were certain that 3^{20} is an integral part of one recension of the Paradise story, it might reasonably be concluded that that recension was continued in 4^{1}, and then in 4^{17-24}. In the absence of complete certainty on that point the larger question must be left in suspense; there is, however, no difficulty in supposing that in the earliest written collection of Hebrew traditions the genealogy was preceded by a history of the Fall in a version partly preserved in ch. 3. The presumption that this was the case would, of course, be immensely strengthened if we could suppose it to be the intention of the original writer to describe not merely the progress of culture, but also the rapid development of sin (so We.).

---

* We. unites v.^{16b} with $^{17-24}$. † *e.g.* Hupfeld, *Quellen*, 126 ff.

‡ יָלַד = 'beget,' ^{18}; גם הוא, ^{22} (*in genealogies*, confined to J, 10^{21} 19^{38} $22^{20.\,24}$ 4^{26}); ושם אחיו, ^{21} (cf. 10^{25}); cf. ^{19} with 10^{25} etc. (Bu. *l.c.*).

2. The fragmentary genealogy of vv.$^{25.26}$ corresponds, so far as it goes, with the Sethite genealogy of P in ch. 5. It will be shown later (p. 138f.) that the lists of 4^{17-24} and 5 go back to a common original; and if the discrepancy had been merely between J and P, the obvious conclusion would be that these two documents had followed different traditional variants of the ancient genealogy. But how are we to account for the fact that the first three names of P's list occur also in the connexion of J? There are four possible solutions. (1) It is conceivable that J, not perceiving the ultimate identity of the two genealogies, incorporated both in his document (cf. Ew. *JBBW*, vi. p. 4); and that the final redactor (R^P) then curtailed the second list in view of ch. 5. This hypothesis is on various grounds improbable. It assumes (see ^{25b}) the murder of Abel by Cain as an original constituent of J's narrative; now that story takes for granted that the worship of Yahwe was practised from the beginning, whereas ^{26b} explicitly states that it was only introduced in the third generation. (2) It has not unnaturally been conjectured that v.$^{25f.}$ are entirely redactional (Ew. Schr. al.); *i.e.*, that they were inserted by an editor (R^P) to establish a connexion between the genealogy of J and that of P. In favour of this view the use of אדם (as a proper name) and of אלהים has been cited; but again the statement of ^{26b} presents an insurmountable difficulty. P has his own definite theory of the introduction of the name יהוה (see Ex. $6^{2ff.}$), and it is incredible that any editor influenced by him should have invented the gratuitous statement that the name was in use from the time of Enosh. (3) A third view is that vv.$^{25.26}$ stood originally before v.^{1} (or before v.^{17}), so that the father of Cain and Abel (or of Cain alone) was not Adam but Enosh; and that the redactor who made the transposition is responsible also for some changes on v.^{25} to adapt it to its new setting (so Sta.) (see on the v.). That is, no doubt, a plausible solution (admitted as possible by Di.), although it involves operations on the structure of the genealogy too drastic and precarious to be readily assented to. It is difficult also to imagine any sufficient motive for the supposed transposition. That it was made to find a connexion for the (secondary) story of Cain and Abel is a forced suggestion. The tendency of a redactor must have been to keep that story as far from the beginning as possible, and that the traditional data should have been deliberately altered so as to make it the opening scene of human history is hardly intelligible. (4) There remains the hypothesis that the two genealogies belong to separate strata within the Yahwistic tradition, which had been amalgamated by a redactor of that school (R^J) prior to the incorporation of P; and that the second list was curtailed by R^P because of its substantial identity with that of the Priestly Code in ch. 5. The harmonistic glossing of v.^{25} is an inevitable assumption of any theory except (1) and (2); it must have taken place after the insertion of the Cain and Abel episode; and on the view we are now considering it must be attributed to R^J. In other respects the solution is free from difficulty. The recognition of the complex character of the source called J is forced on us by many lines of proof; and it will probably be found that this view of the genealogies yields a valuable clue to the structure

of the non-Priestly sections of chs. 2–11 (see pp. 3, 134). One important consequence may here be noted. Eve's use of the name אלהים, and the subsequent notice of the introduction of the name יהוה, suggest that this writer had previously avoided the latter title of God (as E and P previously to Ex. $3^{14ff.}$ and Ex. $6^{2ff.}$). Hence, if it be the case that one recension of the Paradise story was characterised by the exclusive use of אלהים (see p. 53), $4^{25.\,26}$ will naturally be regarded as the sequel to that recension.

3. There remains the Cain and Abel narrative of vv.$^{1-16}$. That it belongs to J in the wider sense is undisputed,* but its precise affinities within the Yahwistic cycle are exceedingly perplexing. If the theory mentioned at the end of the last paragraph is correct, the consistent use of the name יהוה † would show that it was unknown to the author of vv.$^{25.\,26}$ and of that form of the Paradise story presupposed by these vv. Is it, then, a primary element of the genealogy in which it is embedded? It certainly contains notices—such as the introduction of agriculture and (perhaps) the origin of sacrifice—in keeping with the idea of the genealogy; but the length and amplitude of the narration would be without parallel in a genealogy; and (what is more decisive) there is an obvious incongruity between the Cain of the legend, doomed to a fugitive unsettled existence, and the Cain of the genealogy (v.^{17}), who as the first city-builder inaugurates the highest type of stable civilised life.‡ Still more complicated are the relations of the passage to the history of the Fall in ch. 3. On the one hand, a series of material incongruities seem to show that the two narratives are unconnected: the assumption of an already existing population on the earth could hardly have been made by the author of ch. 3; the free choice of occupation by the two brothers, and Yahwe's preference for the shepherd's sacrifice, ignore the representation (3^{19}) that husbandry is the destined lot of the race; and the curse on Cain is recorded in terms which betray no consciousness of a primal curse resting on the ground. It is true, on the other hand, that the literary form of 4^{1-16} contains striking reminiscences of that of ch. 3. The most surprising of these (4^{7b} ‖ 3^{16b}) may be set down to textual corruption (see the note on the v.); but there are several other turns of expression which recall the language of the earlier narrative: cf. $4^{9.\,10.\,11}$ with $3^{9.\,13.\,17}$. In both we have the same sequence of sin, investigation and punishment (in the form of a curse), the same dramatic dialogue, and the same power of psychological analysis. But whether these resemblances are such as to prove identity of authorship is a question that cannot be confidently answered. There is an indistinct-

---

* Cf. יהוה, $^{1.\,3.\,4.\,6.\,9.\,13.\,15.\,16}$; ארור, ^{11}; לבלתי, ^{15}; and obs. the resemblances to ch. 3 noted below: the naming of the child by the mother.

† This uniformity of usage is not, however, observed in 𝔊. In $𝔊^{A}$ Κύριος occurs twice ($^{3.\,15}$), ὁ θεὸς 5 times ($^{1.\,4.\,9.\,10.\,16}$), and Κύριος ὁ θεὸς 3 times ($^{6.\,15.\,15}$) (for variants, see Cambridge LXX).

‡ Even if we adopt Bu.'s emendation of v.^{17}, and make Enoch the city-founder (see on the v.), it still remains improbable that that rôle should be assigned to the son of a wandering nomad.

ness of conception in 4^{1-16} which contrasts unfavourably with the convincing lucidity of ch. 3, as if the writer's touch were less delicate, or his gift of imaginative delineation more restricted. Such impressions are too subjective to be greatly trusted; but, taken along with the material differences already enumerated, they confirm the opinion that the literary connexion between ch. 3 and $4^{1ff.}$ is due to conscious or unconscious imitation of one writer by another.—On the whole, the evidence points to the following conclusion: The story of Cain and Abel existed as a popular legend entirely independent of the traditions regarding the infancy of the race, and having no vital relation to any part of its present literary environment. It was incorporated in the Yahwistic document by a writer familiar with the narrative of the Fall, who identified the Cain of the legend with the son of the first man, and linked the story to his name in the genealogy. How much of the original genealogy has been preserved it is impossible to say: any notices that belonged to it have certainly been rewritten, and cannot now be isolated; but v.^{1} (birth of Cain) may with reasonable probability be assigned to it (so Bu.), possibly also $^{2b\beta}$ (Cain's occupation), and 3^{b} (Cain's sacrifice).—Other important questions will be best considered in connexion with the original significance of the legend (p. 111 ff.).

IV. 1–16.—*Cain and Abel.*

Eve bears to her husband two sons, Cain and Abel; the first becomes a tiller of the ground, and the second a keeper of sheep ($^{1.\ 2}$). Each offers to Yahwe the sacrifice appropriate to his calling; but only the shepherd's offering is accepted, and Cain is filled with morose jealousy and hatred of Abel ($^{3-5}$). Though warned by Yahwe ($^{6f.}$), he yields to his evil passion and slays his brother (^{8}). Yahwe pronounces him accursed from the fertile ground, which will no longer yield its substance to him, and he is condemned to the wandering life of the desert ($^{10-12}$). As a mitigation of his lot, Yahwe appoints him a sign which protects him from indiscriminate vengeance ($^{14f.}$); and he departs into the land of Nod, east of Eden (^{16}).

1–5. Birth of Cain and Abel: their occupation, and sacrifice.—**1.** On the naming of the child by the

1. והאדם ידע] A plup. sense (Ra.) being unsuitable, the peculiar order of words is difficult to explain; see on 3^{1}, and cf. 21^{1}. Sta. (*Ak. Red.* 239) regards it as a proof of editorial manipulation.—The euphemistic use of ידע is peculiar to J in the Hex. (7 times): Nu. $31^{17.\ 18.\ 35}$ (P: cf. Ju. $21^{11.\ 12}$) are somewhat different. Elsewhere Ju. 11^{39} $19^{22.\ 25}$, 1 Sa. 1^{19}, 1 Ki. 1^{4},—all in the older historiography, and some perhaps from the

mother, see Benzinger, *Archæol.*[2] 116. It is peculiar to the oldest strata (J and E) of the Hex., and is not quite consistently observed even there (4^{26} 5^{29} $25^{25f.}$, Ex. 2^{22}): it may therefore be a relic of the matriarchate which was giving place to the later custom of naming by the father (P) at the time when these traditions were taking shape.—The difficult sentence קָנִיתִי אִישׁ אֶת־יְהוָה connects the name קַיִן with the verb קָנָה. But קנה has two meanings in Heb.: (*a*) to (create, or) produce, and (*b*) to acquire; and it is not easy to determine which is intended here.

The second idea would seem more suitable in the present connexion, but it leads to a forced and doubtful construction of the last two words. (*a*) To render אֶת 'with the help of' (Di. and most) is against all analogy. It is admitted that את itself nowhere has this sense (in 49^{25} the true reading is וְאֵל, and Mic 3^{8} is at least doubtful); and the few cases in which the synonym עם can be so translated are not really parallel. Both in 1 Sa. 14^{45} and Dn. 11^{39}, the עם denotes association *in the same act*, and therefore does not go beyond the sense 'along with.' The analogy does not hold in this v. if the vb. means 'acquire'; Eve could not say that she had *acquired* a man along with Yahwe. (*b*) We may, of course, assume an error in the text and read מֵאֵת = 'from' (Bu. al. after 𝔗O). (*c*) The idea that את is the sign of acc. (𝔗J, al.), and that Eve imagined she had given birth to the divine 'seed' promised in 3^{15} (Luther, al.) may be disregarded as a piece of antiquated dogmatic exegesis.—If we adopt the other meaning of קנה, the construction is perfectly natural: *I have created* (or *produced*) *a man with* (the cooperation of) *Yahwe* (cf. Ra.: "When he created me and my husband he created us alone, but in this case we are associated with him"). A strikingly similar phrase in the bilingual Babylonian account of Creation (above, p. 47) suggests that the language here may be more deeply tinged with mythology than has been generally suspected. We read that "Aruru, together with him [Marduk], created (the) seed of mankind": *Aruru zi-ir a-mi-lu-ti it-ti-šu ib-ta-nu* (*KIB*, vi. 1, 40 f.; King, *Cr. Tab.* i. 134 f.). Aruru, a form of Ištar, is a mother-goddess of the Babylonians (see *KAT*[3], 430), *i.e.*, a deified ancestress, and therefore so far the counterpart of the Heb. חַוָּה (see on 3^{20}). The exclamation certainly gains in significance if we suppose it to have survived from a more mythological phase of tradition, in which

---

literary school of J.—[קַיִן] √ קין (Ar. *ḳāna*). In Ar. *ḳain* means 'smith'; = Syr. ܩܝܢܝܐ, 'worker in metal' (see 4^{22} 5^{9}). Nöldeke's remark, that in Ar. *ḳain* several words are combined, is perhaps equally true of Heb. קין (*EB*, 130). Many critics (We. Bu. Sta. Ho. al.) take the name as eponym of the Ḳenites (קֵינִי. קַיִן): see p. 113 below.—[קָנִיתִי] All Vns. express the idea of 'acquiring' (ἐκτησάμην, *possedi*, etc.). The sense 'create' or 'originate,' though apparently confined to Heb. and subordinate

Hawwah was not a mortal wife and mother, but a creative deity taking part with the supreme god in the production of man. See Cheyne, *TBI*, 104, who thinks it "psychologically probable that Eve congratulated herself on having 'created' a man."—That אִישׁ is not elsewhere used of a man-child is not a serious objection to any interpretation (cf. גֶּבֶר in Jb. 3[3]); though the thought readily occurs that the etymology would be more appropriate to the name אֱנוֹשׁ (4[26]) than to קַיִן.

2. *And again she bare, etc.*] The omission of the verb הָרָה is not to be pressed as implying that the brothers were twins, although that may very well be the meaning. The OT contains no certain trace of the widespread superstitions regarding twin-births.—The sons betake themselves to the two fundamental pursuits of settled life: the elder to agriculture, the younger to the rearing of small cattle (sheep and goats). The previous story of the Fall, in which Adam, as representing the race, is condemned to husbandry, seems to be ignored (Gu.).

The absence of an etymology of הֶבֶל is remarkable (but cf. v.[17]), and hardly to be accounted for by the supposition that the name was only coined afterwards in token of his brief, fleeting existence (Di.). The word (= 'breath') might suggest that to a Heb. reader, but the original sense is unknown. Gu. regards it as the proper name of an extinct tribe or people; Ew. We. al. take it to be a variant of יָבָל, the father of nomadic shepherds (4[20]); and Cheyne has ingeniously combined both names with a group of Semitic words denoting domestic animals and those who take charge of them (*e.g.* Syr. ܗܒܠܐ = 'herd'; Ar. *'abbāl* = 'camel-herd,' etc.): the meaning would then be 'herdsman' (*EB*, i. 6). The conjecture is retracted in *TBI*, in the interests of Yeraḥme'el.

3. *An offering*] מִנְחָה, lit. a present or tribute (32[14ff.] 33[10] 43[11ff.], 1 Sa. 10[27] etc.): see below. The use of this word

---

even there, is established by Dt. 32[6], Pr. 8[22], Ps. 139[13], Gn. 14[19. 22].—את] Of the Vns. 𝕿O alone can be thought to have read מֵאֵת (מן קדם); one anonymous Gr. tr. (see Field) took the word as *not. acc.* (ἄνθρωπον κύριον); the rest vary greatly in rendering (as was to be expected from the difficulty of the phrase), but there is no reason to suppose they had a different text: 𝕲 διὰ τοῦ θ., Σ. σὺν κ., 'Ο 'Εβρ. καὶ ὁ Σύρ.: ἐν θ., 𝔙 *per Deum*, 𝕾 ܠܡܪܝܐ. Conjectures: Marti (*Lit. Centralbl.*, 1897, xx. 641) and Zeydner (*ZATW*, xviii. 120): אִישׁ אֹת יַהְוֶה = 'the man of the Jahwe sign' (v.[15]); Gu. אִישׁ אֶתְאַוֶּה = 'a man whom I desire.'

3. מקץ ימים] *After some time*, which may be longer (1 Sa. 29[8]) or shorter (24[55]). To take ימים in the definite sense of 'year' (1 Sa. 1[21] 2[19]

shows that the 'gift-theory' of sacrifice (*RS*², 392 ff.) was fully established in the age when the narrative originated.—*of the fruit of the ground*] "Fruit in its natural state was offered at Carthage, and was probably admitted by the Hebrews in ancient times." "The Carthaginian fruit-offering consisted of a branch bearing fruit, . . . it seems to be clear that the fruit was offered at the altar, . . . and this, no doubt, is the original sense of the Hebrew rite also" (*RS*², 221 and *n.* 3). Cain's offering is thus analogous to the first-fruits (בִּכּוּרִים: Ex. $23^{16. 19}$ $34^{22. 26}$, Nu. 13^{20} etc.) of Heb. ritual; and it is arbitrary to suppose that his fault lay in not selecting the best of what he had for God.—**4.** Abel's offering consisted of *the firstlings of his flock, namely* (see G–K. § 154 *a*, *N.* 1 (*b*)) *of their fat-pieces*] cf. Nu. 18^{17}. Certain fat portions of the victim were in ancient ritual reserved for the deity, and might not be eaten (1 Sa. 2^{16} etc.: for Levitical details, see Dri.-White, *Lev.*, *Polychr. Bible*, pp. 4, 65).—**4b, 5a.** How did Yahwe signify His acceptance of the one offering and rejection of the other? It is

---

20^6 etc.) is unnecessary, though not altogether unnatural (IEz. al.).—הֵבִיא] the ritual use is well established: Lv. $2^{2. 8}$, Is. 1^{13}, Jer. 17^{26} etc. —מִנְחָה: Ar. *minḥat* = 'gift,' 'loan': √ *manaḥa.** On the uses of the word, see Dri. *DB*, iii. 587b. In sacrificial terminology there are perhaps three senses to be distinguished: (1) Sacrifice in general, conceived as a tribute or propitiatory present to the deity, Nu. 16^{15}, Ju. 6^{18}, 1 Sa. $2^{17. 29}$ 26^{19}, Is. 1^{13}, Zeph. 3^{10}, Ps. 96^8 etc. (2) The conjunction of מנחה and זֶבַח (1 Sa. 2^{29} 3^{14}, Is. 19^{21}, Am. 5^{25} etc.) may show that it denotes vegetable as distinct from animal oblations (see *RS*², 217, 236). (3) In P and late writings generally it is restricted to cereal offerings: Ex. 30^9, Nu. 18^9 etc. Whether the wider or the more restricted meaning be the older it is difficult to say.—4. וּמֵחֶלְבֵהֶן] On Meth., see G–K. § 16 *d*. We might point as sing. of the noun (חֶלְבְּהֶן, Lv. $8^{16. 25}$; G–K. § 91 *c*); but 𝔐 has *scriptio plena* of the pl. ומחלביהן.—וישע] 𝔊 καὶ ἔπιδεν (in v.⁵ προσέσχεν); Aq. ἐπεκλίθη; Σ. ἐτέρφθη; Θ. ἐνεπύρισεν (see above); ὁ Σύρ. εὐδόκησεν; 𝔙 *respexit*; 𝔖 ܘܐܬܒܣܡ; 𝔗ᴼ והות רעוא קדם ײ. There is no *exact* parallel to the meaning here; the nearest is Ex. 5^9 ('*look away* [from their tasks] *to*' idle words).—5. חרה] in Heb. always of *mental* heat (anger); 𝔊

---

* Some, however, derive it from נחה = 'direct'; and Hommel (*AHT*, 322) cites a Sabæan inscr. where *tanaḥḥayat* (V conj.) is used of offering a sacrifice (see Lagrange, *Études*, 250). If this be correct, what was said above about the 'gift theory' would fall to the ground.

commonly answered (in accordance with Lv. 9^{24}, 1 Ki. 18^{38} etc.), that fire descended from heaven and consumed Abel's offering (Θ. Ra. IEz. De. al.). Others (Di. Gu.) think more vaguely of some technical sign, *e.g.* the manner in which the smoke ascended (Ew. Str.); while Calv. supposes that Cain inferred the truth from the subsequent course of God's providence. But these conjectures overlook the strong anthropomorphism of the description: one might as well ask how Adam knew that he was expelled from the garden (3^{24}). Perhaps the likeliest analogy is the acceptance of Gideon's sacrifice by the Angel of Yahwe (Ju. 6^{21}).—*Why* was the one sacrifice accepted and not the other? The distinction must lie either (*a*) in the disposition of the brothers (so nearly all comm.), or (*b*) in the material of the sacrifice (Tu.). In favour of (*a*) it is pointed out that in each case the personality of the worshipper is mentioned before the gift. But since the reason is not stated, it must be presumed to be one which the first hearers would understand for themselves; and they could hardly understand that Cain, apart from his occupation and sacrifice, was less acceptable to God than Abel. On the other hand, they would readily perceive that the material of Cain's offering was not in accordance with primitive Semitic ideas of sacrifice (see *RS*², Lect. VIII.).

From the fact that the altar is not expressly mentioned, it has been inferred that sacrifice is here regarded as belonging to the established order of things (Sta. al.). But the whole manner of the narration suggests rather that the incident is conceived as the initiation of sacrifice,—the first spontaneous expression of religious feeling in cultus.* If that impression be sound, it follows also that the narrative proceeds on a *theory* of sacrifice: the idea, viz., that animal sacrifice alone is acceptable to Yahwe. It is true that we cannot go back to

---

wrongly ἐλύπησεν; so 𝔖. On impers. const., see G-K. § 144*b*; cf. $18^{30.32}$ 31^{36} 34^{7}, Nu. 16^{15} etc. The word is not used by P.—For נפל, 𝔖 has ܐܬܟܡܪ (lit. 'became black').

---

* It may be a mere coincidence that in Philo Byblius the institution of animal sacrifice occurs in a legend of two brothers who quarrelled (*Pr. Ev.* i. 10). Kittel (*Studien zur hebr. Archäol.* 103[1]) suggests that our narrative may go back to a time prior to the introduction of the fire-offering and the altar.

a stage of Heb. ritual when vegetable offerings were excluded; but such sacrifices must have been introduced after the adoption of agricultural life; and it is quite conceivable that in the early days of the settlement in Canaan the view was maintained among the Israelites that the animal offerings of their nomadic religion were superior to the vegetable offerings made to the Canaanite Baals. Behind this may lie (as Gu. thinks) the idea that pastoral life as a whole is more pleasing to Yahwe than husbandry.

5b. Cain's feeling is a mixture of anger (*it became very hot to* him) and dejection (*his face fell*: cf. Jb. 29^{24}, Jer. 3^{12}). This does not imply that his previous state of mind had been bad (Di. al.). In tracing Cain's sin to a disturbance of his religious relation to God, the narrator shows his profound knowledge of the human heart.

6–12. Warning, murder, and sentence.—7. The point of the remonstrance obviously is that the cause of Cain's dissatisfaction lies in himself, but whether in his general temper or in his defective sacrifice can no longer be made

---

7. The difficulties of the present text are "the curt and ambiguous expression שְׂאֵת; further, the use of חַטָּאת as masc., then the whole tenor of the sentence, *If thou doest not well* . . . ; finally, the exact and yet incongruous parallelism of the second half-verse with 3^{16}" (Ols. *MBBA*, 1870, 380).—As regards [7a], the main lines of interpretation are these: (1) The inf. שְׂאֵת may be complementary to תֵּיטִיב as a *relative* vb. (G–K. § 120, 1), in which case ׳שׂ must have the sense of 'offer' sacrifice (cf. 43^{34}, Ezk. 20^{31}). So (*a*) 𝔊 *οὐκ ἐὰν ὀρθῶς προσενέγκῃς, ὀρθῶς δὲ μὴ διέλῃς, ἥμαρτες; ἡσύχασον* (reading לְנַתַּח for לַפֶּתַח, and pointing the next two words חָטָאתָ רְבַץ) = 'Is it not so—if thou offerest rightly, but dost not cut in pieces rightly, thou hast sinned? Be still!' Ball strangely follows this fantastic rendering, seemingly oblivious of the fact that נִתַּח (cf. Ex. 29^{17}, Lv. $1^{6.12}$, 1 Ki. $18^{23.33}$ etc.)—for which he needlessly substitutes בִּתֵּר (15^{10})—has no sense as applied to a fruit-offering.—(*b*) Somewhat similar is a view approved by Bu. as "völlig befriedigend" (*Urg*. 204 f.): 'Whether thou make thine offering costly or not, at the door,' etc. ['Whether thou offerest *correctly* or not,' would be the safer rendering].—(2) The inf. may be taken as compressed apod., and ׳ה as an independent vb. = 'do well' (as often). ׳שׂ might then express the idea of (*a*) *elevation of countenance* (= ׳שׂ פנים: cf. Jb. 11^{15} 22^{26}): 'If thou doest well, shall there not be lifting up?' etc. (so Tu. Ew. De. Di. Dri. al.); or (*b*) *acceptance* (׳שׂ ׳פ as Gn. 19^{21}, 2 Ki. 3^{14}, Mal. $1^{8.9}$): so Aq. (*ἀρέσεις*), Θ. (*δεκτόν*), 𝔖 (ܡܩܒܠ), 𝔙 (*recipies*); or (*c*) *forgiveness* (as Gn. 50^{17}, Ex. 32^{32}): so Σ. (*ἀφήσω*), 𝔗^O Jer. and recently Ho. Of these renderings 2 (*a*) or 1 (*b*) are perhaps the most

out. Every attempt to extract a meaning from the v. is more or less of a *tour de force*, and it is nearly certain that the obscurity is due to deep-seated textual corruption (*v.i.*). —8. *And Cain said*] אָמַר never being quite synonymous with דִּבֶּר, the sentence is incomplete: the missing words, *Let us go to the field*, must be supplied from Vns.; see below (so Ew. Di. Dri. al.). That Cain, as a first step towards reconciliation, communicated to Abel the warning he had just received (Tu. al.), is perhaps possible grammatically, but psychologically is altogether improbable.—*the field*] the open country (see on 2^5), where they were safe from observation

---

satisfying, though both are cumbered with the unnatural metaphor of sin as a wild beast couching at the door (of what?), and the harsh discord of gender. The latter is not fairly to be got rid of by taking רֹבֵץ as a noun ('sin is at the door, a lurker': Ew. al.), though no doubt it might be removed by a change of text. Of the image itself the best explanation would be that of Ho., who regards רֹבֵץ as a technical expression for unforgiven sin (cf. Dt. 29^{19}). Jewish interpreters explain it of the evil impulse in man (יֵצֶר הָרָע), and most Christians similarly of the overmastering or seductive power of sin; [7b] being regarded as a summons to Cain to subdue his evil passions.—7b reads smoothly enough by itself, but connects badly with what precedes. The antecedent to the pron. suff. is usually taken to be Sin personified as a wild beast, or less commonly (Calv. al.) Abel, the object of Cain's envy. The word תְּשׁוּקָה is equally unsuitable, whether it be understood of the wild beast's eagerness for its prey or the deference due from a younger brother to an older; and the alternative תְּשׁוּבָה of 𝔊 and 𝔖 (see on 3^{16}) is no better. The verbal resemblance to 3^{16b} is itself suspicious; a facetious parody of the language of a predecessor is not to be attributed to any early writer. It is more likely that the eye of a copyist had wandered to 3^{16} in the adjacent column, and that the erroneous words were afterwards adjusted to their present context: in 𝔖 the suff. are actually reversed (ܘܐܢܬ ܬܫܬܠܛ ܒܗ ܘܗܘ ܢܫܬܥܒܕ ܠܟ).—The paraphrase of $𝔗^O$ affords no help, and the textual confusion is probably irremediable; tentative emendations like those of Gu. (p. 38) are of no avail. Che. *TBI*, 105, would remove v.[7] as a gloss, and make [8a] (reading אחי) Cain's answer to v.[6].

8. אָמַר, in the sense of 'speak,' 'converse' (2 Ch. 32^{24}), is excessively rare and late: the only instance in early Heb. is apparently Ex. 19^{25}, where the context has been broken by a change of document. It might mean 'mention' (as 43^{27} etc.), but in that case the obj. must be indicated. Usually it is followed, like Eng. 'say,' by the actual words spoken. Hence נֵלְכָה הַשָּׂדֶה is to be supplied with 𝔐𝔊𝔖𝔙. $𝔗^J$ but *not* Aq. (Tu. De.: see the scholia in Field): a *Pisqa* in some Heb. MSS, though

(1 Ki. 11^{29}).—**9.** Yahwe opens the inquisition, as in 3^{9}, with a question, which Cain, unlike Adam, answers with a defiant repudiation of responsibility. It is impossible to doubt that here the writer has the earlier scene before his mind, and consciously depicts a terrible advance in the power of sin.—**10.** *Hark! Thy brother's blood is crying to me, etc.*] צְעָק denotes strictly the cry for help, and specially for redress or vengeance (Ex. $22^{22.26}$, Ju. 4^{3}, Ps. $107^{6.28}$ etc.). The idea that blood exposed on the ground thus clamours for vengeance is persistently vivid in the OT (Jb. 16^{18}, Is. 26^{21}, Ezk. $24^{7.8}$, 2 Ki. 9^{26}): see *RS*², 417^{5}. In this passage we have more than a mere metaphor, for it is the blood which is represented as drawing Yahwe's attention to the crime of Cain.—**11.** *And now cursed art thou from* (off) *the ground*] *i.e.*, not the earth's surface, but the cultivated ground (cf. v.[14], and see on 2^{5}). To restrict it to the soil of Palestine (We. Sta. Ho.) goes beyond the necessities of the case.—*which has opened her mouth, etc.*] a personification of the ground similar to that of Sheol in Is. 5^{14} (cf. Nu. 16^{32}). The idea cannot be that the earth is a monster greedy of blood; it seems rather akin to the primitive superstition of a physical infection or poisoning of the soil, and through it of the murderer, by the shed blood (see Miss Harrison, *Prolegomena*, 219 ff.). The ordinary OT conception is that the blood remains *uncovered* (cf. Eurip. *Electra*, 318 f.). The relation of the two notions is obscure.—**12.** The curse 'from off the ground' has two sides: (1) The ground will *no longer yield its strength* (Jb. 31^{39}) to the murderer, so that even if he wished he will be unable to resume his husbandry; and

---

not recognised by the Mass., supports this view of the text. To emend וַיִּשָּׁמֵר (Ols. al.) or וַיֵּמַר, וַיָּמָר (Gk.) is less satisfactory.—9. אֵי] ш אַיֵּה.—10. On the interjectional use of קוֹל, see G–K. § 146 *b*; Nö. *Mand. Gr.* p. 482. —צֹעֲקִים] ш צעק, agreeing with קול (?).—11. אָרוּר . . . מִן] pregnant constr., G–K. § 119 *x*, *y*, *ff*. This sense of מִן is more accurately expressed by מֵעַל in v.[14], but is quite common (cf. esp. 27^{39}). Other renderings, as *from* (indicating the direction from which the curse comes) or *by*, are less appropriate; and the compar. *more than* is impossible.—12. תֹסֵף] juss. form with לֹא (G–K. § 109 *d*, *h*; Dav. §§ 63, *R.* 3, 66, *R.* 6); fol-

(2) he is to be a *vagrant and wanderer in the earth.* The second is the negative consequence of the first, and need not be regarded as a separate curse, or a symbol of the inward unrest which springs from a guilty conscience.

13–16. Mitigation of Cain's punishment.—**13.** *My punishment is too great to be borne*] So the plea of Cain is understood by all modern authorities. The older rendering: *my guilt is too great to be forgiven* (which is in some ways preferable), is abandoned because the sequel shows that Cain's reflexions run on the thought of suffering and not of sin; see below.—**14.** *from Thy face I shall be hidden*] This anguished cry of Cain has received scant sympathy at the hands of comm. (except Gu.). Like that of Esau in 27^{34}, it reveals him as one who had blindly striven for a spiritual good,—as a man not wholly bad who had sought the favour of God with the passionate determination of an ill-regulated nature and missed it: one to whom banishment from the divine presence is a distinct ingredient in his cup of misery.—*every one that findeth me, etc.*] The object of Cain's dread is hardly the vengeance of the slain man's kinsmen (so nearly all comm.); but rather the lawless state of things in the desert, where any one's life may be taken with impunity (Gu.). That the words imply a diffusion of the human race is an incongruity on either view, and is one of many indications that the Cain of the original story was not the son of the first man.

This expostulation of Cain, with its rapid grasp of the situation, lights up some aspects of the historic background of the legend. (1) It

---

lowed by inf. without ל (G-K. § 114 *m*).—נָע וָנָד] an alliteration, as in 1^2. Best rendered in anon. Gr. Vns. (Field): *σαλευόμενος καὶ ἀκαταστατῶν*; 𝔙 *vagus et profugus*; 𝔊 (incorrectly) *στένων καὶ τρέμων*.

13. On עָוֺן (√ *ġawaʸ* = 'go astray': Dri. *Sam.* 134 f.) in the sense of *punishment* of sin, see the passages cited in BDB, *s.v.* 3. נשא ע׳, in the sense of 'bear guilt,' seems peculiar to P and Ezk.; elsewhere it means to 'pardon iniquity' (Ex. 34^7, Nu. 14^{18}, Ho. 14^3, Mic. 7^{18}, Ps. 32^5). This consideration is not decisive; but there is something to be said for the consensus of anc. Vns. (𝔊 *ἀφεθῆναι*; 𝔙 *veniam merear*, etc.) in favour of the second interpretation, which might be retained without detriment to the sense if the sentence could be read as a question.—**14.** אֹתִי] instead of suff. is unlike J. In the next v. אֹתוֹ after inf. was

is assumed that Yahwe's presence is confined to the cultivated land; in other words, that He is the God of settled life, agricultural and pastoral. To conclude, however, that He is the God of Canaan in particular (cf. 1 Sa. 26^{19}), is perhaps an over-hasty inference. (2) The reign of right is coextensive with Yahwe's sphere of influence: the outer desert is the abode of lawlessness; justice does not exist, and human life is cheap. That Cain, the convicted murderer, should use this plea will not appear strange if we remember the conditions under which such narratives arose.

15. What follows must be understood as a divinely appointed amelioration of Cain's lot: although he is not restored to the amenities of civilised life, Yahwe grants him a special protection, suited to his vagrant existence, against indiscriminate homicide.—*Whoso kills Ḳayin* (or 'whenever any one kills Ḳ'), *it* (the murder) *shall be avenged sevenfold*] by the slaughter of seven members of the murderer's clan. See below.—*appointed a sign for Ḳayin*] or *set a mark on Ḳ.* The former is the more obvious rendering of the words; but the latter has analogies, and is demanded by the context.

The idea that the sign is a pledge given once for all of the truth of Yahwe's promise, after the analogy of the prophetic אוֹת, is certainly consistent with the phrase שִׂים . . . לְ: cf. *e.g.* Ex. 15^{25}, Jos. 24^{25} with Ex. o^2 etc. So some authorities in *Ber. R.*, IEz. Tu. al. But Ex. 4^{11a} proves that it may also be something attached to the person of Cain (Calv. *Ber. R.*, De. and most); and that אוֹת may denote a mark appears from Ex. $13^{9.16}$ etc. Since the sign is to serve as a warning to all and sundry who might attempt the life of Cain, it is obvious that the second view alone meets the requirements of the case: we must think of something about Cain, visible to all the world, marking him out as one whose death would be avenged sevenfold. Its purpose is protective and not penal: that it brands him as a murderer is a natural but mistaken idea.—It is to be observed that in this part of the narrative *Ḳayin* is no longer a personal but a collective name. The clause כָּל־הֹרֵג ק׳ (not מִי יַהֲרֹג, or אֲשֶׁר י׳) has frequentative force (exx. below), implying that the act might be repeated many times on members of the tribe Ḳayin: similarly the sevenfold vengeance assumes a kin-circle to which the murderer belongs. See, further, p. 112.

---

necessary to avoid confusion between subj. and obj.—**15.** לָכֵן] *οὐχ οὕτως* (𝔊ΣΘ) implies לֹא כֵן: so 𝔖𝔙; but this would require to be followed by כִּי.—כָּל־הֹרֵג ק׳] see G–K. § 116*w*; cf. Ex. 12^{15}, Nu. 35^{30}, 1 Sa. 2^{13} 3^{11} etc.—יֻקָּם] The subj. might be קַיִן (as v.[24]) or (more probably) impers. (Ex. 21^{21}), certainly not the murderer of Cain.—שִׁבְעָתַיִם] = '7 times': G–K. § 134*r*. Vns.: 𝔊 *ἑπτὰ ἐκδικούμενα παραλύσει*; Aq. *ἑπταπλασίως*

16. *and dwelt in the land of Nôd*] The vb. יָשַׁב is not necessarily inconsistent with nomadic life, as Sta. alleges (see Gn. 13[12], 1 Ch. 5[10] etc.). It is uncertain whether the name נוֹד is traditional (We. Gu.), or was coined from the participle נָד = 'land of wandering' (so most); at all events it cannot be geographically identified. If the last words קדמת עדן belong to the original narrative, it would be natural to regard Ḳayin as representative of the nomads of Central Asia (Knob. al.); but the phrase may have been added by a redactor to bring the episode into connexion with the account of the Fall.

The Origin of the Cain Legend.—The exposition of 4[1-16] would be incomplete without some account of recent speculations regarding the historical or ethnological situation out of which the legend arose. The tendency of opinion has been to affirm with increasing distinctness the view that the narrative "embodies the old Hebrew conception of the lawless nomad life, where only the blood-feud prevents the wanderer in the desert from falling a victim to the first man who meets him."* A subordinate point, on which undue stress is commonly laid, is the identity of Cain with the nomadic tribe of the Ḳenites. These ideas, first propounded by Ew.,† adopted by We.,‡ and (in part) by Rob. Sm.,§ have been worked up by Sta., in his instructive essay on 'The sign of Cain,'‖ into a complete theory, in which what may be called the nomadic motive is treated as the clue to the significance of every characteristic feature of the popular legend lying at the basis of the narrative. Although the questions involved are too numerous to be fully dealt with here, it is necessary to consider those points in the argument which bear more directly on the original meaning of vv.[1-16].

1. That the figure of Cain represents some phase of nomadic life may be regarded as certain. We have seen (p. 110) that in v.[13ff.] the name Cain has a collective sense; and every descriptive touch in these closing vv. is characteristic of desert life. His expulsion from the ארמה and the phrase נע ונד, express (though not by any means necessarily,—

ἐκδικηθήσεται; Σ. ἑβδόμως ἐκδίκησιν δώσει; Θ. δι' ἑβδομάδος ἐκδικήσει; 𝔙 *septuplum punietur*; 𝔖 ܫܒܥܐ ܙܒܢܝ̈ܢ ܢܬܬܒܥ; 𝔗ᴼ לשבעא דרין יתפרע מיניה (hence the idea that Cain was killed by Lamech the 7th from Adam [see on v.[24]]).—16. נוד] 𝔐 נד, 𝔊 Ναΐδ (ניד?) with variants (see Nestle, *MM*, p. 9).—ΣΘ𝔙 (*habitavit profugus in terra*) [𝔗?] take the word as a participle; but the order of words forbids this.—קדמת] see on 2[14]. 'In front of E.' and 'East of E.' would here be the same thing (3[24]).

* Smith, *KM*², 251. † *JBBW*, vi. 5 ff. ‡ *Comp.*² 10 f.
§ *l.c.* ‖ *Ak. Reden*, 229–73.

see below) the fundamental fact that his descendants are doomed to wander in the uncultivated regions beyond the pale of civilisation. The vengeance which protects him is the self-acting law of blood-revenge,—that 'salutary institution' which, in the opinion of Burckhardt, has done more than anything else to preserve the Bedouin tribes from mutual extermination.* The sign which Yahwe puts on him is most naturally explained as the "*shart* or tribal mark which every man bore in his person, and without which the ancient form of blood-feud, as the affair of a whole stock and not of near relations alone, could hardly have been worked."† And the fact that this kind of existence is traced to the operation of a hereditary curse embodies the feeling of a settled agricultural or pastoral community with regard to the turbulent and poverty-stricken life of the desert.

2. While this is true, the narrative cannot be regarded as expressing reprobation of every form of nomadism known to the Hebrews. A disparaging estimate of Bedouin life as a whole is, no doubt, conceivable on the part of the settled Israelites (cf. Gn. 16^{12}); but Cain is hardly the symbol of that estimate. (1) The ordinary Bedouin could not be described as 'fugitives and vagabonds in the earth': their movements are restricted to definite areas of the desert, and are hardly less monotonous than the routine of husbandry.‡ (2) The full Bedouin are breeders of camels, the half-nomads of sheep and goats; and both live mainly on the produce of their flocks and herds (see Meyer, *INS*, 303 ff.). But to suppose Cain to exemplify the latter mode of life is inconsistent with the narrative, for sheep-rearing is the distinctive profession of Abel; and it is hardly conceivable that Hebrew legend was so ignorant of the proud spirit of the full Bedouin as to describe them as degraded agriculturists. If Cain be the type of any permanent occupation at all, it must be one lower than agriculture and pasturage; *i.e.* he must stand for some of those rude tribes which subsist by hunting or robbery. (3) It is unlikely that a rule of sevenfold revenge was generally observed amongst Semitic nomads in OT times. Among the modern Arabs the law of the blood-feud is a life for a life: it is only under circumstances of extreme provocation that a twofold revenge is permissible. We are, therefore, led to think of Cain as the impersonation of an inferior race of nomads, maintaining a miserable existence by the chase, and practising a peculiarly ferocious form of blood-feud.—The view thus suggested of the fate of Cain finds a partial illustration in the picture

---

* *Bedouins and Wahabys*, 148.—The meaning is that the certainty of retaliation acts as a check on the warlike tribesmen, and renders their fiercest conflicts nearly bloodless.

† Smith, *l.c.*—It may be explained that at present the kindred group for the purpose of the blood-feud consists of all those whose lineage goes back to a common ancestor in the fifth generation. There are still certain tribes, however, who are greatly feared because they are said to 'strike sideways'; *i.e.* they retaliate upon any member of the murderer's tribe whether innocent or guilty. See Burck. 149 ff., 320 f.

‡ Nö. *EB*, 130.

given by Burck. and Doughty of a group of low-caste tribes called Solubba or Sleyb. These people live partly by hunting, partly by coarse smith-work and other gipsy labour in the Arab encampments; they are forbidden by their patriarch to be cattle-keepers, and have no property save a few asses; they are excluded from fellowship and intermarriage with the regular Bedouin, though on friendly terms with them; and they are the only tribes that are free of the Arabian deserts to travel where they will, ranging practically over the whole peninsula from Syria to Yemen. It is, perhaps, of less significance that they sometimes speak of themselves as decayed Bedouin, and point out the ruins of the villages where their ancestors dwelt as owners of camels and flocks.* The name קַיִן, signifying 'smith' (p. 102), would be a suitable eponym for such degraded nomads. The one point in which the analogy absolutely fails is that tribes so circumstanced could not afford to practise the stringent rule of blood-revenge indicated by v.[15].—It thus appears that the known conditions of Arabian nomadism present no exact parallel to the figure of Cain. To carry back the origin of the legend to pre-historic times would destroy the *raison d'être* of Sta.'s hypothesis, which seeks to deduce everything from definite historical relations: at the same time it may be the only course by which the theory can be freed from certain inconsistencies with which it is encumbered.†

3. The kernel of Sta.'s argument is the attractive combination of Cain the fratricide with the eponymous ancestor of the Ḳenites.‡ In historical times the Ḳenites appear to have been pastoral nomads (Ex. 2[16ff.] 3[1]) frequenting the deserts south of Judah (1 Sa. 27[10] 30[29]), and (in some of their branches) clinging tenaciously to their ancestral manner of life (Ju. 4[11. 17] 5[24], Jer. 35[7] cpd. with 1 Ch. 2[55]). From the fact that they are found associated now with Israel (Ju. 1[16] etc.), now with Amaleḳ (Nu. 24[21ff.], 1 Sa. 15[6]), and now with Midian (Nu. 10[29]), Sta. infers that they were a numerically weak tribe of the second rank; and from the name, that they were smiths. The latter character, however, would imply that they were pariahs, and of that there is no evidence whatever. Nor is there any indication that the Ḳenites exercised a more rigorous blood-feud than other Semites: indeed, it seems an inconsistency in Sta.'s position that he regards the Ḳenites as at once distinguished by reckless bravery in the vindication of the tribal honour, and at the same time too feeble to maintain their independence without the aid of stronger tribes. There is, in short, nothing to show that the Ḳenites were anything but typical Bedouin; and all the objections to

---

* Burck. 14 f.; Doughty, *Arabia Deserta*, i. 280 ff.

† An interesting parallel might be found in the account given by Merker (*Die Masai*, p. 306 ff.) of the smiths (*ol kononi*) among the Masai of East Africa. Apart from the question of the origin of the Masai, it is quite possible that these African nomads present a truer picture of the conditions of primitive Semitic life than the Arabs of the present day. See also Andree, *Ethnogr. Parall. u. Vergl.* (1878), 156 ff.

‡ The tribe is called קַיִן in Nu. 24[22], Ju. 4[11]; elsewhere the gentilic קֵינִי is used (in 1 Ch. 2[55] קִינִים).

associating Cain with the higher levels of nomadism apply with full force to his identification with this particular tribe. When we consider, further, that the Ḳenites are nearly everywhere on friendly terms with Israel, and that they seem to have cherished the most ardent attachment to Yahwism, it becomes almost incredible that they should have been conceived as resting under a special curse.

4. It is very doubtful if any form of the nomadic or Ḳenite theory can account for the rise of the legend as a whole. The evidence on which it rests is drawn almost exclusively from vv.[13-16]. Sta. justifies his extension of the theory to the incident of the murder by the analogy of those temporary alliances between Bedouin and peasants in which the settled society purchases immunity from extortion by the payment of a fixed tribute to the nomads (cf. 1 Sa. 25[2ff.]). This relation is spoken of as a brotherhood, the tributary party figuring as the *sister* of the Bedouin tribe. The murder of Abel is thus resolved into the massacre of a settled pastoral people by a Bedouin tribe which had been on terms of formal friendship with it. But the analogy is hardly convincing. It would amount to this: that certain nomads were punished for a crime by being transformed into nomads: the fact that Cain was previously a husbandman is left unexplained.—Gu., with more consistency, finds in the narrative a vague reminiscence of an actual (prehistoric) event,—the extermination of a pastoral tribe by a neighbouring agricultural tribe, in consequence of which the latter were driven from their settlements and lived as outlaws in the wilderness. Such changes of fortune must have been common in early times on the border-land between civilisation and savagery; * and Gu.'s view has the advantage over Sta.'s that it makes a difference of sacrificial ritual an intelligible factor in the quarrel (see p. 105 f.). But the process of extracting history from legend is always precarious; and in this case the motive of *individual* blood-guilt appears too prominent to be regarded as a secondary interest of the narrative.

The truth is that in the present form of the story the figure of Cain represents a fusion of several distinct types, of which it is difficult to single out any one as the central idea of the legend. (1) He is the originator of agriculture (v.[2]). (2) He is the founder of sacrifice, and (as the foil to his brother Abel) exhibits the idea that vegetable offerings alone are not acceptable to Yahwe (see on v.[3]). (3) He is the individual murderer (or rather shedder of kindred blood) pursued by the curse, like the Orestes, Alcmæon, Bellerophon, etc., of Greek legend (v.[8ff.]). Up to v.[12] that motive not only is sufficient, but is the only one naturally suggested to the mind: the expression נָע וָנָד being merely the negative aspect of the curse which drives him from the ground.†

* Instances in Merker, *Die Masai*, pp. 3, 7, 8, 14, 328, etc.

† For a Semitic parallel to this conception of Cain, comp. Doughty's description of the wretched Harb Bedouin who had accidentally slain his antagonist in a wrestling match: "None accused Aly; nevertheless the *mesquin* fled for his life; and he has gone ever since thus armed, lest the kindred of the deceased finding him should kill him" (*Ar. Des.* ii. 293, cited by Stade).

(4) Lastly, in vv.[13-16] he is the representative of the nomad tribes of the desert, as viewed from the standpoint of settled and orderly civilisation. Ewald pointed out the significant circumstance, that at the beginning of the 'second age' of the world's history we find the counterparts of Abel and Cain in the shepherd Jabal and the smith Tubal-Cain (v.[20ff.]). It seems probable that some connexion exists between the two pairs of brothers: in other words, that the story of Cain and Abel embodies a variation of the tradition which assigned the origin of cattle-breeding and metal-working to two sons of Lamech. But to resolve the composite legend into its primary elements, and assign each to its original source, is a task obviously beyond the resources of criticism.

IV. 17–24.—*The line of Cain.*

This genealogy, unlike that of P in ch. 5, is not a mere list of names, but is compiled with the view of showing the origin of the principal arts and institutions of civilised life.* These are: Husbandry (v.[2]; see above), city-life ([17]), [polygamy ([19])?], pastoral nomadism, music and metal-working ([20-22]). The Song of Lamech ([23f.]) may signalise an appalling development of the spirit of blood-revenge, which could hardly be considered an advance in culture; but the connexion of these vv. with the genealogy is doubtful.—It has commonly been held that the passage involves a pessimistic estimate of human civilisation, as a record of progressive degeneracy and increasing alienation from God. That is probably true of the compiler who placed the section after the account of the Fall, and incorporated the Song of Lamech, which could hardly fail to strike the Hebrew mind as an exhibition of human depravity. In itself, however, the genealogy contains no moral judgment on the facts recorded. The names have no sinister significance; polygamy (though a declension from the ideal of 2[24]) is not generally condemned in the OT (Dt. 21[15]); and even the song of Lamech (which is older than the genealogy) implies no condemnation of the reckless and bloodthirsty valour which it celebrates.—The institutions enumerated are clearly

* Gu., however (p. 47), considers the archæological notices to be insertions in the genealogy, and treats them as of a piece with the similar notices in 2[15] 3[7. 21. 23].

those existing in the writer's own day; hence the passage does not contemplate a rupture of the continuity of development by a cataclysm like the Flood. That the representation involves a series of anachronisms, and is not historical, requires no proof (see Dri. *Gen.* 68).—On the relation of the section to other parts of the ch., see p. 98 above: on some further critical questions, see the concluding Note (p. 122 ff.).

17. Enoch and the building of the first city.—The question where Cain got his wife is duly answered in *Jub.* iv. 1, 9: she was his sister, and her name was *'Âwân*. For other traditions, see Marmorstein, '*Die Namen der Schwestern Kains u. Abels*,' etc., *ZATW*, xxv. 141 ff.—*and he became a city-builder*] So the clause is rightly rendered by De. Bu. Ho. Gu. al. (cf. 21^{20b}, Ju. 16^{21}, 2 Ki. 15^{5}). The idea that he happened to be engaged in the building of a city when his son was born would probably have been expressed otherwise, and is itself a little unnatural.

That קַיִן is the subj. of וַיְהִי only appears from the phrase כְּשֵׁם בְּנוֹ towards the end. Bu. (120 ff.) conjectures that the original text was כִּשְׁמוֹ, making Enoch himself the builder of the city called after him (so Ho.). The emendation is plausible: it avoids the ascription to Cain of *two* steps in civilisation—agriculture and city-building; and it satisfies a natural expectation that after the mention of Enoch we should hear what *he* became, not what his father became after his birth,—especially when the subj. of the immediately preceding vbs. is Cain's wife. But the difficulty of accounting for the present text is a serious objection, the motive suggested by Bu. (123) being far-fetched and improbable.—The incongruity between this notice and vv.[11-16] has already been mentioned (p. 100). Lenormant's examples of the mythical connexion of city-building with fratricide (*Origines*², i. 141 ff.) are not to the point; the difficulty is not that the first city was founded by a murderer, but by a nomad. More relevant would be the instances of cities originating in hordes of outlaws, collected by Frazer, as parallels to the peopling of Rome (*Fort. Rev.* 1899, Apr., 650–4). But the anomaly is wholly due to composition of sources: the Cain of the genealogy was neither a nomad nor a fratricide. It has been proposed (Ho. Gu.) to remove [17b] as an addition to the genealogy, on the ground that no intelligent writer would put

---

17. On וירע, see on v.[1].—The vb. חָנַךְ appears from Ar. *ḥanaka* to be a denom. from *ḥanak* (Heb. חֵךְ), and means to rub the palate of a new-born child with chewed dates: hence trop. 'to initiate' (Lane, *s.v.*; We. *Heid.* 173). In Heb. it means to 'dedicate' or 'inaugurate' a house, etc. (Dt. 20^{5}, 1 Ki. 8^{63}: cf. חֲנֻכָּה, Nu. 7^{11}, Neh. 12^{27} etc.); and also to 'teach' (Pr. 22^{6}). See, further, on 5^{18}.

city-building before cattle-rearing; but the Phœnician tradition is full of such anachronisms, and shows how little they influenced the reasoning of ancient genealogists.—The name חֲנוֹךְ occurs (besides $5^{18ff.}$, 1 Ch. 1^{3}) as that of a Midianite tribe in 25^{4} (1 Ch. 1^{33}), and of a Reubenite clan in 46^{9} (Ex. 6^{14}, Nu. 26^{5}, 1 Ch. 5^{3}). It is also said that חנך is a Sabæan tribal name (G-B.[12] *s.v.*),* which has some importance in view of the fact that קֵינָן ($5^{9ff.}$) is the name of a Sabæan deity. As the name of a city, the word would suggest to the Heb. mind the thought of 'initiation' (*v.i.*). The city חנוך cannot be identified. The older conjectures are given by Di. (p. 99); Sayce (*ZKF*, ii. 404; *Hib. Lect.* 185) and Cheyne (*EB*, 624; but see now *TBI*, 106) connect it with *Unuk*, the ideographic name of the ancient Babylonian city of Erech.

18. The next four generations are a blank so far as any advance in civilisation is concerned. The only question of general interest is the relation of the names to those of ch. 5.

On the first three names, see esp. Lagarde, *Orientalia*, ii. 33–38; Bu. *Urg.* 123–9.—עִירָד] 𝔊 Γαιδαδ (=עִידָד), 𝔖 עִירָד (the latter supported by Philo), corresponds to יֶרֶד in $5^{15ff.}$. The initial guttural, and the want of a Heb. etymology, would seem to indicate עירד as the older form which has been Hebraized in ירד; but the conclusion is not certain. If the root be connected with Ar. *'arada* (which is doubtful in view of 𝔊's Γ), the idea might be either 'fugitive' (Di. al.), or 'strength, hardness, courage' (Bu.). Sayce (*ZKF*, ii. 404) suggests an identification with the Chaldean city *Eridu*; Ho. with עֲרָד in the Negeb (Ju. 1^{16} etc.).—The next two names are probably (but not certainly: see Gray, *HPN*, 164 f.) compounds with אֵל. The first is given by MT in two forms, מְחוּיָאֵל and מְחִיָּ[י]אֵל. The variants of 𝔊 are reducible to three types, Μαιηλ (מחייאל), Μαουιηλ (מחויאל), Μαλελεηλ (=מהללאל, $5^{13ff.}$). Lag. considers the last original, though the first is the best attested. Adopting this form, we may (with Bu.) point the Heb. מְחַיֵּי אֵל or מְחִיִּי אֵל='God makes me live': so virtually Philo ἀπὸ ζωῆς θεοῦ, and Jer. *ex vita Deus* (cited by Lag.). Both Mass. forms undoubtedly imply a bad sense: 'destroyed (or smitten) of God' (though the form is absolutely un-Hebraic, see Dri. *Sam.* 14).—מְתוּשָׁאֵל is now commonly explained by Ass. *mutu-ša-ili*, 'Man of God,'† though the relative *ša* presents a difficulty (Gray, *l.c.*). The true 𝔊 reading is Μαθουσαλα (=מְתוּשֶׁלַח, $5^{21ff.}$); Μαθουσαηλ occurs as a correction in some MSS—לָמֶךְ] again inexplicable from Heb. or even Arabic. Sayce (*Hib. Lect.* 186) and Hommel connect it with *Lamga*, a Babylonian name of the moon-god, naturalised in S. Arabia.‡

18. On acc. אֶת with pass. see G-K. § 116 *a*, *b*.—יָלַד in the sense of 'beget' is a sure mark of the style of J (see Ho. *Einl.* 99).—מְחוּ] archaic

* Omitted in 13th edition.

† Lenorm. *Orig.*[2] i. 262 f., Di. Bu. al. Che. *EB*, 625. It does not appear that *mutu-ša-ili* occurs as an *actual* name.

‡ Hommel, *Altisrael. Uberl.* 117 n.: "Lamga ist ein babylonischer

19. The two wives of Lamech.—No judgment is passed on Lamech's bigamy, and probably none was intended. The notice may be due simply to the fact that the names of the wives happened to be preserved in the song afterwards quoted.

Of the two female names by far the most attractive explanation is that of Ew. (*JBBW*, vi. 17), that עָדָה means Dawn (Ar. *ġadin*, but 𝔊 has Ἀδα), and צִלָּה (fem. of צל) Shadow,—a relic of some nature-myth (cf. Lenorm. *Orig.*² 183 f.). Others (Ho.) take them as actual proper names of inferior stocks incorporated in the tribe Lamech; pointing out that עדה recurs in 36²ᶠᶠ· as a Canaanite clan amalgamated with Esau. This ethnographic theory, however, has very little foothold in the passage. For other explanations, see Di. p. 100.

20–22. The sons of Lamech and their occupations.—At this point the genealogy breaks up into three branches, introducing (as Ew. thinks) a second age of the world. But since it is nowhere continued, all we can say is that the three sons represent three permanent social divisions, and (we must suppose) three modes of life that had some special interest for the authors of the genealogy. On the significance of this division, see at the close.—**20.** *Yābāl*, son of ʿAdah, *became the father* (*i.e.* originator: 𝔗ᴼ רַב) *of tent- and cattle-dwellers* (*v.i.*); *i.e.* of nomadic shepherds. מִקְנֶה, however, is a wider term than צאן (v.²), including all kinds of cattle, and even camels and asses (Ex. 9³). The whole Bedouin life is thus assigned to Jabal as its progenitor.—**21.** *Yûbāl*, also a

nom. case (G–K. § 90 *o*) of an old Sem. word (also Egypt. according to Erman) מֵת = 'man' (male, husband, etc.): cf. G–B. *s.v.*

20. יֹשֵׁב אֹהֶל וּמִקְנֶה] 𝔊 *οἰκούντων ἐν σκηναῖς κτηνοτρόφων*, perhaps reading אהלי מקנה as in 2 Ch. 14¹⁵ (so Ball). 𝔙 (*atque pastorum*) takes מִקְנֶה as a ptcp.; 𝔖 inserts ܘܡܪ̈ܝ, and 𝔗ᴼ ומרי, before 'cattle'; similarly Kuenen proposed וקנה מקנה. The zeugma is somewhat hard, but is retained by most comm. for the sake of conformity with v.²¹ᶠ·; G–K. § 117 *bb*, 118 *g*.—**21.** וְשֵׁם אָחִיו] cf. 10²⁵ (J) (1 Ch. 7¹⁶).—אבי וגו׳] 𝔊 *ὁ καταδείξας ψαλτήριον καὶ κιθάραν*.—כִּנּוֹר וְעוּגָב] 𝔙 *cithara et organo*; 𝔖 ܩܝܬܪܐ ܘܩܢܢܐ; 𝔗ᴼ כנורא ואבובא (‖ נבלא). See Benzinger, *Archæol.*², 237–246; We. *Psalms* (*Polychr. Bible*), 219 f., 222 f.; Riehm, *Hdwb.* 1043 ff. The כנור is

Beiname des Sin; daraus machten die Sabäer, mit volksetymologischer Anlehnung an ihr Verbum lamaka (wahrsch. glänzen), einen Plural Almâku."

son of ʿAdah, is the father of *all who handle lyre and pipe*; the oldest and simplest musical instruments. These two occupations, representing the bright side of human existence, have ʿAdah (the Dawn?) as their mother; recalling the classical association of shepherds with music (see Lenorm. i. 207).—**22.** Equally suggestive is the combination of *Tûbal-ḳáyin*, the smith, and *Naʿămāh* (ʻpleasant'), as children of the dark Ẓillah; cf. the union of Hephæstos and Aphrodite in Greek mythology (Di. al.).—The opening words of $^{a\beta}$ are corrupt. We should expect: *he became the father of every artificer in brass and iron* (see footnote). The persistent idea that Tubal-cain was the inventor of weapons, *Ber. R.*, Ra. and most, which has led to a questionable interpretation of the Song, has no foundation. He is simply the metal-worker,

certainly a stringed instrument, played with the hand (1 Sa. 16^{23} etc.), probably the lyre (Greek *κινύρα*). The עוגב (associated with the כנור in Jb. 21^{12} 30^{31}: elsewhere only Ps. 150^{4}) is some kind of wind instrument (𝔙𝔗ᴼ),—a flute or reed-pipe, perhaps the Pan's pipe (*σύριγξ*).—**22.** גם הוא] *in genealogies* (as here, 4^{26} 10^{21} 19^{38} $22^{20.\,24}$ [Ju. 8^{31}]) is characteristic of J.—תובל קין] 𝔊 Θοβελ· *καὶ ἦν*. Other Vns. have the compound name, and on the whole it is probable that *καὶ ἦν* is a corruption of Καιν, although the next cl. has Θοβελ alone.—לֹטֵשׁ וגו׳] 𝔊 *καὶ ἦν σφυροκόπος, χαλκεὺς χαλκοῦ καὶ σιδήρου*, 𝔙 *qui fuit malleator et faber in cuncta opera aer. et f.*; 𝔖 ܘܗܘܐ ܦܛܘܫܐ ܕܟܠ ܕܢܚܫܐ ܘܕܦܪܙܠܐ; 𝔗ᴼ רבהון דכל ידעי עיבידת נ׳ וב׳
To get any kind of sense from MT, it is necessary either (*a*) to take לֹטֵשׁ (ʻsharpener' or ʻhammerer') in the sense of ʻinstructor'; or (*b*) take חֹרֵשׁ as neut. (ʻa hammerer of every cutting implement of,' etc.); or (*c*) adopt the quaint construction (mentioned by Bu. 138): ʻa hammerer of all (sorts of things),—a (successful) artificer in bronze,' etc! All these are unsatisfactory; and neither the omission of כל with 𝔊 (Di.), nor the insertion of אבי before it yields a tolerable text. Bu.'s emendation (139 ff.) ויהי למך חֹרֵשׁ וגו׳ [for קין] is much too drastic, and stands or falls with his utterly improbable theory that Lamech and not Tubal-cain was originally designated as the inventor of weapons. The error must lie in the words קין לטש, for which we should expect, הוא היה אבי (Ols. Ball). The difficulty is to account for the present text: it is easy to say that לטש and קין are glosses, but there is nothing in the v. to require a gloss, and neither of these words would naturally have been used by a Heb. writer for that purpose.—בַּרְזֶל] The Semitic words for ʻiron' (Ass. *parzillu*, Aram. פַּרְזְלָ, ܦܪܙܠܐ, Ar. *farzil*) have no Semitic etymology, and are probably borrowed from a foreign tongue. On the antiquity of iron in W. Asia, see Ridgeway, *Early Age of Gr.* i. 616 ff.

an occupation regarded by primitive peoples as a species of black-art,* and by Semitic nomads held in contempt.

On the names in these vv. see the interesting discussion of Lenorm. *Orig.*² i. 192 ff.—The alliterations, *Yābāl—Yûbāl—Tûbal*, are a feature of legendary genealogies: cf. Arab. Habîl and Ḳabîl, Shiddîd and Shaddâd, Mâlik and Milkân, etc. (Lenorm. 192). יבל (𝔊 'Ιωβελ -ηλ) and יובל ('Ιουβαλ) both suggest יָבֵל (Heb. and Phœn.), which means primarily 'ram,' then 'ram's horn' as a musical instrument (Ex. 19^{13}), and finally 'joyous music' (in the designation of the year of Jubilee). On a supposed connexion of יבל with הֶבֶל in the sense of 'herdsman,' see above, p. 103.—תּובַל is a Japhetic people famous in antiquity for metal-working (see on 10^2); and it is generally held that their *heros eponymus* supplies the name of the founder of metallurgy here; but the equation is doubtful. A still more precarious combination with a word for smith (*tumâl*, *dubalanza*, etc.) in Somali and other East African dialects, has been propounded by Merker (*Die Masai*, 306). The compound תובל קין (written in Oriental MSS as one word) may mean either 'Tubal [the] smith' (in which case קין [we should expect הקין] is probably a gloss), or 'Tubal of (the family of) Cain.'† 𝔊 has simply Θοβελ; but see the footnote. Tuch and others adduce the analogy of the Τελχῖνες, the first workers in iron and brass, and the makers of Saturn's scythe (Strabo, XIV. ii. 7); and the pair of brothers who, in the Phœnician legend, were σιδήρου εὑρεταὶ καὶ τῆς τούτου ἐργασίας.—נַעֲמָה (𝔊 Νοεμα) seems to have been a mythological personage of some importance. A goddess of that name is known to have been worshipped by the Phœnicians.‡ In Jewish tradition she figures as the wife of Noah (*Ber. R.*), as a demon, and also as a sort of St. Cecilia, a patroness of *vocal* music (𝔗: cf. Lag. *OS*, 180, 56: Νοεμὶν ψάλλουσα φωνῇ οὐκ ἐν ὀργάνῳ [Nestle, *MM*, 10]).

23, 24. **The song of Lamech.**—A complete poem in three distichs, breathing the fierce implacable spirit of revenge that forms the chief part of the Bedouin's code of honour. It is almost universally assumed (since Herder) that it commemorates the invention of weapons by Tubal-cain, and is accordingly spoken of as Lamech's 'Sword Song.' But the

---

23. The Introd. of the song is imitated in Is. 28^{23} 32^9; cf. also Dt. 32^1. The words הַאֲזִין and אִמְרָה are almost exclusively poetical.—On the form שְׁמַעַן, see G-K. § 46 *f*.—הָרַגְתִּי is perf. of experience (Dav. § 40 (*c*); Dri. *T.* § 12), rather than of single completed action, or of certainty (IEz. De. Bu. al.).—כִּי is not recitative, but gives the reason for the call to attention. —לְפִצְעִי, לְחַבּוּרָתִי] On this use of לְ, see BDB, *s.v.* 5, f.: 𝔊 εἰς τραῦμα [μώλωπα]

---

* See Andree, *Ethnogr. Parall. u. Vergleiche* (1878), 157.

† So Ew., who thinks the קין belongs to each of the three names

‡ Lenorm. 200 f.; Tiele, *Gesch.* i. 265; Baethgen, *Beitr.* 150.

contents of the song furnish no hint of such an occasion (We.); and the position in which it stands makes its connexion with the genealogy dubious. On that point see, further, below. It is necessary to study it independently, as a part of the ancient legend of Lamech which may have supplied some of the material that has been worked into the genealogy.—The vv. may be rendered:

23 Adah and Zillah, hear my voice!
Wives of Lamech, attend to my word!
For I kill a man for a wound to me,
And a boy for a scar.
24 For Cain takes vengeance seven times,
But Lamech seventy times and seven!

23a. Ho. raises the question whether the words 'Adah and Zillah' belong to the song or the prose introduction; and decides (with 𝔙) for the latter view (so Kittel, *BH*), on the ground that in the remaining lines the second member is shorter than the first (which is not clear). The exordium of the song might then read:

Hear my voice, ye women of Lamech!
Attend to my word!—

the address being not to the wives of an individual chieftain, but to the females of the tribe collectively. It appears to me that the alteration destroys the balance of clauses, and mars the metrical effect: besides, strict syntax would require the repetition of the לְ.—**23b.** The meaning is that (the tribe?) Lamech habitually avenges the slightest personal injury by the death of man or child of the tribe to which the assailant belongs. According to the principle of the blood-feud, איש and ילֶד (י׳ is not a fighting 'youth,'—a sense it rarely bears: 1 Ki. $12^{8ff.}$, Dn. $1^{4ff.}$,—but an innocent man-child [Bu. Ho.]) are not the actual perpetrators of the outrage, but any members of the same clan. The parallelism therefore is not to be taken literally, as if Lamech selected a victim proportionate to the hurt he had received. —**24.** Cain is mentioned as a tribe noted for the fierceness

ἐμοί; 𝔙 *in vulnus* [*livorem*] *meum*.—24. כִּי] again introducing the reason, which, however, "lies not in the words immediately after כי, but in the

of its vendetta (7 times); but the vengeance of Lamech knows no limit (70 and 7 times).

The Song has two points of connexion with the genealogy: the names of the two wives, and the allusion to Cain. The first would disappear if Ho.'s division of [23a] were accepted; but since the ordinary view seems preferable, the coincidence in the names goes to show that the song was known to the authors of the genealogy and utilised in its construction. With regard to the second, Gu. rightly observes that glorying over an *ancestor* is utterly opposed to the spirit of antiquity; the Cain referred to must be a rival contemporary tribe, whose grim vengeance was proverbial. The comparison, therefore, tells decidedly against the unity of the passage, and perhaps points (as Sta. thinks) to a connection between the song and the legendary cycle from which the Cain story of [13ff.] emanated.—The temper of the song is not the primitive ferocity of "a savage of the stone-age dancing over the corpse of his victim, brandishing his flint tomahawk," etc. (Lenorm.); its real character was first divined by We., who, after pointing out the baselessness of the notion that it has to do with the invention of weapons, describes it as "eine gar keiner besonderen Veranlassung bedürftige Prahlerei eines Stammes (Stammvaters) gegen den anderen. Und wie die Araber sich besonders gern ihren Weibern gegenüber als grosse Eisenfresser rühmen, so macht es hier auch Lamech" (*Comp.*[2] 305). On this view the question whether it be a song of triumph or of menace does not arise; as expressing the permanent temper and habitual practice of a tribe, it refers alike to the past and the future. The sense of the passage was strangely misconceived by some early Fathers (perhaps by 𝔊𝔙), who regarded it as an utterance of remorse for an isolated murder committed by Lamech. The rendering of 𝔗O is based on the idea (maintained by Kalisch) that Lamech's purpose was to represent his homicide as justifiable and himself as guiltless: 'I have not slain a man on whose account I bear guilt, nor wounded a youth for whose sake my seed shall be cut off. When 7 generations were suspended for Cain, shall there not be for Lamech his son 70 and 7?' Hence arose the fantastic Jewish legend that the persons killed by Lamech were his ancestor Cain and his own son Tubal-cain (Ra. al.; cf. Jer. *Ep. ad Damasum*, 125).*—The metrical structure of the poem is investigated by Sievers in *Metrische Studien*, i. 404 f., and ii. 12 f., 247 f. According to the earlier and more successful analysis, the song consists of a double tetrameter, followed by two double trimeters. Sievers' later view is vitiated by an attempt to fit the poem into the supposed metrical scheme of the genealogy, and necessitates the excision of עדה וצלה as a gloss.

Apart from v.[23f.], the most remarkable feature of the genealogy is

---

second part of the sentence" (BDB, *s.v.* 3, c): cf. Dt. 18^{14}, Jer. 30^{11}.—יֻקַּם on acc., see G-K. § 29 *g*. The Niph. יִקָּם would yield a better sense: 'avenges himself' (Bu. Di. Ho.).

---

* See, further, Lenorm. *Orig.* i. 186 ff.

the division of classes represented by the three sons of Lamech. It is difficult to understand the prominence given to this classification of mankind into herdsmen, musicians, and smiths, or to imagine a point of view from which it would appear the natural climax of human development. Several recent scholars have sought a clue in the social conditions of the Arabian desert, where the three occupations may be said to cover the whole area of ordinary life. Jabal, the first-born son, stands for the full-blooded Bedouin with their flocks and herds,*—the *élite* of all nomadic-living men, and the 'flower of human culture' (Bu. 146). The two younger sons symbolise the two avocations to which the pure nomad will not condescend, but which are yet indispensable to his existence or enjoyment—smith-work and music (Sta. 232). The obvious inference is that the genealogy originated among a nomadic people, presumably the Hebrews before the settlement in Canaan (Bu.); though Ho. considers that it embodies a specifically Ḳenite tradition in which the eponymous hero Cain appears as the ancestor of the race (so Gordon, *ETG*, 188 ff.).—Plausible as this theory is at first sight, it is burdened with many improbabilities. If the early Semitic nomads traced their ancestry to (peasants and) city-dwellers, they must have had very different ideas from their successors the Bedouin of the present day.† Moreover, the circumstances of the Arabian peninsula present a very incomplete parallel to the classes of vv.[20-22]. Though the smiths form a distinct caste, there is no evidence that a caste of musicians ever existed among the Arabs; and the Bedouin contempt for professional musicians is altogether foreign to the sense of the vv., which certainly imply no disparaging estimate of Jubal's art. And once more, as Sta. himself insists, the outlook of the genealogy is world-wide. Jabal is the prototype of all nomadic herdsmen everywhere, Jubal of all musicians, and Tubal (the Tibareni?) of all metallurgists.—It is much more probable that the genealogy is projected from the standpoint of a settled, civilised, and mainly agricultural community. If (with Bu.) we include vv.[2] and [17b], and regard it as a record of human progress, the order of development is natural: husbandmen, city-dwellers, wanderers [?] (shepherds, musicians, and smiths). The three sons of Lamech represent not the highest stage of social evolution, but three picturesque modes of life, which strike the peasant as interesting and ornamental, but by no means essential to the framework of society.—This conclusion is on the whole confirmed by the striking family likeness between the Cainite genealogy and the legendary Phœnician history preserved by Eusebius from Philo Byblius, and said to be based on an ancient native work by Sanchuniathon. Philo's confused and often inconsistent account is naturally much richer in mythical detail than the Heb. tradition; but the general idea is the same: in each case we have a genealogical list

---

* But against this view, see p. 112 above, and Meyer, *INS*, 303 ff.

† Ho. evades this objection by deleting v.[17b], and reducing the genealogy to a bare list of names; but why should the Ḳenites have interposed a whole series of generations between their eponymous ancestor and the origin of their own nomadic life?

of the legendary heroes to whom the discovery of the various arts and occupations is attributed. Whether the biblical or the Phœnician tradition is the more original may be doubtful; in any case "it is difficult," as Dri. says, "not to think that the Heb. and Phœn. representations spring from a common Canaanite cycle of tradition, which in its turn may have derived at least some of its elements from Babylonia" (*Gen.* p. 74).*

IV. 25, 26.—*Fragmentary Sethite Genealogy.*

The vv. are the beginning of a Yahwistic genealogy (see above, p. 99), of which another fragment has fortunately been preserved in 5^{29} (Noah). Since it is thus seen to have

---

* Cf. Eus. *Præp. Ev.* i. 10 (ed. Heinichen, p. 39 ff.). The Greek text is printed in Müller's *Fragm. Hist. Græc.* iii. 566 f. French translations are given by Lenorm. *Orig.* i. 536 ff., and Lagrange, *Études sur les Religions Semitiques*[1], 362 ff. (the latter with a copious commentary and critical introduction).—The passage in Eusebius is much too long to be quoted in full, but the following extracts will give some idea of its contents and its points of similarity with Gen.: Of the two protoplasts Αἰών and Πρωτόγονος, it is recorded *εὑρεῖν δὲ τὸν Αἰῶνα τὴν ἀπὸ τῶν δένδρων τροφήν*.—The second pair, Γένος and Γενεά, dwelt in Phœnicia, and inaugurated the worship of the sun.—Of the race of Αἰών and Πρωτόγονος were born three mortal children, Φῶς, Πῦρ, and Φλόξ: *οὗτοι ἐκ παρατριβῆς ξύλων εὗρον πῦρ, καὶ τὴν χρῆσιν ἐδίδαξαν*.—Then followed a race of giants, of whom was born [Σα]μημροῦμος (=שמי מרום) *ὁ καὶ* Ὑψουράνιος, who founded Tyre. Of him we read: *καλύβας τε ἐπινοῆσαι ἀπὸ καλάμων, καὶ θρύων, καὶ παπύρων· στασιάσαι δὲ πρὸς τὸν ἀδελφὸν Οὔσωον, ὃς σκέπην τῷ σώματι πρῶτος ἐκ δερμάτων ὧν ἴσχυσε συλλαβεῖν θηρίων εὗρε . . . Δένδρου δὲ λαβόμενον τὸν Οὔσωον καὶ ἀποκλαδεύσαντα, πρῶτον τολμῆσαι εἰς θάλασσαν ἐμβῆναι· ἀνιερῶσαι δὲ δύο στήλας . . . αἷμά τε σπένδειν αὐταῖς ἐξ ὧν ἤγρευε θηρίων*.—The further history of invention names (*a*) Ἀγρεύς and Ἁλιεύς, *τοὺς ἁλείας καὶ ἄγρας εὑρετάς*; (*b*) . . . *δύο ἀδελφοὺς σιδήρου εὑρετὰς, καὶ τῆς τούτου ἐργασίας· ὧν θάτερον τὸν* Χρυσὼρ *λόγους ἀσκῆσαι, καὶ ἐπῳδὰς καὶ μαντείας*; (*c*) Τεχνίτης and Γήϊνος Αὐτόχθων: *οὗτοι ἐπενόησαν τῷ πηλῷ τῆς πλίνθου συμμιγνύειν φορυτὸν, καὶ τῷ ἡλίῳ αὐτὰς τερσαίνειν, ἀλλὰ καὶ στέγας ἐξεῦρον*; (*d*) Ἀγρός and Ἀγρούηρος (or Ἀγρότης): *ἐπενόησαν δὲ οὗτοι αὐλὰς προστιθέναι τοῖς οἴκοις σαὶ περιβόλαια καὶ σπήλαια· ἐκ τούτων ἀγρόται καὶ κυνηγοί*; (*e*) Ἄμυνος and Μάγος: *οἳ κατέδειξαν κῶμας καὶ ποίμνας*; (*f*) Μισώρ (מישר) and Συδύκ (צדק): *οὗτοι τὴν τοῦ ἁλὸς χρῆσιν εὗρον*. (*g*) Of Μισώρ was born Τάαυτ, *ὃς εὗρε τὴν τῶν πρώτων στοιχείων γραφήν*; and (*h*) of Συδύκ, the Διόσκουροι: *οὗτοι, φησὶ, πρῶτοι πλοῖον εὗρον*.—After them came others *οἳ καὶ βοτάνας εὗρον, καὶ τὴν τῶν δακετῶν ἴασιν, καὶ ἐπῳδάς*.—It is impossible to doubt that some traditional elements have been preserved in this extraordinary medley of euhemerism and archæology, however unfavourably it may contrast with the simplicity of the biblical record.

contained the three names (Seth, Enos, Noah) peculiar to the genealogy of P, it may be assumed that the two lists were in substantial agreement, each consisting of ten generations. That that of J was not a dry list of names and numbers appears, however, from every item of it that has survived. The preservation of $4^{25f.}$ is no doubt due to the important notice of the introduction of Yahwe-worship (^{26b}), the redactor having judged it more expedient in this instance to retain J's statement intact. The circumstance shows on how slight a matter far-reaching critical speculations may hang. But for this apparently arbitrary decision of the redactor, the existence of a Sethite genealogy in J would hardly have been suspected; and the whole analysis of the J document into its component strata might have run a different course.

25. *And Adam knew, etc.*] see on v.[1] That יָדַע denotes properly the *initiation* of the conjugal relation (Bu.) is very doubtful: see 38^{26}, 1 Sa. 1^{19}.—*And she called*] see again on v.[1].—*God has appointed me seed*] (the remainder of the v. is probably an interpolation). Cf. 3^{15}. Eve's use of אלהים is not 'surprising' (Di.); it only proves that the section is not from the same source as v.[1]. On the other hand, it harmonises with the fact that in $3^{1ff.}$ אלהים is used in dialogue. It is at least a plausible inference that both passages come from one narrator, who systematically avoided the name יהוה up to 4^{26} (see p. 100).

The v. in its present form undoubtedly presupposes a knowledge of the Cain and Abel narrative of 4^{1-16}; but it is doubtful if the allusions to the two older brothers can be accepted as original (see Bu. 154–159). Some of Bu.'s arguments are strained; but it is important to observe that the word עוֹר is wanting in 𝔊, and that the addition of אחר תחת הבל destroys the sense of the preceding utterance, the idea of *substitution* being quite foreign to the connotation of the vb. שִׁית. The following clause כי הרגו קין reads awkwardly in the mouth of Eve (who would naturally have said אשר ה׳ ק׳), and is entirely superfluous on the part of

---

25. אָדָם] here for the first time unambiguously a prop. name. There is no reason to suspect the text: the transition from the generic to the individual sense is made by P only in 5^{1-3}, and is just as likely to have been made by J.—𝔊 reads Εὔαν in place of עוֹד; 𝔖 has both words.—Before ותלד 𝔊𝔖 insert וַתַּהַר.—ותקרא] 𝔰𝔞𝔪. ויקרא.—כִּי] 𝔊 λέγουσα; so 𝔙 and

the narrator. The excision of these suspicious elements leaves a sentence complete in itself, and exactly corresponding in form to the naming of Cain in v.[1]: שת לי אלהים זרע, 'God has appointed me seed' (*i.e.* posterity). There is an obvious reference to 3^{15}, where both the significant words שית and זרע occur. But this explanation really implies that Seth was the first-born son (according to this writer), and is unintelligible of one who was regarded as a substitute for another. How completely the mind of the glossator is preoccupied by the thought of substitution is further shown by the fact that he does not indicate in what sense Cain has ceased to be the 'seed' of Eve.—As a Heb. word (with equivalents in Phœn. Arab. Syr. Jew.-Aram.: cf. Nö. *Mand. Gr.* p. 98) שֵׁת would mean 'foundation' (not *Setzling*, still less *Ersatz*); but its real etymology is, of course, unknown. Hommel's attempt (*AOD*, p. 26 ff.) to establish a connexion with the second name in the list of Berossus (below, p. 137) involves too many doubtful equations, and even if successful would throw no light on the name. In Nu. 24[17] שֵׁת appears to be a synonym for Moab; but the text is doubtful (Meyer, *INS*, 219). The late Gnostic identification of Seth with the Messiah may be based on the Messianic interpretation of 3^{15}, and does not necessarily imply a Babylonian parallel.

26. On the name אֱנוֹשׁ (= ***Man***, and therefore in all probability the *first* member of an older genealogy), see below.—*Then men began to call, etc.*] Better (with 𝔊, etc., *v.i.*): *He was the first to call on the name of Yahwe* (cf. 9^{20} 10^8), *i.e.* he was the founder of the worship of Yahwe; cf. 12^8 13^4 21^{33} 26^{25} (all J). What historic reminiscence (if any) lies behind this remarkable statement we cannot conjecture; but its significance is not correctly expressed when

---

even 𝔗[O].—26. נם הוא] (G-K. § 135*h*) 𝔊 om.—אֱנוֹשׁ] like אדם, properly a coll.: Enôš is a personification of mankind. The word is rare and mostly poetic in Heb. (esp. Jb. Ps.); but is common in other Sem. dialects (Ar. Aram. Nab. Palm. Sab. Ass.). Nestle's opinion (*MM*, 6 f.), that it is in Heb. an artificial formation from אֲנָשִׁים, and that the genealogy is consequently late, has no sort of probability; the only 'artificiality' in Heb. is the occasional individual use. There is a presumption, however, that the genealogy originated among a people to whom אנוש or its equivalent was the ordinary name for mankind (Aramæan or Arabian).—אז הוחל] so Aq. Σ.; אז החל Sam.; 𝔊 οὗτος ἤλπισεν (from √ יחל) implies either זה החל or הוא ה'; so 𝔙 (*iste coepit*) and *Jub* iv. 12; 𝔖 has ܗܢܐ ܫܪܝ. The true text is that read by 𝔊, etc.; and if the alteration of MT was intentional (which is possible), we may safely restore הוא הֵחֵל after 10^8. The Jewish exegesis takes הוּחַל in the sense 'was profaned,' and finds in the v. a notice of the introduction of idolatry (Jer. *Qu.*, 𝔗[OJ], Ra. al.),—although the construction is absolutely ungrammatical (IEz.).—After יהוה 𝔊 adds carelessly τοῦ θεοῦ.

it is limited to the institution of formal public worship on the part of a religious community (De.); and the idea that it is connected with a growing sense of the distinction between the human and the divine (Ew. De. al.) is a baseless fancy. It means that 'Enôš was the first to invoke the Deity under this name; and it is interesting chiefly as a reflexion, emanating from the school of J, on the origin of the specifically Israelite name of God. The conception is more ingenuous than that of E (Ex. 3^{13-15}) or P (6^3), who base the name on express revelation, and connect it with the foundation of the Hebrew nationality.

The expression קרא בשם י׳ (lit. 'call by [means of] the name of Y.') denotes the essential act in worship, the invocation (or rather *evocation*) of the Deity by the solemn utterance of His name. It rests on the widespread primitive idea that a real bond exists between the person and his name, such that the pronunciation of the latter exerts a mystic influence on the former.* The best illustration is 1 Ki. $18^{24ff.}$, where the test proposed by Elijah is *which name*—Baal or Yahwe—will evoke a manifestation of divine energy.—The cosmopolitan diffusion of the name יהוה, from the Babylonian or Egyptian pantheon, though often asserted,† and in itself not incredible, has not been proved. The association with the name of Enoš might be explained by the supposition that the old genealogy of which Enoš was the first link had been preserved in some ancient centre of Yahwe-worship (Sinai? or Kadesh?).

CH. V.—*The Ante-Diluvian Patriarchs* (P).

In the Priestly Code the interval between the Creation (1^1–2^{4a}) and the Flood ($6^{9ff.}$) is bridged by this list of ten patriarchs, with its chronological scheme fixing the duration of the period (in MT) at 1656 years. The *names* are traditional, as is shown by a comparison of the first three with $4^{25f.}$, and of Nos. 4–9 with $4^{17ff.}$. It has, indeed, been held that the names of the Cainite genealogy were intentionally modified by the author of P, in order to suggest certain

* See Giesebrecht, *Die ATliche Schätzung des Gottesnamens*, esp. p. 25 ff., 98 ff.

† W. M. Müller, *AE*, pp. 239, 312; Del. *Babel* [tr. M'Cormack] p. 61 f.; Bezold, *Die Bab.-Ass. Keilinschr.* etc. p. 31 ff.; Oppert, *ZA*, xvii. 291 ff.; Daiches, *ib.* xxii. (1908), 125 ff.; Algyogyi-Hirsch, *ZATW*, xxiii. 355 ff.; Sta. *BTh.* i. 29; Me. *GA*², i. (2te Hälfte), 545 f. Cf., further, Rogers, *Rel. of Bab. and Ass.* (1908), p. 89 ff.

views as to the character of the patriarchs. But that is at best a doubtful hypothesis, and could only apply to three or four of the number. It is quite probable that if we had the continuation of J's Sethite genealogy, its names would be found to correspond closely with those of ch. 5.—The *chronology*, on the other hand, is based on an artificial system, the invention of which may be assigned either to P or to some later chronologist (see p. 136 below).—What is thoroughly characteristic of P is the *framework* in which the details are set. It consists of (*a*) the age of each patriarch at the birth of his first-born, (*b*) the length of his remaining life (with the statement that he begat other children), and (*c*) his age at death.* The stiff precision and severity of the style, the strict adherence to set formulæ, and the monotonous iteration of them, constitute a somewhat pronounced example of the literary tendencies of the Priestly school of writers.

The distinctive phraseology of P (אֱלֹהִים, בָּרָא, דְּמוּת, זָכָר וּנְקֵבָה) is seen most clearly in vv.[1b. 2], which, however, may be partly composed of glosses based on 1[26ff.] (see on the vv.). Note also תּוֹלְדֹת ([1a]), דְּמוּת, צֶלֶם ([3]), הוֹלִיד (throughout), הִתְהַלֵּךְ אֶת־הָאֱלֹהִים ([22. 24], cf. 6[9]); the syntax of the numerals (which, though not peculiar to P, is a mark of late style: see G–K. § 134 *i*; Dav. § 37, *R*. 3); the naming of the child by the father ([3]).—The one verse which stands out in marked contrast to its environment is [29], which is shown by the occurrence of the name יהוה and the allusion to 3[17] to be an extract from J, and in all probability a fragment of the genealogy whose first links are preserved in 4[25. 26].

"The aim of the writer is by means of these particulars to give a picture of the increasing population of the earth, as also of the duration of the first period of its history, as conceived by him, and of the longevity which was a current element in the Heb. conception of primitive times" (Dri. *Gen.* p. 75). With regard to the extreme longevity attributed to the early patriarchs, it must be frankly recognised that the statements are meant to be understood literally, and that the author had in his view actual individuals. The

* Only in the cases of Adam (v.[3]), Enoch ([22. 24]) and Lamech ([28. 29]) are slight and easily explicable deviations from the stereotyped form admitted. The section on Noah is, of course, incomplete.

attempts to save the historicity of the record by supposing (*a*) that the names are those of peoples or dynasties, or (*b*) that many links of the genealogy have been omitted, or (*c*) that the word שָׁנָה denotes a space of time much shorter than twelve months (see Di. 107), are now universally discredited. The text admits of no such interpretation. It is true that "the study of science precludes the possibility of such figures being literally correct"; but "the comparative study of literature leads us to expect exaggerated statements in any work incorporating the primitive traditions of a people" (Ryle, quoted by Dri. p. 75).

The author of P knows nothing of the Fall, and offers no explanation of the 'violence' and 'corruption' with which the earth is filled when the narrative is resumed (6^{12}). It is doubtful whether he assumes a progressive deterioration of the race, or a sudden outbreak of wickedness on the eve of the Flood; in either case he thinks it unnecessary to propound any theory to account for it. The fact reminds us how little *dogmatic* importance was attached to the story of the Fall in OT times. The Priestly writers may have been repelled by the anthropomorphism, and indifferent to the human pathos and profound moral psychology, of Gen. 3; they may also have thought that the presence of sin needs no explanation, being sufficiently accounted for by the known tendencies of human nature.

Budde (*Urgesch.* 93–103) has endeavoured to show that the genealogy itself contains a cryptic theory of degeneration, according to which the first five generations were righteous, and the last five (commencing with Jered [='descent'], but excepting Enoch and Noah) were wicked. His chief arguments are (*a*) that the names have been manipulated by P in the interest of such a theory, and (*b*) that the Samaritan chronology (which Bu. takes to be the original: see below, p. 135 f.) admits of the conclusion that Jered, Methuselah, and Lamech perished in the Flood.* Budde supports his thesis with close and acute reasoning; but the facts are susceptible of different interpretations, and it is not probable that a writer with so definite a theory to inculcate should have been at such pains to conceal it. At all events it remains true that no explanation is given of the introduction of evil into the world.

* The more rapid decrease of life (in ɱ) after Mahalalel ought not to be counted as an additional argument; because it is a necessary corollary from the date fixed for the Flood.

1, 2.—**Introduction**: consisting of a superscription ([1a]), followed by an account of the creation and naming of Adam ([1b. 2]).—**1a.** *This is the book of the generations of Adam*] See the crit. note below; and on the meaning of תּוֹלְדֹת, see on 2[4a].—**1b.** *When God created Man* (or *Adam*) *he made him in the likeness of God*] a statement introduced in view of the transmission of the divine image from Adam to Seth (v.[3]). On this and the following clauses see, further, 1[26ff.].—**2.** *And called their name Adam*] *v.i.*

The vv. show signs of editorial manipulation. In [1a] אָדָם is presumably a proper name (as in [3ff.]), in [2] it is certainly generic (note the pl. suff.), while in [1b] it is impossible to say which sense is intended. The confusion seems due to an attempt to describe the creation of the first man in terms borrowed almost literally from 1[26ff.], where אדם is generic. Since the only new statement is *and he called their name Adam*, we may suppose the writer's aim to have been to explain how אדם, from being a generic term, came to be a proper name. But he has no clear perception of the relation; and so, instead of starting with the generic sense and leading up to the individual, he resolves the individual into the generic, and awkwardly resumes the proper name in v.[3]. An original author would hardly have expressed himself so clumsily. Ho. observes that the heading זה ספר תולדת אדם reads like the title of a *book*, suggesting that the chapter is the opening section of an older genealogical work used by P as the skeleton of his history; and the fuller formula, as compared with the usual אלה תולדת, at least justifies the assumption that this is the first occurrence of the heading. Di.'s opinion, that it is a combination of the superscription of J's Sethite genealogy with that of P, is utterly improbable. On the whole, the facts point to an amalgamation of two sources, the first using אדם as a designation of the race, and the other as the name of the first man.

3–5. **Adam.**—*begat* [*a son*] *in his likeness, etc.*] (see on 1[26]): implying, no doubt, a transmission of the divine image (v.[1]) from Adam to all his posterity.—6–20. The sections on **Seth, Enoš, Ḳenan, Mahalalel,** and **Yered** rigidly

---

1. For אדם 𝔊 has 1° ἀνθρώπων, 2° Ἀδάμ; 𝔙 conversely 1° *Adam*, 2° *hominem*.—**2.** שְׁמָם] 𝔊^L שְׁמוֹ.—**3.** וַיּוֹלֶד] ins. בֵּן as obj. (Ols. al.). הוֹלִיד confined to P in Pent.; J, and older writers generally, using יָלַד both for 'beget' and 'bear.'—בִּדְמוּתוֹ כְּצַלְמוֹ] 𝔊 κατὰ τὴν εἰδέαν αὐτοῦ καὶ κ. τ. εἰκόνα α.—avoiding ὁμοίωσις (see the note on 1[26]).—**4.** ויהיו ימי אדם] 𝔊^L ins. ἃς ἔζησε, as in v.[5]. 𝔖 reads וַיְחִי אדם (but see Ball's note) as in vv.[7. 10] etc. But vv.[3-5] contain several deviations from the regular formula: note אשר חי in v.[5], and the order of numerals (hundreds before tens). The reverse order is observed elsewhere in the chapter.

observe the prescribed form, and call for no detailed comment, except as regards the names.

6–8. *Šēth*: cf. 4^{25}. For the Jewish, Gnostic, and Mohammedan legends about this patriarch, see Lenorm. *Orig.*^{2} 217–220, and Charles, *Book of Jubilees*, 33 ff. — **9–11.** *'Ĕnôš*: see on 4^{26}. — **12–14.** *Ḳênān* is obviously a fuller form of *Ḳáyin* in the parallel genealogy of $4^{17ff.}$; and possibly, like it, means 'smith' or 'artificer' (cf. Syr. ܩܝܢܝܐ: see on 4^{1}). Whether the longer or the shorter form is the more ancient, we have no means of judging. It is important to note that קינן or קנן is the name of a Sabæan deity, occurring several times in inscriptions: see Mordtmann, *ZDMG*, xxxi. 86; Baethgen, *Beitr.* 127 f., 152.—**15–17.** *Mahălal'ēl* (= 'Praise of God') is a compound with the ἅπ. λεγ. מַהֲלָל (Pr. 27^{21}). But there there the Vns. read the participle; and so 𝔊 must have done here: Μαλελεηλ=מְהַלְלְאֵל, *i.e.* 'Praising God.' Proper names compounded with a ptcp. are rare and late in OT (see Dri. *Sam.* 14^{2}; Gray, *HPN*, 201), but are common in Assyrian. Nestle's inference that the genealogy must be late (*MM*, 7 f.) is not certain, because the word might have been borrowed, or first borrowed and then hebraized: Hommel conjectures (not very plausibly) that it is a corruption of *Amil-Arûru* in the list of Berossus (see *AOD*, 29). 'מ is found as a personal or family name in Neh. 11^{4}.—**18–20.** *Yéred* (1 Ch. 4^{18}) would signify in Heb. 'Descent'; hence the Jewish legend that in his days the angels descended to the earth (*Gen.* 6^{2}): cf. *Jub.* iv. 15; *En.* vi. 6, cvi. 13. On Bu.'s interpretation, see p. 129 above. The question whether יֶרֶד or עִירָד be the older form must be left open. Hommel (30) traces both to an original Babylonian '*I-yarad*= 'descent of fire.'

21–24. The account of **Enoch** contains three extraordinary features: (*a*) The twice repeated וַיִּתְהַלֵּךְ אֶת־הָאֱלֹהִים. In the OT such an expression (used also of Noah, 6^{9}) signifies intimate companionship (1 Sa. 25^{15}), and here denotes a fellowship with God morally and religiously perfect (cf. Mic. 6^{8}, Mal. 2^{6} [הָלַךְ]), hardly differing from the commoner 'walk *before* God' (17^{1} 24^{40}) or '*after* God' (Dt. 13^{5}, 1 Ki. 14^{8}). We shall see, however, that originally it included the idea of initiation into divine mysteries. (*b*) Instead of the usual וַיָּמֹת we read וְאֵינֶנּוּ כִּי־לָקַח אֹתוֹ אֱלֹהִים; *i.e.* he was

---

22. ויתהלך—את־האלהים] 𝔊 εὐηρέστησεν τῷ θεῷ (𝔊^{L} adds καὶ ἔζησεν 'Ενωχ), Σ ἀνεστρέφετο, 𝔖 ܫܦܪ ܠܐܠܗܐ, 𝔗^{O} הליך ברחלתא דיי: Aq. and 𝔙 render literally. The art. before 'א is unusual in P (see $6^{9.\,11}$). The phrase must have been taken from a traditional source, and may retain an unobserved trace of the original polytheism ('with the gods').—**23.** ויהי] Rd ויהיו (MSS, 𝔐𝔊, etc.).—**24.** ואיננו] indicating mysterious disappearance ($37^{29f.}$ $42^{13.\,32.\,36}$ [E] 1 Ki. 20^{40}); see G–K. § 152 *m.*—לקח] 𝔊 μετέθηκεν,

mysteriously translated 'so as not to see death' (He. 11^{5}). Though the influence of this narrative on the idea of immortality in later ages is not to be denied (cf. Ps. 49^{16} 73^{24}), it is hardly correct to speak of it as containing a presentiment of that idea. The immortality of exceptional men of God like Enoch and Elijah suggested no inference as to the destiny of ordinary mortals, any more than did similar beliefs among other nations (Gu.). (*c*) His life is much the shortest of the ante-diluvian patriarchs. It has long been surmised that the duration of his life (365 years) is connected with the number of days in the solar year; and the conjecture has been remarkably verified by the Babylonian parallel mentioned below.

The extraordinary developments of the Enoch-legend in later Judaism (see below) could never have grown out of this passage alone; everything goes to show that the record has a mythological basis, which must have continued to be a living tradition in Jewish circles in the time of the Apocalyptic writers. A clue to the mystery that invests the figure of Enoch has been discovered in Babylonian literature. The 7th name in the list of Berossus is Evedoranchus (see *KAT*[3], 532),—a corruption (it seems certain) of Enmeduranki, who is mentioned in a ritual tablet from the library of Asshurbanipal (K 2486 + K 4364: translated in *KAT*[3], 533 f.) as king of Sippar (city of Šamaš, the sun-god), and founder of a hereditary guild of priestly diviners. This mythical personage is described as a 'favourite of Anu, Bel [and Ea],' and is said to have been received into the fellowship of Šamaš and Ramman, to have been initiated into the mysteries of heaven and earth, and instructed in certain arts of divination which he handed down to his son. The points of contact with the notice in Gen. are (1) the special relation of Enmeduranki to the sun-god (cf. the 365 of v.[23]); and (2) his peculiar intimacy with the gods ('walked with God'): there is, however, no mention of a translation. His initiation into the secrets of heaven and earth is the germ of the later view of Enoch as the patron of esoteric knowledge, and the author of Apocalyptic books. In Sir. 44^{16} he is already spoken of as אות דעת לדור ודור. Comp. *Jub.* iv. 17 ff. (with Charles's note *ad loc.*); and see Lenorm. *Orig.*[2] 223; Charles, *Book of Enoch* (1893), *pass.*

25-27. *Methuselah.*—מְתוּשֶׁלַח commonly explained as 'man of the dart (or weapon),' hence tropically 'man of violence,' which Budde (99)

𝔙 *tulit*, but 𝔗^O אמית. The vb. became, as Duhm (on Ps. 49^{16}) thinks, a technical expression for translation to a higher existence; cf. 2 Ki. 2^{10}, Ps. 49^{16} 73^{24}. The Rabbinical exegesis (𝔗^O, *Ber. R.*, Ra.) understood it of removal by death, implying an unfavourable judgment on Enoch which may be due in part to the reaction of legalism against the Apocalyptic influence.

regards as a deliberate variation of מתושאל (4[18]) intended to suggest the wickedness of the later generations before the Flood (see above, p. 129). Lenormant (247) took it as a designation of Saggitarius, the 9th sign of the Zodiac; according to Hommel, it means 'sein Mann ist das Geschoss' (!), and is connected with the planet Mars.* If the 8th name in the list of Berossus be rightly rendered 'man of Sin (the moon-god),' † a more probable view would be that שֶׁלַח is a divine proper name. Hommel, indeed, at one time regarded it as a corruption of *šarraḫu*, said to be an ancient name of the moon-god ‡ (cf. Cheyne, *EB*, 625, 4412).—**28–31.** *Lamech.*—The scheme is here interrupted by the insertion of v.

29. An extract from J, preserving an oracle uttered by Lamech on the birth of Noah.—*This* (זֶה; cf. זאת in 2[23]) *shall bring us comfort from our labour, and from the toil of our hands* [proceeding] *from the ground, etc.*] The utterance seems to breathe the same melancholy and sombre view of life which we recognise in the Paradise narrative; and Di. rightly calls attention to the contrast in character between the Lamech of this v. and the truculent bravo of 4[23f.].

There is an obvious reference backwards to 3[17] (cf. הָאֲדָמָה—אֲרוּרָה, עִצָּבוֹן). The forward reference cannot be to the Flood (which certainly brought no comfort to the generation for whom Lamech spoke), but to Noah's discovery of vine-culture: 9[20ff.] (Bu. 306 ff. al.). This is true even if the hero of the Flood and the discoverer of wine were traditionally

27. After מתושלח 𝔊 ins. ὃς ἔζησεν (cf. v. [5]).—**29.** יְנַחֲמֵנוּ] 𝔊 διαναπαύσει ἡμᾶς: hence Ball, Ki. יְנִיחֵנוּ. The emendation is attractive on two grounds: (*a*) it yields an easier construction with the following מן; and (*b*) a more correct etymology of the name נֹחַ. The harshness of the etymology was felt by Jewish authorities (*Ber. R.* § 25; cf. Ra.); and We. (*De gent.* 38[3]) boldly suggested that נֹחַ in this v. is a contracted writing of נֹחֵם = 'comforter.'—Whether נֹחַ (always written defectively) be really connected with נוּחַ = 'rest' is very uncertain. If a Heb. name, it will naturally signify 'rest,' but we cannot assume that a name presumably so ancient is to be explained from the Heb. lexicon. The views mentioned by Di. (p. 116) are very questionable. Goldziher (*ZDMG*, xxiv. 207 ff.) shows that in mediæval times it was explained by Arab writers from Ar. *nāḥa*, 'to wail'; but that is utterly improbable.—מִמַּעֲשֵׂנוּ] Some MSS and 𝔐 have מִמַּעֲשֵׂינוּ (pl.); so 𝔊, etc.

* *AOD* [1902], 29. Here *Amemphsinus* is resolved into *Amel-Nisin*: formerly (*PSBA*, xv. [1892–3] 245) Hommel propounded the view now advocated by Zimmern (see next note).

† Zimmern, *KAT*[3], 532.

‡ *Aufs. u. Abh.* ii. [1900] 222. Cheyne (*l.c.*) relies on the fact that *šarḫu* ('all-powerful') is an epithet of various gods (De. *Hdwb.* 690 a).

one person; but the connexion becomes doubly significant in view of the evidence that the two figures were distinct, and belong to different strata of the J document. Di.'s objection, that a biblical writer would not speak of wine as a comfort under the divine curse, has little force: see Ju. 9^{13}, Ps. 104^{15}. — In virtue of its threefold connexion with the story of the Fall, the Sethite genealogy of J, and the incident of $9^{20ff.}$, the v. has considerable critical importance. It furnishes a clue to the disentanglement of a strand of Yahwistic narrative in which these sections formed successive stages.—The fragment is undoubtedly rhythmic, and has assonances which suggest rhyme; but nothing definite can be said of its metrical structure (perhaps 3 short lines of 3 pulses each).

32. The abnormal age of Noah at the birth of his first-born is explained by the consideration that his age at the Flood was a fixed datum ($7^{6.\ 11}$), as was also the fact that no grandchildren of Noah were saved in the ark. The chronologist, therefore, had to assign an excessive lateness *either* to the birth of Shem, *or* to the birth of Shem's first-born.

I. *The Chronology of Ch. 5.*—In this chapter we have the first instance of systematic divergence between the three chief recensions, the Heb., the Samaritan, and the LXX. The differences are best exhibited in tabular form as follows (after Holzinger):

	MT.			Sam. (Jub.).			LXX.			Year (A.M.) of Death.		
	First-born.	Remainder.	Total.	First-born.	Remainder.	Total.	First-born.	Remainder.	Total.	MT.	S.	LXX.
1. Adam	130	800	930	130	800	930	230	700	930	930	930	930
2. Seth	105	807	912	105	807	912	205	707	912	1042	1042	1142
3. Enos	90	815	905	90	815	905	190	715	905	1140	1140	1340
4. Kenan	70	840	910	70	840	910	170	740	910	1235	1235	1535
5. Mahalalel	65	830	895	65	830	895	165	730	895	1290	1290	1690
6. Jered	162	800	962	62	785	847	162	800	962	1422	1307	1922
7. Enoch	65	300	365	65	300	365	165	200	365	987	887	1487
8. Methuselah	187	782	969	67	653	720	167*	802*	969	1656	1307	2256
9. Lamech	182	595	777	53	600	653	188	565	753	1651	1307	2207
10. Noah	500	...	...	500	...	...	500	...	...	...	...	...
Till the Flood	100	...	...	100	...	...	100	...	...	...	...	...
Year of the Flood	1656	...	...	1307	...	...	2242	...	...	...	...	...

* So $\mathfrak{G}^L$. $\mathfrak{G}^A$ and other MSS have 187 : 782; but this is a later correction.

These differences are certainly not accidental. They are due to carefully constructed artificial systems of chronology; and the business of criticism is first to ascertain the principles on which the various schemes are based, and then to determine which of them represents the original chronology of the Priestly Code. That problem has never been satisfactorily solved; and all that can be done here is to indicate the more important lines of investigation along which the solution has been sought.

1. Commencing with the MT, we may notice (*a*) the remarkable relation discovered by Oppert * between the figures of the biblical account and those of the list of Berossus (see the next note). The Chaldean chronology reckons from the Creation to the Flood 432,000 years, the MT 1656 years. These are in the ratio (as nearly as possible) of 5 solar years (of 365¼ days) to 1 week. We might, therefore, suppose the Heb. chronologist to have started from the Babylonian system, and to have reduced it by treating each *lustrum* (5 years) as the equivalent of a Heb. week. Whether this result be more than a very striking coincidence it is perhaps impossible to say. (*b*) A widely accepted hypothesis is that of von Gutschmid,† who pointed out that, according to the Massoretic chronology, the period from the Creation to the Exodus is 2666 years: ‡ *i.e.* 26⅔ generations of 100 years, or ⅔ of a world-cycle of 4000 years. The subdivisions of the period also show signs of calculation: the duration of the Egyptian sojourn was probably traditional; half as long (215 years) is assigned to the sojourn of the patriarchs in Canaan: from the Flood to the birth of Abraham, and from the latter event to the descent into Egypt are two equal periods of 290 years each, leaving 1656 years from the Creation to the Flood. (*c*) A more intricate theory has been propounded by Bousset (*ZATW*, xx. 136–147). Working on lines marked out by Kuenen (*Abhandlungen*, tr. by Budde, 108 ff.), he shows, from a comparison of 4 Esd. $9^{38ff.}$ $10^{45f.}$, Jos. *Ant.* viii. 61 f., x. 147 f., and *Ass. Mosis*, 1^{2} 10^{12}, that a chronological computation current in Jewish circles placed the establishment of the Temple ritual in A.M. 3001, the Exodus in 2501, the migration of Abraham in 2071; and divided this last interval into an Ante-diluvian and Post-diluvian period in the ratio of 4 : 1 (1656 : 414 years). Further, that this system differed from MT only in the following particulars: For the birth year of Terah (Gn. 11^{24}) it substituted (with 𝔊 and 𝔪) 79 for 29; with the same authorities it assumed 215 (instead of 430) years as the duration of the Egyptian sojourn (Ex. 12^{40}); and, finally, it dated the dedication of the Temple 20 years after its foundation (as 1 Ki. 6^{1} 𝔊). For the details of the scheme, see the art. cited above.

* *GGN*, 1877, 201–223; also his art. in *Jewish Enc.* iv. 66 f.

† See Nö. *Unters.* 111 ff.; We. *Prol.*[6] 308.

‡ Made up as follows:—1656 + 290 (Flood to birth of Abraham: see the Table on p. 233) + 100 (birth of Isaac: Gn. 21^{5}) + 60 (birth of Jacob: 25^{26}) + 130 (age of Jacob at Descent to Egypt: $47^{9.28}$) + 430 (sojourn in Egypt: Ex. 12^{40}) = 2666.—The number of generations from Adam to Aaron is actually 26, the odd ⅔ stands for Eleazar, who was of mature age at the time of the Exodus

These results, impressive as they are, really settle nothing as to the priority of the MT. It would obviously be illegitimate to conclude that of *b* and *c* one must be right and the other wrong, or that that which is preferred must be the original system of P. The natural inference is that both were actually in use in the first cent. A.D., and that consequently the text was in a fluid condition at that time. A presumption in favour of MT would be established only if it could be shown that the numbers of 𝔖 and 𝔊 are either dependent on MT, or involve no chronological scheme at all.

2. The Sam. Vn. has 1307 years from the Creation to the Flood. It has been pointed out that if we add the 2 years of Gn. 11^{10}, we obtain from the Creation to the birth of Arpachshad 187 × 7 years; and it is pretty obvious that this reckoning by year-weeks was in the mind of the writer of *Jub.* (see p. 233 f.). It is worth noting also that if we assume MT of Ex. 12^{40} to be the original reading (as the form of the sentence renders almost certain), we find that 𝔖 counts from the Creation to the entrance into Canaan 3007 years.* The odd 7 is embarrassing; but if we neglect it (see Bousset, 146) we obtain a series of round numbers whose relations can hardly be accidental. The entire period was to be divided into three decreasing parts (1300 + 940 + 760 = 3000) by the Flood and the birth of Abraham; and of these the second exceeds the third by 180 years, and the first exceeds the second by (2 × 180 =) 360. Shem was born in 1200 A.M., and Jacob in 2400. Since the work of P closed with the settlement in Canaan, is it not possible that this was his original chronological period; and that the systems of MT (as explained by von Gutschmid and Bousset) are due to redactional changes intended to adapt the figures to a wider historical survey? A somewhat important objection to the originality of 𝔖 is, however, the disparity between ch. 5 and $11^{10ff.}$ with regard to the ages at the birth of the first-born.

3. A connexion between 𝔊 and 𝔖 is suggested by the fact that the first period of 𝔊 (2242) is practically equivalent to the first two of 𝔖 (1300 + 940 = 2240), though it does not appear on which side the dependence is. Most critics have been content to say that the 𝔊 figures are enhancements of those of MT in order to bring the biblical chronology somewhat nearer the stupendous systems of Egypt or Chaldæa. That is not probable; though it does not seem possible to discover any distinctive principle of calculation in 𝔊. Klostermann (*NKZ*, v. 208–247 [= *Pent.* (1907) 1–41]), who defends the priority of 𝔊, finds in it a reckoning by jubilee periods of 49 years; but his results, which are sufficiently ingenious, are attained by rather violent and arbitrary handling of the data. Thus, in order to adjust the ante-diluvian list to his theory, he has to reject the 600 years from the birth of Noah to the Flood, and substitute the 120 years of Gn. 6^3! This reduces the reckoning of 𝔊 to 1762 years, and, adding 2 years for the Flood, we obtain 1764 = 3 × 12 × 49.

See, further, on $11^{10ff.}$ (p. 234 f.).

---

* 1307 + 940 (see p. 233) + 290 (as before) + 430 + 40 = 3007.

II. *The Ten Ante-diluvian Kings of Berossus.*—The number *ten* occurs with singular persistency in the traditions of many peoples * as that of the kings or patriarchs who reigned or lived in the mythical age which preceded the dawn of history. The Babylonian form of this tradition is as yet known only from a passage of Berossus extracted by Apollodorus and Abydenus; † although there are allusions to it in the inscriptions which encourage the hope that the cuneiform original may yet be discovered.‡ Meanwhile, the general reliability of Berossus is such, that scholars are naturally disposed to attach considerable importance to any correspondence that can be made out between his list and the names in Gn. 5. A detailed analysis was first published by Hommel in 1893,§ another was given by Sayce in 1899.‖ The first-named writer has subsequently abandoned some of his earlier proposals,¶ substituting others which are equally tentative; and while some of his combinations are regarded as highly problematical, others have been widely approved.**

The names of the Kings before the Flood in Berossus are: 1. Ἄλωρος, 2. Ἀλάπαρος, 3. Ἀμήλων [Ἀμίλλαρος], 4. Ἀμμένων, 5. Μεγάλαρος [Μεγάλανος], 6. Δάωνος [Δάως], 7. Εὐεδώραχος, 8. Ἀμέμψινος, 9. Ὠτιάρτης [Rd. Ὠπάρτης], 10. Ξίσουθρος. Of the suggested Bab. equivalents put forward by Hommel, the following are accepted as fairly well established by Je. and (with the exception of No. 1) by Zimmern: 1. *Aruru* (see p. 102), 2. *Adapa* (p. 126), 3. *Amelu* (=Man), 4. *Ummanu* (='workman'), 7. *Enmeduranki* (p. 132), 8. *Amel-Sin* (p. 133), 9. *Ubar-Tutu* (named as father of Ut-Napištim), and 10. *Ḫasisatra*, or *Atraḫasis* (='the superlatively Wise,'—a title applied to Ut-Napištim, the hero of the Deluge). On comparing this selected list with the Heb. genealogy, it is evident that, as Zimmern remarks, the Heb. *name* is in no case borrowed directly from the Bab. In two cases, however, there seems to be a connexion which might be explained by a *translation* from the one language into the other: viz. 3. אֱנוֹשׁ (=Man), and 4. קֵינָן (='workman'); while 8 is in both series a compound of which the first element means 'Man.' The parallel between 7. חֲנוֹךְ ‖ *Enmeduranki*, has already been noted (p. 132); and the 10th name is in both cases that of the hero of the Flood. Slight as these coincidences are, it is a mistake to minimise their significance. When we have two parallel lists of equal length, each terminating with the hero of the Flood, each having the name for 'man' in the 3rd place and a special favourite of the gods in the 7th, it is too much to ask us to dismiss the correspondence as fortuitous. The historical connexion between the two traditions is still

* Babylonians, Persians, Indians, Phœnicians, Egyptians, Chinese, etc. See Lüken, *Traditionen*, 146 ff.; Lenorm. *Orig.* i. 224 ff.

† Preserved by Eus. *Chron.* [ed. Schœne) i. 7 ff., 31 f. See Müller, *Frag. Hist. Græc.* ii. 499 f.

‡ See Je. *ATLO*², 221 f.

§ *PSBA*, xv. 243–246.

‖ *Exp. Times*, 1899, 353.

¶ *AOD* [1902], 23 ff.

** See Zimmern, *KAT*³, 531 ff.; Dri. *Gen.* 50 f.; Nikel, *Gen. u. Kschrfrsch.* 164 ff.

obscure, and is complicated by the double genealogy of ch. 4; but that a connexion exists it seems unreasonable to deny.

III. *Relation of the Sethite and Cainite Genealogies.*—The substantial identity of the names in Gn. 4[1. 17. 18] with Nos. 3–9 of ch. 5 seems to have been first pointed out by Buttmann (*Mythologus*, i. 170 ff.) in 1828, and is now universally recognised by scholars. A glance at the following table shows that each name in the Cainite series corresponds to a name in the other, which is either absolutely the same, or is the same in meaning, or varies but slightly in form:

Sethite.	Cainite.
1. 'Ādām	
2. Šēth	
3. 'Ĕnôš (Man)	'Ādām (Man)
4. Ḳênān	Ḳáyin
5. Mahălal'ēl	Hănôkh
6. Yéred	'Îrād
7. Ḥănôkh	Mĕḥûyā'ēl
8. Mĕthû-šelaḥ	Mĕthû-šā-'ēl
9. Lémekh	Lémekh
10. Nōăḥ	

Sons of Nōăḥ: Šēm, Ḥām, Yépheth

Sons of Lémekh: Yābāl, Yûbāl, Tûbal-Ḳáyin.

While these resemblances undoubtedly point to some common original, the variations are not such as can be naturally accounted for by direct borrowing of the one list from the other. The facts that each list is composed of a perfect number, and that with the last member the single stem divides into three branches, rather imply that both forms were firmly established in tradition before being incorporated in the biblical documents. If we had to do merely with the Hebrew tradition, the easiest supposition would perhaps be that the Cainite genealogy and the kernel of the Sethite are variants of a single original which might have reached Israel through different channels;* that the latter had been expanded by the addition of two names at the beginning and one at the end, so as to bring it into line with the story of the Flood, and the Babylonian genealogy with which it was linked. The difficulty of this hypothesis arises from the curious circumstance that in the Berossian list of kings, just as in the Sethite list of patriarchs, the name for 'Man' occupies the *third* place. It is extremely unlikely

* Hommel's view (*AOD*, 29 f.) is that the primary list was Chaldean, that the Sethite list most nearly represents this original, and that the Cainite springs from a modification of it under Babylonian influence. It would be quite as plausible to suggest that the Cainite form came through Phœnicia (see the notes on Jabal, Tubal, and Na'amah), and the Sethite from Arabia (Enos, Kenan, Hanokh [?], Methuselah).

that such a coincidence should be accidental; and the question comes to be whether the Assyriologists or the biblical critics can produce the most convincing explanation of it. Now Hommel (*AOD*, 26 ff.) argues that if the word for Man is preceded by two others, these others must have been names of superhuman beings; and he thinks that his interpretation of the Bab. names bears out this anticipation. The first, *Aruru*, is the creative earth-goddess, and the second, *Adapa* (=Marduk) is a sort of Logos or Demiurge—a being intermediate between gods and men, who bears elsewhere the title *zir amiluti* ('seed of mankind') but is not himself a man.* And the same thing must, he considers, hold good of Adam and Seth: Adam should be read אֲדָם, a personification of the earth, and Seth is a mysterious semi-divine personality who was regarded even in Jewish tradition as an incarnation of the Messiah. If these somewhat hazardous combinations be sound, then, of course, the inference must be accepted that the Sethite genealogy is dependent on the Bab. original of Berossus, and the Cainite can be nothing but a mutilated version of it. It is just conceivable, however, that the Bab. list is itself a secondary modification of a more primitive genealogy, which passed independently into Heb. tradition.†

VI. 1–4.—*The Origin of the Nĕphîlîm.*

This obscure and obviously fragmentary narrative relates how in the infancy of the human race marriage alliances were believed to have been formed by supernatural beings with mortal women (vv.[1.2]); and how from these unnatural unions there arose a race of heroes or demi-gods (v.[4]), who must have figured largely in Hebrew folklore. It is implied, though not expressly said, that the existence of such beings, intermediate between the divine and the human, introduced

---

* But against this interpretation of the phrase, see Jen. *KIB*, vi. 1, 362.

† Thus, it might be conjectured that the original equivalent of *Aruru* was not Adam but *Ḥavvah*, as earth and mother-goddess (see pp. 85 f., 102), and that this name stood at the head of the list. That in the process of eliminating the mythological element Ḥavvah should in one version become the wife, in another remain the mother, of the first man (Adam or Enoš), is perfectly intelligible; and an amalgamation of these views would account for the duplication of Adam-Enos in $4^{25f.}$ 5. The insertion of a link (Seth-Adapa) between the divine ancestress and the first man is a difficulty; but it might be due to a survival of the old Semitic conception of mother and son as associated deities (Rob. Sm. KM^2, 298 ff.). It is obvious that no great importance can be attached to such guesses, which necessarily carry us back far beyond the range of authentic tradition.

an element of disorder into the Creation which had to be checked by the special interposition of Yahwe (v.[3]).

The fragment belongs to the class of ætiological myths. The belief in Nĕphîlîm is proved only by Nu. 13^{33} (E?); but it is there seen to have been associated with a more widely attested tradition of a race of giants surviving into historic times, especially among the aboriginal populations of Canaan (Dt. 1^{28} $2^{10.11.21}$ 9^2, Jos. 15^{14}, Am. 2^9 etc.). The question was naturally asked how such beings came to exist, and the passage before us supplied the answer. But while the ætiological motive may explain the retention of the fragment in Gn., it is not to be supposed that the myth originated solely in this reflexion. Its pagan colouring is too pronounced to permit of its being dissociated from two notions prevalent in antiquity and familiar to us from Greek and Latin literature: viz. (1) that among the early inhabitants of the earth were men of gigantic stature;* and (2) that marriages of the gods with mortals were not only possible but common in the heroic age.† Similar ideas were current among other peoples. The Ḳoran has frequent references to the peoples of ʿAd and Thamûd, primæval races noted for their giant stature and their daring impiety, to whom were attributed the erection of lofty buildings and the excavation of rock-dwellings, and who were believed to have been destroyed by a divine judgment.‡ The legend appears also in the Phœnician traditions of Sanchuniathon, where it is followed by an obscure allusion to promiscuous sexual intercourse which appears to have some remote connexion with Gn. 6^2.§

That the *source* is J is not disputed.‖ Di., indeed, following Schrader (*Einl.* 276), thinks it an extract from E which had passed through the hands of J; but borrowing by the original J from the other source is impossible, and the only positive trace of E would be the word נפילים, which in Nu. 13^{33} is by some critics assigned to E. That argument would at most prove overworking, and it is too slight to be considered.—The precise position of the fragment among the Yahwistic traditions

---

* Hom. *Il.* v. 302 f.; Herod. i. 68; Paus. i. 35. 5 f., viii. 29. 3; 32. 4; Lucret. ii. 1151; Virg. *Aen.* xii. 900; Pliny, *HN*, vii. 73 ff. etc. Cf. Lenorm. *Orig.*[2] i. 350 ff.

† Hom. *Il.* xii. 23: ἡμιθέων γένος ἀνδρῶν; Plato, *Cratylus*, 33: πάντες [sc. οἱ ἥρωες] δήπου γεγόνασιν ἐρασθέντος ἢ θεοῦ θνητῆς ἢ θνητοῦ θεᾶς (text uncertain): see Jowett, i. 341.

‡ *Sur.* vii, xv, xxvi, xli, xlvi, lxxxix: see Sale, *Prelim. Disc.* § 1.

§ Euseb. *Præp. Ev.* i. 10 (see p. 124 above): ἀπὸ γένους Αἰῶνος καὶ Πρωτογόνου γεννηθῆναι αὖθις παῖδας θνητούς, οἷς εἶναι ὀνόματα Φῶς καὶ Πῦρ καὶ Φλόξ . . . υἱοὺς δὲ ἐγέννησαν οὗτοι μεγέθει τε καὶ ὑπεροχῇ κρείσσονας . . . ἐκ τούτων, φησίν, ἐγεννήθη Σαμημροῦμος ὁ καὶ Ὑψουράνιος· ἀπὸ μητέρων δέ, φησίν, ἐχρημάτιζον τῶν τότε γυναικῶν ἀνέδην μισγομένων οἷς ἂν ἐ[ν]τύχοιεν.

‖ The literary indications are not absolutely decisive (except יהוה, v.[3]); but the following expressions, as well as the structure of the sentences (in v.[1f.]), are, on the whole, characteristic of J: הֵחֵל, עַל־פְּנֵי הָאֲדָמָה (1), הָיָה בָּאָרֶץ, גִּבּוֹר (4): see Bu. *Urgesch.* 6 ff., 39 A.

cannot be determined. The introductory clause "when mankind began to multiply," etc., suggests that it was closely preceded by an account of the creation of man. There is, however, no reason why it should not have followed a genealogy like that of 4^{17-24} or $4^{25f.}$ (against Ho.), though certainly not that of P in ch. 5. The idea that it is a parallel to the story of the Fall in ch. 3 (Schr. Di. We. Schultz) has little plausibility, though it would be equally rash to affirm that it *presupposes* such an account.—The disconnectedness of the narrative is probably due to drastic abridgment either by the original writer or later editors, to whom its crudely mythological character was objectionable, and who were interested in retaining no more than was needful to account for the origin of the giants.

There remains the question whether the passage was from the first an introduction to the story of the Deluge. That it has been so regarded from a very early time is a natural result of its present position. But careful examination fails to confirm that impression. The passage contains nothing to suggest the Flood as its sequel, except on the supposition (which we shall see to be improbable) that the 120 years of v.[3] refer to an impending judgment on the whole human race. Even if that view were more plausible than it is, it would still be remarkable that the story of the Flood makes no reference to the expiry of the allotted term; nor to any such incident as is here recorded. The critical probability, therefore, is that 6^{1-4} belongs to a stratum of J which knows nothing of a flood (p. 2 ff.). The Babylonian Flood-legend also is free from any allusion to giants, or mingling of gods and men. O. Gruppe, however (*Philologus*, Neue Folge, i. 93 ff.; *ZATW*, ix. 134 ff.), claims to have recovered from Greek sources a Phœnician legend of intermarriages between deities and mortals, which presents some striking affinities with Gn. 6^{1-4}, and which leads up to an account of the Flood. Of the soundness of Gruppe's combinations I am unable to judge; but he himself admits that the Flood is a late importation into Greek mythology, and indeed he instances the passage before us as the earliest literary trace of the hypothetical Phœnician legend. Even, therefore, if his speculations be valid, it would have to be considered whether the later form of the myth may not have been determined partly by Jewish influence, and whether the connexion between the divine intermarriages and the Flood does not simply reproduce the sequence of events given in Gn. That this is not inconceivable is shown by the fact that on late Phrygian coins the biblical name ΝΩ appears as that of the hero of the Deluge (see p. 180 below).

1, 2. The sense of these vv. is perfectly clear. The *sons of God* (בני האלהים) are everywhere in OT members (but probably inferior members) of the divine order, or (using the word with some freedom) *angels* (*v.i.*).

---

1. וַיְהִי כִּי] peculiar to J in Hex.; 26^8 27^1 43^{21} 44^{24}, Ex. 1^{21} 13^{15}, Jos. 17^{13}. See Bu. 6. The apodosis commences with v.[2].—הֵחֵל] see

"The angels are not called 'sons of God' as if they had actually derived their nature from Him as a child from its father; nor in a less exact way, because though created they have received a nature similar to God's, being spirits; nor yet as if on account of their steadfast holiness they had been adopted into the family of God. These ideas are not found here. The name *Elohim* or *sons* (*i.e.* members of the race) *of the Elohim* is a name given directly to angels in contrast with men . . . the name is given to God and angels in common; He is Elohim pre-eminently, they are Elohim in an inferior sense" (Davidson, *Job, Camb. Bible*, p. 6).

In an earlier polytheistic recension of the myth, they were perhaps called אלהים simply. It is only a desire to save the credibility of the record as literal history, that has prompted the untenable interpretations mentioned in the note below.—**2.** These superhuman beings, attracted by the beauty of *the daughters of men* (*i.e.* mortal women) *took to themselves as wives* (strictly implying permanent marriages, but this must not be pressed) *whomsoever they chose.* No sin is imputed to mankind or to their daughters

---

Ho. *Einl.* 97.—על־פני האדמה] see *Oxf. Hex.* i. 187.—**2.** בני [ה]אלהים] Jb. 1^6 2^1 38^7, [Dn. 3^{25}]; cf. ב׳ אלים, Ps. 29^1 89^7. In all these places the superhuman character of the beings denoted is evident,—'belonging to the category of the gods.' On this Semitic use of בן, see Rob. Sm. *KM*², 17; *Pr.*² 85, 389 f. (1) The phrase is so understood by 𝔊 (οἱ ἄγγελοι [also υἱοὶ] τοῦ θεοῦ), Θ, *Jub.* v. 1, En. vi. 2 ff. (Jude ⁶, 2 Pe. 2^4), Jos. *Ant.* i. 73; Fathers down to Cyprian and Lactantius, and nearly all moderns. [𝔖 transliterates ܒܢܝ ܐܠܘܗܝܡ as in Jb. 1^6 2^1.] (2) Amongst the Jews this view was early displaced by another, according to which the 'sons of the gods' are members of aristocratic families in distinction from women of humble rank: 𝔗ᴼᴶ (בני רברביא), Σ (τ. δυναστευόντων), *Ber. R.*, Ra. IEz. [Aq. (υἱοὶ τ. θεῶν) is explained by Jer. as '*deos* intelligens *sanctos* sive *angelos*']. So Spinoza, Herder, al. (3) The prevalent Christian interpretation (on the rise of which see Charles's valuable Note, *B. of Jub.* 33 ff.) has been to take the phrase in an ethical sense as denoting pious men of the line of Seth: Jul. Afr., most Fathers, Luth., Calv. al.: still maintained by Strack. Against both these last explanations it is decisive that בנות האדם cannot have a narrower reference in v.² than in v.¹; and that consequently בני ה׳ cannot denote a section of mankind. For other arguments, see Lenormant, *Orig.*² 291 ff.; the Comm. of De. (146 ff.), Di. (119 f.), or Dri. (82 f.). On the eccentric theory of Stuart Poole, that the sons of God were a wicked pre-Adamite race, see Lenorm. 304 ff.—ויקחו . . . נשים] = 'marry': 4^{19} 11^{29} 25^1 36^2 etc.—מכל אשר] '*consisting of* all whom,'—the rare מן *of explication*; BDB, *s.v.* **3b** (e); cf. G–K. § 119 *w*²: Gn. 7^{22} 9^{10}.

in these relations. The guilt is wholly on the side of the angels; and consists partly, perhaps, in sensuality, partly in high-handed disregard of the rights of God's lower creatures.—It is to be noted, in contrast with analogous heathen myths, that the divine element is exclusively masculine.

3. A divine sentence on the human race, imposing a limit on the term of man's life.—*My spirit shall not*

3. יהוה] 𝔊 Κύριος ὁ θεός.—יָדוֹן] There are two traditional interpretations: (*a*) 'abide': so 𝔊 (καταμείνῃ), 𝔙𝔖𝔗^O; (*b*) 'judge' (Σ. κρινεῖ: so 𝔗^J). The former is perhaps nothing more than a plausible guess at the meaning, though a variant text has been suspected (ילון, ידור, יִכּוֹן, etc.). The latter traces the form to the √ דין; but the etymology is doubtful, since that √ shows no trace of med. ו in Heb. (Nö. *ZDMG*, xxxvii. 533 f.); and to call it a juss. or intrans. form is an abuse of grammatical language (see G–K. § 71 *r*). A Jewish derivation, mentioned by IEz. and Calv., connects the vb. with נָדָן, 'sheath' (1 Ch. 21^{27}),—the body being compared to the sheath of the spirit. The Ar. *dāna* (med. *w*) = 'be humbled' or 'degraded,' yields but a tolerable sense (Tu. Ew. al.); the Egypt. Ar. *dāna*, which means 'to do a thing continually' (Socin; see G–B. *s.v.*), would suit the context well, but can hardly be the same word. Vollers (*ZA*, xiv. 349 ff.) derives it from √ דנן, Ass. *danânu* = 'be powerful'; the idea being that the life-giving spirit shall no longer have the same force as formerly, etc. It would be still better if the vb. could be taken as a denominative from Ass. *dinânu*, 'bodily appearance,' with the sense "shall not be embodied in man for ever."—בָּאָדָם] 𝔊 ἐν τοῖς ἀνθρώποις τούτοις, whence Klostermann restores באדם הַזֶּה,* = 'this humanity,' as distinguished from that originally created,—an impossible exegesis, whose sole advantage is that it gives a meaning to the גַּם in בְּשַׁגָּם (*v.i.*).—לא—לְעוֹלָם (thus separated)] here = 'not . . . for ever,' as Jer. 3^{12}, La. 3^{31}; elsewhere (Ps. 15^{5} etc.) the phrase means 'never.'—בְּשַׁגָּם] so pointed in the majority of MSS, is inf. const. of שָׁגַג, 'err,' with suff. This sense is adopted by many (Tu. Ew. Bu. Ho. al.), but it can hardly be right. If we refer the suff. to הָאָדָם, the *enallage numeri* ('through *their* erring *he* is flesh') would be harsh, and the idea expressed unsuitable. If we refer it to the angels, we can avoid an absurdity only by disregarding the accents and joining the word with what precedes: 'shall not (abide?) in man for ever on account of their (the angels') erring; he is flesh, and,' etc. The sentence is doubly bad in point of style: the first member is overloaded at the end by the emphatic word; and the second opens awkwardly without a connecting part. Moreover, it is questionable if the idea of שגג (inadvertent transgression) is appropriate in the connexion. Margoliouth (*Expositor*, 1898, ii. 33 ff.) explains the obscure

* Already proposed by Egli (cited by Bu.).

[. . . *in*?] *man for ever;* [. . . ?] ***he is flesh, and his days shall be* 120 *years.***

A complete exegesis of these words is impossible, owing first to the obscurity of certain leading expressions (see the footnote), and second to the want of explicit connexion with what precedes. The record has evidently undergone serious mutilation. The original narrative must have contained a statement of the effects on human life produced by the superhuman alliances,—and that opens up a wide field of speculation;*—and possibly also an account of the judgment on the sons of God, the really guilty parties in the transaction. In default of this guidance, all that can be done is to determine as nearly as possible the general sense of the v., assuming the text to be fairly complete, and a real connexion to exist with vv.[1. 2].—(i.) Everything turns on the meaning of the word רוּחַ, of which four interpretations have been given: (1) That רוּחִי is the Spirit of Yahwe as an *ethical* principle, striving against and 'judging' the prevalent corruption of men (as in Is. 63^{10}); so ΣTJ, Luther, al. There is nothing to suggest that view except the particular acceptation of the vb. ידון associated with it, and it is now practically abandoned. (2) Even less admissible is the conception of Klostermann, who understands רוּחִי subjectively of the divine feeling (*Gemüt*) excited by human sin † (similarly Ra.). (3) The commonest view in modern times (see Di.) has been that רוּחַ is the divine principle

word by Aeth. *shegā*='body'; but the proposed rendering, 'inasmuch as their body (or substance) is flesh,' is not grammatically admissible. The correct Mass. reading is בְּשַׁגָּם (*i.e.* גַּם+שֶׁ+בְּ)=***inasmuch as he too.*** The objections to this are (*a*) that the rel. שֶׁ is never found in Pent., and is very rare in the older literature (Ju. 5^7 6^{17} 7^{12} 8^{26}), while compounds like בְּ׳ do not appear before Eccl. (*e.g.* 2^{16}); and (*b*) that the גַּם has no force, there being nothing which serves as a contrast to הוּא. We. observes that בְּ׳ must represent a causal particle and possibly nothing more. The old translators, 𝔊 (διὰ τὸ εἶναι αὐτοὺς) 𝔖𝔙𝔗^O seem to have been of the same opinion; and it is noticeable that none of them attempt to reproduce the גַּם. The conjectures of Ols. ((לָבַשׁ גַּם), Cheyne (בְּמִשְׁכְּנוֹת בָּשָׂר), and others are all beside the mark.—והיו ימיו וגו׳] The only natural reference is to the (maximum) term of human life (so Jos. Tu. Ew. and most since), a man's יָמִים being a standing expression for his lifetime, reckoning from his birth (see ch. 5. 35^{28}, Is. 65^{20} etc.). The older view (𝔗^{OJ}, Jer. Ra. IEz. Calv. al.: so De. Klost.), that the clause indicates the interval that was to elapse before the Flood, was naturally suggested by the present position of the passage, and was supported by the consideration that greater ages were subsequently attained by many of the patriarchs. But these statements belong to P, and decide nothing as to the meaning of the words in J.

* Comp. Cheyne's imaginary restoration in *EB*, 3391, with the reconstructed Phœnician myth of Gruppe in *Philologus*, 1889, i. 100 ff.

† Reading לֹא יָדֹם רוּחִי, 'shall not restrain itself' (lit. '**be silent**'). **See** *NKZ*, 1894, 234 ff. (= *Pent.* [1907] 28 ff.).

of *life* implanted in man at creation, the tenor of the decree being that this shall not 'abide'* in man eternally or indefinitely, but only in such measure as to admit a maximum life of 120 years. There are two difficulties in this interpretation: (*a*) It has no connexion with what precedes, for everything the v. contains would be quite as intelligible apart from the marriages with the angels as in relation to them.† (*b*) The following words הוא בשר have no meaning: as a reason for the withdrawal of the animating spirit they involve a *hysteron proteron*; and as an independent statement they are (on the supposition) not true, man as actually constituted being both flesh and spirit (2^7). (4) The most probable sense is that given by We. (*Comp.*[2] 305 ff.), viz. that רוח is the divine substance common to Yahwe and the angels, in contrast to בָּשָׂר, which is the element proper to human nature (cf. Is. 31^3): so Ho. Gu. The idea will then be that the mingling of the divine and human substances brought about by illicit sexual unions has introduced disorder into the creation which Yahwe cannot suffer to 'abide' permanently, but resolves to end by an exercise of His supreme power.—(ii.) We have next to consider whether the 120 years, taken in its natural sense of the duration of individual life (*v.i.*), be consistent with the conclusion just reached. We. himself thinks that it is not: the fusion of the divine and human elements would be propagated *in the race*, and could not be checked by a shortening of the lives of individuals. The context requires an announcement of the annihilation of the race, and the last clause of the v. must be a mistaken gloss on the first. If this argument were sound it would certainly supply a strong reason *either* for revising We.'s acceptation of [3a], *or* for understanding [3b] as an announcement of the Flood. But a shortening of the term of life, though not a logical corollary from the sin of the angels, might nevertheless be a judicial sentence upon it. It would ensure the extinction of the giants within a measurable time; and indirectly impose a limit on the new intellectual powers which we may suppose to have accrued to mankind at large through union with angelic beings.‡ In view of the defective character of the narrative, it would be unwise to press the antagonism of the two clauses so as to put a strain on the interpretation of either.

4. ***The Nĕphîlîm were*** (or *arose*) ***in the earth in those days***] Who were the נְפִלִים? The name recurs only in Nu. 13^{33},

4. הַנְּפִלִים] 𝔊 οἱ γίγαντες; Aq. οἱ ἐπιπίπτοντες; Σ. οἱ βίαιοι; 𝔖 ܓܢܒܪ̈ܐ; 𝔗^O גבריא. The etymology is uncertain (see Di. 123). There is no

* On this traditional rendering of ידון, see the footnote, p. 143.

† Bu.'s argument that the v. is detachable from its present context is, therefore, perfectly sound; although his attempt to find a place for it after 3^{21} is not so successful (see p. 3 above).

‡ Just as in $3^{22.24}$ man is allowed to retain the gift of illicitly obtained knowledge, but is foiled by being denied the boon of immortality. The

where we learn that they were conceived as beings of gigantic stature, whose descendants survived till the days of Moses and Joshua. The circumstantial form of the sentence here (cf. 12^6 13^7) is misleading, for the writer cannot have meant that the נ׳ existed in those days apart from the alliances with the angels, and that the result of the latter were the גִּבֹּרִים (Lenormant, al.). The idea undoubtedly is that this race *arose* at that time in consequence of the union of the divine 'spirit' with human 'flesh.'—*and also after-*

---

allusion to a 'fall' (√נָפַל) of angels from heaven (𝔗J, Jer.* Ra.), or to a 'fall' of the world through their action (*Ber. R.* Ra.). A connexion with נֵפֶל, 'abortive birth' (from נָפַל, 'fall dead'), is not improbable (Schwally, *ZATW*, xviii. 144 ff.). An attractive emendation of Co. (נְפִילִים מֵעוֹלָם) in Ezk. 32^{27} not only yields a striking resemblance to this v., but supports the idea that the נ׳ (like the רְפָאִים) were associated with the notion of Sheol.—אחרי כן אשר] cannot mean 'after' (as conj.), which would require a perf. to follow, but only 'afterwards, when.' On any view, יָבֹאוּ and וְיָלְדוּ are frequent. tenses.—בוא אל] (as euphemism) is characteristic of JE (esp. J) in Hex. (Bu. 39, *Anm.*). Cf. Rob. Sm. *KM*², 198 ff.—הַגִּבֹּרִים] lit. 'mighty ones' (Aq. δυνατοί; 𝔙 *potentes*; 𝔊Σ𝔖 𝔗O do not distinguish from נפילים). The word is thoroughly naturalised in Heb. speech, and nearly always in a good sense. But pass. like Ezk. $32^{12ff.}$ show that it had another aspect, akin to Ar. *ǧabbār* (proud, audacious, tyrannical). The Ar. and Syr. equivalents are used as names of the constellation Orion (Lane, *Lex.* i. 375 *a*; P. Sm. *Th.* 646).—אשר מעולם] cf. עַם עוֹלָם, Ezk. 26^{20}, probably an allusion to a wicked ancient race thrust down to Sheol.—The whole v. has the appearance of a series of antiquarian glosses; and all that can be strictly inferred from it is that there was some traditional association of the Nephîlîm with the incident recorded in v.$^{1f.}$. At the same time we may reasonably hold that the kernel of the v. reproduces in a hesitating and broken fashion the essential thought of the original myth. The writer apparently shrinks from the direct statement that the Nephîlîm were the offspring of the marriages of vv.$^{1.2}$, and tantalises the curiosity of his readers with the cautious affirmation that such beings then existed. A later hand then introduced a reminder that they existed 'afterwards' as well.—Bu., who omits v.^{3}, restores the original connexion with v.$^{1f.}$ as follows: [והיה כאשר] יבאו בני האלהים . . . [וכן] היו הנפלים בארץ בימים ההם. Some such excellent sentence may very well have stood in the original; but it was precisely this perspicuity of narration which the editor wished to avoid.

---

same point of view appears in 11^{1-9}: in each case the ruling motive is the divine jealousy of human greatness; and man's pride is humbled by a subtle and indirect exercise of the power of God.

* "Et angelis et sanctorum liberis, convenit nomen cadentium."

wards whenever (𝔊 ὡς ἄν) *the sons of the gods came in* . . . *and they* (the women) *bore unto them*] That is to say, the production of Nephîlîm was not confined to the remote period indicated by v.$^{1f.}$, but was continued in after ages through visits of angels to mortal wives,—a conception which certainly betrays the hand of a glossator. It is perhaps enough to remove וְגַם אַחֲרֵי־כֵן as an interpolation, and connect the אֲשֶׁר with בַּיָּמִים הָהֵם; though even then the phrasing is odd (*v.i.*).—*Those are the heroes* (הַגִּבֹּרִים) *that were of old, the men of fame*] (אַנְשֵׁי הַשֵּׁם, cf. Nu. 16^2). הֵמָּה has for its antecedent not אֲשֶׁר as obj. to יָלְדוּ (We.), but הַנְּפִלִים. There is a touch of euhemerism in the notice (We.), the archaic and mythological נְפִלִים being identified with the more human גִּבּוֹרִים who were renowned in Hebrew story.

It is probable that the legend of the Nephîlîm had a wider circulation in Heb. tradition than could be gathered from its curt handling by the editors of the Hex. In Ezk. 32 we meet with the weird conception of a mighty antique race who are the original denizens of Sheol, where they lie in state with their swords under their heads, and are roused to a transient interest in the newcomers who disturb their majestic repose. If Cornill's correction of v.^{27} (גבורים נְפִלִים מעולם) be sound, these are to be identified with the Nephîlîm of our passage; and the picture throws light on two points left obscure in Gen.: viz., the character of the primæval giants, and the punishment meted out to them. Ezekiel dwells on their haughty violence and warlike prowess, and plainly intimates that for their crimes they were consigned to Sheol, where, however, they enjoy a kind of aristocratic dignity among the Shades. It would almost seem as if the whole conception had been suggested by the supposed discoveries of prehistoric skeletons of great stature, buried with their arms beside them, like those recorded by Pausanias (i. 35. 5 f., viii. 29. 3, 32. 4) and other ancient writers (see Rob. Sm. in Dri. *Deut.* 40 f.).

VI. 5–IX. 29.—*Noah and the Flood.*

Analysis of the Flood-Narrative.—The section on the Flood (6^5–9^{17}) is, as has often been observed, the first example in Gen. of a truly composite narrative; *i.e.*, one in which the compiler "instead of excerpting the entire account from a single source, has interwoven it out of excerpts taken alternatively from J and P, preserving in the process many duplicates, as well as leaving unaltered many striking differences of representation and phraseology" (Dri. 85). The resolution of the compound narrative into its constituent elements in this case is justly reckoned amongst the most brilliant achievements of purely literary criticism, and affords a particularly instructive lesson in the art of documentary analysis (comp. the interesting exposition by Gu.[2] 121 ff.). Here it must suffice to give the results of the process, along with a summary of the criteria by which the critical operation is guided and justified. The division generally accepted by recent critics is as follows:

J	6^{5-8}		7^{1-5}		7 (8. 9). 10		12		16b		17b		22. 23
P		9-22		6		11		13-16a		17a		18-21	

J			2b. 3a		6-12		13b		20-22	
P	7^{24}	$8^{1.\ 2a}$		3b-5		13a		14-19		9^{1-17}.

The minutiæ of glosses, transpositions, etc., are left to be dealt with in the Notes. Neglecting these, the scheme as given above represents the results of Bu. (to whom the finishing touches are due: *Urgesch.* 248 ff.) Gu. and Ho. Dillmann agrees absolutely, except that he assigns 7^{17} wholly to J, and 7^{23b} to P; and We., except with regard to 7^{17} (J) $8^{3.\ 13}$, which are both assigned entirely to P. The divergences of Kue. and Co. are almost equally slight; and indeed the main outlines of the analysis were fixed by the researches of Hupfeld, Nöldeke, and Schrader.—This remarkable consensus of critical opinion has been arrived at by four chief lines of evidence: (1) *Linguistic.* The key to the whole process is, of course, the distinction between the divine names יהוה ($6^{5.\ 6.\ 7.\ 8}$ $7^{1.\ 5.\ 16b}$ $8^{20.\ 21}$) and אלהים ($6^{9.\ 11.\ 12.\ 13.\ 22}$ 7^{16a} $8^{1.\ 15}$ $9^{1.\ 6.\ 8.\ 12.\ 16.\ 17}$). Besides this, a number of characteristic expressions differentiate the two sources. Thus J's איש ואשתו (7^{2}) answers to P's זכר ונקבה* (6^{19} $7^{(9).\ 16}$); מחה (6^{7} $7^{4.\ 23}$) to שִׁחֵת and השחית ($6^{13.\ 17}$ $9^{11.\ 15}$); מות (7^{22}) to גָּוַע* (6^{17} 7^{21}); כל־היקום ($7^{4.\ 23}$) to כל־בשר* ($6^{12.\ 13.\ 17}$ 7^{21} and oft.); קל ($8^{8.\ 11}$) and שוב (7^{3a}) to חסר (8^{5}), חרב (8^{13b}) to יבש (8^{14}) [but see on 8^{13b}]; נשמת חיים (8^{22}) to רוח חיים (6^{17}); לְחַיּוֹת (7^{3}) to לְהַחֲיוֹת ($6^{19.\ 20}$); כל־ביתך (7^{1}) to the specific enumerations of 6^{18} $7^{(7).\ 13}$ $8^{16.\ 18}$. (Comp. the list in Ho. *Gen.* p. 68).—(2) *Diversity of representation.* In J clean and unclean animals are distinguished, the former entering the ark by sevens and the latter in pairs (7^{2}, cf. 8^{20}); in P one pair of every kind without distinction is admitted ($6^{19f.}$ $7^{15f.}$). According to J, the cause of the Flood is a forty-days' rain which is to commence seven days after the command to enter the ark ($7^{4.\ 10.\ 12}$ $8^{2b.\ 6}$) —the latter passage showing that the waters began to subside after the 40 days. In P we have (7^{11} 8^{2a}) a different conception of the cause of the Flood; and, in $7^{6.\ 11.\ 13.\ 24}$ $8^{3b.\ 4.\ 5.\ 13a.\ 14}$, a chronological scheme according to which the waters increase for 150 days, and the entire duration of the Flood is one year (see p. 167 ff.).—(3) *Duplicates.* The following are obviously parallels from the two documents: $6^{5-8} \parallel 6^{11-13}$ (occasion of the Flood); $7^{1-5} \parallel 6^{17-22}$ (command to enter the ark, and announcement of the Flood); $7^{7} \parallel 7^{13}$ (entering of the ark); $7^{10} \parallel 7^{11}$ (coming of the Flood); $7^{17b} \parallel 7^{18}$ (increase of the waters: floating of the ark); $7^{22f.} \parallel 7^{21}$ (destruction of terrestrial life); $8^{2b.\ 3a} \parallel 8^{1f.}$ (abatement of the Flood); $8^{13b} \parallel 8^{13a.\ 14}$ (drying of the earth); $8^{20-22} \parallel 9^{8ff.}$ (promise that the Flood shall not recur).—(4) The final confirmation of the theory is that the two series of passages form two all but continuous narratives, which

* Phrases characteristic of the style of P generally.

exhibit the distinctive features of the two great sources of the primitive history, J and P. The J sections are a graphic popular tale, appealing to the imagination rather than to the reasoning faculties. The aim of the writer, one would say, was to bring the cosmopolitan (Babylonian) Flood-legend within the comprehension of a native of Palestine. The Deluge is ascribed to a familiar cause, the rain; only, the rain lasts for an unusual time, 40 days. The picturesque incident of the dove (see 8^{9}) reveals the touch of descriptive genius which so often breaks forth from this document. The boldest anthropomorphisms are freely introduced into the conception of God ($6^{6f.}$ 7^{16b} 8^{21}); and the religious institutions of the author's time are unhesitatingly assumed for the age of Noah.—Still more pronounced are the characteristics of P in the other account. The vivid details which are the life and charm of the older narrative have all disappeared; and if the sign of the rainbow (9^{12-17}) is retained, its æsthetic beauty has evaporated. For the rest, everything is formal, precise, and calculated,—the size of the ark, the number of the persons and the classification of the animals in it, the exact duration of the Flood in its various stages, etc.: if these mathematical determinations are removed, there is little story left. The real interest of the writer is in the new departure in God's dealings with the world, of which the Flood was the occasion,—the modification of the original constitution of nature, 9^{1-7}, and the establishment of the first of the three great covenants, 9^{8-17}. The connexion of the former passage with Gn. 1 is unmistakably evident. Very significant are the omission of Noah's sacrifice, and the ignoring of the laws of cleanness and uncleanness amongst animals.*

The success of the critical process is due to the care and skill with which the Redactor (R^{JP}) has performed his task. His object evidently was to produce a synthetic history of the Flood without sacrificing a scrap of information that could with any plausibility be utilised for his narrative. The sequence of P he appears to have preserved intact, allowing neither omissions nor transpositions. Of J he has preserved quite enough to show that it was originally a complete and independent narrative; but it was naturally impracticable to handle it as carefully as the main document. Yet it is doubtful if there are any actual lacunæ except (*a*) the account of the building of the ark (between 6^{8} and 7^{1}), and (*b*) the notice of the exit from it (between 8^{13b} and ^{20}). The middle part of the document, however, has been broken up into minute fragments,

---

* Traces of P's general vocabulary are very numerous. Besides some of those (marked by *) already enumerated in contrast to J, we have תּוֹלְדֹת (6^{9}); דֹּרֹת (6^{9} 9^{12}); הוֹלִיד (6^{10}); הקים ברית (6^{18} $9^{9.\,11.\,17}$) and נתן ב׳ (9^{12}); אִתּוֹ in enumerations (6^{18} 7^{13} 8^{16} etc.); מין (6^{20} 7^{14}); רֶמֶשׂ, רָמַשׂ (6^{20} $7^{(8).\,14.\,21}$ $8^{17.\,19}$ $9^{2.\,3}$); שֶׁרֶץ, שָׁרַץ (7^{21} 8^{17} 9^{7}); לְאָכְלָה (6^{21} 9^{3}); בעצם היום הזה (7^{13}); מאד מאד (7^{19}); בְּ of specification (7^{21} 8^{17} $9^{10.\,15.\,16}$); פרה ורבה (8^{17} $9^{1.\,7}$); למשפחתיהם (8^{19}); ברית עולם (9^{16}).—Of the style of J the positive indications are fewer: מצא חן (6^{8}); מחה in the sense 'destroy' (6^{7} $7^{4.\,23}$) [see Ho. *Hex.* 101]; עצב (6^{6}); על־פני הארמה ($7^{4.\,23}$ $8^{8\ (?\ 13\ \mathrm{LXX})}$); בעבור ($8^{21}$). See the comm. of Di. Ho. Gu. etc.

and these have been placed in position where they would least disturb the flow of narration. Some slight transpositions have been made, and a number of glosses have been introduced; but how far these last are due to the Redactor himself and how far to subsequent editors, we cannot tell (for details see the notes). Duplicates are freely admitted, and small discrepancies are disregarded; the only serious discrepancy (that of the chronology) is ingeniously surmounted by making J's 40 days count twice, once as a stage of the increase of the Flood (7^{12}) and once as a phase of its decrease (8^{6}).* This compound narrative is not destitute of interest; but for the understanding of the ideas underlying the literature the primary documents are obviously of first importance. We shall therefore treat them separately.

The Flood according to J.

VI. 5–8. The occasion of the Flood:—Yahwe's experience of the deep-seated and incurable sinfulness of human nature. It is unnecessary to suppose that a description of the deterioration of the race has been omitted, or displaced by 6^{1-4} (Ho.). The ground of the pessimistic estimate of human nature so forcibly expressed in v.[5] is rather the whole course of man's development as hitherto related, which is the working out of the sinful knowledge acquired by the Fall. The fratricide of Cain, the song of Lamech, the marriages with the angels, are incidents which, if not all before the mind of the writer of the Flood-story, at least reveal the gloomy view of the early history which characterises the Yahwistic tradition.—5. *the whole bent* (lit. 'formation') *of the thoughts of his heart*] It is difficult to say whether יֵצֶר is more properly the 'form' impressed *on* the mind (the disposition or character), or 'that which is formed' *by* the mind (imagination and purpose—*Sinnen und Trachten*):

5. יהוה] 𝔊 Κύριος ὁ θεὸς (so v.[8]).—וכל־יצר וגו'] 𝔊 loosely: *καὶ πᾶς τις διανοεῖται* (יִצֶּר?) *ἐν τῇ καρδίᾳ αὐτοῦ ἐπιμελῶς ἐπὶ τὰ πονηρά*; 𝔙 *cuncta cogitatio*. Another Gr. rendering (ὁ Ἑβρ., see Field, *ad loc.*) is *φυσικὸν τοῦ ἀνθ.*; but in 8^{21} the same translator has *τὸ πλάσμα τῆς καρ. ἀνθ.* On the later Jewish theologoumenon of the יצר הרע (the evil impulse in man, also called יצר simply) which is based on this passage, and by Jewish comm. (Ra. on 8^{21}) is found here; see Taylor, *Sayings of Jew. Fathers*[2], 37, 148 ff.; Porter, *Bibl. and Sem. Studies by members . . . of Yale*

* The supposition of Hupfeld and Lenormant (*Orig.* i. 415), that the double period occurred in the original J, has no foundation.

cf. 8^{21}, Dt. 31^{21}, Is. 26^{3} (Ps. 103^{14}?), 1 Ch. 28^{9} 29^{18}; *v.i.*—**6.** The anthropopathy which attributes to Yahwe regret (וַיִּנָּחֶם) and vexation (וַיִּתְעַצֵּב) because He had created man is unusually strong. Although in the sense of mere change of purpose, the former is often ascribed to God (Ex 32^{14}, Jer. $18^{7.8}$ $26^{3.13}$, Jl. 2^{13}, Jon. 3^{10} etc.), the cases are few where divine regret for accomplished action is expressed (1 Sa. 15^{11}). The whole representation was felt to be inadequate (Nu. 23^{19}, 1 Sa. 15^{11}); yet it continued to be used as inseparable from the religious view of history as the personal agency of Yahwe.—**7.** God's resolve to *blot out* (מָחָה) the race: not as yet communicated to Noah, but expressed in monologue.—**8.** *But Noah had found favour, etc.*] doubtless on account of his piety; but see on 7^{1}. The Yahwistic narrative must have contained some previous notice of Noah, probably at the end of a genealogy.

VII. 1–5. Announcement of the Flood.—The section is an almost exact parallel to 6^{17-22} (P). V.^{1} presupposes in J a description of the building of the ark, which the redactor has omitted in favour of the elaborate account of P. Not till the work is finished does Yahwe reveal to Noah the purpose it is to serve: v.^{4} is obviously the first intimation that has been given of the approaching deluge. The building of the ark in implicit obedience to the divine command is thus a great test and proof of Noah's faith; cf. Heb. 11^{7}.—**1.** *Thou and all thy house*] J's brevity is here far

---

Univ. (1901), 93 ff.—כל־היום] 'continually'; see BDB, 400 b.—**6.** יהוה] 𝔊 ὁ θεός (so v.^{7}).—ויתעצב] Gn. 34^{7}; cf. Is. 63^{10} (Pi.). Ra. softens the anthrop. by making the impending destruction of the creatures the immediate object of the divine grief.—**7.** אמחה] cf. $7^{4.23}$. **In the full** sense of 'exterminate' (as distinct from 'obliterate' [name, memory, etc.]) the vb. is peculiar to J's account of the Flood; ct. Nu. 5^{23} 34^{11} (P).—The v. is strongly interpolated. The clauses אשר בראתי and מאדם השמים . . . are in the style of P (cf. 6^{20} $7^{14.21}$ $8^{17.19}$ 9^{2} etc.); and the latter is, besides, an illogical specification of האדם. They are redactional glosses, the original text being אמחה את־האדם מעל פני האדמה כי נחמתי כי עשיתים (Bu. 249 ff.; Di. 125).—**8.** מצא חן בעיני] characteristic of, though not absolutely confined to, J: 19^{19} 32^{6} $33^{8.15}$ 34^{11} 39^{4} 47^{25} etc. (Ho. *Einl.* 97 f.).

1. יהוה] 𝔐𝔖 אלהים; 𝔊 Κύριος ὁ θεός.—צדיק] pred. accus.; Dav. § 76.—

more expressive than the formal enumerations of P (6^{18} 7^{13} $8^{16. 18}$). The principle involved is the religious solidarity of the family; its members are saved for the righteousness of its head (cf. 19^{12}).—*thee have I seen* (*to be*) *righteous* (צַדִּיק, see on 6^{9})] Bu. and others take this to be a judgement based on Noah's obedience in building the ark; but that is hardly correct. The verb is not מצא but ראה, which has precisely the same force as the וירא of 6^{5}. Comp. also 6^{8}.—**2.** ***clean*** (טָהוֹר) means, practically, fit for sacrifice and human food; the technical antithesis is טָמֵא, which, however, is here avoided, whether purposely (De. 174) or not it is impossible to say. The distinction is not, as was once supposed (see Tu.), a proof of J's interest in Levitical matters, but, on the contrary, of the naïveté of his religious conceptions. He regards it as rooted in the nature of things, and cannot imagine a time when it was not observed. His view is nearer the historical truth than the theory of P, who traces the distinction to the positive enactments of the Sinaitic legislation (Lv. 11, Dt. 14), and consequently ignores it here. The same difference of standpoint appears with regard to sacrifice, altars, etc.: see $4^{3f.}$ 8^{20} 12^{7} etc.—שִׁבְעָה שִׁבְעָה] *by sevens* (G-K. § 134*q*); *i.e.* '7 (individuals) of each kind' (De. Str. al.), rather than '7 pairs' (*Ber. R.* IEz. Di. Gu. al.),—in spite of the following איש ואשתו. It is a plausible conjecture (Ra. De. Str.) that the odd individual was a male destined for sacrifice (8^{20}).—**3a** presents an impure text (*v.i.*), and must either be removed as a gloss (Kue. Bu. Ho. Gu. al.) or supplemented with 𝔊 (Ba. Ben.).—**3b.** ***to keep seed alive, etc.***] reads better as the continuation of

---

2. For שנים, 𝔐𝔊𝔖𝔙 read שנים שנים,—probably correctly.—איש ואשתו (*bis*)] 𝔐 זכר ונקבה, assimilating J to P.—**3a.** The distinction to be expected between clean and unclean birds is made imperfectly by 𝔐 and 𝔖, which insert הטהור after השמים; and fully by 𝔊, which goes further and adds the words *καὶ ἀπὸ παντῶν τῶν πετεινῶν τ. μὴ καθαρῶν δύο δύο ἄρσεν κ. θῆλυ.* Ball accepts this, thinking the omission in MT due to homoioteleuton. But the phrase זכר ונקבה shows that ^{3a} has been manipulated; and it is on the whole more likely that it is entirely redactional. Birds *may* be included in the הבהמה of v.^{2}; though Bu.'s parallels (Ex. $8^{13f.}$ $9^{9. 22. 25}$, Jer. 32^{43} $33^{10. 12}$ 36^{29}, Ps. 36^{7}) are not quite convincing.—**3b.** לְחַיּוֹת] P uses

^{2} than of ^{3a}.—4. With great rhetorical effect, the reason for all these preparations—the coming of the Flood—is reserved to the end. J knows no other physical cause of the Deluge than the 40 days' rain (cf. v.^{12}).—5. Comp. 6^{22} (P).

7–10, 12, 16b, 17b, 22, 23.—Entrance into the ark and description of the Flood.—J's narrative has here been taken to pieces by the Redactor, who has fitted the fragments into a new connexion supplied by the combined accounts of J and P. The operation has been performed with such care and skill that it is still possible to restore the original order and recover a succinct and consecutive narrative, of which little if anything appears to be lost. The sequence of events is as follows: At the end of the seven days, the Flood comes (v.^{10}); Noah enters the ark (^{7}) and Yahwe shuts him in (^{16b}). Forty days' rain ensues (^{12}), and the waters rise and float the ark (^{17b}). All life on the earth's surface is extinguished; only Noah and those in the ark survive ($^{22f.}$).

The rearrangement here adopted ($^{10. 7. 16b. 12. 17b. 22. 23}$) is due mainly to the acute criticism of Bu. (*Urg.* 258 ff.), who has probably added the last refinements to a protracted process of literary investigation. Some points (*e.g.* the transposition of vv.^{7} and ^{10}) are, of course, more or less doubtful; others (*e.g.* ^{16b}) are seen to be necessary as soon as the components of J have been isolated. The most difficult thing is to clear the text of the glosses which inevitably accompanied the work of redaction; but this also has been accomplished with a considerable degree of certainty and agreement amongst recent comm. The most extensive interpolations are part of v.^{7}, the whole of vv.^{8} and ^{9}, and part of ^{23}. For details see the footnote.

10. *At the end of the 7 days* (cf. v.^{4})] The interval (we may suppose) was occupied in assembling the animals and provisioning the ark.—*the waters of the Flood*] הַמַּבּוּל, a technical name for the Deluge, common to both sources (*v.i.*).—**7.** Noah enters the ark *on account of the . . . Flood*:

Hiph. ($6^{19f.}$).—וָרַע] as Jer. 31^{27}.—4. לְיָמִים] On לְ as denoting the *close* of a term (cf. v.^{10}), see BDB, *s.v.* 6b.—הַיְקוּם] a rare word (only 7^{23}, Dt. 11^{6}), meaning 'that which subsists' (√קום). 𝔊 ἀνάστεμα (other exx. in Field, ἐξανάστασιν), 𝔙 *substantia*, 𝔖 ܟܠ ܩܝܘܡܐ. On the form see Barth, *Nom.-bild.* 181; Kön. ii. 146; G–K. § 85 *d*.

7. וּבָנָיו—אִתּוֹ] The enumeration is in the manner of P (obs. also אִתּוֹ);

hence v.[7] presupposes v.[10]. The same order of events is found in P ([11. 13]) and in the Babylonian legend: "when the lords of the darkness send at evening a (grimy?) rain, enter into the ship and close thy door" (l. 88 f.).—**16b** (which must in any case follow immediately on v.[7]) contains a fine anthropomorphism, which (in spite of the Bab. parallel just cited) it is a pity to spoil by deleting יהוה and making Noah the implicit subject (Klost. *NKZ*, i. 717).—**12.** *forty days and forty nights*] This determination, which in J expresses the entire duration of the Flood, seems to have been treated by R as merely a stage in the increase of the waters (cf. 8[6]). It obviously breaks the connexion of P. The Babylonian deluge lasted only six days and nights (l. 128).—**17b.** Parallel to [18] (P).—**22, 23.** A singularly effective description of the

---

the words either replace וכל־ביתו (as v.[1]), or are a pure insertion;—in either case redactional.—מי המבול] so 7[10] (J), 9[11] (P) (ct. הַמַּ׳ מַיִם, 6[17] 7[6]).—מַבּוּל] 𝔊 κατακλυσμός; 𝔙 *diluvium*; 𝔖 and 𝔗ᴼ טופנא (𝔗ᴶ טובענא). The word has usually been derived from יבל, 'streaming' (see Ges. *Th.*, Di.); but is more probably a foreign word without Heb. etymology (see Nö. *ZDMG*, xl. 732). Del. (*Parad.* 156) proposed the derivation from Ass. *nabâlu*, 'destroy,' which is accepted by König (ii. 153), Ball (p. 53), and others. The Bab. technical equivalent is *abûbu*, which denotes both a 'light-flood' and a 'water-flood': the double sense has been thought to explain P's addition of מַיִם to the word (see on 6[17]). A transformation of the one name into the other is, however, difficult to understand (see *KAT*[3], 495[1], 546[2]). In Ps. 29[10] מבול appears to be used in a general sense without a historic reference to the Noachic Deluge (see Duhm, *ad loc.*).—**8, 9** present a mixed text. The distinction of clean and unclean points to J; but all other features (אלהים [though a reading יהוה seems attested by 𝔐𝔙𝔗ᴶ, and MSS of 𝔊]; זכר ונקבה; the undiscriminated שנים שנים; the categorical enumeration [to which 𝔊 adds the birds at the beginning of v.[8]]) to P. In P the vv. are not wanted, because they are a duplicate of [13-16]: they must therefore be assigned to an interpolator (Bu. al.).—**10.** On the construction of the sentence, see G-K. § 164 *a*, and on v.[6] below.—**12.** גֶּשֶׁם] (√ *ǧasuma*='be massive') commonly used of the heavy winter rain (Ezr. 10[9], Ca. 2[11]): see GASm. *HG*, 64.—**16b.** יהוה] 𝔊 Κύριος ὁ θεός + τὴν κιβωτόν.—**17b.** Since [18] belongs to P (ויגברו, מאד), its duplicate [17b] must be from J, where it forms a natural continuation of [12]. [17a], on the other hand (in spite of the 40 days), must be assigned to P (see p. 164).—**22.** נשמת רוח חיים] is an unexampled combination, arising from confusion of a phrase of J (נשמת חיים, 2[7]) with one of P (רוח חיים, 6[17] 7[15]). The v. being from J (cf. חָרָבָה instead of יַבָּשָׁה; מתו instead of ויגוע, [21]), רוח is naturally the word to be deleted.—**23a** as a whole is J (מחה, יקום, על־פני האדמה); but the clause מארם . . . השמים seems again (cf. 6[7])

effect of the Flood, which is evidently conceived as universal.

VIII. (1b?), 2b, 3a, (4?), 6–12, 13b. Subsidence of the waters. — The rain from heaven having ceased, the Flood gradually abates. [The ark settles on some high mountain; and] Noah, ignorant of his whereabouts and unable to see around, sends out first a raven and then a dove to ascertain the condition of the earth.

The continuity of J's narrative has again been disturbed by the redaction. V.[6a], which in its present position has no point of attachment in J, probably stood originally before [2b], where it refers to the 40 days' duration of the Flood (We. *Comp.*[2] 5). It was removed by R so as to make up part of the interval between the emergence of the mountain-tops and the drying of the ground.—There are two small points in which a modification of the generally accepted division of sources might be suggested. (1) [1b] (the wind causing the abatement of the waters) is, on account of אלהים, assigned to P. But the order [1b] [2a] is unnatural, and transpositions in P do not seem to have been admitted. The idea is more in accord with J's conception of the Flood than with P's; and but for the name אלהים the half-verse might very well be assigned to J, and inserted between [2b] and [3a]. (2) V.[4] is also almost universally regarded as P's (see Bu. 269 f.). But this leaves a lacuna in J between [3a] and [6b], where a notice of the landing of the ark must have stood: on the other hand, [5b] makes it extremely doubtful if P thought of the ark as stranded on a mountain at all. The only objection to assigning [4] to J is the chronology: if we may suppose the chronological scheme to have been added or retouched by a later hand (see p. 168), there is a great deal to be said for the view of Hupfeld and Reuss that the remainder of the v. belongs to J.*—The opening passage would then read as follows:

6a. *At the end of* 40 *days,* 2b. *the rain from heaven was restrained;* 1b. *and Yahwe* (?) *caused a wind to pass over the earth, and the waters abated.* 3a. *And the waters went*

---

to be redactional, and the three words following must disappear with it. [23b] might be assigned with almost equal propriety to J or to P.—וַיִּמַח] (apoc. impf. Qal) is a better attested Massor. reading than וַיִּמָּח (Niph.). It is easier, however, to change the pointing (to Niph.) than to supply יהוה as subj., and the sense is at least as good.—Gu.'s rearrangement ([23aα. 22. 23b]) is a distinct improvement: of the two homologous sentences, that without ו naturally stands second.

3a. הלוך ושוב] G-K. § 113 *u*. 𝔊 has misunderstood the idiom both

---

* It may be noted that in *Jub.* v. 28 no date is given for the landing of the ark.

on decreasing from off the earth, **4.** *and the ark rested on the mountains of Ararat.*—On the landing-place of the ark, see p. 166 below.

6b–12. The episode of the sending out of the birds appears in many forms of the Deluge-tradition; notably in the Babylonian. It is here related as an illustration of Noah's wisdom (Gu.). Tuch quotes from Pliny, vi. 83 (on the Indians): "siderum in navigando nulla observatio; septentrio non cernitur; sed volucres secum vehunt, emittentes sæpius, meatumque earum terram petentium comitantur."—**7.** *He sent out a raven*] The purpose of the action is not stated till v.[8]; partly for this reason, partly because the threefold experiment with the dove is complete and more natural, the genuineness of the v. has been questioned (We. Ho. Gu. al.). Dahse, *ZATW*, xxviii. 5 f., calls attention to the fact that in 𝔊[M] the v. is marked with the obelus. The Bab. account has three experiments, but with different birds (dove, swallow, raven).—**8.** *And he sent out a dove*] perhaps immediately; see 𝔊 below. But if v.[7] be a later insertion, we must supply *and he waited* 7 *days* (see v.[10]).—**9.** The description of the return and admission of the dove is unsurpassed even in the Yahwistic document for tenderness and beauty of imagination.—**10.** *Seven other days*] implying a similar statement before either v.[7] or v.[8].—**11.** *a freshly plucked olive leaf*] The olive does not grow at great altitudes, and was said to flourish even under water (Tu.). But it is probable that some forgotten mythological significance attaches to the symbol in the Flood-legend (see Gu. p. 60). Cf. the classical notices of the olive branch as an emblem of peace: Virg. *Aen.* viii. 116 (*Paciferaeque manu ramum prætendit olivæ*); Livy, xxiv. 30, xxix. 16.—**12.** The third time the dove returns no more; and then at last—

---

here and in v.[7].—7. הערב] on the art. see G–K. § 126 *r*; but cf. Smith's note, *RS*², 126.—𝔊 here supplies *τοῦ ἰδεῖν εἰ κεκόπακεν τὸ ὕδωρ*, as in v.[8].—ויצא יצוא ושוב] 𝔊 *καὶ ἐξελθὼν οὐχ ὑπέστρεψεν*; so 𝔙𝔖 (accepted by Ball): see on [3a].—8. מֵאִתּוֹ] 𝔊 *ὀπίσω αὐτοῦ* (=אַחֲרָיו); assuming that both birds were sent forth on the same day.—10. וַיָּחֶל] cf. וַיִּיָּחֶל, v.[12] (𝔐 has ויחל both times). Both forms are incorrect: read in each case וַיְיַחֵל (Bu. Di. al.).

13b. Noah ventures to remove the *covering* of the ark, and sees that the earth is dry.

20–22. Noah's sacrifice.—J's account of the leaving of the ark has been suppressed. Noah's first act is to offer a sacrifice, not of thanksgiving but (as v.[21] shows) of propitiation: its effect is to move the Deity to gracious thoughts towards the new humanity. The resemblance to the Babylonian parallel is here particularly close and instructive (see p. 177): the incident appears also in the Greek and Indian legends.—**20.** *an altar*] Lit. 'slaughtering-place.' The sacrificial institution is carried back by J to the remotest antiquity (see on 4[3f.] 7[2f.]), but this is the first mention of the altar, and also of sacrifice by fire: see p. 105 above.—עֹלֹת] *holocausts*,—that form of sacrifice which was wholly consumed on the altar, and which was naturally resorted to on occasions of peculiar solemnity (*e.g.* 2 Sa. 24[25]).—**21.** *smelled the soothing odour*] רֵיחַ נִיחֹחַ (*κνίση*, *nidor*)* becomes a technical term of the Levitical ritual, and is never mentioned elsewhere except in P and Ezk. This, Gu. points out, is the only place where Yahwe is actually described as *smelling* the sacrifice; but cf. 1 Sa. 26[19]. It is probably a refinement of the crude eudæmonism of the Bab. story (see p. 177 below); and it is doubtful how far it elucidates primitive Heb. ideas of the effect of sacrifice. That "the pleasing odour is not the motive but merely the occasion of this gracious purpose" (Knobel), may be

—**13b.** מִכְסֶה] possibly described in J's account of the building of the ark. Elsewhere only of the covering of the Tabernacle (P); but cf. מְכַסֶּה, Ezk. 27[7].—חרבו] 𝔊 ins. *τὸ ὕδωρ ἀπό*.

20. ליהוה] 𝔊 *τῷ θεῷ*.—**21.** יהוה] 𝔊 K. *ὁ θεὸς* (*bis*).—ריח הניחח] 𝔖 ܢܝܚܐ ܕܒܣܡܐ ܢܝܚܐ ܕܢܝܚܐ —conflate?—לְקַלֵּל] a different vb. from that used in 3[17] 4[11] 5[29] (ארר). Ho. points out that Pi. of קלל is never used with God as subj. (cf. Gn. 12[3]); and for this and other reasons regards [21a] as an unskilful attempt to link the Noah of the Flood with the prophecy of 5[29]. But [21a] can only refer to the Flood, while the curse of 5[29] belongs to the past: moreover, an interpolator would have been careful to use the same verb. The sense given to קִלֵּל is fully justified by the usage

* *Il.* i. 317: *κνίση δ' οὐρανὸν ἷκεν ἑλισσομένη περὶ καπνῷ*; cf. Ov. *Met.* xii. 153.

sound theology, but it hardly expresses the idea of the passage.—**21b** is a monologue (אֶל־לִבּוֹ).—כִּי יֵצֶר וגו׳ (see on 6^{5}) may be understood either as epexegetical of בַּעֲבוּר הָאָדָם (a reason why Yahwe *might* be moved to curse the ground, though he will not [Ho.]), or as the ground of the promise *not* to visit the earth with a flood any more. The latter is by far the more probable. The emphasis is on מִנְּעֻרָיו, *from his youth*; the innate sinfulness of man constitutes an appeal to the divine clemency, since it cannot be cured by an undiscriminating judgement like the Flood, which arrests all progress toward better things (cf. Is. 54^{9}).—**22.** The pledge of Yahwe's patience with humanity is the regularity of the course of nature, in which good and bad men are treated alike (Mt. 5^{45}). A division of the year into six seasons (Ra.), or even into two halves (De.), is not intended; the order of nature is simply indicated by a series of contrasts, whose alternation is never more to be interrupted by a catastrophe like the Flood. This assurance closes J's account of the Deluge. It rests on an interior resolve of Yahwe; whereas in P it assumes the form of a 'covenant' (9^{11}),—a striking instance of the development of religious ideas in the direction of legalism: cf. Jer. $31^{35f.}$ $33^{20f.\ 25f.}$.

The Flood according to P.

VI. 9–12. Noah's piety; The corruption of the earth.—9. *This is the genealogy of Noah*] The formula is usually taken as the heading of the section of P dealing with the Flood; but see on $9^{28f.}$.—Noah is characterised as

---

of Pual (Ps. 37^{22}, Jb. 24^{18}, Is. 65^{20}).—בעבור] 𝔊 διὰ τὰ ἔργα, as 3^{17}.—כי יצר וגו׳] 𝔊 ὅτι ἔγκειται ἡ διάνοια τ. ἀνθ. ἐπιμελῶς κτλ. See on 6^{5}.—**22.** עֹד] 𝔊 om.; Ball, עַד.—ישבתו] 'come to an end': see on 2^{2}.

9. צדיק תמים] (so Jb. 12^{4}). The asyndeton is harsh; but it is hardly safe to remedy it on the authority of 𝔐 (ותמים) and 𝔙, against 𝔊. To remove צדיק as a gloss from J (7^{1}) (Ball) is too bold. Perhaps the sentence should be broken up into two clauses, one nominal and the other verbal: 'Noah was a righteous man; perfect was he,' etc.—The forensic sense of צדיק given above may not be the original: see S. A. Cook, *JTS*, ix. 632^{1}, who adduces some evidence that it meant what was 'due' among a definite social group, and between it and its gods.

righteous (צַדִּיק) and *faultless* (תָּמִים): on the construction *v.i.* There is perhaps a correspondence between these two epithets and the description of the state of the world which follows; צדיק being opposed to the 'violence,' and תמים to the 'corruption' of v.[11f.]. צדיק, a forensic term, denotes one whose conduct is unimpeachable before a judge; תמים is sacerdotal in its associations (Ex. 12[5], Lv. 1[3] etc.), meaning 'free from defect,' *integer* (cf. 17[1]).—*in his generations* (*v.i.*)] *i.e.* alone among his contemporaries (cf. 7[1]). That Noah's righteousness was only relative to the standard of his age is not implied.*—*walked with God*] see on 5[22]. The expression receives a fuller significance from the Babylonian legend, where Ut-napištim, like the Biblical Enoch, is translated to the society of the gods (p. 177 below).—**11 f.** וְהִנֵּה נִשְׁחָתָה] is the intentional antithesis to the וְהִנֵּה טוֹב מְאֹד of 1[31] (De.).—*All flesh had corrupted its way*] had violated the divinely-appointed order of creation. The result is *violence* (חָמָס, 𝔊 ἀδικία)—ruthless outrage perpetrated by the strong on the weak. A "nature red in tooth and claw with ravin" is the picture which rises before the mind of the writer; although, as has been already remarked (p. 129), the narrative of P contains no explanation of the change which had thus passed over the face of the world.

The fundamental idea of v.[11f.] is the disappearance of the Golden Age, or the rupture of the concord of the animal world established by the decree of 1[29f.]. The lower animals contribute their share to the general 'corruption' by transgressing the regulation of 1[30], and commencing to prey upon each other and to attack man (see 9[5]): so Ra. To restrict כל־בשר to mankind (𝔗O, Tu. Str. Dri. Ben. al.) is therefore

—בְּדֹרֹתָיו] 𝔊 ἐν τῇ γενέσει αὐτ. The f. pl. is highly characteristic of P (Ho. *Einl.* 341); but apparently always as a *real* pl. (series of generations): ct. the solitary use of sg. in P, Ex. 1[6]. Here, accordingly, it seems fair to understand it, not of the individual contemporaries of Noah (Tu. We. Ho. al.), but of the successive generations covered by his lifetime. The resemblance to צדיק בדור הזה (7[1]) is adduced by We. (*Prol.*[6] 390) as a proof of P's dependence on J.—**11.** הָאֱלֹהִים] One of the few instances of P's use of the art. with א׳.—**12.** אלהים] 𝔊 Κύριος ὁ θ.

* So Jerome: "ut ostenderet non juxta justitiam consummatam, sed juxta generationis suæ eum justum fuisse justitiam."

unnecessary and unwarranted. The phrase properly denotes '**all living** beings,' and is so used in 8 out of the 13 occurrences in P's account of the Flood (Dri. *ad loc.*). In 6^{19} $7^{15.16}$ 8^{17} it means animals apart from man; but that in the same connexion it should also mean mankind apart from animals is not to be expected, and could only be allowed on clear evidence.—The difference of standpoint between P and J (6^{5}) on this matter is characteristic.

13–16. Directions for building the ark.—**13.** Announcement in general terms of some vast impending catastrophe, involving *the end of all flesh* (all living beings, as v.[12]).—**14–16.** Description of the Ark.—*An Ark* (chest) *of gopher wood*] probably some resinous wood. In Heb. תֵּבָה is used only of Noah's ark and the vessel in which Moses was saved (Ex. $2^{3.5}$); the name *ark* comes to us through 𝔙 (*arca*), where, however, it is also applied to the ark of the testimony (Ex. 25^{10} etc.). The Bab. Flood-narrative has the ordinary word for ship (*elippu*).—The vessel is to consist internally of *cells* (lit. 'nests'), and is to be coated inside and out with *bitumen* (cf. Ex. 2^{3}).

---

13. בָּא לְפָנַי] not (as Est. 9^{11}) 'has come to my knowledge,' but 'has entered into my purpose.' This is better than (with Di.) to take קֵץ בָּא absolutely (as Am. 8^{2}), and לפני as 'according to my purpose.'—מִפְּנֵיהֶם] *through them*; Ex. 8^{20} 9^{11}, Ju. 6^{6} etc.—מַשְׁחִיתָם] אֶת־הארץ] 𝔊 καὶ τὴν γῆν; 𝔙 *cum terra*; so 𝔖 𝔗^OJ. As Ols. says, we should expect מֵעַל ה' (מֵאֵת [Graetz] is unsuitable). But the error probably lies deeper. Ball emends מַשְׁחִית אֹתָם וְאֶת־ה'; Bu. מַשְׁחִיתָם כי [הם] מַשְׁחִיתִם את־ה'; Gu. וְהִנָּם מַשְׁחִיתִם את־ה'. Eerdmans (*AT Studien*, i. 29) finds a proof of original polytheism. He reads הִנְנוּ מַשְׁחִיתִם וגו': "we [the gods] are about to destroy the earth."—14. תֵּבָה] 𝔊𝔖 κιβωτός; 𝔗𝔗 תיבותא. The word is the Egyptian *ṭeb*(*t*) = 'chest,' 'sarcophagus' (θῖβις, θίβη, in 𝔊 of Ex. $2^{3.5}$): see Ges. *Th.*; Erman, *ZDMG*, xlvi. 123. Jensen (*ZA*, iv. 272 f.), while admitting the Egypt. etymology, suggests a connexion with the Ass. *ilippu ṭi-bi-tum* (a kind of ship). I am informed by Dr. C. H. W. Johns that while the word is written as the determinative for 'ship,' it is not certain that it was pronounced *elippu*. He thinks it possible that it covers the word *tabû*, found in the phrase *ta-bi-e Bêl ilâni Marduk* (Del. *Hwb.* 699 a), which he is inclined to explain of the processional barques of the gods. If this conjecture be correct, we may have here the Bab. original of Heb. תֵּבָה. See *Camb. Bibl. Essays* (1909), p. 37 ff.—עֲצֵי־גֹפֶר] The old trans. were evidently at a loss: 𝔊 (ἐκ) ξύλων τετραγώνων; 𝔙 (*de*) *lignis lævigatis*; Jer. *ligna bituminata*: the word being ἅπ. λεγ. Lagarde (*Sem.* i. 64 f.; *Symm.* ii. 93 f.) considered it a mistaken contraction from גָּפְרִית (brimstone), or rather a foreign word of the same form which meant originally 'pine-wood.' Others (Bochart,

Somewhat similar details are given of the ship of Ut-napištim (p. 176). Asphalt is still lavishly applied in the construction of the rude boats used for the transport of naphtha on the Euphrates (see Cernik, quoted by Suess, *The Face of the Earth*, 27).—**15.** Assuming that the *cubit* is the ordinary Heb. cubit of six handbreadths (about 18 in.: see Kennedy, *DB*, iv. 909), the dimensions of the ark are such as modern shipbuilding has only recently exceeded (see Ben. 140); though it is probably to be assumed that it was rectangular in plan and sections. That a vessel of these proportions would float, and hold a great deal (though it would not carry cannon!), it hardly needed the famous experiment of the Dutchman Peter Janson in 1609–21 to prove (see Michaelis, *Oriental. und Exeget. Bibliot.* xviii. 27 f.).—**16.** The details here are very confused and mostly obscure. The word צֹהַר (ἅπ. λεγ.) is generally rendered 'light' or 'opening for light,'—either a single (square) aperture (Tu.), or "a kind of casement running round the

---

al.) suppose it to contain the root of κυπάρισσος, 'cypress,' a wood used by the Phœn. in shipbuilding, and by the Egypt. for sarcophagi (De.).—קִנִּים] Lagarde's conjecture, קנים קנים (*OS*[1], ii. 95), has been happily confirmed from Philo, *Quæst. in Gen.* ii. 3 (*loculos loculos*: see Bu. 255), and from a Palest. Syr. Lectionary (Nestle, cited by Ho.). On the idiom, see G–K. § 123 *e*.—כֹּפֶר] also ἅπ. λεγ., = 'bitumen' (𝔊𝔙𝔖𝔗^O), Ar. *ḳufr*, Aram. כופרא, Ass. *kupru* (used in the Bab. Flood-story). The native Heb. word for 'bitumen' is חֵמָר (11^3 14^{10}, Ex. 2^3).—**15.** אֹתָהּ] 𝔊 אֶת־הַתֵּבָה.—**16.** צֹהַר] 𝔊 ἐπισυνάγων (rdg. צֹבֵר?); all other Vns. express the idea of *light* (Aq. μεσημβρινόν, Σ. διαφανές, 𝔙 *fenestram*, 𝔖 ܟܘ̈ܐ, 'windows,' 𝔗^O ניהור). They connected it (as Aq. shows) with צָהֳרַיִם, 'noon-day'; but *if* צהרים means properly 'summit' (see G–B.; BDB, *s.v.*), there seems nothing in Heb. to connect the root with the idea of light. The meaning 'back' is supported by Ar. *ẓahr*.—ואל־אמה תְּכַלֶּנָּה מלמעלה] The suff. may refer either to the צהר (whose gender is unknown: cf. Kön. *S.* p. 163) or to the תֵּבָה: the latter is certainly most natural after כַּלָּה. The prevalent explanation—that the cubit indicates either the breadth of the light-opening, or its distance below the roof (see Di.)—is mere guess-work. Bu. (following We.) removes the first three words to the end of the v., rendering: "and according to the cubit thou shalt finish it (the ark)": Di. objects that this would require הָאמה. Ball reads וְאֶל־אָרְכָּהּ תְּכַסֶּנָּה מל', "and for its (the ark's) whole length thou shalt cover it above"; Gu.: ואל־א' תְּגַלֶּנָּה, "and on a pivot (see Is. 6^4) thou shalt make it (the roof) revolve,"—a doubtful suggestion.

sides of the ark (except where interrupted by the beams supporting the roof) a little below the roof" (Dri., so De. Di. al.). Exegetical tradition is in favour of this view; but the material arguments for it (see Di. 141) are weak, and its etymological basis is doubtful (*v.i.*). Others (Ew. Gu. G–B. al.) take it to mean the *roof* (lit. 'back': Ar. *ẓahr*).* The clause *and to a cubit thou shalt finish it above* is unintelligible as it stands: some suggestions are given in the footnote.—The *door* of the ark is to be *in its* (longer?) *side*; and the cells inside are to be arranged in three stories. The ship of Ut-napištim appears to have had six decks, divided into nine compartments (ll. 61–63).

17–22. The purpose of the ark.—Gunkel thinks that v.[17] commences a second communication to Noah; and that in the source from which P drew, the construction of the ark was recorded before its purpose was revealed (as in the parallel account of J: see on 7^1). That, of course, is possible; but that P slurred over the proof of Noah's faith because he had no interest in *personal* religion can hardly be supposed. There is really nothing to suggest that [17ff.] are not the continuation of [13–16].—**17.** *Behold I am about to bring the Flood*] הַמַּבּוּל: see above on 7^7 (J), and in the Note below. —**18.** *I will establish my covenant, etc.*] anticipating $9^{9ff.}$. De. and Gu. distinguish the two covenants, taking that here referred to as a special pledge to Noah of safety in the coming judgement; but that is contrary to the usage of P,

---

17. ואני הנני] cf. Dri. *JPh.* xi. 226.—המבול מַיִם (cf. 7^6)] The מים is certainly superfluous grammatically, but על־הארץ is necessary to the completeness of the sentence. 𝕲 omits מים in 7^6, and inserts it in 9^{11b} (P). Whether it be an explanatory gloss of the unfamiliar מבול (so most), or a peculiar case of nominal apposition (see Dri. *T.* § 188), it is difficult to decide: on the idea that it is meant to distinguish the water-flood from the light-flood, see above, p. 154. The pointing מִיָּם (JDMich. al.) is objectionable on various grounds: for one thing, P never speaks of the Flood as coming 'from the sea.' J's phrase is מי המבול: $7^{7.10}$; cf. 9^{11a} (P). —לְשַׁחֵת] 𝔐𝔰𝔪, לשחית; but elision of ה in Hiph. is unusual: some Sam. MSS have לחשחית (Ball).—יִגְוַע] 'expire,'—peculiar to P in Hex. (cf. 7^{21} $25^{8.17}$

---

* According to Jensen (*KIB*, vi. 1, 487), the Bab. ark had a dome-shaped roof (***mubbu***).

to whom the בְּרִית is always a solemn and permanent embodiment of the divine will, and never a mere occasional provision (Kraetzschmar, *Bundesvorstg.* 197 f.). The entering of the ark is therefore not the condition to be fulfilled by Noah *under* the covenant, but the condition which makes the establishment of the promised covenant possible (Ho.).—*Thou and thy sons, etc.*] The enumeration is never omitted by P except in 8^{1}; cf. 7^{13} $8^{16.\ 18}$: ct. J in 7^{1}.—**19 f.** One pair of each species of animals (fishes naturally excepted) is to be taken into the ark. The distinction of clean and unclean kinds belongs on the theory of P to a later dispensation —**20.** The classification (which is repeated with slight variations in $7^{14.\ 21}$ 8^{19} $9^{2f.\ 10}$) here omits wild beasts (חַיָּה): *v.i.* on v.[19].—יָבֹאוּ does not necessarily imply that the animals came of themselves (Ra. IEz. al.), any more than תָּבִיא (v.[19]) necessarily means that Noah had to catch them.—**21.** *all food which is* (or *may be*) *eaten*] according to the prescriptions of $1^{29f.}$.—**22.** *so did he*] the pleonastic sentence is peculiar to P; cf. esp. Ex. 40^{16} (also Ex. 7^{6} $12^{28.\ 50}$ $39^{32.\ 42f.}$, Nu. 1^{54}, and often).

VII. 6, 11, 13–17a. Commencement of the Flood.—

These vv. (omitting [16b] [J]) appear to form an uninterrupted section of the Priestly narrative, following immediately on 6^{22}.—**6.** Date of the Flood by the year of Noah's life. The number 600 is a Babylonian *ner*; and it has been thought that the statement rests ultimately on a Bab. tradition.—**11.** This remarkably precise date introduces a sort of diary

---

35^{29} 49^{33},—12 t. in all); elsewhere only in poetry (Holz. *Einl.* 341).—**19.** הָחַי] (on anomalous pointing of art. see G–K. § 35*f* (1)). 𝔐 reads החיה as in 8^{17}; and so 𝔊, which takes the word in the limited sense of wild animals, reading [*καὶ ἀπὸ παντῶν τῶν κτηνῶν καὶ ἀ. π. τ. ἑρπετῶν*] *κ. ἀ. π. τ. θηρίων* (see $7^{14.\ 21}$ 8^{19}).—שְׁנַיִם] 𝔊𝔖 שנים שנים as in $7^{9.\ 15}$. So also v.[20].—**20.** מכלרמש] Ins. ו with 𝔐𝔊𝔖𝔙𝔗°; the ו is necessary to the sense.—𝔊 has כל before each class, but MT rightly confines it to the heterogeneous רמש (Ho.). For רמש האדמה, 𝔐 𝔊 have אשר רמש על הא׳.—**21.** לאכלה] see on 1^{29}.—**22.** אלהים] 𝔊 *Κύριος ὁ θ.*

6. On the syntax of the time-relation, see G–K. § 164*a.*—מַיִם] see 6^{17}.—**11.** בשנת—שנה] 'in the year of 600 years'; cf. G–K. § 134*o.*—For '17th day' 𝔊 has '27th'; see p. 167 below.—אֲרֻבֹּת השמים] 8^{2}, Mal. 3^{10}, = א׳ בשמים, 2 Ki. $7^{2.\ 19}$ = א׳ מָּרוֹם, Is. 24^{18}. Apart from these phrases the

of the Flood, which is carried through to the end: see below, p. 167 f. V.^{6}, though consistent with ^{11}, is certainly rendered superfluous by it; and it is not improbable that we have here to do with a fusion of authorities within the Priestly tradition (p. 168).—*the fountains of the Great Deep*] (תְּהוֹם רַבָּה: see on 1^2). Outbursts of subterranean water are a frequent accompaniment of seismic disturbances in the alluvial districts of great rivers (Suess, 31–33); and a knowledge of this physical fact must have suggested the feature here expressed. In accordance with ancient ideas, however, it is conceived as an eruption of the subterranean ocean on which the earth was believed to rest (see p. 17). At the same time *the windows of heaven were opened*] allowing the waters of the heavenly ocean to mingle with the lower. The Flood is thus a partial undoing of the work of creation; although we cannot be certain that the Heb. writer looked on it from that point of view. Contrast this grandiose cosmological conception with the simple representation of J, who sees nothing in the Flood but the result of excessive rain.

Gunkel was the first to point out the poetic character and structure of ^{11b}: note the phrase תהום רבה (Am. 7^4, Is. 51^{10}, Ps. 36^7), and the *parallelismus membrorum.* He considers the words a fragment of an older version of the legend which (like the Babylonian) was written in poetry. A similar fragment is found in 8^2.

13. *On that very day*] continuing v.^{11}. The idea that all the animals entered the ark on one day (J allows a week) has been instanced as an example of P's love of the marvellous (Ho. Gu.).—**14–16.** See on $6^{19f.}$.—**17a.** *the Flood*

---

word 'א is rare, and denotes a latticed opening, Hos. 13^3, Is. 60^8, Ec. 12^3. Here it can only mean 'sluices'; the *καταράκται* of 𝔊 "unites the senses of waterfalls, trap-doors, and sluices" (De.).—**13.** בעצם היום הזה] $17^{23. 26}$, Ex. $12^{17. 41. 51}$, Lv. $23^{14. 21. 28. 29. 30}$, Dt. 32^{48}, Jos. 5^{11} (all P); Ho. *Einl.* 346.—שְׁלֹשֶׁת] irregular gender: G-K. § 97 *c.*—אִתָּם] Better as 𝔊𝔖 אִתּוֹ ($8^{16. 18}$).—**14.** הַחַיָּה] distinguishing wild beasts from domestic (cf. v.^{21}); see on 6^{19}.—כל צפור וגו'] 𝔊 om. Cf. Ezk. 17^{23} 39^4.—**17a.** ארבעים יום] Bu. (264) ingeniously suggests that the last three consonants of the gloss (ארבע[מים]) represent the genuine מַיִם of P (6^{17} 7^6). 𝔊 adds וארבעים לילה. The half-verse cannot be assigned to J, because it would be a mere repetition of v.^{12}.

came upon the earth] as a result of the upheaval, v.[11].—The words *forty days* are a gloss based on 7[4. 12] (*v.i.*); the Redactor treating J's forty days as an episode in the longer chronology: see on v.[12] (J).

18–21, 24. Magnitude and effect of the Flood.—While J confines himself to what is essential—the extinction of life—and leaves the universality of the Flood to be inferred, P not only asserts its universality, but so to speak proves it, by giving the exact height of the waters above the highest mountains.—**18, 19.** *prevailed*] גָּבַר, lit. 'be strong' (𝕲 ἐπεκράτει, Aq. ἐνεδυναμώθη). The Flood is conceived as a contest between the water and the dry land.—**20.** *fifteen cubits*] is just half the depth of the ark. The statement is commonly explained in the light of 8[4]: when the Flood was at its height the ark (immersed to half its depth, and therefore drawing fifteen cubits of water) was just over one of the highest mountains; so that on the very slightest abatement of the water it grounded! The explanation is plausible enough (on the assumption that 8[4] belongs to P); but it is quite as likely that the choice of the number is purely arbitrary.—**24.** 150 *days*] the period of 'prevalence' of the Flood, reckoned from the outbreak (v.[11]): see p. 168.

VIII. 1, 2a, 3b–5, 13a, 14. Abatement of the Flood.—The judgement being complete, God remembers the survivors in mercy. The Flood has no sooner reached its maximum than it begins to abate ([3b]), and the successive stages of the subsidence are chronicled with the precision of a calendar.—**1.** *remembered*] in mercy, as 19[29] 30[22] etc. The inclusion of the animals in the kindly thought of the Almighty is a touch of nature in P which should not be overlooked.—**1b.** The mention of the wind ought certainly to follow the arrest of the cause of the Deluge ([2a]). It is said in defence of the present order that the sending of the wind and the stopping

---

19. וַיְכֻסּוּ] 𝕲 וַיְכַסּוּ, with מַיִם as subj. (better). So v.[20].—**20.** גָּבְרוּ] 𝕲 גָּבְהוּ (ὑψώθη), is preferable to MT (cf. Ps. 103[11]).—הֶהָרִים] 𝕲 (and 𝕾) add τὰ ὑψηλά as in [19].—**21.** וכל האדם] here distinguished from כל־בשר.

1. The addition of 𝕲 καὶ παντῶν τῶν πετεινῶν κ. π. τ. ἑρπετῶν is here very much in place.—וַיָּשֹׁכּוּ] The √ is rare and late: Nu. 17[20] (P),

of the elemental waters are regarded as simultaneous (Di.); but that does not quite meet the difficulty. See, further, p. 155 above.—**3b.** *at the end of* the 150 *days*] (7^{24}). See the footnote.—**4.** The resting of the ark.—*on* (*one of*) *the mountains of 'Ărārāṭ*] which are probably named as the highest known to the Hebrews at the time of writing; just as one form of the Indian legend names the Himalayas, and the Greek, Parnassus. Araraṭ (Ass. *Urarṭu*) is the NE part of Armenia; cf. 2 Ki. 19^{37} = Is. 37^{38}, Jer. 51^{27}. The name *Mount* Araraṭ, traditionally applied to the highest peak (Massis, Agridagh: *c.* 17,000 ft.) of the Armenian mountains, rests on a misunderstanding of this passage.

The traditions regarding the landing-place of the ark are fully discussed by Lenorm. *Or.*[2] ii. 1 ff.: cf. Tu. 133–136; Nö. *Unters.* 145 ff.—The district called Araraṭ or Urarṭu is properly that named in Armenian *Ayrarat*, and is probably identical with the country of the Alarodians of Herod. iii. 94, vii. 79. It is the province of Armenia lying NE of Lake Van, including the fertile plain watered by the Araxes, on the right (SW) side of which river Mt. Massis rises.* Another tradition, represented by Berossus (p. 177 below) and 𝔗ᴼ 𝔖 (קַרְדוּ)†, locates the mountain in Kurdistan, viz. at Ǧebel Ǧûdî, which is a striking mountain SW of Lake Van, commanding a wide view over the Mesopotamian plain. This view is adopted in the Koran (Sur. xi. 46), and has become traditional among the Moslems.—The 'mountain of Niṣir' of the cuneiform legend lies still further south, probably in one of the ranges between the Lower Zab and the next tributary to the S, the Adhem (Radânu) (Streck, *ZA*, xv. 272). Tiele and Kosters, however (*EB*, 289), identify it with Elburz, the sacred mountain of the Iranians (S of the Caspian Sea); and find a trace of this name in the *μέγα ὄρος κατὰ τὴν 'Αρμενίαν Βάρις λεγόμενον* indicated as the mountain of the ark by Nicolaus Damascenus (Jos. *Ant.* i. 95).—What the original Heb. tradition was, it is impossible to say. The writers just named conjecture that it was identical with the Bab., Araraṭ being here a corruption of *Hara haraiti* (the ancient Iranian name of Elburz), which was afterwards confused with the land of Urarṭu. Nö. and Ho. think it probable that 𝔗ᴼ and 𝔖 preserve the oldest name (Ḳardu), and that Araraṭ is a correction made when it was

---

Jer. 5^{26}, Est. 2^{1} 7^{10}.—3b. מקצה חמשים] Rd. מקץ החמשים (Str. Ho. Gk.). 𝔐 מקץ ח׳.—4. For 17th 𝔊 has 27th (7^{11}).

---

* "Ararat regio in Armenia campestris est, per quam Araxes fluit, incredibilis ubertatis, ad radices Tauri montis, qui usque illuc extenditur." Jerome on Is. 37^{38}.

† 𝔗ᴶ has both קרדוניא and ארמניא, as has Berossus.

discovered that the northern mountains are in reality higher than those of Kurdistan.

5. *the tops of the mountains*] *i.e.* (as usually explained) the other (lower) mountains. The natural interpretation would be that the statement is made absolutely, from the viewpoint of an imaginary spectator; in which case it is irreconcilable with v.[4] (cf. Hupf. *Qu.* 16 f.).—**13a, 14.** On New Year's day the earth's surface was uncovered, though still moist; but not till the 27th of the 2nd month was it *dry* (*arefacta*: cf. Jer. 50[38]).

15–19. Exit from the ark: blessing on the animals.—17b. A renewal of the benediction of 1[22], which had been forfeited by the excesses before the Flood. The corresponding blessing on man is reserved for 9[1ff.].—**19.** The animals leave the ark *according to their families*,—an example of P's love of order.

The *Chronology of the Flood* presents a number of intricate though unimportant problems.—The Dates, according to MT and 𝔊,* are as follows:

1. Commencement of Flood	600th year,	2nd mo.,	17th day	(𝔊 27th)
2. Climax (resting of ark)	,,	7th ,,	17th ,,	(𝔊 27th)
3. Mountain tops visible	,,	10th (𝔊 11th),	1st ,,	
4. Waters dried up	601st year,	1st mo.,	1st ,,	
5. Earth dry	,,	2nd ,,	27th ,,	

The chief points are these: (*a*) In 𝔊 the duration of the Flood is exactly 12 months; and since the 5 months between (1) and (2) amount to 150 days (7[24] 8[3]), the basis of reckoning is presumably the Egyptian *solar* year (12 mo. of 30 days + 5 intercalated days). The 2 months' interval between (3) and (4) also agrees, to a day, with the 40 + 21 days

5. היו הלוך וחסור] 'went on decreasing' (G–K. § 113 *u*); less idiomatic than [3a] (J).—*Tenth*] 𝔊 *eleventh*.—13a. After שנה 𝔊 adds לחיי נח (7[11]).

15. אלהים] 𝔊 Κύριος ὁ θ.—17. 𝔪𝔊𝔖 read וְכל־החיה; so v.[19]. — הוצא] Why Qrê substitutes in this solitary instance הַיְצֵא is not clear: see Kön. i. p. 641.—וּפָרוּ וְרָבוּ] 𝔊 וּפְרוּ וּרְבוּ (Impv.), omitting the previous ושרצו בארץ. This is perhaps the better text: see on 9[1ff.] 𝔙 reads the whole as Impv. —19. כל־הרמש—רמש] 𝔊 (better) וכל־הבהמה וכל־העוף וכל הרֶמֶשׂ הרֹמֵשׂ.—למשפחתיהם] (Jer. 15[3]); the pl. of מין (P's word in ch. 1) is not in use (Ho.).

* *Jub.* v. 23–32 (cf. vi. 25 f.) adds several dates, but otherwise agrees with MT, except that it makes the Flood commence on the 27th, gives no date for the resting of the ark, and puts the drying of the earth on the 17th, and the opening of the ark on the 27th day of the 2nd month.

of 8^{6-12} (J). In MT the total duration is 12 mo. + 10 days; hence the reckoning appears to be by *lunar* months of *c.* 29½ days, making up a solar year of 364 days.*—(*b*) The Massoretic scheme, however, produces a discrepancy with the 150 days; for 5 lunar months fall short of that period by two or three days. Either the original reckoning was by solar months (as in 𝔊), or (what is more probable) the 150 days belong to an older computation independent of the Calendar.† It has been surmised that this points to a 10 months' duration of the Flood (150 days' increase + 150 days' subsidence); and (Ew. Di.) that a trace of this system remains in the 74 days' interval between (2) and (3), which amounts to about one-half of the period of subsidence.—(*c*) Of the separate data of the Calendar no satisfactory explanation has yet been given. The only date that bears its significance on its face is the disappearance of the waters on the 1st day of the year; and even this is confused by the trivial and irrelevant distinction between the drying up of the waters and the drying of the earth. Why the Flood began and ended in the 2nd month, and on the 17th or 27th day, remains, in spite of all conjectures, a mystery.‡ (*d*) The question whether the months are counted from the old Heb. New Year in the autumn, or, according to the post-Exilic (Babylonian) calendar, from the spring, has been discussed from the earliest times, and generally decided in favour of the former view (*Jub.*, Jos. *Ant.* i. 80, 𝔗J, Ra. and most).§ The arguments on one side or the other have little weight. If the second autumn month (Marcheŝwan) is a suitable time for the commencement of the Flood, because it inaugurates the rainy season in Palestine and Babylonia, it is for the same reason eminently unsuitable for its close. P elsewhere follows the Babylonian calendar, and there is no reason to suppose he departs from his usual procedure here (so Tu. Gu. al.).—(*e*) The only issue of real interest is how much of the chronology is to be attributed to the original Priestly Code. If there be two discordant systems in the record, the 150 days might be the reckoning of P, and the Calendar a later adjustment (Di.); or, again, the 150 days might be traditional, and the Calendar the work of P himself (Gu.). On the former (the more probable) assumption the further question arises whether the additions were made before or after the amalgamation of J and P. The evidence is not decisive; but the divergences of 𝔊 from MT seem to prove that the chronology was still in process of development after the formation of the Canon.—See Dahse, *ZATW*, xxviii. 7 ff., where it is shewn that a group of Greek MSS

---

* So *Jub.* vi. 32. Cf. Charles's Notes, pp. 54 f. and 56 f.

† That it is a later redactional addition (Ho.) is much less likely.

‡ King (*JTS*, v. 204 f.) points out the probability that in the triennial cycle of Synagogue readings the Parasha containing the Flood-story fell to be read *about* the 17th Iyyar. This might conceivably have suggested the starting-point of the Calendar (but if so it would bring down the latter to a somewhat late period), or a modification of an original 27th (𝔊), which, however, would itself require explanation.

§ See De. 175 f., 183, 184; Di. 129 f.

agree closely with *Jub.*, and argued (but unconvincingly) that the original reckoning was a solar year, beginning and ending with the 27th of the 2nd month.

IX. 1–7. The new world-order.—The religious significance of the Flood to the mind of the Priestly writers appears in this and the following sections. It marks the introduction of a new and less ideal age of history, which is that under which mankind now lives. The original harmonious order of nature, in which all forms of slaughter were prohibited, had been violated by both men and animals before the Flood (see on $6^{11f.}$). This is now replaced by a new constitution, in which the slaughter of animals for human food is legalised; and only two restrictions are imposed on the bloodthirsty instincts of the degenerate creatures: (1) Man may not eat the 'life' of an animal, and (2) human blood may not be shed with impunity either by man or beast.

The Rabbinical theologians were true to the spirit of the passage when they formulated the idea of the 'Noachic commandments,' binding on men generally, and therefore required of the 'proselytes of the gate'; though they increased their number. See Schürer, iii. 128 f.

Vv.$^{1-7}$, both in substance and expression (cf. נתתי לכם, לכם יהיה לאכלה את־כל, and esp. ירק עשב), form a pendant to $1^{29f.}$ We have seen (p. 35) that these vv. are supplementary to the cosmogony; and the same is true of the present section in relation to the story of the Flood. It does not appear to be an integral part of the Deluge tradition; and has no parallel (as vv.$^{8-16}$ have) in J or the Bab. narrative (Gu.). But that neither this nor $1^{29f.}$ is a secondary addition to P is clear from the phraseology here, which is moulded as obviously on $1^{22.\,27f.}$ as on $1^{29f.}$. To treat 9^{4-6} as a later insertion (Ho.) is arbitrary. On the contrary, the two passages represent the characteristic contribution of P to the ancient traditions.

1. An almost verbal repetition of 1^{28}. The wives of Noah and his sons are not mentioned, women having no religious standing in the OT (so v.^{8}). It is perhaps also significant that here (in contrast to 1^{22}) the animals are excluded from the blessing (though not from the covenant—

---

1. 𝔊 adds at end καὶ κατακυριεύσατε αὐτῆς, as 1^{28}.—**2.** בכל—ובכל] 𝔊𝔖 ובכל (*bis*). The בְּ cannot be that of specification (7^{21} 8^{17} $9^{10.\,16}$ etc.), since no comprehensive category precedes; yet it is harsh to take it as continuing the sense of על (𝔊), and not altogether natural to render

vv.[10. 12. 15ff.]).—2. Man's 'dominion' over the animals is re-established, but now in the form of *fear* and *dread* (cf. Dt. 11[25]) towards him on their part.—*into your hand they are given*] conveying the power of life and death (Lev. 26[25], Dt. 19[12] etc.).—3. The central injunction: removal of the prohibition of animal food.—*moving thing that is alive*] an unusually vague definition of animal life.—Observe P's resolute ignoring of the distinction between clean and unclean animals.—4. The first restriction. Abstention from eating blood, or flesh from which the blood has not been drained, is a fundamental principle of the Levitical legislation (Lev. 7[27] 17[10. 14]); and though to our minds a purely ceremonial precept, is constantly classed with moral laws (Ezk. 33[25f.] etc.). The theory on which the prohibition rests is repeatedly stated (Lev. 17[11. 14], Dt. 12[23]): the blood is the life, and the life is sacred, and must be restored to God before the flesh can be eaten. Such mystic views of the blood are primitive and widespread; and amongst some races formed a motive not for abstinence, but for drinking it.* All the same it is unnecessary to go deeper in search of a reason for the ancient Heb. horror of eating with the blood (1 Sa. 14[32ff.]†).—5, 6. The second restriction: sanctity of human life. 'Life' is expressed alternately by דָּם and נֶפֶשׁ.—On לנפשתיכם, *v.i.*—*I will require*] exact an account of, or equivalent for (42[22], Ezk. 33[6], Ps. 9[13] etc.). That God is

'along with' (Di.).—נְתֻנוּ] 𝔐 𝔊 נְתַתִּיו:—3. נתתי לכם את־כל] seems a slavish repetition from 1[29]. We should at least expect the art., which 𝔐 (הכל) supplies.—4. דמו is an explanatory apposition (if not a gloss) to בנפשו; but 𝔊 renders ἐν αἵματι ψυχῆς, and 𝔖 (ܒܢܦܫܗ ܕܡܗ), Σ. (οὗ σὺν ψυχῇ αἷμα αὐτοῦ) as a rel. cl.—5. ואך is suspicious after the preceding אך. 𝔐 (ואת־דמכם) omits.—לנפשתיכם] usually taken as circumscription of gen., emphasising the suff.: '*your* blood, your own'—in contrast with the animals. It is better to render 'according to your persons,' *i.e.* individually;—"dem eloh. Sprachgebrauch entspricht distributive Fassung des ל doch am besten" (De.).—מיד איש אחיו] 'from the hand of

* See *RS*², 234 f.; Frazer, *GB*², i. 133 f., 352 f.; Kennedy, *EB*, 1544.

† It has been thought that the offence warned against is the barbarous African custom of eating portions of animals still alive (𝔗ᴶ, Ra. De. al.); but that is a mistake.

the avenger of blood is to J (ch. 4) a truth of nature; to P it rests on a positive enactment.—*from the hand of every beast*] see Ex. $21^{28f.}$.—**6a** is remarkable for its assonances and the perfect symmetry of the two members: שֹׁפֵךְ דַּם הָאָדָם | בָּאָדָם דָּמוֹ יִשָּׁפֵךְ. It is possibly an ancient judicial formula which had become proverbial (Gu.). The 𝔗𝔗 (*v.i.*) read into the text the idea of judicial procedure; others (Tu. al.) suppose the law of blood-revenge to be contemplated. In reality the manner of execution is left quite indefinite.—**6b.** The reason for the higher value set on the life of man. On the *image of God* see on $1^{26f.}$.—**7.** The section closes, as it began, with the note of benediction.

8–17. The Covenant and its Sign.—In P as in J (8^{20-22}) the story of the Flood closes with an assurance that the world shall never again be visited by such a catastrophe; and in both the promise is absolute, not contingent on the behaviour of the creatures. In P it takes the form of a covenant between God and all flesh,—the first of two covenants by which (according to this writer) the relations of the Almighty to His creatures are regulated. On the content and scope of this Noachic covenant, see the concluding note, p. 173 f.—**9.** *establish my covenant*] in fulfilment of 6^{18}. P's formula for the inauguration of the covenant is always הֵקִים בְּרִית or נָתַן ב׳ (17^2, Nu. 25^{12}) instead of the more ancient and technical כָּרַת ב׳.—**11.** The essence of the covenant is that the earth shall never be devastated by a Flood. Whether its idea be exhausted by this assurance

---

one man that of another.' The full expression would be מיד איש את־נפש אחיו (Ols.); but all languages use breviloquence in the expression of reciprocity. The construction is hardly more difficult than in 15^{10} $42^{25.35}$; and an exact parallel occurs in Zec. 7^{10}. See G–K. § 139*c*; Bu. 283 ff. The ואחיו of 𝔐 𝔖𝔙 makes nonsense; 𝔊 omits the previous ומיד האדם. It would be better to move the Athnach so as to commence a new clause with מיד איש.—**6.** באדם] 𝔙 om.; 𝔗^O בסהדין ממימר דיניא: 𝔗^J is still more explicit.—**7.** ורבו בה] 𝔙 *et implete eam* (as v.[1]). Read ורדו בה after 1^{28} (Nestle in Ball). So 𝔊^L κατακυριευσατε.

10. מכל] 'as many as'; see on 6^2.—לכל חית הארץ] 𝔊 om.—לְכל] perhaps = 'in short': cf. 23^{10}, see G–K. § 143 *e*. The sense of ח׳ ה׳ = 'animals' in general, immediately after the same expression in the sense of 'wild animals,' makes the phrase suspicious (Ho.).—**11.** מבול] 𝔐 המבול;

is a difficult question, on which see p. 173 below.—**12–17.** The sign of the covenant. "In times when contracts were not reduced to writing, it was customary, on the occasion of solemn vows, promises, and other 'covenant' transactions, to appoint a sign, that the parties might at the proper time be reminded of the covenant, and a breach of its observance be averted. Exx. in common life: Gn. 21^{30}, cf. $38^{17f.}$" (Gu.).* Here the sign is a natural phenomenon—the rainbow; and the question is naturally asked whether the rainbow is conceived as not having existed before (so IEz. Tu.). That is the most obvious assumption, though not perhaps inevitable. That the laws of the refraction and reflection of light on which the rainbow depends actually existed before the time of Noah is a matter of which the writer may very well have been ignorant.—For the rest, the image hardly appears here in its original form. The brilliant spectacle of the upturned bow against the dark background of the retreating storm naturally appeals to man as a token of peace and good-will from the god who has placed it there; but of this thought the passage contains no trace: the bow is set in the cloud by God to remind Himself of the promise He has given. It would seem as if P, while retaining the anthropomorphism of the primitive conception, has sacrificed its primary significance to his abstract theory of the covenant with its accompanying sign. On the mythological origin of the symbol, see below.—**14–16.** Explanation of the sign.—^{14b} continues ^{14a}: *and* (*when*) *the bow appears in the cloud*; the apodosis commencing with ^{15} (against De.).—The bow seems conceived as lodged once for all in the cloud (so IEz.), to appear at

---

𝔊 adds מָיִם.—לשחת] 𝔐 להשחית; so v.^{15}.—**12.** אלהים] 𝔊 Κύριος ὁ θ. + (with 𝔖) אל־נח.—**13.** נתתי] hardly historic pf. ('I have set'), but either pf. of instant action ('I do set'), or pf. of certainty ('I will set'); see G–K § 106 *i, m, n.*—**14.** בעַנני ענן] lit. 'when I cloud with cloud'; see G–K. §§ 52 *d* and 117 *r.* — הקשת] 𝔊𝔙 קשתי; so 𝔊 in v.^{16}.—**15.** חיה] 𝔐𝔖 החיה אשר אתכם (cf. v.^{12}).

---

* Hence both of P's covenants are confirmed by a sign: the Abrahamic covenant by circumcision, and this by the rainbow.

the right moment for recalling the covenant to the mind of God.—**16.** *an everlasting covenant*] so $17^{7.13.19}$, Ex. 31^{16}, Lv. 24^{8}, Nu. 18^{19} 25^{13} (all P).

The idealisation of the rainbow occurs in many mythologies. To the Indians it was the battle-bow of Indra, laid aside after his contest with the demons; among the Arabs "Kuzah shoots arrows from his bow, and then hangs it up in the clouds" (We. *Prol.*[6] 311); by Homer it was personified as Ἶρις, the radiant messenger of the Olympians (*Il.* ii. 786, iii. 121; cf. Ov. *Met.* i. 270 f.), but also regarded as a portent of war and storm (xi. 27 f., xvii. 547 ff.). In the Icelandic Eddas it is the bridge between heaven and earth. A further stage of idealisation is perhaps found in the Bab. Creation-myth, where Marduk's bow, which he had used against Tiamat, is set in the heavens as a constellation. (See Je. *ATLO*[2], 248; Di. 155 f.; Gu. 138 f.; Dri. 99).—These examples go far to prove a mythological origin of the symbolism of this passage. It springs from the imagery of the thunderstorm; the lightnings are Yahwe's arrows; when the storm is over, His bow (cf. Hab. 3^{9-11}, Ps. $7^{13f.}$) is laid aside and appears in the sky as a sign that His anger is pacified. The connexion with the Flood-legend (of which there are several examples, though no Babylonian parallel has yet been discovered) would thus be a later, though still ancient, adaptation. The rainbow is only once again mentioned in OT (Ezk. 1^{28} הקשת אשר יהיה בענן ביום הגשם: but see Sir. $43^{11f.}$ 50^{7}), and it is pointed out (by We al.) that elsewhere קֶשֶׁת always denotes the bow as a weapon, never an arc of a circle.

With regard to the covenant itself, the most important question theologically is whether it includes the regulations of vv.[1-6], or is confined to the unconditional promise that there shall no more be a flood. For the latter view there is undoubtedly much to be said (see Valeton, *ZATW*, xii. 3 f.). Vv.[1-7] and [8-17] are certainly distinct addresses, and possibly of different origin (p. 169); and while the first says nothing of a covenant, the second makes no reference to the preceding stipulations. Then, the sign of the covenant is a fact independent of human action; and it is undoubtedly the meaning of the author that the promise stands sure whether the precepts of [1-7] be observed or not. On the other hand, it is difficult to believe that P, to whom the ברית means so much, should have dignified by that name the negative assurance of v.[11]. In the case of the Abrahamic covenant, the ברית marks a new ordering of the relations between God and the world, and is capable of being observed or violated by those with whom it is established. Analogy, therefore, is so far in favour of including the ordinances of [1-7] in the terms of the covenant (so Is. $24^{5f.}$). Kraetzschmar (*Bundesvorstg.* 192 ff.) solves the difficulty by the supposition that the idea of vv.[8-17] is borrowed by P from J, and represents the notion of the covenant characteristic of that document. It is much simpler to recognise the existence of different tendencies within the priestly school;

---

16. לְ[זָכַר] 𝔖𝔗^{O} לִזְכֹּר.—בין אלהים] 𝔊 ביני.

and we have seen that there are independent reasons for regarding vv.$^{1-7}$ as supplementary to the Deluge tradition followed by P. If that be the case, it is probable that these vv. were inserted by the priestly author with the intention of bringing under the Noachic ברית those elementary religious obligations which he regarded as universally binding on mankind.—On the conception of the ברית in J and P, see chs. 15 and 17.

28, 29. The death of Noah.

The form of these vv. is exactly that of the genealogy, ch. 5; while they are at the same time the conclusion of the תולדת נח (6^9). How much was included under that rubric? Does it cover the whole of P's narrative of the Flood (so that תולדת is practically equivalent to 'biography'), or does it refer merely to the account of his immediate descendants in 6^{10}? The conjecture may be hazarded that $6^{9.10}$ 7^6 $9^{28.29}$ formed a section of the original book of תולדת, and that into this skeleton the full narrative of the Flood was inserted by one of the priestly writers (see the notes on 2^{4a}). The relation of the assumed genealogy to that of ch. 5 would be precisely that of the תולדת of Terah ($11^{27ff.}$) to the תולדת of Shem (11^{10-26}). In each case the second genealogy is extremely short; further, it opens by repeating the last link of the previous genealogy (in each case the birth of three sons, 5^{32} 6^{10}); and, finally, the second genealogy is interspersed with brief historical notices. It may, of course, be held that the whole history of Abraham belongs to the תולדת of Terah; that is the accepted view, and the reasons for disputing it are those mentioned on p. 40 f. Fortunately the question is of no great importance.

The Deluge Tradition.

1. Next to cosmogonies, flood-legends present perhaps the most interesting and perplexing problem in comparative mythology. The wide, though curiously unequal, distribution of these stories, and the frequent occurrence of detailed resemblances to the biblical narrative, have long attracted attention, and were not unnaturally accepted as independent evidence of the strictly historical character of the latter.*

---

29. ויהי, Heb. MSS (London Polyglott) and ש ויהיו.

---

* Andree (*Die Flutsagen ethnographisch betrachtet*, 1891), who has collected between eighty and ninety such stories (of which he recognises forty-three as original and genuine, and twenty-six as influenced by the Bab.) points out, *e.g.*, that they are absent in Arabia, in northern and central Asia, in China and Japan, are hardly found anywhere in Europe (except Greece) or Africa, while the most numerous and remarkable instances come from the American continent (p. 125 f.). The enumeration, however, must not be considered as closed: Naville (*PSBA*, 1904, 251–257, 287–294) claims to have found fresh proof of an Egyptian

On the question of the universality of the Deluge* they have, of course, no immediate bearing, though they frequently assert it; for it could never be supposed that the mere occurrence of a legend in a remote part of the globe proved that the Flood had been there. The utmost that could be claimed is that there had been a deluge coextensive with the primitive seat of mankind; and that the memory of the cataclysm was carried with them by the various branches of the race in their dispersion. But even that position, which is still maintained by some competent writers, is attended by difficulties which are almost insuperable. The scientific evidence for the antiquity of man all over the world shows that such an event (if it ever occurred) must have taken place many thousands of years before the date assigned to Noah; and that the tradition should have been preserved for so long a time among savage peoples without the aid of writing is incredible. The most reasonable line of explanation (though it cannot here be followed out in detail) is that the great majority of the legends preserve the recollection of local catastrophes, such as inundations, tidal waves, seismic floods accompanied by cyclones, etc., of which many historical examples are on record; while in a considerable number of cases these local legends have been combined with features due either to the diffusion of Babylonian culture or to the direct influence of the Bible through Christian missionaries.† In this note we shall confine our attention to the group of legends most closely affiliated to the Babylonian tradition.

2. Of the Babylonian story the most complete version is contained in the eleventh Tablet of the Gilgameš Epic.‡ Gilgameš has arrived at the Isles of the Blessed to inquire of his ancestor Utnapištim how he had been received into the society of the gods. The answer is the long and exceedingly graphic description of the Flood which occupies the bulk of the Tablet. The hero relates how, while he dwelt at Šurippak on

---

tradition in a text of the Book of the Dead, containing the following words: "And further I (the god Tum) am going to deface all I have done; this earth will become water (or an ocean) through an inundation, as it was at the beginning" (*l.c.* p. 289).

* On the overwhelming geological and other difficulties of such a hypothesis, see Dri. 99 f.

† See Andree, *l.c.* 143 ff.; Suess, *The Face of the Earth*, i. 18–72 *pass.* Cf. the discussion by Woods in *DB*, ii. 17 ff.; and Dri. *Gen.* 101 ff.—Lenormant, who once maintained the independence of the legends as witnesses to a primitive tradition, afterwards expressed himself with more reserve, and conceded the possibility that the Mexican and Polynesian myths might be distant echoes of a central legend, emanating ultimately from Babylonia (*Orig.*[2] i. 471 f., 488 ff.).

‡ Discovered by G. Smith, in 1872, among the ruins of Asshurbanipal's library; published 1873-4; and often translated since. See *KAT*[2], 55 ff.; Jen. *Kosmologie*, 368 ff.; Zimmern in Gu.'s *Schöpf. u. Chaos*, 423 ff.; Jen. *KIB*, vi. 1, 116 ff. (the translation followed below); Ba. *Light from the East*, 35 ff.; Je. *ATLO*[2], 228 ff.; and the abridgments in Jast. *RBA*[1], 493 ff.; *KAT*[3], 545 ff.; *Texte u. Bilder*, i. 50 ff.

the Euphrates, it was resolved by the gods in council to send the Flood (*abûbu*) on the earth. Ea, who had been present at the council, resolved to save his favourite Utnapištim; and contrived without overt breach of confidence to convey to him a warning of the impending danger, commanding him to build a ship (*elippu*) of definite dimensions for the saving of his life. The 'superlatively clever one' (*Atra-ḫasis*, a name of Utnapištim) understood the message and promised to obey; and was furnished with a misleading pretext to offer his fellow-citizens for his extraordinary proceedings. The account of the building of the ship (l. 48 ff.) is even more obscure than Gn. $6^{14\text{-}16}$: it is enough to say that it was divided into compartments and was freely smeared with bitumen. The lading of the vessel, and the embarking of the family and dependants of Utnapištim (including artizans), with domestic and wild animals, are then described (l. 81 ff.); and last of all, in the evening, on the appearance of a sign predicted by Šamaš the sun-god, Utnapištim himself enters the ship, shuts his door, and hands over the command to the steersman, Puzur-Bel (90 ff.). On the following morning the storm (magnificently described in ll. 97 ff.) broke; and it raged for six days and nights, till all mankind were destroyed, and the very gods fled to the heaven of Anu and "cowered in terror like a dog."

"When the seventh day came, the hurricane, the Flood, the battle-
storm was stilled,
Which had fought like a (host?) of men.
The sea became calm, the tempest was still, the Flood ceased.
When I saw the day, no voice was heard,
And the whole of mankind was turned to clay.
When the daylight came, I prayed,
I opened a window and the light fell on my face,
I knelt, I sat, and wept,
On my nostrils my tears ran down.
I looked on the spaces in the realm of the sea;
After twelve double-hours an island stood out.
At Niṣir * the ship had arrived.
The mountain of Niṣir stayed the ship . . ." (ll. 130–142).

This brings us to the incident of the birds (146–155):
"When the seventh day † came
I brought out a dove and let it go.
The dove went forth and came back:
Because it had not whereon to stand it returned.
I brought forth a swallow and let it go.
The swallow went forth and came back:
Because it had not whereon to stand it returned.
I brought forth a raven and let it go.
The raven went forth and saw the decrease of the waters,
It ate, it . . . it croaked, but returned not again."

---

* See p. 166. † From the landing.

On this Utnapištim released all the animals; and, leaving the ship, offered a sacrifice:

> "The gods smelt the savour,
> The gods smelt the goodly savour
> The gods gathered like flies over the sacrificer" (160 ff.).

The deities then begin to quarrel, Ištar and Ea reproaching Bel for his thoughtlessness in destroying mankind indiscriminately, and Bel accusing Ea of having connived at the escape of Utnapištim. Finally, Bel is appeased; and entering the ship blesses the hero and his wife:

> "'Formerly Utnapištim was a man;
> But now shall Utnapištim and his wife be like to us the gods:
> Utnapištim shall dwell far hence at the mouth of the streams.'
> Then they took me, and far away at the mouth of the streams they made me dwell" (202 ff.).*

3. The dependence of the biblical narrative on this ancient Babylonian legend hardly requires detailed proof. It is somewhat more obvious in the Yahwistic recension than in the Priestly; but there is enough in the common substratum of the two accounts to show that the Heb. tradition as a whole was derived from Babylonia. Thus both J and P agree with the Bab. story in the general conception of the Flood as a divine visitation, its universality (so far as the human race is concerned), the warnings conveyed to a favoured individual, and the final pacification of the deity who had caused the Deluge. J agrees with Bab. in the following particulars: the entry of the hero into the ark *after* the premonitory rain; the shutting of the door; the prominence of the number 7; the episode of the birds; the sacrifice; and the effect of its 'savour' on the gods. P has also its peculiar correspondences (though some of these may have been in J originally): *e.g.* the precise instructions for building the ark; the mention of bitumen (a distinctively Bab. touch); the grounding of the ark on a mountain; the blessing on the survivors.† By the side of this close and marked parallelism, the material differences on which Nickel (p. 185) lays stress—viz. as to (*a*) the chronology, (*b*) the landing-place of the ark, (*c*) the *details* of the

* Two fragments of another recension of the Flood-legend, in which the hero is regularly named Atra-ḫasis, have also been deciphered. One of them, being dated in the reign of Ammizaduga (*c.* 1980 B.C.), is important as proving that this recension had been reduced to writing at so early a time; but it is too mutilated to add anything substantial to our knowledge of the history of the tradition (see *KIB*, 288–291). The other is a mere scrap of twelve lines, containing Ea's instructions to Atra-ḫasis regarding the building and entering of the ark, and the latter's promise to comply (*KIB*, 256–259). See *KAT*³, 551 f.—The extracts from Berossus preserved by Eus. present the Babylonian story in a form substantially agreeing with that of the Gilgameš Tablets, though with some important variations in detail. See Euseb. *Chron.* i. (ed. Schoene, cols. 19–24, 32–34: cf. Müller, *Fr. Hist. Gr.* ii. 501 ff.).

† See more fully Driver, p. 106.

sending out of the birds, (*d*) the sign of the rainbow (absent in Bab.), and (*e*) the name of the hero—sink into insignificance. They are, indeed, sufficient to disprove immediate literary contact between the Heb. writers and the Gilgameš Tablets; but they do not weaken the presumption that the story had taken the shape known to us in Babylonia before it passed into the possession of the Israelites. And since we have seen (p. 177) that the Babylonian legend was already reduced to writing about the time usually assigned to the Abrahamic migration, it is impossible to suppose that the Heb. oral tradition had preserved an independent recollection of the historical occurrence which may be assumed as the basis of fact underlying the Deluge tradition.—The *differences* between the two narratives are on this account all the more instructive. While the Genesis narratives are written in prose, and reveal at most occasional traces of a poetic original (8^{22} in J, 7^{11b} 8^{2a} in P), the Babylonian epic is genuine poetry, which appeals to a modern reader in spite of the strangeness of its antique sentiment and imagery. Reflecting the feelings of the principal actor in the scene, it possesses a human interest and pathos of which only a few touches appear in J, and none at all in P. The difference here is not wholly due to the elimination of the mythological element by the biblical writers: it is characteristic of the Heb. popular tale that it shuns the 'fine frenzy' of the poet, and finds its appropriate vehicle in the unaffected simplicity of prose recitation. In this we have an additional indication that the story was not drawn directly from a Babylonian source, but was taken from the lips of the common people; although in P it has been elaborated under the influence of the religious theory of history peculiar to that document (p. lx f.). The most important divergences are naturally those which spring from the religion of the OT—its ethical spirit, and its monotheistic conception of God. The ethical motive, which is but feebly developed in the Babylonian account, obtains clear recognition in the hands of the Heb. writers: the Flood is a divine judgement on human corruption; and the one family saved is saved on account of the righteousness of its head. More pervasive still is the influence of the monotheistic idea. The gods of the Babylonian version are vindictive, capricious, divided in counsel, false to each other and to men; the writer speaks of them with little reverence, and appears to indulge in flashes of Homeric satire at their expense. Over against this picturesque variety of deities we have in Genesis the one almighty and righteous God,—a Being capable of anger and pity, and even change of purpose, but holy and just in His dealings with men. It is possible that this transformation supplies the key to some subtle affinities between the two streams of tradition. Thus in the Bab. version the fact that the command to build the ark precedes the announcement of the Flood, is explained by the consideration that Ea cannot explicitly divulge the purpose of the gods; whereas in J it becomes a test of the obedience of Noah (Gu. p. 66). Which representation is older can scarcely be doubted. It is true, at all events, that the Bab. parallel serves as a "measure of the unique grandeur of the idea of God in Israel, which was powerful enough to purify and transform in such a manner the most uncongenial and repugnant features" of the pagan myth (*ib.*); and, further, that "the Flood-story of Genesis retains to this day the power to waken the conscience of the world, and was written by the biblical narrator with this pædagogic and ethical purpose" (*ATLO*², p. 252).

4. Of other ancient legends in which some traces of the Chaldean influence may be suspected, only a very brief account can here be given. The *Indian* story, to which there is a single allusion in the Vedas, is first fully recorded in the Çatapatha Brāhmaṇa, i. 8. 1-10.* It relates how Manu, the first man, found one day in the water with which he performed his morning ablution a small fish, which begged him to take care of it till it should attain its full growth, and then put it in the sea. Manu did so, and in gratitude for its deliverance the fish warned him of the year in which the Flood would come, promising, if he would build a ship, to return at the appointed time and save him. When the Flood came the fish appeared with it; Manu attached the cable of his ship to the fish's horn, and was thus towed to the mountain of the north, where he landed, and whence he gradually descended as the waters fell. In a year's time a woman came to him, announcing herself as his daughter, produced from the offerings he had cast into the water; and from this pair the human race sprang. In a later form of the tradition (Mahābhārata, iii. 187. 2 ff.),† the Babylonian affinities are somewhat more obvious; but even in the oldest version they are not altogether negligible, especially when we remember that the fish (which in the Mahābhārata is an incarnation of Brahma) was the symbol of the god Ea.‡—The *Greeks* had several Flood-legends, of which the most widely diffused was that of Deukalion, best known from the account of Apollodorus (i. 7. 2 ff.).§ Zeus, resolved to destroy the brazen race, sends a heavy rain, which floods the greater part of Greece, and drowns all men except a few who escape to the mountain tops. But Deukalion, on the advice of his father Prometheus, had prepared a chest, loaded it with provisions, and taken refuge in it with his wife Pyrrha. After 9 days and nights they land on Parnassus; Deukalion sacrifices to Zeus and prays for a new race of men: these are produced from stones which he and his wife, at the command of the god, throw over their shoulders. The incident of the ark seems here incongruous, since other human beings were saved without it. It is perhaps an

* Translated by Eggeling, *Sacred Books of the East*, xii. 216 ff. See Usener, *Die Sintfluthsagen* (*Religionsgeschichtliche Untersuchungen*, iii.), 25 ff.

† Translated by Protap Chandra Roy (Calcutta, 1884), iii. 552 ff. See Usener, 29 ff.

‡ Usener, however (240 ff.), maintains the entire independence of the Indian and Semitic legends.

§ The earliest allusion is Pindar, *Ol.* 9. 41 ff. Cf. Ovid, *Met.* i. 244-415; Paus. i. 40. 1, x. 6. 2, etc. The incident of the dove (in a peculiar modification) appears only in Plut. *De sollert. an.* 13.—Usener, 31 ff., 244 ff.

indication of the amalgamation of a foreign element with local Deluge traditions.—A *Syrian* tradition, with some surprising resemblances to P in Gen., has been preserved by the Pseudo-Lucian (*De dea Syra*, 12, 13). The wickedness of men had become so great that they had to be destroyed. The fountains of the earth and the flood-gates of heaven were opened simultaneously; the whole world was submerged, and all men perished. Only the pious Deukalion-Sisuthros * was saved with his family in a great chest, into which as he entered all sorts of animals crowded. When the water had disappeared, Deukalion opened the ark, erected altars, and founded the sanctuary of Derketo at Hierapolis. The hole in the earth which swallowed up the Flood was shown under the temple, and was seen by the writer, who thought it not quite big enough for the purpose. In Usener's opinion we have here the Chaldean legend localised at a Syrian sanctuary, there being nothing Greek about it except the name Deukalion.—A *Phrygian* localisation of the Semitic tradition is attested by the epithet *κιβωτός* applied to the Phrygian Apameia (Kelainai) from the time of Augustus (Strabo, xii. 8. 13, etc.); and still more remarkably by bronze coins of that city dating from the reign of Septimius Severus. On these an open chest is represented, bearing the inscription ΝΩΕ, in which are seen the figures of the hero and his wife; a dove is perched on the lid of the ark, and another is flying with a twig in its claws. To the left the same two human figures are seen standing in the attitude of prayer.† The late date of these coins makes the hypothesis of direct Jewish, or even Christian, influence extremely probable.—The existence of a *Phœnician* tradition is inferred by Usener (248 ff.) from the discovery in Etruria and Sardinia of bronze models of ships with various kinds of animals standing in them: one of them is said to date from the 7th cent. B.C. There is no extant written record of the Phœnician legend: on Gruppe's reconstruction from the statements of Greek mythographers see above, p. 141.

5. There remains the question of the origin of this widespread and evidently very popular conception of a universal Deluge. That it embodies a common primitive tradition of an historic event we have already seen to be improbable. If we suppose the original story to have been elaborated in Babylonia, and to have spread thence to other peoples, it may still be doubtful whether we have to do "with a legend based upon facts" or "with a myth which has assumed the form of a history." The mythical theory has been most fully worked out by Usener, who finds the germ of the story in the favourite mythological image of "the god in the chest," representing the voyage of the sun-god across the heavenly ocean: similar explanations were independently propounded by Cheyne (*EB*, 1063 f.) and Zimmern (*ib.* 1058 f.; *KAT*[3], 555). Of a somewhat different order is the astrological theory advocated by Jeremias (249 ff.). The Babylonian astronomers were aware that

---

* Text *Δευκαλίωνα τὸν Σκύθεα*, which Buttmann (*Mythologus*, i. 192) ingeniously emended to Δ. *τ. Σισυθέα*—a modification of the *Σίσιθρος* of Abydenus.

† See the reproductions in Usener, 45, and Je. *ATLO*[1], 131, [2]235.

in the course of ages the spring equinox must traverse the watery (southern) region of the Zodiac: this, on their system, signified a submergence of the whole universe in water; and the Deluge-myth symbolises the safe passage of the vernal sun-god through that part of the ecliptic.—Whatever truth there may be in these theories, it is certain that they do not account for the concrete features of the Chaldean legend; and if (as can hardly be denied) mythical motives are present, it seems just as likely that they were grafted on to a historic tradition as that the history is merely the garb in which a solar or astral myth arrayed itself. The most natural explanation of the Babylonian narrative is after all that it is based on the vague reminiscence of some memorable and devastating flood in the Euphrates valley, as to the physical possibility of which, it may suffice to quote the (perhaps too literal) description of an eminent geologist: "In the course of a seismic period of some duration the water of the Persian Gulf was repeatedly driven by earthquake shocks over the plain at the mouth of the Euphrates. Warned by these floods, a prudent man, Ḥasîs-adra, *i.e.* the god-fearing philosopher, builds a ship for the rescue of his family, and caulks it with pitch, as is still the custom on the Euphrates. The movements of the earth increase; he flees with his family to the ship; the subterranean water bursts forth from the fissured plain; a great diminution in atmospheric pressure, indicated by fearful storm and rain, probably a true cyclone, approaches from the Persian Gulf, and accompanies the most violent manifestations of the seismic force. The sea sweeps in a devastating flood over the plain, raises the rescuing vessel, washes it far inland, and leaves it stranded on one of those Miocene foot-hills which bound the plain of the Tigris on the north and north-east below the confluence of the Little Zab" (Eduard Suess, *The Face of the Earth*, i. 72). See, however, the criticism of Sollas, *The Age of the Earth*, 316.

IX. 18–27.—*Noah as Vine-grower: His Curse and Blessing* (J).

Noah is here introduced in an entirely new character, as the discoverer of the culture of the vine; and the first victim to immoderate indulgence in its fruit. This leads on to an account of the shameless behaviour of his youngest son, and the modesty and filial feeling of the two elder; in consequence of which Noah pronounces a curse on Canaan and blessings on Shem and Japheth.—The Noah of vv.$^{20-27}$ almost certainly comes from a different cycle of tradition from the righteous and blameless patriarch who is the hero of the Flood. The incident, indeed, cannot, without violating all probability, be harmonised with the Flood-narrative at all. In the latter, Noah's sons are married men who take their wives into the ark (so expressly in P, but the same must be presumed for J); here, on the contrary, they are represented as minors living in the 'tent' with their father; and the conduct of the youngest is obviously conceived as an exhibition of juvenile depravity (so Di. Bu. al.). The presumption, therefore, is that vv.[20-27] belong to a stratum of J which knew nothing of the Flood; and this conclusion is confirmed by an examination of the structure of the passage.

First of all, we observe that in v.[24] the offender is the *youngest* son of Noah, and in v.[25] is named Canaan; while Shem and Japheth are referred to as his *brothers*. True, in v.[22] the misdeed is attributed to 'Ham the father of Canaan'; but the words חָם אֲבִי have all the appearance of a gloss intended to cover the transition from [18f.] to [20ff.]; and the clause וְחָם הוּא אֲבִי כְנָעַן in [18b] can have no other purpose. Now [18a] is the close of J's* account of the Flood; and [19] points forward either to J's list of Nations (ch. 10), or to the dispersion of the Tower of Babel.* Vv.[20-27] interrupt this connexion, and must accordingly be assigned to a separate source. That that source is, however, still Yahwistic, is shown partly by the language (יְהוָה, v.[26] [in spite of אֱלֹהִים in v.[27]]; and וַיָּחֶל, v.[20]); and more especially by the connexion with 5[29] (see pp. 3, 133 f.). It is clear, therefore, that a redactor (R^J) has here combined two Yahwistic documents, and sought to reduce the contradiction by the glosses in [18b] and [22].

18, 19. Connecting verses (see above).—Noah's sons are here for the first time named in J, in harmony, however, with the repeated notices of P (5[32] 6[10] 7[13]). On the names see on ch. 10 (p. 195 f.).—**20.** *Noah the husbandman was the first who planted a vineyard*]—a fresh advance in human civilisation. The allusion to Noah as *the* husbandman is

---

19. נפצה כל־הארץ] 'the whole (population of the) earth was scattered.' For the construction cf. 10[5].—נָֽפְצָה] hardly contracted Niph. from √ פצץ [=פוץ] (G-K. § 67*dd*); but from √ נפץ, whether this be a secondary formation from √ פוץ (G-B.[14] 465 f.), or an independent word (BDB, 659). Cf. 1 Sa. 13[11], Is. 11[12] 33[3].—**20.** ויחל וגו'] cf. 4[26] 6[1] 10[8] 11[6] 44[12] (J) 41[54] (E). The rendering 'Noah commenced as a husbandman' (Dav. § 83, *R.* 2) is impossible on account of the art. (ct. 1 Sa. 3[2]): to insert להיות (Ball) does not get rid of the difficulty. The construction with ו cons., instead of inf., is very unusual (Ezr. 3[8]); hence Che. (*EB*, 3426[2]),

---

* Comp. נָֽפְצָה with 10[18] 11[4. 8. 9]; and כָּל־הָאָרֶץ (=the population of the earth) with 11[1. 9] (Bu.); שְׁלֹשָׁה אֵלֶּה בְּנֵי־נֹחַ with 10[29] 22[23] 25[4] (Ho.).

perplexing. If the text be right (*v.i.*), it implies a previous account of him as addicted to (perhaps the inventor of) agriculture, which now in his hands advances to the more refined stage of vine-growing. See the note on p. 185.

Amongst other peoples this discovery was frequently attributed to a god (Dionysus among the Greeks, Osiris among the Egyptians), intoxication being regarded as a divine inspiration. The orgiastic character of the religion of the Canaanites makes it probable that the same view prevailed amongst them; and it has even been suggested that the Noah of this passage was originally a Canaanitish wine-god (see Niebuhr, *Geschichte d. Ebräischen Zeitalters*, 36 ff.). The native religion of Israel (like that of Mohammed) viewed this form of indulgence with abhorrence; and under strong religious enthusiasm the use of fermented drinks was entirely avoided (the Nazirites, Samson, the Rechabites). This feeling is reflected in the narrative before us, where Noah is represented as experiencing in his own person the full degradation to which his discovery had opened the way. It exhibits the repugnance of a healthy-minded race towards the excesses of a debased civilisation.—Since the vine is said to be indigenous to Armenia and Pontus (see De. Di.), it has naturally been proposed to connect the story with the landing of the ark in Ararat. But we have seen that the passage has nothing to do with the Deluge-tradition; and it is more probable that it is an independent legend, originating amidst Palestinian surroundings.

21. *uncovered himself*] the same result of drunkenness in Hab. 2^{15}, La. 4^{21}.—**22.** There is no reason to think (with Ho. and Gu.) that Canaan was guilty of any worse sin than the *Schadenfreude* implied in the words. Heb. morality called for the utmost delicacy in such matters, like that evinced by Shem and Japheth in v.^{23}—**24.** בְּנוֹ הַקָּטָן cannot mean 'his *younger* son' (𝔊𝔙) (*i.e.* as compared with

---

following Kue. (*ThT*, xviii. 147), proposes לַחֲרֹשׁ for אִישׁ: 'Noah was the first to plough the ground.' That reading would be fatal to any connexion of the section with Gn. 3, unless we suppose a distinction between עבר (manual tillage) and חרשׁ. Strangely enough, Ra. (on 5^{29}) repeats the Haggadic tradition that Noah invented the ploughshare; but this is probably a conjecture based on a comparison of 3^{17} with 5^{29}.* —**22.** וַיַּגֵּד] 𝔊 pref. καὶ ἐξελθών.—**23.** הַשִּׂמְלָה] On the art., see G-K. § 126 *r*. That it was *the* 'שׂ which Canaan had previously taken away, and that this notice was deliberately omitted by J (Gu.), is certainly not to be inferred. The 'שׂ is the upper garment, which was also used for sleeping in (Ex. 22^{26} etc.).—**24.** וַיִּיקֶץ] on the irreg. seghol, see G-K.

---

* So Mr. Abrahams, in a private communication.

Shem); still less 'his contemptible son' (Ra.); or Ham's youngest (IEz.). The conclusion is not to be evaded that the writer follows a peculiar genealogical scheme in which Canaan is the youngest son of Noah.—**25–27.** Noah's curse and blessings must be presumed to have been legible in the destinies of his reputed descendants at the time when the legend took shape (cf. 27[28f. 39f.] 49) (on the fulfilment see the concluding note, p. 186 f.). The dominant feature is the curse on Canaan, which not only stands first, but is repeated in the blessings on the two brothers.—**25.** The descendants of Canaan are doomed to perpetual enslavement to the other two branches of the human family.—*a servant of servants*] means 'the meanest slave' (G-K. § 133 *i*).—*to his brethren*] not the other members of the Hamitic race, but (as is clear from the following vv.) to Shem and Japheth.—**26.** *Blessed be Yahwe the God of Shem*] The idea thus expressed is not satisfactory. To 'bless' Yahwe means no more than to praise Him; and an ascription of praise to Yahwe is only in an oblique sense a blessing on Shem, inasmuch as it assumes a religious primacy of the Shemites in having Yahwe for their God. Bu. (294 f.) proposed to omit אֱלֹהֵי and read בָּרוּךְ יַהְוֶה שֵׁם: *Blessed of Yahwe be Shem* (cf. 24[31] 26[29] [both J]). Di.'s objection, that this does not express wherein the blessing consists, applies with quite as much force to the received text. Perhaps a better emendation is that of Graetz בָּרֵךְ י' אָהֳלֵי שֵׁם (יְבָרֵךְ would be still more acceptable): [*May*] *Yahwe bless the tents of Shem*; see the next v.—**27.** *May God expand* (יַפְתְּ) *Yepheth*: a play on the name (יֶפֶת). The use of the generic אלהים implies that the proper name

---

§ 70 *n*.—**26.** לָמוֹ may stand either for לָהֶם (coll.) or לוֹ: see Note 3 in G-K. § 103 *f*. The latter is the more natural here. Ols. (*MBBA*, June 1870, 382) proposed to omit [26b], substituting [27aβ] (וישכן—שם), and retain [27b] with ref. of pl. suff. to אָחִיו. 𝔊 has αὐτοῦ in [26b] and αὐτῶν in [27b].—**27.** יַפְתְּ] 𝔊 πλατύναι, 𝔙 *dilatet*, etc. The √ פתה in the sense 'be spacious' is extremely rare in Heb. (Pr. 20[19] [?24[28]]), and the accepted rendering not beyond challenge. Nö. (*BL*, iii. 191) denies the geographical sense, and explains the word from the frequent Semitic figure of spaciousness for prosperity. This would almost require us to take the subject of the following clause to be God (*v.s.*).

יהוה was the peculiar property of the Shemites.—*and may he dwell*] or *that he may dwell.* The subject can hardly be God (*Jub.* 𝔗^O, *Ber. R.* Ra. IEz. Nö. al.), which would convey no blessing to Japheth; the wish refers most naturally to Japheth, though it is impossible to decide whether the expression 'dwell in the tents of' denotes friendly intercourse (so most) or forcible dispossession (Gu.). For the latter sense cf. Ps 78^{55}, 1 Ch. 5^{10}.—A Messianic reference to the ingathering of the Gentiles into the Jewish or Christian fold (𝔗^J, Fathers, De. al.) is foreign to the thought of the passage: see further below.

The question of the origin and significance of this remarkable narrative has to be approached from two distinct points of view.—I. In one aspect it is a culture-myth, of which the central motive is the discovery of wine. Here, however, it is necessary to distinguish between the original idea of the story and its significance in the connexion of the Yahwistic document. Read in its own light, as an independent fragment of tradition, the incident signalises the transition from nomadic to agricultural life. Noah, the first husbandman and vine-grower, is a tent-dweller (v.[21]); and this mode of life is continued by his oldest and favoured son Shem ([27]). Further, the identification of husbandry and vine culture points to a situation in which the simpler forms of agriculture had been supplemented by the cultivation of the grape. Such a situation existed in Palestine when it was occupied by the Hebrews. The sons of the desert who then served themselves heirs by conquest to the Canaanitish civilisation escaped the protracted evolution of vine-growing from primitive tillage, and stepped into the possession of the farm and the vineyard at once. From this point of view the story of Noah's drunkenness expresses the healthy recoil of primitive Semitic morality from the licentious habits engendered by a civilisation of which a salient feature was the enjoyment and abuse of wine. Canaan is the prototype of the population which had succumbed to these enervating influences, and is doomed by its vices to enslavement at the hands of hardier and more virtuous races.—In the setting in which it is placed by the Yahwist the incident acquires a profounder and more tragic significance. The key to this secondary interpretation is the prophecy of Lamech in 5^{29}, which brings it into close connexion with the account of the Fall in ch. 3 (p. 133). Noah's discovery is there represented as an advance or refinement on the tillage of the ground to which man was sentenced in consequence of his first transgression. And the oracle of Lamech appears to show that the invention of wine is conceived as a *relief from the curse.* How far it is looked on as a divinely approved mode of alleviating the monotony of toil is hard to decide. The moderate use of wine is certainly not condemned in the OT: on the other hand, it is impossible to doubt that the light in which Noah is exhibited, and the subsequent behaviour of his youngest son, are meant to convey an emphatic warning against the moral dangers attending this new step in human development, and the degeneration to which it may lead.

II. In the narrative, however, the cultural motive is crossed by an ethnographic problem, which is still more difficult to unravel. Who are the peoples represented by the names Shem, Japheth, and Canaan? Three points may be regarded as settled: that Shem is that family to which the Hebrews reckoned themselves; that Canaan stands for the pre-Israelitish inhabitants of Palestine; and that the servitude of Canaan to Shem at least *includes* the subjugation of the Canaanites by Israel in the early days of the monarchy. Beyond this everything is uncertain. The older view, which explains Shem and Japheth in terms of the Table of Nations (ch. 10),—*i.e.* as corresponding roughly to what we call the Semitic and Aryan races,—has always had difficulty in discovering a historic situation combining Japhetic dominion over the Canaanites with a dwelling of Japheth in the tents of Shem.* To understand the latter of an ideal brotherhood or religious bond between the two races brings us no nearer a solution, unless we take the passage as a prophecy of the diffusion of Christianity; and even then it fails to satisfy the expressions of the text (Di., who explains the figure as expressing the more kindly feeling of the Heb. towards these races, as compared with the Canaanites). — A number of critics, starting from the assumption that the oracles reflect the circumstances and aspirations of the age when the Yahwistic document originated, take Shem as simply a name for Israel, and identify Japheth either with the Philistines (We. Mey.) or the Phœnicians (Bu. Sta. Ho.). But that the Hebrews should have wished for an enlargement of the Philistines at their own expense is incredible; and as for the Phœnicians, though their colonial expansion might have been viewed with complacency in Israel, there is no proof that an occupation of Israelitish territory on their part either took place, or would have been approved by the national sentiment under the monarchy. The alienation of a portion of Galilee to the Tyrians (1 Ki. 9^{11-13}) (Bu.) is an event little likely to have been idealised in Heb. legend. The difficulties of this theory are so great that Bertholet has proposed to recast the narrative with the omission of Japheth, leaving Shem and Canaan as types of the racial antipathy between the Hebrews and Canaanites: the figure of Japheth, and the blessing on him, he supposes to have been introduced

---

* As regards the former, the expulsion of Phœnician colonists from the Mediterranean coasts and Asia Minor by the Greeks (Di.) could never have been described as enslavement (see Mey. *GA*[1], i. 311 f.); and the capture of Tyre by Alexander, the Roman conquest of Carthage, etc. (De.), are events certainly beyond the horizon of the writer,—unless, indeed, we adopt Berth.'s suggestion (see above), that v.[27] is very late. For the latter, Di. hints at an absorption of Japhetic peoples in the Semitic world-empires; but that would rather be a dwelling of Shem in the tents of Japheth.

after the time of Alexander the Great, as an expression of the friendly feeling of the Jews for their Hellenic conquerors.*—Gu.'s explanation, which is put forward with all reserve, breaks ground in an opposite direction. Canaan, he suggests, may here represent the great wave of Semitic migration which (according to some recent theories) had swept over the whole of Western Asia (*c.* 2250 B.C.), leaving its traces in Babylonia, in Phœnicia, perhaps even in Asia Minor,† and of which the later Canaanites of Palestine were the sediment. Shem is the Hebræo-Aramaic family, which appears on the stage of history after 1500 B.C., and no doubt took possession of territory previously occupied by Canaanites. It is here represented as still in the nomadic condition. Japheth stands for the Hittites, who in that age were moving down from the north, and establishing their power partly at the cost of both Canaanites and Arameans. This theory hardly explains the peculiar contempt and hatred expressed towards Canaan; and it is a somewhat serious objection to it that in 10[15] (which Gu. assigns to the same source as 9[20ff.]) Heth is the *son* of Canaan. A better defined background would be the struggle for the mastery of Syria in the 14th cent. B.C.‡ If, as many Assyriologists think probable, the Ḥabiri of the Tel-Amarna Letters be the עִבְרִים of the OT,—*i.e.* the original Hebrew stock to which Israel belonged,— it would be natural to find in Shem the representative of these invaders; for in 10[21] (J) Shem is described as 'the father of all the sons of Eber.' Japheth would then be one or other of the peoples who, in concert with the Ḥabiri, were then seeking a foothold in the country, possibly the Suti or the Amurri, less probably (for the reason mentioned above) the Hittites.—These surmises must be taken for what they are worth. Further light on that remote period of history may yet clear up the circumstances in which the story of Noah and his sons originated; but unless the names Shem and Japheth should be actually discovered in some historic connexion, the happiest conjectures can never effect a solution of the problem.

CH. X.—*The Table of Peoples* (P and J).

In its present form, the chapter is a redactional composition, in which are interwoven two (if not three) successive attempts to classify the known peoples of the world, and to

* See We. *Comp.* 14 f.; Bu. *Urg.* 325 ff.; Sta. *GVI*, i. 109; Mey. *GA*[1], i. p. 214; Bertholet, *Stellung d. Isr. zu. d. Fremden*, 76 f. Meyer's later theory (*INS*, 220 f.), that Japheth (= Eg. *Kefti*?) stands for the whole body of northern invaders in the 12th cent., to whom the Philistines belonged, does not diminish the improbability that such a prophecy should have originated under the monarchy.

† See Mey. *GA*[1], i. p. 212 ff.; Wi. *GI*, i. 37, 130, 134; Peiser, *KIB*, iv. p. viii.

‡ Already suggested by Ben. (p. 158), who, however, is inclined to identify the Ḥabiri with Japheth.

exhibit their origin and mutual relationships in the form of a genealogical tree.

Analysis.—The separation of the two main sources is due to the lucid and convincing analysis of We. (*Comp.*[2] 6 ff.). The hand of P is easily recognised in the superscription ([1a] אֵלֶּה תּוֹלְדֹת), and the methodical uniformity of the tripartite scheme, with its recurrent opening and closing formulæ. The headings of the three sections are: בְּנֵי יֶפֶת ([2]), וּבְנֵי חָם ([6]), and בְּנֵי שֵׁם ([22]); the respective conclusions are found in [5] (mutilated) [20. 31], v.[32] being a final summary. This framework, however, contains several continuous sections which obviously belong to J. (*a*) [8-12]; the account of Nimrod (who is not even mentioned by P among the sons of Kush) stands out both in character and style in strong contrast to P: note also יָלַד instead of הוֹלִיד ([8]), יהוה ([9]). (*b*) [13f.]: the sons of Mizraim (*v.* יָלַד). (*c*) [15-19]: the Canaanites (יָלַד). (*d*) [21. 25-30]: the Shemites (יֻלַּד [21. 25]; יָלַד [26]).—Duplication of sources is further proved by the twofold introduction to Shem ([21 ‖ 22]), and the discrepancy between [7] and [28f.] regarding חֲוִילָה and שְׁבָא. The documents, therefore, assort themselves as follows:

P: [1a]; [2-5]; [6f. 20]; [22f. 31]; [32]
J: [1b] (?); [8-12]; [13f.]; [15-19]; [21. 25-30].

Vv.[9. 16-18a] and [24] are regarded by We. and most subsequent writers as interpolations: see the notes. The framework of P is made the basis of the Table; and so far as appears that document has been preserved in its original order. In J the genealogy of Shem ([21. 25-30]) is probably complete; that of Ham ([13f. 15ff.]) is certainly curtailed; while every trace of Japheth has been obliterated (see, however, p. 208). Whether the Yahwistic fragments stand in their original order, we have no means of determining.

The analysis has been carried a step further by Gu. ([2] 74 f.), who first raised the question of the unity of the Yahwistic Table, and its connexion with the two recensions of J which appear in ch. 9. He agrees with We. Di. al. that 9[18f.] forms the transition from the story of the Flood to a list of nations which is partly represented in ch. 10; 10[1b] being the immediate continuation of 9[19] in that recension of J (J[j]). But he tries to show that 9[20-27] was also followed by a Table of Nations, and that to it most of the Yahwistic fragments in ch. 10 belong ([8. 10-12. 15. 21. 25-29] = J[e]). This conclusion is reached by a somewhat subtle examination of v.[21] and vv.[15-19]. In v.[21] Shem is the 'elder brother of Japheth,' which seems to imply that Japheth was the *second* son of Noah as in 9[20ff.]; hence we may surmise that the third son was not Ham but Canaan. This is confirmed by the apparent contradiction between [15] and [18b. 19]. In [19] the northern limit of the Canaanites is Ẓidon, whereas in [15] Canaan includes the Ḥittites, and has therefore the wider geographical sense which Gu. postulates for 9[20-27] (see p. 186 above). He also calls attention to the difference in language between the eponymous כְּנַעַן in [15] and the gentilic הַכְּנַעֲנִי in [18b. 19], and considers that this was a characteristic distinction of the two documents. From these premises the further dissection of the Table follows easily enough. Vv.[8-12] may be assigned to J^e because of the peculiar use of הֵחֵל in ^{8} (cf. 9^{20} 4^{26}). V.$^{13f.}$ must in any case be J^j, because it is inconceivable that Egypt should ever have been thought of as a son of Canaan; $^{25-29}$ follow ^{21} (J^e). V.^{30} is assigned to J^j solely on account of its resemblance to ^{19}. It cannot be denied that these arguments (which are put forward with reserve) have considerable cumulative force; and the theory may be correct. At the same time it must be remembered (1) that the distinction between a wider and a narrower geographical conception of Canaan remains a brilliant speculation, which is not absolutely required either by $9^{20ff.}$ or 10^{15}; and (2) that there is nothing to show that the story of Noah, the vine-grower, was followed by a Table of Nations at all. A genealogy connecting Shem with Abraham was no doubt included in that document; but a writer who knows nothing of the Flood, and to whom Noah was not the head of a new humanity, had no obvious motive for attaching an ethnographic survey to the name of that patriarch. Further criticism may be reserved for the notes.

The names in the Table are throughout eponymous: that is to say, each nation is represented by an imaginary personage bearing its name, who is called into existence for the purpose of expressing its unity, but is at the same time conceived as its real progenitor. From this it was an easy step to translate the supposed affinities of the various peoples into the family relations of father, son, brother, etc., between the eponymous ancestors; while the origin of the existing ethnic groups was held to be accounted for by the expansion and partition of the family. This vivid and concrete mode of representation, though it was prevalent in antiquity, was inevitably suggested by one of the commonest idioms of Semitic speech, according to which the individual members of a tribe or people were spoken of as 'sons' or 'daughters' of the collective entity to which they belonged. It may be added that (as in the case of the Arabian tribal genealogies) the usage could only have sprung up in an age when the patriarchal type of the family and the rule of male descent were firmly established (see Rob. Sm. *KM*^{2}, 3 ff.).

That this is the principle on which the Tables are constructed appears from a slight examination of the names, and is universally admitted. With the exception of Nimrod, all the names that can be identified are those of peoples and tribes (Madai, Sheba, Dedan, etc.) or countries (Miẓraim, Ḥavilah, etc.—in most cases it is impossible to say whether land or people is meant) or cities (Ẓidon); some are *gentilicia* (Jebusite, Ḥivvite, etc.); and some are actually retained in the pl. (Rodanim, Ludim, etc.). Where the distinctions between national and geographical designations, between singular, plural, and collective names, are thus effaced, the only common denominator to which the terms can be reduced is that of the eponymous ancestor. It was the universal custom of antiquity in such matters to invent a legendary founder of a city or state;* and it is idle to imagine any other explanation of the names before us.—It is, of course, another question how far the Hebrew ethnographers believed in the analogy on which their system rested, and how far they used it simply as a convenient method of expressing racial or political relations. When a writer speaks of Lydians, Lybians, Philistines, etc., as 'sons' of Egypt, or 'the Jebusite,' 'the Amorite,' 'the Arvadite' as 'sons' of Canaan, it is difficult to think, *e.g.*, that he believed the Lydians to be descended from a man named 'Lydians' (לוּדִים), or the Amorites from one called 'the Amorite' (הָאֱמֹרִי); and we may begin to suspect that the whole system of eponyms is a conventional symbolism which was as transparent to its authors as it is to us.† That, however, would be a hasty and probably mistaken inference. The instances cited are exceptional,—they occur mostly in two groups, of which one ([16ff.]) is interpolated, and the other ([13f.]) may very well be secondary too; and over against them we have to set not only the names of Noah, Shem, etc., but also Nimrod, who is certainly an individual hero, and yet is said to have been 'begotten' by the eponymous Kush (Gu.). The bulk of the names lend themselves to the one view as readily as to the other; but on the whole it is safer to assume that, in the mind of the genealogist, they stand for real individuals, from whom the different nations were believed to be descended.

The geographical horizon of the Table is very restricted; but is considerably wider in P than in J.‡ J's survey extends from the Hittites and Phœnicians in the N to Egypt and southern Arabia in the S; on the E he knows Babylonia and Assyria and perhaps the Kašši, and on the W the Libyans and the south coast of Asia Minor.§ P includes in addition Asia Minor, Armenia, and Media on the N and NE, Elam on the E, Nubia in the S, and the whole

* "An exactly parallel instance . . . is afforded by the ancient Greeks. The general name of the Greeks was Hellenes; the principal subdivisions were the Dorians, the Æolians, the Ionians, and the Achæans; and accordingly the Greeks traced their descent from a supposed eponymous ancestor Hellen, who had three sons, Dorus and Aeolus, the supposed ancestors of the Dorians and Æolians, and Xuthus, from whose two sons, Ion and Achæus, the Ionians and Achæans were respectively supposed to be descended" (Dri. 112).

† See Guthe, *GI*, 1 ff.

‡ Judging, that is, from the extracts of J that are preserved.

§ *Kaphtorim* (v.[14]): according to others the island of Crete.

Mediterranean coast on the W. The world outside these limits is ignored, for the simple reason that the writers were not aware of its existence. But even within the area thus circumscribed there are remarkable omissions, some of which defy reasonable explanation.

The nearer neighbours and kinsmen of Israel (Moabites, Ishmaelites, Edomites, etc.) are naturally reserved for the times when they broke off from the parent stem. It would appear, further, that as a rule only contemporary peoples are included in the lists; extinct races and nationalities like the Rephaim, Zuzim, etc., and possibly the Amalekites, being deliberately passed over; while, of course, peoples that had not yet played any important part in history are ignored. None of these considerations, however, accounts for the apparent omission of the Babylonians in P,—a fact which has perhaps never been thoroughly explained (see p. 205).

From what has just been said it ought to be possible to form some conclusion as to the age in which the lists were drawn up. For P the *terminus a quo* is the 8th cent., when the Cimmerian and Scythian hordes ([2f.]) first make their appearance south of the Caucasus: the absence of the Minæans among the Arabian peoples, if it has any significance, would point to the same period (see p. 203). A lower limit may with less certainty be found in the circumstance that the names פָּרַס and עֲרָב. עַרְבִי (Persians and Arabs, first mentioned in Jer. and Ezk.) do not occur. It would follow that the Priestly List is pre-exilic, and represents, not the viewpoint of the PC (5th cent.), but one perhaps two centuries earlier (so Gu.). Hommel's opinion (*Aufs. u. Abh.* 314 ff.), that the Table contains the earliest ethnological ideas of the Hebrews fresh from Arabia, and that its "Grundstock" goes back to Mosaic times and even the 3rd millennium B.C., is reached by arbitrary excisions and alterations of the names, and by unwarranted inferences from those which are left * (see Je. *ATLO*², 252). — The lists of J, on the other hand, yield no definite indications of date. The S Arabian tribes ([25-30]) might have been known as early as the age of Solomon (Brown, *EB*, ii. 1699),—they might even have been

* It has often been pointed out that there is a remarkable agreement between the geographical horizon of P in Gn. 10 and that of Jer. and Ezk. Of the 34 names of nations in P's Table, 22 occur in Ezk. and 14 in the *book* of Jer.; it has to be remembered, however, that a large part of the book of Jer. is later than that prophet. Ezk. has perhaps 6 names which might have been expected in P if they had been known (פְּקוֹד, פָּרַס, שׁוֹעַ, קוֹעַ, כַּשְׂדִּים, עֲרָב), and Jer. (book) has 5 (מִנִּי, פְּקוֹד, פָּרַס, כַּשְׂדִּים, עֲרָב[י]). The statistics certainly do not bear out the assertion that P compiled his list from these two books between 538 and 526 B.C. (see Di. p. 166); they rather suggest that while the general outlook was similar, the knowledge of the outer world was in some directions more precise in the time of Ezk. than in the Table.

known earlier,—but that does not tell us when they were systematically tabulated. The (interpolated) list of Canaanites ($^{16-18}$) is assigned by Jeremias (*l.c.* 256) to the age of Tiglath-pileser IV.; but since a considerable percentage of the names occurs in the Tel-Amarna letters (*v.i.*), the grounds of that determination are not apparent. With regard to the section on Nimrod ($^{8-12}$), all that can fairly be said is that it is probably later than the Kaššite conquest of Babylonia: how much later, we cannot tell. On the attempt to deduce a date from the description of the Assyrian cities, see p. 212.—There are, besides, two special sources of error which import an element of uncertainty into all these investigations. (*a*) Since only two names (שְׁבָא and חֲוִילָה) are really duplicated in P and J,* we may suppose that the redactor has as a general practice omitted names from one source which he gives in the other; and we cannot be quite sure whether the omission has been made in P or in J. (*b*) According to Jewish tradition, the total number of names is 70; and again the suspicion arises that names may have been added or deleted so as to bring out that result.†

The threefold division of mankind is a feature common to P and J, and to both recensions of J if there were two (above, p. 188 f.). It is probable, also, though not certain, that each of the Tables placed the groups in the reverse order of birth: Japheth—Ham—Shem; or Canaan—Japheth—Shem (see v.^{21}). The basis of the classification may not have been ethnological in any sense; it may have been originally suggested by the tradition that Noah had just three sons, in accordance with a frequently observed tendency to close a genealogy with three names ($4^{19ff.}$ 5^{32} 11^{26} etc.). Still, the classification must follow some ethnographic principle, and we have to consider what that principle is. The more obvious distinctions of *colour*, *language*, and *race* are easily seen to be inapplicable.

The ancient Egyptian division of foreigners into Negroes (black), Asiatics (light brown), and Libyans (white) is as much geographical as chromatic (Erman, *LAE*, 32); but in any case the survey of Gn. 10 excludes the true negroes, and differences of colour amongst the peoples included could not have been sufficiently marked to form a basis of classification. It is certainly noteworthy that the Egyptian monuments represent the Egyptians, Kōš, Punt, and Phœnicians

---

* אַשּׁוּר, כּוּשׁ, מִצְרַיִם and כְּנַעַן do not count, because they are so introduced that the two documents supplement one another.

† For the official enumeration see Zunz, *GdV*², 207; Steinschneider, *ZDMG*, iv. 150 f.; Krauss, *ZATW*, 1899, 6 (1900, 38 ff.); cf. Poznański, *ib.* 1904, 302.

(P's Hamites) as dark brown (Di. 167); but the characteristic was not shared by the offshoots of Kush in Arabia; and a colour line between Shem and Japheth could never have been drawn.—The test of *language* also breaks down. The perception of linguistic affinities on a wide scale is a modern scientific attainment, beyond the apprehension of an antique people, to whom as a rule all foreign tongues were alike 'barbarous.' So we find that the most of P's Hamites (the Canaanites and nearly all the Kushites) are Semitic-speaking peoples, while the language of Elam among the sons of Shem belongs to an entirely different family; and Greek was certainly not spoken in the regions assigned to sons of Javan.—Of *race*, except in so far as it is evidenced by language, modern science knows very little; and attempts have been made to show that where the linguistic criterion fails the Table follows authentic ethnological traditions: *e.g.* that the Canaanites came from the Red Sea coast and were really related to the Cushites; or that Babylonia was actually colonised from central Africa, etc. But none of these speculations can be substantiated; and the theory that true racial affinity is the main principle of the Table has to be abandoned. Thus, while most of the Japhetic peoples are Indo-European, and nearly all the Shemitic are Semites in the modern sense, the correspondence is no closer than follows necessarily from the geographic arrangement to be described presently. The Hamitic group, on the other hand, is destitute alike of linguistic and ethnological unity.—Similarly, when J assigns Phœnicians and Hittites (perhaps also Egyptians) to one ethnic group, it is plain that he is not guided by a sound ethnological tradition. His Shemites are, indeed, all of Semitic speech; what his Japhetic peoples may have been we cannot conjecture (see p. 188).

So far as P is concerned, the main principle is undoubtedly *geographical*: Japheth representing the North and West, Ham the South, and Shem the East. Canaan is the solitary exception, which proves the rule (see p. 201 f.). The same law appears (so far as can be ascertained) to govern the distribution of the subordinate groups; although too many of the names are uncertain to make this absolutely clear. There is very little ground for the statement that the geographical idea is disturbed here and there by considerations of a historical or political order.

The exact delimitation of the three regions is, of course, more or less arbitrary: Media *might* have been reckoned to the Eastern group, or Elam to the Southern; but the actual arrangement is just as natural, and there is no need to postulate the influence of ethnology in the one case or of political relations in the other. Lûd would be a glaring exception if the Lydians of Asia Minor were meant, but that is probably not the case (p. 206). The Mediterranean coasts and islands are appropriately enough assigned to Javan, the most westerly of the sons of Japheth. It can only be the assumption that Shem represents a *middle zone* between N and S that makes the position of Kittîm appear anomalous to Di. Even if the island of Cyprus be meant (which, however, is doubtful; p. 199), it must, on the view here taken, be assigned to Japheth. It is true that in J traces of politico-historical grouping do appear (אַשּׁוּר and בָּבֶל in 8-12; פְּלִשְׁתִּים, כַּפְתֹּרִים in 13f.). — As to the order within the principal groups (of P), it is impossible to lay down any strict rule. Jen. (*ZA*, x. 326) holds that it always proceeds from the remoter to the nearer nations; but though that may be true in the main, it cannot be rigorously carried through, nor can it be safely used as an argument for or against a particular identification.

The defects of the Table, from the standpoint of modern ethnology, are now sufficiently apparent. As a scientific account of the origin of the races of mankind, it is disqualified by its assumption that nations are formed through the expansion and genealogical division of families; and still more by the erroneous idea that the historic peoples of the old world were fixed within three or at most four generations from the common ancestor of the race. History shows that nationalities are for the most part political units, formed by the dissolution and re-combination of older peoples and tribes; and it is known that the great nations of antiquity were preceded by a long succession of social aggregates, whose very names have perished. Whether a single family has ever, under any circumstances, increased until it became a tribe and then a nation, is an abstract question which it is idle to discuss: it is enough that the nations here enumerated did not arise in that way, but through a process analogous to that by which the English nation was welded together out of the heterogeneous elements of which it is known to be composed.—As a historical document, on the other hand, the chapter is of the highest importance: first, as the most systematic record of the political geography of the Hebrews at different stages of their history; and second, as expressing the profound consciousness of the unity of mankind, and the religious primacy of Israel, by which the OT writers were animated. Its insertion at this point, where it forms the transition from primitive tradition to the history of the chosen people, has a significance, as well as a literary propriety, which cannot be mistaken (Di. 164; Gu. 77; Dri. 114).

The Table is repeated in 1 Ch. 1[4-23] with various omissions and textual variations. The list is still further abridged in 𝔊 of 1 Chr., which omits [13-18a] and all names after Arpachshad in [22].—On the extensive literature on the chapter, see especially the commentaries of Tu. (159 f.) and Di. (170 f.). See also the map at the end of *ATLO*.

The Table of P.

1a. Superscription.—*Shēm, Ḥām,* and *Yepheth*] cf. 5[32] (P), 9[18] (J).

On the original sense of the names only vague conjectures can be reported. שֵׁם is supposed by some to be the Heb. word for 'name,' applied by the Israelites to themselves in the first instance as בְּנֵי שֵׁם = 'men of name' or 'distinction'—the titled or noble race (cf. ὀνομαστός): "perhaps nothing more than the ruling caste in opposition to the aborigines." So We. (*Comp.*[2] 14), who compares the name 'Aryan,' and contrasts בני בלי שם (Jb. 30[8]); cf. Bu. *Urg.* 328 f.; al. Gu. (73) mentions a speculation of Jen. that שֵׁם is the Babylonian *šumu*, in the sense of 'eldest son,' who perpetuates the father's *name*.

חָם must, at a certain stage of tradition, have supplanted the earlier כְּנַעַן as the name of Noah's third son (p. 182). The change is easily explicable from the extension of geographical knowledge, which made it impossible any longer to regard the father of the Canaanites as the ancestor of one-third of the human race; but the origin of the name has still to be accounted for. As a Heb. word it might mean 'hot' (Jos. 9[12], Jb. 37[17]): hence it has been taken to denote the hot lands of the south (Lepsius, al.; cf. *Jub.* viii. 30: "the land of Ham is hot"). Again, since in some late Pss. (78[51] 105[23. 27] 106[22]) חם is a poetic designation of Egypt, it has been plausibly connected with the native *keme* or *chemi*='black,' with reference to the black soil of the Nile valley (Bochart, Ebers, Bu. 323 ff.).* A less probable theory is that of Glaser, cited by Hommel (*AHT*, 48), who identifies it with Eg. *'amu*, a collective name for the neighbouring Semitic nomads, derived by Müller (*AE*, 123 ff.) from their distinctive primitive weapon, the boomerang.

יֶפֶת is connected in 9[27] with √ פתה, and no better etymology has been proposed. Che. (*EB*, ii. 2330) compares the theophorous personal name *Yapti-Addu* in TA Tab., and thinks it a modification of יִפְתַּח־אֵל, 'God opens.' But the form פתה (*pitû*) with the probable sense of 'open' also occurs in the Tab. (*KIB*, v. 290 [last line]). The derivation from √ יפה (beautiful), favoured by Bu. (358 ff.), in allusion to the beauty of the Phœnician cities, is very improbable. The resemblance to the Greek *Iapetos* was pointed out by Buttmann, and is undoubtedly striking. Ἰάπετος was the father of Prometheus, and therefore (through Deu-

* Cf. the rare word חוּם, 'black,' 30[32ff.]

kalion) of post-diluvian mankind. The identification is approved by Weizsäcker (Roscher's *Lex.* ii. 55 ff.), who holds that Ἰάπετος, having no Greek etymology, may be borrowed from the Semites (cf. Lenorm. ii. 173–193). See, further, Mey. *INS*, 221.

A curiously complicated astro-mythical solution is advanced by Wi. in *MVAG*, vi. 170 ff.

2–5. **The Japhetic or Northern Peoples**: fourteen in number, chiefly concentrated in Asia Minor and Armenia, but extending on either side to the Caspian and the shores of the Atlantic. It will be seen that though the enumeration is not ethnological in principle, yet most of the peoples named do belong to the same great Indo-Germanic family.

Japheth.

- 1. Gomer.
  - 2. Ashkenaz.
  - 3. Riphath.
  - 4. Togarmah.
- 5. Magog.
- 6. Madai.
- 7. Javan.
  - 8. Elishah.
  - 9. Tarshish.
  - 10. Kittim.
  - 11. Rodanim.
- 12. Tubal.
- 13. Meshech.
- 14. Tiras.

(1) גֹּמֶר (𝔊 Γαμερ): named along with Togarmah as a confederate of Gog in Ezk. 38[6], is identified with the Galatians by Jos., but is really the *Gamir* of the Ass. inscr., the Cimmerians of the Greeks. The earliest reference to the Κιμμέριοι (*Od.* xi. 13 ff.) reveals them as a northern people, dwelling on the shores of the Northern Sea. Their irruption into Asia Minor, by way of the Caucasus, is circumstantially narrated by Herodotus (i. 15, 103, iv. 11 f.), whose account is in its main features confirmed by the Ass. monuments. There the *Gimirrai* first appear towards the end of the reign of Sargon, attacking the old kingdom of Urarṭu (see Johns, *PSBA*, xvii. 223 f., 226). Thence they seem to have moved westwards into Asia Minor, where (in the reign of Sennacherib) they overthrew the Phrygian Empire, and later (under Asshur-bani-pal, *c.* 657) the Lydian Empire of Gyges (*KIB*, ii. 173–7). This last effort seems to have exhausted their strength, and soon afterwards they vanish from history.* A trace of their shortlived ascendancy remained in *Gamir*, the Armenian name for Cappadocia; † but the probability is that the land was named after the people, and not *vice versâ*; and it is not safe to assume that by גֹּמֶר P meant Cappadocia. It is more likely that the name is primarily ethnic, and denotes the common stock of which the three following peoples were branches.

---

* Cf. Wi. *AOF*, i. 484–496; *KAT*[3], 76 f., 101 ff.; Je. *ATLO*[2], 253.

† Cf. Eus. *Chron. Arm.* (ed. Aucher) i. p. 95[2] (*Gimmeri* = Cappadocians), and ii. p. 12 (Γόμερ, ἐξ οὗ Καππάδοκες).

(2) אַשְׁכְּנַז ('Ασχαναζ): Jer. 51^{27}, after Ararat and Minni.* It has been usual (Bochart, al.) to connect the name with the Ascania of *Il.* ii. 863, xiii. 793; and to suppose this was a region of Phrygia and Bithynia indicated by a river, two lakes, and other localities bearing the old name.† Recent Assyriologists, however, find in it the *Ašguza* ‡ of the monn.,—a branch of the Indo-Germanic invaders who settled in the vicinity of lake Urumia, and are probably identical with the Scythians of Herod. i. 103, 106. Since they are first mentioned by Esarhaddon, they might readily appear to a Heb. writer to be a younger people than the Cimmerians. See Wi. *ll.cc.*; *ATLO*², 259 f.

(3) רִיפַת ('Ριφαθ, 'Εριφαθ: but 1 Ch. 1^6 דִּיפַת): otherwise unknown. According to Josephus, it denotes the Paphlagonians. Bochart and Lagarde (*Ges. Abh.* 255) put it further west, near the Bosphorus, on the ground of a remote resemblance in name to the river 'Ρήβαζ and the district 'Ρηβαντία. Che. (*EB*, 4114) favours the transposition of Halevy (פירת), and compares *Bit Burutaš*, mentioned by Sargon along with the Muški and Tabali (Schr. *KGF*, 176).

(4) תֹּגַרְמָה (Θεργαμα, Θοργαμα) = בית תוגרמה, Ezk. 38^6 27^{14}: in the latter passage as a region exporting horses and mules. Jos. identifies with the Phrygians. The name is traditionally associated with Armenia, Thorgom being regarded as the mythical ancestor of the Armenians; but that legend is probably derived from 𝔊 of this passage (Lag. *Ges. Abh.* 255 ff.; *Symm.* i. 105). The suggested Assyriological equivalent *Til-Garimmu* (Del. *Par.* 246; *ATLO*², 260; al.), a city on the frontier of the Tabali mentioned by Sargon and Sennacherib, is not convincing; even though the *Til-* should be a fictitious Ass. etymology (Lenorm. *Orig.*² ii. 410).

(5) מָגוֹג (Μαγωγ): Ezk. 38^2 39^6. The generally accepted identification with the Scythians dates from Jos. and Jer., but perhaps reflects only a vague impression that the name is a comprehensive designation of the barbarous races of the north, somewhat like the *Umman-manda* of the Assyrians. In one of the Tel-Amarna letters (*KIB*, v. 5), a land *Ga-ga* is alluded to in a similar manner. But how the author differentiated Magog from the Cimmerians and Medes, etc., does not appear. The name מגוג is altogether obscure. That it is derived from גוֹג = Gyges, king of Lydia (Mey. *GA*¹, i. p. 558), is most improbable; and the suggestion that it is a corruption of Ass. *Mât Gôg* (*Mât Gagaia*),§ must also be received with some caution.

(6) מָדַי (Μαδαι): the common Heb. name for Media and the Medes; 2 Ki. 17^6 18^{11}, Is. 13^{17} 21^2, Jer. 25^{25} $51^{11.28}$, Est. $1^{3.14.18f.}$ 10^2, Dn. 8^{20} 9^1 [11^1]

---

* Ass. *Mannai*, between lakes Van and Urumia, mentioned along with Ašguza in *KIB*, ii. 129, 147.

† Lag. (*Ges. Abh.* 254) instances Ashken as an Armenian proper name; and the inscription μὴν "Ασκηνος on Græco-Phrygian coins.

‡ Whether the Heb. word is a clerical error for אַשְׁכֻּז (Wi. Jer.), or the Ass. a modification of *Ašgunza*, the Assyriologists may decide (see Schmidt, *EB*, iv. 4330 f.).

§ Del. *Par.* 246 f.; Streck, *ZA*, 321; Sayce, *HCM*², 125.

(Ass. *Madai*). The formation of the Median Empire must have taken place about the middle of the 7th cent., but the existence of the people in their later seats (E of the Zagros mountains and S of the Caspian Sea) appears to be traceable in the monuments back to the 9th cent. They are thus the earliest branch of the Aryan family to make their mark in Asiatic history. See Mey. *GA*[1], i. § 422 ff.; *KAT*[3], 100 ff.; *ATLO*[2], 254.

(7) יָוָן ('Ιωυαν) is the Greek 'ΙάFων-ονες, and denotes primarily the Greek settlements in Asia Minor, which were mainly Ionian: Ezk. 27^{13}, Is. 66^{19}. After Alexander the Great it was extended to the Hellenes generally: Jl. 4^{6}, Zech. 9^{13}, Dn. 8^{21} 10^{20} 11^{2}. In Ass. *Yamanai* is said to be used but once (by Sargon, *KIB*, ii. 43); but the Persian *Yauna* occurs, with the same double reference, from the time of Darius (cf. Æsch. *Pers.* 176, 562). Whether the word here includes the European Greeks cannot be positively determined.*—The 'sons' of Javan are (v.[4]) to be sought along the Mediterranean, and probably at spots known to the Heb. as commercial colonies of the Phœnicians (on which see Mey. *EB*, 3736 f.). Very few of them, however, can be confidently identified.

(8) אֱלִישָׁה ('Ελισα, 'Ελισσα) is mentioned only in Ezk. 27^{7} (אִיֵּי א׳) as a place supplying Tyre with purple. The older verbal identifications with the Αἰολεῖς (Jos. Jer.; so De.), 'Ελλάς (𝔗J), 'Ηλις, etc., are valueless; and modern opinion is greatly divided. Some favour Carthage, because of *Elissa*, the name of the legendary foundress of the city (Sta. Wi. Je. al.); others (Di. al.) southern Italy with Sicily.† The most attractive solution is that first proposed by Conder (*PEFS*, 1892, 45; cf. 1904, 170), and widely accepted, that the *Alašia* of the TA Tablets is meant (see *KIB*, v. 80–92). This is now generally recognised as the name of Cyprus, of which the Tyrian purple was a product:‡ see below on כתים. Jensen now (*KIB*, vi. 1, 507) places אלישה beyond the Pillars of Hercules on the African coast, and connects it with the Elysium of the Greeks.

(9) תַּרְשִׁישׁ (Θαρσις) is identified (since Bochart) with Ταρτησσός (Tartesos), the Phœnician mining and trading station in the S of Spain;§ and no other theory is nearly so plausible. The OT Tarshish was rich in minerals (Jer. 10^{9}, Ezk. 27^{12}), was a Tyrian colony (Is. $23^{1.6.10}$), and a remote coast-land reached by sea (Is. 66^{19}, Jn. 1^{3} 4^{2}, Ps. 72^{10}); and to distinguish the Tarshish of these pass. from that of Gn. 10 (De. Jast. al.), or to consider the latter a doublet of תירס (Che. Mü.), are but counsels of despair. The chief rival theory is Tarsus in Cilicia (Jos.

---

* Against the theory of a second יָוָן in Arabia (which in any case would not affect the interpretation of this pass.), see Sta. *Akad. Red.* 125–142. Cf., further, *ATLO*[2], 255.

† Cf. 𝔗O on Ezk. 27^{7} ממדינת איטליא; and Eus. *Chr. Arm.* ii. p. 13: 'Ελισσά, ἐξ οὗ Σικελοί + et Athenienses [Arm.].

‡ See Müller, *ZA*, x. 257 ff.; *OLz.* iii. 288 ff.; Jen. *ZA*, 379 f.; Jast. *DB*, v. 80 b.

§ Her. i. 163, iv. 152; Strabo, iii. 151; Plin. *HN*, iii. 7, iv. 120, etc.

Jer. al.); but this in Semitic is תרזי (*Tarzi*). Cf. Wi. *AOF*, i. 445 f.; Müller, *OLz*. iii. 291.

(10) כִּתִּים (Κητιοι, Κιτιοι)] cf. Jer. 2^{10}, Ezk. 27^{6}, Is. $23^{1.12}$, Dn. 11^{30}, 1 Mac. 1^{1} 8^{5}, Nu. 24^{24}. Against the prevalent view that it denotes primarily the island of Cyprus, so called from its chief city Κίτιον (Larnaka), Wi. (*AOF*, ii. 422^{1}; cf. *KAT*³, 128) argues that neither the island nor its capital * is so named in any ancient document, and that the older biblical references demand a site further W. The application to the Macedonians (1 Mac.) he describes as one of those false identifications common in the Egypt of the Ptolemaic period. His argument is endorsed by Müller (*OLz*. iii. 288) and Je. (*ATLO*², 261): they suggest S Italy, mainly on the authority of Dn. 11^{30}. The question is obviously bound up with the identity of אלישה—Alašia (*v.s.*).

(11) דֹּדָנִים or רוֹדָנִים (ꝏ𝔊 [Ῥοδιοι] and 1 Ch. 1^{7})] a name omitted by Jos. If 𝔊 be right, the Rhodians are doubtless meant (cf. *Il*. ii. 654 f.): the sing. is perhaps disguised in the corrupt דדן of Ezk. 27^{15} (cf. 𝔊). The MT has been explained of the Dardanians (𝔗^J, De. al.), "properly a people of Asia Minor, not far from the Lycians" (Che. *EB*, 1123). Wi. (*l.c.*) proposes דרנים, the Dorians; and Müller ד(ו)ננים, Eg. *Da-nô-na* = TA, *Da-nu-na* (*KIB*, v. 277), on the W coast of Asia Minor.

(12) תֻּבַל (Θοβελ)] and

(13) מֶשֶׁךְ (Μοσοχ)] are mentioned together in Ezk. 27^{13} (as exporting slaves and copper), 32^{26} (a warlike people of antiquity), $38^{2f.}$ 39^{1} (in the army of Gog), Is. 66^{19} (𝔊); משך alone in Ps. 120^{5}. Jos. arbitrarily identifies them with the Iberians and Cappadocians respectively; but since Bochart no one has questioned their identity with the Τιβαρηνοί and Μόσχοι, first mentioned in Her. iii. 94 as belonging to the 19th satrapy of Darius, and again (vii. 78) as furnishing a contingent to the host of Xerxes (cf. Strabo, XI. ii. 14, 16). Equally obvious is their identity with the *Tabali* and *Muški* of the Ass. Monn., where the latter appear as early as Tiglath-pileser I. (*c.* 1100), and the former under Shalmaneser II. (*c.* 838),—both as formidable military states. In Sargon's inscrs. they appear together; † and during this whole period their territory evidently extended much further S and W than in Græco-Roman times. These stubborn little nationalities, which so tenaciously maintained their identity, are regarded by Wi. and Je. as remnants of the old Hittite population which were gradually driven (probably by the Cimmerian invasion) to the mountainous district SE of the Black Sea.

(14) תִּירָס (Θειρας)] not mentioned elsewhere, was almost unanimously taken by the ancients (Jos. 𝔗^J, Jer. etc.; and so Boch. al.) to be the Thracians (Θρᾶκ-ες); but the superficial resemblance vanishes when the nominative ending *s* is removed. Tu. was the first to suggest the Τυρσ-ηνοί, a race of Pelasgian pirates, who left many traces of their ancient prowess in the islands and coasts of the Ægean, and who were

---

* The city, however, is called כתי in Phœn. inscrs. and coins from the 4th cent. B.C. downwards; see Cooke, *NSI*, pp. 56, 66?, 78, 352.

† See *KIB*, i. 18 f., 64 f., 142 f., ii. 40 f., 56 f.; and Del. *Par*. 250 f.

doubtless identical with the E-*trus*-cans of Italy.* This brilliant conjecture has since been confirmed by the discovery of the name *Turuša* amongst the seafaring peoples who invaded Egypt in the reign of Merneptah (Mey. *GA*[1], i. § 260; W. M. Müller, *AE*, 356 ff.).

6, 7, 20. The Hamitic or Southern Group: in Africa and S Arabia, but including the Canaanites of Palestine.

Ḥam.

1. Kush. 2. Mizraim. 3. Puṭ. 4. Canaan.

5. Ṣeba. 6. Ḥavilah. 7. Ṣabtah. 8. Ra'mah. 9. Ṣabtekah.

10. Sheba. 11. Dedan.

(1) כוש (𝔊 Χους, but elsewhere Αἰθιοπ-ες, -ία)] the land and people S of Egypt (Nubia),—the Ethiopians of the Greeks, the *Kôš* of the Eg. monuments: † cf. Is. 18[1], Jer. 13[23], Ezk. 29[10], Zeph. 3[10] etc. Ass. *Kusu* occurs repeatedly in the same sense on inscrs. of Esarhaddon and Asshurbanipal; and only four passages of Esarhaddon are claimed by Wi. for the hypothesis of a south Arabian *Kusu* (*KAT*[3], 144). There is no reason to doubt that in this v. the African Kush is meant. That the

5. The subscription to the first division of the Table is not quite in order. We miss the formula אלה בני יפת (cf. vv.[20. 31]), which is here necessary to the sense, and must be inserted, not (with We.) at the beginning of the v., but immediately before בארצתם. The clause מאלה—הגוים is then seen to belong to v.[4], and to mean that the Mediterranean coasts were peopled from the four centres just named as occupied by sons of Javan. Although these places were probably all at one time Phœnician colonies, it is not to be inferred that the writer confused the Ionians with Phœnicians. He may be thinking of the native population of regions known to Israel through the Phœnicians, or of the Mycenean Greeks, whose colonising enterprise is now believed to be of earlier date than the Phœnician (Mey. *EB*, 3736 f.).—נפרדו] construed like נפצה in 9[19] (J); ct. 10[32].—איי הגוים] only again Zeph. 2[11]. Should we read איי הים (Is. 11[11] 24[15], Est. 10[1])? אִי (for אֱוִי, perhaps from √ *'awa'*, "betake oneself") seems to be a seafarer's word denoting the place one makes for (for shelter, etc.); hence both "coast" and "island" (the latter also in Phœn.). In Heb. the pl. came to be used of distant lands in general (Is. 41[1. 5] 42[4] 51[5] etc., Jer. 31[10] etc.)

* Thuc. iv. 109; Her. i. 57, 94; Strabo, v. ii. 2, iii. 5: other reff. in Tu. *ad loc.*

† See Steindorff, *BA*, i. 593 f.

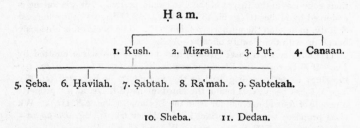

'sons' of Kush include Arabian peoples is quite naturally explained by the assumption that the writer believed these Arabs to be of African descent. As a matter of fact, intercourse, involving intermixture of blood, has at all times been common between the two shores of the Red Sea; and indeed the opinion that Africa was the original cradle of the Semites has still a measure of scientific support (see Barton, *OS*[1], 6 ff., 24).—See, further, on v.[8] (p. 207 f.).

(2) מִצְרַיִם (Μεσραιν)] the Heb. form of the common Semitic name of Egypt (TA, *Miṣṣari*, *Miṣri*, *Mašri*, *Mizirri*; Ass. [from 8th and 7th cent.] *Muṣur*; Bab. *Miṣir*; Syr. ܡܨܪܝܢ; Ar. *Miṣr*). Etymology and meaning are uncertain: Hommel's suggestion (*Gesch.* 530; cf. Wi. *AOF*, i. 25) that it is an Ass. appellative = 'frontier,' is little probable. The dual form of Heb. is usually explained by the constant distinction in the native inscrs. between Upper and Lower Egypt, though מצרים is found in connexions (Is. 11[11], Jer. 44[15]) which limit it to Lower Eg.; and many scholars now deny that the termination is a real dual (Mey. *GA*, i. § 42, An.; Jen. *ZDMG*, xlviii. 439).—On the vexed question of a N Arabian *Muṣri*, it is unnecessary to enter here. There may be passages of OT where that view is plausible, but this is not one of them; and the idea of a wholesale confusion between Eg. and Arabia on the part of OT writers is a nightmare which it is high time to be quit of.

(3) פוּט (Φουδ, but elsewhere Λιβυες)] mentioned 6 times (incl. 𝔊 of Is. 66[19]) in OT, as a warlike people furnishing auxiliaries to Egypt (Nah. 3[9], Jer. 46[9], Ezk. 30[5]) or Tyre (Ezk. 27[10]) or the host of Gog (38[5]), and frequently associated with כוש and לוד. The prevalent view has been that the Lybians, on the N coast of Africa W of Egypt, are meant (𝔊, Jos. al.), although Nah. 3[9] and probably Ezk. 30[5] (𝔊) show that the two peoples were distinguished. Another identification, first proposed by Ebers, has recently been strongly advocated: viz. with the *Pwnt* of Eg. monuments, comprising 'the whole African coast of the Red Sea' (W. M. Müller, *AE*, 114 ff., and *DB*, iv. 176 f.; Je. 263 f.). The only serious objection to this theory is the order in which the name occurs, which suggests a place further north than Egypt (Jen. *ZA*, x. 325 ff.).

(4) כְּנַעַן (Χαναaν)] the eponym of the pre-Israelitish inhabitants of Palestine, is primarily a geographical designation. The etymology is doubtful; but the sense 'lowland' has still the best claim to acceptance (see, however, Moore, *PAOS*, 1890, lxvii ff.). In Eg. monuments the name, in the form *pa-Ka-n-'-na* (*pa* is the art.), is applied to the strip of coast from Phœnicia to the neighbourhood of Gaza; but the ethnographic derivative extends to the inhabitants of all Western Syria (Müller, *AE*, 205 ff.). Similarly in TA Tablets *Kinaḫḫi*, *Kinaḫna*, etc., stand for Palestine proper (*KAT*[3], 181), or (according to Jast. *EB*, 641) the northern part of the seacoast.—The fact that Canaan, in spite of its geographical situation and the close affinity of its language with Heb., is reckoned to the Hamites is not to be explained by the tradition (Her. i. 1, vii. 89, etc.) that the Phœnicians came originally from the Red Sea; for that probably implies no more than that they were connected with

the Babylonians (Ἐρυθρὴ Θάλασσα = the Persian Gulf). Neither is it altogether natural to suppose that Canaan is thus placed because it had for a long time been a political dependency of Eg.: in that case, as Di. observes, we should have expected Canaan to figure as a son of Mizraim. The belief that Canaan and Israel belonged to entirely different branches of the human family is rooted in the circumstances that gave rise to the blessing and curse of Noah in ch. 9. When, with the extension of geographical knowledge, it became necessary to assign the Canaanites to a larger group (p. 187 above), it was inevitable that they should find their place as remote from the Hebrews as possible.

Of the descendants of Kush (v.[7]) a large proportion—all, indeed, that can be safely identified—are found in Arabia. Whether this means that Kushites had crossed the Red Sea, or that Arabia and Africa were supposed to be a continuous continent, in which the Red Sea formed an inland lake (*KAT*[3], 137, 144), it is perhaps impossible to decide.

(5) סְבָא (Σαβα)] Is. 43[3] 45[14], Ps. 72[10]; usually taken to be Meroë* (between Berber and Khartoum). The tall stature attributed to the people in Is. 45[14] (but cf. 18[2.7]) is in favour of this view; but it has nothing else to recommend it. Di. al. prefer the Saba referred to by Strabo (XVI. iv. 8, 10; cf. Ptolemy, iv. 7. 7 f.) on the African side of the Red Sea (S of Suakim). Je. (*ATLO*[2], 265) considers the word as the more correct variant to שׁבא (see below).

(6) חֲוִילָה (Εὐ[ε]ιλα[τ])] often (since Bochart) explained as 'sand-land' (fr. חול); named in v.[29] (J) as a Joktanite people, and in 25[18] (also J) as the eastern limit of the Ishmaelite Arabs. It seems impossible to harmonise these indications. The last is probably the most ancient, and points to a district in N Arabia, not too far to the E. We may conjecture that the name is derived from the large tract of loose red sand (*nefūd*) which stretches N of Teima and S of el-Ǧōf. This is precisely where we should look for the Χαυλοταῖοι whom Eratosthenes (Strabo, XVI. iv. 2) mentions (next to the Nabateans) as the second of three tribes on the route from Egypt to Babylon; and Pliny (vi. 157) gives Domata (= Dûmāh = el-Ǧōf: see p. 353) as a town of the *Avalitæ*. The name might easily be extended to other sandy regions of Arabia, (perhaps especially to the great sand desert in the southern interior): of some more southerly district it must be used both here and v.[29] (see Mey. *INS*, 325 f.). To distinguish further the Cushite from the Joktanite ח׳, and to identify the former with the Ἀβαλῖται, etc., on the African coast near Bab-el-mandeb, is quite unnecessary. On the other hand, it is impossible to place either of these so far N as the head of the Persian Gulf (Glaser) or the ENE part of the Syrian desert (Frd. Del.). Nothing can be made of Gn. 2[11]; and in 1 Sa. 15[7] (the only other occurrence) the text is probably corrupt.

(7) סַבְתָּה (Σαβαθα)] not identified. Possibly Σάβατα, Sabota, the capital of Ḥaḍramaut (see on v.[26]) (Strabo, XVI. iv. 2; Pliny, *HN*, vi. 155, xii. 63),—though in Sabæan this is written שבות (see Osiander, *ZDMG*,

---

* Jos. *Ant.* ii. 249. In i. 134 f. he seems to confuse סבא and שׁבא.

xix. 253; Homm. *SA Chrest.* 119); or the Σάφθα of Ptol. vi. 7. 30, an inland town lying (according to Glaser, 252) W of El-Ḳaṭîf.

(8) רַעְמָה (Ῥεγμα or Ῥεγχμα)] coupled with שׁבא (? and חוילה) in Ezk. 27^{22} as a tribe trading in spices, precious stones, and gold. It is doubtless the רעמת (*Raǵmat*) of a Minæan inscr.,* which speaks of an attack by the hosts of Saba and Ḥaulân on a Minæan caravan *en route* between Ma'ân and Ra'mat. This again may be connected with the Ῥαμμανῖται of Strabo (xvi. iv. 24) N of Ḥaḍramaut. The identification with the Ῥέγ[α]μα πόλις (a seaport on the Persian Gulf) of Ptol. vi. 7. 14 (Boch. al.; so Glaser) is difficult because of its remoteness from Sheba and Dedan (*v.i.*), and also because this appears on the inscr. as *Rǵmt* (Glaser, 252).

(9) סַבְתְּכָא (Σαβακαθα)] unknown. Σαμυδάκη in Carmania † (Ptol. vi. 8. 7 f., 11) is unsuitable both geographically and phonetically. Je. suggests that the word is a duplicate of סַבְתָּה.

(10) שְׁבָא (Σαβα)] (properly, as inscrs. show, סבא: see No. 5 above) is assigned in v.[29] to the Joḳṭanites, and in 25^3 to the Ḳetureans. It is the OT name of the people known to the classical geographers as Sabæans, the founders of a great commercial state in SW Arabia, with its metropolis at *Marib* (Mariaba), some 45 miles due E of San'a, the present capital of Yemen (Strabo, xvi. iv. 2, 19; Pliny, *HN*, vi. 154 f., etc.). "They were the centre of an old S Arabian civilisation, regarding the former existence of which the Sabæan inscriptions and architectural monuments supply ample evidence" (Di. 182). Their history is still obscure. The native inscrs. commence about 700 B.C.; and, a little earlier, Sabæan princes (not kings) ‡ appear on Ass. monuments as paying tribute to Tiglath-pileser IV. (B.C. 738) and Sargon (B.C. 715).§ It would seem that about that time (probably with the help of the Assyrians) they overthrew the older Minæan Empire, and established themselves on its ruins. Unlike their precursors, however, they do not appear to have consolidated their power in N Arabia, though their inscrs. have been found as far N as el-Ǧôf. To the Hebrews, Sheba was a 'far country' (Jer. 6^{20}, Jl. 4^8), famous for gold, frankincense, and precious stones (1 Ki. $10^{1ff.}$, Is. 60^6, Jer. 6^{20}, Ezk. 27^{22}, Ps. 72^{15}): in all these passages, as well as Ps. 72^{10}, Jb. 6^{19}, the reference to the southern Sabæans is clear. On the other hand, the association with Dedan (25^3, Ezk. 38^{13} and here) favours a more northern locality; in Jb. 1^{15} they appear as Bedouin of the northern desert; and the Ass. references appear to imply a northerly situation. Since it is undesirable to assume the existence of two separate peoples, it is tempting to suppose that the pass. last quoted preserve the tradition of an earlier time, before the

---

* Halevy, 535, 2 (given in Homm. *SA Chrest.* 103) = Glaser, 1155: translated by Müller, *ZDMG*, xxx. 121 f., and Homm. *AA*, 322, *AHT*, 249 f.

† Boch.: so Glaser, ii. 252; but see his virtual withdrawal on p. 404.

‡ It is important that neither in their own nor in the Ass. inscrs. are the earliest rulers spoken of as *kings*.

§ Cf. *KIB*, ii. 21, 55.

conquest of the Minæans had led to a settlement in Yemen. $V.^{28}$ (J) however, presupposes the southern settlement.*

(11) דְּדָן (Δαδαν, Δεδαν; but elsewhere Δαιδαν, etc.)] a merchant tribe mentioned along with Sheba in 25^{3} (= 1 Ch. 1^{32}) and Ezk. 38^{13}; with Tema (the modern *Teima*, *c.* 230 miles N of Medina) in Is. 21^{13}, Jer. 25^{23}, and 𝔊 of Gn. 25^{3}; and in Jer. 49^{8}, Ezk. 25^{13} as a neighbour of Edom. All this points to a region in the N of Arabia; and as the only other reference (Ezk. 27^{20})—in 27^{15} the text is corrupt—is consistent with this, there is no need to postulate another Dedan on the Persian Gulf (Boch. al.) or anywhere else. Glaser (397) very suitably locates the Dedanites "in the neighbourhood of Khaibar, el-Ola, El-Hiğr, extending perhaps beyond Teima,"—a region intersected by the trade-routes from all parts of Arabia (see the map in *EB*, iv. 5160); and where the name is probably perpetuated in the ruins of Daidan, W of Teima (Di.). The name occurs both in Minæan and Sabæan inscrs. (Glaser, 397 ff.; Müller, *ZDMG*, xxx. 122), but not in the Greek or Roman geographers.—The older tradition of J (25^{3}) recognises a closer kinship of the Israelites with Sheba and Dedan, by making them sons of Joḳshan and descendants of Abraham through Ḳeturah (*v. ad loc.*). (An intermediate stage seems represented by 10^{25-29}, where S Arabia is assigned to the descendants of ʿEber). P follows the steps of 25^{3} by bracketing the two tribes as sons of Raʿmah: whether he knew them as comparatively recent offshoots of the Kushite stock is not so certain.

22, 23, 31. The Shemitic or Eastern Group.—With the doubtful exception of לוּד (see below) the nations here mentioned all lie on the E. of Palestine, and are probably arranged in geographical order from SE to NW, till they join hands with the Japhethites.

Shem.

1. Elam. 2. Asshur. 3. Arpachshad. 4. Lud. 5. Aram.

(Aram:) 6. Uẓ. 7. Ḥul. 8. Gether. 9. Mash.

(1) עֵילָם (Αἰλαμ)] Ass. *Elamtu*,† the name of "the great plain E of the lower Tigris and N of the Persian Gulf, together with the mountainous region enclosing it on the N and E" (Del. *Par.* 320), corresponding to the later Elymäis or Susiana. The district round Susa was in very

* See Mey. GA^{1}, i. § 403; Glaser, ii. 399 ff.; Sprenger, *ZDMG*, xliv. 501 ff.; Margoliouth, *DB*, i. 133, iv. 479 ff.; Hom. *AHT*, 77 ff., and in *EBL*, 728 ff.; KAT^{3}, 148 ff.; $ATLO^{2}$, 265.

† Commonly explained as 'highland' (Schr. Del. *Hwb.* etc.), but according to Jen. (*ZA*, vi. 170^{2}, xi. 351) = 'front-land,' *i.e.* 'East land.'

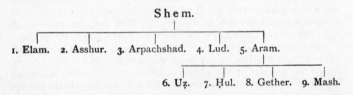

early times (after 3000 B.C.) inhabited by Semitic settlers ruled by viceroys of the Babylonian kings; about 2280 the Anzanite element (of a different race and speaking a different language) gained the upper hand, and even established a suzerainty over Babylonia. From that time onwards Elam was a powerful monarchy, playing an important part in the politics of the Euphrates valley, till it was finally destroyed by Assurbanipal.* The reason for including this non-Semitic race among the sons of Shem is no doubt geographical or political. The other OT reff. are Gn. $14^{1.9}$, Is. 11^{11} 21^{2} 22^{6}, Jer. 25^{25} $49^{34ff.}$, Ezk. 32^{24}, Dn. 8^{2}.

(2) אַשּׁוּר] Assyria. See below on v.[11] (p. 211).

(3) אַרְפַּכְשַׁד ('Αρφαξαδ)] identified by Boch. with the 'Αῤῥαπαχῖτις which Ptol. (vi. 1. 2) describes as the province of Assyria next to Armenia,—the mountainous region round the sources of the Upper Zab, between lakes Van and Urumia, still called in Kurdish *Albâk*. This name appears in Ass. as Arapḫa (Arbaḫa, etc.),† and on Eg. monuments of the 18th dynasty as *'Ararpaḫa* (Müller, *AE*, 278 f.). Geographically nothing could be more suitable than this identification: the difficulty is that the last syllable שׁד is left unaccounted for. Jos. recognised in the last three letters the name of the Chaldeans (כֶּשֶׂד),‡ and several attempts have been made to explain the first element of the word in accordance with this hint. (*a*) The best is perhaps that of Cheyne (*EB*, 318),§ resolving the word into two proper names: ארפך or ארפה (= Ass. *Arbaḫa*) and כֶּשֶׂד,—the latter here introducing a second trio of sons of Shem. On this view the Arpakšad of v.[24] $11^{10ff.}$ must be an error (for כשד?) caused by the textual corruption here. (*b*) An older conjecture, approved by Ges. (*Th.*), Knobel, al., compares the ארפ with Ar. *'urfat* (= 'boundary'),‖ Eth. *arfat* (= 'wall'); ארף כשד would thus be the 'wall (or boundary) of Kesed.' (*c*) Hommel (*AHT*, 212, 294–8) takes the middle syllable *pa* to be the Egyptian art., reading *'Ur-pa-Kesed* = Ur of the Chaldees (11^{28}),—an improbable suggestion. (*d*) Del. (*Par.* 255 f.) and Jen. (*ZA*, xv. 256) interpret the word as *arba-kišādu* = '[Land of the] four quarters (or shores),' after the analogy of a common designation of Babylonia in royal titles.—These theories are partly prompted by the observation that otherwise Chaldea is passed over in the Table of P,—a surprising omission, no doubt, but perhaps susceptible of other explanations. The question is complicated by the mention of an Aramean Kesed in 22^{22}. The difficulty of identifying that tribe with the Chaldeans in the S of Babylonia is admitted by Dri. (p. 223); and if there was another Kesed near Ḥarran, the fact must be taken account of in speculating about the meaning of Arpakšad.

---

* See the interesting historical sketch by Scheil, *Textes elamites-semitiques* (1900), pp. ix-xv [= vol. ii. of de Morgan, *Delegation en Perse: Memoires*]. Cf. Sayce, *ET*, xiii. 65.

† *KIB*, i. 177, 213, ii. 13, 89; cf. Del. *Par.* 124 f.

‡ 'Αρφαξάδης δὲ τοὺς νῦν Χαλδαίους καλουμένους 'Αρφαξαδαίους ὠνόμασεν ἄρξας αὐτῶν: *Ant.* i. 144.

§ A different conjecture in *EB*, 3644; *TBI*, 178.

‖ Note Tu.'s objections, p. 205.

(4) לוּד (ﬢ לד, 𝔊 Λουδ)] usually understood of the Lydians (Jos. Boch. al.), but it has never been satisfactorily explained how a people in the extreme W of Asia Minor comes to be numbered among the Shemites. An African people, such as appears to be contemplated in v.[13], would be equally out of place here. A suggestion of Jen.'s deserves consideration: that לוד is the *Lubdu*,—a province lying "between the upper Tigris and the Euphrates, N of Mt. Masius and its western extension," —mentioned in *KIB*, i. 4 (l. 9 fr. below, rd. *Lu-up-di*), 177 (along with Arrapḫa), 199. See Wi. *AOF*, ii. 47; Streck, *ZA*, xiv. 168; Je. 276. In the remaining refs. (Is. 66^{19}, Jer. 46^{9}, Ezk. 27^{10} 30^{5}), the Lydians of Asia Minor might be meant,—in the last three as mercenaries in the service of Eg. or Tyre.

(5) אֲרָם (Ἀραμ, Ἀραμων)] a collective designation of the Semitic peoples speaking 'Aramaic' dialects,* so far as known to the Hebrews (Nö. *EB*, 276 ff.). The actual diffusion of that family of Semites was wider than appears from OT, which uses the name only of the districts to the NE of Palestine (Damascus especially) and Mesopotamia (Aram-Naharaim, Paddan-Aram): these, however, were really the chief centres of Aramæan culture and influence. In Ass. the *Armaiu* (*Aramu*, *Arimu*, *Arumu*) are first named by Tiglath-pileser I. (*c.* 1100) as dwelling in the steppes of Mesopotamia (*KIB*, i. 33); and Shalmaneser II. (*c.* 857) encountered them in the same region (*ib.* 165). But if Wi. be right (*KAT*[3], 28 f., 36), they are referred to under the name *Aḫlāmi* from a much earlier date (TA Tab.; Ramman-nirari I. [*c.* 1325]; Ašur-rîš-îši [*c.* 1150]: see *KIB*, v. 387, i. 5, 13). Hence Wi. regards the second half of the 2nd millennium B.C. as the period during which the Aramæan nomads became settled and civilised peoples in Mesopotamia and Syria.

In 1 Ch. 1^{17} the words ובני ארם (v.[23]) are omitted, the four following names being treated as sons of Shem:

(6) עוּץ (Ὡς, Οὐζ)] is doubtless the same tribe which in 22^{21} (Ὡξ, Ὡζ) is classed as the firstborn of Naḥor: therefore presumably somewhere NE of Palestine in the direction of Ḥarran. The conjectural identifications are hardly worth repeating. The other Biblical occurrences of the name are difficult to harmonise. The Uz of Jb. 1^{1} (Αὐσιτις), and the Ḥorite tribe mentioned in Gn. 36^{20}, point to a SE situation, bordering on or comprised in Edom; and this would also suit La. 4^{21}, Je. 25^{20} (הָעוּץ!), though in both these passages the reading is doubtful. It is suggested by Rob. Sm. (*KM*[2], 61) and We. (*Heid.* 146) that the name is identical with that of the Arabian god 'Auḍ; and by the former scholar that the OT עוץ denotes a number of scattered tribes worshipping that deity (similarly Bu. *Hiob.* ix.–xi.; but, on the other side, see Nö. *ZDMG*, xl. 183 f.).

(7) חוּל (Οὐλ)] Del. (*Par.* 259) identifies with a district in the neighbourhood of Mt. Masius mentioned by Asshur-nasir-pal. The word (*ḫu-li-ia*), however, is there read by Peiser as an appellative = 'desert' (*KIB*, i. 86 f., 110 f.); and no other conjecture is even plausible.

(8) גֶּתֶר is quite unknown.

---

* οὓς Ἕλληνες Σύρους προσαγορεύουσιν—as Jos. correctly explains.

(9) מַשׁ (ᵐᵗ משא, 𝔊 Μοσοχ, in accord with 1 Ch. 1[17] MT מֶשֶׁךְ)] perhaps connected with Mons Masius,—τὸ Μάσιον ὄρος of Ptol. (v. 18. 2) and Strabo (XI. xiv. 2),—a mountain range N of Nisibis now called Ṭûr-'Abdîn or Ḳerağa Dagh (Bo. Del. *Par.* 259, Di. al.). The uncertainty of the text and the fact that the Ass. monuments use a different name render the identification precarious. Jen. (*KIB*, vi. 1, 567) suggests the mountain *Māšu* of Gilgameš IX. ii. 1 f., which he supposes to be Lebanon and Anti-Libanus. The *Mât Maš* of *KIB*, ii. 221, which has been adduced as a parallel, ought, it now appears, to be read *mad-bar* (*KAT*[3], 191[2]; cf. Jen. *ZA*, x. 364).

31, 32. P's closing formula for the Shemites ([31]); and his subscription to the whole Table ([32]).

The Table of J.

IX. 18a, X. 1b. Introduction. See pp. 182, 188.

A slight discontinuity in v.[1] makes it probable that [1b] is inserted from J. If so, it would stand most naturally after 9[18a] (Di.), not after [19]. It seems to me that [19] is rather the Yahwistic parallel to 10[32] (P), and formed originally the conclusion of J's Table (cf. the *closing* formulæ, 10[29] 22[23] 25[4]).

8–12. Nimrod and his empire.—The section deals with the foundation of the Babylonio-Assyrian Empire, whose legendary hero, Nimrod, is described as a son of Kush (see below). Unlike the other names in the chapter, Nimrod is not a people, but an individual,—a *Gibbôr* or despot, famous as the originator of the idea of the military state, based on arbitrary force.—**8.** The statement that *he was the first to become a Gibbôr on the earth* implies a different conception from 6[4]. There, the Gibbôrîm are identified with the semi-divine Nephîlîm: here, the Gibbôr is a man, whose personal prowess and energy raise him above the common level of humanity. The word expresses the idea of violent, tyrannical power, like Ar. *ğabbār*.

If the כּוּשׁ of v.[6f.] be Ethiopia (see p. 200 f.), it follows that in the view of the redactor the earliest dynasty in the Euphrates valley was founded by immigrants from Africa. That interpretation was accepted even by Tuch; but it is opposed to all we know of the early history of Baby-

---

8. נִמְרֹד (Νεβρωδ)] The Heb. naturally connects the name with the √ מרד = 'rebel' (𝔗J, Ra. al.): see below, p. 209.—הוּא הֵחֵל ל׳] 'he was the

lonia, and it is extremely improbable that it represents a Heb. tradition. The assumption of a S Arabian Kûsh would relieve the difficulty; for it is generally agreed that the *Semitic* population of Babylonia—which goes back as far as monumental evidence carries us—actually came from Arabia; but it is entirely opposed to the ethnography of J, who peoples S Arabia with descendants of Shem ([21. 25ff.]). It is therefore not unlikely that, as many Assyriologists think,* J's כּוּשׁ is quite independent of the Hamitic Kûsh of P, and denotes the *Kaš* or *Kaššu*, a people who conquered Babylonia in the 18th cent., and set up a dynasty (the 3rd) which reigned there for 600 years † (*KAT*[3], 21). It is conceivable that in consequence of so prolonged a supremacy, Kaš might have become a name for Babylonia, and that J's knowledge of its history did not extend farther back than the Kaššite dynasty. Since there is no reason to suppose that J regarded Kaš as Hamitic, it is quite possible that the name belonged to his list of Japhetic peoples.

9. Nimrod was not only a great tyrant and ruler of men, but *a hero of the chase* (גִּבּוֹר צַיִד). The v. breaks the connexion between [8] and [10], and is probably an interpolation (Di. al.); although, as De. remarks, the union of a passion for the chase with warlike prowess makes Nimrod a true prototype of the Assyrian monarchs,—an observation amply illustrated by the many hunting scenes sculptured on the monuments.—*Therefore it is said*] introducing a current proverb; cf. 1 Sa. 19[24] with 10[12]; Gn. 22[14] etc. "When the Hebrews

---

first to become'; see on 4[26] 9[20].—**9.** While Di. regards the v. as an interpolation from oral tradition, Bu. (*Urg.* 390 ff.) assigns it to his J[1], and finds a place for it between 6[4] and 11[1],—a precarious suggestion.—הָיָה[1]] 𝕲 + τοῦ θεοῦ.—לִפְנֵי י׳] 'before Yahwe.' The phrase is variously explained: (1) 'unique,' like לאלהים in Jn 3[3] (Di. al.); (2) 'in the estimation of Y.' (cf. 2 Ki. 5[1] etc.); (3) 'in despite of Y.' (Bu.); (4) 'with the assistance of Y.'—the name of some god of the chase having stood in the original myth (Gu.); (5) 'in the constant presence of Y.'—an allusion to the constellation Orion (Ho.). The last view is possible in [9b], but hardly in [a], because of the היה. A sober exegesis will prefer (1) or (2).

---

* See Del. *Par.* 51–55; Schr. *KAT*[2], 87 f.; Wi. *ATU*, 146 ff.; Jen. *ZA*, vi. 340–2; Sayce, *HCM*[2], 148 ff., etc.

† Remnants of this conquering race are mentioned by Sennacherib (*KIB*, ii. 87). They are thought to be identical with the Κοσσαῖοι of the Greeks (Strabo, XI. xiii. 6, XVI. i. 17 f.; Arrian, *Anab.* vii. 15; Diodorus, xvii. 111, xix. 19, etc.); and probably also with the Κίσσιοι of Her vii. 62, 86, etc. (cf. v. 49, 52, vi. 119). Cf. Del. *Par.* 31, 124, 127 ff.; Mey. *GA*[1], § 129; Wi. *GBA*, 78 ff.; Schr. *KGF*, 176 f.; Oppert, *ZA*, iii. 421 ff.; Jen. *ZDMG*, l. 244 f., etc.

wished to describe a man as being a great hunter, they spoke of him as 'like Nimrod'" (Dri.).—The expression לִפְנֵי יהוה doubtless belongs to the proverb: the precise meaning is obscure (*v.i.*).

A perfectly convincing Assyriological prototype of the figure of Nimrod has not as yet been discovered. The derivation of the name from Marduk, the tutelary deity of the city of Babylon, first propounded by Sayce, and adopted with modifications by We.,* still commends itself to some Assyriologists (Pinches, *DB*, iii. 552 f.; cf. *KAT*³, 581); but the material points of contact between the two personages seem too vague to establish an instructive parallel. The identification with Nazi-Maruttaš, a late (*c.* 1350) and apparently not very successful king of the Kaššite dynasty (Haupt, Hilprecht, Sayce, al.), is also unsatisfying: the supposition that that particular king was so well known in Palestine as to eclipse all his predecessors, and take rank as the founder of Babylonian civilisation, is improbable. The nearest analogy is that of Gilgameš,† the legendary tyrant of Erech (see v.[10]), whose adventures are recorded in the famous series of Tablets of which the Deluge story occupies the eleventh (see p. 175 above, and *KAT*³, 566 ff.). Gilgameš is a true Gibbôr—"two parts deity and one part humanity"—he builds the walls of Erech with forced labour, and his subjects groan under his tyranny, until they cry to Aruru to create a rival who might draw off some of his superabundant energy (*KIB*, vi. 1, 117, 119). Among his exploits, and those of his companion Ea-bani, contests with beasts and monsters figure prominently; and he is supposed to be the hero so often represented on seals and palace-reliefs in victorious combat with a lion (see *ATLO*², 266 f.). It is true that the parallel is incomplete; and (what is more important) that the name Nimrod remains unexplained. The expectation that the phonetic reading of the ideographic *GIŠ. ṬU. BAR* might prove to be the Bab. equivalent of the Heb. Nimrod, would seem to have been finally dispelled by the discovery (in 1890) of the correct pronunciation as Gilgameš (but see Je. *l.c.*). Still, enough general resemblance remains to warrant the belief that the original of the biblical Nimrod belongs to the sphere of Babylonian mythology. A striking parallel to the visit of Gilgameš to his father Ut-napištim occurs in a late Nimrod legend, preserved in the Syrian *Schatzhöhle* (see Gu. *Schöpf.* 146²; Lidz. *ZA*, vii. 15). On the theory which connects Nimrod with the constellation Orion, see Tu. *ad loc.*; Bu. *Urg.* 395 f.; *KAT*³, 581²; and on the late Jewish and Mohammedan legends generally, Seligsohn, *JE*, ix. 309 ff.

---

* Sayce (*TSBA*, ii. 243 ff.) derived it from the Akkadian equivalent of Marduk, *Amar-ud*, from which he thought *Nimrudu* would be a regular (Ass.) Niphal form. We. (*Comp.*² 309 f.) explains the נ as an Aram. impf. preformative to the √ מרד, a corruption from Mard-uk which took place among the Syrians of Mesopotamia, through whom the myth reached the Hebrews.

† So Smith-Sayce, *Chald. Gen.* 176 ff.; Je. *Isdubar-Nimrod.*

10. *The nucleus of his empire was Babylon . . . in the land of Shinʿar*] It is not said that Nimrod founded these four cities (ct. v.[11]). The rise of the great cities of Babylonia was not only much older than the Kaššite dynasty, but probably preceded the establishment of any central government; and the peculiar form of the expression here may be due to a recollection of that fact. Of the four cities, two can be absolutely identified; the third is known by name, but cannot be located; and the last is altogether uncertain.

בָּבֶל (Βαβυλών)] the Heb. form of the native *Bāb-ili*='gate of God' or 'the gods' (though this may be only a popular etymology). The political supremacy of the city, whose origin is unknown, dates from the expulsion of the Elamites by Ḥammurabi, the sixth king of its first dynasty (*c.* 2100 B.C.); and for 2000 years it remained the chief centre of ancient Oriental civilisation. Its ruins lie on the left bank of the Euphrates, about fifty miles due S. of Baghdad.

אֶרֶךְ (Ὀρεχ)] the Bab. *Uruk* or *Arku*, now *Warka*, also on the Euphrates, about 100 miles SE of Babylon. It was the city of Gilgameš (*v.s.*).

אַכַּד (Ἀρχαδ: cf. דַּמֶּשֶׂק and דַּרְמֶשֶׂק)] The name (*Akkad*) frequently occurs in the inscriptions, especially in the phrase 'Šumer and Akkad,' =South and North Babylonia. But a city of Akkad is also mentioned by Nebuchadnezzar I. (*KIB*, iii. 170 ff.), though its site is uncertain. Its identity with the Agadé of Sargon I. (*c.* 3800 B.C.), which was formerly suspected, is said to be confirmed by a recent decipherment. Del. and Zim. suppose that it was close to Sippar on the Euphrates, in the latitude of Baghdad (see *Par.* 209 ff.; *KAT*^{3}, 422^2, 423^8; *ATLO*^{2}, 270).

כַּלְנֵה (Χαλαννη)] Not to be confused with the כלנה of Am. 6^2 (=כַּלְנוֹ, Is. 10^9), which was in N Syria. The Bab. Kalne has not yet been discovered. Del. (*Par.* 225) takes it to be the ideogram *Kul-unu* (pronounced *Zirlahu*), of a city in the vicinity of Babylon. But Jen. (*ThLz.* 1895, 510) asserts that the real pronunciation was *Kullab*(*a*), and proposes to read so here (כַּלְבָה).

שִׁנְעָר (Σεν[ν]αaρ)] apparently the old Heb. name for Babylonia proper (11^2 14$^{1.9}$, Jos. 7^{21}, Is. 11^{11}, Zec. 5^{11}, Dn. 1^2), afterwards ארץ כשדים or simply בבל ['א]. That it is the same as Šumer (*south* Babylonia: *v.s.*) is improbable. More plausible is the identification with the *Šanḫar* of TA Tab. (*KIB*, v. 83)=Eg. *Sangara* (Müller, *AE*, 279); though Wi. (*AOF*, i. 240, 399; *KAT*^{3}, 31) puts it N of the Taurus. *Ğebel Sinğar* (ὁ Σιγγαρος ὄρος: Ptol. v. 18. 2), W of Nineveh, is much too far north for the biblical Shinʿar, unless the name had wandered.

11, 12. The colonisation of Assyria from Babylonia.—

---

11. יָצָא אַשּׁוּר] 'he went out to Asshur' (so 𝔗^J, Cal. and all moderns). The rendering 'Asshur went out' (𝔊𝔙𝔖𝔗^O, Jer. al.) is grammatically

From that land he (Nimrod, *v.i.*) *went out to Assyria*]—where he built four new cities. That the great Assyrian cities were not really built by one king or at one period is certain; nevertheless the statement has a certain historic value, inasmuch as the whole religion, culture, and political organisation of Assyria were derived from the southern state. It is also noteworthy that the rise of the Assyrian power dates from the decline of Babylonia under the Kaššite kings (*KAT*³, 21). In Mic. 5⁵ Assyria is described as the 'land of Nimrod.'

That אשור is here the name of the land (along the Tigris, N of the Lower Zab), and not the ancient capital (now *Ḳal'at Šerkāt,* about halfway between the mouths of the two Zabs), is plain from the context, and the contrast to שנער in v.[10].

נִינְוֵה] (Ass. *Ninua*, *Ninâ*, 𝔊 Νινευη [-ι]) the foremost city of Assyria, was a royal residence from at latest the time of Aššur-bel-kalu, son of Tiglath-pileser I. (11th cent.); but did not apparently become the political capital till the reign of Sennacherib (Wi. *GBA*, 146). Its site is now marked by the ruined mounds of *Nebī Yūnus* (with a village named *Nunia*) and *Kuyunjiḳ*, both on the E side of the Tigris opposite Mosul (see Hilp. *EBL*, 11, 88–138).

רְחֹבֹת עִיר ('Ροωβὼς πόλιν)] has in Heb. appellative significance = 'broad places of a city' (𝔙 *plateas civitatis*). A similar phrase on Ass. monuments, *rêbit Ninâ*, is understood to mean 'suburb of Nineveh'; and it has been supposed that 'ר' ע is a translation of this designation into Heb. As to the position of this 'suburb' authorities differ. Del. (*Par.* 260 f.) thinks it certain that it was on the N or NE side of Nineveh, towards Dûr-Sargon (the modern Khorsabad); and Johns (*EB*, iv. 4029) even identifies it with the latter (cf. *KIB*, ii. 47). Billerbeck, on the other hand, places it at Mosul on the opposite side of the Tigris, as a sort of *tête du pont* (see *ATLO*², 273). No *proper* name at all resembling this is known in the neighbourhood of Nineveh.

כֶּלַח (Χαλαχ, Καλαχ) is the Ass. *Kalḫu* or *Kalaḫ*, which excavations have proved to be the modern *Nimrûd*, at the mouth of the Upper Zab, 20 miles S of Nineveh (Hilp. *l.c.* 111 f.). Built by Shalmaneser I. (*c.* 1300), it replaced Aššur as the capital, but afterwards fell into decay, and was restored by Aššur-nasir-pal (883–59) (*KIB*, i. 117). From that time till Sargon, it seems to have continued the royal residence.

רֶסֶן (Δασεμ, Δασῃ, etc.)] Perhaps = *Riš-îni* ('fountain-head'), an extremely common place-name in Semitic countries; but its site is unknown. A Syrian tradition placed it at the ruins of Khorsabad, 'a parasang above Nineveh,' where a *Rās'ul-'Ain* is said still to be found

---

correct, and gives a good sense (cf. Is. 23[13]). But (1) ראשית (v.[10]) requires an antithesis (see on 1[1]); and (2) in Mic. 5⁵ Nimrod is the hero of Assyria.

(G. Hoffmann in Nestle, *ZDMG*, lviii. 158 ff.). This is doubtless the Riš-ini of Sennacherib (*KIB*, ii. 117); but its identity with רסן is phonetically questionable, and topographically impossible, on account of the definition 'between Nineveh and Kelaḥ.'

The clause הוא העיר הגדלה is almost universally, but very improbably, taken to imply that the four places just enumerated had come to be regarded as a single city. Schr. (*KAT*[2], 99 f.) is responsible for the statement that from the time of Sennacherib the name Nineveh was extended to include the whole complex of cities between the Zab and the Tigris; but more recent authorities assure us that the monuments contain no trace of such an idea (*KAT*[3], 75[4]; Gu.[2] 78; cf. Johns, *EB*, 3420). The fabulous dimensions given by Diodorus (ii. 3; cf. Jon. 3[3f.]) must proceed on some such notion; and it is possible that that might have induced a late interpolator to insert the sentence here. But if the words be a gloss, it is more probable that it springs from the העיר הגדולה of Jn. 1[2], which was put in the margin opposite נִינְוֵה, and crept into the text in the wrong place (*ATLO*[2], 273).*

13, 14.—The sons of Mizraim.—These doubtless all represent parts or (supposed) dependencies of Egypt; although of the eight names not more than two can be certainly identified.—On מִצְרַיִם = Egypt, see v.[6].—Since Mizraim could hardly have been reckoned a son of Canaan, the section (if documentary) must be an extract from that Yahwistic source to which 9[18f.] belong (see p. 188 f.).

(1) לודים (Λουδιειμ: 1 Ch. 1[11] לודיים)] Not the Lydians of Asia Minor (*ATLO*[2], 274), who can hardly be thought of in this connexion; but (if the text be correct) some unknown people of NE Africa (see on v.[22], p. 206). The prevalent view of recent scholars is that the word is a mistake for לוּבִים, the Lybians. See Sta. *Ak. Red.* 141; Müller, *AE*, 115 f.; *OLz*, v. 475; al.

(2) עֲנָמִים (𝔐 עינמים; 𝔊 Aἰν-['Eν-]εμετιειμ[ν])] Müller reads כנמים or (after 𝔊) כנמתים; *i.e.* the inhabitants of the Great Oasis of *Knmt* in the Libyan desert (*Wāḥāt el-Khāriğah*).† For older conjectures see Di.

---

* With the above hypothesis, Schr.'s argument that, since Nineveh is here used in the restricted sense, the passage must be of earlier date than Sennacherib, falls to the ground. From the writer's silence regarding Aššur, the ancient capital, it may safely be inferred that he lived after 1300; and from the omission of Sargon's new residence Dûr-Sargon, it is *probable* that he wrote before 722. But the latter argument is not decisive, since Kelaḥ and Nineveh (the only names that can be positively identified) were both flourishing cities down to the fall of the Empire.

† *OLz*. v. 471 ff.—It should be explained that this dissertation, frequently cited above, proceeds on the bold assumption that almost the best known name in the section (פַּתְרֻסִים, [14]) is an interpolation.

(3) לְהָבִים (Λαβιειμ)] commonly supposed to be the Lybians, the (לוּב) לוּבִים of Nah. 3^9, Dn. 11^{43}, 2 Ch. 12^3 16^8, [Ezk. 30^5?]. Müller thinks it a variant of לוּדִים (1).

(4) נַפְתֻּחִים (Νεφθαλιειμ)] Müller proposes פתנחים = *P-to-n-ḥe*, 'cow-land,'—the name of the Oasis of *Farāfra*. But there is a strong presumption that, as the next name stands for Upper Egypt, this will be a designation of Lower Egypt. So Erman (*ZATW*, x. 118 f.), who reads פתמחים = *p-t-maḥī*, 'the north-land,'—at all periods the native name of Lower Egypt. More recently Spiegelberg (*OLz.* ix. 276 ff.) recognises in it an old name of the Delta, and reads without textual change *Na-patûh* = 'the people of the Delta.'

(5) פַּתְרֻסִים (Πατροσωνιειμ)] the inhabitants of פַּתְרוֹס (Is. 11^{11}, Jer. $44^{1.15}$, Ezk. 30^{14}), *i.e.* Upper Egypt: *P-to-reši* = 'south-land' (Ass. *paturisi*): see Erman, *l.c.*

(6) כַּסְלֻחִים (Χασμωνιειμ)] Doubtful conjectures in Di. Müller restores with help of 𝔊 נסמנים, which he identifies with the Νασαμῶνες of Her. ii. 32, iv. 172, 182, 190,—a powerful tribe of nomad Lybians, near the Oasis of Amon. Sayce has read the name *Kasluhat* on the inscr. of Ombos (see on *Kaphtorim*, below); *Man*, 1903, No. 77.

(7) פְּלִשְׁתִּים (Φυλιστιειμ)] The Philistines are here spoken of as an offshoot of the Kaslûḥîm,—a statement scarcely intelligible in the light of other passages (Jer. 47^4, Am. 9^7; cf. Dt. 2^{23}), according to which the Ph. came from *Kaphtōr*. The clause אֲשֶׁר יָצְאוּ מִשָּׁם פ׳ is therefore in all probability a marginal gloss meant to come after כפתרים.—The Ph. are mentioned in the Eg. monuments, under the name *Purašati*, as the leading people in a great invasion of Syria in the reign of Ramses III. (*c.* 1175 B.C.). The invaders came both by land and sea from the coasts of Asia Minor and the islands of the Ægean; and the Philistines established themselves on the S coast of Palestine so firmly that, though nearly all traces of their language and civilisation have disappeared, their name has clung to the country ever since. See Müller, *AE*, 387–90, and *MVAG*, v. 2 ff.; Moore, *EB*, iii. 3713 ff.

(8) כַּפְתֹּרִים (Χαφθοριειμ)] *Kaphtōr* (Dt. 2^{23}, Am. 9^7, Jer. 47^4) has usually been taken for the island of Crete (see Di.), mainly because of the repeated association of כְּרֵתִים (Cretans?) with the Philistines and the Philistine territory (1 Sa. $30^{14.16}$, Ezk. 25^{16}, Zeph. 2^5). There are convincing reasons for connecting it with *Keftiu* (properly 'the country *behind*'), an old Eg. name for the 'lands of the Great Ring' (the Eastern Mediterranean), or the 'isles of the Great Green,' *i.e.* SW Asia Minor, Rhodes, Crete, and the Mycenian lands beyond, to the NW of Egypt (see Müller, *AE*, 337, 344–53, 387 ff.; and more fully H. R. Hall in *Annual of the British School at Athens*, 1901–2, pp. 162–6). The precise phonetic equivalent *Kptār* has been found on a late mural decoration at Ombos (Sayce, *HCM*^{6}, 173; *EHH*, 291; Müller, *MVAG*, 1900,

---

When this 'cuckoo's egg' is ejected, the author finds that the 'sons' of Egypt are all dependencies or foreign possessions, and are to be sought *outside* the Nile valley. The theory does not seem to have found much favour from Egyptologists or others.

5 ff.). "*Keftiu* is the old Eg. name of Caphtor (Crete), *Keptar* a Ptolemaic doublet of it, taken over when the original meaning of *Keftiu* had been forgotten, and the name had been erroneously applied to Phœnicia" (Hall, *Man*, Nov. 1903, No. 92, p. 162 ff.). In *OLz.*, M. questions the originality of the name in this passage: so also Je. *ATLO*², 275.*

15–19. The Canaanites.—The peoples assigned to the Canaanitish group are (1) the Phœnicians (צִידֹן), (2) the Ḥittites (חֵת), and (3) a number of petty communities perhaps summed up in the phrase מִשְׁפְּחוֹת הַכְּנַעֲנִי in 18b. It is surprising to find the great northern nation of the Ḥittites classed as a subdivision of the Canaanites. The writer may be supposed to have in view offshoots of that empire, which survived as small enclaves in Palestine proper; but that explanation does not account for the marked prominence given to Ḥeth over the little Canaanite kingships. On the other hand, one hesitates to adopt Gu.'s theory that כנען is here used in a wide geographical sense as embracing the main seats of the Ḥittite empire (p. 187). There is evidence, however, of a strong settlement of Ḥittites near Ḥermon (see below), and it is conceivable that these were classed as Canaanites and so inserted here.

Critically, the vv. are difficult. We. (*Comp.*² 15) and others remove 16-18a as a gloss: because (*a*) the boundaries laid down in 19 are exceeded in 17. 18a, and (*b*) the mention of a *subsequent* dispersion of Canaanites (18b) has no meaning after 16-18a. That is perhaps the most reasonable view to take; but even so 18b does not read quite naturally after 15; and what could have induced a glossator to insert four of the most northerly Phœnician cities, passing by those best known to the Hebrews? Is it

---

15. בְּכֹרוֹ] cf. 22^{21} (J).—**18.** אַחַר] adv. of time, as 18^{5} 24^{55} 30^{21} etc. = אַחֲרֵי־כֵן: see BDB, 29 f.—נָפֹצוּ] Niph. fr. √ פוץ; see on 9^{19}: cf. $11^{4.\,8.\,9}$.—מִשְׁפְּחוֹת הַכְּנַעֲנִי] can hardly, even if the clause be a gloss, denote the Phœn. colonies on the Mediterranean (Brown, *EB*, ii. 1698 f.).—**19.** בֹּאֲכָה] 'as one comes' (see G-K. § 144 *h*) might be taken as 'in the direction of' (so Di. Dri. al.); but there does not appear to be any clear case in which the expression differs from עַד־בֹּאֲךָ = 'as far as' (cf. 10^{30} 13^{10} 25^{18} [all J], 1 Sa. 15^{7} with Ju. 6^{4} 11^{33}, 1 Sa. 17^{52}, 2 Sa. 5^{25}, 1 Ki. 18^{46}).—עַד־עַזָּה] 𝔊 καὶ Γάζαν.

---

* V.18f. present so many peculiar features—the regular use of the pl., the great preponderance of quadriliteral names, all vocalised alike—that we can hardly help suspecting that they are a secondary addition to the Table, written from specially intimate acquaintance with the (later?) Egyptian geography.

possible that the last five names were originally given as sons of Heth, and the previous four as sons of Zidon? ^{18b} might mean that the Canaanite clans emanated from Phœnicia, and were *afterwards* 'dispersed' over the region defined by ^{19}.—The change from כנען in ^{15} to הכנעני in $^{18b.\,19}$ is hardly sufficient to prove diversity of authorship (Gu.)

צידן] The oldest of the Phœnician cities; now Ṣaidā, nearly 30 miles S of the promontory of Beirūt. Here, however, the name is the eponym of the Ẓidonians (צידנים), as the Phœnicians were frequently called, not only in OT (Ju. 18^7 3^3, 1 Ki. 5^{20} 16^{31} etc.) and Homer (*Il.* vi. 290 f., etc.), but on the Ass. monuments, and even by the Phœnicians themselves (Mey. *EB*, iv. 4504).

חת (τὸν Χετταῖον)] elsewhere only in the phrases בני ח׳, בנות ח׳ (ch. 23 *pass.* 25^{10} 27^{46b} 49^{32} [all P]); other writers speak of חתי[ם]. The Ḥittites (Eg. *Ḫeta*, Ass. *Ḫatti*) were a northern non-Semitic people, who under unknown circumstances established themselves in Cappadocia. They appear to have invaded Babylonia at the close of the First dynasty (*c.* 1930 B.C.) (King, *Chronicles conc. early Bab. Kings*, p. 72 f.). Not long after the time of Thothmes III. (1501–1447), they are found in N Syria. With the weakening of the Eg. supremacy in the Tel-Amarna period, they pressed further S, occupying the Orontes valley, and threatening the Phœnician coast-cities. The indecisive campaigns of Ramses II. seem to have checked their southward movement. In Ass. records they do not appear till the reign of Tiglath-pileser I. (*c.* 1100), when they seem to have held the country from the Taurus and Orontes to the Euphrates, with Carchemish as one of their chief strongholds. After centuries of intermittent warfare, they were finally incorporated in the Ass. Empire by Sargon II. (*c.* 717). See Paton, *Syr. and Pal.* 104 ff. — The OT allusions to the Ḥittites are extremely confusing, and cannot be fully discussed here: see on 15^{19-21} 23^3. Besides the Palestinian Ḥittites (whose connexion with the people just spoken of may be doubtful), there is mention of an extensive Ḥittite country to the N of Palestine (2 Sa. 24^6 [$\mathfrak{G}^L$], 1 Ki. 10^{29}, 2 Ki. 7^6 al.). The most important fact for the present purpose is the definite location of Ḥittites in the Lebanon region, or at the foot of Hermon (Jos. 11^3 [$\mathfrak{G}^{B,\,al.}$] and Ju. 3^3 [as amended by Mey. al.]), cf. Ju. 1^{26}?). It does not appear what grounds Moore (*Ju.* 82) has for the statement that these Ḥittites were Semitic. There is certainly no justification for treating (with Jast. *EB*, 2094) חת in this v. as a gloss.

The four names which follow are names of Canaanitish clans which constantly recur in enumerations of the aborigines of Palestine, and seldom elsewhere.

(1) היבוסי] The clan settled in and around Jerusalem: Jos. 15^8 18^{28}, Ju. 19^{10}, 2 Sa. 5^{6-9} etc.

(2) האמרי] An important politico-geographical name in the Egyptian and cuneiform documents (Eg. *Amor*, etc., Ass. *Amurru*). In the TA Tablets the 'land of Amurru' denotes the Lebanon region behind the Phœnician coast-territory. Its princes Abd-Aširta and Aziru were then the most active enemies of the Egyptian authority in the north, conducting successful operations against several of the Phœnician cities. It has been supposed that subsequently to these events the

Amorites pressed southwards, and founded kingdoms in Palestine both E and W of the Jordan (Nu. $21^{13ff.}$, Jos. 24^{8} etc.); though Müller has pointed out some difficulties in the way of that hypothesis (*AE*, 230 f.).—In the OT there appears an occasional tendency to restrict the name to 'highlanders' (Nu. 13^{29}, Dt. 1^{7}), but this is more than neutralised by other passages (Ju. 1^{34}). The most significant fact is that E (followed by D) employs the term to designate the pre-Israelite inhabitants of Palestine generally (cf. Am. $2^{9f.}$), whom J describes as Canaanites. Apart from the assumption of an actual Amorite domination, it is difficult to suggest an explanation of E's usage, unless we can take it as a survival of the old Bab. name Amurru (or at least its ideographic equivalent *MAR. TU*) for Palestine, Phœnicia and Cœle-Syria.—See, further, Müller, *AE*, 218 ff., 229 ff.; Wi. *GI*, i. 51–54, *KAT*³, 178 ff.; Mey. *ZATW*, i. 122 ff.; We. *Comp.*² 341; Bu. *Urg.* 344 ff.; Dri. *Deut.* 11 f., *Gen.* 125 f.; Sayce, *DB*, i. 84 f.; Paton, *Syr. and Pal.* 25–46, 115 ff., 147 f.; Mey. *GA*², I. ii. § 396.

(3) הַגִּרְגָּשִׁי] only mentioned in enumerations (15^{21}, Dt. 7^{1}, Jos. 3^{10} 24^{11}, Neh. 9^{8}) without indication of locality. גרגש, גרגשים, גרגשי occur as prop. names on Punic inscrs. (Lidzbarski, *Nord-sem. Epigr.* 405_{4}, $622_{4f.}$, 673_{3}; *Ephem.* i. 36, 308). Ewald conjectured a connexion with NT Γέργεσα.

(4) הַחִוִּי (τ. Εὐαῖον)] a tribe of central Palestine, in the neighbourhood of Shechem (34^{2}) and Gibeon (Jos. 9^{7}); in Ju. 3^{3}, where they are spoken of in the N, הַחִתִּי should be read, and in Jos. 11^{3} Hittites and Hivvites should be transposed in accordance with 𝔊ᴮ. The name has been explained by Ges. (*Th.*) and others as meaning 'dwellers in חַוּוֹת' (Bedouin encampments: cf. Nu. 32^{41}); but that is improbable in the case of a people long settled in Palestine (Moore). We. (*Heid.* 154) more plausibly connects it with חִוְיָה = 'serpent' (see on 3^{20}), surmising that the Hivvites were a snake-clan. Cf. Lagarde, *OS*, 187, 174, l. 97 (Εὐαῖοι σκολιοὶ ὡς ἐπὶ ὄφεις).

The 5 remaining names are formed from names of *cities*, 4 in the extreme N of Phœnicia, and the last in Cœle-Syria.

(5) הָעַרְקִי (𝔐 הערוקי, 𝔊 τ. 'Αρουκαῖον)] is from the city Ἄρκη ἐν τῷ Λιβάνῳ (Jos. *Ant.* i. 138), the ruins of which, still bearing the name *Tell 'Arḳa*, are found on the coast about 12 miles NE of Tripolis. It is mentioned by Thothmes III. (in the form *'r-ka-n-tu*: see *AE*, 247 f.), and in TA letters (*Irkata*: *KIB*, v. 171, etc.); also by Shalmaneser II. (*KIB*, i. 173; along with Arvad and Sianu, *below*), and Tiglath-pileser IV. (*ib.* ii. 29; along with Ṣimirra and Sianu).

(6) הַסִּינִי (τ. 'Ασενναῖον)] inhabitants of סִין, Ass. *Sianu* (*KIB*, *ll.cc.*). Jer. (*Quæst.*) says it was not far from 'Arḳa, but adds that only the name remained in his day. The site is unknown: see Cook, *EB*, iv. 4644 f.

(7) הָאַרְוָדִי (τ. 'Αράδιον)] 'Arwad (Ezk. $27^{8.\,11}$) was the most northerly of the Phœnician cities, built on a small island (Strabo, XVI. ii. 13; *KIB*, i. 109) about 35 miles N of Tripolis (now *Ruād*). It is named frequently, in connexions which show its great importance in ancient times, in Eg. inscrs. (*AE*, 186 f.), on TA Tab., and by Ass. kings from Tiglath-pileser I. to Asshurbanipal (*KAT*², 104 f.; Del. *Par.* 281); see also Her. vii. 98.

(8) הַצְּמָרִי (τ. Σαμαραῖον)] Six miles S of Ruād, the modern village of *Ṣumra* preserves the name of this city: Eg. *Ṣamar*; TA, *Ṣumur*; Ass. *Ṣimirra*; Gr. Σιμυρα. See Strabo, XVI. ii. 12; *AE*, 187; *KAT*^{2}, 105; Del. *Par.* 281 f.

(9) הַחֲמָתִי (τ. Ἀμαθί)] from the well-known Ḥamath on the Orontes; now *Ḥamā.*

The delimitation of the Canaanite boundary in v.^{19} is very obscure It describes two sides of a triangle, from Ẓidon on the N to Gaza or Gerar in the SW; and from thence to a point near the S end of the Dead Sea. The terminus לֶשַׁע (𝔊 Δασα) is, however, unknown. The traditional identification (𝔗J, Jer.) with Καλλιρρόη, near the N end of the Dead Sea, is obviously unsuitable. Kittel, *BH* (very improbably), suggests בֶּלַע (14^{2}). We. (*Comp.*^{2} 15) reads לַשְׁה or לְשֵׁם (Jos. 19^{47} לְשֵׁם) = 'to Dan' (לַיִשׁ), the conventional *northern* limit of Canaan,—thus completing the E side of the triangle.—Gerar was certainly further S. than Gaza (see on 20^{1}); hence we cannot read '*as far as* (*v.i.*) Gerar, up to Gaza,' while the rendering '*in the direction of* Gerar, as far as Gaza,' would only be intelligible if Gerar were a better known locality than Gaza Most probably עַד־עַזָּה is a gloss (Gu. al.).—On the situation of Sodom, etc., see on ch. 19.—On any construction of the v. the northern cities of $^{17.\ 18a}$ are excluded.—𝔐 has an entirely different text: מנהר מצרים עד הנהר הגדול נהר פרת ועד הים האחרון,—an amalgam of 15^{18} and Dt. 11^{24}.

21, 24, 25–30. The Shemites.—The genealogy of Shem in J resolves itself entirely into a classification of the peoples whose origin was traced to ʿEber. These fall into two main branches: the descendants of Peleg (who are not here enumerated), and the Yoḳṭanites or S Arabian tribes. Shem is thus nothing more than the representative of the unity of the widely scattered Hebraic stock: Shemite and 'Hebrew' are convertible terms. This recognition of the ethnological affinity of the northern and southern Semites is a remarkable contrast to P, who assigns the S Arabians to Ḥam,—the family with which Israel had least desire to be associated.

עֵבֶר is the eponym of עִבְרִים (Hebrews), the name by which the Israelites are often designated in distinction from other peoples, down to the time of Saul* (see G-K. § 2 *b*: the pass. are cited in BDB, *s.v.*). It is strange at first sight that while the בני עבר of v.^{21} include all Shemites known to J, the gentilic word is historically restricted to Israelites. The difficulty is perhaps removed by the still disputed, but now widely

* After 1 Sa. it occurs only Dt. 15^{12}, Jer. 34$^{9.\ 14}$, Jon. 1^{9}. But see the cogent criticisms of Weinheimer in *ZATW*, 1909, 275 ff., who propounds the view that Hebrews and Israelites were distinct strata of the population.

accepted, theory that *Ḫabiri* in the TA letters is the cuneiform equivalent of the OT עִבְרִים. The equation presents no philological difficulty: Ass. *ḫ* often represents a foreign ע; and Eerdmans' statement (*AT Studien*, ii. 64), that the sign *ḫa* never stands for ע (if true) is worthless, for *Ḫa-za-ḳi-ya-u*=חִזְקִיָּהוּ shows that Ass. *a* may become in OT *i*, and this is all that it is necessary to prove. The historical objections vanish if the Ḫabiri be identified, not with the Israelitish invaders after the Exodus, but with an earlier immigration of Semitic nomads into Palestine, amongst whom the ancestors of Israel were included. The chief uncertainty arises from the fact that the phonetic writing *Ḫa-bi-ri* occurs only in a limited group of letters,—those of 'Abd-ḫiba of Jerusalem (179, 180 [182], 183, 185). The ideogram *SA. GAS* ('robbers') in other letters is conjectured to have the same value, but this is not absolutely demonstrated. Assuming that Wi. and others are right in equating the two, the Ḫabiri are in evidence over the whole country, occasionally as auxiliaries of the Egyptian government, but chiefly as its foes. The inference is very plausible that they were the roving Bedouin element of the population, as opposed to the settled inhabitants,—presumably a branch of the great Aramæan invasion which was then overflowing Mesopotamia and Syria (see above, p. 206; cf. Wi. *AOF*, iii. 90 ff., *KAT*[3], 196 ff.; Paton, *Syr. and Pal.* 111 ff.). There is thus a strong probability that עברים was originally the name of a group of tribes which invaded Palestine in the 15th cent. B.C., and that it was afterwards applied to the Israelites as the sole historic survivors of the immigrants.—Etymologically, the word has usually been interpreted as meaning 'those from beyond' the river (cf. עֵבֶר הַנָּהָר, Jos. $24^{2f. 14f.}$); and on that assumption, the river is certainly not the Tigris (De.), and almost certainly not the Jordan (We. Kau. Sta.), but (in accordance with prevailing tradition) *the* נהר of the OT, the Euphrates, 'beyond' which lay Ḥarran, the city whence Abraham set out. Hommel's view (*AHT*, 252 ff.) has no probability (cf. Dri. 139^2). The vb. עבר, however, does not necessarily mean to 'cross' (a stream); it sometimes means simply to 'traverse' a region (Jer. 2^6); and in this sense Spiegelberg has recently (1907) revived an attractive conjecture of Goldziher (*Mythos*, p. 66), that עברים signifies 'wanderers'—nomads (*OLz*. x. 618 ff.).*

21. *The father of all the sons of 'Ēber*] The writer has apparently borrowed a genealogical list of the descendants

21. It is doubtful if the text is in order. First, it is extremely likely that the introduction to the section on Shem in J would require modification to prevent contradiction with v.$^{22f.}$ (P). Then, the omission of the logical subj. to יֻלַּד is suspicious. The Pu. of this vb. never dispenses

* In Egyptian texts from Thothmes III. to Ramses IV., the word *'Apuriu* (*'Apriu*) occurs as the name of a foreign population in Egypt; and had been identified by Chabas with the Hebrews of OT. The identification has been generally discarded, on grounds which seemed cogent; but has recently been revived by Hommel (*AHT*, 259), and

of Eber which he was at a loss to connect with the name of Shem. Hence he avoids the direct assertion that Shem begat Eber, and bridges over the gap by the vague hint that Shem and Eber stand for the same ethnological abstraction.—*the elder brother of Yepheth*] The Heb. can mean nothing else (*v.i.*). The difficulty is to account for the selection of Japheth for comparison with Shem, the oldest member of the family. Unless the clause be a gloss, the most obvious inference is that the genealogy of Japheth had immediately preceded; whether because in the Table of J the sequence of age was broken (Bu. 305 f.), or because Japheth was really counted the second son of Noah (Di.). The most satisfactory solution is undoubtedly that of Gu., who finds in the remark an indication that this Table followed the order: Canaan—Japheth—Shem (see p. 188).—**24** is an interpolation (based on 11^{12-14}) intended to harmonise J with P. It cannot be the continuation of [21] as it stands (since we have not been informed who Arpakšad was), and still less in the form suggested below. It is also obviously inconsistent with the plan of P's Table, which deals with

---

with the subj. nor does the Hoph.; the Niph. does so once (Gn. 17^{17} [P]); but there the ellipsis is explained by the emphasis which lies on the fact of birth. Further, a הוא is required as subj. of the cl. אבי וגו׳. The impression is produced that originally עֵבֶר was expressly named as the son of Shem, and that the words הוא אבי וגו׳ referred to him (perhaps ולשם יֻלַּד את־עבר הוא אבי וגו׳). Considering the importance of the name, the tautology is not too harsh. It would then be hardly possible to retain the clause אחי וגו׳; and to delete it as a gloss (although it has been proposed by others: see *OH*) I admit to be difficult, just because of the obscurity of the expression.—נם הוא] cf. 4^{26}.—אחי יפת הגדול] 𝔙 correctly *fratre J. majore*. The Mass. accentuation perhaps favours the grammatically impossible rendering of 𝔊 (*ἀδελφῷ* 'I. *τοῦ μείζονος*), Σ, al.; which implies that Japheth was the oldest of Noah's sons,—a notion extorted from the chronology of 11^{10} cpd. with 5^{32} 7^{11} (see Ra. IEz.). It is equally inadmissible (with IEz.) to take הגדול absolutely (=Japheth the great). See Bu. 304 ff.—**24**. את־שלח] 𝔊 pref. את־קינן וקינן ילד.

(with arguments which seem very convincing) by Heyes (*Bib. u. Aeg.*, 1904, 146 ff.). In view of the striking resemblance to *Ḥabiri*, and the new facts brought to light by the TA Tablets, the hypothesis certainly deserves to be reconsidered (cf. Eerdmans, *l.c.* 52 ff., or *Expos.*, 1909, ii. 197 ff.).

nations and not with individual genealogies (note also יֻלַּד instead of הוֹלִיד).

25. The two sons of Eber represent the Northern and Southern Semites respectively, corresponding roughly to Aramæans and Arabs: we may compare with Jast. (*DB*, v. 82 a) the customary division of Arabia into *Šām* (Syria) and *Yemen*. The older branch, to which the Israelites belonged, is not traced in detail: we may assume that a Yahwistic genealogy (‖ to $11^{16ff.}$ [P]) existed, showing the descent of Abraham from Peleg; and from scattered notices ($19^{30ff.}$ $22^{20ff.}$ $25^{1ff.}$ etc.) we can form an idea of the way in which the northern and central districts were peopled by that family of 'Hebrews.'—On פֶּלֶג, see below.—*For in his days the earth was divided* (נִפְלְגָה)] a popular etymology naturally suggested by the root, which in Heb. (as in Aram. Arab. etc.) expresses the idea of 'division' (cf. the vb. in Ps. 55^{10}, Jb. 38^{25}). There is no very strong reason to suppose that the dispersion (פלוגתא, 𝔗ᴶ etc.) of the Tower of Babel is referred to; it is possible that some other tradition regarding the distribution of nations is followed (*e.g. Jub.* viii. 8 ff.), or that the allusion is merely to the separation of the Yoḳṭanites from their northern kinsmen.

פֶּלֶג (Φαλεκ, Φαλεγ, Φαλεχ)] as a common noun means 'watercourse' or artificial canal (Ass. *palgu*): Is. 30^{25}, Ps. 1^{3} 65^{10}, Jb. 29^{6} etc. Hence it has been thought that the name originally denoted some region intersected by irrigating channels or canals, such as Babylonia itself. Of geographical identifications there are several which are sufficiently plausible: *Phalga* in Mesopotamia, at the junction of the Chaboras and the Euphrates (Knob.); *'el-Falğ*, a district in NE Arabia near the head of the Persian Gulf (Lag. *Or.* ii. 50); *'el-Aflāğ*, S of Ğebel Tuwaiḳ in central Arabia (Homm. *AA*, 222^{2}).

יָקְטָן ('Ιεκταν)] otherwise unknown, is derived by Fleischer (Goldz. *Mythos*, p. 67) from √ *ḳaṭana* = 'be settled.' The Arab genealogists identified him with *Ḳaḥṭān*, the legendary ancestor of a real tribe, who was (or came to be) regarded as the founder of the Yemenite Arabs (Margoliouth, *DB*, ii. 743). On the modern stock of 'el-Ḳaḥṭan, and its sinister reputation in the more northerly parts of the Peninsula, see Doughty, *Arab. Des.* i. 129, 229, 282, 343, 389, 418, ii. 39 ff., 437.

26–30. The sons of Yoḳṭan number 13, but in 𝔊ᴹˢˢ (see on

---

25. יֻלַּד] 𝔪𝔊 ילדו; but שְׁנֵי בָנִים is possibly acc. after pass. as 4^{18} etc. (G-K. § 121 *a, b*)—האחד—אחיו] similarly 22^{21} (J).—**26.** חצרמות] Several western MSS have חצר־מות, as if = 'court of death.'

עובל below) only 12, which may be the original number. The few names that can be satisfactorily identified (*Sheleph*, *Ḥazarmaweth*, *Sheba*, *Ḥavilah*) point to S Arabia as the home of these tribes.

(1) אַלְמוֹדָד (Ἐλμωδαδ)] unknown. The אל is variously explained as the Ar. art. (but this is not Sabæan), as '*Ēl*='God,' and as '*āl*= 'family'; and מודד as a derivative of the vb. for 'love' (*wadda*), equivalent to Heb. יָדִיד (Wi. *MVAG*, vi. 169); cf. Glaser, *Skizze*, ii. 425; *DB*, i. 67.

(2) שֶׁלֶף (Σαλεφ)] A Yemenite tribe or district named on Sabæan inscrs., and also by Arab. geographers: see Homm. *SA Chrest.* 70; Osiander in *ZDMG*, xi. 153 ff., perhaps identical with the Salapeni of Roman writers. Cognate place-names are said to be still common in S Arabia (Glaser).

(3) חֲצַרְמָוֶת (Ἀσαρμωθ)] The modern province of *Ḥaḍramaut*, on the S coast, E of Yemen. The name appears in Sabæan inscrs. of 5th and 6th cent. A.D., and is slightly disguised in the Χατραμωτῖται of Strabo (XVI. iv. 2), the *Chatramotitæ* of Pliny, vi. 154 (*Atramitæ*, vi. 155, xii. 52?).

(4) יָרַח (Ἰαραδ)] uncertain. The attempts at identification proceed on the appellative sense of the word (='moon'), but are devoid of plausibility (see Di.).

(5) הֲדוֹרָם (𝔐 אדורם, 𝔊 Ὀδορρα)] likewise unknown. A place called *Dauram* close to Ṣan'a has been suggested: the name is found in Sabæan (Glaser, 426, 435).

(6) אוּזָל (𝔐 איזל, 𝔊 Αἰζηλ)] mentioned by Ezk. (27[19]: rd. מֵאוּזָל) as a place whence iron and spices were procured. It is commonly taken to be the same as '*Azāl*, which Arab. tradition declares to be the old name of Ṣan'a, now the capital of Yemen. Glaser (310, 427, 434, etc.) disputes the tradition, and locates 'Ûzāl in the neighbourhood of Medina.*

(7) דִּקְלָה (Δεκλα)] Probably the Ar. and Aram. word (*daḳal*, דקלא, ܕܩܠܐ) for 'date-palm,' and therefore the name of some noted palm-bearing oasis of Arabia. Glaser (*MVAG*, 1897, 438) and Hommel (*AA*, 282 f.) identify it with the Φοινικων of Procopius, and the modern *Ğōf es-Sirḥān*, 30° NL (as far N as the head of the Red Sea).

(8) עוֹבָל (𝔐 and 1 Ch. 1[22] עֵיבָל, 𝔊[L] Γαιβαλ)] supposed to be the word '*Abil*, a frequent geographical name in Yemen (Glaser, 427). The name is omitted by many MSS of 𝔊, also by 𝔊[B] in 1 Ch. 1[22] (see Nestle, *MM*, 10), where some Heb. MSS and 𝔖 have עובל.

(9) אֲבִימָאֵל (Ἀβιμεηλ)] apparently a tribal name (='father is God'), of genuine Sabæan formation (cf. אבמעתתר, *ZDMG*, xxxvii. 18), not hitherto identified.

---

* In view of the uncertainty of the last three names, it is worthy of attention that the account of Asshurbanipal's expedition against the Nabatæans (*KIB*, ii. 221) mentions, in close conjunction, three places, *Ḥurarina*, *Yarki*, and *Azalla*, which could not, of course, be as far S as Yemen, but might be as far as the region of Medina. In spite of the phonetic differences, the resemblance to Hadoram, Yeraḫ, and 'Ûzāl is noteworthy. See, however, Glaser, 273 ff., 309 ff.

(10) שְׁבָא] **see on v.**[7] (p. 203). The general connexion suggests that the Sabæans are already established in Yemen; although, if 'Uzāl be as far N as Medina, the inference is perhaps not quite certain.

(11) אוֹפִר (Οὐφειρ)] known to the Israelites as a gold-producing country (Is. 13[12], Ps. 45[10], Jb. 22[24] 28[16], 1 Ch. 29[4] [Sir. 7[18]]), visited by the ships of Solomon and Hiram, which brought home not only gold and silver and precious stones, but almug-wood, ivory, apes and (?) peacocks (1 Ki. 9[28] 10[11. 22]; cf. 22[49]). Whether this familiarity with the name implies a clear notion of its geographical position may be questioned; but it can hardly be doubted that the author of the Yahwistic Table believed it to be in Arabia; and although no name at all resembling Ophir has as yet been discovered in Arabia, that remains the most probable view (see Glaser, *Skizze*, ii. 357–83). Of other identifications the most important are: *Abhira* in India, E of the mouths of the Indus (Lassen); (2) the Sofala coast (opposite Madagascar), behind which remains of extensive gold-diggings were discovered around Zimbabwe in 1871: the ruins, however, have now been proved to be of native African origin, and not older than the 14th or 15th cent. A.D. (see D. Randall-Maciver, *Mediæval Rhodesia* [1906]); (3) *Apir* (originally *Hapir*), an old name for the ruling race in Elam, and for the coast of the Persian Gulf around Bushire (see Homm. *AHT*, 236[4]; Hüsing, *OLz*, vi. 367 ff.; Jen. *ZDMG*, l. 246). If we could suppose the name transferred to the opposite (Arabian) coast of the gulf, this hypothesis would satisfy the condition required by this passage, and would agree in particular with Glaser's localisation. For a discussion of the various theories, see the excellent summary by Che. in *EB*, iii. 3513 ff.; Price, *DB*, iii. 626 ff.; and Dri. *Gen.*[2] XXVI. f., 131.

(12) חֲוִילָה] see p. 202.

(13) יוֹבָב (Ἰωβαβ)] unknown. Halevy and Glaser (ii. 303) compare the Sabæan name *Yuhaibab*.

The limits (probably from N to S) of the Yoḳṭanite territory are specified in v.[30]; but a satisfactory explanation is impossible owing to the uncertainty of the three names mentioned in it (Di.).—מֵשָׁא (Μασσηε) has been supposed to be *Mesene* (ܡܝܫܢ, *Maisān*), within the Delta of the Euphrates-Tigris (Ges. *Th.* 823; Tu.); but the antiquity of this name is not established. Di., following 𝔊, reads מַשָּׂא (see on 25[14]) in N Arabia. This as northern limit would just include Diklah, if Glaser's identification, given above, be correct.—סְפָרָה (Σωφηρα) is generally acknowledged to be *Ẓafār* in the S of Arabia. There were two places of the name: one in the interior of Yemen, N of Aden; the other (now pronounced *'Iṣfār* or *'Isfār*) on the coast of Mahra, near Mirbāt. The latter was the capital of the Himyarite kings (Ges. *Th.* 968; *DB*, iv. 437; *EB*, iv. 4370). Which of the two is here meant is a matter of little consequence.—הַר הַקֶּדֶם] It is difficult to say whether this is an apposition to מוֹשָׁבָם (Tu. al.), or a definition of ספר, or is a continuation of the line beyond ספר. On the first view the 'mountain' might be the highlands of central Arabia (*Neğd*); the second is recommended by the fact that the *eastern* Ẓafār lies at the foot of a high mountain, well adapted to serve as a landmark. The third view is not assisted by rendering בֹּאֲכָה 'in the direction of' (see on v.[19]); for in any case Ẓafār must have been the terminus in a southern direction. The commonly received opinion is that הר הקדם is the name of the Frankincense Mountain between Ḥaḍramaut and Mahra (see Di.).

XI. 1–9.—*The Tower of Babel* (J).

A mythical or legendary account of the breaking up of the primitive unity of mankind into separate communities, distinguished and isolated by differences of language. The story reflects at the same time the impression made on Semitic nomads by the imposing monuments of Babylonian civilisation. To such stupendous undertakings only an undivided humanity could have addressed itself; and the existing disunitedness of the race is a divine judgement on the presumptuous impiety which inspired these early manifestations of human genius and enterprise.

Gu. has apparently succeeded in disentangling two distinct but kindred legends, which are both Yahwistic (cf. יהוה, vv.[5 6. 8. 9. 9]), and have been blended with remarkable skill. One has crystallised round the name 'Babel,' and its leading motive is the "confusion" of tongues; the other around the memory of some ruined tower, which tradition connected with the "dispersion" of the race. Gu.'s division will be best exhibited by the following continuous translations:

A. The Babel-Recension: (1) *And it was, when all the earth had one speech and one vocabulary,* (3a) *that they said to one another, Come! Let us make bricks and burn them thoroughly.* (4aα, γ) *And they said, Come! Let us build us a city, and make ourselves a name.* (6aα) *And Yahwe said, Behold it is one people, and all of one language.* (7) *Come! Let us go down and confound there their language, so that they may not understand one another's speech,* (8b) *and that they may cease to build the city.* (9a) *Therefore is its name called 'Babel'* (Confusion), *for there Yahwe confused the speech of the whole earth*

B. The Tower-Recension: . . . (2) *And when they broke up from the East, they found a plain in the land of Shin'ar, and settled there.* [And they said, Let us build] (4aβb) *a tower, with its top reaching to heaven, lest we disperse over the face of the whole earth.* (3b) *And they had brick for stone and asphalt for mortar.* (5) *And Yahwe came down to see the tower which the sons of men had built.* [And He said . . .] (6aβb) *and this is but the beginning of their enterprise; and now nothing will be impracticable to them which they purpose to do.* (8a) *So Yahwe scattered them over the face of the whole earth.* [?Therefore the name of the tower was called 'Pîẓ' (Dispersion), for] (9b) *from thence Yahwe dispersed them over the face of the whole earth.*

It is extremely difficult to arrive at a final verdict on the soundness of this acute analysis; but on the whole it justifies itself by the readiness with which the various motives assort themselves in two parallel series. Its weak point is no doubt the awkward duplicate (^{8a} ‖ ^{9b}) with which B closes. Gu.'s bold conjecture that between the two there was an etymological play on the name of the tower (פִּיץ or פוּץ) certainly removes the objection; but the omission of so important an item of the tradition is itself a thing not easily accounted for.* Against this, however, we have to set the following considerations: the absence of demonstrable lacunæ in A, and their infrequency even in B; the facts that only a single phrase (אֶת־הָעִיר וְ in v.^{5}) requires to be deleted as redactional, and there is only one transposition (^{3b}); and the facility with which nearly all the numerous doublets (^{3a} ‖ ^{3b}; $^{4a\gamma}$ ‖ ^{4b}; וַיֵּרֶד (^{5}) ‖ נֵרְדָה (^{7}); $^{6a\alpha, \beta}$ ‖ $^{6a\gamma b}$; ^{9a} ‖ $^{8a+9b}$) can be definitely assigned to the one recension or the other. In particular, it resolves the difficulty presented by the twofold descent of Yahwe in ^{5} and ^{7}, from which far-reaching critical consequences had already been deduced (see the notes). There are perhaps some points of style, and some general differences of conception between the two strata, which go to confirm the hypothesis; but these also may be reserved for the notes.

The section, whether simple or composite, is independent of the Ethnographic Table of ch. 10, and is indeed fundamentally irreconcilable with it. There the origin of peoples is conceived as the result of the natural increase and partition of the family, and variety of speech as its inevitable concomitant (cf. ללשנתם, etc., in P, $10^{5.\ 20.\ 31}$). Here, on the contrary, the division is caused by a sudden interposition of Yahwe; and it is almost impossible to think that either a confusion of tongues or a violent dispersion should follow genealogical lines of cleavage. It is plausible, therefore, to assign the passage to that section of J (if there be one) which has neither a Flood-tradition nor a Table of Nations (so We. Bu. Sta. al.); although it must be said that the idea here is little less at variance with the classification by professions of 4^{20-22} than with ch. 10. The truth is that the inconsistency is not of such a kind as would necessarily hinder a collector of traditions from putting the two in historical sequence.

1–4. The Building of the City and the Tower.—(Compare the translation given above.) **1, 2.** The expres-

1. וַיְהִי is not verbal pred. to כל־הארץ, but merely introduces the circumstantial sent., as in 15^{17} 42^{35} etc. (Dav. § 141 and *R.*[1]). Such a sent. is usually followed by וְהִנֵּה, but see 1 Ki. 13^{20}. It may certainly be doubted if it could be followed by another ויהי with inf. cl. (v.^{2}); and this may be reckoned a point in favour of Gu.'s analysis.—If there be any distinction between שָׂפָה and דְּבָרִים, the former may refer to the

* In *Jub.* x. 26, the name of the tower, as distinct from the city, is "Overthrow" (καταστροφή).

sion suggests that in A mankind is already spread far and wide over the earth, though forming one great nation (עָם, v.[6]), united by a common language. In B, on the other hand, it is still a body of nomads, moving all together in search of a habitation (v.[2]; cf. בְּנֵי הָאָדָם, v.[5]).—*broke up from the East*] *v.i.*—*a plain*] the Euphrates-Tigris valley; where Babylon κέεται ἐν πεδίῳ μεγάλῳ (Her. i. 178).—*the land of Shin'ar*] see on 10[10].—3a. With great naïveté, the (city-) legend describes first the invention of bricks, and then (v.[4]) as an afterthought the project of building with them. The bilingual Babylonian account of creation (see p. 47 above) speaks of a time when "no brick was laid, no brick-mould (*nalbantu*) formed": see *KIB*, vi. 1, 38 f., 360.—3b shows that the legend has taken shape amongst a people familiar with stone-masonry. Comp. the construction of the walls of Babylon as described by Her. (i. 179).* The accuracy

pronunciation and the latter to the vocabulary (Di.), or (Gu.) 'שׂ to language as a whole, and 'ד to its individual elements.—דְּבָרִים אֲחָדִים] 'a single set of vocables'; 𝕲 φωνὴ μία (+πᾶσιν=לְכֻלָּם, as v.[6]). Elsewhere (27[44] 29[20] [with יָמִים]) אחדים means 'single' in the sense of 'few'; in Ezk. 37[17] the text is uncertain (see Co.).—On the juxtaposition of subj. and pred. in the nom. sent., see Dav. § 29 (*e*).—2. בְּנָסְעָם מִקֶּדֶם] rendered as above by 𝕲𝕿𝕾𝕿J. Nearly all moderns prefer 'as they wandered in the east' or 'eastward'; justifying the translation by 13[11], which is the only place where מקדם means 'eastward' with a vb. of motion. That 'מק *never* means 'from the east' is at least a hazardous assertion in view of Is. 2[6] 9[11]. נסע (cf. Ass. *nisû*, 'remove,' 'depart,' etc.) is a nomadic term, meaning 'pluck up [tent-pegs]' (Is. 33[20]); hence 'break up the camp' or 'start on a journey' (Gn. 33[12] 35[5. 16. 21] 37[17] etc.); and, with the *possible* exception of Jer. 31[23] (but *not* Gn. 12[9]), there is no case where this primary idea is lost sight of. Being essentially a vb. of departure, it is more naturally followed by a determination of the starting-point than of the direction or the goal (but see 33[17]); and there is no difficulty whatever in the assumption that the cradle of the race was further E than Babylonia (see 2[8]; and cf. Sta. *Ak. Red.* 246, and *n.* 43).—בִּקְעָה] (Syr. ܦܩܥܬܐ, Ar. *baḳ'at*) in usage, a wide, open valley, or plain (Dt. 34[3], Zech. 12[11], Is. 40[4], etc.). The derivation from √ בקע, 'split,' is questioned by Barth (*ES*, 2), but is probable nevertheless.—3. הָבָה] impve. of √ יהב, used interjectionally (G-K. § 69 *o*), as in vv.[4. 7.] 38[16], Ex. 1[10] (all J), is given by Gu. as a stylistic mark of the recension A (J[e]?). Contr. the

* Cf. Jos. *c. Ap.* i. 139, 149; Diod. ii. 9; Pliny, *HN*, xxxv. 51.

of the notice is confirmed by the excavated remains of Bab. houses and temples (*ATLO*^{2}, 279)—**4.** *With its top reaching to heaven*] The expression is not hyperbolical (as Dt. 1^{28}), but represents the serious purpose of the builders to raise their work to the height of the dwelling-place of the gods (*Jub.* x. 19, etc.).

The most conspicuous feature of a Bab. sanctuary was its *zikkurat*,—a huge pyramidal tower rising, often in 7 terraces, from the centre of the temple-area, and crowned with a shrine at the top (Her. i. 181 f.: see Jast. *RBA*, 615–22). These structures appear to have embodied a half-cosmical, half-religious symbolism: the 7 stories represented the 7 planetary deities as mediators between heaven and earth; the ascent of the tower was a meritorious approach to the gods; and the summit was regarded as the entrance to heaven (*KAT*^{3}, 616 f.; *ATLO*^{2}, 52 f., 281 f.). Hence it is probably something more than mere hyperbole when it is said of these *zikkurats* that the top was made to reach heaven (see p. 228 f. below); and, on the other hand, the resemblance between the language of the inscrs. and that of Genesis is too striking to be dismissed as accidental. That the tower of Gn. 11 is a Bab. *zikkurat* is obvious on every ground; and we may readily suppose that a faint echo of the religious ideas just spoken of is preserved in the legend; although to the purer faith of the Hebrews it savoured only of human pride and presumption.—The idea of storming heaven and making war on the gods, which is suggested by some late forms of the legend (cf. Hom. *Od.* xi. 313 ff.), is no doubt foreign to the passage.

4b. *Lest we disperse*] The tower was to be at once a symbol of the unity of the race, and a centre and rallying-point, visible all over the earth (IEz.). The idea is missed by 𝔊𝔙 and 𝔗^J, which render '*ere* we be dispersed.'

---

verbal use 29^{21} 30^1 (both E), 47^{15}, and pl. (הָבוּ) 47^{16}, Dt. 1^{13} 32^3, Jos. 18^4. On the whole, the two uses are characteristic of J and E respectively; see Holz. *Einl.* 98 f.—נִלְבְּנָה לְבֵנִים] Ex. $5^{7.14}$. So in Ass. *labânu libittu* (*KIB*, ii. 48, etc.), although *libittu* is used only of the *un*burned, sun-dried brick. See Nö. *ZDMG*, xxxvi. 181; Hoffmann, *ZATW*, ii. 70.—לִשְׂרֵפָה] dat. of product (Di.); 'שׂ = 'burnt mass' (cf. Dt. 29^{22}, Jer. 51^{25}).—חֵמָר (14^{10}, Ex. 2^3)] the native Heb. name for bitumen (see on 6^{14}).—חֹמֶר] (note the play on words) is strictly 'clay,' used in Palestine as mortar.—**4.** וְרֹאשׁוֹ בַשָּׁמַיִם] בְּ of contact, as in נָגַע בְּ (De.).—וְנַעֲשֶׂה—שֵׁם] 'acquire lasting renown'; cf. 2 Sa. 8^{13}, Jer. 32^{20}, Neh. 9^{10}. The suggestion that שֵׁם here has the sense of 'monument,' though defended by De. Bud. (*Urg.* 375^2), al. (cf. Sieg.-St. *s.v.*), has no sufficient justification in usage. In Is. 55^{13} 56^5 (cf. 2 Sa. 18^{18}), as well as the amended text of 2 Sa 8^{13}

5–9. Yahwe's Interposition.—The turning-point in the development of the story occurs at vv.[5. 6], where the descent of Yahwe is *twice* mentioned, in a way which shows some discontinuity of narration.—On heaven as the dwelling-place of Yahwe, cf. 28[12f.], Ex. 19[11. 20] 34[5] 24[10], 1 Ki. 22[19], 2 Ki. 2[11]; and with v.[5] cf. 18[21], Ex. 3[8].

On the assumption of the unity of the passage, the conclusion of Sta. (*Ak. Red.* 274 ff.) seems unavoidable: that a highly dramatic polytheistic recension has here been toned down by the omission of some of its most characteristic incidents. In v.[5] the name Yahwe has been substituted for that of some envoy of the gods sent down to inspect the latest human enterprise; v.[6] is his report to the heavenly council on his return; and v.[7] the plan of action he recommends to his fellow immortals. The main objection to this ingenious solution is that it involves, almost necessarily, a process of conscious literary manipulation, such as no Heb. writer is likely to have bestowed on a document so saturated with pagan theology as the supposed Bab. original must have been. It is more natural to believe that the elimination of polytheistic representations was effected in the course of oral transmission, through the spontaneous action of the Hebrew mind controlled by its spiritual faith.—On Gu.'s theory the difficulty disappears.

6. *This is but the beginning, etc.*] The reference is not merely to the completion of the tower, but to other enterprises which might be undertaken in the future.—**9.** *Babel*] 𝔊 rightly Σύγχυσις; *v.i.*

(see Dri. *Sam.* 217 f.), the ordinary sense suffices.—נָפוּץ] the word, acc. to Gu., is distinctive of the recension B: cf. vv.[8a. 9b].—**6.** הֵן עַם אֶחָד וגו׳] incomplete interjectional sent. (G–K. § 147 *b*).—וְזֶה הַחִלָּם לַעֲשׂוֹת] lit. 'this is their beginning to act.' On the pointing הַח׳, see G–K. § 67 *w*.—לֹא יִבָּצֵר—יָזְמוּ] imitated in Jb. 42[2].—בצר] lit. 'be inaccessible' (cf. Is. 22[10], Jer. 51[53]); hence 'impracticable.'—יָזְמוּ] contr. for יָזֹמּוּ (G–K. § 67 *dd*).—**7.** נרדה וגו׳] 𝔊 retains the pl. in spite of the alleged reading in *Mechilta* ארדה אבלה (see p. 14 above).—נָבְלָה] (see last note): fr. √ בלל ='mix' (not 'divide,' as 𝔖 [ܢܦܠܓ]).—אֲשֶׁר לֹא] G–K. § 165 *b*.—שמע] ='understand': 42[23], Dt. 28[49], Is. 33[19], Jer. 5[15] etc.—**8.** It is perhaps better, if a distinction of sources is recognised, to point וַיֶּחְדְּלוּ (juss. of purpose: G–K. § 109 *f*), continuing the direct address of [7b].—העיר] 𝔐 pr. את, and (with 𝔊) adds ואת־המגדל.—**9.** קָרָא] '*one* called' (G–K. § 144 *d*).—בָּבֶל] 'mixture' or 'confusion.' The name is obviously treated as a contraction from בַּלְבֵּל, a form not found in Heb., but occurring in Aram. (cf. 𝔖 v.[9], and 𝔗[O] v.[7]) and Arab. On the Bab. etymology of the name, see 10[10].—**9b.**—יהוה] 𝔊 + ὁ θεός.

Origin and Diffusion of the Legends.

1. The double legend is a product of naïve reflexion on such facts of experience as the disunity of mankind, its want of a common language, and its consequent inability to bend its united energies to the accomplishment of some enduring memorial of human greatness. The contrast between this condition of things and the ideal unity of the race at its origin haunted the mind with a sense of fate and discomfiture, and prompted the questions, When, and where, and for what reason, was this doom imposed on men? The answer naturally assumed the legendary form, the concrete features of the representation being supplied by two vivid impressions produced by the achievements of civilisation in its most ancient centre in Babylonia. On one hand the city of Babylon itself, with its mixture of languages, its cosmopolitan population, and its proud boast of antiquity, suggested the idea that here was the very fountainhead of the confusion of tongues; and this idea, wrapped up in a popular etymology of the name of the city, formed the nucleus of the first of the two legends contained in the passage. On the other hand, the spectacle of some ruined or unfinished Temple-tower (*zikkurat*), built by a vast expenditure of human toil, and reported to symbolise the ascent to heaven (p. 226), appealed to the imagination of the nomads as a god-defying work, obviously intended to serve as a landmark and rallying-point for the whole human race. In each case mankind had measured its strength against the decree of the gods above; and the gods had taken their revenge by reducing mankind to the condition of impotent disunion in which it now is.

It is evident that ideas of this order did not emanate from the official religion of Babylonia. They originated rather in the unsophisticated reasoning of nomadic Semites who had penetrated into the country, and formed their own notions about the wonders they beheld there: the etymology of the name Babel (=*Balbēl*) suggests an Aramæan origin (Ch. Gu.). The stories travelled from land to land, till they reached Israel, where, divested of their cruder polytheistic elements, they became the vehicle of an impressive lesson on the folly of human pride, and the supremacy of Yahwe in the affairs of men.

It is of quite secondary interest to determine which of the numerous Babylonian *zikkurats* gave rise to the legend of the Dispersion. The most famous of these edifices were those of E-sagil, the temple of Marduk in Babylon,* and of E-zida, the temple of Nebo at Borsippa on the opposite bank of the river (see Tiele, *ZA*, ii. 179–190). The former bore the (Sumerian) name *E-temen-an-ki* (= 'house of the foundations of heaven and earth'). It was restored by Nabo-polassar, who says that before him it had become "dilapidated and ruined," and that he was commanded by Marduk to "lay its foundations firm in the breast of the underworld, and *make its top equal to heaven*" (*KIB*, iii. 2. 5). The

---

* On its recently discovered site, see Langdon, *Expos.*, 1909, ii. p. 91 ff.

latter expression recurs in an inscr. of Nebuchadnezzar (*BA*, iii. 548) with reference to the same *zikkurat*, and is thought by Gu. ([2] 86) to have been characteristic of E-temen-an-ki; but that is doubtful, since similar language is used by Tiglath-pileser I. of the towers of the temple of Anu and Ramman, which had been allowed to fall gradually into disrepair for 641 years before his time (*KIB*, i. 43). The *zikkurat* of E-zida was called *E-ur-imin-an-ki* ('house of the seven stages (?) of heaven and earth'); its restorer Nebuchadnezzar tells us, in an inscr. found at its four corners, that it had been built by a former king, and raised to a height of 42 cubits; its top, however, had not been set up, and it had fallen into disrepair (*KIB*, iii. 2. 53, 55). The temple of Borsippa is entombed in *Birs Nimrûd*—a huge ruined mound still rising 153 feet above the plain (see Hil. *EBL*, 13, 30 f.)—which local (and Jewish) tradition identifies with the tower of Gn. 11. This view has been accepted by many modern scholars (see *EB*, i. 412), by others it is rejected in favour of E-temen-an-ki, chiefly because E-zida was not *in* but only near Babylon. But if the two narratives are separated, there is nothing to connect the tower specially with the *city* of Babylon; and it would seem to be mainly a question which of the two was the more imposing ruin at the time when the legend originated. It is possible that neither was meant. At Uru (Ur of the Chaldees) there was a smaller *zikkurat* (about 70 feet high) of the moon-god Sin, dating from the time of Ur-bau (*c.* 2700 B.C.) and his son Dungi, which Nabuna'id tells us he rebuilt on the old foundation "with asphalt and bricks" (*KIB*, iii. 2. 95; *EBL*, 173 ff.). The notice is interesting, because, according to one tradition, which is no doubt ancient, though it cannot be proved to be Yahwistic, this city was the starting-point of the Hebrew migration (see below, p. 239). If it was believed that the ancestors of the Hebrews came from Ur, it may very well have been the *zikkurat* of that place which figured in their tradition as the Tower of the Dispersion.

2. In regard to its *religious content*, the narrative occupies the same standpoint as $3^{20.\,22}$ and $6^{1\text{-}3}$. Its central idea is the effort of the restless, scheming, soaring human mind to transcend its divinely appointed limitations: it "emphasises Yahwe's supremacy over the world; it teaches how the self-exaltation of man is checked by God; and it shows how the distribution of mankind into nations, and diversity of language, are elements in His providential plan for the development and progress of humanity" (Dri.). The pagan notion of the envy of the gods,—their fear lest human greatness should subvert the order of the world,—no doubt emerges in a more pronounced form than in any other passage. Yet the essential conception is not mere paganism, but finds an obvious point of contact in one aspect of the prophetic theology: see Is. $2^{12\text{-}17}$. To say that the narrative is totally devoid of religious significance for us is therefore to depreciate the value for modern life of the OT thought of God, as well as to evince a lack of sympathy with one of the profoundest instincts of early religion. Crude in form as the legend is, it embodies a truth of permanent validity—the futility and emptiness of human effort divorced from the acknowledgment and service of God:

hæc perpetua mundi dementia est, neglecto cœlo immortalitatem quærere in terra, ubi nihil est non caducum et evanidum (Calv.).

3. *Parallels.*—No Babylonian version of the story has been discovered; and for the reason given above (p. 226) it is extremely unlikely that anything resembling the biblical form of it will ever be found there.* In Greek mythology there are dim traces of a legend ascribing the diversities of language to an act of the gods, whether as a punishment on the creatures for demanding the gift of immortality (Philo, *De Conf. ling.*), or without ethical motive, as in the 143rd fable of Hyginus.† But while these myths are no doubt independent of Jewish influence, their resemblance to the Genesis narrative is too slight to suggest a common origin. It is only in the literature of the Hellenistic period that we find real parallels to the story of the Tower of Babel; and these agree so closely with the biblical account that it is extremely doubtful if they embody any separate tradition.‡ The difference to which most importance is attached is naturally the polytheistic phraseology ('the gods') employed by some of the writers named (Polyhistor, Abyd.); but the polytheism is only in the language, and is probably nothing more than conscious or unconscious Hellenising of the scriptural narrative. Other differences—such as the identification of the tower-builders with the race of giants (the Nephîlîm of 6^4?), and the destruction of the tower by a storm—are easily explicable as accretions to the legend of Genesis.§ The remarkable Mexican legend of the pyramid of Cholula, cited by Jeremias from von Humboldt,‖ has a special interest on account of the unmistakable resemblance between the Mexican pyramids and the Babylonian *zikkurats*. If this fact could be accepted

* The fragment (K 3657) translated in Smith-Sayce, *Chald. Gen.* 163 ff. (cf. *HCM*[2], 153 f.), and supposed to contain obscure allusions to the building of a tower in Babylon, its overthrow by a god during the night, and a confusion of speech, has since been shown to contain nothing of the sort: see King, *Creation Tablets*, i. 219 f.; Je. *ATLO*[2], 286.

† "Sed postquam Mercurius sermones hominum interpretatus est . . . id est nationes distribuit, tum discordia inter mortales esse cœpit, *quod Jovi placitum non est.*"

‡ Cf. Orac. Sibyll. iii. 98 ff. (Kautzsch, *Pseudepigraphen*, 187); Alexander Polyhistor (Eus. *Chron.* i. 23 [ed. Schoene]); Abydenus (*ib.* i. 33); Jos. *Ant.* i. 118; Eupolemos (Eus. *Præp. Ev.* ix. 17); and *Book of Jub.* x. 18–27. The lines of the Sibyl (iii. 99 f.) may be quoted as a typical example of this class of legends:

ὁμόφωνοι δ' ἦσαν ἅπαντες
καὶ βούλοντ' ἀναβῆναι εἰς οὐρανὸν ἀστερόεντα.
αὐτίκα δ' ἀθάνατος μεγάλην ἐπέθηκεν ἀνάγκην
πνεύμασιν· αὐτὰρ ἔπειτ' ἄνεμοι μέγαν ὕψοθι πύργον
ῥίψαν, καὶ θνητοῖσιν ἐπ' ἀλλήλοις ἔριν ὦρσαν·
τοὔνεκά τοι Βαβυλῶνα βροτοὶ πόλει οὔνομ' ἔθεντο.

§ So Gu.[2] 88 f. On the other side, cf. Gruppe, *Griechische Culte und Mythen*, i. 677 ff.; Sta. *Ak. Red.* 277 f.; Je. *ATLO*[2], 383 ff.

‖ *Vues des Cordilleres* (Paris, 1810), 24, 32 ff.

as proof of direct Babylonian influence, then no doubt the question of a Babylonian origin of the legend and its transmission through non-biblical channels would assume a new complexion. But the inference, however tempting, is not quite certain.

XI. 10–26.—*The Genealogy of Shem* (P).

Another section of the *Tôlĕdôth*, spanning the interval between the Flood and the birth of Abraham. It is the most carefully planned of P's genealogies next to ch. 5; with which it agrees in form, except that in MT the framework is lightened by omitting the total duration of each patriarch's life. In 𝔐 this is consistently supplied; while 𝔊 merely adds to MT the statement καὶ ἀπέθανεν. The number of generations in MT is 9, but in 𝔊 10, corresponding with ch. 5. Few of the names can be plausibly identified; these few are mostly geographical, and point on the whole to NW Mesopotamia as the original home of the Hebrew race.

In 𝔊 the number 10 is made up by the addition of Ḳênān between Arpakšad and Shelaḥ (so 10^{24}). That this is a secondary alteration is almost certain, because (*a*) it is wanting in 1 Ch. $1^{18. 24}$ 𝔊; (*b*) Ḳênān already occurs in the former genealogy ($5^{9ff.}$); and (*c*) the figures simply duplicate those of Shelaḥ. It has been proposed to count Noah as the first name (Bu. 412 f.), or Abraham as the 10th (Tu. De.); but neither expedient brings about the desired formal correspondence between the lists of ch. 5 and $11^{10ff.}$ An indication of the artificial character of these genealogies is found in the repetition of the name Nāḥôr, once as the father, and again as the son, of Teraḥ (see Bosse, *Chron. Systeme*, 7 ff.). It is not improbable that here, as in ch. 5 (corresponding with $4^{25f.}$), P has worked up an earlier Yahwistic genealogy, of which a fragment may have been preserved in vv.$^{28-30}$. We. (*Comp.*^{2} 9, *Prol.*^{6} 313) has conjectured that it consisted of the 7 names left of P's list when Arpakšad and Shelaḥ (see on $10^{21. 24}$) and the first Nāḥôr are omitted (Abraham counting as the 7th). But there is no proof that the Yahwistic genealogy lying behind ch. 5 was 7-membered; and J's parallel to $11^{10ff.}$ could not in any case be the continuation of 4^{16-22}.

10. אַרְפַּכְשַׁד] see on 10^{22}. He is here obviously the oldest son of Shem; which does not *necessarily* involve a contradiction with ch. 10, the arrangement there being dictated by geographical considerations. Hommel (*AA*, 222^{1}), maintaining his theory that Arp. = Ur-Kasdîm, comes to the absurd conclusion that in the original list it was not the name of Shem's son, but of his birthplace: 'Shem *from* Arpakshad'!—שְׁנָתַיִם אַחַר הַמַּבּוּל] The discrepancy between this statement and the chronology of 5^{32} 7^{11} $9^{28f.}$ is not to be got rid of either by wire-drawn arithmetical calculations (Ra. al.), or by the assumption that in the other passages round numbers are used (Tu. De.). The clause is evidently a gloss, introduced apparently for the purpose of making the birth of Arpakšad, rather than the Flood, the commencement of a new era. It fits in admirably with the scheme of the B. of Jub., which gives an integral number of year-weeks from the Creation to the birth of Arp, and from the latter event to the birth of Abraham (see p. 234 below).—**12.** שָׁלַח (Σαλα)] probably the same word which forms a component of מְתוּשֶׁלַח ($5^{21ff.}$), and therefore originally a divine name. This need not exclude a tribal or geographical sense, the name of a deity being frequently transferred to his worshippers or their territory. A place *Ṣalaḥ* or *Salaḥ* in Mesopotamia is instanced by Knobel (Di.). Others regard it as a descriptive name='offshoot' or 'dismissal'; but very improbably.—**14.** עֵבֶר] see on 10^{21}.—**16.** פֶּלֶג] 10^{25}. Hommel (*l.c.*) combines the two names and takes the compound as a notice of Shelaḥ's birthplace: 'Shelaḥ *from* Eber-peleg'=Eber-hannāhār, the region W of the lower Euphrates (see pp. 218, 220 above).—**18.** רְעוּ (Ῥαγαυ)] unknown; certainly not ܐܘܪܗܝ (Edessa). It is possibly abbreviated from רְעוּאֵל (36^4, Ex. 2^{18} etc.: so Homm.); and Mez considers it a divine name. An Aramæan tribe *Ru'ua* is frequently mentioned in Assyr. inscrs. as dwellers on the banks of the Euphrates and Tigris, in or near Babylonia (Del. *Par.* 238 ff.).—**20.** שְׂרוּג (Σερουχ)] a well-known city and district about half-way between Carchemish and Ḥarran, mentioned by Syr. and Arab. writers under the name *Sarūǧ*. The name (*Sarugi*) also occurs several times in the census of the district round Ḥarran (7th cent. B.C.), published by Johns under the title of *An Assyrian Domesday Book*: see pp. 29, 30, 43, 48, 68.—**22.** נָחוֹר (Ναχωρ)] is in J the brother of Abraham (22^{20}; cf. Jos. 24^2); in P he is both the grandfather and the brother (11^{26}). The name must have been that of an important Aramæan tribe settled in or around Ḥarran (27^{43} 28^{10} 29^4). Johns compares the place-name *Til-Naḥiri* in the neighbourhood of Sarugi; also the personal names *Naḥiri* and *Naḥarâu* found in Assyrian Deeds (*l.c.* 71; *Ass. Deeds*, iii. 127; cf. *KAT*^{3}, 477 f.). As a divine name Ναχαρ is mentioned along with other Aramæan deities on a Greek inscription from Carthage (*KAT*^{3}, 477); and Jen. (*ZA*, xi. 300) has called attention to the theophorous name ܒܟܡ ܢܚܝܪ, in the 'Doctrine of Addai,' as possibly a corruption of ܒܟܡ ܢܚܪ.—**24.** תֶּרַח (Θαῤῥα)] is instanced by Rob. Sm.* as a totem clan-name; ܬܪܚܐ (?) being the Syr. and *turâḥû* the Ass. word for 'wild goat.' Similarly Del. (*Prol.* 80), who also refers tentatively to *Til-ša-turâḥi*, the name of a Mesopotamian town in the neighbourhood of Ḥarran. Knobel compares a place *Tharrana*, S of Edessa (Di.); Jen. (*ZA*, vi. 70; *Hittiter und Armenier*, 150 ff. [esp. 154]) is inclined to identify Teraḥ with the Hittite and N Syrian god (or goddess) *Tarḫu*, Ταρκο, etc. (cf. *KAT*^{3}, 484).—**26.** 𝔖 reads 75 instead of 70.

* *KM*^{1}, 220 (afterwards abandoned). Cf. Nöldeke, *ZDMG*, xl. 167 f.: "sicher unmöglich."

The Chronology.—The following Table shows the variations of the three chief recensions (MT, ⅏ and 𝔊), together with the chronology of the Book of Jubilees, which for this period parts company with the Sam., and follows a system peculiar to itself (see p. 134 ff. above):

	MT.		Sam.			LXX.		Jub.
	1st Son.	After.	1st Son.	After.	Total.	1st Son.	After.	1st Son.
1. Shem . .	100	500	100	500	600	100	500	102 ?
2. Arpakšad .	35	403	135	303	438	135	430	66 ?
Καιναν . .	...	...	...	...	...	130	330	57
3. Shelaḥ . .	30	403	130	303	433	130	330	71
4. Eber . .	34	430	134	270	404	134	370	64
5. Peleg . .	30	209	130	109	239	130 [L. 134]	209	61
6. Reu . .	32	207	132	107	239	132	207	59
7 Serug . .	30	200	130	100	230	130	200	57
8 Nāḥôr . .	29	119	79	69	148	79	129 [L. 125]	62
9. Teraḥ . .	70	135	70	75	145	70	135	70
	390	...	1040	...	...	1170 [L. 1174]	...	669
From Flood (or birth of Arp.) to b. of Abr. .	290	...	940	...	...	1070	...	567

The three versions plainly rest on a common basis, and it is not easy to decide in favour of the priority of any one of them. On the application to this period of the general chronological theories described on p. 135 f. it is unnecessary to add much. Klostermann maintains his scheme of Jubilee-periods on the basis of 𝔊, (*a*) by allowing a year for the Flood; (*b*) by adopting the reading of 𝔖, 75 instead of 70, in the case of Teraḥ; and (*c*) by following certain MSS which give 179 for 79 as the age of Naḥor at the birth of Teraḥ. This makes from the Flood to the birth of Abraham 1176 years $=2\times12\times49$. By an equally arbitrary combination of data of MT and 𝔊, a similar period of 1176 years is then made out from the birth of Abraham to the Dedication of the Temple.—The seemingly eccentric scheme of *Jub.* shows clear indications of a reckoning by year-weeks. Since the birth of Arpakšad is said (vii. 18) to have occurred two years after the Flood, we may conclude that it was assigned to A.M. 1309, the 102nd year of Shem. This gives a period of 187 year-weeks from the Creation to the birth of Arp., followed by another of 81 ($567 \div 7$) to the birth of Abraham. We observe further that the earlier period embraces 11 generations with an average of exactly 17 year-weeks, and the later 9 generations with an average of exactly 9: *i.e.*, as nearly as possible one-half: the author accordingly must have proceeded on the theory that after the Flood the age of paternity suddenly dropped to one-half of what it had formerly been.

[It is possible that the key to the various systems has been discovered by A. Bosse, whose paper * became known to me only while these sheets were passing through the press. His main results are as follows: (1) In MT he finds two distinct chronological systems. (*a*) One reckons by generations of 40 years, its *termini* being the birth of Shem and the end of the Exile. In the Shemite table, Teraḥ is excluded entirely, and the two years between the Flood and the birth of Arp. are ignored. This gives: from the birth of Shem to that of Abraham 320 (8×40) years; thence to b. of Jacob 160 (4×40); to Exodus 560 (14×40); to *founding* of Temple 480 (12×40); to end of Exile 480: in all 2000 (50×40). This system is, of course, later than the Exile; but Bo. concedes the probability that its middle section, with 1200 (30×40) years from the b. of Abr. to the founding of the Temple, may be of earlier origin.—(*b*) The other scheme, with which we are more immediately concerned, operates with a Great Month of 260 years (260 = the number of weeks in a five-years' *lustrum*). Its period is a Great Year from the Creation to the *dedication* of the Temple, and its reckoning includes Teraḥ in the Shemite table, but excludes the 2 years of Arpakšad. This gives 1556 years to b. of Shem + 390 (b. of Abr.) + 75 (migration of Abr.) + 215 (descent to Egypt) + 430 (Exodus) + 480 (founding of Temple) + 20 (*dedication* of do.) = 3166. Now $3166 = 12 \times 260 + 46$. The odd 46 years are thus accounted for: the chronologist was accustomed to the Egyptian reckoning by months of 30 days, and a solar year of $365\frac{1}{4}$ days, requiring the interposition of $5\frac{1}{4}$ days each year; and the 46 years are the equivalent of these $5\frac{1}{4}$ days in the system here followed. (For, if 30 days = 260 years, then $5\frac{1}{4}$ days $= \frac{5\frac{1}{4} \times 260}{30} = \frac{21 \times 26}{4 \times 3} = \frac{7 \times 13}{2} = 45\frac{1}{2}$ [say 46] *years*.) The first third of this Great Year ends with the b. of Noah $1056 = 4 \times 260 + 16$ ($\frac{1}{3}$ of 46). The second third *nearly* coincides with the b. of Jacob; but here there is a discrepancy of 5 years, which Bo. accounts for by the assumption that the figure of the older reckoning by generations has in the case of Jacob been allowed to remain in the text.—(2) 𝔊 reckons with a Great Month of 355 years (the number of days in the *lunar* year), and a Great Year of $12 \times 355 = 4260$ years from the Creation to the *founding* of the Temple, made up as follows: 2142 + 1173† + 75 + 215 + 215 + 440‡ = 4260.

* *Die Chronologischen Systeme im AT und bei Josephus* (*MVAG*, 1908, 2).

† Allowing a year for the Flood, and two years between it and the b. of Arpakšad.

‡ See 1 Ki. 6[1] (𝔊).

Significant subdivisions cannot be traced.—(3) ꟿ returns to the earlier Heb. reckoning by generations, its *terminus ad quem* being the measuring out of Gerizim, which, according to the *Sam. Chronicle* published by Neubauer, took place 13 years after the Conquest of Canaan. Thus we obtain 1207 + 1040 + 75 + 215 + 215 + 42 (desert wandering) * + 13 (measurement of Gerizim) = 2807 = 70 × 40 + 7.† —(4) The Book of *Jubilees* counts by Jubilee-periods of 49 years from the Creation to the Conquest of Palestine: 1309 + 567 + 75 + 459 (Exodus) + 40 (entrance to Canaan) = 2450 = 50 × 49.]

XI. 27–32.—*The Genealogy of Teraḥ* (P and J).

The vv. are of mixed authorship; and form, both in P and J, an introduction to the Patriarchal History. In P ([27. 31. 32]), the genealogical framework encloses a notice of the migration of the Teraḥites from Ur-Kasdîm to Ḥarran, to which $12^{4b.\,5}$ may be the immediate sequel. The insertion from J ([28–30]) finds an equally suitable continuation in $12^{1ff.}$, and is very probably the conclusion of J's lost Shemite genealogy. The suppression of the preceding context of J is peculiarly tantalising because of the uncertainty of the tradition which makes Ur-Kasdîm the home of the ancestors of the Hebrews (see concluding note, p. 239)

On the *analysis*, cf. esp. Bu. *Urg.* 414 ff.—Vv.[27] and [32] belong quite obviously to P; and [31], from its diffuse style and close resemblance to P's regular manner in recording the patriarchal migrations (12^5 31^{18} 36^6 46^6: see Hupf. *Qu.* 19 f.), may be confidently assigned to the same source. [28a] presents nothing distinctive of either document; but in [28b] ארץ מולדת is peculiar to JE (see the footnote on the v.). [29] is J because presupposed in $22^{20ff.}$; and its continuation ([30]) brings as an additional criterion the word עֲקָרָה (cf. 25^{21} 29^{31}), which is never used by P.—The extract from J is supplementary to P, and it might be argued that at least [28a] was necessary in the latter source to explain why Loṭ and not Haran went with Teraḥ. Bu. points out in answer (p. 420) that with still greater urgency we desiderate an explanation of the fact that Nāḥôr was left behind: if the one fact is left unexplained, so *a fortiori* might the other.

The formula וְאֵלֶּה תּוֹלְדוֹת does not occur again till 25^{12}; and it is very widely held that in v.[27] it stands as the heading of the section of P

---

* After Jos. 5^6 (𝔊).

† The odd 7 years still remain perplexing (see p. 136). One cannot help surmising that the final 13 was *originally* intended to get rid of it, though the textual data do not enable us now to bring out a round number.

dealing with the life of Abraham. That is wholly improbable. It is likely enough that a heading (א׳ ת׳ אברהם) has been somewhere omitted (so We. Bu. Ho. al.); but the truth is that from this point onwards no consistent principle can be discovered in the use of the formula. The hypothesis that an originally independent book of Tôledôth has been broken up and dislocated by the redaction, is as plausible a solution as any that can be thought of. See, further, on 25^{19}.

27. On the name *Abram*, see on 17^{5}; on *Nāḥôr*, v.^{22} above.—*Haran begat Loṭ*] A statement to the same effect must have been found in J (see 12^{4a}). Haran has no significance in the tradition except as expressing the relationship of Lôṭ, Milkah, and Yiṣkah within the Hebraic group.

That הרן is formed from חָרָן (*v.i.*) by a softening of the initial guttural (We. *Pr.*^{6} 313) is an improbable conjecture (see Bu. 443^{2}). The name occurs elsewhere only in בֵּית־ה׳ (Nu. 32^{36}: cf. בֵּית־הָרָם, Jos. 13^{27})* in the tribe of Gad: this has suggested the view that הָרָן was the name of a deity worshipped among the peoples represented by Lot (Mez: cf. Wi. *AOF*, ii. 499).—The name לוט is also etymologically obscure (? Ar. *lāṭ* = 'cleave to'). A connexion with the Ḥorite clan לוֹטָן in Gn. $36^{20.22.29}$ is probable.

28. The premature death of Haran (which became the nucleus of some fantastic Jewish legends) took place *in the land of his nativity*; *i.e.*, according to the present text, *Ur of the Chaldees*, where his grave was shown down to the time of Josephus (*Ant.* i. 151; Eus. *OS*, 285, 50 ff.).

אור כַּשְׂדִּים (v.^{31} 15^{7}, Neh. 9^{7}: 𝔊 χώρα τῶν Χαλδαίων) is now almost universally identified with the ancient S Babylonian city of *Uru*, whose remains have been discovered in the mounds of *'el-Muḳayyar*, on the right bank of the Euphrates, about 25 miles SE from Erech and 125 from Babylon (see Hilp. *EBL*, 172 ff.). The evidence for this view is

---

28. עַל־פְּנֵי] is *coram* (𝔊 ἐνώπιον), rather than *ante* (𝔙: so Tu.), or 'in the lifetime of' (𝔖 ܒܚܝܘܗܝ); cf. Nu. 3^{4}: see BDB and G-B. *s.v.* פָּנִים.—אֶרֶץ מוֹלַדְתּוֹ] so 24^{7} (J), 31^{13} (E); cf. Jer. 22^{10} 46^{16}, Ezk. 23^{15}, Ru. 2^{11}. A commoner phrase in Pent. is אר׳ ומו׳, 12^{1} 24^{4} 31^{3} 32^{10}, Nu 10^{30} (all J). From the way in which the two expressions alternate, it is probable that they are equivalent; and since מ׳ alone certainly means 'kindred' (43^{7} [J], cf. Est. $2^{10.20}$ 8^{6}), it is better to render 'land of one's parentage' than 'land in which one was born' [𝔖 here and 12^{1}] (cf. Bu. 419^{2}). P has the word, but only in the sense of 'progeny' (48^{6}, Lv. 18^{9} [H]).

---

* Though Wi. (*AOF*, ii. 499) contends that both names are corruptions of חורנים.

very strong. Uru is the only city of the name known from Assyriology (although the addition of the gen. כשדים suggests that others were known to the Israelites: G-K. § 125 *h*): it was situated in the properly Chaldæan territory, was a city of great importance and vast antiquity, and (like Ḥarran, with which it is here connected) was a chief centre of the worship of the moon-god Sin (*KAT*,[2] 129 ff.). The only circumstance that creates serious misgiving is that the prevalent tradition of Gen. points tc the NE as the direction whence the patriarchs migrated to Canaan (see below); and this has led to attempts to find a northern Ur connected probably with the Mesopotamian Chaldæans of 22^{22} (see Kittel, *Gesch.* i. 163 ff.). Syrian tradition identifies it with Edessa (*Urhâi, Urfa*). It is generally recognised, however, that these considerations are insufficient to invalidate the arguments in favour of Uru.—כַּשְׂדִּים]=Bab. *Kašdu*, Ass. *Kaldu* (Χαλδ-αῖοι), is the name of a group of Semitic tribes, distinguished from the Arabs and Aramæans, who are found settled to the SE of Babylonia, round the shore of the Persian Gulf. In the 11th cent. or earlier they are believed to have penetrated Babylonia, at first as roving, pastoral nomads (*KAT*[3], 22 ff.), but ultimately giving their name to the country, and founding the dynasty of Nabopolassar. —By the ancients כשדים was rightly understood of Babylonia (Nikolaos Damasc. in Jos. *Ant.* i. 152; Eupolemos in Eus. *Præp. Ev.* ix. 17; Jer. al.); but amongst the Jews אור came to be regarded as an appellative = 'fire' (*in igne Chaldæorum*, which Jer. accepts, though he rejects the legends that were spun out of the etymology). This is the germ of the later Haggadic fables about the 'fire' in which Haran met an untimely fate, and the furnace into which Abraham was cast by order of Nimrod (*Jub.* xii. 12–14; Jer. *Quæst., ad loc.*; 𝕿J, *Ber. R.* § 38, Ra.).

29. While we are told that Nāḥôr's wife was his brother's daughter, it is surprising that nothing is said of the parentage of Sarai. According to E (20^{12}), she was Abraham's half-sister; but this does not entitle us to suppose that words expressing this relationship have been omitted from the text of J (Ewald). It would seem, however, that tradition represented marriage between near relations as the rule among the Teraḥites (20^{12} $24^{3ff.}$ 29^{19}).

With regard to the names, שָׂרַי seems to be an archaic form of שָׂרָה = 'princess' (see on 17^{15}), while מִלְכָּה means 'queen.' In Bab. the relations are reversed, *šarratu* being the queen and *malkatu* the princess. It cannot be a mere coincidence that these two names correspond to two personages belonging to the pantheon of Ḥarran, where Šarratu was a title of the moon-goddess, the consort of Sin, and Malkatu a title

29. וַיִּקַּח] sing., according to G-K. § 146 *f*.—**30.** עקרה] as 25^{21} 29^{31} (J); not in P (see 16^{1a}).—וָלָד] 𝔐 ילד. Only again as Kethîb of Or. MSS in 2 Sa. 6^{23}. It is possibly here a scribal error, which eventually influenced the other pass.

of Ištar, also worshipped there (Jen. *ZA*, xi. 299 f.; *KAT*[3], 364 f.). It is needless to say that these associations, if they existed, are forgotten in the Hebrew legend.—If, as is not improbable, the tradition contains ethnographic reminiscences, v.[28f.] express (1) the dissolution of an older tribal group, Haran; (2) the survival of one of its subdivisions (Loṭ) through the protection of a stronger tribe; and (3) the absorption of another (Milkah) in a kindred stock.—Of יִסְכָּה nothing is known. The Rabbinical fiction that she is Sarah under another name (implied in Jos. *Ant.* i. 151; 𝔗J, Jer. Ra. IEz. al.) is worthless. Ewald's conjecture that she was the wife of Loṭ is plausible, but baseless.

31, 32. The migration from Ur-Kasdîm to Canaan is accomplished in two stages. Teraḥ, as patriarchal head of the family, conducts the expedition as far as Ḥarran, where he dies. The obvious implication is that after his death the journey is resumed by Abram (12^5); although 𝔐 alone gives a chronology consistent with this view (*v. supra*). Nāḥôr, we are left to infer, remained behind in Ur-Kasdîm; and in the subsequent narratives P (in opposition to J) seems carefully to avoid any suggestion of a connexion between Nāḥôr and the city of Ḥarran.

חָרָן (with virtually doubled ר: cf. 𝔊 Χαρραν; Gr. Κάρραι; Lat. *Carræ*, *Charra*; Ass. *Ḫarrânu*; Syr. and Arab. *Ḥarrān*) was an important centre of the caravan trade in NW Mesopotamia, 60 miles E of Carchemish, situated near the Baliḫ, 70 miles due N from its confluence with the Euphrates. Though seldom mentioned in OT ($12^{4f.}$ [P], 27^{43} 28^{10} 29^4 [J], 2 Ki. 19^{12}, Ezk. 27^{23}†), and now ruined, it was a city of great antiquity, and retained its commercial importance in classical and mediæval times. The name in Ass. appears to be susceptible of several interpretations—'way,' 'caravan' (TA-Tab.), 'joint-stock enterprise' (Del. *Hdwb. s.v.*, *KAT*[3], 29^2)—any one of which might denote its commercially advantageous position at the parting of the route to Damascus from the main highway between Nineveh and Carchemish. Ḥarran was also (along with Ur) a chief seat of the worship of Sin, who had there a temple, *E-ḫul-ḫul*, described by Nabuna'id as "from remote days" a "dwelling of the joy of his (Sin's) heart" (*KIB*, iii. 2. 97), and who was known in NW Asia as the "Lord of Ḥarran" (Zinjirli inscr.: cf. Lidzbarski, *Hb.* 444, *An.*). See, further, Mez, *Gesch. d. St. Ḫarran*; Tomkins, *Times of Abraham*, 55 ff. etc. This double connexion of Abraham with centres of lunar religion is the most

---

31. כלתו] כַּלָּה (Syr. ܟܠܬܐ, Ar. *kannat*) means both 'spouse' and 'daughter-in-law': in Syr. and Ar. also 'sister-in-law,'—a fact adduced by Rob. Sm. as a relic of Baal polyandry (*KM*², 161, 209¹).—ויצאו אתם] gives no sense. Read with 𝔐𝔊 (καὶ ἐξήγαγεν αὐτούς) 𝔙, וַיֹּצֵא אֹתָם, or 𝔖, וַיֵּצֵא אִתָּם.—**32.** יְמֵי־תֶרַח] 𝔊 + ἐν Χαρράν.

plausible argument advanced by those who hold the mythical view of his figure as an impersonation of the moon-god.

It will be observed that while both P and J (in the present text) make Ur-Kasdîm the starting-point of the Abrahamic migration, J has no allusion to a journey from Ur to Ḥarran. His language is perfectly consistent either (*a*) with a march directly from Ur to Canaan, or (*b*) with the view that the real starting-point was Ḥarran, and that באור כשדים is here a gloss intended to harmonise J and P. Now, there is a group of passages in J which, taken together, unmistakably imply that Abraham was a native of Ḥarran, and therefore started from thence to seek the promised land. In $24^{4.7.10}$, the place of A.'s nativity is Aram-Naharaim, and specially the 'city of Nāḥôr'; while a comparison with 27^{43} 28^{10} 29^{4} leaves no doubt that the 'city of Nāḥôr' was Ḥarran. P, on the other hand, nowhere deviates from his theory of a double migration with a halt at Ḥarran; and the persistency with which he dissociates Laban and Rebecca from Nāḥôr (25^{20} $28^{2.5ff.}$) is a proof that the omission of Nāḥôr from the party that left Ur was intentional (Bu. 421 ff.). It is evident, then, that we have to do with a divergence in the patriarchal tradition; and the only uncertainty is with regard to the precise point where it comes in. The theory of P, though consistently maintained, is not natural; for (1) all the antecedents (11^{10-26}) point to Mesopotamia as the home of the patriarchs; and (2) the twofold migration, first from Ur and then from Ḥarran, has itself the appearance of a compromise between two conflicting traditions. The simplest solution would be to suppose that both the references to Ur-Kasdîm in J (11^{28} 15^{7}) are interpolations, and that P had another tradition which he harmonised with that of J by the expedient just mentioned (so We. Di. Gu. Dri. al.). Bu. holds that both traditions were represented in different strata of J (J^1 Ḥarran, J^2 Ur), and tries to show that the latter is a probable concomitant of the Yahwistic account of the Flood. In that he can hardly be said to be successful; and he is influenced by the consideration that apart from such a discrepancy in his sources P could never have thought of the circuitous route from Ur to Canaan by way of Ḥarran. That argument has little weight with those who are prepared to believe that P had other traditions at his disposal than those we happen to know from J and E.* In itself, the hypothesis of a dual tradition within the school of J is perfectly reasonable; but in this case, in spite of Bu.'s close reasoning, it appears insufficiently supported by other indications. The view of We. is on the whole the more acceptable.

---

* The suggestion has, of course, been made (Wi. *AOF.* i. 98 ff.; Paton, *Syr. and Pal.* 42) that E is the source of the Ur-Kasdîm tradition; but in view of Jos. 24^{2} that is not probable.

THE PATRIARCHAL HISTORY.

ABRAHAM.

CHS. XII–XXV. 18.

Critical Note.—In this section of Genesis the broad lines of demarcation between J, E, and P are so clear that there is seldom a serious diversity of opinion among critics. The real difficulties of the analysis concern the composition of the Yahwistic narrative, and the relation of its component parts to E and P respectively. These questions have been brought to the front by the commentary of Gu., who has made it probable that the Yahwistic document contains two main strata, one (J^h) fixing Abraham's residence at Hebron, and the other (J^b) regarding him as a denizen of the Negeb.

1. The kernel of J^h is a cycle of legends in which the fortunes of Abraham and Lot are interlinked: viz. 12^{1-8}; $13^{2.5-18}$; 18; 19^{1-28}; 19^{30-38}. If these passages are read continuously, they form an orderly narrative, tracing the march of Abraham and Lot from Ḥarran through Shechem to Bethel, where they separate; thence Abraham proceeds to Hebron, but is again brought into ideal contact with Lot by visits of angels to each in turn; this leads up to the salvation of Lot from the fate of Sodom, his flight to the mountains, and the origin of the two peoples supposed to be descended from him. In this sequence 12^9–13^1 is (as will be more fully shown later) an interruption. Earlier critics had attempted to get rid of the discontinuity either by seeking a suitable connexion for $12^{9ff.}$ at a subsequent stage of J's narrative, or by treating it as a redactional expansion. But neither expedient is satisfactory, and the suggestion that it comes from a separate source is preferable on several grounds. Now $12^{9ff.}$ is distinguished from J^h, not only by the absence of Lot, but by the implication that Abraham's home was in the Negeb, and perhaps by a less idealised conception of the patriarch's character. These characteristics reappear in ch. 16, which, as breaking the connexion of ch. 18 with 13, is plausibly assigned to J^b. (To this source Gu. also assigns the Yahwistic component of ch. 15; but that chapter shows so many signs of later elaboration that it can hardly have belonged to either of the primary sources.)—After ch. 19, the hand of J appears in the accounts of Isaac's birth (21^{1-7}*) and Abraham's treaty with Abimelech (21^{22-34}*): the latter is probably J^b (on account of the Negeb), while the former shows slight discrepancies with the prediction of ch. 18, which lead us (though with less confidence) to assign

it also to J^b. With regard to ch. 24, it is impossible to say whether it belongs to J^h or J^b: we assign it provisionally to the latter.* The bulk of the Yahwistic material may therefore be disposed in two parallel series as follows:

J^h: 12^{1-8}*; 13^{2-18}*; $18^{1-16.\ 20-22a.\ 33b}$; 19^{1-28}; 19^{30-38};
J^b: 12^9–13^1; 16; 21^{1-7}*; 21^{22-34}*; 24*.†

The Yahwistic sections not yet dealt with are ch. 15* (see above); and the two genealogies, 22^{20-24} and 25^{1-6}, both inserted by a Yahwistic editor from unknown sources. Other passages (13^{14-17} $18^{17-19.\ 22b-33a}$ 22^{15-18}) which appear to have been added during the redaction (RJ or R^{JE}) will be examined in special notes *ad locc.*

2. The hand of E is recognised in the following sections: 15*; 20; 21^{1-7}*; 21^{8-21}; 21^{22-34}*; 22^{1-19} (24*?). Gu. has pointed out that where J and E run parallel to one another, E's affinites are always with J^b and never with J^h (cf. the variants $12^{9ff.}$ ‖ 20; 16 ‖ 21^{8-21}; and the compositions in 21^{1-7} and 21^{22-34}). This, of course, might be merely a onsequence of the fact that E, like J^b, makes the Negeb (Beersheba) the scene of Abraham's history. But it is remarkable that in ch. 26 we find unquestionable Yahwistic parallels to E and J^b, with Isaac as hero instead of Abraham. These are probably to be attributed to the writer whom we have called J^h, who thus succeeded in preserving the Negeb traditions, while at the same time maintaining the theory that Abraham was the patron of Hebron, and Isaac of Beersheba.

Putting all the indications together, we are led to a tentative hypothesis regarding the formation of the Abrahamic legend, which has some value for the clearing of our ideas, though it must be held with great reserve. The tradition crystallised mainly at two great religious centres, Beersheba and Hebron. The Beersheba narratives took shape in two recensions, a Yahwistic and an Elohistic, of which (it may be

---

* Gu. analyses 24 into two narratives, assigning one to each source. The question is discussed in the Note, pp. 340 f., where the opinion is hazarded that the subordinate source may be E, in which case the other would naturally be J^b.

† It is interesting to compare this result with the analysis of the Yahwistic portions of chs. 1–11 (pp. 2–4). In each case J appears as a complex document, formed by the amalgamation of prior collections of traditions; and the question naturally arises whether any of the component narratives can be traced from the one period into the other. It is impossible to prove that this is the case; but certain affinities of thought and expression suggest that J^h in the biography of Abraham may be the continuation of J^e in the primitive history. Both use the phrase 'call by the name of Yahwe' (4^{26} 12^8 [13^4], [but cf. 21^{33} (J^b)]); and the optimistic religious outlook expressed in the blessing of Noah ($9^{26ff.}$) is shared in a marked degree by the writer of J^h. Have we here fragments of a work whose theme was the history of the Yahwe-religion, from its commencement with Enosh to its establishment in the leading sanctuaries of Palestine by Abraham and Isaac? See 12^7 (Shechem), 12^8 (Bethel), 13^{18} (Hebron), 26^{25} (Beersheba).

added) the second is ethically and religiously on a higher level than the first. These were partly amalgamated, probably before the union of J^h and J^b (see on ch. 26). The Hebron tradition was naturally indifferent to the narratives which connected Abraham with the Negeb, or with its sanctuary Beersheba; hence the writer of J^h, who attaches himself to this tradition, excludes the Beersheba stories from his biography of Abraham, but finds a place for some of them in the history of Isaac.

3. The account of P ($12^{4b. 5}$ $13^{6. 11b. 12ab\alpha}$; $16^{1a. 3. 15}$; 17; 19^{29}; $21^{1b. 2b-5}$; 23; 25^{7-11a}; 25^{12-17}) consists mostly of a skeleton biography based on the older documents, and presupposing a knowledge of them. The sole *raison d'être* of such an outline is the chronological scheme into which the various incidents are fitted: that it fills some gaps in the history (birth of Ishmael, death of Abraham) is merely an accident of the redaction. P's affinities are chiefly with J^h, with whom he shares the idea that Hebron was the permanent residence of Abraham. Of the sections peculiar to P, ch. 17 is parallel to 15, and 25^{12-17} has probably replaced a lost Yahwistic genealogy of Ishmael. Ch. 23 stands alone as presumably an instance where P has preserved an altogether independent tradition.

Ch. 14 cannot with any show of reason be assigned to any of the recognised sources of the Pent., and has accordingly been omitted from the above survey. The question of its origin is discussed on pp. 271 ff. below.

CHS. XII. XIII.—*The migrations of Abram* (J and P).

Leaving his home at the command of Yahwe, Abram enters Canaan and erects altars at Shechem and Bethel (12^{1-8}). From Bethel he migrates to the Negeb, and thence, under stress of famine, to Egypt; where by a false representation he enriches himself, but imperils his wife's honour (12^{9}–13^{1}). Laden with wealth, he returns to Bethel, where an amicable separation from his nephew Lot leaves him in sole possession of the promise of the land (13^{2-17}). Abram journeys southward and settles in Hebron (^{18}).

Analysis.—The slender thread of P's narrative is represented by $12^{4b. 5}$ $13^{6. 11b\ 12ab\alpha}$: note the date in 12^{4b}; the form of 12^{5}; רְכוּשׁ, רָכַשׁ, 12^{5} 13^{6}; נֶפֶשׁ, 'person,' 12^{5}; אֶרֶץ כְּנַעַן, 12^{5} 13^{12}; נָשָׂא, 13^{6}; עָרֵי הַכִּכָּר, 13^{12}; and see on the vv. below. These fragments form a continuous epitome of the events between the exodus from Ḥarran and the parting of Abram and Lot. With a slight and inherently plausible transposition ($12^{5. 4b}$; Bu. p. 432) they might pass for the immediate continuation of 11^{32}, if we can suppose that the call of Abram was entirely omitted by P (see Gu. 231). —The rest of the passage is Yahwistic throughout: obs. the consistent use of יהוה; the reference to Paradise, 13^{10}; the anticipation of ch. 19 in $13^{10. 18}$; and the following expressions: מוֹלֶדֶת, 12^{1}; נִבְרְכוּ בְ, 12^{3}; כֹּל מִשְׁפְּחֹת

הָאֲדָמָה, 12^{8}; הִנֵּה נָא ,נָא, $12^{11.13}$ $13^{8.9.14}$; בַּעֲבוּר, $12^{13.16}$; מַה־זֹּאת ע׳, 12^{18}; כִּכַּר הַיַּרְדֵּן, $13^{10.11}$. It falls naturally into three sections: (*a*) $12^{1-4a.6-8}$; (*b*) 12^{10}–13^{1}; (*c*) $13^{2.5.7-11a.12b\beta-18}$; 12^{9} and $13^{3.4}$ being redactional links (RJ) uniting *b* to *a* on the one side and *c* on the other. The purely mechanical connexion of *b* with *a* and *c* was first shown by We. (*Comp.*[2] 24 f.).* The removal of *b* restores the direct and natural sequence of *c* upon *a*, and gets rid of the redactor's artificial theory of a double visit to Bethel with a series of aimless wanderings between. In the main narrative Abram's journey is continuously southward, from Shechem to Bethel (where the separation from Lot takes place), and thence to his permanent abode in Hebron. In the inserted episode (*b*), Abram simply moves down to Egypt from his home in the Negeb and back again.—As to the *origin* of 12^{10-20}, see p. 251 below.

XII. 1–8. The journey to Canaan and the promise of the Land.—**1.** The opening v. strikes a note peculiarly characteristic of the story of Abram—the trial of faith. There is intentional pathos in the lingering description of the things he is to leave: *thy land, thy kindred, and thy father's house*; and a corresponding significance in the vagueness with which the goal is indicated: *to a land which I will show thee.* Obedience under such conditions marks Abram as the hero of faith, and the ideal of Hebrew piety (Heb. $11^{8f.}$).—**2, 3.** The blessings here promised express the aspirations of the age in which the narrative originated, and reveal the people's consciousness of its exceptional destiny among the nations of the world. They breathe the spirit of optimism which is on the whole characteristic of the Yahwistic treatment of the *national* legends, as contrasted with the primitive and cosmopolitan mythology of chs. 2–11, whose sombre tone is only once ($9^{26f.}$) relieved by a similar gleam of hope.—*and will make thy name great*] It has been noticed that the order in which the names of the patriarchs emerge in the prophetic literature is the reverse of that in Genesis, and that Abraham is first mentioned in Ezk. 33^{24}. The inference has been drawn that the figure of

1. לֶךְ־לְךָ (22^{2} [E]; cf. Ca. $2^{10.13}$)] see G-K. § 119 *s*.—On מוֹלֶדֶת (𝔊 συγγένεια) see 11^{28}.—**2.** וֶהְיֵה בְּרָכָה] Impve. expressing consequence (G-K. § 110 *i*) is here questionable, because the preceding vbs. are simple futures. The pointing as consec. pf. (וְהָיָה) was suggested by Giesebrecht

* So Di. Ho. Gu.

Abraham represents a late development of the patriarchal legends (cf. We. *Prol.*[6] 317 f.). But from this promise we may fairly conclude that even in the pre-prophetic period the name of Abraham was famous in Israel, and that in this particular the religious ideas of the people are not fully reflected in prophecy (1 Ki. 18[36] has also to be considered). —The antiquity of the name is now placed beyond doubt by an archæological discovery made by Erman in 1888, but first published by Breasted in 1904. In the Karnak list of places conquered by Sheshonk I., the contemporary of Rehoboam, there is mentioned *pa-ḥu-q-ru-'a 'a-ba-ra-m* = חקל אברם, 'Field of Abram.' It has not been identified; but from its place in the list it must have been in the S of Palestine (see Breasted, *AJSL*, xxi. 35 f.; and cf. Meyer, *INS*, 266).*—*and be thou a blessing* (cf. Zec. 8[13])] Rather: *and it* (the name) *shall be a blessing* (point וְהָיָה, *v.i.*) *i.e.* 'a name to bless by,' in the sense explained by [3b].—3b has generally been rendered *through thee shall all the families of the earth be blessed*] *i.e.* the blessings of true religion shall be mediated to the world through Abram and his descendants (so all Vns.; cf. Sir. 44[21], Ac. 3[25], Gal. 3[8]). The better translation, however, is that of Ra., adopted by most modern comm.: *by thee shall all . . . bless themselves*] the idea being that in invoking blessings on themselves or others they will use such words as 'God make thee like Abram,' etc. (see 48[20], Is. 65[16], Ps. 72[17]; and the opposite,

(*ATliche Schätzung d. Gottesnamens*, 15); see Gu. *ad v.*—3. מְקַלֶּלְךָ] sing.; but the pl. of some MSS, 𝔐𝔊𝔙𝔖 (־ֶיךָ), is more probable; cf. 27[29], Nu. 24[9].—וְנִבְרְכוּ בְךָ] 𝔊 *καὶ εὐλογηθήσονται ἐν σοί*, and so all Vns. The rendering depends on the grammatical question whether the Niph. has pass. or refl. sense. This form of the vb. does not occur except in the parallels 18[18] (with בּוֹ) and 28[14] (בְּךָ—וּבְזַרְעֶךָ). In 22[18] 26[4] it is replaced by Hithp., which is, of course, refl., and must be translated 'bless themselves'; the renderings 'feel themselves blessed' (Tu. KS. Str.), or 'wish themselves blessed' (De.) are doubtful compromises. These passages, however, belong to secondary strata of J (as does also 18[18], and perhaps 28[14]), and are not necessarily decisive of the sense of 12[3]. But it is significant that the Pu., which is the proper pass. of בֵּרַךְ, is consistently avoided; and the presumption appears to be distinctly in favour of the

* See, further, pp. 292 f. below.

Jer. 29[22]). "So the ancient mind expressed its admiration of a man's prosperity" (Gu.). The clause is thus an expansion of [2b]: the name of Abram will pass into a formula of benediction, because he himself and his seed will be as it were blessedness incarnate. The exegetical question is discussed below.—**4a.** The mention of Lot (see on 11[27]) establishes a literary connexion with the Lot narratives of chs. 13. 19.—**5** is P's parallel to [4a] (*v.i.*); the last sentence supplying an obvious gap in J's narrative.—*and they came, etc.*]. This time (ct. 11[31]) the goal is actually reached. On the probable route from Ḥarran to Canaan, see Dri. 146, 300 ff.—**6, 7.** Arrived at Shechem, Abram receives, through a theophany, the first intimation that he has reached the goal of his pilgrimage, and proceeds to take possession of

---

sense given in the text above. The idea is well expressed by Ra.: וזהו פשוטו אדם אומר לבנו תהא כאברהם וכן כל ונברכו בך שבמקרא וזה מוכיח בך יברך ישראל לאמר ישימך אלהים כאפרים וכמנשה (Gn. 48[20]).—4. וַיֵּלֶךְ] 𝔖 ܘܥܒܕ (= וַיַּעַשׂ), adopted by Ba.—5. The parallel to [4a] in the distinctive form (see on 11[31]) and phraseology of P. The vb. רָכַשׁ is peculiar to P (31[18] 36[6] 46[6]); רְכוּשׁ is a word of the later language, found in P (7 t.), in Gn. 14 (5 t.) and as a gloss in 15[14]; in Ch. Ezr. Dn. (15 t.): see Ho. *Einl.* 347. It is supposed to denote primarily 'riding beasts,' like Heb. רֶכֶשׁ, Aram. ܪ̈ܟܫܐ, רִכְשָׁא, Ass. *rukušu* (Haupt, *Hebraica*, iii. 110); then property in general.—נֶפֶשׁ] in the sense of 'person' is also practically confined to P in Hex. (Ho. 345).—עָשׂוּ]='acquired,' as 31[1], Dt. 8[17], Jer. 17[11] etc. The idea of 'proselytising' (𝔗OJ) is rightly characterised by Ra. as Haggada.—אֶרֶץ כְּנַעַן] "ein fast sicheres Kennzeichen für P" (Ho. 340). In JE כנען appears never to be used in its geographical sense except in the story of Joseph (42. 44–47. 50[5]) and Jos. 24[3].—וַיָּבֹאוּ—כְּנַעַן] 𝔊L om., probably from homoioteleuton.—6. בָּאָרֶץ[1]] so 𝔊L, but 𝔊A, al., read לְאָרְכָּהּ (13[17]).—For מוֹרֶה, Σ and 𝔖 read מַמְרֵא. The *convallem illustrem* of 𝔙 is an amalgamation of 𝔊 (τὴν δρῦν τὴν ὑψηλήν [מָרוֹם?]) and 𝔗O (מישרי מורה='plains of M.'); the latter is probably accounted for by aversion to the idolatrous associations of the sacred tree. 𝔗J has מישר דהוו מירי; on which see Levy, *Chald. Wb.* 33. The absence of the art. (ct. גִּבְעַת הַמּוֹרֶה, Ju. 7[1]) seems to show that the word is used as *nom. pr.*—אֵלוֹן] unlike its Aram. equivalents (ܐܝܠܢܐ, אִילָן), which mean tree in general, is never used generically, but always of particular (probably sacred) trees. In the Vns. 'oak' and 'terebinth' are used somewhat indiscriminately (see v. Gall, *CSt.* 24 ff.) for four Heb. words: אֵלוֹן, אַלּוֹן, אֵלָה, אַלָּה (only Jos. 24[26]). The theory has been advanced that the forms with *ê* are alone correct; that they are derivatives from אֵל, 'god,' and denote

the land in the name of Yahwe by erecting altars for His worship. It is, however, a singular fact, that in J there is no record of actual sacrifice by the patriarchs on such altars: see p. l.

The original motive of this and similar legends is to explain the sacredness of the principal centres of cultus by definite manifestations of God to the patriarchs, or definite acts of worship on their part. The rule is that the legitimacy of a sanctuary for Israel is established by a theophany (Ex. 20^{24} [E]). The historic truth is that the sanctuaries were far older than the Hebrew immigration, and inherited their sanctity from lower forms of religion. That fact appears in v.^{6} in the use of the word מָקוֹם, which has there the technical sense of 'sacred place,' as in 22^{4} 28^{11} 35^{1} (𝕲), Ex. 3^{5}, 1 Sa. 7^{16} (𝕲 ἡγιασμένοις), Jer. 7^{12} (cf. Ar. *maḳām*).—Shechem is the first and most northerly of four sanctuaries—the others being Bethel, Hebron (J^{h}), and Beersheba (E, J^{b})—connected with the name of Abraham. The name (*Skmm*, with pl. termination)* occurs in an Eg. inscr. as early as the 12th dynasty. It was an important place in the Tel-Amarna period (see Steuernagel, *Einwanderung*, 120 f.; Knudtzon, *BA*, iv. 127), and figures prominently in OT legend and history. On its situation (the modern *Nābulūs*) between Mts. Ebal and Gerizim, see *EB*, iv. 4437 f.—The אֵלוֹן מוֹרֶה (= 'oracle-giving terebinth') was evidently an ancient sacred tree from which oracles were obtained, and therefore a survival of primitive tree-worship.† Besides Dt. 11^{30} (a difficult pass.,

---

originally the 'sacred tree' without distinction of species.‡ The אַלּוֹן of Gn. 35^{8} is called a palm in Ju. 4^{5}, and אֵילִם (pl. of אֵלָה?) (Ex. 15^{27} etc.) derived its name from 70 palm-trees. But though the Mass. tradition may not be uniformly reliable, אֵלָה and אַלּוֹן appear to be distinguished in Hos. 4^{13}, Is. 6^{13} (Di.); and the existence of a form אַלּוֹן is confirmed by *allânu*, which is said to be an Ass. tree-name (G–B.[14] 36 b). It is probable from Zec. 11^{2}, Ezk. 27^{6} etc., that אַלּוֹן is the oak. With regard to the other names no convincing theory can be formed, but a connexion with אֵל (*ĭlu*) is at best precarious.—6b is probably a gloss: cf. 13^{7b}.—7. וַיֹּאמֶר] 𝔪𝕲𝔙𝔖 add לוֹ.—הַנִּרְאָה אֵלָיו] so 35^{1} (E).

---

* It is possible that this (שכמם) is the oldest form in Heb. also; since 𝕲 often has the pl. Σίκιμα (33^{18} $35^{4.5}$ etc.).

† "Where a tree is connected with a *welī* it was probably the original object of honour" (Curtiss, *Prim. Sem. Rel.*[1] 91). On the obtaining of oracles from trees, see Rob. Sm. *RS*[2], 195. Comp. Ju. 4^{5}, 2 Sa. 5^{24}; and the oak of Zeus at Dodona.—Duhm's brilliant generalisation (*Isaiah*[1], 13 f.), that Abraham was traditionally associated with sacred trees, Isaac and Ishmael with sacred wells, and Jacob with sacred stones, though not literally accurate, has sufficient truth to be suggestive; and may possibly correspond to some vague impression of the popular mind in Israel.

‡ We. *Pr.*[6] 234; Sta. *GVI*, i. 455; v. Gall, *l.c.*; cf. Schwally, *ThLzg.*, 1899, 356.

see Dri. ***ad*** *loc.*, and v. Gall, *Cult-St.* 107 ff.), it seems to be mentioned as one of the sacra of Shechem under other names: הָאֵלָה, הָאַלָּה (a mere difference of pointing, *v.i.*), Gn. 35^{4}, Jos. 24^{26}; אֵלוֹן מְעוֹנְנִים ('terebinth of soothsayers'), Ju. 9^{37}; and אֵ' מֻצָּב ('t. of the pillar' [הַמַּצֵּבָה]) Ju. 9^{6}. The tree is not said to have been planted by Abram (like the tamarisk of Beersheba, 21^{33}),—an additional indication that Abram was not originally the patron or *welī* of the shrine. The sacred stone under the tree (the מֻצָּב of Ju. 9^{6}?) was believed to have been set up by Joshua (Jos. 24^{26}). The sanctuary of Shechem was also associated with Jacob (33^{18} 35^{4}), and especially with Joseph, who was buried there (Jos. 24^{32}), and whose grave is still shown near the village of Balâṭa (*ballûṭ*='oak'): see v. Gall, 117.

8. Abram moved on, nomadic fashion, and *spread his tent* (26^{25} 33^{19} 35^{21}) near *Bethel*, about 20 m. from Shechem; there he built a second altar, and *called by the name of Yahwe*; see on 4^{26}. Luther's rendering: 'predigte den Namen des Herrn,' is absolutely without exegetical warrant; and the whole notion of a monotheistic propaganda, of which Abram was the Mahdi (Je. *ATLO*², 328), is a modern invention unsupported by a particle of historical evidence. It is noticeable that no theophany is recorded here, perhaps because the definite consecration of Bethel was ascribed to Jacob (ch. 28).—Here the parting from Lot took place (ch. 13).

On Bethel (*Beitīn*), see on $28^{10ff.}$ 35^{7}; cf. Jos. 7^{2}. Di. distinguishes the site of Abram's altar (E of Bethel and W of 'Ai) from that of Jacob's pillar, which he takes to have been at Bethel itself. The more natural view is that the local sanctuary lay E of the city (so Gu.), perhaps at *Burǧ Beitīn*, the traditional scene of Abram's encampment (GASm. *EB*, i. 552).—On the somewhat uncertain situation of הָעַי (always with art.=עַיָּה, Neh. 11^{31}, 1 Ch. 7^{28}; and עַיַּת, Is. 10^{28}), see Buhl, *GP*, 177.

XII. 9–XIII. 1.—Abram in Egypt.—The first of three variants of what must have been a very popular story in ancient Israel (cf. 20. $26^{6ff.}$). Whether the original hero was Abraham or Isaac we cannot tell; but a comparison of the three parallels shows that certain primitive features of the legend are most faithfully preserved in the passage before us: note the entire absence of the extenuating circumstances introduced into the other accounts,—the whole subject being treated with a frank realism which

---

8. וַיַּעְתֵּק] intr. Hiph. as 26^{22} (J).

seems to take us down to the bed-rock of Hebrew folklore. —9. *to the Negeb*] The 'dry' region between the Judæan highland and the wilderness of *et-Tīh*, extending from 10 or 12 m. N of Beersheba to the neighbourhood of Ḳadesh (*v.i.*). It is still a suitable pasture ground for camel-breeding Bedouin, and the remains of buildings and irrigation works prove that it was once much more extensively cultivated than at present.—**10.** *the famine was severe* (lit. 'heavy')] emphasising the fact that the visit to Egypt was compulsory. The Nile valley, on account of its great fertility and its independence of the annual rainfall, was the natural resort of Asiatics in times of scarcity; and this under primitive conditions involved an actual sojourn in the country. The admission of Semites to the rich pastures of Egypt is both described and depicted in the monuments (see Guthe, *GI*, 16).* The purchase of corn for home consumption ($42^{1ff.}$) was possible as a temporary expedient at a somewhat more advanced stage of culture.—**11–13.** The speech of Abram to his wife is an instructive revelation of social and moral sentiment in early Israel. The Hebrew women are fairer than all others, and are sure to be coveted by foreigners; but the marriage bond is so sacred that even a foreigner, in order to possess the wife, will kill the husband

---

9. הָלוֹךְ וְנָסוֹעַ] Dav. § 86, *R.* 4; G-K. § 113 *u.* The idea of continuous journeying lies not in נסוע (see on 11^2), but in הלוך (cf. Ju. 14^9).—הַנֶּגְבָּה] 𝔊 ἐν τῇ ἐρήμῳ: Aq. νότονδε: Σ. εἰς νότον. The word, from a √ meaning 'dry,' occurs as a proper name of S Palestine (*Ngb*) in a document of the reign of Thothmes III. (Müller, *AE*, 148; Mey. *ZATW*, vi. 1). Its use to denote the S direction is rare in JE, and apparently confined to later additions (13^{14} 28^{14}, Jos. 18^5). The geographical limits of the region can, of course, only be roughly determined, chiefly from the list of its cities in Jos. 15^{21-32}: on this, and its physical characteristics, see Che. *EB*, 3374 ff.; Palmer, *Desert of the Exodus*, ii. 351 f. (1871).—**10.** לָגוּר שָׁם (Jer. $42^{15ff.}$)] properly 'dwell as a client or protected guest' (גֵּר = Ar. *ğār*: cf. *OTJC*², 342^1). The words, however, are often used in the wider sense of temporary sojourn (15^{13}, Jer. 14^8), and this may be the case here.—**11.** הִנֵּה־נָא] 16^2 $18^{27.31}$ $19^{2.8.19}$ 27^2 (all J). The free use of נָא (*c.* 40 t. in Gen.) is very characteristic of J (Ho. *Einl.* 110).—**13.** אֲחֹתִי אַתְּ] *oratio obliqua* without כִּי, G-K. § 157 *a.* 𝔊, on the contrary, ὅτι

---

* Cf. *Authority and Archæology*, p. 59; *DB*, ii. 531^b (note ‡), 774^b.

first. Hence the dilemma with which Abram is confronted: if Sarai is known as his wife, her life will be safe, but he will probably be slain; if she passes as his sister, her honour will be endangered, but his advantage will be served. In such a case the true Hebrew wife will not hesitate to sacrifice herself for her husband: at the same time she is a free moral agent: Abram's proposal is not a command but a deferential request. Lastly, it is assumed that in the circumstances lying is excusable. There is no suggestion that either the untruthfulness or the selfish cowardice of the request was severely reprobated by the ethical code to which the narrative appealed.—**14, 15.** The stratagem succeeds beyond expectation. Sarai attracts the notice of the courtiers, and is brought into Pharaoh's harem. The incident is characteristic of Oriental despotisms generally: Ebers (*Aeg. u. d. B. Mosis*, 262 f.) cites from the d'Orbiney papyrus an example of the zeal of Egyptian officials in matters of this kind.—**16.** *he treated Abram well, etc.*] cf. v.[13]. This feature of the *reward* is a standing element of the tradition; but in ch. 20 it is only bestowed after the misunderstanding has been cleared up, and in $26^{12ff.}$ its connexion with the incident is loosened.

The gifts enumerated constituted the riches of the patriarchs: 20^{14} 24^{35} 30^{43} $32^{15f.}$ (cf. Jb. 1^{3} 42^{12}), and were perhaps regarded by this narrator as the foundation of Abram's subsequent wealth. The animals mentioned were all known in ancient Egypt (Ebers, 265 ff.), except the

---

ἀδ. αὐτοῦ εἰμί.—בִּגְלָל] In Hex. only 30^{27} 39^{5} (J) and 3 t. in Dt.: elsewhere 4 t.—**15.** פַּרְעֹה] The title of all Egyptian kings mentioned in OT except Shishak (1 Ki. 14^{25}) and Sevé (2 Ki. 17^{4}). It corresponds exactly to Eg. *Per'o* ('Great House'), denoting originally the palace or court, and is not applied to the person of the king earlier than the 18th dynasty (Erman, *LAE*, 58; Griffith, *DB*, iii. 819; Mü. *EB*, iii. 3687). It is needless to go further in search of an etymology, though Renouf, *PSBA*, xv. 421, may be consulted. A confusion of the name here with the "Pir'u king of Muṣuri" mentioned by Sargon (*KIB*, ii. 55, etc.), is too readily suspected by Cheyne (*EB*, 3164, and *TBAI*, 223; cf. Wi. *MVAG*, iii. 2 ff.). Even supposing it proved that this is the proper name of a N Arabian prince, the narrative here must be much older than the time of Sargon; and it is inconceivable that the Heb. designation for the kings of Egypt should have been determined by an isolated and accidental resemblance to a native word.—**16.** After וּבָקָר 𝔐 inserts מקנה כבד מאד, and puts וַעֲבָדִים וּשְׁפָחֹת

camel, which is neither represented nor named in the monuments before the Greek period.* This, Müller supposes, was due to a religious scruple; but, of course, the difficulty remains of thinking that a religiously unclean animal should have been bred in Egypt, or have been gifted by Pharaoh to Abram. The order also—slaves between he-asses and she-asses—is strange; the explanation (Ho. Gu.) that the slaves were intermediate in value between these animals is jejune, and is, besides, contradicted by 24^{35} 30^{43}. It is possible that אֲתֹנֹת וּגְמַלִּים has been added at the end by a glossator; but see 24^{35} 30^{43}, and cf. 𝔐 below.

17. The story reaches its climax. Yahwe interposes at the extreme moment to save Sarai and avert calamity from the patriarchal house. It is noteworthy that Yahwe's intervention is here purely providential: in $20^{3ff.}$ it takes the form of a personal communication, while in the attenuated version of $26^{6ff.}$ it has become superfluous and is omitted.—*smote with great plagues*] severe bodily maladies; cf. 20^{17}, Ex. 11^{1}, Ps. 39^{11} etc. How Pharaoh discovered the cause of his sickness we are left to conjecture; Jos. (*Ant.* i. 164 f.) pretty nearly exhausts the possibilities of the case when he mentions sacrifice, inquiry at the priests, and interrogation of Sarai. Gu. is probably right in suggesting that something has been omitted between [17] and [18].—**18, 19.** To the vigorous expostulation of the Pharaoh, Abram is unable to reply. The narrator evidently feels that morally the heathen king is in the right; and the zest with which the story was related was not quite so unalloyed by ethical reflexions as Gu. (151) would have us believe. The idea of God, however, is imperfectly moralised; Yahwe's providence puts in the wrong the man who is justified at the bar of human conscience; He is not here the absolutely righteous Being proclaimed by the prophets (Am. 3^{2}).—**20.** *Pharaoh gave men charge concerning*

---

before וַחֲמֹרִים.—**17.** וַיְנַגַּע] The Pi. only of smiting with disease: 2 Ki. 15^{5}, 2 Ch. 26^{20} (Pu. Ps. 73^{5}). — גְּדֹלִים] 𝔊 + καὶ πονηροῖς. — וְאֶת־בֵּיתוֹ] possibly a gloss from $20^{17f.}$ (KS. al.); see on 2^{9}.—**19.** וָאֶקַּח] 'so that I took'; Dri. *T.* § 74 *a*, § 116, *Obs.* 2.—אִשְׁתְּךָ] 𝔊 + לְפָנֶיךָ.—**20.** 𝔐𝔊 add at the end וְלוֹט עִמּוֹ, as in MT of 13^{1}: the phrase is interpolated in both places.

---

* Cf. Ex. 9^{3} (J); and see Sayce, *EHH*, 169 (the notice unhistorical); Erman, *LAE*, 493. Ebers' statement as to the name is corrected by Müller, *AE*, 142, *EB*, i. 634.

Abram] *i.e.* provided him with an escort (שִׁלַּח as 18[16] 31[27]). The thought of ignominious expulsion is far from the writer's mind; the purpose of the escort is to see that no further injury is done to the patriarch or his wife (IEz.), bringing fresh judgements on the realm.—**XIII. 1.** The narrative closes with the return of Abram to his home in the Negeb (cf. 12[9]).

Source of 12[10-20].—It has already been pointed out (p. 242 f.) that, though the section breaks the connexion of the main narrative, it is Yahwistic in style; and the question of its origin relates only to its place within the general cycle of Yahwistic tradition. Three views are possible: that it is (1) a secondary expansion of J by a later hand (We.); (2) a misplaced chapter of J's main narrative belonging properly to a subsequent stage of the history; or (3) an excerpt from a separate Yahwistic collection (Gu. [J^b]). To (1) and (2) there are distinct objections: (*a*) the style and moral tone of the narrative, which are those of racy popular legend, and produce the impression of great antiquity; (*b*) the absence from the character of Abram of those ideal features which are prominent in the main narrative, and which later ages tended to exaggerate (*e.g.* ch. 14); especially (*c*) the fact that the home of Abram is not at Hebron but in the Negeb. Gu.'s theory, which is not open to these objections, seems, therefore, to mark an advance in the analysis of J.

2–18. Separation of Abram and Lot.—**2, 5, 7.** The great wealth of the two patriarchs leads to bickering among their retainers. The situation reflects the relations of tribes rather than of private families, quarrels about pastures and watering-places being a common feature of nomadic life and a frequent cause of separation: cf. 21[25] 26[20ff.].—**2.** *Silver and gold*] 24[35] 20[16] 23[16].—**5.** Lot's substance, on the other hand, is purely nomadic: *flocks, herds, and tents.* The last word appears to have the sense of 'people,' 'families'; cf. Ar. *'ahl*, Sab. אהל (Müller, *ZDMG*, xxxvii. 341; Homm. *SA Chrest.* 121).—**3, 4.** A redactional addition (p. 243), bringing the narrative back to Bethel, the traditional scene of the separation.—**6.** P's account of the parting: cf. 36[7]. It has often been noticed that he makes no mention of a quarrel; just as J says nothing of the straitness of the land (*v.i.*).—

---

3. לְמַסָּעָיו] simply 'by stages'; not by the *same* stages by which he had come (𝔊𝔙 Ra.): cf. Ex. 17[1] 40[36. 38] etc.—**5.** וְאֹהָלִים (G–K. §§ 93 *r*, 23 *h*)] 𝔊[A] κτήνη, prob. Gr. corruption of σκηναί (so many MSS).—**6.** נָשָׂא] 𝔐 נשאה—better. Cf. 36[7] (*P*).—6bβ is by some (KS. Ho.) assigned to J,

8, 9. The thought of strife between relatives (אֲנָשִׁים אַחִים) is intolerable to Abram, who, though the older man, renounces his rights for the sake of an amicable settlement. The narrator has finely conceived the magnanimity which springs from fellowship with God. The peaceable disposition ascribed to the patriarchs is characteristic of the old narratives. Jacob substitutes guile for force, but Abraham and Isaac conquer by sheer reasonableness and conciliation.—10, 11a, 12bβ. Lot's choice.—*lifted up his eyes and saw, etc.*] The *Burğ Beitīn* (p. 247), a few minutes SE from the village, is described as "one of the great view-points of Palestine" (GASm. *EB*, 552), from which the Jordan valley and the N end of the Dead Sea are clearly visible.—*the whole Oval of the Jordan*] cf. Dri. *Deut.* 421 f.

כִּכַּר הַיַּרְדֵּן (only here and 1 Ki. 7^{46}=2 Ch. 4^{17}), or הַכִּכָּר simply (v.[12] $19^{17.25.28f}$, Dt. 34^{3}, 2 Sa. 18^{23}), is not (as Di. 230) the whole of the 'Arābāh from the Lake of Galilee to the Dead Sea, but the expansion of the Jordan valley towards its S end, defined in Dt. 34^{3} as 'the plain of Jericho' (see *HG*, 505 ff.; Buhl, *GP*, 112). The northern limit is indeterminate; the southern depends on the site of Zoar (v.[10]), whether N or S of the Dead Sea. It is thus not quite certain whether the term includes the Dead Sea basin; and on this hangs the much more important question whether the writer conceives the Sea as non-existent at the time to which the narrative refers. That is certainly the impression produced by the language of v.[10]. Apart from the assumption of a radical transformation of the physical features of the region, the words *before Yahwe destroyed S. and G.* have no significance. As a mere note of time they would merely show the connexion of the story with ch. 19, and might very well be a gloss (Ols. Di.). See below, pp. 273 f.—*Ẓō'ar* is the S limit of the *Kikkār*, and, if situated at the S end of the Lake (as is most probable), would not be seen from Bethel.

---

but on insufficient grounds (cf. Hupf. *Qu.* 21 f.)—7b. יֹשֵׁב] 𝔐 ישבים.—הַפְּרִזִּי] The name is coupled with הַכְּנַעֲנִי in 34^{30}, Ju. $1^{4.5}$ (J), and often appears in enumerations of the pre-Israelite inhabitants (15^{20} etc.). If, as is probable, it be connected with פְּרָזִי (Dt. 3^{5}, 1 Sa. 6^{18}, Est. 9^{19}), פְּרָזוֹת (Ezk. 38^{11}, Zec. 2^{8}, Est. 9^{19}), it would mean 'hamlet-dwellers' as distinguished from Canaanites, occupying fortified cities (see on הַחִוִּי, 10^{17}). That the P. were remnants of a *pre*-Canaanite population is hardly to be inferred from the omission of the name in $10^{16f.}$, or from its association with the Rephaim in Jos. 17^{15}: this last notice is wanting in $𝔊^{AB}$ and is perhaps a gloss (Moore, *Jud.* 17).—9. הֲלֹא] 𝔊𝔖 וְהִנֵּה.—הַיָּמִין—הַשְּׂמֹאל] Ball suggests the pointing הֵימֵן, הַשְׂמְאֵל (infs. abs.). 𝔐 reads אם השמאלה והימינה ואם הימינה והשמאלה.—10. כֻּלָּהּ] 𝔐 כלו; $𝔊^{L}$ om.—מַשְׁקֶה] in the sense of 'watered region' only again Ezk. 45^{15} (where

like the land of Egypt] coming after *like the garden of Yahwe* (2^{10-14}; cf. Is. 51^{3}) it is an anti-climax, which might be excused (as Di. thinks) because the first comparison was pitched too high. But the last half of the v. seems greatly overloaded, and it is not improbable that both לִפְנֵי—עֲמֹרָה and כא' מ' are to be removed as glosses.—On the luxuriant fertility and abundant water-supply of the district, see *HG*, 483 f.; Buhl, 39; Seetzen, *Reisen*, i. 417.—**11a.** *Lot departed eastward*] see on 11^{2} and the footnote *infra*.—**12b**β. The immediate continuation (in J) of ^{11a}: *and moved his tent up to Sodom*] the intervening words being from P (cf. עָרֵי הַכִּכָּר instead of כ' הַיַּרְדֵּן).—**13.** This notice of the sinfulness of Sodom is another anticipation of ch. 19; but it is introduced here with great effect as showing how Lot had over-reached himself by his selfish conduct.—**14–17.** The promise of the land is now confirmed to Abram.—**14.** *Lift up thine eyes, etc.*] the contrast to Lot's self-interested glance (v.^{10}), while Abram, by his magnanimous surrender of his claims, had unconsciously chosen the good part.—**15.** It is very doubtful if the עַד עוֹלָם can be considered (with Di.) a new element of the promise as compared with 12^{7}.—**16.** *the dust of the earth*] 28^{14}.

This solemn assurance of the possession of the land ($^{14-17}$) is somewhat of a contrast to the simple promises of $12^{2.7}$; and has affinities with a series of passages which appear to represent a later phase of religious reflexion (see on ch. 15, p. 284). Other reasons are adduced for thinking that $^{14-17}$ are the work of a younger hand than the original J. (*a*) It is not the habit of J to cite divine oracles without a specification of the circumstances under which the theophany takes place (but see $12^{1ff.}$). (*b*) The conception of Abram as wandering over the land is not that of J[h], who fixes his permanent dwelling-place at Hebron. (*c*) While Bethel commands a view of the Jordan valley, it affords no

---

the text is corrupt) and Sir. 39^{23}. Should we read מָשְׁקָה?—בְּאֲכָה] see 10^{19}.—צֹעַר] 𝔖 ܨܥܢ = Tanis (צֹעַן) in Egypt (Nu. 13^{22}, Is. $19^{11.13}$ etc.), which is preferred by Ball, but is rather an error caused by the preceding מִצְרַיִם.—**11.** מִקֶּדֶם (cf. 11^{2})] 𝔊 ἀπὸ ἀνατολῶν, 𝔙 *ab oriente*. But the only possible sense here is 'eastward'; hence Sta. (*Ak. Reden*, 292) and Gu. emend to קֵדְמָה.—**11b**, in spite of its resemblance to ^{9a}β, must be assigned to P, being necessary to the completeness of that account, and because it disturbs the connexion of ^{11a} with ^{12b}β.—**16.** אֲשֶׁר]='so that' (G-K. § 166 *b*).—**17.** 𝔊 adds at end καὶ τῷ σπέρματί

wide prospect of the land as a whole. We. (*Comp.*[2] 25 f.) admits that these 'general impressions' are not such as to procure universal assent. In point of fact they are rather overstated; and Di.'s answers may satisfy those who refuse to carry critical operations further than is absolutely necessary. Nevertheless, We.'s impression is probably correct, and has commended itself to KS. Ho. Gu. al.* The vv. may be omitted not only without injury to the context, but with the obvious advantage of bringing out the reference of ^{18} to $^{12f.}$. The redactor has rightly seized the point of the story, which is that by his selfish choice Lot left Abram the sole heir of Canaan.

18. Abram moves his tent to the *terebinth*(*s*) *of Mamre*, in Hebron, and inaugurates the local sanctuary there. In the main narrative of J^h the statement was immediately followed by ch. 18; and it is possible that the theophany recorded at the beginning of that chapter is that which marked the place as holy (see on 12^7).

The site of the tree (or trees, *v.i.*) is not known. There was a Terebinth of Abraham about 15 stadia from Hebron, which was the scene of mixed heathen and Christian worship, suppressed by order of Constantine (Sozomen, *HE*, ii. 4). Josephus (*BJ*, iv. 533) mentions a very large terebinth said to have existed ἀπὸ τῆς κτίσεως μέχρι νῦν, 6 stadia from the city. In spite of the discrepancy as to distance, it is probable that these are to be identified; and that the site was the *Ḥarām Rāmet el-Ḫalīl*, 2 m. N of Hebron. The difficulty in accepting this, the oldest accessible, tradition is that the distance is inconsistent with the statement that the sanctuary was *in* Hebron. And if we suppose the ancient Hebron to have been at *er-Rāme* in the vicinity of the *Ḥarām*, this conflicts with the tradition as to the cave of

---

σου εἰς τὸν αἰῶνα,—approved by Ball.—18. אֵלֹנֵי מַמְרֵא (14^{13} 18^1)] see on 12^6. 𝔊 τὴν δρῦν τὴν Μαμβρήν. 𝔖 also reads the sing., which may be right, though 18^4 cannot be cited in support of it. In J, Mamre is said to be *in* Hebron, in P (where the tree is never mentioned) it is a name of Hebron, and in $14^{13.24}$ it becomes the name of an Amorite chief, the owner of the trees. So 𝔖 here, as shown by the addition of ܐܡܘܪܝܐ.

---

* The only point on which it is impossible to follow We. is his assumption that Hebron is the fixed residence of Abram in *all* strata of J, and that the notion of his migratory life arose from the amalgamation of E (which puts Beersheba in the place of Hebron) with J. There was probably a whole cycle of Yahwistic legends, in which he is represented as living in the Negeb (see already on $12^{9ff.}$). So far as mere literary criticism goes, there is no reason why the addition should not be prior to R^{JE}.

Machpelah, which has as good claims to be considered authentic. The present 'Oak of Abraham,' about 2 m. NW, is as old as the 16th cent. See Robinson, *BR*, i. 216; Buhl, *GP*, 160, 162; Baedeker, *Pal. and Syr.*[3] 138, 142; Dri. *DB*, iii. 224 f.; v. Gall, *CSt.* 52.

Ch. XIV.—*Abram's Victory over Four Kings.*

While Abram was at Hebron, a revolt of five petty kings in the Jordan valley against their over-lord Chedorlaomer of Elam brought from the East a great punitive expedition, in which no fewer than four powerful monarchs took part. A successful campaign—the course of which is traced in detail—ended in the complete defeat of the rebels in a pitched battle in what is now the Dead Sea basin, followed by the sack of Sodom, and the capture of Lot (1–12). Abram, with a handful of slaves, pursues the victorious allies to Dan, routs them in a night attack, and rescues the captives, including Lot (13–16). On his homeward journey he is met by Melchizedek, king of Salem, who blesses him in the name of God Most High, and to whom he pays tithes (18–20); and by the king of Sodom, whose offer of the spoil Abram rejects with proud and almost disdainful magnanimity (17. 21–24).—Such is in brief the content of this strange and perplexing chapter, in its present form and setting. It is obvious that the first half is merely introductory, and that the purpose of the whole is to illustrate the singular dignity of Abram's position among the potentates of the earth. Essentially peaceful, yet ready on the call of duty to take the field against overwhelming odds, disinterested and considerate of others in the hour of victory, reverential towards the name and representative of the true God, he moves as a 'great prince' amongst his contemporaries, combining the highest earthly success with a certain detachment and unworldliness of character.—Whether the picture be historically true or not—a question reserved for a concluding note—it is unfair to deny to it nobility of conception; and it is perhaps an exaggeration to assert that it stands in absolute and unrelieved opposition to all we elsewhere read of Abram. The story does not give the impression that Abram forfeits the character of 'Muslim and prophet' (We.) even when he assumes the rôle of a warrior.

Literary character.—Many features of the chapter show that it has had a peculiar literary history. (*a*) The *vocabulary*, though exhibiting sporadic affinities with P (רְכוּשׁ, [11. 12. 16. 21]; יְלִיד בַּיִת, [14]; נֶפֶשׁ [= 'person'], [21]) or E (האמרי, [7. 13]; בִּלְעָדַי, [24]), contains several expressions which are either unique or rare (see the footnotes): חָנִיךְ, [14] (ἅπ. λεγ.); הֵרִיק, [14]; הַפָּלִיט, [13]; אֵל עֶלְיוֹן קֹנֵה, [18-20. 22]; מִגֵּן, [20]; מָרַד, [4].*—(*b*) The numerous antiquarian *glosses* and *archaic* names, suggesting the use of an ancient document, have no parallel except in Dt. $2^{10-12. 20-23}$ $3^{9. 11. 13b. 14}$; and even these are not quite of the same character. (*c*) The *annalistic* official style, specially noticeable in the introduction, may be genuine or simulated; in either case it marks the passage sharply off from the narratives by which it is surrounded.—That the chapter as it stands cannot be assigned to any of the three sources of Gen. is now universally acknowledged, and need not be further argued here. Some writers postulate the existence of a literary kernel which may either (1) have originated in one of the schools J or E,† or (2) have passed through their hands.‡ In neither form can the theory be made at all plausible. The treatment of documentary material supposed by (1) is unexampled in Gen.; and those who suggest it have to produce some sufficient reason why a narrative of (say) E required to be so heavily glossed. As for (2), we have, to be sure, no experience of how E or J would have edited an old cuneiform document if it had fallen into their hands,—they were collectors of oral tradition, not manipulators of official records,—but we may presume that if the story would not bear telling in the vivid style that went to the hearts of the people, these writers would have left it alone. The objections to P's authorship are equally strong, the style and subject being alike foreign to the well-marked character of the Priestly narration. Ch. xiv. is therefore an isolated boulder in the stratification of the Pent., a fact which certainly invites examination of its origin, but is not in itself an evidence of high antiquity.

1–4. The revolt of the five kings.—1. The four names

---

1. בִּימֵי] 𝕲 ἐν τῇ βασιλείᾳ; 𝖁 *in illo tempore*, reading all the names in the nom. 𝕲 has the first in gen. and the rest nom.; 𝕲[A] further inserts

---

* The singularity of the passage appears to be reflected even in the translation of 𝕲, which has some unusual renderings: ἵππος for רְכוּשׁ, [11. 16. 21] (nowhere else in OT); φάραγξ for עֵמֶק, [3] (not again in Pent.: twice in Jos. and 4 t. in Book of Isa.); περάτης (ἅπαξ λεγ.) for עִבְרִי, [13],—though this might be explained by the unexpected occurrence of the gentilic in this connexion (Aq. περαΐτης).

† So Di. Kittel (*GH*, i. 124, 158 ff.), and (with reserve) Ho., all of whom think of E as the most likely source.

‡ So Wi. *GI*, ii. 26–48, who holds that the original was a cuneiform document of legendary and mythical character, which was worked over first by E and then by J (see below, p. 272).

(see below) do double duty,—as gen. after בִּימֵי and as subj. to עָשׂוּ מ'—a faulty syntax which a good writer would have avoided (*v.i.*). The suggestion that the first two names are gen. and the last two subj.,* has the advantage of putting *Kĕdorlā'omer*, the head of the expedition ([4. 5. 9. 17]), in the place of honour; but it is without warrant in the Heb. text; and besides, by excluding the first two kings from participation in the campaign (against [5. 9. 17]), it necessitates a series of changes too radical to be safely undertaken.—**2.** The group of five cities (*Pentapolis*, Wis. 10[6]) is thought to be the result of an amalgamation of originally independent traditions.

In ch. 19, only Sodom and Gomorrah are mentioned as destroyed (19[24. 28] [18[20]]; so 13[10], Is. 1[9f.], Jer. 23[14] etc.) and Zoar (19[17ff.]) as spared. Admah and Ẓeboim are named alone in Hos. 11[8], in a manner hardly consistent with the idea that they were involved in the same catastrophe as S. and G. The only passages besides this where the four are associated are 10[19] and Dt. 29[22], although 'neighbour cities' of S. and G. are referred to in Jer. 49[18] 50[40], Ezk. 16[46ff.]. If, as seems probable, there were two distinct legends, we cannot assume that in the original tradition Admah and Ẓeboim were connected with the Dead Sea (see Che. *EB*, 66 f.).—The old name of Zoar, בֶּלַע (Destruction?), appears nowhere else.

The four names in v.[1] are undoubtedly historical, although the monumental evidence is less conclusive than is often represented. (1) אַמְרָפֶל ('Αμαρφαλ) is thought to be a faulty transcription of *Ḫammurabi* (*Ammurab*[*p*]*i*), the name of the 6th king of the first Bab. dynasty, who put an end to the Elamite domination and united the whole country under his own sway (*c.* 2100 B.C.).† The final ל is now explained as a transcription of *Hammurapi-ilu*, which once occurs; and the equivalence is

---

καὶ between the second and third. The reading of the Sixtine ed. (first *two* names in gen. coupled by καὶ), which is appealed to in support of Wi.'s construction, has very little MS authority. "I have little doubt that both in H. and P. 19 (which is a rather carelessly written MS) and in 135 the reading is due to a scribe's mistake, probably arising from misreading of a contracted termination and induced by the immediately preceding βασιλέως. How it came into the Roman edition, I do not feel sure." ‡—**2.** בֶּלַע] 𝕲 Βαλλα, etc.—שִׁנְאָב] 𝕲 Σενναάρ.—שֶׁמְאֵבֶר] 𝕲 Συμοβορ, Συμορ, 𝔐 שמאבר ('name has perished'), 𝕾 ܫܡܝܒܪ.—הִיא] the first of the 11 instances of this *Kethîb* in Pent. (see on 2[12]).

---

* Wi. *GI*, ii. 27, 30; Peiser, *MVAG*, 1897, 308 ff.; approved by Gu.

† See Introd. pp. xiv f.

‡ Private communication from Mr. M'Lean.

widely recognised by Assyriologists.* It is, however, questioned by Jen.†, absolutely rejected by Bezold,‡ and pronounced 'problematical' by Mey. *GA*^{2}, I. ii. 551.—(On שִׁנְעָר, see 10^{10}.)—(2) אַרְיוֹךְ (cf. Dn. 2^{14}, Jth. 1^6), it seems, is now satisfactorily identified with *Eri-agu*, the Sumerian equivalent of *Arad-Sin*, a king of Larsa, who was succeeded by his more famous brother, Rîm-Sin, the ruler who was conquered by Ḫammurabi in the 31st year of the latter's reign (*KAT*^{3}, 16, 19). The two brothers, sons of the Elamite Kudurmabug, were first distinguished by Thureau-Dangin in 1907 (*Sumer. und Akkad. Königsinschr.* 210 f.; cf. King, *Chronicles concerning early Bab. Kings*, vol. i. 68^2; Mey. *GA*^{2}, I. ii. p. 550 f.). Formerly the two names and persons were confused; and Schrader's attempt to identify Rîm-Sin with Arioch,§ though accepted by many, was reasonably contested by the more cautious Assyriologists, *e.g.* Jen. (*ZDMG*, 1896, 247 ff.), Bezold (*op. cit.* 27, 56), and Zimmern (*KAT*^{3}, 367). The objections do not hold against the equation *Arioch*=*Eriagu*=*Arad-Sin*, provided Arad-Sin be kept distinct from Rîm-Sin. The discovery by Pinches‖ in 1892 of the name *Eri-*[*E*]*aku* or *Eri-Ekua* stands on a somewhat different footing. The tablets on which these names occur are admittedly late (not earlier than the 4th cent. B.C.); the identity of the names with Eri-Aku is called in question by King;¶ who further points out that this Eri-Ekua is not styled a king, that there is nothing to connect him with Larsa, and that consequently we have no reason to suppose him the same as either of the well-known contemporaries of Ḫammurabi. The real significance of the discovery lies in the coincidence that on these same late fragments (and nowhere else) the two remaining names of the v. are *supposed* to occur.—(3) כְּדָרְלָעֹמֶר (Χοδολλογομορ) unquestionably stands for *Kudur-lagamar*, a genuine Elamite proper name, containing the name of a known Elamite divinity *Lagamar* (*KAT*^{3}, 485), preceded by a word which appears as a component of theophorous Elamite names (*Kudur-mabug*, *Kudur-Nanḫundi*, etc.). It is extremely doubtful, however, if the actual name has yet been found outside of this chapter. The "sensational" announcement of Scheil (1896), that he had read it (*Ku-dur-nu-uḫ-ga-mar*) in a letter of Ḫammurabi to Sinid-innam, king of Larsa, has been disposed of by the brilliant refutation of King (*op. cit.* xxv–xxxix. Cf. also Del. *BA*, iv. 90). There remains the prior discovery of the Pinches fragments, on which there is mentioned thrice a king of Elam whose name, it was thought, might be read *Kudur-laḫ-mal* or *Kudur-laḫ-gu-mal.*** The first element (Kudur)

* See Schr. *SBBA*, 1887, xxxi. 600 ff.; Ungnad, *ZA*, xxii. 8.

† *ZDMG*, 1896, 252.

‡ *Die bab.-ass. Keilinschriften*, etc., 1904, pp. 26, 54.

§ *SBBA*, 1894, xv. 279 ff.

‖ See his *OT in the light*, etc., 223 ff.; cf. Homm. *AHT*, 181 ff.; and Sayce's amended trans. in *PSBA*, 1906, 193 ff., 241 ff.; 1907, 7 ff.

¶ *Letters and Inscrs. of Ḫammurabi*, i. p. liii. Jen., Peiser, and Bezold also pronounce against the identification.

** This reading is questioned by King; see liv–lvi, or the extract in Dri. *Gen.*, *Addenda* on p. 157 *n.* Sayce now (*l.c.* p. 194 ff.) proposes to

is no doubt right, but the second is very widely questioned by Assyriologists.* There is, moreover, nothing to show that the king in question, whatever his name, belonged to the age of Ḫammurabi.† (4) תִּדְעָל (𝔊^{EL} Θαργαλ, 𝔖 ܬܕܥܠ) was identified by Pinches with a "*Tu-ud-ḫul-a*, son of *Gaz*. . . .," who is named once on the tablets already spoken of (see Schr. *SBBA*, 1895, xli. 961 ff.). The resemblance to Tid'al is very close, and is naturally convincing to those who find 'Ariok and Kedorla'omer in the same document; there is, however, no indication that *Tudḫula* was a king, or that he was contemporary with Ḫammurabi and Rîm-Sin (King, *op. cit.*).—גּוֹיִם can hardly be the usual word for 'nations' (𝔊𝔙𝔗), either as an indefinite expression (Tu.) or as a "verschämtes *et cetera*" (Ho.). We seem to require a proper name (𝔖 has ܓܠܝܐ); and many accept the suggestion of Rawlinson, that *Guti* (a people N of the Upper Zab) should be read. Peiser (309) thinks that מֶלֶךְ גּוֹיִם is an attempt to render the common Babylonian title *šar kiššati*.

The royal names in v.[2] are of a different character from those of v.[1]. Several circumstances suggest that they are fictitious. Jewish exegesis gives a sinister interpretation to all four (𝔗^J, *Ber. R.* § 42, Ra.); and even modern scholars like Tu. and Nö. recognise in the first two a play on the words רַע (evil) and רֶשַׁע (wickedness). And can it be accidental that they fall into two alliterative pairs, or that each king's name contains exactly as many letters as that of his city? On the other side, it may be urged (*a*) that the textual tradition is too uncertain to justify any conclusions based on the Heb. (see the footnote); (*b*) the namelessness of the fifth king shows that the writer must have had traditional authority for the other four; and (*c*) *Sanibu* occurs as the name of an Ammonite king in an inscr. of Tiglath-pileser IV. (Del. *Par.* 294, *KIB*, ii. 21). These considerations do not remove the impression of artificiality which the list produces. Since the names are not repeated in v.[8], it is quite possible they are late insertions in the text, and, of course (on that view), unhistorical.—בֶּלַע is elsewhere a royal name (36[32]).

---

read *Kudur-lakhkha-mal*; but the reading appears to be purely conjectural; and, unless it should be corroborated, nothing can be built upon it.

* *e.g.* by King, Zimmern (*KAT*[3], 486[1]), Peiser (who reads it *Kudur-tur-bit*, *l.c.* 310), Jen., Bezold, al.

† There is no doubt some difficulty in finding room for a king Kudur-lagamar alongside of Kudur-mabug (who, if not actually king of Elam, was certainly the over-lord of Arad-Sin and Rîm-Sin) in the time of Ḫammurabi; but in our ignorance of the situation that difficulty must not be pressed. It has, however, induced Langdon (Dri., *Gen*[7], *Add.* xxxii.) to revive a conjecture of G. Smith, that Kudur-mabug and the Kudur-lagamar of this chapter are one and the same person. It does not appear that any fresh *facts* have come to light to make the guess more convincing than it was when first propounded.

3. *all these*] not the kings from the East (Di. Dri.), but (see v.[4]) those of the Pentapolis. That there should be any doubt on the point is an indication of the weak style of the chapter. What exactly the v. means to say is not clear. The most probable sense is that the five cities *formed a league*] of the Vale of Siddim, and therefore acted in concert. This is more natural than to suppose the statement a premature mention of the preparations for battle in v.[8].—*the Vale of Siddîm*] The name is peculiar to this narrative, and its meaning is unknown (*v.i.*). The writer manifestly shares the belief (13^{10}) that what is now the Dead Sea was once dry land (see p. 273 f. below).—*The Sea of Salt*] one of the OT names for the Dead Sea (Nu. 34^3, Dt. 3^{17}, Jos. 3^{16} 15^5 etc.): see *PEFS*, 1904, 64. Wi.'s attempt to identify it with Lake Ḥuleh is something of a *tour de force* (*GI*, ii. 36 f.; cf. 108 f.).—4. *they rebelled*] by refusal of tribute (2 Ki. 18^7 $24^{1.20}$ etc.). An Elamite dominion over Palestine in the earlier part of Ḫammurabi's reign is perfectly credible in the light of the monumental evidence (p. 272). But the importance attributed in this connexion to the petty kings of the Pentapolis is one of the features which excite suspicion of the historicity of the narrative. To say that this is due to the writer's interest in Lot and Sodom is to concede that his conception of the situation is determined by other influences than authentic historical information.

5–7. The preliminary campaign.—One of the sur-

---

3. חברו אל־] apparently a pregnant constr. (G–K. § 119 *ee*)='came as confederates to'; but this is rather harsh. אֶל after חבר naturally refers to that to which one is joined (Ex. 26^3; of a person, Sir. 12^{14}): that being impossible here, חבר must be understood absolutely as Ju. 20^{11} (*v.* Moore or Bu. *ad loc.*) and the אל may have some vague local reference: 'all these had formed a confederacy at (?) the V. of S.'—עֵמֶק הַשִּׂדִּים] 𝔊 τὴν φάραγγα τὴν ἁλυκήν, apparently a conjecture from the context, 𝔙 *vallem silvestrem.* 𝔗^O has חקליא (from שָׂדֶה), 𝔗^J פרדיסיא; 𝔖 'v. of the Sodomites': on the renderings of Aq. and Θ. see Field's Note, p. 30 f. It is evident the Vns. did not understand the word. Nöldeke (*Unters.* 160^8), Renan (*Hist.* i. 116), We. (*Gesch.*[5] 105), Je. (*ATLO*[2], 351), al. think the true form is שֵׁדִים: 'valley of demons.'—4. וּשְׁלֹשׁ] Acc. of time (G–K. § 118 *i*); but 𝔐 ובשלש is better.—מרד] rare in Hex. (Nu 14^9, Jos. $22^{16.18.19.29}$ [P]); and mostly late.—5. אֶת־רְפָאִים] The art. should be supplied, with 𝔐. 𝔊 τοὺς γίγαντας; so 𝔖𝔗^{OJ}.—בְּעַשְׁתְּרֹת ק׳]

prising things in the narrative is the circuitous route by which the Eastern kings march against the rebels. We may assume that they had followed the usual track by Carchemish and Damascus: thence they advanced southwards on the E of the Jordan; but then, instead of attacking the Pentapolis, they pass it on their right, proceeding southward to the head of the Gulf of Aḳaba. Then they turn NW to Ḳadesh, thence NE to the Dead Sea depression; and only at the end of this long and difficult journey do they join issue with their enemies in the vale of Siddim.

In explanation, it has been suggested that the real object of the expedition was to secure command of the caravan routes in W Arabia, especially that leading through the Arabah from Syria to the Red Sea (see Tu. 257 ff.). It must be remembered, however, that this is the account, not of the first assertion of Elamite supremacy over these regions, but of the suppression of a revolt of not more than a few months' standing: hence it would be necessary to assume that all the peoples named were implicated in the rebellion. This is to go behind the plain meaning of the Heb. narrator; and the verisimilitude of the description is certainly not enhanced by Hommel's wholly improbable speculation that the Pentapolis was the centre of an empire embracing the whole region E of the Jordan and the land of Edom (*AHT*, 149). If there were any truth in theories of this kind, we should still have to conclude that the writer, for the sake of literary effect, had given a fictitious importance to the part played by the cities of the Jordan valley, and had so arranged the incidents as to make their defeat seem the climax of the campaign. (See Nöldeke, 163 f.)

The general course of the campaign can be traced with sufficient

---

The reading of the Sixtine and Aldine edd. of 𝔊, Ἀσταρωθ καὶ Καρναιν, which even Di. adduces in favour of a distinction between the two cities, has, amongst the MSS used by the Cambridge editors, the support of only one late cursive, which Nestle maintains was copied from the Aldine ed. It is doubtless a conflation of Καρναιν and the και Ναιν (? Καιναιν) of 𝔊^E, al.^ (Nestle, *ZDPV*, xv. 256; cf. Moore, *JBL*, xvi. 155 f.).—הַזּוּזִים] 𝔊 ἔθνη ἰσχυρά=עַזּוּזִים: so 𝔖𝔗^OJ. Σ. has Ζοιζομμειν=וַמְזֻמִּים.—בְּהָם] 𝔊𝔙𝔖 read בְּהֶם (ἅμα αὐτοῖς, etc.). Some MSS of 𝔪 have בחם, which Jerome expressly says is the real reading of the Heb. text.—6. בְּהַרְרָם] 𝔪𝔊𝔖𝔙 בְּהַרְרֵי. Duplication of ר is rare and doubtful (Ps. 30^8, Jer. 17^3) in sing. of this word, but common in const. pl. Buhl strikes out שֵׂעִיר as an explanatory gloss, retaining בְּהַרְרָם.—אֵיל פָּארָן] 𝔊𝔖 render 'terebinth of Paran,' and so virtually 𝔙𝔗^OJ, which have 'plain' (see on 12^6). If the ordinary theory, as given above, be correct, אֵיל is used collectively in the sense of 'great tree' (here 'palms').—7. For קָדֵשׁ, 𝔖𝔗^OJ (also Saadya) have רקם, apparently identifying it with Petra: see Tuch's Note, p. 271 f.—שְׂדֵה] 𝔊𝔖 שָׂרֵי, 'princes.'

certainty **from the** geographical names of $^{5-7}$; although it does not appear quite clearly whether these are conceived as the centres of the various nationalities or the battlefields in which they were defeated.—עַשְׁתְּרוֹת קַרְנַיִם ('Astarte of the two horns':* Eus. *Præp. Ev.* i. 10; or 'A. of the two-peaked mountain'†) occurs as a compound name only here. A city '*Aštārôth* in Bashan, the capital of Og's kingdom, is mentioned in Dt. 1^{4}, Jos. 9^{10} 12^{4} $13^{12.31}$, 1 Ch. 6^{56} [=בְּעֶשְׁתְּרָה, Jos. 21^{27}]. *Ḳarnaim* is named (according to a probable emendation) in Am. 6^{13}, and in 1 Mac. $5^{26.43ff.}$, 2 Mac. 12^{21}. It is uncertain whether these are two names for one place, or two adjacent places of which one was named after the other ('Aštārôth of [*i.e.* near] Ḳarnaim); and the confusing statements of the *OS* ($84^{5ff.}$ 86^{32} 108^{17} 209^{61} 268^{98}) throw little light on the question. The various sites that have been suggested—Sheikh Sa'd, Tell 'Aštarah, Tell el-'Aš'ari, and El-Muzêrîb—lie near the great road from Damascus to Mecca, about 20 m. E of the Lake of Tiberias (see Buhl, *GAP*, 248 ff.; Dri. *DB*, i. 166 f.; GASm. in *EB*, 335 f.). Wetzstein's identification with Boẓrah (regarded as a corruption of *Bostra*, and this of בְּעֶשְׁתְּרָה, Jos. 21^{27}), the capital of the Ḥaurân, has been shown by Nö. (*ZDMG*, xxix. 431^{1}) to be philologically untenable.—Of a place הָם nothing is known. It is a natural conjecture (Tu. al.) that it is the archaic name of *Rabbath*, the capital of '*Ammon*; and Sayce (*HCM*, 160 f.) thinks it must be explained as a retranscription from a cuneiform source of the word עַמּוֹן. On the text *v.i.*—שָׁוֵה קִרְיָתַיִם is doubtless the Moabite or Reubenite city 'קִר, mentioned in Jer. 48^{23}, Ezk. 25^{9}, Nu. 32^{37}, Jos. 13^{19} (*OS*, Καριαθαειμ, Καριαθα), the modern *Ḳuraiyāt*, E of the Dead Sea, a little S of the Wādī Zerka Ma'īn. שָׁוֵה (only here and v.^{17}) is supposed to mean 'plain' (Syr. ܦܩܥܬܐ); but that is somewhat problematical.—On the phrase הַרְרָם שֵׂעִיר, see the footnote. While שֵׂעִיר alone may include the plateau to the W of the Arabah, the commoner הַר שֵׂעִיר appears to be restricted to the mountainous region E of that gorge, now called *eš-Šera'* (see Buhl, *Gesch. d. Edomiter*, 28 ff.).—אֵיל פָּארָן (*v.i.*) is usually identified with אֵילַת (Dt. 2^{8}, 2 Ki. 14^{22} 16^{6}) or אֵילוֹת (1 Ki. 9^{26}, 2 Ki. 16^{6}), at the head of the E arm of the Red Sea, which is supposed to derive its name from the groves of date-palms for which it was and is famous (see esp. Tu. 264 f.). The grounds of the identification seem slender; and the evidence does not carry us further than Tu.'s earlier view (251), that some oasis in the N of the desert is meant (see Che. *EB*, 3584).‡ The 'wilderness' is the often mentioned 'Wilderness of Paran' (21^{21}, Nu. 10^{12} etc.), *i.e.* the desolate plateau of *et-Tīh*, stretching from the Arabah to the isthmus of Suez. There is obviously nothing in that definition to support the theory that '*Êl-Pârān* is the original name of the later *Elath*.—קָדֵשׁ (16^{14} 20^{1} etc.), or ק' בַּרְנֵעַ (Nu. 34^{4}, Dt. $1^{2.19}$ 2^{14}). The controversy as to the

---

* See Müller, *AE*, 313; Macalister, *PEFS*, 1904, 15.

† Moore, *JBL*, xvi. 156 f.

‡ Trumbull places it at the oasis of *Ḳala'at Naḫl*, in the middle of *et-Tīh*, on the Ḥağğ route halfway between 'Aḳaba and Suez (*Kadesh-Barnea*, p. 37).

situation of this important place has been practically settled since the appearance of Trumbull's *Kadesh-Barnea* in 1884 (see Guthe, *ZDPV*, viii. 183 ff.). It is the spring now known as *'Ain Ḳadîs*, at the head of the Wādī of the same name, "northward of the desert proper," and about 50 m. S of Beersheba (see the description by Trumbull, *op. cit.* 272–275). The distance in a straight line from Elath would be about 80 m., with a difficult ascent of 1500 ft. The alternative name עֵין מִשְׁפָּט ('Well of Judgement') is found only here. Since קָדֵשׁ means 'holy' and מִשְׁפָּט 'judicial decision,' it is a plausible conjecture of Rob. Sm. that the name refers to an ordeal involving the use of 'holy water' (Nu. 5^{17}) from the sacred well (*RS*², 181). The sanctuary at Kadesh seems to have occupied a prominent place in the earliest Exodus tradition (We. *Prol.*⁶ 341 ff.); but there is no reason why the institution just alluded to should not be of much greater antiquity than the Mosaic age.—חַצְצֹן תָּמָר is, according to 2 Ch. 20^2, *'Ēn-gĕdî* (*'Ain Ğidī*), about the middle of the W shore of the Dead Sea. A more unsuitable approach for an army to any part of the Dead Sea basin than the precipitous descent of nearly 2000 feet at this point, could hardly be imagined: see Robinson, *BR*, i. 503. It is not actually said that the army made the descent there: it might again have made a detour and reached its goal by a more practicable route. But certainly the conditions of this narrative would be better satisfied by *Kurnub*, on the road from Hebron to Elath, about 20 m. WSW of the S end of the Dead Sea. The identification, however, requires three steps, all of which involve uncertainties: (1) that ח' תָּמָר = the תָּמָר of Ezk. 47^{19} 48^{28}; (2) that this is the *Thamara* of *OS* (85^3, 210^{86}), the Θαμαρω of Ptol. xvi. 8; and (3) that the ruins of this are found at *Kurnub*. Cf. *EB*, 4890; Buhl, *GP*, 184.

The six peoples named in vv.$^{5-7}$ are the primitive races which, according to Heb. tradition, formerly occupied the regions traversed by Chedorlaomer. (1) The רְפָאִים are spoken of as a giant race dwelling partly on the W (15^{20}, Jos. 17^{15}, 2 Sa. 21^{16}, Is. 17^5), partly on the E, of the Jordan, especially in Bashan, where Og reigned as the last of the Rephaim (Dt. 3^{11}, Jos. 12^4 etc.).—(2) The זוּזִים, only mentioned here, are probably the same as the Zamzummîm of Dt. 2^{20}, the aborigines of the Ammonite country. The equivalence of the two forms is considered by Sayce (*ZA*, iv. 393) and others to be explicable only by the Babylonian confusion of *m* and *w*, and thus a proof that the narrative came ultimately from a cuneiform source.—(3) הָאֵימִים] a kind of Rephaim, aborigines of Moab (Dt. $2^{10f.}$).—(4) הַחֹרִי] the race extirpated by the Edomites ($36^{20ff.}$, Dt. $2^{12.\,22}$). The name has usually been understood to mean 'troglodytes' (see Dri. *Deut.* 38); but this is questioned by Jen. (*ZA*, x. 332 f., 346 f.) and Homm. (*AHT*, 264^2), who identify the word with *Ḫaru*, the Eg. name for SW Palestine.*—(5) הָעֲמָלֵקִי] the Amalekite territory (שְׂדֵה), was in the Negeb, extending towards Egypt (Nu. 13^{29} $14^{43.\,45}$, 1 Sa. 27^8). In ancient tradition, Amalek was 'the firstling of peoples' (Nu. 24^{20}), although, according to Gn. 36^{12} its ancestor was a grandson of Esau.—(6) הָאֱמֹרִי] see on 10^{16}; and cf. Dt. 1^{44}, Ju. 1^{36}.—

* Cf. Müller, *AE*, 136 f., 148 ff.

While there can be no question of the absolute historicity of the last three names, the first three undoubtedly provoke speculation. Rephâîm is the name for *shades* or *ghosts*; 'Emîm probably means '*terrible ones*'; and Zamzummîm (if this be the same word as Zûzîm), 'murmurers.' Schwally (*Leben nach d. Tode*, 64 f., and more fully *ZATW*, xviii. 127 ff.) has given reasons to show that all three names originally denoted spirits of the dead, and afterwards came to be applied to an imaginary race of *extinct giants*, the supposed original inhabitants of the country (see also Rob. Sm. in Dri. *Deut.* 40). The tradition with regard to the Rephaim is too persistent to make this ingenious hypothesis altogether easy of acceptance. It is unfortunate that on a matter bearing so closely on the historicity of Gn. 14 the evidence is not more decisive.

8–12. The final battle, and capture of Lot.—**9.** *four kings against the five*] That the four Eastern kings should have been all present in person (which is the obvious meaning of the narrator) is improbable enough; that they should count heads with the petty kinglets of the Pentapolis is an unreal and misleading estimate of the opposing forces, due to a desire to magnify Abram's subsequent achievement.—**10.** The vale of Siddim was at that time *wells upon wells of bitumen*] The notice is a proof of intelligent popular reasoning rather than of authentic information regarding actual facts. The Dead Sea was noted in antiquity for the production of bitumen, masses of which were found floating on the surface (Strabo, XVI. ii. 42; Diod. ii. 48, xix. 98; Pliny, vii. 65), as, indeed, they still are after earthquakes, but "only in the southern part of the sea" (Robinson, *BR*, i. 518, ii. 189, 191). It was a natural inference that the bottom of the sea was covered with asphalt wells, like those of Hit in Babylonia. Seetzen (i. 417) says that the bitumen oozes from rocks round the sea, "and that (*und zwar*) under the surface of the water, as swimmers have felt and seen"; and Strabo says it rose in bubbles like boiling water from the middle of the deepest part.—**11, 12.** Sodom and Gomorrah are sacked, and Lot is taken captive. The

---

10. בֶּאֱרֹת בֶּאֱרֹת] On the nominal appos. and duplication, see Dav. § 29, *R.* 8; G-K. § 123 *e* (cf. § 130 *e*). 𝔊^L has the word but once.—וַעֲמֹרָה] better as 𝔐𝔊 'וּמֶלֶךְ ע. הֶרָה] On the peculiar ֶ, see G-K. §§ 27 *q*, 90 *i*.—**11.** רְכֻשׁ] 𝔊 ἵππον (*i.e.* רֶכֶשׁ); the confusion appears in [16. 21], but nowhere else in OT.—**12.** בֶּן־אֲחִי אַבְרָם] 𝔊 inserts the words immediately after לוֹט,—an indication that they have been introduced from the margin. It is to be

account leaves much to be supplied by the imagination. The repetition of וַיִּקְחוּ and וַיֵּלֵכוּ in two consecutive sentences is a mark of inferior style; but the phrase בֶּן־אֲחִי אַבְרָם, which anticipates the introduction of Abram in v.[13], is probably a gloss (*v.i.*).

13–16. Abram's pursuit and victory.—The homeward march of the victorious army must have taken it very near Hebron,—Engedi itself is only about 17 m. off,—but Abram had 'let the legions thunder past,' until the intelligence reached him of his nephew's danger.—**13.** *Abram the Hebrew*] is obviously meant as the first introduction of Abram in this narrative. The epithet is not *necessarily* an anachronism, if we accept the view that the Ḫabiri of the Tel Amarna period were the nomadic ancestors of the Israelites (see on 10[21]); though it is difficult to believe that there were Ḫabiri in Palestine more than 600 years earlier, in the time of Ḫammurabi (against Sellin, *NKZ*, xvi. 936; cf. Paton, *Syria and Pal.* 39 ff.). That, however, is the only sense in which Abram could be naturally described as a Hebrew in a contemporary document; and the probability is that the term is used by an anachronistic extension of the later distinction between Israelites and foreigners.—*Mamrē' the Amorite*] see on 13[18]. In J (whose phraseology is here followed) מַמְרֵא is the name of the sacred tree or grove; in P it is a synonym of Hebron; here it is the personal name of the owner of the grove. In like manner *'Eškōl* is a personal name derived from the valley of Eshcol ('grape-cluster,' Nu. 13[23f.]); and *'Anēr* may have a similar origin. The first two, at all events, are "*heroes eponymi* of the most unequivocal character" (Nö. *Unters.* 166),—a misconception of which no contemporary would have been capable.*—

---

noted also that Lot is elsewhere called simply the 'brother' of Abram ([14. 16]).—The last clause is awkwardly placed; but considering the style of the chapter, we are not justified in treating it as an interpolation.

13. הַפָּלִיט] Ezk. 24[26] 33[21] (cf. הַמַּגִּיד, 2 Sa. 15[13]). For the idiom, see G-K. § 126 *r.*—הָעִבְרִי] 𝔊 τῷ περάτῃ (only here), Aq. τῷ περαΐτῃ.—עָנֵר] 𝔐

---

* Di.'s remark (p. 235), that "it makes no difference whether Mamre or the (lord) of Mamre helped Abram," is hard to understand. If

the confederates of Abram (𝔊 συνωμόται)] The expression בַּעֲלֵי בְרִית does not recur; cf. בַּעֲלֵי שְׁבוּעָה, Neh. 6^{18}. Kraetzschmar's view (*Bundesvorstg.* 23 f.), that it denotes the relation of patrons to client, is inherently improbable. That these men joined Abram in his pursuit is not stated, but is presupposed in v.[24],—another example of the writer's laxity in narration.—**14.** As soon as Abram learns the fate of his *brother* (*i.e.* 'relative'), he *called up his trained men* (?: on וַיָּרֶק and חֲנִיכָיו, *v.i.*) and gave chase.—*three hundred and eighteen*] The number cannot be an arbitrary invention, and is not likely to be historical. It is commonly explained as a piece of Jewish *Gematria*, 318 being the numerical value of the letters of אליעזר (15^2) (*Ber. R.* § 43: see Nestle, *ET*, xvii. 44 f. [cf. 139 f.]). A *modern* Gematria finds in it the number of the days of the moon's visibility during the lunar year (Wi. *GI*, ii. 27).—*to Dan*] Now Tell el-Ḳāḍi, at the foot of Hermon.

ענרם, 𝔊 Αὐναν.—**14.** וַיָּרֶק] Lit. 'emptied out,' used of the unsheathing of a sword (Ex. 15^9, Lv. 26^{33}, Ezk. $5^{2.12}$ etc.), but never with pers. obj. as here. Tu. cites the Ar. *ğarrada*, which means both 'unsheath a sword' and 'detach a company from an army' (see Lane); but this is no real analogy. 𝔐 has וַיָּדֶק = 'scrutinize' (Aram.). 𝔊 ἠρίθμησεν (so 𝔙) and 𝔗ᴼ זריז ('equip': so 𝔖 and 𝔗ᴶ) settle nothing, as they may be conjectural. Wi. (*AOF*, i. 102^2) derives from Ass. *diḳu* = 'call up troops'; so Sellin, 937. Ball changes to וַיִּפְקֹד.—חֲנִיכָיו] ἅπ. λεγ., 𝔊 τοὺς ἰδίους, 𝔙 *expeditos*, 𝔖𝔗ᴼ 'young men.' The √ חנך suggests the meaning 'initiated' (see on 4^{17}), hence 'trained,' 'experienced,' etc. Sellin (937) compares the word *ḫanakuka* = 'thy men,' found in one of the Ta'annek tablets. If it comes direct from the ceremony of rubbing the palate of a new-born child (see p. 116), it may have nothing to do with war, but denote simply those belonging to the household, the precise equivalent of יְלִדֵי בַיִת. The latter phrase is found only in P ($17^{12f.\,23.\,27}$, Lv. 22^{11})

Mamre and Eshcol were really names of places, and the writer took them for names of individual men, the fact has the most important bearing on the question of the historicity of the record. The alternative theory, that the names were originally those of persons, and were afterwards transferred to the places owned or inhabited by them, will hardly bear examination. 'Grape-cluster' is a suitable name for a valley, but not for a man. And does any one suppose that J would have recorded Abram's settlement at Hebron in the terms of 13^{18}, if he had been aware that Mamre was an individual living at the time? Yet the Yahwist's historical knowledge is far less open to suspicion than that of the writer of ch. 14.

This name originated in the period of the Judges (Jos. 19^{47}, Ju. 18^{29}); and it is singular that such a prolepsis should occur in a document elsewhere so careful of the appearance of antiquity.—**15.** *He divided himself*] *i.e.* (as usually understood) into three bands,—the favourite tactical manœuvre in Hebrew warfare (Ju. 7^{16}, 1 Sa. 11^{11} 13^{17}, Jb. 1^{17}, 1 Mac. 5^{33}): but see the footnote.—*smote them, and pursued them as far as Hobah*] Hobah (cf. Jth. 15^{5}) has been identified by Wetzstein with *Hoba*, *c.* 20 hours' journey N of Damascus. Sellin (934) takes it to be the *Ubi* of the TA Tablets, the district in which Damascus was situated (*KIB*, v. 139, 63; 146, 12). The pursuit must in any case have been a long one, since Damascus itself is about 15 hours from Dan. It is idle to pretend that Abram's victory was merely a surprise attack on the rearguard, and the recovery of part of the booty. A pursuit carried so far implies the rout of the main body of the enemy.

17, 18–20. Abram and Melkiẓedeḳ.—"The scene between Abram and Melkizedeḳ is not without poetic charm: the two ideals (*Grösse*) which were afterwards to be so intimately united, the holy people and the holy city, are here brought together for the first time: here for the first time Israel receives blessing from its sanctuary" (Gu. 253). **17.** The scene of the meeting is עֵמֶק שָׁוֵה, interpreted as *the king's vale*. A place of this name is mentioned in 2 Sa. 18^{18} as the site of Absalom's pillar, which, according to Josephus (*Ant.* vii. 243), was two stadia from Jerusalem. The situation harmonises with the common view that Šalem is Jerusalem (see below); and other information does not exist.—**18.** *Melkîẓedeḳ, king of Šālēm, etc.*] The primitive

---

and Jer. 2^{14}.—**15.** וַיֵּחָלֵק] (cf. 1 Ki. 16^{21}). The sense given above is not altogether natural. Ball emends וַיִּרְדְּפֵם. Wi. (*GI*, ii. 27^{2}) suggests a precarious Ass. etymology, pointing as Piel, and rendering 'and he fell upon them by night': so Sellin.—מִשְּׂמֹאל] Lit. 'on the left.' The sense 'north' is rare: Jos. 19^{27} (P), Ezk. 16^{46}, Jb. 23^{9}.

17. שָׁוֵה (without art.) must apparently be a different word from that in v.[5]. Hommel and Wi. emend שָׂרֵי (*šarrē*, the Ass. word for 'king').—**18.** מַלְכִּי־צֶדֶק] usually explained as 'King of Righteousness' (Heb. 7^{2}), with *î* as old gen. ending retained by the annexion; but more probably = 'My king is Ẓidḳ,' Ẓidḳ being the name of a S

combination of the kingly and priestly offices has been abundantly illustrated by Frazer from many quarters.* The existence of such priest-kings in Canaan in very early times is perfectly credible, though not historically attested (comp. the *patesis* of Babylonia). *Šālēm* is usually understood to be an archaic name for Jerusalem (Jos. *Ant.* i. 180; 𝕿[OJ], Jer. [*Qu.*], IEz. al.), as in Ps. 76[3], the only other place where it occurs. The chief argument in favour of this view is the typical significance attached to Melkiẓedeḳ in Ps. 110[4], which is hardly intelligible except on the supposition that he was in a sense the ideal ancestor of the dynasty or hierarchy of Jerusalem.

Whether the name was actually in use in ancient times, we do not know. The Tel Amarna Tablets have certainly proved that the name *Uru-Salim* is of much greater antiquity than might have been gathered from the biblical statements (Ju. 19[10], 1 Ch. 11[4]); but the shortened form *Salem* is as yet unattested. It has been suggested that the cuneiform *uru* was misread as the determinative for 'city' (see Sellin, 941).—The identifications with other places of the name which have been discovered—*e.g.* the Salim 8 R. m. from Scythopolis (where, according to Je. [*Ep. ad Evagr.*], the ruins of Melkiẓedeḳ's palace were to be seen)—have no claim to acceptance.

On the name אֵל עֶלְיוֹן (*God Most High*), see below, p. 270 f. —***bread and wine***] comp. 'food and drink' (*akalî šikarî*) provided for an army, etc., in the TA Tablets: *KIB*, 50[22] 207[16] 209[12f.] 242[16] (Sellin, 938).—**19, 20.** The blessing of

---

Arabian and Phœnician deity (Baudissin, *Stud.* i. 15; Baethgen, *Beitr.* 128). That Ẓedeḳ was an ancient name for Jerusalem (see Is. 1[21. 26], Jer. 31[23] 50[7], Ps. 118[19]) there is no reason to believe.—**19.** קֹנֵה has two senses in the OT (if, indeed, there be not two distinct roots. see G-B.[14] *s.v.*): (*a*) 'create' or 'produce' (Ps. 139[13], Pr. 8[22], Dt. 32[6] [? Gn. 4[1]]); (*b*) 'purchase' or 'acquire by purchase' (frequent). The idea of bare possession apart from purchase is hardly represented (? Is. 1[3]); and since the suggestion of purchase is here inadmissible, the sense 'create' must be accepted. That this meaning can be established only by late examples is certainly no objection so far as the present passage is concerned: see on 4[1].—**20.** After וּבֵרְכוּ, 𝕲[L] ins.

---

* *Studies in the Kingship*, 29 ff. "The classical evidence points to the conclusion that in prehistoric ages, before the rise of the republican form of government, the various tribes or cities were ruled by kings, who discharged priestly duties and probably enjoyed a sacred character as descendants of deities" (p. 31).

Melkiẓedeḳ is poetic in form and partly in language; but in meaning it is a liturgical formula rather than a 'blessing' in the proper sense. It lacks entirely the prophetic interpretation of concrete experiences which is the note of the antique blessing and curse (cf. $3^{14ff.}$ $4^{11f.}$ $9^{25ff.}$ $27^{27ff.\ 39f.}$).—*Creator of heaven and earth*] so 𝔊𝔙. There is no reason to tone down the idea to that of mere *possession* ($𝔗^{O}$, al.); *v. infra.*—By payment of the tithe, Abram acknowledges the legitimacy of Melkiẓedeḳ's priesthood (Heb. 7^{4}), and the religious bond of a common monotheism uniting them; at the same time the action was probably regarded as a precedent for the payment of tithes to the Jerusalem sanctuary for all time coming (so already in *Jub.* xiii. 25–27: comp. Gn. 28^{22}).

The excision of the Melkiẓedeḳ episode (see Wi. *GI*, ii. 29), which seems to break the connexion of v.[21] with v.[17], is a temptingly facile operation; but it is doubtful if it be justified. The designation of Yahwe as 'God Most High' in the mouth of Abram (v.[22]) is unintelligible apart from [18f.]. It may rather have been the writer's object to bring the three actors on one stage together in order to illustrate Abram's contrasted attitude to the sacred (Melkiẓedeḳ) and the secular (king of Sodom) authority.—Hommel's ingenious and confident solution (*AHT*, 158 ff.), which gets rid of the king of Sodom altogether and resolves [17-24] wholly into an interview between Abram and Melkiẓedeḳ, is an extremely arbitrary piece of criticism. Sellin's view (p. 939 f.), that vv.[18-20] are original and [17. 21-24] are 'Israelitische Wucherung,' is simpler and more plausible; but it has no more justification than any of the numerous other expedients which are necessary to save the essential historicity of the narrative.

The mystery which invests the figure of Melkiẓedeḳ has given rise to a great deal of speculation both in ancient and modern times. The Jewish idea that he was the patriarch Shem ($𝔗^{J}$, Talm. al.) is thought to be a reaction against mystical interpretations prevalent in the school of Alexandria (where Philo identified him with the Logos), which, through Heb. $7^{1ff.}$, exercised a certain influence on Christian theology (see Jerome, *Ep. ad Evagrium*; cf. *JE*, viii. 450). From a critical point of view the question of interest is whether M. belongs to the sphere of ancient tradition or is a fictitious personage, created to represent the claims of the post-Exilic priesthood in Jerusalem (Well. *Comp.*[2] 312). In opposition to the latter view, Gu. rightly points out that Judaism is not likely to have invented as the prototype

---

יהוה.—[מִגֵּן] only Hos. 11^{8}, Is. 64^{6} (𝔊, etc.), Pr. 4^{9}. The etymology is uncertain, but the view that it is a denom. fr. מָגֵן, 'shield' (√ גנן, BDB) is hardly correct (see Barth. *ES*, 4).

of the High Priesthood a Canaanitish priest-king, and that all possible pretensions of the Jerusalem hierarchy were covered by the figure of Aaron (253). It is more probable that M. is, if not a historical figure, at least a traditional figure of great antiquity, on whom the monarchy and hierarchy of Jerusalem based their dynastic and priestly rights.* To the writer of Ps. 110, M. was "a type, consecrated by antiquity, to which the ideal king of Israel, ruling on the same spot, must conform" (Dri. 167); and even if that Ps. be not pre-Exilic (as Gu. supposes), but as late as the Maccabæan period, it is difficult to conceive that the type could have originated without some traditional basis.—Some writers have sought a proof of the historical character of Melkiẓedeḳ in a supposed parallel between the ἀπάτωρ, ἀμήτωρ, ἀγενεαλόγητος of Heb. 7^{3} and a formula several times repeated in letters (Tel Amarna) of Abdḫiba of Jerusalem to Amenophis IV.: "Neither my father nor my mother set me in this place; the mighty arm of the king established me in my father's house."† Abdḫiba might have been a successor of Melkiẓedeḳ; and it is just conceivable that Hommel is right in his conjecture that a religious formula, associated with the head of the Jerusalem sanctuary, receives from Abdḫiba a political turn, and is made use of to express his absolute dependence on the Egyptian king. But it must be observed that Abdḫiba's language is perfectly intelligible in its diplomatic sense; its agreement with the words of the NT is only partial, and may be accidental; and it is free from the air of mystery which excites interest in the latter. This, however, is not to deny the probability that the writer to the Hebrews drew his conception partly from other sources than the vv. in Gen.

'El 'Elyôn.—'El, the oldest Semitic appellative for God, was frequently differentiated according to particular aspects of the divine nature, or particular local or other relations entered into by the deity: hence arose compound names like אֵל שַׁדַּי (17^{1}), אֵל עוֹלָם (21^{33}), אֵל אֱלֹהֵי יִשְׂרָאֵל (33^{20}), אֵל בֵּית־אֵל (35^{7}), and אֵל עֶלְיוֹן (here and Ps. 78^{35}).‡ עֶלְיוֹן (='upper,' 'highest') is not uncommonly used of God in OT, either alone (Nu. 24^{16}, Dt. 32^{8}, Ps. 18^{14} etc.) or in combinations with יהוה or אלהים (Ps. 7^{18} (?), 47^{3} 57^{3} etc.). That it was in actual use among the Canaanites is by no means incredible: the Phœnicians had a god Ἐλιοῦν καλούμενος Ὕψιστος (Eus. *Præp. Ev.* i. 10, 11, 12); and there is nothing to forbid the supposition that the deity of the sanctuary of Jerusalem was worshipped under that name. On the other hand, there is nothing to prove it; and it is perhaps a more significant fact

* Gu. instances as a historical parallel the legal fiction by which the imperial prestige of the Cæsars was transferred to Charlemagne and his successors.—Josephus had the same view when he spoke of M. as Χαναναίων δυνάστης, and the first founder of Jerusalem (*BJ*, vi. 438).

† Homm. *AHT*, 155 ff.; Sayce, *Monn.* 175; *EHH*, 28 f.; *Exp. Times*, vii. 340 ff., 478 ff., 565 f., viii. 43 f., 94 ff., 142 ff. (arts. and letters by Sayce, Driver, and Hommel).

‡ See Baethgen, *Beitr.* 291 f.—Comp., in classical religion, *Zeus Meilichios*, *-Xenios*, *Jupiter Terminus*, *-Latiuris*, etc.

that the Maccabees were called ἀρχιερεῖς θεοῦ ὑψίστου (Jos. *Ant.* xvi. 163; *Ass. Mosis*, 6[1]).* This title, the frequent recurrence of עֶלְיוֹן as a divine name in late Pss., the name Salem in one such Ps., and Melkiẓedeḳ in (probably) another, make a group of coincidences which go to show that the Melkiẓedeḳ legend was much in vogue about the time of the Maccabees.

17, 21–24. Abram and the king of Sodom.—The request of the king of Sodom presupposes as the usual custom of war that Abram was entitled to the whole of the booty. Abram's lofty reply is the climax to which the whole narrative leads up.—**22.** *I lift up my hand*] the gesture accompanying an oath (Ex. 6[8], Nu. 14[30], Dt. 32[40], Ezk. 20[23], Dn. 12[7] etc.).—*to Yahwe, 'El 'Elyôn*] A recognition of religious affinity with Melkiẓedeḳ, as a fellow-worshipper of the one true God. The יהוה, however, is probably an addition to the text, wanting in 𝔊 and 𝔖, while ⅏ has האלהים.—**23.** *lest thou shouldst say, etc.*] An earlier writer (cf. 12[16]) would perhaps not have understood this scruple: he would have attributed the enrichment of Abram to God, even if the medium was a heathen king.—**24.** The condescending allowance for the weakness of inferior natures is mentioned to enhance the impression of Abram's generosity (Gu.).

The Historic Value of Ch. 14. — There are obvious reasons why this chapter should have come to be regarded in some quarters as a 'shibboleth' between two opposite schools of OT criticism (Homm. *AHT*, 165). The narrative is unique in this respect, that it sets the figure of Abraham in the framework of world-history. It is the case that certain features of this framework have been confirmed, or rendered credible, by recent Assyriological discoveries; and by those who look to archæological research to correct the aberrations of literary criticism, this fact is represented as not only demonstrating the historicity of the narrative as a whole, but as proving that the criticism which resolved it into a late Jewish romance must be vitiated

---

22. הֲרִמֹתִי] On the pf., G–K. § 106 *i*.—**23.** On the אִם of negative asseveration, § 149 *a, c*. The second וְאִם, which adds force to the negation, is not rendered by 𝔊 or 𝔙.—**24.** בִּלְעָדַי] lit. 'not unto me!' (in Hex. only 41[16. 44] [E], Jos. 22[19] [late]). 𝔊𝔙𝔖𝔗[O] seem to have read בִּלְעָדַי רַק as a compound prepositional phrase (= 'except').

---

* Siegfried, *ThLz.*, 1895, 304. On the late prevalence of the title, see also *DB*, iii. 450, *EB*, i. 70 (in and near Byblus), and Schürer, *SBBA*, 1897, p. 200 ff.

by some radical fault of method. How far that sweeping conclusion is justified we have now to consider. The question raised is one of extreme difficulty, and is perhaps not yet ripe for final settlement. The attempt must be made, however, to review once more the chief points of the evidence, and to ascertain as fairly as possible the results to which it leads.

The case for the historic trustworthiness of the story (or the antiquity of the source on which it is founded) rests on the following facts: (1) The occurrence of prehistoric names of places and peoples, some of which had become unintelligible to later readers, and required identification by explanatory glosses. Now the mere use of ancient and obsolete names is not in itself inconsistent with the fictitious character of the narrative. A writer who was projecting himself into a remote past would naturally introduce as many archaic names as he could find; and the substitution of such terms as Rephaim, Emim, Horim, etc., for the younger populations which occupied these regions, is no more than might be expected. Moreover, the force of the argument is weakened by the undoubted anachronism involved in the use of the name Dan (see on v.[14]). The presence of archæological glosses, however, cannot be disposed of in this way. To suppose that a writer deliberately introduced obsolete or fictitious names and glossed them, merely for the purpose of casting an air of antiquity over his narrative, is certainly a somewhat extreme hypothesis. It is fair to admit the presumption that he had really before him some traditional (perhaps documentary) material, though of what nature that material was it is impossible to determine.*—(2) The general verisimilitude of the background of the story. It is proved beyond question that an Elamite supremacy over the West and Palestine existed before the year 2000 B.C.; consequently an expedition such as is here described is (broadly speaking) within the bounds of historic probability. Further, the state of things in Palestine presupposed by the record—a number of petty kingships striving to maintain their independence, and entering into temporary alliances for that purpose—harmonises with all we know of the political condition of the country before the Israelitish occupation, though it might be difficult to show that the writer's knowledge of the situation exceeds what would be acquired by the most cursory perusal of the story of the Conquest in the Book of Joshua.—(3) The consideration most relied upon by apologetic writers is the proof obtained from Assyriology that the names in v.[1] are historical. The evidence on this question has been given on p. 257 ff., and need not be here recapitulated.

---

* It is to be observed that in no single case is the correctness of the gloss attested by independent evidence (see vv.[2. 3. 6. 7. 8. 17]). Those who maintain the existence of a cuneiform original have still to reckon with the theory of Wi., who holds that the basis of the narrative is a Babylonian legend, which was brought into connexion with the story of Abraham by arbitrary identification of names whose primary significance was perhaps mythological. See *GI*, ii. 28 ff. The question cannot be further discussed here.

We have seen that every one of the identifications is disputed by more than one competent Assyriologist (see, further, Mey. *GA*², I. ii. p. 551 f.); and since only an expert is fully qualified to judge of the probabilities of the case, it is perhaps premature to regard the confirmation as assured. At the same time, it is quite clear that the names are not invented; and it is highly probable that they are those of contemporary kings who actually reigned over the countries assigned to them in this chapter. Their exact relations to one another are still undetermined, and in some respects difficult to imagine; but there is nothing in the situation which we may not expect to be cleared up by further discoveries. It would seem to follow that the author's information is derived ultimately either from a Babylonian source, or from records preserved amongst the Canaanites in Palestine. The presence of an element of authentic history in v.[1] being thus admitted, we have to inquire how far this enters into the substance of the narrative.

Before answering that question, we must look at the arguments advanced in favour of the late origin and fictitious character of the chapter. These are of two kinds: (1) The inherent improbability or incredibility of many of the incidents recorded. This line of criticism was most fully elaborated by Nöldeke in 1869 (*Untersuchungen*, 156–172): the following points may be selected as illustrations of the difficulties which the narrative presents. (*a*) The route said to have been traversed is, if not absolutely impracticable for a regular army, at least quite irreconcilable with the alleged object of the campaign,—the chastisement of the Pentapolis. That the four kings should have passed the Dead Sea valley, leaving their principal enemies in their rear, and postponing a decisive engagement till the end of a circuitous and exhausting march, is a proceeding which would be impossible in real warfare, and could only have been imagined by a writer out of touch with the actualities of the situation (see the Notes on p. 261). (*b*) It is difficult to resist the impression that some of the personal names—especially *Bĕra'* and *Birsha'* (see on v.[2]), and *Mamre* and *Eshcol* (v.[13])—are artificial formations, which reveal either the animus of the writer, or else (in the last two instances) a misapprehension of traditional data into which only a very late and ill-informed writer could have been betrayed. (*c*) The rout of Chedorlaomer's army by 318 untrained men is generally admitted to be incredible. It is no sufficient explanation to say that only a rearguard action may have taken place; the writer does not *mean* that; and if his meaning misrepresents what actually took place, his account is at any rate not historical (see p. 267). (*d*) It appears to be assumed in v.[3] that the Dead Sea was formed subsequently to the events narrated. This idea seems to have been traditional in Israel (cf. 13[10]), but it is nevertheless quite erroneous. Geological evidence proves that that amazing depression in the earth's surface had existed for ages before the advent of man on the earth, and formed, from the first, part of a great inland lake whose waters stood originally several hundred feet higher than the present level of the Dead Sea. It may, indeed, be urged that the vale of Siddim was not coextensive with the Dead Sea basin, but only with its shallow southern 'Lagoon'

(S of *el-Lisān*), which by a partial subsidence of the ground might have been formed within historic times.* But even if that were the true explanation, the manner of the statement is not that which would be used by a writer conversant with the facts.—The improbabilities of the passage are not confined to the four points just mentioned, but are spread over the entire surface of the narrative; and while their force may be differently estimated by different minds, it is at least safe to say that they more than neutralise the impression of trustworthiness which the precise dates, numbers, and localities may at first produce.—(2) The second class of considerations is derived from the spirit and tendency which characterise the representation, and reveal the standpoint of the writer. It would be easy to show that many of the improbabilities observed spring from a desire to enhance the greatness of Abraham's achievement; and indeed the whole tendency of the chapter is to set the figure of the patriarch in an ideal light, corresponding not to the realities of history, but to the imagination of some later age. Now the idealisation of the patriarchs is, of course, common to all stages of tradition; the question is to what period this ideal picture of Abraham may be most plausibly referred. The answer given by a number of critics is that it belongs to the later Judaism, and has its affinities "with P and the midrashic elements in Chronicles rather than with the older Israelite historians" (Moore, *EB*, ii. 677). Criticism of this kind is necessarily subjective and speculative. At first sight it might appear that the conception of Abraham as a warlike hero is the mark of a warlike age, and therefore older than the more idyllic types delineated in the patriarchal legends. That judgement, however, fails to take account of the specific character of the narrative before us. It is a grandiose and lifeless description of military operations which are quite beyond the writer's range of conception; it contains no trace of the martial ardour of ancient times, and betrays considerable ignorance of the conditions of actual warfare; it is essentially the account of a Bedouin razzia magnified into a systematic campaign for the consolidation of empire. It has been fitly characterised as the product of a time which "admires military glory all the more because it can conduct no wars itself; and, having no warlike exploits to boast of in the present, revels in the mighty deeds of its ancestors. Such narratives tend in imagination towards the grotesque; the lack of the political experience which is to be acquired only in the life of the independent state produces a condition of mind which can no longer distinguish between the possible and the impossible. Thus the passage belongs to an age in which, in spite of a certain historical erudition, the historic sense of Judaism had sunk almost to zero" (Gu. 255).

It remains to consider the extent and origin of the historic element whose existence in the chapter we have been led to admit. Does it proceed from an ancient Canaanite record, which passed into the Hebrew tradition, to be gradually moulded into the form in which we now find

* Cf. Dri.'s elaborate Note, p. 168 ff.; also Robinson, *BR*, ii. 187 f.; Gautier, *EB*, 1043 f., 1046; Hull, *DB*, i. 576[b].

it? Or did it come directly from an external source into the hands of a late author, who used it as the basis of a sort of historical romance? The former alternative is difficult to maintain if (as seems to be the case) the narrative stands outside the recognised literary sources of the Pentateuch.* The most acceptable form of this theory is perhaps that presented by Sellin in the article to which reference has frequently been made in the preceding pages (*NKZ*, xvi. 929–951). The expedition, he thinks, may have taken place at any time between 2250 and 1750 B.C.; and he allows a long period of oral transmission to have elapsed before the preparation of a cuneiform record about 1500. This document he supposes to have been deposited in the Temple archives of Jerusalem, and to have come into the possession of the Israelites through David's conquest of that city. He thus leaves room for a certain distortion of events in the primary document, and even for traces of mythological influence. The theory would gain immensely in plausibility if the alleged Canaanite parallels to the obscure expressions of vv.[14f.] (חניך, ריק, חלק) should prove to be relevant. At present, however, they are not known to be specifically Canaanite; and whatever be their value it does not appear that they tell more in favour of a Palestinian origin than of a cuneiform basis in general. The assumption that the document was deposited in the Temple is, of course, a pure hypothesis, on which nothing as to the antiquity or credibility of the narrative can be based.

On the other hand, the second alternative has definite support in a fact not sufficiently regarded by those who defend the authenticity of the chapter. It is significant that the cuneiform document in which three of the four royal names in v.[1] are supposed to have been discovered is as late as the 4th or 3rd cent. B.C. Assuming the correctness of the identifications, we have here a positive proof that the period with which our story deals was a theme of poetic and legendary treatment in the age to which criticism is disposed approximately to assign the composition of Gn. 14. It shows that a cuneiform document is not necessarily a contemporary document, and need not contain an accurate transcript of fact. If we suppose such a document to have come into the possession of a Jew of the post-Exilic age, it would furnish just such a basis of quasi-historical material as would account for the blending of fact and fiction which the literary criticism of the chapter suggests. In any case the extent of the historical material remains undetermined. The names in v.[1] are historical; some such expedition to the West as is here spoken of is possibly so; but everything else belongs to the region of conjecture. The particulars in which we are most interested—the figures of Abram and Lot and Melkiẓedeḳ, the importance, the revolt, and even the existence, of the Cities of the *Kikkār*, and, in short, all the details of the story—are as yet unattested by any allusion in secular history.

In conclusion, it should be noticed that there is no real antagonism between archæology and literary criticism in this matter. They deal

* P. 256 above.

with quite distinct aspects of the problem; and the fallacy lies in treating the chapter as a homogeneous and indivisible unity: it is like discussing whether the climate of Asia is hot or cold on conflicting evidence drawn from opposite extremes of the continent. Criticism claims to have shown that the narrative is full of improbabilities in detail which make it impossible to accept it as a reliable contemporary record of fact. All that the archæologist can pretend to have proved is that the general setting of the story is consistent with the political situation in the East as disclosed by the monuments; and that it contains data which cannot possibly be the fabrications of an unhistorical age. So much as this critics are perfectly prepared to admit. Nö., who has stated the case against the authenticity of the chapter as strongly as any man, expressly declined to build an argument on the fact that nothing was then known of an Elamite dominion in the West, and allowed that the names of the four kings might be traditional (*op. cit.* 159 f.).* Assyriology has hardly done more as yet than make good the possibilities thus conceded in advance. It is absurd to suppose that a theory can be overthrown by facts for which due allowance was made before they took rank as actual discoveries.

CH. XV.—*God's Covenant with Abram* (JE).

In a prolonged interview with Yahwe, Abram's misgivings regarding the fulfilment of the divine promises are removed by solemn and explicit assurances, and by a symbolic act in which the Almighty binds Himself by the inviolable ceremonial of the *berîth*.† In the present form of the chapter there is a clear division between the promise of a son and heir ($^{1-6}$) and the promise of the land ($^{7-21}$), the latter alone being strictly embraced in the scope of the covenant.

Analysis.—See, besides the comm., We. *Comp.*² 23 f.; Bu. *Urg.* 416¹; Bacon, *Hebraica*, vii. 75 ff.; Kraetzschmar, *op. cit.* 58 ff.—The chapter shows unmistakable signs of composition, but the analysis is beset with peculiar, and perhaps insurmountable, difficulties. We may begin by

* The same admission was made by We. as long ago as 1889 (*Comp.*² 310). In view of the persistent misrepresentations of critical opinion, it is not unnecessary to repeat once more that the historicity of the names in v.¹ has not been denied by any leading critic (*e.g.* Ew. Nö. Di. We.), even before the discoveries of later years.—For an exposure of Sayce's extraordinary travesty of Nöldeke's arguments, the reader should consult Dri. *Gen.*⁷, *Addenda* to p. 173.

† "Die Berîth ist diejenige kultische Handlung, durch die in feierlicher Weise Verpflichtungen oder Abmachungen irgend welcher Art absolut bindend und unverbrüchlich gemacht wurden" (Kraetzschmar, *Bundesvorstellung*, 40 f.).

examining the solution proposed by Gu. He assigns [1a.* bγ. 2a. 3b. 4. 6. 9. 10. 12aα. b. 17. 18a. bα] to J; [1bαβ. 3a. [2b?] 5. 11. 12aβ. 13a. 14] (to יצאו). [16] to E; and [7. 8. 13b. 14bβ. 15. 18bβ. 19-21] to a redactor. On this analysis the J fragments form a consecutive and nearly complete narrative, the break at v.[7] being caused by R's insertion of [7f.] But (1) it is not so easy to get rid of [7f.] V.[8] is, and [6] is not, a suitable point of contact for [9ff.]; and the omission of [7f.] would make the covenant a confirmation of the promise of an heir, whereas [18] expressly restricts it to the possession of the land. And (2) the parts assigned to J contain no marks of the Yahwistic style except the name יהוה; they present features not elsewhere observed in that document, and are coloured by ideas characteristic of the Deuteronomic age. The following points may be here noted: (*a*) the *prophetic* character of the divine communication to Abram ([1. 4]); (*b*) the address ארני יהוה ([2a] [cf.[8]]); (*c*) the theological reflexion on the nature of Abram's righteousness ([6]: cf. Dt. 6[25] 24[13]); (*d*) the idea of the Abrahamic covenant (found only in redactional expansions of JE, and common in Dt.); to which may be added (*e*) the ideal boundaries of the land and the enumeration of its inhabitants ([18b-21]), both of which are Deuteronomistic (see on the vv. below). The ceremonial of [9f. 17] is no proof of antiquity (cf. Jer. 34[17ff.]), and the symbolic representation of Yahwe's presence in [17] is certainly not decisive against the late authorship of the piece (against Gu.). It is difficult to escape the impression that the whole of this J narrative (including [7f.]) is the composition of an editor who used the name יהוה, but whose affinities otherwise are with the school of Deuteronomy rather than with the early Yahwistic writers. —This result, however, still leaves unsolved problems. (1) It fails to account for the obvious doublets in [2. 3]. [2b] and [3a] are generally recognised as the first traces in the Hex. of the document E, and [5] (a *night* scene in contrast to [12. 17]) is naturally assigned to the same source. (2) With regard to [[12?] 13-16], which most critics consider to be a redactional expansion of J, I incline to the opinion of Gu., that [11. 13-16] form part of the sequel to the E narrative recognised in [3a. 2b. 5] (note האמרי, v.[16]). (3) The renewed introduction of Yahwe in v.[7] forms a hiatus barely consistent with unity of authorship. The difficulty would be partly met by Bacon's suggestion that the proper position of the J material in [1-6] is intermediate between 15[18] and 16[1]. But though this ingenious theory removes one difficulty it creates others, and it leaves untouched what seems to me the chief element of the problem, the marks of lateness both in [1-6] and [7-21].—The phenomena might be most fully explained by the assumption of an Elohistic basis, recast by a Jehovistic or Deuteronomic editor (probably R^JE), and afterwards combined with extracts from its own original; but so complex a hypothesis cannot be put forward with any confidence.

1–6. The promise of an heir (J), and a numerous posterity (E).—1. The v. presupposes a situation of

---

1. אחר[י] הדברים האלה] frequent in E (22[1] 40[1] 48[1], Jos. 24[29]), but also used by J (22[20] 39[7]).—הָיָה דְבַר־יהוה (cf. v.[4])] not elsewhere in the Hex.;

anxiety on the part of Abram, following on some meritorious action performed by him. It is not certain that any definite set of circumstances was present to the mind of the writer, though the conditions are fairly well satisfied by Abram's defenceless position amongst the Canaanites immediately after his heroic obedience to the divine call (Gu.). The attempts to establish a connexion with the events of ch. 14 (Jewish Comm. and a few moderns) are far-fetched and misleading.—*the word of Yahwe came*] On the formula *v.i.* The conception of Abram as a prophet has no parallel in J; and even E, though he speaks vaguely of Abram as a נָבִיא (20^7, *q.v.*), does not describe his intercourse with God in technical prophetic phraseology. The representation is not likely to have arisen before the age of written prophecy. —*in a vision*] probably a night-vision (see v.[5]), in which case the expression must be attributed to E. The mediate character of revelation, as contrasted with the directness of the older theophanies (*e.g.* ch. 18), is at all events characteristic of E.—*thy shield*] a figure for protection common in later writings: Dt. 33^{29}, Ps. 3^4 7^{11} oft., Pr. 2^7 30^5.—*thy reward* [will be] *very great*] a new sentence (𝔊𝔖), not (as 𝔙, EV) a second predicate to אָנֹכִי.—**2.** *seeing I go hence childless*]

found occasionally in the older writings (1 Sa. 15^{10}, 2 Sa. 24^{11}), but chiefly in later prophets and superscriptions: specially common in Jer. and Ezk.—מַחֲזֶה] Only Nu. $24^{4.\ 16}$, Ezk. 13^7. The *word* is thus not at all characteristic of E, though the *idea* of revelation through dreams and visions (מַרְאָה, Nu. 12^6; מַרְאֹת הַלַּיְלָה, Gn. 46^2) undoubtedly is. Considering the many traces of late editing in the chapter, it is highly precarious to divide the phrases of v.[1] between J and E.—הַרְבֵּה (inf. abs.) as pred. is unusual and late (Ps. 130^7, Ec. 11^8). 𝔐 ארבה, 'I will multiply,' is perhaps preferable.—**2.** ארני יהוה] (cf. [8]) is common in the elevated style of prophecy (esp. Ezk.), but rare in the Pss. In the historical books it occurs only as a vocative (exc. 1 Ki. 2^{26}): Jos. 7^7, Ju. 6^{22} 16^{28},—Dt. 3^{24} 9^{26}, 2 Sa. $7^{18.\ 19.\ 20.\ 28.\ 29}$, 1 Ki. 8^{53}. Of these the first three are possibly J; the rest are Deuteronomic.—ובן—אליעור] 𝔊 has *ὁ δὲ υἱὸς Μάσεκ τῆς οἰκογενοῦς μου, οὗτος Δαμασκὸς Ἐλιέζερ*,—a meaningless sentence in the connexion, unless supplemented by *κληρονομήσει με*, as in some MSS of Philo (before *οὗτος*). 𝔖 paraphrases: ܘܒܪ ܡܦܪܢܣܢܘܬܐ ܕܒܝܬܝ ܗܘ ܐܠܝܥܙܪ ܕܡܫܩ. מֶשֶׁק is a *ἅπ. λεγ.*, which appears not to have been understood by any of the Vns. 𝔊 treats it as the name of Eliezer's mother, Aq. (*ποτίζοντος*) as = מַשְׁקֶה; Θ𝔙𝔗^OJ give it the sense

So all Vns., taking הָלַךְ in the sense of 'die' (Ps. 39[14]: cf. Ar. *halaka*), though the other sense ('walk' = 'live') would be quite admissible. To die childless and leave no name on earth (Nu. 27[4]) is a fate so melancholy that even the assurance of present fellowship with God brings no hope or joy.—2b is absolutely unintelligible (*v.i.*). The Vns. agree in reading the names *Eliezer* and *Damascus*, and also (with the partial exception of 𝔊) in the general understanding that the clause is a statement as to Abram's heir. This is probably correct; but the text is so corrupt that even the proper names are doubtful, and there is only a presumption that the sense agrees with [3b].—3. In the absence of children or near relatives, the slave, as a member of the family, might inherit (Sta. *GVI*, i. 391; Benzinger, *Arch.*[2] 113). בֶּן־בַּיִת is a member of the household, but not necessarily a home-born slave (יְלִיד בַּיִת, 14[14]).—5. The promise of a numerous '*seed*' (cf. [3a. 13]) is E's parallel to the announcement of the birth of a bodily heir in J (v.[4]).—*the stars*] a favourite image of the later editors and Deuteronomy (22[17]

---

of 'steward,' which may be a mere conjecture like the *συγγενὴς* of Σ. Modern comm. generally regard the word as a modification of מֶשֶׁךְ (Jb. 28[18]?) with the sense of 'possession'—בֶּן־מֶשֶׁךְ = 'son of possession' = 'possessor' or 'inheritor' (so Ges. Tu. KS. Str. al.); but this has neither philological justification nor traditional support. A √ משק (in spite of מִמְשַׁק, Zeph. 2[9]) is extremely dubious. The last clause cannot be rendered either 'This is Eliezer of Damascus,' or 'This is Damascus, namely Eliezer' (De.). 𝔖 and 𝔗[O] adopt the summary expedient of turning the subst. into an adj., and reading 'Eliezer the Damascene' (similarly 'Ο 'Εβρ. in Field). It is difficult to imagine what Damascus can have to do here at all; and if a satisfactory sense for the previous words could be obtained, it would be plausible enough (with Hitz. Tu. KS. al.) to strike out דַּמֶּשֶׂק [הוא] as a stupid gloss on מֶשֶׁק. Ball's emendation, וּמשֵׁק בֵּיתִי הָא בֶּן־דַּמֶּשֶׂק אֱלִיעֶזֶר, 'and he who will possess my house is a Damascene—Eliezer,' is plausible, but the sing. בֶּן־ with the name of a city is contrary to Heb. idiom. Bewer (*JBL*, 1908, pt. 2, 160 ff.) has proposed the reading—ingenious but not convincing—וּבָנִים בִּקַּשְׁתִּי אֵין לִי זָרַע. [2a] and [3a] are parallels (note the double ויאמר א'), of which the former obviously belongs to J, the latter consequently to E. Since [3b] is J rather than E (cf. יוֹרֵשׁ with v.[4]), it follows that [3a. 2b] must be transposed if the latter be E's parallel to [3b].—3. ירש] in the sense of 'be heir to': cf. 21[10] (E), 2 Sa. 14[7], Jer. 49[1], Pr. 30[23].—4. ממעיך (𝔊 מִמְּךָ?)] of the father, 2 Sa. 7[12] 16[11], Is. 48[19]; of the mother, 25[23] (J), Is. 49[1], Ru. 1[11], Ps. 71[6].—5. החוצה] in J, 19[17] 24[29] 39[12. 13. 15. 18] (Jos. 2[19]?); but also Dt. 24[11] 25[5] etc.—

26[4], Ex. 32[13], Dt. 1[10] 10[22] 28[62]).—**6.** *counted it* (his implicit trust in the character of Yahwe) *as righteousness*] 1 Mac. 2[52]. צְדָקָה is here neither inherent moral character, nor piety in the subjective sense, but a right relation to God conferred by a divine sentence of approval (see We. *Pss.*, *SBOT*, 174).

This remarkable anticipation of the Pauline doctrine of justification by faith (Ro. 4[3. 9. 22], Gal. 3[6]; cf. Ja. 2[23]) must, of course, be understood in the light of OT conceptions. The idea of righteousness as dependent on a divine judgment (חָשַׁב) could only have arisen on the basis of legalism, while at the same time it points beyond it. It stands later in theological development than Dt. 6[25] 24[13], and has its nearest analogies in Ps. 106[31] 24[5]. The reflexion is suggested by the question how Abram, who had no law to fulfil, was nevertheless 'righteous'; and, finding the ground of his acceptance in an inward attitude towards God, it marks a real approximation to the Apostle's standpoint. Gu. (161) well remarks that an early writer would have given, instead of this abstract proposition, a concrete illustration in which Abram's faith came to light.

7–21. The covenant.—7, 8. The promise of the *land*, Abram's request for a pledge (ct. v.[6]), and the self-introduction of Yahwe (which would be natural only at the commencement of an interview), are marks of discontinuity difficult to reconcile with the assumption of the unity of the narrative. Most critics accordingly recommend the excision of the vv. as an interpolation.

So Di. KS. Kraetzschmar, Gu. al. Their genuineness is maintained by Bu. De. Bacon, Ho.; We. thinks they have been at least worked over. The language certainly is hardly Yahwistic. The אני (7) is not a sufficient ground for rejection (see Bu. 439); and although אור כשדים in a J-context may be suspicious, we have no right to assume that it did not occur in a stratum of Yahwistic tradition (see p. 239 above). But לתת—לרשתה is a decidedly Deuteronomic phrase (see *OH*, i. 205): on אדני יהוה, see on v.[2]. On the theory of a late recension of the whole passage these linguistic difficulties would vanish; but the impression of a change of scene remains,—an impression, however, which the interpolation theory does not altogether remove, since the transition from [6] to [9] is very abrupt. Bacon's transposition of the two sections of J is also unsatisfactory.

---

6. והאמין] (on the tense, see Dri. *T.* § 133; G-K. § 112 *ss*): 𝔊𝔙𝔖 add אַבְרָם. The construction with בְּ is usual when the obj. of faith is God (Ex. 14[31], Nu. 14[11] 20[12], Dt. 1[32], 2 Ki. 17[14], 2 Ch. 20[20], Ps. 78[32], Jon. 3[5]): לְ only Dt. 9[23], Is. 43[10].—צְדָקָה] second obj. acc. The change to לצ' (Ps. 106[31]) is unnecessary.

9, 10. The preparations for the covenant ceremony; on which see below, p. 283. Although not strictly sacrificial,* the operation conforms to later Levitical usage in so far as the animals are all such as were allowed in sacrifice, and the birds are not divided (Lv. 1^{17}).—*of three years old*] This is obviously the meaning of מְשֻׁלֶּשׁ here (cf. 1 Sa. 1^{24} [𝔊]: elsewhere = 'threefold,' Ezk. 42^{6}, Ec. 4^{12}). $𝔗^{O}$, which renders 'three' (calves, etc.), is curiously enough the only Vn. that misses the sense; and it is followed by *Ber. R.*, Ra. al. On the number *three* in the OT, see Stade, *ZATW*, xxvi. 124 ff. [esp. 127 f.].—**11.** The descent of the unclean birds of prey (עַיִט), and Abram's driving them away, is a sacrificial omen of the kind familiar to antiquity.† The interpretation seems to follow in $^{13–16}$ (Di. Gu.).—**12.** תַּרְדֵּמָה (𝔊 ἔκστασις) is the condition most favourable for the reception of visions (see on 2^{21}).—*a great horror*] caused by the approach of the deity (omit חֲשֵׁכָה as a gloss). The text is mixed (see below), and the two representations belong, the one to J, and the other to E (Gu.). The scene is a vivid transcript of primitive religious experience. The bloody ceremony just described was no perfunctory piece of symbolism; it touched the mind below the level of consciousness; and that impression (heightened in this case by the growing darkness) induced a susceptibility to psychical influences readily culminating in ecstasy or vision.—**13–16.** An oracle in which is unfolded the destiny of Abram's descendants to the 4th generation. It is to be noted that the prediction relates to the fortunes of Abram's 'seed,' the mention of the land (^{16}) being in-

---

9. גוזל] Dt. 32^{11}† = young of the vulture; but here = 'young dove'; Ar. *ǧauzal*; Syr. ܓܘܙܠܐ.—**10.** וַיְבַתֵּר] a technical term; the vb. only here; cf. בֶּתֶר, Jer. $34^{18.\,19}$—בתוך] Sam. בתור (inf. abs.).—איש בִּתְרוֹ וגו׳] cf. 9^{5}; G–K. § 139 *c.*—**11.** הַפְּגָרִים] $𝔊^{A}$ τὰ σώματα τὰ διχοτομήματα; a conflation of הפגרים and הַגְּזָרִים (v.^{17}).—וַיַּשֵּׁב] Hiph. of נשב only here in the sense of 'scare away': so Aq. (ἀπεσόβησεν) 𝔖𝔙. $𝔗^{O}$ read וַיֵּשֶׁב, which is less expressive; and 𝔊 וַיֵּשֶׁב אִתָּם is quite inadmissible.—**12.** ויהי—לבוא] G–K. § 114 *i*; cf.

---

* So in the covenant between Ašur-nirâri and Mati'ilu (*MVAG*, iii. 228 ff.), the victim is expressly said *not* to be a sacrifice.

† Comp. Virg. *Aen.* iii. 225 ff.

direct and incidental. The passage may therefore be the continuation of the E-sections of [1-6], on the understanding that in E the covenant had to do with the promise of a seed, and not with the possession of the land.—**13.** *a sojourner*] (coll.): see on 12[10].—*400 years*] agreeing approximately with the 430 years of Ex. 12[40] (P).—**15** is a parenthesis, if not an interpolation, reassuring Abram as to his own personal lot (see on 25[8]).—**16.** *the fourth generation*] *e.g.* Levi, Kohath, Amram, Aaron (or Moses) (Ex. 6[16ff.]). To the reckoning of a generation as 100 years (cf. v.[13]) doubtful classical parallels are cited by Knobel (Varro, *Ling. lat.* 6, 11; Ovid, *Met.* xii. 188, etc.).*—*the guilt of the Amorites*] (the inhabitants of Palestine) is frequently dwelt upon in later writings (Dt. 9[5], 1 Ki. 14[24], Lv. 18[24f.] etc. etc.); but the parallels from JE cited by Knobel (Gn. 18[20ff.] 19[1ff.] 20[11]) are of quite a different character.

Vv.[13-16] are obviously out of place in J, because they *presuppose* [18] (the promise of the land). They are generally assigned to a redactor, although it is difficult to conceive a motive for their insertion. Di.'s suggestion, that they were written to supply the interpretation of the omen of v.[11], goes a certain distance; but fails to explain why the interpretation ever came to be omitted. Since [11] is intimately connected with [13-16], and at the same time has no influence on the account of J, the natural conclusion is that both [11] and [13-16] are documentary, but that the document is not J but E (so Gu.). It will be necessary, however, to delete the phrases בִּרְכֻשׁ גָּדוֹל in [14] and תִּקָּבֵר בְּשֵׂיבָה טוֹבָה in [15] as characteristic of the style of P; perhaps also אַרְבַּע מֵאוֹת שָׁנָה in [13]. The whole of [15] may be removed with advantage to the sense.—The text of [12] is not homogeneous, so that as a whole it cannot be linked either with [11] or with [13ff.]. וְתַרְדֵּמָה וגו׳ and וְהִנֵּה אֵימָה וגו׳ are doublets (note the repetition of נפל על); and the poetic חֲשֵׁכָה (only here in Pent.) is doubtless a gloss to אימה. The opening clause וַיְהִי הַשּׁ׳ לָבוֹא is presumably J (in E it is already night in v.[5]). E's partiality for the visionary mode of revelation may be sufficient justification for assigning the תרדמה to him and the אימה to J; but the choice is immaterial.

Jos. 2[5] (J).—**13.** ועבדום] 𝕲 pr. *καὶ κακώσουσιν αὐτ.*; and apparently read וַעֲבָדוּ בָם, avoiding the awkward interchange of subj. and obj.—**16.** ודור רביעי] acc. of condition, 'as a fourth generation' (cf. Jer. 31[8]); G-K. § 118*q*.

---

* Cf. We. *Prol.*[6] 308 (Eng. tr. p. 308), who cites these **vv.** as positive proof that the generation was reckoned as 100 years (see p. 135 above), —a view which, of course, cannot be held unless vv.[13-16] are a unity.

17. *a smoking oven and a blazing torch*] the two together making an emblem of the theophany, akin to the pillar of cloud and fire of the Exodus and Sinai narratives (cf. Ex. 3^2 19^9 13^{21} etc.). The *oven* is therefore not a symbol of Gehenna reserved for the nations (Ra.).—On the appearance of the תַּנּוּר, see the descriptions and illustrations in Riehm, *HWb.* 178; Benzinger, *Arch.*² 65.—*passed between these pieces*] cf. Jer. $34^{18f.}$ (the only other allusion).

On this rite see Kraetzschmar, *op. cit.* 44 ff. Although attested by only one other OT reference, its prevalence in antiquity is proved by many analogies in classical and other writers. Its original significance is hardly exhausted by the well-known passage in Livy (i. 24), where a fate similar to that of the victim is invoked on the violators of the covenant.* This leaves unexplained the most characteristic feature,—the passing between the pieces. Rob. Sm. surmises that the divided victim was eaten by the contracting parties, and that afterwards "the parties stood between the pieces, as a symbol that they were taken within the mystical life of the victim" (*RS*², 480 f.).

18. This ceremony constitutes a *Berîth*, of which the one provision is the possession of 'the land.' A *Berîth* necessarily implies two or more parties; but it may happen that from the nature of the case its stipulations are binding only on one. So here: Yahwe alone passes (symbolically) between the pieces, because He alone contracts obligation.—The *land* is described according to its ideal limits; it is generally thought, however, that the closing words, along with $^{19-21}$, were added by a Deuteronomic editor, and that in the original J the promise was restricted to Canaan proper.

The נְהַר מִצְרַיִם (not, as elsewhere נַחַל מ׳=Wādī el-Arīsh) must be the Nile (cf. Jos. 13^3, 1 Ch. 13^5). On an old belief that the W. el-Arīsh was an arm of the Nile, see Tuch.—הַנָּהָר הַגָּדוֹל וגו׳] cf. Dt. 1^7 11^{24}, Jos. 1^4. The boundary was never actually reached in the history of Israel (the notice

17. ויהי—באה] pf. with sense of plup. (G-K. § 111 *g*).—עֲלָטָה] only here and Ezk. $12^{6.\ 7.\ 12}$. 𝔊 φλὸξ is certainly wrong (לֶהָבָה? לַהַט?).—עָשָׁן] 𝔊𝔙𝔖 read the ptcp., hence Ball emends עָשֵׁן.—הַגְּזָרִים] the noun recurs only Ps. 136^{13}; but cf. the analogous use of the vb. 1 Ki. $3^{25.\ 26}$.

* ". . . tum illo die, Juppiter, populum Romanum sic ferito, ut ego hunc porcum hic hodie feriam, tantoque magis ferito quanto magis potes pollesque." Cf. *Il.* iii. 298 ff. Precisely the same idea is expressed with great circumstantiality in an Assyrian covenant between Ašur-nirâri and the Syrian prince Mati'ilu: see Peiser, *MVAG*, iii. 228 ff.

in 1 Ki. $5^{1. 4}$ is late and unhistorical).—**19–21.** Such lists of pre-Israelite inhabitants are characteristic of Dt. and Dtnic. expansions of JE. They usually contain 5 or 6 or at most 7 names: here there are 10 (see Bu. 344 ff., and Dri.'s analysis, *Deut.* 97). The first three names appear in none of the other lists; and the same is true of the *Rĕphâîm* in 20. The *Ḳenites* (see p. 113) and *Ḳenizzites* (36^{11}) are tribes of the Negeb, both partly incorporated in Judah: the *Ḳadmonites* (only here) are possibly identical with the בְּנֵי קֶדֶם (29^{1}), the inhabitants of the eastern desert.—The *Ḥivvites,* who regularly appear, are supplied here by 𝔐 (after *Girgashites*) and 𝔊 (after *Canaanites*).—On the *Ḥittites,* see p. 215; and, further, on ch. 23 below.

The idea of a covenant (or oath) of Yahwe to the patriarchs does not appear in the literature till the time of Jer. (11^{5}) and Deut. (4^{31} 7^{12} 8^{18}, 2 Ki. 13^{23} etc.): see Kraetzschmar, 61 ff. Of 31 passages in JE where Kr. finds the conception (the list might be reduced), all but three (15^{18} 12^{7} 24^{7}) are assigned to the Deuteronomic (Jehovistic) redaction (see Staerk, *Studien,* i. 37 ff.); and of these three 12^{7} is a mere promise without an oath, while in 24^{7} the words וַאֲשֶׁר נִשְׁבַּע לִי have all the appearance of a gloss. It is, of course, quite possible that $15^{17f.}$ may be very ancient, and have formed the nucleus of the theological development of the covenant-idea in the age of Deut. But it is certainly not unreasonable to suppose that it emanates from the period when Israel's tenure of Canaan began to be precarious, and the popular religion sought to reassure itself by the inviolability of Yahwe's oath to the fathers. And that is hardly earlier than the 7th cent. (Staerk, 47).

CH. XVI.—*The Flight of Hagar and Birth of Ishmael* (J and P).

Sarai, having no hope of herself becoming a mother, persuades Abram to take her Egyptian maid Hagar as a concubine. Hagar, when she finds herself pregnant, becomes insolent towards her mistress, from whose harsh treatment she ultimately flees to the desert. There the Angel of Yahwe meets her, and comforts her with a disclosure of the destiny of the son she is to bear, at the same time commanding her to go back and submit to her mistress. In due course Ishmael is born.

In the carefully constructed biographical plan of the editors the episode finds an appropriate place between the promise of a bodily heir in 15 and the promise of a son through Sarai in 18 (J) or 17 (P). The narrative itself contains no hint of a trial of Abram's faith, or an attempt on his part to forestall the fulfilment of the promise. Its real interest lies in another direction: partly in the explanation of the sacredness of a certain famous well, and partly in the characterisation of the

Ishmaelite nomads and the explication of their relation to Israel. The point of the story is obscured by a redactional excrescence (^{9}), obviously inserted in view of the *expulsion* of Hagar at a later stage. In reality ch. 16 (J) and 22^{8-21} (E) are variants of one tradition; in the Yahwistic version Hagar never returned, but remained in the desert and bore her son by the well Lahai Roi (We. *Comp.*^{2} 22).—The chapter belongs to the oldest stratum of the Abrahamic legends (J^{b}), and is plausibly assigned by Gu. to the same source as 12^{10-20}. From the main narrative of J (J^{h}) it is marked off by its somewhat unfavourable portraiture of Abram, and by the topography which suggests that Abram's home was in the Negeb rather than in Hebron. The primitive character of the legend is best seen from a close comparison with the Elohistic parallel (see p. 324).

Analysis.—Vv.$^{1a. 3. 15. 16}$ belong to P: note the chronological data in $^{3. 16}$; the naming of the child by the father ^{15} (ct. ^{11}); אֶרֶץ כְּנַעַן, ^{3}; and the stiff and formal precision of the style.—The rest is J: cf. יהוה, $^{2. 5. 7. 9. 10. 11. 13}$; שִׁפְחָה, $^{1. 2. 5. 6. 8}$ (also ^{3} [P]); נא, הִנֵּה־נָא, ^{2}.—The redactional addition in $^{9f.}$ (*v.s.*) betrays its origin by the threefold repetition of וַיֹּאמֶר לָהּ מַלְאַךְ יהוה, a fault of style which is in striking contrast to the exquisite artistic form of the original narrative, though otherwise the language shows no decided departure from Yahwistic usage (Di., but see on v.^{10}).

1–6. The flight of Hagar.—1. Hagar is not an ordinary household slave, but the peculiar property of Sarai, and therefore not at the free disposal of her master (cf. 24^{59} $29^{24. 29}$: see Benzinger, *Arch.*^{2} 104 f., 126 f.).*—*an Egyptian*] so v.^{3} (P), 21^{9} (E); cf. 21^{21}. This consistent tradition points to an admixture of Egyptian blood among the Ishmaelites, the reputed descendants of Hagar.†—**2.** *peradventure I may*

1a is assigned to P partly because of אשת אברם (cf. v.^{3}), and partly because the statement as to Sarai's barrenness supplies a gap in that document, whereas in J it is anticipated by 11^{30}.—**1b.** שִׁפְחָה] (from the same √ as מִשְׁפָּחָה) is originally the slave-concubine; and it is a question

---

* "Some wives have female slaves who are their own property, generally purchased for them, or presented to them, before their marriage. These cannot be the husband's concubines without their mistress's permission, which is sometimes granted (as it was in the case of Hagar); but very seldom" (Lane, *Mod. Egypt.* i. 233 [from Dri.]).—On the resemblance to Cod. Ḫamm. § 146, see Introduction, p. xvii.

† The instance is one of the most favourable in Gen. to Winckler's theory that under מִצְרַיִם we are frequently to understand the N Arabian land of Muṣri (Gu.; cf. Che. *EB*, 3164; *KAT*^{3}, 146 f.). Yet even here the case is far from clear. An Egyptian strain among the Bedouin of Sinai would be easily accounted for by the very early Egyptian occupation of the Peninsula; and Burton was struck by the Egyptian physiognomy of some of the Arabs of that region at the present day. (Dri. *DB*, ii. 504^{a}).

be built up—or *obtain children* (*v.i.*)—*from her*] by adopting Hagar's son as her own; cf. 30^{3}.—**3** is P's parallel to $^{2b.\ 4a}$.—**4**. *and went in, etc.* (see on 6^{4})] the immediate continuation of ^{2b} in J.—*was despised*] a natural feeling, enhanced in antiquity by the universal conviction that the mysteries of conception and birth are peculiarly a sphere of divine action.—**5**. *My wrong be upon thee*] *i.e.* 'May my grievance be avenged on thee!'—her injured self-respect finding vent in a passionate and most unjust imprecation.—**6**. *Thy maid is in thy hand*] Is this a statement of fact, or does it mean that Abram *now* hands Hagar back to her mistress's authority? The latter is Gu.'s view, who thinks that as a concubine Hagar was no longer under the complete control of Sarai.—*treated her harshly*] The word (עִנָּה) suggests excessive severity; Hagar's flight is justified by the indignities to which she was subjected (v.[11]).

7–14. The theophany at the well.—**7**. *the Angel of Yahwe*] (see below) is here introduced for the first time as the medium of the theophany. The scene is a *fountain of water* (as yet nameless: v.[14]) *in the desert . . . on the way to Shûr*. Shûr is an unknown locality on the NE frontier of Egypt (see Dri. *DB*, iv. 510^{b}), which gave its name to the adjacent desert: 20^{1} 25^{18}, Ex. 15^{22}, 1 Sa. 15^{7} 27^{8} (*v.i.*).

The מַלְאַךְ יהוה (or מ' אֱלֹהִים) is "Yahwe Himself in self-manifestation," or, in other words, a personification of the theophany. This somewhat subtle definition is founded on the fact that in very many instances the Angel is at once identified with God and differentiated from Him; cp. *e.g.* vv.[10. 13] with [11]. The ultimate explanation of the ambiguity is no doubt to be sought in the advance of religious thought to a more

---

whether the purpose of presenting a newly-married woman with a שִׁפְחָה may not have been to provide for the event of the marriage proving childless. In usage it is largely coextensive with אָמָה, and is characteristic of J against E, though not against P.—הגר] The motive of Hagar's 'flight' may have been suggested by a supposed connexion with Ar. *hağara*, 'flee.' For another etymology, see Nö. *EB*, 1933^{2}.—**2**. אִבָּנֶה] (so only 30^{3}) may be either a denom. from בֵּן (so apparently 𝔊𝔙Σ), or a metaphor from the family as a house (Ex. 1^{21}, 1 Sa. 2^{35}, Ru. 4^{11} etc.).—**5**. חמסי] gen. of obj., G–K, § 128 *h* (cf. Ob. [10]). 𝔊 *ἀδικοῦμαι ἐκ σοῦ*.—וביניך] The point over ׳ indicates a clerical error: rd. (with 𝔐) וּבֵינֶךָ.

7b seems a duplicate of [14b], and one or other may be a gloss. The words בּמדבר—שור are omitted by $𝔊^{L}$ entirely, and partly in several

spiritual apprehension of the divine nature. The oldest conception of the theophany is a visible personal appearance of the deity (ch. 2 f., Ex. 24[10], Nu. 12[6ff.] etc.). A later, though still early, age took exception to this bold anthropomorphism, and reconciled the original narratives with the belief in the invisibility of God by substituting an 'angel' or 'messenger' of Yahwe as the agent of the theophany, without, however, effacing all traces of the primitive representation (Gu. 164 f.). That the idea underwent a remarkable development within the OT religion must, of course, be recognised (see esp. Ex. 23[21]); but the subject cannot be further investigated here. See Oehler, *ATTh.*[3] 203–211; Schultz, *OTTh.* ii. 218–223 [Eng. tr.]; Davidson, *DB*, i. 94; De. *Gen.* 282 ff.

8. The Angel's question reveals a mysterious knowledge of Hagar's circumstances, who on her part is as yet ignorant of the nature of her visitant (cf. 18[2ff.]).—**9, 10** are interpolated
(*v.i.*). — **11, 12.** The prophecy regarding Ishmael (not 12
alone: Gu.) is in metrical form: two triplets with lines of 4 or 3 measures.—*Behold, etc.*] The form of announcement seems consecrated by usage; cf. Ju. 13[5. 7], Is. 7[14].—*Yishmā'ēl*] properly, 'May God hear,' is rendered 'God hears,' in token of Yahwe's regard for the mother's distress (עָנְיֵךְ; cf. וַתְּעַנֶּהָ, [6]). —**12.** *a wild ass of a man*] or perhaps *the wild ass of humanity* (𝔖𝔗[J], IEz. De. al.)—Ishmael being among the families of mankind what the wild ass is amongst animals (Jb. 39[5–8], Jer. 2[24]). It is a fine image of the free intractable Bedouin character which is to be manifested in Ishmael's descendants.—*dwell in the face of all his brethren* (cf. 25[18])] hardly 'to the east of,' which is too weak a sense. עַל־פְּנֵי seems to express the idea of defiance (as Jb. 1[11]), though it is not easy to connect this with the vb. Possibly the

---

cursives: 𝔖 omits על־העין.—שור] ('wall'?) has been supposed (doubtfully) to be a line of fortifications guarding the NE frontier of Egypt. The חגרא of 𝔗[OJ] (if an Arabism) may express שור in the sense of 'wall': 𝔖 has ܓܕܪ (= גְּרָר, 20[1]).—**9, 10** are a double interpolation. The command to return to Sarai was a necessary consequence of the amalgamation of J and E (22[8ff.]); and [10] was added to soften the return to slavery (Gu.). [10] is impossible before [11], and is besides made up of phrases characteristic of redactional additions to JE (cf. 22[17] 32[13]).—הרבָּה] Inf. abs.; G–K. § 75 *ff.*—**11.** וְילַדְתְּ for וְילַדְתְּ] so Ju. 13[5. 7] (G–K. § 80 *d*).—**12.** פרא אדם] see G–K. § 128 *k, l.* 𝔖 has ܥܪܕܐ ܕܒܢ̈ܝܢܫܐ, and 𝔗[J] פרמי לערוד בבני נשא.—

meaning is that Ishmael will be an inconvenient neighbour (שָׁכֵן) to his settled brethren.—**13, 14.** From this experience of Hagar the local deity and the well derive their names. **13.** *Thou art a God of vision*] *i.e.* (if the following text can be trusted) both in an objective and a subjective sense,—a God who may be seen as well as one who sees.—*Have I even here* (? *v.i.*) *seen after him who sees me?*] This is the only sense that can be extracted from the MT, which, however, is strongly suspected of being corrupt.—**14.** *Bĕ'ēr Lahay Rōî*] apparently means either 'Well of the Living One who sees me,' or 'Well of "He that sees me lives"'. The name occurs again 24^{62} 25^{11}.—*between Ḳadesh and Bered*] On Ḳadesh, see on 14^{7}. Bered is unknown. In Arab tradition the well of Hagar is plausibly enough identified with *'Ain-Muweiliḥ*, a caravan station about 12 miles to the W of Ḳadesh (Palmer, *Des. of Exod.* ii. 354 ff.). The well must have been a chief sanctuary of the Ishmaelites; hence the later Jews, to whom Ishmael was a name for all Arabs, identified it with the sacred well Zemzem at Mecca.—**15, 16.** The birth of Ishmael, recorded by P.

The general scope of [13f.] is clear, though the details are very obscure. By a process of syncretism the original numen of the well had come to be regarded as a particular local manifestation of Yahwe; and the attempt is made to interpret the old names from the standpoint of the higher religion. אֵל רֳאִי and לַחַי ראי are traditional names of which the real meaning had been entirely forgotten, and the etymologies here given are as fanciful as in all similar cases. (1) In לַחַי ראי the Mass. punctuation recognises the roots חי, 'live,' and ראה, 'see,' taking ל as circumscribed gen.; but that can hardly be correct. We. (*Prol.*[6] 323 f.), following Mich. and Ges. (*Th.* 175), conjectures that in the first element

---

13. אתה אל ראי] 𝔊 Σὺ ὁ θεὸς ὁ ἐφιδών με, 𝔙 *Tu Deus qui vidisti me*: both reading רֹאִי (ptcp. with suff.).—For אַתָּה, Ba. would substitute אִתָּה, deleting אליה.—The רֹאִי of [13b. 14a] is not the pausal form of the preceding רֳאִי (which would be רֹאִי: 1 Sa. 16^{12}, Nah. 3^{6}, Jb. 33^{21}), but Qal ptcp. with suff. The authority of the accentuation may, of course, be questioned.—**14.** קָרָא] indef. subj., for which 𝔐 substitutes קראה.—בֶּרֶד] 𝔖 ܓܕܪ, 𝔗O חגרא (see on v.[7]). 𝔗J has חלוצא (Elusa), probably *el-Ḥalaṣa*, about 12 miles SW of Beersheba. It has been supposed that בֶּרֶד may be identical with a place Βηρδάν in the Gerar district, mentioned by Eus. (*OS*, 145^{2} [Lag. 299^{76}]), who explains the name as Φρέαρ κρίσεως (= בְּאֵר דִּין): see v. Gall, *CSt.* 43.

we have the word לְחִי, 'jaw-bone' (Ju. 15^{17}), and in the second an obsolete animal name: hence 'Well of the antelope's (?) jaw-bone.' V. Gall (*CSt.* 40 ff.) goes a step further and distinguishes two wells, עַיִן (בְּאֵר) רֳאִי, and בְּאֵר לְחִי, the former peculiar to J and the latter to E (cf. 𝕲 of 24^{62} 25^{11}).—(2) אֵל רֳאִי, whatever its primary significance, is of a type common in the patriarchal narratives (see p. 291). Of the suggested restorations of ^{13b}, by far the most attractive is that of We. (*l.c.*), who changes הלם to אלהים, reads ראי as רָאִיִ, inserts ואחי between ראיתי and אחרי, and renders, "Have I actually seen God and lived after my vision?"—an allusion to the prevalent belief that the sight of God is followed by death (Ex. 33^{20}, Ju. 6^{23} 13^{23} etc.). The emendation has at least the advantage of giving a meaning to *both* elements in the name of the well. Gu.'s objection that the emphatic 'here' is indispensable, is of doubtful validity, for unfortunately הֲלֹם does not mean 'here' but 'hither.'

CH. XVII.—*The Covenant of Circumcision* (P).

To Abram, who is henceforth to be called Abraham (^{5}), God reveals Himself under a new name (^{1}), entering into a covenant with him ($^{2-8}$), of which the sign is the rite of circumcision ($^{9-14}$). The heir of this covenant is to be a son born to Sarai (whose name is changed to Sarah) in the following year ($^{15-22}$). Abraham immediately circumcises all the males of his household ($^{23-27}$).—To the writer of the Priestly Code the incident is important (1) as an explanation of the origin of circumcision, which in his day had become a fundamental institution of Judaism; and (2) as marking a new stage in the revelation of the true God to the world. The Abrahamic covenant inaugurates the third of the four epochs (commencing respectively with Adam, Noah, Abraham and Moses) into which the Priestly theory divides the history of mankind. On the ethnic parallels to this scheme, Gu.'s note (p. 233 ff.) may be consulted.

Source.—The marks of P's authorship appear in every line of the chapter. Besides the general qualities of style, which need not again be particularised, we may note the following expressions: אלהים (throughout, except v.^{1}, where יהוה is either a redactional change or a scribal error); אל שדי, ^{1}; נתן ב׳, הקים ברית, $^{2. 7. 19. 21}$; במאד מאד, $^{2. 6. 20}$; אתה וזרעך אחריך, $^{7. 8. 9. 10. 19}$; לדרתם, $^{7. 9. 12}$; מגרים, ^{8}; ארץ כנען, ^{8}; אחזה, ^{8}; כל־זכר, $^{10. 12. 23}$; מקנה, $^{12. 13. 23. 27}$; בן־נכר, $^{12. 27}$; ונכרתה הנפש וגו׳, ^{14}; פרה ורבה, ^{20}; נשיאם, ^{20}; הוליד, ^{20}; בעצם היום הזה, $^{23. 26}$; see Di. Ho. Gu. References to the passage in other parts of P are $21^{2.4}$ 28^{4} 35^{12}, Ex. 2^{24} $6^{3f.}$ (Lv. 12^{3}?).

The close parallelism with ch. 15 makes it probable that that chapter, in its present composite form, is the literary basis of P's account of the covenant. Common to the two narratives are (*a*) the self-introduction of the Deity (17^{1} ‖ 15^{7}); (*b*) the covenant (17 *pass.* ‖ $15^{9ff.}$); (*c*) the promise of a numerous seed (17^{4} *pass.* ‖ 15^{5}); (*d*) of the land (17^{8} ‖ 15^{18}); (*e*) of a son ($17^{19. 21}$ ‖ 15^{4}); (*f*) Abraham's incredulity (17^{17} ‖ $15^{3. 8}$). The features peculiar to P, such as the sign of circumcision, the etymology of יִצְחָק in v.[17], the changes of names, etc., are obviously not of a kind to suggest the existence of a separate tradition independent of J and E.

1–8. The Covenant-promises.—These are three in number: (*a*) Abraham will be the father of a numerous posterity ($^{2b. 4-6}$); (*b*) God will be a God to him and to his seed ($^{7b. 8b}$); (*c*) his seed shall inherit the land of Canaan (^{8a}). We recognise here a trace of the ancient religious conception according to which god, land, and people formed an indissoluble triad, the land being an indispensable pledge of fellowship between the god and his worshippers (see *RS*², 92 f.).—**1.** *appeared to Abram*] *i.e.*, in a theophany, as is clear from v.[22]. It is the only direct communication of God to Abram recorded in P. P is indeed very sparing in his use of the theophany, though Ex. 6^{3} seems to imply that his narrative contained one to each of the three patriarchs. If that be so, the revelation to Isaac has been lost, while that to Jacob is twice referred to (35^{9} 48^{3}).—*I am 'El Shaddai*] The origin, etymology, and significance of this

---

1. אֵל שַׁדַּי] For a summary of the views held regarding this divine name, the reader may be referred to Baethgen, *Beitr.* 293 ff., or Kautzsch in *EB*, iii. 3326 f. (cf. Che. *ib.* iv. 4419 f.); on the renderings of the ancient Vns., see the synopses of Di. (259), Dri. (404 f.), and Valeton (*ZATW*, xii. 11^{1}).—It is unfortunately impossible to ascertain whether שַׁדַּי was originally an independent noun, or an attribute of אֵל: Nöldeke and Baethgen decide for the latter view. The traditional Jewish etymology resolves the word into שׁ = אֲשֶׁר and דַּי,—'the all-sufficient' or 'self-sufficient' (*Ber. R.* § 46: cf. Ra. אני הוא שיש די באלהותי לכל בריה). Though this theory can be traced as far back as the rendering of Aq. Σ. and Θ. (ἱκανός), it is an utterly groundless conjecture that P used the name in this sense (Valeton). On the other hand, it seems rash to conclude (with Nö. al.) that the Mass. punctuation has no better authority than this untenable interpretation, so that we are at liberty to vocalise as we please in accordance with any plausible etymological theory. The old derivation from √ שדד = 'destroy,' is still the best: it is grammatically unobjectionable, has at

title are alike obscure: see the footnote. In P it is the signature of the patriarchal age (Ex. 6^3); or rather it designates the true God as the patron of the Abrahamic covenant, whose terms are explicitly referred to in every passage where the name occurs in P (28^3 35^{11} 48^3). That it marks an advance in the revelation of the divine character can hardly be shown, though the words immediately following may suggest that the moral condition on which the covenant is granted is not mere obedience to a positive precept, but a life ruled by the ever-present sense of God as the ideal of ethical perfection.—*Walk before me* (cf. 24^{40} 48^{15})] *i.e.*, 'Live consciously in My presence,' 1 Sa. 12^2, Is. 38^3; cf. 1 Jn. 1^7.—*perfect*] or 'blameless'; see on 6^9.—**2.** On the idea and scope of the covenant (בְּרִית), see p. 297 f. below.—**4.** *father of a multitude* (lit. *tumult*) *of nations*] In substance the promise is repeated in 28^3 48^4 (קְהַל עַמִּים) and 35^{11} (ק׳ גּוֹיִם); the peculiar expression here anticipates the etymology of v.[5]. While J (12^2 18^{18} 46^3) restricts the promise to Israel (גּוֹי גָּדוֹל), P speaks of 'nations' in the plural, including the Ishmaelites and Edomites amongst the

---

least some support in Is. 13^6, Jl. 1^{15}, and is free from difficulty if we accept it as an ancient title appropriated by P without regard to its real significance. The assumption of a by-form שׁדה (Ew. Tu. al.) is gratuitous, and would yield a form שָׂדַי, not שַׁדַּי. Other proposed etymologies are: from שַׁד originally = 'lord' (Ar. *sayyid*), afterwards = 'demon' (pointing שֵׁדִי or שַׁדַּי [pl. maj.]: Nö. *ZDMG*, xl. 735 f., xlii. 480 f.); from √ שׁדה (Ar. *ṯadā*) = 'be wet' ('the raingiver': *OTJC*[2], 424); from Syr. ܫܕܐ, 'hurl' (Schwally, *ZDMG*, lii. 136: "a dialectic equivalent of יהוה in the sense of lightning-thrower" [שַׁדַּי]). Vollers (*ZA*, xvii. 310) argues for an original שַׁד (√ שׁוד), afterwards, through popular etymology and change of religious meaning, fathered on √ שׁדד. Several Assyriologists connect the word with *šadû rabû*, 'great mountain,' a title of Bêl and other Bab. deities (Homm. *AHT*, 109 f.; Zimmern, *KAT*[3], 358): a view which would be more plausible if, as Frd. Del. (*Prol.* 95 f.) has maintained, the Ass. √ meant 'lofty'; but this is denied by other authorities (Halevy, *ZKF*, ii. 405 ff.; Jen. *ZA*, i. 251). As to the origin of the name, there is a probability that אֵל שַׁדַּי was an old (cf. Gn. 49^{25}) Canaanite deity, of the same class as *'El 'Elyôn* (see on 14^{18}), whom the Israelites identified with Yahwe (so Gu. 235).—**4.** אֲנִי is *casus pendens* (Dri. *T.* § 197 (4)), not emphatic anticipation of following suff. (as G–K. § 135 *f*).

descendants of Abraham. See, however, on 28^3.—5. Abram's name is changed to *Abraham*, interpreted as 'Father of multitude.' Cf. Neh. 9^7.

The equation אַב הֲמוֹן [גוים]=אַבְרָהָם is so forced that Di. al. doubt if a serious etymology was intended. The line between word-play and etymology is difficult to draw; and all that can safely be said is that the strained interpretation here given proves that אַבְרָהָם is no artificial formation, but a genuine element of tradition. (1) The form אַבְרָם is an abbreviation of אֲבִירָם (Nu. 16^1 etc.: cf. אַבְנֵר, 1 Sa. 14^{51} etc., with אֲבִינֵר, 1 Sa. 14^{50}; אַבְשָׁלוֹם, 2 Ch. $11^{20.21}$, with אֲבִישָׁלוֹם, 1 Ki. $15^{2.10}$), which occurs as a personal name not only in Heb. but also as that of an Ass. official (*Abî-râmu*) under Esarhaddon, B.C. 677 (see *KAT*³, 482)*. (2) Of אברהם, on the other hand, no scientific etymology can be given. The nearest approach to P's explanation would be found in the Ar. ***ruhām*** = 'copious number' (from a √ descriptive of a fine drizzling rain: Lane, *s.v.*).† De. thinks this the best explanation; but the etymology is far-fetched, and apart from the probably accidental correspondence with P's interpretation the sense has no claim to be correct.—With regard to the relation of the two forms, various theories are propounded. Hommel (*AHT*, 275 ff.; *MVAG*, ii. 271) regards the difference as merely *orthographic*, the ה being inserted, after the analogy of Minæan, to mark the long *ā* (אַבְרָהם), while a later misunderstanding is responsible for the pronunciation רָהָם. Strack and Stade (*ZATW*, i. 349) suppose a *dialectic* distinction: according to the latter, אברהם is the original (Edomite) form, of which אברם is the Hebraïzed equivalent.‡ Wi. (*GI*, ii. 26) finds in them two distinct epithets of the moon-god Sin, one describing him as father of the gods (*Sin abu ilâni*), and the other ('father of the strife of peoples') as god of war (*Sin ḳarib ilâni*). The possibility must also be considered that the difference is due to the fusion in tradition of two originally distinct figures (see Paton, *Syr. and*

---

5. את־שמך] G-K. § 121*a*, *b*; but את is omitted in some MSS and in 𝔐.

---

* Hommel's reading of *Abî-râmu* on a contract tablet of Abil-Sin, the grandfather of Ḫammurabi (see *AHT*, 96), has proved to be incorrect, the true reading being *Abî-Eraḫ* (see Ranke, *Personennamen in d. Urk. der Ham.-dynastie*, 1902, p. 48). The name has, however, recently been discovered in several documents of the time of Ammizaduga, the 10th king of the same dynasty. See *BA*, vi. (1909), Heft 5, p. 60, where Ungnad shows that the name is not West Semitic, but Babylonian, that the pronunciation was *Abaram*, and that the first element is an accusative. He suggests that it may mean "he loves the father" (*râma*=רחם), the unnamed subject being probably a god. Comp. *ET*, xxi. (1909), 88 ff.

† The Ar. *kunyā*, *'Abū-ruhm* is only an accidental coincidence: Nö. *ZDMG*, xlii. 484^2.

‡ Similarly v. Gall (*CSt.* 53), who compares Aram. ܒܗܬ, Ar. ***bht***, appearing in Heb. as בוש.

Pal. 41). It is quite a plausible supposition, though the thoroughness of the redaction has effaced the proof of it, that אברם was peculiar to J and אברהם to E.—Outside of Gen. (with the exception of the citations 1 Ch. 1^{27}, Neh. 9^{7}) the form Abraham alone is found in OT.

6. The promise of *kings* among Abraham's descendants is again peculiar to P (35^{11}). The reference is to the Hebrew monarchy: the rulers of Ishmael are only 'princes' (נְשִׂיאִם, v.^{20}), and those of Edom (36^{40}) are styled אַלּוּף.—**7.** *to be to thee a God*] The essence of the covenant relation is expressed by this frequently recurring formula.* It is important for P's notion of the covenant that the correlative 'they (ye) shall be to me a people,' which is always added in other writings (ex. Ezk. 34^{24}), is usually omitted by P (ex. Ex. 6^{7}, Lv. 26^{12}). The *bĕrîth* is conceived as a self-determination of God to be to one particular race all that the word God implies, a reciprocal act of choice on man's part being no essential feature of the relation.—**8.** *land of thy sojourning*] 28^{4} 36^{7} 37^{1} 47^{9}, Ex. 6^{4} (all P).

9–14. The sign of the Covenant.—To the promises of vv.$^{2-8}$ there is attached a single command, with regard to which it is difficult to say whether it belongs to the content of the covenant (v.^{10}), or is merely an adjunct,—an external mark of the invisible bond which united every Jew to Yahwe (^{11}): see p. 297. The theme at all events is the institution of circumcision. The legal style of the section is so pronounced that it reads like a stray leaf from the book of Leviticus (note the address in 2nd p. pl. from ^{10} onwards).—**9.** *And God said*] marks a new section (cf. ^{15}), וְאַתָּה being the antithesis to אֲנִי in ^{4}.—*keep my covenant*] שָׁמַר is opposed to הֵפֵר, 'break,' in ^{14}; hence it cannot mean 'watch over' (Valeton), but must be used in the extremely common sense of 'observe' or 'act according to.' The question would

---

6. [מִמְּךָ] 𝔖 ܟܠ ܥܡܡܐ = מִמֵּעֶיךָ; see on 15^{4}.—**8.** [אֲחֻזָּה] a common word in P; elsewhere only Ps. 2^{8}, Ezk. 44^{28}, 1 Ch. 7^{28}.

---

* The list of passages as given by Dri. (p. 186) is as follows: In P, Ex. 6^{7} 29^{45}, Lv. 11^{45}; in P^{h}, Lv. 22^{33} 25^{38} $26^{12.45}$, Nu. 15^{41}; elsewhere, Dt. 29^{13} (cf. $26^{17f.}$), Jer. 7^{23} 11^{4} 24^{7} 30^{22} $31^{1.33}$, Ezk. 11^{20} 14^{11} 34^{24} 36^{28} $37^{23.27}$, 2 Sa. 7^{24} (= 1 Ch. 17^{22}), Zec. 8^{8}.

never have been raised but for a disinclination to admit anything of the nature of a stipulation into P's idea of the covenant.—**10.** *This is my covenant*] Circumcision is both the covenant and the sign of the covenant: the writer's ideas are sufficiently vague and elastic to include both representations. It is therefore unnecessary (with Ols. and Ball) to read זאת אות בריתי (see v.[13]).—**11.** *for a covenant-sign*] *i.e.*, after the analogy of 9[12f.], a token by which God is reminded of the existence of the covenant. The conception rises out of the extraordinary importance of the rite when the visible fabric of Hebrew nationality was dissolved, and nothing remained but this corporal badge as a mark of the religious standing of the Jew before Yahwe.—**12a.** *at the age of eight days*] connected with the period of the mother's uncleanness: Lv. 12[1. 3]; cf. Gn. 21[4], Lk. 1[59] 2[21], Phil. 3[5]; Jos. *Ant.* i. 214.—**12b, 13** go together (De.), extending the obligation to *slaves*, who as members of the household follow the religion of their master.—The penalty of disobedience is death or excommunication, according as one or the other is meant by the obscure formula: *be cut off from its kindred* (*v.i.*).

---

10. ובין זרעך אחריך] 𝔊 + εἰς τὰς γενεὰς αὐτῶν. The whole is possibly a gloss (KS. Ba. Gu.), due to confusion between the legislative standpoint of [10ff.] with its plural address, and the special communication to Abraham; see, however, vv.[12f.]—המול] inf. abs. used as juss.; G–K. § 113 *cc, gg*: cf. Ex. 12[48], Lev. 6[7], Nu. 6[5].—**11.** וּנְמַלְתֶּם] treated by 𝔗[OJ] as active, from √ נמל, but really abbreviated Niph. of √ מלל (cf. G–K. § 67 *dd*), a rare by-form (Jos. 5[2]) of מול.—והיה] 𝔐𝔖 והיתה, adopted by Ba.—**12.** יליד בית] see 14[14].—מקנת כסף] only vv.[13. 23. 27] and Ex. 12[44].—מורעך is the individualising use of 2nd p. sing., frequently alternating with 2nd pl. in legal enactments. So v.[13].—**14.** ערלתו] 𝔐𝔖𝔊 + ביום השמיני (Ba.).—ונכרתה—מעמיה] So Ex. 30[33. 38] 31[14], Lv. 7[20f. 25. 27] 17[9] 19[8] 23[29], Nu. 9[13],—all in P, who employs a number of similar phrases—'his people,' 'Israel,' 'the congregation of Israel,' 'the assembly,' etc.—to express the same idea (see Dri. 187[2]). עַמִּים is here used in the sense of 'kin,' as occasionally in OT (see 19[38] 25[8]). It is the Ar. '*amm*, which combines the two senses of 'people,' and 'relative on the father's side': see We. *GGN*, 1893, 480, and cf. Dri. on Dt. 32[50] (p. 384); Krenkel, *ZATW*, viii. 280 ff.; Nestle, *ib.* xvi. 322 f.; *KAT*[3], 480 f. With regard to the sense of the formula there are two questions: (*a*) whether it embraces the death-penalty, or merely exclusion from the *sacra* of the clan and from burial in the family grave; and (*b*) whether the punishment is to be inflicted by the com-

15–22. The heir of the Covenant.—The promise of the birth of Isaac is brought into connexion with the main idea of the chapter by the assurance ([19. 21]) that the covenant is to be established with him and not with Ishmael.—**15.** Sarai's name is changed to *Sarah*. The absence of an etymological motive is remarkable (*v.i.*).—**16b.** In 𝔊, *Jub.*, 𝔙 and 𝔖, the blessing on Sarah is by slight changes of text turned into a blessing on the son whose birth has just been foretold (*v.i.*). The MT, however, is more likely to be correct.—**17.** Abraham's demeanour is a strange mixture of reverence and incredulity: "partim gaudio exultans, partim admiratione extra se raptus, in risum prorumpit" is Calvin's comment. It is P's somewhat unnatural clothing of the traditional etymology of Isaac (יִצְחָק, v.[19]); cf. 18^{12} (J), 21^{6} (E).—**18.** The prayer, *O that Ishmael might live before thee!*—under Thy protection and with Thy blessing (Hos. 6^{2})—is a fine touch of nature; but the writer's interest lies rather in the 'determinate counsel and foreknowledge of God,' which overrides human feeling and irrevocably decrees the election

---

munity, or by God in His providence. The interpretation seems to have varied in different ages. Ex. $31^{13f.}$ clearly contemplates the death penalty at the hands of the community; while Lv. $17^{9f.}$ $20^{3.6}$ point as clearly to a divine interposition. The probability is that it is an archaic juridical formula for the punishment of death, which came to be used vaguely "as a strong affirmation of divine disapproval, rather than as prescribing a penalty to be actually enforced" (Dri.). See Sta. *GVI*, i. 421 f.; Ho. p. 127 f.—הֵפַר] pausal form for הֵפֵר (G–K. § 29 *q*).

15. שָׂרַי (𝔊 Σάρα) and שָׂרָה (𝔊 Σάῤῥα)] According to Nö. (*ZDMG*, xl. 183, xlii. 484), ׳ַ is an an old fem. termin. surviving in Syr. Arab. and Eth. On this view שָׂרַי may be either the same word as שָׂרָה, 'princess' (√ שרר), or (as the differentiation of 𝔊 suggests) from √ שרה, 'strive,' with which the name Israel was connected (Gn. 32^{29}, Ho. 12^{4}: see Rob. Sm. *KM*², 34 f. [Nö. dissents]). On Lagarde's (*Mitth.* ii. 185) attempt to connect the name with Ar. *šaraʸ* = 'wild fertile spot,' and so to identify Abraham (as 'husband of Sarai') with the Nabatean god Dusares (*ḏū-ššaraʸ*), see Mey. *INS*, 269 f., who thinks the conjecture raised beyond doubt by the discovery of the name *Šarayat* as consort of Dusares on an inscr. at Bosra in the Ḥaurân. The identification remains highly problematical.—16. וברכתיה] 𝔐 וברכתיו. So 𝔊 *Jub.* 𝔙𝔖, which consistently maintain the masc. to the end of the v.—17. וְאִם—הֲ׳] a combination of the disjunctive question with *casus pendens*; see G–K. § 150 *g*.

of Israel ([19]).—**19a.** Comp. the language with 16[11], and observe that the naming of the child is assigned to the father.—**20.** שְׁמַעְתִּיךָ] a remote allusion to the popular explanation of יִשְׁמָעֵאל, 'May God hear' (cf. 16[11] 21[17]). Ishmael is to be endowed for Abraham's sake with every kind of blessing, except the religious privileges of the covenant.—*twelve princes*] (cf. 25[16]) as contrasted with the 'kings' of [6. 16].—**22.** The close of the theophany.—וַיַּעַל—מֵעַל as 35[13].

23–27. Circumcision of Abraham's household.—**23.** *on that very day* (cf. 7[13])] repeated in v.[26]. Throughout the section, P excels himself in pedantic and redundant circumstantiality of narration. The circumcision of Ishmael, however, is inconsistent with the theory that the rite is a sign of the covenant, from which Ishmael is excluded (Ho. Gu.).—**25.** *thirteen years old*] This was the age of circumcision among the ancient Arabs, according to Jos. *Ant.* i. 214. Origen (Eus. *Præp. Ev.* vi. 11:* cf. We. *Heid.*[2] 175[3]); and Ambrose (*de Abrah.* ii. 348) give a similar age (14 years) for the Egyptians. It is possible that the notice here is based on a knowledge of this custom. Among the modern Arabs there is no fixed rule, the age varying from three to fifteen years: see Di. 264; Dri. in *DB*, ii. 504[b].

Circumcision is a widely diffused rite of primitive religion, of whose introduction among the Hebrews there is no authentic tradition. One account (Ex. 4[24f.]) suggests a Midianite origin, another (Jos. 5[2ff.]) an Egyptian: the mention of flint knives in both these passages is a proof of the extreme antiquity of the custom (the Stone Age).† The anthro-

---

19. אבל] '*Nay, but,*'—a rare asseverative (42[21], 2 Sa. 14[5], 2 Ki. 4[14], 1 Ki. 1[43]) and adversative (Dn. 10[7. 21], Ezr. 10[13], 2 Ch. 1[4] 19[3] 33[17]) particle. See the interesting note in Burney, *Notes on Kings*, p. 11; and cf. König, ii. 265.—לזרעו אחריו] 𝔊 *καὶ τῷ σπέρματι αὐτοῦ μετ' αὐτὸν* appears to imply a preceding clause **εἶναι αὐτῷ θεός**, which is found in many cursives. This is probably the correct reading.—**20.** נשיאם] 𝔊 *ἔθνη*.—**24.** שנה] ɯɯ שנים.—בהמלו] The Niph. is here either refl. or pass.; in [25] it is pass.—**26.** נמול] irreg. pf. Niph.; G–K. § 72 *ee*. 𝔖 takes it as act. (√נמל?) with Ishmael as obj.; and so 𝔊 in v.[27] (**περιέτεμεν αὐτούς**).

---

* Ed. Heinichen, p. 310 f.

† In a tomb of the Old Empire at Sakkara there are wall-pictures of the operation, where the surgeon uses a flint knife: see G. Elliot Smith in *British Medical Journal*, 1908, 732 (quoted by Matthes); and the illustration in *Texte u. Bilder*, ii. p. 126.

pological evidence shows that it was originally performed at puberty, as a preliminary to marriage, or, more generally, as a ceremony of initiation into the full religious and civil status of manhood. This primary idea was dissipated when it came to be performed in infancy; and its perpetuation in this form can only be explained by the inherited belief that it was an indispensable condition of participation in the common cultus of the clan or nation. Passsages like Dt. 10^{16} 30^{6}, Ezk. $44^{7.9}$, show that in Israel it came to be regarded as a token of allegiance to Yahwe; and in this fact we have the germ of the remarkable development which the rite underwent in post-Exilic Judaism. The new importance it then acquired was due to the experience of the Exile (partly continued in the Dispersion), when the suspension of public worship gave fresh emphasis to those rites which (like the Sabbath and circumcision) could be observed by the individual, and served to distinguish him from his heathen neighbours. In this way we can understand how, while the earlier legal codes have no law of circumcision, in P it becomes a prescription of the first magnitude, being placed above the Mosaic ritual, and second in dignity only to the Sabbath. The explicit formulating of the idea that circumcision is the sign of the national covenant with Yahwe was the work of the Priestly school of jurists; and very few legislative acts have exercised so tremendous an influence on the genius of a religion, or the character of a race, as this apparently trivial adjustment of a detail of ritual observance. For information on various aspects of the subject, see Ploss, *Das Kind in Brauch und Sitte der Völker*[2] (1894), i. 342–372; We. *Heid.*[2] 174 f., *Prol.*[6] 338 ff.; Sta. *ZATW*, vi. 132–143; the arts. in *DB* (Macalister) and *EB* (Benzinger); and the notes in Di. 258; Ho. 129; Gu. 237; Dri. 189 ff.; Strack[2], 67; Matthes, *ZATW*, xxix. 70 ff.

The Covenant-idea in P (see also p. 290 f. above). In P's scheme of four world-ages, the word בְּרִית is used only of the revelations associated with Noah and Abraham. In the Creation-narrative the term is avoided because the constitution of nature then appointed was afterwards annulled, whereas the *Bĕrîth* is a permanent and irreversible determination of the divine will. The conception of the Mosaic revelation as a covenant is Jehovistic (Ex. 24^{3-8} $34^{10ff.}$ etc.) and Deuteronomic (Dt. $4^{10ff.}$ $5^{2ff.}$ $9^{9ff.}$ etc.); and there are traces of it in secondary strata of P (Lv. 26^{45} [P^h], Ex. $31^{16f.}$* [P^s]); but it is not found in the historical work which is the kernel of the Code (P^g). Hence in trying to understand the religious significance of the *Bĕrîth* in P^g, we have but two examples to guide us. And with regard to both, the question is keenly discussed whether it denotes a self-imposed obligation on the part of God, irrespective of any condition on the part of man (so Valeton, *ZATW*, xii. 1 ff.), or a bilateral engagement involving *reciprocal* obligations between God and men (so in the main Kraetzschmar, *Bundesvorst.* 183 ff.). The answer depends on the view taken of circumcision in this chapter. According to Valeton, it is merely a sign and nothing

---

* Could this, however, be taken to mean that the Sabbath was a 'sign' of the *Adamic* dispensation conceived as a covenant?

more; *i.e.*, a means whereby God is reminded of the covenant. According to Kraetzschmar, it is both a sign and a constituent of the covenant, forming the condition on which the covenant is entered into. The truth seems to lie somewhere between two extremes. The *Bĕrîth* is neither a simple divine promise to which no obligation on man's part is attached (as in 15^{18}), nor is it a mutual contract in the sense that the failure of one party dissolves the relation. It is an immutable determination of God's purpose, which no unfaithfulness of man can invalidate; but it carries conditions, the neglect of which will exclude the individual from its benefits. It is perhaps an over-refinement when Kraetzschmar (*l.c.* 201) infers from the expressions הֵקִים and נָתַן that for P there is only *one* eternal divine *Bĕrîth*, immutably established by God and progressively revealed to man.

CH. XVIII. *The Theophany at Hebron: Abraham's Intercession for Sodom* (J).

Under the terebinths of Mamre, Abraham hospitably entertains three mysterious visitors ($^{1-8}$), and is rewarded by the promise of a son to be born to Sarah in her old age ($^{9-15}$). The three 'men,' whose true nature had been disclosed by their supernatural knowledge of Sarah's thoughts, then turn towards Sodom, accompanied by Abraham (^{16}), who, on learning Yahwe's purpose to destroy that city ($^{17-21}$), intercedes eloquently on its behalf ($^{22-33}$).

The first half of the chapter ($^{1-16}$) shows at its best the picturesque, lucid, and flexible narrative style of J, and contains many expressions characteristic of that document: יהוה, $^{1.\ 13.\ 14}$; רוּץ לִקְרַאת, ^{2} (only in J 24^{17} 29^{13} 33^{4}); מָצָא חֵן, ^{3}; נָא, $^{3.\ 4}$; עַבְדְּךָ (for 1st per.), $^{3.\ 5}$; כִּי־עַל־כֵּן, ^{5}; לָמָּה זֶּה, ^{13}; השקיף, ^{16}. The latter part ($^{17-33}$) is also Yahwistic (יהוה, $^{20.\ 22.\ 26.\ 33}$; [הִנֵּה־]נָא, $^{27.\ 30\text{ff.}}$; חָלִלָה, ^{25}; הַפַּעַם, ^{32}), but contains two expansions of later date than the primary narrative. We. (*Comp.*² 27 f.) appears to have proved that the original connexion between 18^{15} and 19^{1} consists of $^{16.\ 20-22a.\ 33b}$; and that $^{17-19.\ 22b-33a}$ are editorial insertions reflecting theological ideas proper to a more advanced stage of thought (see below). A more comprehensive analysis is attempted by Kraetzschmar in *ZATW*, xvii. 81 ff., prompted by the perplexing alternation of the sing. ([יהוה] $^{1.\ 3.\ 10.\ 13.\ 14.\ 15.\ 17-21.\ 22b-33}$) and pl. ($^{2.\ 4.\ 5.\ 8.\ 9.\ 16.\ 22a}$) * in the dialogue between Abraham and his guests. The theory will repay a closer examination than can be given to it here; but I agree with Gu. in thinking that the texture of $^{1-16}$ is too homogeneous to admit of decomposition, and that some other explana-

---

* It is important, however, to observe that in 𝔐 (if we except the introductory ^{1a}) the sing. does not appear till ^{10}, but after that regularly up to ^{15}.

tion of the phenomenon in question must be sought than the assumption of an interweaving of a sing. and a pl. recension of the legend (see on v.¹ and p. 303 below).* With Gu. also, we may regard the chapter as the immediate sequel to 13^{18} in the legendary cycle which fixes the residence of Abraham at Hebron (J^h). The conception of Abraham's character is closely akin to what we meet throughout that section of J, and differs appreciably from the representation of him in 12^{10-20} and 16.

1–8. The entertainment of the three wayfarers.—The description "presents a perfect picture of the manner in which a modern Bedawee sheikh receives travellers arriving at his encampment. He immediately orders his wife or women to make bread, slaughters a sheep or other animal, and dresses it in haste; and, bringing milk and any other provisions that he may have at hand, with the bread and the meat that he has dressed, sets them before his guests: if they are persons of high rank he also stands by them while they eat" (Lane, *Mod. Eg.*⁵ i. 364: from Dri.).—**1.** *Yahwe appeared, etc.*] This introductory clause simply means that the incident about to be related has the value of a theophany. In what way the narrator conceived that Yahwe was present in the three men—whether He was one of the three, or whether all three were Yahwe in self-manifestation (De.)—we can hardly tell. The common view that the visitors were Yahwe accompanied by two of His angels does not meet the difficulties of the exegesis; and it is more probable that to the original Yahwist the 'men' were emissaries and representatives of Yahwe, who was not visibly present (see p. 304 f.).—כְּחֹם הַיּוֹם] at the hottest (and drowsiest) time of the day (2 Sa. 4^5).—**2.** *and behold*] The mysteriously sudden advent of the strangers marks them as superhuman beings (Jos. 5^{13}), though this makes no impression on Abraham at the time. The interest of the story turns largely on his ignorance of the real character of his guests.—**3.** The Mass. pointing אֲדֹנָי implies that Abraham recognised Yahwe as one of the three (Tu. De. al.); but this we have just seen to be

1. יהוה] 𝔊 ὁ θεός.—In אליו the suff. may refer back directly to 13^{18} (see on the v.).—באלני ממרא] 𝔊 πρὸς τῇ δρυῒ τῇ M.; see on 13^{18}.—**3.** Read with

* The same solution had occurred to Ball (*SBOT*, 1896), but was rightly set aside by him as unproved.

a mistake. The correct form is either אֲדֹנִי (as $23^{6.\,11}$, etc.: so Di. Dri.), or (better, as 19^{2}) אֲדֹנַי: *Sirs!*—restoring (with 𝔐) the pl. throughout the v.—The whole of Abraham's speech is a fine example of the profuse, deferential, self-depreciatory courtesy characteristic of Eastern manners.—4. *wash your feet*] Cf. 19^{2} 24^{32} 43^{24}, Ju. 19^{21}, 2 Sa. 11^{8}, Lk. 7^{44}, 1 Ti. 5^{10}.—*recline yourselves*] not at meat (Gu.), but during the preparation of the meal. Even in the time of Amos (6^{4}) reclining at table seems to have been a new-fangled and luxurious habit introduced from abroad: ct. the ancient custom 27^{19}, Ju. 19^{6}, 1 Sa. $20^{5.\,24}$, 1 Ki. 13^{20}.—5. *support your heart*] with the food, Ju. $19^{5.\,8}$, 1 Ki. 13^{7}, Ps. 104^{15}; cf. bread the 'staff' of life, Lv. 26^{26}, Is. 3^{1}.—*seeing that, etc.*] Hospitality is, so to speak, the logical corollary of passing Abraham's tent.—**6–8.** The preparation of a genuine Bedouin repast, consisting of hastily baked *cakes* of bread, *flesh*, and *milk* in two forms. On the items, *v.i.*—8. *and they ate*] So 19^{3}—the only cases in OT where the Deity is represented as eating (ct. Ju. $6^{20f.}$ 13^{16}). The anthropomorphism is evaded by Jos. (*Ant.* i. 197: οἱ δὲ δόξαν αὐτῷ παρέσχον ἐσθιόντων; cf. Tob. 12^{19}), 𝔗[J], Ra. al.

9–15. The promise of a son to Sarah.—The subject is introduced with consummate skill. In the course of the conversation which naturally follows the meal, an apparently casual question leads to an announcement which shows

---

𝔐 בעיניכם, תעברו, עבדכם.—5. ואחר תעברו (𝔐𝔊𝔗[OJ]) is the better reading, to which 𝔊 adds εἰς τὴν ὁδὸν ὑμῶν (cf. 19^{2}).—כי־על־כן is not to be resolved into כִּי and עַל־כֵּן, *denn eben desshalb* (G–B.[14], 308 a; De. al.); but is a compound conjunction = *quandoquidem*, 'inasmuch as' (Tu. Di. Dri.), as usage clearly shows; cf. 19^{8} 33^{10} 38^{26} Nu. 10^{31} 14^{43} (all J), Ju. 6^{22}, 2 Sa. 18^{20}, Jer. 29^{28} 38^{4} †; see G–K. § 158 b^{3}; BDB, 475 b.—עברתם על] 𝔊 ἐξεκλίνατε πρός = סַרְתֶּם אֶל ($19^{2f.}$), which is too rashly accepted by Ba.—וַיֹּאמְרוּ] 𝔊 has the sing. wrongly.—6. *Three seahs* would be (according to Kennedy's computation, *DB*, iv. 912) approximately equal to 4½ pecks.—קמח סלת] 𝔊 σεμιδάλεως, [𝔙 *similæ*], which might stand either for קמח (1 Sa. 1^{24}) or סלת (as in every other instance). The latter (the finer variety) is here probably a gloss on קמח.—עגות] (𝔊 ἐγκρυφίας, 𝔙 *subcinericios panes*) are thin round cakes baked on hot stones or in the ashes (Benz. *Arch.*[2] 64).—8. חמאה is the Ar. *laban*, milk slightly soured by fermentation, which is greatly esteemed by the nomads of Syria and Arabia as a refreshing and nourishing beverage (see *EB*, iii. 3089 f.).

superhuman knowledge of the great blank in Abraham's life, and conveys a first intimation of the real nature of the visitors. See Gu.'s fine exposition, 172 f.; and contrast the far less delicate handling of an identical situation in 2 Ki. 4^{13-16}.—**9.** The question shows that Sarah had not been introduced to the strangers, in accordance probably with Hebrew custom (Gu.).—**10.** *I will return*] The definite transition to the sing. takes place here (see on v.^{3}). In the original legend the pl. was no doubt kept up to the end; but the monotheistic habit of thought was too strong for Hebrew writers, when they came to words which could be properly ascribed only to Yahwe.—On כָּעֵת חַיָּה, *v.i.*—*Sarah was listening*] with true feminine curiosity; cf. 27^{5}. The last two words should probably be rendered: *she being behind it* (the tent or the door); cf. the footnote.—**11.** A circumstantial sentence explaining Sarah's incredulity (v.^{12}). —*after the manner of women* (cf. 31^{35})] "quo genere loquendi verecunde menses notat qui mulieribus fluunt" (Calv.); 𝔊 τὰ γυναίκια; 𝔙 *muliebria*.—**12.** *Sarah laughed* (וַתִּצְחַק) *within herself*] obviously a proleptic explanation of

---

9. ויאמרו] 𝔊 ויאמר (wrongly).—אליו] The superlinear points (cf. 16^{5}) are thought to indicate a reading לו.—**10.** כָּעֵת חַיָּה] This peculiar phrase (recurring only v.^{14}, 2 Ki. $4^{16f.}$) is now almost invariably rendered 'at the (this) time, when it revives,' *i.e.*, next year, or spring (so Ra. IEz.; cf. Ges. *Th.* 470; G–B.^{14}, 202 a; BDB, 312 a; Ew. *Gr.* § 337 a; G-K. § 118 *u*; Kö. *S.* § 387 e); but the sense is extremely forced. It is surprising that no one seems to suspect a reference to the period of pregnancy. In NH חַיָּה means a woman in child-birth (so perhaps חָיֶה in Ex. 1^{19} [Ho. *ad v.*]); and here we might point כְּעֵת חַיָּה or כ׳ חָיָה, rendering 'according to the time of a pregnant woman,' or 9 months hence. לַמּוֹעֵד in v.^{14} is no obstacle, for מוֹעֵד is simply the time determined by the previous promise, and there is no need to add הַזֶּה (𝔊 after 17^{21}). 2 Ki. 4^{16} (לַמּ׳ הַזֶּה) does present a difficulty; but that late passage is modelled on this, and the original phrase may have been already misunderstood, as it is by all Vns.: *e.g.* 𝔊 κατὰ τὸν καιρὸν τοῦτον εἰς ὥρας; 𝔗^{O} 'at a time when you are living'; 𝔖 'at this time, she being alive'; 𝔙 *tempore isto, vita comite.* Ba. also points as constr., but thinks חַיָּה an old name for spring.—והנה] 𝔊𝔖 read וְהָיָה.—והוא אחריו] 𝔐 והיא א׳; so 𝔊 οὖσα ὄπισθεν αὐτοῦ. MT is perhaps a neglect of the *Qĕrê perpet* (וְהִוא).—**11.** באים בימים] cf. 24^{1}, Jos. 13^{1} $23^{1.2}$, 1 Ki. 1^{1}.—ארח כנשים] Ba. Kit. more smoothly, כְּאֹרַח נָשִׁים.—**12.** אַחֲרֵי—עֶדְנָה] 𝔊 Οὔπω μέν μοι γέγονεν ἕως τοῦ νῦν presupposes an impossible text בִּלְתִּי הָיְתָה לִי עֶדְנָה. The change is perhaps alluded to in the name יִצְחָק (see on 17^{17}), although the sequel in this document has not been preserved.—*waxed old*] lit. 'worn away,' a strong word used, *e.g.*, of worn out garments (Dt. 8^4 29^4 etc.).—עֶדְנָה (only here), 'sensuous enjoyment' (*Liebeswonne*).—**13.** This leads to a still more remarkable proof of divine insight: the speaker knows that Sarah has laughed, though he has neither seen nor heard her (בְּקִרְבָּהּ, v.[12]). The insertion of Yahwe here was probably caused by the occurrence of the name in the next v.—**14.** *Is anything too strange for Yahwe?*] As the narrative stands, the sentence does not imply identity between the speaker and Yahwe, but rather a distinction analogous to that frequently drawn between Yahwe and the angel of Yahwe (see on 16^7).—**15.** *Sarah denied it*] startled by the unexpected exposure of her secret thoughts into fear of the mysterious guests.

From the religious-historical point of view, the passage just considered, with its sequel in ch. 19, is one of the most obscure in Genesis. According to Gu. (174 ff.), whose genial exposition has thrown a flood of light on the deeper aspects of the problem, the narrative is based on a widely diffused Oriental myth, which had been localised in Hebron in the pre-Yahwistic period, and was afterwards incorporated in the Abrahamic tradition. On this view, the three strangers were originally three deities, disguised as men, engaged in the function described in the lines of Homer (*Od.* xvii. 485 ff.):

> Καί τε θεοὶ ξείνοισιν ἐοικότες ἀλλοδαποῖσιν,
> παντοῖοι τελέθοντες, ἐπιστρωφῶσι πόληας,
> ἀνθρώπων ὕβριν τε καὶ εὐνομίην ἐφορῶντες.*

Dr. Rendel Harris goes a step further, and identifies the gods with the Dioscuri or Kabiri, finding in the prominence given to hospitality, and the renewal of sexual functions, characteristic features of a Dioscuric visitation (*Cult of the Heavenly Twins*, 37 ff.). Of the numerous parallels that are adduced, by far the most striking is the account of the birth of Orion in Ovid, *Fasti*, v. 495 ff.: Hyrieus, an aged peasant of Tanagra, is visited by Zeus, Poseidon, and Hermes, and shows hospitality to them; after the repast the gods invite him to

---

Mechilta on Ex. 12^{40} (see p. 14 above; Geiger, *Urschr.* 439, 442).—אַחֲרֵי בְלֹתִי] Aq. μετὰ τὸ κατατριβῆναί με; Σ. (less accurately) μ. τ. παλαιωθῆναί με.—**14.** היפלא מן] Jer. $32^{17.27}$, Dt. 17^8 30^{11}.

---

* The belief appears to be very ancient. Dr. Frazer cites several primitive rites in which strangers are treated as deities—not always to their advantage (*Golden Bough*, ii. 225, 232, 234 f., and especially 237; *Adonis Attis Osiris*, 21 ff.).

name a wish; and he, being widowed and childless, asks for a son. 'Pudor est ulteriora loqui'; but at the end of ten months Orion is miraculously born. The resemblance to Gn. 18 is manifest; and since direct borrowing of the Bœotian legend from Jewish sources is improbable, there is a presumption that we have to do with variations of the same tale. The theory is rendered all the more plausible by the fact that a precisely similar origin is suggested by the leading motives of ch. 19 (see below).—Assuming that some such pagan original is the basis of the narrative before us, we find a clue to that confusion between the sing. and plu. which has been already referred to as a perplexing feature of the chapter. It is most natural to suppose that the threefold manifestation is a remnant of the original polytheism, the heathen deities being reduced to the rank of Yahwe's envoys. The introduction of Yahwe Himself as one of them would thus be a later modification, due to progressive Hebraïzing of the conception, but never consistently carried through. An opposite view is taken by Fripp (*ZATW*, xii. 23 ff.), who restores the sing. throughout, and by Kraetzschmar, who, as we have seen, distinguishes between a sing. and a pl. recension, but regards the former as the older. The substitution of angels for Yahwe might seem a later refinement on the anthropomorphic representation of a bodily appearance of Yahwe; but the resolution of the *one* Yahwe into *three* angels would be unaccountable, especially in J, who appears never to speak of angels in the plural (see on 19[1]). See Gu. 171, and Che. *EB*, iv. 4667 f.

16–22a. The judgement of Sodom revealed.

The soliloquy of Yahwe in [17-19] breaks the connexion between [16] and [20], and is to all appearance a later addition (see p. 298). (*a*) The insertion assumes that Yahwe is one of the three strangers; but this is hardly the intention of the main narrative, which continues to speak of 'the men' in the pl. ([22a]). (*b*) In [17] Yahwe has resolved on the destruction of Sodom, whereas in [20f.] He proposes to abide by the result of a personal investigation. (*c*) Both thought and language in [17-19] show signs of Deuteronomic influence (see Ho. and Gu.). Di.'s assertion (265), that [20f.] have no motive apart from [17-19] and [23ff.], is incomprehensible; the difficulty rather is to assign a reason for the addition of [17ff.]. The idea seems to be that Abraham (as a prophet: cf. Am. 3[7]) must be initiated into the divine purpose, that he may instruct his descendants in the ways of Yahwe.

16. *and looked out in view of Sodom* (cf. 19[28])] The Dead Sea not being visible from Hebron, we must understand that a part of the journey has been accomplished. Tradition fixed the spot at a village over 3 m. E of Hebron, called by Jerome *Caphar Barucha*, now known as *Beni Naʿim*, but

---

16. סְדֹם] 𝔊 + καὶ Γομόρρας.

formerly *Kefr Barîk*, from which the Sea is seen through gaps in the mountains (see Robinson, *BR*, i. 490 f.; Buhl, *GP*, 158 f.).—**17.** *But Yahwe had said*] *sc.* 'to Himself'; the construction marking the introduction of a circumstance.—**18.** *Seeing Abraham, etc.*] Yahwe reflects, as it were, on the religious importance of the individual beside Him.—*and all nations, etc.*] See the notes on 12³. בו possibly refers not to Abraham but to גוי; cf. 22¹⁸ (We.).—**19.** Comp. Dt. 6¹⁻³.—*For I have known* (*i.e.* 'entered into personal relations with': as Am. 3², Hos. 13⁵) *him in order that, etc.*] There is a certain incongruity between the two parts of the v.: here the establishment of the true religion is the purpose of Abraham's election; in ¹⁹ᵇ the end of the religion is the fulfilment of the promises made to Abraham.—**20.** Resuming v.¹⁶. An earlier form of the story no doubt read ויאמרו instead of ויאמר יהוה.—On the peculiar construction, *v.i.*—**21.** Restoring the pl. as before, the v. reads as a disjunctive question: *We will go down that we may see whether . . . or not: we would know.*

22b-33. Abraham's intercession.

The secondary character of ²²ᵇ⁻³³ᵃ (see p. 298) appears from the following considerations: (*a*) In ²²ᵃ 'the men' (*i.e.* all three) have moved away to Sodom; in ²²ᵇ Yahwe remains behind with Abraham. That

---

17. After אַבְרָהָם 𝔊𝔖 read עַבְדִּי.—**19.** ידעתיו] 𝔐𝔊𝔙 omit the suffix, while 𝔊𝔙𝔖 treat what follows as an obj. cl. (*quod*, etc.), through a misunderstanding of the sense of ידע.—**20.** זעקת] 𝔐 צעקת as v.²¹.—כִּי (*bis*)] 𝔗^O ארי. The particle is ignored by 𝔊𝔙; also by 𝔖, which supplies ܟܠܗ ܡܫܡܥܬܗܘܢ and omits כִּי רַבָּה. If the text be retained the כִּי is either *corroborative* (G-K. §§ 148 *d*, 159 *ee*), or *causal* (BDB, 473 b); but neither construction is natural. Moreover, the parallelism of clauses is itself objectionable; for whether the 'sin' actually corresponds to the 'cry' is the very point to be investigated (v.²¹). This material difficulty is not removed by the addition of שָׁמַעְתִּי (Ols.) or בָּאָה אֵלַי (Kit.). Its removal is the sole recommendation of We.'s proposal to omit וְ before חַטָּאתָם and render, 'There is a rumour about S. and G. that their sin is great, that it is very grievous.'—**21.** Read with 𝔊𝔗^O הַכְּצַעֲקָתָם.—On הַבָּאָה for הַבָּאָה, see G-K. § 138 *k*.—כָּלָה is difficult: cf. Ex. 11¹, another doubtful pass. We. here suggests כֻּלָּה, Ols. כֻּלָּם.

22b contains one of the 18 תִּקּוּנֵי סֹפְרִים (corrections of the scribes). The original reading ויהוה עדנו עמד לפני אב׳ is said to have been changed

Yahwe was one of the three is certainly the view of the later editors (see on 19^{1}); but if that had been the original conception, it must have been clearly expressed at this point. (*b*) In $^{20f.}$ we have seen that the fate of Sodom still hangs in the balance, while in $^{23ff.}$ its destruction is assumed as already decreed. (*c*) The whole tenor of the passage stamps it as the product of a more reflective age than that in which the ancient legends originated. It is inconceivable that the early Yahwist should have entirely overlooked the case of Lot, and substituted a discussion of abstract principles of the divine government. Gunkel points out that the most obvious solution of the actual problem raised by the presence of Lot in Sodom would have been a promise of deliverance for the few godly people in the city; that consequently the line of thought pursued does not arise naturally from the story itself, but must have been suggested by the theological tendencies of the age in which the section was composed. The precise point of view here represented appears most clearly in such passages as Jer. 15^{1}, Ezk. 14$^{14ff.}$; and in general it was not till near the Exile that the allied problems of individual responsibility and vicarious righteousness began to press heavily on the religious conscience in Israel.

23. *Wilt thou even sweep away, etc.*] The question strikes the keynote of the section,—a protest against the thought of an indiscriminate judgement (cf. Jb. 9^{22}).—**24.** *Suppose there should be fifty, etc.*] A small number in a city, but yet sufficient to produce misgiving if they should perish unjustly.—*and not forgive the place*] In OT, righteousness and clemency are closely allied: there is more injustice in the death of a few innocent persons than in the sparing of a guilty multitude. The problem is, to what limits is the application of this principle subject?—**25.** *Shall not the Judge, etc.*] Unrighteousness in the Supreme Ruler of the world would make piety impossible: cf. Ro. 3^{6}.—**27.** *I have ventured*] cf. Jer. 12^{1}. הואיל expresses the overcoming of a certain inward reluctance (Jos. 7^{7}).—*dust and ashes*] an alliterative combination (Jb. 30^{19} 42^{6}, Sir. 40^{3}). As a descrip-

---

out of a feeling of reverence (Ginsburg, *Introd.* 352 f.). The worth of the tradition is disputed, the present text being supported by all Vns. as well as by 19^{27}; and the sense certainly does not demand the suggested restoration (Tu. Di. against KS. Ba. Gu. al.).—**23, 24.** האף] 𝕿^{O} הבירגו, mistaking for אַף = 'anger': so 𝕾𝕿^{J}.—**23** end] 𝕲 + καὶ ἔσται ὁ δίκαιος ὡς ὁ ἀσεβής (^{25a}).—**24.** תשא] *sc.* עָוֹן = 'forgive': Nu. 14^{19}, Is. 2^{9}, Hos. 1^{6} etc.—**25.** חָלִלָה] lit. '*profanum* (*sit*),' construed with מִן, as 44$^{7.17}$, oft. The full formula is ח'ל' מיהוה (1 Sa. 24^{7} 26^{11} etc.).—לא יעשה משפט] 𝖁 (***nequaquam facies judicium hoc***) and 𝕾 (which takes השפט as vocative)

tion of human nature, the phrase recurs only Sir. 10^{9} 17^{32}.—28. בַּחֲמִשָּׁה] lit. 'on account of the 5'; a somewhat paradoxical form of expression.—**30–32.** Emboldened by success, Abraham now ventures on a reduction by 10 instead of 5 (De.); this is continued till the limit of human charity is reached, and Abraham ceases to plead.—**33.** *went*] not to Sodom, but simply 'departed.'—**33b** would be equally appropriate after [33a] or [22a].

XIX. 1–29.—*The Destruction of Sodom and Deliverance of Lot* (J and P).

The three men (see on v.[1]) who have just left Abraham reach Sodom in the evening, are received as guests by Lot ([1–3]), but are threatened with outrage by the Sodomites ([4–11]). Thus convinced of the depravity of the inhabitants, they secure the safety of Lot's household ([12–22]), after which the city is destroyed by fire and brimstone ([23–28]).

Thus far J: cf. יהוה, [13. 14. 16. 24. 27]; [הנה־]נא, [2. 7. 8. 18. 19. 20]; טרם, [4]; כי־על־כן, [8]; לקראת, [1]; פצר, [3. 9]; השקיף, [28].—The summary in [29] is from P: cf. אלהים, ערי הככר, שחת (cf. 6^{17} $9^{11. 15}$).—The passage continues $18^{22a. 33b}$ (J^{h}), and forms an effective contrast to the scene in Abraham's tent (18^{1-15}). The alternation of sing. and pl. is less confusing than in 18; and Kraetzschmar's theory (see p. 298 f.) does less violence to the structure of the passage. Indeed, Gu. himself admits that the sing. section [17–22] (with [26]) is an 'intermezzo' from another Yahwistic author (Gu. 181).

1–3. Lot's hospitality.—Comp. Ju. 19^{15-21}.—**1a.** *the two angels*] Read 'the men,' as 18^{16} [$19^{5. 8}$] [10. 12. 16]; see the footnote.—*in the gate*] the place of rendezvous in Eastern cities for business or social intercourse; Ru. $4^{1ff. 11}$, Jb. 29^{7} etc.—**1b, 2a.** Cf. 18^{2}.—אֲדֹנַי] *Sirs!* See on 18^{3}.

---

mistake the sense.—28. יחסרון] The regular use of the ending ון (G-K. § 47 *m*) from this point onwards is remarkable (Di.). The form, though *etymologically* archaic, is by no means a mark of antiquity in OT, and is peculiarly frequent in Deut. style (Dri. on Dt. 1^{17}).—32. הפעם] see on 2^{23}.

1. שני המלאכים] This word has not been used before, and recurs only in v.[15] (in 𝔐 also v.[12], and in 𝔊 v.[16]). The phrase is, no doubt, a correction for הָאֲנָשִׁים, caused by the introduction of [22b–33a], and the consequent identification of Yahwe with one of the original three, and the other two with His angels (We. *Comp.*[2] 27 f.).—2. הִנֶּה נָּא] so pointed

De.'s inference that Lot's spiritual vision was less clear than Abraham's may be edifying, but is hardly sound. —2b. The refusal of the invitation may be merely a piece of Oriental politeness, or it may contain a hint of the purpose of the visit (18^{21}). In an ordinary city it would be no great hardship to spend the night in the street: Lot knows only too well what it would mean in Sodom.

4–11. The assault of the Sodomites.—**4.** *They had not yet retired to rest when, etc.*] That *all* the men of the city were involved in the attack is affirmed with emphasis (מִקָּצֶה: *v.i.*): an instance of the 'shamelessness' of Sodom (Is. 3^{9}).—**5.** The unnatural vice which derives its name from the incident was viewed in Israel as the lowest depth of moral corruption: cf. Lv. $18^{22ff.}$ $20^{13.\ 23}$, Ezk. 16^{50}, Ju. 19^{22}.—**6–8.** Lot's readiness to sacrifice the honour of his daughters, though abhorrent to Hebrew morality (cf. Ju. $19^{25.\ 30}$), shows him as a courageous champion of the obligations of hospitality in a situation of extreme embarrassment, and is recorded to his credit. Cf. $12^{13ff.}$ —**8.** *inasmuch as they have come under the shadow* (*i.e.* 'protection') *of my roof-tree*] קֹרָה, 'beam' (like μέλαθρα), for 'house.'—**9.** Lot is reminded of his solitary (הָאֶחָד, *der Eine da*) and defenceless position as a *gêr* (see on 12^{10}).—**11.** The divine beings smite the rabble with demonic blindness (סַנְוֵרִים: *v.i.*).

---

only here: G-K. § 20 *d*, 100 *o*.—**3.** פצר] Only again 19^{9} 33^{11} (J), Ju. 19^{7}, 2 Ki. 2^{17} 5^{16}.

4. אנשי סדם] probably a gloss (Ols.).—מקצה] (𝕲 ἅμα) an abbreviation of מִקְצֵה ועד־הקצה (Gn. 47^{21}, Ex. 26^{28}, Dt. 13^{8} etc.)='exhaustively': so Is. 56^{11}, Jer. 51^{31}, Ezk. 25^{9}.—**6.** הפתחה] om. by 𝕲𝔙.—**8.** האל]=הָאֵלֶּה (only again 19^{25} $26^{3f.}$, Lv. 18^{27}, Dt. 4^{42} 7^{22} 19^{11}, 1 Ch. 20^{8}) is an orthographic variant (not in 𝔐), meant originally to be pronounced הָאֵל. See Dri. on Dt. 4^{42}.—כי־על־כן] as 18^{5}.—**9.** גֶּשׁ־הלאה [𝔐 נשה] 𝕲 ἀπόστα ἐκεῖ: 'stand back there'; cf. גְּשָׁה־לִּי, Is. 49^{20}.—וישפט שפוט] Consec. impf. expressing 'paradoxical consequence' (De.); cf. 32^{31} 40^{23}, Jb. 2^{3}: see G-K. § 111 *l*, *m*. The inf. abs. *after* its vb. properly denotes continuance of the action; here its position seems due to the consec. ו, and its force as if it had stood first (G-K. § 113 *r*, *p*).—**11.** סַנְוֵרִים] (2 Ki. 6^{18}†) is related to ordinary blindness (עִוָּרוֹן, Dt. 28^{28}, Zec. 12^{4}†), somewhat as תַּרְדֵּמָה (2^{21}) is to ordinary sleep. If from √ נור ('shine'), it is either a

12–16. The deliverance of Lot.—12. On the construction, *v.i.*—**13.** *Yahwe has sent us*] *i.e.* the 'three' are agents of Yahwe, who is therefore *not* present in person.—**14.** Lot warns his (prospective) *sons-in-law, who were to marry his daughters*: so Jos. *Ant.* i. 202, 𝔙, Tu. Di. Dri. al. Others (𝔊𝔗[J], IEz. De. al.) take לֹקְחֵי as referring to the past, which is possible (cf. 27[46]).—*as one that jested*] see on 21[9]. —**15.** *as the dawn appeared*] The judgement must be accomplished by sunrise ([23f.]); hence the urgency of the summons.—*the angels*] 'the men,' as v.[1].—הַנִּמְצָאֹת] *who are at hand* (1 Sa. 21[4]). — **16.** *he hesitated*] reluctant, and only half-convinced.—*through Yahwe's compassion on him*]. —*left him without the city*] rather suggests, as Gu. (186) holds, that there he is in safety.

17–22. The sparing of Zoar.—17. *the mountain*] the elevated Moabite plateau, which rises steeply to heights of 2500–3000 ft. from the E side of the Sea.—*look not behind thee*] Such prohibitions are frequent in legends and incantations; comp. the story of Orpheus and Eurydice (Ovid, *Met.* x. 51; Virg. *Ge.* iv. 491); cf. also Virg. *Ecl.* viii. 102; Ov. *Fasti*, v. 439.—**20.** *is near enough to flee to*]. —מִצְעָר] *a trifle*: repeated with a view to the etymology of [22b].

---

common oriental euphemism (Kön. ii. p. 404), or dazzling from excess of light (Ac. 9[3]): cf. Hoffmann, *ZATW*, ii. 68[1]. 𝔗[O] שבריריא means both 'brightness' and 'blindness'; and in the Talmud *Shabriri* is a demon of blindness (*JE*, iv. 517 a). 𝔖 ܒܫܘܪ̈ܝܐ, 'hallucinations.'

12. עד מי־לך וגו'] The stiff construction has led to various operations on the text. 𝔊𝔙 seem to have read חֲתָנִים וּבָנִים וּבָנוֹת; 𝔖 has חֲתָנֶיךָ. Di. suggests that the letters ובנ have been accidentally thrust into the word חתניך; Ho. and Gu. omit ו in ובניך (so 𝔐) and commence a new sentence there; Ba. Kit. delete חתן ו. The text may be retained if we take the first cl. as indirect qn.: 'Whomsoever thou hast here as a son-in-law, and thy sons . . . bring forth,' etc.—At end add הַזֶּה with 𝔐𝔊.—**15.** כמו] "rare and poetic" (Di.). Here used as conj. (=כאשר).—הנמצאת] 𝔊 ἃς ἔχεις καὶ ἔξελθε; 𝔙 *quas habes*.—**16.** חמלת] f. inf. const.—16b is omitted by 𝔊[A, al.], but is found in many cursives.

17. ויאמר] 𝔊𝔙𝔖 have pl., which is supported by the previous הוציאם and the following אלהם, though the sing. is maintained in the rest of the section.—תבים] for תַּבֵּט; G–K. § 107 *p*.—המלט] five times repeated in the six vv. is thought by Ba. to be a play on the name לוט.—**20.** ותחי נפשי] 𝔊 + ἕνεκεν σοῦ, a slavish imitation of 12[13].

The city of Ẓō'ar (𝔊 Σηγωρ) was well known, not only in OT times (13^{10} $14^{2.8}$, Dt. 34^{3}, Is. 15^{5}, Jer. 48^{34}), but also in the time of the Crusades, and to the Ar. geographers, who call the Dead Sea the Sea of *Zuġar*. That this mediæval Zoar was at the S end of the lake is undisputed; and there is no good reason to question its identity with the biblical city (see Jos. *BJ*, iv. 482; *OS*[1], 261^{37}). Since Wetzstein, it is usually located at *Ghōr eṣ-Ṣāfiyeh*, about 5 m. SE from the present shore of the Sea (cf. Di. 273; Buhl, *GP*, 271; Smith, *HG*, 505 ff.; and esp. Dri. *DB*, iv. 985b ff.). The situation of the city naturally gave birth to the secondary legend that it had been saved from the fate of the adjacent cities on account of the intercession of Lot; while the name in Heb. readily suggested the etymology of [22b].

23–28. The catastrophe.—Brevity in the description of physical phenomena is in accord with the spirit of the Hebrew legend, whose main interest is the dramatic presentation of human character and action.—**23, 24.** The clause *when Lot entered Zoar*, presupposes [17–22], and, if the latter be from a separate source, must be deleted as an interpolation (Gu.). The connexion is improved by the excision: just as the sun rose the catastrophe took place (G–K. § 164 *b*).—*sulphur and fire* (Ezk. 38^{22}, Ps. 11^{6})] a feature suggested by permanent physical phenomena of the region (see below).—*Yahwe rained . . . from Yahwe*] A distinction between Yahwe as present in the angels and Yahwe as seated in heaven (Di.) is improbable. We must either suppose that the original subject was 'the men' (so Gu.: cf. v.[13]), or that מֵאֵת יהוה is a doublet to מִן־הַשָּׁמָֽיִם: the latter phrase, however, is generally considered to be a gloss (Ols. KS. Ho. Gu. Kit.).—**25.** וַיַּהֲפֹךְ] see on [29].—**26.** Lot's wife transgresses the prohibition of [17], and is turned into a *pillar of salt*.

The literal interpretation of this notice, though still maintained by Strack, is clearly inadmissible. The pillar is mentioned as still existing in WS 10^{7}, Jos. *Ant.* i. 203; the reference obviously being to some curious resemblance to a female figure, round which the popular

---

21. נשאתי פניך] 'have accepted thee' (lit. 'lifted up thy face': opp. השיב פנים)—here in a good sense (as 32^{21}, 2 Ki. 3^{14}, Mal. $1^{8f.}$), more frequent in the bad sense of partiality in judgement (Lv. 19^{15}, Dt. 10^{17}, Mal. 2^{9}, Jb. 13^{10} etc.).

23. יצא] 𝔐 יצאה; cf. 15^{17}.—**25.** האל (v.[8])] 𝔊 + אֲשֶׁר יָשַׁב בָּהֶן לוֹט, as v.[29].—**26.** The v. stands out of its proper position (note the ו consec., and the suffs.), and belongs to [17-22] rather than to the main narrative (Gu.).—

imagination had woven a legend connecting it with the story of Lot. Whether it be identical with the huge cylindrical column, 40 ft. high, on the E side of *Ğebel Usdum*, described by Lynch, is, of course, doubtful.* The fact that Ğ. Usdum is on the SW side of the lake, while Zoar was on the SE, would not preclude the identification: it would simply mean that the whole region was haunted by the legend of Lot. But the disintegration of the rock-salt of which that remarkable ridge is mainly composed, proceeds so rapidly, and produces so many fantastic projections and pinnacles, that the tradition may be supposed to have attached itself to different objects at different periods. See Dri. *DB*, iii. 152.

27, 28. Abraham's morning visit to the spot where he had parted from his heavenly guests forms an impressive close to the narrative.—*and he looked, etc.*] an effective contrast to 18^{16}.—*the smoke of the land* was afterwards believed to ascend permanently from the site of the guilty cities (Wisd. 10^{7}).—The idea may have been suggested by the cloud of vapour which generally hangs over the surface of the Dead Sea (see Di.).

29. (From P: see p. 306.) Gu. conjectures that the v. formed the introduction to a lost genealogy of Lot; and that its original position in P was after 13^{12a}. The dependence of P on J is very manifest.—*the cities in [one of] which Lot dwelt*] as 8^{4}, Ju. 12^{7}.

The destruction of the Cities of the Plain.—The narrative of ch. 19 appears at first sight to be based on vague recollection of an actual occurrence,—the destruction of a group of cities situated in what is now the Dead Sea, under circumstances which suggested a direct inter-

27. וישכם—אל־] preg. constr.—**27b.** must have been interpolated after the expansion of ch. 18 by vv.$^{22b-33a}$.—**28.** ארץ הככר does not occur elsewhere. The variations of 𝔐𝔊𝔖 warrant the emendation כָּל־הַכִּכָּר (Kit.).—כקיטר הכבשן] the same simile in Ex. 19^{18} (also J).—קִיטֹר] Ps. 119^{83} 148^{8}†.—**29.** ההפכה] 'the overthrow,' ἅπ. λεγ. The usual verbal noun is מהפכה (Dt. 29^{22}, Is. 1^{7} [rd. סְדֹם for זָרִים], 13^{19}, Jer. 49^{18} 50^{40}, Am. 4^{11}†), which is never used except in connexion with this particular judgement. The unhebraic form of inf., with the fact that where subj. is expressed it is always (even in Am.) אלהים and not יהוה, justify the conclusion that the phraseology was stereotyped in a heathen version of the story (Kraetzschmar, *ZATW*, xvii. 87 f.). Comp. the use of the vb. $19^{21.25.29}$, Dt. 29^{22}, Jer. 20^{16}, La. 4^{6}.—בהפך] 𝔐 בהפכו is easier. 𝔊 בה׳ יהוה.

* I cannot find the proof of Gu.'s assertion that *this* pillar is now called 'the daughter of Lot.'

position of divine power. It seems unreasonable to suppose that a legend so firmly rooted in Hebrew tradition, so full of local colour, and preserving so tenaciously the names of the ruined cities, should be destitute of historic foundation; and to doubt whether any such cities as Sodom and Gomorrah ever existed in the Dead Sea basin appears an unduly sceptical exercise of critical judgement. It has been shown, moreover, that a catastrophe corresponding in its main features to the biblical description is an extremely probable result of volcanic and other forces, acting under the peculiar geological conditions which obtain in the Dead Sea depression. According to Sir J. W. Dawson, it might have been caused by an explosion of bitumen or petroleum, like those which so frequently prove destructive in Canada and the United States (see *Exp.* 1886, i. p. 74; *Modern Science in Bible Lands*, 486 ff.). A similar theory has been worked out in elaborate and picturesque detail by Blanckenhorn in *ZDPV*, xix. 1–64, xxi. 65–83 (see Dri. p. 202 f.).* These theories are very plausible, and must be allowed their full weight in determining the question of historicity. At the same time it requires to be pointed out that they do not prove the incident to be historical; and several considerations show that a complete explanation of the legend cannot be reached on the lines of physical science. (*a*) It is impossible to dissociate the legend altogether from the current OT representation (13^{10} $14^{3. 10}$) that prior to this event the Dead Sea did not exist,—an idea which geology proves to be absolutely erroneous. It is true that the narrative does not state that the cities were submerged by the waters of the Dead Sea; and it is possible to suppose that they were situated either south of the present margin of the lake, or in its shallow southern bay (which might possibly have been formed within historic times). The fact, however, remains, that the Israelites had a mistaken notion of the origin of the Dead Sea; and this fact throws some suspicion on the whole legend of the 'cities of the Plain.' (*b*) It is remarkable that the legend contains no mention of the Dead Sea, either as the cause of the catastrophe, or as originating contemporaneously with it (Gu.). So important an omission suggests the possibility that the Sodom-legend may have arisen in a locality answering still more closely to the volcanic features of the description (such as the 'dismal *Ḥarras* of Arabia' [Meyer]), and been transferred to the region of the Dead Sea valley. (*c*) The stereotyped term מַהְפֵּכָה (see on v.[29]), which seems to have been imported with the legend, points clearly to an earthquake as the main cause of the overthrow; and there is no mention of an earthquake in any Hebrew version of the story (see Che. *EB*, 4668 f.)—another indication that it has been transplanted from its native environment. (*d*) The most important consideration is that the narrative seems to belong to a widely diffused class of popular tales,

* Physical explanations of the catastrophe were also current in ancient times. Strabo (XVI. ii. 44) says that it took place ὑπὸ σεισμῶν καὶ ἀναφυσημάτων πυρὸς καὶ θερμῶν ὑδάτων ἀσφαλτωδῶν τε καὶ θειωδῶν, in consequence of which the lake burst its bounds, the rocks took fire, and so on. Cf. Jos. *BJ*, iv. 484 f., *Ant.* i. 203; Tacitus. *Hist.* v. 7.

many interesting examples of which have been published by Cheyne in *The New World*, 1892, 239 ff. It is indeed obvious that no physical explanation of the cataclysm furnishes any clue to the significance of the angels' visit to Lot; but a study of the folklore parallels shows that the connexion between that incident and the destruction of Sodom is not accidental, but rests on some mythological motive whose origin is not as yet explained. Thus in the story of Philemon and Baucis (Ovid, *Met.* viii. 625 ff.), an aged Phrygian couple give shelter in their humble dwelling to Zeus and Hermes in human guise, when every other door is closed against them. As a reward for their hospitality they are directed to flee to the mountain, and there, looking back, they see the whole district inundated by a flood, except their own wretched hut, which has been transformed into a temple, etc. The resemblance here is so great that Cheyne (*l.c.* 240) pronounces the tale a secondary version of Gn. 19; but other parallels, hardly less striking, present the same combination of kindness to divine beings rewarded by escape from a destructive visitation in which a whole neighbourhood perishes for its impious neglect of the duties of hospitality.—On these grounds some writers consider the narrative before us to be a Hebrew adaptation of a widespread legend, its special features being suggested by the weird scenery of the Dead Sea region,—its barren desolation, the cloud of vapour hanging over it, its salt rocks with their grotesque formations, its beds of sulphur and asphalt, with perhaps occasional conflagrations bursting out amongst them (see Gu. 188 f.). Dr. Rendel Harris (*Heavenly Twins*, 39 ff.) takes it to be a form of the Dioscuric myth, and thus a natural sequel to 18^{1-15} (see p. 302 above). Assyriologists have found in it a peculiar modification of the Deluge-legend (Jast. *ZA*, xiii. 291, 297; *RBA*[1], 507), or of the World-conflagration which is the astronomical counterpart of that conception (*ALTO*[2], 360 ff.): both forms of the theory are mentioned by Zimmern with reserve (*KAT*[3], 559 f.).—Whatever truth there may be in these speculations, the religious value of the biblical narrative is not affected. Like the Deluge-story, it retains the power to touch the conscience of the world as a terrible example of divine vengeance on heinous wickedness and unnatural lust; and in this ethical purpose we have another testimony to the unique grandeur of the idea of God in ancient Israel.

XIX. 30–38.—*Lot and his Daughters* (J).

This account of the origin of the Moabites and Ammonites is a pendant to the destruction of Sodom, just as the story of Noah's drunkenness ($9^{20ff.}$) is an appendix to the Deluge narrative. Although it has points of contact with $^{1-28}$, it is really an independent myth, as to the origin and motives of which see the concluding Note (p. 314).

Source.—Though the criteria of authorship are slight, there is no reason to doubt that the section belongs to J: note the two daughters, and the mention of Zoar in [30]; and cf. חִיָּה זֶרַע, [32. 34], with 7[3]; and בְּכִירָה, צְעִירָה, [31. 33-35. 37. 38], with 29[26].

30a is a transition clause, connecting what follows with [1-28], esp. with [17-22].—*in the mountain*] of Moab; cf. v.[17].—*he was afraid to dwell in Z.*] lest it should be consumed, though the motive involves a slight discrepancy with [21].—**30b.** *in the cave*] probably a particular cave which was named after Lot (cf. 1 Ki. 19[9]). It is pointed out that לוֹטָן, a possible variant of לוט, is named as a *Ḥōrite* (Troglodyte?) in 36[20. 22. 29]. The habit is said to have persisted till modern times in that region (Di. Dri. after Buckingham, *Travels in Syria* [1825]).—**31.** *there is no man in the earth*] 'We are the survivors of a universal catastrophe.' So Gu., following Pietschmann, *Gesch. der Phönizier*, 115; Jastrow, *ZA*, xiii. 298 (see below). The usual explanations: 'no man in the vicinity' (Di. al.), or 'all men will shrink from us' (Dri.), hardly do justice to the language.—כְּדֶרֶךְ כָּל־הָאָרֶץ] So in the Jewish marriage formula ואנא אעל לותך כאורח כל ארעא (De.).—**32.** The intoxication of Lot shows that the revolting nature of the proposal was felt by the Hebrew conscience. "When the existence of the race is at stake, the woman is more eager and unscrupulous than the man" (Gu. 192).—מֵאָבִינוּ] repeated in [34. 36], anticipating the etymology of [37].—**33, 35.** *he knew not, etc.*] still minimising Lot's culpability (cf. 38[16ff.]).—**37.** מוֹאָב] as if = מֵאָב, '*from a* (my?) *father*' (*v.i.*).—**38.** בֶּן־עַמִּי] not 'son of my people,' which would be

30 end] 𝔐𝔊𝔙 + עמו.—**31.** בוא על'] in this sense only Dt. 25[5].—**32.** לכה] 𝔐 לכי.—**33.** ותשקין] (so [35. 36]); G–K. § 47 *l*.—בלילה הוא] (𝔐 ההוא). On omission of art. with demonstr., see G–K. § 126*y*; cf. 30[16] 32[23] 38[21], 1 Sa. 19[10].—את־אביה] 𝔊 + τὴν νύκτα ἐκείνην.—וּבְקוּמָהּ] 'Appungunt desuper, quasi incredibile'! (Je.). In reality the point probably marks a superfluous letter (cf. v.[35]).—**34.** אבי] 𝔊 אָבִינוּ.—**37.** מוֹאָב] 𝔊 + λέγουσα, Ἐκ τοῦ πατρός μου ([מֵאָבִ[י). For the equivalence of מו and מֵ, cf. Nu. 11[26f.] (מֵידָד = 𝔐 מודד, 𝔊 Μωδαδ), Jer. 48[21] (מֵיפַעַת, Qr. = מופעת, Kt.), etc.: see *ZATW*, xvi. 322 f. The real etymology is, of course, uncertain. Homm. ingeniously and plausibly explains the name as a contraction of אִמּוֹאָב, 'his mother is the father,' after the analogy of a few Assyrian proper names (*Verhand. d. XIII. Orient.-Kong.* 261). The view of Kn. and De. that מו is Aram. מוי (= מַי), 'water,' and that the word meant 'water (*i.e.* *semen*) of a father,' hardly deserves consideration.—**38.** בן־עמי] 𝔊 Ἀμμάν· ὁ υἱὸς τοῦ γένους μου, missing the significance of the בֶּן (*v.s.*).

nothing distinctive of any child, but 'son of my (paternal) kinsman' (see 17^{14}). Note the formal correspondence with בְּנֵי עַמּוֹן, which (and not עַמּוֹן simply) is the invariable designation of the people in OT (exc. Ps. 83^{8}, and MT of 1 Sa. 11^{11} [𝔊 'בְּנֵי ע]). Both etymologies are obviously pointless except as expressing the thought of the mothers, who, as is usual in J, name the children.

Original idea of the legend.—It is very natural to regard this account of the origin of Moab and Ammon as an expression of intense national hatred and contempt towards these two peoples. It has further been surmised (though with little proof)* that incestuous marriages, such as are here spoken of, were customary in these lands, and gave an edge to this Hebrew taunt (so Di.). That the story was so understood by later readers is indeed probable; but how precarious it is to extend this feeling to ancient times appears from ch. 38, where the ancestry of the noble tribe of Judah (held in special honour by J) is represented as subject to a similar taint. The truth seems to be that while incest was held in abhorrence by Israel (as by the ancient Arabs; see We. *GGN*, 1893, 441), it was at one time regarded as justified by extreme necessity, so that deeds like those here related could be told without shame. Starting from this view of the spirit of the narrative, Gu. (190 f.) gives a suggestive interpretation of the legend. It is, he thinks, originally a Moabite legend tracing the common ancestry of Moab and Ammon to Lot, who was probably worshipped at the 'cave' referred to in v.^{30}. V.^{31}, however, presupposes a universal catastrophe, in which the whole human race had perished, except Lot and his two daughters. In the ordinary course the daughters would have been doomed to barrenness, and mankind would have become extinct; and it is to avert this calamity that the women resolve on the desperate expedient here described. That such an origin should have been a subject of national pride is conceivable, though one may fail to find that feeling reflected in the forced etymologies of $^{37f.}$. If Gu.'s theory is anywhere near the truth, we are here on the track of a Moabite parallel to the story of the Flood, which is probably of greater antiquity than the legend of $19^{1ff.}$. Lot is the counterpart of the Hebrew Noah; and just as the Noah of $9^{20ff.}$ steps into the place of the Babylonian Deluge-hero, so the Lot of $19^{30ff.}$ was identified with the entertainer of deity in the heathen myth which probably lies at the basis of $19^{1ff.}$†

* Cf. the similar conjecture with regard to Reuben (p. 515 below). It is difficult to know what to make of Palmer's curious observation that in that region a wife is commonly spoken of as *bint* (daughter): *Desert of the Exodus*, ii. 478; see Dri. 205.

† The connexion with the Deluge-legend was anticipated by Jast. in the art. already cited, *ZA*, xiii. 197 f.—It is a flood of water which destroys the inhospitable people in the parallel from Ovid cited above (p. 312).

Ch. XX.—*Abraham and Sarah at the Court of Gerar* (E).

The chapter deals with an incident closely similar to that recorded in 12^{10-20}. It is indeed impossible to doubt that the two are variants of the same tradition; a view which is confirmed rather than shaken by Strack's enumeration of petty differences. A close comparison (see p. 364 f. below) appears to show that the passage before us is written from a more advanced ethical standpoint than that represented by ch. 12: note the tendency to soften the harsher features of the incident ($^{4.\,6.\,16}$), and to minimise the extent of Abraham's departure from strict veracity.

Source.—The narrative is the first continuous excerpt from E; and contains several stylistic and other peculiarities of that document: esp. [הָ]אֱלֹהִים, $^{3.\,6.\,11.\,13.\,17}$ (^{18} יהוה is a gloss); אָמָה (J שִׁפְחָה), ^{17}; לֵבָב (J לב), ^{5}; see also the notes on נִקָּיוֹן, ^{5}; אָמַר אֶל־, $^{2.\,13}$; נָתַן לְ, ^{6}; אָמְנָה, ^{12} (cf. Di. 279; Ho. 159; Gu. 193).—The appearing of God in a dream is characteristic of E; and the conception of Abraham as a prophet (^{7}) is at least foreign to the original J (but see on 15^{1}). Another circumstance proving the use of a source distinct from J^h or P is that Sarah is here conceived as a young woman capable of inspiring passion in the king (ct. 18^{12} 17^{17}). Lastly, it is to be observed that ch. 20 is the beginning of a section (20–22) mainly Elohistic, representing a cycle of tradition belonging to the Negeb and, in particular, to Beersheba.

1, 2. Introductory notice.—The method of the narrator, Gu. points out, is to let the story unfold itself in the colloquies which follow, vv.$^{1f.}$ containing just enough to make these intelligible.—**1.** *the land of the Negeb*] see on 12^{9}.—*between Ḳādēsh* (14^{7}) *and Shûr* (16^{7}) would be in the extreme S of the Negeb, if not beyond its natural limits. The words וַיָּגָר בִּגְרָר (note the paronomasia) are not a nearer specification of the previous clause, but introduce a new fact,—a further stage of the patriarch's wanderings. There is therefore no reason to suppose that *Gĕrār* lay as far S as Ḳadesh

---

1. וַיִּסַּע] see 11^{2}.—אַרְצָה הַנֶּגֶב] אֶרֶץ הַנּ׳ only 24^{62}, Jos. 15^{19}, Ju. 1^{15} (J), Nu. 13^{29} (E?).—גְּרָר] (10^{19} $26^{1.\,6.\,17}$ [נַחַל גְּרָר], $^{20.\,26}$, 2 Ch. $14^{12f.}$ †) 𝔊 Γεραρα, 𝔖 ܓܪܪ; commonly identified, on the authority of *OS*, $240^{28ff.}$ (ἀπέχουσα Ἐλευθεροπόλεως σημείοις κε πρὸς νότον), with the modern *Umm Ĝerār* ('place of water-pots'), 6 miles SSE of Gaza (so Rowlands, *Holy City*, i. 464; Robinson [who did not find the name], *BR*, ii. 43 f. [cf. i. 189], Ho. Gu.

(*v.i.*).—2. The bareness of the narration is remarkable, and was felt by the Greek translators to be wanting in lucidity (*v.i.*).—*Abimelech, king of Gĕrār*] אֲבִימֶלֶךְ = '*Milk* is [my] father,' is a genuine Canaanite name, compounded with the name of the god *Milk* (see Baeth. *Beitr.* 37 ff.). It occurs as the name of the governor of Tyre (*Abi-milki*) in the TA Tablets (149–156). There is no trace here of the anachronism which makes him a Philistine prince (ch. 26); Gerar is an independent Canaanite kingdom.—*took Sarah*] *sc.* as wife; the same ellipsis as 19^{14}.

3-7. **Abimelech's dream.**—This mode of revelation is peculiar to E ($21^{12.\,14}$ $22^{1ff.}$ 28^{12} $31^{11.\,24}$ 37^{5} 46^{2}, Nu. 12^{6} $22^{9.\,20}$), and probably indicates a more spiritual idea of God than the theophanies of J. It must be remembered, however, that according to primitive ideas the 'coming' of God (so 31^{24}, Nu. 22^{20}) would be as real an event in a dream as in waking experience.—4a. *had not drawn near her*] Not an explana-

---

al.). This suits 26^{1} (according to which it was in Philistine territory), 10^{19} and 2 Ch. 14^{13}; but hardly $26^{17ff.}$, and it is certainly inconsistent with the notice בֵּין קָדֵשׁ וּבֵין שׁוּר. There happens to be a *Wādī Ğerūr*, *c.* 13 miles SW of Ḳadesh, which exactly agrees with this description; and so Trumbull (*Kad.-Bar.* 62 f., 255) and others have decided that this must be the biblical Gerar, while others think there may have been two places of the name (Che. *EB*, ii. 1705 f.). The question really turns on $26^{17.\,21f.}$: so far as the present reference is concerned, we have seen that the argument rests on a misconception; and it is not even necessary to assume (with KS.) that [1a] is a redactional clause, or (with Ho. Gu.) that part of E's narrative has been suppressed between [1a] and [1b]. It is true that מִשָּׁם has no antecedent in E, and it is, of course, conceivable that it was written by R^{E} to connect the following with a previous section of E (Gu.), or by R^{JE} to mark the transition from Hebron (18^{1}) to the Negeb. A redactor, however, would not have been likely to insert the notice 'between Ḳadesh and Shur' unless he had meant it as a definition of the site of Gerar.—2. אָמַר אֶל־] = 'said regarding' is rare: 2 Ki. 19^{32}, Jer. 22^{18} 27^{19}; cf. לְ'א, v.[13], Ju. 9^{54}, Ps. 3^{3} 71^{10}.—After Athnach, 𝔊 inserts ἐφοβήθη γὰρ εἰπεῖν ὅτι Γυνή μού ἐστιν, μή ποτε ἀποκτείνωσιν αὐτὸν οἱ ἄνδρες τῆς πόλεως δι' αὐτήν (from 26^{7b}).

3. על] 𝔐𝔊𝔗 אודת על: cf. 21^{11}, Ex. 18^{8}, Nu. 12^{1} 13^{24} (E), Gn. 21^{25} 26^{32} (J), Jos. 14^{6} (R), Ju. 6^{7}.—בעלת בעל] a married woman, Dt. 22^{22}.—4. To גוי in the indefinite sense of 'people' (*Leute*) we may compare Ps. 43^{1}, Dn. 11^{23}; but the sense is doubtful, and the idea may be that the whole nation is involved in the punishment of the king (Str.). Eerdmans (*Komp. der Genesis*, 41) offers the incredible suggestion that גוי here has

tion of Abimelech's good conscience (which depended solely on the purity of his motives), but of Yahwe's words in [6b]. *Why* he had not come near her, we gather fully from [17].—**4b, 5.** Abimelech protests his innocence.—*innocent folk*]—'such as I am' (*v.i.*).—**5.** בְּתָם־לְבָבִי] 'unsuspectingly'; cf. 2 Sa. 15^{11}, 1 Ki. 22^{34}; in the wider sense of moral integrity the phrase occurs 1 Ki. 9^{4}, Ps. 78^{72} 101^{2}.—**6.** *have kept thee back from sinning* (*i.e.* inexpiably) *against me*] The sin is not mere infringement of the rights of a privileged person (Di.), but the moral offence of violating the marriage bond.—*suffered thee not*] by sickness (v.[17]).—**7.** The situation is altered by this disclosure of the facts to Abimelech: if he *now* retains Sarah, he will be on every ground deserving of punishment.—*he is a prophet*] in a secondary sense, as a 'man of God,' whose person and property are inviolable: cf. Ps. 105^{15}.—On *intercession* as a function of the prophet, Dt. 9^{20}, 1 Sa. 7^{5} $12^{19.23}$, Jer. 7^{16} etc.; but cf. Jb. 42^{8}.—*that thou mayest live*] or 'recover.'

The section ([3-7]) exhibits a vacillation which is characteristic of the conception of sin in antique religion. Sin is not wholly an affair of the conscience and inward motive, but an external fact — a violation of the objective moral order, which works out its consequences with the indifference of a law of nature to the mental condition of the transgressor (cf. the matricide of Orestes, etc.; and see Smend, *ATRG*², 108 f.). At the same time God Himself recognises the relative validity of Abimelech's plea of ignorance ([6]). It is the first faint protest of the moral sense against the hereditary mechanical notion of guilt. But it is a long way from Abimelech's faltering protestation of innocence to Job's unflinching assertion of the right of the individual conscience against the decree of an unjust fate.

8–13. Abimelech and Abraham.—9. *a great sin*] *i.e.*, a state of things which, though unwittingly brought about, involves heavy judgement from God (see on [3-7] above).—*deeds*

---

its late Jewish sense of an individual 'heathen.' Geiger, Graetz, al. regard the word as a gloss or a corrupt dittography. 𝔊 has ἔθνος ἀγνοοῦν καὶ δίκαιον.—**5.** נִקָּיֹן] only here in Hex.; E is addicted to rare expressions. For נ׳ כַּפַּי, cf. Ps. 26^{6} 73^{13}.—**6.** מֵחֲטוֹ] for מֵחֲטֹא; G-K. § 75 *qq*.—נָתַן לְ׳] = 'permit,' 31^{7}, Nu. 20^{21} 21^{23} 22^{13} (E), Ex. 12^{23} (J), 3^{19} (R), Dt. 18^{14}, Jos. 10^{19} (D): see *OH*, i. 192.

8. האנשים] 𝔐𝔊𝔙 pr. כל.—**9.** מה עשית לנו] 𝔖 ܡܢܐ ܥܒܕܬ ܠܟ = מה עשיתי לך,

that are not done] are not sanctioned by the conventional code of morals: cf. 34^{7}, 2 Sa. 13^{12} etc.—To this rebuke Abraham (as in $12^{18f.}$) has no reply, and Abimelech proceeds in—**10** to inquire into his motive for so acting. — מָה רָאִיתָ] '*What possessed thee?*' (*v.i.*).—**11–13.** Abraham's self-exculpation, which is at the same time the writer's apology for his conduct, consists of three excuses: (1) he was actuated by fear for his life; (2) he had not been guilty of direct falsehood, but only of mental reservation; (3) the deceit was not practised for the first time on Abimelech, but was a preconcerted scheme which (it is perhaps implied) had worked well enough in other places. Whether 2 and 3 had any foundation in the Elohistic tradition, or were invented by the narrator *ad hoc* (Gu.), we cannot now determine.—**11.** *There is no piety* (יִרְאַת אֱלֹהִים) *in this place*] Religion was the only sanction of international morality, the *gêr* having no civil rights; cf. 42^{18}: see Bertholet, *Stellung d. Fremden*, 15. Cf. 12^{12}.—**12.** *Besides, she really is my sister*] Marriage with a half-sister on the father's side was frequent among the Semites (Smith, *KM*², 191 f.), and was allowed in ancient Israel (2 Sa. 13^{13}), though prohibited by later legislation (Dt. 27^{22}, Lv. $18^{9.\,11}$ 20^{17}). — **13.** *When God caused me to stray*] The expression is peculiar, as if God had driven him

---

rashly adopted by Ba. Ho. Kit.—חטאתי] 𝔊 ἡμάρτομεν.—**10.** מָה רָאִיתָ] 𝔊 τί ἐνιδών; so 𝔙. Ba. conj. יָרֵאתָ; Gu. רָעִיתָ. The translation given above is taken from Bacher, *ZATW*, xix. 345 ff., who cites many examples from NH of the idiom (lit. 'What hast thou experienced?').—**11.** כִּי] ш כי יראתי.—רק]='[I should act otherwise] *only*,' etc.: a purely asseverative force (BDB) seems to me insufficiently established by Dt. 4^{6}, 1 Ki. 21^{25}, 2 Ch. 28^{10}, Ps. 32^{6}.—**12.** אָמְנָה] ш אמנם[ה?], as 18^{13}, Nu. 22^{37}; but cf. Jos. 7^{20}. These are all the occurrences in Hex.—**13.** הִתְעוּ] ш התעה. The constr. of אֱלֹהִים (*pl. emin.*) with pl. pred. is exceptional, though not uncommon (31^{53} 35^{7}, Jos. 24^{19}), and does not appear to be regulated in our present text by any principle. A tendency to substitute sing. for pl. is shown by 1 Ch. 17^{21} cpd. with 2 Sa. 7^{23}; and it is probable that the change has taken place in many cases where we have no means of tracing it: see Str.² 77; G–K. § 145 *i*. A kindred and equally inexplicable anomaly is the sporadic use of the art. with this word (so vv.$^{6.\,17}$). Both phenomena are probably survivals from a polytheistic form of the legend.—אבי] ш + ומארץ מולדתי (as 12^{1}).—כל־המקום] determined by following relative clause; so Ex. 1^{22} 20^{24}, Dt. 11^{24}.

forth an aimless wanderer (Di.). It proves that in E, as in J and P, Abraham was an immigrant in Canaan.

14–18. Abimelech makes reparation to Abraham.—**14.** The present to Abraham in 12[16] was of the nature of *mōhar* or purchase-price of a wife; here it is a compensation for injury unwittingly inflicted. The restoration of Sarah is, of course, common to both accounts.—**15.** The invitation to dwell in the land is a contrast to the honourable but peremptory dismissal of 12[19f.].—**16.** *see, I give . . . to thy brother*] For injury done to a woman compensation was due to her relatives if unmarried, to her husband if married or betrothed (Ex. 22[15f.], Dt. 22[23ff.]): Abimelech, with a touch of sarcasm, puts Sarah in the former category.—*1000* (shekels) *of silver*] not the money value of the gifts in v.[14] (Str.), but a special present as a solatium on behalf of Sarah.—*a covering of the eyes*] seemingly a forensic expression for the prestation by which an offence ceases to be seen, *i.e.*, is condoned. The fig. is applied in various ways in OT; cf. Jb. 9[24], Gn. 32[21], Ex. 23[8], 1 Sa. 12[3].—The cl. וְאֶת־כֹּל וְנֹכָחַת is obscure, and the text hardly correct (*v.i.*). The general sense is that Sarah's honour is completely rehabilitated.—

---

14. צֹאן] 𝔐𝔊 pr. אלף כסף ׀ (fr.[16]) wrongly.—ועברים ושפחת] probably a gl. fr. 12[16], this being the only instance of שִׁפְחָה in an E context.—**16.** הִנֵּה הוּא—אִתָּךְ] 𝔊 *ταῦτα ἔσται σοι εἰς τιμὴν τοῦ προσώπου σου καὶ πάσαις ταῖς μετὰ σοῦ*; 𝔙 *hoc erit tibi in velamen oculorum ad omnes qui tecum sunt* [*et quocunque perrexeris*]; 𝔖 ܘܗܐ ܐܦ ܗܘ ܢܗܘܐ ܠܟܝ ܚܠܦ ܬܫܘܒܬܐ ܒܥܝܢܐ ܕܟܠ ܕܥܡܟܝ. The difficulties of the v. commence here. The suggestion that הוא refers to Abraham (IEz.) may be dismissed, and also the fantastic idea that Sarah is recommended to spend the money in the purchase of a veil, so that she may not again be mistaken for an unmarried woman (24[65])! The first qn. is, Whose eyes are to be covered?—Sarah's own (לָךְ), or those of the people about her (לְכֹל וגו'), or both (וּלְכֹל [with 𝔐𝔊])? Di. adopts the second view, taking לָךְ as *dat. comm.* To this De. forcibly replies that *dat. comm.* before dat. of reference is unnatural: hence he takes the first view (לָךְ, dat. of ref., and לְכֹל = *bezugs aller*); *i.e.*, "Her credit with her household, which had been injured by her forcible abduction, would be restored, and the malicious taunts or gossip of men and maids would be checked, when they saw how dearly the unintentional insult had been atoned for" (Ba.). A better sense would be obtained if לְכֹל אֲשֶׁר could be taken as neuter: 'all that has befallen thee' (Tu. Ho. al.). That is perhaps

17. *God healed Ab.*] The first explicit intimation (see [4. 6]) that Abimelech had been smitten with a bodily malady, whose nature is indicated by the last word וַיֵּלֵדוּ.—18. A superfluous and inadequate explanation of [17], universally recognised as a gloss; note also יהוה.—עָצַר] see on 16[2].

XXI. 1-21.—*Birth of Isaac and Expulsion of Ishmael* (J, E, and P).

The birth, circumcision, and naming of Isaac are briefly recorded in a section pieced together from the three sources ([1-7]). Then follows a notice of the weaning festival ([8]), to which, by a finely descriptive touch ([9]), is linked the Elohistic version of the origin of the Ishmaelites ([10-21]). A comparison with the Yahwistic parallel (ch. 16) will be found below (p. 324).

Analysis.—[2b-5] are from P (who by the way ignores altogether the expulsion of Ishmael [see on 25[9]]): obs. the naming by the father and the exact correspondence with 16[16] in [3], circumcision ([4]), the chronology ([5]); and the words אֱלֹהִים, [2b. 4]; מוֹעֵד, [2b] (cf. 17[21]); מְאַת שָׁנָה, [5]. [2a] is to be assigned to J (בֵּן לִזְקֻנָיו, *v.i.*); and also, for the same reason, [7]. There remain the doublets [1a] ‖ [1b] and [6a] ‖ [6b]. Since the continuity of P is seldom sacrificed, [1b] is usually assigned to that source (יהוה, a scribal error), leaving [1a] to J (יהוה, פָּקַד). [6b] goes with [7] (therefore J: *v.i.*); and there remains for E the solitary half-verse [6a] (אלהים), which cannot belong to P because of the different etymology implied for יצחק. So Ho. Gu.; Di. Str. differ only in assigning the whole of [6] to E.—The J fragments [1a. 2a. 7. 6b] form a completely consecutive account of the birth of Isaac; which, however, is not the sequel to ch. 18 (see on [6a]), and therefore

---

impossible with the present text; hence Gu.'s emendation אָתָּךְ (pf. √ אתה w. acc.: Jb. 3[25]) is not unattractive.—וְאֵת־כֹּל וְנֹכָחַת] Untranslatable. 𝔊 καὶ πάντα ἀλήθευσον; 𝔙 *quocunque perrexeris: mementoque te deprehensam*; 𝔖 ܘܥܠ ܟܠ ܡܕܡ ܕܚܣܕܬܢܝ ('about all wherewith thou hast reproached me'); 𝔗[O] ועל כל מא דאמרת איתוכחת. The change to וְנֹכַחַתְּ (2 s. pf.) is of no avail, the difficulty being mostly in וְאֵת־כֹּל, which cannot be continuation of אִתָּךְ (Tu. al.), or of לָךְ כְּסוּת עֵינַיִם, but must with MT accents be taken with נ׳. The rendering 'and before all men thou shalt be righted' (Di. De. Dri.) is the best that can be made of the text. The easiest emendation is that of Gu.: וְאַתְּ כֻּלּוֹ נֹכָחַתְּ = 'and thou in all this (affair) art justified,' though the sense given to כלו has no clear example in OT. The more drastic remedies of Ba. do not commend themselves. —18. יהוה] 𝔐𝔖 אלהים

belongs to J^b rather than J^h (Gu.).—$^{8-21}$ is wholly Elohistic: אלהים, $^{12. 17. 19. 20.}$; אמה, $^{10. 12. 13}$; שים לגוי, $^{13. 18}$ (J עשה ל׳, 12^2; P נתן ל׳, 17^{20}); and rare expressions like חמת, $^{14. 15. 19}$; מטחוי קשת, ^{16}; רבה קשת, ^{20}. Further characteristics are the revelation of God by night ($^{12f.}$), and in a voice from heaven (^{17}).

1–7. The birth of Isaac.—2. *a son to his old age*] so v.^{7} 24^{36} 37^3 44^{20} (all J). All the sources emphasise the fact that Isaac was a late-born child; but this section contains nothing implying a miracle (ct. chs. 17, 18).—**3–5.** The naming and circumcision of Isaac, in accordance with $17^{19. 12}$ (P).—**6a.** *God has made laughter for me*] Both here and in ^{6b} laughter is an expression of joy, whereas in $18^{12ff.}$ 17^{17} it expresses incredulity.—**6b, 7** is the Yahwistic parallel. It has been pointed out by Bu. (*Urg.* 224: so Kit. KS. Ho.) that the transposition of ^{6b} to the end of ^{7} greatly improves the sense, and brings out the metrical form of the original (in Heb. 4 trimeters):

> Who would have said to Abraham,
> "Sarah gives children suck"?
> For I have borne him a son in his old age!
> Every one that hears will laugh at me!

8–10. Sarah demands the ejection of Ishmael.—8. The occasion was the customary family feast of the weaning of Isaac (Benz. *Arch.*^{2} 131). The age of weaning in modern Palestine is said to be 2 or 3 years (*ib.* 116); in ancient Israel also it must often have been late (1 Sa. $1^{22ff.}$, 2 Mac.

1a. פקד] never used by P *sensu bono* (Str.).—**2.** אלהים] 𝔊 יהוה.—**3.** הנולד] pointed as pf. with art. (18^{21}).—**6a.** צחק] The √ צחק never occurs outside of Pent., except Ju. 16^{25} (where יְשַׂחֵק should probably be read) and Ezk. 23^{32} (but see Corn. and Toy), the Qal being used only in connexion with Isaac (17^{17} $18^{12. 13. 15}$ 21^6), while Pi. has a stronger sense (19^{14} 21^9 26^8 $39^{14. 17}$, Ex. 32^6). The other form שחק (not in Pent.) is mostly later than Jer. (except Ju 16^{27}, 1 Sa. 18^7, 2 Sa. 2^{14} $6^{5. 21}$): in four cases (Am. $7^{9. 16}$, Jer. 33^{26}, Ps. 105^9) even the name יִצְחָק appears as יִשְׂחָק. It will be seen that in Gn. we have no fewer than 4 (17^{17} 18^{12} $21^{6a. 6b}$) or 5 (21^9?) different suggestions of a connexion of יִצְחָק with √ צחק. Analogy would lead us to suppose that in reality it is a contraction of יִצְחָקאֵל, in all probability the name of an extinct tribe (cf. יִשְׁמָעֵאל, יְרַחְמְאֵל, etc.).—**6b.** יְצַחֵק] see G–K. § 10 *g*.—**7.** מִלֵּל] Aram.; in Heb. rare and poetic.—On the *modal* use of pf. ('would have said'), cf. G–K. § 106 *p*; Dri. *T.* § 19.—בנים] pl. of species; of. Ex. 21^{22}, 1 Sa. 17^{43}, Ca. 2^9 (Di.). 𝔊 has sing.—לזקניו] 𝔊 ἐν τῷ γήρει μου.

$7^{27f.}$).—**9.** *playing with Isaac her son*] The last words are essential to the sense, and must be restored with 𝔊𝔙 (see *Jub.* xvii. 4, with Charles's Note). It is the spectacle of the two young children playing together, innocent of social distinctions, that excites Sarah's maternal jealousy and prompts her cruel demand. The chronology of P, according to which Ishmael was some 17 years old, has for uncritical readers spoiled the effect; and given rise to the notion of Ishmael as a rude lad scoffing at the family joy, or to the still more fanciful explanations current in Jewish circles.*—**10.** *with my son*] If this presupposes an equal right of inheritance as between the sons of the wife and the concubine (Gu.), it also shows a certain opposition to that custom: cf. the case of Jephthah, Ju. $11^{1ff.}$ (see Benz. *Arch.*^{2} 296).—*this slave girl* (אָמָה)] In E, Hagar is not Sarah's maid, but simply a household slave, who has become her master's concubine.

11–13. Abraham's misgivings removed.—**11.** *on account of his son*] whom he loves as his own flesh and blood; for the mother, as a slave, he has no particular affection.—**12.** It is revealed to him (by night: cf. ^{14}) that Sarah's maternal instincts are in accord with the divine purpose.—*shall a seed be called to thee*] *i.e.*, 'in the line of Isaac shall thy name be perpetuated' (Is. 41^8, cf. Ro. 9^7, Heb. 11^{18}). The same idea otherwise expressed in P ($17^{19.\,21}$).—**13.** Hagar's child (still unnamed) is also Abraham's seed, though his descendants are not to be known as such. —*a great nation* (𝔐𝔊𝔖)] cf. 17^{20}.

---

9. מְצַחֵק] 𝔊 παίζοντα μετὰ Ἰσαακ τοῦ υἱοῦ ἑαυτῆς; so 𝔙 (cf. Zec. 8^5, The sense 'mock' ('play with' in a bad sense) would require a following בְּ, but it is doubtful if it actually occurs. $39^{14.\,17}$ may be explained after 26^8; in 19^{14} it means simply 'play' as opposed to serious behaviour (cf. Pr. 26^{19}). See above on v.^{6}.—On the pausal ‑ָ‑, see G-K. § 52 *n.*—**11** end] 𝔊 + Ἰσμαηλ (wrongly).—**12.** זֶרַע] 𝔊 + τὸ ῥῆμα.—**13.** 𝔐𝔊 read האמה הואת לגוי גדול: גָּדוֹל also in 𝔙𝔖.—[ג'] לְגוֹי—שִׂים] so v.^{18} 46^3 (E).

---

* St. Paul's allusion to Ishmael as persecuting Isaac (Gal. 4^{29}, ἐδίωκεν) is based on this מְצַחֵק. For other Haggadic interpretations, see *Ber. R.* § liii; Dri. *DB*, ii. 503b, and *Gen.* 210. Unchastity (cf. $39^{14.\,17}$) idolatry (Ex. 32^6, 𝔗^J Ra), attempted murder (2 Sa. 2^{14}, Pr. 26^{19}), etc., are among the crimes inferred from this unfortunate word.

14–16. Mother and child in the desert.—The sufferings and despair of the helpless outcasts are depicted with fine feeling and insight.—**14.** *a skin of water*] חֵמֶת (*v.i.*), the usual Eastern water-bag, answering to the *ǧirby* of the modern Bedouin (Doughty, *Ar. Des.* i. 227, ii. 585).—*and the boy he placed on her shoulder* (*v.i.*)] cf. $^{15.\,16}$.—*the wilderness of Beersheba* (see on ^{31})] implying that Abraham dwelt *near*, but not necessarily *at*, Beersheba.—**15.** *she cast the boy* (whom, therefore, she must have been carrying) *under one of the bushes*] for protection from the sun (1 Ki. $19^{4f.}$). To save P's chronology, De. and Str. make *cast* = 'eilends niederlegen'—with what advantage does not quite appear. —**16.** *a bowshot off*] out of sight of her child, but within hearing of his cry.—The last cl. should be read with 𝕲; *and the boy lifted up his voice and wept* (v.^{17}): the change of subject being due to the false impression that Ishmael was now a grown lad. Hagar's dry-eyed despair is a more effective picture than that given by MT.

17–19. The Divine succour comes in two forms: a voice from heaven ($^{17f.}$), and an opening of Hagar's eyes (^{19}). —**17.** *God heard*] (twice) preparing for an explanation of יִשְׁמָעֵאל.—While God Himself hears, the medium of His revelation is *the Angel of God* (as 28^{12} 31^{11} 32^{2}, Ex. 14^{19}), who by a refinement peculiar to E (22^{11}) speaks *from heaven*. This goes beyond the primary conception of the Angel: see on 16^{7}.—**18.** Hagar is encouraged by a disclosure of the future greatness of her son.—**19.** *opened her eyes*] cf. $3^{5.\,7}$.

---

14. חמת] Only here ($^{15.\,19}$) = Ar. *ḥamīt* (√ *ḥamita*, 'rancid'?). On the forms חֵמֶת, חֶמֶת, or חֲמַת, חֵמַת, see G–K. § 95 *l*.—שם על־ וגו'] The transposition וְאֶת־הַיֶּלֶד שָׂם עַל־שִׁכְמָהּ was suggested by Ols., and is by far the best remedy for an awkward constr. In MT it would be necessary to take וְאֶת־ה' as second obj. to וַיִּתֵּן, and שם על־שכמה as a parenthetic circumst. cl. (so Di. De. Str.). It is an effort to evade the absurdity of a youth of 17 being carried on his mother's back.—15. השיחם] 'desert shrubs'; see on 2^{5}.—16. הרחק] G–K. § 113 *h*.—כמטחוי קשת] lit. 'as (far as) bowmen do'; 𝕲 ὡσεὶ τόξου βολήν, 𝕾 ܐܝܟ ܫܕܝܐ ܕܩܫܬܐ, hardly imply a different text. On מְטַחֲוֵי (ptc. Pal. √ טחה,—only here), see G–K. § 75 *kk*.—ותשא וגו'] 𝕲 וַיִּשָּׂא [הַיֶּלֶד] אֶת־קֹלוֹ וַיֵּבְךְּ.—17b. אל־קול] MSS and 𝔐 אתק'.—19. באר מים] 𝕲 + חַיִּים,—attractive! (cf. 26^{19}).

The tact of the narrator leaves us in doubt whether the well was now miraculously opened, or had been there all along though unseen. In any case it is henceforth a sacred well.

20, 21. Ishmael's career.—Here we expect the naming of the child, based on v.[17]: this has been omitted by R in favour of J (16^{11}).—**20.** The boy *grew up*, amidst the perils and hardships of the desert,—a proof that *God was with him.*—*he became a bowman*] (pt. רֹבֵה קַשָּׁת: *v.i.*), the bow being the weapon of his descendants (Is. 21^{17}).—**21.** The *wilderness of Pārān* is et-Tīh, bounding the Negeb on the S.—His mother took him a wife *from the land of Egypt*] her own country (v.[9]): see p. 285 above.

Comparison of ch. 16 *with* 21^{1-21}.—That these two narratives are variations of a common legendary theme is obvious from the identity of the leading motives they embody: viz. the significance of the name Ishmael (16^{11} 21^{17}); the mode of life characteristic of his descendants (16^{12} 21^{20}); their relation to Israel; and the sacredness of a certain well, consecrated by a theophany ($16^{7.14}$ 21^{19}).* Each tale is an exhaustive expression of these motives, and does not tolerate a supplementary anecdote alongside of it. Ch. 21, however, represents a conception of the incident further removed from primitive conditions than 16: contrast the sympathetic picture of nomadic life in 16^{12} with the colourless notice of 21^{20}; in 16, moreover, Hagar is a high-spirited Bedawi woman who will not brook insult, and is at home in the desert; while in 21 she is a household slave who speedily succumbs to the hardships of the wilderness. In E the appeal is to universal human sympathies rather than to the peculiar susceptibilities of the nomad nature; his narrative has a touch of pathos which is absent from J; it is marked by a greater refinement of moral feeling, and by a less anthropomorphic idea of God. —See the admirable characterisation of Gu. p. 203 f.

---

20. ויהי רבה קשת] 'and he became, growing up, an archer'; 𝔙 *juvenis sagittarius* (so $\mathfrak{T}^{O}$). But קַשָּׁת is ἅπ. εἰρήμ., the syntax is peculiar, and, besides, the growing up has been already mentioned. The true text is doubtless that given above and implied by 𝔊 ἐγένετο δὲ τοξότης. 𝔖 ܘܪܒܐ ܗܘܐ ܩܫܬܐ also implies קַשָּׁת; but there are further divergences in that Vn. רבה = 'shoot' (not so elsewhere), might be a by-form of רבב (see on 49^{23}; and cf. רב = 'shooter,' in Jer. 50^{29}, Jb. 16^{13}); but it may be a question whether in these three cases we should not substitute רבה for רבב, or whether in this pass. we should not read רֹמֵה קַשָּׁת with Ba. (see esp. Jer. 4^{29}, Ps. 78^{9}). The rendering 'a shooter, an archer' (De.), is clumsy; and the idea that קשת is an explanatory gloss on רֹבֶה (KS.) is not probable.

---

* The well is not identified in E. Gu.'s view, that it was Beersheba, has little to commend it.

XXI. 22–34.—*Abraham's Covenant with Abimelech* (E and J).

Two distinct narratives, each leading up to a covenant at Beersheba, are here combined. (A) In the first, Abraham, acceding to a request of Abimelech, enters into a covenant of permanent friendship with him, from which the place derives its name 'Well of the Oath' ($^{22-24.\ 27.\ 31}$).—(B) In the other, the covenant closes a long-standing dispute about springs, and secures the claim of Abraham's people to the wells of Beersheba, where Abraham subsequently plants a sacred tree ($^{25.\ 26.\ 28-30.\ 32.\ 33}$).

Sources.—The passage, except some redactional touches in $^{32-34}$, has usually been assigned to E (We. Kue. Di. Ho. Str.). Its disjointed character has, however, been felt, and tentative solutions have been proposed by several critics (cf. KS. *Anm.* 92, 93; Kraetz. *Bundvorstg.* 14, 31; v. Gall, *CSt.* 46 f.; *OH.* ii. 30 f.). The most successful is that of Gu., who assigns $^{25.\ 26.\ 28-30.\ 32-34}$ to J, the rest to E: the reasons will appear in the notes. The analysis rests on the duplicates ($^{27a \parallel 30a}$, $^{27b \parallel 32a}$) and material discrepancies of the section; the linguistic criteria being indecisive as between J and E, though quite decisive against P (חֶסֶד, הֵנָּה, ^{23}; כָּרַת בְּרִית, ^{27}; בַּעֲבוּר, ^{30}). But the connexion with ch. 20, and אֱלֹהִים in $^{22.\ 23}$, prove that the main account is from E; while יהוה, ^{33}, and בַּעֲבוּר, ^{30}, show the other to be J. Since the scene is Beersheba, the Yahwistic component must be J^{b}.—$^{32-34}$ have been considerably modified by R. Procksch (10 ff.) holds that in the original E v.$^{22ff.}$ preceded $^{1-20}$; his detailed analysis being almost identical with Gu.'s.

22–24. Abimelech proposes an oath of perpetual amity between his people and Abraham's, and the latter consents (E).—**22.** *Pîkōl* (*v.i.*), *his commander-in-chief*, seems here merely a symbol of the military importance of Gerar: otherwise 26$^{26ff.}$, where P. is a party to the covenant.—**23.** *Swear to me here*] in the place afterwards known as Beersheba (^{31}). Abraham's departure from Gerar, and Abimelech's visit to him in Beersheba, must have stood in E between 20^{17} and 21^{22} (cf. 26$^{13.\ 26}$). — **24.** This unreserved consent is inconsistent with the expostulation of — **25, 26** (J), which pre-

---

22. ופיכל] 𝔊 pr. καὶ Ὀχοζὰθ ὁ νυμφαγωγὸς αὐτοῦ (fr. 26^{26}). Spiegelberg (*OLz*, ix. 109) considers this one of the few Egyptian names in OT =*p*ᶜ*H̯*-*r*(*j*), "the Syrian."—**23.** אם] G–K. § 149 *c.*—נין ונכד] (*proles et soboles*) an alliterative phrase found in Is. 14^{22}, Jb. 18^{19}, Sir. 41^{5} 47^{22}†.—**25.** והוכח] "must be corrected to וְיוֹכַח" (Ba., cf. G–K. § 112 *tt*): 𝔐 ויוכיח. But

supposes strained relations between the parties, and repeated disputes about the ownership of wells. Note (1) the frequentative וְהוֹכִחַ, (2) the pl. 'wells' (retained by 𝔊), (3) the fuller parallel of 26[15. 18ff.], which shows that the right to several wells had been contested.—*And as often as Abraham took Abimelech to task about the wells . . . Abimelech would answer*]—that he knew nothing of the matter (so Gu.).—**27.** Continuing [24] (E). Giving (or exchange?) of presents seems to have been customary when a covenant was made (1 Ki. 15[19], Is. 30[6], Ho. 12[2]). The action would be no suitable answer to v.[26].—**28–30** (J). *the seven ewe lambs* are set apart for the purpose explained in [30]; but the art. shows that they must have been mentioned in the previous context. It is clear from [30] that the lacuna is in J, not in E; while Abimelech's question [29] proves that the lambs were not an understood part of the ceremony (Di.).—**30.** *that it* (the acceptance of the present) *may be a witness, etc.*] so that in future there may be no quarrel about Beersheba.—**31** belongs to E: נִשְׁבְּעוּ, cf. [23f.]; שְׁנֵיהֶם, cf. [27].—בְּאֵר שֶׁבַע = 'seven wells,' is here explained as 'Well of the Oath,' the oath being the central feature of the *berîth*. The etymology is not altogether at fault, since נִשְׁבַּע may mean lit. to 'put oneself under the influence of seven,' the sacred number (Her. iii. 8; Hom. *Il.* xix. 243 ff.; Paus. iii. 20. 9).—**32a.** J's parallel to [27b].*—**33.** The inauguration of the cult of Beersheba (J: cf.

MT is probably right, with freqve. sense of pf. given above. For the following ויאמר (instead of ואמר), see Dri. *T.* § 114 *β*.—באר] 𝔊 *φρεάτων*, *ut sup.*—28. הצאן] 𝔐 (which also omits את־) צאן. De. thinks this one of the few cases (G–K. § 127 *e*) where art. determines only its own word, and not the whole expression.—**29.** Rd. הכבשת with 𝔐 ([30]).—לְבַדֶּנָה (𝔐 לבדהן)]. On suff. cf. G–K. § 91 *f*. The form is chiefly pausal; and though the only other ex. in Pent. (Gn. 42[36]) is E, 30[41] (־ֶנָה) is J, and the form cannot be considered distinctive of E.—**31.** באר שבע] 𝔊 Φρέαρ *ὁρκισμοῦ*, but in [32] Φ. *τοῦ ὅρκου*. The constr. (num. in gen. after sing. noun) has been supposed by Sta. to be Canaanite idiom (cf. קִרְיַת אַרְבַּע, 23[2]).—**33.** אֵשֶׁל] Ar. *'atl*, Aram.

* [32b] would be a natural conclusion to E's narrative (cf. [22]), but for the fact that that source never speaks of a Philistine occupation of Gerar. The last three vv., however, seem to have been altered by a compiler.—It is probable that J gave an explanation of the name of the well, connecting it with the seven lambs; so 𝔗[J] (בירא רשבע חורפן).

26^{25}). Among the *sacra* of that famous shrine there must have been a sacred tamarisk believed to have been planted by Abraham (see on 12^{6}). The planting of a sacred tree is no more a *contradictio in adjecto* (Sta. in v. Gall, 47) than the erecting of a sacred stone, or the digging of a sacred well. The opinion (KS. Ho.) that the subj. is Isaac, and that the v. should stand after 26^{25}, rests on the incorrect assumption that no stratum of J puts Abraham in connexion with Beersheba.—*'El 'Ôlâm*] presumably the pre-Israelite name of the local *numen*, here identified with Yahwe (Gu.: see 16^{13}). Canaanite analogies are Ἦλος ὁ καὶ Κρόνος (Eus. *Præp. Ev.* i. 10, 13 ff.), and Χρόνος ἀγήρατος (Damasc. *Princ.* 123).—34. The assumption that Beersheba was in Philistine territory being incompatible with ^{32b}, the v. must be an interpolation.—On the historical background of these legends, see after 26^{33}.

Beersheba is the modern *Bî'r-es-Sebá'*, in the heart of the Negeb, some 28 miles SW from Hebron, and 25 SE from *Umm el-Ğerār*. Its importance as a religious centre in OT appears not only from its frequent mention in the patriarchal history (22^{19} $26^{23ff.\ 31ff.}$ 28^{10} $46^{1ff.}$), but still more from the fact that in the 8th cent. its oracle (cf. 25^{22}) was resorted to by pilgrims from the northern kingdom (Am. 5^{5} 8^{14}). V. Gall (44 ff.) questions the opinion that it was originally a group of 7 wells, holding that there was but one, whose name meant 'Well of the Oath.' But that "among the Semites a special sanctity was attached to groups of seven wells" is shown by Smith (*RS*², 181 f.: cf. Nö. *ARW*, vii. 340 ff.); and the existence of a plurality of wells at Bi'r es-Seba' has never been disputed. See Rob. *BR*, i. 204 ff.; Smith, *HG*, 284 f.; Robinson, *Bibl. World*, xvii. (1901), 247 ff.; Gautier, *ib.* xviii. 49 ff.; Dri. *ET*, vii. (1896), 567 f.; *Joel and Amos*² (1901), p. 239 f.; Trumbull, *ET*, viii. 89.

CH. XXII. 1–19.—*The Sacrifice of Isaac* (E and R^{JE}).

The only incident in Abraham's life expressly characterised as a 'trial' of his faith is the one here narrated, where the patriarch proves his readiness to offer up his only son

---

אחלא, Ass. *ašlu*; 1 Sa. 22^{6} 31^{13} [in 1 Ch. 10^{12} אֵלָה] †, in both cases probably denoting a *sacred* tree. The word seems to have been strange to Vns.: 𝔊 ἄρουραν, Aq. δενδρῶνα, Σ. φυτείαν, 𝔙 *nemus*, etc. The substitution of אֲשֵׁרָה proposed by Sta. (*v.s.*) is uncalled for, though see *EB*, 4892 f.—עולם] 𝔐 העולם.—34 is wanting in 𝔗ᴶ (ed. Ginsburger).

as a sacrifice at the command of God. The story, which is the literary masterpiece of the Elohistic collection, is told with exquisite simplicity; every sentence vibrates with restrained emotion, which shows how fully the author realises the tragic horror of the situation.

Source.—The original narrative consists of vv.$^{1-14.\ 19}$. In spite of יהוה in $^{11.\ 14}$, this belongs to E: cf. [הָ]אֱלֹהִים, $^{1.\ 3.\ 8.\ 9.\ 12}$; עַר־כֹּה ^{5}; the revelation by night, $^{1ff.}$; the Angel calling from heaven, ^{11}.—On $^{15-18}$ see below. Comp. Di. Ho. Gu.

1–8. Abraham's willing preparation for the sacrifice.—**1.** *God tempted Abraham*] *i.e.*, tested him, to "know what was in his heart" (Dt. 8^{2}),—an anthropomorphic representation: cf. Ex. 16^{4} 20^{20}, Dt. 8^{16} 13^{4} 33^{8} etc. This sentence governs the narrative and prepares the reader for a good ending.—**2.** *thy son—thine only one—whom thou lovest —Isaac*] emphasising the greatness of the sacrifice, as if to say that God knows right well how much He asks.—*the land of Mōriyyāh* (הַמֹּרִיָּה)] All attempts to explain the name and identify the place have been futile.

The prevalent Jewish and Christian tradition puts the scene on the Temple mount at Jerusalem (הַר הַמּוֹרִיָּה, 2 Ch. 3^{1}; τὸ Μώριον ὄρος, Jos. *Ant.* i. 224, cf. 226). But (*a*) the attestation of the name is so late and unreliable that it is a question whether the Chronicler's use of it rests on a traditional interpretation of this passage, or whether it was introduced here on the strength of his notice. (*b*) Even if [הַ]מֹּרִיָּה were a genuine ancient name for the Temple hill, it is not credible that it was extended to the *land* in which it was, and still less that the hill itself should be described as 'one of the mountains' in the region named after it. There is reason to suspect that the name of a land may have been modified (either in accordance with a fanciful etymology [v.^{14}], or on the authority of 2 Ch. 3^{1}) in order that the chief sanctuary of later times

---

1. אחר הד' הא'] 15^{1}.—והאלהים נסה] The reluctance of grammarians to admit that this can be the main sent., and apod. after time determination, is intelligible (De. Di. Gu.), the order being that of the circumst. cl.; but it is difficult, without sophistical distinctions, to take it any other way. As cir. cl. it could only mean 'when God *had* tempted A.,' which is nonsense; and to speak of it as a *Verumständung* of the fol. ויאמר (De.) is to deceive oneself with a word. The right explanation in Dri. *T.* § 78 (3).—אברהם] repeated in 𝔊𝔙; cf. ^{11}.—**2.** המריה] The word was no doubt popularly connected with √ רָאָה as used in ^{14} (cf. 𝔖𝔪 המוראה, Aq. τὴν καταφανῆ, Σ. τῆς ὀπτασίας, 𝔙 *visionis*), though a real derivation from that √ is impossible. 𝔊 τὴν ὑψηλήν (cf. 12^{6}). 𝔖 has ܕܐܡܘܪܝܐ, 𝔗^{O}

might not be altogether ignored in the patriarchal history. The Samaritan tradition identified Moriah with Shechem.* This view has been revived in two forms: (1) that the name is a corruption or variant of מוֹרֶה in 12^6 etc. (Bleek, *SK*, 1831, 520 ff.; Tu., v. Gall [see 𝕲 *inf.*]); and (2) that it is a corruption of חֲמֹרִים ('land of the Ḥamorites' [33^{19}]) (We.). But both these names are too local and restricted to suit the context; and the distance is perhaps too great. Of the attempts to recover the original name, the simplest is א' הָאֱמֹרִי, which would be a natural designation of Palestine in E:† see on 10^{16}. If the legend be very ancient, there is no certainty that the place was in the Holy Land at all. Any extensive mountainous region, well known at the time, and with a lingering tradition of human sacrifice, would satisfy the conditions. Hence, Che.'s suggestion that the land of 'Muṣri' is to be read (*EB*, 3200; Wi. *GI*, ii. 44), is not devoid of plausibility. On Gu.'s solution, see below.

which I will name to thee] *When* this more precise direction was imparted, does not appear.—**3.** While the outward preparations are graphically described, no word is spared for the conflict in Abraham's breast,—a striking illustration of the reticence of the legends with regard to mental states.—**4.** *saw the place afar off*] The spot, therefore, has already been indicated (v.[2]). We are left to imagine the pang that shot through the father's heart when he caught sight of it.—**5.** Another touch, revealing the tense feeling with which the story is told: the servants are put off with a pretext whose hollowness the reader knows.—**6.** "The boy carries the heavier load, the father the more dangerous: knife and fire" (Gu.). It is curious that OT has no allusion to the method of producing fire.—**7, 8.** The pathos of this dialogue is inimitable: the artless curiosity of the child, the irrepressible

---

פולחנא ('worship').—**3.** את־שני נ'] So Nu. 22^{22}. The determination is peculiar. That it means *the* two slaves with whom a person of importance usually travelled (Gu.) is little probable. It is possible that in this legend Abraham was conceived as a man of moderate wealth, and that these were all the servants he had.—**5.** עד־כה] On כה as demonst. of *place*, see BDB, *s.v.* ('rare, chiefly in E'); cf. 31^{37}.—**7.** הנני בני] 'Yes, my son'; the 'Here am I' of EV is much too pompous. 𝕲𝖁 excellently: *τί ἐστιν, τέκνον; Quid vis, fili?*—**8.** השה] 𝔐 𝕲 om. art. (Ba.).

---

* See *ZDPV*, vi. 198, vii. 133.—V. Gall (*CSt.* 112) seems in error when he says this was a *Jewish* tradition.

† But it is doubtful if the restoration can claim the authority of 𝕾, for that Vn. reads ܠܐܪܥܐ ܕܐܡܘܪܝܐ in 2 Ch. 3^1 also.

affection of the father, and the stern ambiguity of his reply, can hardly be read without tears. Note the effect of the repetition: *and they went both of them together* ($^{6. 8}$).—*God will provide*] יִרְאֶה, lit. 'look out'; as 41^{33} [Dt. 12^{13} 33^{21}], 1 Sa. 16$^{1. 17}$. The word points forward to v.^{14}.

9–14. The sacrifice averted.—**9, 10.** The vv. describe with great minuteness the preliminary ritual of the עֹלָה in highly technical language (עָרַךְ, עָקַד, שָׁחַט); *v.i.* —**11, 12.** At the extreme moment Abraham's hand is stayed by a voice from heaven.—**11** is certainly from E; יהוה must therefore be a redactional accommodation to v.^{15} (cf. 𝔖 *inf.*).—The repetition of *Abraham* expresses urgency; as 46^{2}, Ex. 3^{4} (E), 1 Sa. 3^{10}.—**12.** The Angel speaks in the name of God, as 16^{10}, 21^{18}.—*now I know, etc.*] Thus early was the truth taught that the essence of sacrifice is the moral disposition (Ps. 51$^{18f.}$).—**13.** The substitution of the ram for the human victim takes place without express command, Abraham recognising by its mysterious presence that it was 'provided' by God for this purpose.—**14a.** The naming of the place is an essential feature of the legend, and must therefore be assigned to E.—יהוה יִרְאֶה alludes to v.^{8}; but that any sanctuary actually bore this name is scarcely probable. In truth, it seems to be given as the explanation, not of a name, but of a current proverbial saying (Sta. *GVI*, i. 450), which can hardly be the original intention (see below).—**14b.** The words בְּהַר יהוָה יֵרָאֶה yield no sense appropriate to the context.

MT might be rendered: (*a*) 'In the mount of Yahwe he (it) is seen' (Str.), or (*b*) 'In the mount of Y. men appear' [for worship] (Dri. 220, cf. 𝔗^{O} *inf.*), or (disregarding acc.) (*c*) 'In the mount where Y. is

---

9. ערך] of the arranging of the wood on the altar, 1 Ki. 18^{33}, Nu. 23^{4}, Is 30^{33}.—עקד] (ἅπ. λεγ.) in NH means to 'bind the bent fore- and hind-legs of an animal for sacrifice' (Dri.): 𝔊 *συμποδίσας*.—**10.** שחט is technically to cut the throat of a sacrificial victim (Jacob, *ZATW*, xvii. 51).—**11.** יהוה] 𝔖 אֱלֹהִים; so v.^{15}.—**13.** אַיִל אַחַר] 'a ram behind'; so Tu. Di. De. Str. (𝔗^{O}, Σ. in temp. sense). 𝔐𝔊𝔖𝔗^{J}, *Jub.* and Heb. MSS have א' אֶחָד, 'a [certain] ram'; which may be *nichtssagend*, but is preferable to MT (Ho. Gu.).—Rd. also (with 𝔊𝔖) נֶאֱחָז (ptcp.) for pf.—בסבך] 𝔊 *ἐν φυτῷ σαβέκ*, Σ. *ἐν δικτύῳ* (בִּשְׂבָכָה), Aq. *ἐν συχνεῶνι*, 𝔙 *inter vepres*.—**14.** The paraphrase of 𝔗^{O} is interesting: 'And A. worshipped and prayed there

seen': in this case the saying would be יהוה יֵרָאֶה (^{14a}), and ^{14b} would merely mean that it was used in the Temple mount. All these are obviously unsatisfactory. With a slight change (בָּהָר for 'בְּ) the cl. would read 'In the mount Y. appears' (so 𝔊), or (with יִרְאֶה for יֵרָאֶה) 'In . . . Y. sees' (𝔙𝔖).—The text has probably been altered under the same tendency which gave rise to מֹרִיָּה in v.^{2}; and the recovery of the original is impossible. Gu., with brilliant ingenuity, conjectures that the name of the sanctuary was יְרוּאֵל (2 Ch. 20^{16}); this he inserts after הַהוּא; and restores the remainder of the v. as follows: אֲשֶׁר אָמַר הַיּוֹם בָּהָר יִרְאֶה אֱלֹהִים = 'for he said, "To-day, in this mountain, God provideth."

15–19. Renewal of the promises: Conclusion.—15. The occasion seemed to a Jehovistic red. to demand an ampler reward than the sparing of Isaac; hence a supplementary revelation (שֵׁנִית) is appended.—**16.** *By myself I swear*] cf. Ex. 32^{13} (also R^{JE}), elsewhere Is. 45^{23}, Jer. 22^{5} 49^{13}†.—נְאֻם יהוה] lit. 'murmur of Yahwe,' an expression for the prophetic inspiration, whose significance must have been forgotten before it could be put in the mouth of the Angel. Even P (Nu. 14^{28}) is more discriminating in his use of the phrase.—**17.** *occupy the gate of their enemies*] *i.e.*, take possession of their cities (𝔊 πόλεις); cf. 24^{60}.—**18.** *by thy seed . . . bless themselves* (Hithp.)] So 26^{4}; cf. Dt. 29^{18}, Is. 65^{16}, Jer. 4^{2}, Ps. 72^{17}†. See on 12^{3}.—**19.** The return to Beersheba is the close of E's narrative, continuing v.^{14}.

The secondary character of $^{15-18}$ is clear not only from its loose connexion with the primary narrative, but also from its combination of Elohistic conceptions with Yahwistic phraseology, the absence of originality, the improper use of נְאֻם יהוה, etc. Cf. We. *Comp.*^{2} 20; Di. 291; Ho. 165.—The view of De. (324 f.) and Str. (82), that $^{14-18}$ are from a J parallel to 22$^{1-14}$, is untenable.

The difficult question of the *meaning* of this incident is approached from two sides. (1) Those who regard it as a literal occurrence in the life of a man of eminent piety, holding views of truth in advance of his age, are undoubtedly able to give it an interpretation charged with deep religious significance. Familiar with the rite of child-sacrifice amongst the surrounding heathen, the patriarch is conceived

---

(שֵׁם for שָׁם), in that place, saying before the Lord, Here shall generations worship. So it is said at this day, In this mountain A. worshipped before the Lord.'—בְּהַר יהוה יֵרָאֶה] 𝔊 ἐν τῷ ὄρει Κύριος ὤφθη, 𝔙 *in monte Dominus videbit*, 𝔖 ܒܛܘܪܐ ܗܢܐ ܡܪܝܐ ܢܚܙܐ.

16 end] Add מִמֶּנִּי as v.^{12}: so 𝔊𝔙.—18. עקב אשר] elsewhere only 26^{5}, 2 Sa. 12^{6}.

as arrested by the thought that even this terrible sacrifice might rightly be demanded by the Being to whom he owed all that he was; and as brooding over it till he seemed to hear the voice of God calling on him to offer up his own son as proof of devotion to Him. He is led on step by step to the very verge of accomplishing the act, when an inward monition stays his hand, and reveals to him that what God really requires is the surrender of the will—that being the *truth* in his previous impression; but that the sacrifice of a human life is not in accordance with the character of the true God whom Abraham worshipped. But it must be felt that this line of exposition is not altogether satisfying. The story contains no word in repudiation of human sacrifice, nor anything to enforce what must be supposed to be the main lesson, viz., that such sacrifices were to find no place in the religion of Abraham's descendants. (2) Having regard to the origin of many other Genesis narratives, we must admit the possibility that the one before us is a legend, explaining the substitution of animal for human sacrifices in some type of ancient worship. This view is worked out with remarkable skill by Gu. (211–214), who thinks he has recovered the lost name of the sanctuary from certain significant expressions which seem to prepare the mind for an etymological interpretation: viz. אֱלֹהִים יִרְאֶה, [8] (cf. [14]); יְרֵא אֱלֹהִים, [12]; and וַיַּרְא [והנה] אַיִל, [13]. From these indications he concludes that the original name in [14] was יְרוּאֵל; and he is disposed to identify the spot with a place of that name somewhere near Tekoa, mentioned in 2 Ch. 20[16] (יְרִיאֵל in 1 Ch. 7[2] is excluded by geographical considerations). Here he conjectures that there was a sanctuary where the custom of child-sacrifice had been modified by the substitution of a ram for a human being. The basis of Gn. 22 would then be the local cultus-legend of this place. Apart from the philological speculations, which are certainly pushed to an extreme, it is not improbable that Gu.'s theory correctly expresses the character of the story; and that it originally belonged to the class of ætiological legends which everywhere weave themselves round peculiarities of ritual whose real origin has been forgotten or obscured. — An older cultus-myth of the same kind is found in the Phœnician story in which Kronos actually sacrifices his only son 'Ιεούδ (יָחִיד=יחוד?) or 'Ιεδούδ (יָדִיד?) to his father Uranus (Eus. *Præp. Ev.* i. 10, 29). The sacrifice of Iphigeneia, and the later modification in which a hind is substituted for the maiden, readily suggests itself as a parallel (Eurip. *Iph. Aul.* 1540 ff.).

XXII. 20–24.—*The Sons of Nāḥôr* (J,R).

In the singular form of a report brought to Abraham, there is here introduced a list of 12 tribes tracing their descent to Nāḥôr. Very few of the names can be identified; but so far as the indications go, they point to the region E and NE of Palestine as the area peopled by the Naḥorite family. The division into legitimate ([20–23]) and illegitimate

([24]) sons expresses a distinction between the pure-blooded stock and hybrid, or perhaps alien and subjugated, clans (Guthe, *GVI*, 5).

The vv. bear the unmistakable signature of a Yahwistic genealogy. cf. גַּם הִיא [20. 24], w. $4^{22.26}$ 10^{21} 19^{38}; [21a] w. 10^{15}; [23b] w. 9^{19} (10^{29} 25^4); יָלַד [23] (see p. 98). Of P's style and manner there is no trace; and with regard to *'Ûẓ* and *'Ărām*, there is a material discrepancy between the two documents (v.[21] cpd. with $10^{22f.}$). The introductory formula אחרי הד' הא' is not exclusively Elohistic (see on 15^1), and in any case would be an insufficient reason for ascribing (We. *Comp.*[2] 29 f.) the whole section to E. See Bu. *Urg.* 220 ff.—The genealogy appears to have been inserted with reference to ch. 24, from which it was afterwards separated by the amalgamation of P (ch. 23) with the older documents. Its adaptation to this context is, however, very imperfect. Here Abraham is informed of the birth of Nāḥôr's *children*, whereas in the present text of 24 the *grand*children (Laban and Rebekah) are grown up. Moreover, with the excision of the gloss [23a] (*v.i.*), the only point of direct contact with ch. 24 disappears; and even the gloss does not agree with the view of Rebekah's parentage originally given by J (see on 24^{15}). Hence we must suppose that the basis of the passage is an ancient genealogy, which has been recast, annotated, and inserted by a Yahwistic writer at a stage *later* than the composition of ch. 24, but *earlier* than the final redaction of the Pent.

20. מִלְכָּה] see on 11^{29}.—לנחור אחיך] 11^{22}.—**21.** עוּץ] in 10^{23} a subdivision of Aram, is here the principal (בְּכוֹר) Naḥorite tribe (cf. 36^{28}).—בוז (Βαύξ, Βαύζ, etc.)] mentioned in Jer. 25^{23} after Dĕdān and Têmā, is probably the *Bâzu* of Esarhaddon's inscr. (*KIB*, ii. 130 f.), an unidentified district of N Arabia (so Jb. 32^2). — קְמוּאֵל] unknown; see Praetorius, *ZDMG*, 1903, 780.—אֲבִי אֲרָם (πατέρα Σύρων) is possibly a gloss (Gu.), but the classification of the powerful Aramæans (see on 10^{22}) as a minor branch of the Naḥorites is none the less surprising: see p. 334 below.—**22.** כֶּשֶׂד] The eponym of the כַּשְׂדִּים. But whether by these the well-known Chaldæans of S Babylonia are meant is a difficult question. Probability seems in favour of the theory that here, as in 2 Ki. 24^2, Jb. 1^{17}, an Arabian (or rather Aramæan) nomadic tribe is to be understood, from which the Bab. כַּשְׂדִּים may have sprung (Wi. *AOF*, ii. 250 ff.; Gu.). The result has a bearing on the meaning of Arpakšad in 10^{22} (see also on 11^{28}).—חֲזוֹ (Ἀζαῦ)] probably the *Ḫazû* mentioned after *Bâzu* in Esarhaddon's inscr. (above).—פִּלְדָּשׁ and יִדְלָף (Ἰελδάφ, Ἰεδλάφ) are not known. With the former have been compared Palm. פלדשו (Levy, *ZDMG*, xiv. 440) and Sin. פנרשו (Cook, *Gl.* 98; Lidz. *Hdb.* 352), both personal names. — בְּתוּאֵל] as personal name $24^{15ff.}$ (J), 25^{20} $28^{2.5}$ (P). —**23a.** is a gloss (Di. Gu.) excluded by the general scheme of the genealogy and by the number 8 in [23b]. The last consideration is decisive against Di.'s view that the original text was וְאֶת־לָבָן וְאֶת־רִבְקָה.—**24.** וּפִילַגְשׁוֹ] *cas. pend.*: G–K. §§ 111 *h*, 147 *e*. פִּילֶגֶשׁ = παλλακίς (see Sta. *GVI*, i. 380): a Ḥittite origin is suggested by Jensen (*ZDMG*, xlviii. 468 ff., developing a hint of Ew.).—רְאוּמָה] 𝔐 רומה, 𝔊 Ῥεύμα, Ῥεηρά, etc.

—טֶבַח] rightly read by 𝔊𝔖 in 2 Sa. 8^8 (MT מִבְטַח ‖ בֶּטַח, 1 Ch. 18^8), a city of 'Ăram-Ẓôbāh, probably identical with the *Tubiḫi* of TA No. 127, and Pap. Anast., near Ḳadesh on the Orontes (but see Müller, *AE*, 173, 396).—גַּחַם (Ταaμ, Γaaμ, etc.)] unknown.—תַּחַשׁ (Τοχος, Θaaς, etc.)] probably Eg. *Teḫisi*, on the Orontes, N of Ḳadesh (*AE*, 258; Wi. *MVAG*, i. 207).—מַעֲכָה (Μaaχa, Μωχa, etc.)] Dt. 3^{14}, Jos. 12^5 $13^{11.13}$ 2 Sa. $10^{6.8}$, 1 Ch. $19^{6f.}$; an Aramæan tribe and state occupying the modern Ğōlān, S of Hermon, and E of the Upper Jordan.

To the discrepancies already noted (p. 333) between the genealogy and ch. 24, Meyer (*INS*, 239 ff.) adds the important observation that the territorial distribution of the sons of Nāḥôr fits in badly with the theory of J, which connects Nāḥôr and Laban with the city of Ḥarran. He points out that the full-blooded Naḥorites, so far as identified, are tribes of the Syro-Arabian desert, while those described as hybrids belong to the settled regions of Syria, where nomadic immigrants would naturally amalgamate with the native population. Now the Syro-Arabian desert is in other parts of the OT the home of the *Bnê Ḳedem*; and according to E (see on 29^1) it was among the *Bnê Ḳedem* that Jacob found his uncle Laban. Meyer holds that this was the original tradition, and finds a confirmation of it in the geographical background of the list before us. In other words, the Israelites were historically related, not to the civilised Aramæans about Ḥarran, but to nomadic Aramæan tribes who had not crossed the Euphrates, but still roamed the deserts where Aramæans first appear in history (see p. 206). J's representation is partly due to a misunderstanding of the name 'Aramæan,' which led him to transfer the kinsfolk of Abraham to the region round Ḥarran, which was known as the chief seat of Aramæan culture. The genealogy is therefore an authentic document of great antiquity, which has fortunately been preserved by a Yahwistic editor in spite of its inconsistency with the main narrative. It may be added that the Palestinian view-point will explain the subordinate position assigned to the name *Aram*. It can hardly be denied that Meyer's reasoning is sufficiently cogent to outweigh the traces of the names Nāḥôr and Milkah in the neighbourhood of Ḥarran (pp. 232, 237 f.). Meyer's explanation of Nāḥôr as a modification of *Nāhār* (the Euphrates) is, however, not likely to commend itself.

Ch. XXIII. *Purchase of the Cave of Machpelah* (P).

On the death of Sarah at the age of 127 years ($^{1.2}$), Abraham becomes, through formal purchase from the Ḥittites, the owner of the field and cave of Machpelah ($^{3-18}$), and there buries his dead ($^{19.20}$).—This is the second occasion (cf. ch. 17) on which the Priestly epitome of Abraham's life expands into circumstantial and even graphic narration. The transaction must therefore have had a special interest for the writer of the Code; though it is not easy to determine of what nature that interest was (see the closing note).

Source.—That the chapter belongs to P is proved (*a*) by allusions in later parts of the Code ($25^{9f.}$ $49^{29ff.}$ 50^{13}); (*b*) by the juristic formalism and redundancy of the style; (*c*) by the names בני חת, מכפלה, קרית ארבע, ארץ כנען; and the expressions תושב, [4]; אחוזה, [4. 9. 20]; נשיא, [6]; קום, [17. 20]; מקנה, [18] (see the notes; and cf. Di. Ho. Gu.). Against this we have to set the אנכי of v.[4], which is never elsewhere used by P.—At the same time it is difficult to acquiesce in the opinion that we have to do with a 'free composition' of the writers of P. The passage has far more the appearance of a transcript from real life than any other section in the whole of P; and its markedly secular tone (the name of God is never once mentioned) is in strong contrast to the free introduction of the divine activity in human affairs which is characteristic of that document. It seems probable that the narrative is based on some local tradition by which the form of representation has been partly determined. A similar view is taken by Eerdmans (*Komp. d. Gen.* 88), who, however, assigns the chapter to the oldest stratum of Gen., dating at latest from 700 B.C. Steuernagel (*SK*, 1908, 628) agrees that ch. 23 is not in P's manner; but thinks it a midrashic expansion of a brief notice in that document.*

1, 2. The death of Sarah.—**2.** *Ḳiryath-'Arba'*] an old name of Hebron, *v.i.*—וַיָּבֹא] not 'came,' but *went in*—to where the body lay.—*to wail . . . weep*] with the customary loud demonstrations of grief (Schwally, *Leben n. d. Tode*, 20; *DB*, iii. 453 ff.).

---

1. After ויהיו it is advisable to insert שְׁנֵי (Ba. Kit.: cf. $47^{9.\ 28}$). The omission may have caused the addition of the gloss שְׁנֵי חַיֵּי שָׂרָה at the end (wanting in 𝔊).—**2.** קרית ארבע (𝔊 ἐν πόλει 'Αρβόκ)] The old name of Hebron (Jos. 14^{15}, Ju. 1^{10}), though seemingly in use after the Exile

---

* Sayce's contention (*EHH*, 57 ff.), that the incident 'belongs essentially to the early Babylonian and not to the Assyrian period,' is not borne out by the cuneiform documents to which he refers; the correspondences adduced being quite as close with contracts of the later Ass. kings as with those of the age of Ḫammurabi. Thus, the expression 'full silver' (v.[9]) is frequent under Sargon and subsequently (*KIB*, iv. 108 ff.); under the first Babylonian dynasty the phrase is 'silver to the full price' (*ib.* 7 ff.). The formula for 'before' (a witness) is, in the earlier tablets, *maḫar*; in the later, *pân*,—neither the precise equivalent of those here used (בְּאָזְנֵי and לְעֵינֵי). There remains only the expression '*weigh* silver,' which does appear to be characteristic of the older contracts; but since this phrase survived in Heb. till the latest times (Zec. 11^{12}, Est. 3^{9}), it is plain that nothing can be inferred from it. Sayce has not strengthened his case by the arguments in *ET*, 1907, 418 ff.; see Dri. 230, and *Addenda*[7], XXXVII f.

3–7. **The request for a burying-place.**—The negotiations fall into three well-defined stages; and while they illustrate the leisurely courtesy of the East in such matters, they cover a real reluctance of the Ḥittites to give Abraham a legal title to land by purchase (Gu.). To his first request they respond with alacrity: the best of their sepulchres is at his disposal.—3. *arose*] from the sitting posture of the mourner (2 Sa. $12^{16. 20}$).—*the sons of Ḥēth*] see on 10^{15}.

P is the only document in which Ḥittites are definitely located in the S of Canaan (cf. 26^{34} 36^{2}); and the historic accuracy of the statement is widely questioned. It is conceivable that the Cappadocian Ḥittites (p. 215) had extended their empire over the whole country prior to the Heb. invasion. But taking into account that P appears to use 'Ḥēth' interchangeably with 'Canaan' (cf. 26^{34} 27^{46} 36^{2b} w. $28^{1. 8}$ 36^{2a}), it may be more reasonable to hold that with him 'Ḥittite' is a general designation of the pre-Israelite inhabitants, as 'Canaanite' with J and 'Amorite' with E (cf. Jos. 1^{4}, Ezk. 16^{3}). It may, of course, be urged that such an idea could not have arisen unless the Ḥittites had once been in actual occupation of the land, and that this assumption would best explain the all but constant occurrence of the name in the lists of conquered peoples (see p. 284). At present, however, we have no proof that this was the case; and a historic connexion between the northern Ḥittites and the natives of Hebron remains problematical. Another solution is propounded by Jastrow (*EB*, 2094 ff.), viz., that P's Ḥittites are an entirely distinct stock, having nothing but the name in common with either the 'conventional' Ḥittites of the enumerations or the great empire of N Syria. See Dri. 228 ff.

4. *a sojourner and dweller*] so Lv. $25^{35. 47}$, Nu. 35^{15}, and (in a religious sense) Ps. 39^{13} (cf. 1 Pe. 2^{11}). The technical

---

(unless Neh. 11^{25} be an artificial archaism [Mey. *Entst.* 106]). The name means 'Four cities' (see on בְּאֵר שֶׁבַע, p. 326). The personification of אַרְבַּע as *heros eponymus* (Jos. 14^{15} 15^{13} 21^{11}) has no better authority (as 𝔊 shows) than the mistake of a copyist (see Moore, *Jud.* 25). Jewish Midrash gave several explanations of the numeral: amongst others from the 4 patriarchs buried there—Abraham, Isaac, Jacob, and *Adam* (*Ber. R.*; *P. R. Eliezer*, 20, 36; Ra.)—the last being inferred from הָאָדָם הַגָּדוֹל in Jos. 14^{15} (Jer. *OS*, 84^{12}). The addition of אל עמק ᵯᵯᵯ (𝔊 ἥ ἐστιν ἐν τῷ κοιλώματι) seems a corruption of אבי ענק (Ba.) or (with 𝔊) אֵם ע׳ in Jos. 15^{13} 21^{11}.—לספר] In Heb. usage, as in that of all the cognate languages, ספר means 'to wail'; see Mic. 1^{8}.—4. תּוֹשָׁב] IEz. הוא הגר היושב בארץ. According to Bertholet (*Stell. z. d. Fr.* 156–166), the ת׳ is simply a *gêr* (see on 12^{10}) who resides fixedly in one place, without civil rights, and perhaps incapable of holding land; see *EB*, 4818.—5. לֵאמֹר לוֹ (so v.[14]) is an abnormal combination, doubtfully supported by Lv. 11^{1}. The last word

distinction between גֵּר and תּוֹשָׁב is obscure (*v.i.*).—**6.** *O if thou wouldst hear us* (rd. לוּ שְׁמָעֵנוּ, *v.i.*)]. The formula always introduces a suggestion preferable to that just advanced: cf. $^{11. 13. 15}$.—נְשִׂיא אֱלֹהִים is more than 'a mighty prince' (as Ps. 36^{7} 68^{16} 104^{16} etc.); it means one deriving his patent of nobility straight from Almighty God.—*Not a man of us will withhold, etc.*] therefore there is no need to buy. Behind their generosity there lurks an aversion to the idea of purchase.—**7.** The v. has almost the force of a refrain (cf. 12). The first stage of the negotiations is concluded.

8–12. The appeal to ʿEphrôn.—In his second speech Abraham shows his tact first by ignoring tacitly the suggestion of a free gift, and then by bringing the favourable public opinion just expressed to bear on the individual he wishes to reach.—**9.** On *the cave of Makpēlāh*, see at the close.—*in the end of his field*] Abraham apparently does not contemplate the purchase of the whole field: that was thrust on him by ʿEphrôn's offer.—*for full money*] see p. 335 above (footnote). The same expression occurs in 1 Ch. 21$^{22. 24}$.—**10.** *entering the gate, etc.*] *i.e.*, his fellow-citizens, with the right of sitting in public assembly at the gate (cf. יֹצְאֵי שׁ׳ ע׳, 34^{24}).

13–16. The purchase of the field.— With the same tactful persistency, Abraham seizes on ʿEphrôn's expression of goodwill, while waving aside the idea of a gift.—**13.** *If only thou—pray hear me!*] The anakolouthon expresses the polite embarrassment of the speaker.—**14, 15.** ʿEphrôn's resistance being now broken down, he names his price with the affecta-

---

must be joined to v.^{6}, and read either לֹא (as v.^{11}: so 𝔐𝔊), or לוּ (as ^{13}). The last is the only form suitable in all four cases ($^{5. 11. 13. 15}$). On לוּ with impve., cf. G–K. § 110 *e*.—**6.** יִכְלֶה] = יִכְלָא, G–K. § 75 *qq*.

8. את־נפשכם] 'in accordance with your [inner] mind.' Cf. 2 Ki. 9^{15}, 1 Sa. 20^{4}: see BDB, 661 a.—**9.** הַמַּכְפֵּלָה] Elsewhere only 25^{9} 49^{30} 50^{13}; always with art., showing that it retained an appellative sense. 𝔊 (τὸ σπήλαιον τὸ διπλοῦν), 𝔙𝔖𝔗^{OJ} are probably right in deriving it from √ כפל, 'double' (see p. 339).—**10.** לכל] לְ = 'namely' (see on 9^{10}: cf. BDB, 514 b); in ^{18} it is replaced by בְּ = 'among.'—**11.** For לֹא pt. לְא: see on ^{5}.—נתתי לך] 𝔊 om.—נְתַתִּיהָ is perf. of instant action: 'I give it'; G–K. § 106 *m*.

13. For לוּ, 𝔊𝔗^{OJ} (? 𝔖) read לִי, mistaking the idiom.—**14.** לֵאמֹר : לוֹ] as ^{5}. —**15.** 𝔊 (Οὐχί, κύριε, ἀκήκοα γάρ) does not render אֶרֶץ, but the γάρ is odd.

tion of generosity still observed in the East.*—*land* [worth] *400 shekels . . . what is that . . .*?] The word for 'land' is better omitted with 𝔊; it is not the land but the money that ʿEphrôn pretends to disparage.—**16.** Abraham immediately pays the sum asked, and clenches the bargain.—*current with the merchant*] The precious metals circulated in ingots, whose weight was approximately known, without, however, superseding the necessity for 'weighing' in important transactions (Benzinger, *Arch.*[2] 197; Kennedy, *DB*, iii. 420; *ZA*, iii. 391 f.).†

17–20. Summary and conclusion.—17, 18 are in the form of a legal contract. Specifications of the dimensions and boundaries of a piece of land, and of the buildings, trees, etc., upon it, are common in ancient contracts of sale at all periods; cf. *e.g.* *KIB*, iv. 7, 17, 33 (1st Bab. dynasty), 101, and 161 (8th cent. B.C.), 223–5 (6th cent.); the *Assouan Papyri* (5th cent.); and especially the Petra Inscr. cited in *Authority and Archæology*, p. 135.

The traditional site of the Cave of Makpēlāh is on the E side of the narrow valley in which Hebron lies, and just within the modern city (*el-Ḫalīl*). The place is marked by a sacred enclosure (the *Ḥarām*), within which Christians have seldom been admitted. The SE half is occupied by a mosque, and six cenotaphs are shown: those of Abraham and Sarah in the middle, of Isaac and Rebekah in the SE (within the mosque), and of Jacob and Leah in the NW: that of Joseph is just

---

—ואת] better וְאַתָּ (𝔊).—**16.** עבר לסחר] The only other instance of this use of עבר (2 Ki. 12^5) is corrupt (rd. עֶרְכּוֹ, 𝔊).—**17.** קום] = 'pass into permanent possession,' as Lv. 25^{30} $27^{14.\ 17.\ 19}$ (P).—אשר במכפלה] 𝔊 ὅς ἦν ἐν τῷ διπλῷ σπηλαίῳ is nonsense; but 𝔙 *in quo erat spelunca duplex* suggests a reading אֲשֶׁר בּוֹ הַמּ׳ which (if it were better attested) would remove the difficulty of supposing that the name 'double cave' was applied to the district around.—לפני] 𝔐𝔲 על פני as in [19] = 'in front of,' perhaps 'to the E of.'

---

* "The peasants will often say, when a person asks the price of any thing which they have for sale, 'Receive it as a present': this answer having become a common form of speech, they know that advantage will not be taken of it; and when desired again to name the price, they will do so, but generally name a sum that is exorbitant." Lane, *Mod. Eg.*[5] ii. 13 f.

† Cuneiform records recently discovered in Cappadocia seem to prove that shekels "stamped with a seal" were in use in the time of Ḫammurabi. See Sayce, *Contemp. Rev.*, Aug. 1907, p. 259.

outside the Ḥarām on the NW. The cave below has never been examined in modern times, but is stated by its guardians to be double. There is no reason to doubt that the tradition as to the site has descended from biblical times; and it is quite probable that the name Makpēlāh is derived from the feature just referred to. That the name included the field attached to the cave (v.[19] 49[30] 50[13]) is natural; and even its extension to the adjacent district (see on [17]) is perhaps not a decisive objection. — For further particulars, see Robinson, *BR*, ii. 75 ff.; Baedeker, *P. and S.*[3] 141 f.; *PEFS*, 1882, 197–214; Warren, *DB*, iii. 197 ff.; Driver, *Gen.* 228.

Whatever assumption we make as to the origin of this narrative, P's peculiar interest in the transaction is a fact that has to be explained. The motive usually assigned is that the purchase was a pledge of the possession of the land by Abraham's descendants; that view is, indeed, supported by nothing in the passage (see Gu. 241), but it is difficult to imagine any other explanation. It is just conceivable that the elaboration of the narrative was due to a dispute as to the possession of the sacred place between Jews and Edomites in the age of P. It has been held probable on independent grounds that the Edomites had advanced as far north as Hebron during the Exile (see Mey. *Entst.* 106, 114), and from Neh. 11[25] we learn that a colony of Jews settled there after the return. We can at least imagine that a contest for the ownership of the holy place (like those which have so largely determined the later history of Palestine) would arise; and that such a situation would account for the emphasis with which the Priestly jurists asserted the legal claim of the Jewish community to the traditional burying-place of its ancestors. So Gu.[1] 251; *Students' OT*, 99: otherwise Gu.[2] 241 f.

Ch. XXIV.—*Procuring a Wife for Isaac* (J, [E?]).

Abraham on his death-bed (see below) solemnly charges his house-steward with the duty of procuring a wife for Isaac amongst his Mesopotamian relatives ([1–9]). The servant is providentially guided to the house of Nāḥôr, in whose daughter (see on v.[15]) Rebekah he is led to recognise the divinely appointed bride for Isaac ([10–49]). Having obtained the consent of the relatives, and of the maiden herself ([50–61]), he brings her to Canaan, where Isaac marries her ([62–67]).

The chapter is one of the most perfect specimens of descriptive writing that the Book of Gen. contains. It is marked by idyllic grace and simplicity, picturesque elaboration of scenes and incidents, and a certain 'epic' amplitude of treatment, seen in the repetition of the story in the form of a speech (see Dri. 230). These artistic elements so predominate that the primary ethnographic motive is completely submerged. It may be conjectured that the basis of the narrative was a reinforcement of the Aramæan element in the Hebrew stock, as in the kindred story of Jacob and his wives (see Steuernagel, *Einw.* 39 f.). But if such a historical kernel existed, it is quite lost sight of in the graphic delineation of human character, and of ancient Eastern life, which is to us the main interest of the passage. We must also note the profoundly religious conception of Yahwe's providence as an unseen power, overruling events in answer to prayer. All these features seem to indicate a somewhat advanced phase in the development of the patriarchal tradition. The chapter belongs to the literary type most fully represented in the Joseph-narrative (cf. Gu. 220).

Source and Unity of the Narrative.—From the general character of the style, and the consistent use of the name יהוה, critical opinion has been practically unanimous in assigning the whole chapter to J. It is admitted, however, that certain 'unevennesses of representation' occur; and the question arises whether these are to be explained by accidental dislocations of the text, or by the interweaving of two parallel recensions. Thus, the servant's objection that the maiden may not be willing to follow him ([5. 39]), is met by Abraham in two ways: on the one hand by the confident assurance that this will not happen ([7. 40]), and on the other by absolving him from his oath if his mission should miscarry ([8. 41]). In [29f.] Laban *twice* goes out to the man at the well ([29b ‖ 30b]); [28] speaks of the *mother's* house, [23b] of the *father's*: in [50] the servant negotiates with *Laban and Bethuel*, in [53. 55] with the *brother and mother* of the bride; in [51] the request is at once agreed to by the *relatives* without regard to Rebekah's wish, whereas in [57f.] the decision is left to *herself*; in [59] Rebekah is sent away with her *nurse*, in [61a] she takes her own *maidens* with her; her departure is *twice* recorded ([61a ‖ 61b]). These doublets and variants are too numerous to be readily accounted for either by transpositions of the text (Di. al.) or by divergences in the *oral* tradition (*SOT*, 96); and although no complete analysis is here attempted, the presence of two narratives must be recognised. That one of these is J is quite certain; but it is to be observed that the characteristically Yahwistic expressions are somewhat sparsely distributed, and leave an ample margin of neutral ground for critical ingenuity to sift out the variants between two recensions.* The problem has been attacked with great acuteness and skill by Gu. (215–221) and Procksch (14 f.), though with very discordant results. I agree with Procksch that the second component is in all probability E, mainly on the ground that a fusion of J^h and J^b (Gu.) is without parallel, whereas J^b and E are combined in ch. 21. The stylistic criteria are, indeed, too indecisive to permit of a definite conclusion; but the parallels instanced above can easily be arranged in two series, one of which is free from positive marks of J; while, in the other,

* יהוה, [1. 3. 7. 12. 21. 26. 27. 31. 35. 40. 42. 44. 48. 50. 51. 52. 56]; ארם נהרים, [10] (against P's פדן ארם); ארצי ומולדתי, [4] (12[1]); בא בימים, [1] (see on 18[11]); טבת מראה, [16] (26[7], cf. 12[11]); ידע, [16] (see on 4[1]); יש with suff. and ptcp. [42. 49]; טרם, [15. 45]; הצליח, [21. 40. 42. 56] (39[2. 3. 23]); הקרה, [12] (27[20]); רוץ לקראת, [17] (see 18[2]); נא, [2. 12. 14. 17. 23. 42. 43. 45].

everything is consistent with the supposition that Abraham's residence is Beersheba (see p. 241 above).

The Death of Abraham.—It is impossible to escape the impression that in vv.$^{1-9}$ Abraham is very near his end, and that in $^{62-67}$ his death is presupposed. It follows that the account of the event in JE must have occurred in this chap., and been suppressed by the Red. in favour of that of P (25^{7-11}), according to which Abraham survived the marriage of Isaac by some 35 years (cf. 25^{20}). The only question is whether it happened before or after the departure of the servant. Except in $^{14b\alpha}$, the servant invariably speaks as if his master were still alive (cf. $^{12.\ 14b\beta.\ 27.\ 37.\ 42.\ 44b.\ 48.\ 51.\ 54.\ 56}$). In ^{65}, on the other hand, he seems to be aware, before meeting Isaac, that Abraham is no more. There is here a slight diversity of representation, which may be due to the composition of sources. Gu. supposes that in the document to which $^{14b\alpha.\ 36b}$ and ^{65} belong (J^b), the death was recorded after ^{9} (and related by the servant after ^{41}); while in the other (J^h) it was first noticed in connexion with the servant's meeting with Isaac (before ^{66}). Procksch thinks E's notice followed v.^{9}, but doubts whether Abraham's death was presupposed by J's account of the servant's return.—V.^{36b} is thought to point *back* to 25^{5}; and hence some critics (Hup. We. Di. al.) suppose that $25^{1-6\ (11b)}$ originally preceded ch. 24; while others (KS. Ho. Gu.) find a more suitable place for 25^{5} (with or without ^{11b}) between 24^{1} and 24^{2}. See, further, on 25^{1-6} below.

1–9. The servant's commission—**1.** *had blessed, etc.*] His life as recorded is, indeed, one of unclouded prosperity. —**2.** *the oldest* (*i.e.* senior in rank) *servant, etc.*] who, in default of an heir, would have succeeded to the property ($15^{2f.}$), and still acts as the trusted guardian of the family interests; comp. the position of Ziba in 2 Sa. $9^{1ff.}$ $16^{1ff.}$.—*put thy hand, etc.*] Only again 47^{29}—another death-bed scene! It is, in fact, only the imminence of death that can account for the action here: had Abraham expected to live, a simple command would have sufficed (Gu.).

The reference is to an oath by the genital organs, as emblems of the life-giving power of deity,—a survival of primitive religion whose significance had probably been forgotten in the time of the narrator. Traces have been found in various parts of the world: see Ew. *Ant.* 19^{6} [Eng. tr.]; Di. 301; *ATLO*^{2}, 395; and especially the striking Australian parallel cited by Spurrell (^{2}218) from Sir G. Grey.* By Jewish writers

* "One native remains seated on the ground with his heels tucked under him . . .; the one who is about to narrate a death to him approaches . . . and seats himself cross-legged upon the thighs of the other; . . . and the one who is seated uppermost *places his hands under the thighs of his friend*; . . . an inviolable pledge to avenge the death has by this ceremony passed between the two."

it was considered an appeal to the covenant of circumcision (𝔗, Jer. *Qu.*, Ra.; so Tu. Del.). IEz. explains it as a symbol of subjection, (adding that it was still a custom in India); Ew. Di. Ho. al. as invoking posterity (יֹצְאֵי יְרֵכוֹ, 46[26], Ex. 1[5], Ju. 8[30]) to maintain the sanctity of the oath.

3. *God of heaven and of earth*] an expression for the divine omnipresence in keeping with the spiritual idea of God's providence which pervades the narrative. The full phrase is not again found (see v.[7]).—*thou shalt not take, etc.*] The motive is a natural concern for the purity of the stock: see Bertholet, *Stellung*, 67.—5–8. The servant's fear is not that he may fail to find a bride for Isaac, but that the woman may refuse to be separated so far from her kindred: would the oath bind him in that event to take Isaac back to Ḥarran? The suggestion elicits from the dying patriarch a last utterance of his unclouded faith in God.—7. *God of heaven*] *v.i.*—*send his Angel*] cf. Ex. 23[20. 23] 33[2], Nu. 20[16]. The Angel is here an invisible presence, almost a personification of God's providence; contr. the older conception in 16[7ff.].

10–14. The servant at the well.—On the fidelity of the picture to Eastern life, see Thomson, *LB*, i. 261.—**10.** *ten camels*] to bring home the bride and her attendants ([61]). But "such an expedition would not now be undertaken . . .

---

3. לבני] 𝔊 + Ἰσαάκ (as v.[4]); so v.[7].—4. כי] 𝔐 כי אם.—At the end 𝔊𝔙 add מִשָּׁם as v.[7]—5. אָבָה] always with neg., exc. Is. 1[19], Jb. 39[9] (Sir. 6[33]).—7. אלהי השמים] appears only in late books (Jon. 1[9], 2 Ch. 36[23] = Ezr. 1[2], Neh. 1[4f.] 2[4. 20]: אֱלָהּ שְׁמַיָּא is frequent in Aram. parts of Ezr. and Dn.). The words are wanting in one Heb. MS (see Kit.), and may be deleted as a gloss. Otherwise we must add with 𝔊 ואלהי הארץ (cf. [3]).—ואשר נשבע לי] probably interpolated by a later hand (Di.); see p. 284 above.—8. אחריך] 𝔊 + εἰς τὴν γῆν ταύτην.—לא תשב (but 𝔐 תשיב)] juss. with לֹא; G–K. § 109 *d*.

10. Unless we admit a duality of sources, it will be necessary to omit the first וַיֵּלֶךְ (with 𝔊).—וכל־] better וּמִכָּל־ (𝔊𝔙𝔖).—ארם נהרים] Dt. 23[5], Ju. 3[8], Ps. 60[2], 1 Ch. 19[6] †. 𝔗O ארם דעל פרת. The identity of the second element with Eg. *Naharin*, TA. *Naḫrima* (79[14] [rev.], 181[34], 119[32]) is beyond dispute; but it is perhaps too readily assumed that geographically the expressions correspond. The Eg. Naharin extended from E of the Euphrates to the valley of the Orontes (*AE*, 249 ff.); all that can be certainly affirmed about the biblical term is that it embraced *both* sides of the Euphrates (Ḥarran on the E; Pethor on the W [Dt. 23[5]]). Since there is no trace of a dual in the Eg. and Can. forms, it is doubtful if

with any other animals, nor with a less number."—*goodly things*] for presents to the bride and her relations ($^{22.\ 53}$).—On *'Aram Naharaim*, see the footnote.—*the city of Nāḥôr* in J would be Ḥarran (cf. 27^{43} 28^{10} 29^{4}): but the phrase is probably an Elohistic variant to *'Aram Naharaim*, in which case a much less distant locality may be referred to (see on 29^{1}).—**12–14.** The servant's prayer. The request for a sign is illustrated by Ju. $6^{36ff.}$, 1 Sa. $14^{8ff.}$: note הִנֵּה אָנֹכִי [אֲנַחְנוּ] in all three cases. A spontaneous offer to draw for the camels would (if Thomson's experience be typical) be unusual,—in any case the mark of a kind and obliging disposition.—**13.** *the daughters . . . to draw water*] cf. 1 Sa. 9^{11}.

15–27. The servant and Rebekah.—**15.** *who was born to Bethuel, etc.*] cf. $^{24.\ 47}$.

The somewhat awkward phrasing has led Di. al. to surmise that all these vv. have been glossed, and that here the original text ran אֲשֶׁר יָלְדָה מִלְכָּה וגו׳, Rebekah being the daughter of Milkah and Nāḥôr. Comp. 29^{5}, where Laban is described as the son of Nāḥôr. The redactional insertion of Bethû'ēl would be explained by the divergent tradition of P (25^{20} $28^{2.\ 5}$), in which Bethû'ēl is simply an 'Aramæan,' and not connected with Nāḥôr at all (see Bu. 421 ff.). The question can hardly be decided (Ho. 168); but there is a considerable probability that the original J made Laban and Rebekah the children of Nāḥôr. In that case, however, it will be necessary to assume that the tradition represented by P was known to the Yahwistic school before the final redaction, and caused a remodelling of the genealogy of $22^{20ff.}$ (see p. 333). Cf., however, Bosse, *MVAG*, 1908, 2, p. 8 f.

---

the Heb. ending be anything but a Mass. caprice (rd. נהרים?), or a locative term., to be read *-ām* (We. *Comp.*² 45^{1}; Meyer, *ZATW*, iii. 307 f.: cf. G-K. § 88 *c*, and Str. p. 135 f. with reff.). There would in this last case be no need to find a *second* river (Tigris, Chaboras, Baliḫ, Orontes, etc.) to go with Euphrates. The old identification with the Greek Mesopotamia must apparently be abandoned. See, further, Di. 302; Moore, *Ju.* 87, 89; *KAT*³, 28 f.—**12.** הקרה] 'make it occur,' 27^{20} (J).—**14.** הַנַּעֲרָ] Ḳrê. הנערה; so vv.$^{16.\ 28.\ 55.\ 57}$ $34^{3.\ 12}$, Dt. $22^{15f.\ 20f.\ 23-29}$. הנערה is found as Ke. in Pent. only Dt. 22^{19}, but 𝔐 reads so throughout. It is hazardous to postulate an archaic epicene use of נער on such restricted evidence: see BDB, 655 a; G-K. § 17 *c*.—אשקה] 𝔊 + ἕως ἂν παύσωνται πίνουσαι.—הֹכַחְתָּ] *decide, adjudicate*, here = 'allot'; so only v.^{44}. Contr. 20^{16} 21^{25} $31^{37.\ 42}$† (E), Lv. 19^{17}† (P).—ובה] 'and thereby'; G-K. § 135 *p*.

15 After טרם rd. יְכַלֶּה (cf. ^{45}); G-K. § 107 *c*.—𝔐𝔊𝔙 ins. אֶל־לִבּוֹ after

16. Taking no notice of the stranger, the maiden *went down to the fountain* (עַיִן) . . . *and came up*] In Eastern wells the water is frequently reached by steps: ct. Ex. 2[16] (וַתִּדְלֶנָה), Jn. 4[11].—**19, 20.** The writer lingers over the scene, with evident delight in the alert and gracious actions of the damsel.—**21.** The servant meanwhile has stood *gazing at her in silence*, watching the ample fulfilment of the sign.—**22.** The *nose-ring* and *bracelets* are not the bridal gift (Gu.), but a reward for the service rendered, intended to excite interest in the stranger, and secure the goodwill of the maiden. See Lane, *Mod. Eg.*[5] ii. 320, 323; cf. *RS*[2], 453[2].—**23–25.** In the twofold question and answer, there is perhaps a trace of the composition of narratives; *v.i.*—**24.** See on [15]. Read *the daughter of Milkah whom she bore to Nāḥôr* (as 34[1]).—**26, 27.** The servant's act of worship marks the close of the scene.

28–32. Laban's hospitality is inspired by the selfish greed for which that worthy was noted in tradition.—**28.** *her mother's house* cannot mean merely the female side of the family (Di.), for Laban belongs to it, and [53. 55] imply that the father (whether Bethuel or Nāḥôr) is not the head of the house. Some find in the notice a relic of matriarchy (Ho. Gu.); but the only necessary inference is that the father was dead.—**31.** *seeing I have cleared the house*] turning part of

---

לְדַבֵּר ([45]).—**18** end] 𝔊 + ἕως ἐπαύσατο πίνων, omitting the first two words of v.[19].—**20.** השקת] *the* stone trough for watering animals, found at every well (30[38], cf. 30[41], Ex. 2[16]).—**21.** משתאה] not 'wondering' (√ שׁאה; so De.), but 'gazing' (by-form of √ שׁעה) as Is. 41[10]. Constr. before prep.: G–K. § 130 *a*.—**22.** משקלו] Sam. + וישם על אפה, a necessary addition (cf. [47]). נֶזֶם accordingly is here a 'nose-jewel' (Is. 3[21], Pr. 11[22]), in 35[4], Ex. 32[2. 3] (E) an earring.—בקע] = ½ shekel (Ex. 38[26]).—**23–25.** The theory of two recensions derives some little support from the repeated ותאמר אליו of [24. 25]. A mere rearrangement such as Ba. proposes ([23a. 24. 23b. 25]) only cures one anomaly by creating another; and is, besides, impossible if the amendment given above for v.[24] be accepted.—**25.** ללון] Sam. ללין, as v.[23]; but inf. elsewhere is always לִין.—**27.** אנכי emphasises the following acc. suff. (G–K. §§ 143 *b*, 135 *d*, *e*). 𝔖 ܘܢ implies perhaps כִּי אִם (Ba.) or כִּי (Kit.); if not a mistake for ܘܠ.—אחי] Point אָחִי (sing.) with Vns.

28. אִמָּהּ] 𝔖 ܘܐܡܗ (wrongly).—**30.** כראותו (Sam.) is better than MT כראת.—והנה עמד] see G–K. § 116 *s*; Dav. § 100 (*a*).—**31.** פִּנִּיתִי] 'cleared away,'

it into a stable.—**32.** *he* (Laban) *brought the man in* (*v.i.*) . . . *and ungirt the camels*] without removing the pack-saddles.*—*to wash his feet, etc.*] cf. 18^4.

33–49. The servant's narrative. — A recapitulation of the story up to this point, with intentional variations of language, and with some abridgment. 𝕲 frequently accommodates the text to what has gone before, but its readings need not be considered.—**35.** Cf. 12^{16} 13^2.—**36b.** *has given him all that he had*] This is the only material addition to the narrative. But the notice is identical with 25^5, and probably points back to it in some earlier context (see p. 341 above).—**40.** *before whom I have walked*] Cf. 17^1. Gu.'s suggested alteration: 'who has gone before me,' is an unauthorised and unnecessary addition to the *Tikkûnê Sōpherîm* (see 18^{22}).—**41.** אָלָה (*bis*) for שְׁבוּעָה, v.[8]. On the connexion of *oath* and *curse*, see We. *Heid.*[2] 192 f.—**45–47.** Greatly abbreviated from [15–25].—*the daughter of* [*Bethû'ēl the son of*] *Nāḥôr, etc.*] see on [15. 24].—**48.** *daughter of my master's brother*] 'Brother,' may, of course, stand for 'relative' or 'nephew' ($29^{12.\ 15}$); but if Bethuel be interpolated in [15. 24. 47], Rebekah was actually first cousin to Isaac, and such mar-

as Lv. 14^{36}, Is. 40^8 etc.; cf. Ar. √ *fanaʸ* IV. = *effecit ut dispareret.*—**32.** וַיָּבֵא] (𝔙) avoids an awkward change of subj., and is to be preferred (Ols. KS. Gu.). The objection (Di. al.) that this would require to be followed by אֶת־ is answered by the very next cl. Irregularity in the use of אֶת־ is a puzzling phenomenon in the chapter, which unfortunately fits in with no workable scheme of documentary analysis.

33. וַיִּישָׂם] Ḳrê and 𝔐 ויושם (Hoph. √ שׂום), 𝕲𝕾 וַיָּשֶׂם. But Keth. recurs in MT of 50^{26} (וַיִּישֶׂם), again with pass. significance. The anomalous form may be pass. of Qal (G-K. § 73*f*), or metaplastic Niph. from ישׂם or ושׂם (Nö. *Beitr. z. sem. Sprachw.* 39 f.).—ויאמר [2]] 𝔐𝕲𝕾 וַיֹּאמְרוּ, which is perhaps better.—**36.** וקנתה] 𝔐𝕲 וְקָנָהוּ.—**38.** אִם לֹא never has the sense of Aram. אֶלָּא (*sondern*), and must be taken as the common form of adjuration (De.). 𝔐 (*Lond. Pol.*) has כִּי אִם.—**41.** מאלתי] G-K. § 95 *n.*—The v. contains a slight redundancy ([aα ‖ bβ]), but nothing is gained by interposing a cl. between [aβ] and [bα] (KS.).—**46.** מעליה] 𝕲 ἐπὶ τὸν βραχίονα αὐτῆς ἀφ' ἑαυτῆς (conflate?); 𝔙 *de humero* (cf. [18]).

* "The camel is very delicate, and could easily catch a chill if the saddle were taken away imprudently; and on no account can the camel stay out of doors in bad weather. It is then taken into the house, part of which is turned into a stable" (Baldensperger, *PEFS*, 1904, 130).

riages were considered the most eligible by the Naḥorites (29[19]).—49. *that I may turn, etc.*] not to seek a bride elsewhere (Di.), but generally 'that I may know how to act.'

50–61. Departure of Rebekah, with the consent and blessing of her relatives.—50. The relatives, recognising the hand of Providence in the servant's experiences, decline to answer *bad or good*: i.e., anything whatever, as 31[24. 29], Nu. 24[13] etc.

The v. as a whole yields a perfectly good sense: '*we* cannot speak, because *Yahwe* has decided'; and [51] is a natural sequel. It is a serious flaw in Gu.'s analysis of [50ff.], that he has to break up [50], connecting מְיהוה יָצָא הַדָּבָר with [51], and the rest of the v. with [57f.] ('*we* cannot speak: let the *maiden* decide').—On the other hand, לָבָן וּבְתוּאֵל in [50] is barely consistent with אָחִיהָ וְאִמָּהּ in [53. 55]. Since the mention of the father after the brother would in any case be surprising, Di. al. suppose that here again ובתואל is an interpolation; Kit. reads וּבֵתוֹ, and Ho. substitutes וּמִלְכָּה. Gu. (219) considers that in this recension Bethuel is a younger brother of Laban.

51. Here, at all events, the matter is settled in accordance with custom, without consulting the bride.—53. The presents are given partly to the bride and partly to her relatives. In the latter we may have a *survival* of the מֹהַר (34[12], Ex. 22[16], 1 Sa. 18[25]†) or purchase-price of a wife; but Gu. rightly observes that the narrative springs from a more refined idea of marriage, from which the notion of actual purchase has all but disappeared. So in Islam *mahr* and *ṣadaḳ* (the gift to the wife) have come to be synonymous terms for dowry (*KM*², 93, 96): cf. Benzinger, *Arch.*² 106.—55. The reluctance to part with Rebekah is another indication of refined feeling (Gu.). On יָמִים או עָשׂוֹר, *v.i.*—56. The servant's eagerness to be gone arises from the hope of finding his old master still alive.—57, 58. The question here put to Rebekah is not whether she will go now or wait a few days,

---

53. מגרנת (Ezr. 1[6], 2 Ch. 21[3] 32[23]†)] 'costly gifts,' fr. √מגר, Ar. *maǵada* = 'be noble.'—55. וְאָחִיהָ] 𝔊𝔖𝔙 read וְאָחֶיהָ; and so 𝔖𝔙 and many Greek curss. in [53].—ימים או עשור] 'a few days, say ten,' is a fairly satisfying rendering (𝔊 ἡμέρας ὡσεὶ δέκα); 'a year or ten months' (𝔗ᴼ Ra.) is hardly admissible. But the text seems uncertain: 𝔐 ימים או חרש; 𝔖 ܝܪܚ ܝܘܡܬܐ (cf. 29[14]). In deference to 𝔐𝔖 we may insert חֹדֶשׁ before יָמִים: 'a month or at least ten days' (Ols. Ba.).—תֵּלֵךְ] probably 3rd fem. (so all Vns.).

but whether she will go at all. The reference to the wishes of the bride may be exceptional (owing to the distance, etc.); but a discrepancy with [51] cannot easily be got rid of.—**59.** *their sister*] cf. 'your daughter,' 34[8], the relation to the family being determined by that to the head of the house. But it is better to read אַחֹתָהּ (pl.) in [53. 55] with 𝔙𝔖 and MSS of 𝔊.—*her nurse*] see on 35[8].—**60.** The blessing on the marriage (cf. Ru. 4[11ff.]), rhythmic in form, is perhaps an ancient fragment of tribal poetry associated with the name of Rebekah.—*possess the gate*] as 22[17].—**61a** and **61b** seem to be variants. For another solution (KS.), see on [62].—*her maidens*] parallel to 'her nurse' in [59].

62–67. The home-bringing of Rebekah. — **62.** *Now Isaac had come . . .*] What follows is hardly intelligible. The most probable sense is that during the servant's absence Isaac had removed to Beer-laḥai-roi, and that near that well the meeting took place.

The difficulty lies partly in the corrupt מְבוֹא (*v.i.*), partly in the circumstantial form of the sent., and partly in the unexplained disappearance of Abraham. Keeping these points in mind, the most conservative exegesis is that of De.: Isaac (supposed to be living with his father at Beersheba) 'was coming *from a walk in the direction of* B.', when he met the camels; this, however, makes וַיֵּצֵא ([63]) plup., which is hardly right. More recent writers proceed on the assumption that the death of Abraham had been explicitly recorded. Ho. suggests that Isaac had removed to Laḥairoi during his father's life (transposing 25[11b] before 24[2]), and that now he comes *from* that place (reads מִמִּדְבַּר) on hearing of Abraham's death. Di. reads [62a] ויבא[יצחק] אל מדבר ב׳, and finds in these words the notice of Isaac's migration *to* B.—KS., reading as Di., but making the servant implicit subj. of ויבא, puts the chief hiatus between [61a] and [61b]: the servant on his return learned that Abraham was dead;

—**59.** מנקתה] 𝔊 τὰ ὑπάρχοντα αὐτῆς = מִקְנָתָהּ, a word of P.—**60.** אַתְּ is appositional vocative, not subj. to אֲחֹתֵנוּ (*soror nostra es*, 𝔙).—הֲיִי] with abnormal ֲ (G–K. § 63 *q*).—שנאיו] 𝔐 איביו, as 22[17].

62. מְבוֹא] cannot be inf. const. with מִן; the French *il vint d'arriver* (Hupf. 29) has no analogy in Heb. idiom. Nor can it readily be supposed equivalent to מִלְּבוֹא (1 Ki. 8[65]; De. *v.s.*); for the *direction* in which Isaac took his walk is an utterly irrelevant circumstance. 𝔐 and 𝔊 (διὰ τῆς ἐρήμου) read במדבר, from which a fairly suitable text (מִמִּדְבַּר or מִמּ׳) could be obtained (cf. Di. and Ho. *s.*). Gu.'s מְבוֹא (as acc. of direction) has no parallel except the very remote one of מבואה ים, Ezk. 27[3] (of the situation of Tyre). Other suggestions are to delete the word as an uncorrected lapse of the pen; to read מִבְּאֵר with omission of the following בְּאֵר

then ([61b]) took Rebekah and went further; and ([62a]) came to Laḥairoi.—Gu. (operating with two sources) considers [62] the immediate sequel to [61a] in the document where Abraham's death preceded the servant's departure, so that nothing remained to be chronicled but Isaac's removal to Laḥairoi (reads מְבוֹא, 'to the entrance of'). This solution is attractive, and could perhaps be carried through independently of his division of sources. For even if the death followed the departure, it might very well have been recorded in the early part of the ch. (after [10]).

63. לָשׂוּחַ] a word of uncertain meaning, possibly *to roam* (*v.i.*).—*toward the approach of evening*] (Dt. 23^{12}), when the Oriental walks abroad (cf. 3^{8}).—*camels were coming*] In the distance he cannot discern them as his own.—64. At the sight of a stranger Rebekah dismounts (נָפַל as 2 Ki. 5^{21}), a mark of respect still observed in the East (*LB*, i. 762; Seetzen, *Reisen*, iii. 190); cf. Jos. 15^{18}, 1 Sa. 25^{23}.—65. *It is my master*] Apparently the servant is aware, before meeting Isaac, that Abraham is dead.—The putting on of the *veil* (cf. *nubere viro*), the survival of a primitive marriage taboo, is part of the wedding ceremony (see Lane, ME^{5}, i. 217 f.).—67. *brought her into the tent*] The next phrase (שָׂרָה אִמּוֹ) violates a fundamental rule of syntax, and must be deleted as a gloss. Isaac's own tent is referred to. This is the essential feature of the marriage ceremony in the East (see Benz. $Arch.^{2}$ 108 f.).—*comforted himself after* [the death of] *his mother*] It is conjectured (We. al.) that the real reading was 'his father,' whose death had recently taken place. The change would

---

(Lag. Procksch); to substitute מבא[רשבע] ('from Beersheba to': Ba.).—באר לחי ראי] 𝔊 (here and 25^{11}) τὸ φρέαρ τῆς ὁράσεως, omitting לחי; refer to p. 289 above.—63. לָשׂוּחַ] ἅπ. λεγ. commonly identified with שִׂיחַ = 'muse,' 'complain,' 'talk,' etc.; so 𝔊 (ἀδολεσχῆσαι), Aq. (ὁμιλῆσαι), Σ. (λαλῆσαι), 𝔙 (*ad meditandum*: so Tu. De.), 𝔗[OJ] (לצלאה: Ra.); Di. KS. al. think the sense of 'mourning' (for his father) most probable; but? IEz. ('to walk among the shrubs') and Böttcher ('to gather brushwood') derive from שִׂיחַ (21^{15}). 𝔖 ܠܡܬܗܠܟܘ is thought to rest on a reading לָשׁוּט (adopted by Ges. al.), but is rather a conjecture. Nö. (*Beitr. z. sem. Spr.* 43 f.) suggests a connexion with Ar. *sāḥa* = 'stroll' (point לָשׂוּחַ).—הנמלים of ш is wrong (*v.s.*).—65. הַלָּזֶה] 37^{19}†; ш הלז.—הצעיף] $38^{14.\ 19}$† (J). On the art. cf. G-K. § 126 *s*. After Lagarde's brilliant note (*Sem.* 23 ff.), it can scarcely be doubted that the word denotes a large double square wrapper or shawl, of any material.—67. ויבאה] 𝔊 εἰσῆλθεν δέ.—האהלה שרה] art. with const. is violently ungrammatical; G-K. § 127 *f*.—For אמו[2] read מוֹת אָבִיו (Kit.) *v.s.*

naturally suggest itself after J's account of the death of Abraham had been suppressed in accordance with P's chronology. The death of Sarah is likewise unrecorded by J or E.

XXV. 1–6.—*The Sons of Ḳeṭurah* (J? R?).

The Arabian tribes with whom the Israelites acknowledged a looser kinship than with the Ishmaelites or Edomites are here represented as the offspring of Abraham by a second marriage (cf. 1 Ch. $1^{32f.}$).

The names Midian, Sheba, Dedan (see below) show that these Ḳeṭurean peoples must be sought in N Arabia, and in the tract of country partly assigned to the Ishmaelites in v.[18]. The fact that in Ju. 8^{24} Midianites are classed as Ishmaelites (cf. Gn. $37^{25ff.}$) points to some confusion between the two groups, which in the absence of a Yahwistic genealogy of Ishmael it is impossible altogether to clear up. We. (*Comp.*² 29^1) has dropped a hint that Ḳeṭurah may be but a traditional variant of Hagar;* Ho. conjectures that the names in [2-4] are taken from J's lost Ishmaelite genealogy; and Kent (*SOT*, i. 101) thinks it not improbable that Ḳeṭurah was originally the wife of Ishmael. Glaser (ii. 450) considers the Ḳeṭureans remains of the ancient Minæan people, and not essentially different from the Ishmaelites and Edomites. See, further, on v.[18] below.

Source.—(*a*) The genealogy ([1-4]) contains slight traces of J in יָלַד, [3]; כָּל־אֵלֶּה בְּנֵי [4] (cf. 10^{29} 9^{19}); P is excluded by ילד, and the discrepancy with 10^7 as to Sheba and Dedan; while E appears not to have contained any genealogies at all. The vv. must therefore be assigned to some Yahwistic source, in spite of the different origin given for Sheba in 10^{28}.—(*b*) The section as a whole cannot, however, belong to the primary Yahwistic document; because there the death of Abraham had already been recorded in ch. 24, and 24^{36} refers *back* to 25^5.† We must conclude that 25^{1-6} is the work of a compiler, who has incorporated the genealogy, and taken v.[5] from its original position (see on 24^{36}) to bring it into connexion with Abraham's death. These changes may have been made in a revised edition of J (so Gu.); but in this case we must suppose that the account of Abraham's death was also transferred from ch. 24, to be afterwards replaced by the notice of P. It seems to me easier (in view of [11b] and [18]) to hold that the adjustments were effected during the final redaction of the Pent., in accordance with the chronological scheme of P.

---

* So Jewish interpreters: 𝔗J, *Ber. R.*, Jer. *Qu.*, Ra. (but not IEz.).

† The mere transposition of 25^{1-6} before ch. 24 (Hupf. We. al.) does not fully meet the difficulty, there being, in fact, no suitable place for a second marriage of Abraham anywhere in the orginal J (Ho.).

1. *Ḳĕṭûrāh*, called a 'concubine' in 1 Ch. 1^{32} (cf. v.^{6} below), is here a *wife*, the death of Sarah being presupposed. The name occurs nowhere else, and is probably fictitious, though Arabian genealogists speak of a tribe *Ḳaṭūra* in the vicinity of Mecca (Kn.–Di.). There is no 'absurdity' (De.) in the suggestion that it may contain an allusion to the traffic in incense (קְטוֹרָה) which passed through these regions (see Mey. *INS*, 313).—**2–4.** The Ḳeṭurean stock is divided into 6 (𝔊 7) main branches, of which only one, Midian, attained historic importance. The minor groups number 10 (𝔊 12), including the well-known names Sheba and Dedan.

2. זִמְרָן (Ζεβράν, Ζομβράν, etc.) has been connected with the Ζαβράμ [Ζαδραμ?] of Ptol. vi. 7. 5, W of Mecca (Kn.); and with the *Zamareni* of Pliny, *HN*, vi. 158, in the interior; but these are probably too far S. The name is probably derived from זֶמֶר = 'wild goat,' the ending *ān* (which is common in the Ḳeṭurean and Ḥorite lists and rare elsewhere) being apparently gentilic: cf. זִמְרִי, Nu. 25^{14}, 1 Ch. 2^{6} 8^{36} 9^{42}. A connexion with זִמְרִי (𝔖 ܙܡܪܝ), Jer. 25^{25} is very doubtful. On יָקְשָׁן (Ἰεξάν, Ἰεκτάν, etc.) see on v.^{3}—מְדָן (Μαδαίμ)] unknown. Wetzstein instances a Wādī Medān near the ruins of Daidan.—מִדְיָן (Μαδιάμ)] The name appears as Μοδιανα = Μαδιαμα in Ptol. vi. 7. 2, 27 (cf. Jos. *Ant.* ii. 257; Eus. *OS*, p. 276), the *Madyan* of Ar. geogr., a town on the E side of the Gulf of Aḳaba, opposite the S end of the Sinaitic peninsula (see Nö. *EB*, 3081). The chief seat of this great tribe or nation must therefore have been in the northern Ḥiǧāz, whence roving bands ravaged the territory of Moab, Edom (Gn. 36^{35}), and Israel (Ju. 6–8). The mention of Midianites in the neighbourhood of Horeb may be due to a confusion between J and E (see Mey. *INS*, 3 f.); and after the time of the Judges they practically disappear from history. "As to their occupations, we sometimes find them described as peaceful shepherds, sometimes as merchants [Gn. $37^{28.36}$, Is. 60^{6}], sometimes as roving warriors, delighting to raid the more settled districts" (Nö.).—יִשְׁבָּק and שׁוּחַ have been identified by Frd. Delitzsch (*ZKF*, ii. 91 f., *Par.* 297 f.) and Glaser (ii. 445 f.) with *Yasbuḳ* and *Sûḫu* of Ass. monuments (*KIB*, i. 159, 33, 99, 101), both regions of northern Syria. Del. has since abandoned the latter identification (*Hiob*, 139) for phonetic reasons.—3. שְׁבָא and דְּדָן] see on 10^{7}. As they are there bracketed under רַעְמָה, so here under יָקְשָׁן, a name otherwise unknown. The equation with יָקְטָן ($10^{25ff.}$), proposed by Tu. and accepted by Mey. (318), is phonologically difficult. Since the Sabæans are here still in the N, it would seem that this genealogy goes farther back than that of the Yokṭanite Arabs in ch. 10. Between Sheba and Dedan, 𝔊 ins. Θαιμάν (= תֵּימָא, v.^{15}).—3b. The sons of Dedan are wanting in 1 Ch., and are probably interpolated here (note the pl.). 𝔊 has in addition Ραγουήλ (cf. 36^{10}) καὶ Ναβδεήλ (cf. v.^{13}).—אַשּׁוּרִם] certainly not the Assyrians (אַשּׁוּר), but some obscure N Arabian tribe,—*possibly* the אאשר mentioned on two

Minæan inscrs. along with מצר (Egypt), עבר נהרן, and Gaza (Homm. *AHT*, 248 f., 252 f., *AA*, 297 ff.; Glaser, ii. 455 ff.; Winckler, *AOF*, i. 28 f.; König, *Fünf Landschaften*, 9: cf., on the other side, Mey. *ZA*, xi. 327 ff., *INS*, 320 ff.).—לְטוּשִׁם] The personal name לטשו (as also אשורו) has been found in Nabat. inscrs.; see Levy, *ZDMG*, xiv. 403 f., 447, 477 f., where attention is called to the prevalence of craftsmen's names in these inscrs., and a connexion of ל׳ with לֹטֵשׁ in 4^{22} is suggested.—**4.** Five sons of Midian.—עֵיפָה is named along with Midian in Is. 60^{6} as a trading tribe. It has been identified with the *Ḥayapa* (=עֵיפָה?) mentioned by Tiglath-pileser IV. and Sargon, along with some 6 other rebellious Arab tribes (*KIB*, ii. 21, 43): see Del. *Par.* 304, *KAT*[3], 58.—With עֵפֶר, Wetzst. compares the modern *'Ofr* (Di.); Glaser (449), Ass. *Apparu* (*KIB*, ii. 223).—חֲנֹךְ] Perhaps *Hanākiya* near *'Ofr* (Kn.-Di.).—It is noteworthy that these three names—עיפה, 1 Ch. $2^{46f.}$; עפר, 1 Ch. 4^{17} 5^{24}; חנך, Gn. 46^{9}, Ex. 6^{14}, Nu. 26^{5}, 1 Ch. 5^{3}—are found in the Heb. tribes most exposed to contact with Midian (Judah, Manasseh, Reuben). Does this show an incorporation of Midianite clans in Israel? (Nö.).—אֲבִידָע (*'Abî-yada'a*) and אֶלְדָּעָה (*'Il-yeda'* and *Yeda-'il*) are personal names in Sabæan, the former being borne by several kings (*ZDMG*, xxvii. 648, xxxvii. 399; Glas. ii. 449).

5. See on 24^{36}.—**6.** The exodus of the *Bnê Ḳedem* (composed by a redactor).—*the concubines*] apparently Hagar and Ḳeṭurah, though neither bears that opprobrious epithet in Gen.: in 16^{3} Hagar is even called אִשָּׁה. Moreover, Ishmael and his mother, according to J and E, had long been separated from Abraham.—*sent them away from off Isaac*] so as not to be a burden upon him. Cf. Ju. 11^{2}.—***eastward to the land of Ḳedem***] the Syro-Arabian desert.

So we must render, unless (with Gu.) we are to take the two phrases קֵדְמָה and אֶל־אֶרֶץ קֶדֶם as variants. But קֶדֶם in OT is often a definite geographical expression, denoting the region E and SE of the Dead Sea (cf. 29^{1}, Nu. 23^{7}, Ju. $6^{3.33}$ 7^{12} 8^{10}, Is. 11^{14}, Jer. 49^{28}, Ezk. $25^{4.10}$, Jb. 1^{3}); and although its appellative significance could, of course, not be forgotten, it has almost the force of a proper name. It is so used in the Eg. romance of Sinuhe (*c.* 1900 B.C.): see Müller, *AE*, 46 f.; Wi. *GI*, 52 ff.; Mey. *INS*, 243 f.

XXV. 7–11.—*The Death and Burial of Abraham* (P).

$^{7-11a}$ are the continuation of 23^{20} in P. Note the characteristic phrases: יְמֵי שְׁנֵי חַיֵּי, ^{7}; גָּוַע, בְּשֵׂיבָה טוֹבָה, נֶאֱסַף אֶל־עַמָּיו, ^{8}; אֱלֹהִים, ^{11a}; the chronology ^{7}, the reminiscences of ch. 23, and the backward reference in 49^{31}.—^{10} belongs to J.

---

5 end] 𝔐𝔊𝔖+בָּנוֹ.—6. פִּילֶגֶשׁ (see on 22^{24}) is used of a שִׁפְחָה in 35^{22}.—אשר לאברהם] 𝔊 αὐτοῦ.

8. *gathered to his kindred* (see on 17^{14})] Originally, this and similar phrases (15^{15} 47^{30}, Dt. 31^{16} etc.) denoted burial in the family sepulchre; but the popular conception of Sheôl as a vast aggregate of graves in the under world enabled the language to be applied to men who (like Abraham) were buried far from their ancestors.—*Isaac and Ishmael*] The expulsion of Ishmael is consistently ignored by P.—**11a.** Transition to the history of Isaac ($25^{19ff.}$).

^{11b} (like v.^{5}) has been torn from its context in J, where it may have stood after 24^{1} 25^{5}, or (more probably) after the notice of Abraham's death (cf. 24^{62}). Meyer (*INS*, 253, 323) makes the improbable conjecture that the statement referred originally to Ishmael, and formed, along with v.^{18}, the conclusion of ch. 16.

XXV. 12–18.—*The Genealogy and Death of Ishmael* (P).

With the exception of v.^{18}, which is another isolated fragment of J, the passage is an excerpt from the *Tôledôth* of the Priestly Code.—The names of the genealogy ($^{13-16}$) represent at once 'princes' (נְשִׂיאִם: cf. the promise of 17^{20}) and 'peoples' (אֻמֹּת, ^{16}); that is to say, they are the assumed eponymous ancestors of 12 tribes which are here treated as forming a political confederacy under the name of Ishmael.

In the geography of P the Ishmaelites occupy a territory intermediate between the Arabian Cushites on the S (10^{7}), the Edomites, Moabites, etc., on the W, and the Aramæans on the N ($10^{22f.}$); *i.e.*, roughly speaking, the Syro-Arabian desert north of Ǧebel Shammar. In J they extend W to the border of Egypt (v.^{18}).—The Ishmaelites have left very little mark in history. From the fact that they are not mentioned in Eg. or Ass. records, Meyer infers that their flourishing period was from the 12th to the 9th cent. B.C. (*INS*, 324). In OT the latest possible traces of Ishmael as a people are in the time of David (cf. 2 Sa. 17^{25}, 1 Ch. 2^{17} 27^{30}), though the name occurs sporadically as that of an individual or clan in much later times (Jer. $40^{8ff.}$, 2 Ki. 25^{23}, 1 Ch. 8^{38} 9^{44}, 2 Ch. 19^{11} 23^{1}, Ezr. 10^{22}). In Gn. $37^{25ff.}$, Ju. 8^{24}, it is possible that 'Ishmaelites' is synonymous with Bedouin in general (see Mey. 326).

13. נְבָיֹת וְקֵדָר] are the *Nabayati* and *Ḳidri* of Ass. monuments (Asshurbanipal: *KIB*, ii. 215 ff.; cf. Del. *Par.* 297, 299; *KAT*^{3}, 151), and possibly the *Nabatæi* and *Cedrei* of Pliny, v. 65 (cf. vi. 157, etc.). The references do not enable us to locate them with precision, but they must

---

8. ויגוע ויכת] v.^{17} 35^{29}; see on 6^{17}.—ושבע] 𝔐𝔊 better ושבע ימים, as 35^{29}.—ויאסף וגו'] so 25^{17} 35^{29} $49^{29.33}$, Nu. $20^{24.26}$ 27^{13} 31^{2}, Dt. 32^{50} † (all P).—**10.** השדה] 𝔊 + *καὶ τὸ σπήλαιον*.—**11.** לחי ראי] see on 24^{62}.

be put somewhere in the desert E of Palestine or Edom. The Nabatæans of a later age (see Schürer, *GJV*^{3,4}, i. 728 ff.) were naturally identified with נְבָיֹת by Jos. (*Ant.* i. 220 f.), Jer. (*Qu.*), 𝔗J [נבט], as they still are by Schr., Schürer, and some others. But since the native name of the Nabatæans was נבטו, the identification is doubtful, and is now mostly abandoned. The two tribes are mentioned together in Is. 60^7: נְבָיֹת alone only Gn. 28^9 36^3; but קֵדָר is alluded to from the time of Jeremiah downwards as a typical nomadic tribe of the Eastern desert. In late Heb. the name was extended to the Arabs as a whole (so 𝔗J ערב).—אַדְבְּאֵל (Ναβδεήλ: see on v.^{3})] Perhaps an Arab tribe *Idibi'il* which Tiglath-pileser IV. (*KIB*, ii. 21) appointed to watch the Egyptian frontier (not necessarily the border of Egypt proper).—מִבְשָׂם] a Simeonite clan (1 Ch. 4^{25}), otherwise not known.—**14.** מִשְׁמָע follows מבשם in 1 Ch. 4^{25}. Di. compares a *Ğebel Misma'* SE of Kāf, and another near Ḥāyil E of Teima.—דּוּמָה] Several places bearing this name are known (Di.); but the one that best suits this passage is the Dūmah which Arabic writers place 4 days' journey N of Teima; viz. *Dūmat el-Ğendel*, now called *el-Ğōf*, a great oasis in the S of the Syrian desert and on the border of the *Nefūd* (Doughty, *Ar. Des.* ii. 607; cf. Burckhardt, *Trav. in Syr.* 602). It is probably the Δούμαιθα of Ptol. v. 18 (19). 7, the *Domata* of Plin. vi. 157.—מַשָּׂא] See on 10^{30}, and cf. Pr. 31^1. A tribe *Mas'a* is named by Tiglath-pileser IV. along with Teima (v.^{15}), Saba', Hayapa (^{4}), Idibi'il (^{13}), and may be identical with the Μασανοι of Ptol. v. 18 (19). 2, NE of Δούμαιθα.—**15.** חֲדַד] unknown.—תֵּימָא (Is. 21^{14}, Jer. 25^{23}, Jb. 6^{19}) is the modern *Teima*, on the W border of the Neğd, *c.* 250 miles SE of Aḳāba, still an important caravan station on the route from Yemen to Syria, and (as local inscrs. show) in ancient times the seat of a highly developed civilisation: see the descriptions in Doughty, *Ar. Des.* i. 285 ff., 549 ff.—יְטוּר and נָפִישׁ are named together in 1 Ch. 5^{19} among the East-Jordanic tribes defeated by the Reubenites in the time of Saul. יטור is no doubt the same people which emerges about 100 B.C. under the name Ἰτουραῖοι, as a body of fierce and predatory mountaineers settled in the Anti-Lebanon (see Schürer, *GJV*, i. 707 ff.).—Of קֵדְמָה nothing is known. Should we read נוֹדָב as 1 Ch. 5^{19} (Ball, Kit.)?—**16.** בְּחַצְרֵיהֶם] 'in their settlements' or 'villages'; cf. Is. 42^{11} 'the villages that Kedar doth inhabit.'—וּבְטִירֹתָם] טִירָה (Nu. 31^{10}, Ezk. 25^4, Ps. 69^{26}, 1 Ch. 6^{39}) is apparently a technical term for the circular encampment of a nomadic tribe. According to Doughty (i. 261), the Arab. *dīrah* denotes the Bedouin circuit, but also, in some cases, their town settlements.—לְאֻמֹּתָם] 'according to their peoples.' אֻמָּה is the Ar. *'ummat*, rare in Heb. (Nu. 25^{15}, Ps. 117^1 †).—**17.** Cf. vv.$^{7.8}$.

V.^{18} is a stray verse of J, whose original setting it is impossible to determine. There is much plausibility in Ho.'s conjecture that it was the conclusion of J's lost genealogy of Ishmael (cf. $10^{19.30}$). Gu. thinks it was taken from the end of ch. 16: similarly Meyer, who makes ^{11b} (p. 352 above) a connecting link. Di. suggests that the first half may have followed 25^6, the reference being not to the Ishmaelites but to the Ḳeṭureans; and that the second half is a gloss from 16^{12}. But even ^{18a} is not consistent with ^{11b}, for we have seen that the Ḳeṭureans are found E and SE of Palestine, and Shûr is certainly not 'eastward' from where

Abraham dwelt.—If Ḥavîlah has been rightly located on p. 202 above, J fixes the eastern limit of the Ishmaelites in the neighbourhood of the Ğōf es-Sirhān, while the western limit is the frontier of Egypt (on *Shûr*, see on 16^7). This description is, of course, inapplicable to P's Ishmaelites; but it agrees sufficiently with the statement of E (21^{21}) that their home was the wilderness of Paran; and it includes Lahai-roi, which was presumably an Ishmaelite sanctuary. Since a reference to Assyria is here out of place, the words בֹּאֲכָה אַשּׁוּרָה must be either deleted as a gloss (We. Di. Mey. al.), or else read ב׳ אֲשֻׁרָה ; אֲשׁוּר being the hypothetical N Arabian tribe supposed to be mentioned in 25^3 (so Gu.; cf. Homm. *AHT*, 240 f.; Kön. *Fünf Landsch.* 11 ff.), a view for which there is very little justification.—^{18b} is an adaptation of 16^{12b}, but throws no light on that difficult sentence. Perhaps the best commentary is Ju. 7^{12}, where again the verb נָפַל has the sense of 'settle' (= שָׁכַן in 16^{12}). Hommel's restoration עַל־פְּנֵי כֶלַח, 'in front of Kelaḥ' (a secondary gloss on אַשּׁוּר), is a brilliant example of misplaced ingenuity.

THE HISTORY OF JACOB.

CHS. XXV. 19–XXXVI.

SETTING aside ch. 26 (a misplaced appendix to the history of Abraham: see p. 363), and ch. 36 (Edomite genealogies), the third division of the Book of Genesis is devoted exclusively to the biography of Jacob. The legends which cluster round the name of this patriarch fall into four main groups (see Gu. 257 ff.).

A. *Jacob and Esau*:

1. The birth and youth of Esau and Jacob (25^{19-28}). 2. The transference of the birthright (25^{29-34}). 3. Jacob procures his father's blessing by a fraud (27).

B. *Jacob and Laban*:

1. Jacob's meeting with Rachel (29^{1-14}). 2. His marriage to Leah and Rachel (29^{15-30}). 3. The births of Jacob's children (29^{31}–30^{24}). 4. Jacob's bargain with Laban (30^{25-43}). 5. The flight from Laban and the Treaty of Gilead (31^{1}–32^{1}).

C. *Jacob's return to Canaan* (loose and fragmentary):

1. Jacob's measures for appeasing Esau (32^{4-22}).* 2. The meeting of the brothers (33^{1-17}).* 3. The sack of Shechem (34). 4. The visit to Bethel, etc. (35^{1-15}). 5. The birth of Benjamin and death of Rachel (35^{16-20}). 6. Reuben's incest ($35^{21f.}$).

D. Interspersed amongst these are several *cult-legends*, connected with sanctuaries of which Jacob was the reputed founder.

1. The dream at Bethel (28^{10-22})—a transition from A to B. 2. The encounter with angels at Mahanaim—a fragment ($32^{2f.}$). 3. The wrestling at Peniel (32^{23-33}). 4. The purchase of a lot at Shechem (33^{18-20}). 5. The second visit to Bethel—partly biographical (see below) (35^{1-15}).

The section on Jacob exhibits a much more intimate fusion of sources than that on Abraham. The *disjecta membra* of P's epitome can, indeed, be distinguished without much difficulty, viz. $25^{19.\,20.\,26b}$ $26^{34f.}$ 28^{1-9} $29^{24.\,28b.\,29}$ $30^{4a.\,9b.\,22a}$ $31^{18a\beta\gamma\delta b}$ $33^{18a\beta}$ $35^{6a.\,9f.\,11-13a.\,15.\,22b-26.\,27-29}$ 36*. Even here, however, the redactor has allowed himself a freedom which he hardly

* Gu. recognises a second series of Jacob-Esau stories in C. 1, 2; but these are entirely different in character from the group A. To all appearance they are conscious literary creations, composed in a biographical interest, and without historical or ethnographic significance.

uses in the earlier portions of Gn. Not only are there omissions in P's narrative to be supplied from the other sources, but transposition seems to have been resorted to in order to preserve the sequence of events in JE.—The rest of the material is taken from the composite JE, with the exception of ch. 34, which seems to belong to an older stage of tradition (see p. 418). But the component documents are no longer represented by homogeneous sections (like chs. 16. 18f. [J], 20. 22 [E]); they are so closely and continuously blended that their separation is always difficult and occasionally impossible, while no lengthy context can be wholly assigned to the one or to the other.—These phenomena are not due to a deliberate change of method on the part of the redactors, but rather to the material with which they had to deal. The J and E recensions of the life of Jacob were so much alike, and so complete, that they ran easily into a single compound narrative whose strands are naturally often hard to unravel; and of so closely knit a texture that P's skeleton narrative had to be broken up here and there in order to fit into the connexion.

To trace the growth of so complex a legend as that of Jacob is a tempting but perhaps hopeless undertaking. It may be surmised that the Jacob-Esau (A) and Jacob-Laban (B) stories arose independently and existed separately, the first in the south of Judah, and the second east of the Jordan. The amalgamation of the two cycles gave the idea of Jacob's flight to Aram and return to Canaan; and into this framework were fitted various cult-legends which had presumably been preserved at the sanctuaries to which they refer. As the story passed from mouth to mouth, it was enriched by romantic incidents like the meeting of Jacob and Rachel at the well, or the reconciliation of Jacob and Esau; and before it came to be written down by J and E, the history of Jacob as a whole must have assumed a fixed form in Israelite tradition. Its most remarkable feature is the strongly marked biographic motive which lends unity to the narrative, and of which the writers must have been conscious,—the development of Jacob's character from the unscrupulous roguery of chs. 25, 27 to the moral dignity of 32 ff. Whether tradition saw in him a type of the national character of Israel is more doubtful.

As regards the historicity of the narratives, it has to be observed in the first place that the *ethnographic* idea is much more prominent in the story of Jacob than in that of any other patriarch. It is obvious that the Jacob-Esau stories of chs. 25, 27 reflect the relations between the nations of Israel and Edom; and similarly at the end of ch. 31, Jacob and Laban appear as representatives of Israelites and Aramæans. It has been supposed that the ethnographic motive, which comes to the surface in these passages, runs through the entire series of narratives (though disguised by the biographic form), and that by means of it we may extract from the legends a kernel of ancient tribal history. Thus, according to Steuernagel, Jacob (or Ya'ăḳōb-ēl) was a Hebrew tribe which, being overpowered by the Edomites, sought refuge among the Aramæans, and afterwards, reinforced by the absorption of an Aramæan clan (Rachel), returned and settled in Canaan: the events being placed between the Exodus from Egypt and the conquest of Palestine (*Einw.* 38 ff., 56 ff. : cf. Ben. 286). There are indeed few parts of the patriarchal history where this kind of interpretation yields more plausible results; and it is quite possible that the above construction contains elements of truth. At the same time, the method is one that requires to be applied with very great caution. In the first place, it is not certain that Jacob, Esau, and Laban were *originally* personifications of Israel, Edom, and Aram respectively: they may be real historic individuals; or they may be mythical heroes round whose names a rich growth of legend had gathered before they were identified with particular peoples. In the second place, even if they were personified tribes, the narrative must necessarily contain many features which belong to the personifications, and have no ethnological significance whatever. If, *e.g.*, one set of legends describes Israel's relations with Edom in the south and another its relations with the Aramæans in the east, it was necessary that the ideal ancestor of Israel should be represented as journeying from the one place to the other; but we have no right to conclude that a similar migration was actually performed by the nation of Israel. And there are many incidents even in this group of narratives which cannot naturally be understood of dealings between one tribe and another. As a general rule, the ethnographic interpretation must be confined to those incidents where it is either indicated by the terms of the narrative, or else confirmed by external evidence.

XXV. 19–34.—*The Birth of Esau and Jacob, and the Transference of the Birthright* (P, JE).

In answer to Isaac's prayer, Rebekah conceives and bears twin children, Esau and Jacob. In the circumstances of their birth (21–26), and in their contrasted modes of life (27. 28), Hebrew legend saw prefigured the national characteristics, the close affinity, and the mutual rivalry of the two peoples, Edom and Israel; while the story of Esau selling his birthright (29–34) explains how Israel, the younger nation, obtained the ascendancy over the older, Edom.

Analysis.—Vv. 19. 20 are taken from P; note וְאֵלֶּה תּוֹלְדֹת, הוֹלִיד, הָאֲרַמִּי (*bis*), פַּדַּן אֲרָם. To P must also be referred the chronological notice 26b, which shows that an account of the birth of the twins in that source has been suppressed in favour of J. There is less reason to suspect a similar omission of the marriage of Isaac before v. 20.—The rest of the passage belongs to the composite work JE. The stylistic criteria (יהוה, 21 *bis*. 22. 23; עָתַר, 21 *bis*; לָמָּה זֶּה, 22; צָעִיר, 23) and the resemblance of 24-26 to 38 27ff. point to J as the leading source of 21-28; though Elohistic variants may possibly be detected in 25. 27 (Di. Gu. Pro. al.). Less certainty obtains with regard to 29-34, which most critics are content to assign to J (so Di.

We. Kue. Cor. KS. Ho. Dri. al.), while others (*OH*. Gu. *SOT*. Pro.) assign it to E because of the allusion in 27[36]. That reason is not decisive, and the linguistic indications are rather in favour of J (נָא, [30]; לָמָּה־זֶּה, [32] [We. *Comp.*[2] 36]; עַל־כֵּן קרא שמו, [30]).

19, 20. Isaac's marriage.—P follows E (31[20. 24]) in describing Rebekah's Mesopotamian relatives as *Aramæans* (cf. 28[5]), though perhaps in a different sense. Here it naturally means descendants of 'Ărām, the fifth son of Shem (10[23]). That this is a conscious divergence from the tradition of J is confirmed by 28[2]: see Bu. *Urg.* 420 ff.—On *Bĕthû'ēl*, see p. 247 above.—*Paddan 'Ărām*] (28[2. 6. 7] 31[18] 33[18] 35[9. 26] 46[15] [פַּדָּן alone 48[7]]: 𝔊 Μεσοποταμίας) is P's equivalent for 'Ăram Nahăraim in J (24[10]); and in all probability denotes the region round Ḥarran (*v.i.*).

21–23. The pre-natal oracle.—**21.** With the prolonged barrenness of Rebekah, compare the cases of Sarah, and Rachel (29[31]), the mothers of Samson (Ju. 13[2]), Samuel (1 Sa. 1[2]), and John the Baptist (Lk. 1[7]).—*Isaac prayed to Yahwe*] Cf. 1 Sa. 1[10ff.]. No miraculous intervention is

---

19. ואלה ת' יצחק] commonly regarded as the heading of the section (of Gen. or) of P ending with the death of Isaac (35[29]); but see the notes on pp. 40 f., 235 f. The use of the formula is anomalous, inasmuch as the birth of Isaac, already recorded in P, is included in his own genealogy. It looks as if the editor had handled his document somewhat freely, inserting the words יִצְחָק בֶּן in the original heading תולדת אַבְרָהָם (cf. v.[12]).—**20.** פדן] Syr. ܦܕܢ, Ar. *faddān* = 'yoke of oxen'; hence (in Ar.) a definite measure of land (*jugerum*: cf. Lane, 2353 b). A similar sense has been claimed for Ass. *padanu* on the authority of II R. 62, 33 a, b (Del. *Par.* 135). On this view פ' ארם would be equivalent to שְׂדֵה אֲרָם = 'field of Aram' in Ho. 12[13]. Ordinarily, *padanu* means 'way' (Del. *Hwb*, 515 f.); hence it has been thought that the word is another designation of Ḥarran (see 11[31]), in the neighbourhood of which a place *Paddānā* (*vicus prope Ḥarran*: PSm. *Thes.* 3039) has been known from early Christian times: Nöldeke, however, thinks this may be due to a Christian localisation of the biblical story (*EB*, i. 278). Others less plausibly connect the name with the kingdom of *Patin*, with its centre N of the Lake of Antioch (Wi. *KAT*[3], 38).

21. עתר] peculiar to J in Hex.: Ex. 8[4. 5. 24. 25. 26] 9[28] 10[17. 18]. In Ar. *'atr* and *'atīrat* mean animals slain in sacrifice; hence Heb. הַעְתִּיר (Hiph. may everywhere be read instead of Qal) probably referred originally to sacrifice accompanied by prayer, though no trace of the former idea survives in Heb.: "Das Gebet ist der Zweck oder die Interpretation

suggested; and our only regret is that this glimpse of everyday family piety is so tantalisingly meagre.—**22.** During pregnancy the children *crushed one another*] (*v.i.*) in a struggle for priority of birth.

Comp. the story of Akrisios and Proitus (Apol. *Bibl.* ii. 2. 1 ff.), sons of Abas, king of Argos, who *κατὰ γαστρὸς μὲν ἔτι ὄντες ἐστασίαζον πρὸς ἀλλήλους*. The sequel presents a certain parallelism to the history of Esau and Jacob, which has a bearing on the question whether there is an element of mythology behind the ethnological interpretation of the biblical narrative (see pp. 455 f.). Another parallel is the Polynesian myth of the twins Tangaroa and Rongo (Che. *TBI*, 356).

Rebekah, regarding this as a portent, expresses her dismay in words not quite intelligible in the text: *If it* [is to] *be so, why then am I . . .?*] *v.i.*—*to inquire of Yahwe*] to seek an oracle at the sanctuary.—**23.** The oracle is communicated through an inspired personality, like the Arab. *kāhin* (We. *Heid.*² 134 ff.), and is rhythmic in form (*ib.* 135).—*two nations*] whose future rivalries are prefigured in the struggle of the infants.—The point of the prophecy is in the last line: *The elder shall serve the younger* (see on $27^{29.\ 40}$).

24–26. Birth and naming of the twins.—**24.** Cf. 38^{27-30}, the only other description of a twin-birth in OT.—**25.** אַדְמוֹנִי—either *tawny* or *red-haired*—is a play on the name

---

des Opfers, die Begriffe liegen nahe bei einander" (We. 142).—**22.** ויתרצצו] 𝔊 *ἐσκίρτων* (the same word as Lk. $1^{41.\ 44}$), perhaps confusing רוץ, 'run,' with רצץ, 'break.' More correctly, Aq. *συνεθλάσθησαν*; Σ. *διεπάλαιον*.—אם כן למה זה אנכי] 𝔊 *εἰ οὕτως μοι μέλλει γένεσθαι, ἵνα τί μοι τοῦτο;* But the זֶה merely emphasises the interr. (G–K. § 136 *c*), and the latter part of the sentence seems incomplete: 𝔙 *quid necesse fuit concipere?* 𝔖 ܠܡܢܐ ܚܝܐ ܐܢܐ. Graetz supplies הָרָה; Di. Ba. Kit. חַיָּה (cf. 27^{46}); Frankenberg (*GGA*, 1901, 697) changes אנכי to אחיה, while Gu. makes it אָנָּה לִּי (Ps. 91^{10}), with זה as subj.—**23.** לְאֹם] a poetic word; in Hex. only 27^{29} (J).—צעיר] 'the small[er],' in the sense of 'younger,' is characteristic of J ($19^{31.\ 34.\ 35.\ 38}$ 29^{26} 43^{33} 48^{14}, Jos. 6^{26} [1 Ki. 16^{34}] †).

24. תוֹמִים] properly תְּאוֹמִים (so ⅏), as 38^{27}.—**25.** אַדְמוֹנִי] used again only of David, 1 Sa. 16^{12} 17^{42}. It is usually explained of the 'reddish brown' hue of the skin; but there is much to be said for the view that it means 'red-haired' (𝔊 *πυρράκης*, 𝔙 *rufus*: so Ges. Tu. al.). The incongruity of the word with the name עֵשָׂו creates a suspicion that it may be either a gloss or a variant from a parallel source (Di.): for various conjectures see Bu. *Urg.* 217²; Che. *EB*, 1333; Wi. *AOF*, i. 344 f.—עֵשָׂו has no Heb. etymology. The nearest comparison is Ar. *'a'ta^y* (so most) = 'hirsute'

Edom (see on v.[30]); similarly, *all over like a mantle of hair* (שֵׂעָר) is a play on Sēʿîr, the country of the Edomites (36[8]). It is singular that the name *ʿĒsāw* itself (on which *v.i.*) finds no express etymology.—**26a.** *with his hand holding Esau's heel*] (Ho. 12[4]) a last effort (v.[22]) to secure the advantage of being born first. There are no solid grounds for thinking (with Gu. Luther [*INS*, 128], Nowack, al.) that Hos. 12[4a] (בבטן עָקב את־אחיו) presupposes a different version of the legend, in which Jacob actually wrested the priority from his brother (cf. 38[28f.]). The clause is meant as an explanation of the name 'Jacob.'

27, 28. Their manner of life.—**27.** Esau becomes *a man skilled in hunting, a man of the field*] It is hardly necessary to suppose that the phrases are variants from

(also 'stupid'), though that would require as strict Heb. equivalent עָשׁי (Dri.). A connexion with the Phœn. Οὔσωος, brother of *Šamêmrûm*, and a hero of the chase, is probable, though not certain. There is also a goddess ʿ*Asît*, figured on Eg. monuments, who has been thought to be a female form of Esau (Müller, *AE*, 316 f.).—ויקראו] 𝔊𝔖 ויקרא, as v.[26]; but 𝔐 has pl. both times. In any case the subj. is indef.—**26.** יַעֲקֹב is a contraction of יעקבאל (cf. יִפְתָּח, Jos. 15[43], Ju. 11[1ff.] with יִפְתַּח־אֵל, Jos. 19[14. 27]; יִבְנֶה, 2 Ch. 26[6] with יַבְנְאֵל, Jos. 15[11]) which occurs (*a*) as a *place* name in central Palestine on the list of Thothmes III. (No 102: *Yʿḳbʾr*);* and (*b*) as a *personal* name (*Yaʿḳub-ilu*)† in a Bab. contract tablet of the age of Ḫammurabi. The most obvious interpretation of names of this type is to take them as verbal sentt., with ʾĒl as subj.: 'God overreaches,' or 'follows,' or 'rewards,' according to the sense given to the √ עקב (see Gray, *HPN*, 218).‡ They may, however, be nominal sentt.: 'Yaʿḳōb is God' (see Mey. 282); in which case the meaning of the name יַעֲקֹב is pushed a step farther back. The question whether Jacob was originally a tribe, a deity, or an individual man, thus remains unsettled by etymology.—At end of v., 𝔊 adds Ῥεβέκκα,—an improvement in style.

* Mey. *ZATW*, vi. 8; *INS*, 251 f., 281 f.; Müller, *AE*, 162 f.; Luther, *ZATW*, xxi. 60 ff.—The name has since been read by Müller in a list of Ramses II., and (defectively written) in one of Ramses III.: see *MVAG*, 1907, i. 27.—Questioned by Langdon, *ET*, xxi. (1909), p. 90.

† Homm. *AHT*, 96, 112. According to H., the contracted form *Yaḳubu* also occurs in the Tablets (*ib.* 203[1]).

‡ In Heb. the vb. (a denom. from עָקֵב, 'heel') is only used with allusion to the story or character of Jacob (27[36], Ho. 12[4], Jer. 9[3]†: in Jb. 37[4] the text is doubtful), and expresses the idea of insidiousness or treachery. So עָקֵב (Ps. 49[6]†), עָקֹב (Jer. 17[9]), עָקְבָּה (2 Ki. 10[19]†). The meanings 'follow' and 'reward' are found in Arab. (BDB, 784 a).

different documents. Though this conception of Esau's occupation is not consistently maintained (see 33^9), it has doubtless some ethnographic significance; and game is said to be plentiful in the Edomite country (Buhl, *Edomiter*, 43).—Jacob, on the other hand, chooses the half-nomadic pastoral life which was the patriarchal ideal. אִישׁ תָּם, elsewhere 'an ethically blameless man' (Jb. 1^8 etc.), here describes the *orderly*, well-disposed *man* (*Scoticè*, 'douce'), as contrasted with the undisciplined and irregular huntsman. —**28.** A preparation for ch. 27, which perhaps followed immediately on these two verses. V.[27], however, is also presupposed by

29–34. Esau parts with the birthright.—The superiority of Israel to Edom is popularly explained by a typical incident, familiar to the pastoral tribes bordering on the desert, where the wild huntsman would come famishing to the shepherd's tent to beg for a morsel of food. At such times the 'man of the field' is at the mercy of the tent-dweller; and the ordinary Israelite would see nothing immoral in a transaction like this, where the advantage is pressed to the uttermost.—The legend takes no account of the fact that Edom, as a settled state older than Israel, must have been something more than a mere nation of hunters. The contrasted types of civilisation—Jacob the shepherd and Esau the hunter—were firmly fixed in the popular mind; and the supremacy of the former was an obvious corollary.—**29.** Jacob *stewed something*: an intentionally indefinite description, the nature of the dish being reserved as a surprise for v.[34].—**30.** *Let me gulp some of the red—that red there!*] With a slight vocalic change (*v.i.*), we

---

28. כִּי צַיִד בְּפִיו] A curious phrase, meaning 'venison was to his taste.' It would be easier to read (with Ba. al.) לְפִיו; or an adj. (טוֹב?) may have fallen out. 𝔊𝔖 appear to have read צֵידוֹ.

29. ויזר—נזיד] זוד only here in the lit. sense; elsewhere = 'act presumptuously.' The derivative נזיד (2 Ki. 4^{38}, Hag. 2^{12}) with rare prefix ***na*** (common in Ass.).—**30.** הַלְעִיטֵנִי (ἅπ. λεγ.)] a coarse expression suggesting bestial voracity; used in NH of the feeding of cattle.—האדם האדם] The repetition of the same word is awkward, even in an expression of impatient greed. The emendation referred to above consists in reading

may render: *some of that red seasoning* (strictly 'obsonium'). —*'Ĕdōm*] a play on the word for 'red' (אָדֹם). The name is "a memento of the never-to-be-forgotten greed and stupidity of the ancestor" (Gu.).—**31.** Jacob seizes the opportunity to secure the long-coveted 'birthright,' *i.e.* the superior status which properly belonged to the first-born son.

The rare term בְּכֹרָה denotes the advantages and rights usually enjoyed by the eldest son, including such things as (*a*) natural vigour of body and character (Gn. 49[3], Dt. 21[17]: ‖ רֵאשִׁית אוֹן), creating a presumption of success in life, (*b*) a position of honour as head of the family (Gn. 27[29] 49[8]), and (*c*) a double share of the inheritance (Dt. 21[15ff.]). By a legal fiction this status was conceived as transferable from the actual first-born to another son who had proved himself more worthy of the dignity (1 Ch. 5[1f.]). When applied to tribes or nations, it expresses superiority in political might or material prosperity; and this is the whole content of the notion in the narrative before us. The idea of *spiritual* privilege, or a mystic connexion (such as is suggested in Heb. 12[16f.]) between the birthright and the blessing of ch. 27, is foreign to the spirit of the ancient legends, which owe their origin to ætiological reflexion on the historic relations of Israel and Edom. The passage furnishes no support to the ingenious theory of Jacob's (*Bibl. Arch.* 46 ff.), that an older custom of "junior right" is presupposed by the patriarchal tradition.

32. Esau's answer reveals the sensual nature of the man: the remoter good is sacrificed to the passing necessity of the moment, which his ravenous appetite leads him to exaggerate.—הֹלֵךְ לָמוּת does not mean 'exposed to death sooner or later' (IEz. Di. al.), but '*at the point of death now.*'—**34.** The climax of the story is Esau's unconcern even when he discovers that he has bartered the birthright for such a trifle as a dish of lentil soup.—עֲדָשִׁים (2 Sa. 17[28], 23[11], Ezk. 4[9]), still a common article of diet in Egypt and Syria, under the name *'adas*: the colour is said to be 'a darkish brown' (*DB*, iii. 95a).—The last clause implies a certain moral justification of the transaction: if Esau was defrauded, he was defrauded of that which he was incapable of appreciating.

---

the first הָאָדֹם after Ar. *'idām*='seasoning or condiment for bread' (cf. v.[34]): so Boysen (cited in Schleusner[2], i. 969), T. D. Anderson (*ap.* Di.). This is better than (Dri. al.) to make the change in both places. 𝔊 (τοῦ ἑψέματος τοῦ πυρροῦ τούτου) and 𝔙 (*de coctione hac rufa*) seem to differentiate the words.—**31.** כַּיּוֹם]='first of all,' as [33], 1 Sa. 2[16], 1 Ki. 1[51] 22[5] (BDB, 400 b).

Ch. XXVI.—*Isaac and the Philistines* (J, R, P).

The chapter comprises the entire cycle of Isaac-legends properly so called; consisting, as will be seen, almost exclusively of incidents already related of Abraham (cf. esp. ch. 20 f.). The introductory notice of his arrival in Gerar ($^{1-6}$: cf. $20^{1f.}$) is followed by his denial of his marriage with Rebekah ($^{7-11}$ ‖ $12^{10ff.}$ $20^{2ff.}$), his success in agriculture ($^{12-16}$, —the only circumstance without an Abrahamic parallel), his quarrels with the Philistines about wells ($^{17-22}$ ‖ $21^{25f.}$), and, lastly, the Covenant of Beersheba, with an account of the naming of the place ($^{23-33}$ ‖ 21^{22-34}).—The notice of Esau's wives ($^{34f.}$) is an excerpt from P.

Source.—The style, except in $^{34f.}$ and some easily recognised redactional patches ($^{1a\beta\gamma.\ 2a\beta b.\ 3b-5.\ 15.\ 18}$: see the notes), is unmistakably Yahwistic: cf. יהוה ($^{2.\ 12.\ 22.\ 25}$ [even in the mouth of Abimelech, $^{28.\ 29}$]); טובת מראה, ^{7} (24^{16}); השקיף, ^{8}; העתיק, ^{22} (12^{8}); קרא בשם יהוה, ^{25}; אָלָה, ^{28} (24^{41}); בְּרוּךְ יהוה, ^{29} (24^{31}). Some critics find traces of E in $^{1f.}$, but these are dubious.—The relation of the passage to other strata of the J document is very difficult to determine. On the one hand, the extremely close parallelism to ch. 20 f. suggests that it is a secondary compilation based on JE as a composite work, with the name of Isaac substituted for that of Abraham. But it is impossible to imagine a motive for such an operation; and several considerations favour the theory that ch. 26 is a continuation of the source distinguished as J^h in the history of Abraham. (1) The Abrahamic parallels all belong to the Negeb tradition (J^b and E); and it is natural to think that J^h, representing the Hebron tradition, would connect the Negeb narratives with the name of Isaac (whether Abraham or Isaac was the original hero of these legends we cannot well ascertain). (2) The language on the whole confirms this view (cf. השקיף, העתיק, קרא בשם י׳, וירא י׳, and all the phrases of ^{25a}). (3) The ideal of the patriarchal character agrees with that which we find in J^h (magnanimity, peaceableness, etc.). —In any case, it is to be observed that the ch. stands out of its proper order. The Rebekah of $^{7ff.}$ is plainly not the mother of two grown-up sons, as she is at the close of ch. 25; and 27^{1} is the immediate continuation of 25^{34} or ^{28} (see We. *Comp.*[2] 30).

1–6. Isaac migrates to Gerar.—Cleared of interpolations, the section reads: ($^{1a\alpha}$) *There was a famine in the land*; (^{1b}) *and Isaac went to Abimelech, king of the Philistines, to Gerar.* ($^{2a\alpha}$) *And Yahwe appeared to him and said,* (^{3a}) *Sojourn in this land, and I will be with thee and bless thee.* (^{6}) *So Isaac abode in Gerar.*—**1.** Isaac comes probably from

Beer Laḥai-roi, 25^{11}.—On *Abimelech* and *Gerar*, see $20^{1f.}$. The assumption that Gerar was a Philistine kingdom is an anachronism (see on 10^{14}), made also in J^b (21^{32}) but not in E.—**3a.** *and bless thee*] a promise fulfilled in Isaac's successful husbandry ($^{12ff.}$), and other tokens of the divine favour ($^{22.\ 24.\ 28f.}$), with no reference primarily to the blessing of Abraham.

$^{1a\beta\gamma}$ (מלבד—אברהם) is a redactional gloss (R^J or R^{JE}), pointing back to 12^{10}.—$^{2a\beta b}$ (אל־תרד וגו') is obviously inconsistent with ^{3a}, and is best explained as a gloss from the same hand as $^{1a\beta\gamma}$ (KS. Ho.). Di. Gu. al. consider it a variant from a parallel narrative of E (cf. אשר אמר אליך with 22^2), to which Di. quite unnecessarily assigns also $^{1a\alpha}$ and ^{6}; but the evidence is too weak to warrant the improbable hypothesis of a *second* E version of $20^{1ff.}$.—$^{3b-5}$ an expansion in the manner of 22^{15-18}, emphasising the immutability of the oath to Abraham (see on 15^{18}), and showing many traces of late composition.

7-11. Rebekah's honour compromised.—7, 8. Isaac's lie (as 12^{13} 20^2), and the king's accidental discovery of it.—*looked out at a window*] possibly into a court of the palace: cf. 2 Sa. 11^2.—מְצַחֵק אֵת] exchanging conjugal caresses (see on 21^6),—a play on the name Isaac. The vb. is nowhere else construed with אֵת.—**9, 10.** Abimelech's rebuke of Isaac, and the latter's self-exculpation.—*thou mightest have brought guilt*] Cf. 20^9. It is an instance of the writer's timid handling of the theme (see below) that no actual complication arises.—**11.** So stern an injunction would have been in place in ch. 12 or ch. 20, but here it is unmotived.

That the three narratives $12^{10ff.}$ 20, 26^{7-11} are variations of a common theme, appears not only from their close material resemblance, but also

---

3. הארצות] so v.^{4}; 𝔊 *Jub.* read sing. The nearest analogies to this use of pl. (which is rare and mostly late) are 1 Ch. 13^2, 2 Ch. 11^{23}= 'districts' (of Palestine).—האל] see 19^8.—**4a.** The comparison with the stars, as 15^5 22^{17}.—**4b, 5** almost verbally identical with 22^{18}: note esp. the uncommon עקב אשר.—**5b** is made up of Priestly and Dtnic. expressions: cf. Lv. 26^{46}, Dt. 6^2 28^{45} 30^{10} etc.—שמר משמרת denotes chiefly the service of priests in the sanctuary, but is here used in a wider sense (cf. Lv. 18^{30} 22^9, Dt. 11^1, Jos. 22^3, 1 Ki. 2^3, Mal. 3^{14}). The expression is highly characteristic of P (Ho. *Einl.* 344).—אברהם] 𝔐𝔊 + אָבִיךָ.

7. אנשי המקום] cf. 29^{22} 38^{22}, Ju. 19^{16}.—לֵאמֹר] a very rare and questionable use of the word as a real inf. (*dicere*, not *dicendo*). Should אשתי be deleted? 𝔐𝔊 read אִשְׁתִּי הִיא.—**10.** כמעט] G-K. § 106 *p*.—והבאת] cons. pf.; 'thou wouldst (in that case) have brought.'—**11.** העם] 𝔐𝔊 עַמּוֹ.

from particular phrases recurrent in each : *e.g.* אחתי הוא, הרג, מה־זאת עשית לנו, גור, מראה [יפת] טובת, etc. (cf. Kuen. *Ond.* i. 228). Although many good scholars (We. Kue. Ho. al.) are of a different opinion, the present passage appears to be the most colourless and least original form of the tradition. In $12^{10ff.}$ (J^b) the leading features—the beauty of the heroine, the patriarch's fear for his life, his stratagem, the plagues on the heathen monarch, his rebuke of the patriarch, and the rewards heaped on the latter—are combined in a strong and convincing situation, in which each element stands out in its full natural significance. In ch. 20 (E), the connexion of ideas is in the main preserved ; though a tendency to soften the harsher aspects of the incident appears in God's communication to Abimelech, in the statement that no actual harm had come to Sarah, and in the recognition of the half-truth in Abraham's account of his relation to Sarah. In $26^{7ff.}$ (J^h) this tendency is carried so far as to obscure completely the dramatic significance of those features which are retained. Though Isaac is the guest of Abimelech (v.[1]), it is only the 'men of the place' who display a languid interest in his beautiful wife : no one wants to marry Rebekah, least of all the king, who is introduced merely as the accidental discoverer of the true state of affairs, and is concerned only for the morality of his subjects. No critical situation arises ; and the exemplary self-restraint manifested by the men of Gerar affords no adequate basis for the stern injunction of [11], which would have been appropriate enough in ch. 12 or ch. 20. It is, of course, impossible to assign absolute priority in every respect to any one of the three recensions ; but it may reasonably be affirmed that in general their relative antiquity is represented by the order in which they happen to stand—J^b, E, J^h. The transference of the scene from Gerar to Egypt is perhaps the only point in which the first version is less faithful to tradition than the other two.—See the elaborate comparison in Gu. 197 ff.

12–16.—Isaac's successful husbandry.—12. Cultivation on a small scale is still occasionally practised by the Bedouin (see Palmer, *Des. of Ex.* ii. 296). The only other allusions in the patriarchal history are 30^{14} 37^{7}.—**13–16.** Isaac's phenomenal prosperity excites the jealousy of the Philistines, which leads to his enforced departure.—**15.** See on [18] below.

13–16. Gu. thinks the vv. are a pendant to the Rebekah incident, corresponding to the gifts of the heathen king (12^{16} 20^{14}) and the expulsion of Abraham (12^{20}). It is more natural to consider [12ff.] the continuation of [6] ; indeed, it might fairly be questioned whether [7-11] is not a later insertion, interrupting the continuity of the main narrative.—**12.** שערים] 𝔊𝔖 wrongly שְׂעֹרִים, 'barley.' The word is שַׁעַר, meaning 'measure' or 'value' (cf. שָׁעַר = 'reckon,' in Pr. 23^{7}, with allied words in J. Aram. and NH ; esp NH שִׁיעוּר = 'measure').—**13.** וילך הלוך וגדל] G-K. § 113 *u*.

17–22. Isaac's wells.—See on $21^{25f.}$.—**17.** Isaac retires to the *Wādī of Gĕrār*] probably the *Ğurf el-Ğerār*, above (SE) *Umm el-Ğ.*(20^{1}), into which several wādīs converge, including W. er-Ruḥaibeh (v.[22]) and W. es-Sebaʿ.—**19, 20.** The first well is named *ʿEsek* ('annoyance'); the name has not been found.—**21.** *Siṭnāh* ('hostility') is possibly to be sought in the *W. Šuṭnet er-Ruḥaibeh*, close to Ruḥaibeh, though v.[22] seems to imply that the places were some distance apart.—**22.** *Rĕḥôbôth* ('room') is plausibly identified with *er-Ruḥaibeh*, in the wādī of the same name, about 20 m. SW of Beersheba (a description in Palmer, ii. 382 f.).

In the narrative, Isaac himself was represented as the discoverer of these wells, though another tradition (partially preserved in $21^{25f.}$) ascribed the discovery and naming of them to Abraham. Vv.[15. 18] are an ancient gloss, inserted to harmonise the two views by the supposition that the wells had been stopped up by the Philistines,—a practice frequently resorted to in desert warfare (2 Ki. 3^{25}).

23–25. The theophany at Beersheba.—**23.** *went up*] though Bīr es-Sebaʿ lies considerably lower than er-Ruḥaibeh.—**24.** That an *inaugural* theophany (see on 12^{7}) is meant, is clear from v.[25]. According to this narrative, no patriarch had previously visited Beersheba (cf. 21^{33}).—*my servant*] 𝕲 reads 'thy father.' Nowhere else in Gen. is Abraham spoken of as the servant of Yahwe.—**25a.** Note the correspondence of the phraseology with $12^{7f.}$ $13^{4. 18}$.—**25b.** See v.[32].

---

17. ויחן] so (of an individual) 33^{18} (E).—**18.** בימי] 𝔐𝕲𝔙, *Jub.* עַבְדֵי.—ויסתמום] used in the same sense 2 Ki. $3^{19. 25}$, 2 Ch. $32^{3. 4. 30}$. On the masc. suf. (so v.[15]), see G–K. §§ 60 *h*, 135 *o*.—**19.** בנחל] 𝕲 + Γεράρων.—**20.** עשק] ἅπ. λεγ. עסק is common in NH, Tg. in the sense of 'be busy, occupied'; in Syr. it means *durus, asper, molestus, fuit*: hence in Ethpa. *difficilem se præbuit.*—**21.** 𝕲 pr. וַיַּעְתֵּק מִשָּׁם יצחק] (with following vb. in sing.), as v.[22]: cf. 12^{8}.—**22.** ופרינו] 𝕲𝔙𝕿^O וַיַּפְרֵנוּ, cf. 28^{3}.

24, 25aα are regarded by Gu. as an interpolation of the same character as [3b-5]; but the linguistic marks of late authorship which abound in [3b-5] are scarcely to be detected here, and the mention of the altar before the tent is not sufficient to prove dislocation of the text. Nor is it quite correct to say that v.[33] implies a different origin of the sacredness of Beersheba from [24f.]: the consecration of the sanctuary and the naming of the place are separate things which were evidently kept distinct in J^b (21^{33}).—**25.** ויכרו] synonymous with חָפַר in Nu. 21^{18}; elsewhere only used of a grave (50^{5}) or pit (Ex. 21^{33} etc.).

26–33. The treaty with Abimelech.—26. *'Aḥuzzath* (*v.i.*) *his friend*] his confidential adviser, or 'vizier,'—an official title common in Egypt from an early period, and amongst the Ptolemies and Seleucids (1 Mac. 2^{18} 10^{65}; cf. 2 Sa. 16$^{16f.}$, 1 Ki. 4^{5}, 1 Ch. 27^{33}).—*Pîkōl*] see on 21^{22}.—**27.** See vv.$^{14. 16}$.—**28.** The אָלָה is properly the curse invoked on the violation of the covenant; בְּרִית refers to the symbolic ceremony (not here described) by which it was ratified (see on 15$^{17f.}$).—**29.** Abimelech dictates the terms of the covenant: cf. 21^{23}.—**30, 31.** The common meal seems to be a feature of the covenant ceremony (cf. 31$^{53f.}$), though here the essential transaction takes place on the morning of the following day. —**32, 33.** The naming of the well (^{25b}). The peculiar form *Šibʿāh* (*v.i.*) is perhaps chosen as a compromise between שְׁבֻעָה, 'oath' (as Gu. points), and שֶׁבַע, the actual name of the place.

It is possible to recognise in these imperfectly preserved legends a reflexion of historic or pre-historic relations between nomadic tribes of the Negeb (afterwards incorporated in Israel) and the settled population of Gerar. The ownership of certain wells was disputed by the two parties; others were the acknowledged possession of the Hebrew ancestors. In the oldest tradition (J^{b}) the original purpose of the covenant of Beersheba still appears: it was to put a stop to these disputes, and secure the right of Israel at least to the important sanctuary of Beersheba (21^{30}). In the later variations this connexion is lost sight

---

26. אחות] (for the ending, see Dri. *Sam.* 107) has sometimes been mistaken for the noun meaning 'possession' (17^{8}), taken in the sense of a *body holding together* (see Ra. *ad loc.*); so 𝔗^{O} סיעת רחמוהי, '*company* of his friends'; Jer. *collegium amicorum ejus*; Gr.-Ven. *κατοχή τε τοῦ φίλου* (Field).—מרע] a rare word for 'companion,' *sodalis* (Ju. 14$^{11. 20}$ 15$^{2. 6}$, 2 Sa. 3^{8}, Pr. 12^{26} (?) 19^{7}†), whose use in the story of Samson suggested the *νυμφαγωγὸς* of 𝔊 here.—**28.** בינותינו] need not be deleted (𝔊𝔖𝔙, al.). The form בינות (42^{23}, Jos. 22^{34}, Ju. 11^{10}, 2 Sa. 21^{7}, Jer. 25^{16}, Ezk. 10$^{2. 6f.}$†) is always *two-sided*, and is here resolved into the commoner בֵּין . . . וּבֵין, exactly as 2 Sa. 21^{7}. Hence in the first case "us" means all the parties to the covenant, in the second only the Philistine representatives.—**29.** תַעֲשֵׂה] On the ֵ, see G–K. § 75 *hh.*—אתה עתה] 𝔐 אתה עתה, 𝔊 וע' א', a more natural order.—**32.** לו] 𝔊 strangely reads Οὐχ [*εὕρομεν ὕδωρ*].—**33.** אֹתָהּ] 𝔊𝔖 better שְׁמָהּ.—שִׁבְעָה (*ἅπ. λεγ.*)] 𝔊 Ὅρκος; but Aq. Σ. *πλησμονή*, 𝔙 *Abundantiam*, 𝔖 ܣܘܒܥܐ (שִׂבְעָה, Ezk. 16^{49}). In spite of the interchange of sibilants, one is tempted to agree with these authorities: Jerome pertinently asks: 'Quæ enim etymologia est, propterea vocari *juramentum*, quod aquam *non* (cf. 𝔊) invenissent?'—שם] 𝔊𝔖 pr. קָרָא.

of, and the covenant becomes a general treaty of peace and amity, which may also have had historic importance for a later period. In E there is no mention of contested wells at all, nor even a hint that Abraham had dug the well of Beersheba; while J^h seems expressly to bar any connexion between the covenant and the discovery of the well.

34, 35. **Esau's Ḥittite wives (P).**—In P, Esau is represented as still living with Isaac at Mamre (35^{29}).—*Ḥittite* for 'Canaanite': see on 23^3. It is possible, however, that in the case of Basemath the true text was 'Ḥivvite' (so 𝔊𝔖).—On the names, see on $36^{2f.}$.

XXVII. 1–45.—*How Jacob secured his Father's Blessing* (JE).

This vivid and circumstantial narrative, which is to be read immediately after 25^{34} (or 25^{28}), gives yet another explanation of the historical fact that Israel, the younger people, had outstripped Edom in the race for power and prosperity. The clever but heartless stratagem by which Rebekah succeeds in thwarting the intention of Isaac, and diverting the blessing from Esau to Jacob, is related with great vivacity, and with an indifference to moral considerations which has been thought surprising in a writer with the fine ethical insight of J (Di.). It must be remembered, however, that "J" is a collective symbol, and embraces many tales which sink to the level of ordinary popular morality. We may fairly conclude with Gu. (272) that narratives of this stamp were too firmly rooted in the mind of the people to be omitted from any collection of national traditions.

Sources.—The presence of a dual narrative is rendered probable by the following *duplicates* (see We. *Comp.*² 34–36): (*a*) $^{33.34} \parallel {}^{35-38}$. In ^{35} (ויאמר) we are recalled to the same stage as the ויאמר of ^{33}; and ^{34} (Esau's cry) carries us forward to the same point as ^{38}.—(*b*) $^{21-23} \parallel {}^{24-27a}$: here again ויאמר commences two sections which must be alternative, since both lead up to the blessing (ויברכהו).—(*c*) A less obvious doublet may be discovered in $^{11-13.16} \parallel {}^{15}$: in the one case Jacob is disguised by the skin of the kids, in the other by wearing Esau's clothes.—(*d*) $^{30a\alpha} \parallel {}^{30b\beta}$.—(*e*) $^{44b} \parallel {}^{45a\alpha}$ (to ממך).—The language is predominantly that of J, with occasional traces of E; and that the incident was actually recorded in both these documents appears from chs. 32, $35^{3.7}$. In the parallels just enumerated, however, the stylistic criteria are hard to trace; and in the attempt to disentangle them almost everything hangs on the word יהוה in ^{27}. As to (*b*), $^{24-27}$ is certainly J, and $^{21-23}$ consequently E; it will follow that in (*c*) ^{15} belongs to J and $^{11-13.\ 16}$ to E. With regard to (*a*), it is almost impossible to decide which is J's variant and which E's. Gu. assigns $^{35-38}$ to E, on the somewhat subtle ground that in J ($^{33.\ 27}$) Isaac is ignorant who it is that has personated Esau, whereas in E ($^{35.\ 22}$) he knows very well that it is Jacob (so *OH*, *SOT*). Most critics have taken the opposite view, but without any decisive positive reason. See Gu. p. 270 f.; Pro. 19 f.—It is not worth while to push the precarious analysis further: anything else of importance may be reserved for the notes.

1–5. Isaac's purpose to bless Esau: explained by his partiality for his first-born son, and (more naïvely) by his fondness for venison (25^{28}). It is quite contrary to the sense of the narrative to attribute to him the design of frustrating the decree of Providence expressed in the independent legend of 25^{23}.—**1.** Blindness is spoken of as a frequent concomitant of old age (cf. 48^{10}, 1 Sa. 3^{2}, 1 Ki. 14^{4}, Ec. 12^{3}: ct. Dt. 34^{7}).—**3.** *thy quiver* (*v.i.*) *and thy bow*] the latter, the hunter's weapon (Is. 7^{24}; cf. 2 Ki. 13^{15}).—**4.** *that my soul may bless thee*] so $^{19.\ 25.\ 31}$. As if the expiring *nephesh* gathered up all its force in a single potent and prophetic wish. The universal belief in the efficacy of a dying utterance appears often in OT ($48^{10ff.}$ $50^{24f.}$, Dt. 33, Jos. 23, 2 Sa. $23^{1ff.}$, 1 Ki. $2^{1ff.}$, 2 Ki. $13^{14ff.}$).—**5.** *But Rebekah was listening*] cf. 18^{10}.

The close connexion of the blessing and the eating, which is insisted on throughout the narrative, is hardly to be explained as a reward for the satisfaction of a sensual appetite; it rests, no doubt, on some religious notion which we can no longer recover. Ho. compares the physical stimuli by which prophetic inspiration was induced (cf. 1 Sa.

1. וַתִּכְהֶין] On *vav cons.* in the subord. cl., cf. G–K. § 111 *q*.—The last cl. (ויאמר וגו׳) contains a characteristic formula of E (cf. $22^{1.\ 7.\ 11}$ 31^{11}: so v.^{18}), and is probably to be assigned to that source.—**2.** הנה־נא] J; see on 12^{11}.—**3.** תְּלִי] (תליתך ᵐᵘˢ): only here, from √ תלה, 'hang,' is a more suitable designation of the 'quiver' (𝔊𝔙𝔗ᴶ IEz.) than of the 'sword' (𝔗ᴼ Ra.).—צֵידָה Keth. may here be noun of unity (G–K. § 122 *t*)='piece of game' from צַיִד (Qĕrê) (so Tu. De. Di. Gu.). Elsewhere (42^{25} 45^{21} etc.) it means 'provisions,' especially for a journey. This may be explained by the fact that game was practically the only kind of animal food used by the Semites (see *RS*^{2}, 222 f.); but the identity of the √√ is doubted (BDB, 845 a).—**5.** להביא] 𝔊 לְאָבִיו is better, unless both words should be read.

$10^{5f.}$, 2 Ki. 3^{15}); Gu. surmises that a sacrificial meal, establishing communion with the Deity, was originally intended (cf. לפני י׳, v.[7] : see Nu. 23^{1}).

6–17. Rebekah's stratagem.—The mother's jealousy for her favourite son (25^{28}) is aroused by what she has overheard; and she instantly devises a scheme whose daring and ingenuity illustrate the Hebrew notion of capable and quick-witted womanhood.—**7.** *before Yahwe*] in the solemn consciousness of Yahwe's presence: see on v.[4].—**11–13** probably belong to E (see above), and may be omitted from the other narrative, with the effect of making Rebekah's initiative still more apparent: Jacob obeys her without a word.—**11.** *a hairy man*] see 25^{25}. The objection shows just enough shrewdness on Jacob's part to throw his mother's resourcefulness into bolder relief.—**13.** *On me be thy curse*] cf. 16^{5}.—**15.** *the choice clothes*] the festal raiment: the fact that this would have been put on by Esau proves once more that the blessing was a religious ceremony. Since the clothes were in Rebekah's charge, Esau must (as Ho. points out) have been still an unmarried man (ct. P $26^{34f.}$).—**16** goes with [11–13] (E), and may be removed without breach of continuity.—**17.** Rebekah's part being now ended, Jacob is left to his own resources.

18–29. Jacob obtains the blessing.—**20.** *How very quickly thou hast found it, my son!*—] an exclamation rather than a question: the answer being: *Yes, for Yahwe, etc.*—הִקְרָה לְפָנָי] caused the right thing to happen, as 24^{12} (J).—**21–23** may be the direct continuation of [19a] (E); the clause

---

6. בנה] cf. בְּנוֹ, v.[5]; the addition of הַקָּטָן (𝔊) is unnecessary.—**8.** בְּקֹלִי and לַאֲשֶׁר וגו׳ may be variants: acc. to Di. שָׁמַע בְּ is characteristic of E, and שׁמע לְ of J.—**12.** מתעתע (√ תעע)]), properly 'a stammerer' (cf. Ar. *ta'ta'a*) then 'a mocker' (2 Ch. 36^{16}); hence not a mere practical joker (Kn-Di.), but a profaner of religious solemnities (Ho. Gu.).—והבאתי] 𝔖 ܘܐܝܬܝ (2 s.f.).—**13.** אַךְ is given by Di. as a mark of E, in distinction from J's רַק (19^{8} 24^{8}).—**15.** בֶּגֶד being masc. (exc. Lv. 6^{20}), and חֲמֻדֹת in usage a subst., it is best to suppose בִּגְדֵי repeated as *nom. regens* before the gen. (otherwise Dav. § 27).

18. ויאמר וגו׳ [1] is probably to be assigned to E for the same reason as [1b], though something similar must have stood in the other source: Gu., however, makes [19b] the direct sequel of (ויאמר) אל־אביו in [18a] (J), giving [19a] to E.—ויבא] 𝔊𝔙𝔖 וַיָּבֵא (cf. [10. 14. 31]).—**23.** ויברכהו] Another view of the con-

and so he blessed him must have been followed by the words of blessing.—**24–27** bring the parallel narrative (J) up to the same point.—**27a.** The smelling of the garments seems to have a twofold significance: on the one hand it is a final test of Esau's identity (otherwise the disguise v.^{15} would have no meaning), on the other it supplies the sensuous impression which suggests the words of the blessing ^{27b} (so Gu.).

The section, we have seen, is composite (perhaps $^{18. 19a. 21-23. 28}$ = E ‖ $^{19b. 20. 24-27}$ = J); in the primary documents the interview was less complicated, and the movement quicker, than it now appears: but since neither has been preserved intact, we cannot tell how long Isaac's hesitation and Jacob's suspense lasted in each case. In J as it stands, it would seem that Isaac's suspicions are first aroused by the promptness of the supposed hunter's return, and perhaps only finally allayed by the smell of Esau's garments. In E it is the voice which almost betrays Jacob, and the feel of his arms which saves him from detection. For details, see the footnotes.

27b–29. The blessing is partly natural ($^{27b. 28}$), partly political (^{29}), and deals, of course, not with the personal history of Jacob, but with the future greatness of Israel. Its nearest analogies are the blessings on Joseph, Gn. $49^{22ff.}$, Dt. $33^{13ff.}$; and it is not improbable that its Elohistic elements (*v.i.*) originated in N. Israel.—**27b** (J). *the smell of a rich field*] cf.

---

struction, avoiding the division of documents, in Dri. *T.* § 75. The narrator is supposed to "hasten at once to state briefly the issue of the whole, and afterwards, as though forgetting that he had anticipated, proceed to annex the particulars by the same means" (ו̇ cons.). Ew. and Hitz. applied the same principle to several other passages (see *ib.*); but the explanation seems to me not very natural.—**24.** אַתָּה] ɯ האתה.—**25.** מציר בני] 𝔊 מְצֵידְךָ בְּנִי; but see v.^{31}.

27b–29. The critical analysis of the blessing, precarious at the best, depends on such considerations as these: יהוה ^{27b} points decisively to J; האלהים ^{28}, less certainly, to E, which is confirmed by דגן ותירש (cf. ^{37}). $^{29a\alpha}$ (to לאמים) is J because of the last word (25^{23}); and ^{29b} because of the resemblance to 12^{3}. $^{29a\beta}$ (from הוה) is E (cf. ^{37}): (so Gu.). KS. and Ho. differ first in treating $^{29a\beta b}$ as wholly ‖ $^{29a\alpha}$, thus assigning $^{29a\alpha}$ to E and $^{a\beta}$ to J (thus far Pro. agrees with them); then in the inference that ^{37} is J; and, lastly, in the reflex inference that ^{28b} is E.—The metrical structure is irregular. Parallelism appears in ^{28a} and in ^{29} throughout. ^{27b} falls into three trimeters; but ^{29} (also J) can only be scanned in tetrameters. In E trimeters and tetrameters are combined. See Sievers, i. 405, 577, ii. 79, 316.—**27b.** שׂדה] ɯ (ungrammatically) השדה מלא. The מלא, how-

Dt. 33^{23} (*v.i.*).—**28** (E). *fat places of the earth*] for the image cf. Is. 5^{1} 28^{1}, Nu. 13^{20}. "Heaven and earth conspire to give him of their best" (Gu.).—*corn and must*] often combined with 'oil' in pictures of agricultural felicity (Dt. 7^{13}, Ho. $2^{8. 22}$ etc.).—**29a***a* (J). *Peoples . . . nations*] cf. 25^{23}. The reference is to the neighbouring nations subdued by David (2 Sa. 8).—**29a**β (E) resembles a *tribal* blessing (cf. 49^{8}). At all events the mention of *brethren* (pl.) shows that the immediate situation is forgotten.—**29b** (J). Cf. 12^{3}.

30–40. Esau sues in vain for a blessing.—**30.** Both J and E bring out how narrowly Jacob escaped being detected (*v.i.*). **31b.** Esau's address (jussives) is if anything a little more deferential than Jacob's (v.^{19}).—**33.** *Who, then, is he. . . .*?] The words express but a momentary uncertainty; before the sentence is finished Isaac knows on whom the blessing has fallen. The clause is a real parallel to ^{35}, but a difference of conception is scarcely to be thought of (Gu.: see above).—*and blessed he shall be*] Not that Isaac now acquiesces in the ruling of Providence, and *refuses* to withdraw the blessing; but that such an oracle once uttered is in its nature irrevocable.—**34.** *bless me too*] parallel to the same words in ^{38}. Here J's narrative breaks off, and ^{35} (E) resumes from the standpoint of ^{32}.—**36.** *Is it because he was named Overreacher*]—that he must always be overreaching

---

ever, is rendered in 𝔊𝔙, and should perhaps be retained.—**28.** משמני] ‖ מִטַּל, and therefore = שְׁמַנֵּי + מִן (G-K. § 20 *m*), from שָׁמָן (^{39}†).—**29.** וישתחוְ] the final ו should be supplied with Qrê and 𝔖 (see next cl.).—הֱוֵה = הֱוֵה] הוה (הוא) is the common Aram. and NH form of היה (cf. Ph. חוא = חָיָה, חָיָא): in OT Heb. only here, Is. 16^{4}, Neh. 6^{6}, Jb. 37^{6}, Ec. 2^{22} 11^{3}†, and (acc. to Ex. 3^{14}) in the name יהוה. Its occurrence in early Heb., as here, is surprising.—גביר] v.^{37}†.—לְאַחֶיךָ] 𝔊𝔗^{O} לְאָחִיךָ, wrongly.—בני אמך] 𝔊 בְּ' אָבִיךָ after 49^{8}.—On the distributive sing. (אָרוּר, בָּרוּךְ), see G-K. § 145 *l*.

30a contains two variants, of which the second is connected syntactically with ^{30b}. Since the form of ^{a} resembles 18^{33} 24^{22} 43^{2} (all J), we may assign this to J, and the rest of the v. to E.—**31.** יָקֻם] Pt. rather יָקֹם (juss.).—**33.** מִכֹּל] KS. conj. אָכֹל (emphatic inf. abs.).—א' גם ברוך יהיה] The emendation of Hitz. (Ols. Ba.) אֲבָ' גַּם בָּרוּךְ׃ וַיְהִי is hardly suitable: such a sentence would require to be preceded by another action, of which it was an aggravating or supplementary circumstance (cf. 31^{15} 46^{4}, Nu. 16^{13}). It is better (with 𝔖) to read וְגַם, and (with 𝔊) to *insert* וַיְהִי at the beginning of ^{34}.—**36.** הכי] cf. 29^{15}, 2 Sa. 9^{1} (23^{19} ?), Jb. 6^{22}†. The

me?—Note the word-play בִּרְכָתִי : בְּכֹרָתִי.—**37.** Cf. $^{29a\beta.28b}$ (E). All that makes a blessing—political supremacy, and material wealth—has been given away; what remains for Esau?—**38.** *Is that the only blessing thou hast?*] That the blessing can be revoked, Esau does not imagine; but he still hopes that a second (inferior) blessing may be his.—*lifted up . . . wept*] corresponding to ^{34a}. "Those tears of Esau, the sensuous, wild, impulsive man,—almost like the cry of some 'trapped creature,' are among the most pathetic in the Bible" (Davidson, *Hebrews*, 242).—**39, 40a.** His importunity draws forth what is virtually a curse, though couched in terms similar to those of v.^{29}:

> *Away from the fat places of the earth shall thy dwelling be;*
> *And away from the dew of heaven above!*

The *double entendre* in the use of מִן has misled 𝔙 and some comm. into thinking this a *replica* of the blessing of Jacob (cf. Nö. *EB*, 1184). Compare 40^{13} with 40^{19}.—**40a.** *live by thy sword*] by raids on neighbouring territory, plunder of caravans, etc.*—*serve thy brother*] fulfilled in the long subjection of Edom to Israel, from the time of David to that of Joram (2 Ki. $8^{20ff.}$), or even Ahaz (16^6).—**40b.** The prosaic form suggests that this may be a later addition dating from after the emancipation of Edom (Ho. Gu.).—*break his yoke*] a common figure: Jer. 2^{20} 5^5 $28^{2.4.11}$ 30^8, Lv. 26^{13}, Is. 9^3 etc.

The territory of Edom is divided into two parts by the Arabah; that to the E is described by Strabo (XVI. iv. 21) as *χώρα ἔρημος ἡ πλείστη καὶ μάλιστα ἡ πρὸς Ἰουδαίᾳ*. Modern travellers, however, speak of it as

---

rendering above, 'is it that?' etc., satisfies every case (see BDB, 472 a), and is simpler than that given in G–K. § 150 *e*.—Ho. (so Gu.) thinks ^{36a} a redactional expansion; but it has to be considered whether ^{36b} (‖ $^{38a\alpha}$) is not rather a fragment of J.—**38.** ברכני גם אני אבי]=^{34b} (J). On the syntax of אני, see G–K. § 135 *e*.—וַיִּשָּׂא וגו׳] 𝔊$^{A, al.}$ om., but MSS and daughter-Vns. retain, some with the addition *κατανυχθέντος δὲ Ἰσαακ* (וַיִּדֹּם יִצְחָק).—**40.** חָיָה עַל] cf. Dt. 8^3, Ezk. 33^{19}.—תָּרִיד (Jer. 2^{31}, Hos. 12^1 [?], Ps. 55^3, Ju. 11^{37} [em.]†) probably connected with Ar. *rāda*, 'go to and fro' (Nö. *ZDMG*, xxxvii. 539 f.): 'when thou becomest restive.' 𝔐 תארד, 𝔊 *καθέλῃς*=תּוֹרִיד.

---

* Comp. Josephus on the Idumæans: *θορυβῶδες καὶ ἄτακτον ἔθνος αἰεί τε μετέωρον πρὸς τὰ κινήματα καὶ μεταβολαῖς χαῖρον κτλ.* (*BJ*, iv. 231), and *φύσει τε ὠμότατοι φονεύειν ὄντες* (*ib.* 310). Cf. Diod. ii. 48.

extremely fertile (Robinson, *BR*, ii. 154; Palmer, *Des. of Ex.* ii. 430 f.; cf. Buhl, *Edomiter*, 15 f.). Buhl accordingly thinks the curse refers only to the barren plateau W of the Arabah; and this is perhaps better than (with Nö. Dri.) to assimilate the terms of the blessing and the curse.

It is probable that J's narrative contained a form of the curse on Esau, but whether any part is preserved in [39f.] is doubtful. [39] is certainly from the same source as [28] (E); with regard to [40a] the question stands open.—On the metre, see again Sievers, i. 404 f., ii. 78 f., 317. Ba.'s denial of metrical form is based wholly on the doubtful [40b].

41–45. Esau's purpose of revenge.—41. Esau *cherished enmity* (50^{15}) against Jacob.—*the days of mourning* (50^{10})] a period of seven days, within which Esau hoped to accomplish his revenge.—**42.** Thy brother *is going to take satisfaction of thee* (Is. 1^{24}, Ezk. 5^{13}) *by killing thee.*—**44, 45.** *a few days . . . till he forget*] reckoning on Esau's well-known instability, and at the same time making light of the trial of separation.—*bereaved of you both*] The writer has in view the custom of blood-revenge (cf. 2 Sa. 14^{7}), though in the case supposed there would be no one to execute it.

XXVII. 46–XXVIII. 9.—*Isaac's Charge to Jacob* (P).

This short section records the only action attributed to Isaac in the Priestly Code. Two facts are taken over from the earlier tradition (JE): Isaac's blessing of Jacob, and Jacob's visit to Mesopotamia. But the unedifying stories of Jacob's treachery, which were the essential link of connexion between them, are here omitted; and a new motive is introduced, viz., the inadmissibility of intermarriage with the inhabitants of Canaan. By transgressing this unwritten law, Esau forfeits his title to the 'blessing of Abraham,' which is thus transferred to Jacob; and Jacob's flight is transformed into an honourable mission in search of a wife. The romantic interest of Jacob's love-story (ch. 29) is largely

---

43. ברח־לך] 𝔊 + εἰς τὴν Μεσοποταμίαν.—44 f. אחרים] as 29^{20}, Dn. 11^{20}; ct. Gn. 11^{1}.—עַד אשר תשוב and עד־שוב are obviously doublets, though there are no data for assigning either to its proper source. 𝔊 runs both together: ἕως τοῦ ἀποστρέψαι τὸν θυμὸν καὶ τὴν ὀργὴν τ. ἀδ. σου.

discounted by this prosaic representation of the course of events (cf. Gu. 341).

Marks of P's style are abundant : אֵל שַׁדַּי, [3] ; אֱלֹהִים, [4] ; הָאֲרַמִּי, [5] ; פַּדַּן אֲרָם, [2. 5. 6. 7] ; פָּרָה וְרָבָה, [3] ; אֶרֶץ מְגֻרִים, [4] ; בְּנוֹת כְּנַעַן, [1. 6. 8] (J ב׳ הַכְּנַעֲנִי, $24^{3. 37}$) ; קְהַל עַמִּים, [3].

46 is an amplification of 26^{35} (מֹרַת רוּחַ), but attributes to Rebekah an initiative more in the spirit of JE than of P. It may have been supplied by R to facilitate the transition from ch. 27 to 28 (*v.i.*).—**XXVIII. 1.** The language seems modelled on $24^{3. 37}$.—**2.** *thy mother's father*] The earlier affinity between the two families is again ignored by P : see on $25^{19f.}$.—**4.** *the blessing* (𝔊𝔖 'blessings') *of Abraham*] Comp. 17^{8}. Whereas in JE, Isaac is the inspired author of an original blessing, which fixes the destiny of his descendants, in P he simply transmits the blessing attached to the covenant with Abraham.—**9.** *went to Ishmael*] Not to dwell with him permanently, but to procure a wife (see $36^{6f.}$). It is undoubtedly assumed that Ishmael was still alive (Di.), in spite of the chronological difficulties raised by De.

XXVIII. 10–22.—*Jacob at Bethel* (JE).

On his way to Ḥarran, Jacob passes the night at Bethel, where the sacredness of the 'place' is revealed to him by a dream of a ladder leading from earth to heaven. Awaking, he consecrates the stone on which his head had lain, as a 'house of God,'—at the same time naming the place Bethel,—and vows to dedicate a tithe of all he has, in the event of his safe return.

---

46. The objections to assigning the v. to P (Kue. KS. Di. Ho. Gu. al.) are perhaps not decisive. If MT be right, בנות חת agrees in substance with $26^{34f.}$, though in $28^{1ff.}$ P consistently uses ב׳ כנען. 𝔊, however, omits the words מִבְּנוֹת־חֵת כָּאֵלֶּה.—**2.** פדנה] (so [5. 7]) cf. G–K. § 90 *i*. —**3.** קהל עמים] 35^{11} 48^{4} (P), Ezk. 23^{24} 32^{3} ;=הֲמוֹן גּוֹיִם, $17^{4f.}$. In spite of Dt. 33^{3} (Di.), the phrase cannot well denote the tribes of Israel. It seems to correspond to J's 'In thee shall *all nations*,' etc. (12^{3} etc.), and probably expresses some sort of Messianic outlook.—**4.** אלהים] ш יהוה. —**7.** ואל־אמו] perhaps a gloss suggested by $27^{43f.}$ (Di. al.).—**9.** אל־ישמעאל] ш om.—מָחֲלַת] 𝔖 ܡܚܠܬ (cf. 𝔗J) ; see on 36^{3}.

Analysis.—The section consists of a complete Elohistic narrative ($^{11f. 17-22}$), with a Yahwistic insertion ($^{13-16}$). For E, cf. אלהים, $^{12. 17. 20}$; מַצֵּבָה, $^{18. 22}$; the dream, ^{12}; the tithe, ^{22}; and the retrospective references in 31^{13} $35^{3. 7}$. For J, יהוה $^{13\ (bis).\ 16}$; נִצָּב עַל ^{13}, and the resemblances to $12^{3. 7}$ $13^{15f.}$ 18^{18} $22^{15ff.}$ 26^{24} 32^{13}. To J belong, further, ^{10} (חָרָנָה), and (if genuine) ^{21b}, though the latter is more probably interpolated. ^{19a} breaks the connexion of ^{18} and ^{20}, and *may* be taken from J; ^{19b} is an explanatory gloss. (So nearly all recent critics.) Kuenen (*Ond.* i. 145, 247) considers $^{13-16}$ a redactional addition to E, similar to 22^{14-18}, etc., on the ground that J attributes the inauguration of the worship at Bethel to Abraham (12^{8}), and nowhere alludes to the theophany here recorded (so Meyer, *INS*, 236^{3}). But (to say nothing of ^{19a}) the parallelism of ^{16} and ^{17} appears to prove a real amalgamation of primary sources (Di.). Gu. regards ^{14} as secondary, on account of its stereotyped phraseology.

10–12 (E). **Jacob's dream.** — **11.** *he lighted upon the place*] *i.e.*, the 'holy place' of Bethel (see 12^{6}), whose sanctity was revealed by what followed.—*he took* [at haphazard] *one of the stones of the place*] which proved itself to be the abode of a deity by inspiring the dream which came to Jacob that night.—**12.** *a ladder*] or 'stair' (the word only here). The origin of the idea is difficult to account for (see on v.^{17}). Its permanent religious significance is expressed with profound insight and truth in Jn. 1^{51}.—*angels of God*] So (in pl.) only in E (cf. 32^{2}) in the Hex. As always in OT, the angels are represented as wingless beings (cf. En. lxi. 1).

In v.^{11} the rendering 'a certain place' would be grammatically correct (G-K. § 126 *r*); but it destroys the point of the sentence, which is that night overtook the patriarch just at the sacred spot (see Ex. 3^{5}). The idea expressed by the primitive form of the legend is that the inherent sanctity of the place, and in particular of the stone, was unknown till it was discovered by Jacob's dream. It is very probable, as Ho. suggests, that this points to an ancient custom of incubation at Bethel, in which dream-oracles were sought by sleeping with the head in contact with the sacred stone (see Sta. *GVI*, i. 475 f.).

13–16 (J). **The promise.**

In place of the vision of the ladder, which in E constitutes the whole revelation, J records a personal appearance of Yahwe, and an articulate communication to the patriarch. That it was a nocturnal theophany (as in 26^{24}) appears from $^{16a\alpha}$, as well as the word שָׁכַב in ^{13}. The promise is partly addressed to Jacob's special circumstances ($^{13. 15}$), partly a re-

---

11. מראשתיו] Acc. of place (lit. 'at his head-place'), as 1 Sa. $19^{13. 16}$ $26^{7. 11. 16}$, 1 Ki. 19^{6}.—**12.** ויחלם והנה] The usual vivid formula in relating a

newal of the blessing of Abraham ([14]). The latter is not improbably a later amplification of the former (see above).

13. *Yahwe stood by him* (*v.i.*), and announced Himself as one with the God of his fathers. This unity of Yahwe amidst the multiplicity of His local manifestations is a standing paradox of the early religion of Israel: cf. v.[16].—*the land whereon thou liest*] a description peculiarly appropriate to the solitary and homeless fugitive who had not where to lay his head.—**14.** Comp. $13^{14ff.}$ $22^{17f.}$ $26^{4.\ 24}$ 32^{13}.—On [14b] see the note on 12^{3}.—**16.** *Yahwe is in this place, etc.*] The underlying feeling is not joy (Di.), but fear, because in ignorance he had treated the holy place as common ground (𝔗^{OJ}). The exclamation doubtless preserves an echo of the local tradition, more forcibly represented in E (v.[17]). It is the only case in Gen. where a theophany occasions surprise (cf. Ex. 3^{3}).

17–19. Consecration and naming of the place.—**17** follows v.[12] (E) without sensible breach of continuity; even the mention of Jacob's awaking ([16]) is not absolutely indispensable (see [18]). The impression of fear is far more powerfully expressed than in J; the place is no ordinary *ḥarām*, but one superlatively holy, the most sacred spot on earth. Only a N Israelite could have written thus of Bethel.—*a house of God . . . the gate of heaven*] The expressions rest on a materialisation of the conception of worship as spiritual intercourse between God and man.

The first designation naturally arises from the name *Bêth-'ēl*, which (as we see from v.[22]) was first applied to the sacred stone, but was afterwards extended to the sanctuary as a whole. When to this was added the idea of God's dwelling in heaven, the earthly sanctuary became as it were the entrance to the true heavenly temple, with which it communicated by means of a ladder. We may compare the Babylonian theory of the temple-tower as the means of ascent to the dwelling-place

---

dream: 37^{7} (𝔊) ^{9} 40^{9} 41^{1}, Ju. 7^{13}, Is. 29^{8}.—**13.** נצב עליו] 18^{2} 24^{13} 45^{1} (all J). 𝔊𝔙𝔖 take מָקֹם as antecedent to the suff.; but the idea would have been expressed otherwise (מִמַּעַל לו), and the translation loses all its plausibility when the composition of documents is recognised.—Before הארץ, 𝔊 ins. *μὴ φοβοῦ*.—**14.** כעפר הארץ] 𝔊 ὡς ἡ ἄμμος τῆς θαλάσσης, after 32^{13} 41^{49}.—ופרצת] 𝔊 וּפָרַץ: for the word—properly 'break through' [bounds],—cf. $30^{30.\ 43}$, Ex. 1^{12}, Is. 54^{3} etc.—**15.** בכל] 𝔊 + הַדֶּרֶךְ.

of the gods in heaven (see p. 226 above). It is conceivable that the 'ladder' of Bethel may embody cosmological speculations of a similar character, which we cannot now trace to their origin. The Egyptian theology also knew of a 'ladder' by which the soul after death mounted up to 'the gate of heaven' (Erman, *Hdbk.* 96). Whether it has any connexion with the *sillu*, or decorated arch over a palace gate, depicted in *ATLO*², 13, remains doubtful. That the image was suggested by physical features of the locality—a stony hillside rising up in terraces towards heaven—seems a fanciful explanation to one who has not visited the spot; but the descriptions given of the singular freak of nature which occurs near the summit of the slope to the north of *Beitîn* ("huge stones piled one upon another to make columns nine or ten feet or more in height . . .") lend some plausibility to the conjecture (see Peters, *Early Hebrew Story*, 110 ff.).

18. Jacob set up the stone, whose mystic properties he had discovered, as a *maẓẓēbāh*, or sacred pillar (*v.i.*), and *poured oil on the top of it* (35^{14}), in accordance with a custom widely attested in ancient and modern times (see p. 380).—**19a** gives J's account of the naming of the place. If a similar notice occurred in E (as seems implied in 31^{13} 35^{3}), it would naturally have stood later.—**19b** is usually considered a gloss. From Jos. 16^{2} (18^{13}) it appears that *Lûz* was really distinct from Bethel, but was overshadowed by the more famous sanctuary in the neighbourhood.

20–22 (E). **Jacob's vow.**—The vow in OT "consists

---

18. מַצֵּבָה] ('thing *set up*,' Ar. *nuṣb*, Ph. מצבת) is the technical name of the sacred monolith which was apparently an adjunct of every fully equipped Canaanite (or Phœnician) and early Hebrew sanctuary (see Vincent, *Canaan*, 96, 102 f., 140). Originally a fetish, the supposed abode of a spirit or deity,—a belief of which there are clear traces in this passage,—it came afterwards to be regarded as a vague symbol of Yahwe's presence in the sanctuary, and eventually as the memorial of a theophany or other noteworthy occurrence. In this harmless sense the word is freely used by E ($31^{13.\ 45.\ 51.\ 52}$ 33^{20} [em.] 35^{14}, Ex. 24^{4}); but not by J, who never mentions the object except in connexion with Canaanitish worship (Ex. 34^{13}). But that the emblem retained its idolatrous associations in the popular religion is shown by the strenuous polemic of the prophets and the Dtnic. legislation against it (Hos. $10^{1f.}$, Mic. 5^{12}, Dt. 12^{3} etc., esp. 16^{22} [cf. Lv. 26^{1}]); and J's significant silence is probably an earlier indication of the same tendency. It is only at a very late period that we find the word used once more without offence (Is. 19^{19}). See Dri. on Dt. $16^{21f.}$; *RS*², 204 ff., 456 f.; Moore in *EB*, 2974 ff.; Whitehouse in *DB*, iii. 879 ff.—וַיִּצֹק] On this, the usual form, see G-K. § 71.—**19.** ואולם] A strong adversative, found in Pent. only 48^{19},

essentially of a solemn promise to render God some service, in the event of some particular prayer or wish being granted" (Dri.); * hence it falls into two parts: a condition ([20f.]), and a promise ([22]).—**20, 21a**. The conditions correspond with the divine promise in [15] (J)—(*a*) the presence of God; (*b*) protection; (*c*) safe return—except as regards the stipulation for *bread to eat and raiment to wear*. The separation of sources relieves Jacob from the suspicion of questioning the sincerity of an explicit divine promise. On **21b**, *v.i.*—**22**. The promise. *this stone . . . shall be* (𝔊 adds *to me*) *a house of God*] *i.e.* (in the view of the writer), a place of worship. It is to be noted that this reverses the actual development: the stone was *first* the residence of the *numen*, and *afterwards* became a maẓẓēbāh.—**22b**. He will pay a tithe of all his possessions. This and Am. 4[4] are the only pre-Deuteronomic references to the tithe (cf. 14[20]).

In its present setting the above narrative forms the transition link between the Jacob-Esau and the Jacob-Laban cycle of legends. In substance it is, we can hardly doubt, a modification of the cultus-legend of Bethel (now *Beitīn*, situated on an eminence about 10 miles N of Jerusalem, a little E of the road to Nābulus), the founding of which was ascribed to the patriarch Jacob. The concrete features which point to a local origin—the erection of the maẓẓebah, the ladder, the gate of heaven, and the institution of the tithe—are all indeed peculiar to the account of E, which obviously stands nearer to the sources of the native tradition than the stereotyped form of the theophany given by J. From E we learn that the immemorial sanctity of Bethel was concentrated in the sacred stone which was itself the original *Bêth-'ēl*, i.e. the residence of a god or spirit. This belief appears to go back to the primitive stone-

---

Ex. 9[16], Nu. 14[21]. For ואו' לוז, 𝔊 has καὶ Οὐλαμμαύς; cf. Ju. 18[29] (𝔊).—לוז] 35[6] 48[3], Jos. 16[2] 18[13], Ju. 1[23]†. The name Λουζά appears to have been known in the time of Euseb. (*OS*, 135[1]); and Müller (*AE*, 165) thinks it may be identical with *Ruṣa* on Eg. inscr.

21. ושבתי] 𝔊 καὶ ἀποστρέψῃ με, as v.[15].—**21b** can with difficulty be assigned either to the protasis or to the apodosis of the sentence. The word יהוה shows that it does not belong to E; and in all probability the cl. is to be omitted as a gloss (Di. al.). The apod. then has the same unusual form as in 22[1].

---

* But We. (*Heid.*[2] 190) remarks of the Arabian custom: "Die Araber geloben nicht *in eventum*: wenn der und der Fall eintritt, so will ich das tun; sondern sie übernehmen durch das Gelübde eine absolut bindende Pflicht."

worship of which traces are very widely diffused over the surface of the globe.* The characteristic rite of anointing the stone, originally perhaps a sacrifice to the indwelling *numen*, was familiar to classical writers.† The most instructive parallel is the fact mentioned by Pausanias (x. 24, 6), that on a small stone in the sanctuary of Delphi oil was poured every day: we may conjecture that a similar practice was kept up at Bethel long after its original significance was forgotten. Though the monolith of Bethel is not elsewhere explicitly referred to in OT, we may assume that, stripped of its pagan associations and reduced to the rank of a *maṣṣēbāh*, it was still recognised in historic times as the chief religious symbol of that great centre of Hebrew worship.

XXIX. 1–30.—*Jacob's Marriage with Laban's Daughters* (JE, P).

Instead of spending a few days (27^{44}) as Laban's guest, Jacob was destined to pass 20 years of his life with his Aramæan kinsman. The circumstances which led to this prolonged exile are recorded in the two episodes contained in this section; viz. Jacob's meeting with Rachel at the well ($^{1-14}$), and the peculiar conditions of his marriage to Leah

* See Tylor, *Prim. Cult.*[3] ii. 160 ff.; Frazer, *Pausan.* iv. 154 f., *Adonis*, 21; *RS*[2], 204 ff., 232 f. The wide distribution of these sacred objects seems fatal to the theory of Lagrange, that they were miniature reproductions of the Babylonian temple-towers, which again were miniature symbols of the earth conceived as a mountain,—a difficulty of which the author himself is conscious (*Études*[2], 192 ff.).

† On anointed stones (λίθοι λιπαροί, ἀληλιμμένοι, *lapides uncti, lubricati*, etc.), see Clem. Alex. *Strom.* vii. 4, 26; and the remarkable statements of Theophrastus, *Char.* 16; Lucian, *Alexander*, 30; and Arnobius, *Adv. Gentes*, i. 39,—quoted by Frazer, *Pausan.* v. 354.—For Assyriological parallels see *KIB*, i. 44 f., ii. 113, 151, 261.—A curious development of the ancient belief appears in the name Βαίτυλος, Βαιτύλιον, *Betulus*, applied to small stones (aerolites?), supposed to be self-moving and endowed with magical properties, which played a considerable part in the private superstitions of the beginning of the Christian era (Eus. *Præp. Ev.* i. 10, 18; Photius, *Bibl.* [Migne, ciii. 1292 f.]; Pliny, *HN*, xxxvii. 135, etc.). The existence of a Canaanitish deity *Bait-ili* (who can only be regarded as a personification of the temple or the sacred stone) is proved by unimpeachable Assyriological evidence (*KAT*[3], 437 f.; Lagrange, *l.c.* 196). Since Βαίτυλος is also the name of a god in Philo-Byblius, it seems unreasonable to doubt the etymological and material connexion between the ancient Semitic בֵּית־אֵל and the portable betyl of the Græco-Roman period, which was so named as the residence of a spirit; but see the important article of Moore, *Journal of the Archæological Institute of America*, vii. (1903), No. 2, p. 198 ff.

and Rachel ($^{15-30}$). The first, a purely idyllic scene reminding us of 24^{11-33} and Ex. 2^{15-22}, forms a pleasing introduction to the cycle of Jacob-Laban narratives, without a trace of the petty chicanery which is the leading motive of that group of legends.* In the second, the true character of Laban is exposed by the unworthy trick which he practises on Jacob; and the reader's sympathies are enlisted on the side of Jacob in the trial of astuteness which is sure to ensue.

Analysis.—Fragments of P's narrative can be easily recognised in vv.$^{24. 29}$, and probably also in ^{28b}. The separation of J and E is uncertain on account of the close parallelism of the two documents and the absence of material differences of representation to support or correct the literary analysis. Most subsequent critics agree with Di. that v.^{1} belongs to E (see the notes), and $^{2-14}$ to J: cf. רוץ לקראת, ^{13} (18^{2} 24^{17}); עצמי ובשרי, ^{14} (2^{23}). In $^{16f.}$ Rachel appears to be introduced for the first time; hence Di. regards E as the main source of ^{15} (or ^{15b}) $^{-30}$, excluding, however, v.^{26}, where צְעִירָה and בְּכִירָה reveal the hand of J: characteristic expressions of E are משכרת, ^{15} ($31^{7. 41}$); גדלה and קטנה, $^{16. 18}$; יפת תאר וגו׳, ^{17}. So Gu. Pro. nearly. Ball and Corn. assign all from ^{19} onwards to J.

1–14. Jacob's meeting with Rachel.—**1.** *the sons of the East*] Since the goal of Jacob's journey is in J, Ḥarran (28^{10} 29^{4}) and in P, Paddan Aram (28^{7}), it is to be presumed that this third variation comes from E (Di.). Now the בְּנֵי קֶדֶם are everywhere else the tribes of the Syro-Arabian desert, and $31^{21ff.}$ certainly suggests that Laban's home was not so distant from Canaan as Ḥarran (see on $24^{10f.}$ [city of Nahor]). It is possible, therefore, that in the tradition followed by E, Laban was the representative of the nomadic Aramæans between Palestine and the Euphrates (see p. 334 above).—**2.** The well *in the open country* is evidently distinct, even in J, from the town-well of Ḥarran (cf. 24^{13}).—*For . . . they used to water, etc.*] To the end of v.^{3} is an explanatory parenthesis describing the ordinary procedure. The custom of covering the well with a heavy stone is referred to by

1 The curious expression 'lifted up his feet' is found only here.—𝔊𝔙 om. בְּנֵי; and 𝔊 adds to the v. πρὸς Λαβὰν κτλ., as 28^{5b}.—**2.** והאבן גדלה can only mean 'and the stone was great': it is perhaps better to omit

* 𝔗J thinks it necessary to introduce a hint of the coming rivalry into the conversation between Jacob and Rachel (v.^{13}).

Robinson, *BR*, i. 490; Thomson, *LB*, 589; Palmer, *Des. of Ex.* ii. 319 f.; cf. also Diod. ii. 48, xix. 94.—**4.** Jacob accosts the shepherds, and learns that they come *from Ḥarran.* There is nothing else in the narrative to suggest the proximity of a great city; Laban is no city-dweller as in ch. 24, but a nomad sheikh; and the life depicted is everywhere that of the desert. All this confirms the impression that the topography of E (v.[1]) has been modified by J in accordance with the theory that Ḥarran was the city of Nahor.—**5.** *the son of Nāḥôr*] see on 24^{15}.—**7, 8.** Jacob is puzzled by the leisurely ways of these Eastern herdsmen, whom he ironically supposes to have ceased work for the day. He is soon to show them an example of how things should be done, careless of the conventions which they plead as an excuse.—**9.** *a shepherdess*] cf. Ex. 2^{16}. The trait is in accordance with the freedom still allowed to unmarried girls among the Bedouin. Burck. found it an established rule among the Arabs of Sinai that only girls should drive the cattle to pasture (*Bedouin*, i. 351).—**10.** The removal of the stone is a feat of strength which has been thought to belong to a more primitive legend, in which Jacob figured as a giant (Di. Gu. al.): cf. 32^{26}.—**11.** *wept aloud*] 'after the demonstrative fashion of the Oriental' (Ben.),—tears of joy at the happy termination of his journey.—**12.** *brother*] as in v.[15] 13^8 14^{14} (24^{48}?).—**13.** *kissed him repeatedly* (Piel)] The effusive display of affection, perhaps not wholly disinterested, is characteristic of Laban (cf. $24^{29ff.}$).—**14.** *my bone and my flesh*] as 37^{27}, Ju. 9^2, 2 Sa. 5^1 $19^{13f.}$. It is an absurd suggestion that the exclamation is called forth by the recital of Jacob's dealings with Esau, in which Laban recognised a spiritual affinity to himself! The phrase denotes literal consanguinity and nothing more.

---

the art. (with 𝔐).—3. העדרים] 𝔐 הרעים, needlessly substituted by Ba. So also v.[8], where 𝔐 is supported by 𝔊.—6. Before והנה, 𝔊 ins. *ἔτι αὐτοῦ λαλοῦντος* (as v.[9]). An assimilating tendency reappears at the end of the v.; and the variations have no critical value.—9. בָּאָה] perf.; ct. the ptcp. בָּאָה in v.[6].—רעה הוא] 𝔊 + *τὰ πρόβατα τοῦ πατρὸς αὐτῆς*.—10. ויגל] with original *i* in impf. Qal (G-K. § 67 *p*).—13. שמע (𝔊 שֵׁם) = 'the report concerning,' followed as always by gen. obj.—14. חדש ימים] 'a whole month'; see G-K. § 131 *d*.

15–30. Jacob's double marriage.—15. Laban's character begins to unfold itself as that of a man ostensibly actuated by the most honourable motives, but at heart a selfish schemer, always ready with some plausible pretext for his nefarious conduct (see vv.$^{19. 26}$). His apparently generous offer proves a well-laid trap for Jacob, whose love for Rachel has not escaped the notice of his shrewd kinsman. —**16–18a.** An explanatory parenthesis. The manner in which Rachel is introduced, as if for the first time, is thought to mark the transition to another source (Di. al.).—On the names *Lēʾāh* and *Rāḥēl*, *v.i.*—**17.** Leah's eyes were *weak* (רַכּוֹת, 𝔊 ἀσθενεῖς, Aq. Σ. ἁπαλοί): *i.e.* they lacked the lustrous brilliancy which is counted a feature of female beauty in the East.—**18b.** Jacob, not being in a position to pay the purchase price (*mōhar*) for so eligible a bride, offered seven years' service instead. The custom was recognised by the ancient Arabs, and is still met with (We. *GGN*, 1893, 433 f.; Burck. *Syria*, i. 297 f.).—**19.** The first cousin has still a prior (sometimes an exclusive) right to a girl's hand among the Bedouin and in Egypt (Burck. *Bedouin*, i. 113, 272; Lane, *Mod. Eg.*^{5} i. 199).—**22.** Laban proceeds to the execution of his long meditated *coup*. He himself arranges the marriage feast (ct. Ju. 14^{10}), inviting *all the men of the place*, with a view doubtless to his self-exculpation (v.^{26}).—**23.** The substitution of Leah for Rachel was rendered possible by the custom of bringing the bride to the bridegroom veiled (24^{65}). To have thus got rid of the unprepossessing Leah for a handsome price, and to retain his nephew's services for other seven years (v.^{27}), was a master-stroke of policy in the eyes of a man like Laban.—**25.** Jacob's surprise and indignation

---

15. הכי] see on 27^{36}.—מַשְׂכֻּרְתּ] $31^{7. 41}$ (E), Ru. 2^{12} †; שָׂכָר is common to J ($30^{28. 32f.}$) and E (31^{8}, Ex. 2^{9}).—**16.** גדל and קטן are in such connexions characteristic of E (v.^{18} $42^{13. 15. 20. 32. 34}$); see Ho. *Einl.* 104.—רָחֵל means 'ewe' (Ar. *raḫil*=she-lamb); hence by analogy לֵאָה has been explained by Ar. *laʾāt*, 'bovine antelope' (see Nö. *ZDMG*, xl. 167; Sta. *ZATW*, i. 112 ff.), and the names are cited as evidence of a primitive Heb. totemism (*KM*^{2}, 254 f.). Others prefer the derivation from Ass. *liʾat*, 'lady' (see Haupt, *GGN*, 1883, 100).—**18.** ברחל] בְּ *pretii* (G-K. § 119*p*); so $^{20. 25}$.—**20.** ויהיו—אחת] 𝔊^{A} om.—**21.** הָבָה] *Milraʿ* before א (G-K. § 69*o*).—**24.** שפחה] better

are vividly depicted.—**26.** *It is not so done*] cf. 34^{7}, 2 Sa. 13^{12}. Laban no doubt correctly states the local usage: the objection to giving a younger daughter before an older is natural, and prevails in certain countries (Lane, i. 201; cf. *Jub.* xxviii., Ju. $15^{1f.}$, 1 Sa. 18^{17}).—**27, 28.** *Fulfil the week of this one*] *i.e.*, the usual seven days (Ju. 14^{12}, To. 11^{19}) of the wedding festival for Leah. For the bridegroom to break up the festivities would, of course, be a gross breach of decorum, and Jacob has no alternative but to fall in with Laban's new proposal and accept Rachel on his terms.—**30.** Laban's success is for the moment complete; but in the alienation of both his daughters, and their fidelity to Jacob at a critical time ($31^{14ff.}$), he suffered a just retribution for the unscrupulous assertion of his paternal rights.

In Jacob's marriages it has been surmised that features survive of that primitive type of marriage (called *beena* marriage) in which the husband becomes a member of the wife's kin (Rob. Sm. *KM*², 207). Taken as a whole the narrative hardly bears out that view. It is true that Jacob attaches himself to Laban's family; but it does not follow that he did not set up a house of his own. His remaining with Laban was due to his inability to pay the *mōhar* otherwise than in the way of personal service. As soon as the contract expired he pleads his right to 'provide for his own house' (30^{30} J). On the other hand, Laban certainly claimed the right to detain his daughters, and treated them as still members of his family ($31^{26.\ 43}$ E); and it might be imagined that the Elohistic tradition recognised the existence of *beena* marriage, at least among the Aramæans. But it is doubtful if the claim is more than an extreme assertion of the right of a powerful family to protect its female relatives even after marriage.

XXIX. 31–XXX. 24.—*The Birth of Jacob's Children* (JE).

A difficult section, in which the origin of the tribes of Israel is represented in the fictitious form of a family history. The popular etymologies attached to the names are here extremely forced, and sometimes unintelligible; it is remark-

---

לִשְׁ' (𝔐𝔗ᴼ); see v.²⁹.—**26.** הצעירה] distinctive of J; see v.¹⁶.—**27.** וְנִתְּנָה is rather 3rd f. s. pf. Niph., than 1st pl. cohort. Qal (as most). 𝔐𝔊𝔖𝔙 read וְאֶתֵּן.—**28b.** לו לאשה] The double dative is characteristic of P, to whom the whole clause may be assigned along with ²⁹.—**30.** The second גַּם has no sense, and should probably be deleted (𝔊𝔙).

able that, with hardly an exception, they are based on the rivalry between Jacob's two wives. (The names are bestowed by the mothers, as is generally the case in JE.) How far genuine elements of tradition are embodied in such a narrative is a question which it is obviously impossible to answer with certainty. We cannot be wrong in attributing historical significance to the distinction between the tribes whose descent was traced to Jacob's wives and those regarded as sons of concubines; though we are ignorant of the actual circumstances on which the classification depends. It is also certain that there is a solid basis for the grouping of the chief tribes under the names of Leah and Rachel, representing perhaps an older and a later settlement of Hebrews in Palestine (Sta. *ZATW*, i. 112 f.). The fact that all the children except Benjamin are born in Mesopotamia may signify that the leading tribal divisions existed before the occupation of Canaan; but the principle certainly cannot be applied in detail, and the nature of the record forbids the attempt to discover in it reliable data for the history of the tribes. (For a conspectus of various theories, see Luther, *ZATW*, xxi. 36 ff.; cf. Mey. *INS*, 291 f., 509 ff.)

The *sources* are J and E, with occasional clauses from P.—29^{31-35} is wholly from J (יהוה, $^{31. 32. 33. 35}$; עֲקָרָה, ^{31}; הַפַּעַם, $^{34. 35}$), with the possible exception of $^{32b\gamma}$.—30^{1-8} is mainly E (אלהים, $^{2. 6. 8}$; אָמָה, ^{3a}); but $^{3a\beta}$ reminds us of J (16^{2}), ^{4a} is assigned to P (שִׁפְחָה and cf. 16^{3}), and in ^{7} שִׁפְחָה must be either from J (KS. Ba. Gu.) or P (Ho.).—30^{9-13} is again mostly from J (שִׁפְחָה, $^{10. 12}$; cf. ^{9a} with 29^{31} 30^{1} 29^{35}). ^{9b} is P.—30^{14-24} presents a very mixed text, whose elements are difficult to disentangle; note the double etymologies in $^{18.}$ (cf. ^{16}) $^{20. 23f.}$ The hand of E clearly appears in $^{17a. 18. 20a\alpha\beta. 22b\alpha.}$ (^{22a} may be from P: cf. 8^{1}) ^{23}. Hence the parallels $^{14-16. 20a\gamma. 24}$ must be assigned to J, who is further characterised, according to Gu., by the numeration of the sons ($^{17b. 19. 20a\gamma}$). ^{21} is interpolated.

31–35. The sons of Leah.—**31.** *hated*] The rendering is too strong. שְׂנוּאָה is almost a technical term for the less favoured of two wives (Dt. $21^{15ff.}$); where the two are sisters the rivalry is naturally most acute, hence this practice is forbidden by the later law (Lv. 18^{18}). The belief that Yahwe takes the part of the unfortunate wife and rewards her with children, belongs to the strongly marked family religion of

Israel (1 Sa. $1^{2ff.}$).—32. *Rĕ'ûbēn*] The only plausible explanation of the etymology is that it is based on the form רְאוּבֵל (*v.i.*) = רְאוּ־בַעַל, and that יהוה is substituted for the divine name בַּעַל. Most comm. suppose that the writer resolves ראובן into [רָאָ[ה] בְּ[עָ]נְ[יִ]י; but that is too extravagant for even a Heb. etymologist.—33. *Šim'ôn*] derived from שָׁמַע, 'hear,' expressing precisely the same idea as Rĕ'ûbēn. —34. *Lēvî*, as the third son, is explained by a verb for 'adhere' (Niph. √ לוה), on the principle that a threefold cord is not easily broken.—35. *Yĕhûdāh*] connected with a word meaning 'praise' (הוֹדָה: cf. impf. יְהוֹדֶה, Neh. 11^{17}). So in 49^{8}.

XXX. 1–8. Rachel's adopted sons.—1, 2. A passionate scene, showing how Rachel was driven by jealousy of her sister to yield her place to her maid. Her petulant behaviour recalls that of Sarah (16^{5}), but Jacob is less patient than Abraham.—*Am I in God's stead?*] So 50^{19}, cf. 2 Ki. 5^{7}. —3. *bear upon my knees*] An allusion to a primitive ceremony of adoption, which here simply means that Bilhah's children will be acknowledged by Rachel as her own.

On the ceremony referred to, see Sta. *ZATW*, vi. 143 ff.; Ho. 196; Dri. 274. Its origin is traced to a widespread custom, according to which, in lawful marriage, the child is actually brought forth on the father's knees (cf. Jb. 3^{12}; *Il.* ix. 455 f.; *Od.* xix. 401 ff.); then it became a symbol of

---

32. ראובן] 𝔊 'Ρουβην, etc.; 𝔖 ܪܘܒܝܠ; Jos. 'Ρουβηλος. The origin of the name has given rise to an extraordinary number of conjectures (see Hogg, *EB*, 4091 ff.). We seem driven to the conclusion that the original form (that on which the etymology is based: *v.s.*) was ראובל. In that form the name has been connected with Ar. *ri'bāl*, 'lion,' or 'wolf,' in which case Reuben might have to be added to the possibly totemistic names of OT. Another plausible suggestion is that the word is softened from רְעוּ־בעל a theophorous compound after the analogy of רְעוּאֵל.—33. After בֵּן, 𝔊 ins. שֵׁנִי, which may be correct (cf. $30^{7.12.17.19.24}$).—שִׁמְעוֹן] Another supposed animal name, from Ar. *sim'*, a cross between the wolf and hyæna (see Rob. Sm. *JPh.* ix. 80). Ewald regarded it as a diminutive of יִשְׁמָעֵאל, and similarly recently Cheyne (*TBI*, 375).—34. קרא] 𝔐𝔊^{L}𝔖 קָרְאָה; 𝔊^{A} ἐκλήθη.—לֵוִי] We.'s conjecture that this is the gentilic of לֵאָה is widely accepted (Sta. Rob.-Sm. Nö. Mey. al.). Homm., on the other hand, compares S Arab. *lavi'u* = 'priest,' Levi being the priestly tribe (*AHT*, 278 f.; cf. Benz. *Arch.*^{2} 56).

3. בִּלְהָה] (of unknown etymology) is probably to be connected with

the legitimisation of a natural child, and finally a form of adoption generally (50^{23}). Gu., however, thinks the rite originated in cases like the present (the slave being delivered on the knees of her mistress), and was afterwards transferred to male adoption.

obtain children by her] see on 16^{2}.—**6.** The putative mother names the adopted child.—*Dân*] The etymology here given (√ דִּין, 'judge') is very probably correct, the form being an abbreviated theophorous name (cf. *Abi-dan*, Ass. *Asshur-dan*, etc.).—**8.** *wrestlings of God I have wrestled*] The words are very obscure (see Che. 376 ff.). Either 'I have had "a veritable God's bout" (Ba.) with my sister,' or (less probably) 'I have wrestled with God (in prayer) like my sister.'—*and have overcome*] This seems to imply that Leah had only one son at the time (Gu.); and there is nothing to prevent the supposition that the concubinage of Bilhah followed immediately on the birth of Reuben.

9–13. Leah's adopted sons.—**11.** *Gad* is the name of an Aramæan and Phœnician god of Luck (Τύχη), mentioned in Is. 65^{11} (see *Camb. Bible*, *ad loc.*; cf. Baethgen, *Beitr.* 76 ff. 159 ff.). There is no difficulty in supposing that a hybrid tribe like Gad traced its ancestry to this deity, and was named after him; though, of course, no such idea is expressed in the text. In Leah's exclamation the word is used appellatively: *With luck!* (*v.i.*). It is probable, however, that at an earlier time it was current in the sense 'With Gad's help'

---

the Ḥorite clan בִּלְהָן (36^{27}).—**6.** דָּנַנִּי] On the form, see G–K. § 26 *g.*—7aβb must be assigned to J, on account of שִׁפְחָה and בן שני (note also the expression of subj. after *second* vb.).—**8.** נפתולי] ἅπ. λεγ. The vb. has nowhere else the sense of 'wrestle,' but means primarily to 'twist' (cf. Pr. 8^{8}, Jb. 5^{13}, Ps. 18^{27}†); hence נַפְתָּלִי might be the 'tortuous,' 'cunning' one (BDB). But a more plausible etymology derives it from a hypothetical *Naphtal* (from נֶפֶת [Jos. 17^{11}†,—if correctly vocalised], usually taken to mean 'height': cf. כַּרְמֶל fr. כֶּרֶם), denoting the northern highlands W of the Upper Jordan (Mey. *INS*, 539).—The Vns. render the v. more or less paraphrastically, and give no help to the elucidation of the sense.

10. Both here and v.[12] 𝔊 gives a much fuller text.—**11.** בְּגָד] So *Keth.*, 𝔊 Ἐν τύχῃ, 𝔙 *Feliciter.* But *Qrê* בָּא גָד is ancient, being presupposed by S (ܓܕ ܐܬܐ) and 𝔗ᴼᴶ. These Vns. render 'Good fortune comes' (so Ra): another translation, suggested by 49^{19}, is 'A troop (גְּדוּד) comes' (IEz.).

(Ba. Gu.).—**13**. The name *'Āšēr* naturally suggested to Heb. writers a word for happiness; hence the two etymologies: בְּאָשְׁרִי, '*In my happiness*,' and אִשְּׁרוּנִי '(women) *count me happy*.' It is possible that the name is historically related to the Canaanite goddess *'Ăšērāh* (Ba. Ho.), as Gad is to the Aramæan deity. *Aser* appears in Eg. monuments as the name of a district in NW Palestine as early as Seti and Ramses II. (Müller, *AE*, 236 ff.).

14–24. The later children.—14–16. The incident of the love-apples is a piece of folklore, adopted with reserve by the writer (J), and so curtailed as to be shorn of its original significance. The story must have gone on to tell how Rachel partook of the fruit and in consequence became pregnant, while Leah also conceived through the restoration of her marriage rights (see We. *Comp.*[2] 38 f.). How much of this stood in J and has been suppressed in the history of the text we cannot say; we here read just what is necessary to explain the name of Leah's child.—**14**. דּוּדָאִים (*v.i.*) is the round, greenish-yellow, plum-like fruit of *mandragora vernalis*, which in Syria ripens in May—*the days of wheat harvest*—and is still eagerly sought in the East to promote conception (see Tuch's note, 385 ff.). Reuben is named, probably as the only child old enough to follow the reapers in the field (cf. 2 Ki. 4^{18}). The agricultural background shows that the episode is out of place in its present nomadic setting.—**15**. *he shall lie with thee to-night*] Jacob, therefore, had wrongly withheld from Leah her conjugal rights (עוֹנָה, Ex. 21^{10}).—**16**. *I have hired thee* (שָׂכֹר שְׂכַרְתִּיךָ)] Obviously an anticipation of

13. אֹשֶׁר is ἅπ. λεγ.—אִשְּׁרוּנִי] pf. of confidence (G–K. § 106 *n*). It is to be noted that pfs. greatly preponderate in E's etymologies, and impfs. in those of J; the two exceptions ($29^{32f.}$) may be only apparent, and due to the absence of definite stylistic criteria.

14. דּוּדָאִים (Ca. 7^{14}†)] 𝕲 μῆλα μανδραγόρου, 𝕾 ܝܒܪܘܚܐ, 𝕿^OJ^ יברוחין (= Ar. *yabrūh*, explained to be the *root* of the plant). The sing. is דּוּדַי, from the same √ as דּוֹד, 'lover,' and דּוֹדִים, 'love'; and very probably associated with the love-god דודה (Meša, l. 12). Cheyne plausibly suggests (379) that this deity was worshipped by the Reubenites; hence Reuben is the finder of the apples.—**15**. לָהּ] 𝕲 לֵאָה, 𝕾 לה לאה.—וְלָקַחַת (inf.)] Dri. *T.* § 204; but וְלָקַחַתְּ (pf. f.) would be easier.—**16**. תָּבוֹא] 𝔐𝕲 + הַלַּיְלָה.—בַּלַּיְלָה הוּא] see on 19^{33}.—**17a** is from E; but **17b** probably from

J's lost etymology of Issachar.—**18.** E's interpretation of יִשָּׂשכָר, which is, of course, independent of the story of the mandrakes. The name is resolved either into אִישׁ שָׂכָר, 'man of hire,' or into יֵשׁ שָׂכָר, 'there is a reward' (Tu. Di.); or else the י and quiescent שׁ are simply dropped (Gu.): *v.i.*—**20.** Two etymologies of *Zĕbûlûn*; the first from E (אלהים), and the second, therefore, from J: both are somewhat obscure (*v.i.*).—**21.** *Dînāh*] The absence of an etymology, and the fact that Dinah is excluded from the enumeration of 32^{23}, make it probable that the v. is interpolated with a view to ch. 34.—**22-24.** At last Rachel bears a son, long hoped for and therefore marked out for a brilliant destiny—*Yôsēph*.—**23b, 24b.** E derives the name from אָסַף, 'take away'; J more naturally from יָסַף, 'add': *May Yahwe add to me another son!*

XXX. 25–43.—*Jacob enriched at Laban's Expense* (JE).

Jacob, having accomplished his 14 years of service for his wives, is now in a position to dictate terms to Laban,

---

J, on account of the numeral.—18a*β*, while correctly expressing the idea of E, contains the word שִׁפְחָה, which E avoids; and is therefore probably redactional.—**18b.** יִשָּׂשכָר] So Ben Asher regularly, with *Qrê perp.* יִשָּׂכָר: B. Naphtali has יִשְׂשָׂכָר, or יִשְׂשכָר (see Baer-Del. *Gen.* 84 f.; Ginsburg, *Introd.* 250 ff.). The duplication of the שׂ cannot be disposed of as a Massoretic caprice, and is most naturally explained by the assumption that two components were recognised, of which the first was אִישׁ (We. *TBS*, p. v). For the second component We. refers to the שָׂכָר of 1 Ch. 11^{35} 26^{4}; Ba. compares an Eg. deity *Sokar*; while Mey. (*INS*, 536) is satisfied with the interpretation 'man of hire,' corresponding to the description of the tribe in Gn. $49^{14f.}$.—**20.** זְבָדַנִי, זֶבֶד] The √ (except in proper names) is not found in OT, but is explained by Aram. (cf. ܙܒܕܐ, 'dowry'), and is common in Palm. prop. names (BDB, *s.v.*). The interchange of ל and ד is probably dialectic (cf. *dacrima* = *lacrima*), and hardly justifies Cheyne's view that the name in the writer's mind was זַבְדּוֹן (*l.c.* 380).—יזבלני] Another ἅπ. λεγ. apparently connected with זְבֻל, poet. for 'abode': Vns. 'dwell with' (as EVV). This gives a good enough sense here, and is perhaps supported by 49^{13} (see on the v.); but זְבֻלוּן remains without any natural explanation. See Hogg, in *EB*, 5385 ff. Mey. (538) derives it from the personal name זְבֻל (Ju. 9^{28}).—**21** end] 𝕲 + ותעמד מלדת (as 29^{35}).—**24.** יוֹסֵף] Probably a contraction of יוסף־אל, though the *Yšp'r* of the list of Thothmes III. (No. 78)

who, in his eagerness to keep him, invites him to name the price for which he will remain with him. It is interesting to contrast the relative attitudes of the two men with their bearing in $29^{15\text{ff.}}$ Jacob here shows a decision of purpose which causes Laban to adopt an obsequious tone very unlike his former easy assurance. He is overjoyed to find his nephew's demands so reasonable; and correspondingly mortified (31^{2}) when he discovers how completely he has been deceived by Jacob's apparent moderation.—The story, as Gu. reminds us, was originally told to shepherds, who would follow with keen interest the various tricks of their craft which Jacob so successfully applies (and of which he was probably regarded as the inventor). To more refined readers these details were irksome; hence the abridged and somewhat unintelligible form in which the narrative stands.

Sources.—In the earlier vv. ($^{25-31}$) several duplicates show the composition of J and E: $^{25 \parallel 26a}$; $^{26b \parallel 29a}$; $^{28 \parallel 31a}$; ויאמר in ^{27} and ^{28}; אתה ידעת, ^{26b} and ^{29a}. Here $^{25.\,27.\,29-31}$ are from J (יהוה, $^{27.\,30}$; מָצָא חֵן, ^{27}; בִּגְלַל, ^{27}), and $^{26.\,28}$ from E,—each narrative being nearly complete (cf. Di. Gu. Pro.).—In $^{32-36}$ it is quite possible, in spite of the scepticism of Di. and others, to distinguish two conceptions of Jacob's reward (We. *Comp.*² 40 ff.). (*a*) In the first, Jacob is that very day to take out from Laban's flock all abnormally coloured animals: *that* is to be his hire (^{32}). On the morrow (or in time to come), Laban may inspect Jacob's flock: if he find in it any normally coloured animals, Jacob is at once convicted of fraud (^{33}). This account belongs to E (cf. שְׂכָרִי, ^{32}, with ^{28}), though it is doubtful if to the same stratum of E as 31^{7-12}. (*b*) In the other, Laban himself separates the flocks, leaving the *normally* coloured sheep and goats in Jacob's keeping, and removing the others to a distance of three days' journey, under the charge of his sons ($^{32a\beta}$ [from הָסֵר] $^{35\text{f.}}$). Thus Jacob receives for the present nothing at all (^{31} J). The narrative must have gone on to explain that his hire was to consist of any variegated animals appearing in the normally coloured flock now left in his charge (^{36b}); Laban's precautions aim at securing that these shall be few or none. Hence we obtain for J $^{32a\beta.\,35.\,36}$, and for E $^{32a\alpha\delta b.\,33.\,34}$.—$^{37-45}$ is the natural continuation of J's account, but with numerous insertions, which may be either from variants or glosses.—The text here is very confused, and 𝔊 has many variations.

---

is less confidently identified with Joseph than the companion *Y'ḳb'r* with Jacob (cf. p. 360 above; Mey. *INS*, 262; Spiegelberg, *Randglossen*, 13 f.; Müller, *MVAG*, 1907, i. 23, and *JBL*, 1909, 31). But *Yašupili* has been found in contract tablets of the Ḥammurabi period along with *Yaḳub-ili* (Homm. *AHT*, 96 [from Sayce]).

25–31. Jacob proposes to provide for his own house.—A preliminary parley, in which both parties feel their way to an understanding.—**26** (E). *thou knowest with what kind of service, etc.*] E always lays stress on Jacob's rectitude (cf. ^{33}).—**27** (J). *If I have found favour, etc.*] followed by aposiopesis, as 18^{3} 23^{13}.—Laban continues: *I have taken omens* (נִחַשְׁתִּי; cf. $44^{5.15}$, 1 Ki. 20^{33}) *and* (found that) *Yahwe has blessed me, etc.*]—an abject plea for Jacob's remaining with him.—**28** (E). Laban surrenders at once (the answer is in v.^{32}), whereas— **29, 30** in J, Jacob presses for a discharge: his service has been of immense value to Laban, but he has a family to consider.—**31.** *anything at all*] See introd. note above.—*this thing*] which I am about to mention.—*resume herding thy flock*] G–K. § 120 *g*.

32–36. The new contract.—The point in both narratives is that parti-coloured animals form a very small proportion of a flock, the Syrian sheep being nearly all white (Ca. 4^{2} 6^{6}, Dn. 7^{9}) and the goats black or brown (Ca. 4^{1b}). In E, Jacob simply asks this small share as his payment.—**32.** *and it shall be my hire*] The rendering 'and of this sort shall be my hire' (in future), is merely a violent attempt to obliterate

---

26. ואת־ילדי] Not necessarily a gloss; the children might fairly be considered included in Jacob's wages.—**27.** On נִחַשׁ, *v.* 44^{5}.—בגללך] 𝔊 τῇ σῇ εἰσόδῳ, Arm. *in pede tuo* = לרגלך (^{30}).—**28.** 𝔊𝔙 om. ויאמר, smoothing over the transition from J to E.—נקבה] 'designate' (lit. 'prick [off]'): cf. the use of Niph. in Nu. 1^{17}, 1 Ch. 16^{41} etc.—**29.** את אשר] 'the manner in which' (G–K. § 157 *c*); but 𝔖 reads as in v.^{26}.—**30.** לרגלי] contrasted with לפני above. Prosperity has followed Jacob 'wherever he went' (cf. Is. 41^{2}, Jb. 18^{11} etc.). It is unnecessary to emend בִּגְלָלִי (𝔖𝔗^{O}, Che.).—**31.** אשמר] (𝔊𝔖 pr. וְ) must be deleted on account of its awkward position.

32. אעבר, הסר] To get rid of the change of person (and the division of sources) many construe the latter as inf. abs. ('removing'); but the only natural rendering is impve. (cf. ^{35}). 𝔊 has impve. both times.—כל־שה—עזים] 𝔊 πᾶν πρόβατον φαιὸν ἐν τοῖς ἀρνάσιν καὶ πᾶν διάραντον καὶ λευκὸν ἐν ταῖς αἰξίν, a smoother and therefore less original text. The Heb. seems overloaded; Gu. strikes out וְכָל־שֶׂה־חוּם בַּכְּשָׂבִים, and the corresponding cll. in $^{33.35}$.—נָקֹד וְטָלוּא] 'speckled and spotted,' 'parti-coloured.' The words are practically synonymous, both being distinct from עָקֹד ($^{35.39.40}$ $31^{8.10.12}$†), which means 'striped.' If there be a difference, נ׳ ($^{35.39}$ $31^{8.10.12}$†) suggests smaller spots than ט׳ (cf. Ezk. 16^{16}, Jos. 9^{5}, the only places where the √ occurs outside this pass.).—חום] only in this chap.: = 'black'

the difference between J and E.—**33.** *my righteousness shall testify against me*] *i.e.*, the proposal is so transparently fair that Jacob will be as it were automatically convicted of theft if he violates the compact. צְדָקָה, 'unimpeachable conduct,' here means 'fair dealing,' 'honesty.'—*in time to come*] whenever Laban chooses to make an investigation.—**35, 36** (J). *And he* (Laban, see 32aβ) *removed that day, etc.*] Laban's motive in removing the variegated animals to a distance of three days' journey is obvious; he wishes to reduce to a minimum the chance that any such animals should henceforth be born amongst those now entrusted to Jacob.—*white*] Heb. *lābān*, perhaps a play on Laban's name.

37–43. Jacob's stratagem.—The main account is from J, to whose narrative the artifice is essential, but there are many interpolations.—**37–39.** The first step is to work on the imagination of the females by rods of poplar, etc., peeled in such a way as to show patches of white, and placed in the drinking troughs.—**38, 39.** Removing glosses, J's ac-

---

or 'dark-brown.'—**33.** ענה ב] 'testify against' (see 1 Sa. 12[3], 2 Sa. 1[16], Is. 3[9]). An easier sense would be obtained if we could translate 'witness *for*,' but there seem to be no examples of that usage. Dri.'s interpretation: 'there will be nothing whatever to allege against my honesty,' seems, on the other hand, too subtle.—ביום מחר] 'in time to come' (Ex. 13[14], Dt. 6[20]). If we could insist on the literal rendering 'on the morrow,' the proof of divergence between J and E would be strengthened, but the sense is less suitable.—כי—לפניך] 𝔊 *ὅτι ἐστὶν ὁ μισθός μου ἐνώπιόν σου.*—**36.** בינו] 𝔐𝔊 בינם.—𝔐 follows [36] with a long addition based on 31[11-13].

37. לבנה (Ho 4[13] †)] the 'white' tree; according to some, *populus alba* (Di. al.), but very probably *styrax officinalis* (Ar. *lubnaʸ*, so called from its exuding a *milk*-like gum), (Ges. De. Dri. al.).—לוז †] = Aram. לוּזָא, 'almond tree.'—עַרְמוֹן (Ezk. 31[8] †)] *platanus orientalis* (Ass. *irmeânu*).—Instead of the last three words 𝔊 has *ἐφαίνετο δὲ ἐπὶ ταῖς ῥάβδοις τὸ λευκὸν ὃ ἐλέπισεν ποικίλον,*—a very sensible comment, but hardly original. The whole clause '(with) a laying bare (G–K. § 117 *r*) of the white on the rods,' is superfluous, and certainly looks like a variant.—בהן] pl.; מקל being coll. —**38** ff. The text of J, as sifted by We., commends itself by its lucidity and continuity. It is impossible to tell whether the interpolated words are variants from another source (E?) or explanatory glosses.—**38.** רַהַט (v.[41], Ex. 2[16] †)] either 'trough,' fr. Ar. *rahaṭa*, 'be collected,' or 'runnel,' from Aram. רהט = רוץ (see Nö. *ZA*, xii. 187).—שִׁקְתוֹת] const. pl. of שֹׁקֶת, 24[20] †.—The words בשקתות—לשתות divorce לנכח הצאן from its connexion, and must be omitted from the text of J. 𝔊 appears to have changed

count reads: *And he placed the rods which he had peeled in the runnels . . . in front of the flock, and they bred when they came to drink. . . . And the flock brought forth streaked, speckled, and spotted* (young).

The physiological law involved is said to be well established (Dri.), and was acted on by ancient cattle breeders (see the list of authorities in Bochart, *Hieroz.* ii. c. 49; and cf. Jer. *Quæst. ad loc.*). The full representation seems to be that the ewes saw the reflexion of the rams in the water, blended with the image of the parti-coloured rods, and were deceived into thinking they were coupled with parti-coloured males (Jer., We. *Comp.*[2] 41).

40. *And* (*these*) *lambs Jacob set apart . . . and made separate flocks for himself, and did not add them to Laban's stock* (We.).—**41, 42.** A further refinement: Jacob employed his device only in the case of the sturdy animals, letting the weakly ones gender freely. The difference corresponds to a difference of breeding-time (*v.i.*). The consequence is that Jacob's stock is hardy and Laban's delicate.

XXXI. 1–XXXII. 1.—*Jacob's Flight from Laban: their friendly Parting* (J, E).

Jacob perceives from the altered demeanour of Laban and his sons that he has outstayed his welcome ([1. 2]); and, after consultation with his wives, resolves on a secret flight ([3–21]). Laban pursues, and overtakes him at Mt. Gilead ([22–25]), where, after a fierce altercation ([26–43]), they enter into a treaty

---

ויחמנה הצאן to המקלות, rendering thus ([38b]) *ἵνα ὡς ἂν ἔλθωσιν τὰ πρόβατα πιεῖν, ἐνώπιον τῶν ῥάβδων* [*καὶ*] *ἐλθόντων αὐτῶν εἰς τὸ πιεῖν, ἐνκισσήσωσιν* ([39]) *τὰ πρόβατα*.—וַיֵּחַמְנָה] On the unusual pref. of 3 f. pl., see G–K. § 47 *k*.—**39a** is a doublet to the last three words of [38].—ויחמו] *ib.* § 69 *f*; ויחמנה ﬡ.—**40.** 'He set the faces of the flock towards a (*sic*) streaked and every dark one in Laban's flock,' is an imperfect text, and an impossible statement in J, where Laban's cattle are three days distant. 𝔊 vainly tries to make sense by omitting לָבָן, and rendering פְּנֵי = *ἐναντίον*, and אֶל־עָקֹד = *κριὸν* (אַיִל!) *διάλευκον*.—**41.** בכל־] 𝔊𝔖𝔗^O supply עֵת.—**42.** העטפים, הקשרים] 𝔊 *ἐπίσημα, ἄσημα*; but Σ. (paraphrasing) *πρώϊμα ὄψιμα*, and similarly Aq. 𝔙𝔖𝔗^O. It is the fact that the stronger sheep conceived in summer and yeaned in winter, while the weaker conceived in autumn and yeaned in the spring: Pliny, *HN*, viii. 187 ('postea concepti invalidi').

of peace (from which Gilead receives its name), and separate with many demonstrations of goodwill (31^{44}–32^{1}).

Sources.—[1-16] is an almost homogeneous (though perhaps not continuous) excerpt from E: אלהים, [7. 9. 11. 16]; מַשְׂכֹּרֶת, [7] (cf. [41] 29^{15}); מֹנִים, [7] ([41]); מַצֵּבָה, [13]; the revelation by dream, [10f.]; the summons and answer, [11] ($22^{1. 7. 11}$); and the explanation of Jacob's wealth [7ff.]; cf. also the reference to 28^{20-22}. [1] and [3] are from a J parallel: יהוה, [3]; מוֹלַדְתֶּךָ, [3]; the 'sons' of Laban, [1] (cf. 30^{35}).—In [17-54] E still preponderates, though J is more largely represented than some critics (Di. Kue. KS. Dri. al.) allow. The detailed analysis is here very intricate, and will be best dealt with under the several sections.—[18] (except the first four words) is the only extract from P.

1–16. Preparations for flight.—1, 3 (J). The jealousy of Laban's sons corresponds to the dark looks of Laban himself in E (v.[2]); the divine communication is a feature of both narratives (v.[13]).—**4–13.** Jacob vindicates his conduct towards Laban, and sets forth the reasons for his projected flight. The motive of the speech is not purely literary, affording the writer an opportunity to express his belief in Jacob's righteousness (Gu.); it is first of all an appeal to the wives to accompany him: comp. the question to Rebekah in 24^{58}. —**6.** *Ye yourselves know, etc.*] Cf. $30^{26. 29}$. But to repeat the protestation after the work of the last six years implies great hardihood on Jacob's part; and rather suggests that the passage belongs to a stratum of E which said nothing about his tricks with the flock.—**7.** *changed my wages ten times*] Perhaps a round number, not to be taken literally.—**8.** A sample of Laban's tergiversations, and their frustration by God's providence.—**9.** *And so God has taken away, etc.*] The hand of God has been so manifest that Laban's displeasure is altogether unreasonable.—**10–12.** Jacob receives through a dream the explanation of the singular good fortune that has attended him.

In the text vv.[10-12] form part of the same revelation as that in which Jacob is commanded to depart ([13]). But, as We. (*Comp.*[2] 39) asks, "How

---

2. אינֶנּו] 𝔐 אינם (so v.[5]).—**6.** אתנה] only here and thrice in Ezk. (cf. G–K. § 32 *i*).—**7.** והחלף] 𝔐 ויחלף.—עשרת מֹנִים] 𝔊 ('nescio qua opinione ducti' [Jer.]) *τῶν δέκα ἀμνῶν* (so [41]—probably a transliteration, afterwards made into a Gr. word). מֹנִים ([41]†) from $\sqrt{}$ מנה, 'count,' for the usual פְּעָמִים.—אלהים] 𝔐 יהוה (so [9. 16a]).—**9.** את־] 𝔊 אֶת־כָּל־.—אביכם] for אביכן (𝔐);

could two such dissimilar revelations be coupled together in this way?" V.[10] recalls an incident of the past, while [13] is in the sphere of the present: moreover, 'I am the God of Bethel' must surely open the communication. We. solves the difficulty by removing [10] and [12] (assigning them to an unknown source), and leaving [11] as the introduction to [13]: similarly Di. Ho. *OH.* al. Gu. supposes parts of Jacob's speech to have been omitted between [9] and [10] and between [12] and [13].—It is scarcely possible to recover the original sense of the fragment. If the dream had preceded the negotiations with Laban, it might have been a hint to Jacob of the kind of animals he was to ask as his hire (Str. Gu.); but that is excluded by [12b]; and, besides, in v.[8] it is Laban who fixes the terms of the contract. We can only understand it vaguely as an assurance to Jacob that against all natural expectations the transaction will be overruled to his advantage.

13. *I am the God of Bethel*] links this theophany with that of 28[10ff.], and is (in E) the first assurance given to Jacob that his vow (28[20–22]) had been accepted.—**14–16.** Jacob's appeal has been addressed to willing ears: his wives are already alienated from their father, and eagerly espouse their husband's cause.—**14b.** Comp. 2 Sa. 20[1], 1 Ki. 12[16].—**15.** *has sold us*] like slaves.—*consumed our money*] *i.e.*, the price paid for us (cf. Ex. 21[35]). The complaint implies that it was considered a mark of meanness for a man to keep the *mōhar* for himself instead of giving it to his daughters. A similar change in the destination of the *mahr* appears in Arabia before Islam (We. *GGN*, 1893, 434 f.).—**16.** *is ours*

G–K. § 135 *o*.—**13.** האל ביתאל] The art. with constr. violates a well known rule of syntax (G–K. § 127*f*); and it is doubtful if the anomaly be rightly explained by supposing the ellipsis of אֵל or אֱלֹהֵי. The original text may have been הָאֵל [הַנִּרְאָה אֵלֶיךָ בִּמְקוֹם] בֵּיתְאֵל; (so [but without ביתאל] 𝔊, adopted by Ba.); or האל[—ב]ביתאל (𝔗^OJ, Kit.).—ארץ מולדתך] see on 11[28]. It is the only occurrence of מ׳ in E.—𝔊 adds καὶ ἔσομαι μετὰ σοῦ.—**15.** נכריות] 𝔐𝔊𝔖𝔙 כְּנָ׳.—גם אכול] see on 27[33].—**16.** עשר] 𝔊 + καὶ τὴν δόξαν.

17–25. A complete analysis of the vv. cannot be effected. The hand of E is recognised in [19b] (תְּרָפִים, cf. [30] 35[2ff.]), [20] (? הָאֲרַמִּי, as [24]), and especially [24] (אלהים, חֲלֹם; cf. [29. 42]). J betrays its presence chiefly by doublets: [21aβ] ‖ [17] (וַיָּקָם), and [25a] ‖ [23b] (וַיַּשֵּׂג, וַיַּדְבֵּק). The assignment of [21aβ] to J is warranted by the mention of the Euphrates: hence [17] is E. Further than this we cannot safely go. Gu.'s division ([19a. 21-23. 25b] = J; [17. 18aα. 19b. 20. 24. 25a] = E) is open to the objection that it ignores the discrepancy between the seven days of [23a] and the crossing of the Euphrates in [21a] (see on [23] above); but is otherwise attractive. Mey. (235 ff.) gets rid of the geographical difficulty by distinguishing two strata in E, of which the later had been accommodated to the representation of J.—[18] (from

and our children's] E never mentions sons of Laban; and apparently looks on Leah and Rachel as the sole heiresses.

17-25. The flight and pursuit.—**18.** *and drove away all his cattle*] Hence the slowness of his march as compared with Laban's (33^{13b}).—The rest of the v. is from P (cf. 12^{5} 36^{6} 46^{6}).—*to Isaac his father*] 35^{27}.—**19.** *Now Laban had gone to shear his flock*] Sheep-shearing was the occasion of an important festival in ancient Israel ($38^{12ff.}$, 1 Sa. $25^{2ff.}$, 2 Sa. 13^{23}).—With Rachel's theft of the *tĕrāphîm* (the household idol: *v.i.*), cf. Virg. *Aen.* ii. 293 f., iii. 148 f.—**20.** *stole the heart*] (^{26}, 2 Sa. 15^{6}†) 'deceived'; the heart being the seat of intelligence (Ho. 4^{11}): cf. ἔκλεψε νόον, *Il.* xiv. 217.—*the Aramæan* (only here and ^{24})] The emphasising of Laban's nationality at this point is hard to explain. That it is the correction (by E^2) of an older version (E^1), in which Laban was not an Aramæan (Mey. *INS*, 236), is not probable. Bu. (*Urg.* 422^{1}) regards it as a gloss, inserted with a view to v.^{47}—**21.** *crossed the River* (J)] the Euphrates (Ex. 23^{31}, Jos. 24^{2} etc.).—**23.** *his brethren*] his fellow-clansmen. In the sequel Jacob also is surrounded by his clansmen ($^{37.\ 46.\ 54}$),— a proof that tribal relations are clothed in the guise of individual biography.—*seven days' journey*] The distance of Gilead from Ḥarran

---

(וְאֶת־כָּל־רְכֻשׁוֹ) is obviously P.—**17.** *sons and wives*] 𝔐𝔊 'wives and sons.'—18. 𝔊 om. the cl. אֲשֶׁר—קִנְיָנוֹ (so 𝔖); and adds after אֲרָם, καὶ πάντα τὰ αὐτοῦ.—**19.** תְּרָפִים] A pl. of eminence, like אֱלֹהִים, etc.; hence it is doubtful whether one image or several is here referred to. The teraphim was a god (^{30}), its form and size were those of a man (1 Sa. $19^{13.\ 16}$), it was used in private houses as well as in temples (Ju. 17^{5} $18^{14ff.}$, Ho. 3^{4}), and was an implement of divination (Ezk. 21^{26}, Zec. 10^{2}). The indications point to its being an emblem of ancestor-worship which survived in Israel as a private superstition, condemned by the enlightened conscience of the nation (35^{2}, 1 Sa. 15^{23}, 2 Ki. 23^{24}). It seems implied by the present narrative that the cult was borrowed from the Aramæans, or perhaps rather that it had existed before the separation of Hebrews and Aramæans. (See Moore, *Jud.* 379 ff.)—**20.** עַל־בְּלִי] ἅπ. λεγ., is difficult. על for על אשר is rare and poet. (Ps. 119^{136}: BDB, 758 a); בלי (poet. for לא) is also rare with fin. vb. (*ib.* 115 b). Since the following clause is a specification of the preceding, 'wegen Mangels davon dass' (Di.) is not a suitable rendering. We should expect לְבִלְתִּי הַגִּיד, 'in not telling him that,' etc.: 𝔐 has עד בלתי.—**22.** ללבן] 𝔊 + τῷ Σύρῳ.

(*c.* 350 miles as the crow flies) is much too great to be traversed in that time.

If the v. be from J (Gu. Pro.), we must assume (what is no doubt conceivable) that the writer's geographical knowledge was defective. But it is a strong reason for assigning the v. to E, that in that source nothing is said of Ḥarran or the Euphrates, and Laban's home is placed somewhere in the eastern desert (see 29^{1}).

24. God (not the Angel of God, as v.^{11}) warns Laban in a dream to take heed to his words when he encounters Jacob.—*good or bad*] 'anything whatever' (24^{50}, 2 Sa. 13^{22} etc.). Laban did not interpret the prohibition literally (^{29}).—**25.** *in the mountain* . . .] The idea suggested being that Jacob and Laban encamped each on a different mountain, we must suppose the name to have been omitted. The insertion of *Miẓpāh* (v.^{49}) is strongly recommended by Ju. 10^{17} (see Ball, 88).—On the situation of *Mount Gilead*, see p. 402 f.

26–43. The altercation.

The subjects of recrimination are: on Laban's part, (*a*) the secret flight, (*b*) the carrying off of his daughters, and (*c*) the theft of his god; on Jacob's part, (*d*) the hardships of his 20 years' service, and (*e*) the attempts to defraud him of his hire. Of these, *b*, *c*, and *e* certainly belong to E; *a* and *d* more probably to J.—In detail, the vv. that can be confidently assigned to E are: ^{26} (גָּנַב לֵב, as ^{20}), ^{28} (continuation of ^{26}), ^{29} (cf. ^{24}), $^{30.\ 32\text{-}35}$ (תרפים), ^{41} ('ten times'), ^{42} (cf. $^{24.\ 29}$) and ^{43} (because of the connexion with $^{26.\ 28}$): note also אֱלֹהִים, $^{29.\ 42}$; אָמָה, ^{33}. The sequence of E is interrupted by $^{27\ (\parallel 26).\ 31b}$ (the natural answer to ^{27}), $^{36a\ (\parallel 36b)}$: these clauses are accordingly assigned to J; along with $^{38\text{-}40}$ (a parallel to $^{41f.}$). The analysis (which is due to Gu.) yields for E a complete narrative: $^{26.\ 28\text{-}31a.\ 32\text{-}35.\ 36b.\ 37.\ 41\text{-}43}$. The Yahwistic parallel is all but complete ($^{27.\ 31a.\ b.\ 36a.\ 38\text{-}40}$); but we miss something after ^{31} to account for Jacob's exasperation in ^{36}. We may suppose (with Gu.) that Laban had accused Jacob of stealing his flocks, and that $^{38\text{-}40}$ is a reply to this charge.—Procksch's division is slightly different.

26–28. Laban offers a sentimental pretext for his warlike demonstration: in E his slighted affection for his offspring (^{28}); in J his desire to honour a parting guest (^{27}).—**27.** *with mirth and music*] This manner of speeding the parting guest

---

25. אחיו] Better אֹהֳלוֹ (Ba.).—**26, 27.** 𝔊 om. ותגנב את־לבבי, and transp. $^{27a.\ 26b}$.—**27.** ולא] 𝔊 וְלֹא, which is perhaps better than MT.—**28.** נטש] usually 'reject' or 'abandon'; only here = 'allow.'—עשו] for עֲשׂוֹת (G-K.

is not elsewhere mentioned in OT.—**29**. *It is in my power* (*v.i.*) *to do you harm*]—but for the interposition of God.—**30**. *Thou hast gone off forsooth, because forsooth, etc.*] The infs. abs. express irony (Dav. § 86).—*stolen my god*(*s*)] This is a serious matter, and leads up to the chief scene of the dispute.—**32**. Jacob is so sure of the innocence of his household that he offers to give up the culprit to death if the theft can be proved: a similar enhancement of dramatic interest in $44^{9ff.}$.—**33–35**. The search for the teraphim is described with a touch of humour, pointed with sarcasm at a prevalent form of idolatry.—**34**. Rachel had hidden the idol in the *camel's litter* or palanquin (Burck. *Bed.* ii. 85; Doughty, *Ar. Des.* i. 437, ii. 304; BDB, 1124), in which she was apparently resting within the tent, on account of her condition.—**35**. דֶּרֶךְ נָשִׁים = אֹרַח כַּנָּשִׁים (18^{11}, J). Women in this condition were protected by a powerful taboo (cf. Lv. 15^{19} etc.).—**36, 37**. Jacob now turns on Laban, treating the accusation about the teraphim as mere pretext for searching his goods.—**38–40** (J). A fine picture of the ideal shepherd, solicitous for his master's interests, sensitive to the least suspicion of fraud, and careless of his personal comfort.—**39**. *I brought not to thee*] as a witness (Ex. 22^{12}). Jacob had thus gone far beyond his legal obligation.—*made it good*] lit. 'counted it

---

§ 75 *n*.—**29**. יֶשׁ־לְאֵל יָדִי] Mic. 2^1, Pr. 3^{27}, Sir. 5^1 (Dt. 28^{32}, Neh. 5^5). The meaning is certain ('be within one's power'), but the expression is very obscure. The current explanations (both represented in the Vns.) are: (1) That אֵל is an abstract noun = 'power,' and יָדִי gen. (2) That יָדִי is subj. of the sent. and אֵל the word for God: 'my hand is for a God.' The first depends on a singular sense of אֵל; and for the second יש לי ידי לאל would have been more natural. A third view has recently been propounded by Brockelmann (*ZATW*, xxvi. 29 ff.), who renders 'it belongs to the God of my hand,' a survival of a primitive belief in special deities or spirits animating different members of the body (cf. Tylor, *Prim. Cult.*[4] ii. 127).—אביכם, עמכם] 𝔐𝔊 have sing. suff.—**30**. אביך] 𝔊 + ἀπελθεῖν· *καί*. The ו should probably be restored.—**31**. 𝔊 om. כי יראתי.—**32**. The opening words in 𝔊 וַיֹּאמֶר לוֹ יַעֲקֹב may be original, introducing the duplicate from E.—32b is preceded in 𝔊 by the variant *καὶ οὐκ ἐπέγνω παρ' αὐτῷ οὐθέν*.—**33**. לבן] 𝔐 + ויחבש (rd. ויחפש); so 𝔊.—The cl. $^{33a\beta}$ disagrees with what follows, and may be a gloss. 𝔊 reduces the discrepancy by omissions, and a complete rearrangement of clauses.—**36**. מַה[2]] Rd. וּמַה with Heb. MSS 𝔐𝔊𝔖.—**39**. On אֲחַטֶּנָּה for אֲחַטְּאֶנָּה, cf. G-K. § 74 *k* or

missing.'—40. *heat by day and frost by night*] Jer. 36[30]. Under the clear skies of the East the extreme heat of the day is apt to be followed by intense cold at night (see Smith, *HG*, 69 ff.).—**41, 42** (E). *the Fear of Isaac*] The deity feared and worshipped by Isaac ([53]†). That פַּחַד יִצְחָק meant originally the terror *inspired* by Isaac, the local deity of Beersheba (Meyer, *INS*, 254 f.), is a hazardous speculation.—**43.** Laban maintains his right, but speedily adopts a more pathetic tone, leading on to the pacific proposal of [44].—The question *what shall I do to . . .?*] means 'what last kindness can I show them?' (Gu. Dri.); not 'how can I do them harm?' (Di. and most).

44–54. The treaty of Gilead.

Evidences of a double recension appear in every circumstance of the narrative. (*a*) *Two* names are explained: Gilead ([48b]), and Mizpāh ([49a]); (*b*) *two* sacred monuments are erected, a cairn ([46. 48. 51. 52]), and a monolith ([45. 51. 52]); (*c*) the covenant feast is *twice* recorded ([46b. 54]); (*d*) the terms of the covenant are given in *two* forms: (1) Jacob will not ill-treat Laban's daughters ([50]), and (2) the cairn is to mark the boundary between two peoples ([52]); (*e*) God is *twice* called to witness ([49f. 53]). To arrange these duplicates in two parallel series is difficult, because of the numerous glosses and dislocations of the text; but some connecting lines can be drawn. Since J always avoids the word מַצֵּבָה (p. 378), we assume first of all that the monolith (and consequently *Mizpāh*) belongs to E, and the cairn to J. Now the cairn goes with the *frontier* treaty ([51. 52] [removing glosses], J), and Mizpāh with the *family* compact ([49], E). To J we must obviously assign [46. 48], and also (if we may suppose that only the גַּל was spoken of as an עֵד) [44]; while E as naturally claims [45]. At the end, [53b] is E (פחד יצ׳, cf. [42]), and likewise [54] (the feast, ‖ [46], J). [53a] is probably J: note the difference of divine names. Thus: [44. 46. 48. 51-53a] = J; [45. 49. 50. 53b. 54] = E.—The analysis is due to Ho. and Gu.; Pro. practically agrees, with the important difference that the parts of J and E are (quite wrongly, as it seems to me) interchanged. It is superior to the schemes of We. Di. KS. al., which assign the cairn and the mazzebāh to the same sources.—The principal glosses (many of which excite suspicion apart from the analysis) are יעקב in [45] and [46];

---

75 *oo*.—גנבתי יום וג׳ לילה is probably an archaic technical phrase, preserving an old case-ending (G–K. § 90 *l*).—40. On the syntax, see G–K. § 143 *a*.—41. *These twenty years*] The repetition (v.[38]) would, as Di. says, not be surprising in animated speech; and is not of itself evidence of a change of source. But Jacob's oratory is more dignified if relieved of this slight touch of affectation.—זה] not here a pron. but used adverbially, as 27[36] etc. (see BDB, 261 b).—**42.** אלהי אברהם may be a gloss (Gu.): 𝔊 om. אלהי.

vv.[47. 49aα] ; והנה המצבה in [51] ; ועדה המצבה and ואת־המצבה הזאת in [52] : on these *v.i.* Nearly all are retained by 𝔊, where, however, the confusion is increased by a complete change in the order of clauses : [48a. 47. 51. 52a. 48b. 49. 50a. 52b], —[50b] being inserted after [44].—The analysis works out in translation as follows (glosses being enclosed in square brackets, and necessary additions and corrections in ⌜ ⌝) :

J : [44] And now (the speaker is Laban), come, let us make a covenant, I and thou ; . . . and it shall be for a witness between me and thee. [46] And ⌜he⌝ (*i.e.* Laban) [Jacob], said to his brethren, Gather stones ; and they took stones, and made a cairn, and they ate there upon the cairn. [[47] And Laban called it *Yᵉgar Sāhădûthā*, but Jacob called it *Galʿēd.*] [48] And Laban said, This cairn is a witness between me and thee this day ; therefore he called its name ⌜Gilʿad⌝ [[49aα] and Miẓpah, for he said]. [51] And Laban said to Jacob, Behold this cairn [and behold the pillar] which I have thrown up between me and thee—[52] a witness is this cairn [and a witness is the pillar] : I will not pass this cairn to thee, and thou shalt not pass this cairn [and this pillar] to me, with evil intent. [53a] The God of Abraham and the God of Naḥor be Judge between us ! [the God of their father].

E : [45] And ⌜he⌝ (*i.e.* Laban) [Jacob] took a stone and set it up as a pillar. [49aβb] ⌜and he said⌝, May ⌜God⌝ [Yahwe] watch between me and thee, when we are hidden from one another. [50] If thou ill-treat my daughters, or take other wives besides my daughters, no man being with us, see, God is witness between me and thee. [53b] And Jacob swore by the Fear of his father Isaac. [54] And Jacob offered a sacrifice on the mountain and called his brethren to eat bread ; and they ate bread, and spent the night on the mountain.

44. Cf. $21^{23ff.}$ $26^{28ff.}$—The subj. of וְהָיָה cannot be בְּרִית, which is fem., and is rather the fact to be witnessed to than a witness of something else. There must be a lacuna before והיה, where we must suppose that some material object (probably the cairn : cf. [48], J) was mentioned.—45 (E). *And he took a stone*] Since it is Laban who explains the meaning of the stone ([49]), it must have been he who set it up ; hence יַעֲקֹב is to be deleted as a false explication of the implicit

44b. The omitted words (*v.s.*) might be וְנַעֲשֶׂה גַל or some such expression (Ols. Di. Ba. Gu. al.). To the end of the v. 𝔊 appends : *εἶπεν δὲ αὐτῷ* Ἰακ., Ἰδοὺ *οὐθεὶς μεθ' ἡμῶν ἐστίν· ἴδε ὁ θεὸς μάρτυς ἀνὰ μέσον ἐμοῦ καὶ*

subj.—*set it on high as a mazzebāh*] see 28[18. 22]. The monolith may have stood on an eminence and formed a conspicuous feature of the landscape (Di.).—46 (J). *And he* (Laban) *said, etc.*] Here יַעֲקֹב is certainly wrong, for Laban expressly says that the cairn was raised by him ([51]).—*a cairn*] גַּל means simply a heap of stones (*v.i.*), not a rampart (We. Di.). The idea that the גַּל was originally the mountain range of Gilead itself, Laban and Jacob being conceived as giants (We. Gu. Mey.), has certainly no support in the text.—*they ate upon the cairn*] The covenant feast, which may very well have preceded the covenant ceremony; see 26[30].—47. In spite of its interesting and philologically correct notice, the v. must unfortunately be assigned to a glossator, for the reasons given below.—48 (J). Laban explains the purpose of the cairn, and names it accordingly: *cairn of witness.*] The stone heap is personified, and was no doubt in ancient times regarded as animated by a deity (cf. Jos. 24[27]). גַּלְעֵד is, of course, an artificial formation, not the real or original pronunciation of גִּלְעָד.—49 (E). *And* [*the*] *Mizpāh, for he said*] The text, if not absolutely ungrammatical, is a very

---

σοῦ (fr. v.[50]).—46. ויקחו] 𝔊 וַיְלַקְּטוּ.—גַּל] From √ גלל 'roll' (stones, 29[3], Jos. 10[18], 1 Sa. 14[33], Pr. 26[27]). On sacred stone-heaps among the Arabs, see We. *Heid.*[2] 111 f. (with which cf. Doughty, *Ar. Des.* i. 26, 81, 431); Curtiss, *PSR*, 80 (cairn as witness); on the eating *upon* the cairn, Frazer, *Folklore in OT*, 131 ff. — 47. יְגַר שָׂהֲדוּתָא is the precise Aramaic equivalent of Heb. גַּל עֵד, 'heap of witness.' The decisive reasons for rejecting the v. are: (1) It stands out of its proper place, anticipating [48b]; (2) it contradicts [48b], where the *Heb.* name גַּלְעֵד is given by Laban; (3) it assumes (contrary to the implication of all the patriarchal narratives) that the Naḥorites spoke a different dialect from the ancestors of the Hebrews. It may be added that the Aram. phrase shows the glossator to have taken גַּלְעֵד as const. and gen., whereas the latter in [48b] is more probably a sent. 'the heap is witness' (see Nestle, *MM*, 10 f.). The actual name [הַ]גִּלְעָד is usually, but dubiously, explained by Ar. *ǧal'ad* 'hard,' 'firm.'—48. על־כן קרא שמו] so 11[9] 19[22] 29[34f.] (all J), 25[30] (J ?).—49. וְהַמִּצְפָּה] 𝔖 והמצבה, which We. thinks the original name of the place, afterwards changed to המצפה because of the evil associations of the word maẓẓebāh. He instances the transcription of 𝔊 Μασσηφα, as combining the consonants of the new name with the vowels of the old (*Comp.*[2] 44[1]). The argument is precarious; but there seems to be a word-play between the names; and since the opening is evidently corrupt, it is possible that both stood in the text. Ball's restoration והמצבה אשר [הֵרִים

uncouth continuation of [48b], with which in the primary documents it had nothing to do; see further *inf.*—*May God* (read so with 𝔊) *watch*] Miẓpāh means 'watch-post.' On its situation, see p. 403.—**50.** The purport of the covenant, according to E. Jacob swears ([53b]) that he will not maltreat Laban's daughters, nor even marry other wives besides them. The latter stipulation has a parallel in a late Babylonian marriage contract (*KIB*, iv. 187, No. XI.).—*God is witness*] The idea is less primitive than that of J, where the witness is an inanimate object.—We observe how the religious sanction is invoked where human protection fails (cf. 20^{11} 42^{18}, both E).—**51–53a.** The terms of the covenant in J: neither party (people) is to pass the cairn with hostile intent. All the reff. to the maẓẓebāh ([51b. 52a. b]) are to be deleted as glosses. — *The God of Abraham . . . Nāḥôr*] Whether a polytheistic differentiation of two gods is attributed to Laban can hardly be determined. The pl. vb. would not necessarily imply this in E (see 20^{13}), though in J it might.—**53b, 54.** The covenant oath and feast in E.—*The Fear of . . . Isaac*] See on v.[42].—**54.** *his brethren*] not Laban and his companions, but his own fellow-clansmen (v.[37]).—*spent the night, etc.*] Is this part of the religious ceremony? (Gu.).

The Scene of the Treaty.—The name *Gil'ād* (often with art.) in OT is sometimes applied to the whole region E of the Jordan (Jos. 22^9 etc.), but more properly denotes the mountain range (הַר הַגִּלְעָד) extending from

---

אמר [קָרָא הַמִּצְפָּה כִּי] has met with the approval of several scholars (Ho. Str.); but as the sequence to [45] we should rather expect וַיִּקְרָא שְׁמָהּ הַמִּצְפָּה. 𝔊 has καὶ Ἡ ὅρασις, ἣν εἶπεν, following MT.—יהוה] 𝔊 אלהים must be adopted if the v. is rightly ascribed to E.—51. המצבה] 𝔊 + הַזֹּאת (so v.[52]).—אשר יריתי] 'which I have thrown up.' ירה, 'throw,' is most commonly used of shooting arrows, and only here of piling up stones. Once it means to lay (*jacere*) a foundation (Jb. 38^6), but it could hardly be applied to the erection of a pillar. It is an advantage of the analysis given above that it avoids the necessity of retaining the maẓẓebāh as obj. of יריתי and rejecting the cairn.—52. אם—לא (*bis*)] The double negative is contrary to the usage of asseverative sentt. (cf. [50]), but may be explained by an anakolouthon (G–K. § 167 *b*). — את־הגל הזה] 𝔊 om. — 53. ישפטו] ɯɯ𝔊𝔙𝔖 יִשְׁפֹּט.—אלהי אביהם] 𝔊 and Heb. MSS om., ɯɯ א' אברהם, 𝔖 ܠܗܘܢ. Probably a marg. gloss to [53a].—XXXII. 1. וילך וישב] 𝔊 וַיָּשָׁב וַיֵּלֶךְ.

the Yarmuk to the Arnon (2 Ki. 10^{33} etc.), divided by the Jabboḳ into two parts (Jos. 12^{2}), corresponding to the modern *Ğebel 'Ağlūn* and *el-Belḳā*, N and S respectively of the Wādī ez-Zerḳā. The name *Ğebel Ğil'ād* still survives as that of a mountain, crowned by the lofty summit of *Ğebel Ōsha'*, N of es-Salṭ, where are found the ruined cities *Ğil'ād* and *Ğal'aud* (Burckh. *Syria*, 348). It is therefore natural to look here in the first instance for the 'cairn of witness' from which the mountain and the whole region were supposed to have derived their names. The objections to this view are (1) that Jacob, coming from the N, has not yet crossed the Jabboḳ, which is identified with the Zerḳa; and (2) that the frontier between Israel and the Aramæans (of Damascus) could not have been so far S. These reasons have prevailed with most modern authorities, and led them to seek a site somewhere in the N or NE of Ğ. 'Ağlūn. But the assumption that Laban represents the Aramæans of Damascus is gratuitous, and has no foundation in either J or E (see the next note). The argument from the direction of Jacob's march applies only to J, and must not be too rigorously pressed; because the treaty of Gilead and the crossing of the Jabboḳ belong to different cycles of tradition, and the desire to finish off Jacob's dealings with Laban before proceeding to his encounter with Esau might very naturally occasion a departure from strict geographical consistency.*—The site of *Miẓpāh* has to be investigated separately, since we cannot be certain that J and E thought of the same locality. E of the Jordan there was a Miẓpāh (Ju. 10^{17} $11^{11.\,34}$, Ho. 5^{1}) which is thought to be the same as מִצְפֵּה גִלְעָד (Ju. 11^{29}) and רָמַת הַמִּצְפֶּה (Jos. 13^{26}); but whether it lay S or N of the Jabboḳ cannot be determined. The identification with Rāmôth-Gil'ād, and of this with *er-Remte*, SW of the ancient Edrei, is precarious. The name ('watch-post') was a common one, and may readily be supposed to have occurred more than once E of the Jordan. See Smith, *HG*, 586; Buhl, *GP*, 262; Driver in smaller *DB*, *s.v.*; and on the whole of this note, cf. Smend, *ZATW*, 1902, 149 ff.

Historical Background of 31^{44-54}. — The treaty of Gilead in J evidently embodies ethnographic reminiscences, in which Jacob and Laban were not private individuals, but represented Hebrews and Aramæans respectively. The theory mostly favoured by critical historians is that the Aramæans are those of Damascus, and that the

---

* It seems to me very doubtful how far Jacob's route, as described in chs. 32, 33, can be safely used as a clue to the identification of the localities mentioned (Gilead, Miẓpah, Maḥanaim, the Ford, Peniel, Succoth). The writers appear to have strung together a number of Transjordanic legends connected with the name of Jacob, but without much regard to topographical consistency or consecutiveness (see p. 408). The impossibility of the current identifications (*e.g.* those of Merrill and Conder), *as stages of an actual itinerary*, is clearly shown by Dri. in *ET*, xiii. (1902), 457 ff. It is only when that assumption is frankly abandoned that the identification of Gilead with *Ğil'ād*, of Mahanaim with *Maḥne* (p. 405), of the Ford with *Muḫādat en-Nuṣrānīyeh* (p. 408), becomes feasible.

situation reflected is that of the Syrian wars which raged from *c.* 860 to *c.* 770 B.C. (see We. *Prol.*[6] 320 f.). Gu. (p. 312) has, however, pointed out objections to this assumption; and has given strong reasons for believing that the narratives refer to an earlier date than 860. The story reads more like the record of a loose understanding between neighbouring and on the whole friendly tribes, than of a formal treaty between two highly organised states like Israel and Damascus; and it exhibits no trace of the intense national animosity which was generated during the Syrian wars. In this connexion, Meyer's hypothesis that in the original tradition Laban represented the early unsettled nomads of the eastern desert (see p. 334), acquires a new interest. Considering the tenacity with which such legends cling to a locality, there is no difficulty in supposing that in this case the tradition goes back to some prehistoric settlement of territorial claims between Hebrews and migratory Aramæans. It is true that Meyer's theory is based on notices peculiar to E, while the tribal compact belongs to J; and it may appear hazardous to go behind the documents and build speculations on a substratum of tradition common to both. But the only material point in which J differs from E is his identification of Laban with the Aramæans of Ḥarran; and this is not inconsistent with the interpretation here suggested. In any case, his narrative gives no support to the opinion that he has in view the contemporary political relations with the kingdom of Damascus.

XXXII. 2–33.—*Jacob's Measures for propitiating Esau: His Wrestling with the Deity at Peniel* (J, E).

After a vision of angels at Maḥanaim ([2. 3]), Jacob sends a humble message announcing his arrival to Esau, but learns to his consternation that his brother is advancing to meet him with 400 men ([4–7]). He divides his company into two bands, and invokes God's help in prayer ([8–14a]); then prepares a present for Esau, and sends it on in advance ([14b–22]). Having thus done all that human foresight could suggest, he passes a lonely night in the ravine of the Jabboḳ, wrestling with a mysterious antagonist, who at daybreak blesses him and changes his name to Israel ([23–33]).

Sources.—Vv.[2. 3] are an isolated fragment of E (מלאכי אלהים, פָּגַע בְּ [28[11]]); [4-14a] and [14b-22] are parallels (cf. [14a] with [22b]), the former from J (יהוה, [10]; שפחה, [6]; מולדת, [10]; מצא חן, [6]; ct. the implied etymology of מַחֲנַיִם in [8. 9. 11] with E's in [3]): [14b-22] must therefore be E, though positive marks of that writer's style cannot be detected.—On the complicated structure of [23-33] (JE), see p. 407 below.

2, 3. The legend of Maḥanaim.—**2.** *angels . . . met him*] The verb for 'meet,' as here construed (*v.i.*), usually means to 'oppose.'—**3.** *This is God's camp*] or *a camp of gods*. The idea of divine armies appears elsewhere in OT (cf. Jos. 5^{14}), and perhaps underlies the expression 'Host of heaven' and the name *Yahwe Ẓebā'ôth*.—*Maḥanaim* is here apparently not regarded as a dual (ct. $^{8.\,9.\,11}$). On its site, *v.i.*

The brief statement of the text seems to be a torso of a legend which had gathered round the name Maḥanaim, whose original meaning has been lost. The curtailment probably indicates that the sequel was objectionable to the religious feeling of later times; and it has been surmised that the complete story told of a conflict between Jacob and the angels (originally divine beings), somewhat similar to the wrestling of vv.$^{24ff.}$ (Gu. Ben.). The word 'camp' (cf. the fuller text of 𝕲 *inf.*), and the verbal phrase פגע ב both suggest a warlike encounter.

4–14a. Jacob's precautionary measures (J).— **4.** Isaac's death and Esau's settlement in the country afterwards occupied by his descendants are here assumed to have already taken place: otherwise P (36^6).—**5, 6.** We note the extreme servility of Jacob's language:—*my lord . . . thy servant . . . find grace*,—dictated by fear of his brother's vengeance (27^{41}). In substance the message is

---

2. After לדרכו 𝕲 ins. *καὶ ἀναβλέψας τοῖς ὀφθαλμοῖς ἴδεν παρεμβολὴν θεοῦ παρεμβεβληκυῖαν*, enhancing the vividness of the description.—פָּגַע בְּ]= 'encounter with hostility,' Ju. 8^{21} 15^{12} 18^{25}, 1 Sa. $22^{17f.}$, 2 Sa. 1^{15}, 1 Ki. $2^{25ff.}$, Ru. 2^{22};='intercede,' Jb. 21^{15}, Jer. 7^{16} 27^{18}, Ru. 1^{16}. The neutral sense 'meet,' with pers. obj., is doubtfully supported by Nu. $35^{19.\,21}$, Jos. 2^{16}, where hostile intention is evidently implied: elsewhere this is expressed by *acc.* pers. (Ex. 5^{20} 23^4, 1 Sa. 10^5, Am. 5^{19}). Gn. 28^{11} is somewhat different, the obj. being impers. (cf. the use in Jos. 16^7 17^{10} etc.).—**3.** מחנים] an important East Jordanic city and sanctuary, the capital of Ish-bosheth (2 Sa. 2^8), and David's headquarters during the revolt of Absalom (2 Sa. $17^{24.\,27}$), the centre of a fiscal district under Solomon (1 Ki. 4^{14}). The situation of *Mahne* or *Mihne* on *W. el-Ḥimār*, some 14 m. N of the Jabboḳ (see Buhl, *GP*, 257), suits all the other references (cf. Jos. $13^{26.\,30}$—the boundary of Gad and Manasseh), but is too far from the Jabboḳ for this narrative (v.^{23}). But see p. 403 n. On the ending, which is probably no real dual, see on 24^{10}.

4. לפניו] 𝕲 om.—שדה אדום] (cf. Ju. 5^4) is probably a gloss on ארצה שעיר.—**5.** תאמרון] cf. $18^{28ff.}$—וָאֵחַר] for וָאֶאֱחַר (G-K. § 64*h*).—**6** ואשלחה] Cohort. form with vav. consec.—chiefly late; see Dri. *T.* § 69 *Obs.*, § 72; G-K.

nothing but an announcement of his arrival and his great wealth (cf. $33^{12ff.}$) The shepherd, with all his success, is at the mercy of the fierce marauder who was to 'live by his sword' (27^{40}).—**7.** The messengers return with the ominous news that Esau is already on the march with 400 men. How he was ready to strike so far north of his own territory is a difficulty (see p. 415).—**8, 9.** Jacob's first resource is to divide his company into *two camps*, in the hope that one might escape while the other was being captured. The arrangement is perhaps adverted to in 33^{8}. —**10–13.** Jacob's prayer, consisting of an invocation (^{10}), thanksgiving (^{11}), petition (^{12}), and appeal to the divine faithfulness (^{13}), is a classic model of OT devotion (Gu.); though the element of confession, so prominent in later supplications, is significantly absent. — **12.** *mother with* (or *on*) *children*] Hos. 10^{14}; cf. Dt. 22^{6}. A popular saying, —the mother conceived as bending over the children to protect them (Tu.).—**14a.** *spent that night there*] *i.e.*, at Maḥanaim (v.^{22}). We may suppose (with We. Gu.) that an explicit etymology, based on the 'two camps' (vv.$^{8.\,11}$), preceded or followed this clause.

Vv.$^{10-13}$ appear to be one of the later expansions of the Yahwistic narrative, akin to 13^{14-17} 22^{15-18} 26^{3b-5} 28^{14}. They can be removed without loss of continuity, ^{14a} being a natural continuation of ^{9}. The insertion gives an interpretation to the 'two camps' at variance with the primary motive of the division (v.^{9}); and its spirit is different from that of the narrative in which it is embedded. Comp. also חול הים with 22^{17}, לא יספר מרב with 16^{10} 22^{17}. See Gu. 316.

14b–22. The present for Esau (E).—14. *a present*] Not

---

§ 49 *e*.—**8.** וַיֵּצֶר] √ צרר intrans. = 'be cramped'; on the form, cf. G-K. § 67 *p*.—והגמלים] 𝕲^A om. and transp. ואת־הבקר ואת־הצאן.—שני מחנות] That this implies an etymology of Maḥanaim, and that J located the incident there, cannot reasonably be doubted (as by Ho.). The name is obviously regarded as a dual (in contrast to v.^{3}), showing that the current pronunciation is very ancient (Di.).—**9.** האחת] 𝔐 האחד (masc.), which is demanded by the context, as well as by prevailing usage (Albrecht, *ZATW*, xvi. 52).—**11.** קטנתי מן] 'too insignificant for'; G-K. § 133 *c*.—הירדן הזה] The writer apparently locates Maḥanaim in the vicinity of the Jordan; but the allusion, in an editorial passage, has perhaps no great topographical importance.

14. מן־הבא] Art. with ptcp. (not pf.); see G-K. § 138 *k*; Dri. *Sam.*

'tribute' (as often) in acknowledgment of vassalage, but (as 43^{11}, 2 Ki. $8^{8f.}$) a gift to win favour.—**17–20.** By arranging the cattle in successive droves following at considerable intervals, Jacob hopes to wear out Esau's resentment by a series of surprises. The plan has nothing in common with the two 'camps' of v.$^{8f.}$ in J.—**21a.** A repetition of ^{19b}: Jacob lays stress on this point, because the effect would obviously be weakened if a garrulous servant were to let out the secret that other presents were to follow.—**21b.** *Let me pacify him*] lit. 'cover' (or 'wipe clean') his face,—the same figure, though in different language, as 20^{16}. On כִּפֶּר, see *OTJC*², 381; *DB*, iv. 128f.—*see his face*] 'obtain access to his presence': cf. $43^{3.5}$ $44^{23.26}$, Ex. 10^{28}, 2 Sa. $14^{24.28.32}$, 2 Ki. 25^{19}, Est. 1^{14}. The phrase is thought to convey an allusion to *Pĕnû'ēl* (Gu.); see on 33^{10}.—**22.** *spent . . . camp* (בַּמַּחֲנֶה)] cf. ^{14a}. We. (*Comp.*² 46) renders 'in Maḥaneh' (*i.e.* Maḥanaim), but the change is hardly justified.

23–33. The wrestling at Peniel (JE).—**23, 24.** The crossing of the Jabboḳ. The *Yabbōḳ* is now almost univers-

---

57 f.—מנחה] see on 4^3.—**17.** רֶוַח (Est. 4^{14} †)] √ רוח, 'be wide' (1 Sa. 16^{23}, Jb. 32^{20}).—**18.** On the forms יְפָגְשְׁךָ (Ben Napht.), יִפְגָּשְׁךָ (Ben Asher), see G–K. §§ 9 *v*, 10 *g* (*c*), 60 *b*, [and B.-D., *Gen.* p. 85]; and on וּשְׁאֵלְךָ, § 64 *f*.—**20.** ויצו] 𝔊 + τῷ πρώτῳ.—כְּמֹצַאֲכֶם] irreg. inf. for כְּמָצְאֲכֶם (G–K. §§ 74 *h*, 93 *q*).—**21.** יעקב] 𝔐 𝔊𝔗^OJ + בָּא.

23–33. The analysis of the passage is beset by insurmountable difficulties. While most recognise doublets in $^{23f.}$ (*v.s.*), $^{25-33}$ have generally been regarded as a unity, being assigned to J by We. Kue. Corn. KS. Dri. al.; but by Di. to E. In the view of more recent critics, both J and E are represented, though there is the utmost variety of opinion in regard to details. In the notes above, *possible* variants have been pointed out in ^{26a} ‖ ^{26b} (the laming of the thigh) and $^{28.29}$ ‖ ^{30} (the name and the blessing); to these may be added the still more doubtful case ^{31} ‖ ^{32} (Peniel, Penuel). As showing traces of more primitive conceptions, ^{26a} and ^{30} would naturally go together, and also ^{27} for the same reason. Since J prefers the name Israel in the subsequent history, there is a slight presumption that $^{28f.}$ belong to him; and the אלהים of ^{31} points (though not decisively) to E. Thus we should obtain, for E: $^{26a.27.30.31}$; leaving for J: $^{26b.28.29.32}$: v.^{33} may be a gloss. The result corresponds nearly, so far as it goes, with Gu.'s (318 f.). The reader may compare the investigations of Ho. (209 f.), Procksch (32), Meyer (*INS*, 57 f.).—**23.** בלילה הוא (𝔐 ההוא)] as 19^{33} 30^{16}.—יַבֹּק (𝔐 היבק) (Nu. 21^{24}, Dt. 2^{37} 3^{16}, Jos. 12^2, Ju. $11^{13.22}$†) is naturally explained as the 'gurgler,' from √ בקק (Ar. *baḳḳa*), the resemblance to אבק (v.^{25}) being, of course, a popular word-play.—**24b.** Insert כָּל־ before

ally, and no doubt correctly, identified with the *Nahr ez-Zerḳā* (Blue River), whose middle course separates Ğebel ʿAğlūn from el-Belḳā, and which flows into the Jordan about 25 m. N of the Dead Sea. See Smend, *ZATW*, 1902, 137 ff.; and the descriptions in Riehm, *Hwb.*[2] 665; Smith, *HG*, 583–5.—The *ford* referred to cannot be determined; that of *Muḫādat en-Nuṣrānīyeh*, where the road from Ğeraš to es-Salṭ crosses the deep narrow gorge which cleaves the mountains of Gilead, as described by Thomson (*LB*, iii. 583 ff.) and Tristram (*Land of Israel*[3], 549), supplies a more fitting background for the weird struggle about to be narrated than the one in the Jordan valley; but on the difficulties of this identification, see Dri. *ET*, xiii. 459.

The passage of the river seems to be twice described, [24a] and [24b] being apparently doublets. The former continues [23a], which belongs to J (שפחה). Following this clue, we may divide thus: [23a. 24a] = J; [23b. 24b] = E (so Gu.). While E implies that Jacob crossed with his company, the account of J is consistent with the statement of [25a], that after sending the others across he himself was 'left alone.' On any view the action is somewhat perplexing. To cross a ford by night, with flocks, etc., was a dangerous operation, only to be explained by apprehension of an attack from Esau (We.). But Esau is represented as advancing from the south; and Jacob is in haste to put his people and possessions on that side of the river on which they were exposed to attack. Either the narrative is defective at this point, or it is written without a clear conception of the actual circumstances.

25. *a man wrestled with him till the appearing of the dawn*]—Only later does Jacob discover that his unknown antagonist is a god in human form (cf. 18[2] 19[5]).—The rare word (*v.i.*) for 'wrestle' (אבק) is chosen because of the assonance with יַבֹּק.—**26a.** *he saw that he prevailed not*] The ambiguity of the subject extends to the next clause, and leaves two interpretations open (*v.i.*).—*struck the socket of his thigh*] putting it out of joint.—**26b.** *the socket of Jacob's thigh was dislocated as he wrestled with him.*

The dislocation of the thigh seems to be twice recorded (see KS. *An.* 159), and it is highly probable that the two halves of the v. come from

---

אשר (𝔐𝔊𝔖𝔙).—**25.** ויאבק] A vb. used only here and v.[26], distinct from NH התאבק, 'make oneself dusty,' and very probably a modification of חבק, 'clasp' (De. Di.).—**26.** ותקע] √ יקע, lit. 'be rent away' (cf. Jer. 6[8]):

different sources. In [26a] it is a stratagem resorted to by a wrestler unable to gain the advantage by ordinary means (like the trick of Ulysses in *Il.* xxiii. 725 ff.); in [26b] it is an accident which happens to Jacob in the course of the struggle. It has even been suggested that in the original legend the subj. of [26a] was Jacob—that it was he who disabled his antagonist in the manner described (Ho. Gu. Che.: see Müller, *AE*, 163[1]; Luther, *ZATW*, xxi. 65 ff.; Meyer, *INS*, 57). It is possible (though certainly not probable) that this was the view of the document (J or E) to which [26a] belongs, and that it underlies Hos. 12[5].

27. *Let me go, for the dawn is breaking*] Comp. Plautus, *Amphitr.* 532 f., where Jupiter says: "Cur me tenes? Tempus est: exire ex urbe priusquam lucescat volo." It is a survival of the wide-spread belief in spirits of the night which must vanish at dawn (*Hamlet*, Act I. Sc. i.); and as such, a proof of the extreme antiquity of the legend.—But the request reveals to Jacob the superhuman character of his adversary, and he resolves to hold him fast till he has extorted a blessing from him.—**28, 29.** Here the blessing is imparted in the form of a new name conferred on Jacob in memory of this crowning struggle of his life.—*thou hast striven with God*] *Yisrā'ēl*, probably = 'God strives' (*v.i.*), is interpreted as 'Striver with God'; cf. a similar transformation of יְרֻבַּעַל ('Baal contends') in Ju. 6[32]. Such a name is a true 'blessing,' as a pledge of victory and success to the nation which bears it.—*and with men*] This can hardly refer merely to the contests with Laban and Esau; it points rather to the existence of a fuller body of legend, in which Jacob figured as the hero of many combats, culminating

---

𝔊 ἐνάρκησεν, 𝔖 [illegible], 𝔙 *emarcuit*, 𝔗° זע ('gave way'),—all conjectural.—**29.** יִשְׂרָאֵל] A name of the same type as ישמעאל, ירחמאל, etc., with some such meaning as 'God strives' or 'Let God strive'; originally (it has been suggested) a war-cry which passed into a proper name (see Steuernagel, *Einw.* 61). The vb. שׂרה, however, only occurs in connexion with this incident (Ho. 12[4. 5], where read וַיָּשַׂר), and in the personal name שְׂרָיָה; and its real meaning is uncertain. If it be the Heb. equivalent of Ar. *šariya*, Dri. argues that it must mean 'persist' or 'persevere' rather than 'strive' (*DB*, ii. 530), which hardly yields a suitable idea. Some take it as a by-form of שׂרר, either in a denominative sense ('rule,' from שַׂר, prince), or in its assumed primary significance 'shine forth' (Ass. *šarâru*: see Vollers, *ARW*, ix. 184). Some doubt has even been thrown on the traditional Heb. pronunciation by the form *Ysir'r*, found on an inscr. of Merneptah (Steindorff, *ZATW*, xvi. 330 ff.), with which we may compare

in this successful struggle with deity. — **30**. Jacob vainly endeavours to extort a disclosure of the name of his antagonist. This is possibly an older variant of [28f.], belonging to a primitive phase of thought, where he who possesses the true name of a god can dispose of the power of its bearer (Che. *TBI*, 401[1]; *DB*, v. 640). For the concealment of the name, cf. Ju. 13^{18} (the same words). — Gu. thinks that in the original narrative the name of the wrestler was actually revealed.—**31**. *Pĕnî'ēl*] 'Face of God' (*v.i.*). The name is derived from an incidental feature of the experience: that Jacob had seen "God *face* to *face*" (Ex. 33^{11}, Dt. 34^{10}), and yet lived (see on 16^{13}).—The site of Peniel is unknown: see Dri. *ET*, xiii. 457 ff., and *Gen.* 300 ff.—**32**. ***limping on his thigh***] in consequence of the injury he had received ([26b]). That he bore the hurt to his death, as a memorial of the conflict, is a gratuitous addition to the narrative.—**33**. The food-taboo here mentioned is nowhere else referred to in OT; and the Mishnic prohibition (*Ḥullîn*, 7) is probably dependent on this passage. Rob. Sm. explains it from the sacredness of the thigh as a seat of life (*RS*², 380[1]);* and

---

Ass. *Sir-'-lai* (=ישראלי) (see Kittel, *SBOT Chronicles*, p. 58). Comp. also Che. *TBI*, 404.—שרית] 𝔊 ἐνίσχυσας, Aq. ἦρξας, Σ. ἦρξω, 𝔙 *fortis fuisti*, 𝔖 ܐܬܚܝܠܬ, 𝔗^{O} רַב אַתְּ.—**31**. פניאל] 𝔊 Εἶδος θεοῦ, 𝔐𝔖𝔙𝔖 read פנואל as v.[32]. The formal difference arises from the old case-endings of gen. and nom. (G–K. § 90*o*). Strabo (XVI. ii. 16, 18) mentions a Phœnician promontory near Tripolis called Θεοῦ πρόσωπον: it is not improbable that in both cases the name is derived from a fancied resemblance to a face. —**33**. גיד הנשה] נָשֶׁה is to be explained by Ar. *nas*^{an} (for *nasay*^{un}), which means the ***nervus ischiadicus***, or the thigh in which it is found (Ges. *Th.* 921 f.). The question remains whether גיד denotes here a nerve, an artery, a sinew, or a muscle; the first seems by far the most probable. So it seems to have been understood by 𝔖 (ܓܝܕܐ ܕܦܫܝܐ =tetanus-nerve), and by 𝔊 and 𝔙, which appear to have connected נשה with the vb. for 'forget' (Gr.-Venet, τὸ νεῦρον τὸ ἐπιλελησμένον!). The modern Jewish restriction applies, according to De., to the "Spannader, d. h. die innere Ader des sogen. Hinterviertels mit Einschluss der äusseren und der Verästelungen beider."

---

* "The nature of the lameness produced by injury to the sinew of the thigh socket is explained by the Arabic lexx., *s.v. ḥārifat*; the man can only walk on the tips of his toes. This seems to have been a common affection, for poetical metaphors are taken from it."

We. (*Heid.* 168^3) calls attention to a trace of it in ancient Arabia. For primitive parallels, see Frazer, *Golden Bough*, ii. 419 ff., *Folklore in OT*, 142 f. The precise meaning of גִּיד הַנָּשֶׁה is uncertain (*v.i.*).

In its fundamental conception the struggle at Peniel is not a dream or vision like that which came to Jacob at Bethel; nor is it an allegory of the spiritual life, symbolising the inward travail of a soul helpless before some overhanging crisis of its destiny. It is a real physical encounter which is described, in which Jacob measures his strength and skill against a divine antagonist, and 'prevails,' though at the cost of a bodily injury. No more boldly anthropomorphic narrative is found in Genesis; and unless we shut our eyes to some of its salient features, we must resign the attempt to translate it wholly into terms of religious experience. We have to do with a legend, originating at a low level of religion, in process of accommodation to the purer ideas of revealed religion; and its history may have been somewhat as follows: (1) We begin with the fact of a hand-to-hand conflict between a god and a man. A similar idea appears in Ex. $4^{24ff.}$, where we read that Yahwe met Moses and 'sought to kill him.' In the present passage the god was probably not Yahwe originally, but a local deity, a night-spirit who fears the dawn and refuses to disclose his name. Dr. Frazer has pointed out that such stories as this are associated with water-spirits, and cites many primitive customs (*Folklore*, 136 ff.) which seem to rest on the belief that a river resents being crossed, and drowns many who attempt it. He hazards the conjecture that the original deity of this passage was the spirit of the Jabboḳ; in which case the word-play between יַבֹּק and אבק may have greater significance than appears on the surface. (2) Like many patriarchal theophanies, the narrative accounts for the foundation of a sanctuary—that of Peniel. Of the cultus at Peniel we know nothing; and there is very little in the story that can be supposed to bear upon it, unless we assume, with Gu. and others, that the limping on the thigh refers to a ritual dance regularly observed there (cf. 1 Ki. 18^{26}).* (3) By J and E the story was incorporated in the national epos as part of the history of Jacob. The God who wrestles with the patriarch is Yahwe; and how far the wrestling was understood as a literal fact remains uncertain. To these writers the main interest lies in the origin of the name Israel, and the blessing bestowed on the nation in the person of its ancestor. (4) A still more refined interpretation is found, it seems to me, in Ho. $12^{4.5}$: 'In the womb he overreached his brother; and in his prime he strove with God. He strove (וַיָּשַׂר) with the Angel and prevailed; he wept and made supplication to him.' The substitution of the Angel of Yahwe for the divine Being Himself shows increasing sensitiveness to anthropomorphism; and the last line appears to mark an advance in the spiritualising of the incident, the subject being not the Angel (as Gu. and others hold), but Jacob, whose 'prevailing' thus becomes that of importunate prayer.—We may note in a word Steuernagel's ethno-

* But see footnote on p. 410 above.

logical interpretation. He considers the wrestling to symbolise a victory of the invading Israelites over the inhabitants of N Gilead. The change of name reflects the fact that a new nation (Israel) arose from the fusion of the Jacob and Rachel tribes (*Einw.* 61 f.).

CH. XXXIII.—*The Meeting of the Brothers: Jacob's March to Shechem* (JE, P).

The dreaded meeting at last takes place; the brothers are reconciled, and part in friendship; Esau returning to Seir, while Jacob moves on by slow stages first to Succoth and then to Shechem.—It is difficult to characterise the spirit in which the main incident is conceived. Was Esau's purpose friendly from the first, or was he turned from thoughts of vengeance by Jacob's submissive and flattering demeanour? Does the writer regard the reconciliation as equally honourable to both parties, or does he only admire the skill and knowledge of human nature with which Jacob tames his brother's ferocity? The truth probably lies between two extremes. That Esau's intention was hostile, and that Jacob gained a diplomatic victory over him, cannot reasonably be doubted. On the other hand, the narrator must be acquitted of a desire to humiliate Esau. If he was vanquished by generosity, the noblest qualities of manhood were released in him; and he displays a chivalrous magnanimity which no appreciative audience could ever have held in contempt. So far as any national feeling is reflected, it is one of genuine respect and goodwill towards the Edomites.

Sources.—Vv.[1-17] are rightly assigned in the main to J, in spite of the fact that the only divine name which occurs is אלהים, in [5b. 10. 11]. In these vv. we must recognise the hand of E (cf. also [5b] with 48^9, and [10b] with 32^{21}); and, for all that appears, E's influence may extend further. The chief indications, however, both material and linguistic, point to J as the leading source: the 400 men (32^7), the 'camp' in v.[8] (32^8), and the expressions: שפחות, [1. 2. 6]; רוץ לקראת, [4]; מצא חן, [8. 10. 15]; כי־על־כן, [10]. The documents are so deftly interwoven that it is scarcely possible to detect a flaw in the continuity of the narrative.—[18-20] are probably from E, except [18aβ], which is taken from P (see on the vv. below).

1–7. The meeting.—1, 2. Jacob's fears revive at sight

---

2. אחרנים . . . אחרנים] 𝔊 ὀπίσω . . . ἐσχάτους; 𝔖 ܩܕܡܝܐ . . . ܒܬܪܝܗܘܢ.

of the 400 men (32^{7}). He marshals his children (not the whole company, as $32^{8f.}$, though the motive is the same) under their mothers, and in the reverse order of his affection for them.—**3.** *passed on before them*] having previously been in the rear.—He approaches his brother with the reverence befitting a sovereign; the sevenfold prostration is a favourite formula of homage in the Tel Amarna tablets: "At the feet of my Lord, my Sun, I fall down seven and seven times" (38 ff. *pass.*). It does not follow, however, that Jacob acknowledged himself Esau's vassal (Nestle, *MM*, 12; Che. *TBI*, 405); cf. 1 Sa. 20^{41}.—**4.** *fell on his neck*] 45^{14} 46^{29} (J); Lu. 15^{20}.—**5–7.** An interesting picture: the mothers with their little ones come forward in groups to pay their respects to the grim-visaged warrior, whose name had caused such terror in the camp.

8–11. The present.—**8.** Esau remembers another great cavalcade—*camp*—which he had met. The 'present' of $32^{14ff.}$ (E) cannot be referred to, for Esau must have been told repeatedly what *it* was for ($32^{18f.}$). The word מַחֲנֶה points rather to the arrangement of $32^{8f.}$ (J). Gu. somewhat ingeniously explains thus: Esau had met the first division of Jacob's company; and Jacob, ashamed to avow his original motive, by a happy inspiration now offers 'this whole camp' as a present to his brother.—**9.** Esau at first refuses, but, **10, 11,** Jacob insists on his accepting the gift.—*as one sees the*

Read accordingly אחריהם for the first 'א. —**4.** וַיִּשָּׁקֵהוּ] The *puncta extraordinaria* mark some error in the text. Di. observes that elsewhere (45^{14} 46^{29}) 'fell on his neck' is immediately followed by 'wept.' The word should probably be inserted (with 𝔊) after ויחבקהו (so 29^{13}; cf. 48^{10}).—ויבכו] The sing. would be better, unless we add with 𝔊 שְׁנֵיהֶם. ויפל על צוארו ויבך ‖ ויחבקהו וישקהו seem to be variants; of which one or other will be due to E.—**5.** חנן] with double acc., lit. 'has been gracious to me (with) them' (G.-K. § 117 ff.) = 'has graciously given' (so v.^{11}); cf. Ju. 21^{22}, Ps. 119^{29}.—**7.** נִגַּשׁ] Niph. for the previous Qal. Point נָגַשׁ?—יוסף ורחל] 𝔊 transp. as v.^{2}.

10. כִּי־עַל־כֵּן] see on 18^{5}. This and the preceding מצאתי חן mark the v. as J's, in spite of the appellative use of אלהים.—**11a** is a doublet of ^{10a}, and may be assigned to E.—ברכה] 'blessing,' hence the gift which is meant to procure a blessing: 1 Sa. 25^{27} 30^{26}, 2 Ki. 18^{31}.—הֻבָאת] see G–K. § 74*g*; but 𝔐𝔊𝔙𝔖 read better הֵבֵאתִי.

face of God] with the feelings of joy and reverence with which one engages in the worship of God. For the flattering comparison of a superior to the Deity, cf. 1 Sa. 29^{9}, 2 Sa. 14^{17} 19^{28}. It is possible that the phrase here contains a reminiscence of the meaning of Pĕnî'ēl in 32^{31} (We. Di. al.), the common idea being that "at Peniel the unfriendly God is found to be friendly" (Di.). The resemblance suggests a different form of the legend, in which the deity who wrestled with Jacob was Esau—the Usōus of Phœnician mythology (see on 25^{25}; cf. *INS*, 278).

12–17. The parting.—12. Esau, assuming that they are no more to be separated, proposes to march in front with his troop.—**13.** But Jacob has other objects in view, and invents a pretext for getting rid of his brother's company.—עָלוֹת עָלָי] lit. *are giving suck upon me*: *i.e.* their condition imposes anxiety upon me.—**14.** *I will proceed by stages* (? *v.i.*), *gently, according to the pace of the cattle before me*].—*till I come . . . to Sē'îr*] It is, of course, implied that he is to follow in Esau's track; and the mention of Seir as a possible goal of Jacob's journey causes difficulty. Meyer (*INS*, 275 f.) advances the attractive theory that in J Jacob does not cross the Jordan at all, but goes round by Seir and the S of the Dead Sea to Hebron. The question has an important bearing on the criticism of ch. 34.—**15–17.** The offer of an armed escort having been courteously declined, Jacob proceeds but a short

---

13. עלות] √ עול, of which only the ptcp. is in use (1 Sa. $6^{7.10}$, Is. 40^{11}, Ps. 78^{71} †).—ודפקום] better with 𝔐𝔊𝔖 וּדְפַקְתִּים. On the synt. see G-K. § 159 *q*.—**14.** אתנהלה וגו'] 𝔊 *ἐνισχύσω ἐν τῇ ὁδῷ κατὰ σχολὴν τῆς πορεύσεως.* Why Cheyne (405 f.) finds it necessary to resolve the text into a series of geographical glosses is not apparent. התנהל, Hithp. is ἅπ. λεγ., but is a natural extension of the Pi. 'guide [to a watering-place?],' Is. 40^{11} 49^{10}. אַט in the sense of 'gentleness' (2 Sa. 18^{5}, 1 Ki. 21^{27}, Is. 8^{6}, Jb. 15^{11}), and רֶגֶל in the sense of 'pace' are unexceptionable: the ל of *norm* with both words (BDB, 516 b). For מלאכה in the sense of 'property,' we have examples in Ex. $22^{7.10}$, 1 Sa. 15^{9}.—**15.** אצּיגה] lit. 'let me set.' The sense suggested by the context, 'leave behind,' is supported by Ex. 10^{24} (Hoph.).—למה וגו'] The Heb. is peculiar. The obvious rendering would be, 'Why should I find favour, etc.?'; but as that is hardly possible, we must tr. 'Why so? May I find, etc.'—a very abrupt transition. We should at least expect אמצא נא.—**17.** ויעקב] The precedence of subj. indicates contrast, and shows that the v. continues [16] (J).—נסע]

distance, and takes up his quarters at *Sukkôth* (*v.i.*). The name is derived from the *booths*, or temporary shelters for cattle, which he erects there.—*built himself a house*] showing that he contemplated a lengthy sojourn.

Here Esau disappears from the histories of J and E. We have already remarked on the change of tone in this last episode, as compared with the earlier Jacob-Esau stories of chs. 25, 27. Esau is no longer the rude natural man, the easy victim of his brother's cunning, but a noble and princely character, whose bearing is evidently meant to inspire admiration. Jacob, too, is presented in a more favourable light: if he is still shrewd and calculating, and not perfectly truthful, he does not sink to the knavery of his earlier dealings with Esau and Laban, but exhibits the typical virtues of the patriarchal ideal. The contrast betrays a difference of spirit and origin in the two groups of legends. It is conceivable that the second group came from sanctuaries frequented by Israelites and Edomites in common (so Ho. 212); but it is also possible that the two sets reflect the relations of Israel and Edom at different periods of history. It is quite obvious that chs. 25 and 27 took shape after the decay of the Edomite empire, when the ascendancy of Israel over the older people was assured. If there be any ethnological basis to 32. 33, it must belong to an earlier period. Steuernagel (*Einw.* 105) suggests as a parallel Nu. 20^{14-21}, where the Edomites resist the passage of Israel through their territory. Meyer (387^{1}) is disposed to find a recollection of a time when Edom had a powerful empire extending far north on the E of the Jordan, where they may have rendered assistance to Israel in the Midianite war (*ib.* 382), though they were unable ultimately to maintain their position. If there be any truth in either of these speculations (which must remain extremely doubtful), it is evident that chronologically 32 f. precede 25, 27; and the attempt to interpret the series (as a whole) ethnographically must be abandoned.

18–20. Jacob at Shechem.—18. The crossing of the Jordan is not recorded; it is commonly supposed to have

---

see on 11^{2}.—סֻכֹּת was E of the Jordan, but nearer to it than Peniel (Jos. 13^{27}, Ju. $8^{4.5.8}$). The site is unknown (see Smith, *HG*, 585; Buhl, *GP*, 206, 260; Dri. *ET*, xiii. 458 a, *n.* 1). The modern *'Ain es-Sākūt* (9 m. S. of Beisan) is excluded on phonetic grounds, and is besides on the wrong side of the Jordan.

18. שלם עיר שכם] [שלום 𝔊𝔄𝔘] The rendering given above is pronounced by We. to be impossible, no doubt on the ground that שלם, meaning properly 'whole' (Dt. 27^{6}), is nowhere else used in the sense 'safe and sound' of a person. Still, in view of שלום (cf. 28^{21} 43^{27}), and וישלם in Jb. 9^{4}, it may be reasonably supposed that it had that sense. 𝔊 *Jub.* 𝔙𝔖 take שלם as a *nom. pr.*; a view which though it derives some plausibility from the fact that there is still a village *Salim* about 4 m. E of Nābulus (Robinson, *BR*, ii. 275, 279), implies a sense not consonant

taken place at the ford *ed-Dāmiyeh*, a little S of the Jabboḳ, on the road from es-Salṭ to Shechem.—*in safety* (שָׁלֵם)] after his escape from Esau, E not having recorded the lengthened stay at Succoth. On the rendering of שלם as a proper name, *v.i.*—*encamped in front of the city*] in the vale to the E of it, where Jacob's well is still shown (Jn. $4^{6.\ 12}$).—**19.** The purchase of the ground is referred to in Jos. 24^{32} in the account of Joseph's burial. It is significant that Israel's claim to the grave of Joseph is based on purchase, just as its right to that of Abraham (ch. 23).—The *Bnê Ḥămôr* were the dominant clan in Shechem (ch. 34, Ju. 9^{28}).—*a hundred ḳĕsîṭāhs*] an unknown sum (*v.i.*).—**20.** *he set up there an altar*] or more probably (since הִצִּיב is never used of an altar) *a mazzebāh.*—*called it* '*Ēl, God of Israel*] the stone being identified with the deity; cf. 28^{22} 35^{7}, Ex. 17^{15}, Ju. 6^{24}. For heathen parallels, see Mey. *INS*, 295.

Israel is here the name of the nation: cf. Jos. 8^{30}, where Joshua builds an altar on Ebal (E of Shechem) to Yahwe, God of Israel. The stone and its name are undoubtedly historical, and go back to an early time when Shechem (or Ebal?) was the sacred centre of the confederacy of Israelitish tribes (cf. 1 Ki. 12^{1}). We cannot therefore conclude with Di. that the v. refers back to 32^{29}, and comes from the same document.

---

with usage; there being no case of a village described as a 'city' *of* the neighbouring town (De.). We. (*Comp.*² 316^{1}) emends שְׁכֶם: 'Shechem the city of (the man) Shechem.' Procksch accepts the emendation, but regards the words as a conflation of variants from two sources (p. 34). 𝔊 distinguishes the name of the city (Σικίμων, see on 12^{6}) from that of the man (Συχεμ, v.[19] $34^{2ff.}$).—ויחן] as 26^{17}.—**19.** קשיטה (Jos. 24^{32}, Jb. 42^{11} †)] apparently a coin or weight; but the etymology is obscure. 𝔊𝔙𝔗ᴼ render 'lamb'; and it was thought that light had been thrown on this traditional explanation by the Aramaic Assuan papyri, where כבש (lamb) is used of a coin (of the value of 10 shekels?) (so Sayce-Cowley, *Aram. Pap. disc. at Assouan*, p. 23). But Lidzbarski (*Deutsche Lzg.*, 1906, 3210 ff.) holds that the word there should be read כרש (found on a Persian weight: *PSBA*, 1888, 464 ff.).—**20.** Read מצבה for מזבח, and consequently לָהּ for לו (We. al.).—ויקרא וגו'] 𝔊 καὶ ἐπεκαλέσατο τὸν θεὸν 'Ισραήλ.—Except the clause אשר בא' כ' בבאו מפדן ארם in v.[18], which is evidently from P, the whole section 18-20 may safely be assigned to E.

CH. XXXIV.—*The Outrage on Dinah.*

Two narratives are here combined:

I. Shechem, son of Ḥamor, the native princeling, falls in love with Dinah, the daughter of Leah, abducts her, and keeps her in his house ([1-3]*; cf. [26]). He asks her in marriage from her father and brothers, offering to accept any conditions they may impose ([11. 12]). They raise an objection on the score of circumcision ([14]), but eventually consent on terms not expressed in this recension. Shechem complies with the condition, whatever it was ([19]). Simeon and Levi, however, decide that the insult can only be wiped out by blood; they gain access to Shechem's house, slay him, and depart with their sister ([25f.]). Their father, fearing an uprising of the country against him, reproves them for their rash act, which they proudly justify ([30. 31]).—The conclusion is lost.

II. Shechem dishonours Dinah, but lets her return to her family ([1-3]*; cf. [17]); but continuing to love her, he appeals to Ḥamor to arrange a marriage ([4]). Ḥamor comes to speak to Jacob ([6]), and finds him and his sons together ([7]). He proposes not only a marriage between Shechem and Dinah, but a general *connubium* which would legalise all such unions in the future ([8-10]). Jacob's sons agree, on condition that all the clan be circumcised ([13. 15-18]). Ḥamor proceeds to the gate of the city, and persuades his people to undergo the operation ([20-24]). While the fever is on them, the sons of Jacob rush the city, kill all the males, capture the women and children, and carry off the spoil ([27-29]).—The sequel is *perhaps* summarised in 35[5].

This rough analysis * rests mainly on the material incongruities of the narrative, viz.: (*a*) In II., after the seduction Dinah is still in the hands of her relatives, [17]; but in I. she is in Shechem's house and has to be rescued by force, [26]. (*b*) The negotiations are conducted by Ḥămôr alone, [6. 8-10] (II.); but in [11. 12] (I.) Shechem is abruptly introduced pleading his own cause. (*c*) Shechem has already fulfilled the compact, [19] (I.), before the people of the city are consulted, [20-24] (II.). (*d*) Simeon and Levi alone avenge the outrage, and are alone held responsible for the

* The parts left unresolved are vv.[1-3] and [5. 7].—In [1-3], [3a] looks like a first mention of Dinah; and in [2b] וישכב אתה is perhaps ‖ ויקח אתה ויענה; and with a transposition we might read thus: II. [1. 2a] And Dinah . . . and Shechem . . . saw her, [2b] and lay with her. [3bβ] And he comforted the girl . . .: I. [3a] And the soul [of Shechem . . .] clave to Dinah . . . [2b] and he took her and violated her. [3bα] And he loved the girl . . .—[5] and [7] seem to me to belong to II. rather than I.; but the indications are conflicting, and they are possibly redactional vv., inserted to explain the transition from the sing. in [6] to the pl. in [8].—Naturally the redactor has been busy smoothing over discrepancies; and to him may be attributed את־שכם ו in [13a], the whole of [13b. 18b], ושכם בנו in [20a], עירם for עירו in [20b] (cf. [24]), ואל־שכם בנו in [24]; ואת־חמור ו and בנו in [26a]; and the removal of [25b] from [27] (*v.i.*).

consequences, $^{25f.\ 30f.}$ (I.); but all the sons of Jacob are implicated in the sack of the city, $^{27-29}$ (II.).

Sources.—If *style* alone were decisive, I. might safely be identified with J: note רבק ב, ^{3} (2^{24}); נער, $^{3.\ 12}$; מצא חן בע׳, ^{11}; בכנעני ובפרזי, ^{30}. In II., Corn. has pointed out some linguistic affinities with E (see the notes on דבר על לב, ^{8}; ילדה ^{4}; סחר, $^{10.\ 21}$ etc.); but they are insignificant in comparison with the strongly marked Priestly phraseology of this recension: נשיא, ^{2}; טמא, $^{5.\ 13.\ 27}$; נאחז, ^{10}; המל לכם כל זכר, $^{15.\ 22}$; קנין and בהמה, ^{23}; כל זכר, ^{24}; כל יצאי שער עיר ^{24} (*bis*): comp. the list in Kue. *Ges. Abh.* 269 f. These are so striking that Di. and Dri. assign the narrative unhesitatingly to P, and all admit that it has undergone a Priestly redaction (Corn. calls attention to a very similar case in Nu. 31).

But there are grave *material* difficulties in assigning either recension to J or E. (1) In ch. 34, Jacob's children are grown up; and this implies a considerable lapse of time since ch. 33. (2) A bloody encounter with the natives of the land is contrary to the peaceful ideal of patriarchal life consistently maintained by J and (hardly less consistently) by E. (3) Against I. = J, in particular, (*a*) In J the patriarch is generally named Israel after 32^{28}; and here Jacob is used throughout. (*b*) We have seen reason to believe that in J, Jacob was not W of the Jordan at all at this time (p. 414). (*c*) The sons of Jacob would not be found quietly feeding their flocks at Shechem ($37^{12ff.}$) if an incident like this had been of recent occurrence. (4) As regards II. = E, there is less difficulty; but on this hypothesis the amalgamation with J must be due to R^{JE}; and how does it happen that the assumed Priestly redaction is confined to the one component? Moreover, the incident is irreconcilable with 48^{22} (E). (5) Finally, if *Ḥōrite* be the true reading in v.^{2}, we have here a tradition differing from any of the Pent. documents.

These objections are urged with great force by Meyer, who also shows that in Gen. there are sporadic traces of a divergent tradition which ignored the Exodus, and traced the conquest and division of the land directly to Jacob and his sons (chs. 38. 48^{22}). To this (older) tradition ne assigns ch. 34. The first recension must have taken literary shape within the Yahwistic school, and the second may have been current in Elohistic circles; but neither found a place in the main document of the school to which it belonged, and its insertion here was an afterthought suggested by a supposed connexion with 33^{19} (E). This seems to me the best solution, though it leaves the dual recension, the amalgamation, and the Priestly redaction unexplained riddles.—Calling the two narratives J^{x} and E^{x}, we divide as follows:

J^{x} (= I.): $^{3a.\ 2b*.\ 3b\alpha.\ 11.\ 12.\ 14.\ 19.\ 25a.\ 26.\ 30.\ 31}$.
E^{x} (= II.): $^{1.\ 2a.\ 2b*.\ 3b\beta.\ 4.\ 5?.\ 6.\ 7?.\ 8-10.\ 13a.\ 15-18a.\ 20-24.\ 27.\ (25b).\ 28.\ 29}$.

Comp. We. *Comp.*^{2} 45 f., 314 ff.; Kue. *ThT*, 1880, 257 ff. (= *Ges. Abhandl.* 255 ff.), *Ond.* i. 315 f.; Corn. *ZATW*, xi. 1–15; Mey. *INS*, 412 ff.; De. 413; Di. 368 ff.; Ho. 213 ff.; Gu. 326 ff.; Stra. 126 f.; Pro. 35 f.

1–12. Dinah is seduced by Shechem, and afterwards sought in marriage.—2. *the Ḥivvite*] see on 10^{17}; 𝔊 *the*

1. בנות הארץ] 27^{46} (P or R).—2. החוי] 𝔊 החרי. Confusion of ו and ר is

Ḥōrite (*v.i.*).—**3.** *spoke to* (lit. *over*) *the heart*] 50^{21} (E). The phrase means 'to comfort,' not 'to woo'; cf. Ho. 2^{16}, Is. 40^{2}, Ru. 2^{13} etc.—**4.** Comp. $21^{21.\,24}$ 38^{6}, Ju. 14^{2}.—**5.** *kept silence*] took no steps to redress the injury (2 Sa. 19^{11}). **7.** *wrought scandalous folly in Israel*] a standing phrase for crimes of the kind here indicated (Dt. 22^{21}, Ju. $20^{6.\,10}$; cf. Ju. $19^{23f.}$, 2 Sa. $13^{12ff.}$); though 'in Israel' is an anachronism. נְבָלָה is never mere foolishness, but always disgraceful conduct or language.—*such things are not done*] 20^{9} 29^{26}.—**8–10.** Ḥămōr, as prince, takes a broad view: not content with arranging this particular marriage, he proposes an amalgamation of the two races; thinking apparently that the advantage to Jacob would be sufficient compensation for the offence.—**9.** Almost verbally identical with Dt. 7^{3} (cf. Jos. 23^{12}).—**11, 12.** Shechem's offer relates only to his own private affair.—*Ask me ever so much*] lit. 'Multiply upon me.' The Hebrew law of compensation for seduction is given in Ex. $22^{15f.}$—מֹהַר, the price paid to the parents (Ex. $22^{15f.}$, 1 Sa. 18^{25}), and מַתָּן (so only here), the gift to the bride, are virtually distinguished in 24^{53}.

13–17. The answer.—**13a.** *with duplicity*] In this recension (E^{x}) the requirement of circumcision is merely a pretext to render the Shechemites incapable of self-defence.—**14.** Here, on the contrary (J^{x}), the family acts in good faith, and

---

common; but 𝕲 deserves consideration as the harder reading; and also because the only other place where 𝕲 has חרי for MT חוי is Jos. 9^{7}, a passage somewhat similar to this (see Mey. *INS*, 331). It is a slight confirmation of 𝕲 that animal names are frequent among the Ḥorite clans ($36^{20ff.}$), and Ḥămôr means 'he-ass.'—נשיא] a favourite word of P; cf. 17^{20} 23^{6} 25^{16}.—שכב את (v.[7] 35^{22} etc.)] The Mass. always point the את in this phrase as *not. acc.*—**3.** נער] see 24^{14}.—**5.** טִמֵּא] in the sexual sense vv.[13. 27], Ezk. $18^{6.\,11.\,15}$ 22^{11} †; otherwise very frequent in P.—**7.** כשמעם] occupies an unusual position; and there are other small syntactic anomalies in [5. 7].—**8.** חשק ב] Dt. 7^{7} 10^{15} 21^{11}, Ps. 91^{14} †; ct. רבק, v.[3].—On the *casus pendens*, G-K. § 143 *b*.—**9.** התחתן] 'enter into the relation of חֹתֵן and חָתָן' (1 Sa. $18^{21ff.}$, 1 Ki. 3^{1}), and more generally 'form marriage alliance' (Dt. 7^{3}, Jos. 23^{12}, Ezr. 9^{14}).—**10.** סחר] as 42^{34} (E); but cf. 23^{16} (P).—והאחזו] Niph. in this sense peculiar to P (47^{27}, Nu. 32^{30}, Jos. $22^{9.\,19}$).—**12.** מהר ומתן] 𝕲 *τὴν φερνήν*.

13b occupies a syntactically impossible position, and must be deleted as a redactional gloss. וידברו joins on to [15].—**14.** 𝕲 *καὶ εἶπαν αὐτοῖς*

the compact is violated by Simeon and Levi alone.—*that were a reproach to us*] Jos. 5^{9}. Circumcision is regarded as a tribal custom, which it would be a disgrace to infringe. That the custom actually existed from the earliest time among the Hebrews is extremely probable (p. 296 f.); but the fact that both J (Ex. 4^{25}) and E (Jos. $5^{3ff.}$) record its introduction in the age of the Exodus is an additional proof that this chapter follows an independent tradition.—**15.** Continuing ^{13a}.—*Only on this condition will we consent*] referring primarily to the *connubium.*—**16.** *become one people*] A result really desired by the Shechemites, but not seriously contemplated by the sons of Jacob.

18–24. The condition accepted.—**19.** *the most honoured member of his family*] emphasising the greatness of his sacrifice, and the strength of his attachment to Dinah.—**21–23.** Ḥămōr naturally says nothing of the personal matter, but dwells on the advantages the clan will derive from union with the Israelites. The men are already *on friendly terms* with them; the land is *spacious* enough; and by adopting circumcision they will obtain a great accession to their wealth.

25–31. The vengeance of the Hebrews.—**25.** *on the third day*] when the inflammation is said, in the case of adults, to be at its height (De. Di.).—*S. and L., the brothers of Dinah*] cf. 49^{5}. In ch. 29 f., Leah had four other sons who were as much full brothers of Dinah as these two. Was there another tradition, according to which Simeon and Levi were the only sons of Leah (so Mey. *INS*, 286^{1}, 426 f.)?—**26.** לפי חרב] according to the usage of war: without quarter

---

Συμεὼν καὶ Λευὶ οἱ ἀδελφοὶ Δείνας υἱοὶ δὲ Λείας κτλ.—an intelligent anticipation of critical results (cf. ^{25})?—Or is this the original text?—א׳ אשר לו ערלה for 'uncircumcised' does not recur.—**15.** נאות] Either (BDB) impf. Niph., or (G–K. § 72 *h*) intrans. impf. Qal of √אות, 'consent' ($^{22.\,23}$, 2 Ki. 12^{9} †).—להמל וגו׳] as 17^{10}.

19. אֵחַר] G–K. § 64 *d.*—**21.** רחבת ידים (𝕲 *πλατεῖα*)] 'broad on both sides'; Ju. 18^{10}, Is. 22^{18} [33^{21}, 1 Ch. 4^{40}, Neh. 7^{4}, Ps. 104^{25}]†.—**24.** Between וימלו and כל־זכר] 𝕲 ins. *τὴν σάρκα τῆς ἀκροβυστίας αὐτῶν.*—כל־יצאי וגו׳] cf. $23^{10.\,18}$. The repetition of the phrase is avoided by 𝕲.

27–29 are regarded by Di. as a late interpolation; and this is perhaps necessary if the second account is to be identified with P. The

(cf. 2 Sa. 11[25]).—*and went out*] Evidently this is the close of the exploit.—**27.** *came upon the slain*] Cf. 𝔙 *Quibus egressis, irruerunt super occisos cæteri filii Jacob.* That is perhaps the sense intended by the redactor. But, to say nothing of the improbability of two men being able to kill all the males of the city, the second narrative (E^x) must have given an independent account of the attack on Shechem. [25b] must be transferred to this v.; and another word must be substituted for חֲלָלִים (*v.i.*).—**28, 29.** Cf. the similar phraseology of Nu. 31[9. 11] (P).—**30, 31** (continuing [26]). Jacob rebukes Simeon and Levi, not for their treachery and cruelty, but for their recklessness in exposing the whole tribe to the vengeance of the Canaanites.—*I am few in number*] it is the tribal, not the individual, consciousness which finds expression here.

The legend at the basis of ch. 34 reflects, we can scarcely doubt, an incident of the Hebrew settlement in Canaan. Shechem is the eponymus of the ancient city of that name, and Ḥămôr of the tribe dwelling there; Ḥămôr is the father of Shechem, because the tribe is older than its possession of the city. Jacob, in like manner, stands for the Israelites, who are nomads ranging the country round Shechem, and on friendly terms with its inhabitants. Whether Dînāh was a weak Hebrew clan threatened with absorption by the Ḥamorites is not so certain; it is more natural to suppose that a literal outrage of the kind described was the cause of the racial quarrel which ensued.*—There are two historic events which seem to stand in some connexion with the narrative—the Hebrew conquest of Shechem, and the dissolution of Simeon and Levi as tribal entities. (1) The conquest of Shechem is presupposed in Jos. 24; but it is remarkable that it is never mentioned either among the cities captured by the Israelites, or among those which remained independent. The account of its destruction by Abimelech in Ju. 9 appears to imply

---

possibility that the vv. have been glossed by some one who had Nu. 31 in mind is not to be denied.—**27.** חללים] lit. 'pierced,' means either 'slain' (Nu. 19[18] 31[8. 19] etc.), or (rarely) 'fatally wounded' (La. 2[12] etc.); neither sense being suitable here. Gu. suggests חֹלִים, 'sick' ‖ כאבים, v.[25].—**29.** שָׁבוּ וַיָּבֹאוּ] Remove athnach to שבו (√ שבה) and omit ו before את (cf. ɯ𝔊𝔖).—בבית] coll.; but 𝔖 ܕܒܒ̈ܬܐ 𝔊 ἐν τῇ πόλει καὶ ὅσα ἦν ἐν ταῖς οἰκίαις.—**30.** עכר] = Ar. *'akira*, 'be turbid,' in Heb. lit. 'make turbid' = 'undo,'—a strong word; cf. Jos. 6[18] 7[25], 1 Ki. 18[17f.]—מתי מספר] lit. 'men of number,' numerable, and therefore few; Dt. 4[27] 33[6], Jer. 44[28] etc.

---

* A singularly apposite and interesting modern parallel is quoted by Bennett (p. 318 f.) from Doughty, *Arabia Deserta*, ii. 114.

that it had been continuously in the possession of the Bnê Ḥămôr down to that time. On the other hand, the poetic fragment Gn. 48^{22} attributes the conquest to Jacob himself, but as an honourable feat of arms unstained by the treachery which is so prominent in ch. 34. How these conflicting data are to be reconciled, we can hardly conjecture. The differences are too great to justify the opinion that 48^{22} and 34 are merely legendary reflexions of the historic fact recorded in Ju. 9. Yet it is scarcely credible that Shechem was thrice conquered, twice from the same people under circumstances of general similarity. One chief objection to identifying 34 with Ju. 9 is the prominence of Simeon and Levi in J^x. We may either (with Steuernagel) put back the incident (which may after all have been an *unsuccessful* attack on Shechem) to the early days of the Hebrew migration, while Simeon and Levi were independent and still migratory tribes; or (with Mey.) assume that the story of Dinah originated near the Simeonite territory in the S, and was afterwards transferred to Shechem because of certain points of affinity with the historic overthrow of that city under Abimelech.—(2) The dispersion of Simeon and Levi is referred to in the Blessing of Jacob ($49^{6.\ 7}$), as the consequence of deeds of violence, disapproved by the conscience of the nation. It is universally assumed by critics that the two passages are variations of the same theme; hence it is held by many (We. Sta. Gu. Steuernagel, al.) that J^x went on to tell how the Canaanites actually retaliated by the slaughter of Simeon and Levi, while the other brothers escaped. That is just possible; but if so, the narrative departs very widely from the prevailing tradition, according to which S. and L. not only survived, but went down into Egypt with the rest of the family. And there is room for doubt whether the curse on S. and L. in ch. 49 is the result of any particular action of these two tribes (see pp. 516 f.).—The one point, indeed, which stands out with some degree of evidence from these discussions is that there was a form of the patriarchal tradition which knew nothing of the sojourn in Egypt, and connected the story of the conquest with the name of Jacob.

CH. XXXV.—*Jacob in Canaan* (E, J, P).

The compiler's interest in the story of Jacob would seem to have flagged after he had brought him safely back to Canaan; and he hurries to a close with a series of fragmentary excerpts from his sources: a second visit to Bethel, with the death and burial of Deborah, $^{1-15}$; the birth of Benjamin and death of Rachel, $^{16-20}$; Reuben's incest, $^{21.\ 22a}$; a list of Jacob's sons, $^{22b-26}$; the death and burial of Isaac, $^{27-29}$.

Sources.—The P sections are easily recognised by their phraseology, viz. $^{6a*\ 9-13.\ 15.\ 22b-26.\ 27-29}$. The last continuous extract from P was 28^{1-9}; and the connecting links are $29^{24.\ 28b.\ 29}$ $30^{4a.\ 9b.\ 22a}$ $31^{18a\beta\gamma\delta b}$ $33^{18a\beta}$. The natural position of 35^{22b-26} is between 30^{22a} and 31^{18} (see v.[26]); and this transposition is adopted by We. (*Prol.*[6] 327); but perhaps a still better position would be in 37^{2} (see p. 443). A more thorough readjustment is proposed by Gu.: 28^{1-9} $35^{6a.\,11-13a.\,15}$ $29^{24.\,28b.\,29}$ $30^{4a.\,9b.\,22a}$ 35^{22b-26} $31^{18a\beta\gamma\delta b}$ $33^{18a\beta}$ $35^{9.\,10.\,27-29}$. This division of the Bethel-theophany into two, one on the way to Mesopotamia and the other after the return (as in E), is very attractive, and relieves some critical difficulties, as shown in the notes on [9ff.].—To E belong [1-5. 6b-8. 14]: cf. אלהים[ה], [1. 5. 7]; אל, [3. 7]; מצבה, [14]; אלהי הנכר, [2. 4] (cf. Jos. $24^{2.\,20.\,23}$); and the reference in v.[1] to $28^{20ff.}$.—[16-20] are also from E in the main, though perhaps with J variants (מצבה, [20]; cf. the retrospective reference in 48^{7}).—The only purely Yahwistic section is [21. 22a] (ישראל *bis*).

1–8 + 14. Bethel re-visited: the death of Deborah.—**1.** Jacob is reminded of his vow at Bethel ($28^{20ff.}$), and commanded to build an altar there.—*go up*] From Shechem to Bethel there is a continuous ascent of over 1000 ft.—*and dwell there*] It would almost seem that Bethel is to be Jacob's permanent residence; and this (though contradicted by v.[16]) would be in harmony with the tenor of the Elohistic tradition, which closely associates this patriarch with the chief Ephraimite sanctuary.—**2.** Jacob purifies his household for a solemn act of worship.—*Put away the strange gods*] The same words spoken under the same tree by Joshua (24^{23} [E]), point, it would appear, to the memory of a great national renunciation of idolatry at Shechem in the early history of Israel (see v.[4]). A reference to the Teraphim stolen by Rachel (31^{19}) does not exhaust the significance of the notice.—**3.** The use of the old name אֵל here and v.[1] (cf. v.[7]) is noticeable.—**4.** *the earrings* (see on 24^{22})] Objects of superstition, being used as amulets, and in false worship (Ho. 2^{15}, cf. Ju. $8^{24ff.}$).—*the terebinth near Shechem*] See on 12^{6}. The burial of idolatrous emblems under this sacred tree has some traditional meaning which we cannot now explain.—**5.** *a terror of God*] a πανικὸν δεῖμα (De.); cf. Ex. 23^{27}, 1 Sa. 14^{15}, 2 Ch. 14^{13} etc.

V.[5] presupposes an incident like that recorded in ch. 34. The intervening vv.[1-4] are not in keeping with this view of the situation; and the

1. ביתאל] 𝕲 εἰς τὸν τόπον Βαιθήλ is not unlikely to be original (cf. 28^{11} 12^{6}).—**3.** ואעשה] 𝕲 ונעשה.—**4** end] 𝕲 + καὶ ἀπώλεσεν αὐτὰ ἕως τῆς σήμερον ἡμέρας.—**5.** ויסעו] 𝕲 καὶ ἐξῆρεν Ἰσραὴλ ἐκ Σικίμων.—יעקב] 𝕲 Ἰσραήλ.

change of subject from 'Jacob' to 'the sons of Jacob' makes it highly probable that v.^{5} is either redactional (Kue.), or belongs to a different stratum of E.

6a (P). See below.—**7**. The designation of *the place* (*i.e.* the sanctuary: 12^{6} 28^{11}) as *'Ēl Bêth'ēl* is not confirmed by any other OT allusion. Partial analogies may be found in such place-names as Ǎšterôth-Ḳarnaim, Nĕbô, Baal-Ḥăẓôr, Baal-Gad, etc., where the name of the deity is extended to the sacred precincts (Gu. 248); but the text is not above suspicion.—*there the gods had revealed themselves to him*] The pl. vb. together with the use of the art. suggests that the sentence preserves a more polytheistic version of the Bethel-legend than 28^{12},—one in which the 'angels of God' were spoken of as simply אֱלֹהִים.—**8, 14**. The death and burial of Deborah.—*below Bêth'ēl*] means apparently 'to the S of Bethel.'—*under the oak*] or 'sacred tree' (see on 12^{6}).—*tree of weeping*] But *v.i.*—**14**. For the grounds on which this v. is connected with ^{8}, see the footnote *ad loc.*—*set up a maẓẓēbāh*] So v.^{20} at the grave of Rachel. These monuments came to be regarded as simple grave-stones; but were doubtless originally objects of worship, as the next clause indicates.—*poured out a libation on it*] The libation was in the first instance an offering to the dead, according to a custom attested among many ancient peoples,* and found in Catholic countries at the present day.—*poured oil*] 28^{18}.

6a. לוזה] See on 28^{19}. The cl. is an amalgam of P and E.—**7**. למקום] 𝔊 τὸ ὄνομα τοῦ τόπου.—אל ביתאל] 𝔊𝔙𝔖 ביתאל.—**8**. ותקבר] 𝔊 om.—אַלּוֹן] see on 12^{6}.—בכות] 'weeping.' The text is perhaps confirmed by בֹּכִים (weepers), Ju. 2^{5}, which may be the same place. But though בכים might plausibly be regarded as a corruption of בְּכָאִים (2 Sa. $5^{23ff.}$, Ps. 84^{7}), it is difficult to think that בכות is so: 'sacred tree of the baka-trees' is an improbable combination (see v. Gall, *CSt.* 103).

9. עוד] 𝔊 + ἐν Λουζα.—אתו] 𝔐𝔊 + אלהים.—**10**. 𝔊 simplifies by omitting שמך יעקב and ויקרא את שמו ישראל.—**12**. נתתי] 𝔖 נשבעתי (so a schol. in Field).—**14**. The v. cannot possibly be from P, who recognises no maẓẓebās,

---

* Egyptians (Erman, *LAE*, 307), Persians (Her. vii. 43), Greeks (Hom. *Il.* xxiii. 196, *Od.* xi. 26 ff.), Arabs (We. *Heid.*^{2} 182 f.). It is not mentioned in OT, but food-offerings to the dead are referred to in Dt. 26^{14} (To. 4^{18}, Sir. 30^{18}).

The notice of Deborah is in many ways perplexing. The nurse who accompanied Rebekah (24^{59}) is nameless, and there is nothing to lead us to expect that she was to be an important figure in Hebrew legend. How she could have come into Jacob's family is quite inexplicable; and the conjectures that have been advanced on this point are all puerile. Moreover, the sacred tree referred to is in all probability identical with the palm-tree of Deborah 'between Ramah and Bethel' in Ju. $4^{4f.}$. There seems to have been a confusion in the local tradition between the famous prophetess and the nurse; and the chief mystery is how the name of Rebekah got introduced in this connexion at all. If we could suppose with Cheyne (417 f.) that בכות should be בְּכֹרַת and that this is an alternative form of רבקה, so that the real name of the tree was 'Tree of Rebekah,' we might be a step nearer a solution. The identity of the two trees would then have to be abandoned. It is, however, an unsafe argument to say that a 'nurse' could not have been conspicuous in legend: cf. the grave of the nurse of Dionysus at Scythopolis, in Pliny, *HN*, v. 74 (De. Gu.).

9, 10. Jacob's name changed (P).—Comp. $32^{28f.}$ (J).—*when he came from Paddan 'Ărām*] On Gu.'s rearrangement (p. 423 above), there is nothing to suggest Bethel as the scene of the revelation. It is a faint echo of $32^{25ff.}$ from which every element of local tradition, down to the name of the sanctuary, has been eliminated.

6a, 11–13, 15. The blessing transmitted to Jacob: P's parallel to $28^{10ff.}$.—**11, 12.** *'Ēl Shaddai*] see on 17^{1}.—For other expressions in the vv., cf. $17^{6.\,8.\,16}$ $28^{3.\,4}$ 46^{26} 48^{4}.—**13a.** *God went up from him*] as 17^{22}.—**13b** is an awkward continuation, and has probably arisen through dittography from v. [15].—**15.** The naming of the place, as 28^{19}.

That the section refers to Jacob's outward journey, and that [9f.] describe a different theophany on his return, is probable from the following considerations: (1) The analogy of the older tradition (JE). (2) בבאו

---

and no ritual worship of any kind before the Sinaitic legislation. As a part of the Bethel-narrative, it is unintelligible in E, who has already described the origin of the maẓẓebāh there (28^{18}), and still more in J, who does not sanction maẓẓebās at all. The impression that the scene is Bethel depends solely on the words במקום—אתו, which can easily be excised, as a gloss from [15]. The suggestion that the v. continues [8] is due to Cornill (*ZATW*, xi. 15 ff.), and seems the most satisfactory solution of the problem.—נֶסֶךְ] 2 Ki. $16^{13.\,15}$ is the only other instance of the word before Jeremiah, though the vb. appears in 2 Sa. 23^{16}, Ho. 9^{4}. In Jer., Ezk. (20^{28}), and II Isa. it is an accompaniment of heathenish worship; its legalisation for the worship of the temple appe s in Ezk. 45^{17} and P. Its mention here a proof of the great antiquity of the notice (Corn. *l.c.*).

מפדן ארם ([9]) is superfluous after we have read ([6a]) that he had reached a spot בא' כנען. (3) That two consecutive vv. ([10. 11]) should commence with ויאמר לו א' is unnatural even in P (so KS.). (4) The self-disclosure of the divine speaker ([11]) must introduce the revelation (cf. 17^{1}). (5) The עוד of v.[9] (generally treated as redactional) presupposes a former revelation. The one difficulty in this theory of Gu. is to imagine an adequate reason for the dislocation of P.

16–20. Rachel dies in child-birth (E).—**16.** The event took place on the journey from Bethel to *'Ephrāth*, an unknown locality in the later territory of Benjamin (see after v.[20]).—**17.** *This also is a son for thee*] So the nurse cheers the dying woman by recalling her prayer at the birth of Joseph (30^{24}).—**18.** With her last breath Rachel names her son *Ben-'ônî*; but the father, to avert the omen, calls him *Binyāmîn*. The pathos of the narrative flows in sympathy with the feelings of the mother: a notice of Jacob's life-long grief for the loss of Rachel is reserved for 48^{7}.—**19.** *on the way to 'Ephrāth*] The next clause, *that is Bethlehem*, is a gloss (see Sta. *ZATW*, iii. 1 ff.).—**20.** See on v.[14].

The site of Rachel's grave is determined by 1 Sa. 10^{2} (on the border of Benjamin, between Ramah and Gibeah) and Jer. 31^{14} (cf. 40^{1}). Christian tradition places it about a mile N of Bethlehem, in accordance with the gloss at the end of [19]. This, however, rests on a confusion of Ephrath and the better known clan-name אֶפְרָת ־ָה ־ִים, which is always connected with Bethlehem. It is unnecessary to assume a divergence of ancient tradition regarding the site. The beautiful verse of Jeremiah 31^{14} shows how vivid and persistent was the hold of these legends on the popular mind.—The birth of Benjamin in Canaan is interpreted by many critics to mean that this tribe, unlike the rest, was formed after

---

16. ויסעו מביתאל] 𝔊 'Απάρας δὲ 'I. + *ἔπηξεν τὴν σκηνὴν αὐτοῦ ἐπέκεινα τοῦ πύργου Γαδερ* (fr. [21]), showing the influence of the theory that מגדל עדר was at Jerusalem, which Jacob would naturally pass on the way to Bethlehem.—כברת הארץ] 48^{7}, 2 Ki. 5^{19} † (without art.). Apparently a measure of distance (𝔖 a parasang); but nothing is certain. Acc. to Hoffmann (*GGA*, 1890, 23 ff.), 'as far as one can see.'—**17.** בהקשתה (Hi.) ‖ ותקש (Pi.) in [16],—possibly variants from E and J.—Another trace of J is גם זה, pointing back to 30^{24b}.—**18.** בן־אוני] 'son of my sorrow,' from אָוֶן, 'trouble.' Not improbably it is an obsolete proper name, having some connexion with אוֹנוֹ, a city and valley in Benjamin (Ben. 325; Che. 420).—בן־ימין] Usually understood as 'son of good fortune,' the right hand being in antiquity the lucky or fortunate side. The original meaning is probably 'son of the south' (cf. 1 Sa. $23^{19.24}$, **Ps.** 89^{13} etc.), Benjamin being the most southerly of the Rachel tribes.

the conquest of the country (We. Sta. Guthe, al.): Steuern. goes further, and infers that the rise of Benjamin brought about the dissolution of the Rachel tribe. But all such speculations are precarious. The *name* Benjamin, however, does furnish evidence that this particular tribe *was* formed in Palestine (*v.i.* on [18]).

21, 22a. Reuben's incest (J).—**21.** *Tower of the Flock*] Such towers would be numerous in any pastoral country; and the place here referred to is unknown. Mic. 4^8 proves nothing; and the tradition which locates it near Bethlehem rests on this passage. The order of J's narrative (see p. 414) would lead us to seek it E of the Jordan, where the tribe of Reuben was settled.—**22a.** *and when Israel heard*] Probably a temporal clause, of which the apodosis has been intentionally omitted.

The story, no doubt, went on to tell of a curse pronounced on Reuben, which explained his loss of the birthright (so Gu.; otherwise Di.). The crime is referred to in 49^4. The original motive is perhaps suggested by the striking parallel in *Il.* ix. 449 ff. (Gu.):

> ὅς μοι παλλακίδος περιχώσατο καλλικόμοιο·
> τὴν αὐτὸς φιλέεσκεν, ἀτιμάζεσκε δ' ἄκοιτιν,
> μητέρ' ἐμήν· ἡ δ' αἰὲν ἐμὲ λισσέσκετο γούνων,
> παλλακίδι προμιγῆναι, ἵν' ἐχθήρειε γέροντα.

Note that in $30^{14ff.}$ also, Reuben plays a part in the restoration of his mother's conjugal rights.—An ethnographic reading of the legend finds its historic basis in some humiliation inflicted by Reuben on the Bilhah-tribe, or one of its branches (Dan or Naphtali). See on 49^4.

22b–26. A list of Jacob's sons (P).—In two points the list deviates from the tradition of JE (chs. 29. 30): The children are arranged according to their mothers; and the birth of Benjamin is placed in Mesopotamia. Otherwise the order of JE is preserved: Leah precedes Rachel; but Rachel's maid precedes Leah's.—On the position of the section in the original Code, see pp. 423, 443.

22a. The double accentuation means that [22a] was treated by the Mass. sometimes as a whole v., sometimes as a half; the former for private, the latter for liturgical reading (Str. 129; Wickes, *Prose Accents*, 130). Note the 'gap in the middle of the verse,' which 𝕲 fills up with καὶ πονηρὸν ἐφάνη ἐναντίον αὐτοῦ.—ישראל] The name, instead of Jacob, is from this point onwards a fairly reliable criterion of the document J in Gen.—**26.** ילד] 𝔐 and Heb. MSS ילדו.

27–29. The death of Isaac (P).—In JE Isaac was at the point of death when Jacob fled from Esau; whereas, according to the chronology of P, he survived for 80 years. An equally remarkable divergence from the earlier tradition is seen in Esau's living on with his father in Hebron (see on 32^{4}), and the unbroken friendship between him and Jacob.—**27.** *Mamrē*, *Kiryath-'Arba'*, *Ḥebrôn*. See 13^{18} 23^{2}.—**29.** Cf. $25^{8.\,9}$.—Isaac is buried by *Esau and Jacob his sons*] as Abraham by Isaac and Ishmael (25^{9}) P always lays stress on the harmony of the patriarchal family life.

Ch. XXXVI. *Edomite Genealogies, etc.* (partly P).

The chapter consists of seven (or eight) sections: I. Esau's wives and children, $^{1-5}$; II. His migration to Mount Seir, $^{6-8}$; III. A list of Esau's descendants, $^{9-14}$; IV. An enumeration of clans or clan-chiefs of Esau, $^{15-19}$; V. Two Ḥorite lists: a genealogy, $^{20-28}$, and a list of clans, $^{29.\,30}$; VI. The kings of Edom, $^{31-39}$; VII. A second list of clans of Esau, $^{40-43}$.—The lists are repeated with variations in 1 Ch. 1^{35-54}.

The chapter evidently embodies authentic information regarding the history and ethnology of Edom. Whether the statistics were compiled by Israelite writers from oral tradition, or are the scanty remains of a native Edomite literature, it is naturally impossible to determine; the early development of political institutions in Edom makes the latter hypothesis at least credible (see Meyer, *INS*, 329, 383 f.).

Analysis.—A section headed ואלה תלדות would, if homogeneous, be unhesitatingly ascribed to P; but the repetition of the formula (v.^{9}) throws doubt on its unity, and betrays the hand of a redactor. The phraseology of P is most apparent in II. and VII., but can be detected occasionally elsewhere ($^{2a.\,5b.\,10a.\,12b.\,13b.\,30b}$: *i.e.* in I., III., and V.). The crucial difficulty is the contradiction as to Esau's wives between I. and

---

27. קרית הארבע] Rd. perhaps קריתה ארבע (Kit.).—חברון] 𝔊𝔖 + בארץ כנען.—28. יצחק] 𝔊 + אשר חי (as 25^{7}).—29 end] S ܥܣܘ ܘܝܥܩܘܒ ܒܢܘܗܝ.—In P's chronology, Jacob at his father's death had reached the age of 120 years (cf. 35^{28} with 25^{26}); he was 40 years old when he set out for Paddan Aram. The interval of 80 years has to be divided between his sojourn with Laban and his subsequent residence with Isaac; but in what proportions we have no data to determine.

26^{34} 28^{9} (see on vv.[1-5]). On this point I., III., and IV. hang together; and if these sections are excluded, there remains nothing that can be plausibly assigned to P except II. and VII. (so We. Kue. Ho. Gu. al.). The argument for reducing P's share in the chapter to this minimum rests, however, on the assumption that the Code is the compilation of a single writer, who cannot be supposed to lapse into self-contradiction. The facts seem to point to a redactional process and a divergence of tradition within the Priestly school; and I am inclined to think that in I. (?), III., and IV. we have excerpts from the book of Tôledôth incorporated in P, whose main narrative will have included 26^{34} 28^{9}, and in which 35^{29} 36^{6-8} 37^{1} may have read continuously. VII. must then be rejected as a late compilation in which the style of the Tôledôth is successfully imitated (so Meyer).—As regards V. and VI. little can be said. The former might well have been part of the Tôledôth; the latter is unique in Gen., and there are no positive reasons for assigning it to J (so most) or any other source.

1–5. Esau's wives and sons.—The scheme here projected supplies the common framework of the two Edomite genealogies, [9–14] and [15–19], except that in the following sections the second and third wives exchange places. These marriages and births are said to have taken place *in the land of Canaan*, before the migration to Sēʿîr; but the fact that ʾOholibamah is a Ḥorite (see below), indicates an absorption of Ḥorite clans in Edom which would naturally have followed the settlement in Seʿir.—Here we come on a difference of tradition regarding the names and parentage of Esau's wives.

According to 26^{34} 28^{9} (P), the three wives are (*a*) *Yᵉhûdîth* bath-Bᵉʾērî, the Hittite; (*b*) *Bāsᵉmath* bath-ʾĒlôn, the Ḥittite (𝔐𝔊[A]𝔖 Ḥivvite); (*c*) *Maḥălath* bath-Yišmāʿēl, sister of Nᵉbayôth. Here they are (*a*) ʿ*Ādā* bath-ʾElôn, the Ḥittite; (*b*) ʾ*Ohŏlîbāmāh* bath-ʿĂnāh, the Ḥorite; (*c*) *Bāsᵉmath* bath-Yišmāʿēl, sister of Nᵉbāyôth. The confusion is too great to be accounted for naturally by textual corruption, though that may have played a part. We can only conjecture vaguely that vv.[9-14]

1. הוא אדום] probably a gloss (cf. v.[8. 19]); but the persistency with which the equivalence is asserted is itself instructive. Esau and Edom are really distinct names (see p. 359 f.), and P has no legendary identification of them, such as 25^{30}. Hence the connexion is established in two ways: Esau=Edom ([1. 8. 19]); and Esau the father of Edom ([9. 43]).—2. עשו לקח] 'had taken,' as already recorded (26^{34} 28^{9}).—בת צבעון] 𝔐𝔊𝔖 בןצ'; deleted by Ho. and Gu. as a gloss. But in clan names gender is not always carefully distinguished; and the writer probably took ענה as fem. In v.[25] ʾOholibamah is herself one of the *sons* of ʿAnah.—החוי] Rd. הַחֹרִי, *v.s.*—5. יעישׁ] Keth. as v.[14], 1 Ch. 7^{10}; Qrê יְעוּשׁ, as v.[18], 1 Ch.

represent a different tradition from 26^{34} 28^{9}; and that in $^{2-5a}$ a clumsy and half-hearted attempt has been made to establish some points of contact between them. If we accept the החוי of 𝔐, etc., in 26^{34}, the two traditions agree in the main ethnological point, that the Edomite people was composed of Ḥittite (? Canaanite), Ḥivvite (? Ḥorite), and Ishmaelite elements.

On the Names.—(*a*) עדה is the name of one of Lamech's wives: see on 4^{19}.—(*b*) אהליבמה (Ὀλιβεμά, Ἐλιβεμά, etc.). Somewhat similar compounds with אהל are found in Phœnician (אהלבעל, אהלמלך) and Sab. (אהלאל, אהלעתתר) as well as in Heb. (אהליאב, Ex. 31^{6}; אהליבה, Ezk. $23^{4ff.}$) (see Gray, *HPN*, 246^{1}). The first component is presumably Ar. and Sab. *'ahl*, 'family'; the second ought by analogy to be a divine name, though none such is known. It is philologically probable that names of this type were originally clan-names; and 'אה is taken from the old list of Ḥorite clans (v.^{25}, cf. ^{41}).—(*c*) בשמת (for which 𝔐 always reads מחלת, 28^{9}), if from √ בשם, 'smell sweetly,' is likely to have been a favourite woman's name, but recurs only 1 Ki. 4^{15} of a daughter of Solomon. On ענה and צבעון, see on v.^{20}: the obvious connexion with that v. makes it practically certain that חִוִּי in v.^{2} is a mistake for חֹרִי.—On the sons, see below.—It is pointed out by Ho. (187) that both in $^{9-14}$ and $^{15-19}$ the 'Oholibamah branch holds a somewhat exceptional position. This may mean that it represents hybrid clans, whereas the other two are of pure Edomite stock: that it is a later insertion in the lists is less likely.

6–8. Esau's migration to Se'ir.—**6.** Cf. 12^{5} (34^{23}).—*and his daughters*] None are mentioned in $^{2-5}$.—*to the land of Sē'ir*] So we must read with 𝔖.—**7.** The motive for the separation is the same as that which led to the parting of Abraham and Lot (13^{6a}), implying that Esau had lived at Hebron after Jacob's return; contrast J, 32^{4} $33^{14.16}$.—**8.** *the mountain of Sē'ir*] the mountainous country E of the Arabah, the southern part of which is now called *eš-Šera'* and the northern *Ğebāl* (Buhl, *Edom.* 28 ff.). The *land* Se'ir includes the whole Edomite territory as far W as Ḳadesh (Nu. 20^{16}). See on 14^{6} $27^{39f.}$, and below on v.^{20}.

9–14. The genealogy of Esau.—**9, 10.** For the double heading וא' תלדות followed by וא' שמות, cf. $25^{12f.}$.—*Esau the father of Edom*] see footnote on v.^{1}. It is strange that except in these glosses *Edom* is never the eponymus of the

---

1^{35} 8^{39} $23^{10f.}$, 2 Ch. 11^{19}†.—6. אל־ארץ gives no sense, and to insert אַחֶרֶת (𝔗^{O} 𝔙) is inadmissible without a change of text. 𝔐𝔊 מארץ כנען is possible; but it is simplest to follow 𝔖 אל־ארץ שעיר.—מפני] 'on account of, as 6^{13} 27^{4} etc.

nation, although it appears to have been the name of a god
(עבד אדם, 2 Sa. 6¹⁰).—**11 ff.** The total number of the tribes,
excluding the bastard *'Amālēḳ*, is 12, as in the cases of
Israel and Ishmael (25¹²⁻¹⁶). The sons of 'Oholibamah are,
however, put on a level with the grandsons of the other two
wives (so v.¹⁸). The list may be tabulated thus :

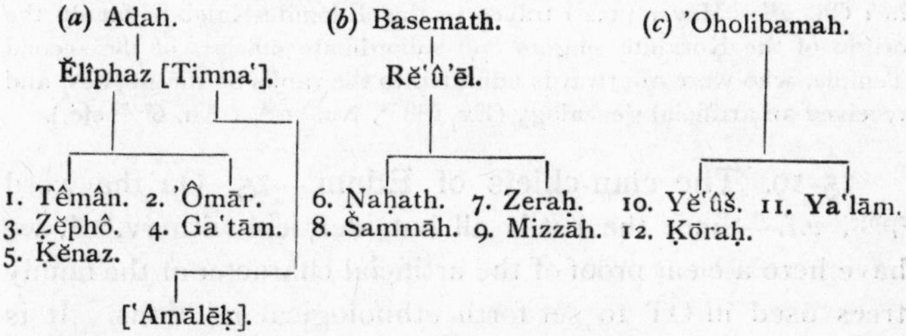

(a) Adah.   (b) Basemath.   (c) 'Oholibamah.

 Ĕlíphaz [Timna']. Rĕ'û'ēl.

1. Têmân. 2. 'Ômār. 6. Naḥath. 7. Zeraḥ. 10. Yĕ'ûš. 11. Ya'lām.
3. Ẓĕphô. 4. Ga'tām. 8. Šammāh. 9. Mizzāh. 12. Ḳōraḥ.
5. Ḳĕnaz.

['Amālēḳ].

The Names.—(a) אליפו] Known otherwise only as the name of the
oldest and wisest of Job's friends (Jb. 2¹¹ etc.), probably borrowed from
this list.—(1) תימן (Θαιμάν)] Frequently mentioned as a district of Edom
(Jer. 49⁷·²⁰, Ezk. 25¹³, Am. 1¹², Ob. ⁹, Hab. 3³), famous for its wisdom,
the home of Eliphaz (Jb. 2¹¹) and of the third king of Edom (v.³⁴). A
village bearing the Greek name, 15 Roman m. from Petra, is mentioned
in *OS*, 260 ; but the site is now lost.—(2) אומר ('Ωμάρ, 'Ωμάν), (3) צפו
(Σωφαρ, 1 Ch. צפי), (4) נעתם (Γοθομ, etc.) are quite unknown, unless
Σωφαρ be the original of Job's third friend.—(5) קנו] the eponym of the
Ḳenizzites, the group to which Kaleb (the ' dog '-tribe, settled in Ḥebron)
and Othniel belonged (Nu. 32¹², Jos. 14⁶·¹⁴ 15¹⁷, Ju. 1¹³ 3⁹·¹¹). The
incorporation of these families in Judah is a typical example of the
unstable political relations of the southern tribes between Israel and
Edom, a fact abundantly illustrated from the lists before us.—The once
powerful people of עמלק (see on 14⁷) is here described as descended from
תמנע, a Ḥorite clan absorbed in Edom (vv.²²·⁴⁰), of which nothing else
is known. The reference may be to an offshoot of the old Amalekites
who had found protection from the Edomites.—(b) רעואל ('Ραγουήλ)]
' Friend of God ' (?) is one of the names of Moses' father-in-law (a
Midianite) (Ex. 2¹⁸, Nu. 10²⁹), also that of a Gadite (Nu. 1¹⁴ 2¹⁴) and of
a Benjamite (1 Ch. 9⁸).—(6) נחת (Ναχοθ, Ναχομ)] cf. 2 Ch. 31¹³.—(7) זרח
(Ζαρε)] (cf. v.³³). Also a clan of Judah (38³⁰) ; cf. Nu. 26¹³ (Simeonite),
1 Ch. 6⁶·²⁶ (Levite).—(8) שמה (Σομε)] cf. 1 Sa. 16⁹ (David's brother), 2 Sa.
23¹¹ (one of his heroes) ; also שמי in Yeraḥmeel (1 Ch. 2²⁸·³²) and Kaleb
(2⁴⁴ᶠ·).—(9) מזה (Μοζε, 'Ομοζε, etc.)] only here. It is pointed out that the
four names form a doggerel sentence : ' descent and rising, there and
here ' (KS. *An.* 178) ; but three of them are sufficiently authenticated ;
and the fact does not prove them to be inventions of an idle fancy.—
(10) יעיש ('Ιε[ο]υς, 'Ιεουλ, etc.)] *v. i.* on v.⁵. As an Israelite name, 1 Ch.
7¹⁰ 8³⁹ (Benjamite), 23¹⁰ᶠ· (Levite), 2 Ch. 11¹⁹ (son of Rehoboam). The

name is thought by some to be identical with that of an Arabian lion-god *Yaġūṯ* (though 𝔊 must have pronounced ع not غ), meaning 'helper,' whose antiquity is vouched for by inscrs. of Thamud (Rob. Sm. *KM*², 254; We. *Heid.*² 19, 146; Nö. *ZDMG*, xl. 168; Fischer, *ib.* lviii. 869; Mey. *INS*, 351 f.; on the other side, Nö. *ZDMG*, xlv. 595; Di. 384; Buhl, *Edom.* 48 f.).—(11) יעלם (Ἰεγλομ, etc.)] possibly an animal name fr. יָעֵל = 'ibex'; but see Gray, *HPN*, 90[5]; cf. יָעֵל, Ju. 4[17ff.] 5[24], and יַעְלָה, Ezr. 2[56].—(12) קרח (Κορε)] a son of Ḥebron, and therefore a Kalebite clan in 1 Ch. 2[43]. Meyer (352[5]) traces to this Edomite-Kalebite family the origin of the Ḳoraḥite singers and subordinate officials of the second Temple, who were afterwards admitted to the ranks of the Levites, and received an artificial genealogy (Ex. 6[21. 24], Nu. 26[58], 1 Ch. 6[7. 22] etc.).

15–19. The clan-chiefs of Edom.—15. On the word אַלּוּף, *v.i.*—Since the list is all but identical with vv.[9–14], we have here a clear proof of the artificial character of the family trees used in OT to set forth ethnological relations. It is not improbable that this is the original census of Edomite 'thousands' from which the genealogy of [9–14] was constructed.—**16.** *ʿAmālēk* is here placed on a level with the other branches (ct. v.[12]).

20–30. Ḥorite genealogies.—20. *the inhabitants of the land*] (Ex. 23[31], Nu. 32[17], Ju. 1[33]); cf. 14[6], Dt. 2[12]. These autochthones are described geographically and ethnologically as sons of *Sēʿîr the Horite*, i.e., a section of the Ḥorite population settled in Mt. Seʿir, Seʿir being personified as the fictitious ancestor of the natives of the country.

---

15. אלוף] 𝔊 ἡγεμών, 𝔙 *dux*, whence EV 'duke.' The word means properly 'chiliarch,' the chief of an אֶלֶף (='thousand' or 'clan'): so Ex. 15[15], Zec. 12[5. 6] 9[7]. Elsewhere it signifies 'friend'; and since the sense 'clan' would be suitable in all the passages cited, it has been proposed to read in each case, as well as in this ch., אֶלֶף as the original text (Rob. Sm. *JPh.* ix. 90; Mey. *INS*, 330). Practically it makes no difference; for in any case the 'chiefs' are but personifications of their clans.—**16.** אלוף קרח] 𝔐 om., probably a gloss from v.[18].—**18.** בת—עשו] 𝔊 om.—**19.** הוא ארום] 𝔊 *οὗτοι εἰσιν οἱ ἡγεμόνες αὐτῶν, υἱοὶ* Ἐδώμ.—**20.** ישבי] 𝔊 sing.—**24b.** הַיֵּמִם] The word is utterly obscure. 𝔊Θ. *τὸν* Ἰαμειν; Aq. *τοὺς ἡμιν* [*ἰμειμ*] (see Field); 𝔐 האימים (Dt. 2[10]: so 𝔗ᴼ גבריא); 𝔗ᴶ 'wild-asses' and 'mules'; 𝔖 ܠܗ ܡܝ̈ܐ (הַמַּיִם?); 𝔙 *aquæ callidæ*. If 𝔙 be right (and it is certainly the most plausible conjecture for sense), [24b] is a fragment of an old well-legend, claiming the proprietorship of these hot springs for the tribe of ʿAnah (cf. Ju. 1[14ff.]). See, further, Haupt, in Ball, *SBOT*, 118.—**30b** is in the style of P.—שעיר] 𝔊 Ἐδώμ.

The name חרי is now generally regarded as a geographical designation, identical with the *Ḫaru* of the Eg. monuments (Müller, *AE*, 137, 149 ff., 240; Jen. *ZA*, x. 332 f., 346 f.; Schw. *ZATW*, xviii. 126; Mey. *INS*, 330 f.), The older theory that the name is derived from חור and means 'cave-dwellers,' is not necessarily discredited by this identification. Even if the Ḥorites were a stratum of population that once covered the region from the Egyptian frontier to the neighbourhood of Damascus, there still seems no reason why they should not have been largely an old troglodyte race, from whom the country derived its name.

The Classification.—According to [20f.] [29f.] there were seven main branches of the Ḥorites in Se'ir, represented by Loṭān, Šôbāl, Ẓib'ôn, 'Ănāh, Dîšôn, 'Ēẓer, and Rîšān (see below). Of these, however, 'Anah and Dišon reappear as subdivisions of Ẓib'on and 'Anah respectively. The duplication has been explained by supposing that parts of these tribes had amalgamated with kindred branches, and thus came to figure both as sons and grandsons of the original ancestor (Di. Gu. al.). It is more likely that 'Anah and Dišon were at first subordinate septs of Ẓib'on (so Mey. 341); that they came into the list of *'allûphîm* ([29f.]) as heads of clan groups; and, finally, obtained a primary position amongst the 'sons' of Se'ir. The relationship as thus reconstructed may be exhibited as follows:

(*a*) Lôṭān (Timna').	(*b*) Šôbāl.	(*c*) Ẓib'ôn.	(*d*) 'Ēẓer.	(*e*) Rîšān.
Ḥōrî, Hēmām.	'Alwān, Mānaḥat, 'Êbāl, Šĕphô, 'Ônām.	'Ayyāh, 'Ănāh, — Dîšôn (Ohŏlîbāmāh), — Ḥemdān, 'Ešbān, Yithrān, Kĕrān.	Bilhān, Za'ăvān [Zû'ān], [Ya]'ăkān.	'Ûẓ, 'Ărān.

The Names.—(*a*) לוטן is plausibly connected with לוט (also a cave-dweller, 19[30]), who may have been originally an ancestral deity worshipped in these regions.—Philologically it is interesting to observe the frequency of the endings *-ān*, *-ōn* in this list, pointing to a primitive *nunation*, as constrasted with sporadic cases of *mimation* in the Edomite names.—חרי (v.[22])] The occurrence of the national name (v.[20]) as a subdivision of itself is surprising. Mey. (339) suspects confusion with another genealogy in which Lôṭan figured as ancestor of the whole Ḥorite race.—הימם (1 Ch. הוֹמָם, 𝔊 Αἱμάν)] cf. הֵימָן, 1 Ki. 5[11], 1 Ch. 2[6], Ps. 89[1].—תמנע, strangely introduced as the 'sister' of Lôṭan, is the same as the concubine of Eliphaz (v.[12]): probably interpolated in both places.—(*b*) שובל (Σωβάλ)] also a Kalebite tribe settled in Ḳiryath-Ye'arim, incorporated in Judah (1 Ch. 2[50. 52] 4[1f.]). The name was connected by Rob. Sm. with Ar. *šibl*, 'young lion.' Ar. ش ought to be שׁ in Heb.; but the objection is perhaps not final in a borrowed name (but see Nö. *ZDMG*, xl. 168; Gray, *HPN*, 109).—עלון (1 Ch. עליָן, 𝔊 Γωλών, Γωλάμ, etc.)] cf. עלוה, v.[40]; otherwise unknown.—מנחת] It cannot be accidental that in

1 Ch. 2[52] the 'half of Manaḥat' is again represented as descended from Šôbāl. These Manaḥathites are further connected with צָרְעָה (v.[53f.]), a notice which We. (Bleek[4], 197) has ingeniously combined with Ju. 13[2], where מָנוֹחַ, the father of Samson, is a native of Ẓor'ah. It seems to follow, not only that מנוח is originally the eponymus of מנחת, but that this Ḥorite clan lived in early times in Ẓor'ah and was included in the mixed tribe of Dan (Mey. 340).—עיבל (Γαιβηλ)] Mey. identifies with the well-known mountain E of Shechem, originally a Ḥorite settlement (?). —שפו (1 Ch. שְׁפִי, 𝔊 Σωφάρ, Σωφάν, Σωφ, etc.)] unknown.—אונם ('Ωμαν, 'Ωναν)] A Yeraḥmeelite name, 1 Ch. 2[26. 28]. The name of Judah's son אונן (Gn. 38[4ff.]) may also be compared.—(*c*) צבעון (Σεβεγών)] Possibly a hyæna-tribe (*ḍabu'*, ܙܒܘܿܥܳܐ, NH, צבוע) (Smith, *KM*[2], 254; Gray, 95).—איה] 'falcon' (Lv. 11[14], Dt. 14[13], Jb. 28[7]); cf. the personal name, 2 Sa. 3[7] 21[8ff.]. —ענה] unknown.—דישן, דישׁן (Δησων, Δαισων)]='mountain-goat' (Dt. 14[5]). —חמדן (Ch. חַמְרָן) and אשבן are not known.—יתרן] Derived from a widely diffused personal name (Heb. Bab. Sab. Nabat.), best known in OT as that of Moses's father-in-law (Ex. 3[1] etc.); also a son of Gideon (Ju. 8[20]), and the Ishmaelite father of Amasa (2 Sa. 17[25] etc.). —כרן (Χαρράν)] only here.—(*d*) אצר] unknown.—בלהן] can scarcely be dissociated from Rachel's handmaid בלהה, whose Ḥorite origin would be somewhat more intelligible if Ḥorite clans were amalgamated in one of her subdivisions (Dan; see on *Manaḥat* above).— זעון (𝔐 ,זעון 𝔊 Ζουκάμ, Ζαυάν=זַעֲוָן)] unknown.—עקן (better יַעֲקָן, as 1 Ch. 1[42])] The tribe is doubtless to be identified with the בְּנֵי יַעֲקָן mentioned in Nu. 33[31f.], Dt. 10[6] as the owners of some wells S of Ḳadesh.—(*e*) דישן (𝔊 Ῥ[ε]ισων)] Rd. דִישׁוֹן or רִישָׁן, to avoid concurrence with the דישן of v.[25f.].—עוץ (Ὦς)] see on 10[23] 22[21].—ארן] Perhaps connected with the Yeraḥmeelite אֹרֶן, 1 Ch. 2[25]. The reading ארם (Heb. MSS, 𝔊𝔙𝔗J) is probably a mistake caused by the proximity of עוץ.

31–39. The kings of Edom.—**31.** ***before there reigned a king of the Israelites*** (*v.i.*)] This may mean either before the institution of the monarchy in Israel, or before any Israelitish sovereign ruled over Edom. The natural *terminus ad quem* is, of course, the overthrow of Edomite independence by David (p. 437 below).—The document bears every mark of authenticity, and may be presumed to give a complete list of Edomite kings. Unfortunately the chronology is wanting. An average reign of 20 years for the eight kings (Meyer) is perhaps a reasonable allowance in early un-

---

31. לבני ישראל] Expression of gen. by ל to prevent determination of the governing noun by the following determinate gen. (G-K. § 129*c*), 'a king belonging to the I.' The second interpretation given above is the only natural one. 𝔊^A ἐν Ιερουσαλήμ, 𝔊^L ἐν Ἰσραήλ,—the latter too readily approved by Ball.

settled times; and the foundation of the Edomite monarchy may be dated approximately from 150 to 200 years before the time of David.—The monarchy was obviously not hereditary, none of the kings being the son of his predecessor; that it was elective (Tu. Kn. Di. De. Dri. al.) is more than we have a right to assume. Frazer (*AAO*, 11^{3}) finds here an illustration of his theory of female succession, the crown passing to men of other families who married the hereditary princesses; but v.^{39} is fatal to this view. The fact that the kings reigned in different cities supports an opinion (Winckler, *GI*, i. 192; Che. 429) that they were analogous to the Hebrew Judges, *i.e.* local chiefs who held supreme power during their life, but were unable to establish a dynasty. A beginning of the recognition of the hereditary principle may be traced in the story of Hadad 'of the seed royal' (1 Ki. 11$^{14ff.}$), who is regarded as heir-presumptive to the throne (Meyer).

32. בלע בן־בעור (𝔊 Βάλακ υἱ. τοῦ Βεώρ)] The name of the first king bears a striking resemblance to בלעם בן־בעור, the soothsayer whom the king of Moab hired to curse Israel (Nu. 22 ff.), and who afterwards died fighting for Midian (Nu. 31^{8} [P]). The identity of the two personages is recognised by (amongst others) Kn-Di. Nö. (*Unters.* 87), Hommel (*AHT*, 153, 222^{1}), Sayce (*EHH*, 224, 229), Che. al., though the legend which places his home at Pethor on the Euphrates (E) is hardly consistent with this notice.—דנהבה (Δενναβα), his city, is not known; acc. to Jerome, *OS*, p. 115,[1] it is *Dannaia*, between Ar Moab and the Arnon, or *Dannaba* near Heshbon (cf. Eus. *OS*, 114^{31}, [p. 249]); Hommel and Sayce suggest Dunip, somewhere in N Syria.—**33.** יובב ('Ιω[α]βάβ, 'Ιώβ, etc.)] identified by 𝔊 (Jb. 42^{18}) with the patriarch Job.—בצרה] A chief city of Edom (Is. 34^{6} 63^{1}, Jer. 48^{24} 49$^{13.\ 22}$, Am. 1^{12}), now *el-Buṣaireh*, 20 m. SE of the Dead Sea.—**34.** חשם ('Ασόμ, 𝔖 ܚܘܫܘܡ = חֻשׁוּם)].—*the land of the Temanite*] see on v.^{11}.—**35.** הדד bears the well-known name of an Aramæan deity, whose worship must have prevailed widely in Edom (see v.^{39}, 1 Ki. 11$^{14ff.}$).—*who smote Midian, etc.*] The solitary historical notice in the list. It is a tempting suggestion of Ewald (*HI*, ii. 336), that the battle was an incident of the great Midianite raid under which Israel suffered so severely, so that this king was contemporary with Gideon (cf. Meyer, 381 f.).—עוית] 𝔊 Γεθθαίμ = עַתַּיִם, on which reading Marquart (*Fundamente*, 11) bases an ingenious explanation of the mysterious name כושן רשעתים in Ju. 3$^{8ff.}$ (חוּשָׁם ראשׁ עַתַּיִם,—a confusion of the third and fourth kings in our list).—**36.** שמלה] 𝔊 שלמה, perhaps the same name as Solomon.—משרקה] A place of this name (Μασρικά) is mentioned in *OS*, 137^{10} (p. 277), in Gebalene, the northern part of Mt. Seir.—37. שאול] The name of the first king of Israel.—רחבות הנהר] so called to distinguish it from other places of the same name (cf. 26[22]), is probably the Ῥωβώθ of *OS*, 145[15] (p. 286), a military post in Gebalene. The river is, therefore, not the Euphrates (although a place *Rahaba* has been discovered on its W side), but some perennial stream in the N of Edom, defined by the city on its banks (cf. 2 Ki. 5[12]).—38. בעל חנן] 'Baal is gracious.' The name of the seventh king is the only existing trace of Baal-worship in Edom.—עכבור] 'jerboa' (Ar. *'akbar*): see Rob. Sm. *KM*[2], 235[1]. Here it is probably a clan-name, but appears as personal in OT (2 Ki. 22[14], Jer. 26[22] 36[12]).—39. הדר] To be read הדד (Heb. MSS, 𝔐𝔖𝔊 partly, and 1 Ch. 1[50]).—For פעו (1 Ch. פעי), 𝔊 has Φόγωρ, *i.e.* פְּעוֹר, the mountain in Moab (Nu. 23[28] etc.).—Why the wife of Hadad II. is named we cannot tell. מהיטבאל ('God does good') is a man's name in Neh. 6[10].—For בת מי זהב it would be better to read בן מ' (𝔊𝔖). But מי זהב (gold-water) is more likely to be the name of a place than of a person; hence Marquart's emendation מן מ' (*l.c.* 10) is very plausible, as is his identification of מי זהב with the miswritten די זהב of Dt. 1[1].

40–43. The chiefs of Esau. — This second list of *'Allûphîm* presents more features of P's style than any other section of the chapter, but is of doubtful antiquarian value. Of the eleven names, more than one half are found in the preceding lists (10–39); the new names, so far as they can be explained, are geographical. It is possible that the document preserves a statistical survey of administrative districts of Edom subsequent to the overthrow of its independence (Ew. Di. Dri. al.); but there is no evidence that this is the case.

40. עלון=עלוה, v.[23].—יתת ('Ιεθέρ, etc.)] probably יִתֶר=יתרן, v.[26].—41. אלה is supposed to be the seaport אילת; see on 14[6].—פינן (Φινες, Φ[ε]ινων)= פּוּנֹן, Nu. 33[42f.], the Φαινών (*Fenon*) of *OS*, 123[9] (p. 299; cf. p. 123), a village between Petra and Zoar, where were copper mines worked by convicts. The name (see Seetzen, iii. 17), and the ruins of the mines have been discovered at *Fenān*, 6 or 7 m. NNW of Šobek (Meyer, 353 f.).—42. מבצר] Acc. to *OS*, 137[11] (p. 277), Μαβσαρά was a very large village in Gebalene, subject to Petra.—43. מגדיאל and עירם are unknown. For the latter, 𝔊 has Ζαφωει[ν]=צפו, v.[11]. It is probable that in the original text both names were contained, as in an anonymous chronicle edited by Lagarde (*Sept-St.* ii.; see Nestle, *Marg.* 12), making the number up to twelve.

It remains to state briefly the more important historical results yielded by study of these Edomite lists. (1) At the earliest period of which we have any knowledge, the country of Se'ir was peopled by a

---

40. למקמתם] 𝔖 לתלדותם.—בשמתם] 𝔊 בארצתם ובגויהם (10[20. 31]).—43. למשבתם] 𝔐 למשפחותם (v.[40]).—הוא עשו] see on v.[1].

supposed aboriginal race called Ḥorites. Though remnants of this population survived only in Se'ir, there are a few traces of its former existence in Palestine; and it is possible that it had once been co-extensive with the wide region known to the Egyptians as *Ḥaru* (p. 433). —(2) Within historic times the country was occupied by a body of nomads closely akin to the southern tribes of Judah, who amalgamated with the Ḥorites and formed the nation of Edom.—(3) The date of this invasion cannot be determined. Se'irites and Edomites appear almost contemporaneously in Egyptian documents, the former under Ramses III. as a nomadic people whom the king attacked and plundered; and the latter about 50 years earlier under Merneptah, as a band of Bedouin who were granted admission to the pastures of Wādī Ṭumīlāt within the Egyptian frontier (*Pap. Harris* and *Anastasi*: see Müller, *AE*, 135 f.; cf. Mey. *INS*, 337 f.). Since both are described as Bedouin, it would seem that the Edomites were still an unsettled people at the beginning of the 12th cent. The land of *Šêri*, however, is mentioned in the TA Tablets (*KAT*[3], 201) more than two centuries earlier.—(4) The list of kings shows that Edom attained a political organisation much sooner than Israel: hence in the legends Esau is the elder brother of Jacob. The interval between Ramses III. and David is sufficient for a line of eight kings; but the institution of the monarchy must have followed within a few decades the expedition of Ramses referred to above. It is probable (though not certain) that the last king Hadad II. was the one subdued by David, and that the Hadad who fled to Egypt and afterwards returned to trouble Solomon (1 Ki. $11^{14ff.}$) was of his family.—(5) The genealogies furnish evidence of the consanguinity of Edomite and Judæan tribes. In several instances we have found the same name amongst the descendants of Esau or Se'ir and amongst those of Judah (see the notes *pass.*). This might be explained by assuming that a clan had been split up, one part adhering to Edom, and another attaching itself to Judah; but a consideration of the actual circumstances suggests a more comprehensive theory. The consolidation of the tribe of Judah was a process of political segregation: the desert tribes that had pushed their way northwards towards the Judæan highlands, were welded together by the strong hand of the Davidic monarchy, and were reckoned as constituents of the dominant southern tribe. Thus it would happen that a Ḥorite or Edomite clan which had belonged to the empire of Edom was drawn into Judah, and had to find a place in the artificial genealogies which expressed the political unity resulting from the incorporation of diverse ethnological groups in the tribal system. If Meyer be right in holding that the genealogies of the Chronicler reflect the conditions of the late post-Exilic age, when a wholesale conversion of Kalebite and Yeraḥmeelite families to Judaism had taken place (*INS*, 300 f.; *Entst. d. Jud.* 114 ff., 130 ff.), a comparison with Gn. 36 yields a striking testimony to the persistency of the minor clan-groups of the early Ḥorites through all vicissitudes of political and religious condition.

JOSEPH AND HIS BRETHREN.

CHS. XXXVII–L.

THE last division of the Book of Genesis is occupied almost entirely with the history of Joseph,—at once the most artistic and the most fascinating of OT biographies. Its connexion is twice interrupted: (*a*) by the story of Judah and Tamar (ch. 38); and (*b*) by the so-called Blessing of Jacob (49^{1-28}): see the introductory notes on these chapters. Everywhere else the narrative follows the thread of Joseph's fortunes; the plan and contents being as follows:

I. Chs. 37. 39–41. Joseph's solitary career in Egypt:—1. Joseph betrayed by his brethren and carried down to Egypt (37). 2. How he maintained his virtue against the solicitation of his master's wife, and was thrown into prison (39). 3. His skill in interpreting dreams discovered (40). 4. His interpretation of Pharaoh's dreams, and his consequent elevation to the highest dignity in Egypt (41).

II. Chs. 42–45. The reunion of Joseph and his brethren:—5. The first meeting of the brethren with Joseph in Egypt (42). 6. The second meeting (43. 44). 7. Joseph reveals himself to his brethren (45).

III. Chs. 46–50. The settlement of the united family in Egypt:—8. Jacob's journey to Egypt and settlement in Goshen (46. 47^{1-12}). 9. Joseph's agrarian policy (47^{13-28}). 10. Joseph at his father's death-bed (47^{29-31} 48). 11. Death and burial of Jacob, and death of Joseph (49^{29-33} 50).

The composition of documents is of the same general character as in the previous section of Genesis, though some peculiar features present themselves. The Priestly epitome (37^{2} 41^{46a} $42^{5.\ 6a}$ $46^{6.\ [8-27]}$ $47^{5*.\ 6a.\ 7-11.\ 27b.\ 28}$ 48^{3-6} $49^{1a.\ 28b-33a\alpha b}$ $50^{12.\ 13}$) is hardly less broken and fragmentary than in the history of Jacob, and produces at first sight the same impression as there, of being merely supplementary to the older narratives,—an impression, however, which a closer inspection easily dispels. Certain late words and constructions have led some critics to the conclusion that the JE passages have been worked over by an editor of the school of P (Giesebrecht, *ZATW*, i. 237, 266^{2}; Ho. 234). The cases in point have been examined by Kue. (*Ond.* i. p. 317 f.), who rightly concludes that they are too few in number to bear out the theory of systematic Priestly redaction.—With regard to the composition of J and E, the most important fact is that the clue to authorship supplied by the divine names almost entirely fails us, and is replaced by the distinction between Israel and Jacob which as names of the patriarch are character istic of J and E respectively (exceptions are 46^{2} $48^{8.\ 11.\ 21}$ [$50^{25?}$]; 46^{5b}). יהוה occurs only in ch. 39 (7 times); elsewhere אלהים is invariably used, sometimes in contexts which would otherwise be naturally assigned to J, though no reason appears why J should depart from his ordinary usage (*e.g.* 42^{28}). It may not always be safe to rely on this characteristic when it is not supported by other indications. Eerdmans, who rejects in principle the theory of a Yahwistic and an Elohistic document, is obliged to admit the existence of an *Israel*-recension and a *Jacob*-recension, and makes this distinction the basis of an independent analysis. A comparison of his results with those commonly accepted by recent critics is instructive in more ways than one.* On the whole, it increases one's confidence in the ordinary critical method.

---

* The Israel-recension (I–R) consists, according to Eerdmans, of 37^{3-24} (J+E), ^{28a} (E), ^{29} (E), $^{30-33}$ (E+J), ^{36} (E); 43 (J); 44 (J); 45^{28} (J), $46^{1.\ 2a}$ (JE), $^{28-34}$ (J); 47^{1-5} (J [v.^{5}, P*]), $^{13-27a}$ (J), ^{27b} (P), $^{29-31}$ (J); 48^{1} (E), ^{2b} (J), $^{8-22}$ (J+E); 50^{1-11} (J), $^{14-26}$ (E*). To the Jacob-recension (J–R) he assigns 37^{2} (P), $^{25-27}$ (J), ^{28b} (J), ^{34} (JE), ^{35} (J); 40; 41; 42 (all E); 45^{1-27} (E*), 46^{2b-5} (E*), $^{6.\ 7}$ (P); 47^{6-11} (P*), ^{12} (E), ^{28} (P); 49^{1a} (P), $^{29-33}$ (P); $50^{12.\ 13}$ (P) (*Komp. d. Gen.* 65–71): the usual analysis is roughly indicated by the symbols within brackets. How does this compare with the generally accepted critical results? (1) No distinction is recognised between P and the other sources; the fragments are mostly assigned to the J–R, but 48^{3-6} is rejected as an interpolation (p. 27). (2) Eerdmans regards ch. 39 (the incident of Potiphar's wife) as the addition of an unintelligent redactor mainly on the ground that it contains the name יהוה (the use of the divine names is thus after all a reliable criterion of authorship when it suits Eerdmans' purpose!). A more arbitrary piece of criticism could hardly be found. (3) Apart from these two eccentricities, and the finer shades of analysis which Eerdmans refuses to acknowledge, it will be seen that except in ch. 37 his division agrees *a potiori* with that of the majority of critics; *i.e.*, the I–R corresponds in the main with J and the J–R with E. (4) In ch. 37, on the contrary, the relation is reversed: I–R = E, and J–R = J. But this divergence turns on a wholly arbitrary and indefensible selection of data. Since the J–R in 45^{5} speaks of a *sale* of Joseph (to the Ishmaelites), it is inferred that $37^{25-27.\ 28b}$ belonged to it. It is conveniently overlooked that 40^{15} (also J–R) refers back to $37^{28a.\ 29f.}$ (the *stealing* of Joseph), that 42^{22} (J–R) presupposes 37^{22} (I–R); to say nothing of the broad distinction that Judah's leadership is as characteristic of one source as Reuben's is of the other. If Eerdmans had duly considered the whole of the evidence, he would have seen first that it is absolutely necessary to carry the analysis further than he chooses to do, and next that the two recensions in ch. 37 must exchange places in order to find their proper connexions in the following chapters. With that readjustment, it is not unfair to claim him as an unwilling witness to the essential soundness of the prevalent theory. With the best will in the world, he has not been able to deviate very far from the beaten track; and where he does strike out a path of his own, he becomes entangled in difficulties which may yet cause him to retrace his steps.

The story of Joseph is the finest example in Genesis, or even in the OT, of what is sometimes called 'novelistic' narrative. From the other patriarchal biographies it is distinguished first of all by the dramatic unity of a clearly conceived 'plot,' the unfolding of which exhibits the conflict between character and circumstances, and the triumph of moral and personal forces amidst the chances and vicissitudes of human affairs. The ruling idea is expressed in the words of E, "Ye intended evil against me, but God intended it for good" (50^{20}; cf. $45^{5.7}$): it is the sense of an overruling, yet immanent, divine Providence, realising its purpose through the complex interaction of human motives, working out a result which no single actor contemplated. To this higher unity everything is subordinated; the separate scenes and incidents merge naturally into the main stream of the narrative, each representing a step in the development of the theme. The style is ample and diffuse, but never tedious; the vivid human interest of the story, enhanced by a vein of pathos and sentiment rarely found in the patriarchal narratives, secures the attention and sympathy of the reader from the beginning to the close. We note, further, a certain freedom in the handling of traditional material, and subordination of the legendary to the ideal element in the composition. The comparatively faint traces of local colour, the absence of theophanies and cult-legends generally, the almost complete elimination of tribal relations, are to be explained in this way; and also perhaps some minute deviations from the dominant tradition, such as the conception of Jacob's character, the disparity of age between Joseph and his older brothers, the extreme youth of Benjamin (suggesting that he had been born since Joseph left home), the allusions to the mother as if still alive, etc. Lastly, the hero himself is idealised as no other patriarchal personality is. Joseph is not (like Jacob) the embodiment of one particular virtue, but is conceived as an ideal character in all the relations in which he is placed: he is the ideal son, the ideal brother, the ideal servant, the ideal administrator.

The close parallelism of J and E, together with the fact that the literary features enumerated above are shared by both, show that it had taken shape before it came into the hands of these writers, and strongly suggest that it must have existed in written form. The hypothesis of B. Luther (*INS*, 141 ff.), that the original author was J, and that he composed it as a connecting link between the patriarchal legends and those of the Exodus, is destitute of probability. The motive suggested is inadequate to account for the conception of a narrative so rich in concrete detail as that before us. Moreover, there is no reason to think that E is dependent on J; and it is certain that in some points (the leadership of Reuben, *e.g.*) E follows the older tradition. Nor is there much foundation for Luther's general impression that such a narrative must be the creation of a single mind. In any case the mastery of technique which is here displayed implies a long cultivation of this type of literature (*ib.* 143); and the matter of the Joseph-narratives must have passed through many successive hands before it reached its present perfection of form.

It is impossible to resolve such a composition completely into its traditional or legendary elements; but we may perhaps distinguish broadly the three kinds of material which have been laid under contribution. (1) The element of tribal history or relationships, though slight and secondary, is clearly recognisable, and supplies a key which may be used with caution to explain some outstanding features of the narrative. That there was an ancient tribe named Joseph, afterwards subdivided into Ephraim and Manasseh, is an item of Hebrew tradition whose authenticity there seems no good reason to question (see p. 533); and the prestige and prowess of this tribe are doubtless reflected in the distinguished position held by Joseph as the hero of the story. Again, actual tribal relations are represented by the close kinship and strong affection between Joseph and Benjamin; and by the preference of Ephraim before Manasseh, and the elevation of both to the status of adopted sons of Jacob. The birthright and leadership of Reuben in E implies a hegemony of that tribe in very early times, just as the similar position accorded to Judah in J reflects the circumstances of a later age. These are perhaps all the features that can safely be interpreted of real tribal relations. Whether there was a migration of the tribe of Joseph to Egypt, whether this was followed by a temporary settlement of all the other tribes on the border of the Delta, etc., are questions which this history does not enable us to answer; and attempts to find a historical significance in the details of the narrative (such as the sleeved tunic of Joseph, the enmity of his brethren, his wandering from Hebron to Shechem and thence to Dothan, the deliverance of Joseph by Reuben or Judah, and so on) are an abuse of the ethnographic principle of interpretation.—For (2) alongside of this there is an element of individual biography, which may very well preserve a reminiscence of actual events. There must have been current in ancient Israel a tradition of some powerful Hebrew minister in Egypt, who was the means of saving the country from the horrors of famine, and who used his power to remodel the land-system of Egypt to the advantage of the crown. That such a tradition should be true in essentials is by no means improbable. There were 'Hebrews' in Palestine as early as the 14th cent. B.C. (p. 218), and that one of these should have been kidnapped and sold as a boy into slavery in Egypt, and afterwards have risen to the office of viceroy, is in accordance with many parallels referred to in the monuments (p. 469); while his promoting the immigration of his kinsfolk under stress of famine is an incident as likely to be real as invented. The figure of Yanḫamu, the Semitic minister of Amenhotep IV. (pp. 501 f.), presents a partial counterpart to that of Joseph, though the identification of the two personages rests on too slender data to be plausible. The insoluble difficulty is to discover the point where this personal history passes into the stream of Israelite national tradition,—or where Joseph ceases to be an individual and becomes a tribe. The common view that he was the actual progenitor of the tribe afterwards known by his name is on many grounds incredible; and the theory that he was the leader of a body of Hebrew immigrants into Egypt does violence to the most distinctive features of the representation. Steuernagel's suggestion (*Einw.* 67), that the story is based on feuds between the *tribe* Joseph and the other tribes, in the course of which *individual* Josephides were sold as slaves to Egypt, illustrates the futility of trying to explain the narrative from two points of view at once. The tribal and the personal conceptions must be kept distinct, each may contain a kernel of history of its own kind; but the union of the two was effected not on the plane of history in either sense, but during the process of artistic elaboration of the theme. (3) There is, lastly, an element of Egyptian folklore, which has been drawn on to some extent for the literary embellishment of the story. The incident of Joseph's temptation (ch. 39) appears to be founded on an Egyptian popular tale (p. 459). The obscure allusions to Joseph as a potent magician are very probably surviving traces of a motive which was more boldly developed in an Egyptian source. The prominence of dreams and their interpretation perhaps hardly falls under this head; it may rather be part of that accurate acquaintance with Egyptian life which is one of the most striking features of the narrative. That in this legendary element there is an admixture of mythical material is very possible; but a direct influence of mythology on the story of Joseph is extremely speculative.—It has been argued with some force that the presence of this Egyptian colouring itself goes far to show that we have to do with genuine history, not with a legend 'woven by popular fancy upon the hills of Ephraim' (Dri. *DB*, ii. 771 *b*). At the same time it has to be considered that the material may have been largely woven in Egypt itself, and afterwards borrowed as drapery for the Israelite hero Joseph. Egyptian folklore might easily have been naturalised in Canaan during the long Egyptian domination, or have been imported later as a result of Egyptian influence at the court of Jeroboam I. It is not difficult to suppose that it was appropriated by the Hebrew rhapsodists, and incorporated in the native Joseph-legend, and gradually moulded into the exquisite story which we now proceed to examine.

CH. XXXVII.—*How Joseph was lost to his Father through his Brethren's Hatred and Treachery* (P, JE).

As the favoured child of the family, and because of dreams portending a brilliant future, Joseph becomes an object of hatred and envy to his brothers (2–11). A favourable opportunity presenting itself, they are scarcely restrained from murdering him by prudential and sentimental considerations urged by one or other of their number (Judah, Reuben); but eventually consent to dispose of him without actual bloodshed (12–30). With heartless cruelty they pretend that Joseph must have been devoured by a wild beast, and witness their father's distress without being moved to confession (31–35).—The chapter is not only full of thrilling human interest, but lays the 'plot' for the highly dramatic story which is to follow. The sudden disappearance of the most interesting member of the family, the inconsolable grief of the father, the guilty secret shared by the brothers, and, above all, the uncertainty which hangs over the fate of Joseph, appeal irresistibly to the romantic instinct of the reader, who feels that all this is the prelude to some signal manifestation of divine providence in the working out of Joseph's destiny.

Sources.—Vv.$^{1.\ 2}$ belong to P (*v.i.*).—The analysis of the rest of the chapter may start from $^{25-30}$, where evidences of a double recension are clearest. In one account, Joseph is *sold* to *Ishmaelites* on the advice of *Judah*; in the other, he is *kidnapped* by passing *Midianites*, unknown to the brethren, and to the dismay of *Reuben*, who had hoped to save him (see the notes). The former is J (cf. $45^{4f.}$), the latter E (40^{15}). Another safe clue is found in the double motive assigned for the envy of the brethren: $^{3.\ 4}$ (the sleeved tunic) ‖ $^{5-11}$ (the dreams): the dream-motive is characteristic of E throughout the narrative, and $^{3f.}$ are from J because of ישראל (cf. ^{13}, and ct. יעקב in ^{34}). Smaller doublets can be detected in $^{12-14}$; in $^{18-20}$, in $^{21f.}$, and in $^{34f.}$. The analysis has been worked out with substantial agreement amongst critics; and, with some finishing touches from the hand of Gu. (353 ff.), the result is as follows: J = $^{3.\ 4.\ 13a.\ 14b.\ 18b.\ 21.\ 23.\ 25-27.\ 28a\gamma}$ (וימכרו to כָּסֶף), $^{31.\ 32a\alpha\gamma b.\ 33a\alpha b.\ 34b.\ 35a}$; E = $^{5-11.\ 13b.\ 14a.\ 15-17.\ 18a.\ 19.\ 20.\ 22.\ 24.\ 28a\alpha\beta}$ (to הבור) $^{b.\ 29.\ 30.\ 32a\beta.\ 33a\beta.\ 34a.\ 35b.\ 36}$. This may be accepted as the basis of the exposition, though some points are open to question, particularly the assumption that all references to a tunic of any kind are to be ascribed to J.

1–11. The alienation between Joseph and his brethren.—1, 2. Three disjointed fragments of P, of which v.^{1} is the original continuation of 36^{6-8} (see p. 429); and $^{2a\alpha}$ is a heading from the Book of *Tôledôth* (see p. 40 f.), which ought to be followed by a genealogy,—perhaps 35^{22b-26},* which we have seen to stand out of its proper connexion (p. 423): $^{2a\beta\gamma b}$ then introduces P's history of Joseph, which has been mostly suppressed by the redactor.—The clause וְהוּא נַעַר is difficult. As a parenthesis (Dri.) it is superfluous after the

---

1. מגורים (17^{8}) and ארץ כנען (but see p. 474) are characteristic of P.—**2.** רעה ב׳] 'like verbs of governing' (Str.); so 1 Sa. 16^{11} 17^{34}.—והוא נער] Gu. suggests וה׳ נֵעֹר על (Niph. √ עור: cf. Jer. 6^{22} etc., and the Hithpal. in Jb. 17^{8}), or וה׳ רֹעֶה (= 'kept company with'),—neither proposal just convincing.—דבתם רעה (so Nu. 14^{37})] lit. 'brought the report of them evil,' ר׳ being second acc., or tertiary pred. (Da. § 76). A bad sense is inherent in דִּבָּה, which is a late word, in Hex. confined to P (Nu. 13^{32} $14^{36f.}$).

---

* Rather than $46^{8ff.}$, as suggested by Kurtz (quoted by Hupf. *Qu.* 216).

definite statement of Joseph's age in $^{2a\beta}$, and leaves us with a wrong identification of the sons of the concubines with the previous אחיו. If it be joined to what follows, Gu. has rightly seen that we want a word expressing something that Joseph was or did in relation to the sons of Bilhah and Zilpah. The meaning probably is that Joseph, while shepherding with (all) his brethren, fell out with the four sons of the concubines.

With this change, Di.'s objections to the unity of v.[2] fall to the ground, and the whole may be safely ascribed to P (note the chronology, the supplementary נשי אביו, and the phrase רבה רעה).—Short as the fragment is, it shows that P's account was peculiar in two respects: (1) He restricts the hostility to the sons of Bilhah and Zilpah, and (2) he traces it to Joseph's reporting their misdeeds to Jacob. It is plain that P is no mere supplementer of the older history, but an independent author, though his account has been sacrificed to the more graphic narratives of J and E.

3, 4 (J). *Now Israel loved Joseph* . . .] These are evidently the opening words of J's Joseph-story, in which the sole motive of the brothers' hatred is the father's favouritism towards the *son of* his *old age* (16^2 44^{20} J). — כְּתֹנֶת פַּסִּים] a shirt or tunic reaching to the extremities (פַּסִּים), *i.e.* the wrists and ankles, whereas the ordinary under-garment was sleeveless, and reached only to the knees. That it was an unusual habiliment appears also from 2 Sa. $13^{18f.}$; but speculations as to its mythological significance (*ATLO*², 384) have no support in either passage.—4. *could not address him peace-*

3. ועשה] 𝔐 ויעש. As the tense can hardly be freq., it is best to restore וַיַּעֲשֶׂה (Ba. Kit.).—כתנת פסים] Cf. Jos. *Ant.* vii. 171: *ἐφόρουν γὰρ αἱ τῶν ἀρχαίων παρθένοι χειριδωτοὺς ἄχρι τῶν σφυρῶν πρὸς τὸ μὴ βλέπεσθαι χιτῶνας.* Except 𝔊 (*χιτῶνα ποικίλον*) and 𝔙 (*tunicam polymitam* [but cf. v.[23]]), all Vns. here support this sense: Aq. χ. *ἀστραγάλων*, Σ. χ. *χειριδωτόν*, 𝔖 ܟܘܬܝܢܐ ܕܒܪ̈ܝܠܐ ('with sleeves'), 𝔗ᴼ כיתונא דפסי, etc. In 2 Sa. 13, 𝔊𝔙 and 𝔖 curiously change sides (χ. *καρπωτός*, *talaris tunica*, ܟܘܬܝܢܐ ܡܫܚܬܐ [= tunica striata]). The real meaning is determined by NH and Aram. פַּס (Dn. $5^{5.\ 24}$) = אֲפְסַיִם, Ezk. 47^3; see Bevan, *Dan.* 100.—4. אחיו ²] Heb. MSS 𝔐𝔊 בניו; 𝔖 ܫܠܡ ܒܡܠܬܗ,.—דַּבְּרוֹ לשלום] On the suff., see G-K. § 115*c*. But no other case occurring of דִּבֶּר with acc. of pers. addressed (Nu. 26^3 is corrupt), Gu. points דְּבָרוֹ ('could not take his matter peaceably'), Kit. em. לְדַבֵּר לוֹ ל' (the ל might be omitted:

ably] or, 'salute him.' The text is doubtful (*v.i.*).—**5–11.** Joseph's dreams (E).—**6, 7.** The first dream—a harvest scene—represents Jacob's family as agriculturists (see on 26^{12}); in vv.$^{2. 13ff.}$ $46^{31ff.}$ they are shepherds. There may be some hint of the immediate cause of its fulfilment, a failure of the harvest (Gu.), though this is questionable.—**8a.** *Wilt thou, forsooth, be king over us?*] The language points beyond the personal history of Joseph to the hegemony of the 'house of Joseph' in N Israel (Ju. $1^{22f.}$).—**9.** The second dream presages Joseph's elevation not only over his brothers, but over his father (Ho.), *i.e.* Israel collectively.—*eleven stars*] Supposed by some to be an allusion to the signs of the Zodiac (De. Gu. al., cf. Je. *ATLO*², 383), the twelfth being either Joseph himself, or the constellation obscured by Joseph as the sun-god. The theory will stand or fall with the identification of Jacob's twelve sons with the Zodiacal signs (see pp. 534 f.); the absence of the art. here makes it, however, at least improbable that the theory was in the mind of the writer.—**11.** *envied* is the appropriate word for E's account, as 'hated' (v.^{4}) is for J's (^{5b} and ^{8b} are redactional).—*his father kept the matter* (in mind)] 𝔊 διετήρησεν. Cf. Lk. $2^{19. 51}$.

While significant dreams bulk largely in E's Joseph-narrative (ch. 40 f.), it is characteristic of this section of the work that the dreams contain no oracular revelations (like $20^{3ff.}$ $31^{11. 24}$), but have a meaning in themselves which is open to human interpretation. The religious spirit of these chapters (as also of ch. 24), both in J and E, is a mature faith in God's providential ruling of human affairs, which is independent of theophanies, or visible interpositions of any kind. It can scarcely be doubted that such narratives took shape at a later period of OT religion than the bulk of the patriarchal legends.

12–17. Jacob sends Joseph to inquire after his brethren.—12, 13a, 14b J ‖ 13b, 14a E (see the analysis

---

see Ex. 2^{3} etc.).—**5b** is out of place *before* the telling of the dream, and is om. by 𝔊.—**7.** Ins. חלמתי at the beginning, with 𝔊.—אֲלֻמִּים] ἅπ. λεγ.; אֲלֻמָּה, Ps. 126^{6}†.—**8b.** Another redactional addition, though found in 𝔊; note the pl. 'dreams' when only one has been told.—**10a.** ויספר—אחיו is an interpolation intended to explain what immediately follows. 𝔊 omits, and seeks to gain the same end by inserting לאביו ו before לאחיו in ^{9}.

12–14 is composite. ישראל shows that $^{12. 13a}$ belong to J; and הנני shows that ^{13b} is from E (cf. $22^{1. 7. 11}$ 27^{1} 31^{11}). Hence ^{14a} is not a specifi-

below). In J, Jacob is dwelling in *the vale of Hebron*; the sons have gone to *Shechem.* If the incident of ch. 34 belonged to the same cycle of tradition, the brethren would perhaps hardly have ventured into the neighbourhood of Shechem so soon (see p. 418); though it has been argued that this very circumstance accounts for Jacob's solicitude. In E we find no indication of either the starting-point or the goal of the journey. **14a** suggests that the flocks were at some distance from Jacob's home: possibly the narrative is based on a stratum of E in which Jacob's permanent residence was at Bethel (see on 35^{1}).—**15–17.** The man who directs Joseph to Dothan is not necessarily a neighbour of the family who knew Joseph by sight (Gu.); nor is the incident a faded version of a theophany (Ho. Ben.): it is simply a vivid description of the uncertainty of Joseph's persistent search for his brethren. —*Dôthān* (2 Ki. $6^{13ff.}$, Jth. 3^{9} 4^{6} 7^{18}) is the modern *Tell Dōthān*, near Ğenīn, about 15 miles N of Shechem. Some local legend may have connected it with the history of Joseph.

$^{15-17}$ would be a sufficiently natural continuation of ^{14b} (J), and Gu.'s conjecture (above) establishes no presumption to the contrary. They may, however, be from E: in this case it is probable that E did not mention Shechem at all, nor J Dothan.

18–30. The plot to murder Joseph frustrated by Reuben (E), or Judah (J).—18a, 19, 20 E ‖ 18b J.

Common to both sources is the proposal to kill Joseph; E develops it most fully, revealing the motive of the crime and

---

cation, but a variant, of ^{13a}, continuing ^{13b}. ^{14b} obviously follows ^{13a}.—**12.** אֶת] with ***puncta extraordinaria***, because for some reason the text was suspected.—**14.** מעמק חברון ($23^{2.\,19}$)] The words might be a gloss based on P (35^{27} $49^{29ff.}$ 50^{13}); but Steuernagel's proposal to remove them (*Einw.* 36) takes too little account of the fragmentariness of J's narrative in ch. 35; and Gu.'s argument that the journey was too long for a young lad is weak.—**17.** שמעתי] 𝔐𝔊 שמעתים.—דתינה, דתן] The form with י is the older (cf. Eg. *Tu-ti-y-na*, Müller, *AE*, 88), the other an accommodation to a common nominal termination. The ending ַיִן is not dual, but an old (Aram.?) locative corresponding to Heb. ַיִם (see pp. 342 f.; Barth, *NB*, 319^{5}; G–K. § 88 *c*).

18a and 18bα are obviously doublets; the analysis adopted above gives the simplest arrangement.—ויתנכלו] 'acted craftily,' only found in late writings (Nu. 25^{18}, Mal. 1^{14}, Ps. 105^{25}†), but the √ occurs in Aram.

the device by which it was to be concealed.—**19.** *yon master-dreamer*] a mocking epithet; cf. [20b].—**20.** *and throw him* (his dead body) *into one of the pits*] The idea would suit either narrative; and we cannot be sure that the indefinite 'one of the pits' does not come from J (see [22]).—**21** J ‖ **22** E. In [21] we must read *Judah* for *Reuben*.—*and delivered him out of their hand*] is premature (v.[23]): the clause might stand more naturally in J between [23] and [25], though the rest of the v. must be left where it is (so Gu.).—*we will not kill him outright*] Judah has as yet no counter-proposal.—**22.** Reuben, on the other hand, has his scheme ready: he appeals to the antique horror of shed blood, which cries for vengeance on the murderer (4^{11}).—*this pit*] a particular cistern which Reuben knew to be empty of water ([24b]). It is probable that one of the numerous pits round Dothan was traditionally associated with the fate of Joseph (Gu.): cf. the *Khan Ğubb Yūsuf* near Safed, incorrectly identified with the Dothan cistern (*BR*, ii. 418 f.).—**24** (E).—**25**-**27**, **28aβ** (J). The fate of Joseph is apparently still undecided, when Judah makes an appeal to the cupidity of his brothers (*what profit*, *etc.* [26]), by proposing to sell him to some passing Ishmaelites. —**25.** *a caravan . . . from Gilead*] The plain of Dothan is traversed by a regular trade route from Gilead through Beisan to Ramleh, and thence (by the coast) to Egypt (Buhl, *GP*, 127). Shechem also lies on several routes from the E of the Jordan to the coast.—The natural products mentioned (*v.i.*) were much in request in Egypt for embalming, as well as

---

and Ass.—On the accus., see G-K. § 117 *w*.—**19.** בעל החלמות] The rendering above is a little too strong; for the use of בעל as 'n. of relation,' see BDB, 127 b.—**21.** נכנו נפש] Second acc. of respect, G-K. § 117 *ll*.—**22.** אל־הבור הזה] 𝕲 εἰς ἕνα τῶν λάκκων, a false assimilation to v.[20].—**23.** את־כתנתו] 𝕲 om. It is impossible to say whether this and the following appositional phrase are variants from E and J respectively, or whether the second is a (correct) gloss on J. 𝔙 combines both in the rendering *tunica talari et polymita*.—**25.** וישבו לאכל־לחם] Assigned by many critics (Di. al.) to E, and certainly not necessary in J. But we still miss a statement in E that the brothers had moved away from the pit.—נכאת (43^{11} †)] supposed to be 'gum-tragacanth'; Ar. *naka'at*.—צֳרִי[ו]=צְרִי] the resinous gum for which Gilead was famous (43^{11}, Jer. 8^{22} 46^{11} 51^{8}, Ezk. 27^{17} †); possibly that exuded by the mastic-tree; but see *EB*, 465 f.

for medicinal and other purposes.—**26**. *cover his blood*] Ezk. 24^{7}, Is. 26^{21}, Jb. 16^{18}.—**28**. *twenty* (shekels) *of silver*] cf. Lv 27^{5} with Ex. 21^{32} (see Dri.).—**28a***a***b, 29, 30** (E). Joseph is kidnapped by trading Midianites, who pass unobserved after the brothers have left the spot.—**30**. Only now does Reuben reveal his secret design of delivering Joseph. It is interesting to note his own later confusion of the intention with the act, in 42^{22}.

That the last section is from another source than $^{25-27}$ appears from (*a*) the different designation of the merchants, (*b*) the absence of the art. showing that they have not been mentioned before, (*c*) Reuben's surprise at finding the pit empty. The composite narrative requires us to assume that the brethren are the subj. of וימשכו ויעלו, against the natural construction of the sentence.

31–36. The deceiving of Jacob.—31, 32. Gu. remarks that the sending of a bloody token is a favourite motive in popular tales. Whether the incident is peculiar to J, or common to J and E, can hardly be determined (*v.i.*)—**33**. *an evil beast has devoured him*] Exactly as v.^{20} (E). A slight change of text in ^{32} (*v.i.*) would enable us to take the words as spoken by the sons to Jacob (so Gu.). **34, 35**. The grief of Jacob is depicted in both sources, but with a difference. E ($^{34a. 35b}$) hardly goes beyond the conventional signs of mourning—'the trappings and the suits of woe'; but J ($^{34b. 35a}$) dwells on the inconsolable and life-long sorrow of

---

—לֹט (43^{11} †)] Gk. λήδανον, Lat. *ladanum*, the gum of a species of cistus-rose (*EB*, 2692 f.). Mentioned amongst objects of Syrian tribute (*ladunu*) by Tiglath-pileser IV. (*KAT*², 151).—**27**. לישמעאלים] 𝔊 + הָאֵלֶּה. The word is apparently used in the general sense of 'Bedouin,' as Ju. 8^{24} (cf. 6^{1} etc.): see on 16^{12}.—בשרנו] 𝔐𝔊𝔖𝔙 prefix ו.—**28b** is assigned to E because of ויביאו, J using הוריד in this connexion (^{25} 39^{1} 43^{11} etc.).—**29**. אין] 𝔊 οὐχ ὁρᾷ.

31. The reason for assigning the v. to J (Gu.) is the precarious assumption that Joseph's coat plays no part at all in E. There is a good deal to be said for the view that it belongs to E (Di. Ho. al.).—**32**. ויביאו] Gu. וַיָּבוֹאוּ, 'and they came' (see on ^{33} above), which would be an excellent continuation of ^{31}: in E they dip the coat in blood, *come* to their father, and *say* 'an evil beast,' etc.; in J they *send* the coat unstained, and let Jacob form his own conclusion.—In any case ויביאו וגו' is E's parallel to J's וישלחו וגו'.—הכר־נא (cf. 38^{25}), and the disjunctive question (cf. 18^{21} 24^{21}) point distinctly to J (Di.).—הַכְּתֹנֶת] G–K. § 100 *l*.—**33**. After בני, 𝔐𝔊𝔖 **ins.** היא.—

the bereaved father. This strain of pathos and subjectivity is very marked in J in the Joseph narratives.—*rent his clothes . . . put on sackcloth*] On these customs, the origin of which is still obscure, see Schw. *Leben n. d. Tode*, 11 ff.; Grüneisen, *Ahnencultus*, 61 ff.; Engert, *Ehe- u. Familienrecht*, 96 ff.—34b. הִתְאַבֵּל, chiefly used in reference to the dead, includes the outward tokens of mourning: Ex. 33^{4}, 2 Sa. 14^{2}; cf. Is. 61^{3}, Ps. 35^{14}.—35. *all his daughters*] There was really only one daughter in the family. A similar indifference to the prevalent tradition in details is seen in the disparity of age between Joseph and his brothers (v.^{3}), and the assumption that Rachel was still alive (^{10}).—*go down . . . as a mourner*] Jacob will wear the mourner's garb till his death, so that in the underworld his son may know how deep his grief had been (Gu.). The shade was believed to appear in *Sheʾōl* in the condition in which it left the world (Schw. 63 f.). —36 (E) resuming ^{28b}. See, further, on 39^{1}.

Ch. XXXVIII.—*Judah and Tamar* (J).

Judah, separating himself from his brethren, marries a Canaanitish wife, who bears to him three sons, ʿEr, ʾÔnān and Shēlāh ($^{1-5}$). ʿEr and ʾOnan become in succession the husbands of Tamar (under the levirate law), and die without issue; and Judah orders Tamar to remain a widow in her father's house till Shelah should reach manhood ($^{6-11}$). Finding herself deceived, Tamar resorts to a desperate stratagem, by which she procures offspring from Judah himself ($^{12-26}$). With the birth of her twin sons, Pereẓ and Zeraḥ, the narrative closes ($^{27-30}$).

The story rests on a substratum of tribal history, being in the main a legendary account of the origin of the principal clans of Judah. To this historical nucleus we may reckon such facts as these: the isolation of Judah from the rest of the tribes (see on v.^{1}); the mixed origin of its leading families; the extinction of the two oldest clans ʿEr and ʾOnan; the rivalry of the younger branches, Pereẓ and Zeraḥ, ending in the

---

טָרֹף טֹרַף] cf. 44^{28}. On inf. abs. Qal used with Pu., see G–K. § 113 *w*.—35. ויקומו] 𝔊 *συνήχθησαν δέ*, adding *καὶ ἦλθον* before לנחמו.—36. והמדנים] Rd. with all Vns. והמדינים as v.^{28}.

supremacy of the former; and (possibly) the superiority of these two (as sons of Judah) to the more ancient Shelah (his grandson). See Steuernagel, *Einw.* 79 f.; where, however, the ethnological explanation is carried further than is reasonable.—It is obvious that the legend belongs to a cycle of tradition quite independent of the story of Joseph. The latter knows of no separation of Judah from his brethren, and this record leaves no room for a reunion. Although P, who had both before him, represents Judah and his sons as afterwards accompanying Jacob to Egypt (46^{12}), there can be no doubt that the intention of this passage is to relate the permanent settlement of Judah in Palestine. Where precisely the break with the prevalent tradition occurs, we cannot certainly determine. It is possible that the figure of Judah here is simply a personification of the tribe, which has never been brought into connexion with the family history of Jacob: in this case the events reflected may be assigned to the period subsequent to the Exodus. It seems a more natural supposition, however, that the legend ignores the Exodus altogether, and belongs to a stratum of tradition in which the occupation of Canaan is traced back to Jacob and his immediate descendants (see pp. 418, 507).—On some touches of mythological colouring in the story of Tamar, see below, pp. 452, 454.

Source.—The chapter is a pure specimen of Yahwistic narration, free from redactional manipulation. The following characteristics of J may be noted: יהוה, $^{7.\,10}$; רע בעיני, $^{7.\,10}$; הבה־נא, ^{16}; הכר־נא, ^{25} (37^{32}); כי־על־כן, ^{26}; ידע, ^{26}; further, the naming of the children by the mother, $^{3-5}$; and the resemblance of $^{27f.}$ to $25^{24f.}$. Since the sequence of 39^{1} on 37^{36} would be harsh, it is probable that ch. 38 was inserted here by R^{JE} (Ho.).

1–5. Judah founds a separate family at Adullam.—1. *went down from his brethren*] Since the chapter has no connexion with the history of Joseph, we cannot tell when or where the separation is conceived to have taken place. From the situation of *'Adullām*, it is clear that some place in the central highlands is indicated. Adullam is *possibly 'Īd el-Mīye* (or *'Aid el-Mā*), on the border of the Shephelah, 12 m. SW of Bethlehem and 7 NE of Eleutheropolis (Buhl, *GP*, 193; Smith, *HG*, 229). It is marked on the Pal. Surv. map as 1150 ft. above sea-level.

The isolation of the tribe of Judah was a fact of capital importance in the early history of Israel. The separation is described in Ju. $1^{3ff.}$; in the song of Deborah (Ju. 5) Judah is not mentioned either for praise or blame; and his reunion with Israel is prayed for in Dt. 33^{7}. The rupture of the Davidic kingdom, and the permanent cleavage between south and north, are perhaps in part a consequence of the stronger

---

1. ויט] 𝔊 ἀφίκετο: the precise force here of נטה, 'turn aside,' is doubtful. The change of עד to אל (Ba.) is unnecessary (cf. 1 Sa. 9^{9}).

infusion of foreign blood in the southern tribe. The verse suggests that the first Judahite settlement was at ʿAdullam, where the tribe gained a footing by alliance with a native clan named Ḥîrāh; but Mey. (*INS*, 435 f.) thinks it presupposes a previous occupation of the region round Bethlehem, and deals merely with an extension towards the Shephelah. It is certainly difficult otherwise to account for the verb ירד (ct. וַיַּעַל, Ju. 1[4]); but were Judah's brethren ever settled at Bethlehem? Gu.'s emendation, וַיִּפֶּר, 'freed himself' (see on 27[40]; cf. Hos. 12[1]), would relieve the difficulty, but is too bold for a plain prose narrative.

2. A more permanent amalgamation with the Canaanites is represented by Judah's marriage with *Bath-Shûaʿ* or *Bath-Shevaʿ* (See on v.[12]). The freedom with which connubium with the Canaanites is acknowledged (ct. 34. 24[3]) may be a proof of the antiquity of the source (Ho. Gu.).—**5b.** *in Kĕzîb, etc.*] It is plausibly inferred that Kĕzîb (= *'Akzîb*, an unknown locality in the Shephelah, Jos. 15[44], Mic. 1[14]) was the centre of the clan of Shelah; though 𝕲 makes all three births happen there.

6–11. Tamar's wrong.—6. *Tamar*, the Heb. word for date-palm, occurs twice as a female name in David's family (2 Sa. 13[1] 14[27]). There is therefore little probability that it is here a personification of the city of the same name on the S border of Palestine (Ezk. 47[19]) (so Steuernagel). A mythological origin is suggested on p. 452 below.—As head of the family, Judah chooses a wife for his first-born (24[3] 34[4] 21[21]), as he is also responsible for the carrying out of the levirate obligation ([8. 11]).—**7.** No crime is alleged against *ʿĒr*, whose untimely death was probably the only evidence of Yahwe's displeasure with him (Pr. 10[27]).—**8–10.** *'Onān*, on the other hand, is slain because of the revolting manner in which he

---

2. וּשְׁמוֹ] 𝕲 וּשְׁמָהּ. See on v.[12].—3. ויקרא] Better as vv.[4. 5] ותקרא (𝔐𝔗 Heb. MSS).—5. שֵׁלָה] 𝕲 Σηλώμ; comp. the gentilic שֵׁלָנִי, Nu. 26[20].—והיה] is impossible, and 𝔐 ויהי little better. Rd. with 𝕲 וְהִיא.—בכזיב] 𝔐 בכזבה, cf. כֹּזֵבָא, 1 Ch. 4[22].—אתו] 𝕲 אֹתָם.—Nothing can be made of the strange renderings of [5b] in 𝕾 and 𝔙: ܘܦܣܩܬ ܗܘܬ ܟܕ ܝܠܕܬܗ; *quo nato parere ultra cessavit* (cf. 29[35] 30[9]).—7. יהוה[2]] 𝕲 ὁ θεός.—8. יַבֵּם] Dt. 25[5. 7] †; denom. from יָבָם, the *term. techn.* for 'husband's brother' in relation to the levirate institution.—9. והיה אם] 'as often as'; G–K. § 159 *o*.—שִׁחֵת (sc. *semen*)] in the sense of 'spoil,' 'make ineffective' (BDB).—נְתָן־ for תֵּת] only again Nu. 20[21]; comp. הֲלֹךְ, Ex. 3[19], Nu. 22[13. 14. 16].—10. אשר עשה] 𝕲, pr. הַדָּבָר.

persistently evaded the sacred duty of raising up seed to his brother. It is not correct to say (with Gu.) that his *only* offence was his selfish disregard of his deceased brother's interests.—**11.** Judah sends Tamar home to her family, on the pretext that his third son Shelah is too young to marry her. His real motive is fear lest his only surviving son should share the fate of ʿEr and ʾOnan, which he plainly attributes in some way to Tamar herself.—*in thy father's house*] according to the law for a childless widow (Lv. 22^{13}, Ru. 1^{8}).

The custom of levirate marriage here presupposed prevailed widely in primitive times, and is still observed in many parts of the world. In its Hebrew form it does not appear to have implied more than the duty of a surviving brother to procure male issue for the oldest member of a family, when he dies childless: the first-born son of the union is counted the son, and is the heir, to the deceased; and although in Dt. $25^{5ff.}$ the widow is said to become the wife of her brother-in-law, it may be questioned if in early times the union was more than temporary. It is most naturally explained as a survival, under patriarchal conditions, of some kind of polyandry, in which the wife was the common property of the kin-group (Smith, *KM*², 146 ff.); and it naturally tended to be relaxed with the advance of civilisation. Hence the law of Dt. 25^{5-10} is essentially a concession to the prevalent reluctance to comply with the custom. This is also illustrated by the conduct of 'Onan: the sanctity of the obligation is so strong that he does not dare openly to defy it; yet his private family interest induces him to defeat its purpose. It is noteworthy that the only other historical example of the law—the analogous though not identical case of Boaz and Ruth—also reveals the tendency to escape its operation.—See Dri. *Deut.* 280 ff. (with the authorities there cited); also Engert, *Ehe- und Familienrecht*, 15 ff.; Barton, *SO*¹, 66 ff.

Judah's belief that Tamar was the cause of the deaths of ʿEr and ʾOnan (*v.s.*) may spring from an older form of the legend, in which she was actually credited with death-dealing power. Stucken and Je. recognise in this a common mythical motive,—the goddess who slays her lovers,—and point to the parallel case of Sara in the Book of Tobit (3^{8}). Tamar and Sara (*šarratu*, a title of Ištar) were originally forms of Ištar (*ATLO*², 381 f.). The connexion is possible; and if there be any truth in Barton's speculation that the date-palm was sacred to Ištar (*SO*¹, 92, 98, 102 ff.), it might furnish an explanation of the name Tamar.

12–19. Tamar's daring stratagem.—**12.** *Bath-Shūaʿ*] See the footnote.—*was comforted*] a conventional phrase for

---

11. וּשְׁבִי ,שְׁבִי] Ba. al. propose וְתֵשֵׁב ,שְׁבִי, after Lv. 22^{13}; but see Is. 47^{8}. —**12.** בת־שׁוּעַ] Apparently a compound proper name, as in 1 Ch. 2^{3} =

the effect of the mourning ceremonies; see Jer. 16^{7}.—The death of Judah's wife is mentioned as a palliation of his subsequent behaviour: "even in early times it was considered not quite *comme il faut* for a married man to have intercourse with harlots" (Gu.).—On the *sheep-shearing*, see 31^{19}.—*Ḥîrāh his associate*] (see $v.^{1}$) is mentioned here because of the part he has to play in the story ($vv.^{20-23}$).—*went up* . . . *to Timnah*] This cannot be the Danite Timnah (Jos. 15^{10} 19^{43}, Ju. $14^{1.\,2.\,5}$), which lies lower than ʿAdullam. Another Timnah S of Hebron (Jos. 15^{57}), but unidentified, might be meant; or it may be the modern *Tibne*, W of Bethlehem, though this is only 4 m. from ʿAdullam, and room has to be found for ʿEnaim between them (but *v.i.* on $v.^{14}$).—**14.** *her widow's garments*] Cf. Jth. 8^{5} 10^{3} 16^{8}.—She assumes the garb of a common prostitute, and sits, covered by *the veil* (see below on $v.^{21}$), by the wayside; cf. Jer. 3^{2}, Ezk. 16^{25}, Ep. Jer. 43. —**15.** *for she had covered her face*] This explains, not Judah's failure to recognise her, but his mistaking her for a harlot (see $v.^{16}$).—**17.** *a kid of the goats*] Cf. Ju. 15^{1}. The present of a kid on these occasions may be due to the fact that (as in classical antiquity) the goat was sacred to the goddess of love (Paus. vi. 25. 2 [with Frazer's Note, vol. iv. 106]; cf. Tac. *Hist.* 2, 3, and Lucian, *Dial. meretr.* 7. 1) (Kn–Di.). —**18.** The master-stroke of Tamar's plot is the securing of a pledge which rendered the identification of the owner

---

בַּת־שֶׁבַע (cf. 1 Ch. 3^{5} with 2 Sa. 11^{3} etc.), through an intermediate בַּת־שׁוּעַ. 𝔊, both here and $v.^{2}$ (but *not* 1 Ch. 2^{3}), gives שוע as the name of Judah's *wife*.—רֵעֵהוּ] 𝔊𝔙 רֹעֵהוּ, 'his shepherd,' wrongly.—**13.** חָם] 'husband's father,' 1 Sa. $4^{19.\,21}$ †. Smith (*KM*², 161 f.) finds in the Arabic usage a distinct trace of baʿal-polyandry; the correlative is *kanna*, "which usually means the wife of a son or brother, but in the Ḥamāsa is used . . . to designate one's own wife."—**14.** וַתְּכַס] so Dt. 22^{12}, Jon. 3^{6}. Read either וַתִּכָּס, Niph. (Gu.), or וַתִּתְכַּס, Hithp., with ܡܢ (as 24^{65}).—בפתח עינים] 𝔖 ܒܦܠܓܗ ܕܐܘܪܚܐ, 𝔙 *in bivio itineris*, and 𝔗ᴼᴶ take the meaning to be 'at the cross-roads' (of which there are several on the short way from ʿAid el-Mā to Tibne). The sense is good, and it is tempting to think that these Vns are on the right track, though their rendering has no support in Heb. usage. If עינים be a proper name it may be identical with the unknown עֵינָם of Jos 15^{34}, in the Shephelah.—וְהִיא לֹא נִתְּנָה לוֹ] 𝔊 וְהוּא לֹא נְתָנָהּ לוֹ, better.—**15** end] 𝔊 + καὶ οὐκ ἐπέγνω αὐτήν.

absolutely certain. *Seal*, *cord*, and *staff* must have been the insignia of a man of rank amongst the Israelites, as seal and staff were among the Babylonians (Herod. i. 195) * and Egyptians (Erman, *LAE*, 228 f.). The *cord* may have been used to suspend the seal, as amongst modern town Arabs (Robinson, *BR*, i. 36), or may have had magical properties like those occasionally worn by Arab men (We. *Heid.* 166). For illustrations of ancient Hebrew seals, see Benzinger, *Arch.*[2] 82, 179 f., 228 ff.

20–23. Judah fails to recover his pledge.—20. It is significant that Judah employs his *fidus Achates* Ḥirah in this discreditable affair, and will rather lose his seal, etc., than run the risk of publicity (v.[23]).—**21.** *Where is that Ḳĕdēshāh?*] strictly 'sacred prostitute,'—one 'dedicated' for this purpose to Ištar-Astarte, or some other deity (Dt. 23[18], Hos. 4[14]†).

This is the only place where קדשה appears to be used of an ordinary harlot; and Luther (*INS*, 180) points out that it is confined to the conversation of Ḥirah with the natives, the writer using זוֹנָה. The code of Ḥammurabi (§ 110) seems to contemplate the case of a temple-votary (*ḳadistu*, *KAT*[3], 423; *ATLO*[2], 380) separating herself for private prostitution; and it is possible that this custom was familiar to the Canaanites, though not in Israel.—That the harlot's *veil* (vv.[14. 19]) was a symbol of dedication to Ištar the veiled goddess (*KAT*[3], 276, 432; *ATLO*[2], 109) is possible, though it is perhaps more natural to suppose that the veiling of Ištar is an idealisation of the veiling of her votaries, which rests on a primitive sexual taboo (cf. the bridal veil 24[65]).

24–26. The vindication of Tamar.—24. As the widow of ʿEr, or the betrothed of Shelah, Tamar is guilty of adultery, and it falls to Judah as head of the family to bring her to justice.—*Lead her out*] a forensic term, Dt. 22[21. 24].—*let her be burnt*] Death by burning is the punishment imposed in Ḥammurabi, § 157, for incest with a mother, and was doubt-

---

21. בקדשה] ɯ𝔊𝔖 המקום (v.[22]). If this reading be accepted, there is no reason to hold that עינים (if a place-name at all) was Tamar's native village.—הִוא] ɯ היא; but see 19[33] etc.—**24.** כמשלש] ɯ more correctly כמשלשת.

---

* Σφρηγῖδα δ' ἕκαστος ἔχει καὶ σκῆπτρον χειροποίητον· ἐπ' ἑκάστῳ δὲ σκήπτρῳ ἔπεστι πεποιημένον ἢ μῆλον ἢ ῥόδον ἢ κρίνον ἢ αἰετὸς ἢ ἄλλο τι· ἄνευ γὰρ ἐπισήμου οὔ σφι νόμος ἐστὶ ἔχειν σκῆπτρον.—Similarly Strabo, XVI. i. 20.

less the common punishment for adultery on the part of a woman in ancient Israel. In later times the milder penalty of stoning was substituted (Lv. 20[10], Dt. 22[23ff.], Ezk. 16[40], Jn. 8[5]), the more cruel death being reserved for the prostitution of a priest's daughter (Lv. 21[9]; cf. Ḫamm. § 110).—**25.** By waiting till the last moment, Tamar makes her justification as public and dramatically complete as possible. Addressing the crowd she says, *To the man who owns these things, etc.*; to Judah himself she flings out the challenge, *Recognise to whom this seal, etc., belong!*—**26.** *She is in the right as against me* (G–K. § 133 *b*[3]; cf. Jb. 4[17] 32[2])] *i.e.*, her conduct is justified by the graver wrong done to her by Judah.

To suppose that incidents like that recorded in [12-26] were of frequent occurrence in ancient Israel, or that it was the duty of the father-in-law under *any* circumstances to marry his son's widow, is to miss entirely the point of the narrative. On the contrary, as Gu. well shows (365 f.), it is just the exceptional nature of the circumstances that explains the writer's obvious admiration for Tamar's heroic conduct. "Tamar shows her fortitude by her disregard of conventional prejudice, and her determination by any means in her power to secure her wifely rights within her husband's family. To obtain this right the intrepid woman dares the utmost that womanly honour could endure,—stoops to the level of an unfortunate girl, and does that which in ordinary cases would lead to the most cruel and shameful death, bravely risking honour and life on the issue. At the same time, like a true mother in Judah, she manages her part so cleverly that the dangerous path conducts her to a happy goal."—It follows that the episode is not meant to reflect discredit on the tribe of Judah. It presents Judah's behaviour in as favourable a light as possible, suggesting extenuating circumstances for what could not be altogether excused; and regards that of Tamar as a glory to the tribe (cf. Ru. 4[12]).

27–30. Birth of Pereẓ and Zeraḥ.—The story closely resembles that of Rebekah in 25[24–26] (38[27b] = 25[24b]), and is probably a variation of the same originally mythical theme (see p. 359).—**28.** The *scarlet* thread probably represents some feature of the original myth (note that in 25[25] 'the first

---

25. On the syntax, see G–K. §§ 116 *u*, *v*, 142 *e*; Dri. *T.* § 166 ff.—לְאִישׁ] st. constr. with cl. as gen.; Ho. al. point לָאִישׁ.—החתמה] fem. only here.—הפתילים] 𝔐𝔊𝔙𝔖𝔗^O הפתיל (as v.[18]).—**26.** כִּי־עַל־כֵּן] see on 18[5].—**28.** ויתן־יד] *sc.* הַנֹּתֵן (G–K. § 144 *e*); 𝔊 + ὁ εἷς.

came out *red*'). The forced etymology of *Zeraḥ* (v.^{30}) could not have suggested it.—**29.** *What a breach hast thou made for thyself!*] The name *Pereẓ* expresses the violence with which he secured the priority.—**30.** *Zeraḥ*] An Edomite clan in $36^{13. 33}$. On the etymology, *v.i.*

To the name Pereẓ, Cheyne (*TBI*, 357) aptly compares Plutarch's account of the birth of Typhon, brother of Osiris: "neither in due time, nor in the right place, but *breaking through with a blow*, he leaped out through his mother's side" (*de Isid. et Os.* c. 12).—The ascendancy of the Pereẓ clan has been explained by the incorporation of the powerful families of Caleb and Jeraḥmeel, 1 Ch. $2^{5. 9}$ (so Sta. *GVI*, i. 158 f.); but a more obvious reason is the fact that David's ancestry was traced to this branch (Ru. 4^{18-22}).

Ch. XXXIX.—*Joseph is cast into Prison* (J).

Joseph is sold by the Ishmaelites ($37^{28. 36}$) to an Egyptian householder, who finds him so capable and successful that ere long he entrusts him with the whole administration of his estate ($^{1-6}$). But his master's wife conceives a guilty passion for him, and when her advances are repelled, falsely accuses him of attempted outrage, with the result that he is thrown into prison ($^{7-20}$). Here again he wins the favour of his superior, and is soon charged with the oversight of the prison ($^{21-23}$).

Source.—With the exception of a harmonising gloss in $^{1b\alpha}$, and a sprinkling of E variants (discussed in the notes), the whole passage is from J. It represents the chief divergence between the two recensions of the history of Joseph. In J, Joseph is first sold to a private Egyptian (איש מצרי, v.^{1}), then cast into the state prison in the way here narrated, where he gains the confidence of the (unnamed) governor, so that when the butler and baker are sent thither they naturally fall under his

---

29. ויהי כְּמֵשִׁיב] An ungrammatical use of the ptcp. Rd. with Ball ויהי כְּמוֹ הֵשִׁיב (cf. 19^{15}).—פרצת—פרץ] cogn. acc. The rendering as a question (מה='why': De. Di. Dri.) is less natural than that given above; and to detach עליך פרץ [𝔐 עלינו] as a separate exclamation ('A breach upon thee!') is worse. 𝔊 (τί διεκόπη διὰ σὲ φραγμός;) 𝔙𝔖 take the vb. in a pass. sense.—ויקרא] 𝔐 𝔖𝔗^J ותקרא (so v.^{30}).—**30.** זֶרַח] as a Heb. word would mean 'rising' (of the sun, Is. 60^3) or 'autochthonous' (=אֶזְרָח). A connexion with the idea of 'redness' is difficult to establish. It is commonly supposed that there is a play on the Aram. זהריתא (which is used here by 𝔖𝔗^O, and is the equivalent of Heb. שָׁנִי), and Bab. *zaḫuritu* (so De. Dri. Gu. al.); but this is not convincing.

charge. In E, Joseph is sold at once to Potiphar (37^{36}), the palace officer in whose house the butler and baker are afterwards confined (40^{3a}); and Joseph, without being himself a prisoner, is told off to wait on these eminent persons (40^{4}). The imprisonment, therefore, is indispensable in J, and at least embarrassing in E.—This conclusion is partly confirmed by the literary phenomena: יהוה, [2. 3. 5]; the Ishmaelites, [1]; הוריד, [1]; הצליח, [3. 23]; מצא חן, [4]; בגלל, [5]. It is somewhat disconcerting to find that none of these occur in the central section, [7-20]; and (We. *Comp.*[2] 56) positively assigns [6-19] to E, because of the phrases יפה תאר ויפה מראה, [6b] (cf. 29^{17}); ויהי אח׳ הדברים ה׳, [7] (cf. 15^{1} $22^{1.20}$ 40^{1} 48^{1}); ראו, [14]; and לאלהים, [9]. These are not decisive (see Di. 403; Ho. 231), and on the whole the material argument must be held to outweigh the dubious linguistic evidence that can be adduced on the other side.—Procksch (42 f.) assigns [7-10] to E and [11-23] to J; but nothing is gained by the division.

1–6. Joseph becomes the controller of an Egyptian estate.—1. *But Joseph had been taken down, etc.*] while his father was mourning over him as one dead ($37^{31ff.}$); the notice resumes 37^{28a}.—*a certain Egyptian*] who is nameless in J (*v.i.*).—**2.** The secret of Joseph's success: a combination of ability with personal charm which marked him out as a favourite of Yahwe (cf. [3. 5. 21. 23]).—*remained in the house, etc.*] under his master's observation, instead of being sent to work in the field.—**4a.** *served him*] *i.e.*, 'became his personal

1. The words פוטיפר—הטבחים are a repetition by R[JE] from 37^{36} (E), in order to harmonise the two sources. But the contradiction appears (1) in the meaningless איש מצרי after the specific designation (this is not to be got rid of by Ebers's observation that under a Hyksos dynasty a high official was not necessarily a native Egyptian), and (2) the improbability of a eunuch being married (though cases of this kind are known [Ebers, 299]).—פוטיפר] 𝔊 Πετεφρη[ς], an exact transcription of Eg. *Pedephrē*='He whom the sun-god gives' (see *DB*, i. 665b; *EB*, 3814); but the long *o* of the Heb. has not been explained. Cf. Heyes, 105–112.—סריס] means 'eunuch' in NH. Aram. Arab. (as is shown by the denom. vbs. ='be impotent'), and there is no case in OT where the strict sense is inapplicable (Ges. *Th.* 973 b). That such a word should be extended to mean 'courtier' in general is more intelligible than the reverse process (so Heyes, 122), in spite of the opinion of several Assyriologists who derive it from *ša rêši*='he who is the head' (Zimmern, *ZDMG*, liii. 116; *KAT*[3], 649).—שר הטבחים] 𝔊 ἀρχιμάγειρος, a title like שר המשקים and ש׳ האופים in ch. 40 (E). Cf. רב הט׳, 2 Ki. $25^{8ff.}$, Jer. $39^{9ff.}$ $40^{1ff.}$ etc., Dn. 2^{14}. The טבחים were apparently the royal cooks or butchers (1 Sa. $9^{23f.}$), who had come to be the bodyguard (Smith, *OTJC*[2], 262[1]).—**2.** איש מצליח] The intrans. Hiph. is thought by Di. Gu. al. to be inconsistent with J's usage (vv.[3. 23] 24^{21}); therefore E.—4. בעיניו] 𝔐𝔊𝔙 בעיני אדניו.—וכל־ישלו] 𝔐 inserts אשר as v.[5 *bis*. 8].—**4a** is wholly assigned to E by

attendant.'—The phrase is a variant from E (cf. 40^4).—**4b.** In J, Joseph's position is far higher, that, namely, of *mer-per* (*mer-pa*, *mer en peri-t*, *etc.*), or superintendent of the household, frequently mentioned in the inscriptions (Ebers, *Aeg.* 303 ff.; Erman, *LAE*, 187 f.).—**6a.** *knew not with him*] (*i.e.* with Joseph [$v.^8$]): 'held no reckoning with him';—a hyperbolical expression for absolute confidence.—**6b** is introductory to $^{7ff.}$.

7–20. Joseph tempted by his master's wife.—7–10. The first temptation. The solicitation of a young man by a married woman is a frequent theme of warning in Pr. 1–9.—**9a.** אֵינֶנּוּ does not mean 'there is none' (which would require אֵין), but 'he is not.'—**9b.** *sin against God*] The name Yahwe is naturally avoided in conversation with a foreigner. All the more striking is the consciousness of the divine presence which to the exiled Israelite is the ultimate sanction of morality.—**11, 12.** The final temptation.—On the freedom of social intercourse between the sexes, see Ebers, 306 f. But the difficulties raised about Joseph's access to the harem do not really arise, when we remember that J is depicting the life of a simple Egyptian family, and not that of a high palace official (see Tu.).—**13–20.** The woman's revenge.—**14.** A covert appeal to the jealousy of the men-servants against the hated Hebrew, and to the fears of the women, whom she represents as unsafe from insult (*to mock us*). An additional touch of venom lurks in the contemptuous reference to her husband as '*he*.' —*Hebrew* may be here a general designation of the Asiatic

Gu.; but וימצא חן pleads strongly for J.—**8.** מה] 𝔐 מאומה ($v.^{23}$).—בבית] 𝔐𝔊𝔖𝔙 בביתו.—**10.** לשכב אצלה and להיות עמה look like variants; but one swallow does not make a summer, and it would be rash to infer an Elohistic recension.—**11.** כהיום הזה] A very obscure expression, see BDB, 400 b. Of the other occurrences (Dt. 6^{24}, Jer. 44^{22}, Ezr. $9^{7.15}$, Neh. 9^{10}†) all except the last are perfectly transparent: 'as [it is] this day,'—a sense quite unsuitable here. One must suspect that the phrase, like the kindred כַּיּוֹם, and כַּיּוֹם הַזֶּה (cf. esp. 1 Sa. $22^{8.13}$), had acquired some elusive idiomatic meaning which we cannot recover. Neither 'on a certain day' (G–K. § 126 *s*) nor 'on this particular day' (BDB) can be easily justified.—**13.** וינס] MSS 𝔐𝔊 + ויצא ($^{12.15}$).—**14.** לְצַחֶק בנו] see on 26^8.—**15.** אצלי] 𝔐𝔖𝔙 (*pallium quod tenebam*) read בידי,—wrongly, since to have said this

Bedouin ($ATLO^2$, 387); but see on 40[15].—**19**. Her distorted
account of the facts has the desired effect on her husband.
—*his wrath was kindled*] against Joseph, of course. There
is no hint that he suspected his wife, and was angry with
her also (De. Di.).—**20**. Imprisonment would certainly not
be the usual punishment for such a crime as Joseph was
believed to have committed; but the sequel demanded it,
Joseph's further career depending on his being lodged in
the *place where the king's prisoners were bound*. That he
became a king's slave (according to Ḥamm. § 129) is not
indicated (against Je. $ATLO^2$, 388). The term for *prison*
(*v.i.*) is peculiar, and recurs only [21. 22. 23] 40[3. 5].

To this episode in Joseph's life there is an Egyptian parallel so
close that we can hardly fail to recognise in it the original of the
Hebrew story. It is the 'Tale of the two brothers' in the d'Orbiney
Papyrus, assigned by Egyptologists to the 19th dynasty. Two brothers
lived together, the older Anpu having a house and wife, and the younger
Batu serving him in the field. One day Batu enters the house to fetch
seed for the sowing, and is tempted by his brother's wife, exactly as
Joseph was by his mistress. Furiously indignant—"like a panther for
rage"—he rejects her advances, out of loyalty to the brother who has
been like a father to him, and expresses horror of the 'great sin'
which she had suggested. Promising silence, he returns to his brother
in the field. In the evening Anpu comes home to find his wife covered
with self-inflicted wounds, and listens to a tale which is a perfect
parallel to the false accusation against Joseph. Anpu seeks to murder
his brother; but being at last convinced of his innocence, he slays his
wife instead. Here the human interest of the story ceases, the remainder being fairy lore of the most fantastic description, containing
at least a reminiscence of the Osiris myth. (See Ebers, 311 ff.; Erman,
LAE, 378 ff.; Petrie, *Egypt. Tales*, ii. 36 ff.; Völter, *Aeg. u. die Bibel*, 50 f.
[who takes the story as a whole to be founded on the myth of Set and
Osiris].) It is true that the theme is not exclusively Egyptian (see the
numerous parallels in Lang, *Myth, Ritual, and Religion*, ii. 303 ff.); but
the fact that the scene of the biblical narrative is in Egypt, and the
close resemblance to the Egyptian tale, make it extremely probable
that there is a direct connexion between them.

21-23. Joseph in prison.—His good fortune and con-

---

would have been to betray herself (De. Di.).—**17** end] 𝔊 + καὶ εἶπέν μοι
Κοιμηθήσομαι μετά σου [𝔊^A Κοιμήθητι μετ' ἐμοῦ].—**18**. וַיְהִי כְּהָרִימִי] 𝔊 ὡς δὲ
ἤκουσεν ὅτι ὕψωσα.—וִינֶס] 𝔊 𝔖 + וַיָּצָא.—**20**. בֵּית הַסֹּהַר] Only in [20-23] 40[3. 5] (J).
The name may be Egyptian (see Ebers, 317 ff.; Dri. *DB*, ii. 768 a, *n.*),
but has not been satisfactorily explained.—מְקוֹם אֲשֶׁר] G–K. § 130 *c*.—
אֲסוּרֵי] so 𝔪 (and also in v.[22]); but rd. with Qrê אֲסִירֵי [22].—**21**. וַיִּתֵּן חִנּוֹ] (as

sequent promotion are described in terms nearly identical with those of vv.[1-6].—In J, the governor of the prison is anonymous, and Joseph is made superintendent of the other prisoners.

Ch. XL.—*Joseph proves his Gift of interpreting Dreams* (E).

Joseph is appointed to wait on two officers of the court who have been put under arrest in his master's house ([1-4]), and finds them one morning troubled by dreams for which they have no interpreter ([5-8]). He interprets the dreams ([9-19]), which are speedily verified by the event ([20-22]). But his eager request that the chief butler would intercede for him with Pharaoh ([14f.]) remains unheeded ([23]).

Source.—The main narrative, as summarised above, obviously belongs to E (see p. 456 f.). Joseph is not a prisoner (as in J 39[20ff.]), but the servant of the captain of the guard (cf. 37[36] 41[12]); the officers are not strictly imprisoned, but merely placed 'in ward' (במשמר) in Potiphar's house ([3. 4. 7]), and Joseph was 'stolen' from his native land ([15a]; cf. 37[28a]), not sold by his brethren as 37[28b] (J).—Fragments of a parallel narrative in J can be detected in [1aβb] (a duplicate of [2]), [3aβ] (from אל־בית ה׳) [b] (Joseph a prisoner), [5b] (the officers imprisoned), and [15b].—In the phraseology note J's המשקה, האפה, [1. 5b] || E's שר המשקים, ש׳ האפים, [2. 9. 16. 20. 21. 22. 23]; J בית הסהר, [3aβ. 5b] || E משמר, [3aα. 4. 7.]; while שר הטבחים, [3. 4], and סרים, [2. 7], connect the main narrative with 37[36] (E).—That in J the turn of Joseph's fortune depended on the successful interpretation of dreams does not explicitly appear, but may be presumed from the fact that he was afterwards brought from the dungeon to interpret them (41[14aβ] J).

1–8. Pharaoh's officers in disgrace: their dreams. —**1.** *the butler . . . the baker*] J writes as if the king had only one servant of each class: his notions of a royal establishment are perhaps simpler than E's. In Babylonia the highest and oldest court offices are said to have been those of the baker and the butler (*ATLO*², 54; cf. Zimmern, *ZDMG*, liii. 119 f.).—**2.** *chief of the butlers . . . . bakers* (E)]

Ex. 3[21] 11[3] 12[36]†) gen. of obj. = 'favour towards him.'—**22.** עֹשִׂים] On omission of subj., see G-K. § 116 *s*.—הוא היה עשה] 𝔊[A, al.] om.—**23.** בידו] 𝔊 πάντα γὰρ ἦν διὰ χειρὸς 'I.—מצליח] 𝔊 + ἐν ταῖς χερσὶν αὐτοῦ.

1. מַשְׁקֵה—והאפה] On the synt., see G-K. §§ 128 *a*, 129 *h*; Dav. § 27 (*b*): cf. v.[5].—**2.** ויקצף is the regular continuation of the time-clause in [1a] (E).—סָרִיסָיו] with so-called *qamez impurum*; so always except in const. st.

The rise of household slaves to high civil dignity seems tc have been characteristic of the Egyptian government under the 19th dynasty (Erman, *LAE*, 105). Titles corresponding to those here used are 'scribe of the sideboard,' 'superintendent of the bakehouse,' etc. (Erman, 187).—**3a.** The officers are not incarcerated, but merely detained in custody pending investigation (Gu.).—**3b** (J). *bound*] *i.e.* 'confined'; cf. $39^{22f.}$.—**4.** Joseph is charged with the duty of waiting on them (שֵׁרֵת as 39^4, 2 Sa. 13^{17}). **5–8** is a skilful piece of narration: the effect of the dreams is vividly depicted before their character is disclosed.—**5.** *each according to the interpretation of his dream*] a sort of *idem per idem* construction, meaning that the dreams had each a peculiar significance.—**5b** (J).—**8.** *no one to interpret it*] No professional interpreter, such as they would certainly have consulted had they been at liberty.—*interpretations belong to God*] The maxim is quite in accord with Egyptian sentiment (Herod. ii. 83), but in the mouth of Joseph it expresses the Hebrew idea that inspiration comes directly from God and is not a מִצְוַת אֲנָשִׁים מְלֻמָּדָה (Is. 29^{13}).

On the Egyptian belief in divinely inspired dreams, see Ebers, 321 f.; Wiedemann, *Rel. of the Ancient Eg.* 266 ff.; Heyes, 174 ff.: on the belief in classical antiquity, Hom. *Il.* ii. 5–34, *Od.* iv. 795 ff.; Cicero, *De divin.* i. § 39 ff. etc.; in modern Egypt, Lane, *ME*[5], i. 330. While this idea was fully shared by the Israelites, the *interpretation* of dreams, as a distinct art or gift, is rarely referred to in OT (only in the case of Joseph, and that of Daniel, which is largely modelled on it). Elsewhere the dream either *contains* the revelation ($20^{3ff.}$ etc.), or carries its significance on its face ($28^{12ff.}$ 37^{10}). See Sta. *BTh.* § 63. 1.

9–19. The dreams interpreted.—9–11. The butler had seen a vine pass rapidly through the stages of its growth; had seemed to squeeze the ripe grapes into a cup and present

(40^7 etc.).—**3.** במשמר] Better perhaps בְּמִשְׁמַר (cf. v.[4]), with בית as acc. of place. So v.[7].—**4.** ימים = 'for some time'; G-K. § 139 *h*.—**6.** זֹעֲפִים] 'be fretful'; elsewhere late (Dn. 1^{10}, Pr. 19^3, 2 Ch. 26^{19} †).—**8.** פֹּתֵר אֵין] On the order, G-K. § 152 *o*.— פתרנים] 𝔊 פִּתְרֹנָם.

10. והיא כפרחת] Not 'when it budded' (𝔖𝔗[O]), for such a use of כְּ with a ptcp. (G-K. § 164 *g*) is dubious even in the Mishnah (*JQR*, 1908, 697 f.). If the text be retained we must render 'as if budding' (Dri. *T.* p. 172^2).

it to Pharaoh,—a mixture of the 'realistic' and the 'fantastic' which belongs to the psychology of the dream (Gu.). It is disputed whether the drinking of the fresh juice is realism or phantasy. "The ordinary interpretation is that the king drank the fresh grape-juice; but as the butler sees the natural process of the growth of the grapes take place with dream-like swiftness, so probably it is taken for granted that the juice became wine in similar fashion" (Ben.; so Gu.). On the other hand, Ebers (*Durch Gosen z. Sinai*², 492) cites two texts in which a beverage prepared by squeezing grapes into water is mentioned.—**12, 13.** The interpretation: the butler will be restored to his office within three days.—*lift up thy head*] Commonly understood of restoration to honour. But in view of the fact that the phrase is used of the baker also, it may be doubted if it be not a technical phrase for release from prison (as it is in 2 Ki. 25^{27}, Jer. 52^{31}).—**14, 15.** Joseph's petition.—*remember me*] On the difficult construction, *v.i.*—*from this house*] Not the prison (as Vns., below), but Potiphar's house, where he was kept as a slave.—**15a** *I was stolen*] cf. $37^{28a\alpha}$ (E).—*the land of the Hebrews*] The ex-

---

Ball emends (after 𝔊 καὶ αὐτὴ θάλλουσα) והיא מַפְרַחַת (cf. Jb. 14^9, Ps. 92^{14}); Kit. כְּפֹרַחַת.—נִצָּהּ] The masc. נֵץ does not occur (in this sense) in bib. Heb., and a contraction of ־ָחָה to ־ָה is doubtful (G-K. § 91 *e*); hence it is better to read נִצָּה as acc.: 'it (the vine) went up in blossom.' It is possible that here and Is. 18^5 נִצָּה means 'berry-cluster'; see Derenbourg, *ZATW*, v. 301 f.—הבשילו] lit. 'cooked'; Hiph. only here.—Note the asyndetous construction, expressing the rapidity of the process.—**13.** יִשָּׂא—אֶת־ראשך] 𝔊 μνησθήσεται . . . τῆς ἀρχῆς σου; similarly 𝔙𝔖𝔗ᴼ.—כַּן] lit. 'pedestal,' used metaphorically as here in 41^{13}, Dn. $11^{7.20.21.38}$ †.—**14.** כי אם־זכרתני] 𝔊 ἀλλὰ μνήσθητί μου, 𝔙 *tantum memento mei*; similarly 𝔖 and 𝔗ᴼᴶ. Something like this must be the meaning; the difficulty is (since a precative pf. is generally disallowed in Heb.) to fit the sense to any known use of the bare pf. (*a*) If it be pf. of certitude, the nearest analogy seems to me to be Ju. 15^7, where כי אם has strong affirmative force, perhaps with a suppressed adjuration, as 2 Ki. 5^{20} (חי יהוה כי אם רצתי): 'thou wilt surely remember me.' To supply a negative sent. like 'I desire nothing [except that thou remember me]' (G-K. § 163 *d*; De. Str.), destroys the idea of pf. of certainty, and is a doubtful expedient for the additional reason that כי אם may mean 'except,' but hardly 'except that.' (*b*) It may be fut. pf., in which case the אם must have its separate conditional sense; and then it is better (with We.) to change כי to אַךְ: 'only, if thou remember me.' The objection (De. Di.) that the remembrance is too

pression is an anachronism in the patriarchal history. It is barely possible that both here and in $39^{14.\,17}$ (41^{12}) there is a faint reminiscence of the historical background of the legends, the early occupation of Palestine by Hebrew tribes.—**15b** (J) was probably followed in the original document by an explanation of the circumstances which led to his imprisonment.—**16–19.** The baker's dream contains sinister features which were absent from the first, the decisive difference being that while the butler dreamed that he actually performed the duties of his office, the baker only sought to do so, and was prevented (Gu.).—**16.** *three baskets of white bread*] The meaning of חֹרִי, however, is doubtful (*v.i.*).—*upon my head*] See the picture of the court-bakery of Rameses III. in Ebers, *Aeg.* 332; Erman, *LAE*, 191. According to Ebers, the custom of carrying on the head (Herod. ii. 35) was not usual in ancient Egypt *except* for bakers.—**17.** *in the uppermost basket*] Were the other two empty (Ho. Ben.)? or were they filled with inferior bread for the court (Gu.)?—*all manner of bakemeats*] The court-baker of Rameses III. "is not content with the usual shapes used for bread, but makes his cakes in all manner of forms. Some are of a spiral shape like the 'snails' of our confectioners; others are coloured dark-brown or red," etc. (Erman, 192).—*while the birds kept eating*] In real life he would have driven off the birds (cf. 15^{11}); in the dream—and this is the ominous circumstance—he cannot.—**19.** *lift thy head from off thee*] In view of the fulfilment, it is perhaps better (with Ball) to remove מעליך as a mistaken repetition of the last word of the v., and to understand the phrase of the baker's release from prison (see on v.[13]). The verb *hang* may then refer to the mode of execution, and not merely (as generally supposed)

---

essential an element of the request to be made a mere condition, has no great weight; and might be met by giving אִם interrogative force (Ho.). See, further, Dri. *T.* § 119 (*δ*).—ועשית־נא] The only case of consec. pf. followed by נא (G-K. § 105 *b*).—מן־הבית הזה] 𝔊𝔙𝔖𝔗ᴼᴶ seem to have read מִן־הַבּוֹר הזה, or מִבֵּית הַסֹּהַר הזה.—**16.** חֹרִי] ἅπ. λεγ., commonly derived from √ חָוַר, 'be white'; so virtually 𝔊 Aq. 𝔙𝔖𝔗ᴶ; but 𝔗ᴼ 'of nobility' (דְּחֵרוּ). Others (Ra. al.) understand it as a characteristic of the baskets: 'perforated' (from חוֹר, 'hole'). The *βαϊνά* (of palm-leaves) of Σ. seems to

to the exposure of the decapitated corpse. Decapitation is said to have been a commoner punishment in Egypt than hanging, but the latter was not unknown (Ebers, 334). The destruction of the corpse by birds must have been specially abhorrent to Egyptians, from the importance they attached to the preservation of the body after death. For OT examples, see Dt. $21^{22f.}$, Jos. 10^{26}, 2 Sa. 4^{12}, and esp. 2 Sa. $21^{9.10}$.

20–23. The dreams fulfilled.—20. That it was customary for the Pharaoh to celebrate his birthday by court assemblies and granting of amnesties, is proved for the Ptolemaic period by the tables of Rosetta and Canopus.—*lifted the head*] see on v.[19].—**23.** The notice of the butler's ingratitude forms an effective close, leaving the reader expectant of further developments.

Ch. XLI. *Joseph becomes Viceroy of Egypt* (JE, P).

Two years after the events of ch. 40, the king of Egypt has a wonderful double dream, which none of his magicians is able to interpret ($^{1-8}$). The chief butler is naturally reminded of his own experience, and mentions Joseph, who is forthwith summoned into the royal presence ($^{9-14}$). Having interpreted the dreams as a prophecy of a great famine ($^{15-32}$), Joseph adds some sage advice on the right way to cope with the emergency ($^{33-36}$); and Pharaoh is so impressed by his sagacity that he entrusts him with the execution of the scheme, and makes him absolute ruler of Egypt ($^{37-46}$). In pursuance of the policy he had foreshadowed, Joseph stores the surplus of seven years of plenty, and sells it during the subsequent famine ($^{47-57}$).

Analysis.—The connexion of this chapter with the preceding appears from ^{1a} and $^{9-13}$: note שר המשקים, ש׳ האפים, ש׳ הטבחים, משמר, קצף (40^2); Joseph

---

rest on Aramaic (Field).—19. מעליך[1]] Om. by two MSS and 𝔙 (Ba. Kit.).—**20.** הלדת את־] as Ezk. 16^5; cf. G–K. § 69 *w*, 121 *b*.—**21.** מַשְׁקֵה] is never elsewhere used of the office of butler: perhaps 'over his [Pharaoh's] drink' (as we should say, 'his cellar'), as Lv. 11^{34}, 1 Ki. 10^{21}, Is. 32^6 (so Ges. *Th.*, Di.).—23. וַיִּשְׁכָּחֵהוּ] Expressing "a logical or necessary consequence of that which immediately precedes" (G–K. § 111 *l*); cf. Dav. § 47.

the servant of the 'ש' הט'; the officers confined in his 'house'; Joseph 'with them' (^{10}, cf. $40^{3.4}$); and comp. ^{11} with 40^{5}. In the first half of the chapter there is no sufficient reason to suspect a second source except in ^{14b} (J); the repetitions and slight variations are not greater than can be readily explained by a desire for variety in the elaboration of detail. The whole of this section (${}^{1-28}$) may therefore be safely assigned to E (cf. ואין־פותר אותם, ^{8}, ופתר אין אתו, ^{15} with 40^{8a}; ^{16} with 40^{8b}).—In the second half, however, there are slight diversities of expression and representation which show that a parallel narrative (J) has been freely utilised. Thus, in ^{33} Joseph recommends the appointment of a single dictator, in ^{34} the appointment of 'overseers'; in ^{34} a *fifth part* is to be stored, in ${}^{35.48}$ *all* the corn of the good years; in ${}^{35b\alpha}$ the collection is to be centralised under the royal authority, in ${}^{b\beta}$ localised in the different cities; צבר בר alternates with קבץ אכל (${}^{35b\alpha.49} \parallel {}^{35a.48}$). Further, ^{38} seems $\parallel {}^{39}$; ${}^{41} \parallel {}^{44}$; and ${}^{45b} \parallel {}^{46b}$; ^{45a} (פוטיפר = פוטי פרע) can hardly be from E, who has employed the name for another person (37^{36}). Some of these differences may, no doubt, prove to be illusory; but taken cumulatively they suffice to prove that the passage is composite, although a satisfactory analysis cannot be given. For details, see the notes below; and consult Ho. 234; Gu. 380 f.; Pro. 43 f.—^{46a} is from P, and ^{50b} is a gloss.

1–8. Pharaoh's dreams.—2. *from the Nile* (*v.i.*)] the source of Egypt's fertility (Erman, *LAE*, 425 ff.), worshipped as 'the father of the gods,' and at times identified with Osiris or Amon-re (Erman, *Handbook*, 14 f., 80 ff.).—*seven cows, etc.*] "According to Diod. Sic. i. 51, the male ox is the symbol of the Nile, and sacred to Osiris, the inventor of agriculture (*ib.* i. 21). . . . The Osiris-steer often appears accompanied by *seven cows*, e.g. on the vignettes of the old and new Book of the Dead" (*ATLO*², 389).—4. The devouring of one set of cows by the other is a fantastic but suggestive feature of the dream; the symbolism is almost transparent.

---

1. ופרעה חלם] Participial cl. as apodosis; see Dri. *T.* § 78 (3).—היאר] An Eg. loan-word (*'iotr*, *'io'r* = 'stream'), used in OT of the Nile and its canals (except Is. 33^{21}, Jb. 28^{10}, Dn. $12^{5ff.}$); found also in Ass. in the form *ya'aru.* See Ebers, 337 f.; Steindorff, *BA*, i. 612 (cf. 171).—2. אחו (41^{18}, Jb. 8^{11}†)] 'Nile-grass' = Eg. *aḥu*, from *aḥa*, 'be green' (Ebers, 338). 𝔊 ἄχει occurs also vv.${}^{3.19}$, Is. 19^{7}, Sir. 40^{16}.—3. ורקות] 𝔐𝔖𝔖 ודקות (so v.^{4}). It is naturally difficult to decide which is right; but Ba. pertinently points to the alliterations as determining the choice: read therefore 'ר in ${}^{3.4.19.20.27}$, but 'ד in ${}^{6.23}$,—in other words, 'ר always of the cows and 'ד always of the ears.—אצל] 𝔊 om., thus making all the 14 cows stand together.—4. ותאכלנה] 𝔊 + שֶׁבַע; so ${}^{7.20.24}$. 𝔊 has many similar variations (which need not be noted), revealing a tendency to introduce uniformity into the description.

—5-7. The second dream is, if possible, more fantastic and at the same time more explicit.—6. *blasted with the east-wind* (𝔊 ἀνεμόφθοροι)] the dreaded sirocco or *Ḥamsīn*, which blows from the SE from February to June, destroying vegetation, and even killing the seed-corn in the clods (Ebers, 340; Erman, *LAE*, 9; Smith, *HG*, 67 ff.).—8. *all the magicians and wise men of Egypt*] The possessors of occult knowledge of all sorts, including the interpretation of dreams (see p. 461); comp. Tac. *Hist.* iv. 83: "Ptolemæus . . . sacerdotibus Ægyptiorum, quibus mos talia intellegere, nocturnos visus aperit"; see Ebers, 341–349. The motive—the confutation of heathen magic by a representative of the true religion—is repeated in the histories of Moses (Ex. 7–9) and Daniel (chs. 2. 5); cf. Is. 47^{12} etc.

9-14. Joseph summoned to interpret the dreams.—9. The butler's ungrateful memory is stimulated by the opportunity of ingratiating himself with his royal master, though this requires him to *make mention of* his old offence. —12. *according to each man's dream he interpreted*] Note the order of ideas as contrasted with v.[11] (40^5): there is a pre-established harmony between the interpretation and the dream, and the office of the interpreter is to penetrate the imagery of the dream and reach the truth it was sent to convey.—13. *I was restored . . . he was hanged*] Lit. 'Me one restored,' etc., according to G–K. § 144 *d, e*. To suppose the omission of *Pharaoh*, or to make Joseph the subj., is barely admissible.—14. *and they brought him hastily from the dungeon*] is a clause inserted from J.—*shaved himself*] his head and beard,—a custom which seems to have been peculiar to the priests under the New Empire (Erman, *LAE*, 219; cf. Herod. ii. 37).

---

8. ותפעם] 'was perturbed'; as Dn. 2^8 (2^1 Hithp.), Ps. 77^5.—חרטמים] Only in this ch., in Ex. 7–9 (P), and (by imitation) in Dn. 2^2. The word is thus practically confined to Egyptian magicians, though no Eg. etymology has been found; and it may be plausibly derived from Heb. חֶרֶט, *stylus*.—אתם] Read with 𝔊 אתו, after חלמו; the dream is 'one' (vv.[25. 26]).—9. את־פרעה] 𝔐 better אל פ׳.—חטאַי] 𝔊 חטאִי (sing.). The resemblance of the cl. ([9b]) to 40^1 does not prove it to be from J (Gu.).—10. אתי] 𝔐 אתם, 𝔊 אתנו.—11. ונחלמה] G–K. § 49 *e*.—12. ויפתר—פתר] 𝔊 καὶ συνέκρινεν ἡμῖν.

15–24. Pharaoh's recital of his dreams.—**15.** *thou canst hear a dream to interpret it*] *i.e.*, 'thou canst interpret a dream when thou hearest it': Heb. subordinates the emphatic clause where we would subordinate the condition.—**16.** Comp. 40^8.—The answer (on the form, *v.i.*) exhibits a fine combination of religious sincerity and courtly deference.—**17–21.** The first dream.—The king gives a vivid subjective colouring to the recital by expressing the feelings which the dream excited. This is natural, and creates no presumption that a parallel narrative is drawn upon. Similarly, the slight differences in phraseology (תאר for מראה, דַּלּוֹת, etc.) are due to the literary instinct for variety.—**22–24.** The second dream.

25–32. The interpretation.—**25–27a.** The general outline of the interpretation: the dream is one; it is a presage of what is to happen; the number seven refers to years. The methodical exposition is meant to be impressive.—**27b** brings the climax: *There shall be seven years of famine* (so Pro. *v.i.*).—**28.** It is uncertain whether הוא refers back to ^{25b} ('This is what [I meant when] I said to Pharaoh'), or to ^{27b}

---

15. תשמע] *Oratio obliqua* after לֵאמֹר (without כי), G–K. § 157 *a*; Dav. § 146, *R.* 1.—**16.** בִּלְעָדַי] lit. 'Apart from me' ($\mathfrak{T}^O$ לא מן חוכמתי), used as 14^{24}. ꞩ𝔊 read בִּלְעֲדֵי אלהים לא יַעֲנֶה = 'Apart from God, one will not be answered,' etc.; cf. 𝔖 ܕܠܡܐ ܣܒܪ ܐܢܬ ܕܒܠܥܕ ܐܠܗܐ ܢܥܢܐ ('Dost thou expect that apart from God one will answer?' etc.). 𝔙 *Absque me Deus respondebit*, shifting the accent. There seems a *double entendre* in the use of יענה: 'answer' and 'correspond': 'God will give an answer corresponding to the welfare,' etc.—**19.** דלות] 'flaccid'; 𝔊 om.—**21.** קִרְבֶּנָה] On the suff. cf. G–K. § 91 *f.*—מראיהן] Sing. (*ib.* § 93 *ss*).—**23.** צנמות] Aram. = 'dried,' 'hardened.' The word is ἅπ. λεγ. in OT, and is omitted by 𝔊𝔙𝔖.—אחריהם] MSS and ꞩ הֶן—. The irregular gender of MT only here in this chapter.

26. פרת] Om. of art. may be justified on the ground that the numeral is equivalent to a determinant (G–K. § 126 *x*); but ꞩ הפרות is much to be preferred.—**27.** הָרֵקוֹת] 'empty.' The pointing is suggested partly by the contrast to מלאֹת (^{22} etc.), partly by the fact that (in MT) רק has not been used of the ears. We ought undoubtedly to read הַדַּקּוֹת (ꞩ𝔖).—יהיו וגו'] The translation above is not free from difficulty; it omits a prediction of unusual plenty preceding the famine, which is, nevertheless, presupposed by what follows. But the ordinary rendering is also weak: why should the seven thin ears alone be fully interpreted? Besides, שִׁבֳּלִים is fem.—**28–32.** The critical difficulties of the ch. commence in this section. Pro. assigns $^{29-31}$ to J (‖ $^{27f.}$ E), instancing כָּלָה (cf. 18^{33} $24^{15.19}$

('This is the announcement I [now] make to Pharaoh'). In any case 29 looks like a new commencement, and may introduce a variant from J (*v.i.*).—31. ולא יִוָּדַע goes back to the ולא נוֹדַע of ^{21}.—32. If the dream is one, why was it twice repeated? Because, says Joseph, the crisis is certain and urgent. So he rounds off his finished and masterly explanation of the dreams.

33–36. Joseph's advice to Pharaoh.—Here Joseph proves himself to be no mere expert in reading dreams, but a man with a large reserve of practical wisdom and statesmanship.—33–35. There is an apparent discrepancy between the appointment of a single official (^{33a}) and that of a commission of 'overseers' (^{34a}); and again between the fifth part (^{34b}) and the whole (^{35a}); we note also the transition from sing. (וחמש) to pl. (ויקבצו, etc.). For attempts at division of sources, see below.—34. The taxing of a fifth part of the crop seems to have been a permanent Egyptian institution (see on 47^{24}), whose origin the Hebrews traced to the administration of Joseph.—35. *under the hand* (*i.e.* the authority) *of Pharaoh*] cf. Ex. 18^{10}, 2 Ki. 13^{5}, Is. 3^{6}.

37–46. Joseph's elevation.—37, 39 (E) ‖ 38 (J).—The *thing* that *was pleasing to Pharaoh, etc.*, is not the interpreta-

---

27^{30} 43^{2} 44^{12}), and כְּבַר (12^{10} 43^{1} $47^{4.\,13}$) as characteristic of J; but they are not decisive. Gu. limits J to $^{29.\,30a.\,32b\beta}$ (‖ $^{27f.\,30b.\,31.\,32ab\alpha}$ E). This is on the whole more satisfying, since ונשכח and ולא יִוָּדַע appear to be doublets (Di.); but a positive conclusion will hardly be reached.

33–36. The passage is certainly composite, and can be resolved into two nearly complete sequences as follows: E = $^{33.\,34b.\,35b\alpha}$ (to פרעה)$^{.\,36a\beta\gamma}$; J = $^{34a.\,35ab\beta}$ (from אֹכֶל)$^{.\,36a\alpha b}$. Characteristic of E are איש, ארץ מצרים, צבר בר, against J's פקידים (with פִּקָּדוֹן), קבץ אכל הארץ; and the only necessary change is יצברו to יצבר. The result corresponds pretty closely with Gu.'s analysis; that of Procksch differs widely.—33. יֵרֶא] see Baer-Del. p. 78; G–K. § 75*p*. Str., however, holds the true reading to be יֵרָא.—34. יעשה] ⅏ ויעש. To the peculiar idiom, De. compares the Latin *fac scribas*; יעשה may, however, mean 'take action,' as 1 Ki. 8^{32}.—וחמש] 𝔊 pl.—35. אכל בערים ושמרו] Ball prefixes וְיִתְּנוּ (as v.^{48}); some such expedient is necessary to make sense of the last word.—For ושמרו, ⅏𝔖 have ישמרו; 𝔊 συναχθήτω (יצברו?).—36. פִּקָּדוֹן] Lv. $5^{21.\,23}$†; obviously suggested here by פקדים in v.^{34}.

37–46. *Analysis.*—To E we may pretty confidently assign $^{37.\,39}$ (נבון וחכם as ^{33}) ^{40}; to J $^{38.\,44.\,45}$. Whether J's parallel to ^{40} commences with ^{41} (Pro.), or is delayed to ^{44} (Gu.), it is hard to decide. ^{41b} reads like a

tion of the dreams, but the practical suggestion with which it was followed up, though it was the former which proved that Joseph was truly inspired. The statement that the policy commended itself comes from E; in J, Pharaoh improves upon it by entrusting the supervision to Joseph himself instead of to the 'overseers' he had proposed.—**38.** *the spirit of God*] here first mentioned in Gen. as the source of inward illumination and intellectual power. The idea that eminent mental gifts proceed from the indwelling of the divine spirit, which is implied in Pharaoh's exclamation, was probably ancient in Israel, although the proofs of it are comparatively late (cf. Ex. 31^{3}, Nu. 27^{18}; see Stade, *BTh.* § 43. 1).—**40.** *over my house*] The dignity may be compared to that of "Mayor of the palace" under the Merovingian kings; cf. 1 Ki. 4^{6} 16^{9}, Is. 22^{15} etc.—**41.** *over all the land of Egypt*] The most coveted civic office in Egypt was that of the *T'ate*, the chief of the whole administration, "the second after the king in the court of the palace" (see Erman, *LAE*, 87 ff., 69). The elevation of Syrian slaves to such dignities is likewise attested for the age of the New Empire (*ib.* 106, 517 f.).—**42.** The form of investiture is specifically Egyptian.—*his signet-ring*] used in sealing documents (Est. 3^{12} 8^{8}), and given as a token of authority (Est. 3^{10} 8^{2}, 1 Mac. 6^{15} etc.).—*fine linen*] the weaving of which was carried to extreme perfection in Egypt; Erman, 448 ff.—*the golden collar*] There is probably an allusion to 'the reward of the gold,' a decoration (including necklets of gold) often conferred in recognition of eminent service to the crown (Erman,

---

formula of investiture accompanying the action of ^{42a}, of which ^{43b} would be the explication. $^{46b\beta}$ would be a natural sequel to ^{43a} (ויעבר). Hence, if a division must be attempted, that of Procksch may be followed, viz., E = $^{40.\ 42b.\ 43a.\ 46b\beta}$; J = $^{41.\ 42a.\ 43b.\ 44.\ 45}$.—38. הנמצא] 1st. pl. impf. Qal.—**40.** ועל־פיך ישק] 𝕲 ἐπὶ τῷ στόματί σου ὑπακούσεται. The meaning 'kiss' being obviously unsuitable, Tu. De. Di. render 'arrange themselves (from Ar. *nasaḳa*); others point יָשֹׁק, 'run'; but no explanation is quite satisfactory. על־פיך may, of course, mean 'at thy command' (45^{21}, Ex. 17^{1} etc.).—רק הכסא] 'only as regards the throne'; G-K. § 118*h*.—**41.** אתך] 𝕲 + σήμερον.—**42.** שֵׁשׁ] Apparently an Egyptian word (Copt. *šens*), replaced in post-Exilic Heb. by בוּץ. It is disputed whether it means cotton alone, or linen alone, or both; see Di.'s exhaustive note

118 ff.: see the engraving, 208*).—**43.** *the second-best chariot*] Horses and carriages first appear on monuments of the 18th dynasty, and must have been introduced "during the dark period between the Middle and the New Empire" (Erman, 490).—*they cried before him* '*Abrēk*] A very obscure word; for conjectures, *v.i.*—**44.** An almost exact parallel (J) to [41] (E).—**45a.** Joseph's marriage.—The conferring of a new name naturally accompanied promotions like that of Joseph (Erman, 144).—*the high priest of* '*Ôn*] was an important personage in the religion and politics of the New Empire (see Erman, *LAE*, 76, 83, 89, and *pass.*), and the priestly college there was reputed the greatest in the country for learning (Herod. ii. 3; Strabo, XVII. i. 29). '*Ôn* (Eg. *Anu*) is Heliopolis, 7 m. NE of Cairo, an ancient seat of the

---

on Ex. 25[4], and *EB*, 2800 f.—הזהב] 𝔐 זהב.—**43.** בְּמִרְכֶּבֶת] G-K. § 85 *h.*—ויקראו] 𝔐𝔊𝔖 ויקרא.—אַבְרֵךְ] The word remains an enigma. The resemblance to Heb. ברך has misled no anc. Vn. except Aq. (*γονατίζειν*) and 𝔙 (*ut genuflecterent*). 𝔖 renders ܐܒܐ ܘܫܠܝܛܐ; 𝔗[O] דין אבא למלכא; 𝔗[J] דין אבא למלכא רב בחכמתא ורכיך בשנייא; 𝔊 has *κήρυξ* as subj. of vb. (𝔙 also has *clamante præcone*). The speculations of Egyptologists are too numerous to mention: see BDB, *s.v.*, or Heyes, 254 ff. The best is that of Spiegelberg (*OLz.* vi. 317 ff.), who considers that it is a call to 'Attention!' (Eg. '*b r-k*; lit. 'Thy heart to thee!'). Frd. Del. (*Parad.* 225) suggested a connexion with Ass. *abarakku* (the title of a high official), which his father declared to be a "neckischer Zufall"! Radical emendations of the text have been proposed by Ball ([ל]אמר כי נתן) and Che. (אַבִּר כינאתן = 'Mighty one of Chuenaten' [Amenophis IV.]: *OLz.* iii. 151 f.); these are wholly unsatisfying, and the latter has not survived the criticisms of Müller (*ib.* 325 f.): see *TBI*, 467.—ונתון] 'thus placing.' As continuation of ויתן in [42a], the inf. abs. is grammatically correct (G-K. § 113 *z*); and though the idiom is infrequent, there is no reason to suspect the text.—**45.** צָפְנַת פַּעְנֵחַ] 𝔊 *Ψονθομφανήχ* (transposing צ and פ? [see Nestle, *ZATW*, xxv. 209 ff.]). The old interpretations follow two lines: (1) 'Revealer of secrets' (Jos. *Ant.* ii. 91; 𝔖𝔗[OJ], Patr.), connecting with Heb. צפן; and (2) 'Saviour of the world' (Copt. *p-sot-om-ph-eneḫ*, De. Ho.); so 𝔙 Jer. *Quæst.* Of modern Egyptological theories the one most in favour seems to be that propounded by Steindorff in *Ztsch. f. Aeg. Spr.* xxvii. 41 f.: that it represents Eg. *De-pnute-ef-onḫ*, and means 'The god speaks and he lives.' It is said (*ib.* 42) that personal names of this type (though with the *proper* name of a deity) are common from the beginning of the 22nd dynasty. See the discussion in Heyes, *op. cit.* 258 ff., who prefers the interpretation

---

* Comp. Heyes, *Bib. u. Aeg.* 248 ff.

worship of the sun-god Ra.—On the other names in the v., *v.i.*—**45b** and **46b** are doublets.—**46a** (P). The chronology is altogether inconsistent with the assumptions of JE regarding the relative ages of Joseph and Benjamin (see Ben. 360).—*stood before Pharaoh*] cf. 47^{7} (P).

47–57.—Joseph's measures for relief of the famine. —**47, 49** (E) ‖ **48** (J). He stores corn during the seven years of plenty.—**50–52** (E ?). Joseph's two sons.—*Mĕnaššeh*] interpreted quite grammatically as 'causing to forget.' The etymology is not to be taken too literally, as if the narrator meant that Joseph had actually forgotten his father's house (cf. Ps. 45^{11}).—**52.** *made me fruitful*] The name of the tribe is generally thought to contain the idea of fruitfulness, from the fertility of the region in central Palestine which it occupied. —**54–57.** The beginning of the famine.—**54, 55** contain a slight discrepancy. According to ^{54b} the Egyptians

---

of Lieblein (*PSBA*, 1898, 202 ff.): *defenti* [or *defenta*]-*pa-anḫ* = "celui qui donne la nourriture de la vie."—אָסְנַת] Explained, with some hesitation, as 'belonging to (the goddess) Neith' (Steindorff, Spiegelberg, al.).—פּוֹטִי פֶרַע] (𝔊 Πετρεφῆ, etc.) is a fuller form of פוטיפר; see on 39^{1}.—It is worthy of remark that, except in the case of Asenath, the suggested Egyptian analogues of these names do not occur, save sporadically, earlier than the 22nd dynasty (that of Shishak).—**45b.** 𝔊 om.—**46.** פרעה מלך מצרים is an amplification in the style of P (Ex. $6^{11.\ 13.\ 27.\ 29.}$ 14^{8}).

47–57. *Analysis.*—Starting from the presumption that the storing of food in the cities and the direct appeal of the famishing people to Pharaoh are not from the same source, the best division seems the following: E = $^{47.\ 49.\ 54a.\ 55.\ 56b}$; J = $^{48.\ 53.\ 54b.\ 56a.\ 57}$ (comp. Gu. and Pro.). $^{50-52}$ are universally assigned to E (on account of אלהים) in spite of the fact that the children are named by the father. P's authorship is perhaps excluded by the explicit etymologies, to which there are no real analogies in that document. The vv. in any case interrupt the context of JE, and may be a supplementary notice inserted by a late hand at what seemed the most suitable place.—**47.** לקמצים] The √ is elsewhere peculiar to P (Lv. 2^{2} 5^{12} 6^{8}, Nu. 5^{26}†); and Ball assigns $^{46-48}$ to that source. But the sense 'by handfuls' is doubtful, and is represented by none of the old Vns. except the clumsy paraphrases of 𝔙 and 𝔗J; so that the text is probably at fault. 𝔊 has δράγματα; 𝔖 and 𝔗O ܟܘܡܪ̈ܝܢ and לאוצרין (with ܘܟܢܫܘܗܝ and וכנשו for ותעש).—**48.** שנים אשר היו] Rd. with 𝔐𝔊 השנים אשר היה הַשָּׂבָע.—**50.** שְׁנַת] 𝔊 τὰ ἑπτὰ ἔτη.—**51.** נַשַּׁנִי] Pi. only here; both the form and the irregular vocalisation (G–K. 52 *m*) are chosen for the sake of assonance with מְנַשֶּׁה.—**54.** היה] 𝔊 οὐκ ἦσαν; so 𝔖—a natural mis-

had no lack of bread, and consequently no need to apply to Joseph, though they were indebted to his forethought. In [55] they are famishing, and have to buy their food from Joseph: this view is connected with $47^{13ff.}$.—56. *opened all that was in them*] Read with 𝔊 'all the granaries,' though the Hebrew text cannot be certainly restored (*v.i.*)—57 prepares for the next scene of the drama (ch. 42).

State granaries, for the sustenance of the army, the officials and the serfs, were a standing feature of Egyptian administration (Erman, *LAE*, 107 f.; cf. 433 f.), and were naturally drawn upon for the relief of the populace in times of scarcity (*ib.* 126). The 'superintendent of the granaries' was a high officer of state, distinct, as a rule, from the vizier or *T'ate* (p. 469); but a union of the two dignities was just as easy under exceptional circumstances as the combination of the Premiership with the Chancellorship of the Exchequer would be with us (see Erman, 89). We can readily understand that such a wise and comprehensive provision impressed the imagination of the Israelites, and was attributed by them to a divine inspiration of which one of their ancestors was the medium (cf. Gu. 384).—Besides these general illustrations of the writer's acquaintance with Egyptian conditions, two special parallels to this aspect of Joseph's career are cited from the monuments: (1) Ameny, a nomarch under Usertsen I. (12th dynasty), records on his grave at Beni-Hasan that when years of famine came he ploughed all the fields of his district, nourished the subjects of his sovereign and gave them food, so that there was none hungry among them. (2) Similarly, on a grave of the 17th dynasty at El-Kab: "When a famine arose, lasting many years, I distributed corn to the city in each year of the famine" (see *ATLO*[2], 390; Dri. 346 f.). For the sale of grain to foreigners, we have the case of Yanḫamu, governor of Yarimutu, in the Amarna letters (see below on $47^{13ff.}$).—It is impossible to desire a fuller demonstration of the Egyptian background of the Joseph-stories than ch. 41 affords. The attempt to minimise the coincidences, and show that "in a more original and shorter form the story of Joseph had a N Arabian and not a Palestinian and Egyptian background, and consequently that 'Pharaoh, king of Egypt,' should be 'Pir'u, king of Miṣrim'" (*TBI*, 454-473), tends to discredit rather than confirm the seductive Muṣri-theory, which is pushed to such an extravagant length.

---

understanding.—56. אשר בהם] 𝔐 אשר בהם בר. The context imperatively demands a noun (𝔊 σιτοβολῶνας, 𝔖 ܐܘܨܪ̈ܐ). Lagarde (*Sym.* i. 57) suggested a Heb. equivalent of Talmud. אִישבורא; We. some derivative of שבר; De. Ba. and Kit. (combining 𝔐 and 𝔖) אוצרות הַבָּר.—וישבר] Pt. וַיַּשְׁבֵּר (Hi.); cf. 42^{6}.—ויחזק וגו'] 𝔊 om.—57. הארץ[1]] Better הארצות as 𝔊 (cf. [54]).

Ch. XLII.—*Joseph's Brethren come to Egypt to buy Food* (E, J)

One thing is still wanting to the dramatic completeness of the story of Joseph: the recognition of his greatness by his family, or (in E) the fulfilment of his youthful dreams. This is the theme of the second part of the history (chs. 42–45), where the writers tax their inventiveness to the utmost in retarding the *dénouement* of the plot. Two visits to Egypt, and not fewer than four interviews with Joseph, are needed to prepare for the final reconciliation; and the hearers' attention is all the while kept on the stretch by the surprising expedients adopted by Joseph to protract the suspense and excite the compunction of his brethren.—In ch. 42 we are told how the ten brothers are brought to Egypt by stress of famine ($^{1-4}$), are recognised by Joseph, and denounced and imprisoned as spies ($^{5-17}$); and how after three days' confinement they are sent home, leaving Simeon behind them as a hostage ($^{18-28}$). Arrived in Canaan, they relate their adventure to Jacob, who bitterly complains of the loss of two children, and refuses to trust Benjamin to their charge ($^{29-38}$). The incident of the money found in the sacks ($^{25.\ 27f.\ 35}$) increases the dread with which they contemplate a return to Egypt.

Analysis.—Ch. 42 belongs *a potiori* to E, and 43. 44 to J (We. *Comp.*^{2} 58 ff.). A distinct difference of representation appears from a comparison of 42^{29-37} (which, *pace* Procksch, is an undiluted excerpt from E) with 43^{3-7} 44^{19-23} (J). "In ch. 42, Joseph secures, by the detention of Simeon, that the brethren shall return under any circumstances, with Benjamin or without; in ch. 43 f., on the contrary, he forbids them to return unless Benjamin is with them" (We.). In J, moreover, the brethren do not volunteer the information that they have a younger brother, but it is drawn out of them by searching questions. It is certain (from doublets and phraseology) that both J and E are represented in 42^{1-14}; though the former is so fragmentary that it is difficult to reconstruct a narrative consistent with $43^{3ff.}$ $44^{19ff.}$. Apparently, the colloquy reproduced in 43^7 44^{20-23} 43^3 must have followed the acknowledgment that they were all one man's sons (^{11a} ∥ ^{13a} E),—a view which seems to fit in with all the literary indications. E's account can easily be traced with the help of $^{29-37}$: it includes the charge of espionage ($^{9.\ 11.\ 14.\ 16.\ 30}$), the imprisonment ($^{17.\ 30}$), the detention of Simeon ($^{19.\ 24.\ 33f.}$), the command to bring down Benjamin ($^{16.\ 20.\ 34}$), and the putting of the money in the sacks ($^{25.\ 35}$).—In

$^{1-14}$, the more obvious doublets are ^{1a} ‖ ^{2a}, ^{5a} ‖ ^{6b}, ^{7a} ‖ ^{8}, ^{11a} ‖ ^{13a}; characteristic phrases of J: ירד, $^{2.3}$; ונחיה ולא נמות, ^{2} (43^{8} 47^{19}); קרא אסון, ^{5} (42^{38} 44^{29}); ישראל ^{5}; אֻכֶל, $^{7.10}$. Possibly also לראות את־ערות הארץ, $^{9b.12b}$, is J's variant for E's מרגלים, $^{9b.11b}$ etc. (cf. $^{30.31.34}$) (Gu.). Hence we may assign to J $^{2.3a.4b.5f.7}$ (except וידבר אתם קשות, which should probably follow ^{9a} in E [Di. KS. Gu.]), $^{9b\beta.10.11a.12}$; and to E all the rest (so Gu. nearly: Procksch, however, very plausibly assigns $^{5.6a}$ to P).—After ^{12} there is no trace of J till we come to $^{27.28ab\alpha\beta}$, an obvious duplicate of ^{35}, containing J's peculiar word אמתחת.—$^{29-37}$ are from E: note the name Jacob, $^{29.36}$; Reuben's leadership, ^{37}; and the words הביאו, ^{34}; תסחרו, ^{34} (37^{28} [? $34^{20f.}$]); פְּלֹנָה, ^{36}. We also obtain some new expressions which may be employed as criteria of E: קשות, ^{30} (cf. ^{7}); כנים, $^{31.33.34}$ (cf. $^{11.19}$); רעבון בתיכם, ^{33} (cf. ^{19}); שׂק, ^{35} (cf. ^{25}).—^{38} belongs to J, but its proper place is after 43^{2} (see on the v.).—A peculiar feature of this and the following chs. is the name ארץ כנען, which is elsewhere in Gen. characteristic of P (see p. 245). From this and some similar phenomena, Giesebrecht and others have inferred a Priestly redaction of the Joseph pericope; but the usage may be due to the constant and unavoidable antithesis between Canaan and Egypt (see p. 438 above).

1–4. The journey to Egypt.—1, 2. Another effective change of scene (cf. 39^{1} 41^{1}), introducing the deliberations in Jacob's family regarding a supply of food; where the energy and resourcefulness of the father is set in striking contrast to the perplexity of the sons.—**4.** Benjamin has taken Joseph's place in his father's affection ($44^{29ff.}$); Jacob's unwillingness to let him out of his sight is a leading motive both in J and E.

5–17. The arrival in Egypt, and first interview with Joseph.—On **5, 6a**, *v.i.*—**6b.** As suspicious strangers the brothers are brought before the viceroy.—*bowed themselves, etc.*] Reminding Joseph of his dreams (v.^{9}). The original connexion in E is broken by the insertion of v.^{7} from J.—

---

1. שֶׁבֶר] of uncertain etymology, is always used of grain as an article of commerce (Am. 8^{5}, Neh. 10^{32}).—יעקב] 𝔊 om.—תתראו] 𝔊 ῥᾳθυμεῖτε (?= תְּאַחֲרוּ, Kit.). Though the Hithpa. occurs elsewhere only in the sense of 'face one another in battle' (2 Ki. $14^{8.11}$ = 2 Ch. $25^{17.21}$), a change of text is uncalled for.—**2.** ויאמר] 𝔊 om.—משם] 𝔊 מעט אכל (as 43^{2}); rd. perhaps משם אכל.—**3.** עשרה] 'ten in number,' acc. of condition.—**4.** יעקב] 𝔊 om.

5a reads like a new beginning, and **5b** is superfluous after $^{1-4}$. Pro. is probably right in the opinion that $^{5.6a}$ are the introduction to P's lost narrative of the visit, a view which is confirmed by the unnecessary explanation of ^{6a}, and by the late word.—**6.** שליט] only Ec. 7^{19} 8^{8} 10^{5} [Ezk. 16^{30}] and Aram. portions of Ezr. and Dn. (Kue. *Ond.* i. p. 318). The resemblance to Σάλατις, the name of the first Hyksos king in Jos.

7 (J) ‖ 8 (E). That Joseph was not recognised by his brethren is natural, and creates a situation of whose dramatic possibilities the narrators take full advantage. The strange mixture of harshness and magnanimity in Joseph's treatment of his brothers, the skill with which he plays alternately on their fears and their hopes, the struggle in his mind between assumed severity and real affection, form the chief interest of the narratives up to the time of the final disclosure. It is unnecessary to suppose that the writers traced in all this the unfolding of a consistent ethical purpose on Joseph's part, and it is certainly an exaggeration to speak of it as an exhibition of 'seelsorgerische geistliche Weisheit' (De.). On the other hand, to say that his object was merely to punish them (Gu.), is clearly inadequate. To the writers, as to the brethren, the official Joseph is an inscrutable person, whose motives defy analysis; and it is probably a mistake to try to read a moral meaning into all the devices by which his penetrating knowledge of the human heart is exemplified.—**9.** *Ye are spies*] A charge that travellers in the East often encounter (see p. 484 below). The eastern frontier of Egypt was fortified and closely watched (Erman, *LAE*, 537 ff.), and a band of ten men seeking to cross it excited suspicion.—*the nakedness of the land*] Not its poverty, but its open and defenceless spots.—**11** (J) ‖ **13** (E). *sons of one man, etc.*] Their eagerness to clear their character betrays them into a disclosure of their family circumstances, which in J is followed up by direct interrogation and a warning that they need not return without their youngest brother (p. 473 above); while in E, Joseph seizes on the reference to Benjamin as a test of their veracity, and threatens that they shall not leave Egypt until he is produced ([15f.]).—*one is not*] It is a fine instance of

---

cont. Ap. i. 77, can hardly be other than accidental.—הוא[2]] 𝔐𝔖𝔗ᴶ והוא.—**9.** עֶרְוַת] lit. *pudenda*, is only here used of defencelessness. Ar. *'aurat* is similarly used of a 'breach in the frontier of a hostile country' (Lane, 2194 c); cf. *Ḳor.* S. 33[13] "our houses are *'aurat*,"—a nakedness, *i.e.* unoccupied and undefended. 𝔊 has τὰ ἴχνη (reading perhaps עקבת [Ba.]); Σ. τὰ κρυπτά.—**10.** ועבדיך] cf. G-K. § 163 *a*: 𝔐𝔊𝔖 om. ו.—**11.** נחנו] So Ex. 16[7. 8], Nu. 32[32], La. 3[42]† (G-K. § 32 *d*); 𝔐 אנחנו.—כנים] lit. 'right men,' is used of persons only in this ch.—**13.** בני איש אחד] 𝔊 om., perhaps

literary tact that Joseph never presses the question as to the fate of the missing brother.—**14.** *This is what I said*] 'It is as I have said' (cf. 41^{28}). Joseph maintains his opinion with well-feigned official obstinacy (Di.).—**15, 16.** *By this shall ye be tested*] The pretext covers a real desire to see Benjamin, which is explicitly avowed in J (44^{21b} 43^{30}).—*By the life of Pharaoh*] In Egypt the king was honoured as a god (Diod. i. 90; Erman, *Handb.* 36 f.); and the oath by his life is attested by an inscription of the 20th dynasty. The OT analogies cited by Kn. (1 Sa. 17^{55}, 2 Sa. 11^{11}) are not in point, since they do not differ from the same formula addressed to private persons (1 Sa. 20^{3} 25^{26}).—**17.** The three days' imprisonment is rather meaningless after v.[16] (see p. 477). Gu. remarks on the prominence of imprisonment in the Joseph narratives, and surmises that a good many Hebrews had known the inside of an Egyptian jail.

18–26. The second interview.—After three days Joseph appears to relent, and to entertain the idea that they may after all be telling the truth. He now proposes to retain only one of them as a hostage, and let the rest carry corn for their starving households.—**18.** *I fear God*] the guardian of 'international religious morality' (Gu.), which is presupposed throughout the patriarchal history; see on 20^{3} 39^{9}.—**21.** *Nay, but we are guilty*] The confession is wrung from them by the distress (צָרָה) which has overtaken them, reminding them of Joseph's distress of soul (צָרַת נפשו) when they left him to die,—*when he pleaded with us*] This touch of pathos is not recorded in ch. 37.—**22.** Reuben had a right to dissociate himself from the confession of guilt, for he had *meant* to save Joseph; but like many another

---

rightly; cf. the ‖ v.[11].—**16.** האסרו] Impv. expressing a determination, G-K. § 110 *c*.—חי פרעה] G-K. § 93 *aa*[1]. The distinction between חַי and חֵי is a Massoretic caprice (Di.).—At the end of the v. 𝔪 inserts a refusal of the condition in the exact terms of $44^{22a\beta}$ (J), which undoubtedly smooths the transition to v.[17], but cannot be original.

18. ואת עשו וחיו] See G-K. § 110 *f*.—**19.** אחד] without art. (האחד 𝔪) *ib.* § 134 *d*; cf. 43^{14}; ct. 42^{33}.—**20.** ויעשו־כן] The words are out of place (cf. [25b]). Did they stand originally after v.[16]?—**21.** אבל] 'Nay, but—,' indicating an affirmation of what one would gladly deny (see on 17^{19}).—

man he claims credit for his good intention rather than for the temporising advice he had actually given (37^{22}).—*his very blood is required*] in spite of the fact that the speaker had kept them trom actual bloodshed.—**23**. *an interpreter*] This is the only place in the patriarchal history where diversity of language appears as a bar to intercourse. —**24**. Joseph is moved to tears by this first proof of penitence.—*Simeon* is chosen as hostage as the oldest next to Reuben, of whose attempt to save him Joseph has just learned for the first time. The effect on the brothers would be the same as in 43^{33}.—**25**. The rest are treated with great generosity; though whether the restoration of the money is pure kindness or a trap, we can hardly say.—*provision for the way*] Hence in E the sacks are not opened till the journey's end (^{35}).

Vv.$^{15-24}$ show a disconnectedness which is unusual in the lucid and orderly Joseph story, and which cannot be explained by discrepancies between J and E. The first proposal—to send one man to fetch Benjamin—leads to no consequences, but is followed, most unnaturally, by the imprisonment of all the ten. This in like manner serves no purpose but to give Joseph time to change his mind. And the colloquy of the brothers ($^{21f.}$) could hardly find a less appropriate place than the moment when hope breaks in on their forebodings. The proper setting for the imprisonment would seem to be their first encounter with Joseph (as v.^{30} 𝔊); and the confession of guilt would stand in a suitable connexion there. It is possible that $^{15f.}$ are a variant to $^{19f.}$, belonging to a somewhat different recension. If Gu. (p. 387) be right in thinking that the earliest form of the legend knew of only one visit to Egypt, it is easy to conceive that in the process of amplification several situations were successively invented, and that two of these have been preserved side by side by an editor, in spite of their imperfect consistency.

26–38. The return to Canaan.—**27, 28**. J's parallel to ^{35} (E).—To leave room for the latter, the account is cut

צרת] 𝔐 בצרת.—אלינו^{2}] 𝔐 עלינו כל.—**25**. ולהשיב] Continuation of vb. fin. by inf. (as here) is very unusual (G-K. § 120*f*).—ויעש] ויעשו? cf. 𝔖𝔙.

27. שקו] Rd. אמתחתו with 𝔊.—מספוא] characteristic of J ($24^{25.32}$ 43^{24}), also Ju. 19^{19} †.—מלון] (√ לון) strictly 'resting-place for the night' (Ex. 4^{24}) or 'night encampment' (Jos. 4^{3}),—perhaps a rude shelter of bushes or canvas (cf. מלונה, 'hut,' Is. 1^{8} 24^{20}) rather than a khan or caravanserai. —כספו] E says צרור כספו ($^{35\ bis}$); so 𝔊 here, wrongly.—אַמְתַּחַת] A word recurring 13 times in chs. 43 f. (J), and nowhere else in OT: 𝔊 invariably μάρσιππος. The √ מתח = 'spread out' (Is. 40^{22}), found in NH. Aram.

short with the opening of the first sack. In J, *each* man found his money at the 'inn' (43^{21}).—**28.** *their heart went out*] 'their courage sank.' Partly from the anticipated accusation of theft (43^{18}), but still more from the superstitious notion that God was bringing trouble upon them.—אַמְתַּחַת] J's peculiar word for 'corn-sack' (*v.i.*).—The last clause, however, *What has God* (אלהים) *done to us?*] is apparently taken from E, probably transposed from the end of ^{35} (KS.).—**29–34.** They recount their experiences to Jacob.—**30.** *treated us as spies*] Better, as 𝔊 (*v.i.*), 'put us in ward as spies.'—**35.** See on $^{27f.}$. The incident explains Jacob's foreboding (v.^{36}) that Simeon and Benjamin are as good as lost.—**36.** *Me have ye bereaved . . . upon me all this has come*] The point of the complaint is that it is *his* children, not their own, that they are throwing away one after another: to which Reuben's offer to sacrifice his two sons is the apt rejoinder.—**37** is E's variant to 43^{9}: here Reuben, there Judah, becomes surety for Benjamin. In E an immediate return to Egypt is contemplated, that Simeon may be released; hence the discussion about sending Benjamin takes place at once. In J the thought of returning is put off to the last possible moment (43^{8}), and the difficulty about Benjamin does not yet arise.—**38** therefore has been removed from its original context: see on $43^{1.2}$.—*bring down . . . to She'ōl*] See on 37^{35}.

Chs. XLIII. XLIV.—*The second Visit to Egypt* (J).

The supply of food being exhausted, another family council is held, at which Jacob's reluctance to part with Benjamin is at last overcome by Judah becoming surety for his safe return: the eleven brethren set out with a present

---

Ar.—**28.** הנה] 𝔐𝔊 add הוא unnecessarily.—חרד אל] Pregn. const.; G–K. § 119*gg*.—**30.** ויתן אתנו] 𝔊 + ἐν φυλακῇ (= בַּמִּשְׁמָר).—**32.** אנחנו אחים] 𝔐𝔊𝔖 transp.—**33.** רעבון] Rd. with 𝔊𝔖𝔗^{O} שבר ר׳, as v.^{19}.—**34.** את־אחיכם] 𝔊𝔖𝔙 pr. ו.—**35.** On the syntax, cf. G–K. § 111*g*.—**36.** כלנה] for כֻּלָּן, as Pr 31^{29} (G–K. § 91*f*). On E's preference for these lengthened suff., see Di. on 41^{21}.

for Joseph and double money in their hand ([1–14]). To their surprise they are received with every mark of honour as the guests of the viceroy; and their fears give place to convivial abandonment at his hospitable table ([15–34]). But Joseph has devised one more trial for them: his silver cup is secretly placed in Benjamin's sack, and on their homeward journey they are overtaken with the accusation of theft. Brought back to Joseph's presence, they offer to surrender their freedom in expiation of some hidden guilt which God has brought home to them (44^{1-16}). But when Joseph proposes to detain Benjamin alone, Judah comes forward and, in a speech of noble and touching eloquence, pleads that he may be allowed to redeem his pledge by bearing the punishment for his youngest brother ([17–34]).

The second journey "brings to light the disposition of the brethren to one another and to their father, thus marking an advance on the first, which only brought them to the point of self-accusation" (Di.). That is true of the narrative as it stands; but since the first journey is taken almost entirely from E and the second from J, the difference indicated is probably due to the different conceptions represented by the two writers, rather than to a conscious development of the plot.

Source.—That the chs. are not the continuation of 42 (E) appears (*a*) from the more reasonable attitude attributed to Joseph, (*b*) from the ignoring of Simeon's confinement, and (*c*) the consequent postponement of the second journey to the last moment, and (*d*) the divergent account of the first meeting with Joseph (p. 473). Positive points of contact with J are (*a*) the discovery of the money at the first halting-place (43^{21}), (*b*) Judah as spokesman and leader ($43^{3ff.\ 8ff.}$ $44^{14.\ 18ff.}$), (*c*) the name Israel ($43^{6.\ 8.\ 11}$), and the expressions: אָכֶל, $43^{2.\ 4.\ 20.\ 22}$ $44^{1.\ 25}$; האיש (of Joseph, without qualification), $43^{3.\ 5.\ 6f.\ 11.\ 13f.}$ 44^{26}; ונחיה ולא נמות, 43^{8}; התמהמה, 43^{10}; ירד and הוריד, $43^{11.\ 15.\ 20.\ 22}$; אמתחת, $43^{12.\ 18.\ 21ff.}$ $44^{1f.\ 8.\ 11f.}$; מלון, 43^{21}; מספוא, 43^{24}; קרה אסון, 44^{29}. The only clear traces of E's parallel narrative are the allusions to Simeon in $43^{14.\ 23b}$. Pro. makes [12a. (‖ 12bα) 13. 14. 15aβb. 16aα. 23b] a continuous sequence from E; but the evidence is conflicting (note האיש, [14]; וירדו, [15b]): see, however, on [12].

1–14. The journey resolved on.—2. Jacob speaks in evident ignorance of the stipulation regarding Benjamin; hence 42^{38} (J) stands out of its proper place. The motive of the transposition is obvious, viz., to account for the seeming rejection of Reuben's sponsorship in 42^{37}.

The original order in J can be recovered by the help of $44^{25ff.}$. After v.[2] there must have been an announcement, in terms similar to 44^{26}, of

the necessity for taking Benjamin with them, to which Jacob replies with the resolute refusal of 43[38] (cf. 44[29]). Then follows ([3ff.]) the more emphatic declaration of Judah, and his explanation of the circumstances out of which the inexorable demand had arisen (see We. *Comp.*[2] 59 f.).

3–5. Judah's ultimatum. On the difference of representation from E, see p. 473 above.—**6.** The reproachful question is intelligible only on the understanding that Jacob has just heard for the first time that he must part with Benjamin.—**7.** *according to the tenor, etc.*] In accordance with the governor's leading questions.—**8–10.** Judah becomes responsible for Benjamin's safety (as in E Reuben, 42[37]).—**9.** *I shall be a sinner, etc.*] For the idea, cf. 1 Ki. 1[21]: guilt is measured not by the moral intention, but by the external consequences, of an action.—**11–14.** Jacob yields to the inevitable; but with characteristic shrewdness suggests measures that may somewhat ease the situation.—**11.** *the produce of the land*] its rarer products, as a token of homage. On זִמְרָה, *v.i.*—On צֳרִי, נְכֹאת, לֹט, see 37[25].—*honey*] may here mean grape-syrup, the *dibs* of modern Syria (see Robinson, *BR*, ii. 81, iii. 381); but there seems no reason to depart from the usual OT sense of the word, viz., the honey of the wild-bee (see Kennedy's careful art. in *EB*, 2104 ff.).—*pistachio-nuts* (*v.i.*) are highly esteemed as a delicacy in Egypt and Syria, although the tree is said to be rarely found in Palestine (according to Rosen, *ZDMG*, xii. 502, not at all).—**12.**

3. בלתי] followed by nom. sent., G–K. § 163 *c*.—Instead of אחכם, 𝔊 has ὁ νεώτερος καταβῇ πρὸς μέ].—**5.** משלח] 𝔊 + τὸν ἀδ. ἡμῶν μεθ' ἡμῶν.—**10.** כי עתה] 'in that case,' as 31[42]; see G–K. § 159 *ee*.—**11.** זִמְרָה] ἅπ. λεγ. 𝔊 καρποί, 𝔙 *optimis fructibus*, 𝔗^O דְּמִשְׁבַּח בארעא, 𝔖 ܫܘܒܚܗ ܕܐܪܥܐ. The meaning is obscure. The derivation from √ זמר, 'praise' [in song] (𝔙𝔗^{OJ}, Tu. al.) is perhaps too poetic to be natural, though it yields a good sense; that from √ זמר, 'prune,' is hardly suitable (see Di.). DHMüller (in Ges. *Hdwb.*[10] p. 983) connects with Aram. ܕܡܰܪ, 'admire': 'admirable products,'—practically the same idea as Tu. (On Ar. *d̲amara*, *d̲imār* [agreeing *phonetically* with Aram. and Heb.], v. Lane, 977 f.)—בטנים] ἅπ. λεγ. Almost certainly nuts of *Pistacia vera*, belonging to the terebinth family (hence 𝔊 τερέμ[β]ινθον, so 𝔙), for which the Syr. name is ܒܛܡܬܐ (Aram. בוטנא, Ar. *buṭm*, Ass. *buṭnu*); see BDB, *s.v.*—**12.** כסף משנה] cf. משנה כסף, v.[15]; and see G–K. § 131 *e*, *q*.—המושב] See Bä-Del.

double money . . . and the money, etc.] can hardly mean double money *besides* that which had been returned; unless (Procksch) the first clause be a variant from E, we must take ו as = 'namely.'—**14.** *'El Shaddai* does not occur elsewhere in J or E (see on 17^{1}), and may be redactional. On the composition of the v., *v.i.*—*as I am bereaved, etc.*] An utterance of subdued resignation: cf. 42^{36}, 2 Ki. 7^{4}, Est. 4^{16}.

15–25. In Joseph's house.—**15.** They first present themselves before Joseph at his official bureau, and are afterwards conducted by the steward to his private residence. The house of a wealthy Egyptian of the 18th dynasty will be found described in Erman, *LAE*, 153, 177 ff.—**16.** Joseph's desire to 'set his eyes on' Benjamin being now gratified, he rewards his brothers by a display of kindness which must have seemed excessive.—*slay and make ready*] In Egypt, accg. to Her. ii. 37, 77, Diod. i. 70, flesh was eaten daily by priests and kings, although the former had to abstain from certain kinds of animal food (Kn-Di.).—**18.** To the simple-minded peasants all this looks like an elaborate military stratagem to overwhelm them by main force and reduce them to slavery.—**19–22.** To forestall the suspicion of theft, they offer to return the money found in their sacks.—*in its full weight*] On the weighing of money, see 23^{16}.—**23.** *your money came to me*] Therefore what you found has nothing to do with it. The steward has entered into Joseph's purpose, and encourages them to

---

p. 79 ('pathachatum uti expresse ait Masora'), G–K. §§ 72 *bb*, 93 *pp*.—**14.** אחר] 𝔐𝔊 האחר. The phrasing is peculiar, and suggests that R^{JE} may have added to J the words אחר ואת־בנימין, at the same time inserting לכם (which 𝔊 om.), to bring about the desired allusion to Simeon.—שָׁכָלְתִּי] Pausal: G–K. § 29 *u*.

16. אִתָּם] 𝔐𝔊𝔙 אֹתָם ו.—בנימין] 𝔊 + אחיו בן־אמו (v.^{29}).—טְבֹחַ] The only case of impve. in *ō* with final gutt. (G–K. § 65 *b*).—**18.** וייראו] 𝔊 וַיִּרְאוּ.—השב] 𝔐 𝔊 הַמּוּשָׁב (v.^{12}).—להתגלל] ἅπ. λεγ. 𝔖$𝔗^{O}$ read להתגרל (see Ba.). 𝔊 τοῦ συκοφαντῆσαι ἡμᾶς, 𝔙 *ut devolvat in nos calumniam.* The text is not to be questioned.—**20.** בִּי] Always followed by ארני (44^{18}, Ex. $4^{10.13}$, Nu. 12^{11}, Jos. 7^{8}, Ju. $6^{13.15}$ 13^{8}, 1 Sa. 1^{26}, 1 Ki. $3^{17.26}$ †). It is commonly derived from √ בעה, 'ask,' or (BDB) Ar. *bayya*, 'entreat': might it not rather be regarded as a shortening of אָבִי (2 Ki. 5^{13}, Jb. 34^{36}) from √ אבה, 'be willing'?—**23.** אביכם] 𝔐𝔊 אבתיכם.

believe that it was a supernatural occurrence, but of auspicious omen, and not, as they had imagined, a calamity.—The notice of Simeon's release is here inserted as the most convenient place, from E.—**24**. Cf. 24^{32}.—**25**. *they had heard, etc.*] In conversation with the steward (cf. v.[16]).

26–34. At Joseph's table.—**27, 28**. Joseph's courteous inquiries as to their welfare and that of their father are a studied prelude to— **29–31**, his profound emotion at the sight of Benjamin,—*his* (full) *brother, the son of his mother.* The disparity in age must have been great (בְּנִי): one wonders whether the narrative does not presuppose that Benjamin had been born since Joseph had been lost.—**30, 31**. For the second time (42^{24}) Joseph's affection finds relief in tears, and again he restrains himself, that he may carry out his plan.—The interlude reveals, as Gu. remarks, a power of psychological observation which is absent from the oldest legends.—**32–34**. The feast brings two more surprises: the arrangement of the brothers in the order of seniority (see on 42^{24}); and the special favour shown to Benjamin.—**32** affords an interesting glimpse of Egyptian manners. Joseph's isolation at table was perhaps due to his having been admitted a member of the priestly caste (41^{45}), which kept itself apart from the laity (Kn-Di.). The Egyptian exclusiveness in intercourse with foreigners, which would have been perfectly intelligible to the later Jews, evidently struck the ancient Israelites as peculiar (Gu.). Cf. Her. ii. 41.—**34**. The custom of honouring a guest by

---

24. האיש—ויתן] 𝔊 om.—**25**. יאכלו] 𝔊 more easily יאכל (of Joseph).

26. ויביאו] On Dagh. or Mappiq in א, see G-K. § 14 *d*.—ארצה] 𝔊 pr. אפים.—**27**. השלום] noun? or adj.? See G-K. § 141 c^4.—**28**. After Athnach 𝔐𝔊 ins. ויאמר ברוך האיש ההוא לאלהים,—a parallel to the benediction on Benj. ([29]): clumsy in expression and hardly original.—**29**. אמרתם] 𝔊 + להביא,—an interesting and perhaps correct addition.—יָחנך] for יָחְנְךָ (as Is. 30^{19}); see G-K. § 67 *n*.—**30**. וימהר ויבקש] 'hastily sought,' though an intermediate clause between the complementary vbs. is very unusual.—אל] 𝔐 על.—**32**. למצרַים] Better לְמִצְרִים: so Vns. Ba.—𝔊 adds *πᾶς ποιμὴν προβάτων*, in mistaken accommodation to 46^{34}.—**34**. וישא] 𝔊𝔖 וישאו.—ידות]='shares' or 'times,' 47^{24}, 2 Ki. 11^7, 2 Sa. 19^{44}, Neh. 11^1, Dn. 1^{20} †.—וישכרו] hardly 'got drunk': שכר of convivial drinking, Hag. 1^6, Ca. 5^1.

portions from the table is illustrated by 2 Sa. 11[8]; cf. Hom. *Il.* vii. 321 f., *Od.* iv. 65 f., xiv. 437.—*five times*].

It is hardly accidental that the number five occurs so often in reference to matters Egyptian (41[34] 45[22] 47[2. 24], Is. 19[18]). Whether there be an allusion to the five planets recognised by the Egyptians (Kn.), or to their ten days' week (Di.), it is impossible to say. Jeremias (*ATLO*[2], 385) connects it with the five intercalary days by which the Egyptian calendar adjusted the difference between the conventionalised lunar year (12 months of 30 days) and the solar year (365 days),—these belonging to Benjamin as the representative of the 12th month! The explanation is too ingenious, and overlooks the occurrence of the numeral where Benjamin is not concerned.

XLIV. 1–17. The cup in Benjamin's sack.—1, 2. This final test of the brethren's disposition is evidently arranged between Joseph and the steward on the evening of the banquet, to be carried out at daybreak (v.[3]).—**1b.** *each man's money, etc.*] Though this seems a useless repetition of 42[25], with no consequences in the sequel, the clause ought scarcely to be omitted (with Gu.) before [2a].—**2.** *the silver cup*] Joseph's ordinary drinking-vessel, but at the same time an implement of divination (v.[5]): therefore his most precious possession. —**3–5.** The trap is skilfully laid: just when they have emerged from the city, and think all danger is left behind, exulting in the fresh morning air, and still unwearied by travel, they are arrested by the steward's challenge, and finally plunged in despair.—**4.** *Why have ye . . . good?*] 𝕲 adds, 'Why have ye stolen my silver cup?' The addition seems necessary in view of the following זֶה.—**5.** *and, moreover, he divines with* (or *in*) *it*] See on v.[15].

On the widely prevalent species of divination referred to (κυλικομαντεία, λεκανομαντεία), cf. August. *De civit. Dei*, vii. 35; Strabo, XVI. ii. 39; Iamblichus, *De myst.* iii. 14. Various methods seem to have been

---

1. 𝕲 ins. Ἰωσήφ as subj.—יוכלון שאת] Ba. plausibly, יוכלו לשאת.—2. גָּבִיעַ] Used of the golden cups of the candlestick (Ex. 25[31ff.] 37[17ff.]); elsewhere only Jer. 35[5], along with the ordinary word for 'cup' (כּוֹס), of the 'bowls' of wine set before the Rechabites.—3, 4. On the synt. of these vv. see G-K. §§ 142 *e*, 156 *f*; Dav. §§ 141, 41, *R.* 3. The addition in 𝕲 runs: *ἵνα τί ἐκλέψατέ μου τὸ κόνδυ τὸ ἀργυροῦν;*.—5. נִחֵשׁ] The derivation of this vb. from נָחָשׁ, 'serpent,' first suggested by Boch. (*Hieroz.* i. 3), is supported by (amongst others) Nö. (*ZVP*, i. 413) and Baudissin (*Stud.* i. 287); on the other hand, see We. *Skizzen*, iii. 147; and Rob. Sm. *JPh*.

employed; *e.g.*, amongst the Babylonians oil was poured into a vessel of water, and from its movements omens were deduced according to a set of fixed rules of interpretation: see Hunger, *Becherwahrsagung bei den Babyloniern nach zwei Keilschriften aus der Hammurabi-zeit* (*Leipziger Semit. Stud.*, 1903, i. 1–80).—An interesting modern parallel is quoted by Dri. (358^1), and Hunger (4), from the Travels of Norden (*c.* 1750), where a Nubian sheikh says: '*I have consulted my cup*, and I find that you are Franks in disguise, who have come to spy out the land.'

6–9. The brethren appeal to their honesty in the matter of the money returned in their sacks, and propose the severest punishment—death to the thief, slavery for the rest—should the missing article be found with them.—**10.** The servant holds them to their pledge, but offers easier terms: the thief alone shall be Joseph's slave.—**11–13.** To the dismay of the brethren the cup is found in Benjamin's sack.—**12.** *beginning . . . youngest*] A calculated strain on the brethren's suspense, and (on the part of the narrator) an enhancement of the reader's interest: cf. 1 Sa. $16^{6ff.}$.—**13.** Their submissiveness shows that no suspicion of a trick crossed their minds; their sense of an adverse fate was quickened by the still unsolved mystery of the money in the sacks, to which they had so proudly appealed in proof of their innocence.—**14–17.** The brethren before Joseph.—**14.** *he was still there*] had not gone out to his place of business (see $43^{15.17}$), but was waiting for them.—**15.** *that a man in my position* (one of the wise men of Egypt) *can divine.*

It is difficult to say how much is implied in this claim of superhuman knowledge on Joseph's part. No doubt it links itself on the one hand to the feeling in the brethren's mind that a divine power was working against them, and on the other to the proofs they had had of the governor's marvellous insight. But whether Joseph is conceived as really practising divination, or only as wishing his brothers to think so, does not appear. Not improbably, as Gu. surmises, the motive comes from an older story, in which the prototype of Joseph actually achieved his ends by means of occult knowledge.

16. *God has found out, etc.*] The exclamation does not

---

xiv. 115.—8. כסף [1] 𝔐 הכסף.—9. אתו] 𝕮 + τὸ κόνδυ.—ומת] 𝔐 יומת, equally good.—12. החל . . . כלה] Infs. abs. (חָחֵל . . . כַּלֵּה) would be more idiomatic than the pf. (so Ball).—16. We. (*Comp.*[2] 60) would omit יהודה and read ויאמרו; but the text is safeguarded by v.[14], and the change is uncalled for. Judah speaks here in the name of all, in [18ff.] for himself.

necessarily imply consciousness of particular guilt (see on 43⁹), and is certainly not meant as a confession of the wrong done to Joseph: at the same time we may be sure that that is the crime to which their secret thoughts gravitate (42[21ff.]).—**17.** Judah's proposal that *all* should remain as slaves is rejected by Joseph, who insists on separating Benjamin's fate from that of the rest. Did he purpose to retain him by his side, while sustaining the rest of the family in their homes?

18–34. Judah's plea for Benjamin.—The speech, which is the finest specimen of dignified and persuasive eloquence in the OT, is perhaps modelled on the style of forensic oratory to which the Hebrews were accustomed in public assemblies at the city gates (ct. the stilted oration of Tertullus in Ac. 24). Sincerity and depth of feeling are not more remarkable than the skilful selection and disposition of the points most likely to appeal to the governor: (1) a recital of the interview in which Joseph had insisted on Benjamin being brought down ([19–23]); (2) a pathetic description of the father's reluctance to part with him, overcome only by the harsh necessity of hunger ([24–29]); (3) a suggestion of the death-stroke which their return without Benjamin would inflict on their aged parent ([30. 31]); and, lastly, (4) the speaker's personal request to be allowed to redeem his honour by taking Benjamin's punishment on himself ([32–34]).—The Massoretes commence a new Parashah with v.[18], rightly perceiving that Judah's speech is the turning-point in the relations between Joseph and his brethren.—**19–23.** On the divergent representations of J and E, see on p. 473 above.—**20.** *to his mother*] See p. 449.—**28.** The words of Jacob enable Judah to draw a veil over the brothers' share in the tragedy of Joseph.—*and I have not seen him till now*] Comp. the rugged pathos of Lowell's

> "Whose comin' home there's them that wan't—
> No, not life-long—leave off awaitin'."

The simple words, with their burden of suppressed emotion,

---

18. כמוך כפ'] G–K. § 161 *c*.—**20.** לאמו] 𝔊 לאביו.—**24.** אבי] 𝔐𝔊𝔙𝔖 אבינו (so 𝔊𝔖 in [27], and 𝔊𝔖𝔙 in [30]).—**28.** ואמר] 𝔊 *καὶ εἴπατε*.

have a meaning for the governor of which the speaker is all unconscious.—**29.** *in trouble to She'ōl*] Cf. 42^{38} 37^{35} 44^{31}.—**30.** *his soul* (not 'life') *is bound up, etc.*] a figure for inalienable affection; as 1 Sa. 18^{1}.

Ch. XLV.—*Joseph reveals himself to his Brethren* (E, J).

The crisis so slowly matured and so skilfully led up to is at last reached, and in a scene of inimitable power and tenderness Joseph makes himself known to his brethren ($^{1-8}$). In a message to his father he discloses his plans for the future, inviting the whole family to settle in Egypt while the famine lasted ($^{9-15}$). The invitation is confirmed by the king ($^{16-20}$); and the brethren depart laden with rich gifts and provision for the journey ($^{21-24}$). Jacob, after a momentary incredulity, is cheered by the prospect of seeing Joseph before his death ($^{25-28}$).

The *sources*, E and J, are here so intimately blended that a complete analysis is impossible. The main fact is the preponderance of E, which appears both from language (אלהים, $^{5.\,7.\,8.\,9}$; יעקב, ^{25}; חרה בעיני, ^{5} [31^{35}]; צדה, ^{21} [42^{25}]; בר, ^{23}; perhaps also מזון, ^{23}; and טענו את־בעירכם, ^{17} [ct. J's ויעמס על־חמרו, 44^{13}]), and representation: ct. v.^{3} with $43^{27f.}$, $^{17-20}$ with 46^{31}–47^{5} (J), where Joseph's kindred are apparently brought under Pharaoh's notice for the first time. Indubitable traces of J are found in $^{4b.\,5a}$ (the *selling* of Joseph), ^{10} (Goshen,—see the notes), ^{28} (ישראל); these are supported by the expressions, התאפק, ^{1a} (as 43^{31}); נעצב, ^{5a}; הוריד, ^{13}; נפל על־צוארי, ^{14}. Thus far in the main We. and Di. More subtle and less reliable criteria are applied by Gu. (402 f., 406), and (with very different results) by Pro. (52 f.). It is probable that ^{3} (E) is ‖ ^{4} (J), and (agt. Pro.) ^{9} (E) ‖ ^{13} (J). But it is very doubtful if the dismissal of the attendants (^{1}) be inconsistent with the overhearing of the weeping (^{2}), or if the latter be necessarily connected with the Pharaoh's invitation ($^{16ff.}$).—Some minor questions, such as the 'waggons' of $^{19.\,21.\,27}$ (cf. 46^{5}), and the authorship of vv.$^{19-21}$, must be reserved for the notes.

1–8. The disclosure.—1, 2. Joseph's self-restraint gives way before Judah's irresistible appeal.—It is pressing matters too far to say that the dismissal of the attendants is a device

---

31. הנער] ɯɯ𝔊𝔙𝔖 + אִתָּנוּ (as v.^{30}).—**32.** אבי] ɯɯ אביו, 𝔖 אבינו.—**34.** אתי] 𝔊 אִתָּנוּ.

1. התודע] Nu. 12^{6}† (E?).—**2.** מצרים] 𝔊 כל־המצרים. The pointing מִצְרַיִם *without* art. (Gu.) is no improvement.—וישמע] 𝔊𝔖 וַיִּשָּׁמַע, as in v.^{16}; so

to keep his relation to the strangers a secret from Pharaoh (see on the sources above).—**3.** *is my father yet alive?*] The question is slightly less natural in the context of J (see $43^{26f.}$ $44^{24ff.}$) than in E, where the absence of any mention of Jacob since the first visit (42^{13}) might leave room for uncertainty in Joseph's mind. But since he does not wait for an answer, the doubt can hardly be real.—*were troubled before him*] Comp. 50^{15-21} (also E).—**4.** J's parallel to v.[3],—probably the immediate continuation of v.[1] (cf. 44^{18}).—**5–8.** With singular generosity Joseph reassures them by pointing out the providential purpose which had overruled their crime for good; cf. 50^{20}. The profoundly religious conviction which recognises the hand of God, not merely in miraculous interventions, but in the working out of divine ends through human agency and what we call secondary causes, is characteristic of the Joseph-narrative amongst the legends of Genesis: see Gu. 404 (cf. ch. 24).—**7.** שְׁאֵרִית] 'remnant,' perhaps in the sense of 'descendants' (2 Sa. 14^7, Jer. 44^7). But the use of פְּלֵיטָה (strictly '*escaped* remnant,' cf. 32^9) is difficult, seeing the whole family was saved (*v.i.*).—**8.** *a father to Pharaoh*] Probably an honorific title of the chief minister (cf. 1 Mac. 11^{32}, Add. Est. 3^{13} 8^{12}); see, further, *inf.*

9–15. Joseph's message to his father.—That both J and E recorded the invitation may be regarded as certain, apart from nice questions of literary analysis: Eerdmans' suggestion that, in J, Jacob conceived the project of going down to Egypt "auf eigene Faust" (*Komp.* 65, 70) being

---

Ho. Gu. The cl., however, is best regarded as a doublet of the preceding, in which case MT is preferable.—3. יוסף [2]] 𝔊 + ὁ ἀδελφὸς ὑμῶν, ὃν ἀπέδοσθε εἰς Αἴγυπτον (as v.[4]).—מפניו] 𝔊 om.—4a. $𝔊^A$ om. entirely.—5. ואל־יחר בעיניכם] (cf. 31^{35}) is E's variant to אל־תעצבו (6^6 34^7 J).—מִחְיָה] In Ju. 6^4 17^{10} the word signifies 'means of subsistence'; in 2 Ch. 14^{12} perhaps 'preservation of life'; and so here if the pointing be right. Ba. plausibly emends מְחַיֶּה, 'preserver of life' (1 Sa. 2^6).—6. חריש וקציר] Ex. 34^{21} (J ?).—7. החיות לפליטה] The want of an obj. after הח' is harsh (cf. 47^{25} 50^{20}). The omission of the ל (𝔐𝔊𝔖 Ols. Ba. al.) improves the grammar, but the sense remains unsatisfying (*v.s.*).—8. אב . . . אדון] That the words are used in their Heb. sense ('father' . . . 'lord') is not to be questioned; in spite of the fact that Brugsch has compared two Egyptian titles, identical in form but altogether different in meaning (see Dri. *DB*, ii. 774; Str. p. 157 f.).

contrary to every natural view of the situation. We may therefore be prepared to find traces of the dual narrative in these vv.—**10.** On *the land of Goshen*, see the footnote.—*be near to me*] The clause is not inconsistent with the preceding; for, as compared with Canaan, Goshen was certainly 'near' to where Joseph dwelt. Nevertheless it is best regarded as a variant from E, continued in ^{11a}. It is only in J that the Israelites are represented as dwelling in Goshen.—**12–15.** The close of Joseph's speech, followed by his affectionate embrace, and the free converse of the brethren.—**13** and **14** (J) are respectively parallel to ^{9} and ^{15} (E).

16–20. Pharaoh's invitation.—This, as already explained, is peculiar to E. It is just possible (though hardly probable) that in this source Joseph's invitation ($^{9-11}$) extended only to his father, while the idea of transplanting the whole family emanated from the king.—**16a.** Cf. v.^{2}.—**18.** *the best*

---

10. גשן] 𝔊 Γέσεμ Ἀραβίας (as 46^{34}). The name is peculiar to J ($46^{28.\,29.\,34}$ $47^{1.\,4.\,6.\,27}$ 50^{8}, Ex. 8^{18} 9^{26}†); P has 'land of Ramses' (47^{11}, cf. Ex. 1^{11} 12^{37}, Nu. 33^{5}); while E uses no geographical designation. That P and J mean the same locality is intrinsically probable (though Naville considers that the land of Ramses was a larger area than Goshen), and is confirmed by recent excavations. The city of Pithom (see on 46^{28}) has been identified by Naville with the modern *Tell el-Maskhuṭa*, 12 m. W of Ismailia, in Wādī Ṭumīlāt, a long and narrow valley leading "straight from the heart of the Delta to a break in the chain of the Bitter Lakes," and therefore marking a weak spot in the natural defences of Egypt (Erman, *LAE*, 525 f.). In the same region, though not quite so far E, excavations at the village of *Ṣafṭ el-Ḥenneh* have established its identity with *Pa-soft* (also called on local inscrs. *Kes*), which is stated to have been the capital of the 20th Nome of Lower Egypt. A rare name of this nome is *Kesem*; and it is at least a plausible conjecture that this is the same as the biblical גֹּשֶׁן (Γέσεμ); and if so the situation of Goshen is fixed as a part of W. Ṭumīlāt surrounding Saft el-Ḥenneh. A confirmation of this may be found in the Ἀραβία of 𝔊, for this in Græco-Roman times (Ptol. iv. 5, 53) was the name of one of the 23 nomes of the Delta, whose capital Φακοῦσσα (cf. Strabo, XVII. i. 26) has long been conjectured to be the ancient *Kes*, preceded by the art. *pa*.—See Naville, *Land of Goshen*, etc. (Fifth Memoir of EEF, 1887), 15 ff., 20; *Store City of Pithom*, etc. (^{4}1903), 4 ff.; Spiegelberg, *Aufenth.* etc. 52; Müller in *EB*, 1758 ff.; and Griffith in *BD*, ii. 232 f.—**11.** כלכל] cf. 50^{21} (E).—פן־תורש] 'lest thou come to want' (lit. 'be dispossessed'); cf. Ju. 14^{15}, Pr. 20^{13} 23^{21} 30^{9}.

17. טען] ἅπ. λεγ. (Aram.); ct. עמס, 44^{13} (J).—בעיר] Ex. 22^{4}, Nu. $20^{4.\,8.\,11}$ (E), Ps. 78^{48}†.—**18.** טוב] = 'best things,' as vv.$^{20.\,23}$ 24^{10}, 2 Ki. 8^{9}; 𝔊

of the land (*v.i.*) . . . *the fat of the land*] The expressions are not altogether inapplicable to Goshen (W. Ṭumīlāt), which was rendered fertile by a canal, and is still spoken of as the best pasture-land in Egypt (Robinson, *BR*, i. 53 f.). But since E never mentions a separate location in Goshen, there is no need to force that sense upon them; the meaning is general: the best of everything that Egypt can afford (*v.i.*). —**19.** The opening words (*v.i.*) throw some doubt on the originality of the v.; and there certainly seems no more reason for ascribing it to J (Gu.) than to E.—The *baggage-waggon* (עֲגָלָה) is said to have been introduced into Egypt from Canaan, with its Semitic name (Eg. *ʿagolt*): Erman, *LAE*, 491.*—**20.** *Let not your eye pity*] The phrase is Deuteronomic, and seems a very strong one for concern about household implements. According to J ($^{10b.\,11b}$ $46^{1.\,32}$) they brought 'all they possessed,' which, if they were half-nomads, would be possible without waggons.

21–28. The brethren return to Canaan.—**22.** Presents of expensive clothes are a common mark of courtesy in the East: cf. Ju. $14^{12f.\,19}$, 2 Ki. $5^{5.\,22f.}$.—*changes of raiment*] such as were substituted for ordinary clothing on festal occasions (see on 27^{15}).—Benjamin receives *five* such suits: see on 43^{34}.—**23.** *of the best* (produce) *of Egypt*] A munificent return

---

πάντων τῶν ἀγαθῶν.—For 'the best *part*,' P uses מֵיטַב ($47^{6.\,11}$).—**19.** ואתה צֻוֵּיתָה] The pass. is awkward in itself, and has no syntactic connexion with the following זאת עשו (hence 𝕾 inserts ܐܡܪ ܠܗܘܢ). Di. Kit. emend ואתה צַוֵּה אֹתָם; Ba. ואתה צוה אתדזאת (after 𝕲 Σὺ δὲ ἔντειλαι ταῦτα; cf. 𝔙); Gu. וְאַתָּה צִוֵּיתִי: the first is best. But it is still difficult to understand the extreme emphasis laid on this point; and a suspicion remains that either the whole v. (Di.), or the introduction, is due to a scribe who wished to make it clear that the waggons were not sent without Pharaoh's express authority: see on v.[21].

21. ויעשו—ישראל] The statement is premature, and furnishes an additional indication that this part of the narrative has been worked over. The repeated ויתן also suggests a doublet or interpolation. In $^{19-21}$, Di. leaves to E only ויתן להם י׳ עגלות ויתן להם צדה לדרך; KS. only the second of these clauses, the rest being redactional.—צדה לדרך] as 42^{25} (E).—**23.** כְּזֹאת] (so pointed only here): 'in like manner' (Ju. 8^8).—מזון] (2 Ch. 11^{23} †) from an Aram. √ זון = 'feed.'—Of the three nouns, בר, לחם, and מזון, 𝕲

---

* Cf. Heyes, *Bib. u. Aeg.* i. 251.

for Jacob's modest complimentary present (43^{11}).—*corn and bread and sustenance for the journey*] cf. v.[20].—**24.** *Do not get excited by the way*] *sc.*, with mutual recriminations,—a caution suggested by 42^{22}.—**25–28.** Jacob's reception of the tidings.—**26.** *his heart became cold*, or *numb*] unable to take in the startling intelligence, as too good to be true.—**27.** But gradually, as they rehearse *the words of Joseph*, and show him the *waggons* as a pledge of his power, *his spirit revived*] he recovered his wonted energy of thought and action.—**28.** From J.—*It is enough*] The father's heart is indifferent to Joseph's grandeur ($^{9.\,11}$) and princely gifts; the fact that his son lives is sufficient consolation for all he has endured (cf. 46^{30}). The psychology of old age could not be more sympathetically or convincingly treated.

XLVI. 1–XLVII. 12.—*The Settlement of Jacob and his Family in Egypt* (J, E, P).

Jacob, encouraged by a night vision at Beersheba, takes his departure for Egypt ($^{1-7}$): (here is inserted a list of the persons who were supposed to accompany him, $^{8-27}$). He sends Judah to announce his arrival to Joseph, who proceeds to Goshen and tenderly welcomes his father ($^{28-30}$). Having instructed his brethren in the part he wishes them to play ($^{31-34}$), Joseph presents five of them before Pharaoh, and obtains permission for them to settle for a time in Goshen (47^{1-6}). Jacob's interview with Pharaoh closes the account of the migration ($^{7-12}$).

Sources.—The narrative of JE is several times interrupted by excerpts from P, whose peculiar style and viewpoint can be recognised in 46^{6-27} $47^{5.\,6a.\,7-11}$ (but see the notes below, p. 439 ff.).—Disregarding these vv.,

---

expresses only לחם. 𝕾 has ܚܡܪܐ, 'wine,' for לחם, but perhaps through dittog. of ܚܡܪ̈ܐ, 'asses.'—**24.** אל תרגזו] 𝕲 *μὴ ὀργίζεσθε*, 𝖁 *Ne irascamini*, 𝕾 ܠܐ ܬܬܚܪܘܢ, 𝕿º לא תתנצון ('quarrel'). But the Heb. verb denotes simply agitation, by whatever emotion produced.—**26.** פוג] In Arab. and Syr. the √ means to be or grow 'cold,' in Syr., also, and NH, fig. 'grow inactive,' 'fail,' 'vanish'; in OT the prevailing idea seems to be that of numbness (BDB); cf. Hab. 1^4 (of *tôrâh*), Ps. 38^9.—**28.** רב] As an exclamation = 'enough!'; cf. Ex. 9^{28}, Nu. $16^{3.\,7}$, Dt. 1^6 2^3 etc.

we have a continuous J narrative from 46^{28}–47^{6} : note ישראל, $^{29.30}$; *Goshen*, $^{28.29.34.1.4.6b}$; the leadership of Judah, ^{28} ; the ignoring of Pharaoh's invitation ($45^{17ff.}$ E) ; נפל על צוארי, ^{29} ; הפעם, ^{30} ; מנעורינו, בעבור, ^{34}.—46^{1-5} is in the main from E, as appears from the night vision, the form of address, ^{2} ; Jacob's implied hesitation, ^{3} (ct. 45^{28}) ; the name *Jacob*, $^{2.5a}$; אלהים, ^{2} ; אֵל, ^{3}.—^{1a} (ישראל) and *possibly* ^{5b} belong to J.—47^{12} is doubtful,—probably E (כלכל, as 45^{11}).—See We. *Comp.*² 60 f.; Di. Ho. Gu. Pro. 54 f. (who assigns 47^{7} to E instead of P and 47^{12} to J).

1–7. Jacob bids farewell to Canaan.—**1.** *came to Be'ersheba'*] There is in E no clear indication of where Jacob lived after his return from Laban (see on 35^{1}). If at Beersheba, the above clause is redactional, written on the assumption that he started from Hebron (37^{14} J). The point would be determined if ^{5b} were the original continuation of ^{5a}, for it is absurd to suppose that the waggons were first put to use in the middle of the journey (We.). But even apart from that, the natural view undoubtedly is that Jacob would not start until his misgivings were removed in answer to his sacrifice, and that consequently his dwelling-place at this time was Beersheba. That he sacrificed at the last patriarchal sanctuary on the way is a much less plausible explanation.—*the God of . . . Isaac*] Isaac is apparently regarded as the founder of the sanctuary, as in ch. 26 (J^{h}) ; an Elohistic parallel to that tradition may have existed, though in 21^{31} (E with J^{b}) its consecration is attributed to Abraham.—**2–4.** The last of the patriarchal theophanies. Comp. $12^{1ff.}$, where the theophany sanctions the occupation of Canaan, as this sanctions the leaving of it (Di.) ; and 26^{2}, where, under circumstances similar to Jacob's, Isaac is forbidden to go down to Egypt.—**3.** *the God of thy father*] As elsewhere in Genesis, אֵל denotes the local *numen*, who here distinguishes himself from other divine beings,—a trace of the primitive polytheistic representation (cf. 31^{13} 35^{1} 33^{20} 21^{33} 16^{13}).—*Fear not, etc.*] The purpose of the revelation is to

---

1. באר שבע] 𝕲 here and v.⁵ τὸ φρέαρ τοῦ ὅρκου (see p. 326).—**2.** לישראל] The word has crept in from v.¹ through an inadvertence of the redactor or a later scribe: "'God said to Israel, Jacob! Jacob!' is a sentence which no original writer would have penned" (We.).—On the form of the v., see on 22^{11}.—**3.** מֵרְדָה] From רְדָה, the rare form of inf. const. of פ״י

remove the misgiving natural to an old man called to leave his hearth and his altar. The thought is confined to E (ct. 45^{28} J).—*for . . . nation*] The words, if genuine, should follow the immediate grounds of comfort in v.^{4}. They are probably to be regarded (with KS. Gu. al.) as an expansion of the same character as $13^{14ff.}$ $22^{15ff.}$ 28^{14} etc.—4. *I will go down with thee*] So in 31^{13} the *'Ēl* of Bethel is with Jacob in Mesopotamia.—*bring thee up*] The reference must be to the Exodus (Ex. 3^{8} 6^{8} etc.), not to Jacob's burial in Canaan ($47^{29f.}$ $50^{5ff.}$).—*lay his hand upon thine eyes*] *i.e.*, close them after death; for classical parallels, cf. Hom. *Il.* xi. 453, *Od.* xi. 426, xxiv. 296; Eurip. *Phœn.* 1451 f., *Hec.* 430; Virg. *Æn.* ix. 487, etc. (Kn–Di.).—6, 7. P's summary of the migration (*v.i.*).

8–27. A list of Jacob's immediate descendants.—The passage professes to give the names of those who went down with Jacob to Egypt, but is in reality a list of the leading clans of the Israelite tribes, closely corresponding to Nu. $26^{5ff.}$. These traditionally numbered *seventy* (cf. the 70 elders, Ex. $24^{1.9}$, Nu. 11^{16}). Closely connected with this was another tradition, that the number of the Israelites at the settlement in Egypt was 70 (Dt. 10^{22}). In the more careful statement of Ex. 1^{5} (P), this means all the *descendants* of Jacob at the time: *i.e.*, it includes Joseph (and presumably his sons, though they were in Egypt already) and, of course, excludes Jacob himself. In the mind of the writer of the present passage these two traditional schemes appear to have got mixed up and confused. As it stands, it is neither an accurate enumeration of Jacob's descendants (for the number 70 includes Jacob and excludes Er and Onan), nor a list of those who accompanied him to Egypt (for it embraces Joseph and his sons: see on $^{26f.}$). When cleared of certain obvious accretions (יעקב ובניו ^{8}; $^{12b\alpha}$; $^{15a\gamma}$; ובנתיו ^{15b}; ששים ושש ^{26} and the whole of ^{27} except the last word שבעים), we find as its nucleus

---

verbs, peculiar to E: see G–K. § 69 m^{2}; Ho. *Hex.* 190.—4. גם עלה] See on 27^{33} 31^{15}. 𝕲 εἰς τέλος.—5. יעקב ^{2}] 𝕲 om.—פרעה] 𝕲 Ἰωσηφ.—6, 7. Cf. 12^{5} 31^{18} 36^{6} (P). Further marks of P: רכש, רכוש, וזרעו אתו ($17^{7.9f.}$ 35^{12}), and the redundant phraseology.

a list of Jacob's sons and grandsons, originally compiled without reference to the migration to Egypt, on the basis of some such census-list as Nu. $26^{5ff.}$

That the section belongs in general to the Priestly strata of the Pent. is seen from its incompatibility with the narrative (and particularly the chronology) of JE; from its correspondence with Nu. $26^{5ff.}$, Ex. $6^{14ff.}$; and from literary indications (ואלה שמות, ^{8} [cf. 25^{13} 36^{10}]; פדן ארם, ^{15}; נפש, $^{15. 18. 22. 25-27}$; יצאי ירך, ^{26}). As regards its relation to the main document of P, three views are possible: (1) That the list was originally drawn up by P, and afterwards accommodated to the tradition of JE by a later editor (Nö. Di. al.). This implies the perfectly tenable assumption that P did not accept the tradition as to the death of Er and Onan, or that of Benjamin's extreme youth at the time of the migration; but also the less probable view that he numbered the sons of Joseph amongst those who 'went down' to Egypt. (2) That the interpolations are due to P, who thus turned an older list of Jacob's children into an enumeration of those who accompanied him to Egypt (Dri.). The only serious objection to this theory is that it makes P (in opposition to Ex. 1^{5}) reckon Jacob as one of the 70. It is nevertheless the most acceptable solution. (3) That the whole section was inserted by a late editor of the school of P (We. Kue. Gu. al.). Even on this hypothesis, the original list will have had nothing to do with the migration to Egypt.—The discrepancy in the computation lies in the first section ($^{8-15}$). The 33 of v.^{15} was in the original list the true number of the *sons* of Leah. The interpolator, whoever he was, had to exclude Er and Onan; to make up for this he inserts Dinah (^{15a}), and reckons Jacob amongst the sons of Leah! Another sign of artificial manipulation of the figures appears in the proportions between the number of *children* assigned to each wife: Leah 32, Zilpah 16, Rachel 14, Bilhah 7 (in all 69); each concubine-wife receiving just half as many children as her mistress. The text of 𝔊 presents some important variations (*v.i.*).

8a. The heading is identical with Ex. 1^{1a}, except the words יעקב ובניו, which are obviously interpolated (see introductory note).—**8b–15.** The sons of Leah: viz. *four* sons of Reuben (v.^{9}), *six* of Simeon (^{10}), *three* of Levi (^{11}), *five* sons and *two* grandsons of Judah (^{12}), *four* sons of Issachar (^{13}), and *three* of Zebulun (^{14}).—**15.** *thirty-three* is thus the correct number of sons, grandsons, and great-grandsons of Jacob by Leah. To preserve this number intact with the omission of Er and Onan, the interpolator was obliged to add Dinah, and to include Jacob himself (see below).

9. Exactly as Ex. 6^{14}, Nu. $26^{5f.}$.—חנוך is also a Midianite tribe (25^{4}); the Reubenites occupied Midianite territory (Jos. 13^{21}).—חצרון] and כרמי] also Judahite clans (see v.^{12} and Jos. 7^{1}).—**10.** (= Ex. 6^{15}). Nu. $26^{12ff.}$

omits אהד and reads נְמוּאֵל for ימואל, and זרח for צחר.—צחר] The name of Ephron's father in 23^{8}.—*the son of the Canaanitess*] representing a clan of notoriously impure stock.—**11.** (= Ex. 6^{16}).—**12.** As Nu. $26^{20f.}$.—The note on the death of Er and Onan is an interpolation (see above).—חצרון] (see on v.[9]) was a town in Judah (Jos. 15^{25}).—חמול] 𝔐 חמואל; 𝔊 'Ιεμουήλ.—**13.** (= Nu. $26^{23f.}$).—תולע] Cf. the judge of the same name, son of פואה, of the tribe of Issachar (Ju. 10^{1}).—פֻּוָּה] 𝔐𝔖 פואה, as 1 Ch. 7^{1}, Ju. 10^{1}.—יוב] 𝔐 and 𝔊 ('Ιασουβ[φ]) read ישוב as Nu. 26: Wi. connects with *Yašub-ilu* under the 1st Babylonian dynasty (*GI*, ii. 68^{3}).—**14.** (Nu. 26^{26}).—אלון a Zebulunite judge in Ju. 12^{11}.—**15.** ואת דינה בתו and ובנתיו are glosses.

16–18. **The sons of Zilpah (Leah's handmaid):** *seven* sons of Gad ([16]), *four* sons, *one* daughter, and *two* grandsons of Asher ([17]): *sixteen* in all ([18]).

16. (As Nu. $26^{15ff.}$, with textual differences).—צפיון] 𝔐𝔊 צפון, as Nu. 26^{15}.—אצבן] 𝔐 אצבעון, 𝔊 Θασοβαν, stands for אזני in Nu. 26^{16}.—**17.** ישוה, a variant of the following ישוי (?), does not appear in Nu. $26^{44f.}$.—The two grandsons חבר and מלכיאל have been connected with the *Ḫabiri* and the (chief) *Milkili* of the Amarna Tablets (Jast. *JBL*, xi. 120).

19–22. The sons of Rachel: *two* of Joseph ([20]) and *ten* of Benjamin ([21]), in all *fourteen*.

20. וַיִּוָּלֵד] 𝔊 + *υἱοί*. But the rel. cl. אשר—און was probably added by the glossator, in which case the בנים of 𝔊 is superfluous.—𝔊 adds, in partial agreement with Nu. $26^{29ff.}$, five names as sons and grandsons of Manasseh and Ephraim.—**21.** In 𝔊 only the first three names are sons of Benjamin, the next six being sons, and the last a grandson, of Bela'. Still another grouping is found in Nu. $26^{38\text{-}40}$.—בכר] (𝔊 Χόβωρ): cf. Sheba' *the Bichrite* in 2 Sa. 20^{1}: in Nu. 26 בכר is an Ephraimite.—גרא] omitted in Nu. 26, is the clan of Ehud (Ju. 3^{15}) and Shimei (2 Sa. 16^{5}).—For the two names אחי וראש, Nu. $26^{38f.}$ has אחירם, for מפים, שפופם or שופם, and for חפים, חוּפָם (see Gray, *HPN*, 35).—נעמן and ארד are sons of בלע in Nu. 26^{40} —**22.** ילד] MSS 𝔐𝔊 ילדה.

23–25. The sons of Bilhah (Rachel's maid): *one* of Dan ([23], in spite of בני), and *four* of Naphtali ([24]): *seven* in all.

23. בני] So Nu. 26^{42}, where for חושים we find שׁוּחָם.—**24.** (as Nu. $26^{48f.}$). —שלם] 𝔐 שלום (as 1 Ch. 7^{13}), 𝔊 Συλλήμ.

26, 27. The final summations.

The original computation (70 = 33 + 16 + 14 + 7) included Er and Onan, but excluded Dinah and Jacob. The secondary figure 66 (= 32 + 16 + 11 + 7) excludes Er and Onan, and Joseph and his two sons, but includes Dinah. To make up the original 70 it was necessary to reckon not only the family of Joseph (3), but Jacob himself.—𝔊, with its 5 additional descendants of Joseph (see on v.^{20}), makes the total 75 (so Ac. 7^{14}), but inadvertently substitutes ἐννέα, instead of ἑπτά, for the שנים of MT ^{27}, overlooking the fact that both Jacob and Joseph have to be reckoned in the 75.—**26.** יצאי ירכו] 35^{11}, Ex. 1^{5}.—**27.** ילד] ɯ ילדו.

28–30. The meeting of Jacob and Joseph.—28. ***to direct before him to Goshen***] The Heb. here gives no tolerable sense. The meaning cannot be that Judah was to guide the travellers to Goshen, for he is sent straight to Joseph; and for the idea that Joseph was to give the needful instructions for their reception in Goshen (Di.), the expression would be extremely harsh. The only natural purpose of Judah's mission was to bring Joseph to meet his father; and the least difficult course is to read (with Vns. *v.i.*): *to appear before him in Goshen*, which had already been indicated by Joseph as the goal of the journey (45^{10}).—**29.** *went up*] Goshen lying somewhat higher than the Nile-valley.—**30.** The v. prepares us for the death-bed scenes ($47^{29ff.}$), which in JE must have taken place soon after, not as in P at an interval of 17 years.

XLVI. 31–XLVII. 12.—Joseph obtains Pharaoh's permission for his brethren to settle in Goshen.—31–34 (J). He prepares his brethren for an introduction to Pharaoh, in the expectation that by laying stress on their herdsmen's calling they may have the desirable frontier dis-

---

28. להורות] ɯ𝔊? 𝔖 לְהֵרָאוֹת (We. לְהֵרֹ֫ת), which is confirmed by וַיֵּרָא in the next v. There is no need to take the לפניו in a temporal sense. The construction is pregnant, but otherwise unobjectionable; the tone of superiority assumed by Jacob towards Joseph is hardly a serious difficulty. Ba. thinks that the συναντῆσαι of 𝔊 implies a reading לְהִקָּרְאוֹת ('to meet'); but the Niph. of קרה would rather mean 'to come upon unexpectedly' (Dt. 22^{6}, 2 Sa. 18^{9}).—גשנה—גשן] 𝔊 καθ' Ἡρώων πόλιν εἰς γῆν Ῥαμεσσή. Heroöpolis has been shown by the excavations of Naville (*Store City of Pithom*, etc.^{4}, 5 ff.; cf. Gillett in *JSBL*, Dec. 1886, p. 69 ff.) to be Pithom (Ex. 1^{11}), now *Tell el-Maskhuṭa* (see p. 488 above). The Bohairic Vn. substitutes *Pethom* for the Ἡρώων of 𝔊. 𝔊 thus makes the meeting take place at the frontier town in the W. Ṭumīlāt towards the desert (so v.^{29}). The reading is noteworthy textually as containing P's name for Goshen.—ויבאו] ɯ𝔙𝔖 ויבא (better).—**29.** על־צואריו עוד] 𝔊 κλαυθμῷ πίονι (var. πλείονι).—The עוֹד is strange; but cf. Ps. 84^{5} (Ru. 1^{14} is not in point).—**30.** פניך] 𝔖 + בני.

31. ואל־בית אביו] 𝔊 om., perhaps rightly.

trict of Goshen assigned to them. It is evident that in J the migration was resolved on without the invitation, or perhaps the knowledge, of the king.—**32.** *for they were cattle-breeders*] a more comprehensive category than *shepherds*. Gu. thinks that the representation made to Pharaoh cannot have been strictly true, or Joseph would not have made such a point of it; * and we must at least suppose that he advises them to emphasise that side of their life which was most likely to gain the end in view. Unfortunately, while he bids them say they are cattle-breeders, they actually describe themselves as shepherds (47^{3}), and yet Pharaoh would make them cattle-overseers (47^{6b}). Some confusion of the two terms may be suspected, but as the text stands, nothing can be made of the distinction.—**34.** *that ye may dwell, etc.*] What motive in the mind of the king is appealed to is not quite clear. If the last clause—*for every shepherd, etc.*—be genuine, it was the Egyptian abhorrence of the class to which they belonged. But such a feeling would be more likely to exclude them from Egypt altogether than to procure their admission to the best pasture-land in the country, where Pharaoh's herds were kept (47^{6b}). Moreover, while there is evidence that swine-herds (Her. ii. 47) and cow-herds (Erman, *LAE*, 439 f.) were looked down on by the Egyptians, the statement that shepherds were held in special abhorrence has not been confirmed; and the clause ($^{34b\beta}$) is probably an interpolation suggested by 43^{32}. See, further, on $47^{3ff.}$.—**XLVII. 1–5a, 6b** (J). Pharaoh grants the request.—**1.** *and behold . . . Goshen*] It is evident that in this narrative Joseph relies on the *fait accompli* to procure a favourable response from Pharaoh. The idea that Pharaoh decided such matters in person may be naïve (Gu.); it is certainly a curious restriction of the absolute authority elsewhere assigned to Joseph.—**2.** *he had taken five, etc.*] On the

32. כי—היו] regarded as a gloss by Di. KS. Ho. Gu. al.—**34.** גשן] 𝔊 Γεσεμ Ἀραβίᾳ.—רעה] 𝔐 (𝔙𝔖𝔗^O) רעי.—**2.** מקצה]=' from the totality of,' as

* So Eerdmans (*Vorgeschichte Israels*, 42; *Exp.*, Aug. 1908, p. 124 f.), who draws the conclusion that, as the Israelites here represent themselves as nomads, they cannot have really been so!

significance of the number, see on 43^{34}.—3, 4. The anticipated question (46^{33}) is answered in accordance with Joseph's instructions, though the phraseology differs by the substitution of רֹעֵי צֹאן for אַנְשֵׁי מִקְנֶה.—It is possible that the repeated ויאמרו is due to the omission between [3] and [4] of a further question by Pharaoh as to the reasons for their coming to Egypt (so Ba. Gu.). The whole leads up to a straightforward request for a temporary domicile in Goshen; and the point may be simply that as herdsmen they had brought their means of subsistence with them, and needed nothing but grazing land, which must have been obtainable in spite of the famine. There is no hint of any aversion to the strangers or their manner of life.—6b. *Let them dwell, etc.*] is the continuation of [5a] in 𝔊 (*v.i.*), whose arrangement of these vv. is obviously more original than that of MT.—As an additional favour, Pharaoh offers to take any capable members of the family into his service as *cattle superintendents* (שָׂרֵי מִקְנֶה),—an office frequently mentioned in the monuments as one of high dignity (Erman, *LAE*, 94 f., 108, 143). The breeding of cattle was carried to great perfection in ancient Egypt (*ib.* 436 ff.).

The admission of pastoral tribes within the frontier of Egypt is an incident twice represented in Eg. inscrs. of the period here supposed. Under Ḥor-em-heb of the 18th dynasty, some barbarians have a definite district assigned to them by a high officer; and reference has already been made (p. 437) to the Edomite nomads who in the time of Merenptah were allowed to pass the fortifications and feed their flocks in "the great pasture-land of Pharaoh"—probably this very Wādī Ṭumīlāt where Goshen was (see *ATLO*[2], 393; Dri. 372).

5, 6a, 7–11. Jacob before Pharaoh (P).—5. The text of 𝔊 (*v.i.*) supplies the following opening to P's account (continuing 46^{7}): *And Jacob and his sons came to Egypt to Joseph; and Pharaoh king of Egypt heard it* ([5a]), *and Pharaoh said to Joseph, etc.*—It is plain that [6b] continues *this* conversation and not that between Pharaoh and the five brethren.—6a. Here Pharaoh himself selects *the best* [part] *of the land* for

---

1 Ki. 12^{31}, Ezk. 33^{2} (otherwise Gn. 19^{4}).—לקח] (plup.) 𝔐 + עִמּוֹ.—3. אחיו] 𝔐𝔊𝔖𝔗[J] אחי יוסף.—רעה] 𝔐 רעי (as 46^{34}).—5, 6. The overlapping of J and P at this point can be proved and corrected from 𝔊. After [5a] (omitting

the Hebrew family to dwell in (see v.[11]).—7. Joseph introduces his father to Pharaoh,—an impressive and dignified scene.—*blessed*], *i.e.* 'saluted' on entering (cf. 1 Sa. 13[10], 2 Ki. 4[29], 2 Sa. 13[25] 19[40]), but recorded, no doubt, with a sense that "the less is blessed of the better" (Heb. 7[7]).—9. *few and evil*] The expression shows that P must have recorded Jacob's long exile with Laban and his protracted sorrow for the loss of Joseph; it is still more interesting as showing that that writer could conceive a good man's life as spent in adversity and affliction.—**11**. *the land of Raʿmses*] The name only here and 𝔊 of 46[28] (see on 45[10]), so called from the city built by Ramses II. (Ex. 1[11]) and named after him 'the house of Ramses,' in the E of the Delta (Erman, *LAE*, 48). The situation is still uncertain; Naville (*Goshen*, 20) was inclined to identify it with Ṣafṭ el-Ḥenneh (see p. 488); but Petrie now claims to have discovered its site at *Tel er-Reṭabeh*, in the middle of W. Ṭumīlāt, 8 m. W of Pithom (*Hyksos and Israelite Cities*, 1906, p. 28 ff.)—**12**. Probably from E ‖ [27a] (J).

XLVII. 13-27.—*Joseph's Agrarian Policy* (J?).

Joseph is here represented as taking advantage of the great famine to revolutionize the system of land-tenure in

---

לאמר) 𝔊 reads [6b]; then ἦλθον δὲ εἰς Αἴγυπτον πρὸς Ἰωσὴφ Ἰακὼβ καὶ οἱ υἱοὶ αὐτοῦ· καὶ ἤκουσεν Φαραὼ βασιλεὺς Αἰγύπτου (=ויבאו מצרימה אל־יוסף יעקב ובניו וישמע פרעה מלך מצרים); then [5a] (repeated) [5b. 6a. 7ff.]. It will hardly be disputed that the text of 𝔊 is here the original, and that P's narrative commences with the additional sentences quoted above. The editor of MT felt the doublet to be too glaring; he therefore omitted these two sentences; and then by transposition worked the two accounts into a single scene. A further phase is represented by Hex. Syr., where [5b] and [6a] are omitted. We have here an instructive example of the complex process by which the sources were gradually worked into a smooth narrative, and one which deserves the attention of those writers who ridicule the minute and intricate operations which the critical theory finds it necessary to attribute to the redactors.—6b. ואם ידעת וְיֶשׁ־] See G-K. § 120 *e*. The הי״ש of 𝔐 is certainly not preferable (Ba.).—**11**. מיטב] v.[6], Ex. 22[4], 1 Sa. 15[9. 15]†. The identification of מ׳ הארץ with the 'land of Ramses' probably rests on a misunderstanding of E's טוב הא׳ (see on 45[18]), and a combination of it with J's גֹּשֶׁן.—**12**. הטף] apparently including here the women: cf. 50[21].

Egypt for the benefit of the crown. In one year the famishing people have exhausted their money and parted with their live-stock, in exchange for bread; in the next they forfeit their lands and their personal freedom. Thus by a bold stroke of statesmanship private property in land (except in the case of the priests) is abolished throughout Egypt, and the entire population reduced to the position of serfs, paying a land-tax of 20 per cent. *per annum* to the king.

Source.—The section $^{13-26}$, dealing as it does with matters purely Egyptian and without interest for the national history of Israel, occupies an anomalous position among the Joseph-narratives, and cannot be confidently assigned to either of the main documents (We. *Comp.*^{2} 61). Linguistic indications are on the whole in favour of J: כבר, ^{13}; נחיה ולא נמות, ^{19} (42^2 43^8); ירות, ^{24} (43^{34}); מקנה הצאן ומקנה הבקר, ^{17} (26^{14}); מצא חן בעיני, ^{25} (see Gu. and Di.). But there are also traces of E's diction: חוק, ^{20}; הבה, הבו, $^{15f.}$ (29^{21} 30^1,—differing from $11^{3.4.7}$) (Di. Ho.); besides some peculiar expressions very unusual in Pent.: להה, ^{13}; אפס, $^{15f.}$; שמם (Qal), ^{19}; הֵא, ^{23} (Di.). It is possible that Ho. (251 f.) and Pro. (54 f.) are right in thinking the passage composite; but no satisfactory analysis can be effected. That it is out of place in its present connexion is generally admitted, but that it finds a more suitable position between chs. 41 and 42 (Di. Gu. al.) is not at all obvious. It is not improbable that a piece of so peculiar a character is a later addition to the original cycle of Joseph-legends, and belongs neither to J nor E.—V.^{27} appears to be from P, with glosses (see the notes).

13, 14. Joseph takes up all the money in Egypt and Canaan. *Canaan* is bracketed with Egypt as far as v.^{15}, after which the situation is purely Egyptian. It is natural to suppose that the references to Canaan are interpolated (Ho. Gu.); but considering the close political relations of the two countries, it would be rash to assume this too easily.—**15–17.** The live-stock is next exhausted.—*horses*] See on 12^{16}.—**18–22.** The people surrender their lands and persons for bread. This is the decisive stroke of Joseph's statecraft, making a return to the old conditions impossible;

---

13. ותלה] 𝔐 ותלא. The √ להה is Aram. ἅπ. λεγ. = לאה, 'languish.' It is one of several rare expressions which occur in this section.—**14.** בשברים] 𝕲 + ויכלכלם (v.^{12}).—**15.** אָפֵס] The vb. only here (and v.^{16}) in Pent.: elsewhere poetic (Is. 16^4 29^{20}, Ps. 77^9†).—כסף] 𝔐 הכסף, 𝕲 כספנו (so v.^{16}).—**16.** לכם] 𝔐𝕲𝔙 + לֶחֶם.—**17.** נהל] Only here in the sense of 'sustain' [with food]; elsewhere, if the √ be the same, it means 'lead' (to watering.

and it is noteworthy that (as if to relieve Joseph of the odium) the proposal is represented as coming from the people themselves.—**18.** *that year . . . the second year*] Not the first and second years of the famine (for we can hardly suppose that the money and cattle were exhausted in a single year), but simply two successive years.—**19.** *buy us and our land*] The only basis of personal independence in a state like ancient Egypt being the possession of land, the peasants know that in parting with their land they sacrifice their freedom as well.—*give seed, etc.*] A temporary provision (see v.[24]) for the time of famine, or perhaps for the first sowing after it was over (Ho.). It is in any case most natural to suppose that these drastic changes took place towards the end of the 7 years.—**21.** *and the people he reduced to bondmen*] Read so with Vns., *v.i.* (Kn. Di. De. al.). The MT: 'he brought them over to the cities' appears to mean that he brought the rural population to the cities where the corn-magazines were (41[35. 48]); but the emphasis on the obj. leads us to expect a parallelism to the appropriation of the land in v.[20] (Di.). A universal redistribution of the inhabitants ($\mathfrak{T}^{O}$, Tu. al.) could not be expressed by the words, and would, moreover, be a senseless measure.—**22.** The priests' property was exempted, because they had a statutory provision of food, and did not need to sell their lands. So the writer explains a privilege which existed in his day (see p. 501 below). Comp. Erman, *LAE*, 129, where Ramses III. is said to have given 185,000 sacks of corn annually to the temples.—**23–26.** Institution of the land-tax.—**23.** *Here is seed for you*] The gift is not to be repeated; hence the incident naturally belongs to the end of the famine.—**24.** *a fifth part*] According to Oriental ideas,

---

place, goal, etc.): see p. 414.—**18.** כי אם] may be rendered equally well (with 𝔊) 'that, if' (protasis to לא נשאר), or with $\mathfrak{T}^{O}$ 'but' [*sondern*] (De. Ho.).—**19.** גם אנחנו גם אדמתנו] 𝔊 avoids the bold zeugma, and substitutes *καὶ ἡ γῆ ἐρημωθῇ*, as at the end of the v.—ונחיה] 𝔊 *ἵνα σπείρωμεν* (ונזרע ?).—**21.** העביר—לערים] MT is supported by $\mathfrak{S}\mathfrak{T}^{OJ}$, while 𝔐𝔊 read העביד—לעבדים, as does the loose paraphrase of 𝔙.—**23.** הֵא] Only Ezk. 16[43] and Aram. Dn. 2[43].—**24.** בתבואת] It seems necessary here to take ת׳ as a noun of action: 'at the bringings in' ($\mathfrak{T}^{O}$ De. Di.), though elsewhere it always

and considering the fertility of Egypt, the impost is not excessive; a much higher percentage being frequently exacted under Eastern governments (cf. 1 Mac. 10[30], and the authorities cited by Di. p. 444). On the severities of taxation under the New Empire, see *LAE*, 122.—**25**. The people gratefully accept the terms.—**26**. The arrangement is fixed by administrative decree, and survives to the time of the writer. **27**. (P, *v.i.*) is the conclusion of the settlement of Israel in Egypt (v.[11]).

The system of land-tenure reflected in vv.[18-26] is supposed by Erman to have actually arisen through the extermination of the old landed aristocracy which followed the expulsion of the Hyksos and the founding of the New Empire (*LAE*, 102 f.). The same writer thus sums up what is known or surmised of social conditions under the New Empire: "The landed property was partly in the hands of the state, partly in those of the priesthood; it was tilled by peasant-serfs; there seem to have been no private estates belonging to the nobility, at any rate not under the 19th dynasty. The lower orders consisted mostly of serfs and foreign slaves; the higher, of officials in the service of the state and of the temples" (*ib.* 129). The peculiar privileges of the priests (and soldiers) are attested by Diod. i. 73 f.; Herod. ii. 168 (but cf. ii. 141): the latter says that every priest and warrior possessed 12 ἄρουραι of land tax-free. Of the amount of the land-tax (one fifth) there appears to be no independent confirmation.—The interest of the biblical account is ætiological. The Hebrews were impressed by the vast difference between the land-tenure of Egypt and that under which they themselves lived; and sought an explanation of the 'abnormal agrarian conditions' (Erman) prevailing in the Nile-valley. Whether the explanation here given rests on any Egyptian tradition, or is due to the national imagination of Israel, working on material supplied by the story of Joseph, remains as yet uncertain (see Gu. 410 f.).

The close connexion between Egypt and Palestine in the matter of food-supply is illustrated by the Amarna letters, where a powerful minister named Yanḫamu is frequently mentioned as holding a position somewhat corresponding to that of Joseph. Yanḫamu, whose name suggests Semitic extraction, was governor of an unknown province

---

means 'increase' or 'produce.' To omit ב (with 𝔊) does not yield a natural construction.—לאכלכם] Ba. happily emends לֶאֱכֹל לָכֶם.—ולאכל לטפכם] Better omitted with 𝔊.—**26**. לחמש] 𝔊 לַחֲמִשׁ. חֹמֶשׁ is not found, and the expression is very awkward. A good sense might be obtained by transposing לַחֲמִשׁ לפרעה (with 𝔊[A, al.]); but whether that is the original text is very doubtful.—**27**. The v. is usually divided between J and P; but ישראל is no sure sign of J, since it denotes the nation. The only characteristic of J is בארץ גשן, which may be very well excised as a gloss: the rest may then quite suitably be assigned to P (cf. נאחז, פרה ורבה).

called Yarimuta, which some have tried (but on the slenderest grounds) to identify with the biblical Goshen (Wi. *Forschungen*, iii. 215; Je. *ATLO*, 391[3]). The references imply that he had control of the state-granaries; and complaints are made of the difficulty of procuring supplies from the high-handed official; in particular, it is alleged that the people have had to part with their sons and their daughters, and the very woodwork of their houses, in return for corn (see Knudtzon, *El-Amarna Tafeln*, p. 407). That this historic figure is the original of some features in the portrait of Joseph (a combination first suggested by Marquart, and approved by Wi. Che. Je. al.) is conceivable enough; though definite points of contact are very restricted, and the historical background of Yanḫamu's activity has completely faded from the biography of Joseph.

An equally striking, and equally unconvincing, parallel is pointed out by Eerdmans (*Vorgeschichte Israels*, 68) from a much later period —the end of the 19th dynasty,—when, according to the Papyrus Harris, Arisu (*'I-'ir-sw*), a Syrian, "in years of scarcity" which followed "the abundant years of the past," "made the whole land tributary to himself alone" (see Petrie, *Hist.* iii. 134). The resemblance vanishes on closer inspection. Arisu is simply a Syrian chief, who, in a time of anarchy, gets the upper hand in Egypt by the help of his companions, oppresses the people, and engages in a crusade against the native religion. To say that "the circumstances of this time correspond in all respects [ganz und gar] to the statements of the Joseph-stories," is a manifest exaggeration.

XLVII. 28—XLVIII. 22.—*Jacob's last Interview with Joseph* (J, E, P).

The death-bed scenes of Jacob are described in great detail by all three narrators, because of the importance of the dying utterances of the last ancestor of all Israel. There are four main incidents: (1) Jacob's charge to Joseph with regard to his burial ($^{28-31}$); (2) the blessing of Joseph and his two sons (48); (3) Jacob's oracles on the future of all the tribes (49^{1-28}); and (4) his instructions regarding his burial in Machpelah ($^{29-33}$).—The first two may be conveniently treated together.

Sources.—The triple thread of narrative is shown by the three beginnings: 47^{28} (P), 47^{29} (J), and 48^{1} (E). To P belong 47^{28} 48^{3-6}: note the chronology and syntax of 47^{28}, the connexion of $48^{3f.}$ with $35^{6a. 11. 12}$; אל שרי, ^{3}; הפרה והרבה, ^{4}; קהל עמים, ^{4}; אחות עולם, ^{4}; הוליד, ^{6}.—Equally decisive are the indications of J in 47^{29-31}; ישראל, $^{29. 31}$; אם מצאתי וגו׳, ^{29}; שים נא ידך וגו׳, ^{29} (24^{2}); חסד ואמת, ^{29} (24^{49} 32^{11}); שכבתי עם־אבתי, ^{30}.—The analysis of $48^{1. 2. 8-22}$ is more doubtful: formerly the passage was treated as a unity and assigned to

E (Hupf., We. *Comp.*^{2} 61 f., Dri. al.), but the evidences of double recension are too numerous to be overlooked. (See Budde, *ZATW*, iii. 56 ff.) Thus, while יעקב, ^{2a}, and אלהים, $^{9.\,11.\,15.\,20f.}$, and האמרי, ^{22}, point to E, ישראל, $^{2b.\,8.\,10f.\,13f.\,21}$, and הצעיר, ^{14}, point to J. A clue to the analysis is supplied by (*a*) the double presentation of Manasseh and Ephraim, ^{10b} ‖ ^{13} (ויגש); and (*b*) the obvious intrusion of $^{15.\,16}$ between ^{14} and ^{17}. $^{13.\,14.\,17\text{-}19}$ hang together and are from J; ^{15} links on to ^{12}, and $^{13f.}$ presuppose ^{10a}. Taking note of the finer criteria, the analysis works out somewhat as follows: E $=^{1.\,2.\,8.\,9.\,10b.\,11.\,12.\,15.\,16.\,20a\beta\gamma b.\,21.\,22}$; J $=^{2b\,(?).\,10a.\,13.\,14.\,17\text{-}19.\,20a\alpha}$ (to ההוא);—deleting ישראל in $^{2b\,(?).\,8.\,11.\,21}$ as a redactional explication. So in general Di. KS. Ho. Gu.; also Pro., who, however, places $^{21.\,22}$ before ^{7} in E's narrative.—The source of ^{7} is difficult to determine; usually it has been assigned to P or R, but by Gu. and Pro. to E (see the notes).

28–31. Joseph promises to bury Jacob in Canaan.—**28** (P). Jacob's age at the time of his death; cf. 47^{9}.—**29–31** (J). Comp. the parallel in P, $49^{29\text{-}32}$.—**29.** On the form of oath, see on 24^{2}.—**30.** *lie with my fathers*] *i.e.*, in She'ôl (see on 25^{8}); cf. Dt. 31^{16}, 1 Ki. 2^{10} etc.—*in their burying-place*] But in 50^{5} (also J) Jacob speaks of "my grave which I have digged for myself." The latter is no doubt the original tradition, and the text here must have been modified in accordance with the theory of P $49^{30f.}$ (We.).—**31.** *bowed over the head of the bed*] An act of worship, expressing gratitude to God for the fulfilment of his last wish (cf. 1 Ki. 1^{47}). Ho.'s conjecture (based on 1 Sa. 19^{13}), that there was an image at the top of the bed, is a possible, though precarious, explanation of the origin of the custom. The mistaken rendering of 𝔊 (*v.i.*) may have arisen from the fact that the oath over the staff was an Egyptian formality (Spiegelberg, *Recueil des Travaux*, xxv. 184 ff.; cf. *EB*, 4779^{1}; Sayce, *Contemp. Rev.*, Aug. 1907, 260).

XLVIII. Adoption and blessing of Joseph's two sons.—**1, 2.** The introduction to all that follows: from

29. ויקרבו—למות] Cf. Dt. 31^{14} (J), 1 Ki. 2^{1}.—**30.** ושכבתי] must be taken as protasis to ונשאתני (Str. Ho. Gu. al.).—בקברתם] Kit. בקברתי, to resolve the contradiction spoken of *supra*. But where intentional manipulation of the text is to be suspected, small emendations are of little avail.—**31.** המטה] 𝔊 τῆς ῥάβδου αὐτοῦ, 𝔖 ܚܘܛܪܗ (= מַטֵּהוּ); cf. Heb. 11^{21}. Other Vns. follow MT, which is undoubtedly right: see 48^{2} 49^{33}.

1. ויאמר] So 1 Sa. 16^{4} 19^{22}. The pl. ויאמרו is more usual in such cases (G-K. § 144 d^{2}): we might also point as Niph. וַיֵּאָמֵר (Jos. 2^{2}).—At end of v. add with 𝔊 ויבא אל־יעקב.—**2.** ויגד] Better וַיֻּגַּד.—**2b** is usually assigned

E.—*took his two sons.*] It seems implied in v.[8] that Jacob had not yet seen the lads,—so soon did his last illness follow his arrival in Egypt.—**3–6.** P's brief account of the adoption of Ephraim and Manasseh. Di. thinks the vv. have been transferred from their original connexion with 49^{28b}, where they were spoken in presence of all the brethren.—**3, 4.** The reference is to the revelation at Luz ($35^{11f.}$), where the promise of a numerous offspring was coupled with the possession of Canaan. On the phraseology, see above.—**5.** *And now*] In view of these promises he elevates Ephraim and Manasseh to the status of full tribes, to share with his own sons in the future partition of the land.—*Ephraim and Manasseh*] The order is the only hint that Ephraim was the leading tribe (cf. v.[20] E); but it is not that usually observed by P (see Nu. $26^{28ff.}$ $34^{23f.}$, Jos. 14^4 16^4 17^1; otherwise Nu. 1^{10}).—*as Reuben and Simeon*] The two oldest are chosen for comparison.—**6.** Later-born sons of Joseph (none such, however, are anywhere mentioned) are to be *called by the name of their brethren, etc.*] *i.e.*, are to be counted as Ephraimites and Manassites.—**7.** The presence of Joseph reminds the dying patriarch of the dark day on which he buried Rachel on the way to Ephrath. The expressions reproduce those of 35^{16-20}.—עָלַי] *to my sorrow*; lit. ('as a trouble) upon me' (cf. 33^{13}).

The notice—one of the most pathetic things in Genesis—is very loosely connected with what precedes, and must in its original setting have led up to something which has been displaced in the redaction. But it is difficult to find a suitable connexion for the v. in the extant portions of any of the three sources. In P (to which the word פַּדָּן at first sight seems to point), De. Di. al. would put it immediately before [ועתה אני נאסף] in 49^{29}; but that view relieves no difficulty, and leads nowhere. A more natural position in that document might be after the mention of the burial of Leah in 49^{31} (v.[32] may be an interpolation); but the form of the v. is not favourable to that assumption, and no good reason can be

---

to J because of ישראל. But the cl. comes very naturally after [2a]; and as there are three other cases of confusion between the two names in this ch. ([8. 11. 21]), the name is not decisive.—**4.** קהל עמים] 28^3; cf. 35^{11}.—לזרעך] 𝔊 ולו׳.—לך אחזת עולם] 17^8.—**7.** פַּדָּן] 𝔊𝔐 + אֲרָם, as in every other case where the name occurs (see on 25^{20}). That the difference is documentary, and points to E rather than P, is a hazardous assumption (Gu.); and to substitute חרן, for the sake of accommodation to J (Bruston, Ba.), is quite

imagined for the transposition. (See Bu. *ZATW*, iii. 67 f.) Bruston (in *ZATW*, vii. 208) puts forward the attractive suggestion (adopted by KS. Ba. Gu. Pro. al.) that the v. introduced a request to be buried in the same grave as Rachel. Such a wish is evidently impossible in P; and Bruston (followed with some hesitation by Ba. KS.) accordingly found a place for it (with the necessary alterations of text) between 47^{29} and ^{30} (J): against this $50^{5.\,11}$ seem decisive. Gu. and Pro. assign it to E, the latter placing it after v.^{22}, which is certainly its most suitable position in E. But is the idea after all any more conceivable in E than in P? The writer who recorded the request, whoever he may have been, must have supposed that it was fulfilled; and it is not just likely that any writer should have believed that Jacob was buried in the grave traditionally known as Rachel's. No satisfactory solution can be given. Hupf. and Schr. consider the v. redactional; so Bu., who thinks it was inserted to correct P's original statement that Rachel was buried in Machpelah (see on 49^{31}).

8, 9. E's narrative is resumed.—Observe that Jacob *sees* the boys (who are quite young children [41^{50}]), whereas in ^{10a} (J) he *could not see*.—**9b** is usually assigned to J, but for no very convincing reason.—**10b, 11** (E). *I had not thought, etc.*] The words are charged with deep religious feeling: gratitude to the God in whose name he is to bless the lads, and whose marvellous goodness had brought his clouded life to a happy end.—**12** (E). *from between his* (Jacob's) *knees*] There must be a reference to some rite of adoption not described, which being completed, Joseph removes the children and *prostrates himself* to receive the blessing (continued in ^{15}).—**10a, 13, 14** (J). Whether this is a second interview in J, or a continuation of that in 47^{29-31}, does not appear; in either case something has been omitted.—**10a.** See on 27^1.—**13 f.** The crossing (*v.i.*) of Jacob's hands has a weird effect: the blind man is guided by a supernatural impulse, which moves unerringly in the line of destiny. The right hand conveys

---

arbitrary.—רחל] 𝔊 + ἡ μήτηρ σου (so 𝔐).—**8.** מי אלה] 𝔐𝔊 + לך.—**9.** ויאמר^2] 𝔊 + Ἰακώβ.—ואברכֶם] (B–D. p. 80). On the pausal seghol, see G–K. §§ 29 *q*, 60 *d*.—**11.** רְאֹה] G–K. § 75 *n* (cf. 31^{28}).—פללתי] Lit. 'had not judged'; only here = 'opine.'—**12.** וישתחו] 𝔐𝔊𝔖 have the pl.—לאפיו] hardly makes sense. Rd. with 𝔊𝔖 לו אַפָּיִם.—**14.** את־ימינו] 𝔐 ins. יד.—שִׂכֵּל] 𝔗^{O} אחכימינין, deriving from √שכל, 'be prudent' (whose Piel does not occur); but 𝔊 ἐναλλάξ, 𝔙 *commutans*, 𝔖 ܡܫܚܠܦ, 𝔗J פרג. These Vns. may be guessing at the sense; but most moderns appeal to Ar. *šakala*, a *secondary* meaning of which is to '*plait* two locks of hair together and *bind* them to the other

the richer blessing.—**15, 16.** The Blessing (E).—The threefold invocation of the Deity reminds us of the Aaronic benediction (Nu. $6^{24ff.}$), which has some resemblance to a feature of Babylonian liturgies (see Je. *Hölle und Paradies*, 30): "in such cases the polytheist names all the gods he worships, the ancient monotheist all the names and attributes of the God he knows" (Gu.).—*before whom . . . walked*] cf. 17^{1}.—*who shepherded me*] Cf. 49^{24}, Ps. 23^{1} 28^{9}, Is. 40^{11}. The image is appropriate in the mouth of the master-shepherd Jacob (Di.).—**16.** *the Angel . . . evil*] The passages in Jacob's life where an angel or angels intervene ($28^{11ff.}$ 31^{11} $32^{2f.}$) all belong to the source E; they are not, however, specially connected with deliverances from evil; and the substitution of 'angel' for 'God' is not explained.—*let my name be named in them*] 'Let them be known as sons of Jacob,' and reckoned among the tribes of Israel.—**17–19.** Continuing 14
(J).—Joseph thinks his father had counted on the elder being on his left (Joseph's right) hand, and will now correct his mistake.—**19.** But Jacob, speaking under inspiration, declares his action to be significant.—*the fulness of the nations*] A peculiar expression for populousness. Cf. Dt. 33^{17} ('myriads of Ephraim'; 'thousands of Manasseh').—**20.** The clause *And he blessed them that day*] is (if not redactional) the conclusion of J's account: the words of blessing are not given. The rest of the v. concludes the blessing of E ($^{15f.}$).—*By thee* (𝔊 *you*) *shall Israel bless*] The formula must have been in actual use, and is said to be still current amongst Jews (Str.).—*he put E. before M.*] If the words are original (E), they call attention to the fact that in the benediction Ephraim had been named first, and find in that slight

---

locks.' In spite of the philological equivalence, Dri. is justly sceptical of so remote an analogy.—כי מנשה הבכור] 𝔊 om.—**15.** את־יוסף] 𝔊 אתם] wrongly, the original connexion being with ^{12b}.—מעודי] (Nu. 22^{30}†) 'ever since I was.' 𝔊𝔖𝔙 'from my youth' (מנעורי?).—**16.** For המלאך, 𝔪 reads המלך.—**19.** ואולם] 'but for all that' (cf. 28^{19}).—**20.** בך] 𝔊 בכם.—יְבָרֵךְ] 𝔊𝔙𝔖 יְבֹרַךְ (Niph.; see on 12^{3}). The most natural form would be Hithpa. יתברך.—**22.** שכם אחד] 𝔊 Σικιμα ἐξαίρετον, Aq. ὦμον ἕνα. For אַחַד instead of אֶחָד, see G–K. § 130 *g*. On כָּתֵף in the sense of 'mountain-slope' (*v.s.*), see Nu. 34^{11}, Jos. 15^{8} [Is. 11^{14}?], etc.

circumstance an augury of the future pre-eminence of Ephr. (Gu.).—**21**, **22**. Closing words to Joseph (E).—**21**. A prediction of the return to Canaan, in terms very similar to 50^{24} (also E). The explicit anticipations of the Exodus are probably all from this document (15^{16} [?] 46^{4} 50^{24}).—**22**. *one shoulder*] The word שְׁכֶם may very well (like the synonymous כָּתֵף) have had in common speech the secondary sense of 'mountain-slope,' though no instance occurs in OT. At all events there is no reasonable doubt that the reference is to the city of Shechem, standing on the 'slope' of Gerizim, the most important centre of Israelite power in early times (see p. 416), and consecrated by the possession of Joseph's tomb (Jos. 24^{32}). The peculiar value of the gift in Jacob's eyes is that the conquest was a trophy of his warlike prowess,—a tradition which has left no trace whatever except in this v. (see below).—*With my sword and with my bow*] Contrast Jos. 24^{12}.

Vv.$^{21.22}$ stand in no organic connexion with each other, or with what precedes. V.^{22}, in particular, not only presupposes a version of the capture of Shechem different from any found elsewhere * (see p. 422 above), but is out of harmony with the situation in which the words are assumed to have been uttered. For it is scarcely credible that Jacob should have referred thus to a conquest which he had subsequently lost, and which would have to be recovered by force of arms before the bequest could take effect. But further, the expression 'above thy brethren' naturally implies that the portions of the other sons had been allotted by Jacob before his death. The verse, in short, seems to carry us back to a phase of the national tradition which ignored the sojourn in Egypt, and represented Jacob as a warlike hero who had effected permanent conquests in Palestine, and died there after dividing the land amongst his children. The situation would thus be parallel to the so-called 'Blessing of Jacob' in ch. 49, which is also independent of, though not quite incompatible with, the final recension of the patriarchal history and the migration to Egypt. For the first statement of this theory, see Meyer, *INS*, 227, 414 f.

XLIX. 1–28a.—*The Blessing of Jacob.*

This important and difficult section—one of the oldest pieces of Hebrew poetry which we possess—consists of a

* Attempts to bring the notice into line with the recorded history, by inserting לא before בחרבי and בקשתי (as Jos. 24^{12}) (Kue.), or by taking לקחתי as a fut.-pf. (Tu. De. Str. al.), are obviously unsatisfactory.

series of oracles describing the characters and fortunes of the twelve tribes of Israel, as unfolded during the age of the Judges and under the early monarchy. That it was composed from the first in the name of Jacob appears clearly from internal indications (vv.[3f. 9. [18]. 26]); but that it was actually uttered by the patriarch on his death-bed to his assembled sons is a hypothesis which several considerations combine to render incredible. In the first place, the outlook of the poem is bounded (as we shall afterwards see) by a particular historical situation, removed by many centuries from the supposed time of utterance. No reason can be imagined why the vista of the future disclosed to Jacob should open during the settlement of the tribes in Canaan, and suddenly close at the reign of David or Solomon; why trivial incidents like the maritime location of Zebulun (v.[13]), or the 'royal dainties' produced by Asher ([20]), or even the loss of tribal independence by Issachar ([15]), etc., should be dwelt upon to the exclusion of events of far greater national and religious importance, such as the Exodus, the mission of Moses, the leadership of Joshua, or the spiritual prerogatives of the tribe of Levi. It is obvious that the document as a whole has historic significance only when regarded as a production of the age to which it refers. The analogy of OT prophecy, which has been appealed to, furnishes no instance of detailed prevision of a remote future, unrelated to the moral issues of the speaker's present. In the next place, the poem is animated by a strong *national* sentiment such as could not have existed in the lifetime of Jacob, while there is a complete absence of the family feeling which would naturally find expression in the circumstances to which it is assigned, and which, in fact, is very conspicuous in the prose accounts of Jacob's last days. The subjects of the oracles are not Jacob's sons as individuals, but the tribes called by their names (see [28a]); nor is there any allusion to incidents in the personal history of Jacob and his sons except in the sections on Reuben and on Simeon and Levi, and even there a tribal interpretation is more natural. Finally, the speaker is not Jacob the individual patriarch, but (as is clear from vv.[6. 7b. 16])

Jacob as representing the ideal unity of Israel (see Kohler, p. 8 f.). All these facts point to the following conclusion (which is that of the great majority of modern interpreters): the poem is a series of *vaticinia ex eventu*, reflecting the conditions and aspirations of the period that saw the consolidation of the Hebrew nationality. The examination of the separate oracles will show that some (*e.g.* those on Issachar and Dan) are certainly pre-monarchic; and that indeed all may be so except the blessing on Judah, which presupposes the establishment of the Davidic kingdom. The process of composition must therefore have been a protracted one; the poem may be supposed to have existed as a traditional document whose origin dates from the early days of the Israelite occupation of Palestine, and which underwent successive modifications and expansions before it took final shape in the hands of a Judæan poet of the age of David or Solomon. The conception of Jacob as the speaker belongs to the original intention of the poem; the oracles express the verdict of the collective consciousness of Israel on the conduct and destiny of the various tribes, an idea finely suggested by putting them in the mouth of the heroic ancestor of the nation. Ultimately the song was incorporated in the patriarchal tradition, probably by the Yahwist, who found a suitable setting for it amongst the dying utterances of Jacob.

Literary Parallels.—Before proceeding to consider the more intricate problems arising out of the passage, it will be useful to compare it with (1) the Song of Deborah (Ju. 5), and (2) the Blessing of Moses (Dt. 33). —1. The former is like an instantaneous photograph: it exhibits the attitude and disposition of the tribes in a single crisis of the national history. It resembles Gen. 49 in the strong feeling of national unity which pervades it, and in the mingling of blame and commendation. It reveals, however, a very different historical background. The chief differences are: the entire ignoring of the southern tribes Judah, Simeon, and Levi; the praise bestowed on Issachar; the substitution of Gilead for Gad; and the division of the unity of Joseph into its constituents Ephraim and Machir (= Manasseh). The importance of these and other divergences for the determination of the relative dates of the two documents is obvious, although the evidence is frequently of a kind which makes it very difficult to form a confident judgement.—2. The Blessing of Moses shows signs (especially in the section on Joseph) of literary dependence on Gn. 49; it is therefore a later composition, written very probably in North Israel after the division of the kingdom (see Dri. *Deut.* 388). It is distinguished from the Blessing of Jacob by its uniform tone of benediction, and its strongly religious point of view as contrasted with the secular and warlike spirit of Gn. 49. Simeon is passed over in silence, while his 'brother' Levi is the subject of an enthusiastic eulogium; Judah is briefly commended in a prayer to Yahwe; the separation of Ephraim and Manasseh is recognised in an appendix to the blessing on Joseph. All these indications point more or less decisively to a situation considerably later than that presupposed by the oracles of Jacob.

Date and Unity of the Poem.—That the song is not a perfect literary unity is suggested first of all by the seemingly complex structure of the sections on Dan (two independent oracles) and Judah (with three exordiums in vv.[8. 9. 10]). We find, further, that a double motive runs through the series, viz., (1) etymological play on the name of the tribe (Judah, Zebulun?, Dan, Gad, Asher?), and (2) tribal emblems (chiefly animal) (Judah, Issachar, Dan, Naphtali, Joseph, Benjamin): one or other of these can be detected in each oracle except those on Reuben and Simeon-Levi. It is, of course, not certain that these are characteristic of two independent groups of oracles; but the fact that both are represented in the sayings on Judah and Dan, while neither appears in those on Reuben and Simeon-Levi, does confirm the impression of composition and diversity of origin. The decisive consideration, however, is that no single period of history can be found which satisfies all the indications of date drawn from the several oracles. Those on Reuben, Simeon, and Levi refer to events which belong to a remote past, and were in all probability composed before the Song of Deborah, while these events were still fresh in the national memory; those on Issachar, Dan, and Benjamin could hardly have originated after the establishment of the monarchy; while the blessing of Judah clearly presupposes the existence of the Davidic kingdom, and must have been written not earlier than the time of David or Solomon. A still later date is assigned by most critics since We. (*Comp.*[3] 320) to the blessing on Joseph, which is generally considered to refer to the kingdom of North Israel and to the Aramæan wars under the dynasties of Omri and Jehu. It is argued in the notes below that the passage is susceptible of a different interpretation from that adopted by the majority of scholars, and may, in fact, be one of the oldest parts of the poem. As for the rest of the oracles, their character is such that it seems quite impossible to decide whether they originated before or after the founding of the kingdom. In any case we hardly get much beyond a broad chronological division into pre-Davidic and post-Davidic oracles; but at the same time that distinction is so clearly marked as to exclude absolutely the hypothesis of unity of authorship.—It has been supposed by some writers (Renan, Kue. al.) that the poem consists of a number of fugitive oracles which had circulated independently among the tribes, and were ultimately collected and put in the mouth of Jacob. But, apart from the general objection that characterisation of one tribe by the rest already implies a central point of view, the inadequacy of the theory is seen when we observe that all the longer passages (Reuben, Simeon-Levi, Judah, Joseph) assume that Jacob is the speaker, while the shorter pieces are too slight in content to have any significance except in relation to the whole.—An intermediate position is represented by Land, who distinguished six stages in the growth of the song: (1) A primary poem, consisting of the two tristichs, vv.^{3} and ^{8}, written at the time of David's victories over the Philistines, and celebrating the passing of the hegemony from Reuben to Judah: to this v.^{4} was afterwards added as an appendix. (2) A second poem on Judah, Dan, and Issachar (vv.$^{9.\ 17.\ 14f.}$: distichs), describing under animal figures the condition of these tribes during the peaceful interval of David's reign in Hebron: to which was appended later the v. on Benjamin (^{27}). (3) The Shiloh oracle (vv.$^{10-12}$), dating from the same period. (4) The decastich on Simeon and Levi (vv.$^{5-7}$), from the time of the later Judges. (5) The blessing of Joseph ($^{22-26}$), a northern poem from about the time of Deborah. (6) The five distichs on Zebulun, Dan, Gad, Asher, and Naphtali (in that order: vv.$^{13.\ 16.\ 19.\ 20.\ 21}$), commemorating the victory of Deborah and Barak over the Canaanites. The theory rests on dubious interpretations, involves improbable historical combinations, and is altogether too intricate to command assent; but it is noteworthy nevertheless as perhaps the first elaborate attempt to solve the problem of the date and integrity of the poem, and to do justice to the finer lines of structure that can be discovered in it.—On the whole, however, the theory of the 'traditional document' (*v.s.*), altered and supplemented as it was handed down from one generation to another, while sufficiently elastic, seems the one that best satisfies all the requirements of the problem (so Gu. 420 f.).

The *order* in which the tribes are enumerated appears to be partly genealogical, partly geographical. The six Leah-tribes come first, and in the order of birth as given in chs. 29 f., save that Zebulun and Issachar change places. Then follow the four concubine or hybrid tribes; but the order is that neither of birth nor of the mothers, the two Zilpah-tribes, Gad and Asher, coming between the Bilhah tribes, Dan and Naphtali. The Rachel-tribes, Joseph and Benjamin, stand last. Geographically, we may distinguish a southern group (Reuben, Simeon, Levi, Judah), a northern (Zebulun, Issachar, Dan?, Gad [trans-Jordanic], Asher, Naphtali), and a central group (Joseph, Benjamin). The general agreement of the two classifications shows that the genealogical scheme itself reflects the tribal affinities and historical antecedents by which the geographical distribution of the tribes in Palestine was in part determined. The suggestion of Peters (*Early Heb. Story*, 61 ff.), that the ages of Jacob's children represent approximately the order in which the respective tribes obtained a permanent footing in Canaan, is a plausible one, and probably contains an element of truth; although the attempt to reconstruct the history of the invasion and conquest on such precarious data can lead to no secure results. It is clear at all events that neither the genealogical nor the geographical principle furnishes a complete explanation of the arrangement in Gn.

49; and we have to bear in mind the possibility that this ancient document may have preserved an older tradition as to the grouping and relations of the tribes than that which is given in the prose legends (chs. 29. 30).—On the question whether a sojourn in Egypt is presupposed between the utterance and the fulfilment of the predictions, the poem naturally throws no direct light. It is not improbable that in this respect it stands on the same plane as 48^{22} (34. 38), and traces the conquest of Palestine back to Jacob himself.

Metrical Form.—See Sievers, *Metrische Studien*, i. 404 ff., ii. 152 ff., 361 ff. The poem (vv.$^{2-27}$) exhibits throughout a clearly marked metrical structure, the unit being the trimeter distich, with frequent parallelism between the two members. The lines which do not conform to this type (vv.$^{7b. 13b. 18}$, and esp. $^{24b-26}$) are so few that interpolation or corruption of text may reasonably be suspected; although our knowledge of the laws of Hebrew poetry does not entitle us to say that an occasional variation of rhythm is in itself inadmissible.

Source.—Since the poem is older than any of the Pentateuchal documents, the only question that arises is the relatively unimportant one of the stage of compilation at which it was incorporated in the narrative of Gen. Of the primary sources, E and P are excluded; the former because of the degradation of Reuben, which is nowhere recognised by E; and the latter by the general tendency of that work, and its suppression of discreditable incidents in the story of the patriarchs. The passage is in perfect harmony with the representation of J, and may without difficulty be assigned to that document, as is done by the majority of critics. At the same time, the absence of literary connexion with the narrative leaves a considerable margin of uncertainty; and it is just as easy to suppose that the insertion took place in the combined narrative JE, perhaps by the same hand which inserted the Blessing of Moses in Deut. (see We. *Comp.*^{2} 62). That it was introduced during the final redaction of the Pent. is less probable, especially if $^{28b\beta}$ (ויברך) was the original continuation of ^{1b} in P (see on v.^{1}).

Monographs on the Song: Diestel, *Der Segen Jakob's in Genes. xlix. historisch erläutert* (1853); Land, *Disputatio de carmine Jacobi* (1858); Kohler, *Der Segen Jakob's mit besonderer Berücksichtigung der alten Versionen und des Midrasch historisch-kritisch untersucht und erklärt* (1867); cf. also Meier, *Geschichte der poetischen National Literatur der Hebräer* (1856), pp. 109–113; Peters, *JSBL*, 1886, pp. 99–116; and see the copious reff. in Tu. or Di.

1, 2. Introduction.—The poem begins with a preamble (v.^{2}) from the hand of the writer who composed or collected the oracles and put them in the mouth of Jacob. ^{1b} is a prose introduction, supplied probably by the editor who incorporated the Song in the narrative of J or JE; while ^{1a} appears to be a fragment of P divorced from its original connexion with [28abβ] by R^{JEP}.—**1b.** *that I may make known, etc.*] The poem is expressly characterised as a prophecy (not, however, as a *blessing* [as [28b]]), which it obviously is as ascribed to Jacob, though the singer's real standpoint is contemporary or retrospective (p. 508 above).—*in the after days*] The furthest horizon of the speaker's vision (*v.i.*).—**2.** A trimeter distich, exhibiting the prevalent metrical scheme of the poem :

Assemble, ye sons of Jacob,
And hearken to Israel your father!

With the call to attention, cf. 4[23], Dt. 32[1], Is. 1[10] 28[14], etc.—Whether in the mind of the poet Israel is the literal or the ideal father of the nation may be doubtful: cf. v.[7], and p. 509 above.

3, 4. Reuben.

3 Reuben! My first-born art thou:
My strength and best of my vigour.
Exceeding in pride and exceeding in fury,
4 Impetuous as water, thou may'st not excel.
For thou wentest up to thy father's bed;
There thou profanedst ⌜the⌝ couch. . . .

The original presents both obscurities and niceties not reflected in the translation; but the general sense is clear. As the first-born, Reuben is endowed with a superabundant vitality, which is the cause at once of his pre-eminence and of his undoing: his energy degenerates into licentious

---

1. באחרית הימים] The phrase occurs 13 times in Heb. OT (Nu. 24[14], Dt. 4[30] 31[29], Is. 2[2], Jer. 23[20] 30[24] 48[47] 49[39], Ezk. 38[16], Hos. 3[5], Mic. 4[1], Dn. 10[14]†), and its Aram. equivalent in Dn. 2[28]. In the prophets it is used technically of the advent of the Messianic age; here and elsewhere (Nu. 24[14] etc.) it has the general sense of the remote future (like Ass. *aḫrat ûmi*: *KAT*[2], 143). That the eschatological sense is primary, and the other an imitation of prophetic style (Gu.), cannot be proved; and there is no justification for deleting either the phrase itself (Staerk, *ZATW*, xi. 247 ff.), or the whole clause in which it occurs (Land).—**2.** The repetition of ושמעו is against the rules of parallelism. We may either omit the word in [2a] (Gu. Sie.), or vary the expression (והקשיבו, והאזינו) in [2b] ($\mathfrak{T}^O$, Ba.). Metrically either expedient would be admissible, but the former is much easier. In $\mathfrak{G}^{B. al.}$ ἀκούσατε is used thrice.

passion, which impels him to the crime that draws down the curse. As a characterisation of the tribe, this will mean that Reuben had a double share of the 'frenetic' Bedouin nature, and wore out his strength in fierce warfare with neighbouring tribes. If the outrage on his father's honour (v.[4]) have historic significance (see below), it must denote some attack on the unity of Israel which the collective conscience of the nation condemned. It is to be noted that the recollection of the event has already assumed the legendary form, and must therefore reach back to a time considerably earlier than the date of the poem (Gu.).—**3b, 4a.** *exceeding . . . excel*] No English word brings out the precise force of the original, where the √ יתר occurs three times in a sense hovering between 'exceed' and 'excel.' The idea of excess being native to the root, the renderings *pride* and *fury* are perhaps preferable to 'dignity' and 'power,' [3c] as well as [4] being understood *sensu malo*, as a censure of Reuben.—**4b.** *Then . . . went up*] A corrupt text:

3a. ראשית אוני (Dt. 21[17], cf. Ps. 78[51] 105[36])] Not *ἀρχὴ τέκνων μου* (𝔊Θ), still less *principium doloris mei* (𝔙 from אָוֶן, 'trouble'; so Aq. Σ.); but 'best part of my virility' (𝔖𝔗o). On ראשית, see p. 12; און as Hos. 12[4].—**3b.** 𝔊 *σκληρὸς φέρεσθαι καὶ σκληρὸς αὐθάδης*; 𝔙 *prior in donis, major in imperio.*—יֶתֶר (abst. pro concr.) might mean 'excess' (Aq. Σ.), or 'superiority' (𝔙), or 'remnant' (𝔖; so Peters, p. 100): whether it is here used in a good sense or a bad (for the latter, cf. Pr. 17[7]) depends on the meaning assigned to the next two words.—שאת] Lit. 'lifting' (𝔊 Aq. ΣΘ𝔖), several times means 'exaltation'; but in Hab. 1[7] it has distinctly the sense of 'arrogance,' the idea preferred above. To read שְׂאֵת, 'turbulence' (Gu.), is unnecessary, and שֵׁאת, 'destruction' (Peters), gives a wrong turn to the thought.—עָז] Pausal for עֹז, 'power,' but the sense of 'fury' is supported by v.[7], Is. 25[3].—**4.** פחז—תותר] 𝔊 *ἐξύβρισας ὡς ὕδωρ, μὴ ἐκζέσῃς*; Aq. *ἐθάμβευσας . . . περισσεύσῃς*; Σ. *ὑπερέζεσας . . . οὐκ ἔσῃ περισσότερος*; 𝔙 *effusus es sicut aqua, non crescas*; 𝔖 ܛܥܝܬ ܐܝܟ ܡܝܐ ܠܐ ܬܘܬܪ. The comparison to water is ambiguous; and it is doubtful if we may introduce the simile of water 'boiling over' (Σ𝔊 and many moderns). The image may be that of a wild rushing torrent,—a fit emblem of the unbridled passion which was Reuben's characteristic (so 𝔗O).—פחז] 𝔐 פחוז. Though the other Vns. also have 2nd pers. we cannot assume that they *read* so; and the analogy of v.[3] leads us to expect another abst. pro concr. The noun is ἅπ. λεγ.; the ptcp. occurs Ju. 9[4], Zeph. 3[4], with the sense 'reckless' or 'irresponsible' (cf. פחזות, Jer. 23[32]). In Arab. the √ means 'be insolent,' in Aram. 'be lascivious': the common idea is

for various suggestions, *v.i.* Gu.'s trans. 'Then I profaned the couch which he ascended,' at least softens the harsh change from 2nd pers. to 3rd.

The 'birthright' of Reuben must rest on some early ascendancy or prowess of the tribe which has left no traces in history. Its choice of a settlement E of the Jordan (Nu. 32, etc.), shows an attachment to nomadic habits, and perhaps an unfitness for the advance to civilised life which the majority of the tribes had to make. In the Song of Deborah, Reuben is still an important tribe, but one that had lost enthusiasm for the national cause (Ju. $5^{15f.}$). In the Blessing of Moses it still survives, but is apparently on the verge of extinction (Dt. 33^{6}). It was doubtless exhausted by struggles like those with the Hagarenes (1 Ch. $5^{10.\ 18ff.}$), but especially with the Moabites, who eventually occupied most of its territory (cf. Nu 32^{37}, Jos. $13^{16ff.}$ with Is. 15, Jer. 48 *pass.*, and Moabite Stone).—The incident to which the downfall of Reuben is here traced ($^{4a\beta b}$) is connected with the fragmentary notice of 35^{22}, and is variously interpreted: (1) According to Rob. Sm. *KM*², 109², Steuer. *Einw.* 16, Ho., it records the fact that Reuben had misused its power as the leading tribe to assail the independence of a weaker member of the confederation (Bilhah, or one of the Bilhah-tribes),—a rather hazardous speculation. (2) Another theory, not necessarily inconsistent with the former (see Rob. Sm. *l.c.*), finds a reference to the persistence in Reuben of an old Semitic custom of marriage with the wives or concubines of a (deceased!) father (Di., Sta. *GVI*, i. 151 f.), which the general moral sense of Israel had outgrown. In this case we must suppose that 49^{4} contains the germ of the legend of which 35^{22}, with its particular mention of Bilhah, is a later phase. (3) It is probable that the *form* of the legend has been partly determined by a mythological motive, to which a striking parallel is found in the story of Phœnix and Amyntor (*Il.* ix. 447 ff.: quoted above, p. 427).—*Metrical Structure.* The oracle is better divided as above into three distichs, than (with MT) into two tristichs (so Land, who assigns each to a separate author). The trimeter measure is easily traced throughout (except l. 3) by following the Heb. accents, supplying Maqqeph after כי and או in v.⁴. Line 3 may be scanned ∪∪′ | ∪′ | ∪′ (Siev.).

---

perhaps 'uncontrollableness' (*ut s.*).—אַל־תּוֹתַר] For the pausal *a*, see G-K. § 53 *n*, and cf. Ru. 2^{14}.—4b. No very acceptable rendering of this difficult clause has been proposed. If we follow the accentuation, יצועי is obj. of עלה, and יצועי עלה a detached sentence: 'Then thou actedst profanely. He went up to my bed'; but apart from the harsh change of person, this is inadmissible, because חִלֵּל is never used intransitively. To read עָלִיתָ with 𝔊 is perhaps a too facile emendation; and to omit עלה with 𝔙 is forbidden by rhythm. On the whole it is best (with Gu.) to point חִלַּלְתָּ, and take עלה as a rel. cl. (*v.s.*). Other suggestions are: ח׳ יצועי עָלֶה (Land); יצועֵי בִלְהָה (Geig. Kit.); י׳ יוֹלַדְךָ (Ba.); but all these are, for one reason or another, objectionable.

5–7. Simeon and Levi.

5 Simeon and Levi—brothers!
    Weapons of ruth are their daggers (?).
6 Into their council my soul would not enter,
    In their assembly my mind would not join:
For in their anger they slaughter men,
    And in their gloating they disable oxen.
7 Accursed be their wrath for it is fierce,
    And their rage for it is cruel!
I will divide them in Jacob,
    And scatter them in Israel.

5a. *brothers*] Hardly ὁμόγνωμοι (schol. in Field) = 'true brother-spirits' (Tu. al.), or 'associates' in a common enterprise. The epithet is probably a survival from an old tradition in which S. and L. were the only sons of Leah (see $34^{1.25}$; cf. Mey. *INS*, 286^1, 426). It is universally assumed that that incident—the treacherous attack on Shechem—is the ground of the curse here pronounced; but the terms of the oracle are perfectly general and in part unsuited to the supposed circumstances; and it seems to me to be the habitual character of the tribes which is denounced, and not any particular action.—**5b.** The transl. is doubtful,

---

5b. 𝔊 *συνετέλεσαν ἀδικίαν ἐξ αἱρέσεως αὐτῶν* (OL. *consummaverunt iniquitatem adinventionis suæ*); Aq. *σκεύη ἀδικίας ἀνασκαφαὶ* [*αὐτῶν*]; 𝔙 *vasa iniquitatis bellantia* [Je. *arma eorum*]; 𝔖 ܡ̈ܐܢܝ ܙܝܢܐ ܒܨܒܝܢܗܘܢ; 𝔗^O בארע תותבותהון עבדו גבורא; 𝔗^J [מאני] ויינא שנינא למחטוב היא כלי׳—.אשתמודעותהון] So Aq. 𝔙𝔖𝔗^J; but 𝔐𝔊𝔗^O כִּלּוּ: 'they accomplished.' מכרתיהם] As to the cons. text, that of 𝔊 cannot be certainly restored; Kethib is supported by Aq. 𝔖𝔗^O (מְכֻרֹת׳: cf. Ezk. 16^3 21^{35} 29^{14}), by 𝔗^J (from √ נכר, see IEz.), and probably 𝔙. The textual tradition must therefore be accepted as fairly reliable. Of the many Heb. etymologies proposed (see Di. 459), the most plausible are those which derive from √ כרר, or (reading מְכֹר׳) from √ כרה, 'to dig.' No √ כרר, 'dig,' is actually found, though it might perhaps be assumed as a by-form of כרה: this would give the meaning 'digging instrument' (cf. *gladio confodere*), which Vollers (*ZA*, xiv. 355) tries to support from Ass. The √ כרר means in Ar. 'to turn' or 'wheel round'; hence Di. conj. that מְכֵרָה may be a *curved* knife or sabre. Some weapon suits the context, but what exactly it is must remain uncertain. How far the exegesis has been influenced by the resemblance to the Gr. *μάχαιρα* (R. Johanan [d. 279 A.D.], cited in *Ber. R.* § 99; Ra.) we cannot tell. Ba. and Gu. take the word to be מְכֻרָה, the former rendering 'plots' (fr. Ar. *makara*, 'to plot')

owing partly to uncertainty of text, and partly to the obscurity of the ἅπ. λεγ. מְכֵרָה (*v.i.*). The rendering above gives a good sense, and Ba.'s objection, that daggers are *necessarily* implements of violence, has no force.—6a. *council . . . assembly*] The tribal gatherings, in which deeds of violence were planned, and sanguinary exploits gloated over. The distich expresses vividly the thought that the true *ethos* of Israel was not represented in these bloody-minded gatherings.—6b. *men . . . oxen*] The nouns are collectives.—*slaughter . . . hough*] Perfects of experience. The latter operation (disable by cutting the sinew of the hind-leg) was occasionally performed by Israelites on horses (Jos. $11^{6. 9}$, 2 Sa. 8^{4}); to do it to a domestic animal was evidently considered inhuman. No such atrocity is recorded of the assault on Shechem (see 34^{28}).*—7b. *in Jacob . . . in Israel*] The speaker is plainly not the individual patriarch, nor the Almighty (Land), but the personified nation.

---

and the latter 'pits' (cf. מִכְרָה, Zeph. 2^{9}); but neither כְּלוּ חָמָס מְכֻרֹתָם (Ba.) nor כְּלֵי וְחָמָס מְכֻרֹתֵיהֶם ['knavery and violence are their pits'] (Gu.) is so good as the ordinary interpretation. Ba., however, rightly observes that מְכֻרֹתָם yields a better metre than ־ֹתֵיהֶם— (so Siev.).—6a. כבדי] Read with 𝕲 כְּבֵדִי, 'my liver,' the seat of mental affections in La. 2^{11} (cf. Ps. 16^{9} 30^{13} 57^{9} 108^{2}: MT כָּבוֹד): cf. *kabittu*, 'Gemüth,' in Ass.—תחד] 𝔐 יחר. Since כָּבֵד is masc., rd. יֵחַד.—6b. רצון] 'self-will,' 'wantonness'; cf. Neh. $9^{24. 37}$, Est. 1^{8} 9^{5} etc.—עִקְּרוּ] On certain difficulties in the usage of the word, see Batten, *ZATW*, xxviii. 189 ff., where it is argued that the sense is general—'make useless.'—שׁוֹר] Aq. Σ𝔖𝔖𝔗^O read שׁוּר, 'wall,' perhaps to avoid the supposed contradiction with $34^{28f.}$. Hence the correct ταῦρον of 𝕲 is instanced in *Mechilta* as a change made by the LXX translators (see p. 14).—7. ארור, ועברתם] 𝔐 אדיר, וחברתם.—עָזָּ] Here pausal form of עַז (ct. v.^{3}).

---

* Zimmern (*ZA*, vii. 162 f.) finds in ^{6b} a reminiscence of the mutilation of the celestial Bull by Gilgameš and Eabani in the Bab. Gilgameš-Epic. Simeon and Levi, like Gilgameš and Eabani, represent the Gemini of the Zodiac; and it is pointed out that the Bull in the heavens is ἡμίτομος, *i.e.* only its fore-half appears as a constellation. The אִישׁ then corresponds to the tyrant Ḫumbaba, who was slain by Gilgameš and Eabani; and Jacob's curse answers to the curse of Ištar on the two heroes for mutilating the Bull.—Whatever truth there may be in this mythological interpretation, it does not relieve us of the necessity of finding a *historical* explanation of the incidents.

The dispersion of these two tribes must have taken place at a very early period of the national history. As regards Simeon, it is doubtful if it ever existed as a separate geographical unit. P is only able to assign to it an inheritance scooped out of the territory of Judah (cf. Jos. 19^{1-9} with $15^{26-32.\ 42}$: see also 1 Ch. 4^{28-33}); and so-called Simeonite cities are assigned to Judah as early as the time of David (1 Sa. 27^{6} 30^{30}, 2 Sa. 24^{7}; cf. 1 Ki. 19^{3}). In the Blessing of Moses it is passed over in silence. Traces of its dispersion may be found in such Simeonite names as Shimeʿi, Shāûl, Yāmîn in other tribes (Rob. Sm. *JPh.* ix. 96); and we may assume that the tribe had disappeared before the establishment of the monarchy (see Steuer. 70 ff.; Meyer, *INS*, 75 ff.).—Very different was the fate of Levi. Like Simeon, it lost its independence and, as a *secular* tribe, ceased to exist. But its scattered members had a spiritual bond of unity in the possession of the Mosaic tradition and the sacred lot (Dt. $33^{8ff.}$), in virtue of which it secured a privileged position in the Israelite sanctuaries (Ju. 17 f.), and was eventually reconstituted on a sacerdotal basis. The contrast between this passage, where Levi is the subject of a curse, and Dt. 33, where its prerogatives are celebrated with enthusiasm, depends on the distinction just indicated: here Levi is the secular tribe, destroyed by its own ferocity, whose religious importance has not yet emerged; there, it is the Priestly tribe, which, although scattered, yet holds the *sacra* and the Tôrāh of the Yahwe-religion (We. *Comp.*[6] 136 ff.).—The *Metre* is regular, except that in the last two lines the trimeters are replaced by a binary couplet. That is no sufficient reason for deleting them as an interpolation (Siev.).

8–12. Judah.

8 Judah! Thee shall thy brethren praise—
    Thy hand on the neck of thy foes—
    Bow down to thee shall thy father's sons.

9 A lion's whelp is Judah,
    From the prey, my son, thou'rt gone up!
He crouched, he couched like a lion,
    And an old lion—who shall arouse him?

10 Departs not the sceptre from Judah,
    Nor staff from between his feet,
Until . . . come. . . . (?),
    And to him the peoples obey.

11 Binding his ass to the vine,
    And his foal to the choicest vine!
He washes his raiment in wine,
    And his clothes in the blood of the grape!
12 With eyes made dull by wine,
    And teeth whitened with milk!

8. *Thee*] The emphasis on the pron. (see G–K. § 135 *e*) is explained by the contrast to the preceding oracles: at last the singer comes to a tribe which he can unreservedly praise. Nowhere else does the poem breathe such glowing enthusiasm and such elevation of feeling as here. The glories of Judah are celebrated in four aspects: (1) as the premier tribe of Israel, [8]; (2) as the puissant and victorious lion-tribe, [9]; (3) as the bearer (in some sense) of the Messianic hope, [10]; (4) as lavishly endowed with the blessings of nature, [11f.].—יְהוּדָה, יוֹדוּךָ] The same fanciful etymology as in 29^{35}.—*thy hand . . . foes*] The image seems to be that of a defeated enemy, caught by the (back of the) neck in his flight, and crushed (Ex. 23^{27}, Ps. 18^{41}, Jb. 16^{12}).—*thy brethren . . . thy father's sons*] The other tribes, who acknowledge the primacy of Judah.—**9.** A vivid picture of the growth of Judah's power; to be compared with the beautiful lyric, Ezk. 19^{2-9}.—*a lion's whelp*] So Dt. 33^{22} (of Dan). The image naturally suggests the 'mighty youth' of the tribe, as its full development is represented by the *lion*, and *old lion* of the following lines. Hence the cl. מִטֶּרֶף—עָלִיתָ is rendered by some (Gu. al.): *On prey, my son, thou hast grown up* (been reared), which is perhaps justified by Ezk. 19^3. But it is better to understand it of the lion's ascent, after a raid, to his mountain fastness, where he rests in unassailable security ([9b]).—*he crouches, etc.*] So (of Israel as a whole) Nu. 24^9.—**10a.** Judah's political pre-eminence.—*sceptre . . . staff*] The latter word (מְחֹקֵק) might be used personally =

8. ידך] Sam. 𝔊 יָדֶיךָ.—**9.** מטרף] 𝔊 ἐκ βλαστοῦ, taking the word as in 8^{11}, Ezk. 17^9.—לביא] 𝔊 σκύμνος, 𝔖 ܓܘܪܝܐ ܕܐܪܝܐ. The common rendering 'lioness' is based on Arab., but it is by no means certain that in Heb. the word denotes specially the female. It is never construed as fem.; and in Ezk. 19^2 the pointing לְבִיָּא shows that the Massoretes considered לָבִיא as masc.—**10a.** שבט and מחקק are found together in Ju. 5^{14}, where מחקק (|| מֹשְׁכִים בְּשֵׁבֶט) has the personal sense of 'commander.' But in Nu. 21^{18}, Ps. 60^9 [$=108^9$] it denotes the commander's staff; and since שבט is always the instrument, the impersonal sense is to be preferred here: hence the ἄρχων of 𝔊 is wrong, and the personal renderings of מח׳ in all Vns. at least doubtful.—מבין רגליו] Sam. מבין דגליו, 'from between his banners,' gives no sense. 𝔊Θ𝔙 interpret after Dt. 28^{57} 'from his

'prescriber [of laws]' ($\mathfrak{GVT}^{OJ}$ al.); but שֵׁבֶט is never so used, and parallelism requires that מחקק should be understood of the commander's *staff* (Nu. 21^{18}, Ps. $60^{9} = 108^{9}$).—*from between his feet*] The chieftain is conceived as seated with his wand of office held upright in front of him. The Bedouin sheikhs and headmen of villages are said still to carry such insignia of authority.

The question arises whether the emblems denote (*a*) kingly authority, or (*b*) military leadership of the other tribes, or merely (*c*) tribal autonomy. Dri. (*JPh.* xiv. 26) decides for (*a*), because (1) שבט, without qualification, suggests a royal sceptre; (2) the last phrase presents the picture of a king seated on a throne; (3) the word ישתחוו in ^{8b} most naturally expresses the homage due to a king (cf. 37^{7}). But in favour of (*c*) it might be urged (1) that מחקק never has this meaning, and (2) that שבט is the word for 'tribe' (*e.g.* vv.$^{16. 28}$), and, if the passage be early, is likely to be used as the symbol of tribal independence. The idea of military hegemony (*b*) is in no way suggested, apart from the connexion with v.^{8}, which is dubious. The point has an important bearing on the exegesis of the next cl. If (*a*) be right, the Davidic monarchy is presupposed, and ^{10b} assigns a term to its continuance; whereas, if (*c*) be right, ^{10b} is possibly (not necessarily) a prophecy of David and his dynasty. See, further, the note at the end of this verse.

10b. The logical relation of the two halves of the v. is clear: the state of things described by ^{10a} shall endure *until*

---

thighs'; and hence $\mathfrak{T}^{O}$ 'from his sons' sons,' $\mathfrak{T}^{J}$ 'from his seed.'—**10b.** עד—שילה] $\mathfrak{G}\Theta$. *ἕως ἂν ἔλθῃ τὰ ἀποκείμενα αὐτῷ* [vars. *ᾧ τὰ ἀποκείμενα* . . ., *ᾧ ἀπόκειται* . . . etc.]; 𝔖 ܥܕܡܐ ܕܢܐܬܐ ܗܘ ܕܝܼܠܗ ܗܘ; 𝔙 *donec veniat qui mittendus est* (reading שָׁלֻחַ: cf. Σιλωάμ (ὃ ἑρμηνεύεται Ἀπεσταλμένος), Jn. 9^{7}); $\mathfrak{T}^{O}$ עד דייתי משיחא דדילה היא מלכותא; $\mathfrak{T}^{J}$ עד זמן די ייתי מלכא משיחא זעיר בנוי. This last curious rendering ('the youngest of his sons') is followed by Ḳimchi and others; and apparently rests on a misunderstanding of שִׁלְיָתָהּ ('afterbirth') in Dt. 28^{57} ($\mathfrak{T}^{O}$ וזעיר בנהא).—עד כי] Only here with impf. With pf. (26^{13} 41^{49}, 2 Sa. 23^{10}) it always marks a limit in the past ('until'); but עַד alone sometimes means 'while,' both with pf. and impf. (1 Sa. 14^{19}, Ps. 141^{10}), and so עַד שֶׁ (Ca. 1^{12}), עד לא (Pr. 8^{26}), and עד אשר לא (Ec. $12^{1. 2. 6}$): see BDB, p. 725 a. The transl. 'as long as' is thus perhaps not altogether impossible, though very improbable.—שילה] MSS and 𝔐 שלה, probably the original text. The *scriptio plena* may have no better foundation than the common Jewish interpretation שִׁילוֹ, 'his son,'—an impossible etymology, since there is no such word as שִׁיל in Heb., and the two forms which appear to have suggested it (viz., NH שִׁלְיל = 'fœtus' and שִׁלְיָה = 'afterbirth' [Dt. 28^{57}†]) are obviously superficial and fallacious analogies. The Mass. vocalisation is therefore

—something happens which shall inaugurate a still more glorious future. Whether this event be the advent of a person—an ideal Ruler—who shall take the sceptre out of Judah's hands, or a crisis in the fortunes of Judah which shall raise that tribe to the height of its destiny, is a question on which no final opinion can be expressed (see below).—*and to him*] Either Judah, or the predicted Ruler, according to the interpretation of $^{10b\alpha}$.—*obedience of peoples*] Universal dominion, which, however, need not be understood absolutely.

The *crux* of the passage is thus $^{10b\alpha}$: עד כי־יבוא שילה. For a fuller statement of the various interpretations than is here possible, see Werliin, *De laudibus Judæ*, 1838 (not seen); Dri. *JPh.* xiv. 1–28 (and

---

open to question, and we are free to try any pronunciation of the *Kethîb* שלה which promises a solution of the exegetical riddle with which we are confronted. In spite of the unanimity of the Vns., the pointing שֶׁלֹּה is suspicious for the reasons given above,—the presence of —שֶׁ in an early document, and the want of a subj. in the relative sentence. On the other hand, the attempts to connect the word with √ שלה, 'be quiet,' are all more or less dubious. (*a*) There is no complete parallel in Heb. to a noun like שִׁילֹה from a ל״ה root. If it be of the type *qîtôl*, the regular form would be שִׁילוֹי; although Kön. (ii. p. 147) argues that as we find בֶּכֶה alongside of בְּכִי, so we might have a שִׁילֹה alongside of שִׁילוֹי. Again, if *ô* be an apocopated form of the nominal termination *ôn*, the √ would naturally be not שלה but שיל (in Arab. = 'flow,' whence *seil*, 'a torrent') or שול. It is true there are a few examples of *un*apocopated nouns of this type from ל״ה verbs (קִיצוֹן, אִיתוֹן [Ezk. 40^{15}?], הֵרוֹן [Gn. 3^{16}†—prob. an error for the reg. הֵרָיוֹן, Hos. 9^{11}, Ru. 4^{13}†]); and the possibility of deriving the form in *ô* from a root of this kind cannot be absolutely excluded (cf. אֲבַדֹּה with אֲבַדּוֹן). (*b*) But even if these philological difficulties could be removed, there remains the objection that שלה (as contrasted with שלם) is in OT at most a negative word, denoting mere tranquillity rather than full and positive prosperity, and is often used of the careless worldly ease of the ungodly. For all these reasons it is difficult to acquiesce in the view that שִׁלֹה can be a designation of the Messiah as the *Peaceful* or the *Pacifier*; while to change the pointing and render till tranquillity (שֶׁלָה) 'come,' is exposed to the additional objection that the וְלוֹ of the following line is left without an antecedent.—יקהת] (Pr. 30^{17}†) *Dag. forte dirimens.* The √ appears in Ar. *waḳiha*, 'be obedient'; Sab. וקה. That a vb. (יִקָּהֲלוּ, יִקָּווּ?) would be more natural (Ba.) is not apparent; the vbs. in 𝔗^OJ paraphrase the sense given above. The √ was evidently not understood by 𝔊Θ (*προσδοκία*), 𝔙 (*expectatio*), Aq. (*σύστημα*), 𝔖 ܣܘܟܝܐ, all of which probably derived from √ קָוָה (Aq. from √ קוה, II.: BDB).

more briefly *Gen.* 410–415); Posnanski, *Schilo Ein Beitrag zur Geschichte der Messiaslehre*: 1 Theil: *Ausleg. von Gn.* 49^{10} *im Altert. bis zum Ende des MA*, 1904; Di. 462 ff.—The renderings grammatically admissible fall into two groups. (i.) Those which adhere to the *text. rec.*, taking שילה as *nom. pr.* (*a*) 'Until Shiloh come' (Shiloh, a name of the Messiah), the most obvious of all translations, first became current in versions and comm. of the 16th cent., largely through the influence of Seb. Münster (1534). Although the Messianic acceptation of the passage prevailed in Jewish circles from the earliest times, it attached itself either to the reading שֶׁלֹּה (ii. below) or to the rendering 'his son' (שִׁיל), or (later and more rarely) to שַׁי לוֹ ('gifts to him'). The earliest trace (if not the actual origin) of Shiloh as a personal name is found in the following passage of the Talmud (*Sanh.* 98*b*): אמר רב לא איברי עלמא אלא לדוד ושמואל אמר למשה ורבי יוחנן אמר למשיח מה שמו דבי ר׳ שילא אמרי שילה שמו שנאמר עד כי יבא שילה (the words are repeated in *Echa Rabba*, with the addition שלה כתיב): "Rab said, The world was created only for the sake of David; but Samuel said, For the sake of Moses; but R. Yoḥanan said, For the sake of the Messiah. What is his name? Those of the school of R. Shela say, Shiloh is his name, as it is said, 'Until Shiloh come.'" The sequel of the quotation is: "Those of the school of R. Yannai say, Yinnôn is his name, as it is said (Ps. 72^{17}), Let his name be for ever, before the sun let his name be perpetuated (יִנּוֹן). Those of the school of R. Ḥaninah say, Ḥanînāh is his name, as it is said (Jer. 16^{13}), For I will give you no favour (חֲנִינָה). And some say Menahem is his name, as as it is said (La. 1^{16}), For comforter (מְנַחֵם) and restorer of my soul is far from me. And our Rabbis say, The leprous one of the school of Rabbi is his name, as it is said (Is. 53^{4}), Surely our sicknesses he hath borne, and our pains he hath carried them, though we did esteem him stricken (*sc.* with leprosy), smitten of God, and afflicted." Now there is nothing here to suggest that Shiloh was already a current designation of the Messiah any more than, *e.g.*, the verb ינון in Ps. 72^{17} can have been a Messianic title. Yet, as Dri. says, it is "in this doubtful company that Shiloh is first cited as a name of the Messiah, though we do not learn how the word was read, or what it was imagined to signify." Subsequently Shiloh as a personal name appears in lists of Messianic titles of the 11th cent. (Posn. 40), and it is so used (alongside of the interpretation שֶׁלּוֹ) by Samuel of Russia (1124). Partly from this lack of traditional authority, and partly from the impossibility of finding a significant etymology for the word (*v.i.*), this explanation is now universally abandoned.—(*b*) 'Until he [Judah] come to Shiloh' (Herder, Ew. De. Di. [hesitatingly] al.). This is grammatically unexceptionable (cf. 1 Sa. 4^{12}), and has in its favour the fact that שילה (שִׁלוֹ, שִׁילוֹ [orig. שִׁילוֹן]) everywhere in OT is the name of the central Ephraimite sanctuary in the age of the Judges (Jos. $18^{1ff.}$, 1 Sa. 1–4 etc.). At the great gathering of the tribes at Shiloh, where the final partition of the land took place (Jos. 18 f.), Judah is imagined to have laid down the military leadership which had belonged to it during the wars of conquest; so that the prophecy marks the termination of that troubled period of the national life. But all this is unhistorical. The account in Jos. 18 belongs to the later idealisation of the conquest of Canaan; there is no evidence that Judah ever went to Shiloh, and none of a military hegemony of that tribe over the others, or of a subjugation of 'peoples' ($^{10b\beta}$), until the time of David, by which time Shiloh had ceased to be the central sanctuary. Even if (with Di.) we abandon the reference to Jos. 18, and take the sense to be merely that Judah will remain in full warlike activity till it has conquered its own territory, it is difficult to see (as Di. himself acknowledges) how that consummation could be expressed by a coming to Shiloh.—(*c*) The translation 'As long as one comes to Shiloh,' *i.e.* for ever (Hitz. Tu.), gives a sense to עד כי which is barely defensible.—(ii.) Those which follow the text underlying all ancient Vns. except 𝔙, viz. אֲשֶׁר לוֹ=שֶׁלֹּה. (*a*) 'Until he comes to that which is his' (Orelli, Br.) involves an improbable use of the acc.; and it is not easy to see how Judah's coming to his own could be the signal for the cessation of any prerogatives previously enjoyed by him.—(*b*) 'Until that which is his shall come' is a legitimate rendering; but the thought is open to the same objection as ii. (*a*).—(*c*). The most noteworthy of this group of interpretations is: 'Until he come whose' [it is], *sc.* the sceptre, the kingdom, the right, etc.; *i.e.* the Messiah. This has the support not only of nearly all Vns., but of Ezk. 21^{32} (where, however, the subj. המשפט is expressed). The omission of the subj. is a serious syntactic difficulty; and this, added to the questionable use of שֶׁ in an early and Judæan passage, makes this widely accepted interpretation extremely precarious. The first objection would be removed if (after a suggestion of We. [see *Comp.*^{2} 320]) we could delete the following ולו as a gloss, and read 'Until he come whose is the obedience,' etc. But metrical considerations preclude this, as well as the more drastic excision of שלה as a gloss on ולו (*ib.* 321).—Of conjectural emendations the only one that calls for notice is that of Ba. (followed by Gressmann), who reads מֹשְׁלֹה: 'Until his ruler (*i.e.* the Messiah) come.'

With regard to the general scope of the v., the question recurs, whether the term fixed by $^{10b\alpha}$ is historic or ideal; whether, in other words, it is a prophecy of the Davidic kingdom or of a future Messiah. (1) The tendency of recent scholars has been to regard v.^{10} as Messianic, but interpolated (We. Sta. Di. Ho. Dri. al.), on the double ground that it breaks the connexion between ^{9} and ^{11}, and that the idea of a personal Messiah is not older than the 8th cent. But (apart from the question whether the subj. in $^{11f.}$ be Judah or the Messiah) the connexion between ^{9} and ^{11} is in any case not so obvious as to justify the removal of ^{10}; and the assumption that the figure of the Messiah is a creation of the literary Prophets is based more on our ignorance of the early religious conceptions of the Israelites than on positive evidence. (2) Accordingly, Gu. (followed by Gressmann, *Ursprung d. Isr.-Jüd. Eschatologie*, 263) finds in the passage proof of a pre-prophetic eschatology, which looked forward to the advent of a Ruler who should found a world-empire, the point of the oracle being that till that great event Judah's dominion should not pass away. It is difficult, however, to believe that the climax of a blessing on Judah is the expectation of a world-ruler who takes the sceptre out of Judah's hands; and though a reference to a

Messianic tradition is quite conceivable, it is probable that it is here already applied to the Davidic monarchy. (3) It seems to me, therefore, that justice is done to the terms and the tenor of the oracle if we regard it as a prophecy of David and his dynasty,—a *vaticinium ex eventu*, like all the other oracles in the chapter. The meaning would be that Judah shall retain its tribal independence (see on [10a]) against all adversaries until its great hero makes it the centre of a powerful kingdom, and imposes his sovereignty on the neighbouring peoples. As for the enigmatic שילה, we may, of course, adopt the reading שֶׁלּוֹ, which is as appropriate on this view as on the directly Messianic interpretation. But if the oracle rests on an early eschatological tradition, it is just possible that שִׁלֹה is a cryptic designation of the expected Ruler, which was applied by the poet to the person of David. Bennett (p. 397) calls attention to the resemblance with שֵׁלָה in ch. 38; and it is a wonder that those who recognise mythical elements in the story of Judah and Tamar have not thought of identifying the שלה of our passage with Judah's third son, of whose destiny the story leaves us in ignorance. Is it possible that this connexion was in the minds of the Jewish authorities (*v.i.*), who render שילה 'his youngest son'? (see Posnanski, 36[3]).

11, 12. As usually understood, the vv. give a highly coloured picture of Judæan life after the conquest, in a land where vines are so common that they are used for tethering the ass, and wine so abundant that garments are washed in it. As a description of the vine-culture for which Judah was famous, the hyperbole is perhaps extreme; and Gressmann (*l.c.* 287) takes the subject to be not the personified tribe, but the Ruler of v.[10], the vv. being a prediction of the ideal felicity to be introduced by his reign. Whether this be the original sense of the passage or not is hard to decide; but Gr. is doubtless right in thinking that it supplied the imagery for the well-known picture of the Messianic king in Zec. 9[9].—**12.** 𝕲𝖁 take the adjs. as comparatives: 'brighter than wine (*v.i.*) . . . whiter than milk': but this is less natural.

---

11. אסרי] with archaic case-ending: cf. בני below, and perhaps חכלילי in v.[12].—שׂרקה] ἅπ. λεγ. = שֹׂרֵק, Is. 5[2], Jer. 2[21] [שָׂרֹק, Is. 16[8]]; probably from the *red* colour of the best grapes.—סותה] 𝔐𝔖 כסותה, 'covering' (Ex. 21[10] etc.). סות (√ סָוָה?) does not occur elsewhere.—**12.** חכלילי] In Pr. 23[29] חַכְלִלוּת עינים means '*dulness* of eyes,' the effect of excessive drinking. This is the only sense justified by etymology (Ass. *akâlu*, 'be gloomy'; Ar. *ḥakala*, IV, 'be confused': see BDB, *s.v.* חכל), and must be retained here, although, of course, it does not imply reproach, any more than שׁכר in 43[34]. 𝕲 χαροποί[οί], 'glad-eyed'; and similarly 𝖁𝕾.

The section on Judah lacks the unity of the first two oracles, and is very probably composed of strophes of diverse origin and date. V.^{8} opens with a play on the name, like vv.$^{16. 19}$, while v.^{9} starts afresh with an animal comparison, like vv.$^{14. 17. 27}$ (see Introd. Note, p. 510). The impression of discontinuity is partly confirmed by the poetic form; v.^{8} being an irregular tristich, and the remainder a series of 7 perfect trimeter distichs. The dekastich $^{10-12}$ seems distinct from what precedes (note the repetition of the name in ^{10}), but is itself a unity. The proposal to remove v.^{10} as a late Messianic interpolation, and to make v.^{11} the continuation of v.^{9}, does not commend itself; and the excision of the third line in v.^{10} (Meier, Fripp) merely avoids an exegetical difficulty by sacrificing the strophic arrangement.

13–15. Zebulun and Issachar.

13 Zebulun shall dwell by the shore of the sea,
And . . . shore of ships (?),
And his flank is on Ẓidon.

14 Issachar is a bony ass
Crouching between the panniers (?):
15 And he saw that rest was good,
And that the land was sweet;
So he bent his shoulder to bear,
And became a labouring drudge.

13. *shall dwell*] An allusion to the etymology in 30^{20}. It is plausibly conjectured that יִשְׁכֹּן has been substituted by mistake for the original יִזְבֹּל (Gu. al.).—The second and third lines are unintelligible, and the text is probably corrupt. The comparison of Zebulun to a recumbent animal, with 'itself' (וְהוּא) towards the sea-coast, and its hind-parts towards Ẓidon (Di. Gu. al.), is unsatisfying and almost grotesque. Dt. 33^{19b} shows that it is the advantageousness of Zebulun's geographical position which is here celebrated. —*Ẓîdôn*] may be a name for Phœnicia, in whose commercial pursuits it has been surmised that Zebulun became more and more involved (Sta. *GVI*, i. 171).—**14.** *bony*] *i.e.* strong-

---

13. חוף ימים] Ju. 5^{17}; cf. ח' הים, Dt. 1^{7}, Jos. 9^{1}, Jer. 47^{7}, Ezk. 25^{16}†: חוף is never found with any other gen. except in the next line.—והוא וגו'] One is tempted to construe prosaically thus: 'And *that* a shore for ships, with its flank on Ẓidon'; but this would entail elision of לְ, to the detriment of the rhythm: besides, the repetition of חוף and the unique combination ח' אנית are suspicious. Ba. reads יגור for לחוף (after Ju. 5^{17}), and deletes the last line.—על] 𝔐𝔊𝔙𝔖𝔗^{OJ} עד.—**14.** חמר גרם] 𝔐 ח' גרים, 'ass

limbed. Issachar had strength enough, but preferred ease to exertion.—הַמִּשְׁפְּתָיִם] The common interpretation 'sheep-pens' has no appropriateness here, and may be a conjecture based on Ju. 5^{16}. Equally unsuitable are the renderings of the old Vns. ('boundaries,' etc.), and the 'fire-places' or 'ash-heaps' which the Heb. etymology would suggest. The form is dual, and one naturally thinks of the 'panniers' carried by the ass (*v.i.*).—**15.** מְנוּחָה] A technical term for the settled, as contrasted with the nomadic, life (Gu.).—*a labouring drudge*] Lit. 'became a toiling labour-gang'; cf. Jos. 16^{10}. מַס is a levy raised under the system of forced labour (*corvée*). That a Heb. tribe should submit to this indignity was a shameful reversal of the normal relations between Israel and the Canaanites (Jos. 16^{10} 17^{13} [= Ju. 1^{28}], Ju. $1^{30. 33. 35}$).

The two northern Leah-tribes found a settlement in Lower Galilee, where they mingled with the Canaanite inhabitants. According to Jos. 19^{10-16}, Zebulun occupied the hills north of the Great Plain, being cut off from the sea both by Asher and by the strip of Phœnician coast. We must therefore suppose that the tribal boundaries fluctuated greatly in early times, and that at the date of the poem Zebulun had access at some point to the sea. The almost identical description on Ju. 5^{17} is considered by Gu. to have been transferred from Zebulun to Asher,—a view which, if it can be substantiated, affords a reliable criterion of the relative dates of the two oracles. The district of Issachar seems to have been between the Great Plain and the Jordan, including the Vale of Jezreel,—a position in which it was peculiarly difficult for a Hebrew tribe to maintain its independence. The tribe is not even mentioned in the survey of Ju. 1, as if it had ceased to be part of Israel. Yet both it and Zebulun had played a gallant part in the wars of the Judges (Ju. $4^{6. 10}$ $5^{14. 18}$ 6^{35} 5^{15}). The absence of any allusion to these exploits lends colour to the view that this part of the poem is of older date than the Song of Deborah.

---

of sojourners' (unless גֵּרִים be an adj. fr. גרם). 𝔊 τὸ καλὸν ἐπεθύμησεν (= חָמַד גֶּרֶם: Ginsb. *Introd.* p. 254); 𝔖 ܓܢܒܪܐ ܓܒܪܐ, Aq. and 𝔙 support on the whole MT.—בין המשפתים] Ju. 5^{16}†, but cf. Ps. 68^{14}. The three pass. are somehow interrelated, although no sense will suit them all. Vns. mostly render 'territories,' or something equivalent, both here and in Ju. But the διγομίας of 𝔊 in Ju. (see Schleusner) is noteworthy, and shows that the rendering above has some show of authority. So the late Gr.-Ven. ἡμιφόρτια. For the rest, see Moore on Ju. 5^{16}.—**15** טוב] ɯɯ טובה.—למס עבד] 𝔊 ἀνὴρ γεωργός (Ginsb. *l.c.*).—On מס, see DBD, and Moore, *Jud.* p. 47.

16–21. Dan, Gad, Asher, and Naphtali.

16 Dan shall judge his people,
    As one of the tribes of Israel.
17 Be Dan a serpent on the way,
    A horned snake on the path,
That bites the hoofs of the horse,
    And the rider tumbles backwards!

18 [I wait for thy salvation, Yahwe!]

19 Gad—raiders shall raid him,
    But he shall raid their rear!

20 Asher—his bread shall be fat,
    And he shall yield dainties for kings.

21 Naphtali is a branching terebinth (?)
    Producing comely tops (?).

16. *Dân . . . judge*] See on 30^{6}.—*his people*] Not Israel, but his own tribesmen. The meaning is not that Dan will produce a judge (Samson) as well as the other tribes ($\mathfrak{T}^{OJ}$), nor that he will champion the national cause (Ew. De. Di. al.); but that he will successfully assert an equal status with the other tribes. Note that in Ju. $18^{2.\ 11.\ 19}$ the Danites are spoken of as a 'clan' (מִשְׁפָּחָה).—**17.** The little snake, concealed by the wayside, may unhorse the rider as effectually as a fully armed antagonist: by such insidious, but not ignoble, warfare Dan in spite of his weakness may succeed.—שְׁפִיפֹן] ἅπ. λεγ. is probably the *cerastes cornutus*, whose habits are here accurately described (see Dri., and Tristram, *NHB*, 274).—**18.** An interpolation, marking (as nearly as possible) the middle of the poem (so Ols. Ba. Siev. al.). The attempts to defend its genuineness as a sigh of exhaustion on Jacob's part, or an utterance of the nation's dependence on Yahwe's help in such unequal conflicts as those predicted for Dan, are inept.—Dan was one of the weakest of the tribes, and perhaps the latest to secure a permanent settlement (Ju. $1^{34f.}$, Jos. 19^{47}, Ju. 18). Its migration northward, and conquest of Laish, must have

---

17. שפיפן] 𝕲 ἐνκαθήμενος, taking the ἅπ. λεγ. as an adj.—ויפל] Ba. נִפַּל (after 𝕾 ܡܦܝܠܐ).

taken place early in what is known as the Judges' period; and is apparently presupposed here and in Ju. 5^{17}.—**19.** Strictly: 'A marauding band shall attack him, but he shall attack their heel' (rdg. עֲקֵבָם, *v.i.*); *i.e.*, press upon them in their flight. The marauders are the warlike peoples to the E, specially the Ammonites (1 Ch. $5^{18ff.}$, Ju. 10 f.), who at a later time dispossessed the tribe (Jer. 49^{1}). As yet, however, Gad maintains its martial character (cf. 1 Ch. 12^{8-15}), and more than holds its own.—**20.** Asher settled in the fertile strip along the coast, N of Carmel. The name occurs as a designation of Western Galilee in Eg. inscrs. of the time of Seti and Ramses II. (see Müller, *AE*, 236 ff.).—*fat*] Probably an allusion to the oil (Dt. 33^{24}) for which the region was, and still is, famous.—*royal dainties*] fit for the tables of Phœnician kings (cf. Ezk. 27^{17}).—**21.** The verse on Naphtali is ambiguous. Instead of אַיָּלָה, 'hind,' many moderns read אֵילָה ('a spreading terebinth'). The following cl.: 'giving fair speeches,' suits neither image; on the one view it is proposed to read 'yielding goodly lambs' (אִמְּרֵי), on the other 'producing goodly shoots' (אֲמִרֵי). No certain conclusion can be arrived at.

---

19. גָּד] The name is here (otherwise than 30^{11}) connected with גדוד, 'band' (1 Sa. $30^{8.15.23}$, 1 Ki. 11^{24}, 2 Ki. 5^{2} 6^{23} etc.), and with √ גוד, 'assail' (Hab. 3^{16}, Ps. 94^{21}†).—עקב] Rd. עקבָם, taking the ם from the beginning of v.[20].—**20.** מאשר] Read with 𝔊𝔖𝔙 אָשֵׁר.—שמנה] 𝔐𝔖 שמן.—**21.** אַיָּלָה שלחה] So Aq. 𝔙 (Jer. *Qu.*). 𝔖 and 𝔗J probably had the same text, but render 'a swift messenger.' On Jerome's *ager irriguus* (*Qu.*) and its Rabbinical parallels, see Rahmer, *Die hebr. Traditionen in den Werken des Hier.* p. 55. 𝔊 *στέλεχος* seems to imply אֵילָה; but Ba. dissents.—הנתן] After either אַיָּלָה or אֵילָה, נֹתְנָה would be better.—אִמְרֵי] 'words,' is unsuitable, and caused 𝔖 and 𝔗J to change the metaphor to that of a messenger. An allusion to the eloquence of the tribe is out of place in the connexion. The reading אֲמִרֵי, 'topmost boughs,' has but doubtful support in Is. 17^{6} (see the comm.). אִמֵּר, 'lamb,' is not Heb., but is found in Ass. Phœn. Aram. and Ar. 𝔊 *ἐν τῷ γενήματι* is traced by Ba. to בִּפְרִי; but?—שֶׁפֶר] *ἅπ. λεγ.*—Ba. argues ingeniously, but unconvincingly, that אַיָּלָה belongs to v.[22], and that the פרת of that v. stood originally in [21]. His amended text reads:

נפתלי פֹּרָת שְׁלֻחָה	*Naphtali is a branching vine,*
הנתנה פְּרִי שפר	*That yieldeth comely fruit*

22–26. Joseph.

22 A fruitful bough (?) is Joseph—
  A fruitful bough by a well (?).
  . . .
23 And . . dealt bitterly with him,
  And the archers harassed him sorely.
24 Yet his bow abode unmoved,
  And nimble were the arms of his hands.
Through the hands of the Mighty One of Jacob,
  Through the ⌜name⌝ of the Shepherd of the Israel-Stone,
25 Through thy father's God—may he help thee!
  And El Shaddai—may he bless thee!
Blessings of heaven above,
  Blessings of Tĕhôm ⌜ ⌝ beneath,
Blessings of breast and womb,
26 Blessings of . . . (?),
Blessings of the eternal ⌜mountains⌝,
  ⌜Produce⌝ of the everlasting hills—
Be on the head of Joseph,
  And on the crown of the consecrated one of his brethren.

The section is full of obscurities, and the text frequently quite untranslatable. Its integrity has naturally not passed unquestioned. We may distinguish four stages in the unfolding of the theme: (1) The opening tristich (^{22}), celebrating (as far as can be made out) the populousness and prosperity of the central double-tribe. (2) Joseph's contest with the 'archers' ($^{23.\ 24a}$). (3) A fourfold invocation of the Deity (^{24b} $^{25a\alpha\beta}$). (4) The blessing proper ($^{25a\gamma\delta b.\ 26}$), which closely resembles the corresponding part of the Blessing of Moses (Dt. 33^{13-16}), the two being probably variants of a common original. Meyer (*INS*, 282 ff.) accepts (1), (2), and (4) as genuine, but rejects (3) as a later addition, which has displaced the original transition from the conflict to the blessing. Fripp (*ZATW*, xxi. 262 ff.) would remove (3) and (4) ($^{24b-26}$), which he holds to have been inserted by an Ephraimite editor from Dt. 33: Ho. seems in the main to agree. Sievers also (II. 362) questions the genuineness of $^{24b-26}$ on metrical grounds. But we may admit the northern origin of some of the vv., and the resemblance to Dt. 33, and even a difference of metre, and still hold that the whole belongs to the earliest literary recension of the Song to which we have access. The warm enthusiasm of the eulogy, and the generous recognition of Joseph's services to the national cause, are no doubt remarkable in a Judæan document; but such a tone is not unintelligible in the time of David, when the unity of the empire had to be maintained by a friendly and conciliatory attitude to the high-spirited central tribes.

22. On the ordinary but highly questionable rendering,

---

22. בן פרת] בֵּן is const. st.: the rhythmic accent forbids the usual shortening of the vowel with Maqqeph (בֶּן).—פֹּרָת] Contracted from פֹּרִיָּה,

the image is that of a young thriving vine planted by a fountain and thus well supplied with water, whose tendrils extend over the wall.—*a fruitful bough*] Or 'A young fruit-tree': lit. 'son of a fruitful [tree' or 'vine']. There is probably an etymological allusion to Ephraim (אֶפְרַת = פֹּרָת: We.).—**23, 24.** The figure is abruptly changed: Joseph is now represented as beset by troops of archers, whose attack he repels.—*dealt bitterly* . . .] The following word וָרֹבּוּ requires some amendment of text (*v.i.*).—**24.** *abode unmoved*] or 'constant.' Taken with the next line, this suggests a fine picture: the bow held steadily in position, while the hand that discharges the arrows in quick succession moves nimbly to and fro (Gu.). The expressions, however, are peculiar, and a different reading of the second line given in

---

'fruitful' (Is. 17[6] 32[12], Ezk. 19[10], Ps. 128[3]), or פֹּרִיָּת, with archaic fem. termination. פֹּארָה, 'bough' (Ezk. 17[6] 31[5. 6]), might be thought of, but would be hardly suitable as gen. after בן.—Down to עין the Vns. have substantially the same text.—בנות צעדה עלי שור] defies explanation. Lit. *filiæ discurrerunt super murum* (𝔙). But בנות = 'tendrils,' has no analogy; צעד means 'march' or 'stride,' but not 'extend'; and the discord of number is harsh (notwithstanding G–K. § 145*k*). The Vns. reveal early corruption of the text, without suggesting anything better. 𝔊 *υἱός μου νεώτατος* (= 𝔐 בני צעירי) *πρός μὲ ἀνάστρεψον* (= עֲלַי שׁוּב). 𝔖 ܒܢܝܢܐ ܡܣܥܪܐ ܕܣܠܩ ܥܠ ܫܘܪܐ (בִּנְיָן סָעַר הָעֹלֶה שׁוּר ?).—Zimmern's zodiacal theory, which identifies Joseph with the sign Taurus, finds two tempting points of contact in the consonantal text: reading פרת = פָּרָה, 'juvenca,' at the beginning, and שׁוֹר, 'ox,' at the end. But the reconstruction of the text on these lines, with the help of Dt. 33[17] (see *ZA*, vii. 164 ff.; *ATLO*[2], 399), has no title to respect: against it see Ba. p. 116.—**23.** וָרֹבּוּ] From √ רבב, a by-form of רבה,* 'shoot,' with intrans. pf. (G–K. § 67 *m*). The simple pf. between two consec. impfs. being suspicious, the least change demanded is וַיָּרֹבּוּ. 𝔐𝔊 (*ἐλοιδόρουν*) and 𝔙 (*jurgati sunt*) read וַיְרִיבֻהוּ, 'strove with him.' Parallelism suggests a noun as subj. to וַיָּ׳; we might read רַבִּים, 'bowmen' (Jer. 50[29]), or (since the line is too short) רֹבֵי קֶשֶׁת (21[20]).—**24a.** 𝔊 *καὶ συνετρίβη μετὰ κράτους τὰ τόξα αὐτῶν* [= וַתִּשָּׁבֵר בְּאֵיתָן קַשְּׁתָּם].—ותשב] 𝔖 ܘܬܒܬ = וַתָּשָׁב. The sense 'abide' for ישב is justified by Lv. 12[4], 1 Ki. 22[1], Ps. 125[1], and nothing is gained by departing from MT.—באיתן] Lit. 'as a permanent one' (בְּ *essentiæ*).—ויפזו] 2 Sa. 6[16]†. 𝔊 *καὶ ἐξελύθη*, 𝔖 ܘܐܬܪܦܝܘ may represent ויפורו (see Ba.).—[𝔊 יָדָם] זרועי ידיו] is a hard

---

* But see above on 21[20].

some Vns. is approved by several scholars (*v.i.*).—*Strong One of Jacob*] A poetic title of Yahwe, recurring Is. 49^{26} 60^{16}, Ps. $132^{2.5}$, and (with Israel for Jacob) Is. 1^{24}. See, further, the footnote below.—*Through the name*] מִשֵּׁם, the reading of 𝔖 and $𝔗^{O}$, though not entirely satisfactory, is at least preferable to the meaningless מִשָּׁם of MT.—*the Shepherd of the Israel-Stone*] A second designation of Yahwe as the Guardian of the Stone of Israel,—either the sacred stone of Bethel, or (better) that of Shechem (Jos. $24^{26f.}$), which was the religious rendezvous of the tribes in early times (see p. 416): so Luther, *INS*, 284^{1}. Both text and translation are, however, uncertain (*v.i.*).—**25, 26.** The construction is ambiguous: it is not clear whether the lines beginning with *Blessings* are a series of accusatives depending on the וִיבָרְכֶךָּ of ^{25a} ('may he bless thee *with* blessings,' etc.), or subjects to תִּהְיֶיןָ in ^{26b}. The second view is adopted above; but the ambiguity may be an intentional refinement.—**25aαβ.** *'Ēl Shaddai*] For the reading, *v.i.*; and see on 17^{1}.—**25aγδb,**

---

combination, but perhaps not too bold.—**24b.** אֲבִיר] occurs only in the pass. cited above. It is reasonably suspected that the Mass. changed the punctuation to avoid association of ideas with אַבִּיר, 'bull,' the idolatrous emblem of Yahwe in N Israel. Whether the name as applied to Yahwe be really a survival of the bull-worship of Bethel and Dan is another question; אַבִּיר (strong) is an epithet of men (Ju. 5^{22}, Jb. 24^{22} 34^{20}, Je. 46^{15}, 1 Sa. 21^{8} etc.), and horses (Jer. 8^{16} 47^{3} 50^{11}) much more often than of bulls (Ps. 22^{13} 68^{31} 50^{13}, Is. 34^{7}), and might have been transferred to Yahwe in its adj. sense. On the other hand, the parallelism with 'Stone of Israel' in the next line favours the idea that the title is derived from the cult of the Bull at Bethel, which may have had a more ancient significance than an image of Yahwe (cf. Mey. *INS*, 282 ff.; Luther, *ZATW*, xxi. 70 ff.). The further inference (Nö. Lut. Mey.) that Jacob was the deity originally worshipped in the bull is perhaps too adventurous.—מִשָּׁם] So 𝔊𝔙; but $𝔖𝔗^{O}$ מִשֵּׁם.—אבן ישראל] Cf. צור יש׳, 2 Sa. 23^{3}, Is. 30^{29}; also א׳ הָעֵזֶר, 1 Sa. 4^{1} 5^{1} 7^{12}. The translation above agrees with 𝔖; MT puts רֹעֶה in apposition with א׳ י׳ (so 𝔙); 𝔊 ἐκεῖθεν ὁ κατισχύσας Ἰσρ. omits אבן, and may have read עזר (Ba.). The line is too long for the metre, but אבן is the one word that should *not* be omitted. —**25** ויעזרך . . . ויברכך] Cf. Ps. 69^{33}, and see Ew. § 347 *a*.—ואת־] Read with 𝔐𝔊 (ὁ θεὸς ὁ ἐμός), 𝔖 וְאֵל: though שַׁדַּי alone (Nu. $24^{4.16}$) would be suitable in an ancient poem.—רבצת] Metrically necessary in Dt. 33^{13}, but here redundant; probably, therefore, a gloss from the other recension (Siev.).—**26.** אביך גברו על־ברכת הורי עד] There are two stages of corruption.

26a. The blessings, arranged in three parallel couplets,—the first referring to the fertility of the soil.—*Blessings of heaven above*] Rain and dew, the cause of fertility (so Dt. 33^{13} em.). —*Tĕhôm . . . beneath*] The subterranean flood, whence springs and rivers are fed: see on 1^{2}.—*Blessings of breasts and womb*] Contr. the terrible imprecation, Hos. 9^{14}.—**26a.** Passing over the first four words as absolutely unintelligible (*v.i.*), we come to the third pair of blessings: . . . *of the eternal mountains . . . of the everlasting hills* (Dt. 33^{15}, Hab. 3^{6})] In what sense the mountains were conceived as a source of blessing is not clear,—perhaps as abodes of deity; cf. the 'dew of Hermon' (Ps. 133^{3}).—The word rendered *produce* is uncertain; we should expect 'blessings,' as 𝔊 actually reads (*v.i.*).—**26b.** *Be on the head*] as in benediction the hand is laid on the head (48^{14}): cf. Pr. 10^{6} 11^{26}.—נְזִיר אֶחָיו] So Dt. 33^{16}. The נָזִיר is either the *Nazirite* —one 'consecrated' to God by a vow involving unshorn hair (Ju. $13^{5.7}$ etc.)—or the *prince* (so only La. 4^{7}). For the rendering 'crowned one' there are no examples. The second interpretation is that usually adopted by recent scholars; some explaining it of the Northern monarchy, of

---

one remediable, the other not. The last line is to be restored with 𝔊 ברכת הַרֲרֵי עַד, 'blessings of the eternal mountains' (Dt. 33^{15}, Hab. 3^{6}). But the first three words, though represented by all Vns., must be wrong; for to put ברכת under the regimen of על destroys the parallelism, and the vb. גָּבְרוּ cuts off תהיין from its subj. What is obviously required is a line parallel to ברכת שדים ורחם. Gu.'s suggested emendation, though far from satisfying, is the best that can be proposed: ברכת אָב אַךְ גֶּבֶר וָעָל = 'Blessings of father, yea, man and child.'—אביך] 𝔐𝔊 + ואמך, suggested no doubt by the previous line.—הורי] 𝔙𝔖𝔗^{OJ} render 'my progenitors,' by an impossible derivation from √ הרה, 'be pregnant.'—תאות] EV 'utmost bound' (so De., fr. √ תאה or תוה; see BDB), has no real philological or traditional justification. If the text were reliable, it might be the common word 'desire,' from √ אוה (𝔊$^{curs.}$ 𝔏𝔙𝔗^{OJ}), in the sense of 'desirable things.' With some hesitation I follow above Ols. Gu. al., reading תבואת after Dt. 33^{14}. But 𝔊^{B} ברכת has great weight (all the greater that the translator has lost the thread of the thought), and ought perhaps to be preferred.—נזיר] is not necessarily a derivative from the noun נֵזֶר, 'diadem,' = 'the crowned one'; more probably it comes from the vb. directly,—נזר = 'dedicate' (cf. נדר)—which admits various shades of meaning. Of the Vns. 𝔊𝔗^{J} represent the idea of 'prince' or 'ruler, 𝔗^{O} 'the separated one,' 𝔙 Saad. 'the Nazirite,' 𝔖 'the crown' (נֵזֶר).

which the Joseph-tribes were the chief part; though others think it merely ascribes to Joseph a position of princely superiority to his brethren. The other view is taken by Sellin (*Beitr.* ii. 1, 132 ff.) and Gu., who conceive the ancient Nazirite as a man like Samson, dedicated to single-handed warfare against the foes of Israel (cf. Schw. *Kriegsalterthümer*, 101 ff.), and hold that Joseph is so designated as being the foremost champion of the national cause. The interpretation is certainly plausible; but it derives no support from the word קָדְקֹד (‖רֹאשׁ), which is never used in connexion with the Nazirite, and is quite common in other connexions (see Dt. 33^{20}).

The opinion confidently entertained by many scholars (see We. *Comp.*[3] 321), that the Blessing of Joseph presupposes the divided kingdom, rests partly on this expression, and partly on the allusion to an arduous struggle in [23f.]. But it is clear that neither indication is at all decisive. If נָזִיר could mean only 'crowned one,' we should no doubt find ourselves in the time of the dual monarchy. In point of fact, it never denotes the king, and only once 'princes'; and we have no right to deny that its import is adequately explained by the leadership which fell to the house of Joseph in the conquest of Canaan (Ju. $1^{22ff.}$). Similarly, the 'archers' of v.[23] *might* be the Aramæans of Damascus, in which case Joseph would be a name for the Northern kingdom as a whole; but they may as well be the Midianites (Ju. 6 ff.) or other marauders who attacked central Israel between the settlement and the founding of the monarchy, and whose repeated and irritating incursions would admirably suit the terms of the description. The general considerations which plead for an early date are: (1) The analogy of the rest of the poem, some parts of which are earlier, and none demonstrably later, than the age of David or Solomon. (2) The incorporation of the blessing in a Judæan work is improbable at a time when Israel was a rival kingdom. (3) Although Joseph sometimes stands for the Northern kingdom, it can hardly do so here in an enumeration of the tribes. Consequently it takes us back to the time when Joseph was still a single tribe, or when at least the separation of Ephraim and Manasseh was not clearly recognised: the addition in Dt. 33^{17b} is instructive in this regard (see Gu., and Sellin, *l.c.* 134).

27. Benjamin.

27 Benjamin is a ravening wolf:
In the morning he devours the prey,
And at eve divides the spoil.

---

27. זאב יטרף] Descriptive impf., see Dav. § 44, *R.* 3, § 142. On pausal *ā*, see G-K. § 29 *u.*—עד]='booty,' Is. 33^{23}, Zeph. 3^{8} [? Is. 9^{5}]; 𝔊 ἔτι.

Benjamin is praised for its predatory instincts, and its unflagging zest for war. The early history contains a good deal to justify the comparison: its fight with Moab (Ju. $3^{15ff.}$), its share in the struggle with the Canaanites (Ju. 5^{14}), its desperate stand against united Israel (Ju. 19 f.); it was famous for its skill in slinging and archery (Ju. 20^{16}, 1 Ch. 8^{40} 12^{2}, 2 Ch. 14^{7} 17^{17}). But a special reference to the short-lived reign of Saul is probable: the dividing of spoil reminds us of the king who clothed the daughters of Israel with scarlet and ornaments (2 Sa. 1^{24}).—The contrast between this description and the conception of Benjamin in the Joseph-stories is an instructive example of how tribal characteristics were obscured in the biographical types evolved by the popular imagination.

28ab*a* (to אביהם) is the subscription to the poem; the remainder of the v. belongs to P, and probably continued ^{1a} in that source.—*the tribes of Israel, twelve* in number] The division into 12 tribes is an artificial scheme, whose origin is uncertain (see Luther, *ZATW*, xxi. 33 ff.; Peters, *Early Heb. Story*, 55 ff.). It obtained also amongst the Edomites, Ishmaelites, and other peoples; and in Israel betrays its theoretic character by the different ways in which the number was made up, of which the oldest is probably that followed in the Song of Jacob. In Dt. 33, Simeon is omitted, and Joseph divided into Ephraim and Manasseh; in P (Nu. 2) Joseph is again divided, to the exclusion not of Simeon, but of Levi.

The recently revived theory of a connexion between the original sayings of the Blessing and the signs of the Zodiac calls for a brief notice at this point. The most striking correspondences were set forth by Zimmern in *ZA*, vii. (1892), 161 ff.; viz., Simeon and Levi = Gemini (see p. 517); Judah = Leo, with the king-star Regulus on its breast (בין רגליו); and Joseph = Taurus. This last comparison, it is true, rests on Dt. 33 rather than Gn. 49, and is only imported into this passage by a violent reconstruction of v.^{22} (p. 530). Other possible combinations mentioned by Zimmern are Issachar = Aselli (in Cancer), Dan = Serpens (N of Libra), Benjamin = Lupus (S of Scorpio), and Naphtali = Aries

---

28. שבטי ישראל] 𝔊 *υἱοὶ* Ἰακώβ.—איש אשר כ׳] Such a construction is impossible. We must either omit the rel. (Vns.) or read **איש איש** (Ols. De. KS. Gu. al.).

(reading אַיִל for אַיָּלָה). Stucken (*MVAG*, 1902, 166 ff.), after a laboured proof that Reuben corresponds to Behemoth (hippopotamus), an old constellation now represented by Aquarius, completed the circle after a fashion, with the necessary addition of Dinah = Virgo as the missing sign; and his results are adopted by Jeremias (*ATLO*², 395 ff.). A somewhat different arrangement is given by Winckler in *AOF*, iii. 465 ff. These conjectures, however, add little to the evidence for the theory, which must in the main be judged by the seven coincidences pointed out in Zimmern's article. That these amount to a demonstration of the theory cannot be affirmed; but they seem to me to go far to show that it contains an element of truth. It is hardly accidental that in each series we have one double sign (Gemini, Simeon-Levi) and one female personification (Virgo, Dinah), and that all the animal names occurring in the Song (lion, ass, serpent, ram?, ox?, wolf) can be more or less plausibly identified with constellations either in the Zodiac or sufficiently near it to have been counted as Zodiacal signs in early times. The incompleteness of the correspondence is fairly explained by two facts: first, that the poem has undergone many changes in the course of its transmission, and no longer preserves the original form and order of the oracles; and second, that while the twelve-fold division of the ecliptic goes back to the remotest antiquity, the traditional names of the twelve signs cannot all be traced to the ancient Babylonian astronomy. It may be added that there is no *prima facie* objection to combinations of this sort. The theory does not mean that the sons of Jacob *are* the earthly counterparts of the Zodiacal constellations, and nothing more. All that is implied is that an attempt was made to discover points of resemblance between the fortunes and characteristics of the twelve tribes on the one hand, and the astro-mythological system on the other. Such combinations were necessarily arbitrary, and it might readily happen that some were too unreal to live in the popular memory. Where the correspondence is plausible, we may expect to find that the characterisation of the tribe has been partly accommodated to the conceptions suggested by the comparison; and great caution will have to be observed in separating the bare historical facts from the mythological allusions with which they are embellished. In the present state of the question, it may be safely said that the historical interpretation must take precedence. The Zodiacal theory will have to be reckoned with in the interpretation of the Song; but it has as yet furnished no trustworthy clue either to the explanation of obscure details, or to the restoration of the text.

XLIX. 28b–L. 26.—*The Death and Burial of Jacob; and the Death of Joseph* (P, J, E).

Jacob charges his sons to bury him in the family sepulchre at Machpelah, and expires ($^{28b-33}$). Joseph causes the body to be embalmed; and, accompanied by his brethren and an imposing *cortège*, conveys it to its last resting-place in

Canaan (50^{1-14}). He pacifies and reassures his brethren, who fear his vengeance now that their father is gone ($^{15-21}$). He dies in a good old age, after exacting an oath that his bones shall be carried up from Egypt when the time of deliverance comes ($^{22-26}$).

Sources.—$49^{28b\beta-33}$ belongs to P, with the possible exceptions of ^{32} (a gloss), and the clause $^{33a\beta}$; note the reference to ch. 23 and the identical phraseology of the two passages; also the expressions נוע, אחזה, נאסף אל־עמיו (*bis*).—In ch. 50, vv.$^{12. 13}$ are from P (Machpelah, etc.: note also that the suff. in בניו refers back to 49^{33}). Vv.$^{1-11. 14}$ are mainly J (ישראל, ^{2}; מצא חן בע׳, ^{4}; גֹּשֶׁן, ^{8}; הכנעני, ^{11}: note the reference [$^{5f.}$] to Joseph's oath [47^{29-31}]); and $^{15-26}$ E (אלהים, $^{19. 20. 24. 25}$; כלכל, ^{21} [45^{11} 47^{12}]; התחת אלהים אני, ^{19} [30^{2}]: the resemblance to $45^{5. 7}$; and the backward reference in Ex. 13^{19}, Jos. 24^{32}). The analysis might stop here (Di. We. Dri. al.); but a variant in ^{10} (^{10b} ‖ $^{10a\beta}$), and the double name of the place of burial suggest that there may be two accounts of the funeral (see KS. *An.* 242). Ho. Gu. Pro., however, seem to me to go too far in the attempt to establish a *material* difference of representation (*e.g.*, that in E's account Joseph's brethren did not go up with him to the burial). Traces of J in $^{15-26}$ are equally insignificant (see the notes).

28b–33. Jacob's charge to his sons.—28bβ. The sequel to ^{1a} in P. Note the close formal parallel to 28^{1} (P): *And . . . called . . . and blessed . . . and charged . . . and said . . .—each with a special blessing*] *v.i.*—**29, 30.** See on ch. 23.—**31.** *Abraham and Sarah his wife*] 25^{9} 23^{19}. The burying-place of Isaac (35^{29}) is not elsewhere specified; and the burials of Rebekah and Leah are not recorded at all.—On the possibility that the notice of Rachel's burial (48^{7}) stood here originally, see p. 504 f.—**32.** Probably a gloss (*v.i.*).—**33.** *drew up his feet into the bed*] The clause may have been inserted from J; cf. 48^{2b}.—As in the case of all the patriarchs except Joseph, the actual account of the death is left to P.

L. 1–14. The burial of Jacob.—1. The forms in which

---

29. ויצו אותם] 𝔊 om.—אל־עַמָּי] Read אל־עַמָּי (cf. ^{33}): see on 25^{8}.—**30.** For בשרה המ׳, 𝔊 has simply במכפלה, and for the following השרה, המערה.—**31.** קברתי] 𝔊 קָבְרוּ.—At the end of the v. Bu. would add ואת־רחל as P's original statement (*ZATW*, iii. 82).—**32.** The v. has no syntactic connexion with the preceding, the construction is cumbrous in the extreme, and the notice superfluous after ^{30b}. It should probably be deleted as a marginal variant to ^{30b} (so De. Gu.).—מקנה] 𝔊 במ׳.

Joseph's grief expressed itself were doubtless conventional, though they are not elsewhere alluded to in OT.—**2.** The Egyptian practice of embalming originated in ideas with which the Hebrew mind had no sympathy,—the belief that the *ka* or ghostly double of the man might at any time return to take possession of the body, which consequently had at all costs to be preserved (Erman, *LAE*, 307). In the cases of Jacob and Joseph (v.[26]), it is merely an expedient for preserving the body till the burial could take place. On the various methods employed, see Herod. ii. 86–88; Diod. i. 91; and Budge, *The Mummy*, 160 ff., 177 ff.—*the physicians*] In Egypt the embalmers formed a special profession.—**3.** *forty days . . . seventy days*] The process of embalming occupied, according to Diod., over 30 days, according to Herod., 70 days; exact data from the monuments are not yet available (Erman, 315, 319 f.; Budge, 179). The mourning for Aaron and Moses lasted 30 days (Nu. 20^{29}, Dt. 34^{8}); the Egyptians (who are here expressly mentioned) are said to have mourned for a king 72 days (Diod. i. 72).—**4–6.** Joseph seeks Pharaoh's permission to absent himself from Egypt. Why he needed the court to intercede for him in such a matter does not appear.—**5a.** Cf. $47^{29ff.}$.—*have digged*] The rendering 'have purchased' is possible, but much less probable (cf. 2 Ch. 16^{14}). The confused notice Ac. 7^{16} might suggest a tradition that Jacob's grave was in the plot of ground he bought near Shechem (33^{19} E), which is the view maintained by Bruston (*ZATW*, vii. 202 ff.). On any view the contradiction to 47^{30} remains.—**7–9.** The funeral procession is described with *empressement* as a mark of the almost royal honours bestowed on the patriarch. Such processions are frequently depicted on Egyptian tombs: Erman,

2. חנט] v.[26], Ca. 2^{13}†. Apparently a Semitic √, meaning in Arab. 'become mature,' applied in Heb. Aram. and Arab. to the process of embalming.—3. חֲנֻטִים] ἅπ. λεγ.; abstr. pl. = 'embalming.'—4. בכיתו] The fem. only here, for בְּכִי. The suff. prob. gen. obj. (weeping *for* Jacob).—דברו־נא] Add with 𝔊 עָלָי.—5. השביעני] 𝔐𝔊$^{A, al.}$ + לפני מותי.—הנה אנכי מת] 𝔊 om. The phrase occurs in E 48^{21}, and (without הנה) 50^{24}.—כריתי] 𝔊𝔙𝔗^{J} 'have digged'; 𝔖 'have purchased,' 𝔗^{O} אַתְקֵנִת = 'have prepared.' The first sense preponderates in usage (the second, Dt. 2^{6}, Hos. 3^{2}, Ib. 6^{27} 40^{30}†),

320 f.; Ball, *Light from the East*, 119 f.—*horsemen*, however, never appear in them: "We have no representations of Egyptians on horseback; and were it not for a few literary allusions, we should not know that the subjects of the Pharaoh knew how to ride" (Erman, *LAE*, 492 f.).—**10, 11.** The mourning at the grave.—*Gōren hā-Āṭād*] 'the threshing-floor of the bramble'; the locality is unknown (*v.i.*).—**11.** *Ābēl Miẓraim*] one of several place-names compounded with אָבֵל = 'meadow' (Nu. 33^{49}, Ju. 11^{33}, 2 Sa. 20^{15}, 2 Ch. 16^{4}); here interpreted as אֵבֶל מִצְרַיִם, 'mourning of Egypt.' The real name 'meadow of Egypt' may have commemorated some incident of the Egyptian occupation of Palestine; but the situation is unknown.—The record of the actual burying in J and E has not been preserved.

It is difficult to say whether *Gōren hā-Āṭād* and *Ābēl Miẓraim* are two different places, or two names for one place. Jerome (*OS*, $85^{15ff.}$) identifies the former with Bethagla (='*Ain Ḥağla*, or *Ḳaṣr Ḥağla*, S of Jericho [Buhl, *GP*, 180]), but on what authority we do not know. The conjecture that it was in the neighbourhood of Rachel's grave depends entirely on a dubious interpretation of 48^{7}. Since there appears to be a doublet in v.^{10} ($^{10a\beta \parallel 10b}$), it is natural to suppose that one name belongs to J and the other to E, and therefore there is no great presumption that the localities are identical ('בנ' הא in ^{11} may be a gloss). According to the present text, both were E of the Jordan ($^{10a\ 11b}$); but such a statement if found in one document would readily be transferred by a redactor to the other; and all we can be reasonably confident of is that one or other was across the Jordan, for it is almost inconceivable that א' בע' הירדן should be an interpolation in *both* cases. Since it is to be assumed that in J and E the place of mourning was also the place of burial, and since the theory of a *détour* round the Dead Sea and the E of Jordan to arrive at any spot in W. Palestine is too extravagant to have arisen from a fanciful etymology, it would seem to follow that, according to at least one tradition, Jacob's grave was shown at some now unknown place E of the Jordan (Meyer, *INS*, 280 f.). Meyer's inference that Jacob was originally a transjordanic hero, is, however, a doubtful one; for the East is dotted with graves of historic personages in impossible places, and we have no assurance that tradition was more reliable in ancient times.

---

and is here to be preferred.—את־אבי] 𝔖 + כאשר השביעני.—**10.** אטד] The word for 'bramble' in Jotham's parable from Gerizim, Ju. $9^{14f.}$ (only Ps. 58^{10} again). Can there be an allusion to the threshing-floor of this passage at Shechem?—**11.** בנ' האמר] Possibly a gloss from v.^{10}. If so, שמה (𝔖 שמו), referring to גרן (whose gender is uncertain), must have been substi-

12, 13. The account of the actual burial (from P).—It is significant that here the Egyptians take no part in the obsequies: the final redactor may have assumed that they were left behind at the mourning place E of the Jordan.—See further on $49^{29ff.}$.—**14** (J). The return to Egypt.

15–21. Joseph removes his brethren's fears.—The vv. contain a variation of the theme of $45^{5ff.}$ (Gu.), as if to emphasize the lesson of the whole story, that out of a base intent God brought good to His people.—**15.** *saw*] *i.e.* 'realised,'—took in the full significance of the fact (cf. 30^{1}). If it were meant that they 'learned' for the first time that their father was dead, the inference would surely be not merely that the brethren had not been present at the funeral (Gu.), but that E had not recorded it at all.—**16, 17.** They send a message to Joseph, recalling a dying request of their father (not elsewhere mentioned).—*the servants of the God of thy father*] Religion is a stronger plea than even kinship (Gu.).—**18.** Cf. 44^{16}. The v. may have been inserted from J (*v.i.*).—**19.** *am I in God's stead?*] (30^{2}): to judge and punish at my pleasure.—**20.** Cf. $45^{5.7.8}$.—**21.** The continuance of the famine seems presupposed, in opposition to the chronology of P (47^{28}).

22–26. Joseph's old age and death.—**22.** *a hundred and ten years*] Cf. Jos. 24^{29}. It is hardly a mere coincidence, but

---

tuted for שם המקום (so 𝔙𝔗J, Gu.).—**12.** בניו לו] The suff. find no suitable antecedents nearer than 49^{33}, the last excerpt from P.—כאשר צום] $𝔊^{B, al.}$ *καὶ ἔθαψαν αὐτὸν ἐκεῖ*.—**13.** שרה] 𝔊 *τὸ σπήλαιον*, and so again for את־השרה.—**14.** אחרי—אביו] 𝔊 om.

15. לו ונו׳] Cond. sent. with suppressed apodosis, G–K. § 159 *y*.—**16.** ויצוו] 𝔊 *καὶ παρεγένοντο*, and 𝔖 ܘܩܪܒܘ, seem to have read וַיִּגְּשׁוּ, which if correct would make the excision of v.[18] from E almost imperative (see on the v.). But the sense of צִוָּה, 'to commission,' is justified by Ex. 6^{13}, Jer. 27^{4}, Est. 3^{12} etc.; and נגש would not properly be followed by לאמר.—**17.** אָנָּא] a strong particle of entreaty; in Pent. only Ex. 32^{31}.—**18.** גם—לפניו] 𝔊 om.—For וילכו, Ba. (after Vatke) reads ויבכו, which would give point to the following גם. But the change is not necessary: וילכו would mean 'they went away' only if they had previously been present. That certainly seems implied in [17b] (apart from the reading of 𝔊𝔖 in [16]); and hence there is much to be said for assigning v.[18] to J (Di. Ho. Pro.).—**19b.** 𝔊 reads *τοῦ γὰρ θεοῦ ἐγώ εἰμι*.—**20.** אלהים] 𝔐 והא׳: 𝔊𝔖𝔙 also have the copula.—**21.** ועתה] 𝔊 *εἶπεν δὲ αὐτοῖς*.—**22.** ובית] 𝔊 *καὶ οἱ ἀδελφοὶ αὐτοῦ*

rather an instance of the Egyptian affinities of the narrative, that 110 years is at least three times spoken of as an ideal lifetime in Egyptian writings (Stern, *Z. Aeg. Spr.*, 1873, 75 f.). —**23.** Joseph lived to see his great-grandchildren by both his sons,—another token of a life crowned with blessing (Ps. 128[6], Pr. 13[22] 17[6] etc.). The expressions used of Ephraim's descendants are somewhat difficult (*v.i.*).—*Mākîr*] the most powerful clan of Manasseh, in the Song of Deborah (Ju. 5[14]) numbered among the tribes of Israel, and possibly therefore an older unit than Manasseh itself (see Meyer, *INS*, 507, 516 f.).—The expression *born on Joseph's knees* implies the adoption of Machir's sons by Joseph (see on 30[3]), though the action does not seem to have any tribal significance.—**24, 25.** Joseph predicts the Exodus (as did Jacob, 48[21]), and directs his bones to be carried to Canaan. For the fulfilment of the wish, see Ex. 13[19], Jos. 24[32].—*his brethren* are here the Israelites as a whole (v.[25]).—**26.** The death of Joseph.—*in a coffin*] or mummy-case, the wooden inner shell, shaped like the mummy, which was placed in the stone sarcophagus (see Erman, *LAE*, 315 f.; Ball, *Light from the East*, 121). A mythological allusion to the 'coffin' of Osiris (Völter, 55) is not to be thought of.

"This 'coffin in Egypt,'" remarks Delitzsch, "is the coffin of all Israel's spiritual satisfaction in Egypt." Gu. shows sounder judgement and truer insight when he bids us admire the restful close of the narrative, and the forward glance to the eventful story of the Exodus.

καὶ πᾶσα ἡ πανοικία.—**23.** בני שלשים] 𝔐 בנים ש׳: so 𝔊𝔖𝔗[OJ]. שִׁלֵּשִׁים means 'great-grandchildren' (Ex. 34[7]); hence בני ש׳ ought to mean 'great-great-grandchildren' (not, of course, of Ephraim, but of Joseph in Ephraim's line). But there being no reason why the descent should be carried further in the line of Ephraim than in that of Manasseh, we must understand 'great-grandchildren,' whether we read with 𝔐, or take בני ש׳ as appositional gen. (see Di.).—על־ברכי] 𝔐 בימי, 'in the days of,—'a bad correction' (Ba.), supported by no other Vn.—**24.** נשבע] 𝔊 + ὁ *θεὸς τοῖς πατράσιν ἡμῶν.*—**25** end. Add with Heb. MSS 𝔐𝔊𝔖𝔙 אִתְּכֶם, 'with you.'—**26.** ויישם] 𝔐 ויושם. See on 24[33].

INDEXES.

I. ENGLISH.

II. HEBREW

PRINTED BY MORRISON AND GIBB LTD., EDINBURGH AND LONDON